Adrian Frutiger – Typefaces. The Complete Works

Swiss Foundation
Type and Typography

ADRIAN FRUTIGER
THE

TYPEFACES.
COMPLETE WORKS

Edited by
Heidrun Osterer and Philipp Stamm

Birkhäuser
Basel · Boston · Berlin

Content

Kurt Weidemann
Adrian Frutiger – The standard-setter

With Gutenberg's invention of the adjustable hand mould, no less was achieved than the industrial-scale production of a commodity – metal type – in any desired quantity and with consistent quality, effectively ushering in the modern era. Master scribes were replaced by master printers. This invention would last half a millennium before it, in turn, was pushed aside by photosetting, by information being transmitted at the speed of light. The end result, however, was still a printed letter on a page. Unfortunately a correspondingly fast improvement in human comprehension has not been forthcoming. The composition of our brains is basically unchanged since the time of Adam & Eve. An a is an a, and always will be.

At the threshold of this new era in printing technology, one name stood out: Adrian Frutiger. The measurer and standard-setter of all things typographic. In his 1951 diploma submission, Adrian Frutiger produced nine wooden panels on which he had engraved, letter by letter, examples of Western alphabets – from Greek inscriptional capitals to humanistic minuscules and cursives. It was already apparent in this work that he was a master of space, proportion and order. It was clear even then that his career path would be characterised by his passion for the criteria of legibility and the beauty of form. During his time in France, typefaces such as *Méridien, Serifa, Iridium* and *Linotype Centennial* were produced, typefaces that captured the zeitgeist, and which are still proving their worth today.

Around the middle of the last century work began on the production of a typeface family with the name *Univers.* A system ordered and classified into 21 members was a totally new approach at the time. These 21 members would find their application in every area of use: from gracing posters to appearing on the smallest packaging leaflet. The first step in the generation of every printed product developed by a highly specialised profession is the choice of a typeface and its design. As much for movable type as for photosetting and the compositor, this typeface is still the lynchpin at the end of those 500 years. It represents both the end of an era and the beginning of a new one. If survival down the ages is an important criterion for art, then this is also true for the art of typography. And it is all the more true for a typographic art that neither displays nor has need of modish showiness.

With Adrian Frutiger there has always been a seamless transition between applied and fine art. The glyphs of his Indian typeface and of his logotypes have also been applied in his sculptures, reliefs and woodcuts in a free and unique manner. They spring from the same sense of form and strength of expression as his applied art. Everything that takes and assumes shape in his works has been filtered through his depth of knowledge and his power of thought. However, Adrian Frutiger has always remained a great, yet modest man, a man who, in his dedication to his work in the service of type and the word, and in his ceaseless invention in the form and material of his fine art works has been, and will remain, a standard-setter.

Adrian Frutiger
A typeface is a tool

Working with hot metal was my first experience of the power of type to make the whole world of thought legible simply by re-arranging the same letters over and over again. This made it clear to me that optimum readability should always be foremost when developing a typeface. But then we found ourselves in an era in which type was no longer set using lead characters, but with beams of light. Transforming the typefaces of the old masters from the old to the new process was the best learning experience for me. But when it came to the grotesques, I had an idea of my own. And from that idea arose the *Univers* family. Technical progress took a great leap forward. Moving typefaces to electronic representation brought with it the jaggies and later the vectorisation of the outlines. Given my sense of form, it was quite a painful experience. Now, though, with font creation programmes and their resolution-independent Bézier curves, and with lasersetting, it looks to me like our journey through the desert is finally over.

Other tasks fell to me. *OCR-B* set me the problem of designing characters that were readable not only to the human eye, but also to mechanical ones – something that stirred up, shall we say, an aesthetic conflict that taught me how to think about things in a different way. With the signage concepts for the airports and the Paris Métro I worked on large-scale typefaces. That's how I came to realise that, in all sizes, readability follows the same rules about counters and sidebearings. When I was asked to think about the Indian typefaces, this uncharted territory amazed me. Only when I began to write and draw the characters, did I become aware of the deep-seated connections between the Indo-European cultures. It took only a short time for me to grasp that my task consisted of imparting 500 years of Western experience in setting and printing technology. My Indian colleagues would have to find their own way forward from there.

The evolution of these letters – this continual simplification from symbol to sound – is something that has always preoccupied me. I was always fascinated by the symbol as the expression of a signature, a brand, and above all, a cipher. This connection between letters and symbols brought me into the commercial world of the logo as an area of operation. In the course of my working life I built up knowledge and skill. To impart those achievements and experiences to the next generation became the most important thing. In May 1968 the intellectual climate changed. In their impetuousness, the students pushed their craft to one side and tried to solve problems simply by force of intellect. I could never express myself only through words, without using my hands and the tools of my trade. So I have chronicled my legacy in my books, through my writing and my drawing.

On my career path I learned to understand that beauty and readability – and up to a certain point, banality – are close bedfellows: the best typeface is the one that impinges least on the reader's consciousness, becoming the sole tool that communicates the meaning of the writer to the understanding of the reader.

from *Adrian Frutiger. Denken und Schaffen einer Typographie*

The book that you are holding is the result of many conversations between myself and friends from the profession, conducted over a period of two years at my studio in Bremgarten near Bern. Erich Alb, Rudolf Barmettler and Philipp Stamm used their subtle but – at the same time – direct questioning and discussing to awake in me memories that, for years, had been deeply buried. For that I am grateful to them. We met once a month, and talked about my typeface design work in chronological order. It was almost like living my professional life all over again, beginning with the school in Zurich, through my time at Deberny &Peignot and then on to Linotype.

Without the discussions between specialists, my friends in the profession, and other advisors, this book would never have happened. My thanks go to Heidrun Osterer, Philipp Stamm, my above-mentioned colleagues, and to Silvia Werfel, who transformed the transcripts into proper German.

Introduction
How we made this book

This book is the product of a series of factors and happy coincidences. In 1999 Erich Alb, publisher of Syndor Press approached us to carry out the design of a book about the typographical work of Adrian Frutiger. We gladly agreed, little realising what the project would become – a task that would define our working lives for the next decade.

The project began in 1994, at a dinner held to celebrate a Linotype typeface competition, during the course of which Friedrich Friedl suggested during a conversation with Adrian Frutiger that he write his professional memoirs. Frutiger rose to the challenge and Syndor Press, publishers of Frutiger's books between 1996 and 2001, undertook the planning of a multi-volume edition. The first volume, which dealt with Frutiger's fine art works, appeared in 1998 under the title *Forms and Counterforms.* The content of the second volume, containing his typographical works, had burgeoned so much that we were brought in as designers.

During the development of the design concept we were faced with many questions regarding content, simply because our involvement in Adrian Frutiger's typeface creation runs so deep. Between 2001 and 2003, in a series of intensive discussions with Adrian Frutiger, Erich Alb, Rudolf Barmettler and Philipp Stamm analysed and examined the origins and development of each of his typefaces. These conversations were recorded on tape. In 2001 we undertook a month-long research journey through France, England and Germany, to gather as much material as possible from libraries, museums and antiquarian booksellers, as well as from public and private collections. We also sought out people who had worked with Adrian Frutiger or who were still in contact with him, and during the course of some long and wide-ranging interviews we deepened our knowledge of Adrian Frutiger's life's work.

In our discussions with Erich Alb we tried to exert a little more influence over the book's concept. This wasn't always successful, but the project was making progress – until the moment at the end of 2001 when Syndor Press was forced into liquidation. At that time we were already far more familiar with the deeper material, and after securing Erich Alb and Adrian Frutiger's agreement, decided to carry the project forward ourselves, becoming the book's authors as well as its designers.

The collected documents pertaining to Adrian Frutiger's work were transferred from Syndor Press in Cham to our offices in Basel, so that we would always have the originals at our disposal for consultation and reproduction. In order to get an overview of the material and to see how we were going to organise the chapters in the book, we began to form an archive of all the documents from Adrian Frutiger, as well as those that we had collected on our travels. The question was, of course, what would ultimately become of all this material? And so, starting in October 2002, during many meetings over the course of two years, a group of six people prepared the establishment of Swiss Foundation Type and Typography, whose founding member was to be Adrian Frutiger.

The work on the book continued in parallel. We started, basically, at the beginning, throwing out a lot of original concepts, and completely reworking the ideas for the design and contents. Only the size format of the first volume of the originally planned series was retained. We presented our ideas to Adrian Frutiger, Erich Alb and Rudolf Barmettler. The reaction was very positive, and, above all, Adrian Frutiger was grateful that his typographical work would be so comprehensively documented.

The setting up of the Foundation was well under way, and took up a lot of time and energy, so much so that the book was pushed somewhat into the background. But further research travels and interviews were also being conducted that enabled us to answer questions that were becoming ever more exacting and searching. The Linotype company opened up its archive and entrusted us with the remaining original design drawings of Adrian Frutiger's typefaces for Swiss Foundation Type and Typography. We undertook research into type design and history and re-appraised the material we had on hand. We had Adrian Frutiger's hot metal typefaces recast at Rainer Gerstenberg's in Darmstadt,

then set them as alphabets at a hand compositor's in Basel and printed them on barite paper. Our colleagues scanned in these typefaces and, over many hours, prepared them for the examples in the book. New typefaces by Adrian Frutiger for Linotype necessitated an ongoing enlargement of the book's scope. We also needed to find a publisher for the book and draw up a contract. And still the questions rolled in, and the discussions continued. There were many delays, and many clarifications were necessary – including the question of who was actually now the author of the book. Many people had a claim on that particular honour.

The book's continued existence was assured when the Foundation agreed to take on part of the costs – our design office had already almost come to a standstill because of it. The transcriptions of the interviews were edited by us before being sent to Silvia Werfel, a specialist journalist, who took Adrian Frutiger's words and translated them into flowing prose. In summer 2007, the publishing contract with Birkhäuser was finally signed, and we began to compose the ancillary texts that would frame Adrian Frutiger's typefaces against a background of typographic history and contemporary typographic design. As Silvia Werfel's texts came in, we gave them the finishing touches. At this point, with the solid support of our co-workers, the available material for the chapters had already been sounded out, sorted, and built into the layout.

That the project has come to a successful conclusion with the book you are now holding is due to many people. First and foremost, we must thank the extreme patience and good will of Adrian Frutiger, who read every chapter and gave his input on each of them. Furthermore, we would like to thank the Foundation, which continuously held our work up to scrutiny, but, in the end, backed us financially; Linotype, in whose company archives we were allowed to research at any time without hindrance; Silvia Werfel, who captured the nuances of Adrian Frutiger's speech, and whose transcripts provided an excellent foundation for the chapters; Erich Alb and Bruno Pfäffli, who scrupulously proofread the book using two very different approaches; the translators and proofreaders of the English and French editions, in particular Paul Shaw, who read the chapters in the already translated English version with a critical and scholarly eye – and who made small improvements here and there; Birkhäuser Verlag, for their appreciation and support of our work; and, naturally, our colleagues and co-workers, who, in spite of little compensation, have given us their committed support, and who transformed our ideas and supplemented them with their own. And let us not forget the worldwide support – be it moral or in the form of further information and documents – that we have encountered everywhere, and which gave us the strength to bring together the three available language editions of this work. It was planned to be published in time for Adrian Frutiger's 80th birthday in the spring of 2008 – but at least we managed it by autumn of the same year.

Basel, July 2008
Heidrun Osterer and Philipp Stamm

Introduction
How to use this book

Book structure
This book is divided into three sections: typeface chapters, explanations of typesetting technologies, and pages dedicated to logos. They have been ordered chronologically. In order to follow the development of Adrian Frutiger's type designs clearly, the typeface chapter sequence is based on the year of the design of the typeface, not of its publication or production; in many cases the dates are very widely separated. Since the designs are seldom dated, and the correspondence does not always provide the relevant information, in some cases the sequence cannot be definitively verified. In addition, many typefaces were developed in parallel.

Typeface chapter structure
The structure within the chapters themselves is largely chronological, from the conception of a typeface through to its development, publishing and marketing. For the analysis at the end of every chapter (sample text, typeface dimensions, typeface comparison, height comparison), the digital version of the typeface was used, since it contains the character sets of every available weight.

Chapter titles
Lowercase letters are not available in every one of Adrian Frutiger's typefaces. To maintain visual cohesion throughout the book all chapter titles were set in capitals.

Column titles
Adrian Frutiger's typefaces are classified as book typefaces, jobbing typefaces, signage typefaces, corporate typefaces and type-design projects. This classification can be found next to the page number. Additionally, logos, wordmarks and typeface production are similarly annotated.

Typesetting technology pages
Adrian Frutiger developed many of his typefaces in light of the then-current typesetting technologies, beginning with *Egyptienne F* through to *OCR-B* and to *Frutiger Neonscript*. So that readers who are not overly familiar with the technology may better understand the reasons behind a particular typeface design, the most important typesetting technologies have been given short descriptions in this book. Each technique is introduced before the typeface chapter where it is first used.

Logo pages
The myriad logos and wordmarks produced by Adrian Frutiger and his co-workers are extremely hard to date. Often the companies are no longer in business, or they do not keep an archive or record of such things. Often it is simply not possible to find out for whom a particular logo was designed, and whether it was indeed ever used. For this reason the logos are gathered together in unequal time periods on a single page. The arrangement and descriptions are as precise as the available information allows.

Wide text columns
These contain Adrian Frutiger's own words from the conversations with Erich Alb, Rudolf Barmettler und Philipp Stamm. The editors have checked the accuracy of the names, dates and other facts as far as possible, and have also expanded the information where necessary. Additionally, where necessary, the text has been supplemented with quotations by Frutiger from other sources.
The first-person text has been set in *Egyptienne F*. By doing this, this typeface – which had fallen somewhat out of fashion when it was chosen in 2002 – should reach a new audience. Indeed, in the last few years it has become a popular body text for magazines in Switzerland.

Narrow text columns
The text in these columns is set in the sober, geometric *Avenir*. Written by the editors, it illuminates the further interrelation of Adrian Frutiger's type design work with reference to context, creation and use. It also contains each typeface's history and technology.

Character set comparison
Each chapter contains a comparison of the character set in the original setting technology and in the digital font.

Sample text
As an illustration of the text image, each typeface available in digital form is given a page with trilingual sample text in various point sizes. The sizes are adjusted from chapter to chapter for optical consistency. The kerning and leading are harmonised with each other. The respective details are found underneath the sample text.

Typeface measured analysis
For typefaces with several weights, the proportions of height to width of the normal face are given as well as the black and oblique. For the calculation of the proportions a fixed cap height of 10 cm was chosen. The letter proportions of H n o were measured, along with the weight of vertical and horizontal strokes.

Typeface comparison
This compares Adrian Frutiger's typeface with two other similar typefaces from different designers. The choice of comparison typefaces was made according to similarities in character and form, as well as the year of creation. The printing typeface classification plays only a subsidiary role. Using the chosen characters, the differences between Adrian Frutiger's typefaces and the others are demonstrated.

Height comparison
In the more comprehensive chapters the typeface comparison is supplemented by a height comparison. For the measurement of typeface height (red figures), a cap height of 1 cm was used. Additionally, the proportional relationship of ascenders and descenders to the x-height is given (black figures).

Career path
Adrian Frutiger's teachers and mentors

Starting out

Adrian Frutiger was born on 24 May 1928 in Unterseen near Interlaken in Switzerland. He grew up as the second-youngest child, with his sister Charlotte and his brothers Roland and Erich. His mother, Johanna, a baker's daughter, raised the children and ran the household. His father Johann, son of a carpenter, was at this time employed in a draper's in Unterseen.[1] The village itself is cut off from Interlaken by the river Aare, and lies on the valley floor between Lake Brienz in the east and Lake Thun in the west. Towards the south stands the imposing mountain panorama of the Berner Alps, with the Eiger, Mönch and Jungfrau peaks; towards the north the foothills of the Alps proper dominate the horizon. The wider world seems distant, yet the proximity of fashionable Interlaken means it is never far away. In 1934 Adrian Frutiger's father opened a handloom workshop there, the Oberländer Webstube, whereupon the family moved to the health resort. Their house stood directly by the train tracks. To the rear could be seen a gasworks with its coal silos and loading cranes, and a little further away, the base station of a mountain cable car could be seen. Adrian Frutiger liked to look at this scenery through the window. With hindsight he has stated that this daily contact with all things mechanical – his passion for model traction engines and the interest in electricity that this awoke in him from an early age – proved to be a natural education. Even the simple Jacquard loom that his father inherited aroused his interest. This machine allowed semi-automatic weaving and, with the help of homemade punch cards, they were able to produce versions of the weaving samples that his father had collected over the years with a much finer warp and weft. Under its later name of Frutiger Heimtextil, the shop continued to be run by Frutiger's younger brother Erich until 2006. In the mid 1980s Adrian Frutiger designed the logo for the family company /01/, one of almost 100 logos and wordmarks he made during his career.

Frutiger's education began in 1935. His first school year did little to fire his enthusiasm. Adolescence, however, brought about a great transformation: he discovered the joys of reading, drawing and painting. The children's books of Ernst Eberhard, with their hand-drawn ink illustrations, especially captivated him. One of these stories centred on a boy who inherited a great deal of money through his willingness to help other people. This legacy enabled the boy to attend the Kunstgewerbeschule (School of Applied Arts) in Bern, and the story ended with the boy continuing his studies in far-off Italy. This story captured Adrian Frutiger's imagination so strongly that he wrote to Ernst Eberhard, who lived in Unterseen and worked as a secondary school teacher. The reply he received, with its invitation to visit, was written in a beautiful script that Adrian Frutiger started immediately to imitate. Eberhard advised him to observe more closely while drawing from nature. Through yearly visits to Eberhard, Adrian Frutiger's drawings received critical dissection. This father figure became his first mentor. In 1948, while Frutiger was working on his *Die Kirchen am Thunersee*, a deep friendship also developed with his former primary school teacher Franz Knuchel and his wife Leny. Inspired by them, he started reading classic literature. The works of Herman Hesse, particularly *Steppenwolf, Narcissus and Goldmund* and *The Glass Bead Game,* left a lasting impression on him. Even as a youth, Frutiger already displayed a desire to travel further and wider, although home still remained important to him. After living in Paris for nearly 20 years, he still gladly designed the dust jacket for the *Jahrbuch vom Thuner- und Brienzersee 1971*[2], at the request of Franz Knuchel.

At the end of secondary school, Adrian Frutiger's interest in type took firm root. Something in him rebelled against the stiff up-and-down strokes of the *Hulliger Schrift* /02/. This style of handwriting, developed by the Basel teacher Paul Hulliger was introduced into Basel schools in 1926, and by 1936 had been adopted by ten of Switzerland's 25 cantons. It is a reworking of Ludwig Sütterlin's handwriting style that had been used in German schools since 1911. Frutiger straightened the joined, rightward-sloping script, and modelled his own rounder, more flowing hand on the writing of Ernst Eberhard /03/.

At the age of 15, Adrian Frutiger decided on his career path, but his father was firmly set against the profession of a 'starving painter'. There was also no money available for a

Logo for Frutiger Heimtextil, designed in 1985 for the family weaving and cloth business in Interlaken.

/02/
At secondary school Frutiger learnt the Hulliger Schrift handwriting system, which was introduced in 1926 by the Basel schoolteacher Paul Hulliger.

/03/
Adrian Frutiger's handwriting at age 13 (top) and 15 (bottom) – it became more upright, more rounded and more fluid.

/04/
Die Kirchen am Thunersee –
*cover and double-page spread from
Adrian Frutiger's final submission
for his diploma in typesetting, 1948.*

Die Kirche von Leißigen

Wenn wir nun die einzelnen Gotteshäuſer am Thunerſee kurz betrachten wollen, ſo iſt es wohl am nützlichſten, wenn wir ſie ihrer geographiſchen Reihenfolge nach beſuchen.

Am obern Ende des Thunerſees, dem Morgenberghorn zu Füßen, liegt das ſchmucke Dörflein Leißigen. Mitten aus ſeinen Dächern und Baumkronen hervor erhebt ſich der ſtattliche Turm einer in vortrefflichem Stile erbauten Kirche. In ihrer einfachen und gefälligen Form diente ſie ſeinerzeit als Vorbild für die Kirchen der Schweizerdörfer an der Landesausſtellung in Genf 1896 und an der Weltausſtellung in Paris 1900.

Die Kirche von Leißigen zählt zu den älteſten im Bereiche des Thunerſees. Wohl iſt der heutige Bau erſt im Jahre 1675 entſtanden, aber er wird, wenn nicht in den Ausmaßen, ſo doch in ſeiner Form dem alten Vorbild nachgebaut worden ſein. Die Geſchichte dieſes Gotteshauſes und ſeines Kirchenſatzes reicht bis zurück in das 10. Jahrhundert. Sie ſoll 933 von König Rudolf II. von Burgund und ſeiner Gemahlin, der frommen Bertha von Alemannien, geſtiftet worden ſein als eine der zwölf Tochterkirchen von Einigen, deren gemeinſame Geſchichte wir ſpäter betrachten werden.

Den erſten Beſitzer dieſes Kirchenſatzes finden wir urkundlich im Jahre 1289 unter dem Namen Heinrich von Strättligen; dieſer verſchenkte ihn 1312 dem Kloſter Interlaken. In den Dokumenten-Büchern von Interlaken leſen wir Folgendes über dieſe Schenkung: „Johann, Heinrich und Ulrich von Strättligen, Herren zu Spiez, als wahre Patrone der Kirche zu Leuzingen, übergeben das Patronatsrecht dieſes Kirchenſatzes, um Gotteswillen und zu ihrem und aller Vorfahren

12

Schloßkirche Spiez

DIE
KIRCHEN
AM
THUNER
SEE

scholarship. The then-current economic uncertainty was surely at the forefront of his father's mind when he told his son, "first you learn a trade, then you can do what you want."[3] Adrian Frutiger had been supplementing his pocket money running errands for the Confiserie Deuschle in Interlaken, so it seemed an obvious choice to ask the owner for an apprenticeship. However, Eberhard persuaded him to take up a more artistic profession. Frutiger applied to Ernst Jordi, a friend of Eberhard, and head of the Otto Schlaefli Buch und Kunstdruckerei AG (a book and fine art printer) in Interlaken and was taken on. It shows a certain normality, that in neutral Switzerland in the middle of the Second World War, a 15-year-old could decide against an already set apprenticeship as a pastry maker. Adrian Frutiger accepted readily, but once again he met with opposition from his father, who thought that all members of the printing trades belonged to the ranks of 'the socialists'.

/05/
Textbook for typesetters from 1945, co-authored by Walter Zerbe, Adrian Frutiger's teacher at the Gewerbeschule in Bern.

During the four-year typesetting apprenticeship Adrian Frutiger visited the Gewerbeschule in Bern. On the recommendation of the school's governing body, the Otto Schlaefli Buch und Kunstdruckerei AG agreed to grant him an additional day a week at the school to study drawing and woodcuts. Adrian Frutiger stood out, "due to his conscientious approach to work, his remarkable creative faculties and his extraordinary initiative."[4] His typography teacher was Walter Zerbe, already well known for his book *Satztechnik und Gestaltung* /05/, written with Leo Davidshofer. Published in 1945 by the Bildungsverband Schweizerischer Buchdrucker (The Swiss Book Printers' Educational Association),[5] it was for many years the foremost Swiss textbook on typesetting.

During his apprenticeship Adrian Frutiger had already produced two publications. In the fourth year he produced *Die Rede des jungen Hediger*.[6] In the spring of 1948, at the Gewerbeschule, he presented as his final submission for his typesetting apprenticeship *Die Kirchen am Thunersee* /04/. Ernst Jordi, head of the printing company wrote the introduction: "This little work before you must be judged, first and foremost, as an independent creation in words and pictures – his journeyman's piece, as it were – of our young friend and colleague, Adrian Frutiger. On his journeys and walks, he has turned time and again to the homely, yet most beautiful building our small corner of the world, the church on Lake Thun. With much love and dedication he has drawn it, made woodcuts of it, and then immersed himself in its history. It fills us with joy and pride to be present at the birth of this small volume, and to have been able to lend a hand in its printing. We express the hope that with it, this young craftsman will have taken a first step, upon which he can further build, gradually to take his place in the realm of the arts. That he succeeds in this, I wish him with all my heart. God bless Art!"[7] The book was handset in Rudolf and Paul Koch's blackletter typeface *Claudius*.[8] Accompanied by Adrian Frutiger's 12 woodcuts, it was printed in a run of 1000 copies, 25 of which were bibliophile editions, linen-bound, individually numbered and coloured by hand. Additionally Adrian Frutiger also added the book's title in calligraphy by hand.[9]

/06/
Willow branch, designed by Adrian Frutiger in 1949 in the style of Chinese and Japanese woodcuts.

After the successful conclusion of his typesetting apprenticeship Adrian Frutiger took up a six-month position as a hand compositor at the well known printing plant Gebr. Fretz AG in Zurich. However, his goal was still entry into the Kunstgewerbeschule in the same city.

Enrichment

Shortly before his 21st birthday in early 1949, Adrian Frutiger began his further education. After Max B. Kämpf,[10] Frutiger was the second student at the Kunstgewerbeschule in Zurich who wanted to study type design. (Another, earlier Zurich student who went on to become a type designer had been Hans Eduard Meier, whose *Syntax Antiqua* was issued in 1968.) During the week, Frutiger attended various type design courses given by Alfred Willimann. After a short time, he asked that his timetable be changed to enable him to attend Walter Käch's courses for lettering as well. In addition he attended classes in other specialist areas, like still life, life and perspective drawing. But he was most drawn to Karl Schmid's

/07/
Inscriptional capitals, carved in stone in 1949 by Adrian Frutiger during his further education as a type designer in Zurich.

Nicolas Jenson's roman typeface from 1470 – the balance of the text image was an example for Adrian Frutiger.

qui omnibus ui aquarum submersis cum filiis suis simul ac nuribus mirabili quodā modo quasi semen huāni generis conseruatus est:quē utinā quasi uiuam quandam imaginem imitari nobis contingat:& hi quidem ante diluuium fuerunt:post diluuium autem alii quorū unus altissimi dei sacerdos iustitiæ ac pietatis miraculo rex iustus lingua he‑ bræorū appellatus est:apud quos nec circuncisionis nec mosaicæ legis ulla mentio erat . Quare nec iudæos(posteris eni hoc nomen fuit)neq; gentiles:quoniam non ut gentes pluralitatem deorum inducebant sed hebræos proprie noiamus aut ab Hebere ut dictū est:aut qa id nomen transitiuos significat.Soli qppe a creaturis naturali rōne & lege inata nō scripta ad cognitionē ueri dei trāsiere:& uoluptate corporis cōtépta ad rectam uitam pueniisse scribunt:cum quibus omibus præclarus ille totius generis origo Habraam numerādus est:cui scriptura mirabilem iustitiā quā non a mosaica lege(septima eim post Habraā generatione Moyses nascitur)sed naturali fuit ratione consecutus sūma cum laude attestatur.Credidit enim Habraam deo & reputatū est ei in iustitiam. Quare multarum quoq; gentium patrem diuina oracula futurū:ac in ipso benedicēdas oés gentes hoc uidelic& ipsum quod iam nos uideūs aperte prædictum est:cuius ille iustitiæ perfectioém non mosaica lege sed fide cōsecutus est:qui post multas dei uisiones legittimum genuit filium:quem primum omnium diuino psuasus oraculo circūcidit:& cæteris qui ab eo nascerétur tradidit:uel ad manifestum multitudinis eorum futuræ signum:uel ut hoc quasi paternæ uirtutis isigne filii re‑ tinétes maiores suos imitari conaret':aut qbuscūq; aliis de causis.Non enim id scrutādum nobis modo est.Post Habraam filius eius Isaac in pietate successit:fœlice hac hæreditate a parétibus accæpta:q uni uxori coniunctus quum geminos genuisset castitatis amore ab uxore postea dicitur abstinuisse.Ab isto natus é Iacob qui ,ppter cumulatū uirtutis prouétum Israel etiam appellatus est duobus noibus ,ppter duplicem uirtutis usū.Iacob eim athletā & exercétem se latine dicere possumus: quam appellatione primū habuit:quū practicis operatioibus multos pro pietate labores ferebat.Quum auté iam uictor luctando euasit:& speculationis fruebat'bonis:tūc Israelem ipse deus appellauit æterna premia beatitudinéq; ultimam quæ in uisione dei consistit ei largiens: hominem enim qui deum uideat Israel nomen significat. Ab hoc.xii. iudæorum tribus ,pfectæ sūt.Innumerabilia de uita istorum uirorum fortitudine prudentia pietateq; dici possunt:quorum alia secundum scripturæ uerba historice considerantur:alia tropologice ac allegorice interpretāt':de qbus multi cōscripserūt:& nos in libro quē inscripsiūs

76

botanical drawings and woodcuts /06/. In autumn 1949, Frutiger began engraving inscriptional capitals in smoothly worn pebbles from the river Sihl /07/.

Adrian Frutiger's calligraphy teacher, Alfred Willimann, was a sculptor, graphic artist and typographical designer who had been lecturer for drawing and lettering at the Kunstgewerbeschule in Zurich since 1930. He was also deeply involved in the well known photography class given by Hans Finsler.[11] Willimann was self-taught in several fields. Due to financial and familial constraints he could only complete one year at the Kunstgewerbeschule in Zurich. In his notes Adrian Frutiger wrote: "When I presented Alfred Willimann with my little book about the churches, he greeted me with a good-natured smile and said something like: 'you really are from the old typesetters' guild, and are spoiling it already for the artists'. He ignored me for a week after that … I followed him anyway to all four preparation classes that were held every four hours and were obligatory for each student. I listened to him, and looked over his shoulder when he was explaining calligraphy to the others at their desks. I was astounded at this glimpse into a new world of understanding lettering, so very different from what I had learned as a compositor at the Gewerbeschule. My first weeks in Zurich were like being in a maze. Everything that I had learned as a compositor and woodcut artist seemed so squalid and naïve, parochial and, well, a bit kitschy. My first encounter with Willimann had left my youthful pride in my work severely dented; I only realised later that he did it on purpose, to give me a wake up call, to get me fired up from the very start."[12] Alfred Willimann's teaching built on the history of lettering, which he illustrated with examples. He drew the historic scripts with a piece of chalk held flat against the board, imitating a broad-nib pen and then explained the pen grip, the drawing of the stroke and the rhythm of the various script examples. For him calligraphy meant a sort of two-dimensional architecture, as Frutiger once described it. For Alfred Willimann the essence of calligraphy was not building up the black, but rather covering the white, so that the light of the white page remains alive. That light, that white from the counters and sidebearings, would, in time, become an important aspect of Adrian Frutiger's entire work as a type designer. Under Willimann's teaching he also learned to understand the quality of the downstrokes. So that these contain tension and life, pressure must be applied at both the beginning and end of the stroke, without the stroke ends becoming flat. /12/. The result of this waisted stroke can also be found in some of Adrian Frutiger's type designs.

In contrast to Alfred Willimann, Walter Käch /13/ graduated from a course of several years study in graphic design at the Kunstgewerbeschule in Zurich after completion of an apprenticeship as a lithograph. Towards the end of his studies in 1920, three of the greatest European personalities, who brought about the definitive upheaval in typographic teaching and education at the beginning of the 20th century, were lecturing in Zurich. It was a singular stroke of luck for Walter Käch that Fritz Helmut Ehmcke, Rudolf von Larisch and Anna Simons were in Zurich for one year. Thanks to Anna Simons, a former student of Edward Johnston, Johnston's seminal 1906 work, *Writing and Illuminating and Lettering*,[13] was available in German after 1910. Anna Simons' translation was titled *Schreibschrift, Zierschrift & Angewandte Schrift*.[14] The Austrian Rudolf von Larisch was also responsible for many books on calligraphy and lettering, amongst them the standard work *Unterricht in ornamentaler Schrift*[15] first published in 1905. The title emphasises Larisch's basic approach to writing: understanding letters as a medium for graphic expression. Edward Johnston and Anna Simons put more emphasis on the role of readability in calligraphy. The graphic artist and type designer Fritz Helmut Ehmcke, from Germany like Anna Simons, was well known as an author of books on lettering. One of them was *Ziele des Schriftunterrichts*,[16] published in 1911. At the end of the 1921 academic year, Walter Käch accompanied Ehmcke to the Kunstgewerbeschule in Munich, and stayed there for a year as his assistant. From 1925 to 1967 (with a break between 1929 to 1940) Walter Käch lectured in Zurich on type and lettering.[17] He subsequently published two standard works on type design: in

/09/
Alfred Willimann, Adrian Frutiger's teacher in the history and practice of lettering at the Kunstgewerbeschule in Zurich.

/10/
Wordmarks by Alfred Willimann for the carpenter and joiner Karl Steiner (top), for Lignoplast (middle) and for the paint manufacturer Gromalto (bottom).

ALT,
RÓMISCHE
PORTRÄT
PLASTIK

/11/
Poster title by Alfred Williman for a 1953 exhibition on Roman portrait sculpture at the Kunsthaus Zurich, designed using inscriptional capitals.

In Vereinbarung, allen dasselbe bedeutend, fügen sich Zeichen zu Wort und Satz, einem Gedanken zugeordnet. Andernfalls bedeuten die Zeichen im Raum, — zum Bild das immer konkret eine Massbeziehung darstellt.

Das Schreibwerkzeug, die Breitfeder, ex wenn fein ~~~ zu breit, zeichnet je nach Federstellungswinkel den Typ. gewicht ausgleichend bei 25°, verhält sich Vertikal — zu Horizontal — Zug, wie Stamm zu Ast.

Federstellung steil mittel flach Die Feder, ohne Druck geführt, zeigt im Freilauf einen leichten Einzug, ihrer konstruktion entsprechend, dadurch entstehen sichere, kräftige Flächen

auswirkend von Stützfuss — mit Druck fliessen die

fangen an, es entsteht ein Senkfuss, die Flächen wirken weich und wankend. durch die auszeichnenden charakterisierenden Serifen (Ober + unter Endungen) sind

Akzente und reflektieren je nach Einsatz mit starker oder schwacher Resonanz,

ebenso aktiv auf die Gelenke, es sind Angeln. zentral, versteckt umwindend, abgleitend

Vom Einsatz aus sind die Schriften aktiv, sie bilden und regulieren als Widerstände das vorgesehene Lichtbild.

Situation ist der Raum, komponiere sind Senkrechte, Waagrechte, Quadrat, Punkt, Strich, Zeichen, Wort, Zeilen. Kolumnen sind Einheiten, die kompress LINIE HALTEN oder ausgeglichen LINIE HALTEN auf Titel oder mehreren Satz angewendet, ordnend wirken. Bild-Teil um Buch-Teil fertigen, das ist die Gegenwart, das Wirksame beachten in Berücksichtigung des Einzelwerk auf das Gesammte.

/12/
Instructions for correct lettering by
Alfred Willimann, from his lettering
course at the Kunstgewerbeschule
in Zurich.

ADRIAN FRUTIGER   17

1949, as Frutiger's further education was beginning, the ring-bound *Schrift Lettering Écritures /17/*, and in 1956, *Rhythmus und Proportion in der Schrift / Rhythm and Proportion in Lettering /14/*.[18]

Walter Käch divided the text sections of his first book into chapters on written script and drawn script. For the drawn scripts he demonstrated the tracing of the outlines of a script using illustrated examples. Using Roman Imperial capitals as a model, he contrasted correctly and incorrectly drawn sans serif capitals /16/. Adrian Frutiger adopted many of the form-giving principles described in the book. They were instrumental in shaping his canonical forms. He also fell back on his teacher's knowledge and insight when it came to the optical rules governing his letter shapes, refining them gradually, and culminating in 1953's *Univers*. However, Adrian Frutiger and Walter Käch did not always see eye to eye. "One thing that always stirred up confrontation was the concept of rhythm in a line of text. Referring to an enlargement of Nicolas Jenson's antiqua, I tried to demonstrate that the counters and sidebearings were of equal weight," Frutiger later said. "It seemed to me that Jenson, like Gutenberg, had adopted a grid system as a framework. Käch didn't agree. He taught that the sidebearings should be kept narrower, which is certainly valid for signwriting. My thoughts, however, lay in the direction of typefaces for reading. I later drew all my serif typefaces according to this concept, to avoid irregularity in the text flow."[19] Frutiger's appreciation for Nicolas Jenson's roman /08/, designed in Venice in 1470, was a result of his study under Alfred Willimann. For Frutiger it was the regularity of the text image and not the individual letter shapes that is paramount. The quality lies in the interplay of form and counterform. "The letters should stand next to each other like links in a chain,"[20] he has said.

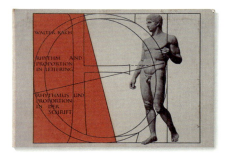

Both Willimann and Käch had a different outlook on type design, said Adrian Frutiger. Both, however, based their principles on the history of lettering. Alfred Willimann often drew his wordmarks and titles on type in a linear sans serif /10/. His historical reference point was the antique Greek and Roman inscriptional capitals from the 5th to the 2nd century BC, based on the elementary shapes of circle, square, triangle and double square /11/. Walter Käch followed a completely different path in his teaching of lettering. He used as a model the Roman uncial and half-uncial of the 4th and 5th centuries AD, the letter widths of which exhibit a unifying principle /15/. This harmonisation of the proportions can also be found in the sans serifs of the 19th century, such as *Akzidenz Grotesk*. Walter Käch defined the symmetry of a letter on a grid to be a guiding principle. Stylistically, these were static scripts with square, oval and triangle as their elementary forms. The stroke contrast in the scripts is more pronounced than in the inscriptional letters. As with the uncials – drawn with a shallow pen angle – the curves terminate the letter shape. The curve ending in Käch's letters are therefore horizontally terminated /17/, which was a novelty in contrast to the majority of the grotesques that existed at the time. It is a characteristic that can also be seen in Adrian Frutiger's sans serif design /19/, drawn in 1950–51, under Käch's supervision. In 1953 at Deberny & Peignot in Paris, this design formed the basis for the *Univers* typeface concept. "In my head, I always had this idea of completeness. And that had already started forming under Käch. Käch had taught us how to think in terms of typeface families."[21] With his first grotesque, Frutiger had gone beyond Käch's ideas. He changed and considerably refined the typeface and, at Emil Ruder's suggestion, opened out the counters. With his second grotesque, *Concorde*, designed 1961–64 in conjunction with André Gürtler, the differentiated letter proportions owed more to Alfred Willimann's understanding of lettering.

Adrian Frutiger brought his further education at the Kunstgewerbeschule in Zurich to a close with his final diploma submission, which he had worked on for nearly a year. Like Max B. Kämpf he took as his subject the history of lettering, and cut 15 historical scripts, reversed out on nine wooden plates /18/. In order to get the stress of the strokes exactly right, he first drew the scripts in the usual manner on well-sized paper, then fixed

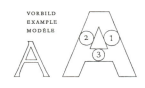

Cover and inner pages of Walter Käch's 1949 textbook Schriften Lettering Écritures, showing drawn sans serifs.

/18/
Adrian Frutiger's 1951 final diploma submission for the Kunstgewerbeschule in Zurich – woodcut (top, reduced by approx. 50 %), accompanying booklet (left).

/19/
Sans serif design in three weights by Adrian Frutiger, produced during 1950–1951 under the direction of Walter Käch – india ink on Bristol board, original size.

hf ff

f f f

pimq

y y y y

nzxy

Febr. 1950

Nomenst

anse

budong p

bdpqg

vomwar

this onto the beech wood boards and transferred the images of the letters onto the wood by applying pressure in an etching press. In 1951 this diploma submission was published in Zurich by the Bildungsverband Schweizerischer Buchdrucker, under the title *Schrift Écriture Lettering,* with a short introductory text by Alfred Willimann in three languages. This work, printed as an accordion book, formed the second stage – in attaining the wish expressed by Ernst Jordi – that Adrian Frutiger could subsequently build upon. The diploma submission enabled him to take his first step into the future – to Paris. He sent the work out to specialists in the field and also as an example of his work to various type foundries in Europe. He received a contract for a year's employment from Charles Peignot, owner of Fonderies Deberny & Peignot in Paris. At that time Adrian Frutiger had no idea that Peignot was in need of a type designer who could contribute to the development of the Lumitype photosetting machine. In the end he would spend more than eight years at Deberny & Peignot and, altogether, 40 in France.

Passing the baton

Late in the summer of 1952 Adrian Frutiger started his job as a type designer at Deberny & Peignot, which was, at that time, one of the most respected type foundries in Europe. *Méridien,* his first major text typeface, was designed between 1954 and 1957 after *Initiales Président,* his first jobbing typeface, and several type designs that were never completed. *Méridien* was a latin style. Charles Peignot and his son, Rémy, encouraged Frutiger in the direction of this French typeface style. It was a very intense period for Frutiger: for one thing, he was able to put to use everything that he had learned, and for another, it gave him the opportunity continually to broaden his knowledge and experience in typeface production, first in hot metal, and then, from 1954 onwards, in phototypesetting.

In 1952, while he was still employed at Deberny & Peignot, Adrian Frutiger started teaching at the École Estienne, a vocational college for the graphic arts. The head of the school, Robert Ranc, was a friend of Charles Peignot, and employed Frutiger at the beginning to give an evening course. Later, the teaching of type and typography was expanded, and in addition Frutiger also found himself teaching at the École Nationale Supérieure des Arts Décoratifs. Altogether, it came to a day and a half teaching per week. Frutiger divided his teaching into three areas: the history of lettering and writing, drawing typefaces, and the design of signs and symbols. This teaching eventually gave rise to the *Signs and Symbols* trilogy [23] /23/, edited by Horst Heiderhoff, which offered an introductory discussion about symbols. In the first volume, published in 1978, Frutiger wrote, "… symbols that do not have enclosed areas awake in us more abstract feelings, while those with enclosed areas awake in us memories of objects."[24] To press the point home, he used the cross as an example of an abstract symbol that allows no spatial interpretation. He contrasted this with the square, which immediately offers a representation of an enclosure or cube /22/. Frutiger shared his knowledge in many other books such as *Type Sign Symbol*[25] /23/ (1980). In addition there have been countless articles and many lectures by Frutiger, all characterised by an easily understandable and succinct presentation of the subject. This quality has always marked his thinking. At the same time, there is a simplicity and directness in his books, even when detail and depth are needed.

Adrian Frutiger first became known internationally with the *Univers* typeface concept, which, beginning in 1953, he had derived from his earlier design for a grotesque /19/. For the first time, a typeface family had been developed at one time. Emil Ruder, the well-known typographer, teacher, and later director of the Allgemeine Gewerbeschule Basel (School of Applied Art), acted as mentor to Adrian Frutiger during this family's creation. Frutiger had already met him during his further education, in the course of an exchange of ideas and critical appraisals of work and projects. Ruder, became for Frutiger another mentor and father figure. "His influence on my work as a type designer was decisive. At each one of our meetings, he was my point of reference," Frutiger has said. "In appreciation and

criticism he was always constructive, encouraging, but always with an eye to what he termed classical. His goal was to always respect the deep humanity of the past, to refrain from overly personal touches, to always work towards the possibility of purity, which still retained something for the future. Emil Ruder knew this and was able to achieve it, and I'm eternally grateful to him for it. It gave me joy and satisfaction when, years after the meetings about my first designs, he brought out all of them in typographical creations in hot metal."[26] Together with his students in the typography course at the Kunstgewerbe-schule in Basel, Emil Ruder contributed much to the success of *Univers*. Another contributor was Rudolf Hostettler, the editor of the magazine *Typographische Monatsblätter,* which was published by the printing union. The typeface concept was comprehensively covered in the *Univers Special Edition* 1/1961 /21/. Beginning with this edition, the Monotype version of *Univers* was adopted as the sole typeface for *TM,* and remained so for many years. Emil Ruder's standard work, *Typographie – ein Gestaltungslehrbuch / Typography – A Manual of Design,* published in 1967 in three languages, was also set using *Univers.* Frutiger wrote the foreword.

Adrian Frutiger has subsequently gone on to further expand his wealth of experience in the field of type design. He has always been involved in the most important new type-setting technologies, be it with the Lumitype photosetting machine, for which he reworked classic typefaces and designed his own, or with the ECMA,[28] for whom, starting in 1963, he developed the machine-readable typeface *OCR-B,* or with the strike-on types for IBM's golfball Selectric Composer, or, from 1968 onwards, with the various digital typesetting procedures at Linotype. At age 42, challenges, like the development of the signage and orientation systems at Charles de Gaulle airport at Paris-Roissy, set in motion a fundamental analysis of symbol recognition. The typeface *Alphabet Roissy* first appeared in 1970, and became the benchmark for all other signage typefaces. In 1976 Linotype released it in a reworked form as *Frutiger.* In conjunction with his co-workers and the various typeface manufacturers, there have appeared, to date, 12 jobbing and 27 body typefaces, eight signage typefaces and five corporate typefaces. An important part of Frutiger's body of work also consists of designs that never made it into production.

The typefaces – especially the body typefaces – of Adrian Frutiger exhibit recurrent traits that are characteristic of him. Above all it is the text image that is characterised by balance and symmetry. As he has said in conversation, "You could call it a style, a personal form convention, that I can't encapsulate; neither can I say, without difficulty, where it actually comes from. A mixture of the cross between the two personalities who were my teachers, and of course, my personality is in there somewhere. A mix. And the luck, that the mixing of the Germanic with the Latin produced such a personal expression."[29]

Production of type
Handsetting

With his invention in 1455 of setting and printing moveable type (known in Korea since the 14th century), Johannes Gutenberg revolutionised the very nature of type design and printing, a technological shift that started in Germany. His method of producing letters and printing was hardly improved upon until well into the 19th century. It created a whole new industry – printing – which divided itself into further sub-industries over time: type foundries appeared, along with case rooms, printing plants and other sub-contractors, who, amongst other things, produced printing presses, papers, inks and related tools.

At Deberny & Peignot, Frutiger's employers, typeface production started with original drawings /01/. They were produced with a cap height of around 10 cm, right-reading, with India ink on white bristol board. Every character received the necessary width and weight. As a test of quality and overall impression, the original drawings would be photographically reduced and assembled into words. Then the original drawings would be corrected with opaque white paint and India ink until the reduced sample would meet all expectations in terms of potential word combinations and form a perfect image.

In the next stage of the process, the matrix – the master mould for the cast letters – was prepared. There were three different production methods for this stage. In the first, the punched matrix, the final artwork, was photographically reduced to the final letter size, etched onto a zinc plate. Then, using a transparent sheet of gelatine, its mirror image would be transferred onto the raw, polished face of the steel slug. Finally, the letter contours were directly hand-engraved on the steel slug, and the raised letter produced using files, gravers and counterpunches. To check the appearance of the letter, a smoke proof was prepared. The steel letter, known as a punch, was held over a candle flame to blacken it. Pressed onto a sheet of paper, it gave a precise image of the letter. If this passed muster, the hardening of the punch took place. It was then punched into a block of copper /04/. The result was the master mould of the letter: the matrix. This is a variation on the oldest form of matrix production.

The second method, known as a galvanic matrix, began with hand engraving of the letter image onto a soft lead slug. Since the face could not be struck into metal, the 'master punch' with the definitive face was then suspended in a galvanic nickel bath. The application of an electric current caused metallic nickel to be deposited onto the letter shape /07/. The resulting negative letter shape was cast into a zinc block and thus turned into the matrix for letter casting /08/. This is the method that Frutiger encountered at Deberny & Peignot.

In the third procedure, the drilled matrix (a brass plate), onto which the letter image has been engraved, served as the template. The brass plate was clamped into a pantograph, with a metal slug at its other end. The deep outline of the letter, engraved into the brass template, would be traced using the pantograph's guide stylus, and a sharp drill would cut the corresponding letter into the metal slug. The

/01/
Original drawing for Univers (India ink on bristol board) with guide lines for hand setting by Deberny & Peignot.

/02/
Photographic enlargement of the original drawing, glued to card stock, and a brass template taken from the cardboard template.

/03/
By tracing the brass template with a pantograph, the letter image is replicated as a reduced-scale matrix.

/04/
Drilled and cleaned-up steel punches, struck and finished copper matrices and cast letters (right to left).

desired point size of the resulting letter could be dialled into the pantograph beforehand. Several point sizes could be produced from a single template. This method was extremely common, since it was very economical. It brought with it technical compromises, however. No matter how fine the drill, it was not possible to cut right or acute angles with full precision. These would have to be worked on later by hand /06/. Raised letter images could also be cut with a pantograph. These could then be sent for galvanising to produce matrices. An embossed brass block served as a template /05/.

Once produced, the matrices were adjusted to ensure that the negative impressions had a uniform depth across the matrix and the baseline was parallel to the narrow edge of the lead slug. The matrix had to be worked to an accuracy of 100th of a millimetre. Here a gauge needle provided much-needed help for making sensitive measurements.

After the matrices were prepared, the casting of the lead letters took place. In the mid-19th century me-chanical casting machines replaced the earlier hand-casting methods. Eventually, fully automatic casting machines appeared, which could not only cast the letters at great speed, but also automatically ejected the sprue and cleaned and polished the edges of the cast letter. Such a machine could produce up to 40000 letters a day Overshoots (letters that extended beyond the lead slug) were still difficult to cast and to set, since they broke so easily. They were useful for letter kerning, so that there was not too much whitespace between the letters. These were employed particularly in the italics, but also in single letters of regular typefaces, for example T or f.

The cast letters were ready to be set. An alphabet for hand composition consisted of some 120 characters. Normally, a compositor could set around 1500 characters at 10 pt in an hour. This performance was reduced with smaller point sizes or with complex texts. In time, methods were sought to improve the speed of hand composition. Larger type drawers as well as the ordering of the character compartments according to letter frequency contributed to an increase in output. Additionally, not only ligatures were cast, but also logotypes, i.e. commonly used words and syllables on a single slug. In the Wiener Staats-druckerei a system was used that required 1248 separate compartments on the type drawer. In Gutenberg's time, the setters were capable of a far lower output. However, with a type tray comprising 290 characters, including varying weights and accented characters, as well as ligatures for letter pairs, a subtler level of typography was possible.

Frutiger also authored an article on letter-punch production at Deberny & Peignot (see page 99).

/05/
The shape of the letter is traced around the raised template; and then the punch is cut by milling.

/06/
The corners of the pantograph-milled punch have to be cleaned up by hand using a graver.

/07/
Galvanic matrix: master type punch (left) and raw matrix after ten-day galvanic nickel bath (right).

/08/
Reverse-cast and cleaned nickel matrix (left) and cast letter slugs (right).

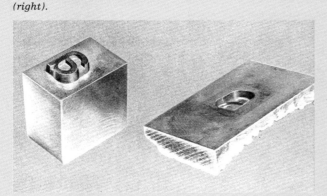

Name of typeface	Commissioned by	Designer	Design | Publication	Typesetting technology	Manufacturer	Weights
Initiales Président	Deberny & Peignot	Adrian Frutiger	1952 | 1954	Handsetting	– Deberny & Peignot	1
President•				Photon-Lumitype photosetting	– Deberny & Peignot | Photon Inc.	1
				CRT and laser digital typesetting	– D. Stempel AG | Linotype•	1
				PostScript digital typesetting	– Linotype•	1
					URW++•	1

PRÉSIDENT

I arrived in Paris with a lust for life and a backpack full of knowledge in the late summer of 1952. That was quite some luggage that Alfred Willimann and Walter Käch had given me during my time at the Kunstgewerbeschule (School of Arts and Crafts) in Zurich. I had sent my diploma thesis[1] to around a dozen major European type foundries. Thus Charles Peignot employed me and I received a contract for a year.

When I started at Deberny & Peignot, the foundry depended 80% on *Futura,* which at that time was called *Europe* in France. There were also many fantasy typefaces, shaded and outlined ones. What was missing was a new business card typeface. The salesmen said that such a typeface had to be designed first, because all the old ones were worn out, although they remained one of the safest investments. Smaller printers in particular had a steady demand for them. At the time the mostly all capitals business card typefaces were known in France as 'Initiales'.[2] That was the first kind of typeface I made for D&P.

There were around ten different Latin faces[3] in the D&P type specimen book. I oriented myself around the *Latins Larges /09/* for my design for *Président.* Something other than a Latin was out of the question. I worked intensively on it, as I didn't yet know the shapes but found them fascinating. Latins were used primarily for jobbing type, particularly for letterheads and business cards but also for shop front signs /04/. It almost became fashionable for grocery shops to use Latins /03/. Their advantage was that one could engrave or paint them broad or narrow, thick or thin. Like sans serif typefaces they were easy to modify. Latins originated around the mid-19th century as a softer kind of *Didot.* Their serifs weren't placed at right angles, they had a concave bracket. In the Art Nouveau era there were numerous variations with much frippery, including at D&P. The lowercase c for example had an inward-facing hook, and wherever possible letters had tails curling inward /09/.

Président is a kind of remake. It wasn't about trying to invent a new style of typeface. Deberny & Peignot basically needed a cleanly cut business card typeface with a regular, almost strong weight. The contrast between thick and thin strokes in *Président* is somewhat less than that of a Latin – business card typefaces do require a certain amount of strength. Charles Peignot let me get on with it. He did, however, request letter variations right from the start /22/. A typesetter must be allowed some space to play, he would say. He also wanted ligatures, superiors for abbreviations and logotypes; in other words, for frequent use, blocks cast for terms such as 'Rue', 'Avenue', 'Boulevard' or 'Place' /01/. That was something new – he really cared about making typesetters' work easier.

First I drew a few letters on tracing paper with a sharp pencil, an H, two to three vowels, three to four consonants. There was no 'OHamburgefons' like there was later in Germany. The designs were roughly 24 point size. At that size I could control the shape at a glance. That became my typical way of working. Next to my studio was the block makers'

About Président   With his very first alphabet, the all-capitals *Initiales Président,* Adrian Frutiger created an enduring and mature work. The name of the typeface, chosen by Charles Peignot, is hardly presumptuous when compared with those of other typefaces; the Flinsch foundry[4] had the likes of *Aristokrat, Baron, Baronesse, Kavalier,* and the Haas'sche Schriftgiesserei AG had one called *Chevalier.*

The *Initiales Président* shapes are based on those of Latin typefaces. Frutiger names them *Latins Larges /09/.* It is also worth referring to the *Caractères Antiques Latinés /08/,* a kind of sans serif with triangular reinforced terminals. Like *Président,* it has little stroke contrast.

In Francis Thibaudeau's 1924 type classification /07/, Latins are classed as a subdivision of Elzévirs[5], which encompassed all the venetian and transitional romans. The neoclassical romans named after Didot comprise the second of four principle groups. The two other principle groups, Egyptienne and Grotesque – the latter called Antique[6] in France – represent (along with Latins) the considerable innovations in type creation of the 19th century.

'Elzévirs' is also used in the illustration for the index title page 'Latins' in volume 2 of the type specimen book *Spécimen Général* of the Fonderies Deberny & Peignot from 1926.[7] The reference to the index of the same name in volume 1 shows, however, that Latin types, as improvements on neoclassical romans, represented a return to the older art of type creation. Latins can, in part, be regarded in the context of the neo-renaissance reform movement[8] that in the 19th century sought to move away from dispassionate, classicist-influenced book typography.

In German-speaking countries, Latins played no role whatsoever by the time of Frutiger's apprenticeship in the 1940s and 50s. In France, however, they remained up to date. *Initiales Président,* made as a jobbing typeface by Deberny & Peignot for foundry type in 1954 and adapted in 1965 to Photon-Lumitype photosetting is not Frutiger's only Latin typeface. Today it is sold in digital form by the type manufacturers Linotype as well as by URW++ under the name of *President.*

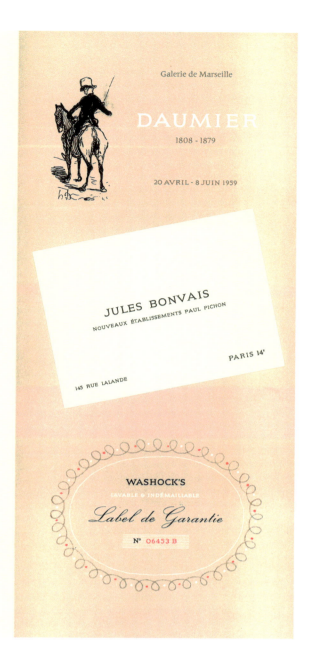

LA NATURE EST UN TEMPLE
OU DE VIVANTS PILIERS LAISSENT PARFOIS SORTIR
DE CONFUSES PAROLES: L'HOMME Y PASSE
A TRAVERS DES FORÊTS DE SYMBOLES QUI L'OBSERVENT
AVEC DES REGARDS FAMILIERS.

CHARLES BAUDELAIRE

c 24   **SERVICES**

c 20   **EXÉCUTION**

c 16   **LES CAVALIERS**

c 12 - 1   **BIEN COMPRENDRE**

c 12 - 2   **UNE PERFECTION DANS**

c 12 - 3   **UN ÉQUIPEMENT RATIONNEL**

c 8 - 1   **DES CARACTÈRES JUDICIEUSEMENT**

c 8 - 2   **FONDEURS CONSCIENCIEUX ET EXPÉRIMENTÉS**

c 8 - 3   **PAREILLEMENT ÉQUIPÉ VOUS AUREZ UN RENDEMENT ACCRU**

Dans le corps 8 œils 2 et 3 pour faciliter la composition et améliorer
les approches nous avons fondus les noms blocs suivants:

RUE	AVENUE	BOULEVARD	PLACE
double	supérieures	sortes crénées	
LA	EILMORST	A V V W Y	

Galerie de Marseille

DAUMIER
1808 - 1879

20 AVRIL - 8 JUIN 1959

JULES BONVAIS
NOUVEAUX ÉTABLISSEMENTS PAUL PICHON

PARIS 14ᵉ

145 RUE LALANDE

WASHOCK'S
LAVABLE & INDÉMAILLABLE
Label de Garantie
Nº 06453 B

/01/
*Inside pages of the four-page
brochure* Le Président *from 1958
with specimen text, available
weights and an example of use.*

/02/
*Deberny & Peignot stall at
the TPG trade fair of 1956 in Paris –
lettering in* Initiales Président.

/04/
*Wide, high-contast Latin typeface
from the 19th century on
a wall in Paris – 'Bill posters
prohibited'.*

ÉPICERIE - COMESTIBLES
Volailles & Gibiers

/03/
*In the late 19th century
Latin typefaces were very popular
for company stationery and for
shop fronts.*

department, there they also had repro equipment. I normally asked if I could quickly stick my sketches in the enlarger. Afterwards I would trace the shapes by hand with India ink on board, correcting with white opaque paint. Always without a compass. These black and white drawings were at least 10 cm in size. Any smaller would have been too fiddly to manage. They had to be roughly the size of an apple or other fruit to be really workable. That's what I was taught by Walter Käch at the Kunstgewerbeschule in Zurich.

With *Président* I had everything reduced to 24 point, which I then stuck together in order to see if it worked. I would straight away determine character width, side bearings and optical baseline, once again a discipline that Walter Käch had taught me. So I delivered clean drawings for about ten test letters, after which one brass template was engraved for the small to medium font sizes and another one for the large ones. They were drawn differently; the small sizes were a bit heavier and the larger ones a bit thinner. Then steel punches would be pre-cut using a pantograph, and smoke proofs made, which I would check with Marcel Mouchel, director of the engraving department. One could still correct mistakes at this point because the steel wasn't yet hard. Finally the punch was hardened, the matrix punched, justified and put in the casting machine. Unlike German type foundries, they still used steel engraving in France. In Germany they were changing over to drilling matrices, even in smaller point sizes (for more about the manufacture of matrices see page 24 manual typesetting and page 129 machine type casting).

Starting with these ten basic letters I drew the entire alphabet. For three or four months I worked daily until everything was ready, with French and Nordic ligatures and accents. *Initiales Président* has caps and small caps only. These were produced from the

Latins, Runic, Etienne, Renaissance The interest in Latins – a type form from the 19th century with pointed serifs – must have been considerable, as they appeared almost simultaneously and in near-identical form in France, England, Germany and Holland. The oldest example, found by the Dutch type expert Gerrit W. Ovink, is a type specimen page of *Latines grasses*[9] from 1854 from the Laurent & Deberny type foundry of Paris. Another early example from the same type foundry is shown in the book, *Nineteenth Century Ornamented Typefaces* by Nicolete Gray. This is *Lettres Latines*[10] from 1855, identified in the *Spécimen Général* of the Fonderies Deberny & Peignot type specimen book from 1926 as *Initiales Latines Noires*.

Despite this early evidence from Paris, the origin of Latins still cannot be solved conclusively, especially as the *Handbuch der Schriftarten* (Manual of Types)[11] from 1926 dates a *Schmale Renaissance* of the W. Woellmer type foundry, Berlin, to 1830. Known in France as Latines, these typefaces are called Latin, Antique or Runic in Britain, Latin or Runic in the US, and Etienne, Renaissance or Latines in Germany. The only common features of Latin typefaces are their pointed serifs /05/ and proportionally adjusted widths. Other than that there are significant differences. Thus Latins may be jobbing or headline faces but also text faces. Similarly, the stroke contrast may vary; very pronounced like a neoclassical roman, yet also very subtle like a sans serif /06/.

/06/
Latins can vary from narrow
to wide and high to low-contrast
(vertical to horizontal stroke
proportion).

/07/
Francis Thibaudeau's classification
of printing types from 1924 has
Latins as a subdivision of Elzévir
faces.

Whereas the French Latines have always had bracketed transitions from the stem to the serif and only slightly concave serifs, the English runic and antique serifs are mostly very concave. The English Latins are headline faces with accentuated triangular serifs and flat bases. Well-known examples are *Latin Condensed* and *Latin Wide*, still available today. Unfortunately serif shapes cannot be determined by names, as there is no formal system for doing so. The same is true in Germany; similar or even identical typefaces may be given different descriptions depending on the foundry.

Deberny & Peignot's type specimen book from 1926 has thirteen fonts described as Latins next to the *Caractères Antiques Latinés* /08/. They are called 'Latines' in the female plural and 'Latins' in the male plural, depending on whether 'Lettres', or for instance, 'Initiales' or 'Caractères' precede them. The Latin spectrum ranges from light through regular to bold, and from condensed, narrow, and regular to expanded. Only two Latins are sloping. The type specimen book *compo dp* from 1961 includes the remaining half of the original Latins /09/ and five new ones in the form of *Méridien, Initiales Président, Tiffany*[12] /18/, *Cristal* and *Phoebus*.

/08/
Possible sources of inspiration for Président: Caractères Antiques Latinés *from the two-volume type specimen book by D&P, 1926 and* Latins Larges *(below).*

CARACTÈRES ANTIQUES LATINÉS   3ᵉ Catégorie.

MUSICALE
Charmes

DÉTONATION
2 Rapière 3

GÉNÉRALISATEUR
Air majestueux

OUTIL DE MÉCANICIEN
Forme 456 Usage

NOS VEDETTES DU CASINO
Quatre années de succès

FONDERIES DEBERNY & PEIGNOT, 14, RUE CABANIS, PARIS

/09/
Older Latins still in use in the foundry type specimen book compo dp *by Deberny & Peignot, c.1961.*

LATINS NOIRS

ABCD course
EFGHIJ rampant
KLMNOP évolutions
QRSTUVXY péremptoire
ZABCDEFGHIJ minerais de fer
VOIX AGRÉABLES une grande famille
MAUVAISE PENSION démonstration de joie
DISTRIBUTEUR OFFICIEL nos sentiments distingués
UNE AFFECTATION SINCÈRE expérience sur le sentiment
LES OBLIGATIONS DE LA VIE nombreux accidents de la route
DEUX EXPLOSIONS FORMIDABLES très nombreuses formes du danger
CARACTÈRE DOMINANT DE LA MUSIQUE quelques appréciations sur les faits divers

1234567890123456789 0

70

LATINS NOIRS SERRÉS

boutons ABCDEF
constructif GHIJKLM
couleur rouge NOPQRSTUV
communications XYZABCDEFGHI
moteur pour bateau GRANDE RÉFORME
trois langues étrangères RÉGIONS DE FRANCE
la publication d'une revue d'art COURS D'ARTS GRAPHIQUES
société de libraires et imprimeurs REPRODUCTIONS DES TABLEAUX
exposition nationale du livre et du papier LES OUVRAGES DE VULGARISATION
anciennes marques des corporations de lyon LES NOUVELLES ÉCOLES D'ENSEIGNEMENT
notions pratiques sur la construction du bâtiment PUBLICATION ILLUSTRÉE D'ART CONTEMPORAIN

1234567890123456789 0

71

LATINS LARGES

48 ABC orne
36 DEFG denier
28 HIJKL décision
20 MNOPQR étonnantes
14 STUVXYZAB arbre superbe
12 JOLIE PORTION la transformation

1234567890123456789 0

LATINS ÉTROITS

48 ABCDE tendeur
36 FGHIJKL volontaire
24 MNOPQRSTUV photographies
18 XYZABCDEFGHIJ formule courante
14 OUVRAGES D'ARTISTES ouvriers et artistes d'art
12 LE ROYAUME DES FRANÇAIS fermeture hebdomadaire du bar

1234567890123456789 0

74

LATINS NOIRS LARGES

ABC amis
DEFG gitane
HIJKL dernier
MNOPQR énervant
STUVXYZ obligations
AMUSEMENT belle manière
TRANSPIRATION travail très précis
DES JOLIS PAYS belle présentation
UN CHEMIN DE FER sensations nouvelles
CONCURRENT LOYAL tapissier-décorateur
LES LOUPS ET LES RENARDS pour résister à l'opinion publique
LA PHOTOTYPIE EN COULEURS les célèbres demeures historiques

1 2 3 4 5 6 7 8 9 0

76

/10/
*Frutiger's design for a business
card typeface based upon the cross-
hatched* Initiales Typogravure,
c.1952/53.

Business card typefaces Well-known business card typefaces still available today include *Chevalier*, by Emil A. Neukomm 1944, *Monotype Spartan*[13], *Copperplate Gothic* by Frederic W. Goudy 1903, and *Engravers Roman*[14] by Robert Wiebking 1899. Business card typefaces intend to radiate dignity; they are supposed to appear elegant and respectable. The epitome of fine type and printing would have to be engravers' fonts and copperplate engraved writing paper and business cards, more than a few of which involve some intricate embossing. Type foundries liked to emulate this quality, giving rise to an abundance of business card typefaces that are often placed in separate indexes in catalogues.

Adrian Frutiger's 'Rhone' design /10/ sought to give the appearance of an engraver's font. However, this Latin – some of it cross-hatched – was never completed as the sleeker *Président* took its place. The extended character shapes, as well as setting in caps and small caps only, are typical of Latin and sans serif-style business card typefaces.

Deberny & Peignot's brochure from c.1948 /18/ has popular English scripts like *Calligraphiques Noires*, outlined or cross-hatched typefaces such as *Initiales Typogravure* and a few sans serifs, including *Simples Larges*. The only Latin face is *Initiales Tiffany*. Other Latin faces no longer seemed to meet the demands of the day as contemporary business card typefaces.

/11/
*Three basic ampersand shapes;
roman capital shape (left),
italic capital shape (middle) and
italic lowercase shape (right).*

/12/
*Calligraphic and drawn ampersand
shapes; Aldus, 1954 by the calligrapher and type designer Hermann
Zapf (left) –* Président *(right).*

/13/
*Roman capital & of
Clearface Gothic, 1907 with numeral-
like shape (left), italic capital
shape of Goudy Sans, 1929 (right).*

/14/
*Frutiger achieves his typical
ampersand by matching strokes
and counters with other
alpha-numerical characters.*

/18/
*A six-page folded card showing
examples of jobbing typefaces
in use – Deberny & Peignot, c.1948.*

/15/
*The ampersand by Zurich teacher
Walter Käch compared to
that of his student Adrian Frutiger.*

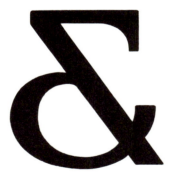

/16/
In contrast to Président, *the*
Univers *ampersand has the shape
of the lowercase t, and has two
right angles in the lower counter.*

/17/
*André Gürtler, Frutiger's co-worker
in the 1960s, designed an ampersand
based on the uncial E-shape for his
Egyptienne 505 in 1966.*

Basic forms of & The ampersand, a ligature of the letters e and t is used in Latin texts to denote the word 'et' (and) and also occasionally to substitute the letters e and t within words. According to the *Duden* dictionary, ampersands may only be used in German for trade names[15] – a rule that barely anyone adheres to. In the US, Webster simply defines it as a character standing for the word and. There are three predominant basic ampersand shapes in typefaces /11/. Most romans have the looped roman capital shape; italic in addition have the italic capital and italic lowercase shapes. Needless to say there are multiple variations.[16]

Type designers are sometimes trying to create a shape that looks more drawn as opposed to written. This should be simple and sleek like the curves and counters of letters and numerals. An example of this form – loop-oriented but simplified – is *Clearface Gothic* /13/ from c.1907 by Morris Fuller Benton. It was a shape taught by Walter Käch, Adrian Frutiger's tutor at the Kunstgewerbeschule in Zurich /15/. In contrast, Frederic W. Goudy chose the italic capital shape /13/ for his *Goudy Sans* in 1929. Frutiger too uses the italic capital for his ampersand. Unlike Goudy, however, he closes the lower counter, thereby creating a modern shape – his characteristic trademark.

same template in principle. The 12 point for instance had three visual sizes, oeil 1, 2 and 3 /21/. For an initial letter one would use 12 point oeil 1, and for the remaining letters of a name 12 point oeil 2 with a smaller size. Inserting small caps was normal in France, clients would insist upon it. At the end a test sentence would be cast from the finished capital letters and some of that would be set. Naturally Charles Peignot had to approve it himself. There was no further discussion about the shapes, I wouldn't have shown anything I wasn't sure about. I did, however, experiment a lot, especially with the ampersand. I was never keen on the classical shape, I found its lines too complicated. I wanted all characters to have the same style /14/, and eventually discovered this special new shape. First Peignot had to agree to it, seeing as the ampersand is particularly important in French. '& Cie.' is always written using an ampersand. Of course I checked Jan Tschichold's book *Formenwandlungen der et-Zeichen* (Shape Variations of the Ampersand) to see what shapes there were to start with. For me the whole thing was above all a question of the counter shapes. These were supposed to be comparable to those of a B. I wanted the & to have a discreet and almost strict design, whereas for Hermann Zapf for example, being a type designer and calligrapher working at the same time as me, it provided a great chance to let his fantasy run free /12/.

The H and O are about the same height and width optically. The numerals were meant to have the same character as the letters, only very slightly narrower. Therefore there's no great difference between the capital O and the zero, both adhere to the same principle /34/. I wanted as much white space as possible, that's why the 2 is drawn so tall – maybe somewhat schoolboy-like. The wide A clearly shows a Latin influence. The K doesn't quite

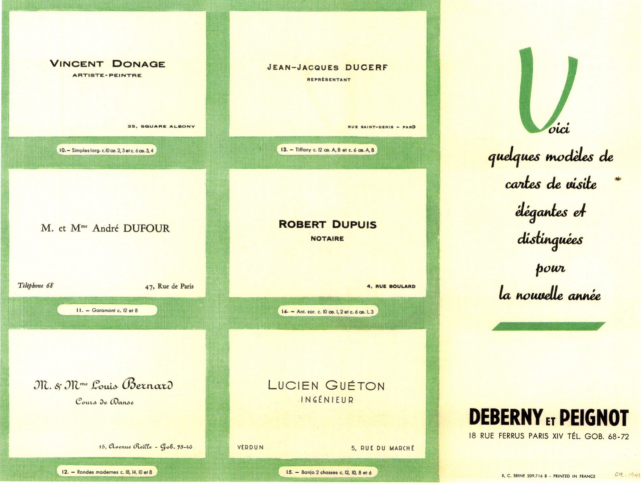

conform, it's different from Latin Ks /25/. Its arms are the same length optically and don't touch the stem. This, too, is a question of counter spaces and movement. I never have attached strokes that look like they've been stuck on. They always flow from another stroke /28/. Perhaps this is typical for the Alfred Willimann school. He regarded Greek lapidary script with its very simple clear shapes as the one true type. However, I didn't bother too much about the history of type to start with. That only happened two years later when I had to copy all the classical typefaces for the Lumitype photosetting machine.

In the end *Initiales Président* was available in 8, 12, 16, 20 and – it was unusual but had commercial reasons – 24 point. The 8 and 12 point font sizes respectively consisted of oeil 1, 2 and 3 /21/. Additional lighter and bolder weights were superfluous in this case. They did, however, include ligatures such as LA, and on my request even overhangs, called 'sortes crénées' /22/, were cast for combinations like VA, something that was otherwise only normal for italic fonts. I suggested it because I was taught by Käch and Willimann that the space between letters is important, maybe even more so than the counter spaces. The type founders accepted this at once, after I showed them how ungraceful it looks when a V with no overhang is next to an A – there's a massive hole. Needless to say there's a normal V for the other combinations.

Initiales Président was very well received in France. Charles Peignot came up with the name. Back then I was still too unaccustomed to the French way of life. I had my first taste of it, which was really quite an emotional experience for me. I had the great fortune to learn my trade in a Swiss German, Germanic-based environment and then ply it in a Latin-based one, which can probably be detected in all of my typefaces.

Additions to Président Adrian Frutiger remembers[17] that alternative characters were made for *Initiales Président* at Charles Peignot's request. He mentions narrow and expanded letter variations, for instance for E and U. It was probably just a partial addition. There is an alternative V shape /26/, round at the bottom and thus halfway between U and V. Also, in the type specimen book *compo dp* there are two Rs and Os pictured, although the narrow O is in fact the zero /19/. Real narrow and expanded shapes were not included in *Président*.
On the other hand, words cast on blocks in corps size 8 use oeil 2 and 3. *Le Président*, a brochure from 1958 shows the four words 'Rue', 'Avenue', 'Boulevard' and 'Place'. The A and V are very tightly kerned /01/. The kerning is much less on the same four words in the *Initiales Fantaisies* brochure from 1956 /22/. It may just be a case of simply hand-set words rather than words cast on blocks. Neither brochure shows them well spaced.
Superior letters (supérieures) are very commonly used in French typography /22/. Abbreviations such as MME, MLLE, N[O], S[T], 1[ER] and 2[EME] are set using these. Particular care needs to be taken with the typography for business cards and writing paper, as they serve a representative function. Unusually hole-tearing letter combinations are irritating. Characters with overhangs (sortes crénées), letters which are wider than the body /20/, ought to prevent this from happening. The example here, the business card in the *Le Président* brochure /01/, once

/19/
Initiales Président *from the type specimen book* compo dp; *two different Rs in the first line, two different Os in the third line.*

HÉLIOGRAVURE
FORMIDABLEMENT
BONNES INTERPRÉTATIONS

/20/
Capitals with large side bearings were also cast with overhangs, for better fit.

/22/
D&P delivered commonly used words cast on blocks, superior characters (supérieures) and capital letters with overhangs (sortes crénées).

/21/
Type in 12 and 8 point body size was available in three visual sizes, 'oeil 1, 2, 3'.

c. 12 œil 1
BIEN COMPRENDRE
c. 12 œil 2
UNE PERFECTION DANS
c. 12 œil 3
POUR FACILITER SON LABEUR

c.12 œil 1   c.12 œil 2   c.12 œil 3

/23/
The smaller visual sizes within a given point size produced the small caps of the next bigger visual size.

again lacks well-balanced word shapes. It is not enough to deal with pairs of letters full of holes simply by setting them tightly. If pairs are too tight they must be letter-spaced, extended.

Initiales Président was cast in 24, 20, 16, 12 and 8 corps sizes. However, the typeface is notably larger than usual, as *Président* has no lowercase, and therefore no ascenders and descenders. Capitals fill the entire extent of the body: 12 and 8 point each have three visual sizes (oeil 1, 2, 3) **/21/**. A process – other manufacturers use it for their business card faces – which enables the capitals to be set with small caps and then again with more small caps for those. When the same body size is used for all three 'œils', the baseline will remain constant without requiring extra lead to be placed above and below **/23/**. 'œil 3' is used for the 'am' in place names such as Frankfurt am Main, for example.

For me it was a really nice job because it was always about the highest quality. *Président* was supposed to be a means of expression for personalities and as beautiful and balanced as possible. I quickly forgot about it, with all that followed. Now though, when I look at it again, I'm quite astonished. It already clearly demonstrates my style – a mixture of both my teachers' influence and my very own personal idea of form. I don't mean convention or an ideal, that would be too philosophical. If a typeface looked good I simply felt real satisfaction. The tiniest mistake instantly hit my eye. I feel that the 'look' of type was complete inside me when I left the Kunstgewerbeschule. Of course I was to learn a lot more, but the style was already there.

/24/
Frutiger's design principle was already established with his first typeface – no spur on the G, the counter is not interrupted by the tail of the Q.

/25/
The K-shape of Président *is typical of Frutiger's typefaces – but atypical of Latins with the two strokes to the right not offset.*

/26/
Originally there was an alternative letter shape halfway between U and V, which is no longer available.

/27/
Photosetting text specimen, 1964/65: It took more than ten years after its hot metal version for Président *to be made available for Photon-Lumitype.*

GQ K K UVV

LE VIEUX JUGE BLONI
PIPE A TETE SCULPTE
DE TEMPS A AUTRE, S
TREMPE SES LEVRES I
POSE DEVANT LUI SUF

/28/
In contrast to Italian Old Style *by Frederic W. Goudy, M, R and W are created from one movement in* Président.

/29/
One original was used to engrave the three sizes 12 pt œil 1 (left), œil 2 (centre) and œil 3 (right) – here all brought to the same size.

/30/
The capital A (brown) compared to the enlarged small caps A (black) of the digital Président *by Linotype.*

MRW MRW AAA A

/31/
Both hot metal R shapes with vertical and virtually diagonal downstroke, as well as its current shape in the Linotype Library.

/32/
Comparison of the Œ ligature in hot metal and digital setting – its shape is noticeably wider in the original version.

/33/
The curve of the J is more delicate in its current version, while the K's inner space is tighter and the top left serif of the N is noticeably thinner.

RRR ŒŒ

JKN JKN

Typeface comparison   *Président* is compared both to
Augustea by Alessandro Butti and Aldo Novarese, and
to *ITC Friz Quadrata* by Ernst Friz. All three have serif
forms found among Latin faces. They also share similar
character shapes and a very slight contrast between the
thick and thin strokes. The three typefaces are classed
in the Incised group, which itself stems from inscriptions
in stone and metal.

Président possesses the even character widths typical
of a Latin typeface. In contrast, the principle of proportion of *Augustea* visibly evokes Imperial Roman capitals.
E, F and S are narrow, while H, N and O verge on square
and circle. *Friz Quadrata* has an equally variable character pitch, though not according to roman principles. The
S is set wider, the N somewhat narrower.

The axis of contrast runs vertically in *Augustea* and *Président*, whereas it is slightly slanted in *Friz Quadrata*. In
general *Augustea* and *Friz Quadrata* seem more dynamic
due to the extended terminals of the K and R. This is
made even stronger by the asymmetry of the Y.

Augustea and *Président* are capitals-only typefaces, *Friz
Quadrata* also has lowercase. For this typeface comparison *Augustea Open* was transformed into a 'Plain' weight,
since the regular weight of *Augustea* is unavailable digitally.

ABCDEFGHIJKLMN
OPQRSTUVWXYZ&
ABCDEFGHIJKLMNOPQR
STUVWXYZ123456789

/35/
*Although the letter shapes are
relatively similar, the test word
'Hofstainberg' clearly shows
Président's width.*

HOFSTAINBERG

Augustea
Alessandro Butti / Aldo Novarese
1951

K M Q R S Y 4 8

HOFSTAINBERG

Président
Adrian Frutiger
1954

K M Q R S Y 4 8

K	M	Q	R	S	Y	4	8
Serifs concave, legs not connected, with bottom serif	Splayed stems, top shoulder with serifs	Wide oval shape, tail in the centre with horizontal finish	Downstroke swerves out of the top bowl	Fairly wide form, rather shallow curve	Short stem, symmetrical shape with top serifs	Slightly flattened top, deep horizontal stroke with a half-serif	Double-decker form, slender waist

HOFSTAINBERG

Friz Quadrata
Ernst Friz
1965

K M Q R S Y 4 8

Font production:
Digitised by Linotype

Font format:
PostScript Type 1

Also available:
TrueType
OpenType Com

ABCDEFGHIJKLMN
OPQRSTUVWXYZ&
ABCDEFGHIJKLMNOPQR
stuvwxyz1234567890

ÅBÇDÈFG
HIJKLMÑ
ÔPQRŚTÜ
VWXYZ&
ÆŒ¥$£€
1234567890
ÅBÇDÉFGHIJ
KLMÑÔPQRŚ
TÜVWXYZ SS
FI FL Æ Œ Ø Ł Đ
[. , : ; · ' / - – —]
(¿ ¡ " « ‹ › » " ! ?)
{ § ° % ⓐ ‰ * † }

Regular

You may ask
why so many di
fferent typefaces. Th

EY ALL SERVE THE SAME PURPOSE BU

t they express man's diversity. It is the same diversi ty we find in wine. I once saw a list of Médoc wines f eaturing sixty different Médocs all of the same ye ar. All of them were wines but each was different from the others. It's the nuances that are importan

t. The same is true for typefaces. Pourquoi tant d'Alphabets différents! Tous servent au même but, mais aussi à exprimer la diversité de l'homme. C'est cette même diversité que nous retrouvons dans les vins de Médoc. J' ai pu, un jour, relever soixante crus, tous de la même année. Il s'agissait certes de vins, mais tous étaient différents. Tout est dans la nuance du b ouquet. Il en est de même pour les caractères! Sie fragen sich warum es notwendig ist, so viele Schriften zur Verfügung zu haben. Sie dienen alle

zum selben, aber machen die Vielfalt des Menschen aus. Dies e Vielfalt ist wie beim Wein. Ich habe einmal eine Weinkarte studiert mit sechzig Médoc-Weinen aus dem selben Jahr. Das ist ausnahmslos Wein, aber doch nicht alles der gleiche Wei n. Es hat eben gleichwohl Nuancen. So ist es auch mit der Sc hrift. You may ask why so many different typefaces. They al l serve the same purpose but they express man's diversity. It is the same diversity we find in wine. I once saw a list of Mé

doc wines featuring sixty different Mé docs all of the same year. All of them were wines but each was different from the others. It's the nuances that are im portant. The same is true for typefaces. Pourquoi tant d'Alphabets différents! Tous servent au même but, mais aussi à e xprimer la diversité de l'homme. C'est c ette même diversité que nous retrouvons dans les vins de Médoc. J'ai pu, un jour,

68 pt | –30   54 pt | –15   36 pt | –10   24 pt | –5   15 pt | 19 pt | –5   10.5 pt | 13 pt | –3   8 pt | 10.2 pt | 5   6 pt | 8 pt | 10

Type-design project
Delta
1952

noismileno

noismetiskonteram

noismet skonteram

nois

vom wahren sinn des

Incomplet sera complete
Insuffisant augmente

Incomplet sera comlete
Insuffisant augmente

Incomplet sera complete
Isuffisant augmente

Incomplet sera complete
Insuffisant augmente

Insuffisant augmente
Incomplet sera complete

Monsieur le Baron Despont

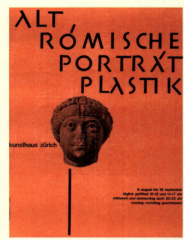

/01/
*Alfred Willimann's poster
from 1953 employs archaic Roman
capitals.*

/02/
*Two undated pencil drawings
of a single case typeface (original
size), c.1952/53 – it was originally
intended to have five weights.*

/03/
*Undated study of the single case
typeface with combinations
of different shapes of upper- and
lowercase letters.*

delta delta DELTA Delta Delta

/04/
*Based on Adrian Frutiger's 'Delta'
type-design project, Joan Barjau
created the Jeune Adrian font,
1991–97.*

abcdefghijklmnopqrst
uvwxyz1234567890
{[(.,;:?!$€-*)]}äöüåøœçß

tiens, mon unique
enfant, mon fils,
prends ce breuvage.
sa chaleur te rendra
ta force et ton
courage. la mauve,
le dictame, ont avec
les pavots mêlé leurs
sucs puissants qui
donnent le repos :

tiens, mon unique
enfant, mon fils,
prends ce breuvage.
sa chaleur te rendra
ta force et ton
courage. la mauve,
le dictame, ont avec
les pavots mêlé leurs
sucs puissants qui
donnent le repos:

/05/
*'Delta' paste-up in two versions:
A and E have been swapped;
m, n and u have rounder arcs
(right).*

36 TYPE-DESIGN PROJECT

The 'Delta' style *'Delta'*, one of Adrian Frutiger's first typeface designs /05/ is in the style that he felt came most naturally to him. When comparing the two designs for this single case typeface, one notices that only the a and e actually change shapes from upper- to lowercase. Nevertheless, there is an impression that the alphabet on the left is uppercase and the one on the right is lowercase. The rounder character shapes of the right-hand version contribute to this sense.

Already, at an early stage of the design, Frutiger looked at several weights and widths /02/, a discipline that he learnt as a student of Walter Käch in Zurich.

Charles Peignot's desire to create a unicase typeface led to a meeting between Frutiger and Cassandre, in order to produce some tests using the Lumitype machine /06/, based on Cassandre's own *Peignot* /07/ typeface. The uppercase version (top) was kept slightly more open, the middle version had lowercase letters added to match it, while the lower variant mixed upper-and lowercase, with some new character shapes. The Lumitype process was still in its experimental phase: the uppercase I of the top version and the m of the middle version appear to have suffered a spacing mistake.

The Delta style accompanied Frutiger throughout his life, until *Nami* (see page 402), based on it, was finally produced by Linotype in 2007.

I've always been especially interested in the development of the transition of uppercase into lowercase shapes. With *'Delta'* /05/, one of my earliest designs, I had in mind the reduction to one alphabet, such as existed in the 5th century.[1] A line of letters ought to have a lowercase feel, in spite of the 'capital' G, R and T in it. I sketched different shapes for some of the letters /03/. I named the typeface *'Delta'* because I liked the word; it sounded classical and fit the shapes. Its style – one could call it an uncial sans serif – has stuck with me throughout my whole life.

Charles Peignot had always dreamt of a new kind of typeface that would unite upper- and lowercase in one alphabet. He thought *Peignot* /07/ was marvellous, yet wanted to go further and so brought A.M.Cassandre and myself together. I guess he figured that A.M. Cassandre's genius and my typographic knowledge would come up with something. Thus we met three or four times in 1954/55.

In my opinion a new typeface had to be built on the foundations of a classical typeface. I imagined, based on *Peignot,* transforming uncial and semi-uncial shapes into a contemporary typeface. Cassandre didn't follow, he didn't really act on my suggestions. We always kind of talked at cross-purposes. Cassandre was an artist; he would take letters and play around with them. Even the way he talked was like an artist who has a head full of ideas. His *Bifur* typeface is in fact like a picture /07/. On the other hand I was the typographer who saw a skeleton within letters, related to other characters. There are three samples with a text by Charles Baudelaire /06/. These were photosetting tests using Lumitype, which were produced after the conversations with Cassandre. However, he wasn't happy with any of the results.

LA NATURE EST UN TEMPLE OU DE VIVANTS PLERS
LABSENT PARFO6 SORTR DE NOMBREUSES PAROLES
LES HOMMES Y PASSENT A TRAVERS DES FORETS DE SYMBOLES
QUI LES OBSERVENT AVEC DES REGARDS FAMLERS
COMME DE LONGS ECHOS QUI DE LON SE CONFONDENT
DANS UNE TENEBREUSE ET PROFONDE UNITE
LES PARFUMS ET LES COULEURS ET LES SONS SE REPONDENT

CHARLES BAUDELARE

La Nature est un temple o de vivants piliers
laissent parfois sortir de nombreuses paroles
Les hommes y passent travers des forts de symboles
qui les observent avec des regards familiers
comme de longs chos qui de loin se confondent
dans une tnbreuse et profonde unit
les parfums et les couleurs et les sons se rpondent

charles baudelaire

La nature est un temple ou De vivants piliers
Laissent parfois sortir De nombreuses paroles
Les hommes y passent a travers Des forets De symboles
qui les observent avec Des regards familiers
comme De longs echos qui De loin se confonDent
Dans une tenebreuse et profonDe unite
Les parfums et les couleurs et les sons se reponDent

charles bauDelaire

/06/
Proof of a sans serif face based on Peignot *with upper- and lowercase variants.*

ABCDEFGHILMNOPQRSTUVY
abcdefghilmnopqrstuvy
abcDefghilmnopqrstuvy

ABCDEFGHIJKLM
NOPQRSTUVWXYZ
abcdefghijklmnopqrs
tuvwxyz 1234567890

ABCDEFGHIJKLM
NOPQRSTUVWXYZ
abcdefghijklmnopqrs
tuvwxyz 1234567890

BIFUR

Name of typeface	Commissioned by	Designer	Design | Publication	Typesetting technology	Manufacturers	Weights
Initiales Phoebus	Deberny & Peignot	Adrian Frutiger	1953 | 1953	Handsetting	– Deberny & Peignot	1
				Photosetting Starlettograph	– Deberny & Peignot	1

PHOEBUS

Compared to *Initiales Président*, which took a long time to complete, *Initiales Phoebus* was very quick. When work started on it I already had a co-worker who did the drawings according to my sketches. It was merely an uppercase alphabet, so basically not too much work. Charles Peignot simply wanted something for the swash section of his type specimen book.[1] That was the fashion at the time; one has only to think of *Graphique* by Hermann Eidenbenz for example /08/. Peignot was aware of that typeface and asked me to try something in that direction. He was always looking for something unusual to liven up the otherwise very classical selection that Deberny & Peignot had to offer.

I don't remember whether I studied similar typefaces, but I do recall *Luna* /08/; maybe I used the *Encyclopaedia of Typefaces*[2] for some ideas, I'm not sure any more. It wasn't that Charles Peignot was set on having a shadow typeface. He just asked me for a few suggestions for a new fantasy typeface, in order to compete with Fonderie Olive. I also drew a shaded narrow sans serif as a test, 'Rodin hat uns'/05/. In the end though, I found it too conventional. To make it more special, one would have had to add an italic, a semibold and so on. The italic latin shape took my fancy a good deal more; all the up- and downstrokes presented an opportunity to add a little triangle.

I started to sketch a titling face with deep shadows, but it looked somewhat banal standing straight up, so I tried an italic. The typeface gained a lot in dynamic thanks to the slanting character shapes against the slant of the deep shadows. I saw the letter shapes in my inner eye and sketched those deep shadows directly, off the cuff. It worked – a larger shadow would have been too bulky, anything thinner and the letters wouldn't have stood out enough. It was really a matter of feeling, of intuition. It was clear that it had to be with serifs, and equally that it was to be a latin-style typeface, serifs slanting right at the bottom and left at the top. The capital I for example would collapse without the little triangle at the top. *Phoebus*, being without contours and whose shapes are completed by the eye itself, was quite to Peignot's taste. He liked the fact that the typeface was entirely composed of shadows and seemed somehow to hover in the air. Nevertheless, the letter shapes are perfect, one can see that with a word such as 'Lumineux'/03/.

The final artwork – India ink on Bristol board – was, as I said before, by my co-worker. She was very efficient. She probably made herself a template to make sure the angles were all the same. Other than that, the process was the same as it was for *Président*. Each letter was first reduced photographically, then everything was cut out and glued together. One could easily see in the prints whether any strokes were too thick or too thin, and whether they were too narrow or too wide. Strokes that indicated character width and lines had to be very thin so that one could cut very precisely using a sharp scalpel and steel ruler to achieve an accurate composition. This remained my own special work technique. I cut out

About Phoebus There are no any remaining designs or final artwork left for *Initiales Phoebus*. There is, however, one remaining study for a narrow, semibold sans serif. The 'Rodin hat uns' /05/ design consists of some shadow type without contours. As opposed to *Gill Shadow* or *Memphis Luna* /08/, Adrian Frutiger matched the shadow depths with the same widths to the spacing between characters. Another interesting aspect of this design is the variation of single letters. Adrian Frutiger drew two different N shapes, an uppercase and a lowercase one, and matched the A shape to that of the latter. It has a similarity of shape to the *Phoebus* A, which is rounded at the top left-hand corner. The M and N shape variations can also be found in *Phoebus*.

Advertisements were commonly placed in trade publications by type manufacturers to publicise new typefaces. A special kind of marketing strategy can be found in the journal *Caractère*[3]. In the editorial section Rémy Peignot now and again presents an overview of newly released typefaces by Deberny & Peignot, under the title 'Parade typographique' /02/. Over four to six pages, using specially designed examples, he demonstrates how the advertised typefaces can be employed /12/. A very nice use of *Phoebus* can be seen on the front page of *Caractère* 12, 1954 /01/. Presumably Rémy Peignot was responsible for this design, but there is no reference to its author anywhere in the publication.

An article in the German trade journal *Der Polygraph* from 1955/56 states that *Initiales Phoebus* was released in 1953, with *Président* and *Ondine* following in 1954. Taking into account documents that were consulted and conversations with Adrian Frutiger, we can assume that he drew *Président* first and then *Phoebus* and *Ondine*, suggesting we ought to give preference to the latter order.[4] The name 'Phoebus' is not spelled consistently by Deberny & Peignot. In one advertisement from 1954 /12/ it is without the œ dipthong, while another from 1955 /11/ has the œ dipthong.

On the initiative of Erich Alb and financed by Linotype, Bruno Maag produced a digital Beta version of *Phoebus* specially for this book. The font is intended to be completed and released.

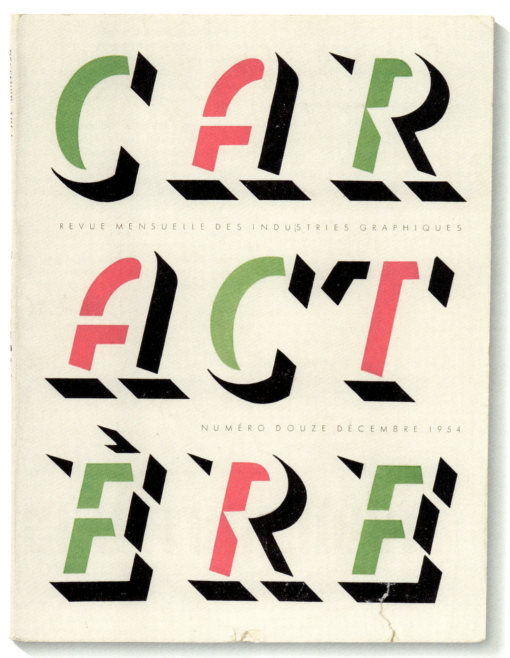

/01/
*Cover page of the small-format
French trade journal
Caractère, no.12, 1954, designed by
Rémy Peignot.*

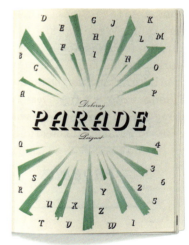

/02/
*Deberny & Peignot's column
'Parade typographique', edited and
designed by Rémy Peignot –
Caractère, no.3, 1955.*

LUMINEUX

/03/
*The character shapes appear well
balanced, quiet and distinct in
spite of their unusual distribution
of black and white.*

a lot, and if I cut something wrong I'd just have to go and do it again. For me that was the quickest and best way. I would never have dared to go straight to the type foundry with the final artwork. First I needed to secure an overall impression for myself. I would assemble letters together into words and whole sentences – I wanted to see how they worked together.

Phoebus had a couple of alternate letters: I designed an upper- and lowercase shape for M and for N /13/. V and W are also somewhat lowercase in shape as they're not pointed /14/. That arose from the basic premise of the *Peignot* typeface by A.M.Cassandre, who played around with this mix very consistently. Of course *Phoebus* was only usable in larger point sizes – it was cut in 48, 36, 30, 24 and 18 point; any smaller size was meaningless.

I worked on it for roughly two months. I was working on other things at the same time, as I was already busy with *Méridien*. I was at the company office from around 9 to 6 and at home I would continue the search. I kept going constantly. I wasn't even aware of it at the time. Then there was photosetting with Lumitype. I kept going stronger, and new discoveries brought about new insights and new possibilities.

When I started, Deberny & Peignot must have had some 450 people total working there. At the time being I was the only type designer. There were at least 15 engravers, around 100 type-casters and a whole hall full of women packing type for shipping, using all the letters in the required amounts. In addition there were the people in the block-making factory, and on the top floor was the workshop for blind embossing and foil stamping. The École Estienne was a great school for engraving. There Charles Peignot soon trained ten young engravers, as it was his desire to create a pool of experts who could also cut type

Swashes Along with classical text faces, Deberny & Peignot introduced some cutting-edge jobbing typefaces by important designers into their typeface selection. Typefaces mentioned are *Bifur* 1929, *Acier Noir* 1936 and *Peignot* 1937, all three by A.M.Cassandre; *Initiales Film* /06/ 1934, a sans serif shadow face on a grid background by Marcel Jacno; and *Initiales Floride* 1939 by Imre Reiner.

Frutiger's *Initiales Phoebus* from 1953 must surely count as one of the most cutting edge swash faces of the 20th century. At the same time it continues the tradition of shadow latin faces from the 19th century. In the 'Caractères Éclairés' index in volume 2 of Deberny & Peignot's type specimen book from 1926, there are around two dozen shadow or outlined typefaces, nearly half of them latins. Yet there are no faces which are shadow-only apart from *Initiales Phoebus* in either that book or in the *compo dp* type specimen book from 1961.

Well known shadow-only faces available today would be the two sans serif faces *Gill Sans Shadow* /08/ by Eric Gill 1936, which previously existed in three versions,[5] and *Umbra*[6] /23/ from 1935 by Robert H.Middleton. In 1937 Rudolf Wolf designed *Memphis Luna*[7] /08/, based on his own slab serif *Memphis*, for the D.Stempel AG type foundry. One year prior to *Phoebus*, *Stridon* /09/ from the Paris type foundry Fonderie Warnery et Cie was released. In contrast to the above-mentioned typefaces, *Stridon* – like *Phoebus* – is a slanting shadow-only typeface.

/04/
Deberny & Peignot monogram,
presumably designed by Rémy
Peignot; advertisement heading in
La France Graphique, *no. 45, 1950.*

/05/
Uncompleted design for
a jobbing typeface by
Adrian Frutiger; photostat,
c.1953.

RODIN HAT UNS

INITIALES ORIENTALES ÉCLAIRÉES

- GLORIEUX SOUVENIR
- PETIT ÉTABLISSEMENT
- UNE EXPOSITION DE JOUETS
- ÉTUDES SUR UN AUTEUR RUSSE
- UNE GRANDE VICTOIRE DE NAPOLÉON
- RAYONS SPÉCIAUX D'ARTICLES DE MÉNAGE
- MŒURS ET COUTUMES DANS LA GRANDE ILE DE BORNÉO

1 2 3 4 5 6 7 8 9 0 1 2 3 4 5 6 7 8 9 0

INITIALES ANTIQUES FILETÉES

- LE PETIT POUCET
- UN PARISIEN A TURIN
- HISTORIETTE POUR FERNAND
- BELLE FÊTE SPORTIVE A GRENOBLE
- MATINÉE CHEZ LA BARONNE DE REBENDART

1 2 3 4 5 6 7 8 9 0

148

INITIALES OMBRÉES

GRATIS
BIBELOTER
ÉTUDE
BARON
DEVIS

149

INITIALES FILM

ROBE
MATIN
COUDRE
LIVRAISON
L'APRÈS-MIDI
BELLE EXCURSION
123 456 789

152

/06/
Selections from the wide range
of older shadow faces in
the compo dp *type specimen*
book, 1961.

Of particular interest in connection with *Phoebus* is the monogram d & p /04/ in an advertisement by Deberny & Peignot, which appeared in the *La France Graphique* trade publication, no. 45 from 1950. Like Adrian Frutiger's *Phoebus* the monogram has italic latin shadow letters, although these are lowercase letters with outlined three-dimensional shapes. The angle is virtually the same, and even the shadow shapes have the same angle and dimension. There is no full alphabet for it, as they were probably characters drawn by Rémy Peignot. Whether or not they served to inspire Frutiger remains unanswered.

for other foundries. With this in mind he sought to make contact with German firms. He found it stupid for each foundry to have its own specialists. It was only because we had so many good engravers that *Univers* was completed so quickly. Unfortunately, these wonderful experts would later lose their jobs because nothing became of this pool. However, when photosetting came along, draftspeople had to be employed.

The name *Phoebus* probably comes from Rémy Peignot. He would have been looking for a description which had something to do with light. *Umbra* or *Luna* for example – all of these typeface names have to do with light. *Phoebus* isn't exactly common in French, but one gets the gist of its historical background. 'Phoebus' is the name of the god Apollo in Greek mythology and means 'the pure one, the light one'.

There were also the cinema posters by Jan Tschichold from the '20s for the Phoebus-Palast, a cinema in Munich.[8] At the time Tschichold was still propagating 'New Typography' and sans serif type. Later he would do a complete U-turn, which was his every right. I would go so far as to say that it shows he was a very generous person in doing so. He lost his position as teacher of typography and calligraphy at the Meisterschule für Deutschlands Buchdrucker, Schule der Stadt München und des Deutschen Buchdrucker-Vereins in Munich in 1933 – the National Socialists were responsible for his dismissal – and emigrated to Basel. He worked at the Benno Schwabe publishing house and had a small teaching job at the Kunstgewerbeschule in Basel, then after that at the Birkhäuser publishing house, at Penguin Books in London, and then in Basel again at the pharmaceutical company Roche. When I first met him he had changed over entirely to the classical side. One can never know what goes on inside someone's mind. Jan Tschichold simply felt more at

ABCDEF
GHIJKLM
NOPQRS
TUVWXYZ
1234567
890

/07/
Initiales Cristal *by Rémy Peignot, made in 1953 for Typophane transfer sheets, and for handsetting in 1955.*

/09/
Stridon *made in 1952 by the Fonderie Warnery (Paris); advertisement in* Bulletin Officiel des Cours professionnels, *no. 138, 1955.*

/08/
Selection of shadow faces from the 1930s and 40s; Gill Sans Shadow *and* Memphis Luna *without contours,* Ricardo *and* Graphique *with contours,* Profil *with an additional outline.*

Gill Shadow
LUNA
RICCARDO
GRAPHIQUE
PROFIL

ETRE AU SERVICE DE
LA TYPOGRAPHIE

STRI
STRID
STRIDO
STRIDON
DU CORPS 20 AU CORPS 77

W
Fonderie WARNERY et Cⁱᵉ
8, rue Jean-Dolent, PARIS-XIV
GOB. 04-62

/10/
Advertisement for the Starlettograph headline setting machine for setting continuous sizes on photographic material – Caractère, 1963.

/11/
Advertisement with marketing text for Initiales Phœbus *– Bulletin Officiel des Cours professionnels, no. 138, 1955.*

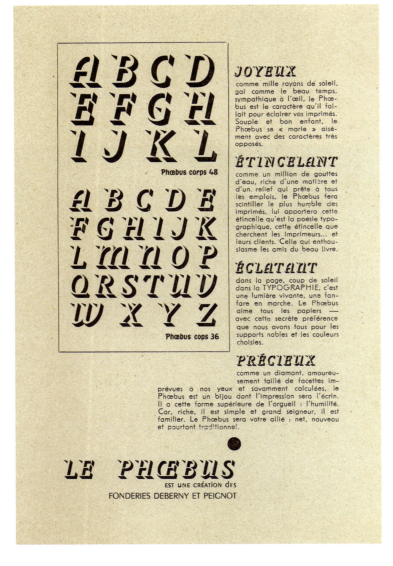

/12/
Pages of 'Parade typographique' by Deberny & Peignot with newly released foundry and Typophane typefaces – Caractère, no. 3, 1954.

Typophane transfer sheets Adrian Frutiger's early jobbing typefaces *Initiales Président, Initiales Phoebus* and *Ondine* are all produced by hot metal setting. Other jobbing faces made by Deberny & Peignot were released as Typophane transfer sheets, which may be regarded as forerunners of the successful Transfer Lettering by Letraset and Mecanorma (see Transfer setting technique, page 223).

Typophane presented the graphic studios and advertising agencies with an easy means for headline setting. Charles Peignot was quick to recognise this and believed in the success of the various new setting methods. He started publicising them with adverts and articles in the French trade publications, in addition to appearances at trade fairs.

The first four typefaces on offer for Typophane transfer sheets by Deberny & Peignot were *Initiales Cristal* **/07/** by Rémy Peignot 1953, *Améthyste* and *Bolide* by Georges Vial 1954, and *Chaillot* 1954 by Marcel Jacno **/12/**. *Initiales Cristal* was released 1955 in addition for hot metal setting and was later – as were *Initiales Phoebus* and *Méridien*, among others – marketed for photosetting for the Starlettograph headline setting machine **/10/**. This machine is, in fact a Starsettograph, made by H. Berthold AG of Berlin, of which D&P had the rights of sale in France. A later model, Staromat, was also put on the French market by Deberny & Peignot.

home with the classics towards the end. For me classical typography is something lasting. Nevertheless I was wholly on Emil Ruder's side, typographically speaking, at that time. I'm sure that stemmed from my upbringing and schooling – under Williman, no less – even though my apprenticeship was steeped in the classics. Although we had different precepts, I got on very well with Jan Tschichold, though I probably appreciated him more than he did me.

Designing *Phoebus* was fun, but success was not forthcoming. It didn't sell as well as expected. It did however enrich Deberny & Peignot's range of typefaces. All in all it was a busy year for work. I also found time to help Rémy Peignot with the final artwork for his titling typeface *Initiales Cristal* **/07/**. This very delicate typeface works well in larger point sizes, though unfortunately it's seldom used as a headline face. At least it meant Rémy had his own typeface, that was enough for him and it made me happy. I was glad to help him, after all of the many times he had helped me.

/13/
As alternatives to the angular upper-case shapes of M and N, round lowercase shapes (somewhat similar to uncials) were included.

/14/
The rounded uppercase A V W and the lowercase M and N shapes give the font a handwritten character.

/15/
The angularity of the serif shapes of the capitals is combined with the serif orientation of the lower case (left at the top, right at the bottom).

/16/
Like the alternative shape of Initiales Président, *the V from* Initiales Phoebus *is designed with a round vertex.*

/17/
Phoebus *has a clear stroke contrast between the downstrokes and the hairline strokes – the stroke width itself is not uniform.*

/18/
The typical Frutiger ampersand also radiates authority in the shaded Phoebus.

/19/
Président, Phoebus *and* Cristal *all have contrasting upper and lower counter spaces in the numerals 5 and 2.*

/20/
The uppercase I and the numeral 1 have identical shapes in Phoebus, *as do the uppercase O and the zero.*

/21/
M character of Initiales Phoebus *in 36 pt size – in 2006 the typeface was recast from original Deberny & Peignot matrices.*

ABCDEFGHIJKLMMN
OPQRSTUVWXYZ&
1234567890

Typeface comparison The 19th century was rife with various kinds of shadow typefaces. However, there is no shadow face without an outline depicted in Nicolete Gray's benchmark book *Nineteenth Century Ornamented Typefaces*. Thus it is possible that the three sans serif shadow faces from around 1930, *Plastica* from 1929, *Gill Sans Shadow* from 1932/1936 /08/, and *Umbra* from 1935 /23/, plus the slab serif *Memphis Luna* from 1937, belong to the first generation of this genre.[9]

The three typefaces shown below also have something else fundamentally different about them. In *Umbra* the reversed-out stroke width is very fine, but casts an even deeper shadow. On the other hand, *Memphis Luna* has an even balance between relief and shadow depth. Along-side its emphasised serifs and other characteristics, this makes it very distinct. In *Phoebus* the stroke widths vary and the shadow depth is halfway between that of the other two typefaces. In addition, Frutiger chose triangular serifs and also inclined the typeface /22/. The printing elements have been kept simple and are tilted once at most. They are always two-dimensional and never linear. The quality of Adrian Frutiger's work can be particularly appreciated in K. The end of the upper arm is highlighted by the serif, without creating too complex an inner space.

Comparing the original to the digital Beta version of *Phoebus* shows the newer version to be inaccurate in its detail.[10]

/23/
The only one of the three typefaces
available as a digital font is Umbra;
Memphis Luna *is shown here*
as a scan and Phoebus *as a digital*
Beta version.

HOFSTAINBERG

Umbra
Robert Hunter Middleton
1932

HOFSTAINBERG

Memphis Luna
Rudolf Wolf
1937

HOFSTAINBERG

Phoebus
Adrian Frutiger
1954

A	G	K	M	O	S	5	6
Asymmetrical shape, rounded top	Spurless stem	Arms do not touch the stem	Slightly spread legs, visible stroke contrast in up- and down-strokes	Inner and outer shadows overlap	Continuous shadow on the diagonal stroke	Bar with serif	Diagonal shape, circle appears geometrically linear

Font production:
Beta version
Dalton Maag / Linotype

Font format:
OpenType

Phoebus™
Linotype
1 weight

ABCDEFGHIJKLMMN NOPQRSTUVWXYZ& 1234567890

ABCDEFG
HIJKLMM
NNOPQRSTU
VWXYZ&
1234567890
Regular

YOU MAY ASK

WHY SO MANY DIFFER

ENT TYPEFACES. THEY ALL S

ERVE THE SAME PURPOSE BUT THEY

EXPRESS MAN'S DIVERSITY. IT'S THE SAME DIVERSITY
WE FIND IN WINE. I ONCE SAW A LIST OF MÉDOC WINES
FEATURING SIXTY DIFFERENT MÉDOCS ALL OF THE SA
ME YEAR. ALL OF THEM WERE WINES BUT EACH WAS
DIFFERENT FROM THE OTHERS. IT'S THE NUANCES TH

AT ARE IMPORTANT. THE SAME IS TRUE FOR TYPEFACES. POURQUOI TANT D'ALPHA
BETS DIFFÉRENTS! TOUS SERVENT AU MÊME BUT, MAIS AUSSI À EXPRIMER LA DIVE
RSITÉ DE L'HOMME. C'EST CETTE MÊME DIVERSITÉ QUE NOUS RETROUVONS DANS
LES VINS DE MÉDOC. J'AI PU, UN JOUR, RELEVER SOIXANTE CRUS, TOUS DE LA MÊME
ANNÉE. IL S'AGISSAIT CERTES DE VINS, MAIS TOUS ÉTAIENT DIFFÉRENTS. TOUT EST
DANS LA NUANCE DU BOUQUET. IL EN EST DE MÊME POUR LES CARACTÈRES! SIE FRA
GEN SICH, WARUM ES NOTWENDIG IST, SO VIELE SCHRIFTEN ZUR VERFÜGUNG ZU HA

BEN. SIE DIENEN ALLE ZUM SELBEN, ABER MACHEN DIE VIELFALT DES MENS
CHEN AUS. DIESE VIELFALT IST WIE BEIM WEIN. ICH HABE EINMAL EINE WEI
NKARTE STUDIERT MIT SECHZIG MÉDOC-WEINEN AUS DEM SELBEN JAHR. DA
S IST AUSNAHMSLOS WEIN, ABER DOCH NICHT ALLES DER GLEICHE WEIN. ES
HAT EBEN GLEICHWOHL NUANCEN. SO IST ES AUCH MIT DER SCHRIFT. YOU M
AY ASK WHY SO MANY DIFFERENT TYPEFACES. THEY ALL SERVE THE SAME
PURPOSE BUT THEY EXPRESS MAN'S DIVERSITY. IT'S THE SAME DIVERSITY.
WE FIND IN WINE. I ONCE SAW A LIST OF MÉDOC WINES FEATURING SIXTY DI

FFERENT MÉDOCS ALL OF THE SAME YEAR. ALL
OF THEM WERE WINES BUT EACH WAS DIFFERE
NT FROM THE OTHERS. IT'S THE NUANCES THA
T ARE IMPORTANT. THE SAME IS TRUE FOR TY
PEFACES. POURQUOI TANT D'ALPHABETS DIFFÉ
RENTS! TOUS SERVENT AU MÊME BUT, MAIS A
USSI À EXPRIMER LA DIVERSITÉ DE L'HOMME.
C'EST CETTE MÊME DIVERSITÉ QUE NOUS RETR
OUVONS DANS LES VINS DE MÉDOC. J'AI PU, UN
JOUR, RELEVER SOIXANTE CRUS, TOUS DE LA M

66 pt | –35   40 pt | –25   31 pt | –10   23 pt | –5   15.5 pt | 19 pt | 0   10 pt | 13 pt | 2   7 pt | 10.2 pt | 10   5.7 pt | 8 pt | 10

Type-design project
Element-Grotesk

1953

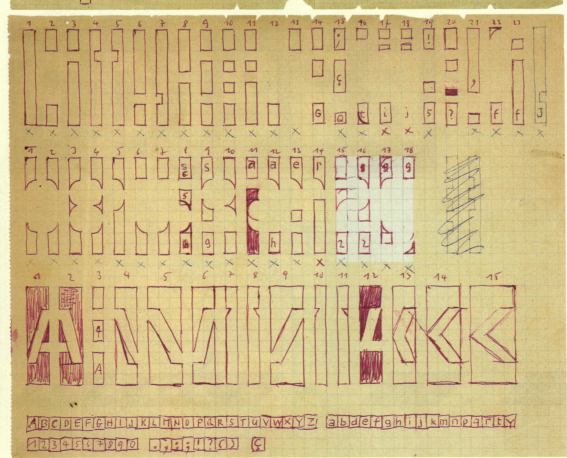

/01/
Sketch of an alphabet composed of elements (above); and sketch of the negative shapes of the elements (below).

/02/
Test showing how the widths of characters could be changed by simply adding more of the same elements in the middle of each one.

/03/
The elements also make it possible to join letters.

A new approach to type This alphabet design composed of elements is a search for a headline face to comply with Charles Peignot's desire to create an entirely new sort of typeface. The demand brought about by advertising agencies for individual headline faces called for such a typeface, spurring Adrian Frutiger on to try out new designs.

An early sketch /01/ shows the letters divided into vertical elements, transformed at a later stage into negative shapes. Diagonal lines were a problem, as they cannot be extended with elements. Adrian Frutiger tried different widths for K and different elements for M, but in doing so drifted away from the initial concept. By test casting a few elements, words like 'Houtife' /02/ could be set. Joining letters offers interesting choices, giving them the appearance of logos /03/.

This typeface design has similarities to the 'Rodin hat uns' design from the same time for a headline face, which evolved into *Initiales Phoebus* (see page 40).

The details of '*Element-Grotesk*'[1] were never elaborated, no doubt for financial as well as technical reasons. The questions regarding standardising shapes or character spacing remain unsolved.

Charles Peignot always encouraged me to scale new heights in my search for new ideas for alphabets. During my first period working for Deberny & Peignot I was free from all constraints and allowed to search in all directions. This is how I came up with this idea. It was to design a stencil face for headline setting. Marcel Jacno, who had drawn several alphabets for Deberny & Peignot, had done a similar alphabet that was very successful.[2] It was released in 1954 as *Chaillot* /04/ – but only for Typophane transfer sheets (for more about the technology transfer sheets see page 223).

The squares on graph paper gave my design the possibility of making letters using construction elements. I sketched the entire alphabet with upper- and lowercase letters on such paper /01/, in order to see into how many and into what type of elements one could divide the letters. On a second sheet I then put the individual elements together. It presented a whole new possibility of setting different widths by repeating individual basic elements /02/. I showed Charles Peignot a few words I'd pieced together, and along with Marcel Mouchel, our engraver, I tried engraving a couple of these stick-like individual elements from which proofs were then made /02/.

The x-height became equal to the cap height /07/, which at this point had nothing to do with the search for a uni-case typeface. The shapes of individual characters, round on the outside and square on the inside, arose from the system. Some of the upper- and lowercase letters could be set using the same elements /06/, which reduced the huge amount of individual elements somewhat. In the end, however, it didn't become a stencil face. The typeface was never produced either. It is pretty daring to break up letters into their constituent components. More than anything, the typesetters wouldn't have had much fun with it.

/04/
Chaillot by Marcel Jacno, a typeface produced for Typophane transfer sheets, released by Deberny & Peignot, 1954.

/05/
Gill Cameo Ruled 1930, a foundry typeface by Eric Gill, in which the vertical lines are a purely decorative element.

/07/
Positive and negative letters constructed from the elements in the sketch on the left page without space between them.

/06/
Elements combined into letters (right), sorted by shapes (below) and numbered according to the sheet on the preceding page.

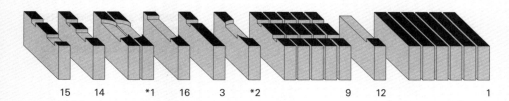

15   14   *1   16   3   *2   9   12   1

Type-design project
Federduktus
1953

l'incomplet sera complété

le courbe redressé

le creux rampli

l'usé renouvelé

l'insuffisant augmenté

l'excès dissipe

/01/
*Typeface sketch written with a
broad quill c.1953–54 – two lines of
text are also included in the
design for 'Delta'.*

/02/
*Adrian Frutiger in his office at
Deberny & Peignot in Paris, 1955 –
on his desk are a sketch for
'Federduktus' and Jan Tschichold's*
Meisterbuch der Schrift.

kirchhofer's casino gallery

/03/
*Logotype from the early 1950s
for Kirchhofer watches and jewelery
in Interlaken, Switzerland –
still in use today.*

Adrian Frutiger searched in many directions for new type designs for Deberny & Peignot. The source for most of his studies and designs were historical forms of writing. He had already studied them under Alfred Willimann – which led to his diploma thesis (see page 20) – and they also served as the basis for the 'Federduktus' design. As with historical uncials and semi-uncials, upper- and lowercase shapes are mixed together on his calligraphic page /01/.

When transforming the written draft into a working typeface, Adrian Frutiger picked only the lowercase forms of the characters /04/. In the draft version, only the r and s are altered slightly. On the whole this version has slightly taller ascenders and a lighter weight. However, it was not the lively script face that Charles Peignot was looking for.

It is interesting to compare the line 'l'incomplet sera complété' /01/ written in broad pen with the same line for the design of 'Delta' (see page 36). As opposed to script, which Frutiger learnt under Alfred Willimann, drawn type is used here, a subject he learnt under Walter Käch. Rhythm and stroke contrast are purposefully set parameters in the pencil drawn version, rather than a result of the position of the pen, as it is in 'Federduktus'.

This design, based on broad pen writing, dates from my early years at Deberny & Peignot. The search for new jobbing faces led me to try a pen, with which I wrote a few lines /01/. The impetus arose from Charles Peignot's desire to have script fonts in the style of Roger Excoffon's *Mistral,* released by Fonderie Olive. Being a salesman, Charles Peignot wanted to give printers the opportunity to offer their clients something new, seeing as the purchase of a minimum[1] was fairly cheap. However, it was never realised.

It was a painstaking search. I couldn't base it around Art Nouveau and its plethora of typefaces, as these were regarded as old-fashioned. I always came back to the classical forms. I never managed to produce a lively script typeface such as Peignot had imagined. I wasn't capable of designing anything comparable to Excoffon's typefaces. Also, I prefer pens to brushes. The experiments with a broad pen produced the uncial and semi-uncial shapes. I made a paste-up /04/ of the best characters, which differ only in details, in order to test them. I hung a design on the wall behind my desk /02/. All of these experiments eventually led to *Ondine,* which was produced in 1954.

The logo for the company of an acquaintance from my home town of Interlaken dates from this period of writing experiments /03/. Other characters were added later. I'm not sure whether a whole alphabet was ever produced for Kirchhofer, but at any rate the logo is still in use to this day.

ainsi amour inconstament me meine
et quand je pense avoir plus de douleur
sans y penser je me treuve hors de peine
puis quand je croy ma joye estre certeine
et estre au haut de mon desire heur
il me remet en mon premier malheur

acdehijlmn
opqrstuvy

/04/
Undated proofs of 'Federduktus' with alternates and overviews of the characters used in each.

commencez d'abord par me dire combien
les hommes de votre globe ont de sens! nous
en avons soixante et douze, dit l'académicien,
et nous nous plaignons toujours du peu;
notre imagination va audelà de nos besoins,
malgrès toute notre curiosité nous avons

abcdeghijlm
noprstuvxyz

Name of typeface	Commissioned by	Designer	Design	Publication	Typesetting technology	Manufacturer	Weights
Ondine	Deberny & Peignot	Adrian Frutiger	1953	1954	Handsetting	– Deberny & Peignot	1
Formal Script 421•				Digital CRT and Laser	– D. Stempel AG | Linotype	1
				Digital PostScript	– Adobe | Linotype	1
					Bitstream•	1
					URW++	3

ONDINE

In my second year in Paris, Charles Peignot commissioned me to design a sturdy script face in the style of *Mistral* /05/. Roger Excoffon's typeface had been released in 1953 by Fonderie Olive in Marseille and was an immediate success. Peignot wanted to counter it with something unique, seeing as the classically oriented Deberny & Peignot range was lacking such a decorative alphabet.[1] Up to that point in time I hadn't dealt with script faces, but from my apprenticeship I recalled *Legende* /05/ by F.H.Ernst Schneidler very well. With that in mind, I did some first drafts with a broad pen, trading ideas with Peignot's son Rémy.

I didn't want to show Charles Peignot my first designs. I picked the shapes that worked best. To finish those with opaque white and black ink would have taken me too long, so I wrote the letters with a broad pen on tracing paper and put them in the enlarger (the capital letters then had a height of some 20 cm). I produced precise drawings from these, used white transfer paper to copy the type to black card, and then cut the letters out with scissors. That way I could spread them out in front of me. If a detail was incorrect I would cut something off or do letters again if need be. That way I quickly produced black and white originals, my speedy method for final artwork. Rémy Peignot alone knew that I worked in this manner, as his office where he designed the specimens was next to mine.

Cutting out things seems to be in my blood. After all, my name refers to the Frutig valley in the Bernese Oberland where scissor work is traditional. All of my uncommissioned artistic work[2] was cut from paper. I was always happiest cutting rather than doing finished drawings. Of course I also worked very precisely with pencils. Cutting out works fine for a round fantasy script like *Ondine,* but as soon as serifs come into the equation scissors won't do.

I then composed words for Charles Peignot, cleanly mounted on card with both baseline and width marked. He immediately decided to test it by having the typeface engraved. What he liked most of all were the wide and narrow letter variations /13/ and also the Qu ligatures /14/. Engraving was easy, nothing like it was for my first typeface *Président.* Nevertheless I could see from the first casting that the correct optical positioning of the lowercase baseline was difficult. I had to alter the pointed terminals, in particular the sharp ones of m and n, pointing downward, at least three times. In the end *Ondine* was also cut and cast in larger point sizes. For fantasy scripts one would gladly go up to five Cicero, that is 60 pt /03/, for example when setting for small posters. There weren't any wooden letters for *Ondine,* although we did have some at Deberny & Peignot that weren't, however, made by us.

Interestingly, foundations for later typefaces can be seen in the first drafts for *Ondine* /02/. It hints at the italic shapes of *Méridien.* This must simply be my own style, my 'handwriting'. A photo inspired Rémy Peignot to name it *Ondine.* It shows a young woman with

About Ondine   Undine, or Ondine in French, is a term for water nymphs. Presumably a creation of the late Middle Ages, it was first mentioned by Paracelsus in the mid-16th century in his book *Liber de Nymphis*.[3]

The squared-off appearance connects Adrian Frutiger's *Ondine* to the late Middle Ages. There are, however, many historical traits and references apparent, from the majuscule italic of Roman antiquity and the semi-italic to the late gothic italic /04/. Consequently *Ondine* is not a replica of any specific historical letterform; rather it can be regarded as stylistic pluralism.

In contrast to influential script fonts of the 1950s such as *Mistral, Choc* and *Bolide* /07/ with their individual spontaneous forms of expression, *Ondine* seems somewhat rigid and harsh. This is due in part to the pointed, sharp-edged terminals, but also to the unconnected and, unusually for script fonts, upright appearance.

Adrian Frutiger drew the character shapes of *Ondine* with a broad pen. He then enlarged them and cut them out of black card stock with scissors. This is perhaps one of the reasons why nearly all of the closed character shapes have openings. In addition to the standard characters, Frutiger designed some alternative shapes /13/ which are unfortunately no longer available in today's versions of the face.

Ondine, made as a jobbing face in foundry type in 1953 by Deberny & Peignot, was available in eight sizes from 12 to 60 Didot point /03/, as it still is to this day.[4] Even though it was initially unsuccessful, it was taken over in 1981 by D. Stempel AG in Frankfurt am Main and adapted for the photosetting machines of the Mergenthaler Linotype group, as well as for all other new setting methods. Frutiger himself only started to release historically based script fonts in the 1990s, starting with the project Type-before-Gutenberg (see page 370).

Ondine is available now as a standard character set and also as a CE Font (Central European) from Linotype and Adobe. URW++ have it as three variants: a regular, an outline and a relief version. Bitstream's unlicensed version is called *Formal Script 421*. Some of the characters differ wildly from each other in each manufacturer's version, as well as from the original.

/02/
Typeface design from the early 1950s related in form to both Ondine *and* Méridien *italique.*

Hynomelipas

bcdfw nomelipas

ghjkrtuvxyz

ONDINE

particulièrement plus robuste	DÉLICIEUSE SENSATION	12
promenade dans les bois	VNE BELLE OPÉRETTE	14
produits nouveaux	AUTOMATIQUES	18
déformations	STVVXYZAB	24
admission	NNOPQR	30
distances	HIJKLM	36
laveur	DEFG	48
soute	ABC	60

1234567890 1234567890

53116 D

133

/01/
After sketching Ondine *with a broad quill and enlarging it, it is cut out from black card stock.*

/03/
Presentation of Ondine *with fruit still life from the type specimen book* compo dp *by Deberny & Peignot, 1961.*

long flowing hair in the water, a water nymph, an undine. That same picture was put on the front page of the brochure /08/, which was later often reproduced in trade magazines.

Ondine is a mix of different forms. I used uncials /04/ as a starting point for the capital letters, although I also designed alternative letters which are based on early Roman hand-written capitals. The lowercase letters have elements of uncials, Carolingian and Gothic minuscules in addition to a certain semblance to Schneidler's *Legende* /05/, which in my opinion remains one of the best typefaces of its kind. A typical trait of *Ondine* is the attempt to draw lowercase letters as open gestures where possible. Apart from b and p this worked for all lowercase and, needless to say, for numerals. The inner spaces of the letters are a special detail of *Ondine*. Only uppercase A B D, the 8 and the & /17/ have closed shapes. Really I wanted all characters to have an opening. I wanted air to enter them. That was practically impossible for B and D, but the O, an equally typically closed shape, has a gap at the top left. I found it let the typeface breathe more easily.

As I say, *Ondine* also had alternative letters; there were two Es (uncialis and capitalis rustica), and I drew two widths for uppercase M N U V /13/. It was a lot of fun for me to develop something like that, and Charles Peignot loved such things. Nowadays text faces in a handwritten style are designed with several alternative characters, so as to emulate handwriting as closely as possible. Such considerations played no part when it came to *Ondine*. I never felt the need to design a connected handwritten font. For foundry type it was extremely laborious and around three times as costly as normal fonts. Excoffon made his *Mistral* /05/ in that manner, with connectors that fit together with pinpoint accuracy. It was quite a work of art for its day. For me however, a text face was always composed of

Formal derivation of Ondine *Ondine*'s several historical sources go back to antiquity, to the very beginnings of written Latin. Therefore some shapes correspond to Roman cursive capitals /04/, for instance M and N. One of the main starting points for the uppercase shapes is uncials /04/. A feature typical of this is the round shape of the E, which also has an alternative shape for the foundry version of *Ondine* /10/.

Uncials, a development from the roman cursive capitals were part of the transition from capitals to minuscules.[5] This can clearly be seen in the subtle hints of ascenders and descenders and in a few lowercase shapes such as a and d.

Particularly pertinent to the lowercase, and all the more so to the general appearance of *Ondine*, are written Carolingian minuscules and Gothic cursives, as well as the *Civilité A2* typeface by Robert Granjon /04/. The downstrokes with pointed terminals and the swelling of the curves in the latter are features it shares with Frutiger's typeface, as are its dark appearance and strong stroke contrast.

With its many formal references, *Ondine* could be described as a historicised typeface, although precisely for that reason it should be regarded as an independent one.

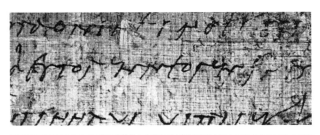

/05/
Well known and successful script faces: Legende *by F.H.E.Schneidler, 1937 and* Mistral *by R.Excoffon, 1953.*

/04/
Historical scripts: Roman cursive capitals, 2nd century, uncial, early form, 4th/5th century, semi-italic, c.700, Gothic cursive, mid-15th century, Civilité, printing type, mid-16th century.

/06/
Other script faces (e.g.):
Brush *by R.Smith, 1942*
Bravo *by E.A.Neukomm, 1945*
Impuls *by L.Zimmermann, 1954*
Choc *by R.Excoffon, 1955*

Brush

Bravo

Impuls

Choc

One trend of the 1940s and 1950s was towards the flighty spontaneity of written type. These light-hearted and individual seeming typefaces sought to break with the austere uniformity and order of the Second World War and post-war period. The brush became the relevant tool, the popular and much-used writing instrument of the time.[6]
Frutiger, however, looked to historical forms written with a broad quill for his *Ondine* designs, thus setting himself apart from the trend. *Ondine* could not compete with the popular brush-like fonts *Mistral* /05/ and *Choc* /06/ by the Fonderie Olive. It is only since the 1990s that it has been used a lot, mostly for company branding and shop fronts of Asian and Arabic origin.
At the same time as *Ondine*, Deberny & Peignot released the brush fonts *Bolide* and *Améthyste* /07/ by Georges Vial. The *compo dp* type catalogue from 1960 contains other typefaces in a handwritten style alongside *Ondine* such as *Scribe* /09/, *Jacno* and *Contact* /07/. The brush faces mentioned above are not included, as they were not made as foundry type. Instead they were produced for Typophane[7], which was much faster and cheaper to produce. It would appear that Deberny & Peignot meant to test these fonts first using the simpler technology. Possibly they were specifically aimed at a market outside of printing offices.

individual, unconnected elements. Roger Excoffon worked completely differently from the way I did. As it happens, we were good friends and would always meet in Paris at the bistro next door, but the 'old timers' weren't supposed to know that. He was a painter and graphic designer and only came to type design through his stepfather[8]. Unburdened by theoretical and historical specialist knowledge, he would design using his own creativity and came up with dynamic brush-style letters based on his handwriting for jobbing faces such as *Mistral* and *Choc* /06/, but also an unusual sans serif like *Antique Olive* (see page 355), with its idiosyncratic proportions.

Ondine was released to the market very quickly. To be honest, I was never very comfortable with that. I always had the feeling I was harming my teachers, Willimann even more so than Käch. My type conscience plagued me. I told Peignot that I simply mustn't get ahead of myself and that he shouldn't require anything of me that I couldn't do. I worked on *Ondine* for six weeks at the most. I basically regarded it as a waste of time and effort. I knew it wouldn't compete with *Mistral,* not in France, but Peignot didn't mind, he merely wanted a handwritten font. Indeed, *Ondine* didn't manage to stand up to the tough competition. Somehow it was alien to the French. They didn't know that style of writing with a broad pen. French calligraphy continued along the lines of *Calligraphiques noires* /12/, which were produced in the 19th century using a pointed pen.[9]

I didn't want to design a historical type at all, instead I wanted to create something modern which flowed from the development of type that I had internalised. The lowercase letters were the most important thing for me, it was a case of matching the uppercase letters to their rhythm. Funny that the capitals should later be employed more often. *Ondine*'s

/07/
*From the Deberny & Peignot
typeface library:*
Jacno *by M. Jacno, 1950*
Contact *by I. Reiner, 1952*
Bolide *by G. Vial, 1954*
Améthyste *by G. Vial, 1954*

/08/
Cover of the four-page Ondine *type
specimen brochure from 1956
with character set and sample text.*

lack of success was no great *misfortune* for the foundry. Nobody criticised me in any way. The only company to choose *Ondine* for its corporate design in the end was a mustard factory in Dijon, which used it on their tubes. I've always laughed about that and called it my mustard typeface.

It's interesting that the typeface is so successful now. *Ondine* can't be properly classified, it has too many quirks, but that seems to be exactly what people now like about it. Free typefaces with a written style appear to be in fashion, a trend towards casual, personal typefaces.

Deberny & Peignot market segments   Traditionally, the mainstay of the type range at Deberny & Peignot was fonts for handsetting of long copy. However, the appearance of typesetting machines by Mergenthaler Linotype and Monotype increasingly ate up that market in the 20th century. In addition, from the 1950s onwards design work started shifting away from the printers to the design studios. Deberny & Peignot reacted to this with two measures:

For one thing, they invested in typesetting technology with the adoption of the Photon-Lumitype photosetting machine (see page 58) and the introduction of the Typophane letter transfer sheets (see page 223).

For another, they tried to promote jobbing headline typefaces to compete with those of their competitor, the Fonderie Olive in Marseille, which led the market. For this important field alphabets were produced by different designers for Deberny & Peignot.

An advertisement from 1956 /09/ shows: at this time Deberny & Peignot had other areas of enterprise alongside type, among them the sale of printing machines, typesetting and printing equipment and furniture by manufacturers in Europe and the USA. Also, typesetting for clients was offered in their very own 'Atelier de composition', as was the manufacture of printing plates (Sicoplast).

/09/
Full page advertisement by Deberny & Peignot showing comprehensive range in La France Graphique, *1956.*

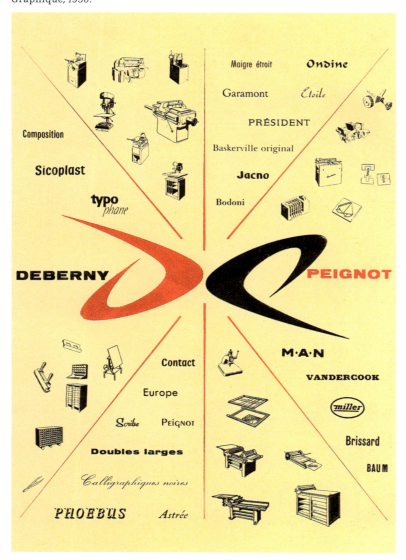

/10/
Proof from the Haas'sche type foundry from September 11, 1975 showing character widths, with alternate characters and ligatures.

/11/
The shortened character width markers to the right of the lowercase f and the ff ligature demonstrate the only two overhangs (kerns) in Ondine.

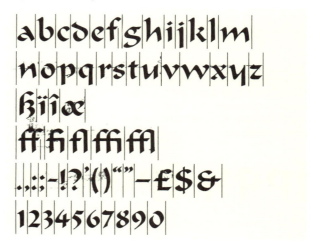

/12/
Inside double-page spread of the four-page Ondine / Calligraphiques Noires *brochure, 1956.*

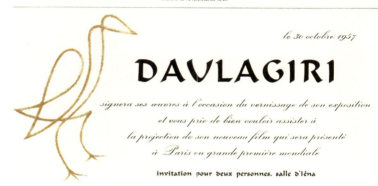

/13/
Detail from the back page of the Ondine type specimen from 1956: UVEMN were additionally available as alternative letters.

UVV EE MM NN
MENV MENV MENV

/14/
Unfortunately, both Qu ligatures are no longer available in the current versions by Bitstream and Linotype.

/15/
Three versions of the Œ diphthong: The foundry original has an uncial E while the Bitstream and Linotype versions use a roman capital E.

/16/
The fl ligature by Linotype is not an independent form, but simply f and l joined together.

/17/
Only a few characters have closed counters. The numerals are significantly smaller than the uppercase letters.

/18/
The Bitstream version is closer to the original (left), while the Linotype version is more pointed, its angles are more acute and the bowl of its p is separated.

/19/
Matching the pointed ends of the downstrokes to the optical baseline of other characters was quite a challenge.

Characters of Ondine
*for foundry type
by Deberny & Peignot, Paris.*

ABCDEFGHIJKLMN
OPQRSTUVWXYZ&
abcdefghijklmnopqrs
tuvwxyzß1234567890

Typeface comparison The DIN 16518 classification for printing types has two groups of typefaces with a derived from writing: Group VIII Schreibschriften (scripts) and Group IX Handschriftliche Antiqua (script-like serif faces). "Scripts is what they call the Latin school and chancellery types that had been turned into printing typefaces." "Script-like serifs are those typefaces that come from traditional serifs or their italics, changing the alphabet by adding a personal, hand-written touch." [10] Classifying typefaces with written properties is extremely difficult, even for the experts. Hans Rudolf Bosshard's *Technische Grundlagen der Satzherstellung* puts *Legende* into the script category, *Ondine*, however, into script-like serifs – in spite of its lowercase, which are obviously much closer to a roman serif. The difference here is supposed to be the capitals, drawn with the flourish of a decorative script in *Legende*, while *Ondine*'s caps look like a handwritten version of a normal printing type. Bosshard is aware of the problem in general and suggests a new classification model [11], proposing to merge the two groups.

All three broad pen scripts shown below appear upright and have similar characters. *Ondine* comes across as very regular, as opposed to *Legende* and *Palomba*; the difference in shape between capitals and lowercase is not very pronounced, the x-height is rather tall, as is typical for Frutiger.

/21/
Compared to these other script faces Ondine *appears very even and rather static.*

Hofstainberg

Legende
F. H. Ernst Schneidler
1937

D K W a d k n 5 8

Hofstainberg

Palomba
Georg Trump
1954

D K W a d k n 5 8

Hofstainberg

Ondine
Adrian Frutiger
1954

D K W a d k n 5 8

D	**K**	**W**	**a**	**d**	**k**	**n 5**	**8**
Vertical, strict appearance	Downstroke ends obliquely, diagonal top bent bade	Very wide, diagonal stroke a little concave on the left	Diagonal form, large x-height, counter open at the bottom	Uncial form, counter open	Ascender above cap-height, unconnected shape	Downstrokes almost terminate in a point, light strokes	Top counter open

Font production:
Adobe Font digitised by
Linotype

Font format:
PostScript Type 1

Also available:
TrueType
OpenType Com

ABCDEFGHIJKLMN
OPQRSTUVWXYZ&
abcdefghijklmnopqrs
tuvwxyzß1234567890

ÅBÇDÈFG
HIJKLMÑ
ÔPQRŠTÚ
VWXYZ&
ÆŒ¥$£€
1234567890
åbçdéfghij
klmñôpqr
štŭvwxyzß
fi fl æ œ ø ł ð
[.,:;·'/--—]
(¿¡"‹›»"!?)
{§°%@‰*†}

Regular

Pourquoi tant
d'Alphabets différ
ents! Tous servent au mêm
e but, mais aussi à exprimer la diversit
é de l'homme. C'est cette même diversité que nous retro
uvons dans les vins de Médoc. J'ai pu, un jour, relever s
oixante crus, tous de la même année. Il s'agissait certes
de vins, mais tous étaient différents. Tout est dans la n
uance du bouquet. Il en est de même pour les caractère
s! Sie fragen sich, warum es notwendig ist, so viele Schriften zur Verfügung
zu haben. Sie dienen alle zum selben, aber machen die Vielfalt des Menschen
aus. Diese Vielfalt ist wie beim Wein. Ich habe einmal eine Weinkarte studiert
mit sechzig Médoc-Weinen aus dem selben Jahr. Das ist ausnahmslos Wein,
aber doch nicht alles der gleiche Wein. Es hat eben gleichwohl Nuancen. So ist
es auch mit der Schrift. You may ask why so many different typefaces. They
all serve the same purpose but they express man's diversity. It is the same dive

rsity we find in wine. I once saw a list of Médoc wines featuring sixt
y different Médocs all of the same year. All of them were wines but ea
ch was different from the others. It's the nuances that are important.
The same is true for typefaces. Pourquoi tant d'Alphabets différents! T
ous servent au même but, mais aussi à exprimer la diversité de l'hom
me. C'est cette même diversité que nous retrouvons dans les vins de
Médoc. J'ai pu, un jour, relever soixante crus, tous de la même année.
il s'agissait certes de vins, mais tous étaient différents. Tout est dans l

a nuance du bouquet. Il en est de même p
our les caractères! Sie fragen sich, waru
m es notwendig ist, so viele Schriften zur
Verfügung zu haben. Sie dienen alle zum
selben, aber machen die Vielfalt des Mens
chen aus. Diese Vielfalt ist wie beim Wein.
Ich habe einmal eine Weinkarte studiert
mit sechzig Médoc-Weinen aus dem selbe
n Jahr. Das ist ausnahmslos Wein, aber d
och nicht alles der gleiche Wein. Es hat e

75 pt | −10   56 pt | −3   38 pt | 0   26 pt | 0   18 pt | 19 pt | 5   12.5 pt | 14 pt | 5   9 pt | 10.5 pt | 10   7.5 pt | 8.2 pt | 15

Production of type
Lumitype photosetting

The Lumitype photosetting machine was invented by the French engineers René Higonnet and Louis Moyroud and was developed in Paris and Cambridge, Massachusetts. In the United States it was known as the Photon.

René Higonnet was a patent lawyer and amateur photographer. He conceived the idea for a photosetting machine in 1944 during a visit to an offset printing shop where text set in hot metal was used for the exposure of the printing plate. The hot metal text, transferred to barite paper and recorded on film using a repro camera, served as a template for the exposure.

Higonnet had the idea of mounting the letters on a glass plate. During the exposure this plate would turn quickly and precisely. As a photographer, he knew that a flash exposure could last for only a millionth of a second. A plate with a diameter of 20 cm and a speed of 600 RPM would move 6 µm in a millionth of a second. This would result in a blurring which would be imperceptible to the human eye. If

the stroboscopic flash exposed at least one letter per revolution, then 36 000 exposures an hour would be possible. In this manner, Lumitype outstripped machine setting, which could cast up to 5700 characters an hour. In Louis Moyroud, Higonnet found an extremely hardworking partner, full of ideas. In 1944 they registered their first patent in France.

The inventors soon realised that more was needed than a stable, high-speed exposure of a single character on a revolving plate. A whole series of characters would need to be processed quickly. Furthermore, they would need to be sharply captured in the correct order, aligned precisely on the baseline. The letters and words of differing, pre-defined widths must sit together cleanly, and must be justified over the entire width of the line. The precise identification of the desired character, and the rapid calculation of its size presented a particular problem. It needed a calculating device that could convert relative values into absolute ones, which the machine could then transpose into various point sizes. Higonnet and

Moyroud developed the solution to this problem from 1946 to 1948, which represented one of their most important inventions.

With the help of Vannevar Bush and Bill Garth and his Lithomat company (later Photon, Inc.), they pressed ahead with development in the United States. Financed by members of the American Newspaper Association (ANPA), The Graphics Arts Research Foundation began its research programme on the development of the photosetting machine. Now, instead of wanting an easy, quick and reasonably priced machine, the backers at ANPA put forward a catalogue of 19 requests meant to produce a then unparalleled typographical performance. For example, they stipulated an easy method of combining various typefaces and a change in point size relative to the baseline. This actually slowed down development, and made the resulting machine expensive and prone to break down.

In 1951 the Photon 100 was launched in the USA /06/. The input station (keyboard) and the output station

/01/
Page from Louis Moyroud's workbook – attached are the first test exposures with stroboscopic flash, May 1944.

/02/
Industrial prototype of the Photon-Lumitype from 1949 – the cover of the exposure unit is raised.

/03/
This construction schematic shows the path of the light flash in the first Industrial prototype of the Photon-Lumitype.

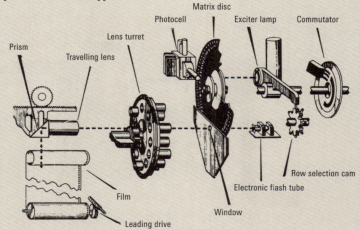

/04/
The lens disc of the Photon-Lumitype with 12 lenses for the exposure of type sizes from 5 up to 48 pt.

/05/
The Lumitype typeface disc contained 14 type weights on seven rings, with special characters on an eighth.

/06/
Right-hand view into the open exposure unit of a 1954 Photon 100, with the swappable typeface disc (left).

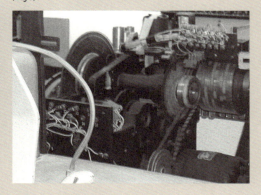

(the exposure unit) were separate units. The input station consisted of a control panel, a paper tape punch and a typewriter. In the exposure unit there was a rotating glass plate (later replaced with a synthetic one), which acted as the matrix plate /05/. The stroboscopic flash was so targeted and focused that it would hit the chosen letter precisely. Twelve lenses, behind which were mounted movable prisms, steered the light beam onto a film roll and exposed the image of the letter.

Fixed and movable prisms behind 12 objective lenses directed the light beam onto a roll of film and exposed the letter image. One glass plate held 16 (or in the Lumitype, 14) interchangeable alphabets so, altogether, 17 280 characters were on each one, which offered then unheard-of typographical possibilities. Through collaboration with the well-established French type foundry of Deberny & Peignot both the throughput and output quality were subsequently improved. Unfortunately, the French Lumitype company and American Photon, Inc. ceased collaboration, and instead independently worked on the further development of the device.

In general, Cambridge, Massachusetts-based Photon placed less emphasis on the typographic quality than did Lumitype in Paris. While in Cambridge metal types were copied and released under different names, in Paris the creation of new typefaces and an appropriate redrawing of original ones was encouraged. Final designs for the Lumitype were produced with a cap height of 11 cm, in contrast to those for the Photon, which were taller but did not allow for accents on uppercase letters, since such accents are rarely needed in the American newspaper market.

Whereas the designer was limited to an 18-unit division for each of the characters when designing typefaces for photosetting on Monotype or Linotype systems, 36 units, i.e. twice as many, were available on the Lumitype. Overshooting characters were no longer a problem either. However, when producing original drawings, the characteristics of the photosetting system had to be taken into account: sharp incisions in the letter shapes always had to be made a little wider, since these had a tendency to fill in. In contrast, insufficient illumination of the type negative could result in the rounding-off of right-angled corners. By pulling out the corners into points, the type designer could mitigate this effect. Very fine hairlines could also pose problems, since they might not receive sufficient blackness during exposure, and could break off when copying the matrices. They needed to be drawn thicker. The camera that exposed the characters on the matrix was mounted on a vibration-proof block of granite. Two to three hours of concentrated work were necessary until a plate – each character adjusted by hand – was exposed and developed. Each plate was produced individually, and each client could choose their own combination of typeface and characters.

/07/
The Lumitype system with the input unit in the middle and exposure unit on the right-hand side.

/08/
Table of levels and positions for character placement, drawn by Adrian Frutiger for Lumitype.

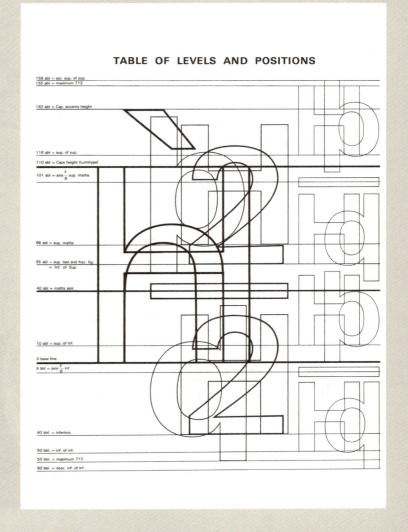

Name of typeface	Commissioned by	Designer	Design | Publication	Typesetting technology	Manufacturer	Weights
Méridien	Deberny & Peignot	Adrian Frutiger	1953 | 1957	Lumitype photosetting	– Deberny & Peignot	4
Latine•				Photon photosetting	– Photon Inc.•	4
Meridien••				Handsetting	– Deberny & Peignot	3|4
Latin 725•••				CRT and laser digital typesetting	– D. Stempel AG | Linotype••	6
				PostScript digital typesetting	Adobe | Linotype••	6
					Bitstream•••	6

MÉRIDIEN

The impetus for *Méridien* came from Rémy, Charles Peignot's son, in 1953. Once we had *Président,* a modern Latin jobbing typeface, in our repertoire, a Latin face for setting shorter text was to be designed in addition. Rémy said it was a pity for me to be designing fantasy typefaces and that my talents would be better spent on classical type. One of the main reasons for including such a face may have been that the competition in Marseille, the Fonderie Olive, had brought out *Vendôme* /02/ by François Ganeau in 1951; a modern, good, strong and also successful text face with a few Latin touches. However, it appears somewhat harsh; with its straight lines, the elegance of Latin typefaces is not expressed. In comparison, *Méridien* is much finer and more elegant.

Drawing this beautiful classical typeface was a wonderful task. The first year at Deberny & Peignot was one of getting to know each other, feeling our way. Charles Peignot, a man of vision, had engaged me in 1952 because he already intended to take over the Lumitype production for Europe. So he needed somebody to be responsible for type design for the newfangled phototypesetting machines. This was the reason he brought me to Paris, although he didn't tell me so. In the meantime I was occupied with all sorts of 'gap-fillers': drawing a script, fantasy typefaces, and working on the hot metal text typeface *Méridien.*

First I developed the normal, so-called light weight between January and May 1954.[1] I had discussed the character of the typeface with Rémy a great deal – we also studied old fonts together – so that I already had the typeface completed in my head when I began sketching, as ever, around 24 point size, on tracing paper with a very hard pencil for the outlines and a softer one for filling in. The first letters were a couple of tricky ones: 'mondegvr' and uppercase H and O. I used a sharp knife to make corrections; I never used an eraser, I always scratched and scraped. I had a trick for final artwork with an x-height of 8 cm. Instead of drawing the same downstrokes umpteen times, I made one perfect downstroke, prepared a block and had around a hundred copies made on art paper at the proofing press. I then cut out and stuck together what I needed, using black paint on cardboard to clean up the joins.

After the *Méridien* regular weight, I started redrawing the classical hot metal typefaces such as *Bodoni* and *Garamont*[2] for the Lumitype photosetting machine. This meant I didn't have enough time to complete the bold and semi-bold *Méridien* weights myself. So, along with the director of the engraving department, Marcel Mouchel, I determined the basic letters and the weights. He then completed the entire character set. An italic was initially made for Lumitype only; one for hot metal was added later.

As early as 1949 the first prototype of a photosetting machine was unveiled in the USA by its inventors, René Higonnet and Louis Moyroud.[3] It was named Photon. In France the

About Méridien   The name 'Méridien' was chosen by Rémy Peignot, lending it an association with the South. 'Méridien' (meridian in English) commonly means pertaining to midday or also to a circle on the Earth's surface passing through the equator and connecting the poles.[4] Rémy Peignot designed the beautiful publicity brochures for *Méridien* on that theme in the late 1950s showing a globe of the Earth opened up, defined by lines of longitude that extend beyond the Earth and reach out to the edge of the page. /39/

The first design drafts /03–08/ should not be regarded merely in relation to *Méridien,* but also as containing important steps on the way to defining Frutiger's type design. The influence of humanist roman typefaces can clearly be seen in the lowercase letters /03/. Ascenders and descenders are highly pronounced. The small counters of a and e, as well as the face's rhythm and proportions are typical features. The unaccented beginning of the curve of the a has its origins in humanist roman typefaces. In the lowercase a one can also discern the influence of Walter Käch by the round transition of the bowl into the stem. However, in designing *Méridien,* Frutiger overcame this influence and instead followed the example of the humanist minuscule /10/. On the whole he found his own shape for the a by drawing the bowl bigger, thus making both counters of equal size. This a became a hallmark of all of Frutiger's text faces.

Also interesting is Frutiger's search for serif shapes which, alternately pointing to one side in the 'novipa' design /08/, brings to mind *Phoebus.* This design with its shortened descenders and angular join of the a curve to the stem may be regarded as a precursor to *Méridien.*

In 1954 work began on the foundry version of *Méridien.* The three upright weights were not completed until 1959, the italic not until 1966. On the other hand, all four weights for Lumitype photosetting were already finished in 1957. After Deberny & Peignot was liquidated,[5] D. Stempel AG expanded *Méridien* to six weights for Linotype photosetting. Today it is available as a digital font in PostScript, TrueType and OpenType formats. Bitstream has it in a plagiarised version as *Latin 725.*

At gravis ut fundo vix tandem redditus im
Jam senior, madidaque fluens in veste
Summa petit scopuli, siccaque in rupe res
Illum et labentem Teucri, et risere natan
Et salsos rident revomentem pectore fluct
Hic læta extremis spes est accensa duobu
Sergesto, Mnestheique, Gyan, superar
Sergestus capit ante locum, scopuloque
Nec tota tamen ille prior præeunte carina :
Parte prior; partem rostro premit æmu
At media socios incedens nave per ipsos

/01/
Text sample of foundry type
Méridien *demi-gras (enlarged): the*
capitals appear integrated into the
text, thanks to the low cap height.

/02/
Foundry type type specimen
compo dp *by Deberny & Peignot,*
1961: title page in Méridien;
specimen pages of Vendôme *by*
their competitor, Fonderie Olive,
Marseille.

/03/
*Pencil drawing, undated
(original size): lowercase e and
a have very small counters,
atypical of Frutiger.*

mintrcoulphdafvbqswzxy

nomelipnas

/04/
*Pencil drawing, undated
(reduced): design for an italic
including features of
the later Méridien italique.*

/05/
*Pencil drawing, undated
(reduced): this typeface design
shows similarities to both
Ondine and Méridien italique.*

/06/
*Blueprint, c.1953 (greatly reduced):
only a few early drawings
show Frutiger's search for his
typical a-shape.*

elida

Hynomelipas

bcdfw nomelipas

ghjkrtuvxyz

/07/
*Pencil drawing (slightly reduced):
Méridien gras, drawn with a
soft pencil for the shape and a hard
one for the outline.*

TPAGKUJ

HEDRO

/08/
*Pencil drawing, undated
(greatly reduced): design for a
Méridien-like typeface in
eight weights – the serifs of the
uprights are asymmetrical.*

novipa   novipa

novipa   novipa

novipa   novipa

novipa   novipa

The first book in Europe produced on Lumitype, *La Folle Journée ou Le Mariage de Figaro* was set in *Méridien* /09/. The choice of text was no coincidence; it is a comedy from 1775–78 by Pierre Augustin Caron de Beaumarchais[6], a polemic against the politics and society of the 'Ancien régime' in France, hence it was banned by the king and only premiered in 1784. The book too, like so many on the eve of the French Revolution, underwent several changes by the censors before it was printed in 1785. Like the play, it was a huge success on release[7] and just one year later was adapted to become the opera *Le nozze di Figaro* by Wolfgang Amadeus Mozart, whereby the piece is still world famous to this day.

Thus, a book of rebellious content was chosen to present a revolutionary typesetting method (around 1454 Gutenberg printed the book of books, the Bible, to present his revolutionary method of publishing). That a new typeface like *Méridien* should be chosen ahead of a classic one for this new technology corresponds to the progressive thinking of the people involved.

Photon was adapted for the European market by Deberny & Peignot and called 'Lumitype', with preparations beginning in the fall of 1953. It took many attempts before it could be presented at the Salon International des Techniques Papetières et Graphiques three years later. For the machine's introduction to Europe,[8] Deberny & Peignot wanted to present a new font of their very own, *Méridien,* in addition to the classical ones. We began work on the Lumitype version during the course of 1955. It still appeared a bit thin. We subsequently 'fattened' it a little. The specialist book printers Berger & Levrault in Nancy bought the first Lumitype and quickly presented a book set in Lumitype *Méridien* – Beaumarchais' *Le Mariage de Figaro* /09/ – at the machine's official inauguration in 1957.

When it came to *Méridien* there were a couple of fundamental considerations about form and character. The starting point on the one hand was the Latins with their triangular serifs. Due to its arched serifs, the sometimes slighty curvy strokes of the capitals /18/ and the minimally concave stems, *Méridien* is actually closer to written text and is both more elegant and more legible than traditional Latins (see page 29). The venetian oldstyle by Nicolas Jenson (c.1470) was the other starting point /14/, being an important precedent for me. Alfred Willimann had always raved about it. Its even rhythm fascinated me from the start. It's a question of stroke width and proportion. The hardest thing about a new typeface is finding the right proportions between black and white. The old Gothic typefaces are a prime example of balance /11/. Even the curves end in vertical strokes – which makes it hard to read – producing a uniquely even grid with consistent white spacing /13/. One can also find attempts among the typefaces of the Renaissance to align the white contrast of counters and spaces between letters. This was my aim for *Méridien* too.

/09/
Dust jacket and inside page of
Le Mariage de Figaro, *1957: the first book set on Lumitype in* Méridien *romain, italique and demi-gras.*

I had enlarged *Jenson,* drawn lines down the middle of the vertical strokes and seen that it too produced an even grid. Walter Käch, who, as a lettering artist, spent no time with printing types, always had a different opinion regarding spacing. His proof using the Golden Section /15/ was very complicated.[9] Käch said that the counter spaces of the letters ought to be greater than the spaces between letters, while I contested that that wasn't possible for a text typeface. His great model was the Imperial Roman capitals. They have a completely different rhythm from text faces and are also less vertically stressed. The spaces between letters have to be narrower in larger point sizes compared to smaller ones. This was also done in casting type for large sizes. However, *Méridien* was supposed to be a text typeface for setting long copy. The lowercase n and the o I placed in a precisely proportioned rectangle /19/. If there wasn't enough space, the reader would instantly find the type too tight. Like *Jenson*, and basically like the Carolingian minuscules or semi-uncials /10/ before it, *Méridien* is fairly wide.

I wanted to avoid giving it too much of a rigid character. That's why there are no really straight stems. They're slightly concave, in other words they become slightly stronger at the top and bottom /18/. These barely noticeable swells are a lively expression of natural growth and, in my opinion, stop the reader from tiring too quickly. In order to further support the reading flow, *Méridien* has relatively strong serifs. The serifs and terminals on curves (such as f and j) have an individual, consistent character /20/. I wanted neither the Art Nouveau-style curly pig's tail of the Latins – that was out of place by the '50s – nor the teardrop shapes. I really hated those. They seemed to me to be plump foreign objects. Perhaps I was trying to be too consistent, I made no differences at all between the individual

Rhythm and proportion Graphic designer Walter Käch, who taught Frutiger lettering at the Kunstgewerbeschule in Zurich, studied Ancient Roman capitals in detail and wrote general thoughts on the subject in his book *Rhythm and Proportion in Lettering.* He writes, "Thus in the balanced word-picture we notice that the inner spaces of the letters reveal the proportion of the Golden Mean. The letter O should be considered as a basis for the width of all the other letters as well as for inner spaces. (…) Rhythm and proportion together form the basis for the harmonious aspect of the page."[10]

Käch's drawing /15/ shows the Golden Section for constructing the o and, using the letter sequence 'rom', for counters and spaces. Frutiger did not agree with Käch's ratios for text typefaces: "The ideal face seemed to me to be 'Jenson' typeface which, despite all the technical deficiencies of a 15th century typeface, may serve as the quality model of a perfect overall appearance. In order to better explain the secret of these laws, let us make a few basic reflections on the structure of a typeface. The true model of such a well balanced appearance we find in Gutenberg's pages of text set in his black letter type. His type is called 'Textur' because the page of type gives the appearance of a texture made of equal mashes. (…) The type designers of the Latin faces of the renaissance period maintained and further developed these structural qualities by giving equal white value (deliberately or guided by their feeling for style) to all space within

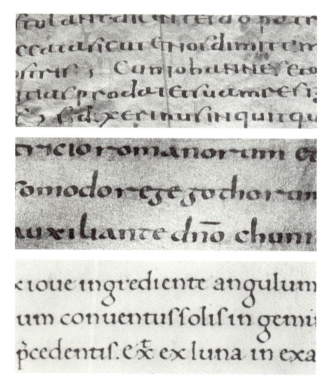

/10/
Historical scripts: semi-uncials, early 6th century, Carolingian minuscule, 8th century, humanist minuscule, 15th century.

/11/
Although they have different shapes, both Gutenberg's textura and Jenson's roman typeface (right-hand page) have an evenly balanced text appearance.

/12/
The symmetry of strokes in gothic script and roman typefaces is made evident by using a grid – Old English, Adobe Jenson, Méridien.

/13/
Evenness of counters and spaces in gothic script, diversification in roman typefaces.

the characters (…). This is one of the paramount rules of the typographic aesthetics of a serifed typeface." [11]
Thus, according to Frutiger, the spaces between letters ought to be equal to the counters, rather than being based, as Käch argued, on the Golden Section. When it comes to serif faces for text setting, Frutiger's objection is understandable. Walter Käch's method is, however, better for sans serifs. There is no contradiction here, as the spaces between letters should be smaller for sans serifs than for serif faces (see page 92), according to both Käch and Frutiger. In fact, Frutiger never employed the Golden Section in his typeface design.
Today there are new problems in type-design. Optimum readability means that operators have to adjust tracking; the smaller the type, the bigger the spaces between letters. There is no fixed tracking for digital fonts. The basic proviso for a harmonious text appearance is, in any case, that the font be fitted properly by the designer or manufacturer. [12]

serif shapes: a serif is a serif. Now, with the hindsight of lots of experience, I would probably choose the classical teardrop shapes. One looks at *Garamond,* its absolutely natural-seeming teardrops contain something like an ideal form, a truly simple, clear point-shaped terminal /20/.

From this point of view I would have to describe the y as a transgression of youth. At the time I just didn't get it together to let the y end in a teardrop, while all other serifs are more or less pointed. So I placed a normal serif on the downstroke /21/. Another peculiarity of *Méridien* is its low cap height. This stems cames from my discussions with Emil Ruder in Basel. He was convinced that a typeface ought to appear the same in any language, whether it be an English text with few capitals or a German text full of them. The reduction in cap height reflects this desired optical adaptation. Today I'm no longer so sure about the merits of such equalisation. Diversity is where real wealth lies. Making these characteristic differences valid is better than adapting everything to fit one another. An early Latin text sample of *Méridien* demonstrates just how harmoniously the few short capitals blend in /01/. Of course Latin text samples always look the nicest because there are very few diagonals in a line. K W and Z were only added to the alphabet later on, while X was seldom used. I must stress, however, that the most harmonious line is not automatically the most legible one. Only the diversity of individual letters with ascenders and descenders, with straight or diagonal strokes or curves guarantees the best legibility. With later text samples I always insisted on showing German texts alongside French ones. That way one can see straight away whether a typeface is sufficiently versatile to meet different demands.

/14/
The evenly balanced rhythm of Nicolas Jenson's roman typeface from 1471 remains a model today.

/16/
Compared to oldstyle typefaces, the pointed serifs of Latins produce simpler counter shapes.

/17/
Concave serifs appear more elegant than ones with a flat base – serifs with a protruding base appear lumpy and misshapen.

/18/
Straight strokes appear technical, while tapered strokes look more sensitive and natural.

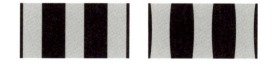

/15/
Walter Käch's study for a typeface written with a broad pen, showing construction and proportion based on the Golden Section.

/19/
Méridien has mostly tapered strokes, slightly inclined stress and evenly sized counters.

Let's look at the individual letters of *Méridien.* I purposely inclined the P stem slightly to the left /22/. I wanted to avoid it from leaning forward. I did the same thing with the r. These things are details that one sorts out in one's head, although they're not really justi- fied. The diagonal downstroke of the R doesn't meet the stem but the arc, which is normal with Latin characters /23/. The search for the right a shape can be seen on the 'elida' /06/ blueprint. The boldly swinging connection I discarded quickly; it's simply another shape altogether. Käch had drawn such a shape with his pen – which looked wonderful – but they don't appear in any classical typefaces, which all have an angled connection. I asked myself, why couldn't the a flow as nicely at the top as the e does at the bottom? I didn't want a teardrop shape because those don't exist in capitals, except maybe in the J. That was an intellectual decision. For reasons of legibility it would have been wiser to terminate the top of the a like the c, with a semi-serif /24/. I felt very strongly that the arc of the n should meet the stem on the curve /25/, which comes from my time spent drawing plants at school in Zurich under my teacher Karl Schmid.[13] It was only in later life that I became conscious that there's a new stroke in those places, that the stroke is simply attached straight to the stem.

The most difficult letter is the g, it has slightly too large an upper bowl in the regular weight of the hot metal *Méridien.* The spaces of the upper bowl, middle and loop were intended to be the same optically. That way the g looks a bit scrunched up. It's more bal- anced in the bold and semi-bold weights /31/, going back to Marcel Mouchel, the engraver. The f and j are purposely kept narrow, as I was still very influenced by type founding /20/. Overhangs were always a little problematic. Even though no ligatures were necessary for

The multitude of originals *Méridien,* Adrian Frutiger's first text typeface, unites many of the substantial design findings that mark his entire work. He created a strict – he calls it purist – typeface that has a rather angular ex- pression (typical of Latins) made apparent by its pointed serifs /20/ and further reinforced by the absence of the teardrop shape. At the same time it hints at a sensitive introverted touch thanks to a subtle diagonal stress, slightly concave serifs /17/ and downstrokes that taper in the middle /18/. These are details of shape that stem from Frutiger's time writing with a broad-edged pen in Alfred Willimann's classes in Zurich.

Méridien was made for foundry type and photosetting at the same time. Four weights: romain, italique, demi- gras and gras were made for Lumitype photosetting in 1957. Photon, the American company, which released the typeface under the name of *Latine* at the same time, named the same weights Medium, Medium Italic, Bold and Extrabold.

The regular weight was given yet another name for found- ry type, 'normal'. It was released in 1957; the bold fol- lowed in 1958 and the semi-bold in 1959. The italic did not exist until 1966, even though it was advertised in the *Typografische Monatsblätter* as early as 1958.[14]

The individual characters of *Méridien* sometimes vary strongly between handsetting and photosetting, but also within photosetting between Lumitype and Photon. There are also major differences between early versions and

---

/20/
Compared to Adobe Garamond *(left),* Méridien *looks very uniform and hard with semi-serifs on its terminals.*

Hcjrfs Hcjrfs

/21/
Adobe Garamond *with teardrop shape at end of y – horizontal foot serifs are more of an exception:* Bembo *italic,* Candida, Méridien.

y γ y y

/22/
For foundry type (left) the two letters Pr are slightly inclined to the left; this was changed for Linotype.

Pr Pr

/23/
As is the norm for Latins, the diago- nal downstroke of R connects to the bowl, although unusually in this case it connects to a straight line rather than a curve.

R

/24/
The start of the a stroke is identical to the curve end without the semi-serif on e and c – for Linotype lowercase c was straightened.

aec c

/25/
The transition from stem to curve is round, the counter is vertically centered, making lowercase n appear rather static.

n

/26/
Méridien *has no reversed or mirrored shapes, b and q have a corner in the counter, while d and p are round.*

bq dp

/27/
The original Méridien *has very short descenders – these were later made longer for Linotype.*

pp

/28/
The connection of long s and round s is more apparent in the original version (left) than in the Linotype version.

ß ß

/29/
Diareses in foundry type differ in size; this was corrected for Linotype, where they are also not so close.

Ä ä Ä ä

/30/
Changes of shape may have technical or aesthetic reasons – the cedilla by Linotype (below) is a product of convenience.

Æ æ Ç
Æ æ Ç

subsequent adaptations by Linotype and Bitstream. The differences can be seen especially clearly in lowercase f, on the one hand in the shape and width of the curve, but also in the quality of the cross-stroke. The f curve, which was drawn protruding only slightly by Adrian Frutiger, in the Photon version appears pared down to a caricature. Likewise in the regular weight of the digital version by Linotype, the curve is far too tight, while slightly better by Bitstream **/34/**. The cross-stroke is also different. In the 'originals' (foundry type, Lumitype, Photon) Adrian Frutiger tapers the cross-stroke towards both sides, like the shape of the serifs. Sadly there is none of this in the digital adaptations; it is now a stroke with parallel sides **/34/**.

The shapes are more diverse still in the *Méridien* italics. The diagram of lowercase b d f p q shows different curve shapes and angles, long or short upstrokes, sometimes with stressed terminals 'only' on the descenders, and sometimes with pronounced serifs **/35/**.

The likely reason for the various shapes and angles, and therefore for the differentiated character widths, is the adaptation to the width units of the different systems. Whether or not questions of design came into it, can no longer be gleaned after so many years.

this narrow f, I drew them anyway and they became totally independent shapes **/33/**. When it came to the fi ligature, I naturally allowed myself to set a teardrop shape, because it was an i-dot. Nevertheless I have to say that looking at it properly now for the first time, it's still a very nice f. The two downstrokes of the fi ligature should have at least the same space as the m. Perhaps it was a bit on the wide side, but I didn't want to interrupt the rhythm of the type by making it any narrower. Ligatures, which developed due to technical type-casting constraints, became increasingly narrow over the years, so that they almost looked like single letters. To my eyes they are often clearly too narrow.

The most important thing about *Méridien* for me was its even rhythm. However, the overall impression wasn't supposed to be rigid, but lively and organic and therefore reader-friendly. I wanted readers to have the feeling they were strolling through a forest, rather than through a suburb with dour, straight houses.

/31/
The upper bowl of the g is too large in the regular weight for foundry type (left); this was corrected for Linotype.

/32/
Along with Frutiger's typical italic uppercase shape, the classic roman uppercase shape is also available as an alternative for foundry type.

/33/
The f ligatures are based on the width of the m; the digital version has only two of the original five.

ggg ggg

&&

/34/
f in regular, semi-bold and bold: from top to bottom – foundry type, Lumitype and Photon photosetting, PostScript Linotype and Bitstream.

/35/
Italics with and without serifs, from top to bottom: foundry type, Lumitype and Photon photosetting, PostScript Linotype and Bitstream.

/36/
Final artwork, undated: designs were made for a narrow Méridien *for Lumitype that was never produced.*

fff
fff
fff
fff
fff

bdfpq
bdfpq
bdfpq
bdfpq
bdfpq

peuple a bien voulu
le nouveau monde
de demain

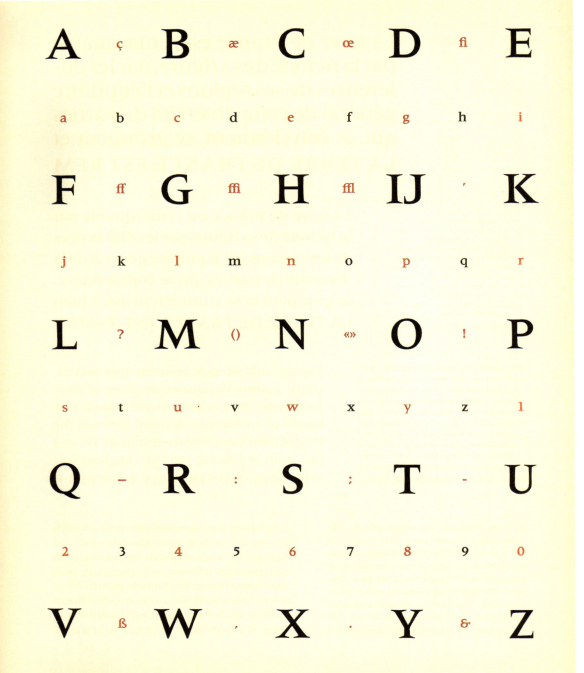

/37/
Second page of the four-page type specimen for foundry type Méridien demi-gras by Deberny & Peignot, Paris 1959.

/38/
Jacket design by Adrian Frutiger from 1964 set in Méridien – pocket book series Miroirs de l'art by Editions Hermann, Paris.

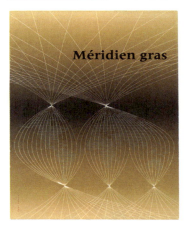

/39/
Title pages of Méridien type specimens for foundry type: regular, gras 1958, demi-gras 1959 – the design is by Rémy Peignot.

*Characters of Méridien normal
for foundry type by
Deberny & Peignot, Paris.*

ABCDEFGHIJKLMN
OPQRSTUVWXYZ&
abcdefghijklmnopqrs
tuvwxyzß1234567890

Dualism of shapes in nature Frutiger's first text type-face *Méridien* – indeed all of his type design – was influenced by shapes in nature and people. In the *Typografische Monatsblätter* he wrote, "A stroke in type that is not straight and taut but alive allows alternative forms to emerge from the white spaces between the black elements. This gives rise to a dualism that the eye is used to seeing in nature. For example, we think of the shapes of trees, and see the same fine curves in a forest that reach from root to bough, leaving convex empty spaces between trees that we do not consciously take in, yet they are part of our visual perception."[15] /18/
The human foot is also considered (instep and arch of the sole). He wrote of serif shapes that, "the triangular extension of a serif visually reinforces the line better than the classic form of parallel serifs. It has to be noted that two pointed serifs opposite one another make for a more consistent overall appearance by using the white spaces within or between letters better than thick, angular serifs that protrude cone-like into the inner space sculpture, thus breaking the uniformity of a chain sequence."[16] /17/

*Full page advertisements
(1957 below, 1966 right):* Méridien
*for foundry type was initially
only released in three weights –
the italic only followed, unlike the
Lumitype version, in 1966.*

Font production:
Adobe Font digitisec by
Linotype

Font format:
PostScript Type 1

Also available:
TrueType
OpenType Std
XSF

Meridien™
Linotype
6 weights

ABCDEFGHIJKLMN
OPQRSTUVWXYZ&
abcdefghijklmnopqrs
tuvwxyzß1234567890

Sie fragen sich
warum es notwen
dig ist, so viele Schriften zu
r Verfügung zu haben. Sie dienen alle z

um selben, aber machen die Vielfalt des Menschen aus. Di
ese Vielfalt ist wie beim Wein. Ich habe einmal eine Wein
karte studiert mit sechzig Médoc-Weinen aus dem selben
Jahr. Das ist ausnahmslos Wein, aber doch nicht alles der
gleiche Wein. Es hat eben gleichwohl Nuancen. So ist es

auch mit der Schrift. *You may ask why so many different typefaces.* They all serve the sa
me purpose but they express man's diversity. It is the same diversity we find in wi
ne. I once saw a list of Médoc wines featuring sixty different Médocs all of the sam
e year. All of them were wines but each was different from the others. It's the nua
nces that are important. The same is true for typefaces. *Pourquoi tant d'Alphabets diff
érents!* Tous servent au même but, mais aussi à exprimer la diversité de l'homme. C'
est cette même diversité que nous retrouvons dans les vins de Médoc. J'ai pu, un j

our, relever soixante crus, tous de la même année. Il s'agissait certes de v
ins, mais tous étaient différents. Tout est dans la nuance du bouquet. Il e
n est de même pour les caractères! *Sie fragen sich, warum es notwendig ist, so
viele Schriften zur Verfügung zu haben.* Sie dienen alle zum selben, aber ma
chen die Vielfalt des Menschen aus. Diese Vielfalt ist wie beim Wein. Ich
habe einmal eine Weinkarte studiert mit sechzig Médoc-Weinen aus de
m selben Jahr. Das ist ausnahmslos Wein, aber doch nicht alles der gleic
he Wein. Es hat eben gleichwohl Nuancen. So ist es auch mit der Schrift.

You may ask why so many different typefaces. Th
ey all serve the same purpose but they expr
ess man's diversity. It is the same diversity w
e find in wine. I once saw a list of Médoc wi
nes featuring sixty different Médocs all of t
he same year. All of them were wines but ea
ch was different from the others. It's the nu
ances that are important. The same is true f
or typefaces. *Pourquoi tant d'Alphabets différen
ts!* Tous servent au même but, mais aussi à e

72 pt | –40   54 pt | –30   36 pt | –15   24 pt | –10   16 pt | 19 pt | –5   11 pt | 13 pt | 0   8 pt | 10.2 pt | 5   6.5 pt | 8 pt | 15

ÅBÇDÈFG
HIJKLMÑ
ÔPQRŠTÜ
VWXYZ&
ÆŒ¥$£€
1234567890
åbçdéfghij
klmñôpqrš
tüvwxyzß
fi fl æ œ ø ł ð
[.,:;·'/-–—]
(¿¡"«‹›»"!?)
{§°%@‰*†}

Roman

*ÅBÇDÈFG
HIJKLMÑ
ÔPQRŠTÜ
VWXYZ&
ÆŒ¥$£€
1234567890
åbçdéfghij
klmñôpqrš
tüvwxyzß
fi fl æ œ ø ł ð
[.,:;·'/-–—]
(¿¡"«‹›»"!?)
{§°%@‰*†}*

Italic

ÅBÇDÈFG
HIJKLMÑ
ÔPQRŠTÜ
VWXYZ&
ÆŒ¥$£€
1234567890
åbçdéfghij
klmñôpqrš
tüvwxyzß
fi fl æ œ ø ł ð
[.,:;·'/-–—]
(¿¡"«‹›»"!?)
{§°%@‰*†}

Medium

*ÅBÇDÈFG
HIJKLMÑ
ÔPQRŠTÜ
VWXYZ&
ÆŒ¥$£€
1234567890
åbçdéfghij
klmñôpqrš
tüvwxyzß
fi fl æ œ ø ł ð
[.,:;·'/-–—]
(¿¡"«‹›»"!?)
{§°%@‰*†}*

Medium Italic

**ÅBÇDÈFG
HIJKLMÑ
ÔPQRŠTÜ
VWXYZ&
ÆŒ¥$£€
1234567890
åbçdéfghij
klmñôpqrš
tüvwxyzß
fi fl æ œ ø ł ð
[.,:;·'/-–—]
(¿¡"«‹›»"!?)
{§°%@‰*†}**

Bold

***ÅBÇDÈFG
HIJKLMÑ
ÔPQRŠTÜ
VWXYZ&
ÆŒ¥$£€
1234567890
åbçdéfghij
klmñôpqrš
tüvwxyzß
fi fl æ œ ø ł ð
[.,:;·'/-–—]
(¿¡"«‹›»"!?)
{§°%@‰*†}***

Bold Italic

Typeface comparison Independence is what distinguishes the three typefaces shown below. They do not really fit into old style (pointed serifs) nor Latins in the sense of typefaces evolved from the classical model (diagonal stress).

The Latin-like *Vendôme* by François Ganeau is used to compare with *Méridien*. It has long triangular serifs. Also shown is *Trump Mediaeval* by Georg Trump, basically a humanist typeface with angular, almost rigid shapes. Its serifs are relatively strong, their triangular shape and length form the connecting element here as well.

Méridien oozes symmetry and calm, due to the even balance of the counters. This is particularly noticeable in the lowercase a which, in contrast to *Vendôme*, has a small bowl compared to the upper counter. The symmetry of the a shape in *Trump Mediaeval* is interrupted by the flattened top.

Méridien gets its restrained feel from its concave serifs and curved stems, whereas the lively dynamic of *Vendôme* is mainly due to its characters veering slightly to the right, as well as its tapered lines (e.g. R and J). *Trump Mediaeval* is brought to life chiefly by the previously mentioned breaks in its curves, visible in a e and n.

/42/
Measurements of stroke widths and proportions of the Méridien *regular weight.*

Roman					
	Hh = 10.00 cm	nh = 7.23 cm	oh = 7.78 cm	Hh : Hw = 1 : 0.74	nh : nw = 1 : 0.87
	Hw = 7.43	nw = 6.33	ow = 7.43	Hw : Hs = 1 : 0.18	nw : ns = 1 : 0.19
	Hs = 1.36	ns = 1.21	os = 1.43	Hs : Hq = 1 : 0.45	nh : oh = 1 : 1.08
	Hq = 0.62	nq = 0.62	oq = 0.34		nw : ow = 1 : 1.17

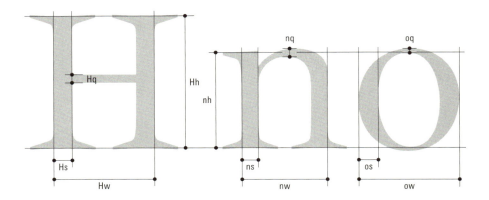

/43/
Compared to the other two type-faces Méridien *appears more delicate; it has fewer idiosyncratic letter shapes and a larger x-height.*

Hofstainberg

Vendôme
François Ganeau
1951

BJKabpy37

Hofstainberg

Méridien
Adrian Frutiger
1954

BJKabpy37

B	J	K	a	b	p	y	3 7
Hollow horizontals	Arch ends in a half-serif	Oblique down-stroke without curve	Arch without serif or drop, hollow serif	No serif at bottom counter	Round connection, symmetrical counter	Horizontal serif at bottom	Open shape, diagonal

Hofstainberg

Trump Mediaeval
Georg Trump
1954

BJKabpy37

*Comparison showing the
different weights and angle of
the italics.*

	Hh	Hw	Hs	Hq
Roman	10.00 cm	7.43 = 1	1.36 = 1	0.62 = 1
Medium	10.00	8.32 = 1.12	1.82 = 1.34	0.86 = 1.39
Bold	10.00	9.50 = 1.28	2.42 = 1.78	1.07 = 1.72
Italic	10.00	7.13 = 0.96	1.09 = 0.80	0.62 = 1

13.5°

/45/

*Height comparison showing the
differences of x-heights to
ascenders and descenders – the cap
height is the starting point.*

cm **Vendôme**
43.2 pt

cm **Méridien**
45.8 pt

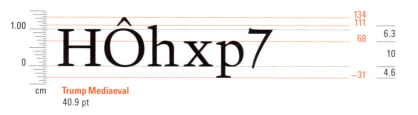

cm **Trump Mediaeval**
40.9 pt

Name of typefaces	Commissioned by	Designer	Design | Publication	Typesetting technology	Manufacturer	Weights
Garamont, Janson, Baskerville, Caslon, Perpetua, Times, Bodoni, Sphinx etc.	Deberny & Peignot	Adrian Frutiger, Ladislas Mandel and others	starting 1954 | starting 1957	Lumitype photosetting	– Deberny & Peignot	40–50

Caractères Lumitype

In New York in 1949, Frenchmen Louis M. Moyroud and René A. Higonnet presented their prototype for an electromechanical photosetting machine /35/. Thereupon, the Graphic Arts Research Foundation was founded in Cambridge, Massachusetts, in order to fund its development.[1] Charles Peignot, who knew about the Photon-Lumitype project, decided to take over its manufacture and sale in Europe. However, before the contract was signed a few things needed sorting out.[2]

When Peignot employed me in 1952 he already knew that he would soon be wanting somebody to design typefaces for this new machine. In March 1954 the first Photon delivered to Paris started to be assembled, whose individual components were sent directly from America. Deberny & Peignot unveiled this machine in May 1954 at the Salon International des Techniques Papetières et Graphiques (TPG) in Paris /43/. In one advertisement it was called 'La Composeuse Photographique Lumitype (Photon aux USA)'. It wasn't a Lumitype, it was an American Photon.[3] We couldn't yet develop a machine plus typesetting disc for the French market because that was a major undertaking. Besides which some of the parts had to be adapted to European standards, for instance the character layout and the keyboard. Those sort of things were different on the American Photon and the French Lumitype. Overall they were the same, hence the term Photon-Lumitype was often used. The first Lumitype made in France was presented at the Salon TPG in Paris in 1956 /44/ and again a year later in Switzerland at Graphic 57 in Lausanne. On this occasion Charles Peignot founded the Association Typographique Internationale (ATypI).[4]

We had the Photon at Deberny & Peignot and experimenting with it led to adjustments. The Photon typesetting discs contained eight rows with two fonts each, making sixteen fonts altogether. With twelve possible point sizes, that meant one disc had over 17000 characters available at any time. For the Lumitype we put special characters and flying accents on the innermost row, so a disc consisted of fourteen alphabets plus one row of special characters /01/. One had a proper little composing room with fantastic possibilities for setting complicated textsetting and mixing type of any kind. Photosetting brought about far-reaching changes to the printing presses and composing rooms. One typesetting disc replaced many cases full of lead type, which weighed tons, film exposure replaced metal setting.

Charles Peignot determined the type selection for Lumitype, and I was responsible from the start for redrawing the typefaces; he trusted in me completely. He had other things to attend to and was happy to leave the whole type bazaar to me. The very first thing I did was to develop a numbering system /03/, because names were out of the question. I was familiar with the classification using stylistic descriptions by Maximilien Vox /04/, and it was a great idea of his to simply give them names. – For an international business,

About Lumitype The idea of setting type by photographic means was formulated by American Michael Alisoff as early as 1870, and the first patent for photosetting was given to Arthur Ferguson in England in 1893. Numerous experiments and patents followed, most notably for the Uher-Type by Edmund Uher, which was installed in a few composing rooms and for which Jan Tschichold designed some typefaces in the 1930s. The Rotofoto by George Westover was ready for production in the 1940s, but was never put on the market. Westover already wanted to adapt the Monotype system for photosetting in the 1930s, but the company was not interested. They only came round to the idea in 1944, putting Monophoto on the market in 1952. The Fotosetter by Intertype is another machine that was commercialised. Between 1950 and 1955 around 100 of them were sold in America. All of these machines were based on substituting lead with photographic templates. These so-called 'first generation' phototypesetting machines ceased to exist in the 1960s.

The second method was based on the developments of new techniques for type storage using changeable media and simple binary systems for controlling commands. Higonnet and Moyroud were involved in this 'second generation' when developing the Photon-Lumitype. In 1944 they were given their first patent. In due course over 80 more patents would follow, many of them after they emigrated to the United States in 1948.

In 1951 the Photon 100 was launched. A year later it was used to produce the first book *The Wonderful World of Insects* to be set entirely on a photosetting machine.[5] Such a machine was also delivered to Deberny & Peignot in Paris, and formed the basis for the development of the French Photon-Lumitype.[6] The Lumitype 200 followed in 1956, first installed at Berger-Levrault in Nancy. Then came the punch-tape controlled Version 500, in addition to further improved models. Also worth mentioning are the Lumizip (1959), the fastest machine, which set 1–2 million characters per hour, and the bestselling Pacesetter. New models were constantly adapted to new technological developments such as the laser and the cathode ray tube (CRT).

Photon was the market leader for a brief period, but its financial situation was dire. In 1975 Photon was bought by Dymo Graphic Systems.[7]

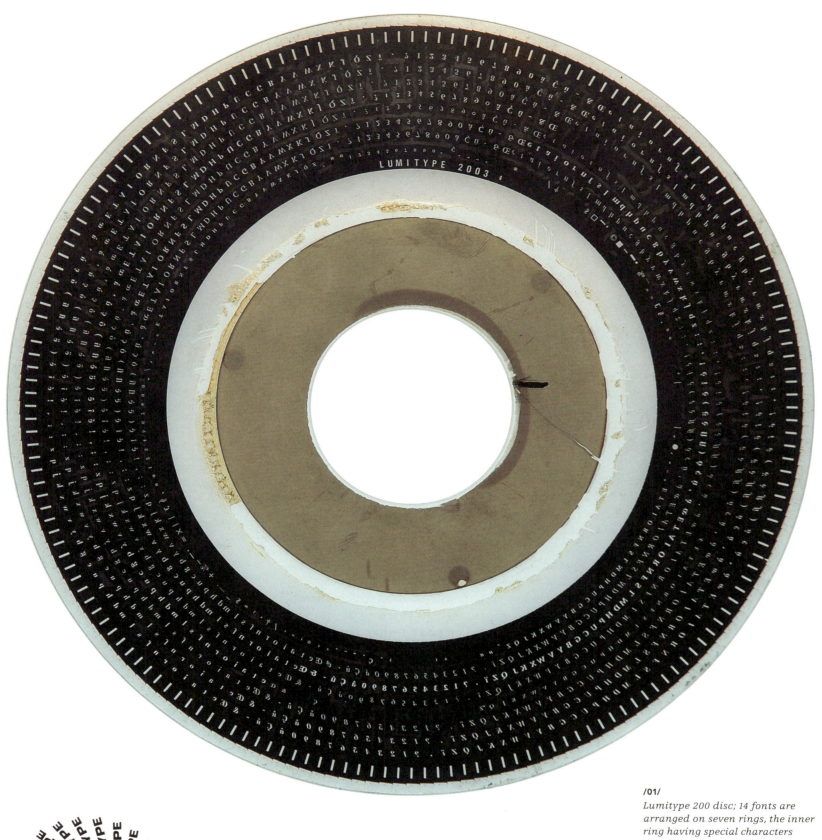

/01/
Lumitype 200 disc; 14 fonts are arranged on seven rings, the inner ring having special characters and flying accents.

/02/
The Lumitype logo recalls the photosetting lens and also the font disc – design by Rémy Peignot, 1960.

however, it just wasn't practical. To Germans or Englishmen terms like 'Garalde' or 'Didone'[8] meant nothing. Clearly naming the individual weights was a problem. Monotype had a numbering system that nobody could understand and that was a real mess. The Photon's numbering system wasn't much better either. It was important for my numbering system that, for example, humanistic and neoclassical romans be easily differentiated. So instead of descriptions I used numbers. Peignot thought it a pity that Vox's stylistic descriptions /04/ were no longer employed, yet he straight away conceded that another possibility had to be found for easily understandable international communication. I also went along to the salesmen and explained to them how my numbering system was constructed. They immediately grasped that orders and correspondence would work well using it. They thought it ideal as a sales technique.

I had finished the numbering system when I arranged the fonts. – It consisted of three plus two digits /03/. The first digit of the three-digit number denoted the classification group. Group 100 was intended for all handwritten romans including broken (blackletter) typefaces. Group 200 was for humanist typefaces. All Renaissance romans were placed in group 300, all transitional typefaces in 400 and neoclassical romans in 500. Group 600 was egyptians, 700 was sans serif, 800 was incised typefaces and 900 was script fonts. The second and third digits of the three-digit number divided the typefaces into classic ones and new ones. Numbers 01 to 50 were for classic typefaces, 51 to 99 for new ones. The two-digit number after the hyphen denoted width, weight and slant. So the regular weight of Renaissance Antiqua *Garamont,* for example, was given the number 301-55, its italic was 301-56 /13/.

Lumitype classification The most important document for understanding Lumitype type classification, dated 6.14.1954, is a note by Adrian Frutiger with calculations of the font sizes for Lumitype and with his numerical type classification /03/. The document[9] confirms that the famous *Univers* system stemmed from that of Lumitype. In his numbering system, Frutiger designated each font weight with a three-digit and a two-digit number. The first digit of the three-digit number stands for the typeface style, for example 500 for the 'Didone' group (Neoclassical or 'Modern'). This meant that each typeface style could have up to 99 typefaces. The second and third digits from 01 to 50 were reserved for classic typefaces, with 51 to 99 for new ones. The sequence of production, although not always precise, can thus be identified.

The two-digit number after the hyphen describes the width, weight and slant of a font. The first digit denotes weight; from 30 ultralight to 80 extra bold. 90 is decorative weights, for instance. The last digit denotes width and slant, from 1 narrow to 9 expanded. Odd numbers stand for upright fonts, even ones for italics.

Without the above mentioned document, the Lumitype classification would not be totally comprehensible, as the Lumitype catalogue from 1961 does away with any stylistic descriptions in favour of the numbering system /13/. However, only five out of the nine groups in the catalogue contain fonts. In hindsight, it is not always

/04/
Typeface classification by Maximilien Vox from 1954 with ten groups, the basis for Frutiger's Lumitype classification.

Médièves	Typefaces of the Middle Ages and earlier
Humanes	Typefaces of the Jenson type
Garaldes	Typefaces of the Aldus and Garamond type
Réales	Typefaces of the Fournier and Baskerville type
Didones	Typefaces of the Didot and Bodoni type
Simplices	Typefaces without serifs
Mécanes	Typefaces with emphasised serifs
Incises	Typefaces based on inscriptions
Manuaires	Typefaces with handwritten character
Scriptes	Typefaces based on scripts

/03/
Typeface classification for Lumitype with nine groups; letter from Adrian Frutiger, dated June 14, 1954.

CLASSIFICATION DES CARACTÈRES LUMITYPE

Il est évident que chaque caractère LUMITYPE doit porter un numéro d catalogue.

Il semble indispensable de créer, dès le début, un système permettan de classer logiquement tous les caractères, quelle que soit l'extension des futurs spécimens LUMITYPE.

Voici les principes du système adopté :

Chaque alphabet porte deux numéros : un numéro de série (style) en 3 chiffres, et un numéro d'adjectif (graisse, pente, chasse, etc...) en 2 chiffres.

I) NUMÉRO DE SÉRIE (STYLE)

Nous avons pris comme base la classification faite par Mr. VOX pour énumérer les différents groupe de "Style" de caractères d'imprimerie et minuscrits :

NOMS DONNÉS PAR VOX	EXEMPLES	NUMÉRO DU GROUPE de STYLE.
MANUAIRES	LIBRA, JACNO, caractères GOTHIQUES, etc.....	100
HUMANES	VIEUX ROMAIN, VERONESE, MICHEL-ANGE, etc	200
GARALDES	GARAMONT, PLANTIN, JENSON, POLIPHILE, etc...	300
RÉALES	BASKERVILLE, COCHIN, TIMES,etc	400
DIDONES	DIDOT, BODONI, NORMANDES, etc..	500
MÉCANES	dit EGYPTIENNES comme BETON, PHARAON, MEMPHIS, etc...	600
LINÉALES	dit ANTIQUES comme FUTURA, KABEL, ERBAEGROTESK, etc...	700
INCISES	dit LATINES comme AUGUSTEA, ALBERTUS, etc...	800
SCRIPTES	ETOILE, RONDO, SCRIBE, TRAFTON-SCRIPT, etc...	900

Chaque groupe de style se divise en 99 séries.
Nous avons pris les numéros de I à 50 pour énumérer les séries classiques redessinées pour la LUMITYPE et de 5I à 99 pour des nouvelles créations. Ainsi nous avons trouvé, pour donner un exemple, le numéro de série 30I pour le GARAMONT, 40I BASKERVILL 75I nouvelle ANTIQUE, etc.....

2°) – NUMÉRO D'ADJECTIF –

Pour distinguer dans une série (Famille) les différents alphabet gras, étroit, italique, etc... un deuxième numéro s'ajoute au premier. Il est composé de deux chiffres : les dizaines pour distinguer les différentes graisses et les unités pour distinguer les pentes et les chasses. Les adjectifs normaux, c'est-à-dire la graisse normale et la chasse normale, portent le numéro situé au milieu de l'échelle 50 et 5. Les maigres et les étroites se situent en-dessous, c'est-à-dire de 40 à IO et de 4 à I ; les gras et les larges se situent au-dessus, c'est-à-dire de 60 à 90 et de 7 à 9. Les romains se terminent avec un chiffre impair et les italiques avec un chiffre pair.

Voici le tableau des numéros d'adjectifs :

GRAISSES	Numéro	PENTES ET CHASSES	Numéro
		SERRÉ ROMAIN	1
		" ITALIQUE	2
FIN	30	ETROIT ROMAIN	3
MAIGRE	40	" ITALIQUE	4
NORMALE	50	ROMAIN	5
I/2 GRAS	60	ITALIQUE	6
GRAS	70	LARGE ROMAIN	7
DOUBLE-GRAS	80	" ITALIQUE	8
ECLAIRÉS, OMBRÉS, etc...	90	DOUBLE LARGE ROMAIN...	9

clear when a typeface is described as classic or as new. Hence Eric Gill's *Perpetua* from 1928 is categorised as classic, while Stanley Morison's *Times Roman* from 1932 and *Clarendon* (number 653), originally a 19th century typeface, are classed as new.

Adrian Frutiger's numerical font classification is based on that of Maximilien Vox from 1954, though it contains only nine instead of ten groups. While Maximilien Vox has two groups, 'Médièves' and 'Manuaires' /04/, Frutiger puts them together in one group. Moreover, he names some of the styles differently /03/. Vox's classification from the following year, 1955, also has nine groups /05/. The stylistic descriptions also coincide with Frutiger's, apart from 'Manuaires' which is first in Frutiger's and second to last in Vox's. Thus Vox abandons his original historical sequence with gothic faces as the earliest typefaces in the first group, seeing as broken type (blackletter) was hardly in use by the mid 20th century. The 'Vox Classification' /06/ from 1963, revised once again, forms the basis for several national typeface classifications, among them the classification of the German industry standard, DIN 165´8 /07/.[10]

So first there was the numbering system for Lumitype. Later I happily modified it for *Univers.* I gave one of my first lectures at the École Estienne in Paris. When I introduced the numbering system for *Univers* there was a great round of applause. Then I got to the system for classification and there was an uproar. Oh dear, the things that were said; it was called 'blockheaded' and 'unrealistic'. The French were of the opinion that Vox's classification was the best in the world.

The point was reached with Lumitype where I couldn't do everything by myself and had to employ other people, as there were so many classic fonts to adapt for Lumitype. Lucette Girard, a student of mine from the first course I taught at the École Estienne, was one of my first co-workers. I recognised her talent and was able to send her to Walter Käch in Zurich for half a year, so that she could receive the same training as I'd had. Together we drew all the regular weights for *Univers,* using india ink and opaque white the way it used to be done. In late 1954 Ladislas Mandel started at Deberny & Peignot and he introduced an entirely new method of drawing, using scraper boards. I used that method because I could see that it worked well. Another of the first co-workers was Albert Boton. He started on the narrow *Univers,* as it was easier to draw. Later he would become one of my best draftsmen. We also had Robert Meili and Annette Celsio, my secretary's sister. At first she was more of a dogsbody and only filled in the drawings with india ink, but in time she became really skilled. Together we were quite a team.

The first typefaces we did for Lumitype were classics such as *Garamont* and *Bodoni.* After that came *Baskerville* and *Janson* as well as *Caslon* and *Perpetua* /13/. Although sans serifs were asked after pretty early on, we put them off for a while. In my head, of course,

CLASSIFICATION MAXIMILIEN VOX

Groupes	HUMANES	GARALDES	RÉALES	DIDONES	MÉCANES	LINÉALES	INCISES	MANUAIRES	SCRIPTES
formes des empattements, pieds et extrémités des lettres									
Aspects généraux de la lettre capitale	IS	IC	IS	IC	IS	NES NES	ERSI PASC	LAC ESU	OE ED
romain et italique	TS	IC	IS	IE	IN	ICA ICA	AUG NES	POLK BAM	DH BB
Aspects généraux de la lettre bas de casse	ica	aie	ier	ien	icn	sodi sodi	abce abcm	cisel renoi	ersi en ei
romain et italique	nic	aic	aic	aiu	inc	onde onde	nord nose	lona chou	ec en en ie
Études morphologiques de la lettre									
Caractères appartenant à chacun des groupes									

/05/

Typeface classification by Maximilien Vox from 1955 with nine groups; 'Médièves' are included under 'Manuaires'.

/06/

Typeface classification by Vox from 1963 with nine groups, but arranged differently and with the order changed slightly.

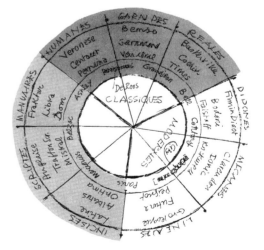

/07/

DIN classification 16518 from 1964 with eleven groups, based on the 'Vox Classification', although the names are different.

I	Venezianische Renaissance-Antiqua (Typus Jenson)	
II	Französische Renaissance-Antiqua (Typus Aldus / Garamond)	
III	Barock-Antiqua (Typus Fournier / Baskerville)	
IV	Klassizistische Antiqua (Typus Didot / Bodoni)	
V	Serifenbetonte Linear-Antiqua (Egyptienne)	
VI	Serifenlose Linear-Antiqua (Grotesk)	
VII	Antiqua-Varianten	
VIII	Schreibschriften (Schönschriften)	
IX	Handschriftliche Antiqua	
X	Gebrochene Schriften	Xa Gotisch (Textura)
		Xb Rundgotisch (Rotunda)
		Xc Schwabacher
		Xd Fraktur
		Xe Fraktur-Varianten
XI	Fremde Schriften (nicht lateinische Schriften)	

Photon, INC.
Cambridge, Mass.

TYPE FACE & MACHINE DATA

TYPE FACES:

The following type faces are now available for composition
on Photon machines:

1. Baskerville
2. Baskerville Italic
3. Bodoni
4. Bodoni Italic
5. Bodoni Bold
6. Bodoni Bold Italic
7. Bookman Old Style
8. Bookman Old Style Italic
9. Bruce Old Style
10. Cambridge Garamond (similar to American Garamond)
11. Cambridge Garamond Italic (similar to American Garamond It.)
12. Caslon Old Style #1
13. Century Expanded
14. Cheltenham Wide
15. Gothic Condensed
16. Ionic
17. Modern #1
18. Old English
19. Scotch
20. Scotch Italic
21. Stymie Bold #1 (similar to Rockwell)
22. Techno Medium (similar to Spartan, Futura & 20th Century)
23. Techno Heavy (" " " " " " ")

February 23, 1955

/08/
*List of fonts available for the
American Photon Inc. photosetting
machine in February 1955.*

/09/
*Font weights from the brochure
La Lumitype, c.1957, showing
Photon rather than Lumitype fonts.*

Techno Extrabold corps 12 set 12	**Un seul disque peut contenir seize styles**
Techno Extrabold Ital. corps 12 set 12	***Un seul disque peut contenir seize styles***
Techno Heavy corps 12 set 12	Un seul disque peut contenir seize styles
Techno Heavy Ital. corps 12 set 12	*Un seul disque peut contenir seize styles*
Techno Medium corps 12 set 12	Un seul disque peut contenir seize styles
Techno Medium Ital. corps 12 set 12	*Un seul disque peut contenir seize styles*
Garamond corps 12 set 10,75	Un seul disque peut contenir seize styles
Garamond ital. corps 12 set 10,75	*Un seul disque peut contenir seize styles*
Baskerville corps 12 set 12	Un seul disque peut contenir seize styles
Baskerville Ital. corps 12 set 12	*Un seul disque peut contenir seize styles*
Century Schoolbook corps 12 set 12,50	Un seul disque peut contenir seize styles
Century Schoolbook Ital. corps 12 set 12	*Un seul disque peut contenir seize styles*
Bodoni corps 12 set 12	Un seul disque peut contenir seize styles
Bodoni Ital. corps 12 set 12	*Un seul disque peut contenir seize styles*
Bodoni Bold Ital. corps 12 set 12	***Un seul disque peut contenir seize styles***
Bodoni Bold corps 12 set 12	**Un seul disque peut contenir seize styles**

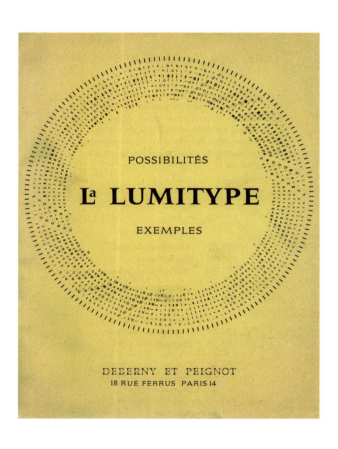

POSSIBILITÉS

La LUMITYPE

EXEMPLES

DEBERNY ET PEIGNOT
18 RUE FERRUS PARIS 14

/10/
*Title page and inside page of the
Lumitype brochure (undated,
c.1957); apart from Méridien only
Photon fonts are used.*

LE STYLE et le corps du caractère ayant été choisis,
la justification et l'interlignage ayant été détermi-
nés, l'opératrice travaille comme sur un clavier
de machine à écrire normal. Elle a sous les yeux
une frappe de machine à écrire ordinaire
qui lui sert de témoin. Toute erreur de frappe peut être corrigée par retour du chariot
devant la lettre erronée. Il suffit alors d'en-
foncer la touche correction puis celle correspondant à la lettre correcte. Cette
correction n'implique pas la nécessité
de recomposer la ligne. S'il y a trop
d'erreurs de frappe, la ligne entière
peut être annulée par pression sur
une touche spéciale.

Texte composé sur 3 justifica-
tions différentes avec initiale
de départ suivie de petites capitales.

Annuaire du Téléphone. Le nombre correct
de points de conduite nécessaire en vue de
la justification a été calculé et inséré auto-
matiquement par la machine.

OVERLAPPING CHARACTERS

Ta Te To Ti Tr Tu Tw Ty Va Ya Ye
Yo YA FA PA TA VA Wa We WA

Ta Te To Tr Tu Tw Ty Va Ya Ye Yo
YA FA VA TA VA Wa We Wo WA

VIASPHALTE
ROUTES-AERODROMES
Les spécialistes des fondations et revêtements en empierrements stabilisés
TRANSFORMATION DES MATÉRIAUX PAR CONCASSAGE MOBILE
TRAITEMENT AU TRAVEL-PLANT
— (12 Ingénieurs A. et M.) —

2, Rue Villegaignon   62, Bd Malesherbes   Avenue de Valmy
ALGER   PARIS-8e   ORAN
Téléphone: Alger 165-81   Téléphone: LABorde 35-00   Téléphone: Oran 221-27

/11/
*Mixed type using 14 alphabets
from 5 to 28 pt at the same time –
sample text from the 1961
catalogue.*

Dans une même **ligne,** *tous les styles*
que comporte *le disque*
peuvent être mélangés **dans tous les**
corps sans altérer ni *la justification*
ni l'alignement de base des lettres

Possibilities of Photon-Lumitype "This disc replaces three tons of matrices (…), it weighs 1000 grammes and has a diameter of 20 cm."[12] This quote from the *La Lumitype* brochure /10/ makes plain the fantastic potential of Photon-Lumitype. 16, or 14, fonts could be combined at the same time and automatically aligned on the base line in 5 to 28 pt size /11/. With 80 characters per font and by reducing the tracking, specimens could be set. The earliest use in print of Lumitype fonts was not before 1956 or even 1957, which is what the records imply. The cover of the Lumitype brochure shows the French character set of the typesetting disc. These are, however, Photon fonts. The typesetting examples do not include any Lumitype fonts either /10/. Only Frutiger's *Méridien* is included in romain and demi-gras weights, as examples and as text.

Understandably, French typesetting requires a different character set from its English counterpart, both on the typesetting disc and on the keyboard. In particular, a sizeable amount of accented letters had to be accomodated, which could not be achieved without excluding several characters. Among others, the f ligatures were dropped. These were reinstated on Lumitype 200 /13/, and flying accents[13] enabled other Western European languages to be set.

I started working on them during this period. The most pressing task was transferring the most used fonts, which took at least two years. I would normally use the Monotype lead versions as models.[11] I found those to be the best fonts at the time, as opposed to those of Linotype. Those had aesthetic restrictions due to the double matrices, whereby the regular weight was combined with the italic or semi-bold on one matrix, giving them the same width. It was Hermann Zapf who laid the foundations for Linotype as a good setting machine with his book faces *Palatino* and *Aldus.* To this day many German paperbacks are still set in *Aldus.*

When it came to *Garamont* /16/ (spelled with a t at Deberny & Peignot[14]), I took the house-cut Deberny & Peignot version as a master. That came from Georges Peignot, Charles Peingot's father. The italic is beautiful, surely one of the best in the world. I learned a lot working on these classic fonts. They all had to be redrawn for that new technology. When copying and correcting them, a little bit of my own form perception crept in subconsciously, even though I regarded myself as a worker who had to adapt fonts to a very particular system, and not at all as an 'artist'. With hindsight I have to say that I wasn't really the right man to draw classic fonts for photosetting. That only occured to me later when I was asked to redraw classic fonts for the photosetting machines for D. Stempel AG / Linotype. I proposed they use the *Baskerville,* which I had already redrawn for Lumitype /13/. Horst Heiderhoff, the artistic director at D. Stempel AG, showed me a sheet that compared their *Baskerville* to mine and told me there was too much 'Frutiger' in my version. He was right, one could tell that my one didn't smell of the 18th century, it was too wide and open.

Deberny et Peignot
18 rue Ferrus Paris 14
Port-Royal 79-79

/12/
Inside title page of the Caractères Lumitype *font catalogue, 1961 – the photo shows a section of the disc with* Univers.

/13/
Font index from 1961 of available Lumitype fonts; the numbering is also the typeface classification.

LISTE DES CARACTÈRES LUMITYPE

Ce catalogue est appelé à se compléter d'année en année. Mais il convient de préciser que nous pouvons mettre sur disque toutes séries de caractères désirées par un client, dont il aura obtenu du créateur les droits de reproduction, conformément aux dispositions de l'Association Typographique Internationale.

301-55	Garamont romain		501-67	Bodoni demi-gras étroit
301-56	*Garamont italique*		501-75	**Bodoni gras**
			501-76	***Bodoni gras italique***
302-55	Janson romain			
302-56	*Janson italique*		502-83	**Sphinx gras romain**
302-65	**Janson demi-gras**		502-84	***Sphinx italique***
302-66	***Janson demi-gras italique***			
			651-55	Egyptienne romain
351-55	Méridien romain		651-56	*Egyptienne italique*
351-56	*Méridien italique*		651-75	**Egyptienne gras**
351-65	**Méridien demi-gras**			
351-75	**Méridien gras**		751-45	Univers romain maigre
			751-46	*Univers italique maigre*
401-55	Baskerville romain		751-47	Univers étroit maigre
401-56	*Baskerville italique*		751-48	*Univers étroit italique maigre*
			751-49	Univers serré maigre
402-55	Caslon romain		751-53	Univers large
402-56	*Caslon italique*		751-55	Univers romain
402-65	**Caslon demi-gras**		751-56	*Univers italique*
402-66	***Caslon demi-gras italique***		751-57	Univers étroit
			751-58	*Univers étroit italique*
403-55	Perpétua romain		751-59	Univers serré
403-56	*Perpétua italique*		751-63	**Univers large demi-gras**
403-65	**Perpétua demi-gras**		751-65	**Univers romain demi-gras**
451-55	Times romain		751-66	***Univers italique demi-gras***
451-56	*Times italique*		751-67	**Univers étroit demi-gras**
451-65	**Times demi-gras**		751-68	***Univers étroit italique demi-gras***
			751-73	**Univers large gras**
501-55	Bodoni romain		751-75	**Univers romain gras**
501-56	*Bodoni italique*		751-76	***Univers italique gras***
501-65	**Bodoni demi-gras**		751-83	**Univers large double gras**
501-66	***Bodoni demi-gras italique***			

I always looked to the future. I didn't study the historical originals precisely enough like, for instance, Robert Slimbach, who compared old typefaces at the Plantin Moretus Museum in Antwerp for his *Adobe Garamond*. It's perhaps worth pointing out that in 1988/89 Slimbach had superior technology at his disposal in the form of outline software. Lumitype was photosetting in its infancy. With its technical conditions, all the details that are important to historians would never have come to light. One could say that I wasn't satisfied with much, and yet I felt I had done my work properly. The Lumitype results were pretty good if one bears in mind the vectorised steps of the cathode-ray faces from the 1970s (see page 275).

When drawing classic fonts I tried to be as considerate as I could, and was keen to get the best out of the new technology. Nevertheless, the fonts don't have any historical worth. It would be wrong to make comparisons, because it was only thirty years later that producing beautiful classic fonts was made possible again thanks to drawing software. I preferred to look ahead, the beauty of *Univers* was more important to me than that of classic fonts. I had a hard time making *Univers* too. To think of the sort of aberrations I had to produce in order to see a good result on Lumitype! V and W needed huge crotches in order to stay open /29/. I nearly had to introduce serifs in order to prevent rounded-off corners – instead of a sans serif the drafts were a bunch of misshapen sausages!

The order of work was like this: first of all one of the typesetters at Deberny & Peignot would set the alphabet in question for me in 10 pt. Then 1 pt brass rules were placed in this alphabet set in order to make the character width visible. 10 pt was a good size because Lumitype was set up for text fonts. For the time being one could set 5 to 28 pt, even up to

Lumitype font range There was never any agreement about font selection between the American Photon Inc. and Deberny & Peignot, although *Méridien*, under the name *Latine*, and *Univers* were taken on by Photon, classic typefaces such *Garamont*, *Caslon*, *Baskerville* and *Bodoni* had distinct versions that corresponded to each one's national habits. A letter sent by Photon refers to their *Garamond* as *Cambridge Garamond* /09/, as opposed to Lumitype's *Paris Garamont*[15] /13/. *Times Roman* went the other way, going from Photon to Lumitype.[16] For this reason there was no concordance about the uniform cap height of Lumitype fonts.[17] Both manufacturers, including Lumitype's succesor, the International Photon Corporation, constantly expanded their range of typefaces. Mostly they consisted of text fonts, but also agate fonts for very small point sizes, as well as non-latins.[18]

Exactly who redrew what is now almost impossible to say of classic fonts for Lumitype. Apart from Adrian Frutiger, who was responsible for the quality of font adaptions in his role as artistic director and who himself redrew a few fonts, others active at D&P in the mid-50s and who participated were: Lucette Girard, Ladislas Mandel, Annette Celsio, Albert Boton and Robert Meili.[19]

Adrian Frutiger says in conversation that originals by Deberny & Peignot and Monotype were used as the basis for redrawing classic fonts. That George Peignot's *Garamont* was used is obvious. Lumitype *Bodoni*, on the

12 Les premiers hommes, témoins des mouvements convulsifs de la terre, encore récents et très fréquents, n'ayant que les montagnes pour asiles contre les inondations, chassés souvent de ces mêmes asiles par le feu des volcans, tremblants sur une terre qui tremblait sous leurs pieds, nus d'esprit et de corps, exposés aux injures de toutes les
ABCDEFGHIJKLMNOPQRSTUVWXYZ ABCDEFGHIJKLMNOPQRSTUVWXYZ AB 1234567890

12 *Les premiers hommes, témoins des mouvements convulsifs de la terre, encore récents et très fréquents, n'ayant que les montagnes pour asiles contre les inondations, chassés souvent de ces mêmes asiles par le feu des volcans, tremblants sur une terre qui tremblait sous leurs pieds, nus d'esprit et de corps, exposés aux injures de tous les éléments, victimes de la fureur des ani*
ABCDEFGHIJKLMNOPQRSTUVWXYZ ABCDEFGHIJKLMNOPQRSTUVWXYZ 1234567890

12 LES PREMIERS HOMMES, témoins des mouvements convulsifs de la terre, encore récents et très fréquents, n'ayant que les montagnes pour asiles contre les inondations, chassés souvent de ces mêmes asiles par le feu des volcans, tremblants sur une terre qui tremblait sous leurs pieds, nus d'esprit et de corps, exposés
ABCDEFGHIJKLMNOPQRSTUVWXYZ ABCDEFGHIJKLMNOPQRSTUVWXYZ AB 1234567890

12 *Les premiers hommes, témoins des mouvements convulsifs de la terre, encore récents et très fréquents, n'ayant que les montagnes pour asiles contre les inondations, chassés souvent de ces mêmes asiles par le feu des volcans, tremblants sur une terre qui tremblait sous leurs pieds, nus d'esprit et de corps, exposés aux injures de tous les*
ABCDEFGHIJKLMNOPQRSTUVWXYZ ABCDEFGHIJKLMNOPQRSTUVWXYZ ABCD 1234567890

/14/
Garamont *301-55 and 301-56,*
and also Janson 302-55 with small
caps and 302-56 from the 1961
Lumitype *catalogue.*

/16/
Comparison between Garamont *for handsetting by Deberny & Peignot (top) and* Lumitype *Garamont, roman and italic.*

/15/
Comparison between the American Photon Garamond *(left) and the French Lumitype* Garamont.

Un seul disque peut contenir seize
Un seul disque peut contenir seize

Un seul disque peut contenir seize
Un seul disque peut contenir seize

HAMBOURG Hambourg
HAMOURG Hamour

HAMBOURG Hambourg
HAMBOURG Hamourg

other hand, bears no real relation to that of any manufacturer; some key letters are very different. AMS are more open /17/, G is angular and not round in the transition from the arc to the downstroke /18/, the diagonal of the N is slightly offset downwards on the left and does not end in a point on the right, which balances the proportions of both triangular counters /19/. Also, the W does not have the usual crossed V shapes /21/. These are all features that visibly mirror Frutiger's understanding of shape. Another difference is the 4, where the serif at the end of the cross-stroke is missing, as is the terminal curl of the 5 /23/. The Lumitype *Bodoni* italic g is very unusual in that it does not have the typical double loop shape /22/. Did Adrian Frutiger study Bodoni's *Manuale Tipografico* of 1818? That contains the single loop g shape, albeit seldom.[20]

The Lumitype version of *Bodoni* is balanced and linear, cool and elegant. The grace typical of Giambattista Bodoni's typefaces is, however, not achieved. That goes for most adaptations, unfortunately.[21]

48 pt before the appearance of the Lumitype catalogue in 1961. Finally, together with the technical draftsman and photographer responsible for the typesetting discs, Monsieur Bernard, I would work on the enlargements that served as masters for the disc.

Secondly I would determine the cap heights. All Lumitype fonts, both wide and narrow, were to have the same H-height. This wouldn't have been possible with lowercase letters, the x-heights varied too much, it would have given a false appearance. I chose 11 units as a predetermined size for the cap heights. Together with ascenders and descenders there were 18 height units and with the 18 width units this made a square /25/. The typeface with the widest dimensions from the hot metal catalogue was *Sphinx*, a very bold neoclassical face /27/. The narrowest must have been some sans serif or other. I took the average of both and determined the height as 11 cm. 12 cm would have been too much for the widest and 10 cm too little for the narrowest. It was important to me that I use a grid (one unit equal to 1 cm). All Lumitype fonts were made to fit into this grid. This was me being logical, as it also made enlarging easier.

The system of units of all new typesetting machines was at the time based on the 18-unit system, following the example of Monotype. So it was for Photon. However, I found it was too few and so I spoke to the engineer René Gréa about it, telling him one couldn't get a nice image with 18 units. I explained to him that f t r and sometimes even I had the same number of units on Monotype, and that that just couldn't be right. René Gréa was an understanding man with a feel for artistic subtleties. He thought for a moment about my desire to have half units and then said that it wasn't a problem, he would simply build in another little cog. After a day spent experimenting we had our half units and that was a

12 LES PREMIERS HOMMES, témoins des mouvements convulsifs de la terre, encore récents et très fréquents, n'ayant que les montagnes pour asiles contre les inondations, chassés souvent de ces mêmes asiles par le feu des volcans, tremblants sur une terre qui tremblait sous leurs pieds, nus d'espr ABCDEFGHIJKLMNOPQRSTUVWXYZ ABCDEFGHIJKLMNOPQRSTUVWXYZ ABC 1234567890

12 *Les premiers hommes, témoins des mouvements convulsifs de la terre, encore récents et très fréquents, n'ayant que les montagnes pour asiles contre les inondations, chassés souvent de ces mêmes asiles par le feu des volcans, tremblants sur une terre qui tremblait sous leurs pieds, nus d'espr ABCDEFGHIJKLMNOPQRSTUVWXYZ ABCDEFGHIJKLMNOPQRSTUVWXYZ 1234567890*

12 Les premiers hommes, témoins des mouvements convulsifs de la terre, encore récents et très fréquents, n'ayant que les montagnes pour asiles contre les inondations, chassés souvent de ces mêmes asiles par le feu des volcans, tremblants sur une terre qui tremblait sous leurs pieds, nus ABCDEFGHIJKLMNOPQRSTUVWXYZ ABCDEFGHIJKLMNOPQRSTUVWXYZ 1234567890

12 Les premiers hommes, témoins des mouvements convulsifs de la terre, encore récents et très fré quents, n'ayant que les montagnes pour asiles contre les inondations, chassés souvent de ces mê mes asiles par le feu des volcans, tremblants sur une terre qui tremblait sous leurs pieds, nus ABCDEFGHIJKLMNOPQRSTUVWXYZ ABCDEFGHIJKLMNOPQRSTUVWXYZ 1234567890

/20/
Three weights of Bodoni 501 *and also* Bodoni 504 *with slightly strengthened hairlines and serifs.*

/17/
Compared to Bodoni's original or the Berthold Bodoni *(left), the letters* AMS *of Lumitype* Bodoni 501-65 *appear very wide and open.*

AMS AMS

/18/
The angular transition from the curve to the leg in the counter is not typical of Bodoni, *but it is of Frutiger.*

G G

/19/
Frutiger evens the counters in the N by displacing the diagonal line downwards and not letting it run up to the tip at the right.

N N

/21/
According to Frutiger, crossed V shapes do not correspond to the original form of capital alphabets.

W W

/22/
The sleeker italic form of Lumitype Bodoni *is unusual – it appears very rarely in Bodoni's* Manuale Tipografico *(1818).*

g g g g

/23/
Frutiger omits the serif on the cross-stroke of the 4, while the cross-stroke of the 5 is barely bent towards the left.

45 45

real advantage, because that way one could work much finer nuances. We started with four units for the i, four and a half units for the f and five units for the t /28/. We also made the u slightly narrower than the n, which is better aesthetically because light flows in from above in the u.

Thanks to the half units we could work on flying accents. I drew the accents in such a way that they always stood exactly in the middle, whether they were wide, narrow or italics. The idea of having half units wasn't there from the beginning. René Gréa's labour consisted chiefly of organising the construction and adapting the machine for European requirements, that took some two years. Mike Parker, who at that time was responsible for redrawing fonts as Director of Typographic Development at Mergenthaler Linotype, told me ten or fifteen years later that it had been dumb not to have realised that 18 units weren't enough to produce good typography with. The 36 units of the 1950s were a real step forward.

Em square and units   The basic measurement for typography is the em square, a square the size of the body, i.e. the type size. The em square has a fixed proportion, but no fixed width. It grows and shrinks with the point size and that is its very advantage.

In Monotype machine setting and in photosetting the em square is divided into units. Initially these were 18 units. Lumitype had 36. Such low divisions of the em square necessitated compromising the design in order to achieve a well-balanced appearance. The characters have to deviate from their intended form or from the original and be drawn wider or narrower; serif widths have to be adjusted – or optically even spacing has to be forgone. This becomes most obvious with typewriter faces where all the characters have to fit onto the same-size unit.

When redrawing foundry types for photosetting, changes to the letter shapes cannot be avoided, as letters for handsetting have individual widths. Today, with 1000 units per em square, this restriction does not apply anymore.

In order to define a common cap height for all Lumitype faces, Adrian Frutiger based it on the most important foundry types – on the one hand the widest letter W /26/, on the other, the greatest vertical distance from ascender to descender /33/. This resulted in a cap height of 11 units.

/24/
Compared to the Photon Baskerville t (top), the Lumitype Baskerville t has a better fit, thanks to the use of half units.

/25/
Character width diagram of Lumitype with 36 half units as opposed to the 18 units of Photon and other photosetting machines.

/26/
The cap height of Lumitype was based on the width of the W in the most important text faces.

/27/
In wide typefaces such as Sphinx the W is bigger than the 18 units or 36 half units of the em quad.

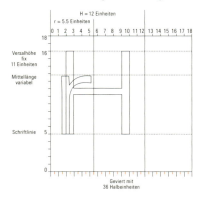

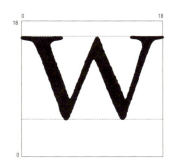

/28/
Univers light italic 751-46; height and stroke width dimensions are at the top, with half-unit character width table below.

/29/
The corners and incisions are exaggerated in order to keep the counters open and the corners from being rounded off in photosetting.

/30/

Some weights of Times, Egyptienne *and* Univers *have the same tracking, as the table demonstrates.*

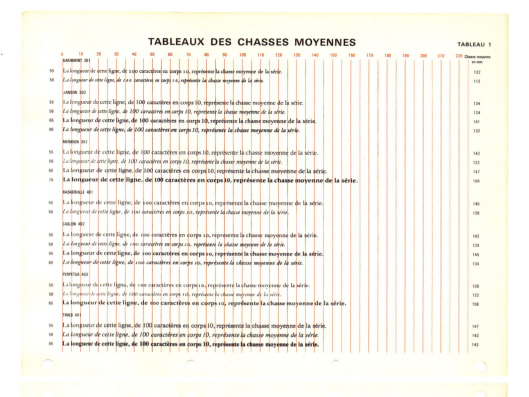

/31/

Garamont and Sphinx compared: The same caps height produces visibly different ascenders, x-heights and descenders.

Garamont (Lumitype)

Sphinx (Lumitype)

/32/

The maximum possible height determines the size of a Photon font; there is no height uniformity.

/33/

The greatest distance from ascender to descender determines the size of the cap height of Lumitype fonts.

/34/

Lumitype fonts generally have a cap height of 110 mm in the final artwork – accents hover above the em quad.

/35/
R.Higonnet and L.Moyroud's prototype of the Photon-Lumitype from 1948 is now in the Musée de l'imprimerie in Lyon.

/36/
A look at the inside of the Photon 100 reveals its mechanical and electronic parts as well as its rotating disc.

/37/
Fonts are selected by pressing a key on the keyboard at the right – some of the font names can still be read.

/39/
From left to right: Bill Garth, Louis Moyroud and René Higonnet with the first industrial prototype of the Photon-Lumitype in 1949.

/40/
René Higonnet (second from left), joint inventor of the Photon, explaining the newly arrived photo-setting machine to Charles Peignot (third from left) in 1954.

/38/
The Photon model 1 was delivered to Deberny & Peignot in 1954 from the USA – today it is in the Gutenberg museum in Mainz.

/43/

The Photon 100, first presented at the 4th Salon International des Techniques Papetières et Graphiques TPG in 1954.

/44/

Charles Peignot showing the French Lumitype 200 to an interested audience at the 5th Salon TPG in Paris, 1956.

/41/

René Grea, engineer at D&P, at the 'keyboard' of the Lumitype, with Charles Peignot in the background explaining the exposure unit.

/42/

Adrian Frutiger (seated) with Robert Meili – behind them is final artwork of Lumitype Caslon (ink on board, c.1958).

/45/

The first Lumitype 200 by Fonderies Deberny & Peignot can be seen at the Musée de l'imprimerie in Lyon.

Production of type
Machine setting – Single-letter casting

Univers
Page 88

Devanagari
Page 206

Tamil
Page 212

American engineer Tolbert Lanston began work on the development of the Monotype setting and casting machine in 1887. Ten years later, it appeared on the market. The processes of casting type and setting it were housed in separate units. The link between the two was an 11-cm-wide punched tape that was produced by the setting machine /01/ – the 'keyboard apparatus'. The pattern of holes on this roll contained all the typographical information necessary to allow for the automatic operation of the casting machine. With the invention of the casting frame /05/, Lanston had got around the complicated handling of individual matrices, which is necessary with Linotype machines.

The keyboard of a Monotype machine contained 334 keys, 30 of which were justification keys. This large number resulted from six alphabets: an alphabet pair (upper- and lowercase) for regular weights, and two further pairs for italic and semibold (or, alternately, for a small caps alphabet). If the order of the keys was changed, this would have an effect on the matrix frame, the intermediate frame, and, with a change of typeface, on the unit setting. This would further affect the set or justifying drum. This light metal cylinder was divided into even fields, each of which contained two figures. At the end of the line, the justification pointer would point to one of these fields. After the compositor had transferred the figure shown onto the red keys of his or her keyboard, the resulting set of holes on the punch tape would send to the caster the width of the justification wedge to be cast.

Due to this important, time-saving justification mechanism, the em widths were constrained to a system of 18 units since the associated adding-indication mechanism worked on this mathematical principle. The second reason for the choice of an 18-unit system was the automated, mechanical regulation of the width of the casting nozzle.

The 18 units are a relative, not an absolute, measure. They depend on the body size, measured in typographic points (p). All glyphs fall into one of 12 unit groupings, with widths from 4 to 18 units. While the drawings are made, the division of the units is resolved on an alphabet-by-alphabet basis. It has to be considered, however, that for each group of units, only a limited number of glyphs is possible.

After casting, the letters were automatically lined up into ready-justified lines. The caster checked the text on the line and the setter then placed line after line together on a printing plate. The casting speed depended on the body size of the typeface being cast. An hourly rate of around 10 000 letters in 10 pt has to be viewed in relation to an arithmetical text capture of 6 500 characters.

/01/
The Monotype keyboard apparatus with over 300 keys for six alphabets and 30 additional justification keys.

/02/
The Monotype caster cast typefaces in sizes from 5 to 14 pt, with a large-slug apparatus for up to 36 pt.

/03/
Detail of the keyboard apparatus – above is the punched tape and in front is the justifying drum which displayed the justification units.

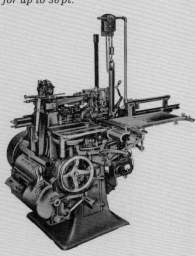
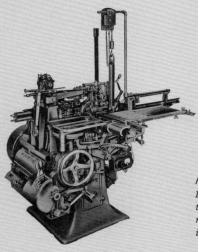

/04/
Detail of the casting machine with the punched tape for controlling the matrix case – in front is the lead ingot to be melted.

/05/
The matrix case contained up to 272 interchangeable individual matrices (top) – in each row all the matrices had to have the same unit modules.

Production of type
Monophoto photosetting

Univers
Page 88

Apollo
Page 138

**Univers
Greek**
Page 103

In 1955 the Monotype Filmsetter, the first photosetting machine from Monotype, came onto the market /01/. It was based on the technology of the Monotype hot metal machine, so each em was still divided into 18 units. The keyboard apparatus was constructed with little modification, and instead of controlling the casting, the punch tape now controlled the exposure. The exposure mechanism and removable film drum replaced the type metal pot, mould and pump. The matrices were now made out of film material instead of metal. As with the hot metal machines, only one width was available for each unit row. If there were more glyphs than spaces available, a further row with matrices of the same width needed to be added on.

During exposure the matrix case /04/ – the grid – moved accurately, using well-established technology, to the area to be exposed. The chosen letter was then exposed onto the film with the aid of a flash tube and an optical system with two rotating mirrors /02/. By rotating the mirror, the letters were set one after the other in a line. The line feed was made possible by the film's controllable transport rollers. The performance matched more or less that of the hot metal machines. Text could be set from 6 to 24 pt with a maximum line width of 56 cicero (252.6 mm). The film matrix case held 255 replaceable single matrices /04/. For most typefaces two matrix sets were available: from 6 to 7pt and from 8 to 24 pt. There were, however, matrices that contained the entire range of point sizes for a particular typeface, as was the case with Frutiger's *Apollo*. The setting performance was equal across all point sizes and averaged around 10 000 characters an hour. A disadvantage in comparison with Monotype's hot metal machines was that corrections could not be made as quickly. Instead of simply exchanging the wrong character, now the whole film had to be corrected by paste-up.

Monotype produced a clear leap forward in performance with its 1969 Model 600. Instead of a single matrix, this filmsetting machine had four matrix plates, each of which contained 100 matrices in point sizes from 6 to 14. It also contained a word buffer so that corrections could be carried out before the paper tape was punched. The keyboard was also connected to an illuminated scale, which showed the distance remaining to the end of the line. The em had been changed over to ciceros, so that conversion into units was no longer necessary.

Thanks to its four matrix plates, the Model 600 had various design sizes of the same typeface simultaneously available. It thus employed the principle of optical scaling. This changed the stroke weights according to point size: in light and regular weights, the strokes of smaller point sizes were made heavier, while in small sizes of bold weights the counters had more white space.

/01/

The Monophoto setting machine worked by controlling the matrices according to the same principle as its hot-metal forebear.

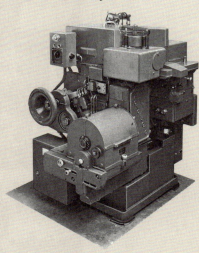

/02/

This construction schematic shows the path of the light beam from its source to the film in the film drum.

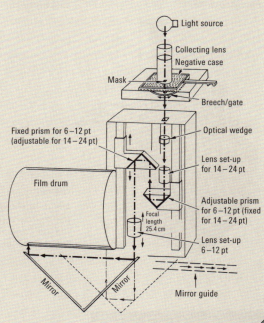

Light source
Collecting lens
Negative case
Mask
Breech/gate
Fixed prism for 6–12 pt (adjustable for 14–24 pt)
Optical wedge
Film drum
Lens set-up for 14–24 pt
Adjustable prism for 6–12 pt (fixed for 14–24 pt)
Focal length 25.4 cm
Lens set-up 6–12 pt
Mirror
Mirror
Mirror guide

/03/

Example of a matrix case layout with a specification of 5 to 18 unit widths in each row.

/04/

In the Monophoto system the metal matrices were replaced by photographic negatives – the matrix case remained unchanged.

Name of typeface	Commissioned by	Designer	Design | Publication	Typesetting technology	Manufacturer	Weights
Univers	Deberny & Peignot	Adrian Frutiger	1953 | 1957	Handsetting	– Deberny & Peignot	20
Swiss 722 | Zurich*				Photon-Lumitype photosetting	– Deberny & Peignot	20 | 21
Linotype Univers**				Machine setting | photosetting	– Monotype	21
				CRT and laser digital typesetting	– D. Stempel AG | Linotype	21
				PostScript digital typesetting	– Adobe | Linotype	27
					Bitstream*	22
					Linotype**	63

UNIVERS

As work on the Lumitype progressed and the first classic fonts had been drawn, we turned our attention to sans serif fonts. Charles Peignot was in no doubt that the foundry's best-selling typeface, *Futura* – known in France as *Europe* – ought to be included in the range. I suggested another project to him because I felt that *Europe* was no longer contemporary. In the 'Univers special edition' of *TM* 1/1961 /33/ I stated my reasons:

"[...] The simple rhythm of classical architecture is reflected in the typefaces of the time; inner spaces and blank spaces have the same value, their arrangement is determined by one unit of space. Modern architecture seeks new rhythms. Even sans serifs no longer possess the classical equal space for counters and right side bearings; the counters are more open and the spaces between letters narrower. This is one of the most pressing questions of design asked of new sans serifs. The influence sans serif type has had on typography has gone hand in hand with all other kinds of revolutions over the course of the last hundred years. Lithographic business card fonts were cut by most type foundries at the end of the last century. Some of these old sans serifs have had a real renaissance within the last twenty years, once the reaction of the 'New Objectivity', with its geometrical principles of construction, had been overcome. A purely geometrical form of type is unsustainable over a larger period of time. The eye sees horizontal lines thicker than vertical ones, a perfect circle looks misshapen when used as an O in a word. Our time seems to have found its expression in concrete. Modern concrete buildings aren't necessarily geometrical; their forms have tension and liveliness. Type has to have these things too. [...]"[1]

I had learned as a student under Walter Käch in Zurich to model sans serif shapes on those of classical antiquas. My first drafts of a sans serif face date from this period (see page 21). As a continuation of these studies I finished the first drawings for *Univers* in winter 1953 with the word 'monde' /16/, which I sent to Emil Ruder, the typography teacher at the Allgemeine Gewerbeschule in Basel, for his opinion. He suggested minimally widening the characters /06/. He also thought that the letter shapes should be oriented around classical – antiquas. We determined that "in the regular weight, applying the roman principle to the capitals would be desirable, that is narrow letters with two square shapes on top of one another (B E F P R S) in contrast to the wide shapes that touch on being square (O C G N H). Looking to the planned narrow and expanded weights, all letters would have to be more or less evenly balanced."[2] So I came up with some designs based on Capitalis Monumentalis /09/, because even the M with its spread legs /15/ wasn't consistent in the various degrees of width and boldness. The classical double loop shape of the g was rejected for similar reasons, it looks forced in narrow, small and italic weights.

Before I started drawing the typeface I designed a construction diagram for myself /12/. These are only sketches, as I wanted to know first of all whether it was doable to go

About Univers   *Univers* owes its existence to the courage and progressive spirit of Charles Peignot, who had the foresight to back such an unprecented project. For the first time ever a large typeface family was launched without first testing a few weights on the market.[3] Frutiger's sans serif design from his time as a student at the Kunstgewerbeschule in Zurich in 1950/51 served as the starting point.[4] (see page 21). Made easier by new inexpensive type production methods for Lumitype photosetting, 21 weights /01/ were conceived in the sense and knowledge of a demand for a functional, contemporary typeface.

In the *Swiss Typographic Magazine TM/STM* 5/1957, Emil Ruder writes that "it seemed hopeless to embark upon such a huge venture that would try the endurance of both the designers and the company. What convinced us that it would be a success? We believe in the need for a big step in the field of type design. One can feel the urge to rise above the superficiality of the day and create something of real substance. Moreover we believe in a sans serif renaissance."[5]

Emil Ruder is talking about sans serif in the sense of a universal typeface for all kinds of uses including book and newspaper setting. He thought *Univers* was proving versatile enough to fit the bill, and it was proved so when TM editor, Rudolf Hostettler, started setting his magazine entirely in *Univers* from 1961 onward. Other exemplary designs and publications followed, particularly from the Basel school, giving *Univers* ever more exposure and so contributing to the worldwide reputation of 'Swiss Typography'. Special merit goes to Emil Ruder and some of his Basel students who would go on to be famous typographers: Fritz Gottschalk, Hans-Jürg Hunziker, Hans-Rudolf Lutz, Bruno Pfäffli and Helmut Schmid to name but a few.[6]

In the plain, objective, unembellished world of 'Swiss Typography', asymmetrically arranged and set in only a few, contrasting weights and point sizes, the elegance of *Univers* was especially noticeable. *Univers* brought international fame to Adrian Frutiger. It showed that a great type designer was at work.

/01/
Bruno Pfäffli's display of the original 21 Univers weights is clever and concise.

kjyHOLIE
Fz stuchr
flambe
winxov

/02/
*First artwork of Univers 55
for Deberny & Peignot, 1953/54 –
the curves are rounder and
smoother in the finished version.*

/03/
*Adrian Frutiger (seated) inspects
the final artwork of Univers 83
by Ladislas Mandel, with Lucette
Girard in the foreground.*

/04/
*Paste-up of Univers 49 with photo-
graphic reductions of the hand-
drawn originals – the upper-case X
has been stuck on upside down.*

vez-vous gouté le fameux whisky que j'ai beaucoup

vendu

ABCDEFGHIJKLMNOPQRSTUVWXYZ

ÆæŒœfiflß—&–&ÂÄÅáàâåÈèÉÊêëËÑñÜüûÔöï

1234567890% ::,(†)‹*›'! çc;ÇØø:$

*Montage de texte
Univers 49
1954*

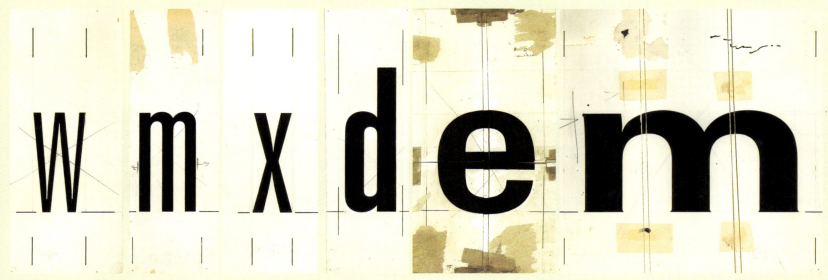

/05/
Final artwork with baseline and widths marked – black ink on card with corrections in pencil.

/06/
Widened counters, at Emil Ruder's suggestion, made by cutting the card and inserting a strip.

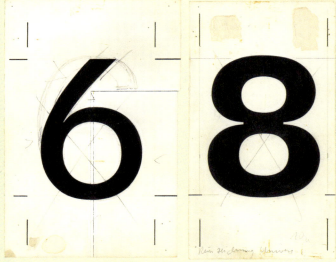

/07/
The diagonal 6 was rejected, the deep cuts in the 8 for photo-setting make it appear like a caricature.

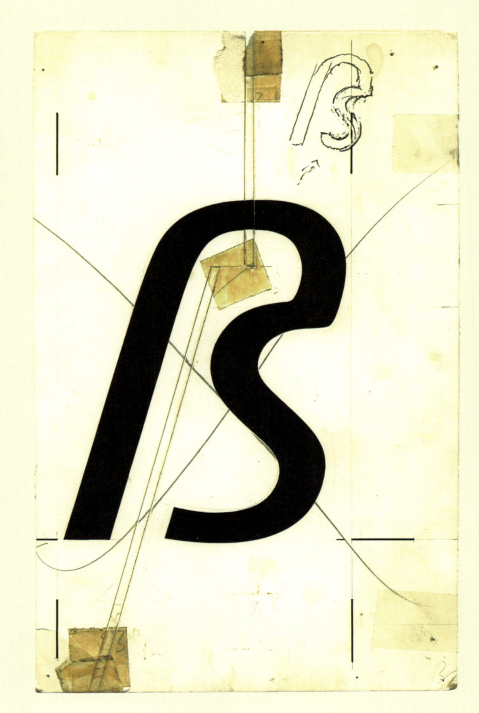

/08/
The curved end was drawn according to the sketch, but the transition from the long s to the round s is much smoother.

from tight, fine letters to wide, bold ones. I just wanted to check the whole spectrum. I decided that the vertical axis should be the right side of the stem. The line had to be the same for each weight. The stroke width was on the left, it was exactly the same within each weight. On the right were the widths, from narrow to wide. This 'accordion' wasn't mathematical, I determined the stroke widths of the single weights and also the letter widths by feel. The letters became almost equally wide in their corresponding widths. That means that an n from the light weight had – from the right edge of the first to the right edge of the second downstroke – almost the same width as an n from the bold weight. This diagram represents the idea, the whole thing isn't identical to the finished *Univers* shapes. I used the n for the diagram published in *TM* 5/1957, but I changed it to h in later publications because of its ascender. There too the letter widths were presented as being mathematically identical, which looked more scientific **/33/**.[7]

During my first visit to Photon Inc. in the USA, who, after *Méridien,* had also taken on *Univers,* one of the people responsible for type came up to me and showed me a whole batch of films with *Univers* letters. He laid them one on top of each other on a light box and confronted me with lots of calculations. He was looking for a mathematical connection between boldness and width and couldn't figure out how I'd calculated it. Some of his results coincidently led to a connection with the Golden Section. When I told him that I had worked out the basic type grid by intuition, he was nonplussed, not to say disappointed.

I constructed *Univers* on a horizontal-vertical axis. That was my starting point. All the different weights of width and boldness came from this cross, even the terminals fit inside in **/33/**. *Univers* has horizontal terminals at the ends of the curves like uncials **/09/**. I was aware that in the regular weight a diagonal, classic curved end would have been nicer, but I wanted to make 21 weights and I couldn't cut the narrow weights diagonally, it just didn't look good. The horizontal ending was a matter of consistency for me, with respect to the whole font family. The t is an exception. The t arc ends vertically rather than horizontally **/11/**. All letters with a tight radius have this ending, that's f j r and t. The slanted cut of the t demonstrates my respect for writing with a pen. I never liked it horizontal, a t is not a cross. I didn't do a slanted cut in the ampersand **/28/**, because to me that character is composed of two capitals, E and T.

Much later, in the 70s, there was a further diagram **/14/**. This study for the Linotype company, with the title 'The Definition of Medium' had the following problem: readers are used to a certain proportion between black and white. As soon as that proportion changes a bit, readers find it unpleasant. It's a subconscious thing. A lot of foundries had to add another weight, the so-called 'book', to the regular one because of that. They'd seen that

Historical background Greek lapidary script **/09/** is the origin of sans serif type. The idea was seized upon some 2000 years later for typefaces in the early 19th century. In France, sans serifs are known as antiques, in reference to their ancient origin, and some contemporary typefaces include it in their names, such as *Antique Olive* by Fonderie Olive, or *Antique Presse* by Deberny & Peignot **/40/**. *Univers* too, prior to being named, was known simply as Antique **/15/** at Deberny & Peignot.[8]

The Roman form principle of letters, based on square, circle, triangle and upright double square **/09/**, may seem an ideal archetype for *Univers*, but impractical for planning a typeface family made up of four different widths and two slopes. Frutiger brought the cap widths into line like Greek lapidary script and unlike *Futura*, which is based on the Roman principle of Capitalis Monumentalis. In doing this, he conformed to the neoclassical sans serif proportions of the 19th century.

Uncials originated in the 3rd century AD. The use of parchment paper and pen changed the shapes of capitals. They became rounder and softer, and some ascenders and descenders started to appear. Small letters began to emerge from the capitals. This was perfected in the Irish-Roman semi-uncials **/09/**, where the stroke ends are broader with horizontal terminals. This is what Adrian Frutiger is referring to when he speaks of uncial terminals in *Univers* **/11/**.

Adrian Frutiger always lets his visual intuition guide him, and only afterwards does he try to find principles to explain the facts. A comparison he made between the proportions of classic and modern typefaces relates them to classic and modern architecture (Greek temples, Bauhaus) **/10/**. The missing serifs mean that sans serif faces do not have equal spaces for counters and side bearings any more as they had before. The counters are more open, the spaces between letters (sidebearings) narrower. This reflects the thoughts of his tutor, Walter Käch. Some of the essential form principles of *Univers* were adopted by Frutiger from Walter Käch.[9]

/09/
Historical scripts:
Greek lapidary, 5th–4th century BC;
Roman Capitalis Monumentalis,
1st century AD; Anglo-Irish
semi-uncials, 8th century.

/10/
The downstrokes are evenly spaced
in serif typefaces – sans serifs
have a more varied rhythm like
modern architecture.

mundi

mundi

/11/
Adrian Frutiger talks of uncial
terminals since uncial is the
only historical script with letters
that sometimes have horizontal
curved ends.

their first version was too delicate or too strong for a text face. That's why I found it interesting to define what a regular weight is. I laid a grid over the letters of classic typefaces and could later see exactly what relationship there was between both parts. I now had the means to apply this ratio to a sans serif typeface. Converted into a grid with units it gives a lowercase n with the stroke width of one unit a counter width of three units and one unit each for left and right side bearing. A whole letter is then five units wide, with a relation of five and a half units in height.

I determined the regular weight of *Univers* together with Emil Ruder. He was a great help to me. We looked at it in the reduction and discussed it for a long time, how the width should be in relation to height and white space. He'd written his corrections, like opening the counters, on card in the final artwork. That's how *Univers* was made, after many constructive discussions with Emil Ruder. *Univers* 55 is my most successful 'Medium'.

The choice of name was important commercially. It was talked about early on, when the project was first laid on the table and journalists started to write about it. By 1956 it couldn't simply be called the 'the new sans serif by Deberny & Peignot' any longer. General director Stanislas Boyer, Charles and Rémy Peignot and I chose the name.[10] We started with my test word 'monde' – after *Europe* we were anxious to branch out further than Europe – I was sure that 'monde' wouldn't work, because it would be understood as 'Mond' (moon) in German. Boyer suggested 'Galaxy', and Rémy came up with 'Universal'. If we were talking large dimensions, then why not go all the way? So Charles Peignot turned it into 'Univers', French for the universe.

To represent the 21 weights of the *Univers* font family I used uppercase H and E and the word 'monde' in my diagram /16/. I would show the regular weight first and put the four bold weights next to each other. At the bottom I put the narrower weights and right at the very bottom I added the wide ones. I quickly realised that the wide weights belonged at the top instead /17/. Then I mirrored the whole diagram and turned it 90 degrees, so that the bolds were at the bottom, the lights at the top and the wides on the left with the narrows on the right. That's how the weights were numbered in ascending order /18/.

As already mentioned in the 'Caractères Lumitype' chapter, there was trouble in naming the weights /16/. I had already introduced a numbering system for Lumitype fonts in order to make ordering easier (see page 76). That served as the basis for the *Univers* numbering, the first digit stands for the stroke width and the last digit is width and slope. Uneven last digits are upright weights, evens are italics. *Univers* is constructed like a star. "55 was the starting point; its black-white relation is meant for book setting. Its neighbours to the left and right (all the fifties) have exactly the same stroke thickness. What changes are the inner spaces and side-bearings, which result in the narrow and compressed weights

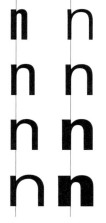

/13/
Identical stroke widths in different widths and near-identical widths in different weights of Univers *by Deberny & Peignot.*

/14/
Frutiger's definition of the Medium (1970s) showing the ratios of the x-height to stroke width, counter and character width –
Univers 55 *is behind it in grey.*

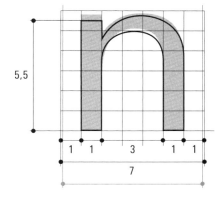

/12/
Schematic diagram in four weights – development of curves and counters of the compressed, condensed, regular and extended typefaces.

15

First type sample of Univers *from 1954 with text in four weights – the uppercase M still has spread legs.*

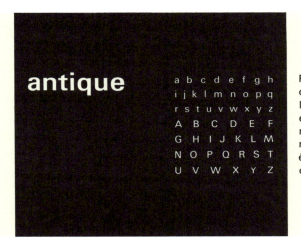

Les périodes de grandes architectures correspondent à des sommets de la civilisation et c'est un lieu commun que d'apprécier les nuances de la forme des civilisations au style de leur architecture respective. Mais l'architecture d'une époque reste, en tant que moyen d'expression d'un idéal, celui d'un groupe d'hommes, d'une communauté, d'un peuple. La typographie est un moyen d'expression non moins complet.

antique

a b c d e f g h
i j k l m n o p q
r s t u v w x y z
A B C D E F
G H I J K L M
N O P Q R S T
U V W X Y Z

Rien de surprenant au fait que le graphisme d'une époque, correspondant à une évolution de la culture chez un peuple, détermine, révèle ou exprime un tempérament ou une tendance dominante de la culture de ce peuple. Il est notoirement évident que la typographie allemande a été très longtemps marquée par la gothique, considérée comme caractère représentatif

a B c D e

Le vingtième siècle cherche son expression typographique; sans doute attend-t-il l'intervention des machines à composer photographiques qui ne manqueront pas d'influencer le graphisme de la deuxième moitié du siècle. Enfin il faut considérer qu'il existe aussi une typographie dont le rythme de renouvellement accéléré correspond aux appétits démesurés de la publicité

Les périodes de grandes architectures correspondent à des sommets de la civilisation et c'est un lieu com mun que d'apprécier les nuances de la forme des civi lisations au style de leur architecture respective Mais l'architecture d'une époque reste, en tant que moyen d'expression d'un idéal, celui d'un groupe d'hommes, d'une communauté, d'un peuple La typographie est un moyen d'expression non moins

Rien de surprenant au fait que le graphisme d'une époque, correspondant à une évolution de la culture chez un peuple, détermine, révèle ou exprime un tempérament ou une tendance dominante de la culture de ce peuple. Il est notoirement évident que la typographie allemande a été très longtemps marquée par la gothique, considérée comme caractère représentatif

Le vingtième siècle cherche son expression typographique; sans doute attend-t-il l'intervention des machines à composer photographiques qui ne manqueront pas d'influencer le graphisme de la deuxième moitié du siècle. Enfin il faut considérer qu'il existe aussi une typographie dont le rythme de renouvellement accéléré correspond aux appétits démesurés de la publicité

Il existe une évolution de la typographie parallèle à celle de l'architecture, sa puissance d'expression est plus subtile sans doute mais évidente. Elle se manifeste dans tous les domaines et ce serait une erreur que de rechercher la typographie exclusivement dans les livres édités à l'intention des bibliophiles. La lettre est par définition une création spirituelle

Il existe une évolution de la typographie parallèle à celle de l'architecture, sa puissance d'expression est plus subtile sans doute mais évidente. Elle se manifeste dans tous les domaines et ce serait une erreur que de rechercher la typographie exclusivement dans les livres édités à l'intention des bibliophiles. La lettre est par définition une création spirituelle

F g g m *H* **n**

16

First Univers *diagram c.1955 with descriptions of the 21 weights in French and English, but still unnumbered.*

Second Univers *diagram from 1956 with horizontal arrangement – the typeface is still nameless.*

The 'HE monde' diagram **/16/** shows the 21 *Univers* weights in a first undated slightly rough depiction. The handwritten names of each weight in two languages are still numberless on the yellowed photographic print. Two slightly reworked diagrams in English titled 'Universal family' and 'Sanseri' **/17/** probably followed soon after, accompanying a memorandum by Louis Rosenblum from February 1956. The weights have different names in all three samples, which shows how problematic the definitions were. In the same note some names are mooted about for the new 'Sans Serif' by Deberny & Peignot. 'Universal', 'Constellation' and 'Cosmos' are suggested.[11]

In *TM/STM* 5/1957 there is an improved, more clearly arranged version.[12] It is the first to include Adrian Frutiger's (Lumitype) numbering system, integrated in the 'monde' diagram **/18/**. This weights diagram would become a sort of trademark for *Univers*. D&P, ATF, and, later on, Haas foundry used it for type samples and advertisements. Rémy Peignot in particular created innovative versions of this diagram: sometimes the rectangles are frames, sometimes they are black or coloured areas, and sometimes they serve as a window to the universe **/37/**. Rémy was also responsible for the 'univers' **/19/** diagram with empty spaces for possible extensions of the type family. It served to demonstrate the dimensions of the *Univers* concept.[13]

Bruno Pfäffli, typographic designer and colleague (later to be studio partner) of Adrian Frutiger's, also made a *Univers* diagram **/01/** which later became a real trademark of *Univers*. Designed for American Type Founders ATF in 1962, it was first displayed in *Monotype Newsletter* 130/1963. Reduced to the essentials, with only the letter u in all weights, he takes on the task of designing the arrangement of the diagram. What stands out is the 16° incline of the *Univers* italic weight, unusual for a sans serif.[14] Along with its large variety of weights, this eye-catching italic became one of the main typographic merits of *Univers*, as can be seen in the advertisements for Monotype by Hans-Rudolf Lutz **/36/**,[15] but also as a working typeface. Words set in *Univers* italics can be found most easily in text bodies, which, sadly, is normally not the case with other sans serifs.

appear semi-bold and bold. In the extended weights, on the other hand, this makes them look thin. This principle was applied to all weights. For this reason it was necessary to attach a bold 80 for the extended widths and a 30 for the compressed ones."[16] The 83 appears nearly as bold as the 75. The same goes for 39 in comparison with 47. Later I asked myself whether it was right that this way a light stroke width appeared to become a regular stroke width in a compressed weight, or whether it would have been better to adapt the stroke width optically. I happened to have it like that in my diagram, and figured if I corrected anything the grading wouldn't be right anymore. In the end it was more of a matter of logic for me than harmony. It could be regarded as an error, but I did it consciously. In later adaptations for photosetting this was changed.

Initially *Univers* was intended for Lumitype. Nevertheless I did my final artwork independently of photosetting methods, on Bristol board with opaque white paint. For me the only way was to deliver drawings ready for cutting and casting. At that time I already had colleagues to help with the final artwork. My best helper was Lucette Girard. I finished all the regular weights with her, based on the drawings stuck together, which Emil Ruder had reviewed. Ladislas Mandel tackled the wide weights **/03/**. He introduced new working methods, scraperboards and stencils for drawing curves. Albert Boton, who was new in the studio, did the narrow weights, which were slightly easier to draw. Only once the final artwork was ready were the optical corrections for photosetting addressed. The regular weight was more or less okay, but the bold and compressed weights were pretty bad. I had to draw some awful caricatures, put serifs on and make huge cuts in the angles so that the type would look right when exposed **/07/**. It was one heck of an ordeal!

The fact that Charles Peignot had taken on the *Univers* project was an enormous gift for me. It took quite some courage on his part to decide to make it for hot metal too. I worked out that there were 35000 punches to cut. Peignot saw that sales of *Europe* were dwindling rapidly and that the foundry was in danger of going down. *Univers* gave the many engravers much-needed work and the foundry could survive another few years.[17]

When manufacturing the lead characters, we determined that *Univers* had a good set on Lumitype, so we kept the character widths. So that they always remained the same, I devised a system of steel templates. They were inserted in the casting device with the corresponding width and then the letter was cast. The casters worked in the morning when they were still sober and tidy. In the afternoons there were some who filled their bellies with a few litres of wine. Unfortunately I left too much right side bearing and they had to be recast.

Of the originally planned 21 weights for hot metal setting, 20 were made, though not the 49 weight under 10 pt. There were only 20 weights for Lumitype photosetting, the 39

/18/

The diagram from TM *5/1957 has the correct arrangement of the 21* Univers *weights, which are numbered accordingly.*

/19/

Rémy Peignot's Univers *diagram from 1957 – published in* TM *11/1963 – shows possible extensions to the 21 weights.*

weight was missing as it led to problems with exposure. The entire range was completed for Monotype and Monophoto. The vast number of font weights – the first time for ones based on the same basic concept – enabled the designers to fit the 'clothing' to the content and not the other way round. Something light and dainty could be set in light condensed, something very heavy in black extended *Univers*. Later Linotype and other manufacturers added more weights – whatever they may be called, they're not all mine. I felt like the sorceror's apprentice who forgets the magic word.

One of the things to decide about shape was the size of the capitals. The different cap heights was just theory in the *Univers* project /33/, it would have complicated the whole hot metal production. The engravers would tell me that it was out of the question for a caster to take an E that wasn't on the base line, it had never occured in their lifetimes. I instantly backed down. However, Emil Ruder thought it was good to draw the uppercase letters slightly smaller than the ascender, which was also discarded because of the relatively tall x-height. He was of the opinion that a text image ought to look roughly the same in any language, no matter if it was German with lots of capitals or a romance language with few of them /35/. In TM 1/1961 Ruder demonstrates a text in three languages – German, French and English – and says that *Univers* works for all of them, which is not entirely true in my opinion. Anyway I've changed my views on it with the passage of time, because the reader benefits from a clear distinction between upper- and lowercase. The capitals aren't conspicuous in *Univers* because of the white spaces. In M and N, for example, the leg isn't covered by the main stem, it's next to it. This sideways shift allows as much light to enter as possible. There is no concentration of black, due also to the conical shape of the downstrokes /33/. This was important for the project as a whole and for the gray areas of the text. *Univers* doesn't form patches in print, like *Akzidenz Grotesk* for example, because the uppercase letters are only drawn slightly bolder than the lowercase.

I made myself stencils in order to get the curves, like the o exactly right. I remembered just how much time we used to spend drawing under Walter Käch until he was satisfied. I would draw an o and cut a stencil out of tracing paper from the best quarter. I would then hold the tracing paper against the edge of the table and sand it until the curve was perfect. I drew my o using this stencil, both inner and outer shapes. I also drew g p q d b the same way. The inner shapes of both round and half-round letters were the same in principle. What varied, on the other hand, were the curves in the stem connections. As long as the counters were equally round, that was the main thing. Ascender and descender were just added. It doesn't require different letter widths. It's simply like a knitting mesh, and each square in the mesh is the same. I always stuck to this basic principle. Apart from the c, which I drew narrower. Because of the white entering it, the narrow c looks as wide as the o.

To begin with, sans serifs were jobbing faces for posters, advertisements and packaging, mostly in bold or bold condensed type, always capitals only. Outline and shadow varieties appeared early on. In 1834 the first sans serif face with lowercase appeared, Thorowgood's bold condensed *Seven-line Grotesque*.[18] The leap from jobbing fonts to text fonts would take another forty years. In 1870 Schelter & Giesecke in Leipzig released *Breite Magere Grotesk* and in 1880, *Breite Fette Grotesk*.[19] Despite the width implied by their names, both typefaces have normal widths – in the lowercase at any rate – and are only wide compared to other sans serifs, which were mostly bold condensed. The Schelter grotesque is the mother of all static grotesques. *Royal Grotesk* by Ferdinand Theinhardt was very important to the next generation. It, too, was released in 1880, and has been available as *Akzidenz Grotesk* light from Hermann Berthold in Berlin since 1908.[20]

The British, German and American static grotesque typefaces from the 19th century and early 20th century that are still well-known, such as *Akzidenz Grotesk, Monotype Grotesque, Venus Grotesk, Franklin Gothic, News Gothic* etc. all feature the same diagonally cut curve ends /22/. There was, however, no consistency. In old type specimens, horizontally and diagonally cut curve ends alternate, even within the same character set /21/. The ends are inconsistent in both upper- and lowercase. This comes as no surprise, because fonts by several different manufacturers were slung together to form a 'family'. There is yet no sign of the uniformity that was to become so characteristic of sans serif design in the 1950s.

It was this essential aspect that split Swiss designers forever into two camps. Emil Ruder extolled the advantages and optical measurements of *Univers* in *TM/STM* 5/1957 and in the special edition 1/1961, /33/ and let

/20/
Breite Magere Grotesk *by*
Schelter & Giesecke *around 1870 –*
the version shown is by
Haas'sche Schriftgiesserei.

BÖRNE: Hätte die Weltgeschichte ein Sachregister, wie ihr Namensverzeich- nis, so könnte man sie besser benützen.

/21/
The a shapes of the original
Akzidenz Grotesk *vary greatly in comparison to* Univers, *which was conceived of as one family.*

aaaa aaa aaaa
aaaa aaaa aaa

/22/
Sans serif faces from the first half of the 20th century have diagonally cut curved ends – they look as though they have not been properly executed yet.

Akzidenz Grotesk
News Gothic
Venus Grotesk
Monotype Grotesque
Record Gothic
Reform Grotesque

/23/
Sans serif faces from 1954–62 have horizontally cut curved ends and are more balanced and matter-of-fact.

Univers
Helvetica
Folio
Mercator
Recta
Permanent

/24/
The uppercase M of Maxima
by Gert Wunderlich has spread legs like the original Univers *design.*

Maxima

students experiment with *Univers*. On the other hand, some designers – for example the Zurich school – regard it alongside Berthold *Akzidenz Grotesk* or *Helvetica*. They deem *Univers* too smooth and conformist. The same goes for former Basel students Karl Gerstner – who designed a system for *Akzidenz Grotesk*[21] – and Wolfgang Weingart. The latter, who taught typography at the Schule für Gestaltung in Basel from 1968, prefer the lively, more archaic character of original sans serifs. Weingart writes; "Univers became an untouchable, almost sacred institution, while Akzidenz Grotesk lay forgotten in dusty old cases."[22]

It would appear that Swiss type design had not achieved a great deal in the intervening fifty years when Emil Ruder wrote, "One has the impression that most of these typefaces weren't made to last. Type design often runs dangerously parallel to fashion crazes and the restlessness of our times. Thus we see more than a few typefaces whose style is dated long before their technical application is. This hunger for change and for all things unusual is a genuine need, and to some degree we ought to honour that. However, in the face of changing fashions we have to create something really durable, in our case a standard typeface."[23]

Folio, *Mercator* and *Neue Haas Grotesk* (which was taken over by D. Stempel AG in 1961 and named *Helvetica*) were released at the same time as *Univers* in 1957. *Recta* followed in 1958 and *Permanent* in 1962. All of these typefaces have horizontally cut curve ends in common.[24] A *Univers*-like face called *Maxima* was released in East Germany in 1970. *Univers* was also one of the starting points for *Haas Unica*, a reconceived version of *Helvetica* in 1980.[25]

I made the numerals narrow on purpose. Their character widths vary in the hot metal version, but for Lumitype photosetting they're all 10 units. This is most noticeable with the zero, which is impossible to confuse with the O. My numerals were always narrower than the uppercase alphabet. This is also the case with classic typefaces, apart from old style numerals, of course. On Lumitype we only had lining figures to start with because there wasn't enough room on the Lumitype disk. So there was only one 1. Monotype made an alternative narrow version with less side bearing.

There are differences to other typefaces in the *Univers* individual letters. With Capitalis Monumentalis /09/ in mind, I attached the Q tail to the exterior shape. I didn't want to disturb the counter. The fact that the tail emerges horizontally from the Q is one of my characteristics, it's in most of my typefaces. The curved indent in the upstroke of the 1, like in *Akzidenz Grotesk* /29/, was something alien to me. An upstroke is something simple and not so fanciful, horizontal with a bump in it. Accordingly, my 1 is simple, like the 7 is too. I always clearly distinguished symbols, numerals and letters. The same goes for the question mark /27/; its curve is cut vertically at the top, and not horizontally like the numerals and letters. On the printed page it should look more like an exclamation mark and less like a 2. My ampersand /28/ was adopted by the European typesetting systems; only when Linotype took over my *Univers* for photosetting for the American market did it get swapped for the looped 'meat-hook ampersand'. The Americans were radical, they didn't want my ampersand at all. The diaereses on ä, ö, ü /32/ were designed with technical considerations in mind. They're arranged by cap height for reasons of even alignment. The Germans criticised this, because diaeresis and letter are always one unit to them where everything has to be close together. However, I couldn't set the dots any lower because although the x-height for all Lumitype fonts was variable, the position of flying accents was set to a specific height.

The best *Univers* remains the hot metal one cast by Deberny & Peignot. All the other adaptations are something of a sorry tale. In 1959 the contract with Monotype was signed – a wise move for Peignot because the expansion of these machines was a worldwide sensation. Stanley Morison made the decision for Monotype. He said that *Univers* was the least bad sans serif face. In their adverts advertisements they wrote, "Univers – a synthesis of Swiss thoroughness, French elegance and British precision in pattern manufacture."[24] The version for machine setting from 1960, where I even had some influence, is already incoherent. There were technical difficulties. Transferring the 36 unit system of Lumitype to the 18 Monotype units didn't work very well. The small f, the t, the capitals – they all seem squashed. I would discuss it for hours with John Dreyfus and the technicians. I could point out that they needed to be wider than the t, but nothing could be done about

---

/25/
Univers was consulted for the reworking of Helvetica *into* Haas Unica *by A. Gürtler, Ch. Mengelt and E. Gschwind.*

Unica

/26/
ß is a ligature of the long s and the round s – in Adobe Caslon *(left and middle) the long s is included in the character set.*

ſs ß ß

/27/
One of the few inconsistencies of Univers *– in two weights the curve is cut vertically, while in the others it is horizontal.*

????

/28/
Because his ampersand was largely unaccepted, Frutiger designed a traditional looped one as an alternative.

/29/
Compared to Akzidenz Grotesk *(left) and* Helvetica *(right),* Univers *(middle) has the simplest form.*

111
777

/30/
Univers (below) appears more harmonious and much smoother than the earlier sans serif faces like Akzidenz Grotesk *(top).*

GKR
GKR

/31/
Curve endings have been unified on Univers *lowercase – they are cut off horizontally at the same height.*

acegs
acegs

/32/
The heights of the letters are not uniform in Akzidenz Grotesk *(above), whereas in* Univers, *unusually, even the accents are aligned.*

H5äliè
H5äliè

Top left facsimile

TM   Typographische Monatsblätter
SGM   Schweizer Graphische Mitteilungen
RSI   Revue suisse de l'Imprimerie
Nr. 1 Januar/Janvier 1961 80. Jahrgang
Herausgegeben vom Schweizerischen Typographenbund
zur Förderung der Berufsbildung
Edité par la Fédération suisse des typographes
pour l'éducation professionnelle

typographischemonatsblätter

typographische monatsblätter
(repeated in decreasing and increasing sizes)

typographischemonatsblätter

/33/

*TM 1/1961 is devoted entirely to
Univers – A. Frutiger, E. Ruder and
P. Heuer write about its conception
and production over 60 pages.*

Right page (top)

Der Werdegang der Univers
Adrian Frutiger, Paris

Über die Grotesk im allgemeinen. Meine erste Begegnung mit der Lapidarschriftform geht zurück in den Anfang meiner Schriftsetzerlehrzeit. Die Mengen Bleibuchstaben verschiedener Formen und Arten waren für mich noch gegebene Dinge, welche mit richtighandhabt werden. Der Sinn für ihr ordnendes Zusammensetzen fehlte mir ganz; ich fühlte keine schöpferische Anregung, die Buchstaben als Bauelemente zu erkennen und damit zu gestalten, mit andern Worten: ich war kein Typograph.

Dagegen fühlte ich von Anfang an eine große Lust zum Schriftschreiben. Nicht eigentlich im Sinne des kalligraphischen Viel- und Schönschreibens, sondern im Sinne des Schreibvorganges an sich, in der notwendigen Handhabung des Werkzeuges zur Gestaltung einer authentischen Form.

Die eingelebte Methode, den Schriftunterricht mit Groteskformen zu beginnen, habe ich erst viele Jahre später als völlig falsch erkannt. Im Unterbewußtsein fühlte ich aber schon damals, bei unzähligen Ansätzen zum «Schönschreiben», die Unlust, welche in einem Werkzeug liegt, das nicht vom Material her geformt wurde, sondern eine intellektuelle Erfindung ist. Diese kleine, runde Fläche, die in jeder Richtung Balken von gleicher, unsensibler Dicke zieht mit runden, unklaren Ansätzen, bleibt mir in unangenehmer Erinnerung. Meine erste Begegnung mit Grotesk war also eine schlechte; sie hat mir aber später viel geholfen zur Erkenntnis, daß Schriftformen nur dann gut sind, wenn Material und Werkzeug treu und richtig gehandhabt werden.

Als ich später selbst dazu kam, Schriftunterricht zu erteilen, ersetzte ich die Vorübung das Papier durch flachgestrichene Tonerde und die Feder durch eine Zweipunktreglette. Die einfachste Formgebung durch den Eindrücken ergibt volle Konzentration auf die Bestimmung der Innen- und Zwischenräume, von welchen die Schönheit einer Schrift zum großen Teil abhängt. (1)

Die Lapidarschrift oder Grotesk ist in ihrem eigentlichen Wesen eine geritzte oder gemeißelte Form. Ihre Strenge und Reinheit liegt im Widerstand, den das Material (Schiefer, Stein) dem Werkzeug (Griffel, Meißel) beim Arbeitsvorgang leistet. Je größer der Widerstand ist, desto klarer werden die Formen. Die einheitliche Formgebung eines gleichmäßigen Striches ist das elementare und natürlichste Ausdrucksmittel: mit einem Stecken oder Stein ritzen, mit Kohle oder Kreide schreiben. Auch Bleistift und Kugelschreiber haben diese Eigenschaften, und sie sind unsere meistgebrauchten Schreibzeuge. (3)

Diese Liebe zur Urform und dieser Hang zur klarsten, strengsten Art, Schriftformen auszudrücken, wurden in mir wach bei der Begegnung mit der Kunstgewerbeschule Zürich. Seine große Einsicht über Formenwerte, sein strenges Aufbauen, seine schöpferische Kraft überhaupt waren für mich grundlegende Erfahrungen. (2)

In Gegenwart von antiken oder auch modernen Kunstwerken großer Reinheit suchte ich oft verzweifelt nach einer Druckschrift, welche auch dem Text Ausdruckskraft verleihen könnte. Die Lust fehlte nicht, neue Schriften zu gestalten, die dem Bilde näher kommen. Dazu ist es nicht möglich, anders vorzugehen, als auf den Ursprung zurückzugreifen. Das Problem Groß- und Kleinbuchstaben taucht dabei auf. Die formal und intellektuell komplizierte Verbindung zweier so grundverschiedener Elemente macht es von Anfang an schwer, an einen klaren, einheitlichen Formenaufbau zu schreiten. Seit Anfang des Jahrhunderts ist es stets «puristes» gegeben, welche entweder nur mit Großbuchstaben oder nur mit Kleinbuchstaben arbeiten. Charles Peignot und Cassandre hatten den Mut, ein neues Alphabet zu schaffen, in welchem Groß- und Kleinbuchstaben sich vereinigt finden; Ausgangspunkt war der geschichtliche Hintergrund der Halbunziale und Karolinger Minuskel.

In Gegenwart allen technischen Fortschritte, man sich, ob es noch der rechtfertigt sei, daß ein Satz eines normalen Textes fünf verschiedene Alphabete zu verwenden: Versalien, Gemeine (geradestehend und kursiv) und Kapitälchen. Teleschreiber und -setzer arbeiten in direkter Linia um die ganze Erde; ihre Ausdrucksmittel sind beschränkt; beschränken heißt nicht verarmen; oft sind aus der Vereinfachung neue, lebendige, der Zeit angepaßte Werte und Formen entstanden. (4)

Bottom left page

monde *monde*

Gaumont *Baskerville*

Römer Intention   spannende Grenzen

378

Die Grotesk als Drucktype. Eine Druckschrift ist aufgebaut auf eine alte geschichtliche und technische Tradition. Als klassische, das heißt dauernde Schriftformen können diejenigen bezeichnet werden, welche auf richtige Grundlage der historischen Schriftentwicklung aufgebaut sind und zugleich materialgerecht gearbeitet wurden. Diese beiden Bedingungen schließen allzu persönliche Ansichten des Schriftgestalters in Hinsicht der Formgebung aus.

Der formale Ausdruck der bildenden Künste jeder Epoche wurde von den verwendeten Materialien beeinflußt. Im Altertum sind es roher Stein und Holz; später wurden die Steine poliert und das Holz gehobelt; das Metall kam dazu; heute sind es Beton, Glas, Plastic usf., welche die Konstruktionsmöglichkeiten unendlich erweitern. – In jedem Zeitalter hat das bearbeitete Material auch der Schrift Rhythmus und Form verliehen: Stein – Lapidarschrift, Marmor – Kapitalis, Pergament – von der Rustika bis zur Textur, Stahlstempel und Blißguß – Medievalschriften, Kupferstich – Antiqua und Schreibschrift, Litho – alle Phantasieschriften und auch die ersten Groteskformen.

Jede Schrift trägt das Wesentliche ihrer Zeit in sich. Die gediegene Form der Karosse aus dem 18. Jahrhundert harmoniert sehr gut mit den Schriften der gleichen Zeit; die Formen waren richtig in ihrer Zeit. Die richtige Funktion hat dem Düsenflugzeug seine Form gegeben; seine Schönheit sollte sich in den Schriften der Gegenwart wiederfinden. (6)

Der einfache Rhythmus der klassischen Architektur spiegelt sich wider in den zeitentsprechenden Schriften; Innenräume und Zwischenräume haben gleichen Wert, die Gliederung ist von *einer* Raumeinheit bestimmt. Die moderne Architektur sucht nach neuen Rhythmen. Auch die Grotesk hat nicht mehr der klassischen, gleichwertigen Raum für Punzen und Fleisch; die Punzen sind offener, die Zwischenräume zwischen Buchstaben enger gehalten. Dies ist eine der wichtigsten Gestaltungsfragen, die einer neuen Grotesk gestellt sind. (7)

Der Einfluß der Groteskschrift auf die Typographie hat sich in den letzten hundert Jahren ganz allmählich und Hand in Hand mit allen andern Umwälzungen abgespielt. Die lithographischen Kartenschriften wurden Ende des letzten Jahrhunderts von den meisten Schriftgießereien in Druckschrift geschnitten. Einige dieser ersten Grotesken erlebten in den letzten zwanzig Jahren eine richtige Renaissance, nachdem die Reaktion der «Neuen Sachlichkeit» mit ihren geometrischen Konstruktionsprinzipien überstanden worden war.

Eine rein geometrische Schriftform ist auf die Dauer nicht haltbar. Das Auge sieht horizontale Striche dicker als vertikale, der perfekte Zirkelkreis als O scheint unförmig und sticht im angespannten Wort heraus. – Unsere Zeit scheint ihren Ausdruck im Beton gefunden zu haben. Der moderne Betonbau ist aber nicht unbedingt geometrisch; die Formen sind gespannt, lebendig. Die Schrift muß es auch sein. Auf geometrische Grundlagen aufgebaut, können die Linien frei spielen, zum Zwecke, daß sich die einzelnen Buchstaben in ihrem Ausdruck finden und sich in Wort, Zeile und Seite zu einer zusammenhangenden Struktur verbinden.

Bottom middle column

5
Der moderne Betonbau hat neue, lebendige, gespannte Formen gebildet. Vergleich mit Schriftzeichnungen. Oben: Geometrische Schriftformen. Mitte: Innenaufnahme des Guggenheimmuseums, Neuyork (Architekt Frank Lloyd Wright). Unten: Auf geometrischer Grundlage aufgebaute freigezeichnete Schriftzeichnungen.

6
Jede Schrift trägt das Wesen ihrer Zeit in sich

7
Vergleich zwischen Rhythmen der klassischen und der modernen Architektur (Versailles, Petit-Trianon. Le Corbusier; Le couvent Sainte-Maria de la Tourette). In gleichem Sinne hat die Grotesk nicht mehr den klassischen, gleichwertigen Raum für Punzen und Fleisch (Beispiel Baskerville); die Punzen sind offener, die Zwischenräume enger

8
Die Alltagsbilder unserer Zeit zeigen neue, gute Formen. Der Ausdruck unserer Schriftform sucht mit ihnen in Einklang zu stehen

9
Übersicht der 21 diversen Schnitte der Univers

10
Schematische Darstellung der Übereinstimmung zwischen den verschiedenen Schnitten von eng bis breit und von mager bis fett

5
Le béton a créé de nouvelles formes non géométriques et vivantes en architecture. Comparaison avec le dessin de la lettre. En haut: Conception géométrique de la lettre. Milieu: Vue d'intérieur du musée Guggenheim à New York (architecte Frank Lloyd Wright). En bas: Dessins de lettres tracés librement sur une base géométrique

6
Chaque caractère porte en soi l'expression essentielle de son époque

7
Comparaison des rythmes de l'architecture classique et moderne (Versailles, Petit-Trianon. Le Corbusier: Le couvent Sainte-Maria de la Tourette). De même, un caractère antique n'est plus construit avec des espaces égaux comme contrepoinçons et approches, ce qui est le cas dans le caractère classique de gauche (Baskerville); les contrepoinçons sont plus ouverts, au détriment des espaces entre les lettres

8
Chaque jour, de nouvelles images et de nouvelles formes frappent nos yeux. Nos formes de caractères cherchent à être en accord avec cette nouvelle expression

9
Tableau d'ensemble des 21 séries de l'Univers

10
Dessin schématique montrant la concordance entre les différentes séries, de l'étroit au large et du maigre au gras

11
En haut: Mauvaise proportion entre le blanc des contrepoinçons et le blanc des approches. En bas: Les contrepoinçons sont plus larges, les espaces plus étroits

5
Modern concrete building has created new and dynamic shapes. Comparison with type design. Top: Geometrically designed type. Middle: Interior of the Guggenheim Museum of Modern Art, New York (Frank Lloyd Wright). Bottom: Type design based on geometrical patterns, but with curves traced in a free hand

6
Each type face reflects essential features of its period of origin

7
If we compare the rhythm of classic and modern architecture (Versailles, Petit-Trianon. Le Corbusier: convent of Sainte-Marie de la Tourette) with type design, we notice a change in optical conceptions! The classic, well balanced spacing in counters and between letters (Baskerville) is superseded by more open counters and less space between letters

8
Type design endeavours to fall in line with contemporary industrial design, architecture and landscape planning and development which reveal new and attractive shapes

9
The 21 different founts of Univers

10
This illustration shows how the different weights and widths are synchronised

11
Top: The space within the counters is not in good proportion with the spacing between letters. Bottom: Wider counters, less space between letters

Bottom right page

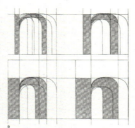

monde
monde

univers (type specimen grid)

Die Univers. Im Jahre 1954 wurde mir die Aufgabe gestellt, die Schriftauswahl für den europäischen Markt der Lumitype-Photon zu treffen und die Zeichnungen auszuführen. Beim Kapitel Grotesk wußte ich, daß es notwendig war, dem gegenwärtigen Bedürfnis nach verschiedenen Varianten von Fette und Breite nachzukommen. Ich erinnere mich, als Setzer stets ein Gefühl von Verworrenheit gehabt zu haben vor der Verschiedenheit in Herkunft, Form und Ausführung aller Groteskarten, welche sich im gleichen Betrieb vorfanden. Aus diesem und andern Überlegungen entstand der Gedanke, eine Synthese der meistverwendeten Schnitte zu machen. (9)

Die ersten Bemühungen gingen dahin, die richtigen Fetten zu finden. Fette heißt Dicke des Striches *und* ihr Verhältnis zum Weißraum. Die 55 war der Ausgangspunkt; ihr Schwarz-Weiß-Verhältnis ist für Buchsatz gedacht. Die Nachbarn links und rechts der 55 (alle Fünfziger) haben genau die selbe Strichdicke; was sich ändert, sind die Innen- und Zwischenräume, welche in schmalen und engen Schnitten ein halbfettes und fettes Bild ergeben, in den breiten hingegen ein mageres. (10) Dieses Prinzip würde in allen verschiedenen Dicken durchgesetzt. Aus diesem Grunde war es auch nötig, eine Fette 80 für die Breiten und eine 30 für die Engen anzuschließen. Alle Schnitte sind dadurch verwandt; sie beziehen ihre Formen aus einer Basisform. Die verschiedenen Fetten sind mit Zehnerstellen, die verschiedenen Breiten und Lagen mit Einerstellen bezeichnet. Ungerade Ziffern bedeuten geradestehende Schnitte, gerade Ziffern Kursivschnitte. In der Tabelle sind die drei Schnitte normaler Breite gerade und kursiv in vier Fetten: mager (45, 46), normal (55, 56), halbfett (65, 66) und fett (75, 76). Links sind die breiten Schnitte: normal (53), halbfett (63), fett (73) und doppeltfett (83), rechts die schmalen Schnitte gerade und kursiv: mager (47, 48), normal (57, 58) und halbfett (67, 68). Ganz rechts außen befinden sich die engen Schnitte: fein (39), mager (49) und normal (59). Wichtige optische Probleme, die beim Schriftentwerfen stellen, mußten im Hinblick auf die Gesamtplanung gelöst werden. Im Normalschnitt wäre die Anwendung des römischen Prinzips in den Versalien wünschenswert, das heißt schmale Buchstaben mit zwei Quadratformen übereinander (B, E, F, P, R, S) in Kontrastwirkung zu den breiten Formen, die auf einer quadratischen Form beruhen (O, C, G, N, H). Im Hinblick aber auf die neben dem normalen Schnitt geplanten schmalen und fetten Schnitte mußten alle Buchstaben mehr oder weniger gleichwichtig gehalten werden. Aus ähnlichen Gründen wurde auf die klassische Form des «Univers» reizvoll gehalten wäre. Für alle weiteren Schnitte wäre diese Lösung nicht anwendbar gewesen. Um die Versalien im deutschsprachigen Satz mit in anderen Sprachen ungewohnten Häufung von Versalien ist das Verhältnis von Versalien zu Gemeinen von großer Bedeutung. Es ist möglich, die Versalien niederer als die Oberlängen zu halten, was im Normalschnitt der des «Univers» reizvoll gewesen wäre.

12

13

14

15

16

17

18

Column 1 (page 12)

zu stark werden zu lassen, entschloß man sich für eine verhältnismäßig große n-Höhe, was in allen Schnitten durchgeführt werden kann. Dadurch erhält sich die Schrift in den kleinsten Graden eine gute Lesbarkeit; die Schrift hat das sogenannte große Bild. Gegenüber der knappen Oberlänge ist die Unterlänge noch einmal verkürzt. Dieses Verhältnis ist in allen Schnitten dasselbe. Die Versalien sind nur wenig fetter als die Gemeinen, was sehr viel zu einem ruhigen Schriftbild beiträgt, selbst bei einer Häufung von Versalien. (12)

Die Ziffern sind auf Versalhöhe in der Fette der Gemeinen gezeichnet, um den relativ kleinen Innenräumen der Ziffern Rechnung zu tragen. Bei der Planung der verschiedenen Fetten und Lagen stellte sich im weiteren die Frage, ob die Abschlüsse von c, s und e schräg oder waagrecht zu halten seien. Es hat sich gezeigt, daß die einzige Lösung für alle Schnitte der waagrechte Abschluß im Sinne der Unzialschrift ist. (13)

Die Art der Reihung der Buchstaben zum Wort ist entscheidend. Das Weiß in den Buchstaben steht in Beziehungen zum Weiß zwischen den Buchstaben. In den ersten Versuchen zur 'Univers' ist diese Beziehung von der üblichen und gebräuchlichen Art; die beiden Weiß sind sich zu ähnlich; das Licht dringt zu stark zwischen die Buchstaben und gefährdet die Bandwirkung der Zeile. Dieser Fehler wurde behoben. Die Buchstaben sind verbreitert worden und damit auch die weißen Innenflächen; das Weiß zwischen den Buchstaben ist verengert worden. Die beiden Weiß stehen in einem Mengenkontrast zueinander; die Punzen sind expressiver geworden. Durch das gegenseitig sich wie die Glieder einer Kette, die Zeile ist dichter und die Führung der Buchstaben in der Zeile besser geworden. (11) Balken, die sich zusammenfügen, sind leicht konisch gezeichnet. Das freie Balkenende ist leicht verdickt, das andere Ende verdünnt, um die Schwarzanhäufung aufzulockern und das Zuschmieren zu verhindern. (14)

Die Versalhöhe ist leicht differenziert. Versalien, die mit der Schmalseite der Balken die Höhe begrenzen (H), sind größer als solche, die mit der Breitseite der Balken die Höhe einnehmen (E). (15)

Die Dicke eines Striches ist wohl optisch von einem Buchstaben zum andern identisch, praktisch wurden aber an kompakten Zeichen, wie B, R, M usf., die Dicke verringert, wodurch einem dunkleren Hervorstechen in der Zeile vorgebeugt wird. (16)

Die Kursivalphabete wurden von den Geradestehenden abgewandelt. Auf einer horizontalen Mittellinie dreht sich die Vertikale zur Schräge. Der gewählte Winkel ist ziemlich groß, damit der Unterschied zwischen Geradestehender und Kursiv besser betont ist. Mit diesem Konstruktionsprinzip hat die Kursiv genau die gleiche Weite wie die Geradestehenden, und die Grauwirkung ist die selbe. (17)

Der Fotosatz stellt noch andere Forderungen an die Zeichnung eines Buchstabens. Die Matrizenscheibe der Lumitype dreht sich mit 8 Umdrehungen in der Sekunde. Die Buchstaben werden durch die sich drehende Scheibe hindurch mit einem Blitz von der Dauer von 5 Millionstel einer Sekunde. Dabei muß die Lichtstärke sehr groß sein. Das fotografische Gesetz ist, daß durch

12

Column 2 (page 12)

eine kleine Öffnung proportional weniger Licht durchgeht als durch eine große Öffnung. Es ist also notwendig, daß zum Beispiel i-Punkte und Punkturen, hauptsächlich in mageren Schriften, sehr stark verdickt werden müssen. Dagegen müssen Verdichtungen, wie zum Beispiel in W, in einer schmalfetten Serie sehr stark geöffnet werden, aber auch nur so viel, daß im großen Graden die Übertreibungen nicht als Fehler gesehen werden. (18)

12 verschiedene Grade werden von der gleichen Scheibe fotografiert; die Zeichnung muß also so angelegt sein, daß sie im Corps 5 nicht zufließt, dagegen im Corps 28 auch nicht einen auseinandergezerrten Eindruck macht. Dazu kommt, daß sich an die Fotografie des Films die Kopie auf Offsetplatte oder Kupferzylinder anschließt. Heikle Stellen können in einem Falle zufließen, im andern aufweiten oder brechen! Ein weiteres Problem ist dasjenige der Breitenbestimmung der Buchstaben. 23 Einheiten stehen in der Lumitype zur Verfügung, ein ganzes Alphabet von i bis W zu gestalten.

Das Schriftgestalten ist nicht ausschließlich ein ästhetisches Problem, sondern zum großen Teil im Verstehen der technischen Gegebenheiten, auf welchen die Formen aufgebaut werden. Und die Schrift ist dann schön, wenn sie richtig im Dienste einer strengen Gesetzmäßigkeit durch leichte Auslaßungen steht.

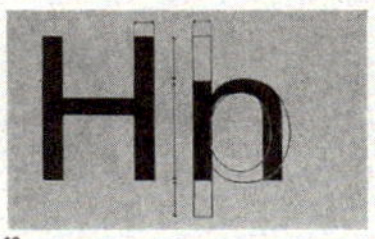

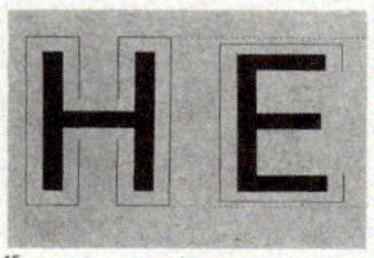

Column 3 (page 12), French

12
Le différence de grandeur entre capitales et bas-de-casses est réduite au minimum pour obtenir une composition sans rupture
13
Les boucles de c, a, s, etc. ont une terminaison horizontale, comme dans l'onciale. Ce principe a été appliqué dans toutes les séries
14
Les traits aà un autre sont légèrement coniques pour éviter une accumulation de noir dans les angles intérieurs
15
La graisse à hauteur des lettres ne sont pas à égard d'après des lois mathématiques mais d'après des lois optiques
17
Les italiques sont dérivées des romains. Sur une ligne médiane horizontale, la verticale pivote
16
Exagérations nécessaires pour le dessin d'une écriture destinée à la photo-composition. Les angles intérieurs sont très ouverts et certains angles extérieurs sont renforcés par un léger empattement
12
The difference in height between capitals and lower case characters is small, and this ensures a well-balanced composition
13
The end strokes of c, a, s, etc. are horizontal (like those of uncials). This applies to all founts
14
Joining strokes are very slightly thickened. Patchminesss avoided by slightly conical strokes on a tapering end
15 16
Weight and height of letters is governed by optical instead of mathematical rules
17
Italics are directly derived from upright founts. A horizontal line in the middle of the x-height serves as an axis
18
Such exaggerations as are necessary in type design are needed for filmsetting. The interior of acute angles is opened up considerably, while the outside is slightly strengthened

Column 4 (page 13), German

12
Der Größenunterschied zwischen Groß- und Kleinbuchstaben ist ziemlich gering, damit wir ein ruhiges Satzbild erhalten
13
Die Abschlüsse von c, e, s usf. sind waagrecht im Sinne der Unzialschrift. Das Prinzip wurde in allen Schnitten durchgehalten
14
Balken, die sich zusammenfügen, sind leicht konisch eigen ausßen, wodurch Schwarzanhäufungen aufgelockert werden
15 16
Fette und n-Höhe der Buchstaben sind nach optischer und nicht nach mathematischen Regeln bestimmt
17
Die Kursiven sind von den Geradestehenden abgewandelt. Auf einer horizontalen Mittellinie dreht sich die Vertikale zur Schräge
18
Notwendige Übertreibungen beim Zeichnen einer Schrift für den Fotosatz. Innenwinkel sind sehr stark geöffnet. Außenwinkel sind teilweise verstärkt durch leichte Auslaßungen

Das Grundprinzip des Fabrikationsprozesses eines Bleibuchstabens wurde im der ersten Gießern des 15. Jahrhunderts erfunden und erlebte seither keine fundamentale Änderung, außer derjenigen, welche zur direkten Matrizenbohrung führte.

Das Endprodukt ist ein erhabener Buchstabe. Er entsteht als Mengenprodukt, indem eine Metallegierung in ein Mutterstück, die Matrize, gegossen wird. Eine künstlerischen Gefühlsmäßigkeit und aus verschiedenen technischen Vorwänden ist es richtiger, diese Matrize mit Hilfe eines erhabenen Originalmodells, des Stempels, herzustellen, als sie direkt vertieft zu bohren. Warum? Es ist schwer und handwerklich kompromißvoll, in verkehrter Arbeitsweise in der Vertiefung zu gestalten, was erhaben erscheinen soll. Die feinste Fräse erlaubt es nicht, rechte und spitze Winkel bis aufs Äußerste auszuarbeiten. Zudem ist Retuschieren in der Matrize unmöglich. Letzte Feinheiten können aber nur richtig und sauber ausgearbeitet werden in der definitiven Größe des geschnittenen Grades. Der Rauchabzug des Stempels oder des Zeugschnittes ist eine unfehlbare Kontrollmöglichkeit vor der Fabrikation. Aus diesen Gründen hat die Gießerei Deberny & Peignot mit der alten Tradition nicht brechen wollen und ist auch in den jüngsten Schriftschnitten dem Stahlstempel treu geblieben.

Eine neue Schrift entsteht logischerweise zuerst im Kopfe des Gestalters. Bevor der erste Strich überhaupt skizziert wird, muß Klarheit über ganz bestimmte Punkte herrschen. Außer der elementaren Stilfrage ist zuerst diejenige des Zweckes zu beantworten: Handelt es sich um eine Linie um eine Textschrift, um eine Auszeichnungsschrift? In welchem Druckverfahren muß die Schrift am besten reproduktionsfähig sein? Ist mechanischer Blei- oder Fotosatz vorzusehen? usw. Die Bedingungen all dieser Fragen umgrenzen schon von Anfang an das Bild der zu schaffenden Schrift.

Die ersten Skizzen sind für die formal wichtigsten Buchstaben erstellt: i, o, n, v, p, d, H, O, A, mit welchen sofort Worte gebildet werden, um die Schrift von Beginn an im Wortbild zu gestalten.

Die ersten Schwarzweißzeichnungen (1), die ungefähr 10 cm hoch ausgeführt sind, werden mit Hilfe eines Mikrofilmapparates auf einen mittleren Grad verkleinert. Die Fotabzüge werden genau auf der vorausbestimmten Breiten den Hilfslinien nach ausgeschnitten und zu einem Text zusammengeklebt. (2) Das Ganze wird auf die kleineren Grade weiter verkleinert. Oft kommt es so weit, daß man von solchen Probesatz ein Strichklische und dritten Klebesatz, werden Vergrößerungen der Zeichnungen angefertigt. Diese großen Fotografien werden auf Karton aufgezogen, der Karton auf eine Metallplatte aufgeleimt und die Buchstaben in mit aller Sorgfalt von Hand aus dem Karton ausgeschnitten. Diese Arbeit geschieht mit einer Präzision von zwei Zehntelmillimetern. Von dieser Originalschablone wird

Column 5 (page 13), German

eine Fabrikationsschablone in drei- bis fünffacher Verkleinerung auf dem Pantographen in eine Messingplatte gefräst. (3) Nach dieser Messingschablone werden auch mit Hilfe des Pantographen die Originalstempel und -zeugschnitte hergestellt, in Reduktionen von 5 bis 15, je nach Grad. (4) Die vorerwähnten Toleranzen von zwei Zehntelmillimeter sind automatisch in der richtigen Stellung vor dem Gießmund. Der Gießer braucht nur noch die angegebene Dickte einzustellen. (7)

Von jedem Schriftzeichen und von allen Graden wird ein Probeguß angefertigt. Davon werden Probesätze hergestellt, auf Grund deren letzte Korrekturen angebracht werden als Gut zum Gießen erteilt wird. Der Guß erfolgt mit erprobten Legierungen, die nach Größe verschieden sind. Die Legierung bezieht die Mitarbeiter zur Widerstand größer oder kleiner Flächen, feiner, grober oder auch überhängender Formen. Der fertige Guß wird mit Fehlertoleranzen von 1 bis 3 Hundertstelmillimeter kontrolliert, je nach Schriftart und Schriftgrad.

Ich möchte diese Gelegenheit nicht unbenützt lassen, die Mitarbeiter zu erwähnen, welche an der Entstehung der ersten Schnitte beteiligt waren: Lucette Girard und Ladislas Mandel als Schriftzeichner und Marcel Mouchel als Leiter der Gravurabteilung Deberny & Peignot.

13

Bottom column 1 (page 18), German

Die Druckschriften historischer Prägung. Viele unserer noch heute im Gebrauch stehenden Druckschriften vergangener Epochen sind Schrifttypen von hohen Qualitäten, die das Überdauern der Jahrhunderte begreiflich machen. Die Antiqua der italienischen Renaissance, die Barock- und die klassizistische Antiqua, scheinen in funktioneller wie formaler Hinsicht unübertrefflich. Der richtig dosierte Fettenwechsel, das gute formkünstlerische Wohl an Mittel-, Ober- und Unterlängen und die schöne Grauwirkung der älteren Antiqua erscheinen bei nicht nur als eine schöne, sondern auch eine mühelos lesbare Schrift, und es fehlt nicht an Stimmen, welche in der Mediäval alle Tugenden einer Druckschrift vereinigt finden. Oft hört man die Ansicht, die Mediäval sei der nicht mehr zu übertreffende Endpunkt aller Druckletternentwicklung.

Bei aller objektiven Würdigung unbestreitbarer Qualitäten darf nicht übersehen werden, daß Schriften wie die Bembo, die Garamond, die Caslon, die Baskerville oder die Bodoni Schriften *vergangener* Epochen sind. Diese Schriften sind zudem mit ihren Nationen eng verknüpft. Die Baskerville, in englischer Sprache gesetzt, zeigt dort ihre volle Wirkung, und im deutschen Satz verändert sich ihr Charakter. Häufung der Versalien und enge Wortbilder bewirken eine spürbare Abwertung ihrer formalen Qualitäten. Diese Beurteilung ist allgemein verbreitet und umfaßt Anforderungen, die heute an eine Schrift gestellt werden müssen, nicht genügen. Sie wurzelt in einer Zeit, für die Werbung und Publizistik unbekannte Dinge waren, und ihre ursprüngliche Form zeigt nur eine Normalbreite, mageren und kursiven Schnitt. Ihr Wesen ist Intimität, und nicht ohne Bedenken kann sie für Werbedrucksachen und für Arbeiten in größeren Format eingesetzt werden. Die Vergrößerung der Garamond zum Beispiel über die Typengröße hinaus ist ihrer Wirkung abträglich. Wir benötigen heute große Buchstaben, halbfette, fette, schmale, breite, kursive und normale Schnitte. Derartige Ansprüche kann nur die Linear-Antiqua, die Grotesk erfüllen, nicht irgendeine Grotesk — eine gute Grotesk.

Die Groteskschriften vor der Univers. England schuf die ersten Endstriche, welche bei ihrem Auftreten auf dem Kontinent die bekannten Schockwirkungen auslösten. Die Schriftbezeichnung Grotesk — absonderlich, lächerlich ist so erklärbar. Bis auf den heutigen Tag wurde diese Bezeichnung beharrlich auf die Schrift angewandt, und es ist offensichtlich, daß der diffamierende Name an ihr festhaftet. An dieser Einstellung ist Schrift wesentlich beteiligt. Für den Buchdrucker besteht das typische Merkmal der Grotesk immer noch darin, daß ihr etwas *fehlt*: die Endstriche und der Fettenwechsel. Diese Beurteilung ist allgemein verbreitet und sich wohl kaum bewußt, daß sie mit diesem oberflächlichen und nur im Negativen verharrenden Urteil mit zur Verfemung der Grotesk beitragen. Der Wert einer Sache kann nie darin bestehen, daß ihr etwas mangelt. Paul Renner schrieb in der Einführung zu seiner Futura: «Unsere Zeit zieht eine Schrift vor, die technische Form, jeder Kunst vor.» Sympathie und Verständnis für diese Formulierung dürfen nicht hindern,

Bottom column 2 (page 18), German

auch hier wieder das Negative herauszuhören. Für Renner ist es darum, den Ballast vergangener Jahrhunderte abzuwerfen und sich vom Diktat klassischer Schriften zu befreien.

In den ersten Schnitten der Futura waltet weitgehend das Prinzip der Konstruktion, wenn auch Renner in den späteren Futura-Schnitten einsehen mußte, daß optische Korrekturen unumgänglich sind. Die Futura bleibt aber das Beispiel der weitgehend konstruktiven Grotesk, und der aufmerksame Betrachter wird im freien Schnitt des Versal U ohne große Mühe dort den optischen Knickwirkung schon, wo es fehlt nicht an Stimmen, aufstoßen.

Die Futura wurzelt im Konstruktivismus in Architektur und Kunst der zwanziger Jahre, und mit diesen gemeinsam demonstrierte sie für eine Überwindung des Individuellen (in dem Künstlerschriften des Buchdrucks) mittels der Konstruktion. Der demonstrative Charakter und ihre enge Verflechtung mit dem positiven, aber auch negativen Zeichen ihrer Zeit haben bewirkt, die Bedeutung der Futura für unsere Zeit in Frage zu stellen. Die Drucktype, welche das Auge als richtig empfinden soll, kann nicht konstruiert sein. Das menschliche Auge hat die Tendenz, alle waagrecht gelagerten Werte zu vergrößern, die senkrechten Teile als schwächer zu registrieren; im rechten oder spitzen Winkel aufeinanderstoßende Balken müssen konisch verjüngt und verdünnt werden; diese hilft die Zudunklung einzelner Teile vermeiden. Der geometrischen Ebene der Konstruktion ist die Ebene der Empfindung überlagert, auf welcher im Gegeneinander von Schwarz und Weiß die definitive Form gefunden wird.

In der Schweiz fanden Gestalter und Drucker in der Akzidenzgrotesk der Jahrhundertwende die Tugenden, welche der Futura mangelten: Sachlichkeit, undemonstrative und unpersönliche Haltung, Robustheit in der Strichstärke, großes Bild und starke Offenhaltung der Punzen bis in die kleinsten Grade. Diese Eigenschaften gewährleisten eine Verwendung auf fast allen Gebieten, und die Akzidenzgrotesk hat ihre Brauchbarkeit bewiesen, ist sie doch seit zwei Jahrzehnten die bevorzugte Grotesk des Gestalters.

Es mag in ihrer neutralen und zurückhaltenden Art begründet sein, daß die offensichtlichen Mängel der Akzidenzgrotesk nicht zu erklären. Ihr Mangel an Sensibilität erklärt sich aus der Zeit ihrer Entstehung. In der Zeitspanne von 1850 bis 1900 entstanden Typen barbarer Art bis zu solchen schlimmster Entartung, und es ist eigentlich erstaunlich, wie gut sich die Akzidenzgrotesk hält. Jener Zeit mangelte vor allem die Einsicht, daß auch die Drucktype vom geschriebenen Buchstaben abzuleiten sei und daß eine Schrift des Schreibens, obwohl verändert durch die Technik des Stempelschnittes, doch niemals ganz in Widerspruch geraten darf mit ihrem Ursprung. Der Fettenwechsel in der Akzidenzgrotesk ist mehr oder weniger willkürlich und nicht durch den Fettenwechsel der Schreibfeder bedingt. In jeingen Graden und Schnitten sind die Versalien im Verhältnis zu den Gemeinen zu groß, was vor allem im deutschen Satz zu schlechten Satzbildern führt.

18

Bottom column 3 (page 19), German

Die Univers. Mit der Univers wird eine neue Wertung der Grotesk eingeleitet. Ihre Formen greifen weder auf alte Groteskschnitte zurück, noch haben sie den demonstrativen Zug einer Schrift, die gegen die Vergangenheit rebelliert. Die Univers wurde aus einem gründlichen Wissen heraus um die Schriftformen der Vergangenheit geschaffen. In ihr ist die Erkenntnis wirksam, daß Schrift ein von unseren Vorfahren übernommenes Kulturgut ist, welches weiter vernachlässigt noch gewaltsam geändert werden darf und das wir in guten Zustande wieder übergeben werden soll. Es reichnet sich an die Möglichkeit ab, den Gegensatz Antiqua Grotesk zu überbrücken, ja ihn illusorisch zu machen.

Die bisherige negative Deutung der Grotesk, ihr Wesen bestehe im Weglassen, wird durch eine positive ersetzt: *Die Formen der Grotesk zeigen das Wesentliche einer Schrift.* Keine Endstriche oder anderweitige Auszierungen lenken das Auge von den wesentlichen Form ab, die außerordentlich empfindlich ist und kleinste formale Verstöße registriert. Anstelle eines sturen Konstruktionsprinzips waltet in allen Buchstaben der Univers ein vielfältiges Spiel von optischen Werten. Die verhältnismäßig große n-Höhe gibt selbst in den kleinsten Graden das große Bild und trägt zu einem ruhigen Schriftbild bei, auch dem die großen Versalien nicht hervorstechen. Die Weite der Buchstaben regelt das Verhältnis der weißen Räume in und zwischen den Buchstaben. Die Weißmenge im Buchstaben ist deutlich größer als das Weiß zwischen den Buchstaben. Die Typen halten sich so gegenseitig wie die Glieder einer Kette; die Zeile ist dicht und führt den Blick in der Leserichtung. Schwarzanhäufungen sind durchweg, selbst in den schmalsten und fettesten Schnitten, aufgelockert, was das Zuschmieren verhindert.

Reich differenziert sind die Fetten, von denen grundsätzlich drei wirksam sind; der senkrechte Balken ist der fetteste, der waagrechte der dünnste, und die Fette der Diagonale liegt in der Mitte. Diese drei Werte haben in E und etwas dünner als die einzige Querbalken beim H. Bei kleinen Punzen (B) sind alle Striche dünner als bei großen Punzen (O). Der Balken des I ist etwas fetter, damit sich der Buchstabe neben den andern behaupten kann.

In einem größeren Grade ist leicht erkennbar, daß die Buchstaben ein- und ausfließen. Einläufe sind an oberster Partien von a, g, m, n, p, q und u, Ausläufe in den unteren Partien von a, b, d und u.

Das c ist schmäler als das o, damit es durch das von rechts einfließende Weiß nicht leichter scheint. u und n wirken im gleicher Breite, weil das beim n unten einfließende Weiß aktiver ist als das von unten einfließende beim n.

Zum ersten Male in der Geschichte des Buchdrucks wurde eine reich verzweigte Schriftfamilie nicht auf Grund der ersten erfolgreichen Schnitte, sondern von Beginn an planmäßig aufgebaut. Ausgangspunkt und wichtigster Schnitt ist der normale (Univers 55), von dem aus alle weiteren entwickelt worden sind. Wichtige optische Probleme mußten immer in Hinblick auf die Gesamtplanung gelöst werden.

Bottom column 4 (page 19), German

Die Einwirkungen der Univers auf die Typographie unserer Zeit. Die Univers entzieht sich der bis heute üblichen minderen Bewertung der übrigen Groteskschnitte. Sie ist gleichgewichtiger Partner der übrigen Druckschriften. Ihre graphischen Werte befruchten ihre Verwendung in subtilen Druckwerken selbst intimen Charakters. In ihr ist der Fettenwechsel, Verbundenheit mit der traditionellen Schriftentwicklung und Offenhaltung der Punzen in den kleinsten Graden werden eine gute Lesbarkeit gewährleistet. Die Univers gibt den Anlaß zu einer Überprüfung der von Vorurteilen etwas verbauten Frage, ob eine Grotesk in größer Menge (im Buche beispielsweise) mühelos gelesen werden könne.

Die Qualität der einzelnen Type bedingt eine Kompositionsart, in der sich die Schrift frei entfalten kann. Eine banale Schrift mit wenig künstlerischen Werten wird den Typographen immer wieder dazu verleiten, entweder die Schrift nur als Grauwert einzusetzen, ihre eine dekorative Rolle zuzuweisen, oder aber mit einer virtuosen Kompositionsart die Schwäche der Schrift zu übertönen. Die Typographie der Bauhauszeit in den Arbeiten von El Lissitzky, Moholy-Nagy, Joost Schmidt, Paul Renner und anderen spricht sich allenig in der Kompositionsart aus, in der Asymmetrie, den dynamischen Flächenbeziehungen und in den Richtungskontrasten. Die Typen, grobe oder geistlose Antiqua- und Groteskschnitte der Jahrhundertwende, waren vom Elan jener Zeit nicht erfaßt, und ihre Qualitäten standen weit unter derjenigen der Komposition. Die Degradierung der Drucktypen zu Grauwerten ist nicht einmal bei Schriften minderer Qualität gerechtfertigt. Es soll nicht bestritten werden, daß jede Schrift und Satzart ihre Grauwerte besitzen, die von guten Satzgestalter registriert und richtig eingesetzt werden: daß die Wertung der formal und funktionell richtige Satzart. Es ist ein Symptom beruflicher Unreife und modernistischen Gebarens, die Graufläche als Ausgangspunkt und Basis der Gestaltung zu nehmen, eine Fläche, der sich die Typographie zu fügen und zu unterordnen hat. Eine Druckschrift, im der Größe von 6 Punkt auf eine Breite von 40 Cicero gesetzt, ergibt ein schönes und vielleicht sogar kostbares Grau und ist trotzdem ein typographisches Gebilde mit schweren funktionellen und formalen Mängeln.

Die große Mittellänge und die vergleichsweise kleinen Ober- und Unterlängen zeitigen nebst dem großen Bild im kleinen Grad ein weiteres, höchst erwünschtes Ergebnis: Die Versalien sind weder zu groß noch zu fett und brechen nicht aus dem Satzbild aus. Dieses Größenverhältnis von Versalien zu den Gemeinen gestattet den Satz in verschiedenen Sprachen, ohne daß sich das Satzbild entscheidend ändert. Im Beispiel 1 wurde der deutsche Text von Adalbert Stifter mit starker Versalanhäufung keineswegs zu einer fleckigen Satzwirkung, die sich bei betonten Versalien sofort einstellen würde. Der französische und der englische Text, aus der selben Schrift gesetzt, ergeben ähnlich angeordnete die gleiche Satzstruktur, und es kann daraus gefolgert werden, daß sich die Univers in den verschiedenen Sprachen ohne Qualitätseinbuße bewähren wird.

19

Ende 1962 dürften die vier erwähnten Grundschnitte mit Kursiv in den meisten Graden zwischen 6 und 48 Punkt zur Verfügung stehen, und zwar mit sämtlichen europäischen Akzenten und in den Kleinkegelgraden mit liniehaltenden Bruchziffernligaturen, hoch- und tiefstehenden Ziffern und Buchstaben und den üblichen Spezialzeichen.

AGJrvwyz *ACJOWgirvwxyz* **AJVXaegwxy**

/34/
Monotype Univers *in TM 1/1961 (above) and some characters with side bearing corrected in TM 1/1962 (below).*

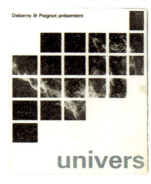

/37/
Publicity material by Deberny & Peignot for Univers *– designed by Rémy Peignot in the 1950s and '60s, it shows a spiral galaxy.*

/36/
Advertisements by Hans-Rudolf Lutz from the 1960s for Monotype showing the spatial modulation of Univers.

/38/
Otl Aicher's corporate design for the 1972 Olympic Games in Munich used Univers *throughout.*

/35/
Texts in different languages appear homogenous in Univers, *unlike* Futura *(left) – the relation of x-height to ascenders and descenders is the key.*

Sie fragen sich, warum es notwendig ist, so viele Schriften zur Verfügung zu haben. Sie dienen alle zum selben, aber machen die Vielfalt des Menschen aus. Diese Vielfalt ist wie beim Wein. Ich habe einmal eine Weinkarte studiert mit sechzig Médoc-Weinen aus dem selben Jahr.

You may ask why so many different typefaces. They all serve the same purpose but they express mans diversity. It is the same diversity we find in wine. I once saw a list of Médoc wines featuring sixty different Médocs all of the same year. All of them were wines but each was different.

Pourquoi tant d'Alphabets différents! Tous servent au même but, mais aussi à exprimer la diversité de l'homme. C'est cette même diversité que nous retrouvons dans les vins de Médoc. J'ai pu, un jour, relever soixante crus, tous de la même année. Il s'agissait certes de vins, mais tous étaient différents.

Sie fragen sich, warum es notwendig ist, so viele Schriften zur Verfügung zu haben. Sie dienen alle zum selben, aber machen die Vielfalt des Menschen aus. Diese Vielfalt ist wie beim Wein. Ich habe einmal eine Weinkarte studiert mit sechzig Médoc-Weinen aus dem selben Jahr.

You may ask why so many different typefaces. They all serve the same purpose but they express mans diversity. It is the same diversity we find in wine. I once saw a list of Médoc wines featuring sixty different Médocs all of the same year. All of them were wines but each was different.

Pourquoi tant d'Alphabets différents! Tous servent au même but, mais aussi à exprimer la diversité de l'homme. C'est cette même diversité que nous retrouvons dans les vins de Médoc. J'ai pu, un jour, relever soixante crus, tous de la même année. Il s'agissait certes de vins, mais tous étaient différents.

Dieu dit: Voici, je v[o]

qui se trouve sur la

et tout arbre qui a e[]

ce sera votre nourri[]

A toute bête sauvag[e]

à tout ce qui bouge[]

je donne toute herb[]

Il en fut ainsi.

Dieu vit tout ce qu'i[]

/39/
*Excerpt from the book 'Genesis',
set by Bruno Pfäffli in hot metal
Univers and illustrated with woodcuts by Adrian Frutiger (heavily
enlarged).*

it, the character set in the die case just wouldn't allow it. Some things were corrected in 1962, but it still wasn't optimal /34/. Nevertheless *Univers* was influenced by Monotype in the end because many small foundries simply cast the Monotype matrices, used it for hand composition as well, even though it was a poor second-hand copy to start with.

The *Univers* versions for the various photo- or lasersetting systems, be they Compugraphic, Linotype, Adobe or Bitstream, are all based on the inferior Monotype matrices. The best *Univers* adaptation is by Günter Gerhard Lange, initially for Diatype by Berthold. It comes very close to the original *Univers,* even though Lange allows himself some minimal liberties.

Linotype's early adaptations, on the other hand, were a catastrophe. I can vividly recall the fruitless discussions at D.Stempel AG when the first *Univers* adaptations for Linofilm were produced. The uppercase italics were just slanted uprights with no reworking whatsoever. There wasn't enough room on the master for italics. The tilt angle, which was originally 16°, became 12°. The reduced tilt angle was for linecasting. The original angle of 16°, however, came from Lumitype photosetting. The first time it didn't matter technically whether there was an overshoot or not. I found that for photosetting, having no physical body, one could try a completely different slope, so that it would really show a clear contrast. *Univers* came about at the same time that PR and advertising agencies emerged – that's why I wanted a snappy typeface, and that's why there are so many weights and such a strong tilt angle. Maybe I went a bit too far, that's arguable, 15° might have been sufficient, but it's precisely the 16° that has become one of the features of *Univers*. At Deberny & Peignot I could also insist upon the 16°. The sharp inclination was immediately criticised. They said it was on the verge of falling over, it was always a topic of discussion. Some of them thought it was fun, while to others it was a thorn in their side. I stuck to my opinion that there ought to be a real difference between an upright and an oblique.

At Linotype *Univers* was for a long time a necessary evil, an orphan that nobody really cared for. I really suffered for it. *Helvetica,* however, was preened and constantly improved, so becoming a top successful product. It was only Bruno Steinert, managing director at Linotype, who initiated the reworked *Linotype Univers* in 1994, which actually went back to the hot metal originals. The impetus for renewal came from Deutsche Bank, who were changing their corporate design. The agency responsible for the corporate design chose the *Univers* – like Anton Stankowski – as their inhouse typeface. They choose the Berthold version, but that wasn't available worldwide, so they turned to Linotype. Thereupon I was invited to work on it by Bruno Steinert and Otmar Hoefer. I was overwhelmed and felt a certain amount of satisfaction. They asked me to help determine the extreme poles. Interpolating was easy, but extrapolating was impossible. I corrected the slanted fonts by

Antique Presse and Univad   In the early 1960s, *Antique Presse* was made as foundry type after requests from the sales department at Deberny & Peignot. It is an extension of *Univers*. It says in the *Antique Presse* brochure that clients had complained they had no fonts for large scale newspaper headline setting, and so they had to make their own photographic enlargements and photo-engraved plates.

An article about Ladislas Mandel in *Etapes Graphiques* states: "Antique Presse, 1964. This is the first creation by Mandel." [26] A design from 1963 titled 'Antique Presse, Mandel' /40/ shows clear differences to later versions, for example S and C, and in the whole arrangement. Mandel explains that he designed non-classical shapes for a, S and G, so as to fill the empty spaces and achieve a homogenous colour. [27] The design was rejected, and it was reworked along the lines of *Univers*. The undated 'Univers bis' sheet /40/ shows the reworked version. *Antique Presse* was made in three weights with upper- and lowercase letters from 48 to 94 pt. The lowercase 69 and 89 were omitted after being transferred to the Haas'sche type library. The typeface disappeared altogether with the demise of hot metal setting. Linotype did not make it for photosetting. Adrian Frutiger included *Antique Presse* in a list of his own creations for the first and only time in 1988. [29] In conversation dated 28 May, 2001 he has reaffirmed the attribution.

Another relative of *Univers* is *Univad* /41/, a typeface designed by Ladislas Mandel in 1974 for photosetting on Photon in the smallest point sizes. The counters are as open as possible in order to be acceptably legible in such small sizes. Its increased stroke contrast and widening of letters also improved legibility. As a result, *Univad* 55 looks like *Univers* 55 but is strictly speaking a 53.

The shapes of some letters were altered from those of *Univers*. R has a straight downstroke, W is steeper, 5, 6 and 9 are more open. Q, like *Antique Presse,* has a slightly downward offset cross-stroke. This typeface has been unavailable since photosetting stopped being used.

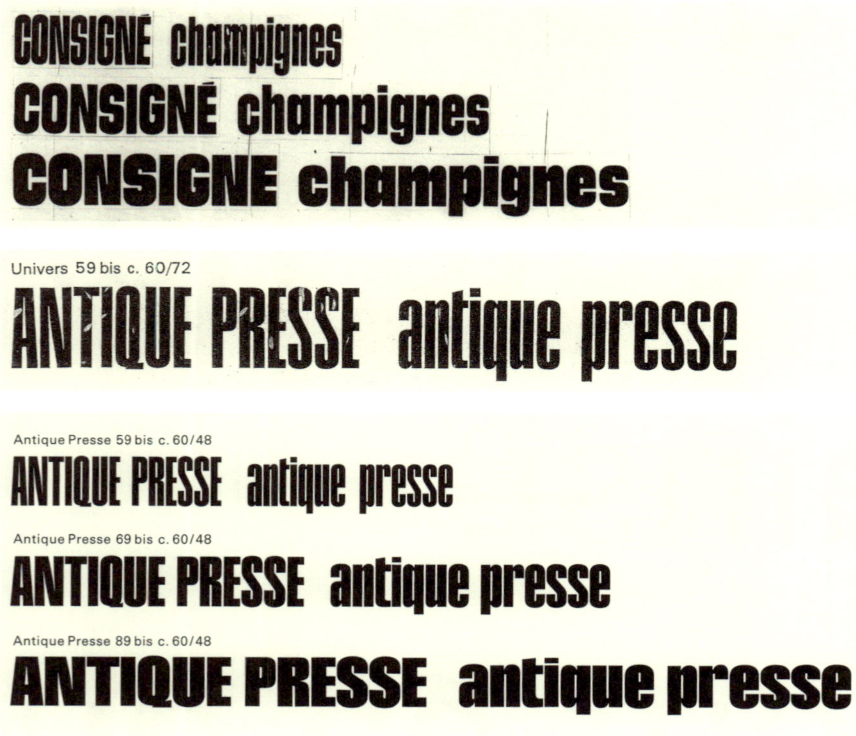

CONSIGNÉ champignes
CONSIGNÉ champignes
CONSIGNE champignes

Univers 59 bis c. 60/72

ANTIQUE PRESSE antique presse

Antique Presse 59 bis c. 60/48

ANTIQUE PRESSE antique presse

Antique Presse 69 bis c. 60/48

ANTIQUE PRESSE antique presse

Antique Presse 89 bis c. 60/48

ANTIQUE PRESSE antique presse

THE QUICK BROWN FOX JUMPS
OVER THE LAZY DOG
the quick brown fox jumps
over the lazy dog

ABCDEFGHIJKLMNOPQRSTUVWXYZ
ÆŒ & 1234567890° £$% §†ßfiflæœ
abcdefghijklmnopqrstuvwxyz
[!?...'_.:-.;-'—·] (¼½¾) Ç@©*

Univers 55

THE QUICK BROWN FOX JUMPS
OVER THE LAZY DOG
the quick brown fox jumps
over the lazy dog

ABCDEFGHIJKLMNOPQRSTUVWXYZ
ÆŒ & 1234567890° £$% §†ßfiflæœ
abcdefghijklmnopqrstuvwxyz
[!?... .:-.;-'—·] (¼½¾⅜⅝⅛⅓) Ç@©*

Univad 755-55

THE QUICK BROWN FOX JUMPS
OVER THE LAZY DOG
the quick brown fox jumps
over the lazy dog

ABCDEFGHIJKLMNOPQRSTUVWXYZ
ÆŒ & 1234567890° £$% §†ßfiflæœ
abcdefghijklmnopqrstuvwxyz
[!?...'_.:-.;-'—·] (¼½¾) Ç@©*

Univers 63

THE QUICK BROWN FOX JUMPS
OVER THE LAZY DOG
the quick brown fox jumps
over the lazy dog

ABCDEFGHIJKLMNOPQRSTUVWXYZ
ÆŒ & 1234567890° £$%
abcdefghijklmnopqrstuvwxyzæœflfi
[!?...'_.:-.;-'—·] (¼½¾⅜⅝⅛⅓) @©*§†

Univad 755-65

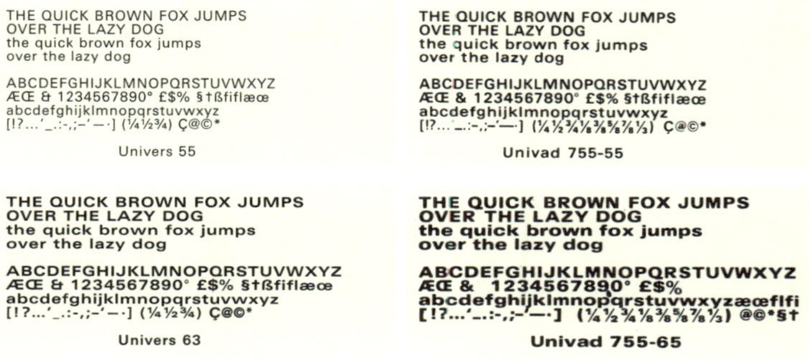

/41/

Univad *(right), a* Univers *designed by Ladislas Mandel for agate sizes – here in 5 pt – was made in 1974 for photosetting on Photon machines.*

/40/

Design by Ladislas Mandel, 1962/63 (top), Univers-*style corrected version* (middle), *finished version of* Antique Presse *from an undated brochure* (bottom).

Non-latin typefaces   In the 20th century there was increasing modernisation of non-Latin typefaces, whose shapes were simplified to sans serif shapes. They were based on roman models in proportion, rhythm, stroke contrast and also form. Among others, *Univers* is the source of many adaptations.

From 1973–76, Frutiger drew what was to be *Univers Cyrillic* /43/ together with Alexei Chekoulaev for Stempel foundry. Seeing as only a few letters coincide between the Cyrillic and Latin (roman) alphabets, Adrian Frutiger explained in a letter to Walter Greisner that he regarded this design as a new creation.[30] Compugraphic made a new version too, which led to an issue of copyright infringement.[31]

Ladislas Mandel had already designed a Cyrillic version of *Univers* in 1967 called *Mir* /42/ for the International Photon Corporation. He took his cue from the Cyrillic cursive script, whose letter shapes often vary greatly from the printed forms. Adrian Frutiger consulted this typeface before working on his, but was critical of Mandel's stance because "in my opinion 15–20 of the shapes are unusual for the reader."[32] He decided to stick with the more common printed upright alphabet.[33]

Given that Greek lapidary script /09/ is the basis of sans serif faces, it is interesting to note Frutiger's adaptation of *Univers* to the Greek alphabet. The O of *Univers Greek* /44/, drawn by Adrian Frutiger around 1967 for Monotype[34] is oval, whereas in lapidary script it is a circle.

In 1968 Asher Oron[35] designed *Oron* /45/, a Hebrew typeface based on *Univers*. He adapted his typeface to match the *Univers* widths. The traditionally strong horizontal strokes of Hebrew were made thinner than the vertical strokes, following the Latin rhythm.[36] Yet the Hebrew alphabet has little in common with its Latin counterpart. It runs along two lines only, with some exceptions. Having *Oron* adjusted to *Univers*' x-height makes it appear a little small next to it. The square basic shapes of its characters are hard to reconcile with the proportions of *Univers*. It seems appropriate that this typeface is not called 'Univers Hebrew' since their differences are so great.

rounding off the outer shapes with scissors and drawing strokes with a felt-tip pen on the insides. This *Univers* enlargement was, despite help from software programs, a mammoth task. After two years of intensive work with Reinhard Haus, the monumental project was complete. The new *Linotype Univers* is, on the whole, better than most other versions, but to be frank I find it a little exaggerated to develop such a huge family.

A stolen version was released by Bitstream. They gave *Univers* a different name: *Swiss 722*[37]. Today it's called *Zurich*. All the different adaptations for various systems are a real muddle. What should young designers do when confronted by them? I just hope they have an educated eye, so they can see and feel the differences intuitively, and not with their heads.

/42/
Cyrillic Univers *for photosetting called* Mir *from 1967 by Ladislas Mandel for the International Photon Corporation.*

АБВГДЕЖЗИКЛМНОПРСТУФХЦ
ЧШЩЪЫЬЭЮЯѴЙ
абвⰂгдежзийклмнопрстуфхц
чшщъыьэюя

/43/
Linotype digital font Univers Cyrillic *by Adrian Frutiger and Alexei Chekoulaev in four weights with corresponding Oblique.*

АБВГДЕЖЗИЙКЛМНОПРСТУФХЦ
ЧШЩЪЫЬЭЮЯ
абвгдежзийклмнопрстуфхцчшщъыьэюя
Алфавет Алфавет **Алфавет Алфавет**
Алфавет Алфавет ***Алфавет Алфавет***

/44/
Univers Greek upright and oblique, drawn by Adrian Frutiger for English Monotype in 1967.

ΑΒΓΔΕΖΗΘΙΚΛΜΝΞΟΠΡΣΤΥΦΧΨΩΣ
αβγδεζηθικλμνξοπρστυφχψωςϚϞϠ
ἠὐὑὒὓὔὕὖὗὒὗ

ΑΒΓΔΕΖΗΘΙΚΛΜΝΞΟΠΡΣΤΥΦΧΨΩΣ
αβγδεζηθικλμνξοπρστυφχψωςϚϞϠ
ἠὐὑὒὓὔὕὖὗὒὗ

/45/
The Israeli graphic designer Asher Oron designed the Hebrew sans serif typeface family Oron, *which matches* Univers, *in 1968.*

אות עברית זאת,הראשונה שעוצבה **This type face, the first**
בארבעה משקלות,הותאמה במיוחד **in Hebrew to be available**
לשימוש עם סדרת יוניברס הלטינית. **in four weights, is also**
זאת הפעם הראשונה שאות עברית **the first designed specially**
הותאמה לאותיות הקטנות באלף בית לטיני **to align with the lower case**
כך שיתאימו במיוחד, זו בצד זו, לטקסטים **of a Latin type face, for use**
דו לשוניים ארוכים, בהם השימוש באותיות **together in bilingual printing**
הגדולות (caps) בלבד יפגע מאוד בקריאות. **of extended texts.**

/46/
Stuck-on 'daggers' from Haas'sche Schriftgiesserei, used to prevent corners of their photosetting fonts from being rounded off during exposure.

Univers extensions Further weights were added to the initial 21, *Univers* 69 for Photon in 1965, and later on *Univers* 93 by Haas for photosetting **/47/**. It was a very different story over at Linotype, even though Adrian Frutiger worked almost exclusively for Linotype from the end of the '60s. In 1984, fifteen years after the first *Univers* weights were released by Linotype, there were still only 19 weights in their type specimen, including *Univers* 65 reversed. Compugraphic also had two reversed weights, Berthold had three outline weights. In 1987 the extra-black *Univers* 85 was re-released, *Univers* 93 followed five years later, but *Univers* 83 is still missing. Only in 1990 was the *Univers* family extended by Adobe/Linotype for PostScript technology with four new wide italics **/48/**. Altogether there have been 35 weights produced by various manufacturers,[38] not including *Univers* 55 phonetic **/53/**, which is no longer available.

Adobe went back to the Linotype version when digitising the typefaces for PostScript. Unfortunately this tends to be the case with manufacturers, because users want the same fonts they were used to from the previous version, but at the same time they need them adapted quickly for the new technology. Repeated adaptations make typefaces differ from the originals, as is the case with *Univers*. The oblique weights changed the most. Linotype made two versions[39] prior to PostScript, one with a 12° tilt (which was used for the PostScript version since it was the only one that included narrow obliques) and

Univers 39
hamburg
HAMBURG
1245-6780

Univers 69
hamburg
HAMBURG
1234-5780

Univers 93
hamburg
HAMBURG
1245-6758

/47/
Univers 69 was made in 1965 for Photon – much later, Haas'sche Schriftgiesserei produced weights 39, 69 and 93 for their own photosetting machine.

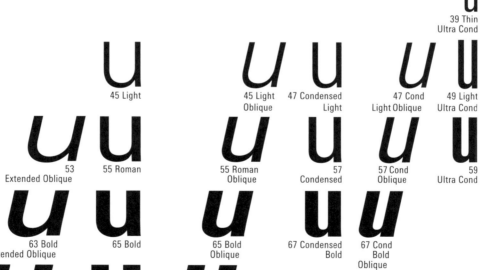

/48/
27 weights of the digital Univers LT by Linotype – the numbers for roman and oblique are the same, as the obliques are only inclined at 12°, unlike the original.

39 Thin Ultra Cond

45 Light

45 Light Oblique · 47 Condensed Light · 47 Cond Light Oblique · 49 Light Ultra Cond

53 Extended

53 Extended Oblique · 55 Roman

55 Roman Oblique · 57 Condensed · 57 Cond Oblique · 59 Ultra Cond

63 Bold Extended

63 Bold Extended Oblique · 65 Bold

65 Bold Oblique · 67 Condensed Bold · 67 Cond Bold Oblique

66 Bold Italic

73 Black Extended

73 Black Extended Oblique · 75 Black

75 Black Oblique

/49/
The only Linotype TrueType font to retain the original 16° angle is the 66 Bold Italic.

85 Extra Black · 85 Extra Black Oblique

93 Extra Black Extended · 93 Extra Black Extended Oblique

a second one with the original 16°. The naming of the 12° oblique weights is good, even though they are actually given incorrect odd numbers, and so is the added oblique /48/.

The first PostScript version of *Univers* by Adobe from 1987 is full of mistakes.[40] Hans-Jürg Hunziker intervened at Adobe, and in 1994 a slight reworking was finally undertaken. The result was more or less the same as the current *Univers* by Adobe/Linotype /48/.

In 1993 Linotype agreed to Adrian Frutiger's proposal to undertake a TrueTypeGX character extension for *Univers*, similar to *HelveticaGX* with 596 characters instead of the usual 256 for PostScript.[41] The extension is done in part by using existing characters for photosetting such as the special I and a for use in schoolbooks /51/, small caps /52/ and the different varieties of ampersand, and also by using new characters. Extended characters include old-style figures (like small caps still in demand), more f ligatures[42], the most frequently used accents in European languages, as well as swashes and mathematical symbols. Whether Adrian Frutiger had *Univers Flair* /50/ in mind[43] for the swashes is unclear from the letter. The typeface *Geschriebene Initialen zur Grotesk* (Written Initials for Grotesque) (see page 400) is enclosed as an alternative, combined with *Kabel* by Rudolf Koch.

Univers Flair
aa AAAAAABBBCC GDDDE HH HHHHH HHIIIIIIJJJJJJTT KLLLJLLLLMMMMMMMM MM MMNNnnnnnnnnnNN

/50/
*Univers Flair by American
Phil Martin (Alphabet Innovations)
for the VGC Photo-Typositor
photosetting machine, 1970s.*

/51/
*Linotype final artwork for the 12 pt
design size of schoolbook and
phonetic characters in* Univers 55.

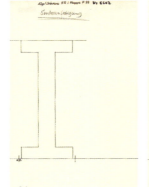

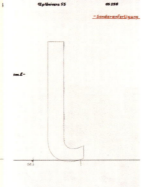

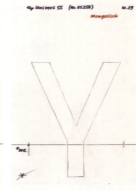

Italy Italy Italy Italy

/52/
Small caps for Univers 55
*are available from Monotype and
Linotype; the latter also has
alternative shapes for 4,6 and 9.*

/53/
*Linotype final artwork of
letters from the international
phonetic alphabet corresponding
to* Univers 55.

Nn NR 469

/54/
*Adrian Frutiger in his studio
in 1996 busy cutting, sticking and
retouching the artwork for the
new Linotype Univers.*

Linotype Univers In 1996, *Univers* finally received the attention it deserved at Linotype, and was painstakingly reworked using the original hot metal templates from 1957.

Reinhard Haus, artistic director at Linotype, took on the job together with Adrian Frutiger. Not only was the typeface extended from 27 weights and widths to 59 + 4, but the relationships of weights and widths were optimised **/62/**. The basis for that was the weight diagram for *Neue Helvetica*.[44] The extension of *Univers* is in keeping with the *zeitgeist,* which also produced such superfamilies as *Thesis* and *Fago.*

Frutiger drew the boldest and lightest weights, all the others in between were interpolated. While he was busy reworking the interpolated weights by cutting them out of black paper, remounting them and filling in missing parts with a felt-tip pen (and placing points for digitisation) **/54/**, Reinhard Haus was digitising the masters **/55/**. All of the weights were reworked in that manner.

The star-shaped numbering system of the many weights became problematic. The renumbering from 1997 (55 became 550, the boldest weight was 1050) was not accepted by users. In 1998 the current entirely three-digit system was established.[45] It starts in the top left hand corner with the narrowest weight 110, and runs to the right in width up to 140 and down in boldness up to 940. The third position defines the slope; 0 is upright, 1 is oblique.

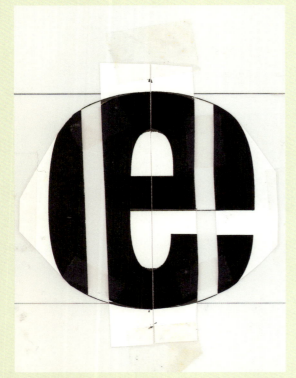

/55 /
*Retouched paste-up designs
with markings for digitising the
new Linotype Univers
920 condensed extra black.*

/56/
The regular weight of Univers LT
(left) is slightly heavier than
the new Linotype Univers *(right).*

Univers

Univers

Univers   Univers

Univers   Univers

Univers   Univers

Univers   Univers

Univers   Univers

Univers   **Univers**

/57/
The title page, designed by Leonardi/
Wollein, is based on communist
portraits that Hans-Rudolf Lutz
'drew' in Univers *in 1967.*

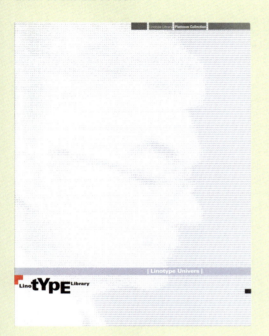

/58/
In the Linotype Univers *brochure*
from 2000/2001 some notable
differences to the old Univers LT
are clearly illustrated.

---

6 Linotype Univers

The Big Picture
Is Revealed
in the Small Points

Im Kleinen
zeigt sich
die Größe

Les détails
font la
différence

Quality is often visible only on second glance. Subtle changes to certain letters, only noticeable when enlarged – such as refinements of the proportions in the stroke weights, or a slight taper in the exit strokes, or alterations in the curves – lend Linotype Univers a contemporary character and contribute to a homogenous form.

Oft erschließt sich Qualität erst auf den zweiten Blick. Feine, erst in der Vergrößerung sichtbare Veränderungen der Einzelbuchstaben – wie die Verbesserung der Proportionen in den Strichstärken oder leichte Verjüngungen in den Ausläufen und Änderungen an den Rundungen – verleihen der Linotype Univers einen zeitgemäßen Charakter und tragen zu einem homogenen Gesamtbild bei.

La qualité ne se remarque souvent pas au premier regard. Aussi, des modifications subtiles à certaines lettres, uniquement visible une fois agrandies – telles, par exemple, que le raffinement des épaisseurs de traits, de légères diminutions des déliés ou des altérations aux courbes – ont fait de la Linotype Univers une police moderne aux formes homogènes.

85
Linotype Univers
930

Single characters are most noticeable different in the condensed weights. The curves of the vertical strokes are extremely prominent. These new typefaces share very little in common with the old Univers condensed, but fit in far better with the form of the entire family.

Besonders in den schmalen Schriftschnitten wurden die einzelnen Zeichen deutlich verändert. Die Rundungen der vertikalen Striche sind hier sehr markant. Es entstanden neue Typen, die nur noch wenige Gemeinsamkeiten mit der alten, schmalen Univers besitzen und sich jetzt wesentlich besser in den Schriftcharakter der Gesamtfamilie einfügen.

La différence est particulièrement notable dans les polices condensées. Les courbes de l'Univers sont très prononcées. La nouvelle Univers compressée a très peu en commun avec l'ancienne version; fait à remarquer, elle se marie cependant beaucoup mieux avec les autres tailles de la famille.

Recognizable contrasts in the strokes emphasize the new Linotype Univers' humanist character. Simultaneously, the taper of the typeface prevents stroke thickening in smaller type sizes and improves legibility.

Deutlichere Kontraste in den Strichstärken betonen den Antiquacharakter der neuen Linotype Univers. Gleichzeitig verhindert die Öffnung der Verdickungen das Zulaufen der Schrift in kleineren Schriftgraden und verbessert die Lesbarkeit.

Des contrastes plus nets dans les traits confirment à la nouvelle Linotype Univers son caractère humaniste. Simultanément, l'épurement du style de la police prévient l'épaississement des traits à faible grandeur, ce qui a pour effet d'améliorer la lisibilité.

Univers
39/49/59
Linotype Univers
210/310/410

The italic weights, following the original Univers design, slope once again at 16° instead of at 12°. Every character was reworked individually, and the character widths were adjusted optically for a better fit.

Die kursiven Schnitte sind nun in Anlehnung an den Originalentwurf der Univers wieder um 16° statt um 12° geneigt. Auch hier wurden alle Zeichen individuell überarbeitet und die Laufweiten optisch angepaßt.

Les caractères italiques sont de nouveau inclinés de 16°, au lieu de 12°, comme dans l'ébauche originale de l'Univers. Chaque caractère a été individuellement revu: pour obtenir une meilleure composition, leurs largeurs ont été fixées à visuellement.

Univers
86

Linotype Univers
731

12°   16°

65
Linotype Univers
460

Slight tapering and an accent in the curves contributes to a balanced typographic form.

Leichte Verjüngungen und eine Akzentuierung der Kehlungen führen zu einem ausgewogenerem Schriftbild.

De légères atténuations des traits et une accentuation des courbes donnent aux caractères tout leur équilibre.

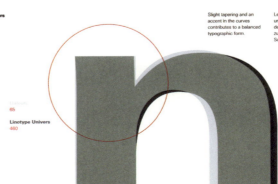

Width relation of digital Univers LT – Univers 59 has a heavier stroke width than the other weights; the laws of optics were ignored.

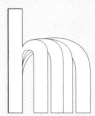

Univers original versus digital When Deberny & Peignot was taken over in 1971, its matrices went to Haas, and in the course of being taken over by Linotype in 1989 they went to Walter Fruttiger AG, where they remain today.[46] The rights have been owned since then by Linotype.

Although the original *Univers* was consulted, *Linotype Univers* diverges from the original in some important areas. The stroke widths of each weight are no longer mathematically equal.

Linotype Univers has slightly less stroke width in the narrow weights than in the wide ones in order to guarantee an even colour **/60/**. In the compressed weights the round letters no longer have straight vertical strokes, which integrates them better into the character of the family **/58/**. Moreover, the stroke width contrast in the boldest weights has been raised to further accentuate the roman character **/58/**. To complete the extension, five totally new weights have been added **/62/**.

When comparing the foundry type original with the two digital fonts *Univers LT* and *Linotype Univers* **/63/**, it becomes apparent that the alterations are more noticeable the narrower or wider the weight. In 630 one can see particularly well how *Linotype Univers* reverts to the original. This weight was clearly too narrow in *Univers LT*, aside from the fact that certain characters, like c, were insufficient in shape.

/60/
Unlike the original concept, the stroke widths of the new digital Linotype Univers *are made to match the widths optically.*

/62/
Constant outline shapes of the individual weights through digital interpolation and subsequent drawing.

/61/
The concept of width remaining almost the same in different weights – measured from the right edge of the downstroke – was retained.

/63/
Comparison of weight, width and slope between Univers *by Deberny & Peignot for handsetting,* Univers LT *and* Linotype Univers.

Profondeurs
Profondeurs
Profondeurs

Univers 45, Univers LT 45, Linotype Univers 330

Perspektive
Perspektive
Perspektive

Univers 55, Univers LT 55, Linotype Univers 430

Maschinen
Maschinen
Maschinen

Univers 65, Univers LT 65, Linotype Univers 630

Boxkampf
Boxkampf
Boxkampf

Univers 75, Univers LT 75, Linotype Univers 730

Luftkurorte
Luftkurorte
Luftkurorte

Univers 56, Univers LT 55 Obl., Linotype Univers 431

Kalksteinhöhle
Kalksteinhöhle
Kalksteinhöhle

Univers 57, Univers LT 57, Linotype Univers 520

Kartoffelernte
Kartoffelernte
Kartoffelernte

Univers 58, Univers LT 57 Obl., Linotype Univers 521

Wasserkraftwerke
Wasserkraftwerke
Wasserkraftwerke

Univers 59, Univers LT 59, Linotype Univers 510

Univers adaptations *Univers* was an enormous success, produced by countless manufacturers for countless typesetting machines. Made for photosetting on Lumitype and Photon in 1957, the foundry version followed in 1958 by Deberny & Peignot. In 1961 Monotype released two parallel versions, one for their hot metal casting machines and one for photosetting. 1961 was also the date of the American Type Founders foundry version, and another in 1970 (in anticipation of the Olympic games in Munich 1972) **/38/** by Ludwig & Mayer.

As early as 1963 people other than printers could use the typeface, thanks to Letraset; and IBM Composer *Univers* (see page 190) was available on typewriters. *Univers* was released for line-casting by the British company Matrotype in 1967. Just seven years later Mergenthaler Linotype followed suit with a line-casting version with only three weights, although the company had produced the typeface for photosetting from 1969 on, albeit hesitantly. Frutiger was involved in this work. He wasn't, however, involved in adaptations by other manufacturers, as he had pledged himself to Linotype early on. Compugraphic's 1967 version was drawn by André Gürtler. Both Harris and Linotype prepared *Univers* for CRT setting, and Hell did so for its Digiset laser setter in 1977.

At the beginning of the new millennium the situation was only slightly less confusing, with six different digital versions by several suppliers. In the meantime there are three alternative versions of *Univers* available.

Foundry type

Deberny & Peignot | 1958
American Type Founders | 1961
Ludwig & Mayer | 1970
Haas | 1971
Stempel | 1973

Machine setting
Single character casting

Monotype | 1961
Ludlow

Machine setting
Line casting

Matrotype | 1967
Neotype
Mergenthaler Linotype | 1974

Transfer sheets

Letraset | 1963
Mecanorma

Composer setting

IBM | 1964
Varityper

Photosetting

Lumitype | 1957
Photon | 1957
Monophoto | 1961
Compugraphic | 1967
Mergenthaler Linotype | 1969
Alphatype
Berthold
Dr. Böger
Graphic Systems
Haas
Intertype
Microtype
Singer
Stempel
Wang

CRT setting

Linotype | 1969
Harris
Hell

Laser setting

Hell
Linotype
Scangraphic

Digital setting

Adobe / Linotype | 1987
Bitstream | 1990
Berthold*
Scangraphic*
URW*
Linotype | 1996

* no longer available

Metal typesetting

Deberny & Peignot – Foundry type
Univers 55/56

CKMaghrst
CKMaghrst

Monotype – Single character casting
Univers Medium 689

CKMaghrst
CKMaghrst

Matrotype – Line casting
Univers 55/56

CKMaghrst
CKMaghrst

Transfer sheets

Letraset (Deberny & Peignot)
Univers 55/56

CKMaghrst
CKMaghrst

Mecanorma (Deberny & Peignot)
Univers 55/Italic 56

CKMaghrst
CKMaghrst

Photosetting

Lumitype 200
Univers 751-55/751-56

CKMaghrst
CKMaghrst

Photon
Univers Medium/Medium Italic

CKMaghrst
CKMaghrst

Monophoto
Univers Medium 689

CKMaghrst
CKMaghrst

Berthold
Univers 55/56

CKMaghrst
CKMaghrst

Compugraphic MCS 8600
Univers Medium/Medium Italic

CKMaghrst
CKMaghrst

Mergenthaler V·I·P
Univers 55/Italic 56

CKMaghrst
CKMaghrst

Digital setting

Adobe/Linotype
Univers LT 55 Roman/55 Oblique

CKMaghrst
CKMaghrst

URW
Univers Regular/Regular Italic

CKMaghrst
CKMaghrst

Berthold
Univers BQ Regular/Italic

CKMaghrst
CKMaghrst

Scangraphic
Sh Univers Roman/Italic

CKMaghrst
CKMaghrst

Bitstream
Zurich BT Roman/Italic

CKMaghrst
CKMaghrst

Linotype
Linotype Univers 430 Basic Regular/431 Basic Regular Italic

CKMaghrst
CKMaghrst

Linotype Univers™
Linotype
63 weights

Å B Ç D È F G
H I J K L M Ñ
Ô P Q R Š T Ü
V W X Y Z &
Æ Œ ¥ $ £ €
1 2 3 4 5 6 7 8 9 0
å b ç d é f g h i j
k l m ñ ô p q r š
t ü v w x y z ß
fi fl æ œ ø ł ð
[. , : ; · ' / - – —]
(¿ ¡ " « ‹ › » " ! ?)
{ § ° % @ ‰ * † }

110 UltraLight Compressed

Å B Ç D È F G
H I J K L M Ñ
Ô P Q R Š T Ü
V W X Y Z &
Æ Œ ¥ $ £ €
1 2 3 4 5 6 7 8 9 0
å b ç d é f g h i j
k l m ñ ô p q r š
t ü v w x y z ß
fi fl æ œ ø ł ð
[. , : ; · ' / - – —]
(¿ ¡ " « ‹ › » " ! ?)
{ § ° % @ ‰ * † }

210 Thin Compressed

Å B Ç D È F G
H I J K L M Ñ
Ô P Q R Š T Ü
V W X Y Z &
Æ Œ ¥ $ £ €
1 2 3 4 5 6 7 8 9 0
å b ç d é f g h i j
k l m ñ ô p q r š
t ü v w x y z ß
fi fl æ œ ø ł ð
[. , : ; · ' / - – —]
(¿ ¡ " « ‹ › » " ! ?)
{ § ° % @ ‰ * † }

310 Light Compressed

Å B Ç D È F G
H I J K L M Ñ
Ô P Q R Š T Ü
V W X Y Z &
Æ Œ ¥ $ £ €
1 2 3 4 5 6 7 8 9 0
å b ç d é f g h i j
k l m ñ ô p q r š
t ü v w x y z ß
fi fl æ œ ø ł ð
[. , : ; · ' / - – —]
(¿ ¡ " « ‹ › » " ! ?)
{ § ° % @ ‰ * † }

410 Compressed

Å B Ç D È F G
H I J K L M Ñ
Ô P Q R Š T Ü
V W X Y Z &
Æ Œ ¥ $ £ €
1 2 3 4 5 6 7 8 9 0
å b ç d é f g h i j
k l m ñ ô p q r š
t ü v w x y z ß
fi fl æ œ ø ł ð
[. , : ; · ' / - – —]
(¿ ¡ " « ‹ › » " ! ?)
{ § ° % @ ‰ * † }

510 Medium Compressed

/64/

*This comparison shows the
different weights and the angle
of the italics.*

	Hh	Hw	Hs	Hq
130 UltraLight	10.00 cm	6.71 = 0.86	0.27 = 0.21	0.27 = 0.26
230 Thin	10.00	7.03 = 0.90	0.58 = 0.45	0.50 = 0.49
330 Light	10.00	7.35 = 0.94	0.89 = 0.68	0.74 = 0.72
430 Regular	10.00	7.77 = 1	1.30 = 1	1.02 = 1
530 Medium	10.00	8.19 = 1.05	1.72 = 1.32	1.32 = 1.29
630 Bold	10.00	8.65 = 1.11	2.17 = 1.67	1.63 = 1.60
730 Heavy	10.00	8.98 = 1.15	2.59 = 1.99	1.76 = 1.72
830 Black	10.00	9.34 = 1.20	3.07 = 2.36	1.89 = 1.85
930 ExtraBlack	10.00	9.98 = 1.28	3.99 = 3.07	2.15 = 2.11
431 Italic	10.00	7.40 = 0.95	1.25 = 0.96	1.04 = 1.02

16.3°

Å B Ç D È F G
H I J K L M Ñ
Ô P Q R Š T Ü
V W X Y Z &
Æ Œ ¥ $ £ €
1 2 3 4 5 6 7 8 9 0
å b ç d é f g h i j
k l m ñ ô p q r š
t ü v w x y z ß
fi fl æ œ ø ł ð
[. , : ; · ' / – —]
(¿ ¡ " « ‹ › » " ! ?)
{ § ° % @ ‰ * † }

120 UltraLight Condensed

Å B Ç D È F G
H I J K L M Ñ
Ô P Q R Š T Ü
V W X Y Z &
Æ Œ ¥ $ £ €
1 2 3 4 5 6 7 8 9 0
å b ç d é f g h i j
k l m ñ ô p q r š
t ü v w x y z ß
fi fl æ œ ø ł ð
[. , : ; · ' / – —]
(¿ ¡ " « ‹ › » " ! ?)
{ § ° % @ ‰ * † }

121 UltraLight Condensed Italic

Å B Ç D È F G
H I J K L M Ñ
Ô P Q R Š T Ü
V W X Y Z &
Æ Œ ¥ $ £ €
1 2 3 4 5 6 7 8 9 0
å b ç d é f g h i j
k l m ñ ô p q r š
t ü v w x y z ß
fi fl æ œ ø ł ð
[. , : ; · ' / – —]
(¿ ¡ " « ‹ › » " ! ?)
{ § ° % @ ‰ * † }

220 Thin Condensed

Å B Ç D È F G
H I J K L M Ñ
Ô P Q R Š T Ü
V W X Y Z &
Æ Œ ¥ $ £ €
1 2 3 4 5 6 7 8 9 0
å b ç d é f g h i j
k l m ñ ô p q r š
t ü v w x y z ß
fi fl æ œ ø ł ð
[. , : ; · ' / – —]
(¿ ¡ " « ‹ › » " ! ?)
{ § ° % @ ‰ * † }

221 Thin Condensed Italic

Å B Ç D È F G
H I J K L M Ñ
Ô P Q R Š T Ü
V W X Y Z &
Æ Œ ¥ $ £ €
1 2 3 4 5 6 7 8 9 0
å b ç d é f g h i j
k l m ñ ô p q r š
t ü v w x y z ß
fi fl æ œ ø ł ð
[. , : ; · ' / – —]
(¿ ¡ " « ‹ › » " ! ?)
{ § ° % @ ‰ * † }

320 Light Condensed

Å B Ç D È F G
H I J K L M Ñ
Ô P Q R Š T Ü
V W X Y Z &
Æ Œ ¥ $ £ €
1 2 3 4 5 6 7 8 9 0
å b ç d é f g h i j
k l m ñ ô p q r š
t ü v w x y z ß
fi fl æ œ ø ł ð
[. , : ; · ' / – —]
(¿ ¡ " « ‹ › » " ! ?)
{ § ° % @ ‰ * † }

321 Light Condensed Italic

Å B Ç D È F G
H I J K L M Ñ
Ô P Q R Š T Ü
V W X Y Z &
Æ Œ ¥ $ £ €
1 2 3 4 5 6 7 8 9 0
å b ç d é f g h i j
k l m ñ ô p c r š
t ü v w x y z ß
fi fl æ œ ø ł ð
[. , : ; · ' / – —]
(¿ ¡ " « ‹ › » " ! ?)
{ § ° % @ ‰ * † }

130 UltraLight

Å B Ç D È F G
H I J K L M Ñ
Ô P Q R Š T Ü
V W X Y Z &
Æ Œ ¥ $ £ €
1 2 3 4 5 6 7 8 9 0
å b ç d é f g h i j
k l m ñ ô p q r š
t ü v w x y z ß
fi fl æ œ ø ł ð
[. , : ; · ' / – —]
(¿ ¡ " « ‹ › » " ! ?)
{ § ° % @ ‰ * † }

131 UltraLight Italic

Å B Ç D È F G
H I J K L M Ñ
Ô P Q R Š T Ü
V W X Y Z &
Æ Œ ¥ $ £ €
1 2 3 4 5 6 7 8 9 0
å b ç d é f g h i j
k l m ñ ô p q r š
t ü v w x y z ß
fi fl æ œ ø ł ð
[. , : ; · ' / – —]
(¿ ¡ " « ‹ › » " ! ?)
{ § ° % @ ‰ * † }

230 Thin

Å B Ç D È F G
H I J K L M Ñ
Ô P Q R Š T Ü
V W X Y Z &
Æ Œ ¥ $ £ €
1 2 3 4 5 6 7 8 9 0
å b ç d é f g h i j
k l m ñ ô p q r š
t ü v w x y z ß
fi fl æ œ ø ł ð
[. , : ; · ' / – —]
(¿ ¡ " « ‹ › » " ! ?)
{ § ° % @ ‰ * † }

231 Thin Italic

Å B Ç D È F G
H I J K L M Ñ
Ô P Q R Š T Ü
V W X Y Z &
Æ Œ ¥ $ £ €
1 2 3 4 5 6 7 8 9 0
å b ç d é f g h i j
k l m ñ ô p q r š
t ü v w x y z ß
fi fl æ œ ø ł ð
[. , : ; · ' / – —]
(¿ ¡ " « ‹ › » " ! ?)
{ § ° % @ ‰ * † }

330 Light

Å B Ç D È F G
H I J K L M Ñ
Ô P Q R Š T Ü
V W X Y Z &
Æ Œ ¥ $ £ €
1 2 3 4 5 6 7 8 9 0
å b ç d é f g h i j
k l m ñ ô p q r š
t ü v w x y z ß
fi fl æ œ ø ł ð
[. , : ; · ' / – —]
(¿ ¡ " « ‹ › » " ! ?)
{ § ° % @ ‰ * † }

331 Light Italic

Å B Ç D È F G
H I J K L M Ñ
Ô P Q R Š T Ü
V W X Y Z &
Æ Œ ¥ $ £ €
1 2 3 4 5 6 7 8 9 0
å b ç d é f g h i j
k l m ñ ô p q r š
t ü v w x y z ß
fi fl æ œ ø ł ð
[. , : ; · ' / – —]
(¿ ¡ " « ‹ › » " ! ?)
{ § ° % @ ‰ * † }

140 UltraLight Extended

Å B Ç D È F G
H I J K L M Ñ
Ô P Q R Š T Ü
V W X Y Z &
Æ Œ ¥ $ £ €
1 2 3 4 5 6 7 8 9 0
å b ç d é f g h i j
k l m ñ ô p q r š
t ü v w x y z ß
fi fl æ œ ø ł ð
[. , : ; · ' / – —]
(¿ ¡ " « ‹ › » " ! ?)
{ § ° % @ ‰ * † }

141 UltraLight Extended Italic

Å B Ç D È F G
H I J K L M Ñ
Ô P Q R Š T Ü
V W X Y Z &
Æ Œ ¥ $ £ €
1 2 3 4 5 6 7 8 9 0
å b ç d é f g h i j
k l m ñ ô p q r š
t ü v w x y z ß
fi fl æ œ ø ł ð
[. , : ; · ' / – —]
(¿ ¡ " « ‹ › » " ! ?)
{ § ° % @ ‰ * † }

240 Thin Extended

Å B Ç D È F G
H I J K L M Ñ
Ô P Q R Š T Ü
V W X Y Z &
Æ Œ ¥ $ £ €
1 2 3 4 5 6 7 8 9 0
å b ç d é f g h i j
k l m ñ ô p q r š
t ü v w x y z ß
fi fl æ œ ø ł ð
[. , : ; · ' / – —]
(¿ ¡ " « ‹ › » " ! ?)
{ § ° % @ ‰ * † }

241 Thin Extended Italic

Å B Ç D È F G
H I J K L M Ñ
Ô P Q R Š T Ü
V W X Y Z &
Æ Œ ¥ $ £ €
1 2 3 4 5 6 7 8 9 0
å b ç d é f g h i j
k l m ñ ô p q r š
t ü v w x y z ß
fi fl æ œ ø ł ð
[. , : ; · ' / – —]
(¿ ¡ " « ‹ › » " ! ?)
{ § ° % @ ‰ * † }

340 Light Extended

Å B Ç D È F G
H I J K L M Ñ
Ô P Q R Š T Ü
V W X Y Z &
Æ Œ ¥ $ £ €
1 2 3 4 5 6 7 8 9 0
å b ç d é f g h i j
k l m ñ ô p q r š
t ü v w x y z ß
fi fl æ œ ø ł ð
[. , : ; · ' / – —]
(¿ ¡ " « ‹ › » " ! ?)
{ § ° % @ ‰ * † }

341 Light Extended Italic

/65/
Characters of Univers 55
for foundry type by
Deberny & Peignot, Paris.

A B C D E F G H I J K L M N
O P Q R S T U V W X Y Z &
a b c d e f g h i j k l m n o p q r s
t u v w x y z ß 1 2 3 4 5 6 7 8 9 0

Frutiger's thoughts on the new Linotype Univers "The astonishing thing is Linotype's position towards this new typeface family, which had its heyday and is still rated today. This in a period of time I would define as being a focal point of mighty worldwide change. [...] The young generation today is motivated by looking to the future [...] it's not surprising that they often push the boundaries of reason. The older generation looks on in horror, criticising graffiti-sprayed walls, closing their ears to the sound of loud dance music, and their eyes to the sight of posters full of blurry stencil fonts, bad typewriter fonts and letters twisted to the point of illegibility. They forget that today's generation is the gateway between a world which is coming to an end and a future which will be very different. [...] The electronic age will have different requirements. New ways will forge a new world. [...] Why criticise it instead of trying to understand it? Garamond has been one of the bestselling typefaces for some time (after thirty years of Times). Doesn't that sound confident? I imagine a return to calm in a few decades, perhaps to the love of designing a beautiful typeface on a white piece of paper."[47]

/66/
Characters of Univers LT 55
by Linotype for
digital typesetting.

A B C D E F G H I J K L M N
O P Q R S T U V W X Y Z &
a b c d e f g h i j k l m n o p q r s
t u v w x y z ß 1 2 3 4 5 6 7 8 9 0

/67/

Comparison between
Univers *for handsetting (top),*
Univers LT *(middle)*
and Linotype Univers *(bottom)*
in regular and bold weights.

Der Grundcharakter einer Schrift wird von einheitlichen Formmerkmalen aller Buchstaben eines Alphabets bestimmt. Er allein besagt noch nichts über das Niveau einer Druckschrift und die Qualität des Satzgefüges. Das Erscheinungsbild ist etwas Komplexes, das sich aus vielen Einzelheiten, wie Form, Proportionen, Duktus, Rhythmus

Der Grundcharakter einer Schrift wird von einheitlichen Formmerkmalen aller Buchstaben eines Alphabets bestimmt. Er allein besagt noch nichts über das Niveau einer Druckschrift und die Qualität des Satzgefüges. Das Erscheinungsbild ist etwas Komplexes, das sich aus vielen Einzelheiten, wie Form, Proportionen, Duktus, Rhythmus

Der Grundcharakter einer Schrift wird von einheitlichen Formmerkmalen aller Buchstaben eines Alphabets bestimmt. Er allein besagt noch nichts über das Niveau einer Druckschrift und die Qualität des Satzgefüges. Das Erscheinungsbild ist etwas Komplexes, das sich aus vielen Einzelheiten, wie Form, Proportionen, Duktus, Rhythmus

Der Grundcharakter einer Schrift wird von einheitlichen Formmerkmalen aller Buchstaben eines Alphabets bestimmt. Er allein besagt noch nichts über das Niveau einer Druckschrift und die Qualität des Satzgefüges. Das Erscheinungsbild ist etwas Komplexes, das sich aus vielen Einzelheiten, wie Form, Proportionen

Der Grundcharakter einer Schrift wird von einheitlichen Formmerkmalen aller Buchstaben eines Alphabets bestimmt. Er allein besagt noch nichts über das Niveau einer Druckschrift und die Qualität des Satzgefüges. Das Erscheinungsbild ist etwas Komplexes, das sich aus vielen Einzelheiten, wie Form, Proportionen

Der Grundcharakter einer Schrift wird von einheitlichen Formmerkmalen aller Buchstaben eines Alphabets bestimmt. Er allein besagt noch nichts über das Niveau einer Druckschrift und die Qualität des Satzgefüges. Das Erscheinungsbild ist etwas Komplexes, das sich aus vielen Einzelheiten, wie Form, Proportionen

Font production:
Digitised by Linotype

Font format:
PostScript Type 1

Also available:
TrueType
OpenType Com
XSF

A B C D E F G H I J K L M N
O P Q R S T U V W X Y Z &
a b c d e f g h i j k l m n o p q r s
t u v w x y z ß 1 2 3 4 5 6 7 8 9 0

You may ask w

hy so many differen

t typefaces. They all serve th

e same purpose but they express man's

diversity. It is the same diversity we find in wine. I once saw
a list of Médoc wines featuring sixty different Médocs all of
the same year. All of them were wines but each was differ
ent from the others. It's the nuances that are important. The
same is true for typefaces. *Pourquoi tant d'Alphabets différe*

nts! Tous servent au même but, mais aussi à exprimer la diversité de l'homme. C'est
cette même diversité que nous retrouvons dans les vins de Médoc. J'ai pu, un jour, re
lever soixante crus, tous de la même année. Il s'agissait certes de vins, mais tous étai
ent différents. Tout est dans la nuance du bouquet. Il en est de même pour les caractè
res! *Sie fragen sich, warum es notwendig ist, so viele Schriften zur Verfügung zu hab
en.* Sie dienen alle zum selben, aber machen die Vielfalt des Menschen aus. Diese Vie
lfalt ist wie beim Wein. Ich habe einmal eine Weinkarte studiert mit sechzig Médoc-W

einen aus dem selben Jahr. Das ist ausnahmslos Wein, aber doch nicht alle
s der gleiche Wein. Es hat eben gleichwohl Nuancen. So ist es auch mit der
Schrift. *You may ask why so many different typefaces.* They all serve the sam
e purpose but they express man's diversity. It is the same diversity we find
in wine. I once saw a list of Médoc wines featuring sixty different Médocs a
ll of the same year. All of them were wines but each was different from the
others. It's the nuances that are important. The same is true for typefaces.
Pourquoi tant d'Alphabets différents! Tous servent au même but, mais aussi

à exprimer la diversité de l'homme. C'est cette
même diversité que nous retrouvons dans les
vins de Médoc. J'ai pu, un jour, relever soixante
crus, tous de la même année. Il s'agissait certe
s de vins, mais tous étaient différents. Tout est
dans la nuance du bouquet. Il en est de même
pour les caractères! *Sie fragen sich, warum es
notwendig ist, so viele Schriften zur Verfügung
zu haben.* Sie dienen alle zum selben, aber ma
chen die Vielfalt des Menschen aus. Diese Vielf

65 pt | −25   48 pt | −20   32 pt | −2   22 pt | 0   14.5 pt | 19 pt | 8   10 pt | 13 pt | 11   7.2 pt | 10 pt | 17   5.8 pt | 7.8 pt | 23

Å B Ç D È F G
H I J K L M Ñ
Ô P Q R Š T Ü
V W X Y Z &
Æ Œ ¥ $ £ €
1 2 3 4 5 6 7 8 9 0
å b ç d é f g h i j
k l m ñ ô p q r š
t ü v w x y z ß
fi fl æ œ ø ł ð
[. , : ; · ' / - – —]
(¿ ¡ " « ‹ › » " ! ?)
{ § ° % @ ‰ * † }

420 Condensed

*Å B Ç D È F G
H I J K L M Ñ
Ô P Q R Š T Ü
V W X Y Z &
Æ Œ ¥ $ £ €
1 2 3 4 5 6 7 8 9 0
å b ç d é f g h i j
k l m ñ ô p q r š
t ü v w x y z ß
fi fl æ œ ø ł ð
[. , : ; · ' / - – —]
(¿ ¡ " « ‹ › » " ! ?)
{ § ° % @ ‰ * † }*

421 Condensed Italic

Å B Ç D È F G
H I J K L M Ñ
Ô P Q R Š T Ü
V W X Y Z &
Æ Œ ¥ $ £ €
1 2 3 4 5 6 7 8 9 0
å b ç d é f g h i j
k l m ñ ô p q r š
t ü v w x y z ß
fi fl æ œ ø ł ð
[. , : ; · ' / - – —]
(¿ ¡ " « ‹ › » " ! ?)
{ § ° % @ ‰ * † }

430 Regular

*Å B Ç D È F G
H I J K L M Ñ
Ô P Q R Š T Ü
V W X Y Z &
Æ Œ ¥ $ £ €
1 2 3 4 5 6 7 8 9 0
å b ç d é f g h i j
k l m ñ ô p q r š
t ü v w x y z ß
fi fl æ œ ø ł ð
[. , : ; · ' / - – —]
(¿ ¡ " « ‹ › » " ! ?)
{ § ° % @ ‰ * † }*

431 Italic

Å B Ç D È F G
H I J K L M Ñ
Ô P Q R Š T Ü
V W X Y Z &
Æ Œ ¥ $ £ €
1 2 3 4 5 6 7 8 9 0
å b ç d é f g h i j
k l m ñ ô p q r š
t ü v w x y z ß
fi fl æ œ ø ł ð
[. , : ; · ' / - – —]
(¿ ¡ " « ‹ › » " ! ?)
{ § ° % @ ‰ * † }

440 Extended

*Å B Ç D È F G
H I J K L M Ñ
Ô P Q R Š T Ü
V W X Y Z &
Æ Œ ¥ $ £ €
1 2 3 4 5 6 7 8 9 0
å b ç d é f g h i j
k l m ñ ô p q r š
t ü v w x y z ß
fi fl æ œ ø ł ð
[. , : ; · ' / - – —]
(¿ ¡ " « ‹ › » " ! ?)
{ § ° % @ ‰ * † }*

441 Extended Italic

Linotype Univers™
Linotype
63 weights

ÅBÇDÈFG
HIJKLMÑ
ÔPQRŠTÜ
VWXYZ&
ÆŒ¥$£€
1234567890
åbçdéfghij
klmñôpqrš
tüvwxyzß
fi fl æ œ ø ł ð
[.,:;·'/ - – —]
(¿¡"«‹›»"!?)
{§°%@‰*†}

520 Medium Condensed

ÅBÇDÈFG
HIJKLMÑ
ÔPQRŠTÜ
VWXYZ&
ÆŒ¥$£€
1234567890
åbçdéfghij
klmñôpqrš
tüvwxyzß
fi fl æ œ ø ł ð
[.,:;·'/ - – —]
(¿¡"«‹›»"!?)
{§°%@‰*†}

521 Medium Condensed Italic

ÅBÇDÈFG
HIJKLMÑ
ÔPQRŠTÜ
VWXYZ&
ÆŒ¥$£€
1234567890
åbçdéfghij
klmñôpqrš
tüvwxyzß
fi fl æ œ ø ł ð
[.,:;·'/ - – —]
(¿¡"«‹›»"!?)
{§°%@‰*†}

620 Bold Condensed

ÅBÇDÈFG
HIJKLMÑ
ÔPQRŠTÜ
VWXYZ&
ÆŒ¥$£€
1234567890
åbçdéfghij
klmñôpqrš
tüvwxyzß
fi fl æ œ ø ł ð
[.,:;·'/ - – —]
(¿¡"«‹›»"!?)
{§°%@‰*†}

621 Bold Condensed Italic

ÅBÇDÈFG
HIJKLMÑ
ÔPQRŠTÜ
VWXYZ&
ÆŒ¥$£€
1234567890
åbçdéfghij
klmñôpqrš
tüvwxyzß
fi fl æ œ ø ł ð
[.,:;·'/ - – —]
(¿¡"«‹›»"!?)
{§°%@‰*†}

720 Heavy Condensed

ÅBÇDÈFG
HIJKLMÑ
ÔPQRŠTÜ
VWXYZ&
ÆŒ¥$£€
1234567890
åbçdéfghij
klmñôpqrš
tüvwxyzß
fi fl æ œ ø ł ð
[.,:;·'/ - – —]
(¿¡"«‹›»"!?)
{§°%@‰*†}

721 Heavy Condensed Italic

ÅBÇDÈFG
HIJKLMÑ
ÔPQRŠTÜ
VWXYZ&
ÆŒ¥$£€
1234567890
åbçdéfghij
klmñôpqrš
tüvwxyzß
fi fl æ œ ø ł ð
[.,:;·'/ - – —]
(¿¡"«‹›»"!?)
{§°%@‰*†}

530 Medium

ÅBÇDÈFG
HIJKLMÑ
ÔPQRŠTÜ
VWXYZ&
ÆŒ¥$£€
1234567890
åbçdéfghij
klmñôpqrš
tüvwxyzß
fi fl æ œ ø ł ð
[.,:;·'/ - – —]
(¿¡"«‹›»"!?)
{§°%@‰*†}

531 Medium Italic

ÅBÇDÈFG
HIJKLMÑ
ÔPQRŠTÜ
VWXYZ&
ÆŒ¥$£€
1234567890
åbçdéfghij
klmñôpqrš
tüvwxyzß
fi fl æ œ ø ł ð
[.,:;·'/ - – —]
(¿¡"«‹›»"!?)
{§°%@‰*†}

630 Bold

ÅBÇDÈFG
HIJKLMÑ
ÔPQRŠTÜ
VWXYZ&
ÆŒ¥$£€
1234567890
åbçdéfghij
klmñôpqrš
tüvwxyzß
fi fl æ œ ø ł ð
[.,:;·'/ - – —]
(¿¡"«‹›»"!?)
{§°%@‰*†}

631 Bold Italic

ÅBÇDÈFG
HIJKLMÑ
ÔPQRŠTÜ
VWXYZ&
ÆŒ¥$£€
1234567890
åbçdéfghij
klmñôpqrš
tüvwxyzß
fi fl æ œ ø ł ð
[.,:;·'/ - – —]
(¿¡"«‹›»"!?)
{§°%@‰*†}

730 Heavy

ÅBÇDÈFG
HIJKLMÑ
ÔPQRŠTÜ
VWXYZ&
ÆŒ¥$£€
1234567890
åbçdéfghij
klmñôpqrš
tüvwxyzß
fi fl æ œ ø ł ð
[.,:;·'/ - – —]
(¿¡"«‹›»"!?)
{§°%@‰*†}

731 Heavy Italic

ÅBÇDÈFG
HIJKLMÑ
ÔPQRŠTÜ
VWXYZ&
ÆŒ¥$£€
1234567890
åbçdéfghij
klmñôpqrš
tüvwxyzß
fi fl æ œ ø ł ð
[.,:;·'/ - – —]
(¿¡"«‹›»"!?)
{§°%@‰*†}

540 Medium Extended

ÅBÇDÈFG
HIJKLMÑ
ÔPQRŠTÜ
VWXYZ&
ÆŒ¥$£€
1234567890
åbçdéfghij
klmñôpqrš
tüvwxyzß
fi fl æ œ ø ł ð
[.,:;·'/ - – —]
(¿¡"«‹›»"!?)
{§°%@‰*†}

541 Medium Extended Italic

ÅBÇDÈFG
HIJKLMÑ
ÔPQRŠTÜ
VWXYZ&
ÆŒ¥$£€
1234567890
åbçdéfghij
klmñôpqrš
tüvwxyzß
fi fl æ œ ø ł ð
[.,:;·'/ - – —]
(¿¡"«‹›»"!?)
{§°%@‰*†}

640 Bold Extended

ÅBÇDÈFG
HIJKLMÑ
ÔPQRŠTÜ
VWXYZ&
ÆŒ¥$£€
1234567890
åbçdéfghij
klmñôpqrš
tüvwxyzß
fi fl æ œ ø ł ð
[.,:;·'/ - – —]
(¿¡"«‹›»"!?)
{§°%@‰*†}

641 Bold Extended Italic

ÅBÇDÈFG
HIJKLMÑ
ÔPQRŠTÜ
VWXYZ&
ÆŒ¥$£€
1234567890
åbçdéfghij
klmñôpqrš
tüvwxyzß
fi fl æ œ ø ł ð
[.,:;·'/ - – —]
(¿¡"«‹›»"!?)
{§°%@‰*†}

740 Heavy Extended

ÅBÇDÈFG
HIJKLMÑ
ÔPQRŠTÜ
VWXYZ&
ÆŒ¥$£€
1234567890
åbçdéfghij
klmñôpqrš
tüvwxyzß
fi fl æ œ ø ł ð
[.,:;·'/ - – —]
(¿¡"«‹›»"!?)
{§°%@‰*†}

741 Heavy Extended Italic

ÅBÇDÈFG ÅBÇDÈFG   ÅBÇDÈFG ÅBÇDÈFG   ÅBÇDÈFG ÅBÇDÈFG
HIJKLMÑ HIJKLMÑ   HIJKLMÑ HIJKLMÑ   HIJKLMÑ HIJKLMÑ
ÔPQRŠTÜ ÔPQRŠTÜ   ÔPQRŠTÜ ÔPQRŠTÜ   ÔPQRŠTÜ ÔPQRŠTÜ
VWXYZ& VWXYZ&   VWXYZ& VWXYZ&   VWXYZ& VWXYZ&
ÆŒ¥$£€ ÆŒ¥$£€   ÆŒ¥$£€ ÆŒ¥$£€   ÆŒ¥$£€ ÆŒ¥$£€
1234567890 1234567890   1234567890 1234567890   1234567890 1234567890
åbçdéfghij åbçdéfghij   åbçdéfghij åbçdéfghij   åbçdéfghij åbçdéfghij
klmñôpqrš klmñôpqrš   klmñôpqrš klmñôpqrš   klmñôpqrš klmñôpqrš
tüvwxyzß tüvwxyzß   tüvwxyzß tüvwxyzß   tüvwxyzß tüvwxyzß
fi fl æ œ ø ł ð fi fl æ œ ø ł ð   fi fl æ œ ø ł ð fi fl æ œ ø ł ð   fi fl æ œ ø ł ð fi fl æ œ ø ł ð
[.,:;·'/-– —] [.,:;·'/-– —]   [.,:;·'/-– —] [.,:;·'/-– —]   [.,:;·'/-– —] [.,:;·'/-– —]
(¿¡"«‹›»"!?) (¿¡"«‹›»"!?)   (¿¡"«‹›»"!?) (¿¡"«‹›»"!?)   (¿¡"«‹›»"!?) (¿¡"«‹›»"!?)
{§°%@‰*†} {§°%@‰*†}   {§°%@‰*†} {§°%@‰*†}   {§°%@‰*†} {§°%@‰*†}

820 Black Condensed — **821 Black Condensed Italic** — **920 ExtraBlack Condensed** — **921 ExtraBlack Cond Italic** — Typewriter Regular — Typewriter Regular Italic

ÅBÇDÈFG ÅBÇDÈFG   ÅBÇDÈFG ÅBÇDÈFG   ÅBÇDÈFG ÅBÇDÈFG
HIJKLMÑ HIJKLMÑ   HIJKLMÑ HIJKLMÑ   HIJKLMÑ HIJKLMÑ
ÔPQRŠTÜ ÔPQRŠTÜ   ÔPQRŠTÜ ÔPQRŠTÜ   ÔPQRŠTÜ ÔPQRŠTÜ
VWXYZ& VWXYZ&   VWXYZ& VWXYZ&   VWXYZ& VWXYZ&
ÆŒ¥$£€ ÆŒ¥$£€   ÆŒ¥$£€0 ÆŒ¥$£€0   ÆŒ¥$£€ ÆŒ¥$£€
1234567890 1234567890   123456789 123456789   1234567890 1234567890
åbçdéfghij åbçdéfghij   åbçdéfghij åbçdéfghij   åbçdéfghij åbçdéfghij
klmñôpqrš klmñôpqrš   klmñôpqrš klmñôpqrš   klmñôpqrš klmñôpqrš
tüvwxyzß tüvwxyzß   tüvwxyzß tüvwxyzß   tüvwxyzß tüvwxyzß
fi fl æ œ ø ł ð fi fl æ œ ø ł ð   fi fl æ œ ø ł ð fi fl æ œ ø ł ð   fi fl æ œ ø ł ð fi fl æ œ ø ł ð
[.,:;·'/-– —] [.,:;·'/-– —]   [.,:;·'/-– —] [.,:;·'/-– —]   [.,:;·'/-– —] [.,:;·'/-– —]
(¿¡"«‹›»"!?) (¿¡"«‹›»"!?)   (¿¡"«‹›»"!?) (¿¡"«‹›»"!?)   (¿¡"«‹›»"!?) (¿¡"«‹›»"!?)
{§°%@‰*†} {§°%@‰*†}   {§°%@‰*†} {§°%@‰*†}   {§°%@‰*†} {§°%@‰*†}

830 Black — **831 Black Italic** — **930 ExtraBlack** — **931 ExtraBlack Italic** — Typewriter Bold — Typewriter Bold Italic

ÅBÇDÈFG ÅBÇDÈFG   ÅBÇDÈFG ÅBÇDÈFG
HIJKLMÑ HIJKLMÑ   HIJKLMÑ HIJKLMÑ
ÔPQRŠTÜ ÔPQRŠTÜ   ÔPQRŠTÜ ÔPQRŠTÜ
VWXYZ& VWXYZ&   VWXYZ& VWXYZ&
ÆŒ¥$£€ ÆŒ¥$£€   ÆŒ¥$£€0 ÆŒ¥$£€0
1234567890 1234567890   123456789 123456789
åbçdéfghij åbçdéfghij   åbçdéfghij åbçdéfghij
klmñôpqrš klmñôpqrš   klmñôpqrš klmñôpqrš
tüvwxyzß tüvwxyzß   tüvwxyzß tüvwxyzß
fi fl æ œ ø ł ð fi fl æ œ ø ł ð   fi fl æ œ ø ł ð fi fl æ œ ø ł ð
[.,:;·'/-– —] [.,:;·'/-– —]   [.,:;·'/-– —] [.,:;·'/-– —]
(¿¡"«‹›»"!?) (¿¡"«‹›»"!?)   (¿¡"«‹›»"!?) (¿¡"«‹›»"!?)
{§°%@‰*†} {§°%@‰*†}   {§°%@‰*†} {§°%@‰*†}

840 Black Extended — **841 Black Extended Italic** — **940 ExtraBlack Extended** — **941 ExtraBlack Extd Italic**

Typeface comparison The fact that *Univers, Helvetica* and *Folio* (all shown below) were released practically at the same time demonstrates that there was a real need for a modern sans serif face.[48] *Univers*, unlike *Helvetica* and *Folio*, was conceived of and developed as a large family right from the beginning.[49]

All three typefaces have similar characters to traditional 19th-century sans serif faces. The closed shape of the curves, which is unlike other existing sans serifs, is a typical feature, as are the consistently balanced character widths and ascenders reduced to the cap height throughout the typeface. The x-height of *Univers* is halfway between that of *Helvetica* and *Folio*, although all three have rather tall x-heights /70/. *Helvetica* regular is slightly heavier than *Univers*, whereas *Folio* is lighter. The fact that there is no *Folio* roman weight has to be taken into account. In the example shown *Folio* light is used. That *Univers* has something lively about it in spite of its static appearance is due to its stroke width contrast, which is highly pronounced. On the whole, *Univers* is the most balanced typeface of the three, due not only to its optimal black and white relationship, but also to its clear shapes free of excess elements, most clearly visible in G K a and y.

/68/
Measurements of stroke widths and proportions of the Linotype Univers *430 Basic Regular weight.*

Regular				
Hh = 10.00 cm	nh = 6.99 cm	oh = 7.31 cm	Hh : Hw = 1 : 0.77	nh : nw = 1 : 0.85
Hw = 7.77	nw = 5.96	ow = 6.90	Hw : Hs = 1 : 0.16	nw : ns = 1 : 0.20
Hs = 1.30	ns = 1.21	os = 1.31	Hs : Hq = 1 : 0.78	nh : oh = 1 : 1.06
Hq = 1.02	nq = 0.93	oq = 0.89		nw : ow = 1 : 1.16

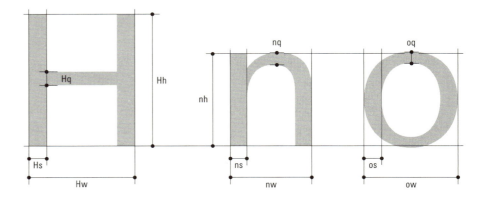

/69/
The black and white relation of Univers *is optimally balanced when compared with the other two typefaces.*

Hofstainberg

Linotype Univers
Adrian Frutiger
1957

G K Q a t y ß 1 2

G	K	Q	a	t	y	ß	1 2
Angular connection to the stem, stem without spur	Legs come to an angle	Horizontal tail with slightly concave shape	Straight connection into stem	Oblique start, end of loop is vertical	Horizontal terminal	Ligatureform long s and round s	Upstroke on 1 slightly hollow; arc on 2 with straight finish

Hofstainberg

Folio
Konrad F. Bauer / Walter Baum
1957

G K Q a t y ß 1 2

Hofstainberg

Neue Helvetica
Max Miedinger
1957

G K Q a t y ß 1 2

/70/

*Height comparison showing the
differences of x-heights to
ascenders and descenders – the cap
height is the starting point.*

Linotype Univers
39.5 pt

Folio
40 pt

Neue Helvetica
40 pt

Name of typeface	Commissioned by	Designer	Design | Publication	Typesetting technology	Manufacturer	Weights
Egyptienne	Deberny & Peignot	Adrian Frutiger	c.1956 | c.1958	Fotosatz Lumitype | Photon	– Deberny & Peignot | Photon Inc.	3|6
Egyptienne F*				Lichtsatz CRT, Lasersatz	– D. Stempel AG | Linotype*	4
Humanist Slabserif 712**				Digitalsatz PostScript	– Adobe | Linotype*	4
					Bitstream**	4

EGYPTIENNE F

Egyptienne is easily explained – it was made for one reason: publishers were using *Bodoni* for their classic literature; however, they complained that their books set in Lumitype *Bodoni* didn't look the same as the hot-metal versions. Printers also complained that *Bodoni* ended up too thin or too pointed if it wasn't properly exposed **/17/**. I told them it was useless trying to make a *Bodoni* with bolder hairline strokes and bolder serifs. I would have to design a new typeface. For this reason I designed *Egyptienne*. The name is silly because the serifs were never as strong as the Egyptienne kind, it was just named like that. Maybe it has a certain kinship to *Clarendon* **/10/**, which also has rounded serifs. *Egyptienne* is a sort of strong neo-classical typeface, half way between a classical Antiqua and an Egyptienne, simply a strong book face.

The typeface was used a lot by publishers for a time; they were glad to have a *Bodoni*-style typeface that they could rely upon to look good in print. So the typeface came about due to technical, rather than aesthetic considerations. Charles Peignot **/02/** wanted to include the whole palette on his typesetting disk: classic fonts, an Egyptienne, a sans serif. He wanted to use all fourteen alphabets that were possible on the machine. *Egyptienne* was never made for hot-metal setting. I did try a few test castings of two or three letters with Marcel Mouchel, director of the engraving department. Peignot also thought it might be an interesting typeface for the foundry, but then along came *Univers* and took over everything, with the crazy task of cutting 35,000 punches. To my eyes *Egyptienne* is not a particularly important typeface. Although to be fair, in the relatively short period of half a decade so much work had to be somehow pulled out of a hat so that the new machine could have the type it needed. The fact that not everything was perfect never bothered me, I just closed the book on it.

One of the first drafts of *Egyptienne* **/01/** stems from my first year at Deberny & Peignot, that would be 1952/53. There's still a lot of Walter Käch in there and it's very student-like. One can see that in the lowercase a with its rounded shape, and the G with its spur, untypical of me, or the f with its hard top – it makes me surprised that it was really me who did it. I was experimenting so much at that time, every morning I'd arrive at the type foundry with a new idea. I was a free spirit. Apart from Charles Peignot's requests, the business card face and later on the fantasy typefaces, nobody ever told me what to do. I was free to put my feelers out in any direction.

When the *Bodoni* problems with exposure arose I developed the preliminary designs using paste-ups **/03/** and envisaged three weights from the start – like the Lumitype *Bodoni* itself – although in the end only two were realised.

In *Egyptienne* the lowercase ascenders are taller than the uppercase letters. I allowed myself to go my own way there **/18/**. Emil Ruder's theory was behind that idea, that capitals

A first typeface for photosetting   *Egyptienne*, the first typeface designed exclusively for Lumitype, was displayed in the Lumitype catalogue in 1961 in three weights; romain **/16/**, italique and gras. The first year of its appearance varies from source to source. The brochure for the *Graphismes by Frutiger* exhibition at Monotype House in 1964[1] has it as 1960. The brochure *Typefaces designed by Adrian Frutiger* (D. Stempel AG, 1983) says 1956 or 1958[2], and in 'Forms and Counterforms'[3] in the *Gutenberg-Jahrbuch* of 1985, Horst Heiderhoff lists the year of *Egyptienne*'s appearance as 1955/56.

Adrian Frutiger himself explains that *Egyptienne* came about due to exposure problems **/17/** with *Bodoni 501*. Therefore it cannot have been produced before the installation of the first Lumitype machine in 1957. He cites 1958 as the likely date.

Bodoni book C 504 for Photon-Lumitype (see page 81) also arose as a reaction to exposure problems which users had complained about. Thus this can only have appeared after 1961, as it is not included in the catalogue of the same year. We can therefore assume that *Egyptienne*, made as a substitute for *Bodoni*, was adopted as a typeface in its own right, and that *Bodoni* received a second makeover in the end.

It is a fact that Charles Peignot wanted to complement his classic typeface range with some new ones.[4] This was reason enough to include *Egyptienne* in the range – alongside *Méridien* and *Univers* – as a new typeface, especially as Deberny & Peignot's existing slab serif typefaces were somewhat dated by then.[5] In fact *Egyptienne* was the only slab serif face in the 1961 catalogue.

It is interesting to note the similarity between *Egyptienne* and *Univers*. Walter Greisner of D. Stempel AG in Frankfurt noticed this kinship and in 1973 had the idea of incorporating *Egyptienne* as a text typeface with serifs into the *Univers* family.[6] In 1976 Frutiger's typeface was taken on by D. Stempel AG under the name of *Egyptienne F* (F stands for Frutiger) for Linotype photosetting, in four weights out of a total of six available on Photon. It is available as a digital font from Linotype and under the name of *Humanist Slabserif 712* also from Bitstream.

ABÇDEFGHJKLMNOP
QRSTUVWXYZŒ
abçdefghijklmnopqrs
tuvwxyzœß
1234567890 &£

/01/
Undated paste-up by Adrian Frutiger – design for a slab serif face showing features of the later Egyptienne F.

/03/
Paste-up on card – design for Egyptienne for Lumitype photosetting, probably mid 1950s.

HOE phomtgave

HOE phomtgave

HOE phomtgave

HOE phomtgave

/02/
Businessman Charles Peignot – final artwork in the background is for Egyptienne by Adrian Frutiger for Lumitype photosetting.

ought to be small, making them more easily integrated. Nowadays I'm no longer so sure that Ruder's theory is right. The x-height in practically all my early working typefaces is relatively tall, but the proportions remain about the same. If you lay the typefaces over one another, you can see that clearly (see page 410). The fact that the proportions of my typefaces were similar wasn't due to any concept. When you draw as much type as I did at Alfred Willimann, it becomes second nature. My x-height is merely my personality, though I also like classic typefaces with their clearly smaller lowercase, their tall ascenders and large capitals. They just aren't my preference. It has to do with people and space. I find that a person has a very defined vitality, the sort of person who just stands there with feet spread firmly on the ground. Not squarely like an Albrecht Dürer picture, just naturally like a living person with their gait and their manner. I can't express in numbers how I arrived at these proportions, it's all a matter of feel. Numbers meant nothing to me. My eye always told me whether something was right or wrong.

For Lumitype I always started by making the cap height 11 cm (see page 83), no matter whether it was a light, bold or condensed face. I had determined that height for all weights, and based on that I then determined the x-height optically. I couldn't always make those the same. If the serifs were bold I had to raise the x-height a bit so that the inner shapes would seem large enough, while I'd have to lower it for small typefaces. The lowercase x-height of *Egyptienne*, for instance, was slightly taller than that of *Univers*, precisely because I wanted the inner spaces to be more open /18/. I'd rather have used the x-height instead of the cap height as a standard, that way there would have been fixed consistency, but as soon as the serifs grew bolder there were problems. I kept the proportions of classic

Origins of Egyptian typefaces   Industrialisation first started in England in the late 18th century. Mechanical production lead to a surplus of products, giving rise to widespread advertising and marketing, which sought to distinguish products between competitors. This meant there was an abundance of printed advertisements and a broad spectrum of new jobbing typefaces.
At the same time both Britain and France were plundering Egypt's antiquities, unleashing wild enthusiasm for Ancient Egypt at home.[7]
Both events left their mark on the output of English type foundries. The first slab serif face appeared in 1815, *Two Lines Pica Antique* /04/ by the Vincent Figgins type foundry. It had unbracketed serifs. Figgins also produced the first clarendon-like typeface[8] in 1815/17, with bracketed serifs. The name 'Egyptian' was first applied in 1816, albeit to a sans serif.[9] The Robert Thorne type foundry introduced a slab serif 'Egyptian' in 1820, *Two Line Great Primer Egyptian* /05/ with unbracketed serifs. In 1843 the Alexander Wilson type foundry made an 'Egyptian' with bracketed serifs /06/.
The term 'Egyptian' was thus applied to a sans serif face and to some slab serif faces (mostly with unbracketed serif connections). In the 20th century 'Egyptienne' generally refers to slab serif fonts or to their classification group.

/04/
Square serif transition: Two Lines Pica Antique, *Vincent Figgins, 1815/17.*

/05/
Square serif transition: Two Line Great Primer Egyptian, *Robert Thorne (W. Thorowgood), 1820.*

/06/
Serifs with concave stem transitions: Eight Line Egyptian Condensed, *Alexander Wilson, 1843.*

/07/
Serifs with concave stem transitions: Double Pica Ionic, *Henry Caslon, 1844.*

/08/
Serifs with concave stem transitions: Two Lines English Clarendon, *William Thorowgood, 1848.*

/09/
Recut of the English Antique *by Blake & Stephenson, c.1838 – available from Bitstream as* Egyptian 710 BT.

/10/
Ionic, *recut by C.H. Griffith, 1926;* Clarendon, *recut by Hermann Eidenbenz, 1951–53;* Egizio *by Aldo Novarese 1955.*

Ionic
Clarendon
Egizio

/11/
Rockwell *and* Memphis *from the 1930s were based on the early Egyptian faces from the 19th Century.*

Rockwell
Memphis

/12/
Precursor of a new style of type – matter of fact expression without drop shapes: Schadow *by Georg Trump, 1937.*

Schadow

/13/
Static typefaces with reinforced serifs and concave transitions: Melior *1952 by Hermann Zapf and* Egyptienne F.

Melior
Egyptienne F

Antique No.5

Problems of photosetting   Neoclassical typefaces such as *Bodoni* caused problems for photosetting due to their very fine serifs and hairlines. The danger that these fine details would not be reproduced in print was great. Nevertheless, this is a chain of problems which cannot entirely be attributed to photosetting alone: the process of photosetting for offset printing was more complex than the direct process of hot metal setting for letterpress. There were more production stages that could potentially reduce the quality of reproduction. Problems arose due to the short time of exposure, contamination of the developer and fluctuations in duration and temperature for developing and fixing photographic material. The same problems could recur in plate-making. Another factor is that thin offset printing ink on smooth paper changed the appearance of type, compared to letterpress printing on uncoated paper.

The difficulty for type design lay in the fact that in photosetting, one character had to serve for continuous scaling from 4 up to 36 or even 72 pt. It was only in a later phase of photosetting that a solution was sought – particularly for neo-classical typefaces – by having three design sizes[10] for small, regular and large point sizes. However, photosetting never attained the quality of foundry type, because each single point size in the latter method was cut for maximum legibility, and the set width adjusted accordingly.

/14/
'Egyptienne' as a description is for slab serifs in general, and certainly not for a precise kind of serif form.

/15/
Drop-shaped serifs in Bodoni *and* Clarendon *compared to the angular serifs of* Méridien *and* Egyptienne F.

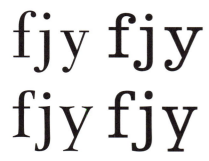

/18/
In relation to classic typefaces – Linotype Bodoni *is shown here – Univers and* Egyptienne F *have a high x-height / cap height ratio.*

Lumitype - Deberny et Peignot, 18, rue Ferrus, Paris 14   Egyptienne romain   651-55

6 Les premiers hommes, témoins des mouvements convulsifs de la terre, encore récents et très fréquents, n'ayant que les montagnes pour asiles contre les inondations, chassés souvent de ces mêmes asiles par le feu des volcans, tremblants sur une terre qui tremblait sous leurs pieds, nus d'esprit et de corps, exposés aux injures de tous les éléments, victimes de la fureur des animaux féroces, dont ils ne pouvaient éviter de devenir la proie; tous également pénétrés du sentiment commun d'une terreur funeste; abcdefghijklmnopqrstuvwxyz abc LES PREMIERS HOMMES, TÉMOINS DES MOUVEMENTS CO

7 Les premiers hommes, témoins des mouvements convulsifs de la terre, encore récents et très fréquents, n'ayant que les montagnes pour asiles contre les inondations, chassés souvent de ces mêmes asiles par le feu des volcans, tremblants sur une terre qui tremblait sous leurs abcdefghijklmnopqrstuvwxyz abcdefghijklmnopqrstuv LES PREMIERS HOMMES, TÉMOINS DES MOUVEME

8 Les premiers hommes, témoins des mouvements convulsifs de la terre, encore récents et très fréquents, n'ayant que les montagnes pour asiles contre les inondations, chassés souvent de ces mêmes asiles par le feu des volcans, tremblants sur une terre qui tremblait sous leurs pieds, nus d'esprit et de corps, exposés aux injures de abcdefghijklmnopqrstuvwxyz abcdefghijklmnopqrstuvwxyz abcdefg LES PREMIERS HOMMES, TÉMOINS DES MOUVEMENTS CONV

9 Les premiers hommes, témoins des mouvements convulsifs de la terre, encore récents et très fréquents, n'ayant que les montagnes pour asiles contre les inondations, chassés souvent de ces mêmes asiles par le feu des volcans, tremblants sur une terre qui abcdefghijklmnopqrstuvwxyz abcdefghijklmnopqrstuvwxyz ab LES PREMIERS HOMMES, TÉMOINS DES MOUVEMENTS

10 Les premiers hommes, témoins des mouvements convulsifs de la terre, encore récents et très fréquents, n'ayant que les montagnes pour asiles contre les inondations, chassés souvent de ces mêmes asiles par le abcdefghijklmnopqrstuvwxyz abcdefghijklmnopqrstuvwxyz abcdefghijklmnopqrstuvwxyz abcdefghijklmno LES PREMIERS HOMMES, TÉMOINS DES MOUVEMENTS CONVULSIFS DE LA TERRE, ENCORE RÉC

12 Les premiers hommes, témoins des mouvements convulsifs de la terre, encore récents et très fréquents, n'ayant que les montagnes pour asiles contre les inondations, chassés souvent de abcdefghijklmnopqrstuvwxyz abcdefghijklmnopqrstuvwxyz abcdefghijklmnopqrstuvwxyz a ABCDEFGHIJKLMNOPQRSTUVWXYZ ABCDEFGHIJKLMNOPQRSTUVWXY 1234567890

14 Les premiers hommes, témoins des mouvements convulsifs de la terre, encore récents et très fréquents, n'ayant que LES PREMIERS HOMMES, TÉMOINS DES MOUVEMENTS CONVULSIFS

18 Les premiers hommes, témoins des mouvements convulsifs de LES PREMIERS HOMMES, TÉMOINS DES MOUVEMENTS

24 Les premiers hommes, témoins des mouvemen LES PREMIERS HOMMES, TÉMOINS DES

28 Les premiers hommes, témoins des mou LES PREMIERS HOMMES, TÉMOINS

36 Les premiers hommes, témoins LES PREMIERS HOMMES,

48 LES premiers hommes,

/16/
Sample setting of Egyptienne F romain 651-55 *from the* Caractères Lumitype *typeface catalogue by* Deberny & Peignot, 1961.

/17/
This text sample of Lumitype Bodoni 501-55 *demonstrates the problem of hairlines breaking up in photosetting.*

Les premiers hommes, témoins des mouvements convulsifs de la terre, encore récents et très fréquents, n'ayant que les montagnes pour asiles contre les inondations, chassés souvent de ces mêmes asiles par le feu des volcans, tremblants sur une terre qui tremblait sous leurs pieds, nus d'esprit et de corps, exposés aux injures de tous les éléments, victimes de la fureur des animaux féroces, dont ils ne pouvaient éviter de devenir la proie; tous également pénétrés

typefaces absolutely intact, though even there I always started with a cap height of 11 cm. I would never have let myself alter a *Bodoni.* The above goes only for my own typefaces.

I worked for around one and a half months on the regular and black weights of *Egyptienne,* after which I made a proper italic with an italic g shape /26/. *Egyptienne* must have been one of the first typefaces on Lumitype. Later it was extended to six weights. Stempel / Linotype adapted *Egyptienne* in 1976, naming it *Egyptienne F* /23/. I didn't have a great deal to do with that, I only went there once a month, and when I did we mainly discussed new typefaces. We took the Lumitype type specimen and added the bold, the 65, to it /20/. The Stempel type people had tremendous high standards of quality. I could learn a lot from them about details. If a Stempel worker asked me whether they could change a letter slightly, I immediately consented. I knew they could do it better than me. They really improved the italic. The lowercase k and p are still very student-like in the Lumitype version. Stempel added more of a handwritten character with the swinging lower k arc and the flat initial stroke of the p /26/. Unfortunately, the serifs in today's DTP version are no longer concave, meaning that much of its liveliness disappears /22/, but I've never cared to argue about such matters.

I discovered much Universness in the typeface – I was apparently still trapped in the world of *Univers* and my teacher Walter Käch. The e end stroke, for example, has a typically thickened *Univers* terminal, which is absolutely unnecessary; in a classic typeface the e ought to have a thin end /16/. And the terminal at the top of the a is square, I could have made it round. Perhaps it would've been wiser to try and make a slighly stronger *Bodoni*? It certainly would have been possible to make the serifs and hairlines slightly

Development / adaptation of Egyptienne F Although Adrian Frutiger had conceived four weights (55, 56, 65, 75) for *Egyptienne* right from the start /03/, only 55, 56 and 75 were initially produced for photosetting on Photon-Lumitype.

Later the bold 65 weight was added, plus the regular weight was extended to include small caps. In the undated International Photon Corporation font catalogue (itself based on the Lumitype catalogue from 1961) there is an *Egyptienne 656* next to *Egyptienne 651*. It is the same typeface; although all four weights have the same character width, they have simply been duplexed. The black 75 weight is missing. Instead there is the additional 65 weight.

The American company Dymo Graphic Systems took over the five weights 55, 56, 65, 66 and 75 from Photon-Lumitype. In an undated 'Temporary specimen' issued by the company an additional sixth weight, *Egyptienne 651-76*, is shown.

Frutiger reworked the four originally conceived weights /03/ for Stempel photosetting in 1976, which were to be readapted for new techniques and machines repeatedly. A new variant was made for f and j for the Linotron 505 /23/, these are narrow letters without kerning. The curve of the f was narrowed, while the terminal serif of the j was simply cut off.

/19/

Extension of Egyptienne *from three to six weights for photosetting by the International Photon Corp. and Dymo Graphic Systems.*

/20/

Letter and accompanying drawings of Egyptienne F *65 with corrections from Adrian Frutiger to Linotype, 1977.*

/21/

Comparison of diaereses and i-dot between Egyptienne F *and* Humanist Slabserif 712 *(bottom) – the circular shapes are incongruous and clearly too small.*

/22/

Clear differences in the strokes, serif shapes and serif thickness between the three weights from Linotype (grey) and Bitstream.

Formal differences between the versions *Egyptienne* has a distinct similarity of shape to *Univers.* Despite its serifs, the counters appear to be the same size due to the x-height being raised **/18/**. On the other hand, the uppercase proportions of Adrian Frutiger's *Egyptienne* are more diverse.

Compared to the first draft **/01/** the produced version has a more dynamic expression, particularly the upper-case letters. The stroke contrast is slightly greater, D O Q are slightly wider and thus appear less square. The serifs of the round letters flow from the curves. Single characters like G R a f g r t 3 6 7 9 have redesigned shapes (for instance the g has a double loop).

The serifs of Frutiger's original *Egyptienne* for Photon-Lumitype are slightly curved **/16/**. This makes them appear less rigid than those of many slab serifs. The *Egyptienne F* reworking of the typeface by D. Stempel AG / Linotype in 1976 maintained the appearance of the original form and indeed improved the italics. This version is distinguished by a more pronounced handwritten touch, which can also be found in the later PostScript version, along with an asymmetrical counter space in the lowercase p **/26/**. Unfortunately, the bases of the serifs were straightened when reworking the Adobe PostScript version, but not for the Bitstream version **/21/**. Even so, the latter has slightly stronger and more symmetrical serifs **/22/**, and the upstroke seems flatter **/26/**. More apparent differences can be discerned with the number 5 **/24/**.

bolder. However, even if I had maintained the character of *Bodoni,* it still wouldn't have been *Bodoni* anymore, and one couldn't have called it as such. I probably did the *Univers*-style thickening because I simply didn't like the drop shape, it always seemed alien to me. There is a certain consistency to it, one can also see that in the f and j **/15/**. It's not as un-considered as it first appeared to me after all. The y is a total mistake, but there, too, I just didn't manage to do the drop shape. It was supposed to have a strong terminal at the bottom, there's still a lot of *Méridien* in there.

In the end, *Egyptienne* is no substitute for *Bodoni,* and I don't think the clients were entirely satisfied with the solution. Yet it's still a useful text face, as the baseline is very good, distinctive and stable under any exposure. It's a shame it never received a proper name.

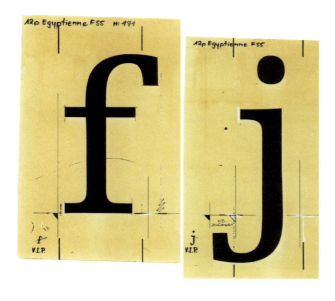
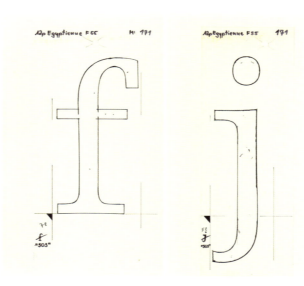

/23/
Working drawings for the Linotype V.I.P typesetting machines (left) with overshot serifs, and also for 505 without overshots.

/24/
The Lumitype 5 (top) has a downstroke, Linotype (middle) only has it in black, Bitstream does not have it at all.

/25/
The Linotype (middle) and Bitstream (bottom) R is wider, its right leg has a square end; 6 has a different arc shape.

/26/
Linotype's italic (middle) appears more elegant and dynamic than the original – it has retained the asymmetric foot serif on p.

/27/
Bitstream's version has an obvious error in lowercase u, the left downstroke is bolder than the one on the right.

55 5   R6   egkpm   u

5555   R6   egkpm

5555   R6   egkpm

While Adrian Frutiger's *Egyptienne* is considered to be a static typeface, it does not necessarily create this impression. The curves on C G S appear slightly asymmetrical and the connections to the semi-serifs have no spurs on them. The leg of the capital R is extended diagonally, adding movement to the face. On the whole Frutiger's *Egyptienne* possesses varied and exciting rhythm.

In the reading sizes the open appearance of *Egyptienne* with its accentuated base line promises to be extremely readable. The serifs are by no means dominant. *Egyptienne* is more like a robust serif than a slab serif typeface. In the display sizes, the character of the face and the beauty of its shapes comes to the fore. Its appearance is succinct, the serifs deliver a strong expression.

The widths of Linotype's *Egyptienne F* are better fitted than to Bitstream's *Humanist Slabserif 712*, which appears rather uneven /30/. As far as the curved serifs go, however, this cloned version is closer to the Lumitype original. The regular weight is distinguished by a more pronounced human touch, as the new given name implies. When looking at the individual character shapes, the qualities are distributed unevenly between the two versions. Thus the Q tail of Bitstream's regular weight flows more delicately out of the curve /29/, while the circular diareses /21/ disappear when set in smaller point sizes /30/.

/28/
Characters of Egyptienne romain *751-55 for Lumitype photosetting by Deberny & Peignot.*

ABCDEFGHIJKLMN
OPQRSTUVWXYZ&
abcdefghijklmnopqrs
tuvwxyzß1234567890

/29/
Adrian Frutiger's Egyptienne *in the digital version,* Humanist Slabserif 712 *by Bitstream.*

ABCDEFGHIJKLMN
OPQRSTUVWXYZ&
abcdefghijklmnopqrs
tuvwxyzß1234567890

/30/
Readability comparison between Egyptienne Lumitype *(top),* Egyptienne F Linotype *(middle) and* Humanist Slabserif 712 Bitstream *(bottom).*

Les premiers hommes, témoins des mouvements convulsifs de la terre, encore récents et très fréquents, n'ayant que les montagnes pour asiles contre les inondations, chassés souvent de ces mêmes asiles par le feu des volcans, tremblants sur une terre qui abcdefghijklmnopqrstuvwxyz abcdefghijklmnopqrstuvwxyz ab

Les premiers hommes, témoins des mouvements convulsifs de la terre, encore récents et très fréquents, n'ayant que les montagnes pour asiles contre les inondations, chassés souvent de ces mêmes asiles par le feu des volcans, tremblants sur une terre qui abcdefghijklmnopqrstuvwxyz abcdefghijklmnopqrstuvwxyz ab

Les premiers hommes, témoins des mouvements convulsifs de la terre, encore récents et très fréquents, n'ayant que les montagnes pour asiles contre les inondations, chassés souvent de ces mêmes asiles par le feu des volcans, tremblants sur une terre qui abcdefghijklmnopqrstuvwxyz abcdefghijklmnopqrstuvwxyz ab

Les premiers hommes, témoins des mouvements convulsifs de la terre, encore récents et très fréquents, n'ayant que les montagnes pour asiles contre les inondations, chassés souvent de ces mêmes asiles par le feu des volcans, tremblants sur une terre abcdefghijklmnopqrstuvwxyz abcdefghijklmnopqrstuvwxyz ab

Les premiers hommes, témoins des mouvements convulsifs de la terre, encore récents et très fréquents, n'ayant que les montagnes pour asiles contre les inondations, chassés souvent de ces mêmes asiles par le feu des volcans, tremblants sur une terre qui abcdefghijklmnopqrstuvwxyz äbcdëfghijklmnöpqrstüvwxyz ab

Les premiers hommes, témoins des mouvements convulsifs de la terre, encore récents et très fréquents, n'ayant que les montagnes pour asiles contre les inondations, chassés souvent de ces mêmes asiles par le feu des volcans, tremblants sur une terre qui abcdefghijklmnopqrstuvwxyz äbcdëfghijklmnöpqrstüvwxyz ab

Font production:
Adobe Font digitised by
Linotype

Font format:
PostScript Type 1

Also available:
TrueType
OpenType Com
XSF

ABCDEFGHIJKLMN
OPQRSTUVWXYZ&
abcdefghijklmnopqrs
tuvwxyzß1234567890

Sie fragen sich
warum es notwen
dig ist, so viele Schriften z
ur Verfügung zu haben. Sie dienen all

e dem selben, aber machen die Vielfalt des Menschen aus. Diese Vielfalt ist wie beim Wein. Ich habe einmal eine Wei nkarte studiert mit sechzig Médoc-Weinen aus dem selbe n Jahr. Das ist ausnahmslos Wein, aber doch nicht alles d er gleiche Wein. Es hat eben gleichwohl Nuancen. So ist e

s auch mit der Schrift. *You may ask why so many different typefaces.* They all serve t he same purpose but they express man's diversity. It is the same diversity we find in wine. I once saw a list of Médoc wines featuring sixty different Médocs all of the sam e year. All of them were wines but each was different from the others. It's the nuance s that are important. The same is true for typefaces. *Pourquoi tant d'Alphabets différ ents! Tous servent au même but, mais aussi à exprimer la diversité de l'homme. C'est cette même diversité que nous retrouvons dans les vins de Médoc. J'ai pu, un jour, rel*

ever soixante crus, tous de la même année. Il s'agissait certes de vi ns, mais tous étaient différents. Tout est dans la nuance du bouque t. Il en est de même pour les caractères! *Sie fragen sich, warum es notwendig ist, so viele Schriften zur Verfügung zu haben.* Sie dien en alle zum selben, aber machen die Vielfalt des Menschen aus. Die se Vielfalt ist wie beim Wein. Ich habe einmal eine Weinkarte studi ert mit sechzig Médoc-Weinen aus dem selben Jahr. Das ist ausnah mslos Wein, aber doch nicht alles der gleiche Wein. Es hat eben gle

ichwohl Nuancen. So ist es auch mit der S chrift. *You may ask why so many differe nt typefaces.* They all serve the same pur pose but they express man's diversity. It is the same diversity we find in wine. I on ce saw a list of Médoc wines featuring si xty different Médocs all of the same year. All of them were wines but each was diff erent from the others. It's the nuances th at are important. The same is true for typ

ÅBÇDÈFG
HIJKLMÑ
ÔPQRŠTÜ
VWXYZ&
ÆŒ¥$£€
1234567890
åbçdéfghij
klmñôpqrš
tüvwxyzß
fi fl æ œ ø ł ð
[.,:;·'/-–—]
(¿¡"«‹›»"!?)
{§°%@‰*†}

55 Roman

ÅBÇDÈFG
HIJKLMÑ
ÔPQRŠTÜ
VWXYZ&
ÆŒ¥$£€
1234567890
åbçdéfghij
klmñôpqrš
tüvwxyzß
fi fl æ œ ø ł ð
[.,:;·'/-–—]
(¿¡"«‹›»"!?)
{§°%@‰†}*

56 Italic

ÅBÇDÈFG
HIJKLMÑ
ÔPQRŠTÜ
VWXYZ&
ÆŒ¥$£€
1234567890
åbçdéfghij
klmñôpqrš
tüvwxyzß
fi fl æ œ ø ł ð
[.,:;·'/-–—]
(¿¡"«‹›»"!?)
{§°%@‰*†}

65 Bold

ÅBÇDÈFG
HIJKLMÑ
ÔPQRŠTÜ
VWXYZ&
ÆŒ¥$£€
1234567890
åbçdéfghij
klmñôpqrš
tüvwxyzß
fi fl æ œ ø ł ð
[.,:;·'/-–—]
(¿¡"«‹›»"!?)
{§°%@‰*†}

75 Black

66 pt | −40　　52 pt | −15　　35 pt | −10　　23 pt | 0　　15 pt | 19 pt | 0　　10 pt | 13 pt | 2　　8 pt | 10.2 pt | 15　　6.5 pt | 8 pt | 20

Typeface comparison   All three typefaces below are based on the neoclassical model, each showing vertical stress. However, they have a low thick-thin contrast and have strong serifs with bracketed connections to the stems. They also appear less static than most typefaces of this class due to varying capital widths.

Because of their strong serifs *Egyptienne F* and *Egyptian 505* may be classed as slab serif typefaces. On the whole though, classification is not straightforward, as there are various models of classification. In the book *Technische Grundlagen zur Satzherstellung*, the typefaces *Melior* and *Egyptienne F* are placed in the Clarendon sub-group of slab serif linear roman fonts.[11] In the brochure *Wegweiser Schrift*, Hermann Zapf's *Melior* is in the newspaper font subgroup of static roman fonts, while *Egyptienne F* is in static egyptienne fonts.[12]

In general *Melior* has a higher stroke contrast and more angular curves which sets it apart from the other two typefaces shown below. *Egyptienne F* and *Egyptian 505* have more in common with each other, which is not so surprising seeing as the designer of *Egyptian 505*, André Gürtler, spent six years working in Frutiger's studio before teaching type design at the Basel School of Design. *Egyptian 505* started life as part of a student project in room 505 of the Basel school.

/31/

Measurements of stroke width and proportions of Egyptienne F *regular weight.*

Roman				
Hh = 10.00 cm	nh = 6.97 cm	oh = 7.28 cm	Hh : Hw = 1 : 0.79	nh : nw = 1 : 0.87
Hw = 7.91	nw = 6.10	ow = 7.38	Hw : Hs = 1 : 0.17	nw : ns = 1 : 0.20
Hs = 1.34	ns = 1.25	os = 1.36	Hs : Hq = 1 : 0.72	nh : oh = 1 : 1.04
Hq = 0.97	nq = 0.81	oq = 0.73		nw : ow = 1 : 1.21

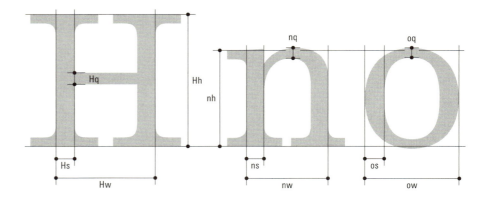

/32/

Compared to the other two slab serifs Melior *and* Egyptian 505, Egyptienne F *is the strongest and most balanced.*

Hofstainberg

Melior
Hermann Zapf
1952

Q R S a g y & 2 5

Hofstainberg

Egyptienne F
Adrian Frutiger
1958

Q R S a g y & 2 5

Q
Oval shape, horizontal tail on baseline

R
Wide serif, extended leg

S
Narrow form

a
Horizontal terminal

g
Round connection, counter symmetrical

y
Horizontal foot serif

&
Italic capital shape with connected cross-stroke

2 5
Horizontal terminals

Hofstainberg

Egyptian 505
André Gürtler
1966

Q R S a g y & 2 5

Comparison showing the
different weights and angle of
the italics.

	Hh	Hw	Hs	Hq
Roman	10.00 cm	7.72 = 1	1.35 = 1	0.89 = 1
Bold	10.00	7.82 = 1.07	1.95 = 1.44	0.98 = 1.10
Black	10.00	8.40 = 1.15	2.43 = 1.80	1.28 = 1.44
Italic	10.00	7.39 = 1.02	1.38 = 1.02	0.91 = 1.02

13.2°

Heights comparison showing the
differences of x-heights to
ascenders and descenders – the cap
height is the starting point.

Melior
41.4 pt

Egyptienne F
43.9 pt

Egyptian 505
47 pt

Logos and wordmarks

1957–1960

Georges Johannet
architect
Paris (F)
Design: André Gürtler

Deberny & Peignot
type foundry
Paris (F)

Éditions Scientifiques Hermann
scientific literature
publishing house
Paris (F)

Pierre Berès
publisher
Paris (F)

Libraire Scientifique Hermann
scientific literature booksellers
Paris (F)

kirchhofer

Kirchhofer
watches and jewelery
Interlaken (CH)

SCIENCES

Sciences
scientific publication
Paris (F)

Production of type
Machine Setting – Line-casting

Opéra
Page 130

Concorde
Page 150

In 1884 Ottmar Mergenthaler, a watchmaker born in Germany, brought his first typesetting machine to market in the United States. In 1886 the name 'Linotype' was introduced. The setting, casting and distribution mechanisms were united in a single machine /01/. The magazine with the matrices was located in the upper part of the machine, while the distributor mechanism was underneath.

The matrices /02/ are the key part of Mergenthaler's invention. They serve as a setting medium instead of lead characters, and are stored in a magazine above the keyboard. Released by a key press, they align themselves in the assembler into a line of text /02/. The typesetter can read the typed text represented by the assembled matrices and make any necessary corrections by hand.

Cone-shaped justification wedges were introduced into the spaces between words. Before casting could begin, these would be forced up between the letter groups, justifying the line and holding the matrices solid. A simple lever press took the matrix line to

the casting nozzle, where they were cast. Complete lines were produced this way. The machine then automatically worked the cast matrices to an exact line height and body size, and would place them on the make-up galley /05/. Directly after casting, a part of the machine known as the elevator transported the used matrices up to the distributor /03/ where the single matrices were resorted back into their appropriate slots in the magazine through identification by combination teeth, unique to each matrix. In this way they were ready to be used on the next line of text to be set.

The characters were not subject to any limitation in units. However, a duplex matrix /02/ had to have two glyphs of equal width on its casting edge. Usually these were a roman, and either the italic or semibold cut of the same typeface. Therefore, the italic version had to be adjusted to the roman, and the angle of inclination was made steeper. In addition, this setting technology did not allow for any kerning. All matrices must have a minimum wall thickness and there-

fore the sidebearing must not vary by more than +/– 0.1 mm.

At the end of the 19th century, Linotype used pantographs and pantographic milling machines for the production of their matrices. Engraved brass templates, 10–20 cm in size, were prepared for the punch-cutting machines. Using the pantograph's pointer, the punch cutter would trace out the outline of the letter in order to mill it, with a prepared reduction factor, into the blank punch clamped at the other end. After the preparation of the master type punch, the actual matrix production could begin. In a process of over 60 stages, the characteristic Linotype matrix was produced from a block of brass.

In the USA matrices were produced only by Linotype themselves, D. Stempel AG exclusively sold Linotype matrices in Germany. Matrotype in England and Sofratype in France also offered Linotype matrices, usually in combination with copies of Linotype typefaces.

/01/
Linotype Europa Quick line setting and casting machine – in the centre is the keyboard and above it the matrix magazine.

/02/
Duplex matrices in normal and semibold – for correct sorting each matrix has a distinctive tooth pattern.

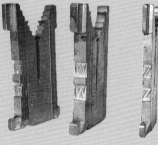

/03/
The toothed rod over the magazine holds the matrices in place until they are sorted and fall back into their respective magazine channels.

/04/
The obverse characters on the rear face of the matrices allowed the compositor to check the line of type before it went to casting.

/05/
The newly cast line hardened immediately and was then laid next to the previously cast lines on the make-up galley.

OPÉRA

I designed *Opéra* in 1958 at the request of Alfred Devolz. It was his ambition to have his small company Sofratype, which made matrices for line-casting, offer a newspaper typeface of their very own. French newspapers were dominated by *Excelsior,* which was distributed by Linotype. Linotype was the main player for newspaper printers at the time; Monotype was pretty insignificant, and consequently *Times* was seldom used, not even once Linotype got a licence for it and sold it themselves.

I patiently set about drawing a proper newspaper typeface, clean and as good as I could muster, but to be frank I wasn't really excited enough about it. It all happened very quickly. I simply did what I could with so little time and delivered the sketches **/03/**, while a colleague executed them. Although he showed me the drafts and we discussed them a little, we didn't really go into the finest details. My colleague worked very independently, as well as he deemed fit. An upright weight was produced with matching small caps, an italic and a semibold, all from 8 to 12 pt.[1] There was no special headline size. I determined that the character should follow the semibold weight as it had to share a matrix with the regular weight **/05/** – the uniform spacing of fonts for technical reasons, always together on one matrix, was ever the shortcoming of Linotype fonts.

The italic is a cross between a real italic and a slanted upright. Instead of drawing real tails I made do with putting straight little feet on the end of the downstrokes **/08/**. The numerals are on the narrow side; they were tabular figures to be used for setting stock exchange prices. The small caps look pretty narrow too, they appear to be almost independent. I made a compromise with the lowercase shapes: for a c f j and r I chose the usual teardrop shape. It would have seemed strange to use unusual ideas for a newspaper typeface. The short descenders are also typical for use in newspapers, they're normally much longer in my typefaces. Nevertheless there are a few details that perhaps recall Latin faces or *Méridien* in particular, such as the uppercase J. I had to give a little of myself after all.

The result was fine, but Sofratype was a small company and one couldn't demand the very highest quality. So the serifs aren't concave, as that would have been too much for the engravers. I just couldn't have asked for it. However, Devolz was happy with it, and when the French daily paper *Le Figaro* bought *Opéra* he was also proud. Only one page of *Le Figaro* was set in it. It didn't look any worse than other typefaces, but nor did it look any better – it was just an ordinary newspaper face.

Alfred Devolz was responsible for naming it, he wanted to name his own typefaces after major squares in Paris. *Opéra* was the starting point and springboard for *Concorde* (see page 150), but that's another story altogether.

Development of Opéra   Alfred Devolz approached Frutiger's employer Deberny & Peignot about producing a newspaper typeface. Devolz, from Switzerland, owned a company in Paris, Sofratype, which manufactured matrices for line-casting machines. Charles Peignot agreed to allow his famous artistic director to work for another company under two conditions: first, that the name Adrian Frutiger be used only in connection with Deberny & Peignot, and second, that any designs by Adrian Frutiger be personally approved by Peignot himself.[2]
Alfred Devolz was very happy with this amicable accord to the problem mentioned, but not elaborated upon in a letter following the oral agreement.[3] It is interesting to note that Adrian Frutiger sent a letter to Alfred Devolz from his private address two days prior to the agreement between Sofratype and Deberny & Peignot, containing a drawing of the first three test letters for engraving **/03/**.[4]
Frutiger himself produced a sketch of *Opéra* in 1958 **/02/**, after which his colleague Ladislas Mandel produced the final artwork **/04/**. The test engravings made after the final artwork were discussed between Frutiger and the Sofratype engraver.
In July 1960 *Opéra* was advertised as a typeface in a marginal note in the French trade publication *Informations TG*. Despite having the same character width in the romain and gras weights, it looks unconstrained, and Frutiger even manages the impossible by designing an italic which is not merely slanted. *Opéra* was declared to have excellent legibility.[5] *Opéra* was presented by Sofratype in a four-page leaflet, designed by Bruno Pfäffli, showing the testword 'Êhpà' in three weights: romain, italique and gras. A sample setting and a character showing are, however, only shown for romain and italique.
Sofratype was bought by Mergenthaler Linotype in the USA in the mid-1960s under the aegis of Mike Parker. *Opéra* was never adapted to other typesetting systems.

Opéra

/01/

*Title page of the Sofratype
type specimen brochure for the
newspaper typeface* Opéra –
early 1960s.

OPÉRA   131

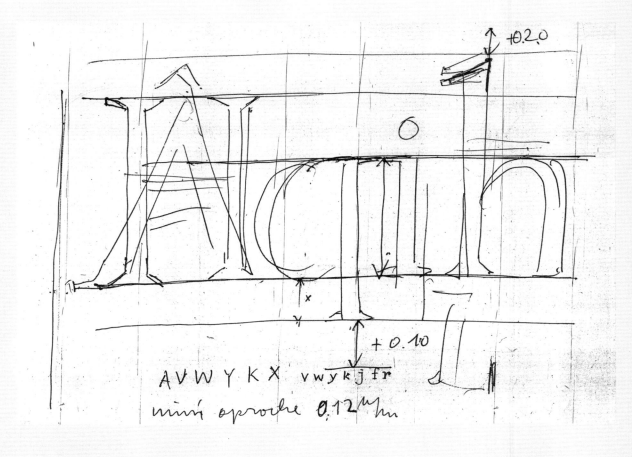

/02/
Letter sketch showing heights for what was to become Opéra – the extremely short descenders in comparison to the ascenders are noteworthy.

/03/
Design of the first three characters for test-casting Opéra – capital with accent, lowercase letters with ascender and descender.

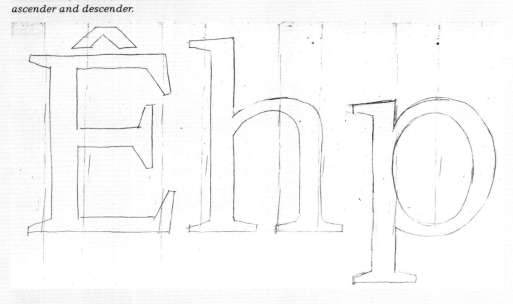

/04/
Pencil drawings of Opéra on tracing paper and sketches of different letters with hatching between them.

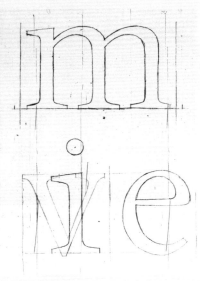
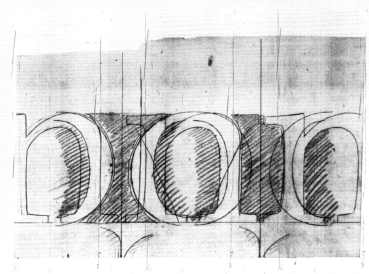

Formal characteristics There are three special formal characteristics of *Opéra*. Two of them are atypical of Frutiger's typeface design. One is its irregular appearance; in particular the capital V and lowercase v seem narrow, whereas the lowercase k is wide and awkward in the regular weight **/07/**. The other is the angular connection of the curve to the stem in lowercase h m n u **/06/**, a feature unusual in Frutiger's work as they are normally rounded. Furthermore, Frutiger uses teardrop shapes, after having emphatically spurned them in *Méridien*. However, he breaks the classical principle in the only capital with the teardrop shape, the J: here he opts for a semi-serif to match the other characters **/07/**. Hence the teardrops only appear in lowercase, although not the s, as is often the case.

Apart from these special characteristics, *Opéra* is a typical Frutiger typeface with similarities in shape to *Méridien*. Its general appearance is open and wide and contemporary, as opposed to that of the antiquated *Excelsior* **/07/**. A noticeable feature of *Opéra* is that its lowercase italic has feet pointing in the reading direction which give it a more dynamic appearance compared to a sloped typeface **/08/**.

Due to its very tall x-height, even for a newspaper typeface **/10/**, *Opéra* can be set small to save space without impairing its readability.

/05/
Diagram of Opéra – *all three weights have the same character width, since two weights of a character are engraved on one linecasting matrix at a time.*

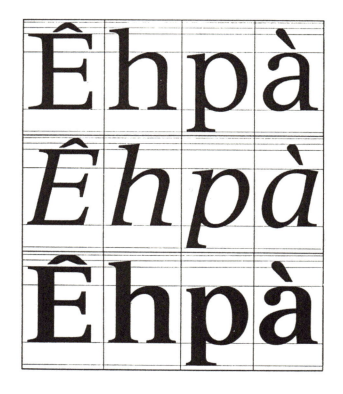

/06/
Rather atypically of Frutiger and unlike Méridien, *the curve connections to the stems are angular in* Opéra *(right).*

/07/
The three Opéra *weights with additional narrow small caps in regular (right) and* Excelsior *(below).*

ABCDEFGHIJKLM
NOPQRSTUVWXYZ
abcdefghijklm
nopqrstuvwxyz
1234567890

/08/
The italics of serif typefaces Perpetua, Times, Melior *and* Opéra *have different terminal shapes: serif, tail and foot respectively.*

nnnn

/09/
Specimen of Opéra *in 8 pt in romain (top) and italique (middle) – in comparison with* Excelsior *in 8.8 pt (bottom).*

Ehpa Ehpa Ehpa Ehpa

/10/
Compared with Excelsior, Times *and* Melior *(from left),* Opéra *has a noticeably larger x-height, but shorter descenders.*

ABCDEFGHIJKLMNOPQRSTUVWXYZ
abcdefghijklmnopqrstuvwxyz
1234567890
ABCDEFGHIJKLMNOPQRSTUVWXYZ
ABCDEFGHIJKLMNOPQRSTUVWXYZ
abcdefghijklmnopqrstuvwxyz
1234567890
OPERA
ABCDEFGHIJKLMNOPQRSTUVWXYZ
abcdefghijklmnopqrstuvwxyz
1234567890

OPÉRA vous propose un jeu de capitales accentuées plein œil, vous assurant ainsi dans votre texte, une image régulière, dans laquelle les accents se placent avec aisance. Vous y remarquerez en plus, l'importance du corps de la lettre, l'équilibre des volumes, qui font

OPÉRA vous propose un jeu de capitales accentuées plein œil, vous assurant ainsi dans votre texte, une image régulière, dans laquelle les accents se placent avec aisance. Vous y remarquerez en plus, l'importance du corps de la lettre, l'équilibre des volumes, qui font

OPÉRA vous propose un jeu de capitales accentuées plein œil, vous assurant ainsi dans votre texte, une image régulière, dans laquelle les accents se placent avec aisance. Vous y remarquerez en plus, l'importance du corps de la lettre, l'equilibre des volumes, qui font

Name of typeface	Commissioned by	Designer	Design | Publication	Typesetting technology	Manufacturers	Weights
Alphabet Orly	Aéroport de Paris Orly Sud	Adrian Frutiger	1959 | 1961	3d Neon Lettering Adhesive (letter set backlit)	Unknown	2

ALPHABET
ORLY

The first designs for *Alphabet Orly* were created in 1959 for the opening of the new Aéroport d'Orly-Sud in 1961[1] /01/. Orly used to be a small airport in the south of Paris but after its extension it became the most important. The airport's director – I don't remember his name – an elderly gentleman and friend of Charles Peignot, contacted him to ask whether he could take care of the signage. Peignot then commissioned me with the design of the new alphabet specifying that I should design a signage face based on the typeface *Peignot*, which was named after him. The result was a kind of narrow *Peignot*, a pure capital letter typeface, which has much in common with *Univers.*

Additionally, Charles Peignot started to speak of colours: everything to do with departures should have blue letters on a light blue background and everything to do with arrivals should have red letters on a pink background. But there were constantly new additions: 'Arrivées' got a dark blue background to differentiate itself from 'Départs' with a light blue one. He tried to build a system but in the end he got everything mixed up /06/. I had no influence on the use of colours. I had absolutely no say in the matter. With his coloured boards Peignot acted a bit like an artist. In the end I thought it was akin to a bunch of flowers. This was Charles Peignot's project. I only followed his instructions. The basic layout of the boards was done by me, and Bruno Pfäffli then created the templates with the right order of text. The panels, however, were done by different sign painters. One day one worker came, the next day another. And you know what it's like: the lettering starts on a particular day and then it continues for years without you being present all the time. I wasn't in Orly on a daily basis to control the work. I was quite unhappy about it all because I could see that it was neither beautiful nor what the airport really needed. But exactly what it really needed I didn't know at the time.

My criticism is this: capitals are too big for a signage system. If you have gigantic boards, then you can read capitals well, but you can never fit enough text on smaller boards. Regarding the space problem Charles Peignot asked me to develop two alphabets, a wider one and a narrower one. If they had lots of space, they took the wider one; if they had little space they chose the narrower one /06/. The second point of criticism is the differentiation of the two languages: French in regular and English in italics using the same colours; that really wasn't a good decision.

At that time I wasn't interested at all in the problem of signage. The change from hot metal setting to phototypesetting, the adaptation of book- and newsprint to the new technology – that was what fully occupied me. Only ten years later, for the large Roissy / Charles de Gaulle Airport in the north of Paris, was I really prepared to think about the problem of signage. There was nothing left of the original system at Orly when they took over *Alphabet Roissy* (see page 224). But *Orly* still exists as façade signage – Orly Sud, Orly-Ouest /02/.

A signalisation without a system   The first signage project in which Adrian Frutiger participated is marked by memories of failure. Photographs from the archive at Airport Paris-Orly[2] from the 1960s and 1970s /06/ clearly show a lack of consistency in implementation.

The typography on the panels in the two base colours – blue and red with a light or dark background – is inconsistent, thus creating confusion rather than helping orientation. There are left-aligned as well as centred layouts with different letter-spacing. Even the two languages are not positioned the same way throughout. The French is above or – in the case of short words – to the left of the English. Furthermore, there are panels of varying sizes and proportions with one, two or three lines of text, as well as differently shaped arrows and several different fonts.

Another confusing aspect of the panels with Frutiger's typeface is the different widths of the letters. It remains unclear whether this is due to the existence of a condensed and expanded font, since narrow and wide letter shapes are mixed inconsistently in the panels. The differing stroke contrast of the typefaces is confusing too. *Alphabet Orly* exists on microfilm /05/ as capitals in regular and italic cuts only, including the respective numerals.[3]

Alphabet Orly is based not only on the typeface *Peignot* /04/ by Adolphe Jean-Marie Mouron (more commonly known as Cassandre) but also on *Univers*. There was, however, another sans-serif signage face before the introduction of *Alphabet Orly*.[4] The pictured typeface /03/ is likely to be this predecessor, and therefore could be regarded as another source of forms for Adrian Frutiger's typeface, which can be seen in the shape of the G in *Alphabet Orly* /05/.

Based on these examples – and at least in normal width and with generous letter-spacing – an elegant and beautifully shaped typeface with a clear stroke contrast has been created; but not an ideal signage face. Because of the majuscules, *Alphabet Orly* needs generous letter-spacing and that means a lot of space. In addition, the counters are too closed, which can result in a somewhat messy appearance. The fine hairlines tend to blend into each other when lit from behind, leading to additional limitations in character recognition.

Photo laboratoire ADP

Photo lab...

/01/
*Façade signage from 1961 for the
airport – called at the time* Aéroport
de Paris *– in* Alphabet Orly *and
in 1977 combined with Frutiger's logo.*

/02/
*Preserved façade signage in
three-dimensional neon letters at
Orly airport in* Alphabet Orly.

Signage at Orly airport – presumably the board (left) does not show
Frutiger's typeface but an older
sans-serif.

PORTES **3̶1**
GATES
PORTES **31**
GATES

/04/
Cassandre's Peignot *(above)*
and Frutiger's Univers
form another basis for Alphabet
Orly.

/06/
*Inconsistent signage system – set
in Alphabet Orly in various widths,
letter spacing and layouts.*

/05/
Frutiger's Alphabet Orly *in regular
and italic – the G features the
base shape of the former signage
face at Orly.*

ABCDEFGHIJKLM
NOPQRSTUVWXYZ
1234567890

ABCDEFGHIJKLM
NOPQRSTUVWXYZ
1234567890

/07/
*Preserved signage in the elevator
area on the wall on the
first floor of Aéroport de Paris,
Orly Sud.*

"Type is like a spoon: if I remember in the evening the shape of the spoon with which I ate my soup at lunch, then it was a bad spoon."
Adrian Frutiger

Name of typeface	Commissioned by	Designer	Design | Publication	Typesetting technology	Manufacturer	Weights
Apollo	Monotype	Adrian Frutiger	1960 | 1964	Photosetting	– Monotype	3
		John Dreyfus		Digital PostScript	– Monotype	3

APOLLO

Apollo was the first typeface that Monotype had designed for their new Monophoto photosetting machine. Up to that point they had only adapted foundry types for it. I already knew John Dreyfus well, so one day he asked me whether I'd be prepared to draw a new typeface for Monophoto. I was still employed by Deberny & Peignot, but Charles Peignot was glad to help his friend in London, and a contract was made. Monophoto was a mistake in my opinion. It worked according to the mechanical principle of the old Monotype casting machine, only using film matrices instead of metal. It still had only 18 units for the widths, and the text was still stored on punched tape.[1] Afterwards the characters were photographically exposed, instead of casting each letter like the casting machine. At any rate, other manufacturers were further advanced in the early '60s, not to mention Lumitype.[2]

John Dreyfus wanted a strong typeface that could withstand any photosetting complication – that was the job description. He was no typeface designer himself, and he let me get on with the design by myself, but not the execution. John would sit with me for hours on end as we discussed every single shape. He was a diligent type expert who knew exactly what he wanted. Before work started on production, test exposures of my drafts were made, always under his watchful, controlling eye. I was his 'tool', his hand. I suppose it was like *Times* and Stanley Morison, who would also tell his draftsman how he wanted everything. Sometimes I had the impression that John wished to make himself a little monument, as Morison had done with *Times*. For me it was just a regular grind. I was probably a bit phlegmatic and didn't think it was worth the effort to argue with John, I wasn't interested in giving the typeface my personal touch. John's willpower was probably greater than my aesthetic feeling. Nevertheless, *Apollo* has a few of my typical details, even though I've never regarded this serif face as being truly mine. It's really a joint effort by John Dreyfus and myself.

I did the final artwork together with Ladislas Mandel in Paris /01/. It was done, as usual, with ink on thick white card with a cap height of 11 cm. The draftsmen at Monotype in Salfords would draw the 'sheets' in pencil from this. The masters for exposure – known as friskets – cut from masking film, were made from these drawings, around 27 cm in size. One of the difficulties was that one master was used for exposing the typeface in all sizes from 6 to 24 pt. This affected the stroke widths. I discussed the stroke widths at length with John Dreyfus, but I can't remember anymore how we arrived at these weights. John was very sure of what he wanted in the details and I just followed his instructions. In the end the semibold should have been bolder when you compare it to the regular weight. Both weights are perhaps a bit too similar /08/. Actually, the semibold is used very little for text display type, instead the italic is used. The semibold is more often applied to headlines and initials.

Production stages of Apollo Following the adoption of *Univers* for Monotype and the Monophoto system, type manufacturers Monotype and Deberny & Peignot reached a further agreement. John Dreyfus, Stanley Morison's successor as typographic advisor at Monotype and co-founder of ATypI with Charles Peignot, wanted a typeface made exclusively for the Monophoto photosetting machine. He wanted Adrian Frutiger to design it, as he was one of the few designers with knowledge and experience of photosetting.

After *Egyptienne*, the first typeface specific to Photon-Lumitype photosetting, Adrian Frutiger turned his attention to Monophoto with *Apollo*. Prior to that only existing typefaces had been adapted for the machine, as was usual.

The test stage of *Apollo* began on 25 March 1960 with test exposures /02/ based on Frutiger's first 14 drawings. On 5 January 1961 Monotype obtained a large number of originals /01/, a total of 69 characters in roman, 66 in italic and 12 in semibold, but no complete character set. Characters were reworked where necessary until early autumn, adapted to the inflexible 18 unit matrix, which Frutiger disliked. Production of *Apollo* was halted at the end of September 1961 in order to give precedence to another exclusive typeface, *Albertina* by Chris Brand. Monotype production records do not state why.[3]

Work resumed on *Apollo* in April 1962, with greater continuity and more test exposures, drawings, reworkings and adaptations to the 18 unit system. On several occasions Monotype draftsmen designed letters, not always to Frutiger's satisfaction. He particularly disliked the ß /14/. Monotype was also unhappy that things were proceeding so slowly. Frutiger was occasionally re-correcting characters that had already been approved. In autumn 1964, four and a half years after work commenced on it, yet still before *Albertina*, the three weights were completed. The roman includes small caps, which are also available in the PostScript fonts. All three *Apollo MT* weights include oldstyle figures.

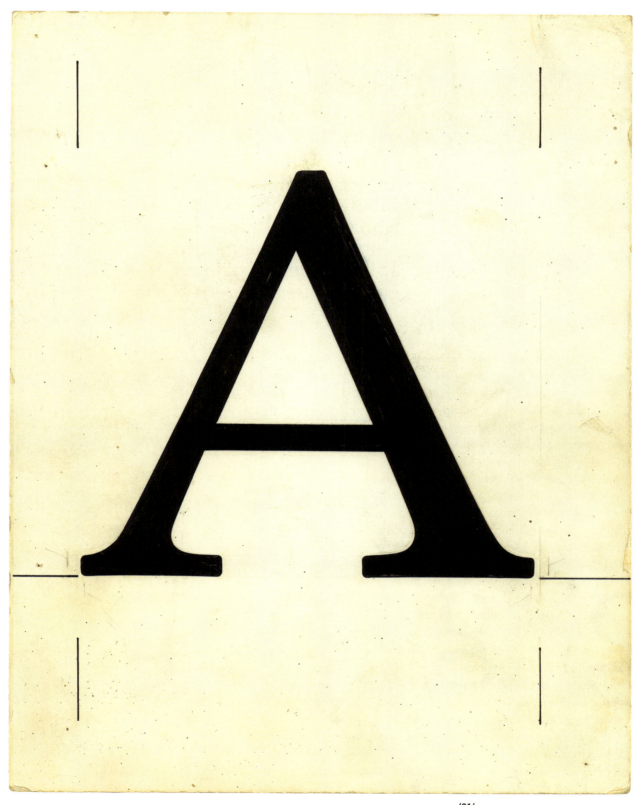

/01/
Final artwork, ink on white card (original size) – the production of Apollo, *including interruptions, took over four years to complete.*

/02/
*Test exposure of the first 14
characters of Apollo with an alternative C and shorter descenders
for g and p.*

C45-24pt.

an aegean afghan in again agfa apian Cepea Cepea
Change Change Chief Chief engine fain feign gin
Haha hinge Happening CHOOCHC CHOOCHC
neigh pane One an aegean afghan in again agfa
apian Change Change Cepea Cepea Chief Chief
engine fain feign gin Haha hinge Happening CHO

C45-24pt. on 22 pt.

an aegean afghan in again agfa apian Cepea Cepea
Change Change Chief Chief engine fain feign gin
Haha hinge Happening CHOOCHC CHOOCHC
neigh pane One an aegean afghan in again agfa
apian Change Change Cepea Cepea Chief Chief
engine fain feign gin Haha hinge Happening CHO

CHO   aefghinp

C g p

not checked
3.5.60

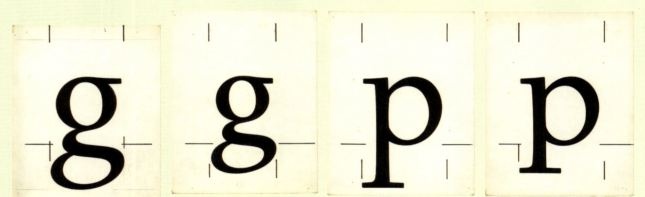

/03/
*Final artwork on card (greatly
reduced) – alternative versions of
lowercase g j p q y with shorter
descenders were offered.*

/04/
*Apollo capital C has the same
basic shape as lowercase c – the
alternative version (right)
with additional bottom semi-serif
was not produced.*

/05/
*Frutiger redrew the descender of
lowercase y to be like j, thereby
changing it from the shape used for
Méridien and Opéra.*

Adrian Frutiger designed the *Apollo* regular weight to be quite heavy, to ensure consistency under exposure and also printed offset on smooth paper. In this respect it is similar to *Egyptienne* /08/, made for Photon-Lumitype. It looks similar in shape, however, to *Méridien*.

Apart from *Méridien*, oldstyle *Apollo* also recalls Frutiger's favourite historical model *Jenson* /06/. This is due to its strokes being curved on one side, asymmetrical serifs, long descenders and absence of true teardrop shapes. All of these attributes add to a written feel. For Adrian Frutiger this is an essential requirement of a good text typeface.

What was new to Frutiger's work was the design of an alternative descender depth. The final artwork for the very first 14 characters and their test exposures /02/ already included shortened descenders for lowercase g and p /03/. Whether this was due to Frutiger or to John Dreyfus is not noted in the production records of the Monotype Type Drawing Office. In the end both versions were released, the more elegant standard version with long descenders, and the more economical 'modified' version with shorter descenders.[4] The current digital *Apollo MT* has the long descenders, meaning it can be set with minimum leading.

On closer inspection there are a couple of peculiarities in *Apollo*. For example, the fact that the transitions from stroke to serif in the lowercase letters are angular on the right but round on the left /07/. I wanted to create movement which would give the typeface a certain elegance. Like *Méridien,* the stems aren't rigidly vertical. This can only be seen in the larger point sizes. In the smaller sizes one can only feel a degree of softness, which may be a characteristic of mine. I don't like the right end of the stroke of a /10/. The hard point bothers me, it looks down because the stem isn't curved to the right before the serif connects to it. On the other hand, I like the really small counters of a and e, which recall *Garamond.* I find them elegant. I didn't use the same drawing for the counters of b d p q, as I normally would /11/. You can do that with a sans serif but not with an oldstyle. The q is a little wide, but b I find very nice. K embodies my style /12/. Another typical trait of mine is the alignment of the horizontal middle strokes in E and F /13/. I've never liked them to be too short. Horizontals are always roughly the same width in my typefaces, with the bottom stroke the longest and the middle the shortest. G J W, R with its straight downstroke in all weights, S and lowercase a are all visibly cooked up by me.

The italic has different angles of inclination /20/, as was usual in the French school. A *Garamond* italic always dances a little. The tiny end of the italic g is special, the ear, it looks somewhat shrivelled /18/. On the whole, the text appearance of the italic is rather uneven.

Apollo is a very classical typeface – although perhaps a bit boring. In my opinion some other Monotype text faces do have a lot more character. Moreover, there are irregularities in some letters. These aren't expressions of my personality, they're more likely

/06/
Nicolas Jenson's roman of 1471 has asymmetric serifs and in part has strokes that are concave on one side.

/07/
Asymmetric placing of stem and serif – Bruce Rogers' Centaur *(left), based on* Jenson, *and* Apollo.

/08/
Apollo (middle) is related in shape to Méridien *(top), while sharing its dark appearance on the page with* Egyptienne F *(bottom).*

/09/
Compared to Méridien *(left) and* Opéra *(middle),* Apollo *clearly has longer descenders.*

Ehpa Ehpa Ehpa

On the greatest and most useful of all inventions, the invention of **alphabetical writing,** Plato did not look with much complacency. He seems to have thought that the use of letters had operated on the human mind *as the use of the go-cart* in learning to walk.

On the greatest and most useful of all inventions, the invention of **alphabetical writing,** Plato did not look with much complacency. He seems to have thought that the use of letters had operated on the human mind *as the use of the go-cart* in learning to walk.

On the greatest and most useful of all inventions, the invention of **alphabetical writing,** Plato did not look with much complacency. He seems to have thought that the use of letters had operated on the human mind *as the use of the go-cart* in learning to walk.

/10/
Differering of open and close counter spaces in Garamond *(left) – adjusted counters in* Apollo *(right).*

/11/
Different curve shapes and connections are commonplace in dynamic typefaces like the oldstyle face Apollo.

/12/
The principle of balance and simplicity: no spur for G, serifs instead of teardrops for J, clear triangles for K and W.

/13/
The arms of E and F typically have similar lengths in Frutiger's typefaces – this is especially noticeable in Apollo.

ae ae   bdpq   GJKRSW   EF

irregularities due to photosetting methods and the small number of units. Still, *Apollo* was used quite a lot,[5] and it was advertised properly. 'The first lettering for phototypesetting' – John Dreyfus made sure that the fanfares were blown. It was released in 1964, at the same time that an exhibition of my work was shown at Monotype in London, called *Graphismes by Frutiger.*[6] Among others, drawings for *Apollo* were displayed there. This typeface was my only commission for Monotype.

Apollo as a book typeface   The British Monotype Corporation was famous for the good quality of its typefaces. They were particularly often used in book typography – especially as foundry type was often unaffordable for extensive typesetting jobs. The Monophoto photosetting machine, too, was aimed at book typesetting, and with *Apollo* the company sought to target its traditional market sector.[7]

To match the requirements of subtle book typography, the three weights were supplemented with small caps and oldstyle figures. This is uncommon for Frutiger's typefaces. Some of the *Apollo* letters have inharmonious proportions. The counters of q and b do not correspond in the roman weight /21/, and a in the italic is too wide compared with e and c /17/. The rigid 18 unit system is to blame. Frutiger's lowercase c, for example, was made much narrower in the process. Generally though, letters tended to be made wider rather than narrower when transferred from original drawings to the 18 unit system, which is true of the a. Moreover, whole rows of units were shifted, for instance from 14 to 15 units, meaning that *Apollo* retains an open, generous feel typical of Frutiger's typefaces, in spite of its solid text appearance.

/14/
Test print of an interim version of Apollo *from 1962 – M is clearly too wide, Æ Œ are too narrow, the ß shape does not fit.*

ABCDEFGHIJKLMNOPQRSTUVWXYZÆŒ&
ABCDEFGHIJKLMNOPQRSTUVWXYZÆŒ
abcdefghijklmnopqrstuvwxyzæœijß
ABCDEFGHIJKLMNOPQRSTUVWXYZÆŒ &
abcdefghijklmnopqrstuvwxyzæœijß

/15/
In the current digital version Apollo MT, *the ligature widths have been corrected and* ß *has the curvy shape.*

ÆŒ æœ ß CGS

/16/
The semi-serif in capital C of Apollo *is slightly diagonal and longer in comparison to G and S.*

/17/
When adapted to the 18 unit system of Monophoto, a was widened (too much) and c compressed.

ace

/18/
The ear of lowercase italic g is too thin compared to the upstroke; very wide and idiosyncratic shape of k.

gk

/19/
Although Apollo and Méridien *are similar in appearance, formal differences are equally easy to spot.*

aegktvxz
aegktvxz

/20/
The downstrokes of italic Apollo *have different angles; character spacing is optimised in the case of f.*

fhlt

/21/
q is too wide due to the Monophoto 18 unit system; this has not been corrected in the current Apollo MT *digital version.*

qbm

/22/
Rounded transition from stem to curve in n of the digital Apollo MT *Regular, and h of* Apollo *Semi-Bold.*

nmh **nmh**

/23/
Monophoto Filmsetter Faces, *undated type catalogue with* Apollo *645 (right).*

'Monophoto' Apollo 645

Film Matrix-case A size for all sizes

6 Point 5¾ Set

THE FIRST THING TO REMEMBER ABOUT A FILMSETTER IS THAT IT
The first thing to remember about a filmsetter is that it is a camera and that its function is to present language in all its beauty, variety and intricacy. Its products are more versatile than those of casting machines, and they open up to the typographer a whole new vista of design, liberating him
The first thing to remember about a filmsetter is that it is a camera and that its function is to present language in all its beauty, variety and intricacy. Its products are more versatile than those of casting machines, and they open up to the
THE FIRST THING TO REMEMBER ABOUT A FILMSETTER

7 Point 6¾ Set

THE FIRST THING TO REMEMBER ABOUT A FILMSETTER IS THAT IT
The first thing to remember about a filmsetter is that it is a camera and that its function is to present language in all its beauty, variety and intricacy. Its products are more versatile than those of casting machines, and they open up to the typographer a whole new vista of design, liberating him
The first thing to remember about a filmsetter is that it is a camera and that its function is to present language in all its beauty, variety and intricacy. Its products are more versatile than those of casting machines, and they open up to the
THE FIRST THING TO REMEMBER ABOUT A FILMSETTER

8 Point 7½ Set

THE FIRST THING TO REMEMBER ABOUT A FILMSETTER IS THAT IT
The first thing to remember about a filmsetter is that it is a camera and that its function is to present language in all its beauty, variety and intricacy. Its products are more versatile than those of casting machines, and they open up to the typographer a whole new vista of design, liberating him
The first thing to remember about a filmsetter is that it is a camera and that its function is to present language in all its beauty, variety and intricacy. Its products are more versatile than those of casting machines, and they open up to the
THE FIRST THING TO REMEMBER ABOUT A FILMSETTER

9 Point 8¾ Set

THE FIRST THING TO REMEMBER ABOUT A FILMSETTER IS THAT IT
The first thing to remember about a filmsetter is that it is a camera and that its function is to present language in all its beauty, variety and intricacy. Its products are more versatile than those of casting machines, and they open up to the typographer a whole new vista of design, liberating him
The first thing to remember about a filmsetter is that it is a camera and that its function is to present language in all its beauty, variety and intricacy. Its products are more versatile than those of casting machines, and they open up to the
THE FIRST THING TO REMEMBER ABOUT A FILMSETTER

10 Point 9¾ Set

THE FIRST THING TO REMEMBER ABOUT A FILMSETTER IS THAT IT
The first thing to remember about a filmsetter is that it is a camera and that its function is to present language in all its beauty, variety and intricacy. Its products are more versatile than those of casting machines, and they open up to the typographer a whole new vista of design, liberating him
The first thing to remember about a filmsetter is that it is a camera and that its function is to present language in all its beauty, variety and intricacy. Its products are more versatile
THE FIRST THING TO REMEMBER ABOUT A FILMSETTER

11 Point 10¾ Set

THE FIRST THING TO REMEMBER ABOUT A FILMSETTER IS THAT IT
The first thing to remember about a filmsetter is that it is a camera and that its function is to present language in all its beauty, variety and intricacy. Its products are more versatile than those of casting machines, and they open up to the
The first thing to remember about a filmsetter is that it is a camera and that its function is to present language in all its
THE FIRST THING TO REMEMBER ABOUT A FILMSETTER

12 Point 11½ Set

THE FIRST THING TO REMEMBER ABOUT A FILMSETTER IS THAT IT
The first thing to remember about a filmsetter is that it is a camera and that its function is to present language in all its beauty, variety and intricacy. Its products are more versatile
The first thing to remember about a filmsetter is that it is a camera and that its function is to present language in all its
THE FIRST THING TO REMEMBER ABOUT A FILMSETTER

14 Point 13¾ Set

THE FIRST THING TO REMEMBER ABOUT A FILMSETTER IS THAT IT
The first thing to remember about a filmsetter is that it is a camera and that its function is to present language in all its
The first thing to remember about a filmsetter is that it is a camera and that its function is to present language in all its

abcdefghijklmnopqrstuvwxyz£1234567890.,:;"'!?-0[]—
ABCDEFGHIJKLMNOPQRSTUVWXYZ
ABCDEFGHIJKLMNOPQRSTUVWXYZ&
abcdefghijklmnopqrstuvwxyz£1234567890.,:;"'!?()
ABCDEFGHIJKLMNOPQRSTUVWXYZ&

16 Point 15¾ Set

abcdefghijklmnopqrstuvwxyz£1234567890
ABCDEFGHIJKLMNOPQRSTUVWXYZ.,:;"'!?-0[]—
ABCDEFGHIJKLMNOPQRSTUVWXYZ&
abcdefghijklmnopqrstuvwxyz£1234567890.,:;"'!?()
ABCDEFGHIJKLMNOPQRSTUVWXYZ&

/24/
Characters of Apollo *645 normal
for photosetting by
the Monotype Corporation.*

ABCDEFGHIJKLMN
OPQRSTUVWXYZ&
abcdefghijklmnopqrs
tuvwxyz ß 1234567890

Marketing Apollo At the same time as *Apollo*'s release, an exhibition of Frutiger's graphic work opened at Monotype House in London. In the exhibition brochure the typeface is introduced across a double page under the heading 'New face for filmsetting' and all of its weights are displayed a few pages later.[8] It was also promoted in the *Monotype Recorder* and the *Monotype Newsletter*, Monotype's customer magazines, and continued to be mentioned there for many years.[9]

Allen Hutt was referring to a text in the *Monotype Recorder* when he wrote in the *British Printer:* "The Monotype Corporation announce Apollo as a 'bread and butter' face; if so, it's deliciously exotic French bread and creamy Norman butter. The description is in fact misleading. Apollo is a face of chic, of panache; it will, in Morison's phrase, demonstrably 'confer distinction, authority, elegance' to the texts it presents."[10]

In 1971 the *Gutenberg-Jahrbuch* was set in *Apollo*, with additional special characters made for it. Among others, a long s was required for historic texts.[11]

The 1971 *Gutenberg-Jahrbuch* also poetically expounds upon the origin of the name 'Apollo' with a full page advertisement for Monotype **/25/**. A small detail: directly on the page opposite, the caption notes the "use of the typeface 'Apollo' by Albert [sic!] Frutiger".[12]

/25/
The photosetting typeface Apollo
*was named after Apollo,
the ancient Greek god of light,
reason and youth.*

/26/
*Typesetting sample from 6 to
9 pt from the* Monotype Recorder
*No.1/1979 with a text about the
creation of* Apollo *by John Dreyfus.*

APOLLO SERIES 645

'Monophoto' Apollo was the earliest design commissioned especially for filmsetting by 'Monotype'. The decision to obtain a new design from Adrian Frutiger was influenced by two factors: first, because he was one of the first type designers to have tackled the problem of adapting and creating typefaces for phototypesetting while working for Deberny Peignot in Paris on typefaces for the Photon/Lumitype machine; and second, because 'Monotype' had learnt from first-hand experience while collaborating with him on the joint manufacture of Univers that he was a type designer of quite exceptional gifts. The main problems he had to resolve in producing his 'Monophoto' Apollo design were of proportion and weight. First it was required of him that he should supply drawings which would ensure that a single set of matrices would yield satisfactory results in all sizes from 6 to 24 point. Secondly the weight of the design had to be sufficiently heavy to produce a good impression when printed by photolithography on smooth paper, whilst at the same time keeping

it light enough to contrast with Apollo semi-bold which was deliberately made not so heavy as to preclude its use independent of the normal weight. Originally 'Monophoto' faces where supplied in three separate forms to suit the smallest sizes, the middle range of sizes, and the larger display sizes. But as printers were not prepared to buy three sets of matrices to cover the range from 6 to 24 point, it became clear that the best service would be provided by creating a set of matrices that would span the entire range. The solution was to create a typeface with open counters and a particularly sharp line, which together produce an attractive, crisp and easily read text. The height of the capitals was kept relatively low, so as to avoid a spotty effect, particularly when setting languages such as German in which every noun starts with a capital letter. The resultant design is unmistakably modern in appearance, but without

any idiosyncrasies which prevent it from being used for a wide range of work. It is an all-purpose face (or as printers used to say 'a bread-and-butter type'), suited equally to bookwork, catalogues and jobbing work. As it was first manufactured at a time when hot-metal was still extensively used, and before filmsetting machines were as sophisticated as they have since become, it was looser than has since become fashionable. But with the facilities now available for adjusting 'Monotype' filmsetters to produce tighter inter-character spacing, Apollo can now be set much tighter and to great advantage. In recent years 'Monophoto' Apollo has been very extensively used for the setting of fine art catalogues produced by the Tate Gallery and by the British Museum, as well as for publications

issued by the BBC and the National Trust. Its virtues have come to be increasingly recognised and its place in the repertoire of good twentieth-century filmsetting faces is thoroughly assured. Adrian Frutiger has also designed typefaces for an extremely wide variety of needs, including computers, airport signing, the Indian continent, and an astonishing range of seriffed as well as sans serif types.

Apollo von »Monotype«

Was wäre die Antike ohne ihn gewesen?
Für die Hellenen waren die hell erklingenden drei Silben mehr
als ein Name. Als Gott des Lichtes, der Vernunft und der Jugend,
als Schutzherr der Musen und der Heilkunde reichte seine Macht weit;
seinem Schutz waren die Herden ebenso anvertraut wie die Schiffe.

Apoll, der Reine und Strahlende
bestimmte das Denken und Fühlen von den Toren des Herakles
bis zum Ganges. Münzen, Vasen und Plastiken zeugen
noch immer von ihm. Der völkerversöhnende Geist Olympias
entsprang seiner Epoche.

Das Apollinische galt und gilt noch immer
als das irdische Maß für Harmonie, als Wertmaßstab
abendländischer Kultur. Die Gestalt des Apoll von Olympia
war viele Generationen Inbegriff des Schönen.
Ein Ideal, das kaum verblaßte, weil es nah und doch zugleich
unerreichbar fern erschien.

Von Apoll zu Apollo,
welch ein gewaltiger Bogen spannt sich hier
aus der Vergangenheit zur unmittelbaren Gegenwart,
mit ihren kühnen Eroberungen des Weltraums,
jenem Triumph von Wagemut und technischem Kalkül,
dessen vorläufiger aber gewiß nicht endgültiger Höhepunkt
die Landung auf dem Mond gewesen ist.

Apolls Geist
folgt so der stürmisch vorwärtseilenden
Menschheit mühelos. Gestern, heute und morgen.
Warum sollte eine Schrift nicht seinen Namen tragen?
Ausdruck und Gleichmaß,
Schwung und Schönheit zeichnen die »Monophoto« Apollo aus.
Beherrscht und zugleich beherrschend
präsentiert sie sich als Fleisch des Geistes den Lesern
des Gutenberg-Jahrbuches. »Monophoto« Apollo – gezeichnet von
Adrian Frutiger, dem Schöpfer der Univers-Grotesk.

»Monophoto« Filmsatz

Setzmaschinen-Fabrik Monotype Gesellschaft m. b. H.
Frankfurt am Main und Berlin

Font production:
Adobe Font

Font format:
PostScript Type 1

Also available:
TrueType
OpenType Std

ABCDEFGHIJKLMN
OPQRSTUVWXYZ&
abcdefghijklmnopqrs
tuvwxyzß1234567890

Sie fragen sich
warum es notwen
dig ist, so viele Schriften zu
r Verfügung zu haben. Sie dienen alle zu

m selben, aber machen die Vielfalt des Menschen aus. Diese Vielfalt ist wie beim Wein. Ich habe einmal eine Weinkarte s tudiert mit sechzig Médoc-Weinen aus dem selben Jahr. Das ist ausnahmslos Wein, aber doch nicht alles der gleiche Wein. Es hat eben gleichwohl Nuancen. So ist es auch mit der Schr

ift. *You may ask why so many different typefaces.* They all serve the same purpose bu t they express man's diversity. It is the same diversity we find in wine. I once saw a list of Médoc wines featuring sixty different Médocs all of the same year. All of th em were wines but each was different from the others. It's the nuances that are im portant. The same is true for typefaces. *Pourquoi tant d'Alphabets différents!* Tous se rvent au même but, mais aussi à exprimer la diversité de l'homme. C'est cette même diversité que nous retrouvons dans les vins de Médoc. J'ai pu, un jour, relever soix

ante crus, tous de la même année. Il s'agissait certes de vins, mais tous étaient différents. Tout est dans la nuance du bouquet. Il en est de mê me pour les caractères! *Sie fragen sich, warum es notwendig ist, so viele Schriften zur Verfügung zu haben.* Sie dienen alle zum selben, aber mach en die Vielfalt des Menschen aus. Diese Vielfalt ist wie beim Wein. Ich habe einmal eine Weinkarte studiert mit sechzig Médoc-Weinen aus d em selben Jahr. Das ist ausnahmslos Wein, aber doch nicht alles der gl eiche Wein. Es hat eben gleichwohl Nuancen. So ist es auch mit der Sc

hrift. *You may ask why so many different typef aces.* They all serve the same purpose but th ey express man's diversity. It is the same div ersity we find in wine. I once saw a list of M édoc wines featuring sixty different Médocs all of the same year. All of them were wines but each was different from the others. It's t he nuances that are important. The same is tr ue for typefaces. *Pourquoi tant d'Alphabets di fférents!* Tous servent au même but, mais aus

ÅBÇDÈFG
HIJKLMÑ
ÔPQRŠTÜ
VWXYZ&
ÆŒ¥$£€
1234567890
åbçdéfghij
klmñôpqrš
tüvwxyzß
fi fl æ œ ø ł ð
[.,:;·'/-–—]
(¿¡"«‹›»"!?)
{§°%@‰*†}
Regular

ÅBÇDÈFG
HIJKLMÑ
ÔPQRŠTÜ
VWXYZ&
ÆŒ¥$£€
1234567890
åbçdéfghij
klmñôpqrš
tüvwxyzß
fi fl æ œ ø ł ð
[.,:;·'/-–—]
(¿¡"«‹›»"!?)
{§°%@‰*†}
Italic

ÅBÇDÈFG
HIJKLMÑ
ÔPQRŠTÜ
VWXYZ&
ÆŒ¥$£€
1234567890
åbçdéfghij
klmñôpqrš
tüvwxyzß
fi fl æ œ ø ł ð
[.,:;·'/-–—]
(¿¡"«‹›»"!?)
{§°%@‰*†}
Semibold

1234567890
ÅBÇDÉFGHIJ
KLMÑÔPQRŠ
TÜVWXYZ&
Oldstyle Figures & Small Caps

ff fi fl ffi ffl
½ ⅓ ⅔ ¼ ¾
⅛ ⅜ ⅝ ⅞
Expert

1234567890
Italic Oldstyle Figures

ff fi fl ffi ffl
½ ⅓ ⅔ ¼ ¾
⅛ ⅜ ⅝ ⅞
Italic Expert

1234567890
Semibold Oldstyle Figures

ff fi fl ffi ffl
½ ⅓ ⅔ ¼ ¾
⅛ ⅜ ⅝ ⅞
Semibold Expert

76 pt | −15   58 pt | −5   38 pt | −5   26 pt | −5   17 pt | 20 pt | −5   12 pt | 13 pt | 2   9 pt | 10.2 pt | 5   7 pt | 8 pt | 15

Typeface comparison There are only a few typefaces like *Apollo,* made at the beginning of the photosetting era exclusively for that method. Chris Brand's *Albertina* was also made for photosetting only, although it was originally designed for foundry type.[13] *Bembo* was based on a typeface by Francesco Griffo cut during the Incunabula and adapted by Monotype for single letter casting in 1929. All three book faces are oldstyles and were available on Monophoto.

Apollo seems rounder than the other two typefaces, due to its flat upstrokes and rounded transitions from curve to stem, plus the q without a spur. The curved left sides of its stems add to this impression of roundness. *Albertina* was also designed with slightly concave stems, but they were straightened during production by Monotype.[14]

The stroke width contrast of *Apollo* is lower than that of *Bembo* and *Albertina;* thus it looks fairly dark on the page. Asymmetrical serifs and the curved terminal of n give both *Bembo* and *Apollo* a semblance of writing. The *Albertina* n, on the other hand, has nothing very handwritten about it, although the 5 does.

Apollo is wider than the other two, but only wider than *Albertina* if brought to the same x-height.

/27/

Measurements of stroke widths and proportions of the Apollo *regular weight.*

Roman					
	Hh = 10.00 cm	nh = 6.99 cm	oh = 7.51 cm	Hh : Hw = 1 : 0.81	nh : nw = 1 : 0.85
	Hw = 8.15	nw = 5.94	ow = 7.24	Hw : Hs = 1 : 0.18	nw : ns = 1 : 0.20
	Hs = 1.46	ns = 1.20	os = 1.45	Hs : Hq = 1 : 0.55	nh : oh = 1 : 1.07
	Hq = 0.80	nq = 0.92	oq = 0.54		nw : ow = 1 : 1.22

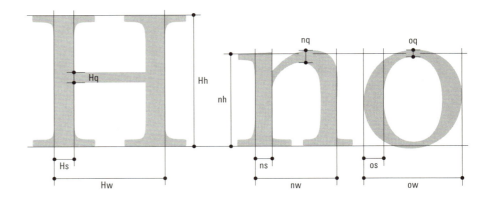

/28/

A look at details of Apollo *in comparison with two other related typefaces from Monotype –* Bembo *and* Albertina.

Hofstainberg

Bembo
Monotype (Francesco Griffo)
1929 (1496)

CRWafnq56

Hofstainberg

Apollo
Adrian Frutiger
1964

CRWafnq56

C	R	W	a	f	n	q	5 6
Diagonal axis of contrast, upward curve at bottom	Straight downstroke with semi-serif	V-shapes do not overlap, no middle serif	Curve ends in a point, main stem leans slightly to the left	Inside curve symmetrical, vertical semi-serif	Asymmetric serif connections, bracketed on one side	No spur, smooth connection to stem	Curve terminates horizontally

Hofstainberg

Albertina
Chris Brand
1965

CRWafnq56

Comparison showing the
different weights and angle of
the italics.

	Hh	Hw	Hs	Hq
Roman	10.00 cm	8.15 = 1	1.46 = 1	0.80 = 1
Semibold	10.00	8.71 = 1.07	2.01 = 1.38	0.81 = 1.01
Italic	10.00	7.93 = 0.97	1.34 = 0.92	0.73 = 0.91

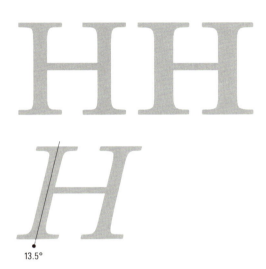

13.5°

/30/

Height comparison showing the
differences of x-heights to
ascenders and descenders – the cap
height is the starting point.

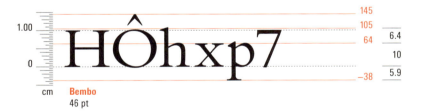

Bembo
46 pt

Apollo
49.8 pt

Albertina
43.8 pt

Type-design project
Alphabet Entreprise Francis Bouygues
1961

/01/
*Alphabet for Enterprise
Francis Bouygues with alternate-
capital shapes.*

aABCDEFGHIJKLMM
NNOPQRSTUVWXYZ

EFLTZK41
7DBPR&JI
235689O
QCGSUNH
AVWXMY

/02/
*Design of a wide, slab serif roman
from student days, c.1950;
basis for the EFB typeface design.*

/04/
*Logo with connected, slightly
modified shapes – the counters of
the B are rectangular and
the letters narrower in general.*

/05/
*Suggestions for logos for
two business areas of Enterprise
Francis Bouygues.*

TUVWX
YZJ 1234
56789&0

/03/
*A Clarendon-like typeface
by Walter Käch, from his 1949
typedesign textbook
Schriften Lettering Écritures.*

STATEL
STIM

Collaboration After the failed attempt by Charles Peignot to set up an internal graphic design studio, Adrian Frutiger became self-employed in 1961. He got a few jobs through the Parisian advertising agency Synergie, among them that of designing an alphabet for Enterprise Francis Bouygues /01/, today one of the biggest businesses in France.

Adrian Frutiger suggested a constructed typeface apt for a construction company, the basis of which he adapted to optical criteria. Thus the stroke widths are not all the same, the vertical lines are thicker than the horizontals, easily recognisable by the fine guidelines, which can still be made out in one reproduction /06/. There are optical corrections in the details worth noting; the upper serif of the C, for example, is lower than the bottom one; the cross-stroke of the G is finer than the other horizontal lines.

Adrian Frutiger had already drawn a slab serif typeface in his student days /02/. This design shows the influence of his teacher Walter Käch, even though Frutiger made it outside of the classroom. He frequently worked at the school's composing room, where he also engraved the design in lead. Particularly the J, ampersand and numerals have typical Käch shapes /03/. This alphabet formed the basis of the Bouygues typeface design, with such typical Frutiger traits such as the spurless G and the sharp-angled K.

We were already in our studio at the Place d'Italie when I was contacted by the construction company Enterprise Francis Bouygues. They needed a company logo, and as ever when I did a logo, I suggested designing their own company typeface. I surprised them with one of those placards which are used in the construction industry: "Ici nous construisons pour la maison..." was written on it for instance. This was a design with letters around 20 cm in size, cut out of black paper and stuck on a yellow background.

The character of the typeface was based on elements like beams, steel girders and metal construction. I was also thinking of concrete moulds with their slightly rounded edges. It was in the style of the time – the fifties and its 'Frigidaire style'[1] was still influential. The EFB word mark /04/ was meant to look like a picture. The B has rectangular counters to match those of E and F. In the alphabet they're slightly rounded so as to be more legible /01/. The very long serifs recall I-beams, everything looks very technical as it was intended to. I mixed the upper- and lowercase shapes, with a uniform height. Lowercase a m n are more harmonious than the uppercase obliques and are absolutely legible. Once again Charles Peignot's influence can be discerned. From an historical point of view it goes back to uncials (see page 52), like all my one-alphabet attempts. I also designed an outline typeface /07/. I fancied drawing a light typeface so that the managers' letterheads would have finer, more elegant letters.

I don't think the alphabet was actually used as a company typeface. I've certainly never seen it in use.[2] There are just a few words that I cut out and stuck together /08/. I drew the basics of this typeface while still at the Kunstgewerbeschule in Zurich, a design in the Egyptienne style /02/.

/06/
Enlargement (bottom) of the figure on the left – construction and optical correction are visible thanks to the guidelines.

/08/
Test setting with the letters F and B in outline form, representing Francis Bouygues' initials.

/07/
Design of an outline version for lighter, more elegant use such as management letterheads.

à la mesure
d'aujourd'hui
pour le repos et
le com ort

de qualité
de la orêt de
rim orion

Name of typeface	Client	Designer	Design | Publication	Typesetting technology	Manufacturer	Weights
Concorde	Sofratype	Adrian Frutiger André Gürtler	1961 | 1964	Machine line casting	– Sofratype	3

CONCORDE

After the newsprint type *Opéra* (see page 130), we did another typeface, *Concorde,* for the Paris-based company Sofratype, who manufactured matrices for line casting machines. Alfred Devolz, the company's director, was keen to have his own sans serif, and so he came to me. Usually, he would take over the typefaces from other typesetting machine manufacturers. But he was of the opinion that there was no decent grotesque for the line casting machines. He wanted a jobbing type for newsprint but it shouldn't be a copy of *Univers.* This would have been impossible anyway since the rights were with Deberny & Peignot and thus its use would have incurred royalties.

Concorde was always meant to have only three cuts; therefore I had much more freedom with the shapes during the design compared to *Univers* with its 21 cuts. I felt I was on the right track with this grotesque; it was a truly novel typeface. It wasn't as close to the classical form as *Syntax* /09/ by Hans Eduard Meier, which was developed at the same time but only released in 1968. But it wasn't meant to be too far removed from *Univers* either; the round junctures at the stem, for instance, were maintained. It was important to me to remain within the right shape of grotesque with little stroke contrast. I was looking for elegance and I wanted a connection to the round style of the 1950s.

I only drew one finial myself /03/. Everything else was taken over by André Gürtler. He'd had good training. He'd been a student of Emil Ruder's in Basel and he'd gained practical experience at Monotype in England. But he received his final training for drawing typefaces from me. In 1959 I employed him as typographer for Deberny & Peignot. When Devolz gave us his commission in 1961, I handed the task to André. I myself was still bound to Deberny & Peignot. It took him two years to complete *Concorde* at Sofratype – he remained my employee but was paid by Devolz. He always came to my studio for meetings. We completely trusted each other and he immediately understood what I wanted to achieve with *Concorde.* André took over the implementation including the punchcutting – that was some tedious detailed work.

Concorde was designed for job composition in newsprint. It was introduced in a special sample setting in the body text sizes 8 pt and 10 pt /01/. The three originally envisaged cuts – regular, italic and bold – were developed simultaneously. This was important because of the adjustments. They had to have the same letter-spacing since the regular and bold cuts, and the regular and italic cuts respectively, were on the same matrix. The regular cut, therefore, appears to be a bit loosely tracked. We also deliberately kept it fairly fine; through the mechanics of high pressure there was always a certain percentage of ink gain, called slur, which resulted in a slight increase in stroke weight. Finding the absolutely perfect stroke weight in relation to the letter-spacing is the most difficult part in designing a typeface. The reader is very sensitive regarding this point. He has a clear feeling for

The development of Concorde The start of work on *Concorde* is documented by a 1961 letter from Alfred Devolz to Deberny & Peignot, in which he confirms the agreement regarding a sans-serif typeface.[1] This letter demonstrates that Frutiger – although self-employed with his own studio since 1960 – was still closely connected to Deberny & Peignot through his role as external art director.

André Gürtler, who was significantly involved in the design of *Concorde*, remembers: "At some point Adrian said to me: Would you like to design a typeface? I already had quite a lot of experience with typefaces under his direction of course. He really whetted my appetite when he showed me a sheet with a curved terminal. It was a so-called whisky-sketch. Every now and again a whisky was had in the studio and then the atmosphere loosened up a bit. He showed me the sheet and I instantly understood, not 90%, but 100% what he meant to do with this terminal /03/. Although this style didn't exist in grotesques at the time, except for *Gill Sans.* When he showed me how he would draw it, something wonderful happened, an energetic current flowed through me. He trusted me and I knew what he wanted. That was something really special. I did identify strongly with Adrian Frutiger; he was a father figure for me."[2]

Gürtler created all drawings with a soft pencil on tracing paper using a cap height of 135 millimetres (5.3 in). It took him a long time to develop the minuscule g /02/. His suggestion to try out a classical g as in *Gill Sans* was accepted by Frutiger. Gürtler was delighted because he thought that the classical g "is the most awesome letter to write with a broad pen because it is a powerful shape, historically as well as in terms of calligraphy". With the so-called last smoke proof[3] his work at Sofratype was finished after two years.

The name 'Concorde' was used for another typeface as well. In 1968, Günter Gerhard Lange, art director at Berthold, used it for a robust transitional typeface designed for hand, machine and phototypesetting. He was referencing the *Concorde*, the novel supersonic aircraft that was being developed at the time. However, if he had known that the name was already in use, he would have chosen a different one.[4]

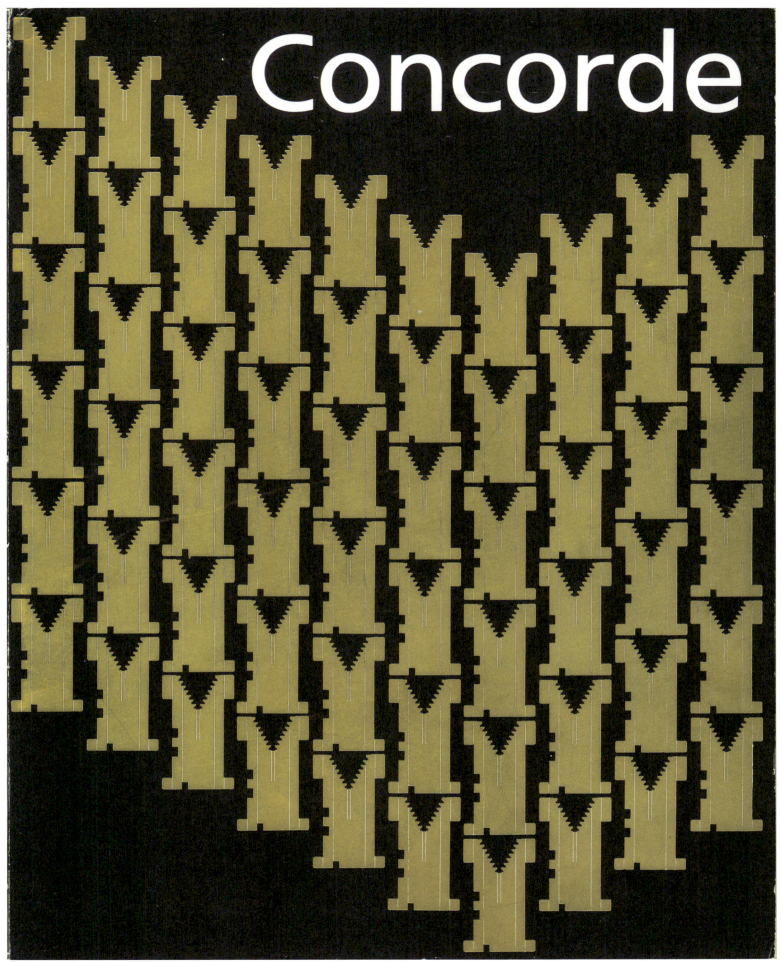

Concorde

/01/
*Cover of the four-page sample setting
by Sofratype using the regular
and bold cuts of Concorde, circa 1964,
design Bruno Pfäffli.*

/02/
Original designs for the g
in three cuts by André Gürtler –
the simple shape was rejected
for Concorde.

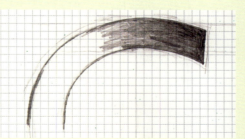

/03/
Initial sketch as a design idea for
Concorde – drawn by André Gürtler
from memory of the 'whisky-sketch'
curve ending.

A dynamic sans serif With his 1915/16 sans serif **/05/** for London Transport, Edward Johnston created the basis for two new styles of typefaces, the geometric (see page 330) and the dynamic sans serif. The difference between these two styles becomes obvious in the S-shapes. The majuscule S features diagonally cut circles and the minuscule s has long flat curves.

As opposed to Johnston's sans serif, *Gill Sans* (1928) **/07/** by his former student and colleague[5] Eric Gill was no longer dominated by a circular shape but by a written impression. The dynamic style is obvious in the regular font but even more so in the cursive, a true Italic with a narrower ductus and varying minuscule shapes. From 1931 onwards, the Dutch designer Jan van Krimpen developed a first type family with *Romulus Serif* and the sample cut of *Romulus Sans Serif* **/08/**. Since its implementation was terminated, it is almost unknown.[6] Also very little known is *Stellar* **/06/** by Robert Hunter Middleton from 1929. Its strokes are tapered and – similar to the 1968 *Syntax* **/09/** by Hans Eduard Meier – its curves and diagonal strokes are angular. *Syntax* clearly displays a relationship to the dynamic Renaissance antiqua. The glyph widths vary considerably, the curve of the n is clearly asymmetrical and features an angular joint with the stem; with the e, it points to the next letter.[7]

the right relationship between white and black. When *Univers* was transferred to photo-typesetting at Linotype, I did calculations concerning this point as well as numerous studies (see page 93). I think I did the stroke weight quite well with *Univers,* and also with *Concorde* it's about right when I look at it now.

Concerning *Concorde,* the classical minuscule g is worth mentioning. There were different designs for that **/02/**. The r runs remarkably wide **/09/**. This hasn't got anything to do with the matrix. First, it benefited the bold version and secondly, I simply liked the wide r, even if it might cause a little gap in some words. For optical reasons, the upper curve of the p is slightly lowered and thus a bit lower than in the a and h. In the bold cut it goes up higher **/11/**.

As opposed to the later *Frutiger* typeface, *Concorde* features a splayed M **/09/**, which has a classical feel to it, although Roman Imperial capitals did not influence me in this case **/04/**. The U is slightly narrower than the N; this is usually done that way. The V might be a bit too wide; if you look at the interior and exterior whitespace, then it could definitely be a bit narrower. The S, too, is designed quite wide; if it was narrower, it would appear contrived.

The numerals, on the other hand, are fairly narrow compared to the capitals. They all stand on a half-unit, a half em in other words, and therefore have a narrower spacing than, for example, the *Frutiger* numerals. This was pre-determined for technical reasons, mainly due to the tabular setting. However, not only in these three cuts, but in all typefaces, columns of figures should stand evenly below each other – we even talked about full stops and commas, which should stand on a quarter em. The looped numeral 8 **/13/** has got its very

/05/
*Edward Johnston's geometrical
sans serif (1916) – the minuscules
however are not geometrical
but dynamic.*

/04/
*Capitalis Monumentalis,
1st century BC – square, circle,
triangle and vertical double square
result in heavily varying widths.*

/07/
Gill Sans with a true Italic – from
1928 onwards Eric Gill designed one
of the most significant dynamic
sans serifs.

AFGMNOSUV abefghprst
AFGMNOSUV abefghprst

/08/
*A first type family –
the Renaissance antiqua* Romulus
and Romulus Sans Serif
by Jan van Krimpen (1931–37).

AFGMNOSUV abefghprst
AFGMNOSUV abefghprst

/09/
*Typefaces by two Willimann
students – Adrian Frutiger's* Concorde
(1964, top) and Hans Eduard Meier's
Syntax *(1968, bottom).*

AFGMNOSUVabefghprst
AFGMNOSUV abefghprst

/06/
Robert H. Middleton's Stellar *(1929)
has tapered strokes as well as
rectangular-cut terminals in the
curves and diagonals.*

Stellar

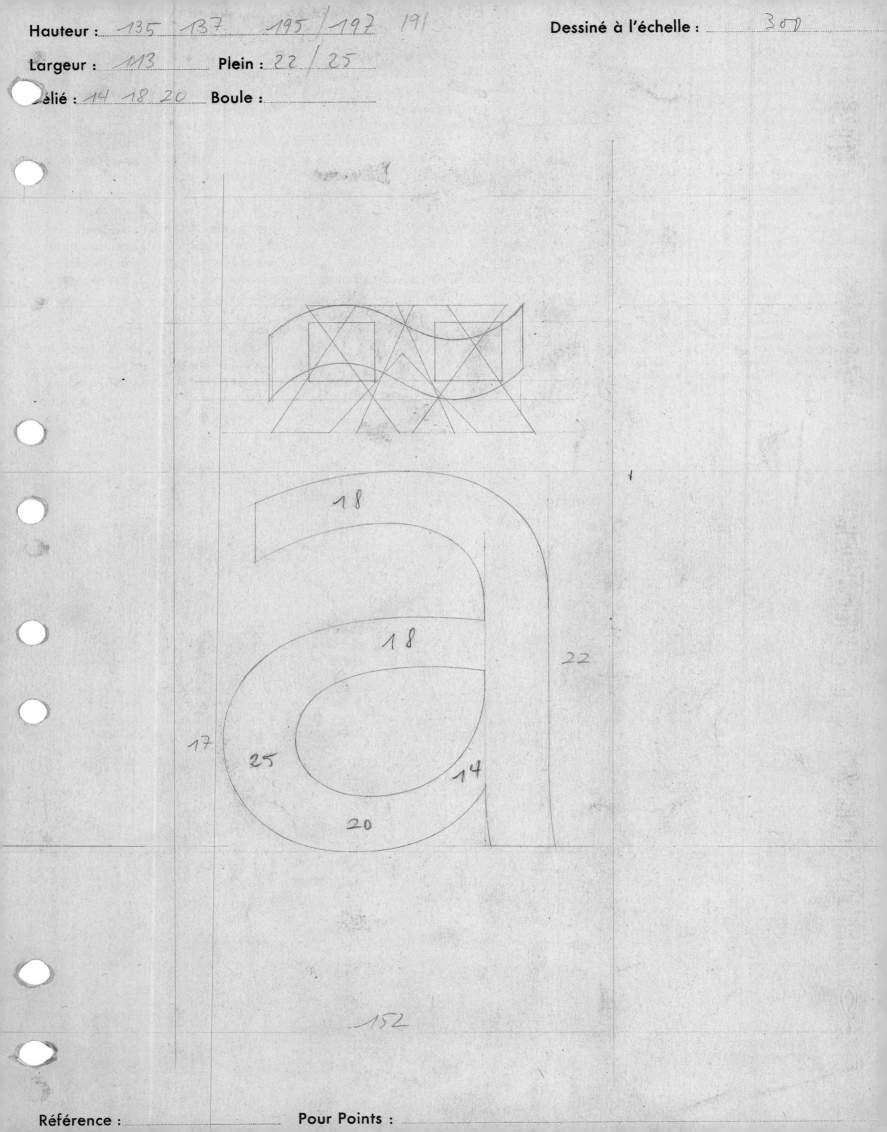

18

18

22

17

25

14

20

The static aspects in the dynamic Concorde Concorde has dynamic but also static aspects. Compared, for instance, to *Gill Sans* and the later *Syntax* it features a less dynamic expression. The differences in the widths of its majuscules are less significant and – not quite understandably – also more unsystematic. This becomes apparent when looking at the letters based on a circle, such as C D G O and Q /14/. Unlike the G, the O does not have a round but an oval shape and the S is not half the width of the O but almost the same. The already mentioned proportional relationships can be found in the F and G. André Gürtler drew the M according to a Renaissance antiqua with spread legs although he considered this as unsuitable for a sans serif. Frutiger, however, who would have liked to use the spread shape in *Univers* (see page 94), was delighted to be able to use it in this case.
With the minuscules, the curves join the stem in a round form and therefore appear almost symmetrical and only slightly dynamic. Totally static, and devoid of any written impression, are the mirrored or rotated letters b d p q, the stresses of which are vertical and the counters oval. The dynamic style thus becomes only truly apparent in the flat curve endings of a c e and s.
The numerals, too, are clearly dynamic; the looped 8, for instance, demonstrates an origin in handwriting /13/.

own design without any reference to *Univers*; the same is true for the common ampersand, which is better suited to newsprint than my otherwise preferred unique version.

The cursive *Concorde,* which was never finished, isn't a true italic. We put some effort into designing it as beautifully as possible in terms of shape but on no account did we want to imitate a classical cursive. I've always preferred simply to set a grotesque type at an oblique angle. My oblique sans serifs are corrected in terms of shape, of course, but they don't have a narrower letter-spacing than the regular ones. This has been consistently implemented with all my grotesque typefaces. That wasn't coincidence, however, it was well considered. I did studies and drew other grotesque shapes, which were closer to a cursive, but for me that simply didn't feel right. With a grotesque, the oblique version for me is just an enforced necessity. That's different with the classical typefaces. There has always been the concept of a cursive in its own right. I've calligraphed the humanist cursives often enough, they were in my hand and in my head, but I wouldn't have been able to transform them into a grotesque form. I would have had to make too many compromises. Grotesque and antiqua are simply two different worlds.

The name of the typeface refers to Place de la Concorde in Paris, in the same way as *Opéra* is named after Place de l'Opéra. *Concorde* was finished in 1964 but it was only released in the romain (regular) and gras (bold) cuts. Only a few years later, at the end of the 1960s, Sofratype was taken over by the typesetting machine manufacturer Mergenthaler. They weren't aware of the fact that with *Concorde* they had a totally up-to-date typeface. It silently disappeared with the sale.

/10/
Riveted brass stencils of Concorde *as templates for the engraving of the punches with the pantograph.*

Principe de construction du « Concorde », caractère dessiné par Adrian Frutiger et André Gürtler.

/11/
Proportional template of Concorde – *the upper curve of the p in the regular and oblique cuts is slightly below the guide.*

Oh là là elle avale le savon
Envol Happe Élan Hosanna Opale
kann Hans sehen

HOHOEŒEOHEHE

O *Oh là là elleal avale le savon
Envol Happe Élan Hosanna Opale
kann Hans lesen*

HHE HOHO EHE

**Oh là là elle avale le savon
Envol Happe Élan Hosannna Opale
kann Hans lesen**

HE HOHO EHE

/12/
Smoke proof of some letters of Concorde romain, italique *and* gras *in order to check the engraved punches.*

8 8

/13/
As opposed to Univers *(left), the numerals of* Concorde *have a half-em width and the 8 has a dynamic, looped shape.*

a b c d e f g h i j k l m n o p q r s t u v w x y z é à è ù â ê î ô û ç
A B C D E F G H I J K L M N O P Q R S T U V W X Y Z
É È Ê Ë Æ Œ Ç & 1 2 3 4 5 6 7 8 9 0

/14/
Alphabet (without punctuation marks) of Concorde romain *in 10 pt from the four-page sample setting by Sofratype.*

/15/
Minuscule a of Concorde romain *with all diacritics – final artwork with measurements in millimetres (opposite page).*

/16/
Text string from the sample setting by Sofratype – only the regular and bold cuts of Concorde *were implemented.*

Avant même d'avoir regardé, comme si depuis long-temps, inconsciemment, cette pensée couvait en moi et n'attendait que l'instant d'éclore, j'avais deviné! Debout auprès d'un quinquet, à l'entrée de la roulotte, le jeune personnage inconnu avait défait son bandeau et jeté sur ses épaules une pèlerine. On voyait, dans la

Avant même d'avoir regardé, comme si depuis long-temps, inconsciemment, cette pensée couvait en moi et n'attendait que l'instant d'éclore, j'avais deviné! Debout auprès d'un quinquet, à l'entrée de la roulotte, le jeune personnage inconnu avait défait son bandeau et jeté sur ses épaules une pèlerine. On voyait, dans la

Type-design project
Serifen-Grotesk
1962

An inscriptional roman for text setting   In his 1962 designs for 'Serifen-Grotesk' Frutiger drew on Copperplate Gothic /03/ by Frederic W. Goudy, which was cut in by American Type Founders. Similar to a grotesque, this very popular stationery typeface shows hardly any stroke contrast; its short, fine endings have their very own charisma. Formally it belongs to the group of inscriptional romans, i.e. to the engraved types.

Copperplate Gothic comprises eight majuscule alphabets. Frutiger, however, designed minuscules. His interesting approach was that of an inscriptional roman for text setting with waisted strokes. The sample setting 'une pomme du monde' /04/ gives a first impression. About thirty years later, in May 1993, Adrian Frutiger sent a reworked and extended version of 'Serifen-Grotesk' to Gerhard Höhl of Linotype.[1] In the accompanying letter it is referred to by the working title 'Cooperline'[2]. The minuscule alphabet was almost completely present, and of the majuscules the sample set contained D H V /02/. They were slightly thinner than in the 1962 design. Due to the short, fine endings the typeface appears hard in spite of the waisted strokes. Furthermore, it leaves a somewhat unsteady, messy impression. The reason for this might be a lack of stroke contrast in the e and o, for instance; the o is also too big and the w too strong. The special shape of the comma, and the round dots on the i presumably add to this impression. According to Frutiger it was the right decision that this design was never implemented.

/01/
Belonging to the group of inscriptional romans, 'Serifen-Grotesk' has very short endings, waisted strokes, little stroke contrast and almost vertical bowl endings.

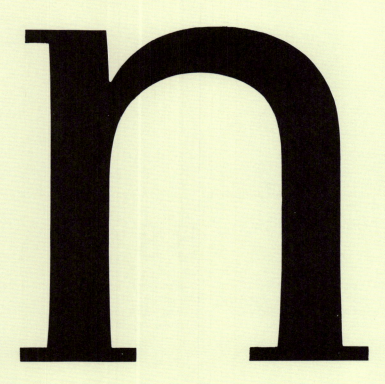

/02/
Extended typeface design with the working title 'Cooperline' – included in a 1993 letter to Linotype, in which Frutiger suggested it as a potential project.

Doch wie jenen erreicht, ringsum die Versammlung durchwandelnd, der das erwartete warf in einen Helm, den er hielt in der Hand und hinein warfs nahend der Herold.

/03/
The name of Goudy's inscriptional roman Copperplate Gothic *as well as its very short, fine endings derive from copperplate engraving.*

COPPERPLATE GOTHIC

/04/
Typeface design 'Serifen-Grotesk' from 1962 in three cuts – the inclined cut lacks the character of a real italic.

une pomme du monde
une pomme du monde
une pomme du monde

Type-design project
Gespannte Grotesk
1962

universite	*universite*	universite
universite	*universite*	universite
universite	***universite***	**universite**
universite	***universite***	

universite

/05/
Template of 'Gespannte Grotesk' from 1962 – the twelve cuts of this dynamic grotesque are ordered according to the Univers template.

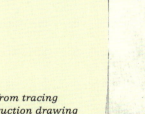
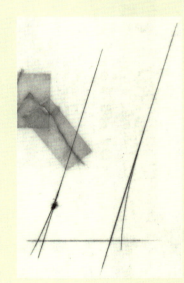

/06/
n-shape cut out from tracing paper and construction drawing of the pronounced ending of the inclined down stroke.

/07/
Pronounced endings and concave down strokes can be found in Clearface Gothic 1910, Colonia 1938, Optima 1958 and Post Marcato 1963.

/08/
According to Adrian Frutiger, 'Gespannte Grotesk' is not so much related to Optima (top) but rather to Syntax (bottom).

/09/
The cuts of the 1962 designs of 'Gespannte Grotesk' form the basis for the shapes of 'Serifen-Grotesk' (opposite page).

Clearface Gothic
Colonia
Optima
Post Marcato

du monde
du monde

une pomme du monde
une pomme du monde
une pomme du monde

When drawing the designs called *'Serifen-Grotesk'* and *'Gespannte Grotesk'* my aim was to get away from the hard design of *Univers* and to create some slightly more lively typefaces – a type of *Copperplate Gothic* /03/ with short, fine serifs as well as a softer grotesque. Both designs were created in 1962 and are based on the same basic shape; the down strokes are not straight but waisted, and the bowls end vertically. These typefaces embody the Willimann spirit and not the principles of Walter Käch as was the case with *Univers* – because drawing all down strokes straight and cutting off the rounded endings horizontally had always repelled me. It didn't conform to my innermost feeling for form.

The project *'Serifen-Grotesk'*, which I later called *'Cooperline'*, is firmly rooted in the world of aesthetics and technology. It is a hybrid, half antiqua and half grotesque – a typical product of the early 1960s. I'm glad it wasn't implemented because it lacks harmony. It looks loveless. The o is too dark, the stroke contrast isn't distinct enough /02/ and the e lacks a fine serif at the end of the curve. If you compare it to the designs of *'Serifen Grotesk'* /04/ and *'Schmale Méridien'* (see page 67), the lack of quality becomes obvious. It looks too arty with its waisted strokes and short serifs.

Just like *Univers*, *'Gespannte Grotesk'* is designed as an extended family. The concept included twelve cuts here: four weights in normal width with the respective italics, three condensed cuts and one expanded extra bold cut /05/.

The success of *Univers* had put me in a spin, it had made me slightly greedy. I wanted more of the same. I was only 30 years old and within five or six years I had had this success. From an inner, personal point of view it was difficult to get to grips with that. You think it's going to last forever, that it'll keep going on like this. With every new task I

The humane in the grotesque Adrian Frutiger's main concern is a humane typeface – this is also particularly true for the grotesques. With *Univers* he demonstrated a consideration for human optical perception through subtle differences in stroke contrast; with the 1962 design of *'Gespannte Grotesk'* he took that concept a clear step further by additionally using waisted down strokes /09/. He had already used this approach in 1954 with *Méridien*, his first typeface for text setting.

The best-known example of typefaces with waisted terminals is *Optima* /08/ by Hermann Zapf from 1958. In terms of approach, however, *Optima* is a sans-serif antiqua with distinct stroke contrast and additionally waisted stroke endings, and not a linear grotesque.

With the twelve cuts of *'Gespannte Grotesk'* Frutiger designed another large font family /05/ as he had done before with *Univers*. He developed this design of his own accord – there was no client brief or specified setting technology. Since he had opened his own studio at the beginning of 1961 he had to find sponsors for his design ideas in order to be able to realise them, which, at that time, was all but impossible at Deberny & Peignot.[3]

On the one hand, *'Gespannte Grotesk'* formed the basis for *'Serifen-Grotesk'*, also from 1961, with its short endings and a slightly less pronounced waisting /02/; on the other, there were several reworkings of the typeface, which Adrian Frutiger called a 'softer' grotesque, in the following thirty years.

Hamburgo Hamburgo
Hamburgo Hamburgo

/10/
1991 design of 'University' *for a multiple-master typeface – the bowl ending of the a is diagonal, the transitions from the stem to the bowl or shoulder in b g m r u are angular.*

/11/
Adrian Frutiger 1995 in his studio with designs for a waisted grotesque on the wall.

/12/
Shape comparison – e of 'Gespannte Grotesk' *(top left), a of* 'University' *(bottom left) and a trio of e a of* 'Primavera' *(right).*

/13/
Comparison of bowl or curve endings and transitions in the a and e of Univers 1957, Frutiger 1976 and Vectora 1990 (from left to right).

e eee eee
a aaa aaa

Although the designs look similar at first glance, they differ in quite essential aspects that contribute to their overall character. In terms of style, 'Gespannte Grotesk' belongs to the dynamic grotesques; the e and f feature flat bowl shapes – and therefore open counters – and the bowls end vertically. The shape of the counters, however, appears static because the transition from the stem to the bowl is round and the stress is vertical. Frutiger's second version from 1991, called 'University', /10/ is very different due to its diagonally cut bowl endings and the angular transition from the stem to the bowl. Here, its relationship to Vectora from 1990 becomes apparent (see page 352). A third version from 1993 with the working title 'Primavera' can be categorised as a static grotesque. The bowl shapes are round and closed, and the bowl endings are horizontal /14/ or, in one instance, diagonal /16/. The transitions from the stem to the bowl are here round again. It is interesting to look at the minuscule a in one of the three 'Primavera' versions, the projecting tail is atypical for Frutiger's typefaces /14/.
Surprisingly, Frutiger has never succeeded in realising his project of a softer grotesque,[4] although all his sans-serifs have been extremely successful and there would be room enough for another waisted linear grotesque in addition to Optima.

thought that something big might come of it. But when I look at proofs of 'Gespannte Grotesk' now, I realise that I used the 1960s to come to terms with that success, to get back to myself.

'Gespannte Grotesk' is more closely related to Syntax /08/ by Hans Eduard Meier, who was a student of Alfred Willimann's – like myself. It has less in common with Optima by Hermann Zapf. In the sample setting 'une pomme du monde' the regular cut looks quite good actually, but the italic version is a mess. The same is true for the italics of 'Serifen-Grotesk' /04/. The project wasn't implemented. But I couldn't quite let go of this humane form of a grotesque, even much later on I still couldn't.

At the beginning of the nineties I returned to the designs for 'universite' and showed it to Otmar Hoefer and Reinhard Haus from Linotype under the working title 'University'. Since this project was just a suggestion, I only used the word 'Hamburgo' as a sample setting /10/. Compared to the original designs, the letters were either expanded or condensed. I had drawn them in four cuts – as a basis for a computer-generated typeface family – because I had planned this project for the new multiple-master-programme. The sample settings represented the four cornerstones for all continuous interim steps – in the horizontal axis from expanded to condensed and in the vertical axis from thin to bold. In 1993, I tried again to place my designs with Linotype. First, a slightly revised serif version, the earlier mentioned 'Cooperline' /02/, and second, an altered sans version with the working name 'Primavera' /14/. Yet again I was unsuccessful with my suggestions. It simply wasn't meet to be.

/14/
Typeface design 'Primavera' *from 1993 with horizontal bowl endings compared to vertical ones in* 'Cooperline' *and* 'Gespannte Grotesk'.

Doch wie er jenen erreicht, ringsum die Versammlung durchwandelnd, der das bezeichnete warf in einen Helm, den er hielt in der Hand und hinein warfs nahend der Herold.

/15/
Design for a waisted grotesque – meant as part of an extended family including Linotype Centennial *(top), from the 1990s (no date).*

/16/
Typeface design (no date) with diagonal curve or bowl endings for a c e s and vertical ones for r; rounded transition from down stroke to bowl / curve.

Am Brunnen vor dem Tore da steht ein Lindenbaum, in seinem kühlen Schatten hatt' ich so manchen Traum.

Domverbau
Domverbau

Name of typeface	Client	Designer	Design | Release	Typesetting technology	Manufacturer	Weights
Algol	Éditions Hermann	Adrian Frutiger	1963 | 1963	Lumitype photosetting	– Deberny & Peignot	2

ALPHABET
ALGOL

I designed *Algol* for a single book.[1] It was about a new programming language. I suggested developing a new alphabet because this technical language was something special. At that time I was already working on the OCR typeface, but had heard about these things and had a pretty good idea of what we would have to deal with.

Usually you had to design 110 glyphs for one alphabet but for *Algol* there were fewer: capitals and lowercase letters, the numerals and a few mathematical symbols. There were no diacritics for different languages. The designs for *Algol* were done quickly. I sort of had my own technique: pasting lines instead of drawing them, or instead of creating many bowl shapes just drawing one and using the same one all over again. One of the draftsmen then implemented the designs. All that took three months at most including the manufacturing of the font disc. Two cuts of the typeface, thin and semibold, were created for Lumitype; the font disc was manufactured at Deberny & Peignot but the drawings were done in my studio. Initially I was thinking of setting the whole book in *Algol* but it soon turned out that it wasn't suitable as a typeface for reading. It was suitable for formulae that had to stand out from the text. The whole book was full of them, there were as many formulae as there was text **/01/**. A formula isn't read in the same way as a word, it is read symbol by symbol and the more clearly they differentiate themselves from each other the better.

In terms of style I wanted to change something mechanical into something logical; logical in the sense of unity of thought. I knew *Microgramma*[2] but *Algol* couldn't be a grotesque typeface – that would have been too naked, a formula has to hang together like a word. I also thought that a kind of *Egyptienne F* wouldn't be suitable either because that was a pure text typeface but I was looking for a very particular type of 'fantasy typeface'. After several trials I decided on these angular curves and slab serifs because they connect the formulae. I thought the angular and square-edged appearance was succinct and attractive. This interplay between the ends of the serifs and the angular curves was beneficial for the formulae. It should also be clearly recognisable when compared with other slab serif typefaces. The straight terminals for example with the a and t suited that too. I don't know how I arrived at these shapes; I had lots of ideas. There were loads of things flowing through my head and out of my pencil … Somehow I was 'feeling' the construction of the typeface, which is somewhat close to a mathematical problem, but to describe this feeling is actually quite difficult; I could have easily had little incisions at the top and bottom of the g but that would have looked too conservative, although I wanted to remain a bit classical.

Reductions were quite fashionable at the time. *Algol* was my personal fashion of deliberately leaving the normal classic play behind. That was quite characteristic for the time. To get away from the classical but remain legible. I would say that's actually the typical Swiss graphic design: this grid-like, cube-like appearance.

Typeface for a computer language   Only a few years after the development of *Univers*, which was a typeface for universal application in many languages and typesetting technologies, and which had met with general approval and international success, Frutiger drew a typeface for one single language.

'Algol', the abbreviation for 'algorithmic language', is the name for a family of programming languages that had been developed from 1958 onwards. Algol 60 was developed from 1958 to 1963: the '60' stands for the year of 'almost-completion', the final version was created in 1963. Algol 60 represents a milestone in the history of programming languages and served as a foundation for many subsequent languages such as Pascal, C, Ada and even Java.[3]

Shortly after the completion of the final version of Algol 60, the book *algol* was published in 1964 by Éditions Hermann in Paris, a publishing house specialising in scientific publications.[4] Adrian Frutiger had been working for Éditions Hermann[5] since 1956 when it was taken over by Pierre Berès. He mainly designed covers for existing books that were being republished. In 1957 Marcel Nebel, Frutiger's first co-worker, a graduate from the Basel School of Arts and Crafts, assisted him for half a year. Adrian Frutiger also directed the design work for the newly founded scientific magazine *sciences,* the four-volume monumental work *Art de France* and the paperback series *Miroirs de l'art* (see page 68).[6]

Exclusively for the design of the book *algol*, Adrian Frutiger developed the typeface of the same name, which was used for setting the mathematical formulae and comments. In addition to the 92 glyphs, which included capitals and lowercase letters, numerals and a few mathematical symbols, whole words such as 'valeur', 'Boolean' or 'alors' were produced **/02/**. Altogether, *Algol* thus comprises 116 glyphs.[7] The oft-used *Bodoni*, which was available on Lumitype early on, was selected for the text of the book *algol*. It was a revised version, called *Bodoni book C 504-55*, which had been adapted to the technical problems of phototypesetting and included its italic and bold cuts.

The production of *Algol* for Lumitype took three months from idea to phototypesetting the book.[8] This was considerably shorter than using traditional hot metal typesetting and also less costly, which made it possible to develop a typeface for a single book.

/01/
*Cover and interior page of
the publication* algol *by
Éditions Hermann, Paris 1964.*

/02/
*Some additional glyphs
including numerals,
mathematical symbols and
words.*

0|1|2|3|4|5|6|7|8| 9|
+|−|X|/|÷|↑
<|≤|=|≥|> ≠
≡|⊃|V|∧|¬
aller a|si|alors|sinon|pour|faire
remanent|Booleen|entier|reel|
tableau|aiguillage|procedure

debut C≔RAC2 (AXA+BXB);
    D ≔ ARCTAN (B/A);
    C ≔ LOG(C);
    si A < 0 **alors** D ≔ D + 3.1415927
fin;

Remarque : *Puisque* A *et* B *ont été indiqués dans la partie valeur, si les paramètres effectifs correspondants sont des expressions compliquées, celles-ci ne seront calculées qu'une fois.*

2. *Résolution d'une équation du deuxième degré :*

procedure EQUA2 (A,B,C, X1R, X1I, X2R, X2I, IMPOSS, INDET);
   valeur A,B,C; **reel** A,B,C, X1R, X1I, X2R, X2I;
   etiquette IMPOSS, INDET;
debut reel DELTA; **si** A ≠ 0 **alors aller a** NORMAL;
                    si B = 0 **alors aller a si** C ≠ 0 **alors**
                    IMPOSS **sinon** INDET;
  X1R ≔ X2R ≔ −C/B; **aller a** FORCAGE A ZERO;
  NORMAL: DELTA ≔ B↑2 − 4 X A X C;
                si DELTA > 0 **alors aller a** SOLUTION REELLE;
  COMPLEXE: X1R ≔ X2R ≔ X2R ≔ − B/2/A;
          X1I ≔ RAC2 (−DELTA) /2/A;
          X2I ≔ X1I; **aller a** FIN;
  SOLUTION REELLE: X1R ≔ (−B + (**si** B>0 **alors** −1 **sinon** 1) X RAC2 (DELTA))
                                      /2/A;
          X2R ≔ C/A/X1R;
  FORCAGE A ZERO: X1I ≔ X2I ≔ 0;
  FIN : **fin** EQUA2;

Remarque : *Si l'on n'avait pas mis A, B, C dans la partie valeur, les paramètres effectifs correspondants seraient recalculés chaque fois que ces lettres apparaissent dans le corps de la procédure.*

3. *Résolution numérique d'une équation :*
procedure BISSECTION (F) INITIAL: (X1, D1) PRECISION: (DO)
      RESULTATS : (XP, XL);
commentaire. Cette procedure determine les nombres XP et XL (dont la difference est inferieure a DO) qui encadrent un zero de la fonction F(X) a derivee positive. F(X) est calculee pour X1, X1+D1 et ainsi de suite pour des valeurs equidistantes de X jusqu'au passage du zero (ce passage est indique par B≔**vrai**). On utilise ensuite la methode de bissection. XP est la valeur finale et XL la valeur anterieure au passage par zero;

valeur DO; **reel** XL, XP, X1, D1, DO; **reel procedure** F;
debut Booleen A, B, C; **reel** X, D;
    A ≔ B ≔ **faux**; X ≔ X1; D ≔ D1;
    L : C ≔ (SIGNE (F(X)) = SIGNE (D));

82

ABCDEFGHIJKLMNO
PQRSTUVWXYZabcdef
ghijklmnopqrstuvwxyz

/03/
*The horizontal bowl shapes
without incisions and the
right-angled joints are typical
of the typeface* Algol.

Name of typeface	Designer	Design | Publication	Typesetting technology	Manufacturers	Weights
Serifa	Adrian Frutiger	1963 | 1967	Handsetting	– Bauersche Giesserei	2
			Photosetting	– D. Stempel AG | Linotype	9
				Compugraphic	10
			PostScript digital typesetting	– Adobe | Linotype	6
				Bitstream	9
				Elsner+Flake	8
				Scangraphic	8
				URW++	11

SERIFA

In the early 1960s I briefly had less work for my colleagues, so I asked André Gürtler in 1963 whether he'd like to do a study for an Egyptienne to complement *Univers,* but based on its style. The outcome consisted of eight weights with the name *'Champion'* /05/. Max Caflisch, type adviser to the Bauer type foundry, knew about the project. He had a lot of curiosity, and always wanted to know everything. One day he suggested my design to Bauer. Walter Greisner was managing director there at the time and he was looking for a modern slab serif typeface. Even though the art director, Konrad Friedrich Bauer, wasn't too keen on the typeface, a contract was drawn up. He named it *Serifa.*

It was no big deal for Charles Peignot that *Serifa* wasn't released by Deberny & Peignot. I was no longer employed by them (from 1960 to 1963 I was the outside art director there, while still doing my own studio work), and they weren't interested in new typefaces anymore; plus Charles Peignot was no longer there anyway. René-Paul Higonnet, son of René Higonnet, one of the two inventors of Photon-Lumitype, had taken over as director and kicked him out.[1]

Serifa was constructed like *Univers,* and I thought it would be similarly successful. I expected every new project to turn into something really big. Each time it was used I thought it would be really big. After the huge success of *Univers,* I found it difficult to readjust. This expressed itself in my being very restless, full of ideas and anxious to achieve even more. Working on *Serifa* was relatively easy; the *'Champion'* designs were already there. Of course, it wasn't a case of simply adding on serifs in order to achieve the aim of making an Egyptienne that corresponded to *Univers.* The whole typeface had to be rethought /09/. However, it was no epic task. *Serifa* was quite clearly a modern typeface.

I never compared it to any historical typefaces, but nevertheless it's possible that it was subconsciously influenced by existing slab serif faces. After all, the Egyptian style had been around since the early 19th century (see page 120). Compared to other slab serif faces such as *Rockwell* and *Memphis* /25/, *Serifa* was always something of an outcast child. It wasn't really comparable to those new, geometrically constructed slab serifs; and the older Egyptians like *Ionic* or *Clarendon* /23/ had a classical foundation.

So I drew the first weights of *Serifa,* light and semibold, for foundry type. There were moulds made for all sizes of these two alphabets, and a test was carried out /01/. The hot metal version was released in 1967, but by then the foundries were aware that their time was up. Some of them reoriented themselves, but the Bauer type foundry was liquidated in 1972. The foundry range was taken on by Wolfgang Hartmann, director of the Fundición Tipográfica Neufville[2] in Barcelona, who also oversaw the licensing of the Bauer fonts. Hartmann showed some interest in *Serifa.* He sold licences to companies that had already started photosetting, but he didn't produce any typefaces for photosetting himself. *Serifa*

Beginning of Serifa André Gürtler, who was employed as a lettering artist from 1959 to 1965 by Adrian Frutiger, worked out the range of weights for *Serifa* in 1963 /05/. When asked about the beginnings of the typeface he said that there "wasn't enough work around at the time, so Adrian gave me a word and told me we were going to make an Egyptienne. I went and transformed the word into a family. Regular, regular italic, semibold, bold, there were around eight weights of this word; it was sort of a way to pass the time. It interested him to see what could be done with an Egyptienne. Whilst working on that project – it was only a pre-project – the *Univers* shape crept in, which I went along with naturally."[3]
Adrian Frutiger offered the typeface to ATF[4], who were interested, but pulled out shortly before sealing the contract. *Serifa* was put on the shelf.[5] Max Caflisch, type advisor at the Bauer type foundry, drew managing director Walter Greisner's attention to the *'Champion'* family. Greisner was looking for a *Memphis*-style typeface with a modern feel.[6] Starting in 1966, the typeface was produced in two weights.[7] The reason that Konrad F. Bauer was not particularly enthusiastic about *Serifa* may be due to the fact that Bauersche already had two slab serifs in their range: *Volta,* a *Clarendon*-like typeface by Konrad F. Bauer and Walter Baum from 1957, and also *Beton,* created by Heinrich Jost in 1930 /25/.
D. Stempel AG had Frutiger adapt *Serifa* for photosetting. The light weight was renamed regular. It was shown in five weights – regular, italic, semibold, bold and semibold condensed – in an advertisement in *Typografische Monatsblätter* in 1977.[8] The typeface was expanded to nine weights with the addition of thin, thin italic, light and light italic.[9] In later years Linotype[10] dropped both thin weights and the semibold condensed weight for digital readaptation. Adobe sold *Serifa* in the same six weights, while Elsner+Flake and Scangraphic have the two thin weights in their range. URW++ have *Serifa* in thin, light, regular, semibold and bold upright weights, plus a unique stencil weight. Bitstream has it under its proper name in all nine original Stempel weights.

SerifaABCDEFGHIJK

Serifa ABCDEFGHIJKLM

Serifa ABCDEFGHIJKLMNO

Serifa ABCDEFGHIJKLMNOPQ

Serifa ABCDEFGHIJKLMNOPQRS

Serifa ABCDEFGHIJKLMNOPQRSTUVV

Serifa ABCDEFGHIJKLMNOPQRSTUVWXY

Serifa ABCDEFGHIJKLMNOPQRSTUVWXYZABCI

Serifa ABCDEFGHIJKLMNOPQRSTUVWXYZABCDEFGHI

Serifa ABCDEFGHIJKLMNOPQRSTUVWXYZABCDEFGHIJKLMN

Serifa ABCDEFGHIJKLMNOPQRSTUVWXYZABCDEFGHIJKLMNOP

Serifa ABCDEFGHIJKLMNOPQRSTUVWXYZABCDEFGHIJKLMNOPQRSTUVWX

Serifa ABCDEFGHIJKLMNOPQRSTUVWXYZABCDEFGHIJKLMNOPQRS

Serifa ABCDEFGHIJKLMNOPQRSTUVWXYZABCDEFGHIJKL

Serifa ABCDEFGHIJKLMNOPQRSTUVWXYZABCDEFGHI

Serifa ABCDEFGHIJKLMNOPQRSTUVWXYZABCI

Serifa ABCDEFGHIJKLMNOPQRSTUVWXY

Serifa ABCDEFGHIJKLMNOPQRSTUVV

Serifa ABCDEFGHIJKLMNOPQRS

Serifa ABCDEFGHIJKLMNOPQ

Serifa ABCDEFGHIJKLMNO

SerifaABCDEFGHIJK

Serifa ABCDEFGHIJKLM

Serifa ABCDEFGHIJKLMNO

Serifa ABCDEFGHIJKLMNOPQ

Serifa ABCDEFGHIJKLMNOPQRS

no no n nn

Design sketches for Serifa – pencil
on tracing paper, original size,
undated.

/03/
Study for Serifa in three widths –
pencil on tracing paper, mounted on
card, undated.

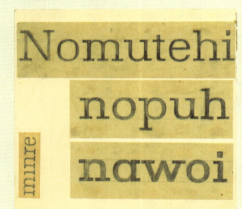

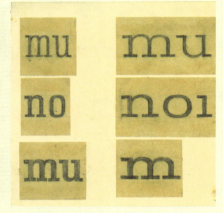

/04/
Design for Serifa – unlike the
design on the left, the a has the
roman shape and the arc is
open and dynamic.

nim
nomap

/05/
Overall concept of what was to
become Serifa – diagram with eight,
or nine, intended variants in five
weights and three widths.

Breit	Normal	Normal - Kursiv	Schmal
	champion		
champion	champion	*champion*	
	champion		champion
	champion		
champion			

Eine Schmal-magere
für Nachschlage-
werk-Satz wie
Adressbücher, Fahr-
plan etc. ?

Guter Kontrast.

Serifen
zu dick

Gross buchstaben versuch
(vielleicht nur Kersal gross für Advertising)

HEH Emon

HEH Emon

Gesamt plan für eine
neue Egyptienne Familie
Sommer 1963
At.

Serifa designs As usual, the first designs were made in pencil on tracing paper /02/ with an x-height of between 7.5 and 15 millimetres. And, as usual, several weights were designed. A study of what was to become *Serifa* shows three weights with three respective widths /03/. The lowercase italic a is noteworthy; it is like its counterpart in the geometrical *Memphis*. A later design shows the a with a roman shape, typical of Frutiger /04/. Here, too, one can recognise the search for the typeface's characteristic form and the dynamic shape of the a, similar to the 'Serifen-Grotesk' design from 1962 (see page 156). In *Serifa* /06/ however, the closing, static bow shape is given precedence, which is found in *Univers* and in the 'Champion' design /05/ from 1963.

The design encompasses eight weights, while a possible ninth is referred to. Apart from the two wide weights, the project appears to be based around earlier slab serif faces like the *Schadow Antiqua* typeface family by Georg Trump for the C.E. Weber type foundry /26/. This typeface also has four weights in regular width with just one oblique and a bold condensed version. The wide, ultra bold design of *Serifa* veers more towards the extra bold weight of *Rockwell*. However, the wide weights were never produced, although the sloped weights were developed by D. Stempel AG /30/.

was available for a handful of headline setting machines, but the transfer sheets sold better.[11] Seeing as I had a proper contract with Bauer, taken over by Hartmann, I still received royalties for 25 years.

After the first two hot metal cuts, it was extended to nine weights for photosetting /30/. Walter Greisner, who in the meantime had finished at Bauer and become managing director at D. Stempel AG, wanted a proper typeface family. He couldn't get anywhere with a mere two weights. So along with three further weights, italic versions were also made of the thin, light and regular weights. *Serifa* doesn't have a true italic, but rather an oblique, that is, it's slanted /10/. You can tell that by the way the serifs are placed, just like in the upright version. Plus, the cursive shapes of a and g, for example, look different in an italic. But watch out: a slanted typeface has to be reworked too. I would never have let the shapes simply be sloped. I redrew all the curves. If you tilt a round o like that, it becomes strangely oval. It needs correcting.

The skeleton of *Serifa* corresponds to *Univers*. I had two basic structures. They're like two lines running through me: one follows the *Univers* skeleton, where every letter has roughly the same width, while the other follows the more classical principle with differing letter widths. This shows the old dilemma between Walter Käch and Alfred Willimann. The pair of them had completely different concepts of type (see page 16). In any case, the classical skeleton is better than the one with consistent widths when it comes to reading flow. *Univers*, however, would have been unthinkable without a constant width skeleton, it was only the concept of systematic widths that made the many varieties possible. I guess there are two spirits inside me, and they've probably always been slightly in conflict.

/06/
Inner page of the six-page test sampler for Serifa *light and semibold by Bauersche Giesserei in 1967, with a text by Emil Ruder.*

/07/
Back page of the first Serifa *specimen with a text by typeface designer and typographer Hermann Zapf (title page see page 163).*

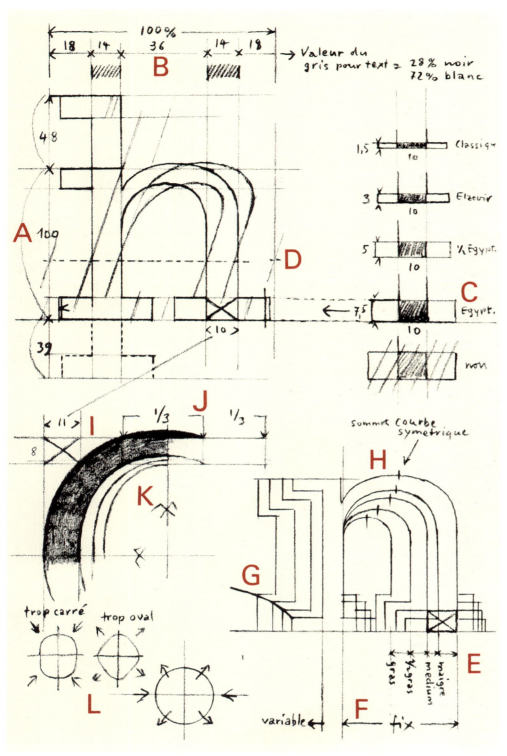

The German design magazine *Gebrauchsgraphik* from June 1968 includes some basic considerations by Adrian Frutiger regarding the design of text faces, illustrated with three sketch pages for *Serifa*, dated 3 September 1963 and 28 January 1964. These construction drafts were integrated into one illustration in Adrian Frutiger's 1980 book *Type Sign Symbol* and commented upon thus:

"There is relatively little room for play in the search for a new text face. The first movement towards a new type image is, in any case, not a spontaneous creative act (as, for example, in calligraphic exercises) but an intellectual process aimed at recognising the connections during the reading process. The typesetting technique envisaged and the requirements of the market must, accordingly, be included in the planning. These components make it possible for the type designer to reach new conclusions. The following basic considerations are included in a sketchbook for the design of the Egyptian face *Serifa*: A. Determination of the character height and the proportions of ascenders and descenders. – B. Proportioning of the black and white values of the basic design, together with the harmonisation of the total width with the character height. – C. The thickness of the horizontal strokes and serifs is the main factor for the definition of the type style. – D. The pivoting point and degree of slope of the italics are defined on the basis of the roman face. – E. Logical grading of the various styles. – F. The

/09/
Although similar in shape,
Serifa (top) has noticeably wider
proportions than Univers
(bottom).

Hamburg
Hamburg

/08/
Diagram depicting the form
principles for Serifa –
1979 reworking of the original
drawings from 1963/64.

/10/
Egyptienne F *(top) italic*
has a true italic form,
where as Serifa *(bottom) has*
an oblique form.

/11/
Unusual features for Frutiger are
the spur on the G and the offset leg
of lowercase k in Serifa *(bottom) –*
Egyptienne F *(top).*

/12/
Typical Frutiger features:
triangular K, Q with a horizontal
tail, R with a curved leg –
Egyptienne F *(top),* Serifa *(bottom).*

/13/
Unlike Egyptienne F *(top),*
Serifa *(bottom) does not have the*
characteristic ß and & shapes
of Adrian Frutiger.

agn *agn*
agn *agn*

Gk
Gk

KQR
KQR

ß &
ß &

stroke thicknesses in relation to counters and letter-spaces follow definite rules. – G. The length of the serifs does not follow the same criteria as those for the thickness of strokes. – H. The construction of the curve of the n provides the plan for a symmetrical construction of all other curves. – I. Convex and concave outlines of the curves are affected by matching with the basic plan. – J. The curves are higher than the straight lines. – K. The curves of the various weights are related in form. – L. The geometry of curves is the primary consideration for the determination of a style. *Serifa* is not built up from the perfect circle; it is slightly oval and only a little angular."[12]

In addition to the two publications referred to above, six points for typeface design are listed by means of six detailed illustrations of individual *Serifa* characters /14/: "1. Precise balancing of stroke thicknesses, horizontal and vertical. – 2. The serifs are not parallel but slightly tapered inwards. – 3. Displacements necessary for the achievement of good optical spacing. – 4. The inner angles are opened up where possible, to avoid filling-in of black. – 5. Incisions of standard depth are indispensable for good legibility. – 6. All curves are in harmonious accord."[13]

Serifa is very suitable for headline typesetting, but not for text composition. It doesn't flow properly, besides which it's too wide. It's much wider than *Univers* or *Egytienne*. I don't think I was entirely true to myself with *Serifa*. For instance, there's the G with its spur /11/, which has always been a thorn in my side, so why didn't I stop myself from using it? The legs of lowercase k are displaced /11/, which was necessary with *Serifa*, otherwise both serif connections at the bottom would have been much too acute. Nevertheless, it still pained me to displace the legs like that. I didn't do it with uppercase K /12/. Neither ß nor & is my style /13/; though in Germany my typical ß would never have been accepted. I did stay true to myself with uppercase R for example, where the freestanding leg is slightly curled. Even my special Q was accepted /12/, and the £ symbol is very much in my style /17/. The diaereses are interesting /18/. In the Bauer hot metal version the uppercase diaereses have the same cap height, they were incorporated into the letters: Ü on the inside, Ä and Ö on the outside. That was at the type founders' request; they didn't want any overshots. This was changed later for the photosetting version by Stempel / Linotype.

What I find really baffling with hindsight is the slightly curved diagonal stroke of the 7 /15/. I did the same thing later with *OCR-B*, for reasons of recognition, but I'm at a loss as to why I did it with *Serifa*. There are different designs for the dollar symbol. In an early pasted-up version of the reduced final artwork the S has a vertical stroke going through it /29/; this way the counters are very small and the character becomes too black. Later I just added a stroke above and below the S /17/, the Americans accepted the dollar symbol in this form straight away. Otherwise the salesmen would have complained about it, because it's an important symbol for them.

1

2

3

4

5

6

/14/
Details of the original Serifa *drawings with important optical principles for type design*

/15/
Straight diagonal stroke of the Egyptienne F 7, *increasing slightly in thickness towards the bottom (top); slight curve in* Serifa 7 *(bottom).*

/16/
Stymie (top) has varying widths, like the classical principle of proportion. Serifa *(bottom) has regularized widths.*

/17/
The sleek £ shape of the original foundry type Serifa *(top) has been retained in the digital version by Linotype (bottom), but the $ has been changed.*

/18/
Diaereses and ring accents are placed at cap height in Serifa *foundry type (top); in the Linotype digital version (bottom) they are above the capitals.*

Z7
Z7

ECHOS
ECHOS

£$
£$

/19/

*Renaissance slab serif
(dynamic style)
with high stroke contrast –
Joanna 1930.*

Joanna

/21/

*Baroque slab serifs with high
stroke contrast –* Century
Schoolbook *1917,* Excelsior *1931,*
Candida *1936.*

Schoolbook
Excelsior
Candida

/23/

*Neoclassical slab serifs
(static style) with high stroke
contrast –* Schadow *1937,*
Clarendon *1951,* Impressum *1963.*

Schadow
Clarendon
Impressum

/25/

*Geometric slab serifs
with low stroke contrast –*
Beton *1931,* Rockwell *1934,*
Memphis *1935.*

Beton
Rockwell
Memphis

/27/

*Static slab serif (derived from
neoclassical types) with low stroke
contrast –* Venus Egyptienne
before 1950, Serifa *1967.*

Venus Egyptienne
Serifa

/28/

*Dynamic slab serif
(derived from Renaissance types)
with low stroke contrast –*
PMN Caecilia *1990.*

PMN Caecilia

/20/

*The transitions from stem to
serif differ between concave and
angular, which is not synonymous
with right angled.*

/22/

As opposed to Memphis *(left),
both* Clarendon *(middle) and* Serifa
*(right) have a consistency of form
throughout the different weights.*

rrrr rrr rrrrr

/24/

*Basic forms of slab serifs – high
stroke contrast: renaissance, baroque,
neoclassical; low stroke contrast:
geometric, static, dynamic (l to r).*

/26/

Georg Trump's Schadow-Antiqua
*1937 introduced the era of
static Egyptians with its angular-
oval arc forms.*

ABCDEFGHIJKLMNO
PQRSTUVWXYZ
abcdefghijklmnopqrs
tuvwxyz1234567890

**ABCDEFGHIJKLMN
OPQRSTUVWXYZ
abcdefghijklmnopqrs
tuvwxy 1234567890**

ABCDEFGHIJKLMNOPQ
RSTUVWXYZ
abcdefghijklmnopqrstuvw
xyz1234567890

**ABCDEFGHIJKLMNO
PQRSTUVWXYZ
abcdefghijklmnopqrs
tuvwxy1234567890**

*ABCDEFGHIJKLMNO
PQRSTUVXYZ
abcdefghijklmnopqrstu
vwxyz1234567890*

**ABCDEFGHIJKLMNOPQRSTUVW
XYZ1234567890
abcdefghijklmnopqrstuvwxyz**

Slab serif typeface group Egyptienne, or slab serif, typefaces are characterised by their strong serifs. There is no rule to determine how thick serifs have to be in order to be classed as slab serifs.[14] This can lead to much confusion in type specimens and instruction texts.[15] As a guide, the regular weight should have a serif thickness which is at least 50 per cent of the stem width.

In order to do justice to the multitude of slab serifs, Hans Rudolf Bosshard in 1980 suggested dividing the group into subgroups.[16] He called the first subgroup Egyptienne and the second one Clarendon. Both have a historic basis (see page 120), but nevertheless this leads to confusion because on the one hand Egyptienne is commonly used to describe the main group, and on the other hand both terms are names of typefaces. This becomes particularly confusing when typefaces with the name 'Egyptienne', such as *Egyptienne F*, are classed in the Clarendon subgroup due to their stem to stem transitions being concave. Serif shape alone is not enough for a satisfactory classification.

A different approach is taken in the student's manual *Schriften erkennen*. Slab serif faces are placed in four subgroups: those derived from Renaissance or old style typefaces, newspaper faces and constructed faces.[17] Hans Peter Willberg published a reworked division into four groups in 2001 in *Wegweiser Schrift*; dynamic, static, geometric and decorative Egyptienne.[18] In this book we have chosen a division that makes the connecting and

separating characteristics visibly clear. The groups have a historical basis. However, they do not refer to the development of Egyptian faces.

Slab serif Renaissance faces /19/ are derived from Renaissance old style faces; their style is dynamic. Their uppercase letters have differentiated proportions, the curve of the e points to the letters that follow and the stress is diagonal /24/.

Neoclassical faces derived from classic old style faces are characterised by even proportions, an arc shape that closes in on itself and a vertical stress /23/. Baroque slab serifs /21/ have features of both groups. The clear stroke contrast is a common feature of all three of these groups. On the other hand, serif shape and angular or concave transitions from stem to serif are not taken into consideration /22/.

Slab serif faces with a low stroke contrast are divided into three further groups. One can distinguish geometric /25/ (based on circles) /24/ static with a vertical stress /27/ and dynamic with a slightly diagonal stress /28/. The latter were first produced in the 1980s in the Netherlands.[19]

Serifa is one of my worst attempts at a typeface, I think it's fair to say. Not because of the characters that were unusual for me, but because my idea of a constructivist slab serif face was wrong for the eye. I always wanted to make readable typefaces. And *Serifa* just isn't comfortable to read, it doesn't flow well enough because of its wide fit. One could use it for posters. *Serifa* is pretty meaningless and yet it endures. That's the tragic thing about typefaces, they stick around and always will. Once you design one you have to be able to stand by it. In the six-page article of the *Gebrauchsgraphik* trade magazine from June 1968 it said that at least *Serifa* was released at the right time, seeing as Egyptian faces were increasingly being used by graphic designers.[20] I only hope they used it properly.

/29/
Testing 'setability' was achieved by sticking together photographic reductions of the original drawings.

/30/
The Stempel/Linotype brochure *Schriften von Adrian Frutiger 1983* shows all nine Serifa *variants for photosetting.*

55235   35 thin/fein/extra-maigre 12   9 pt/3,50 mm

The basic character in a type design is deter mined by the uniform design characteristics of all letters in the alphabet. However, this al one does not determine the standard of the t ypeface and the quality of composition set wi th it. The appearance is something complex which forms it self out of many details, like for

56235   36 thin italic/kursiv fein/italique extra-maigre 12

Der Grundcharakter einer Schrift wird von ei nheitlichen Formmerkmalen aller Buchstabe n eines Alphabets bestimmt. Er allein besagt noch nichts über das Niveau einer Druckschr ift und die Qualität des Satzgefüges. Das Ersc heinungsbild ist etwas Komplexes, das sich a us vielen Einzelheiten, wie Form, Proportio

02235   45 ligth/leicht/maigre 12

L'aspect de chaque caractère d'imprimerie est une chose complexe, où forme mouveme nt et rythme, et donc aussi les proportions, le réglage des approches, etc., ne se laissent pl us dissocier. Dans tous les rapports formels et autres relations il s'agit de phénomènes o ptiques irréductibles aux règles mathémathi

11235   46 light italic/kursiv leicht/italique maigre 12

The basic character is a type design is deter mined by the uniform design characteristics of all letters in the alphabet. However, this al one does not determine the standard of the typeface and the quality of composition set with it. The appearance is something compl ex which forms itself out of many details, like

05235   55 roman/normal/romain 12

Der Grundcharakter einer Schrift wird v on einheitlichen Formmerkmalen aller Buchstaben eines Alphabets bestimmt. Er allein besagt noch nichts über das Niv eau einer Druckschrift und die Qualität des Satzgefüges. Das Erscheinungsbild ist etwas Komplexes das sich aus vielen

13235   56 italic/kursiv/italique 12

L'aspect de chaque caractère d'imprimer ie est une chose complexe, où forme mou vement et rythme et donc aussi les propo rtions, le réglage des approches, etc., ne se laissent plus dissocier. Dans tous les ra pports formels et autres relations il s'agit de phénomènes optiques irréductibles au

07235   65 bold/halbfett/demi-gras 12

The basic character in a type design is determined by the uniform design char acteristics of all letters in the alphabet. However, this alone does not determin e the standard of the typeface and the q uality of composition set with it.The ap pearance is something complex which

09235   75 black/fett/gras 12

Der Grundcharakter einer Schrift wir d von einheitlichen Formmerkmalen aller Buchstaben eines Alphabets bes timmt. Er allein besagt noch nichts ü ber das Niveau einer Druckschrift und die Qualität des Satzgefüges. Das Ers cheinungsbild ist etwas Komplexes d

24235   67 bold condensed/schmal halbf./étroit demi-gras 12

L'aspect de chaque caractère d'imprimerie est une chose complexe où forme mouvement et rythme, et donc aussi les proportions, le réglage des approche s, etc., ne se laissent plus dissocier. Dans tous les rapports formels et autres relations il s'agit de phé nomènes optiques irréductibles aux règles mathé matiques et que seule pourra percevoir et fixer la

Serifa was the last typeface to be included in the Bauersche Giesserei collection, and it was advertised intensely. In 1967 a six-page teaser appeared **/01/**. This depicted the light weight in thirteen point sizes from 6 to 48 pt and semibold in eight sizes from 12 to 48 pt. The 6 to 10 pt sizes were still in production. Some advertisements appeared, chiefly in the print magazine *Deutscher Drucker* in 1968. The modern character of *Serifa* is repeatedly alluded to, reinforced in part by a design inspired by *Univers*. Bruno Pfäffli, one of Adrian Frutiger's studio colleagues, designed the specimen and the advertisements. The ad with the repetitive sequence of the typeface name clearly demonstrates its typographic language **/32/**. Articles in the trade press also served to publicise the typeface, such as the exhaustive trilingual article 'Aus der Werkstatt einer Schriftgiesserei' ('From a type foundry's workshop') by Hans Kuh in *Gebrauchsgraphik* of June 1968.[21]

/31/
Characters of Serifa *light for foundry type by Bauersche Giesserei, Frankfurt.*

ABCDEFGHIJKLMN
OPQRSTUVWXYZ&
abcdefghijklmnopqrs
tuvwxyzß1234567890

Die Bauersche bringt Frutigers Serifa

/32/
Serifa *for foundry type – advertisement by Bauersche Giesserei in* Deutscher Drucker, *29 February 1968.*

BAUERSCHE GIESSEREI
FRANKFURT A·M
HAMBURGER ALLEE 45

Warum Serifa? Weil ein unentbehrlicher Schrifttypus hier seine reife, endgültige Prägung erhielt. Weil mit ihr sauber, kühn und klar vorgetragen wird, was ausgesagt werden soll. An ihr ist nichts zufällig oder austauschbar. Die Serifa steht fest auf ihren Füßen. Schwüngchen, Häkchen und unausgegorenes Beiwerk wird man nicht finden und ganz gewiß nicht vermissen. Aber ein reiches Spiel optischer Wirkung ist in ihren Formen lebendig.

/33/
Serifa *for foundry type – advertisement by Bauersche Giesserei in* Deutscher Drucker, *11 November 1968.*

Weil sie nicht der Befriedigung einer modischen Laune dient, weil sie nicht auf historische Vorlagen zurückgreift, weil sie in gründlicher und zeitgemäßer Auseinandersetzung mit der Form in Optik und Lesbarkeit die Serifen bewußt einsetzt: deshalb ist Adrian Frutigers Serifa

anders als die anderen

BAUERSCHE GIESSEREI 6 FRANKFURT AM MAIN 90 HAMBURGER ALLEE 45

/34/
Serifa *for foundry type – advertisement by Bauersche Giesserei in* Deutscher Drucker, *30 May 1968.*

Font production:
Adobe Font digitised by
Linotype

Font format:
PostScript Type 1

Also available:
TrueType
OpenType Std

Serifa®
Linotype – 6 weights
Bitstream – 9 weights

A B C D E F G H I J K L M N O P Q R S T U V W X Y Z &

a b c d e f g h i j k l m n o p q r s t u v w x y z ß 1 2 3 4 5 6 7 8 9 0

Pourquoi tan

t d'Alphabets dif

férents! Tous servent au m

ême but, mais aussi à exprimer la dive

rsité de l'homme. C'est cette même diversité que nous re trouvons dans les vins de Médoc. J'ai pu, un jour, relever soixante crus, tous de la même année. Il s'agissait certes de vins, mais tous étaient différents. Tout est dans la nua nce du bouquet. Il en est de même pour les caractères! *Si*

e fragen sich, warum es notwendig ist, so viele Schriften zur Verfügung zu ha ben. Sie dienen alle zum selben, aber machen die Vielfalt des Menschen aus. Diese Vielfalt ist wie beim Wein. Ich habe einmal eine Weinkarte studiert mi t sechzig Médoc-Weinen aus dem selben Jahr. Das ist ausnahmslos Wein, ab er doch nicht alles der gleiche Wein. Es hat eben gleichwohl Nuancen. So ist es auch mit der Schrift. *You may ask why so many different typefaces.* They a ll serve the same purpose but they express man's diversity. It is the same di

versity we find in wine. I once saw a list of Médoc wines featuring sixty different Médocs all of the same year. All of them were wines but each was different from the others. It's the nuances that are im portant. The same is true for typefaces. *Pourquoi tant d'Alphabets différents!* Tous servent au même but, mais aussi à exprimer la div ersité de l'homme. C'est cette même diversité que nous retrouvons dans les vins de Médoc. J'ai pu, un jour, relever soixante crus, tous de la même année. Il s'agissait certes de vins, mais tous étaient dif

férents. Tout est dans la nuance du bouqu et. Il en est de même pour les caractères! *Sie fragen sich, warum es notwendig ist, so viele Schriften zur Verfügung zu haben.* Sie dienen alle zum selben, aber machen die Vielfalt des Menschen aus. Diese Vielfalt i st wie beim Wein. Ich habe einmal eine W einkarte studiert mit sechzig Médoc-Wein en aus dem selben Jahr. Das ist ausnahm slos Wein, aber doch nicht alles der gleich

70 pt | −20   52 pt | −15   34 pt | −15   23 pt | −5   15 pt | 19 pt | 0   11 pt | 14 pt | 10   8 pt | 10.2 pt | 15   6.5 pt | 8 pt | 15

Å B Ç D È F G
H I J K L M Ñ
Ô P Q R Š T Ü
V W X Y Z &
Æ Œ ¥ $ £
1 2 3 4 5 6 7 8 9 0
å b ç d é f g h i j
k l m ñ ô p q r š
t ü v w x y z ß
fi fl æ œ ø ł ð
[. , : ; · ' / - – —]
(¿ ¡ " « ‹ › » " ! ?)
{ § ° % @ ‰ * † }

Thin – Bitstream

Å B Ç D È F G
H I J K L M Ñ
Ô P Q R Š T Ü
V W X Y Z &
Æ Œ ¥ $ £
1 2 3 4 5 6 7 8 9 0
å b ç d é f g h i j
k l m ñ ô p q r š
t ü v w x y z ß
fi fl æ œ ø ł ð
[. , : ; · ' / - – —]
(¿ ¡ " « ‹ › » " ! ?)
*{ § ° % @ ‰ * † }*

Thin Italic – Bitstream

Å B Ç D È F G
H I J K L M Ñ
Ô P Q R Š T Ü
V W X Y Z &
Æ Œ ¥ $ £ €
1 2 3 4 5 6 7 8 9 0
å b ç d é f g h i j
k l m ñ ô p q r š
t ü v w x y z ß
fi fl æ œ ø ł ð
[. , : ; · ' / - – —]
(¿ ¡ " « ‹ › » " ! ?)
{ § ° % @ ‰ * † }

45 Light

Å B Ç D È F G
H I J K L M Ñ
Ô P Q R Š T Ü
V W X Y Z &
Æ Œ ¥ $ £ €
1 2 3 4 5 6 7 8 9 0
å b ç d é f g h i j
k l m ñ ô p q r š
t ü v w x y z ß
fi fl æ œ ø ł ð
[. , : ; · ' / - – —]
(¿ ¡ " « ‹ › » " ! ?)
*{ § ° % @ ‰ * † }*

46 Light Italic

Å B Ç D È F G
H I J K L M Ñ
Ô P Q R Š T Ü
V W X Y Z &
Æ Œ ¥ $ £ €
1 2 3 4 5 6 7 8 9 0
å b ç d é f g h i j
k l m ñ ô p q r š
t ü v w x y z ß
fi fl æ œ ø ł ð
[. , : ; · ' / - – —]
(¿ ¡ " « ‹ › » " ! ?)
{ § ° % @ ‰ * † }

55 Roman

Å B Ç D È F G
H I J K L M Ñ
Ô P Q R Š T Ü
V W X Y Z &
Æ Œ ¥ $ £ €
1 2 3 4 5 6 7 8 9 0
å b ç d é f g h i j
k l m ñ ô p q r š
t ü v w x y z ß
fi fl æ œ ø ł ð
[. , : ; · ' / - – —]
(¿ ¡ " « ‹ › » " ! ?)
*{ § ° % @ ‰ * † }*

56 Italic

Typeface comparison   All three typefaces shown below belong to the slab serif (Egyptian) classification group. According to Hans Peter Willberg they should be placed in the 'static' subgroup. Their origins can be traced back to classic typefaces, noticeable by their vertical stress and even character widths.[22]

Schadow by Georg Trump is the oldest of the three typefaces. It has a strong stroke width contrast, and its serifs have angular transitions to the stem. *Venus Egyptienne*,[23] on the other hand, has curved transitions and barely has any stroke width contrast. *Serifa* has features of both typefaces. It has a very low stroke width contrast like *Venus Egyptienne*, and its serifs have angular stem transitions like *Schadow*. Its broad appearance looks altogether geometric, comparable to *Rockwell* or *Memphis*, putting it in danger of landing in the wrong classification group. Its even character widths, however, plainly demonstrate that it pertains to the static Egyptian typeface group.

The basic shape of the curves of the three typefaces can be seen in uppercase G. In *Serifa* its curves are slightly pulled into the corners, in accordance with Frutiger's basic design principle **/08/**. This is much more pronounced in *Schadow*. In contrast, *Venus Egyptienne* has a clearly defined oval shape.

/35/
Measurements of stroke widths and proportions of the Serifa regular weight.

Roman					
Hh = 10.00 cm	nh = 6.97 cm	oh = 7.28 cm	Hh : Hw = 1 : 0.79	nh : nw = 1 : 0.87
Hw = 7.91	nw = 6.10	ow = 7.38	Hw : Hs = 1 : 0.17	nw : ns = 1 : 0.20
Hs = 1.34	ns = 1.25	os = 1.36	Hs : Hq = 1 : 0.72	nh : oh = 1 : 1.04
Hq = 0.97	nq = 0.99	oq = 0.99		nw : ow = 1 : 1.21

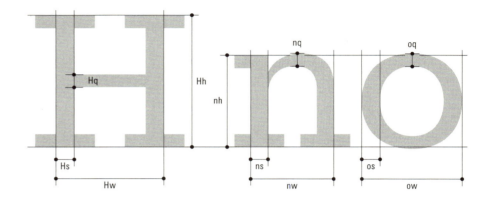

/36/
Serifa's *broad proportions and strong serifs create well-defined lines.*

Hofstainberg

Schadow
Georg Trump
1937

E G R ä g k m 2 5

Hofstainberg

Venus Egyptienne
Bauersche Giesserei / H. Berthold AG
before 1950

E G R ä g k m 2 5

Hofstainberg

Serifa
Adrian Frutiger
1967

E G R ä g k m 2 5

E	G	R	ä	g	k m	2	5
Middle horizontal stroke has terminal serif	Stem with spur, cross stroke optically symmetrical	Diagonal right leg, terminal semi-serif	Rectangular diaeresis, drop-shaped counter	Single loop shape, flat descender, with ear	Offset legs, symmetrical serifs	Terminal serif, straight diagonal stroke	Inclined vertical stroke

/37/

*Comparison showing the
different weights and angle of
the obliques.*

	Hh	Hw	Hs	Hq
Light	10.00 cm	7.42 = 0.94	0.85 = 0.63	0.66 = 0.68
Roman	10.00	7.91 = 1	1.34 = 1	0.97 = 1
Bold	10.00	8.53 = 1.08	2.11 = 1.57	1.44 = 1.48
Black	10.00	9.34 = 1.18	2.48 = 1.85	1.82 = 1.88
Italic	10.00	7.71 = 0.97	1.36 = 1.01	0.98 = 1.01

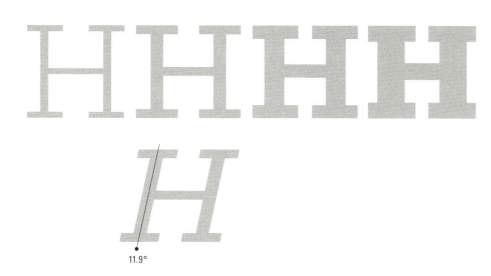

11.9°

/38/

*Height comparison showing the
differences of x-heights to
ascenders and descenders – the cap
height is the starting point.*

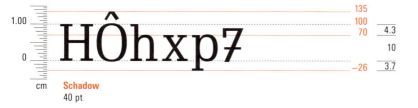

Schadow
40 pt

Serifa
43.7 pt

Venus Egyptienne
42.9 pt

ÅBÇDÈFG
HIJKLMÑ
ÔPQRŠTÜ
VWXYZ&
ÆŒ¥$£€
1234567890
åbçdéfghij
klmñôpqrš
tüvwxyzß
fiflæœøłð
[.,:;·'/-–—]
(¿¡"«‹›»"!?)
{§°%@‰*†}

65 Bold

**ÅBÇDÈFG
HIJKLMÑ
ÔPQRŠTÜ
VWXYZ&
ÆŒ¥$£€
1234567890
åbçdéfghij
klmñôpqrš
tüvwxyzß
fiflæœøłð
[.,:;·'/-–—]
(¿¡"«‹›»"!?)
{§°%@‰*†}**

75 Black

ÅBÇDÈFG
HIJKLMÑ
ÔPQRŠTÜ
VWXYZ&
ÆŒ¥$£
1234567890
åbçdéfghij
klmñôpqrš
tüvwxyzß
fiflæœøłð
[.,:;·'/-–—]
(¿¡"«‹›»"!?)
{§°%@‰*†}

Bold Condensed – Bitstream

" The skeleton of a letter is like a keyhole engraved on the reader's memory.
The letter that is read is the key that seeks and finds its lock. When the designer strays
too far from the base form, then you get friction, frustration or unreadability."
Adrian Frutiger

Production of type
OCR technology

OCR-B
Page 176

Documenta
Page 218

Thanks to special typefaces, Optical Character Recognition (OCR) machines for typesetting were able automatically to recognise text and encodings written by typewriters. These OCR machines transferred the scanned data offline (either on punched or magnetic tape) or online (via cable) to a computer downstream that set the text. The data were then prepared for further processing so that the desired text could be set using either hot metal or phototype.

OCR machines were preceded in the 1950s by mechanical document processing systems. These systems were needed to read payment forms, cheques, prescriptions, aeroplane tickets, pay slips, material receipts etc. However, the large quantity of documents to be processed outstripped the capacity of the mechanical systems and they were soon superseded by the OCR machines, which had a processing capacity of over 100 000 documents an hour.

In order to guarantee correct machine reading at high processing speeds, the producers of documents had to take into account a whole slew of factors regarding paper, ink, printing and design. To ensure this workflow, IBM, one of the pioneers in the field of plain text reading, set up a test lab. The quality of the symbols as well as the design and shape of forms were tested along with the composition of the paper and the spectral-isometric measurement of ink ratios. The human brain's flexibility in recognition cannot be fully matched by OCR machines. However, through standardisation (the extensive curtailing of differences between the glyphs of a particular class) and stylisation (choosing a character's form according to criteria of recognisability for OCR machines), this lower flexibility could be mitigated.

Machine-readable typefaces are placed in the optical and magnetic typeface classification group. *OCR-A* (DIN 66008) belongs to the first group, and is composed of only uppercase characters in addition to numbers and some special glyphs. The code is composed of 13 elements (10 vertical and 3 horizontal strokes arranged on a grid). Far less stylised is the later *OCR-B* /01/, designed by Adrian Frutiger in collaboration with European Computer Manufactures Association (ECMA). It is little different from the then-current typewriter and printing typefaces. The character set is composed of numbers, special characters and upper- and lowercase characters. In 1973 *OCR-B* was declared a worldwide standard in ISO 1073-2. Alongside *OCR-A* and *OCR-B* there are still a number of other optically readable typefaces, like *Farrington 12L/12F*. Within the group of magnetic typefaces, *CMC-7* (DIN 66007) and *E-13-B* are notable. Both are printed with ink containing iron oxide allowing the data to be captured by magnetic scanning heads.

/01/
This original drawing of OCR-B appears to be a book face.

/02/
After various tests and corrections the central line was derived from the shape of the book face.

/03/
The central line became the guideline for the engraving of the typewriter typeface with a constant stroke weight.

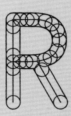

/04/
The measuring points placed on the central line and the outline served as reference points for the digitising of the typeface.

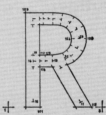

/05/
A 1974 machine for reading OCR-B typescript – the reading speed could reach 500 characters a second.

/06/
Coordinate table produced by measurements of the letter R of OCR-B – the five XY columns are for the three proportional variations.

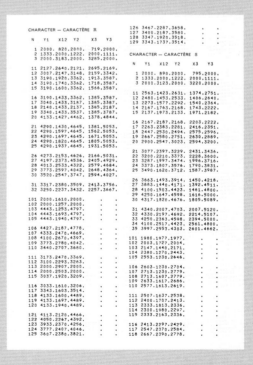

Name of typeface	Client	Designer	Design | Publication	Typesetting technology	Manufacturer	Weights
OCR-B	European Computer Manufacturers Association	Adrian Frutiger	Since 1963 | since 1965	Letterpress, Computer Composition, Typewriter Composition PostScript digital typesetting	– Several computer and typewriter manufacturers – Adobe | Linotype Bitstream Elsner+Flake	1

OCR-B

In 1961 thirteen computer and typewriter manufacturers founded the 'European Computer Manufacturers Association' – ECMA – based in Geneva.[1] The main objective for its founding members was the creation of an international standard for optical character recognition to be used, for instance, in payment transactions. But most of all they wanted to avoid the wider adoption of *OCR-A* /02/ – we used to call it 'robot type' – in Europe. It was one of the first machine-readable typefaces that came from the United States. For the European OCR manufacturers it was a given that the shape of its capitals would never be accepted over here, and they were intent on coming up with a European answer, *OCR-B*, that would be aesthetic and pleasant to the human eye. In 1963 I was approached by Robert Ranc, director of the École Estienne, and Gilbert Weill[2], an engineer from the R&D department at Compagnie des Machines Bull, asking me to develop *OCR-B*. In a first meeting they explained their goals: they wanted to suggest an international standard using a non-stylised form of the alphabet. The problem with this task was that all companies that were members of ECMA had developed their own readers and each of those worked in a different way; some read the counter, others the contours and yet others the centreline.

Over a space of five years we would meet up every three months at one of the companies' offices. First they had to agree on a common grid. Then, at one of the following meetings, they gave me a template and said the typeface would be read according to these points. The cells were only a few millimetres big and the system was considerably finer than the matrix of *OCR-A* with its 5 by 9 cells /03/. I would always draw curves in my designs. The engineers said that adjusting them to the grid wasn't the task of the designer, it was the task of the computer. In my studio we created hundreds of drawings, all filled in with black. The grid was only superimposed later for copying purposes, so that the manufacturers could read the character's mass precisely. If a cell was more than half full it counted as a plus, if it was less than half full it counted as a minus. Initially only horizontal steps were possible but later the cells could also be divided diagonally. The resulting computations were done by the computer firms. They looked after legibility and the typewriter manufacturers looked after the execution of the typeface. The characters had a consistent line weight and the most important thing was to determine the form-giving 'centreline'. It was needed for the milling of the typewriter face /01/.

Since I insisted, it was agreed to develop a differentiated 'letterpress font' for book printing in addition to the font with the consistent weight. Up until this point only numerals and capitals had been important but now we also had to deal with lower case characters. As far as the letterpress shapes were concerned, it was important that I built them up from the centreline. The shape of the type around it, the difference between fine and bold, didn't matter in technological terms. The discussion revolved around the question

Worldwide standardisation Since the beginning of the 20th century many countries have devised national standards – for electrical sockets or paper sizes, for example. Due to growing globalisation an increasing need emerged to make these national standards compatible with each other. This resulted in the foundation of the International Organisation for Standardisation – ISO in 1947.[3]

It is this organisation to which ECMA[4] submits its applications for the certification of worldwide standards. The increasing use of computers, which were being produced by a growing number of manufacturers to their own standards, created the need to standardise basic operating technologies for software applications. With the main objective of coordinating the different computer standards, three companies – Compagnie des Machines Bull, IBM World Trade Europe Corporation and International Computers and Tabulators Limited – initiated a meeting of all major European computer manufacturers that led to the foundation of ECMA in 1961, a private standards organisation for the standardisation of information and communication systems.

One of ECMA's projects dealt with automatic character recognition. Adrian Frutiger developed two versions of *OCR-B*: the first one featured constant stroke weight and round terminations. In the second, called *'Letterpress'*, the stroke weight was adapted according to optical criteria and the terminations were angular. Initially *OCR-B* was monospaced. Additionally the width of the glyphs varied, i.e. it was a proportional typeface.

Besides the drawing and manufacture of the typeface, the technology for reading and processing information was important. The computer manufacturers agreed on the 'system curve of merit' as a common basis for the differentiation of individual characters.

OCR-B, which was initially developed for typewriter setting, was swiftly adapted to other typesetting systems (for example Monotype in 1971)[5] and is still used in contemporary computerised technologies. Frutiger was one of the first designers worldwide who – with regards to machine-readable typefaces – dealt with questions of aesthetics in combination with technology. This led to his giving numerous talks on the subject, the first of which took place in 1967 in Paris at the ATypI conference. After a first recommendation by the ISO committee in 1966, *OCR-B* was declared a worldwide standard in 1973.

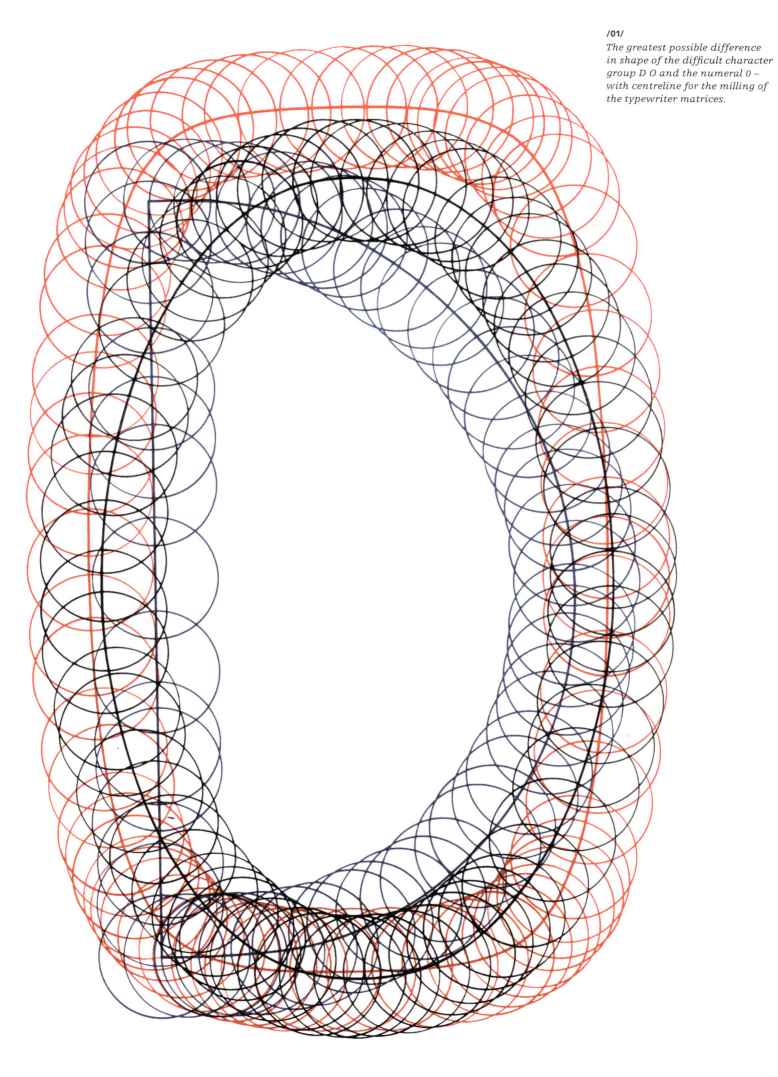

/01/
*The greatest possible difference
in shape of the difficult character
group D O and the numeral 0 –
with centreline for the milling of
the typewriter matrices.*

of what machine-readers would be able to read in the future: only typewriter faces or also typefaces for book work or even handwriting? The people responsible at the time understood that there were two different worlds: the simpler shapes of letters typed on a typewriter – that was the reality we were dealing with – and the more complicated typographic shapes in bookprinting. Back in the 1960s, being able to machine-read books was still a dream. But we all agreed that this would be ideal. There was a fountain of ideas, we were even talking about automatic translation. But even the most far-sighted engineers wouldn't have been able to predict desktop publishing.

In the meetings I would always hand out photocopies of the drawings produced in my studio to each participant. Each of them would then go off and do their own maths in their respective companies and come up with a different result. Initially it was just some impenetrable gobbledygook for me when the engineers were discussing all their paper computer print-outs full of numbers, but after a while I began to understand what they were talking about. I never interfered with the finer details of the engineers' work. If they came to the conclusion that part of a shape was too wide, too narrow, too high or too low, we would note the changes with a pencil on the drawings right there and then in the meeting. The translation into coordinates /20/ was carried out by the participating firms.

For the readers the distance between the characters was very important /16/, each character had to be clearly separated from the next one. The shapes had to be clearly distinguishable too /11/. To check this there was the so-called 'system curve of merit': each character was compared with every other in the computer by superimposing them two-by-two /10/ based on the centreline /08/.

Machine-readable typefaces Initially the shapes of OCR typefaces (optical character recognition) were solely determined by the reading technology of computers. They had to be simplified or stylised. The only criterion was that of correct recognition.

The numerals face E13B (MICR) of the American Bankers Association /04/ was part of the 'first generation' of stylised, machine-readable typefaces. It was based on a matrix of 7 by 10 cells. Another typeface for magnetic readers was CMC-7 (Caractères Magnétiques Codés) /04/, developed in 1961 by the French Compagnie des Machines Bull. Its numerals and capitals were each constructed using seven strokes of constant weight whereas the counters varied.

In 1961 a committee of the USA Standards Institute (USASI) agreed on the creation of OCR-A /02/ as a national standard for machine-readers. This typeface with its still extremely stylised shape based on a matrix of 5 by 9 cells /03/ belonged to the 'second generation'. OCR-A was preceded by fonts from different manufacturers, including Farrington, NCR (National Cash Register) and IBM /05/. Initially it only contained numerals, capitals and a few special characters but was later extended to include lowercase letters as well. Together with OCR-B it was recommended by ISO in 1966.

Like Adrian Frutiger's typeface, Farrington 12L/12F /07/ belonged to the 'third generation' featuring a look that was more pleasing to the human eye.

/02/
The standard character set of OCR-A *developed in the USA from 1961 onwards and given USASI standard status in 1966.*

ABCDEFGHIJKLMNOPQRSTUVWXYZ
ÄÖÜÆŒÅØÑ£$¢¥0123456789.,:;
!?-{}*&+='"/%∫Чн|

/03/
The computer-readable shape of the numeral 8 is based on a matrix of 5 by 9 cells in OCR-A, *and 14 by 19 cells in* OCR-B.

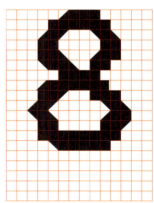

/04/
Stylised characters for the printing of banking forms with magnetic ink – E13B *(top) USA and Canada;* CMC-7 *(bottom) Europe.*

0123456789⑾⑿

0123456789
ABCDEFGH
IJKLMNOPQ
RSTUVWXYZ

/05/
Progenitors of the numerals in OCR-A: Farrington 12F1, RCA, NCR C6000, IBM X9A-120, Remington Rand NS-69-8, Burroughs B2A, GE 59A-04, Farrington 7BI.

1234567890
1234567890
1234567890
1234567890
1234567890
1234567890
1234567890
1234567890

/06/
Machine-readable numerals and capitals, based on a grid of 7 by 9 cells – manufacturer unknown.

0123456789
ABCDEFGHIJ
KLMNOPQRST
UVWXYZÆŒ⊞

/07/
Farrington 12L/12F Selfchek – *machine-readable character set by the credit card company Farrington Manufacturing Company.*

0123456789
ABCDEFGHIJKL
MNOPQRSTUVWX
YZ △ᎩΓ┐├┘
-+/.,$ ∎|
'():;&#?¶"=—

Character recognition The formal principle of *OCR-B* was based on the premise that each character must differ from another by at least 7 per cent in the worst possible case. To check this, two characters were superimposed in such a way that they covered each other optimally **/08/**. Additionally, this test was carried out using two different printing weights: a fine weight caused by weak pressure on the keys of the typewriter keyboard or through a lack of ink on the typewriter ribbon, as well as a fat, squashed weight caused by strong pressure on the keys or by bleeding ink. Even if the fine and fat weights were superimposed – the original weight could be fattened by a factor of up to 1.5 – the difference of 7 per cent still had to be guaranteed **/12/**. A test print demonstrates the principle **/10/**. It shows a vastly fattened N and a thin M, which the computer had to clearly identify as such based on the difference (shown in red). Generous character spacing was needed to guarantee correct processing **/31/**; serifs, on the other hand, were rather detrimental to performance since they increased the coverage ratio of the characters **/09/**. Furthermore, the paper should not be reflective and the type should not bear any stains.

There followed a period of rapid technological progress: by 1970 standard typewriter faces were machine-readable, as are books, newsprint and handwriting today.

While the width of each single character was the same for all manufacturers, the height would partly differ **/18/**. Following the demands of the bigger companies, we would eventually have three heights **/19/**, since it was cheaper to adapt the typeface than to change the production of the machines. It made no difference to us, we just had to do the work three times over. For one year we were practically fully occupied with the development of these matrices. André Gürtler was part of the team at the time and in 1964 Nicole Delamarre joined us as well. Of utmost importance was the difference between capitals and numerals. For a long time we experimented with identical heights but there would always be pairs that didn't work. The B-8 combination caused us some major headache: specifically, the machines that read the counter would never recognise the difference correctly. Eventually I came up with the idea to keep the numerals higher than the capitals – that was the solution **/23/**. Since the numerals were of correct proportions right from the start and thus formed the basis for the standard, all the capitals of the typeface were eventually scaled down.

For the typewriters all characters had to be of even width, these were monospaced faces. Therefore we had to draw a narrow m **/25/**. I staunchly refused to introduce any serifs if it wasn't absolutely necessary. But with i j and I we had no choice, because of the danger of them being confused **/15/**; the l got a curve at the bottom. That the D eventually turned out to be a bad shape might have been due to technical issues. In the first version it is very beautiful **/24/**, in the final one it seems to be narrower **/26/**. The C too turned out far too narrow in the end. With the K, the arm and tail don't come to an acute point on the stem. I've never done that anywhere else but there was no other option technically. If there had been a gap in the centreline, the reader would possibly have read the K as a stroke and a chevron.

/08/
All characters, here H and T, are compared according to their greatest overlapping area.

/09/
Serifs increase the similarity between characters and are therefore less suitable for machine-readers.

/10/
The computer printout shows the difference (in red) – it has to be at least 7% in order to clearly differentiate the fine M from the N.

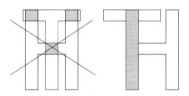

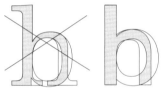

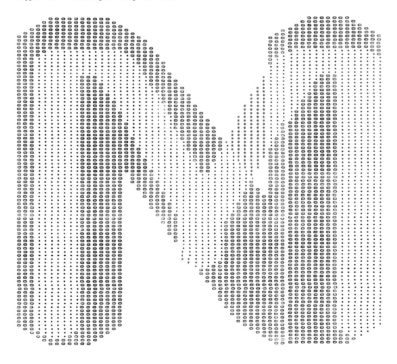

/11/
In the design, it is important to strive for the greatest possible differentiation whilst avoiding a stylised look.

/12/
The differentiation, and thus correct recognition, must still be guaranteed in the worst possible case where a character is fattened by a factor of 1.5.

/13/
B 8 & are difficult to differentiate for a machine-reader – very similar in Univers *(top) compared to* OCR-B *(bottom).*

/14/
With Univers *(top), the majuscules are wider and higher than the numerals; the opposite is true for* OCR-B *(bottom).*

/15/
Characters that are very similar in shape get a serif, horizontal bar or curved stroke in OCR-B *(bottom).*

/16/
In contrast to the letters and to Univers *(top), the numerals of* OCR-B *(bottom) feature dynamic curves.*

B8& CDOQ0 1Iijl!) 2359

B8& CDOQO 1Iijl!) 2359

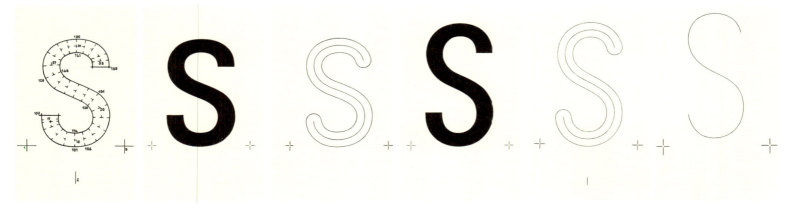

/17/
OCR-B 1965 – Size I: Reference point drawing, Letterpress version with stroke contrast and outlined skeleton letter shape with centreline.

/18/
OCR-B 1965 – Size II: Letterpress (angular) and linear version (round) with taller proportions – neither was developed further.

/19/
OCR-B 1965 – Size III: Centreline of the capital S in the linear version with even greater vertical scaling.

/20/
Cover and interior page of the ECMA manual from 1965 – the table lists the coordinates of the reference points for R and S in µm.

/21/
The numeral 1 leans slightly to the right – construction drawing of the 'Constant stroke width font' according to ECMA-11.

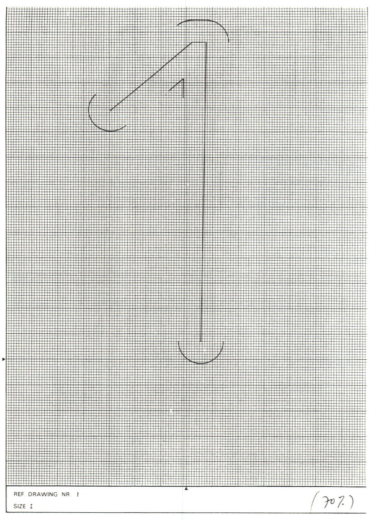

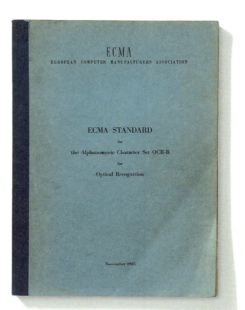

/22/
Correct character recognition of the skeleton line and contour in spite of interference caused by squashing or staining.

/23/
Comparison method – point resolution for data capture in black; final artwork and difference between B and 8 in colour.

24

First test version of OCR-B
*from 1963 with dynamic curved
strokes for b g q, alternative m and
similar shapes for capital O and
the numeral 0.*

Designing OCR-B   The first test version of *OCR-B* dates from 1963[6] and contained 109 characters **/24/**. The bowl shapes of the majuscules were static, while there are two types of bowl shapes in the minuscules: a round, static bowl, for instance in c d p, and a flat, dynamic one in b g q. All numerals had dynamic shapes but the curves varied: flat curves in 2 3, leaning towards the diagonal in 5 and clearly diagonal in 6 9. Initially Frutiger designed the majuscules so they were of the same height as the numerals, but for the first test version the former were scaled down to differentiate them more clearly.

The version published as Standard ECMA-11 in 1965 contained 112 characters including three additional letters with diacritics **/25/**. Some characters had undergone considerable correction. This is obvious with the W, whose outer diagonals became curved; with the numeral 0, which received a more oval shape to differentiate itself better from the capital O; with j, which now had a normally placed dot; as well as with the aforementioned b g q, which now featured static bowl shapes. The same was true for the $ sign. The @ had obviously changed, whereas the slight incline in the numeral 1 was hardly visible. Altogether the typeface now had a more consistent shape compared to the test version.

A further extension and correction phase took place from 1969 onwards **/26/**. Five more characters were added: the section mark §, the two Dutch ligatures IJ ij, the German esszett ß and the Japanese currency symbol ¥.

25

First published version of OCR-B
*from 1965 with curved diagonals for W,
greater difference between O and zero
and different crossing for 8.*

5.3   Sub-set 3 : Extended alphanumeric sub-set

This sub-set comprises 98 characters, in particular those of the ISO 7-bit coded character set (ISO 646:1991) :   /7/

| SPACE

5.4   Sub-set 4 : Options sub-set

This sub-set comprises 16 capital national letters, 16 small national letters, 11 diacritical signs and 4 further characters :

/8/

NOTE : The special forms of the national letters À Á Ñ Ö Ü å in this subset should not be used for new font implementations; see clause 7.3

OCR-B *from 1971 with horizontal bar
for j, curved descender for y,
very wide B, and altered shapes for
capital O, lower case o and zero.*

*Extension of the alphabet from
1994 with additional accents and
diacritics for several European
languages.*

The British pound sign £ was changed considerably. There were still problems in differentiating D O 0 and B 8 &. With the D, the curved stroke now started directly at the stem, the O was more oval; the zero, on the other hand, had become more angular. The Q was adapted in shape to the O and the tail of the Q was altered. The B now featured a markedly wider shape that resolved the conflict with the 8, whereas the ampersand & got a smaller lower bowl at the expense of the upper one. The j was changed yet again and, similar to the i, it now had a horizontal bar while the y received a curved descender. Additionally, with the Ü, the trema was changed slightly and so were the comma and the semicolon. Eventually all corrections – those that are listed here and others – were not beneficial in terms of shape; instead Frutiger had acknowledged the overarching goal of character recognition.

Even with the international standard ISO 1073/II in 1976 the *OCR-B* project had not yet come to a close. Instead the number of characters was successively extended. From 121 characters in 1976 the font grew to 147 by 1994 **/27/**. The additional characters were mainly due to the inclusion of special characters for different languages. Some character shapes of Linotype's digitised version of *OCR-B* are not identical to the ECMA original – there is more similarity in Berthold's, but only in the typewriter version **/33/**.[7]

The different national special characters were added successively **/27/**. Every now and again the secretary general of ECMA, Dara Hekimi, asked us whether we wanted to draw the ligatures for a particular country. These characters were no longer controlled by the whole ECMA committee, they were defined as either legible or illegible by the respective country. They were also no longer subject to that complicated comparison process. Special national characters were only available in the respective countries. The ij ligature for instance can only be found in Dutch machines. The French ligature œ was added in the nineties **/27/**. The æ however had been integrated earlier **/24/**, this ligature was important for the Nordic languages. In French, on the other hand, it wasn't seen as a mistake when ae and oe were separated. Contrary to today, œuvre without ligature was totally acceptable.

I've always slightly regretted that eventually only the numerals remained so open in their shapes **/13/**. The rest appears to be fairly *Univers*-like, among other things because of the horizontal termination, although the first drafts of the *OCR-B* actually looked quite different **/24/**. One could have given the C endings, the bottom of the g and also the S a vertical instead of a horizontal termination. This would certainly have been possible in terms of technology and recognition. Although I already had experimented with open letter shapes, as for example in the designs for '*Delta*' and '*Gespannte Grotesk*', I remained close to the *Univers*-style when designing *OCR-B*. The open shape was already there but I only became aware of its better legibility when I carried out the numerous legibility studies for the signage face *Roissy*. From that point onwards I felt the stroke endings of *Univers* were too closed. But when all's said and done, I'm pleased that at least the numerals of the *OCR-B* are useable because these are the characters that get used almost exclusively.

Le principal goulot d'étranglement dans la suite des opérations de traitement réside dans l'obligation de préparer manuellement, à partir de documents conçus pour l'homme (états imprimés, fiches, registres) des documents directement exploitables par la machine, tels que des cartes perforées. Depuis de nombreuses années, les constructeurs de matériel électronique s'efforcent de

Les origines exactes de l'alphabet restent indistinctes. Les caractères romains, qui sont à la base de notre alphabet actuel, s'apparentent aux caractères grecs lus, à l'origine, alternativement de droite à gauche et de gauche à droite.

/28/
OCR-B as a proportional font in the Letterpress version (top) and as a monospaced font in the constant-stroke version for typewriters (bottom).

/32/
In 1973 OCR-B was declared an international standard by the International Standards Organisation (ISO) and was subsequently updated.

/29/
The search for an unambiguous shape – the numeral zero (top) and the capital O (bottom) in comparison from 1963, 1965 and 1971.

000
000

/30/
The digital 'Letterpress' version by Linotype (left) and the digital 'constant-stroke' version by Berthold.

EK EK

/31/
A generous letter spacing is needed for machine-readable characters – the characters must not touch each other.

xylon

/33/
Slight incline of the 1 in the original (left) and in the digital version by Berthold (right), but not in Linotype's version (centre).

111

/34/
The numeral 6 appears to be wider in the diagonal in the digital version by Linotype (centre) – original (left), Berthold (right).

666

/35/
The digital version of the lower case c by Linotype (centre) is rounder than the original version from 1976 (left) and the Berthold version.

CCC

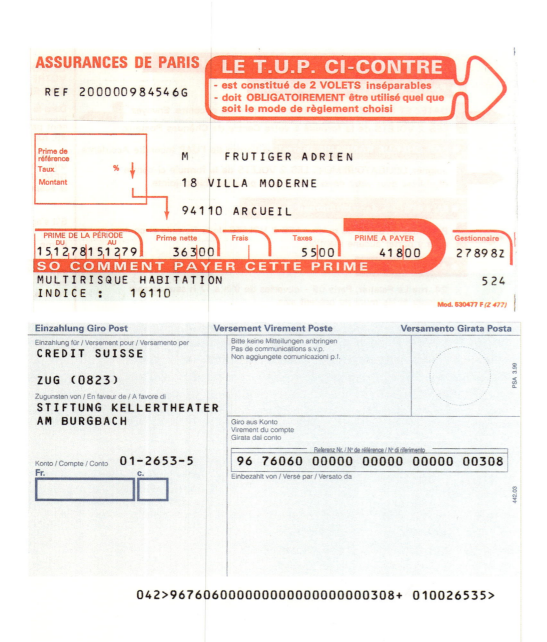

Applications Since the 1960s machine-readable typefaces have been used for data recognition and processing. They can be found on cheques, bank statements, postal forms and credit cards. They are, however, increasingly being replaced by typefaces for typewriters and newsprint or bookwork since those are now equally readable, and because data are no longer transferred via printed type, but stored on magnetic strips or chips. Adrian Frutiger's *OCR-B* can be found on paying-in forms in some countries, for instance in France and Switzerland, */36/* but in the latter case it has, for some years now, only been used in the encoding line. There are also three encoding lines printed on the back of Swiss ID cards */39/*. Furthermore, the barcode numbers on the price tags of consumer goods are often set in *OCR-B* */37/*.

A totally different application for Frutiger's typeface could be found – up until the 1980s – in text processing. For example the IBM golfball typewriter could read texts typed in *OCR-B* – so-called typoscripts – so they did not have to be phototypeset a second time at the printer's. But this application disappeared with the arrival of data exchange via floppy discs. *OCR-A* and *OCR-B* eventually found their fashionable expression in the graphic design of the 1990s where they were seen as techno, cool and trendy.

/37/
Barcode EAN-13 of a book with ISBN number and stock number set in OCR-B.

/36/
Use of OCR-B *in a French paying-in form from 1978 and a Swiss post office form from 1999.*

/38/
Adrian Frutiger giving a talk on OCR-B *in the Unesco building in Paris at the ATypI conference, 10 November 1967.*

/39/
Swiss Confederation ID card – with three encoding lines on the back in Adrian Frutiger's typeface OCR-B.

zu tauchen in diesen Schlund hinab.*PT.*PT.^-

Die haben wir heute nicht mehr, die Rittersmänner und Knappen.
Dafür haben wir einen Haufen mindestens so mutige Bürodamen
und Knäppinnen, wo¤¤sowie Büromänner und Büroknappen. Alle
müssen sie edelster Abstammung sein, bei dem Mut, den sie
tagtäglich beweisen, wenn sie mit dem Lift den Schlund hinauf-
tauchen, direkt dem modernen Drachenungeheuer<¤ <Computer<<
in den Rachen. Schaurig hallt es durch die geweihten Hallen,
wenn er allmorgendlich sein Opfer sucht. Die modernen Ungeheuer fressen ihre Opfer nicht gerade auf, nein nein, aber
sie verwandeln durch ihren papierenen, Zahlengespickten¤¤
zahlengespickten Output die Bpr¤¤Büromänner und Damen auf
eigenartige Weise. Plötzlich wird ein sonst so munterer und
freundlicher Knappe oder eine ebensolche Knäppin, den der
Drache in seinen Bann gezogen hat, so merkwüri¤dig. Mit irrem
Blick, unverständliches Zeug über die Lipöe¤¤Lippen flüsternd
oder rufend (je nach Stadium), wandeln sie durch die Gänge.
Meistens steuern sie, einem untrüglichen Instinkt folgend,
direkt auf des Ungeheuers Filiale, das Büro des <EDV-Knappen<<
zu. Mit papierenen Tatsachen, diese durch wort- j¤und gestein¤¤
gestenreiche Tiraden unterstützt, verlangen sie Abhilfe,
auf dass der <EDV-Knappe<<, schwächlich und untern¤ernährt
wie er ist, sofort mit stumpfem Schwert das Ungeheuer zur Räs-
on bringe.^-

Meistens wird die Wut des Drachen durch die falsche Fütterung

/40/
Original typescript in OCR-B; suitable
for OCR data capture – mistakes
like the one in line four are flagged
with deletion symbols.

/41/
Character register of OCR-B,
*reproduced using final artwork
by ECMA from 1976.*

ABCDEFGHIJKLMN
OPQRSTUVWXYZ&
abcdefghijklmnopqrs
tuvwxyzß1234567890

Typeface comparison   The three typefaces below demonstrate the progress in OCR technology. While with *OCR-A* the only decisive parameter concerning its design was simple machine-reading technology, *OCR-B* profits from a more sophisticated recognition technology, thus allowing for a shape that is closer to the optical criteria for human readability. Frutiger's *OCR-B* was the direct basis for *OCRBczyk* from 1994. It features a much finer visual character but still remains true to the aesthetics of the OCR typeface from the 1960s, although this is no longer necessary in technological terms; it is geared towards the zeitgeist.[8]

Both typefaces are so-called 'monospace' faces, while *OCRBczyk* is a proportional typeface. This particularly benefits the m, which no longer appears so squeezed. The difference in shape between *OCR-A* and *OCR-B* becomes obvious in the curved strokes. Whereas in *OCR-A* almost all curves are transformed into angles, they are rounded in *OCR-B* – if not always in a harmonious way. It is also interesting to look at the implementation of the tremata: in *OCR-A* the capitals are scaled down so that – together with the tremata – they conform to the cap height. With *OCR-B*, the cap height remains and the oblong tremata are positioned above the cap height. In the case of *OCRBczyk* the capitals are slightly scaled down and the tremata – here as horizontal rectangles – move above the cap height too.

/42/
*The aesthetics of the computer
typefaces from the 1960s still had
a following at the end of the
20th century.*

Hofstainberg

OCR-A
USA Bureau of Standards
1968

Hofstainberg

OCR-B
Adrian Frutiger
1971

Ä Consistent height of capitals, vertical trema

D The curve traces almost a semi-circle

W Slightly curved outer diagonals

e Sharply foreshortened finial

f Mathematically equal cross lengths on right and left side

g Flattened curved stroke

m Narrow shape

2 0 Open shape, varying round forms

Hofstainberg

OCRBczyk
Alexander Branczyk (Adrian Frutiger)
1994

Font production:
Adobe Font digitised by
Linotype

Font Format:
PostScript Type 1

Also available:
TrueType
OpenType Std

ABCDEFGHIJKLMN
OPQRSTUVWXYZ&
abcdefghijklmnopqrs
tuvwxyzß1234567890

Pourquoi tan
t d'Alphabets diff
érents! Tous servent au mê

me but, mais aussi à exprimer la divers

ité de l'homme. C'est cette même diversité que nous retro
uvons dans les vins de Médoc. J'ai pu, un jour, relever so
ixante crus, tous de la même année. Il s'agissait certes d
e vins, mais tous étaient différents. Tout est dans la nua
nce du bouquet. Il en est de même pour les caractères! Sie

fragen sich, warum es notwendig ist, so viele Schriften zur Verfügung zu haben. S
ie dienen alle zum selben, aber machen die Vielfalt des Menschen aus. Diese Vie
lfalt ist wie beim Wein. Ich habe einmal eine Weinkarte studiert mit sechzig Méd
oc-Weinen aus dem selben Jahr. Das ist ausnahmslos Wein, aber doch nicht alles
der gleiche Wein. Es hat eben gleichwohl Nuancen. So ist es auch mit der Schrift.
You may ask why so many different typefaces. They all serve the same purpose but
they express man's diversity. It is the same diversity we find in wine. I once sa

w a list of Médoc wines featuring sixty different Médocs all of the same
year. All of them were wines but each was different from the others. It's
the nuances that are important. The same is true for typefaces. Pourquo
i tant d'Alphabets différents! Tous servent au même but, mais aussi à ex
primer la diversité de l'homme. C'est cette même diversité que nous ret
rouvons dans les vins de Médoc. J'ai pu, un jour, relever soixante cru
s, tous de la même année. Il s'agis sait certes de vins, mais tous étaie
nt différents. Tout est dans la nuance du bouquet. Il en est de même nua

nce du bouquet. Il en est de même pour les
caractères! Sie fragen sich, warum es not
wendig ist, so viele Schriften zur Verfü
gung zu haben. Sie dienen alle zum selben,
aber machen die Vielfalt des Menschen au
s. Diese Vielfalt ist wie beim Wein. Ich h
abe einmal eine Weinkarte studiert mit se
chzig Médoc-Weinen aus dem selben Jahr.
Das ist ausnahmslos Wein, aber doch nicht
alles der gleiche Wein. Es hat eben gleich

ÅBCDEFG
HIJKLMÑ
OPQRSTÜ
VWXYZ&
Æ ¥$£€
1234567890
åbcdefghij
klmnopqrs
tuvwxyzß
æ ø
[.,:;.'/-]
(" "!?)
{§ %@ *†}

Regular

ÅBÇDÈFG
HIJKLMÑ
ÔPQRŠTÜ
VWXYZ&
ÆŒ¥$£€
1234567890
åbçdéfghij
klmñôpqrš
tüvwxyzß
fifl æœøłð
[.,:;.'/-—]
(¿¡"‹‹ ‹ ›››"!?)
{§°%@‰*†}

Alternate

68 pt | −210   50 pt | −210   34 pt | −210   22 pt | −190   15 pt | 19 pt | −180   10 pt | 13 pt | −160   7.2 pt | 10 pt | −155   5.8 pt | 7.8 pt | −115

OCR-B   **187**

" The great stroke of luck in my life is to have been blessed
  first with an artistic feeling for shapes,
  and second with an easy grasp of technical processes and of mathematics."
  Adrian Frutiger

Production of type
Strike-on composition

From 1887 on there were several attempts to use typewriters as composing machines. Some of the machines created between 1920 and 1940 were the Typary, the Orotype machine and the Varityper. The Varityper, based on the Hammond typewriter, was manufactured by the Frederick Hepburn Company. In 1947 it incorporated differentially spaced characters. In the 1940s the International Business Machines company (IBM) joined the field as it began manufacturing typewriters with typesetting capabilities. Their machines had four proportional typeface widths; and were capable of typing left- or right-aligned text with ragged margins or fully-justified text (achieved by spacing out words on a line). Typewriter setting gradually took over areas previously served by small-run offset printing (e.g. press releases, brochures, or circulars).

IBM was the leader in this field. In 1966 the company launched a much-improved desktop typesetter, the IBM Magnetic Tape Selectric Composer /03/, as well as the IBM Composer System /05/, with the golf-ball typehead (which the company had developed in 1961) /04/. The 9-unit proportional system bridged the gap between a traditional typewriter with a single, monospaced font and the higher-quality systems used in photosetting and hot-metal typesetting that had 18 or more units. However, only seven of the Composer's nine units were usable (units 3 to 9) compared to the 13 (of 18) usable character widths in hot metal and photosetting. Consequently, line composition suffered due to the absence of fine typographic adjustments.

A further limitation was the narrow range of point sizes. Typefaces for the Composer were available only in sizes between 6 and 12 pt. Headlines could be produced either by user other typesetting technologies, or by subsequent enlargement with a repro camera. An advantage of the golfball machines over traditional typewriters was that the typeface could be changed quickly by switching out the golfball. At first, five typefaces were available, but more were continually added.

The typed text was used in one of two ways: either it was saved for further processing on punched-paper or magnetic tape, or it was output as readable text, printed on barite paper or on a special film. Barite paper could be used as a starting point in repro for offset printing. The film could, according to its particular specification, take 10 000 to 30 000 direct copies, and was used for less typographically demanding printing.

When drawing typefaces for the Composer, one needed to remember that the fixed character width in each typeface had to be adopted. Consequently, a g remained 5 units wide, no matter if it formed part of *Press Roman* (i.e. *Times New Roman*) or *Univers*. Likewise, the number of characters per unit was also fixed, which presented a special problem for the adaptation of non-latin typefaces. Following the rapid acceptance of personal computers starting in the mid-1980s, the Composer's prominence began to wane. The last iteration – the IBM Personal Selectric – was introduced in 1983.

/01/
The type cylinder from the 1895 Blickensderfer No. 5 typewriter already presages the later golfball.

/02/
The 1961 IBM Selectric was the first electric golfball typewriter from the company. The golfball allowed the typeface to be changed.

/03/
The IBM-72 Composer was able to cheaply produce repro-ready text in small and medium point sizes.

/05/
The IBM Magnetic Tape Selectric Composer allowed the simultaneous recording of keystrokes on tape as the operator typed.

/04/
Detail of the mechanism of a golfball typewriter – the golfball easily permits the typeface to be swapped out.

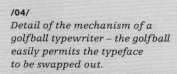

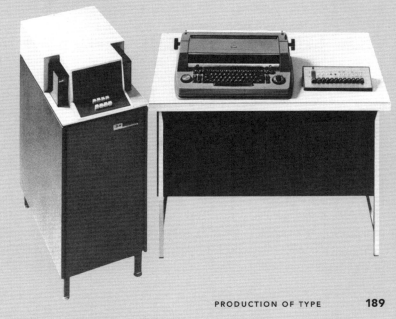

Name of typeface	Client	Designer	Design | Publication	Typesetting technology	Manufacturer	Weights
Univers	International Business Machines IBM	Adrian Frutiger	1964 | 1966	Typewriter	– International Business Machines IBM	8

Univers

IBM Composer

In 1964 a representative of the European headquarters of IBM appeared at my studio and asked me to cooperate in the design of a typeface for a machine, the name of which was still being kept secret. First of all I had to sign a non-disclosure agreement (NDA). Then he pulled out another sheet of paper and asked: do you know this typeface? That was pretty easy for me, it was *Times.* Fritz Kern then explained to me that *Univers* had also been selected for their new golfball typewriter. Two weeks later the contract was signed and I was invited over to the factory in Lexington (Kentucky), where the typewriters were manufactured. When I arrived there I was presented with yet another NDA. Stanley Morison, who was in Lexington before me, hadn't signed this paper. If they didn't trust him, he didn't want to see anything, he's quoted as saying. So they took him straight back to the airport without showing him anything. I had no problem with the NDA and so I signed. Then a golfball was brought in /01/ and a secretary typed something on a big, wide typewriter. They gave me the completed sheet of paper. It was *Times* all right. To see a typed *Times* instead of the usual monospaced faces for typewriters was like a miracle to me, simply extraordinary. During the course of the day I was given a tour of the factory where they showed me everything in a very detailed way including the golfball made of nickel-plated plastic – a miracle of mechanical engineering, which was very difficult to manufacture.

There was a bit of a problem with the copyrights for the typefaces. For *Times,* the IBM guys didn't have a licence from Monotype, so it appeared under the name *Press* /02/. Concerning *Bodoni,* they said it was a reproduction by IBM based on the original by Giambattista Bodoni. *Pyramid*[1] was introduced as IBM's egyptienne version and *Aldine* was an adaptation of Monotype's *Bembo.* But with *Univers* /04/ my name was registered. Its rights lay with Deberny & Peignot, and I recall very clearly the deal that was struck with René-Paul Higonnet, the new director. I already knew about the IBM project but wasn't allowed to say anything. The young Higonnet wanted to give a licence for *Univers* to the English company Matrotype, a company that – just like Sofratype in France – produced matrices for typesetting machines. I took advantage of the situation and suggested that I would waive my licensing fees for the Matrotype *Univers* if he in turn would grant me the right to use *Univers* for a machine by IBM that was still under wraps. And that's what we did.

My task was to adapt *Univers* to the new IBM Composer technology, which had nine units. That's half of the 18 Monotype units, I thought immediately. The advantage compared to Monotype was that there were no limits concerning the number of letters per unit. But the biggest problem was that each letter of the alphabet was given a fixed unit, no matter which typeface was used /06/. They had used *Times* as the basis, and texts that were typed using a classic typeface didn't look like they were done on a typewriter – they printed well. With egyptienne and grotesque typefaces, i.e. with all other styles, however, there was a

Cooperation with IBM Adrian Frutiger and IBM had cooperated even before his reworking of *Univers* for the Composer. As a member of ECMA[2], IBM had adopted Frutiger's machine-readable typeface *OCR-B* (developed from 1963 onwards) for its typewriters (see page 176). This project was, however, managed by another department of the company and had no influence on subsequent projects.

A milestone on the way to the Composer typesetting machine was the 1961 development of the electric 'golfball' typewriter, which would supplant the traditional typewriter with typebars. Three years later it was fitted with magnetic tape for the memory unit. Eventually in 1966, after seven years of development, IBM introduced the Selectric Composer and the Magnetic Tape Selectric Composer. These typesetting machines allowed for setting text with ragged margins flush left or right, centred or justified.[3] While IBM targeted the office market with its golfball typewriters, the Composer was aimed at small-format offset printing shops that would accept a reduction in printing quality in favour of a quick and low-cost production process.

Max Caflisch, a Swiss typographer and typography expert, who was also working as a typography consultant to IBM World Trade in New York and Lexington (Kentucky), was instrumental in the selection of typefaces for the Composer. One typeface each was picked from the five classification groups renaissance, transitional, neoclassical, slab serif and sans serif /02/.[4] In 1964 it was decided to use *Univers* as the sans serif face.

Adrian Frutiger was asked to carry out the reworking of *Univers* himself. His studio was also commissioned to adapt non-Latin alphabets such as Greek, Cyrillic /13/, Arabic, Hebrew and Thai for the golfball, which Frutiger regarded as an extremely difficult task. For this job, he was even given a one-day private seminar in Thai.[5] Frutiger was also charged with training employees in Lexington and at the French factory in Orléans. Additionally, he gave talks on type design and manufacturing, aesthetics and proportion as well as on the history of typography and printing for IBM employees around the world.[6]

Adrian Frutiger worked for IBM until 1981, in particular in the USA, France and Germany.[7]

/01/
'Golfballs' made of nickel-plated plastic (about 32 mm in diameter) showing different languages in monospace or proportional fonts.

problem. Let's take the s for instance: in *Times* it's relatively narrow, but in a grotesque like *Univers* it's wide /09/. And that's exactly where it started to get difficult. The *Univers* s should have had five instead of the allocated four units. The g is too narrow as well. The classic g has a narrow form but the grotesque g has a wide one, just like a d or q. The crippled g is a typical characteristic of the Composer-*Univers* /03/. But it was worse with the F and T. You can clearly see the big gaps. The condensed *Univers* looks a lot better than the regular cut because it was overall closer to an antiqua /04/. For the IBM Composer a humanistic grotesque in the style of Sofratype's *Concorde* (see page 150) would have been better, actually. But IBM wanted *Univers* and at that time *Concorde* only existed in my and André Gürtler's heads. I only discovered the qualities of that typeface later.

In order to get a better idea about the problem of units I eventually conducted a study into this issue on my own. I compared the classic Lumitype and Monotype faces with each other /07/ and calculated the average values for individual letters. On the basis of these calculations I defined seven different glyph widths /08/. I put all that down in writing to get a better idea myself but also to explain to the experts what the problem was. This was acknowledged at IBM but it was impossible to change anything. The whole machine would have had to be rebuilt. Another problem was that not all letters were printed using the same force of impact. Although the spring system would allow for three different impact levels, some letters were simply too fine /11/. We drew these letters a bit fatter. Furthermore, the impact of the golfball would not hit the right position with all letters. The s, for instance, which had the longest way to go until it reached the paper, was always a bit off-centre and stuck to the following letter /04/. I suggested slightly moving letters with that kind of

Typesetting and typeface quality When compared to traditional constant-width typewriter faces, IBM's typewriter faces with their nine units and seven glyph widths respectively represented a substantial improvement.[8] But in relation to print and compared to *Univers* for phototypesetting with its 36 units for the Lumitype and 18 for the Monophoto, this represented another massive loss in quality. Adrian Frutiger accepted this challenge in full knowledge of the fact that he would not be able to meet the demands for a mature typesetting face with his adaptation for the IBM Composer. IBM, however, deliberately used the comparison with existing typesetting technologies in their brochures: "On the one hand: hot metal setting and phototypesetting with high print quality and offering all typographic possibilities – but often inefficient, for example in small-format offset printing. On the other hand: typewriter setting, quick and cost-effective but with limited print quality, and often insufficient for high typographic demands. This situation has now changed. Here is a new typesetting machine: the IBM Magnetic Tape Composer. It fills the gap between hot metal and typewriter setting. It unites many of the benefits of these technologies but stays clear of their disadvantages. We incorporated all those elements from typewriter setting that facilitate usage and lower costs and all those of hot metal and phototypesetting that enable the selection of beautiful typefaces and typographic options."[9]

/02/

The first typefaces, including Univers, *implemented for the IBM Composer: (from top to bottom)* Press (Times), Aldine (Bembo), Bodoni, Pyramid.

ABCDEFGHIJKLMNOPQRSTUVWXYZ
abcdefghijklmnopqrstuvwxyz
1234567890$.,-'':;!?*½¼¾–()[]=†/+%&@
Press Roman is a unique type face highlighting both appearance and fine legibility. Characteristically, Press Roman has no pronounced thick and thin strokes as are found frequently in other type faces. The short ascenders and descenders help to create a large lower

ABCDEFGHIJKLMNOPQRSTUVWXYZ
abcdefghijklmnopqrstuvwxyz
1234567890$.,-'':;!?*½¼¾–()[]=†/+%&@
Aldine Roman has a delicate beauty of letter which makes it an outstanding face. Throughout its general design, there is a harmonious balance between thin and thick strokes. This face is especially characterized by ascending and descending letters which are finely

ABCDEFGHIJKLMNOPQRSTUVWXYZ
abcdefghijklmnopqrstuvwxyz
1234567890$.,-'':;!?*½¼¾–()[]=†/+%&@
Bodoni Book is an upright, well delineated type face. It is especially characterized by distinctly contrasting thick and thin strokes. Its serifs are also distinctive, with a perfectly flat line. The strong vertical accent in the construction of each letter marks it clearly as a

ABCDEFGHIJKLMNOPQRSTUVWXYZ
abcdefghijklmnopqrstuvwxyz
1234567890$.,-'':;!?*½¼¾–()[]=†/+%&@
Pyramid is a uniquely designed face featuring a square serif. Because of its outstanding ability to hold the reader's attention, it lends itself particularly well to material requiring special emphasis. Although it often is used for subheads in printed material, it can also be

/03/

A golfball contains 88 symbols with varying key configurations – American (top), German (bottom).

ABCDEFGHIJKLMNOPQRSTUVWXYZ
abcdefghijklmnopqrstuvwxyz
1234567890$.,-'':;!?*½¼¾–()[]=†/+%&@

ABCDEFGHIJKLMNOPQRSTUVWXYZÄÖÜ
abcdefghijklmnopqrstuvwxyzäöüß
1234567890.,-'':;!? =+§%/&*()–

/04/

The regular cut of Univers IBM *in 10pt (top) and the condensed cut in 11pt (bottom) feature the same line length.*

This example of Univers, a precisely defined sans-serif type face, was created by Adrian Frutiger for the IBM "Selectric" Composer. It has an elegant simplicity of style, giving a clean, clear type impression. Univers is a firm type face without typographical eccentricities.

This example of Univers, a precisely defined sans-serif type face, was created by Adrian Frutiger for the IBM "Selectric" Composer. It has an elegant simplicity of style, giving a clean, clear type impression. Univers is a strong type face, minus typographical eccentricities.

/05/

In order to guarantee a harmonious text image in the various sizes and weights, the force of impact is altered.

This example of Univers, a precisely defined sans-serif face, was created by Adrian Frutiger for the IBM "Selectric" Composer. It has an elegant simplicity of style, giving a clean,

This example of Univers, a precisely defined sans-serif face, was created by Adrian Frutiger for the IBM "Selectric" Composer. Univers is

/06/

Widths table of the IBM Composer with 9 units and 7 widths respectively – UVXqux *are missing, as are all numerals.*

3	4	5	6	7	8	9
i ;	I (	J	P y	B	A Y	M
j '	f)	a	S *	C	D w	W
l '	r !	c	b †	E	G ¾	m
. -	s /	e	d $	F	H ½	
,	t	g	h +	L	K &	
	:	v	k =	T	N %	
		z	n]	Z	O @	
		?	o ›		Q ¼	
		[	p ;		R –	

As far as printing quality was concerned, typewriter setting could not compete with hand or phototypesetting. The text – especially in *Univers* – appeared messy due to letter combinations that either looked lumpy or exhibited gaps. The counters were not always harmonious either. The P for instance featured a distinctly smaller counter than the R; the g was clearly too small as well and the y, on the other hand, appeared too open /03/.

Given that the width was pre-determined by *Press*, the choice of *Univers* was not ideal because its principle – like that of static typefaces in general – is based on the adjustment of letter width and not on their differences. Therefore, a dynamic sans-serif, i.e. a typeface based on a Renaissance roman such as Adrian Frutiger's 1962 design 'Gespannte Grotesk' or *Gill Sans* by Eric Gill, would have been better suited. Frutiger integrated the latter in his study of character width /07/. It is not known whether Max Caflisch, who was responsible for the selection of typefaces for the IBM Composer, was also considering the use of *Gill Sans*.

Initially, thirteen golfballs were manufactured for eight cuts and three sizes of *Univers* /12/. Later there were at least twenty-two in five sizes from 7 to 12 point.[10] If a change of typeface was necessary, the golfballs – weighing only nine grammes – were easily and quickly exchangeable.

problem within the unit. But, my, did that set off the technologists. These were ideas typical of an artist, they said, that kind of thing wasn't allowed. The problem had to be solved technologically, not through drawing. On that point they were right, though.

Eight cuts were developed for this machine: the normal and condensed versions each in light, medium, medium italic and bold /12/; we didn't use the expanded and extra condensed cuts, that would have been difficult. There were up to four, and later five, sizes per cut. They were roughly one point smaller than the ones for handsetting.

IBM didn't hire me only as a type designer – I also had a consulting contract. Up until 1981 I went to Lexington every three months and stayed for about a week. This also included training the employees. The IBM draftsmen were specialising in typewriter faces after all, and therefore mainly drew typefaces with a constant width and stroke contrast. I taught them a bit about the history of typography, about printing machines and technologies and about handsetting, machinesetting and phototypesetting. But most of all I wanted them to know what a metal letter looks like. I couldn't, however, give comprehensive lectures on drawing typefaces, but everyone had to draw a letter according to the typographic laws at least once. That was how I trained the employees at the factory; I always had two days of my stay allocated to that. At IBM's French factory in Orléans I did similar training.

Univers is the only one of my typefaces that was used by IBM. Although I suggested a modern, semi-condensed semi-egyptienne /14/, which was tuned to the width system of the Composer and was very similar to a classic face. A golfball was even manufactured and a sample set created – it never sold, it simply remained an internal trial.

/07/

Width comparison of 40 alphabets (Lumitype and Monotype) with a calculation of average values in units per em.

/08/

Representation of average values from the analysis shown opposite divided into 9 units – IBM did not use this.

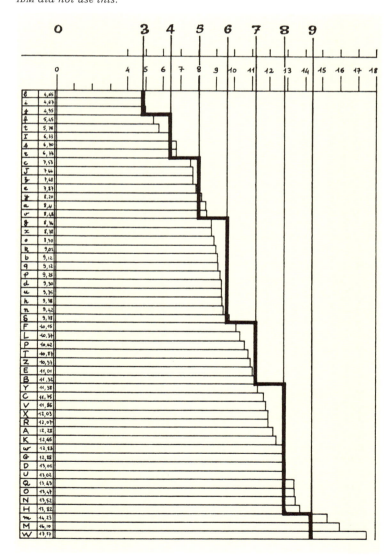

The defined units per character for the Composer require adjustments in width.

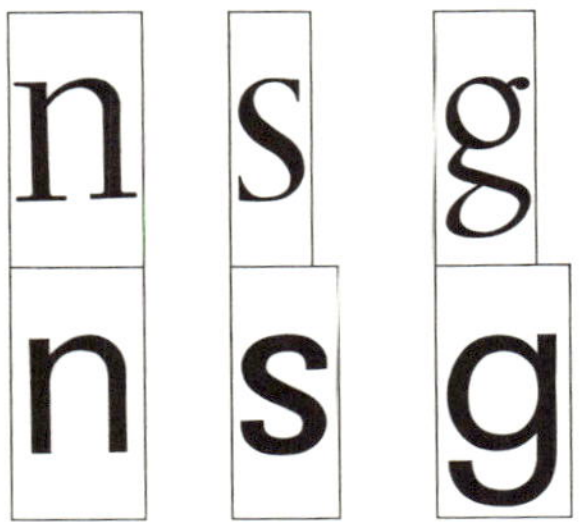

Not only sans-serif but also italic letters have different widths compared to a regular antiqua.

The i of the regular cut of Univers for the Composer – the three different forces of impact significantly change the weight.

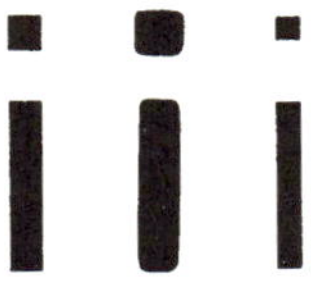

IBM Composer-Schriften

IBM

/12/

This early typeface sample (no date) for the IBM Composer features Univers in 8 cuts besides Press, Bodoni, Aldine and Pyramid.

11 Punkt, mager

ABCDEFGHIJKLMNOPQRSTUVWXYZ
abcdefghijklmnopqrstuvwxyz
1234567890$.,-'':;!?*½¼¾—()[]=†/+%&@

This example of Univers, a precisely defined sans-serif face, was created by Adrian Frutiger for the IBM "Selectric" Composer. Univers is a very useful face, well suited for advertising and technical literature. It is effectively used

11 Punkt, schmallaufend mager

ABCDEFGHIJKLMNOPQRSTUVWXYZ
abcdefghijklmnopqrstuvwxyz
1234567890$.,-'':;!?*½¼¾—()[]=†/+%&@

This example of Univers, a precisely defined sans-serif type face, was created by Adrian Frutiger for the IBM "Selectric" Composer. It has an elegant simplicity of style, giving a clean, clear type impression. Univers is a strong type face, minus typographical eccentricities.

11 Punkt, normal

ABCDEFGHIJKLMNOPQRSTUVWXYZ
abcdefghijklmnopqrstuvwxyz
1234567890$.,-'':;!?*½¼¾—()[]=†/+%&@

This example of Univers, a precisely defined sans-serif face, was created by Adrian Frutiger for the IBM "Selectric" Composer. Univers is a very useful face, well suited for advertising and technical literature. It is effectively used for direct mail pieces, brochures and folders.

11 Punkt, schmallaufend normal

ABCDEFGHIJKLMNOPQRSTUVWXYZ
abcdefghijklmnopqrstuvwxyz
1234567890$.,-'':;!?*½¼¾—()[]=†/+%&@

This example of Univers, a precisely defined sans-serif type face, was created by Adrian Frutiger for the IBM "Selectric" Composer. It has an elegant simplicity of style, giving a clean, clear type impression. Univers is a strong type face, minus typographical eccentricities.

11 Punkt, normal kursiv

ABCDEFGHIJKLMNOPQRSTUVWXYZ
abcdefghijklmnopqrstuvwxyz
1234567890$.,-'':;!?*½¼¾—()[]=†/+%&@

This example of Univers, a precisely defined sans-serif face, was created by Adrian Frutiger for the IBM "Selectric" Composer. Univers is a very useful face, well suited for advertising and technical literature. It is effectively used

11 Punkt, schmallaufend normal kursiv

ABCDEFGHIJKLMNOPQRSTUVWXYZ
abcdefghijklmnopqrstuvwxyz
1234567890$.,-'':;!?*½¼¾—()[]=†/+%&@

This example of Univers, a precisely defined sans-serif type face, was created specially for the IBM "Selectric" Composer by Adrian Frutiger. It is a practical face, well suited to advertising and technical literature. It can be used for brochures, folders and direct mail.

11 Punkt, halbfett

ABCDEFGHIJKLMNOPQRSTUVWXYZ
abcdefghijklmnopqrstuvwxyz
1234567890$.,-'':;!?*½¼¾—()[]=†/+%&@

This example of Univers, a precisely defined sans-serif face, was created by Adrian Frutiger for the IBM "Selectric" Composer. Univers is a very useful face, well suited for advertising and technical literature. It is effectively used

11 Punkt, schmallaufend halbfett

ABCDEFGHIJKLMNOPQRSTUVWXYZ
abcdefghijklmnopqrstuvwxyz
1234567890$.,-'':;!?*½¼¾—()[]=†/+%&@

This example of Univers, a precisely defined sans-serif type face, was created specially for the IBM "Selectric" Composer by Adrian Frutiger. It is a practical face, well suited to advertising and technical literature. It can be used for brochures, folders and direct mail.

Typeface design for the Composer In 1969 Frutiger designed a new typeface that was adjusted to the unit widths of the Composer /14/. He drew a semi-egyptienne, which was typical for a typewriter face. This choice becomes understandable when considering *Pyramid*, then the only egyptienne for the Composer. Frutiger's typeface is slightly less strong than *Pyramid,* and it is more harmonious and less messy. With *Pyramid* it is noticeable that the serifs are not finer than the terminals, as should be the case. This can be seen in the A M and N for instance /02/ (this clearly shows how necessary Frutiger's seminars were for the typeface designers at IBM).

The semi-egyptienne was developed comprehensively and comprised the whole alphabet with numerals, diacritics and special characters. Exactly why it was never implemented remains unclear given its obvious improvements over *Pyramid*. In an undated letter Emil Ruder, then director of the Kunstgewerbeschule Basel, listed the qualities of this typeface.[11] On the evidence of this letter, the working title 'Delta' can be confirmed. A formal relationship to the design 'Delta' (see page 36) from the beginning of the 1950s cannot, however, be established. 'Delta' is clearly similar to Adrian Frutiger's *Egyptienne* (see page 118). The only significant difference is that 'Delta' is available as an oblique with inclined shapes, whereas *Egyptienne* features a true italic.

The effort that went into the manufacturing of the golfball was enormous since the technologists wanted absolute precision. The final artwork was one hundred times bigger than the golfball. At IBM each drawing was additionally checked with a magnifying glass. There I learned what exaggerated quality means. The better part of the final artwork was done in my studio. I had to hire another employee, Silvain Robin, who – together with Nicole Delamarre and later also with Hans-Jürg Hunziker – did the drawings for the Composer. André Gürtler finished his work on the normal cut in Switzerland because he had started teaching type design at the Kunstgewerbeschule Basel. Together with Henry Friedlaender, the adaptation of his Hebrew scripts was carried out.

Overall, the Composer was an ingenious invention at the time. But eventually it was overtaken by the rapid pace of technological development, and so it remained only a transitional phenomenon.

/14/
Inclined semi-egyptienne in 10 pt
with the working title 'Delta',
and adjusted to the seven character
widths of the Composer.

/13/
Character map, test setting and
spacing sample – Cyrillic italic with
manual corrections by Adrian
Frutiger.

D-10-I   *Essonnes March 11, 1969*

ABCDEFGHIJKLMNOPQRSTUVWXYZ &   1234567890
abcdefghijklmnopqrstuvwxyz   [(.:,;`'?!†—-+=$*@/%¼½¾)]
£§ÅÄØÖåäàøöÜüßçÇçÑñ»¿ ¡ ´`ˆˇ«» ÆÆæéœ

IN SPITE OF THE INCREASING INTEREST IN THE
HISTORY OF PRINTING A KNOWLEDGE OF STAN-
dards among the rank and file of printers is still greatly
lacking. To the average printer of to-day, type is type.
Nous vivons dans un monde de la chose imprimée. Notre
éducation s'est faite grâce aux livres. De la même façon
les journaux nous apportent le récit et les images du monde.
Über Jahrhunderte hinweg bleibt die Schrift Träger aller
menschlichen Äußerungen. Örtlich bedingt fühlt jede der
Nationen die Form in ihrer Gesamtheit einheitlicher.

HHOHOH&	¿PPOPOHPH?	iioionin.fifi	rroronrn
ΠOIOHIH*	¡BBOBOHBH!	`llolonln´flfl	ttotontnftft
TTOTOHTH	(RROROHRH)	hhohohn	ffofonfn`ff´
JJOJOHJH	[KKOKOHKH]	nnono	jjojonjngjgj
LLOLOHLH	ESKIMO	uuouonun	vvovonvn
FFOFOHFH		mmomonmn	wwowonwn
EEOEOHEH			xxoxonxn
	UUOUOHUH		yyoyonyn
	MMOMOHMH		zzozonzn
	NNONOHNH	»oonon»	
OOHOH	ZZOZOHZH	ccoconcn	ääoäonän
QQOQOHQH	SSOSOHSH	«eeoeonen»	ååoåonån
CCOCOHCH		aaoaonan	ààoàonàn
GGOGOHGH		ssosonsn	ææoæonæn
DDODOHDH			ççoçonçn
	AAOAOHAH		ééoéonén
	AAOAOHAH		ıɪoɪonɪn
	ÆÆOÆOHÆH	bbobonbn	ññoñonñn
AAOAOHAH	EEOEOHEH	ddodondn	ööoöonön
VVOVOHVH	NNONOHNH	ppoponpn	øøoøonøn
WWOWOHWH	ÖÖOÖOHÖH	qqoqonqn	œœoœonœn
XXOXOHXH	ØØOØOHØH	ggogongn	ßßoßonßn
YYOYOHYH	UUOUOHUH	kkokonkneskimo	üüoüonün

310 hp @ 2965 RPM 78¼+40½=118¾ §2/5 £9–8 10%

010203040506070809000   áàãâ éèêë íîî óòôö úùûü

Logos and wordmarks
1961–1964

Jacqueline Iribe
Textile Designer
Paris (F)

Scripta Pantographes
machine tool manufacturer
Paris (F), Düsseldorf (D),
Milan (I)

Brancher Frères
printing ink manufacturers
Vélizy (F)
Design not implemented

Agence Information et Entreprise
Public Relations Agency
Paris (F)

Centre International de
Généralisation du Mont Canisi
organisers of symposia
for heavy industry
France

Club Europe Industrie
union of European industrialists
Paris (F)
Design not implemented

Europe Industrie
union of European industrialists
Paris (F)

Agence Arma Publicité
advertising agency
Paris (F)

Association de fabricants
d'encres d'imprimerie
printing ink manufacturers
association
Paris (F)

Éditions Tallandier
book and magazine publisher
booksellers
Paris (F)

Imprimerie Hofer
printing firm
Paris (F)
Design: André Gürtler

Hang Druck
printing firm
Frankfurt am Main (D)

Dernières Nouvelles de Colmar
newspaper
Colmar (F)
Design: Bruno Pfäffli

mills-K –
Constructions tubulaires
scaffolding construction firm
Paris (F)

Druckerei Winterthur
printing firm
Winterthur (CH)
Design: Bruno Pfäffli

Jean Cartier-Bresson
printing agency
Paris (F)

CUSENIER

Cusenier liqueurs
liqueur and spirits distillery
France

CANTADOR

Cantador Watch
watchmaker
Switzerland

IПΓEIG

Institut professionel
de recherches et d'études des
industries graphiques
research institute for the
graphic industry
Paris (F)

MELPOMENE

Mélpomène
architectural students' magazine,
École Nationale Supérieure des
Beaux-Arts
Paris (F)

*Ministry of the interior –
National External Trade Centre
France*

*Ministry of the interior –
Society for Agricultural Research
France*

*Ministry of the interior –
National Centre for Small- to
Medium-sized Businesses
France*

*Compagnies Bancaires
union of credit institutes
France*

*Henowatch
watchmaker
Interlaken (CH)*

*Villeroy & Boch
articles for kitchen, table and
bathroom
Mettlach (D)*

*Urbanisation du
District de Paris
urbanisation and planning
for the Paris region
Paris (F)*

*Formus
design agency
Paris (F)
Design: Bruno Pfäffli*

*Electricité de France
et Gaz de France
national electricity and gas
companies
France*

*Compagnie Générale de
Télégraphie Sans Fil
wireless telecommunications
company
Paris (F)*

*Atelier Frutiger
typographic studio
Arcueil (F)*

*American Type Founders
New Jersey (USA)
Design: Bruno Pfäffli*

*Prache – Auger – de Franclieu
commercial bookbinder,
specializing in spiral binding
Choisy-le-Roi (F)*

*Éditions du Griffon
publishing house
Neuenburg (CH)*

*Prache – Auger – de Franclieu
commercial bookbinder,
specialising in spiral binding
Choisy-le-Roi (F)
Design not implemented*

*Beaufour
pharmaceutical laboratory
Dreux (F)*

*Europe
economics magazine
Paris (F)*

*Europrint
printing company
Paris (F)
Design: André Gürtler*

Name of typeface	Client	Designer	Design | Publication	Typesetting technology	Manufacturer	Weights
Alphabet EDF-GDF	Électricité de France	Adrian Frutiger	1964 | 1967	Transfer lettering	– Esselte Letraset Ltd.	2

ALPHABET
EDF-GDF

The monogram EDF-GDF is well-known to the French people. Consciously or subconsciously they associate it with their main energy suppliers. But which concrete images are conjured up in consumers' minds by those letters? How is it possible to make it clear to them that all the facilities of the different sectors are parts of one single service enterprise, and how is it possible to communicate that this public company also has an industrial and commercial personality with a highly developed dynamic?[1] This problem represented the start of my project for the French energy supplier Électricité de France (EDF)/Gaz de France (GDF) at the beginning of the 1960s. Under the direction of Jacques Veuillet I designed a monogram logotype /02/, the form of which was subject to clearly defined guidelines. Apart from other aspects, it had to be suited to three-dimensional representation on office and factory façades /03/. Right from the beginning, we also created full-length company name logos with the wordmarks 'Électricité de France' and 'Gaz de France' in their very own typeface /04/.

The differentiated inner structure of this gigantic corporation very soon required an extension of the EDF typeface to include the whole alphabet in order to be able to signify not only, for example, the geographic areas of a sector, but also the functions of a large power plant. So I started to develop the capitals with the help of André Gürtler /05/. All individual letters were constructed on the basis of a rectangle; the round movements were divided into vertical and horizontal ones and the angles rounded. In terms of legibility this is not a good thing. This project, however, wasn't mainly concerned with the reading process but with architectural signage and the titling of print material – the written word became a monumental ornament in its own right.

In terms of proportions, the first EDF alphabet is comparable to a fairly bold cut. It was necessary to create enough space in the stroke itself to be able to build in light sources. For use in print material, the typeface was extended with lowercase letters, numerals and symbols /05/. But for subtitles or subcategories it was regarded as too bold and so EDF asked for an additional thin version. Unfortunately, it's a bit naked. During the following years condensed characters were added as well /06/.

Every now and again we also did some small jobs for the group, such as different print materials, exhibition lettering or signage /09/. And of course there was a lot to update such as the building signage in the whole of France /03/ and the letterheads /04/ for each site – we had quite a lot to do and worked together with Veuillet until the end of the 1970s. During the 1980s EDF changed to another typeface, something 'modern': EDF as a cursive and additionally positioned in a rectangle /01/.[2] What that looks like on the buildings I don't dare to imagine. But when you've come to the end of your tenure, then you should call it a day really.

Architecture and typography   One of the guidelines for the typographic branding of EDF was its adaptability to the architectural sphere.[3] EDF owned different types of buildings. On the one hand, there were the monumental, electricity-producing power plants situated in the countryside, and also the first gigantic nuclear power plants were being planned; on the other, there was the modern, light-flooded architecture of the public buildings.

Adrian Frutiger picked up the already existing letterform /01/ with rounded angles and from this basis developed the logotype EDF-GDF with the two monograms positioned vertically one above the other /02/.[4] Applied to the light-flooded public buildings it signified the monumental power plants. On the façades of the power plants, however, only the monogram EDF was used in combination with the logogram /01/, a thunderbolt framed by a circle.

In terms of signage for the public buildings, it was not so much about the compact EDF-GDF sign but about the line-forming wordmarks /03/. Their harmonious letters, which hardly differed in width, formed a mutual rhythm with the structure of the fenestration.

There were different stages of the typeface development over a long period of cooperation. When exactly the lowercase letters and numerals, and the thin and condensed fonts were created cannot be established. The typeface was supplied in the form of rubdown sheets that were used to create printing templates for brochures, letterheads and the like. *Univers* by Deberny & Peignot was selected for running text.[5]

EDF was the project owner but Gaz de France, a company in its own right, also participated in it. At the level of directorate general and public buildings, the two companies appeared as a single entity; concerning the service sectors and products, however, they acted separately. Although EDF wanted a coherent branding, there were a number of inconsistencies. The G sometimes had a horizontal bar and different G-shapes could even be found on the same building /03/. The R appeared with a diagonal leg on one building. Expanded versions were created, and sometimes the A was condensed /03/. Also, the letter spacing was not always consistent. But in spite of all this, EDF – virtually a monopoly – was groundbreaking in France as far as its efforts for a uniform branding were concerned.

Logo development for the public enterprise Électricité de France (founded 1946) – (from left to right) 1958, 1967, 1987, 2005.

/02/
The logotype monogram with white letters on a blue background is used as neon signage on building façades.

/03/
In the façade signage the shapes of A F G R vary and in places differ significantly from Frutiger's typeface.

/04/
Letterhead Électricité de France – Gaz de France set in Alphabet EDF-GDF *and combined with* Univers.

Alphabet EDF-GDF *gras and maigre* – the black font also contains the logogram by Giulio Confalonieri.

ABCDEFGHIJKLMNOPQRST UVWXYZ ÉÈÊË 1234567890 abcdefghijklmnopqrstuvwxyz éèêë .,:;'!?- −/«»*%()=×+

ABCDEFGHIJKLMNOPQRST UVWXYZ ÉÈÊË 1234567890 abcdefghijklmnopqrstuvwxyz éèêë .,:;'!?- −/«»*%()=×+

/06/

Condensed version of the logotype in the regular font – a complete alphabet cannot be found.

ELECTRICITE DE FRANCE
électricité de france

/07/

Wordmark 'information' – implemented in an inclined, version of the light font of Alphabet EDF-GDF.

information

/08/

EDF-GDF documented their new branding – architecture, interior design and typographic styles – in a 1968 book.

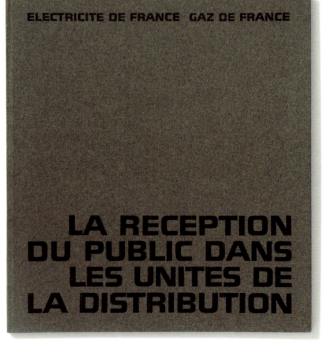

/09/

Signage – the information is engraved on the aluminium plate and then coloured black.

/10/

Table sign made of acrylic glass featuring the black font of Alphabet EDF-GDF and the logotype monogram in a circle.

"I make the bricks, I am not the architect.
I just make good bricks that graphic artists can build with."
Adrian Frutiger

ABCDEFGHIJKLMNOPQRSTUVWXYZ
abcdefghijklmnopqrstuvwxyz
1234567890

ABCDEFGHIJKLMNOPQRSTUVWXYZ
abcdefghijklmnopqrstuvwxyz

/01/
Typeface design 'Katalog' with a horizontal spur for a and half serifs for fjr (top); teardrop serifs for afjr (bottom).

Hanna vom neuen dom muss dem dummen Hans neue Hosen anpassen und dann den neun dosen pseudo Hunden von dem Hovades vasen senden

Hanna vom neuen dom muss dem dummen Hans neue Hosen anpassen und dann den neun dosen pseudo Hunden von dem Hovades vasen senden

Hanna vom neuen dom muss dem dummen Hans neue Hosen anpassen und dann den neun dosen pseudo Hunden von dem Hovades vasen senden

Hanna vom neuen dom muss dem dummen Hans neue Hosen anpassen und dann den neun dosen pseudo Hunden von dem Hovades vasen senden

/02/
1965 adhesive letter set comprising ten letters in four cuts – the serifs of the oblique are clearly asymmetrical.

/03/
Several versions of the cursive lowercase n between 1965 and 1969 with changes in angle, serifs and overall shape.

A strong typeface for newsprint The uniform letterspacing of all fonts in the 1965 adhesive letter set **/02/** points to the intended use in line casting. Therefore a relationship with Sofratype would have been possible, but with *Opéra* (see page 130) they already had a typeface for newsprint. Two years later, Frutiger's design was the subject of a discussion with D. Stempel AG and a note dated 18 December 1967 contains the main points made by Walter Greisner und Erich Schulz-Anker in relation to the *'Cheltenham'* project.[1] An interest in short ascenders and descenders was noted as well as in a maximum number of characters per line and a true cursive. A point that was taken up by Frutiger as is confirmed by another adhesive letter set with integrated oblique and italic fonts **/05/**. In 1968, the complete alphabet of this design was available under the name *'Katalog'*.[2] In contrast to the 1965 design, a f j and r now featured teardrop serifs **/01/**. In a letter dated 23 January 1969 **/08/** Erich Schulz-Anker, art director of Stempel, critically reviewed[3] the sample alphabet that was completed at the end of 1968 **/06/**.[4] Presumably the project was stopped thereafter – maybe also because two newsprint faces were already in development at Linotype at the time: Matthew Carter's *Olympian* from 1970 and Arthur Ritzel's *Rotation* from 1971 **/09/**.[5] Further versions of *'Katalog'* are set in the sample string 'une pomme du monde' **/07/**. All four designs using this string (see also pages 156/157) are titled 'Konzept 1969' – none of them was ever implemented.[6]

Without any client commission I started out to design a strong typeface with good legibility for newsprint. I wanted it to be similar in form to *Cheltenham* **/09/**.[7] This timeless, valuable typeface is neither a pure antiqua nor an egyptienne – it lies somewhere in between the two. It has been used a lot in the USA. With its clear shapes and narrow letter-spacing it is well suited for newsprint. It does, however, also contain a few bizarre forms such as the lowercase g, therefore you tend to think of it as an old-fashioned typeface.

The project was discussed with Walter H. Cunz, the co-owner of D. Stempel AG. But he soon dropped it since he was convinced that it wouldn't be successful. The partner company Linotype didn't seem to see the point either. A new typeface for newsprint had to be really good because it had to be accepted by readers on a daily basis. Maybe it was a mistake to use *Cheltenham* as a starting point. I would have had to develop a wider ductus even if my typeface was meant to be narrower than the longstanding number one of newsprint faces from Linotype, *Excelsior* **/09/**. A narrow newsprint face was something new indeed.[8] If I look at the adhesive letter set **/06/** now, I can see it's all right but not extraordinary. The weight of the main strokes is too strong by ten per cent and the short serifs are ungraceful. The whole thing doesn't 'breathe' properly, there's no life in it. The small caps, however, are interesting. I should have continued working on it, should have improved the design. Why wasn't I able to create a harmonious typeface? I didn't succeed in bringing all aspects of a good newsprint face together: the right stroke weight, a breathing text image, open punches, and a narrow letter-spacing. Maybe the whole spirit of newsprint wasn't my thing really. With the grotesques, I could draw on rich resources but with the antiquas I was only able to do that later when I designed *Iridium* and *Linotype Centennial*.

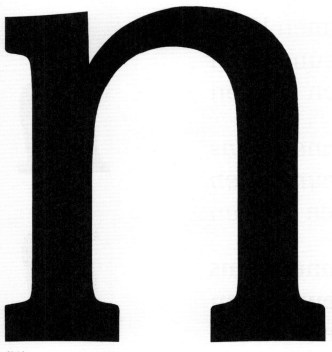

/04/
Reproduction on film –
the shoulder and the transition to
the serifs were subsequently
filled in with ink.

/06/
Comparison of Adrian Frutiger's
newsprint face with (from top
to bottom) Excelsior, Melior *and*
Candida *– set in body type, 1968.*

Homburger sturm auf Oberammergauer
Homburger sturm auf Oberammergauer
Homburger sturm auf Oberammergauer
Homburger sturm auf Oberammergauer

/05/
Adhesive letter set from c.1968
with integrated oblique and italic
fonts – the a of the regular version
features a teardrop shape whereas
it is horizontal in the oblique.

Jede Planung ist ein schöpferisch aktiver Vorgang und setzt die Mitarbeit zahlreicher Betriebsangehöriger voraus. Diese Planung kann nie der Initiative eines einzelnen überlassen werden. Alle Mitarbeiter sollen sich *Hand in Hand* auf ihrem Spezialgebiet ständig über neue Hilfsmittel und Arbeitsmethoden auf dem laufenden halten *und von den* eigenen Unternehmungen entsprechende Vorschläge erfordern. Nur so kann der eigene Betrieb **von dem anpassenden Handel** und dem Einfluss einer gewissen Betriebsblindheit und der damit verbundenen überheblichkeit bewahrt werden.

ABCDEFGHIJKLMNOPQRSTUVWXYZ
hahbhchdhehfhghhhihjhkhlhmhnhohphqhrh
hshtnunvnwnxnynzn

/07/
The 1969 version with very strong,
short serifs and with slightly finer
and longer ones – static e in contrast
to Frutiger's 'Serifen-Grotesk'.

une pomme du monde
une pomme du monde
une pomme du monde
une pomme du monde
une pomme du monde
une pomme du monde

D. STEMPEL AG

Schriftgießerei
Messinglinienfabrik
Linotype-Matrizenfabrik
Maschinenfabrik

Der Betrieb befindet sich in Frankfurt am Main Süd, Hedderichstraße 106–114

D. Stempel AG · 6 Frankfurt am Main 70 · Postfach 701160

Herrn
Adrian Frutiger
23, Villa Moderne
94 Arcueil
FRANCE

Ihre Zeichen	Ihre Nachricht vom	Unsere Zeichen	Hausapparat	6 Frankfurt am Main 70
		SchA/mcv	284	23. Januar 1969

Lieber Herr Frutiger,

nachdem ich Ihnen auf Ihren Brief bisher nur einen kurzen Zwischenbescheid gab, möchte ich mich heute zu dem Schriftversuch (Probeschnitt) etwas ausführlicher äußern.

Ich hatte mir bei der ersten flüchtigen Durchsicht des Abzuges spontan einige Randnotizen gemacht, die ich hier zunächst unfrisiert wiedergebe:

1) Schrift ist insgesamt zu fett.

2) Mittellängen entschieden zu hoch (es kommt nicht darauf an, einen schmalen Eindruck zu erzielen, sondern einen schmalen Lauf.)

3) Die abgerundeten kurzen Serifen erwecken etwas den Eindruck, als sei die Schrift "abgequetscht". ???
Bei der "Cheltenham" gehört das abgerundet Stumpfhafte zum Charakter der Schrift, daher entsteht dort nicht dieser Eindruck. Bei der F-Schrift ist die Zeichnung selbst sonst so exakt – daher rührt möglicherweise die optische Täuschung.
Die "Cheltenham" hat übrigens sehr niedrige Mittellängen.

Aus Ihrem Brief entnehme ich nun, daß unsere Meinungen hierzu im Prinzip konform gehen. Hochovale o- und e-Formen (und das würde sinngemäß für c, b, d, p und q gelten) sind immer problematisch, wenn Lesbarkeit vordergründig ist wie bei einer Zeitungstextschrift, da sich die Formen sonst zu wenig von n, m, u, h usw. unterscheiden. Werden sie aber bei solch hohen Mittellängen kreisförmiger gehalten, wird die Schrift für eine Zeitung zu breit, also gibt es nur die Möglichkeit niedrigerer Mittellängen.
Ich merkte bereits an, daß ein schmaler Eindruck nicht notwendig sei – ich möchte ergänzen: im Gegenteil. Eine Zeitungsschrift sollte so selbst-

verständlich unauffällig sein wie nur möglich (also auch nicht betont schmal wirken). Die Excelsior ist eine solch unscheinbare Type und als Zeitungsschrift bisher kaum erreicht.

Zu der Anmerkung 3), daß die Schrift etwas "abgequetscht" wirke, machte ich drei Fragezeichen. Das sollte heißen "wie kommt das?" ich finde nämlich die kurzen Serifen gut, sie bringen etwas Neues und zwar nicht nur formal, sondern möglicherweise auch funktional, wenn die Mittellängen kürzer und die Schrift leichter wird. Wenn man natürlich auch noch nichts Definitives sagen kann, so glaube ich doch, daß es sich lohnt, diesen Ansatz weiter zu verfolgen. Auf jeden Fall bin ich gespannt auf das Ergebnis des nächsten Schrittes.

Daß H, g und s zu schmal sind und das t oben etwas zu kurz – diese Meinung teile ich mit Ihnen. Überhaupt glaube ich, weitgehendst mit Ihnen übereinzustimmen, soweit es das Problem einer Zeitungsschrift betrifft.

Ob das allerdings zum Phänomen Druckschrift allgemein gilt, weiß ich nicht. Aus gelegentlichen Unterhaltungsfragmenten, einigen Passagen Ihres Briefes an Prof. Gürtler und vor allem aus einer analytischen Betrachtung Ihrer Schriften "Meridien" und "Serifa" komme ich zu dem Eindruck gewisser unterschiedlicher Auffassungen. Ich würde es daher begrüßen, wenn wir uns darüber gelegentlich etwas eingehender unterhalten könnten.

Da es sich dabei um Prinzipielles, d.h. um unterschiedliche Denkansätze zu handeln scheint, will ich vorab einige Gedankengänge niederschreiben, die meines Erachtens das Grundproblem berühren.

Sie erwähnen in dem Brief an Herrn Gürtler, daß Sie bei der "Meridien" als Mediäval das Prinzip "mehr Einheit in eine Schrift" hineinzubringen durchführen konnten. Ich vermag nur sehr bedingt zuzustimmen, daß das anzustreben richtig ist, wenn man darunter die äußeren Merkmale einer Schrift versteht. Ich glaube nämlich, daß das zwar hinsichtlich eines einheitlichen Formprinzips einer Schrift (Stil) zutrifft, nicht jedoch für eine so weitgehende Homogenisierung der äußeren Details. Ich bin vielmehr der Meinung, daß das Geheimnis einer guten Druckschrift (das ist: Klarheit plus Funktion als Lese-Zeichen plus ästhetische Sensibilität der Form) in einem hohen Grad an Komplexität liegt, d.h. in einer großen Vielfalt an Formelementen innerhalb einer stilistischen Einheit. Würden Sie zustimmen, wenn ich sage, Formklarheit ist nicht das alleinige Ziel einer Druckschrift und nicht das einzige Kriterium für ihre Qualität? Klarheit einer Schrift ist meines Erachtens ein vornehmlich form-technisches Moment, das bei Kenntnis der optischen Phänomene mit den Mitteln der heutigen Techniken und Verfahren relativ leicht zu lösen ist, aber sie ist nicht der Kern des

ästhetischen Problems. (Wenn ein Vergleich erlaubt ist: Das klarste Wasser ist destilliertes Wasser, aber es ist ohne Würze).

Manche heutigen Schriften kranken einfach daran, daß ihre Zeichen einander zu ähnlich und deren Einzelheiten zu homogen sind. (Der frühere Handschnitt brachte wenigstens eo ipso Differenzierungen in die Details. Klassisches Beispiel: Garamond, Janson). Bei den heutigen Verfahren, Originalzeichnungen faksimilegetreu zu übertragen, besteht die Gefahr der Perfektion besonders, wenn nicht im Entwurf genügend unterschiedliche Details eingearbeitet sind – denn letztlich ist Schrift doch mehr als nur eine Ansammlung perfekter Zeichen. Dieses Problem hat übrigens Tschichold meines Erachtens in der Sabon-Antiqua hervorragend gelöst. Die Schrift ist durchaus sachlich, vielleicht sogar ein bißchen trocken, aber sie enthält eine Fülle feinster Formnuancen in vergleichbaren Elementen. Da ist z.B. der Ansatz links oben beim n anders als jeder der beiden beim u. Oder: Beide Z z haben oben andere Serifen als unten, und was es dergleichen mehr an subtilen Dingen gibt. Das sind natürlich – im Grunde genommen – Garamond-Figuren, aber sie sind mit heutigen Mitteln unpersönlich interpretiert.

Ich möchte heute nicht in Details gehen – darüber können wir einmal sprechen – ich wollte nur andeuten, was ich meine, wenn ich in der äußeren Angleichung der Formen und Einzelelemente nicht das zentrale Problem einer Schrift zu sehen vermag. Das war schon mein Einwand gegen das dem Gürtler-Versuch zugrunde liegende Konzept, das ein grafisches Prinzip ist, aber kein schriftspezifisches. Das eigentliche Problem eines jeden ästhetischen Objektes – und das ist ja die Schrift in hohem Maße – liegt – wie bereits gesagt – in der Komplexität.

Nun habe ich eigentlich schon mehr geschrieben als ich wollte, ohne daß ich mich wohl richtig verständlich machen konnte – das ist in einem Brief bei einem solchen Problemkreis doch schwierig.

Zu Ihrem Jonic-Versuch kann und möchte ich nichts sagen, da ich erstmals durch Ihren Brief davon hörte. Das gleiche gilt für das Bodoni-Walbaum-Projekt, über das ich nicht informiert bin. Auch weiß ich nicht, welche "neuen Schriftprobleme" Sie meinen, von denen Sie schreiben.

Wann sind Sie wieder einmal in Frankfurt? Es wäre schön, wenn wir dann unsere Anschauungen abtasten, diskutieren und besser klären könnten. Da auch Sie offenbar den Wunsch dazu haben, freue ich mich auf ein solches Gespräch.

Inzwischen grüße ich Sie herzlichst,
Ihr

Erich Schulz-Anker
D. STEMPEL Aktiengesellschaft
Künstlerische Leitung

/08/
Letter by Erich Schulz-Anker, art director of D. Stempel AG, commenting on Frutiger's design and typographic work.

Cheltenham, 1896 – Bertram G. Goodhue
Hand in Hand auf ihrem Spezialgebiet ständig über neue Hilfsmittel und Arbeitsmethoden auf dem laufenden halten *und von den* eigenen Unternehmungen entsprechende Vorschläge

Century Expanded, 1900 – Morris F. Benton
Hand in Hand auf ihrem Spezialgebiet ständig über neue Hilfsmittel und Arbeitsmethoden auf dem laufenden halten *und von den* eigenen Unternehmungen entsprechende Vorschläge

Century Schoolbook, 1917 – Morris F. Benton
Hand in Hand auf ihrem Spezialgebiet ständig über neue Hilfsmittel und Arbeitsmethoden auf dem laufenden halten *und von den* eigenen Unternehmungen entsprechende Vorschläge

Ionic No. 5, 1925 – Mergenthaler Linotype
Hand in Hand auf ihrem Spezialgebiet ständig über neue Hilfsmittel und Arbeitsmethoden auf dem laufenden halten *und von den* eigenen Unternehmungen entsprechende Vorschläge

Excelsior, 1931 – Chauncey H. Griffith
Hand in Hand auf ihrem Spezialgebiet ständig über neue Hilfsmittel und Arbeitsmethoden auf dem laufenden halten *und von den* eigenen Unternehmungen entsprechende Vorschläge

Times New Roman, 1932 – Stanley Morison
Hand in Hand auf ihrem Spezialgebiet ständig über neue Hilfsmittel und Arbeitsmethoden auf dem laufenden halten *und von den* eigenen Unternehmungen entsprechende Vorschläge

Corona, 1941 – Chauncey H. Griffith
Hand in Hand auf ihrem Spezialgebiet ständig über neue Hilfsmittel und Arbeitsmethoden auf dem laufenden halten *und von den* eigenen Unternehmungen entsprechende Vorschläge

Melior, 1952 – Hermann Zapf
Hand in Hand auf ihrem Spezialgebiet ständig über neue Hilfsmittel und Arbeitsmethoden auf dem laufenden halten *und von den* eigenen Unternehmungen entsprechende Vorschläge

Gazette (Imperial), 1957 – Edwin W. Shaar
Hand in Hand auf ihrem Spezialgebiet ständig über neue Hilfsmittel und Arbeitsmethoden auf dem laufenden halten *und von den* eigenen Unternehmungen entsprechende Vorschläge

Concorde, 1968 – Günter Gerhard Lange
Hand in Hand auf ihrem Spezialgebiet ständig über neue Hilfsmittel und Arbeitsmethoden auf dem laufenden halten *und von den* eigenen Unternehmungen entsprechende Vorschläge

Schriftentwurf ‹Katalog›, 1969 – Adrian Frutiger
Hand in Hand auf ihrem Spezialgebiet ständig über neue Hilfsmittel und Arbeitsmethoden auf dem laufenden halten *und von den* eigenen Unternehmungen entsprechende Vorschläge

Olympian, 1970 – Matthew Carter
Hand in Hand auf ihrem Spezialgebiet ständig über neue Hilfsmittel und Arbeitsmethoden auf dem laufenden halten *und von den* eigenen Unternehmungen entsprechende Vorschläge

Rotation, 1971 – Arthur Ritzel
Hand in Hand auf ihrem Spezialgebiet ständig über neue Hilfsmittel und Arbeitsmethoden auf dem laufenden halten *und von den* eigenen Unternehmungen entsprechende Vorschläge

Times Europa, 1974 – Walter Tracy
Hand in Hand auf ihrem Spezialgebiet ständig über neue Hilfsmittel und Arbeitsmethoden auf dem laufenden halten *und von den* eigenen Unternehmungen entsprechende Vorschläge

/09/
Comparison of typefaces for newsprint – Rotation was created almost simultaneously to Frutiger's design and implemented at D. Stempel AG.

/10/
*Drawing of the 'Katalog' a
with measurements and corrections –
ink, opaque white and pencil on
satin paper, original size.*

Name of typeface	Client	Designers	Design | Publication	Typesetting technology	Manufacturer	Weights
Dev-nagari, New-nagari, Tamil Linear	National Institute of Design, India	Adrian Frutiger Mahendra Patel	1967–72 | 1967–72 | sample cast 1973 1970–72 |	Machine composition – Letterpress	– Monotype	1

देवनागरी · தமிழ்
DEVANAGARI   TAMIL

It was due to Armin Hofmann, a faculty member at the Kunstgewerbeschule in Basel, that I worked in India. In 1965, he was teaching at the National Institute of Design (NID)[1] in Ahmedabad for six months.[2] The students were supposed to acquire a basic knowledge of Western design so that they could use it within the Indian cultural context and thus give Indian design a fresh boost. Hofmann had observed that the Indian scripts, which had such beautiful predecessors in calligraphy, were in bad shape. He said it needed an expert to try and renew Indian typography similar to European typeface development. He took this issue to Gira Sarabhai, co-founder of NID and director of the design department, and suggested asking me to teach at the school, too. Armin Hofmann himself had come to NID through her. Her family had built up a chemical enterprise in Ahmedabad, which had partner companies all over the world. Therefore Gira was at Geigy in Basel quite often. There she noted the beautifully designed corporate print materials. She wanted the same quality for Indian graphic design.

At my first, three-day-long visit to NID in 1965 (on my way back from Japan – the last meeting to complete *OCR-B* had taken place there) I spontaneously gave a lecture on European typographic development. Two years later, in February 1967, I came to Ahmedabad for five weeks. I was supposed to give a lecture and a seminar and to try to create something useful in the modern world out of the old script. Thirty students attended my lecture. In the seminar I taught a selected group to write with a broad-edged pen and I did a number of calligraphic exercises with them. My two best students were Mahendra Patel and Vikas Satwalekar. Both of them later returned to NID as faculty members and held various leading positions. Mahendra has a studio for typography in Ahmedabad. He was a very talented and hardworking student.

India has thirteen different typographic cultures /05/.[3] The most important one is Devanāgarī /11/, the holy script of the gods, which is mainly found in the north of India. It is used for Sanskrit. Its basic principle is the straight, horizontal line above each letter. This is very intelligent, since you can see at a glance where one word ends and the next one begins.[4] What I was trying to do was a formal simplification in the sense of the shapes of *Univers*. While I was doing this, I noticed right away that something was wrong but I didn't know what it was and therefore couldn't do anything about it at first. Then I had the idea to write a classical script first using the Calam,[5] a type of antiqua suitable for the pen /13/. I had to learn this first and Mahendra and Vikas were my teachers. The positioning of the pen is different to how we use it here. When writing in Devanāgarī the hand is less flexed towards the back than when writing a Latin script. Therefore the writing angle is turned by ninety degrees, which produces diagonals that descend towards the right and to the empty spaces at the bottom left and top right of the curves /13/. With a Latin alphabet it's

Scripts of the Indian cultures   Adrian Frutiger described his thoughts about trying, as a European, to renew Indian scripts and the questions he came across during that work in his book *Type Sign Symbol:* "In the western world, typeface design has shared in the process of technical development. In the developing countries we are now faced with the problem of adapting scripts in such a way that they can keep pace with the communication media of the West. Commissioned by the National Institute of Design in Ahmedabad, India, I was given the job of studying the typographical basis of Devanagari (the script of Ancient Sanskrit and today the official Indian script) with the aim of making it better accessible to modern typesetting and reproduction techniques. Can the sacred script of India be modernised? – Indian culture is still largely based on an oral tradition. [...] The written word has never been regarded as indispensable, either for instruction or for public information. We know, however, how extremely important the written word and prayer are in all oriental religions as a sacramental means of expression. For this reason, writing has remained a privilege of the learned and wise. This explains why, in India, the script has been fixed in its ancient calligraphic form and is today split into countless regional variations. This state of affairs could almost be compared with the Western epoch before Charlemagne, when every European land cultivated its own script in complex, ornamental style (uncials and half-uncials). But so far no 'Indian Carolingian minuscule' has been developed to give an impetus to the synthesis of expression. On the other hand, the new printing techniques, which in the West have trimmed [...] the original calligraphic forms of our scripts, have so far had absolutely no active influence on the forms of Indian letters. [...] Today, however, Indian typography needs a new image just as badly as India needs a new road network and mechanised agriculture. But is it possible to achieve artificially a similar outcome to the effect of 500 years of punchcutting, matrix-making, casting and printing on our own original alphabet?"[6]

*Reworked and simplified glyph –
the letter ka, written with a Calam,
received a symmetric form.*

/02/
*An attempt to renew the
Devanāgarī script – the linear
strokes lend it a more
contemporary expression.*

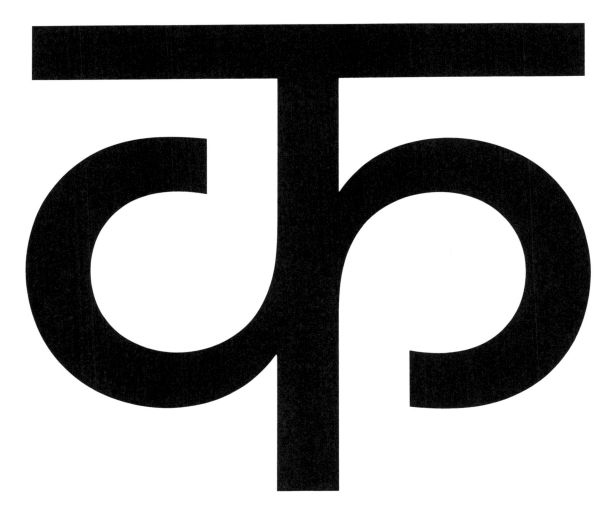

/03/
*Parallels in architecture –
historical ruin in central India (top),
modern architecture by Louis Kahn
in Ahmedabad (bottom).*

the other way round. They made me do exercises for a few days /13/, criticised, corrected and explained. That was a rich experience. From these trials I tried to develop a grotesque. I did what I could but my intuition told me that there was something wrong. I didn't say anything though. The people at the Institute were obviously excited about the *Univers* principle. My design was reviewed at the highest levels. Gira announced my visit at the university of Benares[7] where a commission of influential dignitaries would review my designs. Without an OK from Benares there was no point in continuing, Gira said. So I prepared a sample script comparison with Mahendra: on the one side we had the normal newsprint type and on the other we presented our attempt at a linear script in 8 pt. I handed out the copies to the circle of wise men and women and explained my approach. They looked at them through their magnifying glasses and compared them. After a longer discussion the president came towards me, shook my hand and then she said: "It's all right." What a relief.

During the remaining time of my stay we designed the templates for the expanded and bold fonts /17/. I gave it everything, but when the five weeks were over, we came to the conclusion that it could not be up to me to renew Indian typography, this had to be done by an Indian. Therefore I asked Gira whether Mahendra could come over to my studio in Paris and continue the work there. During four weeks in 1968 he then developed the conceptual approach for the typeface in my studio. This took place during his holidays since he was actually in Basel to learn how to teach type design and typography, because he was supposed to start teaching in Ahmedabad. Two and a half years later he returned for thirteen months to finish *Devanagari* and to adjust it to Monotype's 18-unit system. Mahendra

Indo-European scripts The Indian and European scripts have a common root: Phoenician script /06/. Based on 22 consonantal symbols, it is one of the earliest alphabetic scripts. First evidence of its existence can be traced to the 9th century BC around the eastern coast of the Mediterranean – the Levant. It flourished from the 7th century BC until the 7th century AD. With the rise of Islam, the Phoenician script was replaced by Arabic. The Aramaic alphabet developed from the Phoenician, /06/ and spread throughout the East as far as India. It is assumed that the basis of the Brāhmī script evolved from the Aramaic alphabet /06/. All Indian scripts can be derived from the Brāhmī. This is also true for Devanāgarī, in which Sanskrit – the holy language of Hinduism – is written. Deva means god and Nāgarī means city. The residence of the gods is Benares, today called Varanasi, one of the holiest places of Hinduism and a centre of traditional Hindu culture and science. Alongside the Indian scripts, the Hebrew, Arabic and Greek scripts are also based on the Phoenician alphabet; the Greeks, however, introduced additional symbols for vowels. Taken over by the Etruscans and passed on by the Romans, it eventually led to our contemporary Latin alphabet.

/04/
Geographical areas of the eleven most important scripts of modern India using the example of the letter ka.

KASHMIRI

GURMUKHI

Delhi

ASAMIYA

BENGALI

Ahmedabad   Varanasi

GUJARATI   DEVANAGARI

Calcutta

Mumbai   ORIYA

TELUGU

KANNADA

Chennai

TAMIL

MALAYALAM

/05/
Of the 22 languages listed in the constitution, 13 are represented in 11 different scripts on Indian banknotes.

/07/
Linear jobbing types drawn especially by graphic designers in a style to fit the images – newspaper advertisement from 1967.

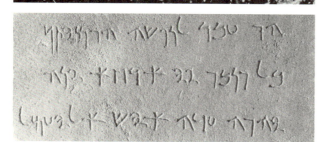

/06/
Predecessors of the Devanāgarī script – Phoenician, 9th BC (top), Aramaic, 5th BC (centre) and Brāhmī, 3th BC (bottom).

Indian scripts The different regions of India have their own languages and usually also their own scripts. 22 languages are listed in its Constitution,⁹ but no single script – and on the currency notes 13 languages are represented in 11 different scripts /05/. Based on the Brāhmī script, /06/ Indian scripts developed in different formal directions, dependent on the material to which the script was applied. The scripts of the North such as Devanāgarī, Bengali, Gurmukhī and Assami, which represent the Indo-Arian languages (part of the Indo-European language family), were carved in tree bark. This resulted in angular shapes. The scripts of the South such as Telugu, Tamil, Malayāḷam, Kannada and Oriyā, which represent the Dravidic languages, are carved in palm leaves. Their shapes are round because the carving of horizontal lines would have split the leaves. The common root of Indian scripts can be clearly observed in the symbol क /04/. In almost all of the scripts, the base of the symbol is formed by a bowl on the left, an open curve on the right and a horizontal bar, which in the southern scripts tends to be round as well. Just like European scripts – but unlike their Phoenician and Aramaic predecessors – Indian scripts are written from left to right.

had to draw the complete set of characters /21/. We had a lot of discussions about each single glyph – a good piece of work at the end of our studies of Devanāgarī.

A sample cast of the *Univers*-based *Devanagari* was made in 1973 at Monotype in 12 and 24 pt. The company had secured the rights, hoping that the Indian market would need this typeface. The sample copies were named 'Monotype *Devanagari Univers* Medium, Serie 731' /23/. Essentially an honest name but pretty stupid at the same time. It would be possible to think of a Greek or Cyrillic *Univers* but there is no such thing as a *Devanagari Univers* or 'Univagari' as it was referred to by its detractors. Monotype never put this typeface on the market; the salespeople thought it was still too early, and thus it never got beyond the sample cast. The typeface was never published.

I was at NID twice, altogether. My main task was to transfer the Western experience of five hundred years of typesetting and printing technologies. But I had my doubts. Could we achieve in India what had slowly developed here over a period of five hundred years? After a thorough deliberation of the cultural aspects I noted in my letter from India: "1. The typefaces do not yet have true principles of well-established forms; everything is still in flux; there are still study commissions tasked to define the alphabets, to reduce the number of glyphs, ligatures and diacritics and to define the basic outline of the letters. – 2. Sanskrit partly evolved from the same sources as Greek, from which our Latin alphabet is derived. – 3. In Sanskrit as well as in occidental scripts the calligraphy of the pen follows the respective rules thus forming a contrast between descender and ascender, straight lines and curves. – 4. The laws of legibility and the aesthetic qualities of the alphabet remain the same: values and shapes of the punches have to be in a precise relation to the

/08/
Phonetic segmentation of
Devanāgarī *in five different*
vocal groups (1–5) and
three additional groups (6–8).

/09/
Basic shape of the letter क
with different additional forms
and combinations set
in Monotype Devanagari.

/10/
Indian numerals (Devanāgarī)
and contemporary Arabic numerals,
European numerals from
the Middle Ages and from today
(from top to bottom).

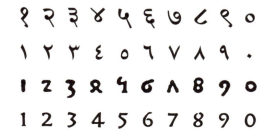

/11/
Sample sheet of Monotype
Devanagari *from 1959 – in places*
the forms are clearly different
from Frutiger's version.

'MONOTYPE' DEVANAGARI
SERIES No. 155

/12/
Asymmetrical shape of क in
Monotype Devanagari –
*the angular-cut horizontal stroke
is typical for a typeface.*

Working on the new Devanagari   Adrian Frutiger introduced a reduction in the calligraphic ductus. The overall basis of the symbols later followed more clearly a horizontal-vertical principle; diagonal movements were avoided where possible and organic shapes were channelled typographically, as it were /16/. There were also changes in shape in Frutiger's *Devanagari*. In a calligraphic study, for instance, he changed the asymmetric loop of the क to a symmetrical one /13/.

The next step comprised the drawing of the symbols /14/. As is common with typefaces for hot metal setting – and for technological reasons – the oblique imprint of the reed pen was replaced by square-cut stroke endings. Mahendra Patel called this typeface with stroke contrast 'Devanagari in the classical style'. Final artwork was produced for the medium and bold cuts.[10]

In a third step Frutiger reduced the stroke contrast /15/. Similar to *Univers*, a matrix was created that contained a sample string in five numbered weights and widths and even some decorative types /17/. Patel drew the medium, bold and bold condensed cuts of 'New-nagari in the linear style' /22/. He worked for slightly over a year on the original designs /21/, which were created with ink and opaque white on cardboard and were 20 cm (about 7.9 inches) in height.[11] In 1973 Monotype produced sample matrices of the regular cut of *Devanagari Univers* in 12 and 24 pt /23/. There were 180 glyphs per cut, including all ligatures and diacritics.

/13/
*Calligraphic study by
Adrian Frutiger – the usually
asymmetrical loop of the क is given
a symmetrical form.*

को सामातक ।धाम आत्मोया क्षेपस्तको तक सामो

/14/
*'Dev-nagari in the classical style' –
the script appears more typographic
than in other Devanāgarī
typefaces.*

की अभिव्यक्ति

/15/
*'New-nagari in the linear style' –
stroke contrast is clearly reduced,
the bowls and curves display
similarities to* Univers.

की अभिव्यक्ति

/16/
*From the traditional handwritten
form to the simplified drawn one,
which is easier to change in
weight and width.*

/17/
*Matrix of 'New-nagari' in five
weights and four widths and in an
outlined, filleted, cursive and
shadowed version.*

देवनागरी	देवनागरी	देवनागरी	देवनागरी	देवनागरी
देवनागरी	देवनागरी	देवनागरी	देवनागरी	देवनागरी
देवनागरी	देवनागरी	देवनागरी	देवनागरी	देवनागरी
देवनागरी	देवनागरी	देवनागरी	देवनागरी	देवनागरी
देवनागरी				

/18/
*Syllables listed according to
similarities in shape –
'Dev-nagari' is shown below the line,
'New-nagari' above.*

Sample setting of 'Dev-nagari' medium and bold in the classical style with simplified shapes and stroke contrast.

हिंदी भाषा की प्रसार-वृद्धि करना उसका विकास करना ताकि वह भारत की सामाजिक संस्कृति के सब तत्वों की अभिव्यक्ति का माध्यम हो सके तथा उसकी आत्मीयता में हस्तक्षेप किए बिना हिंदुस्तानी और अष्टम अनुसूची में उल्लिखित अन्य भारतीय भाषाओं के रूप

हिंदी भाषा की प्रसार-वृद्धि करना उसका विकास करना ताकि वह भारत की सामाजिक संस्कृति के सब तत्वों की अभिव्यक्ति का माध्यम हो सके तथा उसकी आत्मीयता में हस्तक्षेप किए बिना हिंदुस्तानी और अष्टम अनुसूची में उल्लिखित अन्य भारतीय भाषाओं के रूप

/20/
Hot metal version of Devanagari Univers *24 pt by Monotype – the kerned letter is neccesary for accent marks.*

/21/
Mahendra Patel, 1971 in Frutiger's studio in Arcueil – with final artwork showing variations on the Devanagari Univers *on the wall.*

/22/
Sample setting of 'New-nagari' in medium, bold and bold condensed with reduced stroke contrast similar to a sans-serif antiqua.

हिंदी भाषा की पसार-वृद्धि करना उसका विकास करना ताकि वह भारत की सामाजिक संस्कृति के स तत्वों की अभिव्यक्ति का माध्यम हो सके

हिंदी भाषा की प्रसार-वृद्धि करना उसका विकास करना ताकि वह भारत की सामाजिक संस्कृति के तत्वों की अभिव्यक्ति का माध्यम हो सके

हिंदी भाषा की प्रसार-वृद्धि करना उसका विकास करना ताकि वह भारत की सामाजिक संस्कृति के सब तत्वों की अभिव्यक्ति का माध्यम हो सके

/23/
Character sheet of the sample matrices for Devanagari Univers *medium in 24 pt from 1973 – also created in 12 pt.*

Trial No. 3	'MONOTYPE'	16-8-73
Devanagari: Univers Medium		Series No. 731—24 point
Display		Order No. E784

Typ 5578   Nos. 50, 52, 58, 83, 92, 102, 103, 111, 112, 115, 116, 136, 219, 228, 233, 234, 253, 256, 315, 471 Added

Modification Order F200   Nos. 119, 120, 121, 125 Redesigned

आपको "मोनोटाइप" मशीन की ग्राह्यकता हैं

अ इ उ ऊ ए क ग घ च ज झ ट ठ ड ढ ण त

थ द न प फ ब म य र ल व ष स ह ळ क्ष ज्ञ

black of the sensitive lines that surround them."[12] The second project on which Mahendra worked together with me in Paris was *Tamil* /27/, which is used in the south of India. The Tamil script was originally written on palm leaves /24/. It has round shapes since angular forms would have split the leaves. Mahendra drew the typeface after a magnification of such a palm leaf /25/. First we conducted a study on how to draw a fine skeleton script from such a palm script and how to then make it thicker without changing its style /28/. The shoulders are therefore finer than the fat descenders. Here too, I only gave some directions and Mahendra created the designs. Just as with *Devanagari,* he adjusted the script to the Monotype system. When his time in my studio had come to an end, he returned to India to teach and to develop his own typefaces. He always drew templates first in the classical style using the Calam according to how we had discussed it; then he made them fatter and on that basis developed a type of sans serif. What I did at the Institute and in my cooperation with Mahendra was to provide support, consulting and direction. It has been said that I had designed a new Indian script and that it had been implemented – this is wrong! I carried out some initial trials for a renewal and then I was a consultant who created the basis from which my Indian colleagues and friends independently developed their own work. I'm happy that I was able to achieve something in this cooperation. That's all.

A linear Tamil type   In 1980 Adrian Frutiger wrote: "The next script group to be considered by Mahendra Patel and myself was that of South India. This group has a fundamentally different structure from that of the North. The alphabets are, indeed, phonetically formed in the same way and there are even analogies in letterforms, but the principal difference between North and South is in the material used. In North India, a hollow pen is used for writing on paper, but in the South the dried palm-leaf is still in use [...]. For this reason the South Indian scripts are much rounder and more connected than those of the North. The formation of the strokes is absolutely fibre-like. Note the few but very elongated horizontals, which have that appearance because they lie in the fibre direction of the leaf and are consequently difficult to discern. The manuscript is made legible by dusting it with a black powder, which remains in the crevices and makes the writing visible. As a basic study, the characters were uniformly drawn in skeletal form and the line-movement was regulated into a uniform stroke. The interior and exterior spaces were balanced and the long horizontals shortened as far as possible. We then modelled the actual printing typeface around this skeleton and designed the characters as single elements suitable for typesetting. The *Tamil* alphabet was initially planned in a light and a medium version."[13]

/24/
Original 'pages' of a Tamil book – the glyphs are carved into palm leaves, which are then sprinkled with black powder to render the symbols visible.

/25/
Shape carved into a palm leaf, handwritten shape, skeleton and linear forms of a character from the Tamil *type (from left to right).*

/27/
Sample setting of the light version of Mahendra Patel's Tamil *type in the linear style.*

ஹிந்தி பாஷை பரவுவதற்கு ஆவன செய்தலும்,
இந்தியாவின் பலகூறுடைய பண்பாட்டின்
சகல அம்சங்களாயும் வெளீயிடுவதற்கேற்ற
கருவியாகப்பயன்படுமாறு அதை அபிவிருத்தி
செய்தலும், அதனுடைய தனிப்பண்பிற்கு

/26/
An attempt to open the closed punches during the design process for the linear Tamil *type.*

/28/
Sample text of the Tamil *type in the linear style in three weights: light, bold and bold condensed.*

ஸா ஸி ஸீ ஸு ஸூ ஸெ ஸே ஸை ஸ்
ஸா ஸி ஸீ ஸு ஸூ ஸெ ஸே ஸை ஸ்

தபஸிலில் குறிப்பிட்ட மற்றைய இந்திய
தபஸிலில் குறிப்பிட்ட மற்றைய இந்திய
தபஸிலில் குறிப்பிட்ட மற்றைய இந்திய

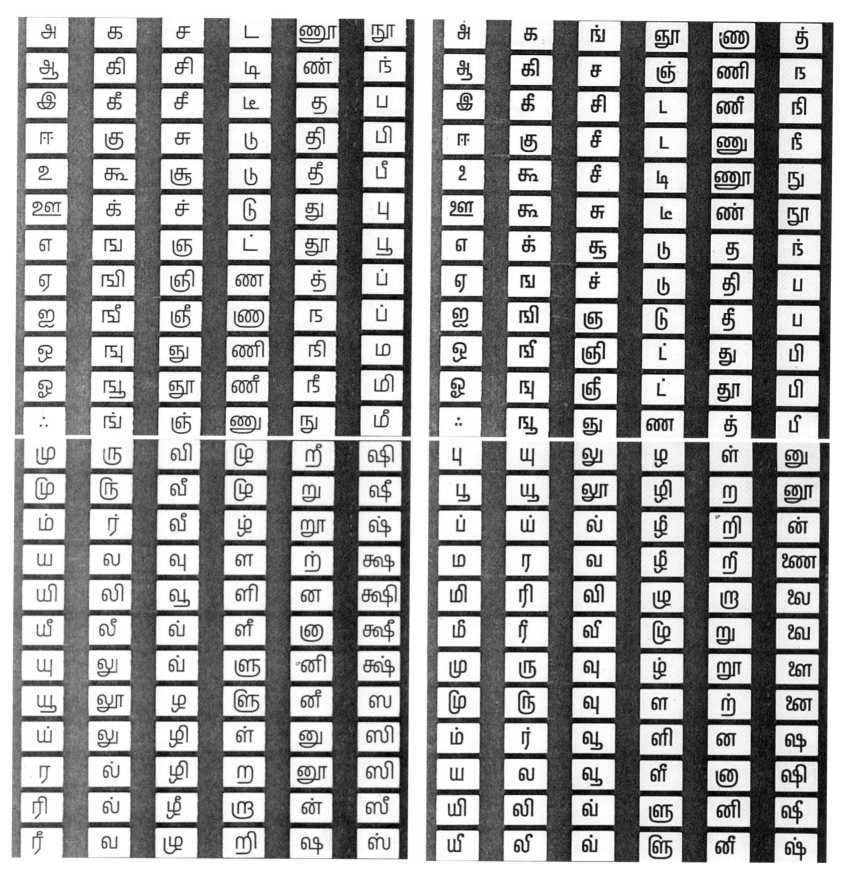

/29/
Final artwork for Tamil Linear by Mahendra Patel in a thin and semibold cut – recorded on microfilm.

Name of typeface	Client	Designer	Design | Publication	Typesetting technology	Manufacturer	Weights
Alpha BP	Crosby/Fletcher/Forbes (British Petroleum Co.)	Adrian Frutiger	1968 | 1969	Phototypesetting	– Conways	2

ALPHA BP

During 1968 I was approached by the agency Crosby/Fletcher/Forbes. It was founded in London in 1965; since 1972 it's been known as Pentagram.[1] They had to develop a new branding for British Petroleum and among other things BP wanted their own typeface to help improve their image. They had been using *Helvetica* so far and this typeface was so omnipresent in the 1960s that they decided to get one of their own. Initially, the new typeface was meant to be derived from the *'Universal'* alphabet /05/ by the Bauhaus artist Herbert Bayer. The glyphs, however, were too abstract. So eventually Colin Forbes came to see me. He complained about BP's insistence on *Futura* /06/, which he thought was too 'fiddly'. Could I design an improved *Futura* for them? With 'fiddly' he was referring to the optical corrections that are necessary for a typeface for text setting: tapered bowl or curve joints to open up counters, or differences in the width of strokes. The construction of the shapes has been watered down through small interventions everywhere.

Alpha BP /09/ is not a typeface that I invented from scratch: it is an attempt to create a more geometrical *Futura*. On the basis of its bold cut, two new versions were created, a bold and a semibold. I'd done some distinctly geometric designs /01/ of my own at first but that was out of the question. The lettering had to be rather neutral and absolutely classic. It wasn't possible to bring an oval shape to the O and so I adopted the 'circular' form of *Futura* /07/. But there is a lot of difference in the details; this is most significant in the numerals. The 1, for instance, has received a longer and more diagonal serif and the terminals for 6 and 9 are rounder and wider. Some capitals such as B E F T have a wider spacing, the S is more open. With the lowercase letters, the ascenders are a bit shortened and the j has a curve at the bottom /09/. This project was interesting but also quite difficult; on the one hand you had pure construction and on the other you were trying to create an easily legible, harmonious typeface. Colin Forbes knew that he could talk about the tiniest detail with me. We got on well and had long conversations. I did at least three, four designs with small changes that were hardly visible. The work on *Alpha BP* took about a year. I came up with the name, by the way. It was actually a mistake; I had jotted 'Alpha BP' on a note instead of 'Alphabet BP'. Forbes immediately thought that this was a brilliant name.

At that time another constructed typeface was being created – by Herb Lubalin. It was a characteristic feature of the magazine Avant Garde from 1968 onwards and was released in 1970 as *Avant Garde Gothic* by Tom Carnase, who had extended it to a typeface for text setting. I hold this typeface in very high regard; it is a true 'création', a creative achievement. The capitals with their alternative shapes and the ligatures /08/, all these invitations to play around, that was a gift for graphic designers. I was glad something good was emerging from the USA as a counterbalance to the omnipresent Swiss graphic design. I don't mean that in a bad way – but a bit of movement must be allowed, mustn't it?

A better Futura or a typeface in its own right? In 1968 Adrian Frutiger was commissioned to design a corporate typeface for British Petroleum. His actual client was the London design studio run by Theo Crosby, Alan Fletcher and Colin Forbes. According to Alan Fletcher, they contacted Frutiger because his studio only worked with the best designers. Colin Forbes reported how he had received a 45-minute lecture on type design and legibility when he asked Frutiger for a typeface with a circular O. Georg Staehelin from the design studio's Zurich office also participated in the meetings in Paris two or three times.[2]

Even before Adrian Frutiger was contacted, discussions about the new corporate typeface were being held.[3] A majuscule alphabet adapted to the logo was under consideration as a design approach but was immediately discarded since it had an old-fashioned appeal and poor legibility /02/. The circle, however, represented a clear contrast in shape when compared to the pointed serifs of the rather narrow Latin face used in the logo. The purest circular faces can be found at the Bauhaus, among others Herbert Bayer's *'Universal'* alphabet from 1925 /05/. (The idea of a universal type – Bayer spoke of a supra-national and versatile 'world type' – had thus been around long before *Univers*.)[4] But all of the typefaces developed at the Bauhaus remained as exploratory designs. However, Paul Renner's *Futura* /06/ – a text type with the classic proportions of the Imperial Roman Capitals – was issued in 1927 by Bauersche Giesserei in Frankfurt.

Frutiger's study of a solely constructed typeface demonstrates a variety of possibilities /01/. There are variations in the terminals of c e r s t, which exist in diagonal, vertical or horizontal forms, and in a m r and u there are also differences in the joints of the curves or shoulders, in the upper part of the stems and in the shapes of the curves themselves. Eventually the diagonal terminals were chosen, which represent a clear contrast to *Futura*.[5] With *Alpha BP* Adrian Frutiger designed a typeface in its own right in two weights /09/: a bold cut for the company name and for product names /11/ as well as a medium cut for additional information at petrol stations, for instance.

In 1989 BP's branding was redesigned by Wolff Olins and Frutiger's typeface replaced by one designed by Michael Harvey, which itself is no longer in use.

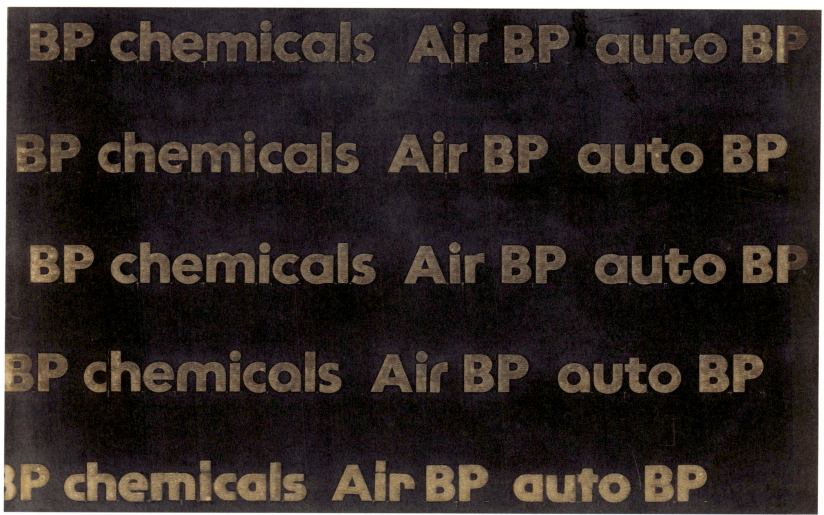

/01/
First designs for Frutiger's corporate type for British Petroleum – a variation of approaches for a constructed typeface.

/02/
A typeface developed from the logogram before Frutiger joined the project was rejected as too old-fashioned.

 **BP SUPER**

/03/
One of the first designs for Alpha BP was seen as too radical due to the missing half serifs for the lowercase a n p r u.

**air BP
super
vanellus**

/04/
Samples for Alpha BP in three weights – the ultra bold version (left) was not implemented.

**ABCDEFG
abcdefgh
12345678**

**BP regular
BP super**

**24 hours
Pay here**

**abcdefghi
jklmnopqr
s tuvwxyz**

/05/
Initial design of 'Universal' (1925) – some individual glyphs of this solely constructed alphabet were later reworked by Herbert Bayer.

ABCDEFGHIJKLMN OPQRSTUVWXYZ abcdefghijklmnop qrstuvwxyz012345 6789(.,:;-)!?&

/06/
Starting point in terms of shape for BP's type is the bold version of Futura *by Paul Renner (1928).*

/07/
The comparison shows that neither the majuscule O of Futura *(left) nor that of Alpha BP (right) are circular.*

ABCDEFGHIJKLMN OPQRSTUVWXYZ abcdefghijklmnop qrstuvwxyz012345 6789(.,:;-)!?/&

ABCDEFGHIJKLMN OPQRSTUVWXYZ abcdefghijklmnop qrstuvwxyz012345 6789(.,:;-)!?/&

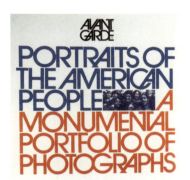

/08/
Cover design for the magazine Avant Garde by art director Herb Lubelin – set in his typeface Avant Garde Gothic (1971).

/09/
Alpha BP in bold and medium cuts – in contrast to Futura *all the terminals are diagonal.*

/10/
Inconsistent labelling – the two cans on the left are set in Alpha BP, the one on the right in Futura.

/11/
The bold cut of Alpha BP was used for all company and product names – almost exclusively in minuscules.

"The realisation that the balance of the counters was responsible
for the actual beauty of a typeface was, for me, a revelatory experience."
Adrian Frutiger

DOCUMENTA

/01/
OCR-B *(top) with horizontal stroke endings*, Documenta *(bottom) with vertical ones.*

/02/
Closed shapes in Univers *(top) and open shapes* Frutiger *(bottom).*

/03/
Monospace typeface Documenta – *definition of the sidebearing (top) and sample text (bottom).*

CGS
CGS

CGS
CGS

HAHBHCHDHEHFHGHIHJHKHLHMHNHOHPH
HQHRHSHTHUHVHWHXHYHZH & ÅØÆŒÄÖÜ
hahbhchdhehfhghihjhkhlhmhnhohph
hqhrhshthuhvhwhxhyhzh ß éèêëåñøæœ
1234567890
.,:;'?!--*†«»()[]
$£§% +×=/º<>.

/04/
In OCR-B *(top)* i *and* l *are different in shape; in* Documenta *(bottom) they are the same.*

/05/
Letters with different shapes – OCR-B *(top) and* Documenta *(bottom).*

i l r
i l r

D M Q R W
D M Q R W

DIE SCHRIFT FÜR OPTISCHE LESBARKEIT

Das Alphabet ist das Ergebnis einer
Normungsstudie, deren Ziel darin
bestand, eine Formenreihe fest-
zulegen, die sowohl fehlerlos von
elektronischen Lesern wie auch
mit Wohlgefallen vom menschlichen
Auge erkannt werden kann. Die
Bestimmung dieser Schrift zwang zu
Kompromißlösungen.

/06/
In addition, some of the numerals have different shapes – OCR-B *(top),* Documenta *(bottom).*

2 4 5 7
2 4 5 7

/07/
Final artwork for the minuscule o *based on 12 units – all glyphs are set to this width.*

A harmonious OCR typeface   At the end of the
1960s, Fritz Sutter from the Basel *National Zeitung* asked
Adrian Frutiger to develop an OCR typeface exclusively
for his company.[1] Fritz Sutter spoke of a parallel design
to *OCR-B* but with added quality.[2]

Documenta[3] is a monospace face based on twelve units
of glyph width.[4] It therefore featured wider letterspacing
than *OCR-B*. The most obvious difference can be found
in the basic concept of the typeface: while *OCR-B* has
horizontal stroke endings similar to those of *Univers,* and
Documenta has vertical ones **/01/**.

Individual glyphs featured a more typical Adrian Frutiger
design – there was no need to take into account the conditions dictated by a number of different manufacturers.
The D therefore has a more angular shape in the curves
/05/, the M features slightly spread legs, the tail of the
Q does not cross into the counter and the leg of the R
has a gentle curve at the top. The most striking difference
in the lowercase letters can be found in the l **/04/**. With
OCR-B it features a curved stroke, whereas in *Documenta*
it has serifs.

On the basis of Adrian Frutiger's instructions, a special
grid for Linotron 505 from Mergenthaler Linotype was
developed.[5] The Linotron was set up at *National Zeitung*
from 1969 to 1983. The grid has unfortunately been lost.

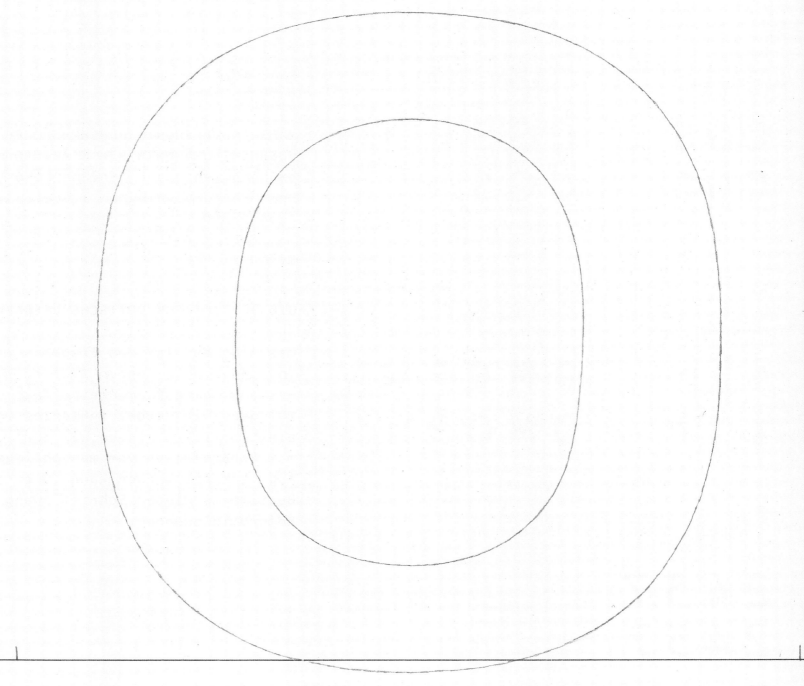

Dokumenta
Mappe F 54

12

Name of typeface	Client	Designer	Design | Publication	Typesetting technology	Manufacturer	Weights
Alphabet Facom	Facom	Adrian Frutiger	1970 | 1971	Phototypesetting	– H. Berthold AG	1

ALPHABET

For about twelve years the tool manufacturer Facom was our 'bread and butter'.[1] The cooperation started in 1963, initially with the design of their catalogue – there was no mention of a typeface yet. A big, fat Bentley drove into our little backyard at Place d'Italie and Monsieur Mosès[2], the owner of Facom, climbed out of the car. I've always wondered why, of all people, he picked us,[3] but at this time there weren't that many studios like ours. Presumably word got round about what we did. Monsieur Mosès introduced his company, showed us the current catalogue and asked whether we were prepared to take on the design of the catalogue pages. He had a very clear idea about this. "We don't have salespeople who sell and explain everything. The catalogue is our shop window!" All garages and ironmongeries had the Facom catalogue. It had a print run of 250 000 to 300 000 copies. There were two editions, a French one and a German one.

So then our task was to design the layout of the catalogue as if it were a shop window. The contents were to hand. Bruno Pfäffli instantly realised that there were quite a few issues with the current catalogue that we could improve on. First of all, he suggested using *Univers* for the body copy. For the drawings, or the stylistic treatment respectively, of the overview pages we asked the painter Rudolf Mumprecht, a friend of ours, for ideas. But Mumprecht looked at everything from the perspective of an artist. Each drawing was a little piece of art, not geared towards technology but towards beauty. And of course, Facom promptly criticised the illustrations as being too stylised. We had to admit that Mumprecht had gone too far. For a period of about one year Bruno worked on nothing else but the catalogue.[4] Altogether we did four catalogues for Facom.

Before the design of the alphabet in 1970 **/02/**, I first drew the numerals.[5] That was because I was able to convince Monsieur Mosès that it was a good idea to keep the page and reference numbers in the catalogue in the same style as the wordmark Facom. The wordmark consists of caps and a lowercase m, all at the same height **/01/**. An acute M wouldn't have been harmonious. When I saw the wordmark I thought: such a good logo in France? It turned out that the designer was Lucette Girard.[6] I already knew her from my time at Deberny & Peignot and, even before that, from École Estienne – so it was clear where the quality came from. Based on the wordmark I then designed the alphabet together with my draftswoman Nicole Delamarre. She took over the implementation. In keeping with the wordmark, we drew different versions of the letters A and M as well as of a and f – something that had become second nature to me since my time at D&P. Compared to the first version, the numerals 1, 2 and 7 were later changed **/03/** to adapt better to the alphabet. We then ordered a Diatype font disc from H. Berthold AG.[7] The typesetting was done by a company that specialised in headline composition, but the Diatype disc remained the property of Facom. Today Facom still uses a similar typeface.[8]

Catalogue design and corporate typeface   Facom sell their comprehensive range of tools solely through their catalogue. Due to the wide variety of articles on offer,[9] the connection between manufacturer and hardware stores is best achieved through print.[10] Catalogue design demands the greatest possible functionality. For Horst Heiderhoff, the 1973 Facom catalogue – designed by Studio Frutiger & Pfäffli – is an example of how it should be done.[11]

The flyleaf shows an overview of the different tool categories, similar to a shop window **/04/**. For this first interaction by the user, heavily stylised drawings were created in order to prevent users from getting sidetracked by unnecessary detail, and instead let themselves be guided by the product categorisation. The page numbers within the segments refer to the starting page of individual categories. If the respective category page is opened, another overview page with similar layout is shown **/04/**, this time with a narrower categorisation of tools. The representation of the articles then changes to photographs supported by short descriptions and schematic drawings with measurements. The pages designed by Bruno Pfäffli are well structured, with a clear layout.

Heiderhoff writes: "A normal user of the Facom catalogue will not notice the use of a corporate Facom alphabet. The designers don't see this as a drawback but rather an advantage: a good typeface should not be 'noticed' – a 'construction' will always have a disruptive effect. It should, however, without the reader noticing, lead them into an environment where people feel at ease (quality, trust, beauty) and to where they would like to return because of their positive memories."[12] Adrian Frutiger used the letter shapes of the Facom wordmark as a starting point and designed a corporate typeface with capitals and lowercase letters **/02/**. The gentle curves of the horizontal strokes and bowl shapes communicate the idea of smooth technology, and are reminiscent of the tools' tactile handles. In comparison to the wordmark, the typeface was narrowed in order to make it suitable for shorter texts. In spite of its strong composition, it has good legibility in body text sizes.

/01/

*Pictogram and logogram
by Lucette Girard – the letters are
wider than in the later
alphabet by Adrian Frutiger.*

AABCDEFGHIJKLMMNOPQRST UVWXYZ ÁÀÂÄÅÇÑØ ÆŒ &

aαbcdefꞙghijklmnopqrstuvwxyz
áàâäåçñø æœ ß £$¢ 1234567890
.,:;!?¡¿-—/„""°(«»)*[%]=×+

/02/

*The corporate typeface Alphabet
Facom, with the alternative
letters A M a f, is an extension of the
logogram Facom.*

127&

/03/

*In the first version, the numerals 127
have a stronger diagonal expression
and the T of the ampersand still
features the small caps form.*

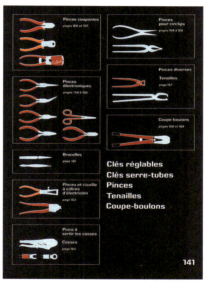

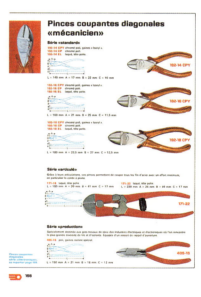

/04/

*Facom catalogue from 1973 – from
'shop window' to required article in
three steps: (from left to right)
tool categories, product groups
and individual articles.*

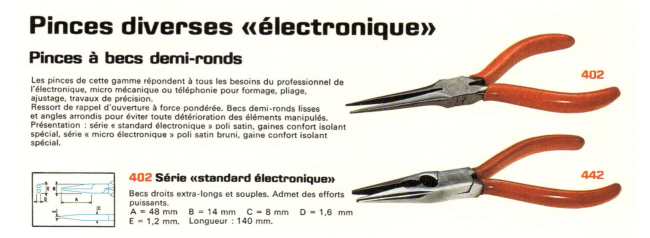

Pinces diverses «électronique»

Pinces à becs demi-ronds

Les pinces de cette gamme répondent à tous les besoins du professionnel de
l'électronique, micro mécanique ou téléphonie pour formage, pliage,
ajustage, travaux de précision.
Ressort de rappel d'ouverture à force pondérée. Becs demi-ronds lisses
et angles arrondis pour éviter toute détérioration des éléments manipulés.
Présentation : série « standard électronique » poli satin, gaines confort isolant
spécial, série « micro électronique » poli satin bruni, gaine confort isolant
spécial.

402 Série «standard électronique»
Becs droits extra-longs et souples. Admet des efforts
puissants.
A = 48 mm   B = 14 mm   C = 8 mm   D = 1,6 mm
E = 1,2 mm.   Longueur : 140 mm.

402

442

/05/

*Article names and numbers are
set in Alphabet Facom; detailed tool
descriptions in Univers.*

" The work of a type designer is just like that of a dressmaker:
clothing the constant, naked human form."
Adrian Frutiger

Production of type
Transfer type

An early form of rub-down type was used in France at the beginning of the 1950s. In 1954 Deberny & Peignot introduced the Typophane /01/ process, offering it as an extension of its foundry types, which would enable printers to follow the fashions of the time without large investments. Initially there were four jobbing typefaces available (see page 43).
The typefaces were printed onto a transparent, self-adhesive celluloid carrier film. The characters were individually cut out with a scalpel, released from the carrier film and placed on a sheet of paper. Pressing down with the thumb made the letters stick, but they could be lifted up again for corrections or other purposes. Guidelines printed underneath the characters helped to maintain alignment.
In 1956 Letraset in England developed a 'wet' transfer process and it was superseded by a dry method. Mecanorma developed a similar process. In the Letraset process, rubbing the letter made it come away from the carrier sheet and stick to the surface underneath /02/. This prevented the cut edges from

appearing and the characters from falling off. They could not, however, be moved again without being destroyed.
In order to set transfer type properly, letters have to be positioned very precisely on their baselines, which is not easy, in spite of the guides provided. Spacing characters optically is another issue for the untrained eye. And letters can easily be damaged when rubbing them down if the carrier sheet slips or is lifted up too soon.
As with foundry type, a synopsis provided different amounts for individual characters on each transfer sheet, according to their average occurence. Apart from different typefaces, sizes and colours, there were also sheets with graphic symbols, as well as custom sheets with special typefaces /03/, company logos, pre-spaced words, or individual illustrations. Production was very elaborate and the sheets were rather expensive. Transfer lettering was used well into the 1990s by graphic designers, typographer, engineers and fine artists; and also by non-profes-

sionals who needed to prepare originals for printing in a short time.
The process was used in many countries. In the former East Germany (GDR) it was called 'Typofix', for example. The range of available typefaces and the worldwide availability of transfer type were comparable to those from Monotype or Linotype. The typefaces were produced under licence, but there were also exclusive libraries.
Transfer sheets are still available but have suffered considerably in popularity c since the introduction of desktop publishing. They are still used for non-professional applications, but even there only marginally.

/01/
The Typophane process requires the printed, self-adhesive carrier film to be cut out and released from the protective sheet.

/02/
With proper transfer type, characters can be released from the carrier film by rubbing it down with a burnisher or other blunt tool.

/03/
A transfer sheet exclusively made for the airport Charles-de-Gaulle in Paris with Alphabet Roissy *by Adrian Frutiger.*

/04/
Apart from large libraries of typefaces, the manufacturers' product ranges included transfer sheets with a variety of subjects.

Name of typeface	Client	Designer	Design | Publication	Typesetting technology	Manufacturer	Weights
Alphabet Roissy	Aéroport de Paris	Adrian Frutiger	1970–72 | 1972	Foil Stamping | Transfer lettering	– not known | Letraset	1
Alphabet Roissy-Solaris		AF | Hans-Jürg Hunziker	1973–74 | 1974	Flip-Blades	– Solaris	1
Caractères TVP		Adrian Frutiger	1978–79 | 1979	CathodeRayTube (CRT) Monitor	– Thomson-CSF	1

ALPHABET
ROISSY

I had my first experience in designing a signage face in 1959/60 for Orly airport (see page 134). But back then I wasn't really mature enough for such a task. In 1970/71 the architect Paul Andreu asked me whether I would design a signage face for the airport Charles-de-Gaulle in Paris-Roissy. Everybody must have thought I would use *Univers* for this since it was well-known among experts. But I realised that I had to draw a new typeface. I had come to the conclusion that *Univers* was a good typeface for reading but it wasn't suited for reference books, which are more consulted than read – and nor for signage, where it's all about instant recognition.

Initially, there was a somewhat naive idea to use a geometrical grotesque like *Futura* /05/ since the airport was – at least on the architectural plans – circular. But you can only see that when you are in an aircraft directly above the airport. A circular o is a pure symbol but it isn't just about the o, it's about the interplay of all letters. Therefore *Futura* was out. But definitely a sans serif since serifs would only have created noise, an unnecessary humming. What was important was total clarity – I would even call it nudity – an absence of any kind of artistic addition. It was pretty obvious, however, that it had to be a typeface with caps and lowercase letters since the resulting word images are recognised quicker. Eventually *Concorde* (see page 150), which I had drawn together with André Gürtler in the 1960s for Sofratype's line casting matrices, became the starting point for my design. There is already a first indication of *Alphabet Roissy* in there. The caps are deliberately smaller than the ascenders of the lowercase letters /15/. The most important glyphs, however, were the numerals; they can be found on each panel. Each numeral therefore had to have the same clarity as an arrow.

The signage in the airport had to be bilingual and was supposed to be differentiated by colour. For this, we had a colour expert[1] on the team who told us right from the start that the contrast must not be too strong. He then mixed a dark yellow, positioned a black and a white letter one above the other on this background and showed us that the contrast was the same in both instances. The idea was good: illuminated from within, the French text should be set in black against the dark yellow background and below it, in white, the English text /02/. We all agreed to the idea of the yellow colour; we didn't imagine at the time how difficult it would be to always produce the same shade of yellow. Unfortunately, the first design of *Roissy* using the words 'Départ' and 'Departure' was lost during an exhibition. I had made it together with my colleague Nicole Delamarre. We'd cut the letters from black cardboard and the yellow background respectively. It took us a long time to find the right colour foils from Letraset. We had to put many layers on top of each other to get the dark yellow, at least four layers of foil. Light yellow, light grey, pink … for the presentation we created a small panel adding words in *Univers* for comparison; I held it

Projects involving flying   Alphabet Roissy (1970) was Adrian Frutiger's second signage project, an exclusive signage face for the airport Roissy-Charles-de-Gaulle in the north of Paris. Based on his almost two decades of experience as a type designer and the insights gained from the majuscule alphabet developed for Paris-Orly, Frutiger's signage face *Alphabet Roissy* was instantly recognised internationally as an excellent standard. Frutiger was part of an expert team directed by the architect Paul Andreu, who was the overall project leader. The signage system was implemented in cooperation with draftsmen and technologists from the company Aéroport de Paris; the director was Jacques Berthaut.[2]

In 1974, Adrian Frutiger and Horst Heiderhoff, director of the typography and advertising department at D. Stempel AG, gave a comprehensive report on the new signage face in *form*, the German design magazine.[3] Three years later *Typografische Monatsblätter* /04/ published a similar article in German, English and French.[4] At that time *Alphabet Roissy* – then reworked and extended to become the typeface family *Frutiger* – was celebrating further successes (see page 250).

In addition to *Alphabet Roissy* a monospace version named *Roissy-Solaris* was developed in 1973/74 for the airport's flip board displays /24/. In 1979 a special screen type called *Caractères TVP* was added /26/. Adrian Frutiger was also responsible for some architectural artwork. Ropes that had been set into the concrete walls during the construction of the airport's train station left 'stripe symbols' when they were taken out.[5] He also developed a logo for Aéroport de Paris (see page 274). The monogram, however, did not meet with broad approval – AP usually stands for 'Assistance Publique', i.e. social services, and it was thus abandoned a few years later.[6]

Another client from the context of the airport was the airline Air France. Together with Bruno Pfäffli, Adrian Frutiger was responsible for the re-design of their flight schedule.

Bruno Pfäffli designed a functional typography that saved space and costs. It was set in various fonts of *Univers*. Typographic illustrations were positioned throughout.[7] As opposed to the airport signage which did not use any pictograms at all, Frutiger developed linear symbols – which were 22 mm (about 0.86 in) in size – for the flight schedule.[8]

/01/
For better legibility when panels are slightly tilted Roissy *features large word spacing; the letter-spacing, however, is a little too narrow.*

/02/
Signage (1972) in Roissy *(top); today's signage by Jean Widmer in* Frutiger *(bottom).*

/03/
White, and especially backlit, type on a dark background has to be finer since it would appear optically fatter otherwise.

slightly askew just like the passengers in the airport would see it and it became immediately clear which one was easier to read.

Initially, we developed the typeface mainly for the interior signage. The size of the letters was dependent on the reading distance: for a distance of 20 metres (about 65 feet) we chose a height of 10 centimetres (about 4 inches), for 2 metres (about 6.5 feet) we chose 1 centimetre (about 0.4 inches). I used the lowercase c as a template for the word spacing. You didn't have to measure anything, you just put it in and took it away again. I decided on the c because I thought: too much is better than not enough. Unfortunately, I didn't stick to that concept when it came to letter-spacing. Therefore there is one serious point of critique regarding the airport signage: the *Roissy* signage is set too narrow, it has at least 15% too little whitespace between the letters. We did some testing, but it wasn't optimal. We put up a panel at a distance of 100 metres (about 109 yards) and compared two versions with each other. 100 metres, however, isn't a good distance. Within the airport it more or less works but for the exterior road signage the letter-spacing is definitely too narrow. To be honest, I have to say I recognised that too late. Unfortunately, Jean Widmer adopted the spacing for the motorway signage.[9]

I also did various studies with regard to individual glyphs. All these studies were concerned with the French and English culture respectively. Americans, for instance, write the 7 without the horizontal crossbar and the 1 without a half-serif – which I think is best – but Europeans think that there is a danger of confusion with the lowercase l. So eventually I decided on the version with the very short half-serif /12/; it is at least closer to the American way than the one with the long one. I did several studies for the y as well and then

Legibility and choice of typeface   In *Typografische Monatsblätter* /04/ the following considerations concerning a signage face can be found: "Written directional signs consist, for the most part, of single or compound words, seldom of complete sentences. One can easily come to the conclusion that the sign is not 'read', i.e. it does not create consecutive images in the way that book or newspaper texts do, but that it is 'spelled out'. As recently as ten years ago was it thought that people in airports 'spelled' in this way. Consequently all words used to be written entirely in uppercase letters, since they permitted each letter to retain its individuality; whereas lowercase letters, which have become drastically simplified through centuries of use, are not so easily recognised in isolation. They tend to cling to each other to form units of easy and rapid comprehension for the reader to 'photograph'."[10]

"A condensed face was briefly considered for its compactness but discarded because of its poor legibility. Tall, stretched letters provide no contrast between round and straight elements. Enlarging vertically does not make the letter bigger or more legible at a distance. On the contrary, the emphasis on verticality produces a grid effect, which can be ornamentally restful and handsome (in a black-letter face for instance) but which sometimes estranges the word."[11]

/04/
Cover for Frutiger's article in TM/STM from the series 'Zeitschriften-Plagiate' (magazine plagiarism) by Hans-Rudolf Lutz.

/05/
None of the tested types is satisfactory – they are either too individual, too strongly historically influenced or do not have good legibility.

douane
douane
douane

/08/
Compared to the circular o, the oval o-shape results in better-connected word images – adhesive letter design by Adrian Frutiger.

/06/
Narrow typefaces have clearly reduced legibility since round and straight glyphs look too similar.

douane
~~douane~~

/07/
Study of the ideal stroke weight for Alphabet Roissy – too fine (top), correct (centre), too fat (bottom).

douane
douane

douane

ODBEFHIJKLMN
PQURSTVWCG
QU WA &YXZJ

Notes of details (in case of some being overlooked or in case of slight inattention)   height of letters = 1"   width of stem = ⅛"   the curves of (E C) &c. slightly less than ⅛"   OQCGS& are a little taller than 1" and project slightly above & below top & foot lines   J projects slightly below foot line   K is as wide as W, fall slightly below foot line

Note : the 2nd QU to be cut together as one   WITH CARE, INK NOT waterproof.

obdcepqɔuɡas
aɑhijklmnrsek
tvwxyz   ɡɡ
1234567890
ɔupqjyɡ

/09/
In Edward Johnston's signage face (1916) for London Transport the numeral 1 has no upper serif but the top of the stroke is oblique; the minuscule l ends in a curve.

Unambiguous symbol recognition *Alphabet Roissy* features open letterforms similar to the 1964 typeface *Concorde*. However, some changes specific to a signage face had been implemented. For example a one-storey version of the minuscule g was chosen since this simpler form integrated better into the word image. The vertical majuscule M is also less obtrusive. The opposite is true for the Q; through the diagonally positioned tail a characteristic element of the symbol is being emphasised /17/.

Altogether, *Alphabet Roissy* is slightly darker than *Concorde* since signage faces have stronger strokes than typefaces in order to guarantee good legibility of a single word or numeral under busy or even stressful environmental conditions. Additional factors regarding the quality of a signage face are: sufficient symbol size, generous kerning, letter-spacing and leading, as well as enough distance to the edge of the background. Different lighting situations such as backlit or lit panels as well as sunlight, but also shiny surfaces, a large reading distance, a limited field of vision, an unfavourable point of view and the movement of the reader/viewer have a strong influence on the perception and legibility of signage. Comprehensive tests are therefore necessary; the blur test, for instance, clearly demonstrates the quality of the numerals 6 and 9, which are neither too diagonal nor too vertical. /18/.

decided that for *Roissy* it would get a curve at the bottom /11/. This has an aesthetic softness, it is closer to the American expression. The letters b d p q, which are similar in terms of shape, are mirrored or rotated forms respectively. I thought that the difference between p and q is sufficiently clear if one letter has the stroke on the left and the other on the right. In sans-serif typefaces the glyphs I l and 1 are a topic in terms of shape: in German signage faces the majuscule I often gets a serif at the top and bottom and the minuscule l has a curve at the bottom in order to make it easier to differentiate the two letters /16/. To be honest, I don't think that's necessary. As far as I'm concerned these signs have to be naked. For a similar reason I chose the one-storey version for the g. Since the Renaissance there has been the one-storey g in the cursive. Therefore both forms have always been of equal value to me. With longer texts the two-storey g is helpful for reading even if it represents a dissonance, as it were – it is the only letter with three counters. Signage, however, isn't read like a book, it is taken in at one single glance. So the only solution for me was the one-storey g. The numerals 6 and 9 could be more open but I thought that it would better fit the overall rhythm of the typeface as it is /18/.

The arrow is a very important symbol. In Gestalt psychology the arrow is one of the most significant symbols; its appearance can be traced back far into the history of humankind. It is the only non-verbal sign that was used at the Paris-Roissy airport. The arrow had to be neither acute-angled like a weapon nor obtuse-angled like a snowplough. The right-angled form was the right one /20/, not with parallel strokes however, but with tapered ones /21/. Furthermore, the arrow should be the same in each direction without changing the weight.

/10/
Study of the ideal letter-spacing – too narrow (top), normal (centre), and, according to the prevailing view at the time, too wide (bottom).

douane
douane
douane

/13/
The manual Signalisation sur les aéroports *(1976) lists the width of the minuscule c as the measure for the whitespace between words.*

/11/
Letters are not read the same way in each country – the y (top right) seems ideal for English.

Roissy Roissy
Roissy Roissy

Riencàcdéclarer
Rien à déclarer

/12/
Only a short serif for the 1 (far right) so that people from English-speaking countries do not confuse the numerals 1 and 7.

12 12 12 12 12 12

/14/
The use of pictograms is rejected since the clarity of expression seems questionable without international conventions.

 Bar
 Selfservice
 Snack
 Restaurant

/15/
A slightly taller ascender and a finer stroke differentiate the minuscule l from the majuscule I in Roissy.

Illinois

/16/
Clear distinction between I and l in a grotesque – DIN-Mittelschrift, *Erik Spiekermann's* Officina, Vialog *of Werner Schneider, Helmut Neuss.*

Illinois
Illinois
Illinois

/17/
Different letter shapes and proportions in Concorde *(top) compared to Alphabet Roissy (bottom).*

MQ grsy
MQ grsy

/18/
Legibility study – the numerals 6 and 9 of Alphabet Roissy can still be clearly differentiated when heavily blurred.

69 69 69

For the airport's large display boards Hans-Jürg Hunziker additionally drew a monospace majuscule alphabet in 1973/74 /24/. The implementation, however, turned out to be difficult. First we made a few trials with a dotted typeface or with glyphs constructed from seven segments, as is the case with hand-held calculators. But none of those were suitable. The airport passenger only feels safe with a 'normal' typeface. Therefore we settled on a flip board system. But using the Solaris technology /25/ cost a shed-load of money. The little blades were printed in silkscreen and then cut. A tricky thing to do. If the blades only moved a tiny bit it instantly resulted in a visible flaw. The printing technology partly influenced the shapes of the glyphs. Acute incisions, as with the M for instance, are smeared in silkscreen so the incisions had to be slightly obtuse. Altogether however, the Solaris type was meant to maintain the *Roissy* character. Well, with the M the centre triangle doesn't go all the way down to the baseline, it was supposed to have as much light as possible flowing into it /24/.

Altogether I was working for almost a decade on the various tasks for the Paris-Roissy airport. I was still a member of the commission for the airport's extension, Roissy 1 and Roissy 2, and after that I stopped. The typeface for Roissy airport is very important to me. There was also one very important situation in the context of the Roissy project: the architects were bending over the plans and were able to spatially imagine the passageways. This was impossible for me. Then I had an epiphany: my talent is mainly rooted in the two-dimensional.

Information technologies From the start there have been large display boards /27/ and dice-shaped information displays to inform passengers about departure and arrival times at the airport Paris-Roissy. For these elements, the specifically designed *Roissy-Solaris* was used /24/. The printing of the monospace type onto the flip blades and the manufacture of the whole system was carried out by the Italian company Solaris at Udine. Each single unit /25/ contained the complete set of characters on flip blades including capitals, numerals and the punctuation marks full-stop, dash and stroke.

Apart from the information boards, there are also the monitors of the internal TV system where departure and arrival times can be obtained. Presumably a standard typeface had been used during the first few years before Adrian Frutiger's screen type *Caractères TVP* /26/ was implemented since a sheet showing detail corrections is dated 17 May 1979.[12]

The height of the majuscules and numerals comprises 13 cells based on a rectangular grid of 16 by 16 cells. There are, however, different proportions in the design drawings: 82 by 122 millimetres (3.3 by 4.8 inch) in an undated letter-set and 48 by 96 millimetres (1.9 by 3.8 inch) – equivalent to a vertical double cell – on an attachment to the dated sheet /26/.

Today, *Alphabet Roissy* is no longer used for the signage. It has been replaced by *Frutiger*, which has also been implemented on the monitors /28/.

/19/
*Special manufacture of
the Letraset sheets in the exclusive
typeface* Alphabet Roissy *for
Aéroport de Paris.*

/20/
*Weapon, direction sign, snow plough? –
The weapon is acutely angled,
the direction sign right angled and
the snow plough obtusely angled.*

/21/
*Construction drawing of the
Frutiger arrow for Roissy –
the strokes are tapered towards
the apex.*

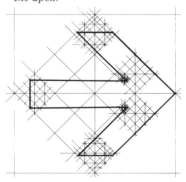

/22/
*Precise instructions for the
positioning of text and arrow –
the horizontally cut arm sits
on the mean-line.*

/23/
*Ratio of type size to leading –
half of the x-height defines the
ascender height and the distance to
the ascender of the following line.*

/24/

The redesign of the alphabet as the monospace type Roissy-Solaris was carried out by Hans-Jürg Hunziker.

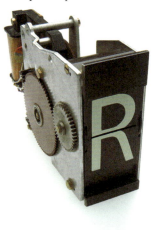

/25/

Each single, and very sturdy, unit of the electro-mechanical Solaris technology contains the complete alphabet.

/26/

Frutiger's design variations and study (1979, top) for Caractères TVP, *a cathode ray monitor typeface (bottom).*

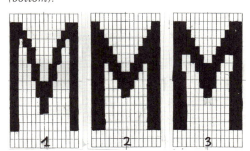

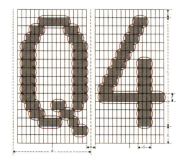

/27/

Departure board of the Paris-Roissy airport with flip-blade technology by the Italian company Solaris and with the monospace alphabet from 1973/74.

/28/

Today's vastly improved monitor technology allows the use of Frutiger as a screen type.

ALPHABET
BRANCHER

We really enjoyed the projects for the printing inks manufacturer G. et P. Brancher Frères. We had, as early as 1960, already worked for them through the in-house graphic studio of Deberny & Peignot. Shortly after I opened my own design studio in 1961 Brancher became our client. Over the course of many years we regularly designed print material for the Parisian firm /06/.

Louis Brancher took over the company in 1880 and he chose a beehive for the company logo as a symbol of an active family community creating a quality product. In 1958, more than one hundred years after its formation, the beehive logo was still in the letterhead /03/. This logo was literally calling out for a more stylised representation, and that happened in 1960 /04/. During the redesign, Pierre Brancher, then the company president, told me that the aspects of quality and industriousness were very important to him. I thought the comparison with busy bees, quality honey and good colour wasn't bad at all. In 1971, after Pierre Brancher's retirement, his son took over the company, but from then onwards we mainly worked together with Pierre's grandson Olivier.

Due to the extension of the company with a new factory and subsidiaries abroad, we carried out a further comprehensive redesign of its branding in 1971 /05/. In spite of its new size, the family character of the enterprise was supposed to be maintained. We kept the beehive as a pictogram; in order to achieve colour effects, however, it was no longer a line drawing. Instead we used block colour. I liked the fact that – although it was even further stylised – you could still recognise the beehive. Then we were looking for the most harmonious connection between pictogram and company name. We came up with the idea to integrate the shape of the beehive, which was reminiscent of an A, into a wordmark. For this reason, the other letters received the same chunky expression. Through the rounded edges and the eight colours we also tried to establish an association with viscous printing inks.[1] Based on my wordmark, Hans-Jürg Hunziker drew further capitals one by one in the studio, depending on which letters were needed for the various product names. During a three-year continuous development, almost all letters of the alphabet were created and so it made sense to complete the set.

Practically, the whole studio was involved in the design of Brancher's new branding. Bruno Pfäffli, for instance, designed the letterheads /05/, Hans-Jürg Hunziker the product packaging and Nicole Delamarre the brochures /06/. As a variation on the design, we used only elementary, geometrical shapes beside the typeface. The colour tins got wavy lines, products for rolls received circles as an indicator and cleaning products featured linear contrasts. All printing material, products and the complete advertising material could thus be given a uniform and clearly recognisable image.

A typeface as viscous as honey   In the minds of the consumers, the over one-hundred-year-long connection between Brancher and the beehive brings together the ideas of industriousness and the viscous fluids honey and printing ink. A 1975 manuscript by Horst Heiderhoff states: "This fact was the reason that during the first redesign in 1960 the beehive was kept, although the association appeared to be slightly 'outdated' at first. On closer inspection, however, the benefits of this time-honoured connection, which had firmly established itself in people's minds, outweighed all the more modernistic designs, and the image of the beehive prevailed."[2] This first redesign of the logo was carried out by Frutiger in the in-house typographic studio at Deberny & Peignot. According to Adrian Frutiger, this studio only lasted for about half a year, since clients thought that the invoices generated were too expensive. Therefore, when Frutiger opened his own studio, he was able to take over Brancher as a client. Among other things, Bruno Pfäffli redesigned the product packaging /06/.[3]

A second redesign from 1971 comprises the design of an eight-colour wordmark in addition to the logo, and, gradually, of a whole majuscule alphabet. It represents Frutiger's fifth corporate typeface and the fourth in a row of related typefaces of similar shape. A common characteristic of these four corporate typefaces is a rectangular base shape with rounded edges for the majuscule O. This is true for the serif design of the corporate alphabet for Francis Bouygues (see page 148) as well as for the three sans serifs for EDF-GDF (see page 198), Facom (see page 220) and Brancher.[4] *Alphabet Brancher* is almost identical in shape and proportion to *Alphabet EDF-GDF*. It is, however, significantly stronger and features rounded corners for all glyphs.

The above-mentioned style of type was quite common for corporate typefaces during the mid-20th century.[5] It projected a neutral, cool, robust and durable feel. Thus, the technological and industrial aspects of an enterprise were emphasised. For Brancher, the 'family' idea was maintained through a consistent implementation of the wordmark on facades, signage, door handles, work uniforms and even on the crockery for visitors.[6] Today, the wordmark is used in a modified version; the alphabet is no longer in use.[7]

/01/
The 1961 logo design by Bruno Pfäffli for the printing inks manufacturer Brancher Frères was not implemented.

/02/
The rounded corners of the letter shapes of Alphabet Brancher trigger an association with viscous colour.

ABCDEFGHIJKLMNOPQR
STUVWXYZ0123456789

03/
Logo of Brancher Frères until 1960 – symbol of an active family community that creates a quality product.

/04/
Redesign of the Brancher Frères logo at Deberny & Peignot – designs and implementation (1960) by Adrian Frutiger.

/05/
The beehive was integrated into the new wordmark in a heavily stylised, block-colour form – design from 1970.

BRANCHER

SOCIÉTÉ DES ENCRES G. ET P. BRANCHER FRÈRES

Fabrique d'encres d'imprimerie fondée en 1840	Zone industrielle B.P. 80	3 et 5, rue Paul Dautier 78140 - Vélizy	Téléphone 946 00-10 Télex 69 720

/06/
Adrian Frutiger's logos from 1960 (left) and 1970 (right) in use – advertisements not by Studio Frutiger.

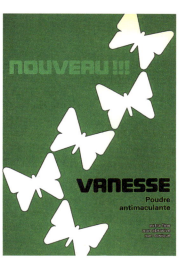

/07/
Labels (left) by Bruno Pfäffli with the 1960 logo – brochure (right) by Nicole Delamarre with Alphabet Brancher.

Logos and wordmarks
1965–1971

Pierre Disderot Luminaires
lighting manufacturers
Cachan (F)

Rencontres – Centre de Sornetan
Protestant union of Switzerland
Lausanne (CH)

Totem
public relations agency
Paris (F)

Caisse Nationale de Retraite
des Ouvriers
workers retirement savings fund
France

Euralair
private airline company
Le Bourget (F)

Tissages Normands Réunis
upholstery fabric manufacturer
Paris (F)

Boutique du Palais Royal
luxury goods shop
Paris (F)

Laboratoires Peloilles
pharmaceutical company
Paris (F)

Hadlaub Verlag
publishing house
Winterthur (CH)
Design: Bruno Pfäffli

Evangelische Gesellschaft des
Kantons Bern
Christian organisation
Bern (CH)

Traduction Œcuménique
de la Bible – Édition du Cerf
publishing house
Paris (F)

Banque Européenne
d'Investissement
European Investment Bank
Brussels (B)
Design: Bruno Pfäffli

Demy Frères
manufacturer of concrete silos
Paris (F)

Bull-General-Electric
computer manufacturer
Paris (F)

Grif – Société Filiale du Groupe Prache
concept and implementation
of company publications
Paris (F)
Design: Bruno Pfäffli

jet-guide
magazine masthead for Air France
Paris (F)
Design not implemented

Brancher Frères
printing ink manufacturers
Paris (F)

Inodep – Institut Œcuménique
pour le Développement des Peuples
Ecumenical Institute
for Human Development
Paris (F)

Mills
scaffolding construction firm
Le Bourget (F)

Pictogram for
Air France flight schedules
France

Production of type
Linofilm photosetting

In 1954 Mergenthaler Linotype Company introduced the Linofilm, a photocomposing system that superseded traditional hot metal line-casting technology. The Linofilm system consisted of four parts: a keyboard unit **/01/**, a photo unit **/02/**, a correction unit **/03/** and a composer **/06/**.

The Linofilm keyboard unit comprised an electric typewriter with a special keyboard **/01/** and two switches that transmitted command data from the punched tape to the photo unit. Above the keyboard there was a scale showing character widths – each font had a width card with printed circuits.

The Linofilm photo unit exposed captured text to right-reading positive film or light-sensitive photo paper. 18 interchangeable grids **/04/**, which each contained the negatives for 88 characters **/05/**, could be accessed at the same time. In order to expose the size range from 6 to 36 pt, three grids or frames were needed. For each grid, type sizes were defined by a system of automatically changing lenses. An electronic flash tube provided 12 exposures a second.

That resulted in a theoretical output of 43 000 characters per hour.

The frame needed for the punch tape was inserted and automatically positioned in front of the lens system and kept there until the tape was finished or the font had to be changed. Individual characters were singled out by the lenses and the aperture. The aperture consisted of eight metal plates with interlocking openings that moved in both directions, accessing one character at a time. The punched tape instructed the aperture situated behind the frame to project the selected character onto the film. A moving mirrored reflector added one character next to another according to its width.

The Linofilm correction unit **/03/** did most of its work automatically. It was based on the register punches – identical for each size – that were made when the photo unit **/02/** exposed a line. Punching out faulty lines and splicing on corrected ones did not result in thicker film material.

The Linofilm composer **/06/** was the last piece in the production chain. It could reduce or enlarge lines of type between 4 and 216 pt and set them at a length of up to 90 cicero (96 pica) at any height. Enlargements and reductions required for ads or jobbing work were achieved by a system of moving mirrors. The negative holder, lenses and film material remained in place. The size and position of the type could be seen through a translucent layout sheet that worked like a screen with the image projected from behind.

/01/
Keyboard unit for the Linofilm photosetting system with the control unit (left) and the backlit keys for font selection (right).

/02/
Text is captured on punched tape and exposed onto photographic film or light-sensitive paper within the Linofilm photo unit.

/03/
The Linofilm corrector cut out faulty lines in the film and spliced in new text.

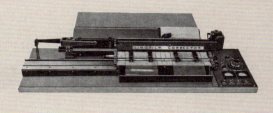

/06/
The Linofilm composer could scale lines of type, slant them and move them horizontally and vertically.

/04/
The Linofilm's revolving font magazine held 18 grids for parallel operation.

/05/
A grid consisted of a metal frame with glass negatives, each carrying 88 characters.

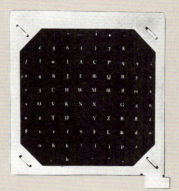

Name of typeface	Client	Designer	Design | Publication	Typesetting technology	Manufacturer	Weights
Iridium	D. Stempel AG	Adrian Frutiger	1972 | 1972	Phototypesetting Digital Typesetting PostScript	– D. Stempel AG | Linotype – Linotype	3 3

IRIDIUM

Iridium was my first typeface design for D. Stempel AG, and in 1972 it was one of the first typefaces the company commissioned especially for phototypesetting. However, our co-operation had already started earlier. After my talk on *OCR-B* at the ATypI conference in 1967 in Paris, I was invited over to Frankfurt by Walter Greisner. Due to my experience with the design of *OCR-B* and the Lumitype designs for phototypesetting, Walter Greisner, Walter Cunz and Heinrich Vallée – all in leading roles at Stempel – asked me whether I was interested in helping set up their matrix manufacturing department. They wanted to do a consulting contract with me. It was clear that I needed a home for my work, and I said to myself, if it can't be Paris – which would have been my favourite – then it's Frankfurt am Main. After we'd finalised the contract I flew to America first, to look at the whole business of typeface manufacture over there. I stayed for four days. The art director Mike Parker and Matthew Carter at Mergenthaler Linotype made sure that all doors were open for me. That kind of trust did me good. For me, a company that trusted me was the basis for everything else. There were others too, in America, who wanted to work with me; one of them held a cheque under my nose. I found that a bit fishy. At Stempel, however, everything was done correctly. When I returned from America, I made a plan as to how to proceed since the whole department for matrix manufacturing had to be set up from scratch.

D. Stempel AG was in the business of manufacturing typefaces for handsetting, and since 1900 they had been exclusively producing the line-casting matrices for Linotype's European distribution.[1] When, from 1967[2] onwards, Linotype also built phototypesetting machines in Germany, Stempel was commissioned with the production of these typefaces as well. Walter Greisner was in charge of that. When I joined, they were just setting up a new camera that was designed by an engineer from the American Mergenthaler Linotype – it was a gigantic monster. A three-metre-long piece of granite served as a base.[3] Back then, this camera had a focal length of several metres.

I had already experienced the change from one technology at Lumitype to another, newer one. Now there was a similar thing happening at Stempel. The basis was the original artwork that had been used for more than half a century as a master for the templates and punches of the Linotype matrices. So first of all it was about creating negatives of these drawings. The biggest problem was adapting the typefaces to 18 units. Also the accents for the European market created a lot of headaches for us because – as opposed to Lumitype – automatic centring wasn't possible in this case. Overall, the Lumitype was much more advanced than the Linofilm. These early days at Stempel were a real pain for me!

The first adaptations for phototypesetting at Stempel were typefaces that existed for handsetting as well as machinesetting, such as *Palatino* by Hermann Zapf. Further developed into *Aldus* it was one of the most-used typefaces in Europe, and in Germany almost

The origin of Iridium   The term *Iridium* comes from the Greek 'iris', meaning rainbow. It is the name of a chemical element and refers to a silvery-white, very hard and brittle precious metal that belongs to the group of platinates. It is also the chemical element with the highest density. Since it is resistant to acids, it is often used in the manufacture of appliances and machines as a hardening additive in platinum.[4]

Walter Greisner had chosen a suitable name[5] for this typeface, which was designed by Adrian Frutiger for phototypesetting.

Produced in 1972 by D. Stempel AG for the matrix plates of the Linotype phototypesetting machines, it was suggested that *Iridium* be used for Linotype's line-casting machines as well. Although Stempel had been setting up the production of photographic matrices since 1968, the casting of metal type and Linotype matrices remained an important part of the business.[6]

Linotype was doing well; there was a constant demand for line-casting machines in Europe. They had also had some success in the business of phototypesetting in Europe. The magazine *Deutscher Drucker* from 1970 contains a report about Linotype GmbH and their sales record when introducing the first phototypesetting machine produced in Germany – the 'Linofilm Europa'.[7]

Although adapted to Linotype's different phototypesetting machines, *Iridium* received little attention for a long time until, in 1993, it disappeared altogether due to the eventual abandonment of the photocomposing system. In conversation with Walter Greisner, he expressed his belief that *Iridium* would probably have had more success had it been produced for line-casting machines as well. Linotype, however, had favoured *Helvetica* and *Syntax*, and *Iridium* was put on the backburner due to a lack of resources.[8]

Only in 2002, when Linotype decided to publish all of Adrian Frutiger's typefaces, did it eventually become available as a PostScript font.

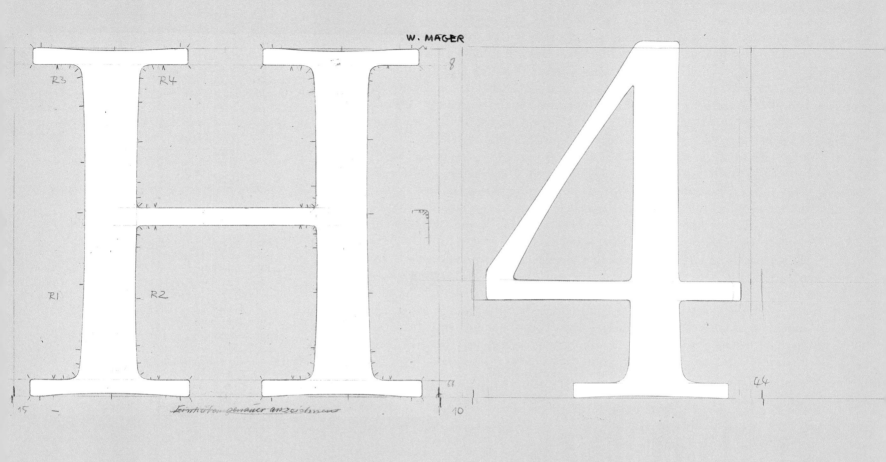

/01/

*After 1972 Adrian Frutiger drew
small capitals and oldstyle
numerals in addition to the regular
font of* Iridium.

every single paperback was set in *Aldus.* We didn't have much time for these adaptations because the new machines needed a selection of matrix plates pretty quickly. It wasn't only Hermann Zapf's beautiful typefaces that had to suffer: in the heat of the moment it had completely escaped me to consult him. There were ill feelings that put our friendship to the test. The adaptation of *Univers,* too, was a problem. The idea was to directly transfer it from Lumitype but that didn't work because of the 36 units. So eventually I had to redraw it all. Apart from that, it was necessary to set the obliques at 12° instead of 16° because the same drawings were used for phototypesetting as well as line-casting, and it would have been too wide for the line-casting matrices otherwise.[9]

During the first year or two, the photo masks – called friskets – **/05/**, were created at my studio by my colleagues until the department in Frankfurt was fully equipped. The setting up, however, moved ahead quite quickly and soon it was much more practical over there than at our place in Paris. The draftsmen, for instance, got rotatable light tables. The cutting of the friskets from rubylith foil[10] was thus much more comfortable than at our studio, where everything was done using a normal table.

One particular situation has stuck in my memory. At Stempel we were talking about the adaptation of *Baskerville* for phototypesetting. For hot metal setting they had the so-called *Original-Baskerville Antiqua.* I suggested using the drawings for the Lumitype *Baskerville.* The response was that the Lumitype *Baskerville* 'had too much Frutiger' in it. And suddenly it became totally clear to me: they were absolutely right. When working for Lumitype, I really had a tendency to give everything the Frutiger treatment. I wasn't really good at adapting classic typefaces, but I only realised that fairly late.

The noble form in a typeface "Design the most beautiful typeface you're capable of." Walter Greisner's demand formed the basis for *Iridium-Antiqua,* which – according to Erich Schulz-Anker – is a typeface developed specifically for phototypesetting and based on neoclassical styles.[11] However, its classification in this group is debatable.

A typical characteristic of neoclassical typefaces is fine serifs **/03/** and a strong stroke contrast. The latter is not particularly pronounced in the phototypesetting face *Iridium,* in order to minimise the risk of its printing too finely in offset printing – especially since the reproduction templates were produced in only one design scale for all point sizes.[12]

A further characteristic of neoclassical typefaces is the equalised widths of the capitals. Regarding this aspect, however, Frutiger's *Iridium* follows more closely a transitional typeface by using different widths **/06/**. There is no explicitly vertical stress and the bowl shape – for instance in the lowercase e – is half open **/07/**. Additionally, the round shapes feature soft and mediating transitions between the main strokes and the hairlines. On the other hand, the well-pronounced teardrop shapes are a typical – but not necessarily obligatory – characteristic of a neoclassical antiqua. **/09/**

As opposed to the regular font with its upright stress and, therefore, static bowl shapes for b d p and q **/10/**, these same letters feature an asymmetric, dynamic shape in

/02/
Representation of a neoclassical typeface – handsetting for book printing, phototypesetting in offset and photogravure.

/03/
Comparison of serifs – the transitional Baskerville *(left), the neoclassical typefaces* Bodoni *(centre) and* Iridium *(right).*

/04/
Iridium *(bottom) has a more condensed look than* Baskerville *(top) but appears more open and sleek than* Bodoni *(centre).*

charakteristischen Merkmale einer klassizistischen Form durch die reproduktionstechnische Bearbeitung besonders für den Offsetdruck nicht verändern dür-

charakteristischen Merkmale einer klassizistischen Form durch die reproduktionstechnische Bearbeitung besonders für den Offsetdruck nicht verändern dür-

charakteristischen Merkmale einer klassizistischen Form durch die reproduktionstechnische Bearbeitung besonders für den Offsetdruck nicht verändern dür-

/05/
Based on outline drawings, Adrian Frutiger cut Iridium *freehand into the masking film for reproduction.*

the italic. Thus, the lowercase italic letters bear a relationship to the group of renaissance antiquas and to *Méridien* /15/.

Although one can find the characteristics of a number of different styles in *Iridium*, its overall shape feels well-balanced and natural. All individual shapes and counter-shapes form a harmonious, indigenous whole, and the typeface seems to glow from within. When trying to create 'the most beautiful' typeface, Frutiger chose – and anything else would have been a surprise – a tapered stroke, a characteristic typical of most of his serifs. The feet of the serifs are concave and the upper serifs are slightly curved. As always his glyphs are of a clear, open and simple shape. But nonetheless, there are many differences compared to his earlier serifs. There is a richness of shapes apparent in *Iridium* that cannot be observed in any of Frutiger's earlier typefaces. For the first time ever, Frutiger chose a teardrop shape for the majuscule J, /08/ thus abandoning completely his earlier dislike of teardrop shapes as expressed in *Méridien. Opéra* has teardrops as well but only in the lowercase. With *Iridium*, the strict principles of *Méridien* have eventually given way to a natural generosity and serenity.

Unfortunately, however, the small capitals and oldstyle numerals /01/ are missing in the digital font of this sleek and elegant typeface. The best versions of the various ones produced for phototypesetting have not always been chosen either /20/.

During the re-drawing of the existing typefaces at Stempel we started talking about the problem with neoclassical typefaces in phototypesetting /02/. Walter Greisner soon realised he wanted a 'real' typeface, one that was especially designed for phototypesetting. He came to me and said: "Design the most beautiful typeface you're capable of." He already had a name for it as well: Iridium – like the precious metal, which is even more rare than platinum and, by the way, also more resilient. He didn't explicitly ask for a neoclassical antiqua but he wanted a noble, extremely easy-to-read, and beautiful typeface. Nonetheless, *Iridium* has a strong neoclassical undertone. But it isn't as hard as *Bodoni*. With Lumitype, this problem resulted in the design of *Egyptienne,* which, however, has never been a replacement for a neoclassical typeface. The question was: How far can the term 'neoclassical' be stretched? I developed different designs and talked to Greisner a lot. Maybe the issue of neoclassical typefaces for phototypesetting wasn't such a big problem in Germany as it was in France because they weren't used as much in Germany.[13]

We drew *Iridium* in my studio, then photographically reduced the letters and put them together into text samples to check the results. Finally, we used pencil to create a big clean outline drawing of each glyph /01/. The experts at Stempel helped with the spacing. I also had the chance to work with Arthur Ritzel, the director of the typeface department, for a few years. He was a real dictator, but he knew his business extraordinarily well. He also had an unfailing eye for the exact spacing of a typeface. There are still some pencil drawings of *Iridium* on tracing paper that bear his corrections and signature /22/. He was almost over-anal, most of the time it was about a hundredth of a millimetre. More often than not I didn't agree with him. I put a rubylith foil over the final artwork and cut

/06/
Iridium (right) references the proportions of the transitional Baskerville *(left), not those of the neoclassical* Bodoni.

/07/
With Iridium *(right), the finial of the e and the curve of the n resemble transitional designs.*

MORS MORS MORS

eon eon eon

/08/
For the first time, Adrian Frutiger designed a typeface with a teardrop shape for the J but he discarded the looped form for the cursive k.

/09/
The teardrop shape, which is not yet very obvious in Baskerville, is pronounced as a ball shape in neoclassical typefaces such as Bodoni *and* Iridium *(from left to right).*

/10/
In contrast to Baskerville *(left), the lowercase b in* Bodoni *(centre) and* Iridium *(right) features a serif.*

J *kk*

acj acj acj

bpq bpq bpq

/11/
Comparison of Baskerville, Bodoni, Walbaum *and* Iridium *(from left to right) – the horizontal link in the k is atypical for Frutiger*

/12/
As is common, the two Ss are the same in the regular font; in the Italic font the lowercase s gets a teardrop.

/13/
Except for p and q, the descenders of Iridium *italic feature a teardrop –this is also true for the ligatures.*

KKKK

SsSs

fjy fi fl ß

/14/
When compared, Baskerville *italic has the most curved form,* Bodoni *is slightly less curved and* Iridium *features the least curved shapes.*

/15/
The asymmetrical forms of Iridium *(right) p and q are more reminiscent of* Méridien *than of* Baskerville *or* Bodoni.

nz nz nz

pq pq pq pq

out the friskets on the light table /05/. I did this manually in order to set something against the high definition reproduction of phototypesetting.

Just as with some other typefaces, real heart and soul went into *Iridium*. I really gave my all to create a beautiful typeface. The base strokes swell and shrink almost unnoticeably and the foot of the serifs is very slightly arched. The widths of the capitals, which are normally equalised in the neoclassical style, are very carefully harmonised here. I drew the M wide, but didn't extend the vertex to the baseline – once again I was concerned about the harmony between the counters and the sidebearings /06/. This was also the reason I couldn't use my typical version of the K with its detached angle. *Bodoni* does have that angle that touches the stem, but the disadvantage is that the counters become very narrow. With *Iridium*, however, it is connected to the stem via a short crossbar. This creates bigger counters /11/. *Walbaum* has a similarly attached angle. It is a very beautiful typeface anyway. If I had to look to examples, *Walbaum* would be a beautiful one – not so much as regards the detailing, but rather concerning its overall appearance.

In spite of everything else, with *Iridium* it wasn't all about the technology of setting and exposure: it was first of all about the creation of a beautiful, noble typeface – the technology came second. It is stable and delicate at the same time, and for a neoclassical typeface it is soft and full of life. You don't immediately see that, but you can feel it instantly. This is due to its overall construction. Everything plays with everything else. The effect of this typeface comes from its whole not from its details. I still find it beautiful when I look at it now.

D. Stempel AG   In addition to handsetting and the production of line-casting matrices for the Linotype machines in Europe,[14] Stempel set up another successful line of business in 1967: the manufacture of typefaces for photosetting and digital printing.[15] Typefaces were often produced for more than one printing technology. Since 1963, Arthur Ritzel[16] had been heading the departments of typeface design and punchcutting. He also stayed in the USA often to oversee the manufacture of matrix plates.

In 1967, the new board member Walter Greisner initiated the manufacture of grids for phototypesetting. He took over as chairman from Heinrich Vallée in 1973 after the latter had, four years earlier, replaced the long-serving Walter H. Cunz.[17]

The position of art director at D. Stempel AG was held jointly from 1947 to 1956 by Hermann Zapf[18] and Georg Kurt Schauer. In 1950, Gotthard de Beauclair, joined as a third art director. Subsequently, Erich Schulz-Anker took over as sole art director. With his articles on *Iridium-Antiqua* /23/ he conveyed some interesting points on the thinking behind this typeface for phototypesetting.[19] Further important contributions are owed to the cooperation between Frutiger and Horst Heiderhoff. The latter was assistant to Schulz-Anker from 1963 and then became art director himself from 1976 to 1981.[20] The result was several comprehensive accounts of Frutiger's design work as well as *Der Mensch und seine Zeichen* /25/[21].

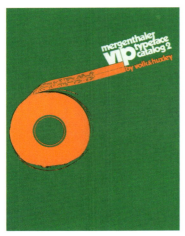

/16/
1980 catalogue of typeface samples for the VIP phototypesetting machine by American Mergenthaler including the three Iridium *fonts.*

/17/
Linotype Fotosatz Schriften –
part 1 – brochure of Mergenthaler
Linotype GmbH including Iridium
in three fonts from 6 to 48 pt.

/18/
Shortening serifs creates space for the diareses in phototypesetting (centre) – in the later digital design they are placed above the letter.

UÜ Ü

/19/
Different positioning of the dots for i and j – Linotron 505 (left), Linofilm VIP (centre) and PostScript (right).

ij ij ij

/20/
Curve shapes in f and j – Linotron 505 version without overlap (left), version with overlap (centre) and PostScript version (right).

fj fj fj

/21/
Strongly differing widths in the lowercase a for the phototypesetting machines Linotron 505 (black) and Linofilm Quick (blue).

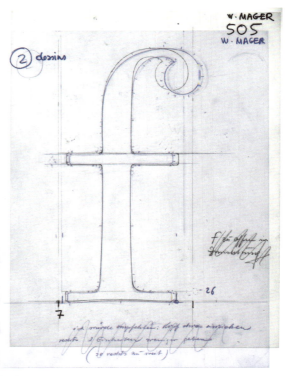

/22/
Working drawing of lowercase f without overlap for Linotron 505 (black) and with overlap (blue) – implementation not known.

D. Stempel AG
6000 Frankfurt am Main 70
Postfach 701160
Telefon (0611) 6068-1

Iridium-Antiqua

Die Konzeption einer spezifischen Fotosatzschrift

(Beitrag aus Druck Print, Heft 3/1973)

ABCDEFGHI
JKLMNOPQR
STUVWXYZ
abcdefghijklm
nopqrstuvwxyz
1234567890

*ABCDEFGHI
JKLMNOPQR
STUVWXYZ
abcdefghijklm
nopqrstuvwxyz
1234567890*

ABCDEFGHI
JKLMNOPQR
STUVWXYZ
abcdefghijklm
nopqrstuvwxyz
1234567890

Der Fotosatz hat sich – soweit es die Werkschriften betrifft – trotz seiner völlig neuen Technologie bisher meist damit begnügt, vorhandene Schriftschnitte des Bleisatzes in das Fotosatz-Schriftenprogramm zu übernehmen. Schon bald hatte sich allerdings erwiesen, daß die unveränderte »Übernahme« zu keinen befriedigenden Ergebnissen führt. Die für ein anderes Verfahren entworfenen Schriften mußten überarbeitet und den neuen materialen und technischen Bedingungen angepaßt werden.

Die Art und das Ausmaß der Adaption richtet sich nach der besonderen Struktur der Zeichen, nach dem Stil der Schrift. Manche Schriften sind besonders empfindlich gegen die reproduktionstechnischen Veränderungen im Fotosatz. Das gilt vor allem für Schriften mit starken Fett/Fein-Kontrasten, z. B. solchen im Stil einer Bodoni-, Walbaum- oder Didot-Antiqua. Die Aufgabe und das Problem, die klassizistische Antiqua dem Fotosatz zu erschließen, diese Weise unter optimalen Bedingungen bereits im Entwicklungsstadium ein fotosatzgerechtes Ergebnis gesichert werden.

Die Konzeption der »Iridium«

Die besondere Aufgabe, die sich *Frutiger* mit der »Iridium« gestellt hatte, geht jedoch darüber hinaus: sie betrifft den Ausdruck und die Anmutungsqualitäten der Schrift. Klassizistische Schriften sind von der Konstruktion her meist streng, nüchtern und kühl. Das sollte bei der »Iridium« gemildert werden.

Nun bewirkt jedoch die gestochen scharfe Reproduktion der Schriftzeichen im Fotosatz gerade jenen Eindruck, der hier bewußt vermieden werden sollte. So mußte dieser Tendenz mit geeigneten Mitteln entschieden entgegengearbeitet werden. *Frutiger* hat das Problem auf zweifache Art gelöst: einmal durch eine entsprechende Formanlage, dann aber auch durch den eigenhändig-freihändigen Schnitt der großen Reproduktionsvorlagen.

Die Konzeption der »Iridium«: Ausgangsbasis ist, dem Entwurfsziel entsprechend, die klassizistische Grundform mit ihrer Eleganz im Ausdruck. Gegenüber den historischen Vorbildern sind jedoch die Mittellängen zugunsten eines etwas größeren Schriftbildes leicht erhöht, der Duktus ist weniger streng, alle Formelemente sind sensibel moduliert. Das betrifft die Grundstriche wie die An- und Abschwellungen, die verbindenden Feinelemente wie die abschließenden Serifen. Was für die Einzelheiten gilt, gilt auch für die Gesamtstruktur und den Ausdruck der Schrift: das Erscheinungsbild der »Iridium« hat die Klarheit und Eleganz der klassizistischen Schrift, und es ist zugleich angenehm geschmeidig.

Die Qualitäten einer Fotosatzschrift sind nicht allein das Ergebnis der Konzeption und des zeichnerischen Entwurfs, sondern auch der adäquaten Ausführung der Reproduktionsvorlagen. Bei der »Iridium« übernahm der Entwerfer selbst die Herstellung der großen Vorlagen, der sogenannten Friskets. Das heißt, *Adrian Frutiger* schnitt die Schriftzeichen anhand der korrigierten Entwürfe selbst, und zwar freihändig in das dafür üblicherweise verwendete zweischichtige Folienmaterial. So ist die endgültige Formgebung ganz von den Intentionen und der werkzeugführenden Hand des Designers bestimmt.

Mit der »Iridium« hat die D. Stempel AG dem Fotosatz den klassizistischen Schriftcharakter in einer modernen Variante erschlossen. Sie steht in den Garnituren mager, Kursiv und halbfett für die Fotosetzmaschinen der Mergenthaler-Linotype-Gesellschaften zur Verfügung.

Erich Schulz-Anker

Bodoni-Antiqua

ist durch die bloße Adaption einer historischen« Type kaum befriedigend zu lösen.
So hat die *D. Stempel AG* von vornherein einen anderen Weg gewählt und mit der »Iridium« von *Adrian Frutiger, Paris*, eine *eigenständige klassizistische Fotosatzschrift* entwickelt und herausgebracht. Dieser Auftrag ermöglichte es dem Entwerfer, bereits bei der Konzeption der Schrift eine fotosatzspezifische Lösung anzustreben und die Entwurfszeichnungen darauf auszurichten.

Iridium-Antiqua

Anders als beim Bleisatz werden im Fotosatz bei vielen Systemen meist sämtliche mit den betreffenden Maschinen möglichen Schriftgrade von einer Schriftgröße durch Verkleinerung oder Vergrößerung erzielt. Um dennoch die für eine klassizistische Schrift notwendige kontrastreiche Wiedergabe in allen Graden zu gewährleisten, bedarf es einer sorgfältigen Ermittlung und Festlegung der Strichverhältnisse durch die experimentelle Erprobung. Hierfür standen bei der Entwicklung der »Iridium« die perfekt ausgestatteten Fertigungslabors der *D. Stempel AG* zur Verfügung. In engster Zusammenarbeit zwischen *Adrian Frutiger* und den Schriftexperten des Hauses konnte auf

Neue Schriften

in unserem Blei- und Fotosatzprogramm

48 **Helvetica**Outline
36 **Helvetica**Outline
28 **Helvetica**Outline
24 **Helvetica**Outline
20 **Helvetica**Outline
16 **Helvetica**Outline **für Schwarz-Weiß-Kontraste**

3/6 ABCDEFGHIJKLMNOPQRSTUVWXYZ
abcdefghijklmnopqrstuvwxyz

4/6 ABCDEFGHIJKLMNOPQRSTUVWXYZ
abcdefghijklmnopqrstuvwxyz

5/6 ABCDEFGHIJKLMNOPQRSTUVWXYZ
abcdefghijklmnopqrstuvwxyz

6 ABCDEFGHIJKLMNOPQRSTUVWXYZ
abcdefghijklmnopqrstuvwxyz

7/8 ABCDEFGHIJKLMNOPQRSTUVWXYZ
abcdefghijklmnopqrstuvwxyz

8 ABCDEFGHIJKLMNOPQRSTUVWXYZ
abcdefghijklmnopqrstuvwxyz

9/10 ABCDEFGHIJKLMNOPQRSTUVWXYZ
abcdefghijklmnopqrstuvwxyz

10 ABCDEFGHIJKLMNOPQRSTUVWXYZ
abcdefghijklmnopqrstuvwxyz

Helvetica extrabreit leicht

12 ABCDEFGHIJKLMNOPQRSTUVWXYZ
abcdefghijklmnopqrstuvwxyz

14 ABCDEFGHIJKLMNOPQRSTUVWXYZ
abcdefghijklmnopqrstuvwxyz

16 ABCDEFGHIJKLMNOPQRSTUVWXYZ
abcdefghijklmnopqrstuvwxyz

20 ABCDEFGHIJKLMNOPQRSTUVWXYZ
abcdefghijklmnopqrstuvwxyz

/23/

Characters of Iridium *for phototypesetting on Linofilm VIP by D. Stempel AG.*

ABCDEFGHIJKLMN
OPQRSTUVWXYZ&
abcdefghijklmnopqrs
tuvwxyzß1234567890

'Der Mensch und seine Zeichen' Adrian Frutiger has shared his knowledge of type in many seminars worldwide and through his teaching at two Paris schools. Initiated by Charles Peignot, his first engagement was at École Estienne, the vocational college for the graphic design trade, as early as 1952. He taught courses on type design there until 1960.

From 1954 onwards 1966, his second teaching stint at École Nationale Supérieure des Arts Décoratifs became his main focus as a teacher. One afternoon a week he taught the students the fundamentals of design, the history of type, and complemented this by calligraphic studies according to the Alfred Willimann school. Additionally, he would put up signs and symbols for discussion and analysis – an area that has always been of particular interest to him.[22] After 1966, Frutiger did hardly any teaching any more; his seminars were taken over by Bruno Pfäffli.[23] The accumulated teaching materials and notes ended up in a box and were filed away.

One day, when Adrian Frutiger showed this box to Horst Heiderhoff, art director of D. Stempel AG, the latter was excited by the content and variety of the material and, on his initiative, it was used as the basis of a series of three books produced by the company in 1978, 1979 and 1981 as giveaways. The original publications were set in *Iridium* /25/, which was replaced by *Linotype Centennial* in later editions, where the original three volumes were combined into one book.[24]

/25/
Covers of the first edition of Der Mensch und seine Zeichen, *originally published in three volumes, and interior page from the first volume with drawings by Helena Nowak.*

der Zeitablauf, in dem sich der Mensch augenblicklich befindet, wird im Grunde symmetrisch empfunden: hinten = die Vergangenheit, vorne = die Zukunft, der Mensch in der Gegenwart, in der Mitte, im Jetzt). Eigentlich sind wir auch sehr beruhigt oder versichert, wenn wir eine symmetrische Figur oder Konstruktion sehen, obwohl wir wissen, daß ihr Innerstes aus funktionellen Gründen asymmetrisch angeordnet ist. Ein symmetrisch gebautes Schloß etwa (45) weist mit aller Wahrscheinlichkeit eine asymmetrische Gliederung im Inneren auf; eine symmetrische Aufteilung könnte in diesem Falle innenarchitektonische Konflikte erzeugen (z. B. zwei Küchen, zwei Säle, zwei WC etc.). Einzige Ausnahmen wären vielleicht Kirchen, Theater, Kinos, welche eine zentrale Funktion besitzen.

45

Wir möchten betonen, daß der Mensch sich eigentlich in steter Auseinandersetzung mit einer symmetrischen Außenwelt und einem asymmetrischen Funktionieren in seinem Inneren befindet (46). Sein Herz schlägt nicht in der Mitte des Körpers, er arbeitet mit der rechten Hand, im modernen Leben muß er lernen, in einem Automobil das Lenkrad links zu betätigen, aber auf der rechten Seite der Straße zu fahren. Es stellt sich letztlich die Frage: Ist der Mensch *mitte-los* geworden?

46

Der Verlauf der westlichen geschriebenen Sprachen ist asymmetrisch. Wir lesen von links nach rechts, mit einem bestimmten Zeitablauf: Anfang – Ende. Dabei sind innerhalb unseres aus 26 Buchstaben bestehenden Alphabets einige symmetrisch und andere asymmetrisch angelegt (47). Es wird uns während des Lesens oder Schreibens von Großbuchstaben nicht mehr bewußt, daß A oder O symmetrische und B, C oder D asymmetrische Formen haben. (Eigenartigerweise sind mit Ausnahme des E alle Vokale symmetrisch: A I O U Y.)

47

Wir wissen heute, daß die Phönizier und sogar noch die ersten griechischen Benutzer des Alphabets in symmetrischer Weise geschrieben haben: auf eine von links nach rechts gehende Linie folgte eine von rechts nach links gehende Linie, dann wieder eine von links nach rechts etc. (48). (Dies glich den Bewegungen eines Bauern, der mit dem Pflug das Feld beackert.) Die Buchstaben mußten demzufolge auf jeder Linie erneut »umgedreht« werden, und daraus ergab sich, daß asymmetrische Buchstaben einmal rechtsherum und ein andermal linksherum geschrieben wurden. Im Laufe der Zeit wurde dieses Vorgehen mit der Form des Buchstabens, der sich als Urtyp (archetype) in den

48

30

Font production:　Font format:　Also available:
Digitised by Linotype　PostScript Type 1　TrueType

ABCDEFGHIJKLMN
OPQRSTUVWXYZ&
abcdefghijklmnopqrs
tuvwxyzß1234567890

Sie fragen sich
warum es notwen
dig ist, so viele Schriften zu
r Verfügung zu haben. Sie dienen alle z

um selben, aber machen die Vielfalt des Menschen aus. Di
ese Vielfalt ist wie beim Wein. Ich habe einmal eine Weinka
rte studiert mit sechzig Médoc-Weinen aus dem selben Jah
r. Das ist ausnahmslos Wein, aber doch nicht alles der gleic
he Wein. Es hat eben gleichwohl Nuancen. So ist es auch m

it der Schrift. *You may ask why so many different typefaces.* They all serve the same pur
pose but they express man's diversity. It is the same diversity we find in wine. I once s
aw a list of Médoc wines featuring sixty different Médocs all of the same year. All of th
em were wines but each was different from the others. It's the nuances that are import
ant. The same is true for typefaces. *Pourquoi tant d'Alphabets différents!* Tous servent
au même but, mais aussi à exprimer la diversité de l'homme. C'est cette même diversit
é que nous retrouvons dans les vins de Médoc. J'ai pu, un jour, relever soixante crus, to

us de la même année. Il s'agissait certes de vins, mais tous étaient di
fférents. Tout est dans la nuance du bouquet. Il en est de même pour
les caractères! *Sie fragen sich, warum es notwendig ist, so viele Schrift
en zur Verfügung zu haben.* Sie dienen alle zum selben, aber machen
die Vielfalt des Menschen aus. Diese Vielfalt ist wie beim Wein. Ich
habe einmal eine Weinkarte studiert mit sechzig Médoc-Weinen aus
dem selben Jahr. Das ist ausnahmslos Wein, aber doch nicht alles de
r gleiche Wein. Es hat eben gleichwohl Nuancen. So ist es auch mit d

er Schrift. *You may ask why so many differ
ent typefaces.* They all serve the same pur
pose but they express man's diversity. It i
s the same diversity we find in wine. I onc
e saw a list of Médoc wines featuring sixty
different Médocs all of the same year. All
of them were wines but each was different
from the others. It's the nuances that are
important. The same is true for typefaces.
Pourquoi tant d'Alphabets différents! Tous

ÅBÇDÈFG
HIJKLMÑ
ÔPQRŠTÜ
VWXYZ&
ÆŒ¥$£€
1234567890
åbçdéfghij
klmñôpqrš
tüvwxyzß
fi fl æ œ ø ł ð
[.,:;·'/-–—]
(¿¡"«‹›»"!?)
{§°%@‰*†}
Regular

*ÅBÇDÈFG
HIJKLMÑ
ÔPQRŠTÜ
VWXYZ&
ÆŒ¥$£€
1234567890
åbçdéfghij
klmñôpqrš
tüvwxyzß
fi fl æ œ ø ł ð
[.,:;·'/-–—]
(¿¡"«‹›»"!?)
{§°%@‰*†}*
Italic

**ÅBÇDÈFG
HIJKLMÑ
ÔPQRŠTÜ
VWXYZ&
ÆŒ¥$£€
1234567890
åbçdéfghij
klmñôpqrš
tüvwxyzß
fi fl æ œ ø ł ð
[.,:;·'/-–—]
(¿¡"«‹›»"!?)
{§°%@‰*†}**
Bold

69pt|–70　　53pt|–30　　35pt|–25　　23pt|–20　　15pt|20pt|–10　　10pt|13pt|0　　8pt|10.2pt|5　　6.5pt|8pt|15

Typeface comparison   Although the transitional *Photina*, designed by José Mendoza y Almeida for Monotype, and the neoclassical antiqua *Basilia* by Frutiger's former colleague André Gürtler are in different classification groups, *Iridium* shares commonalities with both of them.

All three typefaces were designed at almost the same time. Gürtler completed his *Basilia* as early as 1970 with four cuts for hot metal setting at Haas'sche Schriftgiesserei AG, but it was only published in 1978, in an adapted version for phototypesetting, at Autologic Switzerland and USA.[25] Just like *Iridium*, *Photina* – which was published by Monotype in 1971 in a roman and semibold font – is, indicated by its name, a typeface especially developed for phototypesetting.

Photina features an oblique stress, which gives it a lively expression. Frutiger achieved the same effect for *Iridium* through the use of tapered strokes. *Basilia*, however, with its upright stress, pointed half serifs and rectangular transition from the serifs to the stem, appears rather hard.

Iridium's softness, which is achieved through – for a neoclassical typeface – the moderate stroke contrast and subtle transitions from base stroke to hairline in the bowl shapes, makes it the sleekest of these three typefaces.

/26/
Measurements of stroke width and proportions of the Iridium *regular weight.*

Roman				
Hh = 10.00 cm	nh = 6.34 cm	oh = 6.75 cm	Hh : Hw = 1 : 0.79	nh : nw = 1 : 0.89
Hw = 7.91	nw = 5.67	ow = 6.47	Hw : Hs = 1 : 0.18	nw : ns = 1 : 0.21
Hs = 1.41	ns = 1.20	os = 1.47	Hs : Hq = 1 : 0.37	nh : oh = 1 : 1.06
Hq = 0.53	nq = 0.70	oq = 0.35		nw : ow = 1 : 1.14

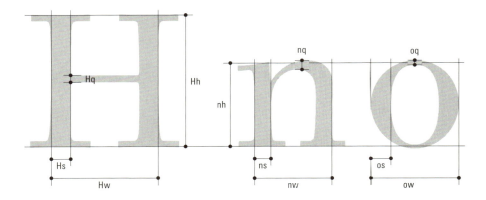

/27/
Rare in a classical typeface, Iridium*'s relatively heavy hairlines prevent them from disappearing during phototypesetting.*

Hofstainberg

Photina
José Mendoza y Almeida
1971

G J K a b g n 5 9

Hofstainberg

Iridium
Adrian Frutiger
1972

G J K a b g n 5 9

G
Wide shape, beard with angular transition into curve

J
Curve terminates in teardrop serif

K
Bridge between stem and vertex

a
Curve terminates in teardrop serif, curved serif at right

b
Stem slightly curved, rising top serif

g
Ear with teardrop serif, oval lower counter

n
Dynamic shape

5 9
Curves end with different-sized teardrop serifs

Hofstainberg

Basilia
André Gürtler
1978

G J K a b g n 5 9

Comparison showing the
different weights and angle of
the italics.

	Hh	Hw	Hs	Hq
Roman	10.00 cm	7.91 = 1	1.41 = 1	0.53 = 1
Bold	10.00	8.59 = 1.08	2.10 = 1.49	0.57 = 1.07
Italic	10.00	8.03 = 1.01	1.25 = 0.89	0.50 = 0.94

17°

/29/

Height comparison showing the
differences of x-heights to
ascenders and descenders – the cap
height is the starting point.

Photina
43.5 pt

Iridium
41.3 pt

Basilia
43.3 pt

Name of typeface	Client	Designer	Design | Publication	Typesetting technology	Manufacturer	Weights
Alphabet Métro	Régie Autonome des Transports Parisiens (RATP)	Adrian Frutiger	1973 | 1973	Phototypesetting Starsettograph	– H. Berthold AG	1

ALPHABET
MÉTRO

The director of the RATP, Monsieur Ebeling, had asked me to design a new typeface for the Paris Métro. The contact with Ebeling came via Paul Andreu, with whom I had already worked together on the Roissy Airport project (see page 224). He was responsible for the modernisation of the Métro stations and he was thinking of something new, like the airport typeface. First, however, I carried out a study on the existing typefaces, and for the first time I walked through the Métro with my eyes wide open and equipped with a camera. Usually, I would use it without paying particular attention to the typefaces. But now I photographed each individual signage board and in the end I had collected a proper historical series of about sixty photos. I could identify about fifty different typefaces, many of which only differed in small details and most of which were truly awful. They were mainly narrow grotesques in white lettering on a blue background /03/.

In my study I came up with the following insight: the Métro is like an old lady. You can't simply transform her into a modern creature. In over one hundred years it has experienced a part of the history of typographical development. The Métro entrances from the Art Nouveau /01/ period are wonderful and have been purposely maintained as cultural heritage. Therefore, I was thinking of a soft, step-by-step modernisation.

Equipped with a template of the typeface *Roissy* and the photographs, I went to a meeting of the project team, which was headed by Ebeling. I asked him to put himself in the shoes of a Métro user. He should imagine how he would feel if all of a sudden a Métro line was designed using *Roissy*. After all, the Métro user identifies with the station signage that has been in use for centuries, and then, all of a sudden – basically overnight – something totally new appears with lowercase letters and perhaps even in a different colour. That would be a shock! Besides, replacing the complete network signage would have taken years and during this long period, the Métro user would have been confused by the use of two different styles of signage. I then created a first design, a template with white paper on a blue background and based on the existing panels. I suggested developing a modernised version based on the existing style. The director understood the points I was making. I still remember the happy expression on his face when he realised the positive economic aspect of my proposal to go for a soft modernisation. This way, it became possible to use the maintenance budget for the Métro: every time a panel broke, it would be replaced with the new version.

So I designed an alphabet with capitals, numerals and a few special characters /06/. Additionally, there were the ligatures LA, LT and TT. The colour scheme was adopted from the existing signage: white letters on a blue background for station names and signs such as Sortie, Départ and so on; and blue letters on a white background for the connection lines /07/. I created blueprints and cut them apart as usual, then I glued them back together

The Métro in Paris, the Tube in London The Parisian underground railway system (the 'Métropolitain' or simply 'Métro', English 'Metro') was opened to coincide with the 1900 World's Fair. The Métro is – after London (1863), Glasgow (1896) and Budapest (1896) – the fourth-oldest underground system in the world. In these ambitious cities, the new mass-transport systems were, from the start, an overwhelming success (except for Glasgow where there were technical challenges to overcome). But how were the new operating companies to communicate with their passengers? How would the users find the Underground?

London Underground identified the entrances to their stations – as did other businesses at that time – with monumental lettering on the facades.[1] In 1908, under the direction of Frank Pick, chief executive of London Underground, a uniform visual identity first appeared in the form of a circular logo with horizontal cross-bar designed by Harold Stabler. In 1916, Edward Johnston[2] was contracted by Frank Pick to re-design the logo. In addition, he developed the typeface *Johnston Railway Sans*, which, with only a few modifications, is still in use today.[3]

In Paris, the lettering used in the Métro was an integral part of the whole architectural concept. The entrances to the Métro stations were visual markers in Art Nouveau /01/, the prevailing style of the times. The lettering on these entrances was in a correspondingly florid style. Both were designed by the architect Hector Guimard,[4] whose artistic credo was the indivisible unity of architecture, furniture and decoration.

The Métro rapidly expanded until the start of the 1930s. After the Second World War its operation was taken over by the RATP. In contrast, however, to London – where almost since its inception, logos and lettering had been the underpinnings of visual communication – in Paris the lettering, as well as the designs of the stations, had been dictated by the individual architects responsible and by current architectural fashion. This had resulted in a mishmash of lettering and building styles, each of which had its own individual personality. In the period between 1930 and 1970, in spite of rising passenger numbers and heavier use, the Métro fell into neglect. By 1971, it was clear that measures had to be taken. So the work began of building new lines, as well as renovating the existing ones. The architect Paul Andreu – among others – was brought in, and he, in turn, brought in Frutiger.

/01/
First signage for the Paris Métro (1900) by Hector Guimard in Art Nouveau style.

/02/
The change to a constructed grotesque (square-cornered counters with rounded exterior corners).

/03/
Narrow grotesque with narrow letter spacing – sign built from individual tiles.

/04/
From 1973 onwards, staggered introduction of signage – based on Univers – by Adrian Frutiger.

/05/
Signage by Jean-François Porchez – the first with lowercase lettering – has been in use since 1996.

/06/
Symbol schedule for Alphabet Métro, including numerals, punctuation, accents and ligatures.

ABCDEFGHIJKLMNOPQR
STUVWXYZ   LA LT TT
Â É È Ê Ç Ü   .,'-_.
1234567890   AOÛT 1973

with modified heights and corrected them /11/. These were used by my colleague Brigitte Rousset to create the final artwork /13/. She wasn't a trained type designer, but she was a very exact person. If you gave her precise instructions, she would carry them out equally precisely.

Métro is a compromise based on a selection of predecessor typefaces. But it also embodies the spirit of *Univers.* I just couldn't help myself. In terms of width it is between *Univers* 67 and *Univers* 75 /10/, the stroke weight is slightly stronger than in the 65-cut. Compared to *Univers,* M and W are fairly wide because in the negative type there absolutely shouldn't be any white blobs. I drew the numerals 6 and 9 in an even more reduced and open style because it was a signage face /10/. I wanted a harmonious line of numerals with good legibility.

My decision to use only capitals was mainly based on the fact that the existing signage was set in caps only /02/03/. The stations were named after places, monuments or personalities, and the typical French way of emphasising names is through capitalisation. Besides, I wanted to keep the production fairly simple because the workers who were to manufacture the signs did not have any typographic training. I had observed how they worked and thought about what I could do to help them do the right thing – not in a thoughtless manner but with confidence. So I came up with the 'idiotproof' letter spacing system using the set-width bar /09/. Below each glyph there was a bar with an arrowhead pointing to the left; pushed into each other it would guarantee the correct letter spacing. For difficult letter combinations, both L and T received a second arrow /14/. Then I defined the instructions for the word spacing, leading and whitespace around the panel /15/. On site, in the

Univers as the basis for Métro   Adrian Frutiger took several existing typefaces used in the Métro as the foundation for the creation of *Alphabet Métro*. He therefore defined an all caps semi bold sans serif typeface to be used in reverse. On the basis of this, he decided to design a font somewhere between *Univers* 67 and 75 /10/. He then took blueprints of the Berthold cut of *Univers* 67, using the usual cut-and-paste method to produce his first samples of *Métro* /11/.

The *Alphabet Métro* that resulted from this process is a departure in several areas from *Univers*. The counters of A G P R 4 5 are kept larger; those of 6 and 9, thanks to the diagonal sweep of the curve, are larger as well. The bowl terminals of C and G are slightly shortened, giving the letters a more open appearance and the diagonal of the 7 is slightly curved. The crotches have blunt incisions /12/, so that the form remains clear and open when the letters are rendered in enamel.

The contrast in stroke weight of C D G L M N X is diminished compared to *Univers*, while that of A P R Y Z is slightly increased. The comparison between M and N is interesting with regards to the distribution of contrast in stroke weight: in *Univers* the vertical strokes are stronger than the diagonals while in *Métro* it is exactly the opposite. Frutiger had chosen the classical distribution of stroke weight that arises naturally as a result of writing with a quill or broad-edged pen.

/07/
Signage boards in the corridors of the Métro, in both positive and negative versions, mounted at eye level.

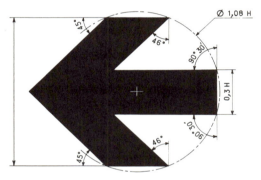

/08/
Drawing of the arrow designed to match the form of the letters.

/09/
System for signage fabrication with width bar to ensure correct letter spacing.

MÉTRO 679
MÉTRO 679
MÉTRO 679

/10/
Alphabet Métro *sandwiched between* Univers 67 and 75, *showing the diagonal curve in 6 and 9, and the curved diagonal of the 7.*

/11/
Blueprints of Berthold Univers 67 – *cut, rearranged and pasted as first sample of* Alphabet Métro.

/12/
The diagonal of the N in Alphabet Métro is heavier than the vertical strokes – in Univers 67 and 75 *the situation is reversed.*

The arrow An important symbol in the design of *Alphabet Métro* was the arrow /08/. The three strokes are so precisely balanced that they appear optically equal, although both the diagonals are about 7% finer than the horizontal. The height and width of the arrow was conceived so that all its corners (with the exception of the point) lie on the circumference of an overlaid circle. This principle was also used for the arrow for *Alphabet Roissy* (see page 228). Both arrows feature horizontally terminated diagonals, to match the Roman letters. This horizontal termination underscores the direction of the arrow, so that the symbol gains the utmost clarity. Adrian Frutiger adjusted the proportion of each arrow to its corresponding typeface. The lines of the *Métro* arrow are therefore shorter and thicker than those of the *Roissy* arrow. While the *Métro* arrow is based on the cap height, that of *Alphabet Roissy* is around one-and-a-half times the cap height. The signage at *Roissy* hangs in wide, high-ceilinged spaces, and the reading distance is greater than that of the *Métro* signage, which in the tunnels is often fixed at eye level /07/. In addition, the capitals and lowercase letters of *Alphabet Roissy* give a line of text a lighter and more open appearance than the semibold capitals of *Alphabet Métro*. The necessary counterbalance between the arrow and the other glyphs in *Alphabet Roissy* is a product of weight and size. In *Alphabet Métro*, the distinction is achieved only through weight.

workshop, I showed the workers how to compose a panel. Sometimes I stayed there for several days to support them.

The panels are made of enamel – this is still a French speciality. During the enamelling process there is a risk of blurring when the colour is applied. But I wanted to be sure of maintaining a clear style. Therefore, there are obtuse incisions in the angles, for instance with the B R or the 8 /13/. This juncture shouldn't be blurred but should be firm and clear, also when copying or, in this case, when enamelling. For the Métro, enamel really is the best material, although it's an expensive product. Such a panel will last twenty years and even graffiti can be washed off easily.

But my work didn't stop there. In the Métro carriages there is a long panel near the doors showing each single station name on the respective line. For such small text, I had a font disk manufactured by Günter Gerhard Lange at Berthold AG, so the text could be composed via phototypesetting. Altogether I worked on this project for about two years, and I enjoyed it.

In the mid-nineties, Jean-François Porchez developed a new signage /05/ with capitals and lowercase letters, something very individual and modern. His thinking isn't wrong at all. The Métro can be modern. Maybe it's also that the era of reverence for the historical is simply over? It might also be a question of age: when I drew *Métro,* I was about 45. I certainly won't criticise a young type designer who is making his own way today. It's just a shame that the typeface isn't as legible as you might expect from a lowercase font.

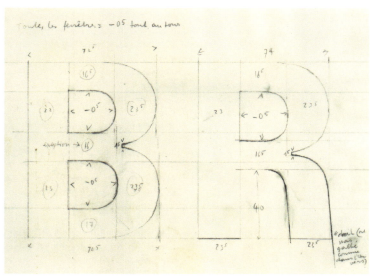

/13/
Working drawings of B and R, showing the obtuse cuts in the acute angles to prevent the glyphs from filling-in during the production of the enamel signs.

/14/
For the setting of critical letter pairs, L and T are provided with a second arrow for the kerning specification.

**GALLIENI _ PONT DE LEVALLOIS
MIROMESNIL
CARREFOUR PLEYEL · PORTE DE CLICHY**

/15/
Exact layout of word spacing for a signage board based on the length of the longest line.

Name of typeface	Client	Designer	Design | Publication	Typesetting technology	Manufacturer	Weights
Centre Georges Pompidou, CGP	Visual Design Association Jean Widmer, Ernst Hiestand	Adrian Frutiger Hans-Jürg Hunziker	1974 | 1976	Transfer lettering Die cut lettering Phototypesetting Digital typesetting PostScript	– Mecanorma – Not known – Linotype – André Baldinger	1 1 2 2

ALPHABET
CENTRE POMPIDOU

Jean Widmer[1] from Paris commissioned me to develop this typeface in the typewriter style with the working title *Beaubourg*. Together with Ernst Hiestand[2] he had been charged in 1974 with developing a corporate identity for the new cultural centre at Place Beaubourg in Paris /01/, which was just being built at the time. During the building works it was re-named after the French president as the 'Centre Georges Pompidou'.[3] The same was true for the typeface, which then was called *Centre Georges Pompidou* or *CGP* for short.[4]

It was clear from the beginning that *Alphabet Beaubourg* should be a typewriter face to be written as vertical lines. These two important criteria inevitably led to some studies concerning the typeface's legibility in order to find the ideal shape. The criterion of legibility derives from a feeling for a well-known or familiar shape. Since it was the vertical that had to be accentuated, the letters couldn't be too wide in order to generate unambiguous word images /03/.

The typographic expression of a typewriter face refers to fast communication such as addresses, letters or circulars. For the initial project we used a typeface with four units written on the IBM-Direction[5] /02/. If such a typeface with all its shortcomings is blown up to signage size – in other words if it's taken out of its context – it appears obsolete. When we implemented the prototypes for the signage, we became aware of this problem and we decided to draw each letter in its individual width and adapted to its natural need for space.

The final artwork was created in my studio. But I didn't do it myself. It was my then-colleague Hans-Jürg Hunziker. In 1978, a year after the opening of the Centre, I wrote: "The first step was the definition of the stroke weight. For several reasons it was defined with-in the limits of a thin typeface because, contrary to popular belief, a bold letter does not always have better legibility than a thin one. The vertical direction of the typeface has a strong signalling effect within its environment, and it was not necessary to search for a typeface characterised by its boldness. *Alphabet Beaubourg* is therefore similar in appear-ance to a typeface of medium weight, based upon a good typewriter face. The stroke width looks uniform. In reality, however, the reader perceives the horizontal strokes differently to the vertical ones, and it is this fact that the change between serifs and downstrokes is based upon. The construction of each glyph is based on this difference in stroke width. With *Alphabet Beaubourg*, however, this optical law seems to falter due to the vertical reading direction. The perception of the blackness is slightly compromised; a minimal correction to account for this was carried out during implementation. The typographic law, which guarantees optimal legibility, is the one where the whitespace within the letters and the whitespace between them is such that a harmonious whole is created from the chain of individual elements."[6]

The typeface Centre Georges Pompidou CGP   The development of a corporate identity for the Centre Georges Pompidou started with a competition. About twenty international agencies who had had experience in the area of public signage systems were invited.[7] The project that was eventually selected by Jean Widmer and Ernst Hiestand suggested a corporate identity without a logo,[8] and the use of a typewriter face as a symbol for fast communication, which would be adapted to the sim-plicity of the wayfinding system[9] /01/. In order to meet the unusual demands on legibility best, Adrian Frutiger was commissioned to implement the alphabet.[10]

The starting point was *Fine Line* by IBM with four units /02/. In large sizes, however, the typical characteristics of a typewriter face come to the fore in a rather negative way and therefore it was redesigned into the proportion-al typeface *Centre Georges Pompidou CGP* at Adrian Frutiger's studio /02/. Slightly fatter than the original, the serifs are shorter and the overall typeface is less wide. Oldstyle figures replaced the lining figures and some individual glyphs such as 1 3 4 and 0 were additionally modified in shape /02/. The g too was changed; it re-ceived a wider bowl. Although the shape of the Q with its curved tail as well as the round terminal of the leg in the R were atypical for a Frutiger typeface, they were brought over unchanged, together with G K and d. After completion of the alphabet in 1975, the typographer responsible, Hans-Jürg Hunziker, changed jobs to work for Centre Pompidou.[11]

Final artwork was produced in a size of approximately 25 cm (matching the IBM typefaces). Initially *Alphabet CGP* was scaled photographically to the sizes of 95, 70 and 32 mm, which were the sizes used in the signage system, and was then transferred onto the panels via silk screen printing. Later, the letters were transferred direct-ly to the panels using an adhesive character set produced by foil stamping. For brochures and small print works transfer characters[12] at the cap heights of 5, 8 and 13 mm /04/ were used initially. In 1975, Hunziker redrew the type-face for phototypesetting on the Linotype VIP using 18 units, and in 1995 he designed a semibold cut.[13] Both cuts were digitised by André Baldinger in 1997. A new corporate identity was designed three years later by Intégral Ruedi Baur et associés. *Alphabet CGP* was re-placed (but not totally abandoned) by *DIN*.[14]

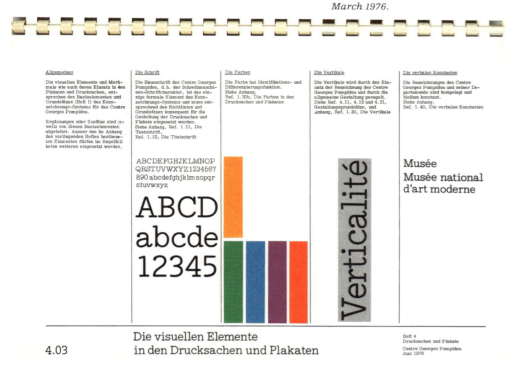

/02/
Fine Line *(enlarged, top) and the digital version of* Centre Georges Pompidou CGP *normal (centre) and bold (bottom) from 1997.*

ABCDEFGHIJKLMNOPQRS
TUVWXYZabcdefghijklmno
pqrstuvwxyz1234567890

ABCDEFGHIJKLMNOPQRS
TUVWXYZabcdefghijklmno
pqrstuvwxyz1234567890

**ABCDEFGHIJKLMNOPQRS
TUVWXYZabcdefghijklmno
pqrstuvwxyz1234567890**

/04/
Folded flyer with monthly programme, photoset in Centre Georges Pompidou *on Linotype VIP.*

Name of typeface	Client	Designer	Design | Publication	Typesetting technology	Manufacturer	Weights
Frutiger	D. Stempel AG	Adrian Frutiger	1974 | 1976	Photosetting	– D. Stempel AG | Linotype	8
Humanist 777*				Digital Setting CRT and Laser	– D. Stempel AG | Linotype	16
Frutiger Next**				Digital Setting PostScript	– Adobe | Linotype	14 | 19
					Bitstream*	14
					Linotype**	21

FRUTIGER

The *Frutiger* typeface is the print version of the *Roissy* signage font. It is plain to see that *Frutiger* is based on *Roissy* (see page 224), which in turn is based on *Concorde* (see page 150). When Mike Parker first saw the signage in the *Roissy* typeface at Charles de Gaulle airport (in Paris-Roissy), it was clear to him that it needed to be turned into a typeface for print. I still remember clearly how he came to me with the proposal in 1974. Mike Parker was at that time typographical director of the American Mergenthaler Linotype Company. He had a bloodhound's nose for trends and at the type selection meetings at Linotype he was influential.

The starting point for *Frutiger* was some enlargements of *Roissy*. From the very beginning we conceived it for photosetting. For that we needed new original drawings. Back then – in the seventies and eighties – I was so snowed under with projects that I could only do the sketches. It was impossible for me to draw a typeface from A to Z myself, although I would have done it gladly. I had to delegate a lot. So Hans-Jürg Hunziker[1] got the first originals for *Frutiger* together. He's an unbelievably good draughtsman. He was at Mergenthaler Linotype for four years in Brooklyn, New York, before he came to our studio at Arcueil in 1971, and he stayed with us until 1975. The characters were drawn large-format, and then, for control purposes, reduced to text size. But Hans-Jürg didn't trace the outlines, instead he drew new curves using the samples as a guide. Of course, a few minor corrections were necessary. When I was designing *Roissy*, I had no idea that one day a text type would come out of it. I drew the curves and terminals as distinct as possible; the letters and numerals had to be as clear and unambiguous as an arrow. All the fine details that belong in a printing typeface I left to one side because signage typefaces and printing typefaces are two different worlds. With signage typefaces, the letters and numerals are more stand-alone, whereas with a typeface for printing, the whole alphabet has to play together. For *Frutiger*, therefore, Hans-Jürg chose more high-contrast terminals /01/, closer to an antiqua, I would say.

To tell the truth, I made a mistake with the adjustment of the stroke weights. The normal typeface, *Frutiger* 55, is a little too bold /02/. Actually, Hans-Jürg and I set up a logical system of how the weighting varies; but *Frutiger* 55 still came out a little too bold for a print font, probably because it was still a little too heavily influenced by *Roissy*. But I had a bit of luck at the same time, since *Frutiger* 45 was and is even more regularly deployed, especially in mass composition. It still is a little heavier than is normal. The contrast between thin and semibold is excellent. No one could have foreseen that a light typeface would have such a huge success – 45 and 65 really have been a resounding success. With the weight adaptation the following might have probably occurred: the stroke weight of *Frutiger* 55 we probably based on the common n of *Univers* 55. The common n

A signage type becomes a text type *Frutiger* is one of the most popular and successful typefaces by Adrian Frutiger. In 2007, the international font distributor Font Shop published a list of the top 100 best typefaces based on sales figures and several other lists from the previous decade, as well as on the opinion of an expert jury. *Frutiger* was placed at number 3 behind *Helvetica* and *Garamond*. Adrian Frutiger's first sans serif typeface, *Univers*, was among the top ten at number 10 and *Avenir* among the top one hundred at number 65.[2]

Frutiger, released in 1976 by Linotype as a typeface for photosetting, has outstanding legibility. It works well in both small and large sizes. This is due to its two predecessors: the text type *Concorde* and the signage face *Alphabet Roissy*, which was redesigned to become *Frutiger*. Through its open, but rather sturdy composition it is particularly convincing in small sizes. Up until 2005, *Frutiger* was even used for newspapers: for the masthead, the headlines and the body text of the Dutch quality daily *Trouw*.[3]

In the reading sizes, however, *Frutiger* 55 appears slightly too dark and the oblique version 56, which Linotype wrongly called 'Italic' /21/, does not correspond to the 1990s fashion of dynamic sans serifs with their true cursives. For these two reasons, in 1997, after the release of the extended *LT Univers*, Linotype Library suggested Adrian Frutiger also redesign the typeface that bears his name. From Linotype, the art director Reinhard Haus, head of marketing Otmar Hoefer and managing director Bruno Steinert participated in the discussion. Haus, together with the freelancers Silja Bilz and Erik Faulhaber,[4] developed the new version from 1998 onwards. It was first used in a preliminary version of the narrow fonts for the signage of the Munich Alte Pinakothek museum.[5] In 2001, the typeface was released under the name *Frutiger Next*. It is very different from the original and in many points does not correspond to Frutiger's understanding of type design.

Both digital versions are available at Linotype as Open-Type fonts: *Frutiger LT*, which meanwhile has been extended to 19 fonts, and *Frutiger Next* with an extended character set in 21 fonts. The few benefits of *Frutiger Next* are to be found in the additional small capitals and several types of figures.

gives the fundamental note. The n of *Univers,* however, has finer junctures than in *Frutiger* **/03/**. The interplay between bold and thin in *Frutiger* is therefore not as marked, and it all comes across as a bit darker. It used to happen to every foundry that the regular typeface would come out either too bold or too light; so then, you'd cut a so-called book cut, or you'd use the thin as the regular. Often I'd watch the punchcutters at Deberny & Peignot. The first thing they'd do was put all the lowercase letters between two ms. Using m, n and u, the type founders would check their values. They'd do that with m as well. At Stempel AG, using this method, we'd check whether the letters were too heavy or too light, and whether the spacing was OK **/05/**.

From the beginning we had planned eight fonts for *Frutiger,* four regular and four oblique. These were drawn, not photographically inclined. The slant amounted to 12 degrees. Later we added the condensed fonts. The 47 and 77 fonts, that is, the condensed thin and the condensed bold versions, were drawn by us. The two intermediate fonts, 57 and 67, were interpolated. Because the machine interpolation produced junctures that were a little too fine, we had to rework those **/08/**. The shape itself remained unchanged. I photocopied the completed outline drawings before every handover. In 1989, the ultrafine and fine fonts, 25 and 35, appeared for the laser-setting machines from Linotype **/06/**. I drew the ultrafine myself. The Americans Herb Lubalin and Tom Carnase were the first to market in 1970 with an ultrafine typeface, *Avant Garde Gothic* X-Lite. That really made an impact. It was only photosetting that made it at all possible. But it was also to do with the times: in the eighties, ultralight faces were really in fashion. Then the somewhat coarse Swiss Style was replaced by the New Wave, with its fine colour gradients and those really

Frutiger for phototypesetting   Work on the development of a text type based on the signage face *Roissy* started in 1974. The redesign, in terms of shape and the extension to eight fonts, was carried out by Hans-Jürg Hunziker. In 1976, the four weights 45, 55, 65, 75 and the oblique fonts 46, 56, 66 and 76 were released. In addition, an adhesive letter set designed in 1975 contained a narrow-thin font, which was only implemented in 1983. Initially, it was planned to release four fonts: the 47 and the 77 were drawn, and the fonts in between, i.e. the 57 and 67 were developed by interpolation **/07/** after a test run using a narrower *Frutiger* 55 showed that electronic generation needed only small amendments. Eventually, five narrow fonts were implemented, including *Frutiger* 87. Also in 1985, the extra bold 95 font was released.[6] In the correspondence it was initially still called 85 but it is not clear whether the font was meant to be less bold or whether the naming changed since the increase in weight was greater than in the other fonts.

A further extension was implemented by Linotype in 1989 with *Frutiger* 25 and 35 **/06/**. They were available as laser fonts for Linotype's typesetting computers. This, however, lasted only a few years, since the shift towards the personal computer was already in full swing. Additionally, at the end of the 1980s, thin and light fonts – set far too narrow as usual at the time – **/04/**, were no longer fashionable.

Sie fragen sich, warum es notwendig ist, so viele Schriften zur Verfügung zu haben. Sie dienen alle zum selben, aber machen die Vielfalt des Menschen aus. Diese Vielfalt ist wie beim Wein. Ich habe einmal eine

Sie fragen sich, warum es notwendig ist, so viele Schriften zur Verfügung zu haben. Sie dienen alle zum selben, aber machen die Vielfalt des Menschen aus. Diese Vielfalt ist wie beim Wein. Ich habe einmal eine

Sie fragen sich, warum es notwendig ist, so viele Schriften zur Verfügung zu haben. Sie dienen alle zum selben, aber machen die Vielfalt des Menschen aus. Diese Vielfalt ist wie beim Wein. Ich habe einmal eine

/02/
Pleasing optical grey in LT Univers *(top) – Frutiger 55 is somewhat dark (centre) and thus Frutiger 45 is often used (bottom).*

/03/
Bowl shape and juncture are clearly stronger in the slightly heavier Frutiger 55 (red) *than in* LT Univers 430 (grey).

Frutiger. Typography on the move.

■ About 10 years ago, construction work started on the new Paris (Charles de Gaulle) airport complex. The chief architect, Paul Andreu, was aware of the importance of a good system of indication and signalisation for the smooth running of the airport, and he asked me to take on this responsibility. When the matter of specifying a type-style came up, I realised that the use of a face like Univers, for example, would not suit either the general aesthetic and architectural concept or the principles of optimum legibility... ...The characters of Univers are a little too 'smooth' for sufficiently rapid and accurate reading on indicator panels. For example, letters such as c, e, s, or v, y, and also b, d, p, q, g are too similar in appearance. There is also the point that the reader of indicator panels is usually on the move: in a car, on an escalator, walking or even running. This factor has a strong influence on the conditions for optimum legibility, because the word-image, as seen by the reader, is constantly changing or blurring...

...The law of type design calls for obedience to other criteria, not only intellectual ones, because, to the reader, type-matter is above all a *written* image, i.e. one which has originated from the free movement of the hand. Since the process of reading takes place through the recognition of complete word-images, a relationship of form between all the letters is absolutely indispensable. Consequently, between the bare 'realism' of Futura or Kabel and the strongly modelled harmony of Helvetica and Univers, there is room for a type design which has the freehand rhythm of writing as opposed to 'constructivism' but at the same time avoids the 'uncial' style of rounded characters, so as to allow the appearance of clearly identifiable characters within the harmonious word-image... ...These are the motives which I can describe to you as having led to the creation of the new sans serif. Commissioned by D. Stempel AG of Frankfurt, I have adapted it to make a typeface family, consisting of four weights accompanied by four italics, for phototypesetting on equipment supplied by the Mergenthaler-Linotype Group... ...I am delighted by your comment: 'From our point of view it's the first new and original sans family to appear on the market for some years', and I thank you for the interest that you have shown in the typeface. ▮▮

When the man who designed Univers puts his name to a typeface, it must be special. Adrian Frutiger can also claim Egyptienne, Apollo, Serifa, Glypha and the standard OCR B typefaces among his many achievements. Designed for total legibility, Frutiger is truly a new sans, and is available now in four weights plus italics for display setting on typositor and on the VIP with Advanced Typography Program for computerised textsetting.

/04/
Frutiger flyer from London typesetters Conways – typical of the typography of the 1980s is the too-tight letterspacing.

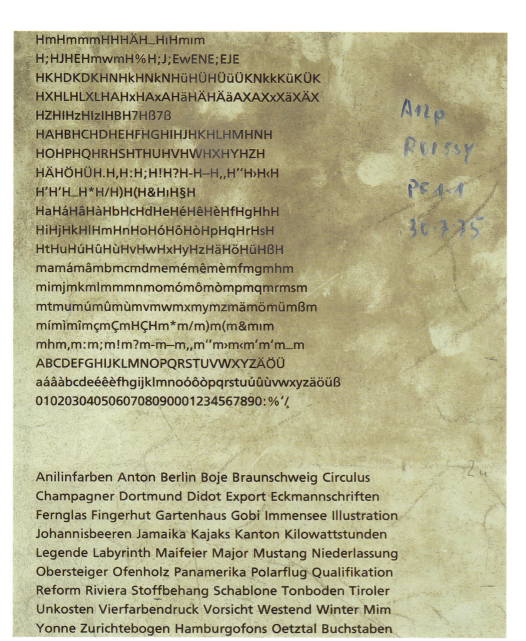

HmHmmmHHHÄH_HıHmım
H;HJHEHmwmH%H;J;EwENE;EJE
HKHDKDKHNHkHNkNHüHÜHÜüÜKNkkKüKÜK
HXHLHLXLHAHxHAxAHäHÄHÄäAXAXxXäXÄX
HZHIHzHIzIHBH7Hß7ß
HAHBHCHDHEHFHGHIHJHKHLHMHNH
HOHPHQHRHSHTHUHVHWHXHYHZH
HÄHÖHÜH.H,H:H;H!H?H–H––H,,H''H›H‹H
H'H'H_H*H/H)H(H&HıH§H
HaHáHâHàHbHcHdHeHéHêHèHfHgHhH
HiHjHkHlHmHnHoHóHôHòHpHqHrHsH
HtHuHúHûHùHvHwHxHyHzHäHöHüHßH
mamámâmbmcmdmemémêmèmfmgmhm
mimjmkmlmmmnmomómômòmpmqmrmsm
mtmumúmûmùmvmwmxmymzmämömümßm
mímìmîmçmÇmHÇHm*m/m)m(m&mım
mhm,m:m:m;m!m?m-m–m–,,m''m»m‹m'm'm_m
ABCDEFGHIJKLMNOPQRSTUVWXYZÄÖÜ
aáâàbcdeéêèfhgijklmnoóôòpqrstuúûùvwxyzäöüß
010203040506070809000123456789 0:%'/

Anilinfarben Anton Berlin Boje Braunschweig Circulus
Champagner Dortmund Didot Export Eckmannschriften
Fernglas Fingerhut Gartenhaus Gobi Immensee Illustration
Johannisbeeren Jamaika Kajaks Kanton Kilowattstunden
Legende Labyrinth Maifeier Major Mustang Niederlassung
Obersteiger Ofenholz Panamerika Polarflug Qualifikation
Reform Riviera Stoffbehang Schablone Tonboden Tiroler
Unkosten Vierfarbendruck Vorsicht Westend Winter Mim
Yonne Zurichtebogen Hamburgofons Oetztal Buchstaben

/05/
A sample exposure from 1975 on photo paper as a test for the spacing of the typeface Frutiger 55 in 12 pt.

abcdefghijklmn
opqrstuvwxyz
ABCDEFGHIJKLMN
OPQRSTUVWXYZ&
1234567890.,:;?
!()-''——$¢%//£·[]*§†‡ı
áàâäãăăçāinj
‹›«»‰œŒ¿¡ƒ""„
nßæÆåÅøØfifl+−×=n

abcdefghijklmn
opqrstuvwxyz
ABCDEFGHIJKLMN
OPQRSTUVWXYZ&
1234567890.,:;?
!()-''——$¢%//£·[]*§†‡ı
áàâäãăăçāinj
‹›«»‰œŒ¿¡ƒ""„
nßæÆåÅøØfifl+−×=n

/06/
First type samples of Frutiger 25 and 35 from 1989; exposure at 2450 dpi on photopaper with laser typesetter Linotronic 300.

/08/
Character produced by interpolating Frutiger 47 and 67 (left), re-edited working drawing for typeface 67 (right).

/07/
Minutes of a meeting from 3 November 1983 about the new typeface projects at D. Stempel AG, among them Frutiger 47, 57, 67, 77 and 85.

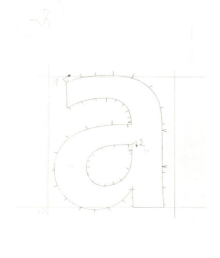

elegant, fine typefaces. Of the laser fonts, *Frutiger* Ultralight and Light weren't, however, taken into the program of PostScript typefaces /21/ – probably because of the sales figures. When a typeface is bought only twice in two years, then it's simply dropped. Such outcomes are outside my sphere of influence. Those were business decisions.

There were some details that I absolutely insisted be brought under my control even with my heavy workload – that I wouldn't leave up to the typeface manufacturer; for example the acute, grave and circumflex accents. Very often, I also chose the form of the cedilla myself /17/; my designer's understanding tells me that it shouldn't be connected to the letter itself, but should instead be offset like an acute or grave accent. However, this idea wasn't taken up by Linotype, since there's a typographical rule that states that it has to be attached, otherwise a foreign speaker wouldn't recognise it. The arguments we had over that! It was only with my signage typefaces *Roissy* and *Métro* (see page 244), and also with those for Deberny & Peignot, like *Méridien* and *Univers* for hot metal setting and Lumitype, where everything was under my control, that I was able to push my version through. However, for Linotype, my simplified accents and special characters were never even considered. It even came to a falling-out with the Americans, since they went behind my back as the designer, and changed the letterforms. Mergenthaler Linotype in the USA always stood there like giants and looked down on us as tiny dwarves. It was always: "The typeface must sell". What could I do about it? The only thing in *Frutiger* that we could implement was the £-sign /19/.

Internally, *Frutiger* was at first called *Roissy,* since D. Stempel AG's rights included the use of the name.[7] The typeface now carries my name for legal reasons.[8] Mike Parker

Comparison between Concorde, Roissy, Frutiger   Of the three related typefaces *Concorde* (see page 150), *Alphabet Roissy* (see page 224) and *Frutiger, Concorde* has the finest and *Roissy* the strongest stroke weight in the regular font /09/. The curves are more open in *Concorde* /10/ and the letters are generally wider, which produces a lighter appearance. At the same cap height there are only minimal differences in the dimensions of ascender, x-height and descender /20/.

Frutiger, a typeface for the photosetting of text and headline composition, features a 7% reduction in stroke weight compared to the signage face *Roissy.* Additionally, there are also markedly deeper cuts in the acute angles, for example in the capital M /12/. There is a basic difference in the shape of the curves. In *Frutiger,* they are more pronounced towards the end /10/. The terminals of the curves are also cut differently: vertical in *Concorde,* slightly diagonal in *Roissy* and *Frutiger.* Only the minuscule e of *Frutiger* is cut vertically /16/.

It is interesting to look at the differences in the widths of the majuscules in *Roissy* and *Frutiger.* In *Frutiger,* A and F are slightly narrower /11/. The S is markedly narrower and more diagonal in the middle /15/ while the U is clearly wider. The differences become most obvious when comparing S T and U, which appear to be almost of the same width in *Roissy* but are clearly different in *Frutiger* /15/.

/09/
Comparison of the stroke weight and proportion of the n of Frutiger *(black) – left* Concorde *(brown), right* Roissy *(brown).*

/10/
Comparison of the curve shape of the C of Frutiger *(black) – left* Concorde *(grey), right* Roissy *(grey).*

/11/
Roissy *(top) is altogether somewhat heavier, also A and F are somewhat broader than in* Frutiger.

AFGH
AFGH

/12/
The legs of Concorde *(left) are splayed; in contrast to* Roissy *(centre),* Frutiger *has deeper incisions (right).*

/13/
The tail of Concorde *(left) is horizontal – varying diagonals in* Roissy *(centre) and* Frutiger *(right).*

/14/
Concorde *(left) and* Roissy *(centre) have a same-width, although differently curved S; in* Frutiger *(right), it is narrower.*

/15/
S and U exhibit different widths – in contrast to Roissy *(top) the S of* Frutiger *is narrower, while the U is wider.*

MMM   QQQ   SSS sss

STU
STU

/16/
Differing curve shapes and different terminations of the curve ends: Concorde, Roissy, Frutiger *(from left to right).*

/17/
Only Frutiger *(right) has the – atypical for Adrian Frutiger – standard joined* ç; Concorde, Roissy, Frutiger *(from left to right).*

/18/
The curve juncture of the r in Concorde *(left) and in* Frutiger *(right) is more sharply tapered than in* Roissy *(centre).*

aaa
eee

ÇÇÇ   rrr

/20/
For the same cap heights, Concorde *(left) and* Frutiger *(right) possess the same x-height –* Roissy *(centre) is somewhat shorter.*

/19/
The pound sign in Frutiger *is simple; the non-curving horizontal stroke at the foot sits directly on the stem.*

£

Ehpa Ehpa Ehpa

Frutiger LT PostScript It is slightly surprising not to find *Frutiger* among the first 42 typefaces of the Post-Script collection published by Adobe in cooperation with Linotype. The *Schriftenhandbuch* (Type Manual) of Lino-type Library from 1988 only contains Frutiger's *Univers* with eight, *Univers* Condensed with six and *Glypha* with four fonts.[9] In the same year, however, *Frutiger* was published in five regular and four oblique fonts.

The 1989 laser fonts in the weights of 25 and 35 were not transferred to the new technology **/21/**.

Only in 1991 were 14 of the original 16 *Frutiger* fonts – the regular narrow versions – published again for digital type-setting. In 2006, a new addition was released with the narrow oblique fonts. Thus, Frutiger's typeface was extended with fonts in the LT version that had not existed before and were not part of the reworked *Frutiger Next* **/37/** either.

In 1983, Adrian Frutiger drew a stroke weight template for the narrow fonts **/23/**. It does not show a mathematically derived construction of the stroke weights, but one that is based on intuition and experience. Therefore, there are no regular steps. The same is true for the *Frutiger LT* fonts in regular widths **/22/**. There is an almost regular increase in the 45, 55 and 65 fonts but not in the 75 and 95 ones. This is due to the fact that, in a linear accession, the increase is perceived to be less in the bold fonts than in the fine ones.

realised quickly that this typeface would be copied. The American type manufacturers had the practice of writing in their type sample books 'similar to …', so 'similar to *Times*' and so on. A judge had decided, however, that you couldn't do this regarding a person. A personal name cannot be misused. So when a work carried the name of its creator, it could be protected. 'Similar to …' couldn't then be used. Explaining this to me, Mike Parker convinced me to call the typeface *Frutiger*. This principle of legal protection extended to the person is the only reason why it has that name. And now all the imitations have names that begin with 'Fr' – that's where you'll find them in the type sample books, under those initial letters. But every type expert knows that behind them all, there's *Frutiger*. And the use of these knock-offs is pretty widespread, since the Linotype originals were expensive.

A normal body type isn't usually protected by copyright. In Washington we had to go to court because of a copy. The judge's decision was: a normal typeface is in the public domain, it's a tool like a hammer, like a saw, like a scythe. As long as a typeface keeps its head down, stays 'normal', it's a tool. Basically, I think that's right. We tried, therefore, by means of various examples, to show how definitively our typeface differed from others, for example we overlaid the characters; but the judge couldn't see any difference. As soon as you make an exotic typeface, with conspicuous curlicues, serifs and the like, then it can be protected like a brand. Even in Germany there were some legal skirmishes between D. Stempel AG and some other firm. Reinhard Haus really expended an immense amount of effort – comparisons, overlays – but the decision of the judge was always the same: a layman wouldn't be able to tell the difference; he'd only see whether a typeface is readable or not.

Frutiger
25 ultra light

Frutiger
35 thin

Frutiger LT
45 Light

Frutiger LT
46 Light Italic

Frutiger LT
47 Light Cond.

Frutiger LT
48 Light Cond. Italic

Frutiger LT
55 Roman

Frutiger LT
56 Italic

Frutiger LT
57 Condensed

Frutiger LT
58 Condensed Italic

Frutiger LT
65 Bold

Frutiger LT
66 Bold Italic

Frutiger LT
67 Bold Cond.

Frutiger LT
68 Bold Cond. Italic

Frutiger LT
75 Black

Frutiger LT
76 Black Italic

Frutiger LT
77 Black Cond.

Frutiger LT
78 Black Cond. Italic

Frutiger LT
87 Extra Black
Cond.

Frutiger LT
88 Extra Black
Cond. Italic

Frutiger LT
95 Ultra Black

/21/
PostScript fonts of the Frutiger LT *family of typefaces, which comprises some 19 members – the lasersetting typefaces 25 and 35 (left) are no longer available.*

/22/
Overlaying the fonts of Frutiger LT *shows that the individual character design is not based on a schematic principle.*

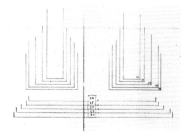

/23/
Weight increments for the narrow font of Frutiger: *the unit specification underneath corresponds to the minuscule n.*

The magazine *form* has used the narrow cut of *Frutiger* as its basic typeface since 1981. In 1995 the publisher had a typeface developed between 45 and 55 by the young Dutchman Lucas de Groot. This book typeface had, furthermore, a different form for the esszett (ß) /27/. The ß is a special character. Jan Tschichold said that the ß isn't formed from a long s and a z, rather from a long s and a round s. That influenced me, so I incorporated Jan Tschichold's proposal in *Univers.* In *Frutiger,* however, I consciously drew the bellied B-form. For a grotesque typeface, this is an easier character, one that better fits in.[10] Lucas de Groot then designed for *form* an ß comprised of a long s and a round s. I find this ß-form beautiful. Shame it's not one of mine. In a light version like that, it looks really elegant. But it's something else entirely when you have to transfer such a form into the bold. I always had in my head the idea of the whole right from start. From my studies under Walter Käch I had already learned to think in terms of the typeface families. I liked calling this a landscape: the landscape where different typefaces unfold. The *Frutiger F* for *form* was also slightly reworked. All this happened, mind you, without consultation with Linotype. Reinhard Haus complained about the situation in an internal memo to Dr Volker Stückradt, Linotype's lawyer. In his memo, he noted everything that had changed, included a sample, and said that they should question me about it. I saw the revisions, but couldn't see any points of contention. With that, as far as I was concerned, the matter was closed. If I'd got myself worked up over something like that every time it happened, I'd be long dead. If the copy had actually got worse, then I would have been annoyed, but it was well done.

As early as three years previously, Robert Slimbach and Carol Twombly's *Myriad* /32/ had already caused an exchange of letters. When I first saw this sans serif, I thought: "my

Frutiger for *form* and the Post Office In 1981, the German design magazine *form* changed its text type from *Helvetica* thin to *Frutiger* 45 citing the following reason: "Compared to the sans serifs, which are most used and even overused today, *Frutiger* is more individual in its single shapes and thus there is more contrast between individual glyphs. It avoids having totally even lines of text; it is 'rougher' to the eye, more vibrant and tactile. Word images can be perceived better as a whole. Reading large amounts of text is less tiring."[11] Even when redesigning the layout in 1995, the magazine stuck with *Frutiger* /25/ but switched from the light font to the book font /26/, which was developed by the type designer Lucas de Groot.[12] Since this was done without any agreement with Linotype Hell AG, art director Reinhard Haus suggested in an internal memo that they intervene at *form*.[13]

As early as 1987, the Dutch post office PTT used an interpolation of *Frutiger* as their corporate type. It was designed by Lucas de Groot and commissioned by Studio Dumbar.[14] It seemed like Frutiger was the corporate type of the Post Office in general. The German Post and, since 1980, the Swiss PTT have also been using *Frutiger*. It appeared even earlier on the Swiss postal vehicles, where it was introduced in 1978. Together with the typesetter responsible, Kurt Wälti, Adrian Frutiger designed several figurative and word marks for the post offices.[15]

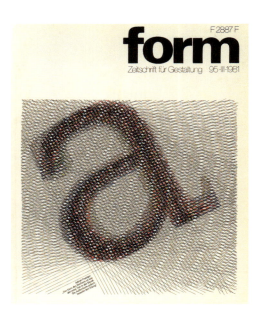

/24/
Starting with the 95-III-1981 issue, the design magazine form *changed its text typeface from* Helvetica *narrow to* Frutiger *45.*

Sie fragen sich, warum es notwendig ist, so viele Schriften zur Verfügung zu haben. Sie dienen alle zum selben, aber machen die Vielfalt des Menschen aus. Diese Vielfalt ist wie beim Wein. Ich habe einmal eine

Sie fragen sich, warum es notwendig ist, so viele Schriften zur Verfügung zu haben. Sie dienen alle zum selben, aber machen die Vielfalt des Menschen aus. Diese Vielfalt ist wie beim Wein. Ich habe einmal eine

Sie fragen sich, warum es notwendig ist, so viele Schriften zur Verfügung zu haben. Sie dienen alle zum selben, aber machen die Vielfalt des Menschen aus. Diese Vielfalt ist wie beim Wein. Ich habe einmal eine

/26/
In 1995, Lucas de Groot created the F Frutiger Book *for* form *magazine (centre), a font between* Frutiger LT 45 *(top) and 55 (bottom).*

/27/
Comparison of the regular and inclined fonts of Frutiger LT *(left),* F Frutiger Book *(centre) and* Frutiger Next *(right).*

ßß ßß ßß

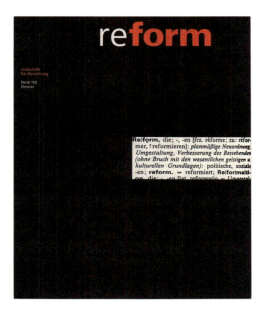

/25/
The supplement to form *issue 150-2-1995 contained the* F Frutiger Book – *interpolated by Lucas de Groot – and also an interview with Adrian Frutiger.*

A true cursive in addition to the grotesque In conversation,[16] Adrian Frutiger made his opinion absolutely clear: for him, a grotesque should only have an inclined – an oblique – cut. He could not see any historical reference for having a true cursive – an italic – in a sans serif and he failed to see any advantages to that either. You do not have to share this opinion, because an italic is usually better suited for accentuation than an oblique. But we have to respect Frutiger's opinion. The people responsible at Linotype, however, were lacking in respect in terms of the italic of *Frutiger Next*. Although Adrian Frutiger did not argue his point in a forceful fashion in his fax */29/* and letter */31/*, he nonetheless made it absolutely clear that he did not see the italic as a basic font but rather as an additional one at most. It is typical of him that he did not simply object, but was trying to find a way forward. Linotype, however, sacrificed Frutiger's opinion to the fashion of the 1990s, even though – with *Linotype Ergo* and *Linotype Projekt* – they already had exclusive types with true italics in their collection.[17] The fashion for having a sans serif italic was started in the 1980s with typefaces such as *Lucida Sans*, *ITC Stone Sans*, *Today Sans Serif* and *Meta* */32/*. In 1992, *Myriad* followed */32/*. Linotype regarded its regular cut as an imitation of *Frutiger*,[18] which is not true. In 1999, there was the opposite situation: *Frutiger Next* was in parts inspired by *Myriad* Italic.

Sie fragen sich, warum es notwendig ist, so viele Schriften zur Verfügung zu haben. Sie dienen alle zum selben, aber machen die Vielfalt des Menschen aus. Diese Vielfalt ist wie beim Wein. Ich habe einmal eine

Sie fragen sich, warum es notwendig ist, so viele Schriften zur Verfügung zu haben. Sie dienen alle zum selben, aber machen die Vielfalt des Menschen aus. Diese Vielfalt ist wie beim Wein. Ich habe einmal eine

Sie fragen sich, warum es notwendig ist, so viele Schriften zur Verfügung zu haben. Sie dienen alle zum selben, aber machen die Vielfalt des Menschen aus. Diese Vielfalt ist wie beim Wein. Ich habe einmal eine

/28/
Frutiger Next *Light (top), Regular (centre) and Medium (bottom) in comparison with* Frutiger LT *(left side).*

/30/
Sample from 1998 of Frutiger *as a Multiple Master font, with four poles and the intermediate steps on two axes.*

/31/
In contrast to Frutiger LT *(top),* Frutiger Next *(bottom) has a true cursive, in a similar fashion to* Myriad *(centre).*

/32/
Frutiger LT, Meta, Myriad, Thesis Sans *and* Frutiger Next *(top to bottom) – in the latter the counter shapes of the roman and italic are particularly different.*

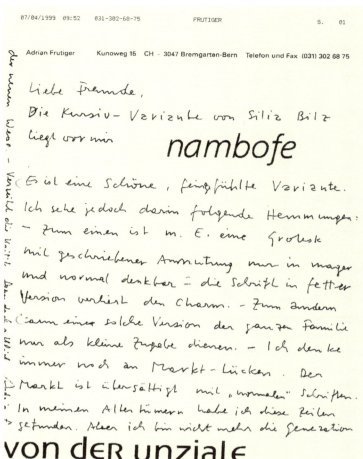

/29/
Negative reaction from Adrian Frutiger to the sample characters of the cursive Frutiger Next – *fax dated 7 April 1999.*

Sie fragen sich, warum es notwendig ist, so viele Schriften zur Verfügung zu haben. Sie dienen alle zum selben, aber machen die Vielfalt des Menschen aus. Diese Vielfalt ist wie beim Wein. Ich habe einmal eine

Sie fragen sich, warum es notwendig ist, so viele Schriften zur Verfügung zu haben. Sie dienen alle zum selben, aber machen die Vielfalt des Menschen aus. Diese Vielfalt ist wie beim Wein. Ich habe einmal eine

Sie fragen sich, warum es notwendig ist, so viele Schriften zur Verfügung zu haben. Sie dienen alle zum selben, aber machen die Vielfalt des Menschen aus. Diese Vielfalt ist wie beim Wein. Ich habe einmal eine

abefginps   *abefginps*
abefginps   *abefginps*
abefginps   *abefginps*
abefginps   *abefginps*
abefginps   *abefginps*

typeface has gained a little cousin – and it's not badly done, either." When Reinhard Haus sent me a side-by-side comparison of *Frutiger* and *Myriad,* I wrote back: "between business partners, I think this has gone a little bit too far."[19] By 'business partners' I meant Adobe. That Adobe, in 1992, would bring out a similar typeface to *Frutiger* – and despite their having taken over all the Linotype typefaces as PostScript fonts – I found that a little inappropriate. Nevertheless, I wouldn't write such a letter today. My perspectives have widened; of course that's got something to do with age – you get more easygoing. Why shouldn't a good typeface be developed further by a third party? When I see today that someone has taken my thoughts and developed them further, I'm even proud of that. So what if *Myriad* has a round dot over the i and a true cursive. I've got nothing against that. I still feel, however, that a grotesque is far removed from a serif font, and doesn't really need a true cursive /32/. The thing about a grotesque is, you can design it right away from very narrow to very wide, which you can't do with a classical typeface. You can imagine a narrow *Garamond,* but everything else would be humbug, a miscarriage. Even with a sans serif antiqua, like Hans Eduard Meier's *Syntax,* it wouldn't be possible without a drop in quality. But with a grotesque, it's completely different. It's inescapable, that a typeface based on the horizontal-vertical principle, gives you more possibilities for expansion and compression than a typeface where the oblique is based on writing with a pen. In the latin type likewise, everything was there (see page 29) for going from narrow to wide typefaces. It just worked.

I also see a difference in the application of grotesque and antiqua. Grotesques get used primarily in advertising, corporate identity and for job printing. That they also get

Is Frutiger Next really a Frutiger? Like *LT Univers, Frutiger Next* /37/ is part of the Linotype Platinum Collection. This collection contains a number of typeface classics, which are available in a totally new digital version. Most of the typeface families have been considerably extended and the different fonts have been transformed into a more harmonious set. The shapes of the glyphs have also been reworked.

In general, Linotype's approach of reworking the classic typefaces has to be supported because most digitisations have not been based on the original drawings but on adaptations from later technologies. More often than not, any mistakes and technological shortcomings have been transferred from one technology to the next and can be found again, including some new, additional flaws, in the PostScript fonts. Furthermore, typefaces have usually been extended in a rather piecemeal fashion over time as new fonts and glyphs are added.

With the new digital versions, we have to ask the question, however, of whether the new typeface does justice to the original concept, the original design. And if there are potential improvements, which of these are true to the spirit of the designer? Today, if possible, Linotype consults the original type designers for these redesigns, as opposed to the adaptations created for phototypesetting at the end of the 1960s. Hans Eduard Meier, for instance, drew the fonts for the extension of *Linotype Syntax* himself on the computer and Hermann Zapf kept

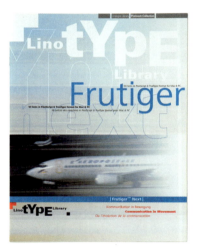

/33/
Front cover of the 16-page brochure for Frutiger Next (2001) – the typeface is part of the Linotype Library Platinum collection.

/34/
Compared to LT Univers 430 (top), Frutiger Next *Regular (bottom) has a lighter and clearly narrower form.*

Sie fragen sich, warum es notwendig ist, so viele
Schriften zur Verfügung zu haben. Sie dienen alle zum
selben, aber machen die Vielfalt des Menschen aus.
Diese Vielfalt ist wie beim Wein. Ich habe einmal eine

Sie fragen sich, warum es notwendig ist, so viele
Schriften zur Verfügung zu haben. Sie dienen alle zum
selben, aber machen die Vielfalt des Menschen aus.
Diese Vielfalt ist wie beim Wein. Ich habe einmal eine

/35/
Letter of 14 April 1999 from Adrian Frutiger to Bruno Steiner following the previous fax about the cursive in Frutiger Next.

/36/
Stroke-weight comparison of the same cap heights: Frutiger LT 55 Roman, Frutiger Next *Regular,* LT Univers 430 *Basic Regular (top to bottom).*

a critical eye on Akira Kobayashi[20] when his typefaces *Aldus Nova, Optima Nova* and *Palatino Nova* were extended.

Adrian Frutiger was involved in the redesigns of *Linotype Univers, Frutiger Next* and *Avenir Next*. As regards *Frutiger Next*, however, the reworking did not follow his understanding of type design. This was not true for the italic, as Erik Faulhaber stated,[21] but overall. Faulhaber's book title *Frutiger: Die Wandlung eines Schriftklassikers* (Frutiger: the transformation of a typeface classic) does not bode well. The whole construction of the typeface had been changed. The fact that the stroke weight of *Frutiger Next* Regular is finer than that of *Frutiger LT* 55 was the only change based on Adrian Frutiger's own criticism. Today, however, it appears slightly too light **/34/**. It is indeed finer than the perfect stroke weight of *LT Univers* 430 **/34/**. There was not only a totally new and systematic concept for the (unnumbered) weight grades of *Frutiger Next* **/37/**; the proportions of the letters were also changed. Compared to the majuscules, the minuscules received a slightly increased x-height as well as slightly longer ascenders and descenders **/42/**. *Frutiger Next* also features a much more pronounced stroke contrast **/44/**. Overall *Frutiger Next* therefore appears unusually narrow, especially since Frutiger's typefaces tend to run rather wide.

These are all reasons not to use *Frutiger Next* for the sample strings on page 263 but the older *Frutiger LT*.

used in the meantime as text type these days for scientific or reference books, is acceptable. But for literature and poetry, there's really no substitute for a classical typeface. The whole reading process functions more easily, to my eyes, with antiqua than with grotesque. The serifs help the words to hang together. I wouldn't like to state that only classical typefaces will do as text types. To someone with a scientific education, the clarity of a grotesque is more trustworthy and agreeable. It's probably even more welcome than a serif typeface, since it works with notations that otherwise don't appear in literature, with formulae that have to be clearly and exactly presented. Antiqua and grotesque both have their strong points, but their use remains different. A certain rapprochement between the robust grotesque and the classical antiqua typefaces is, however, perfectly possible.

Frutiger was also converted for non-latin alphabets. In 1985 *Frutiger Cyrillic* was released in 14 weights (see page 413), from thin to bold, and with the corresponding italics. There was also an ultrablack and five condensed faces. In 2007 Linotype's *Frutiger Arabic* also appeared. Released in four weights, it was the work of the Lebanese designer Nadine Chahine.

A really tricky episode was *Frutiger Next* **/37/**. This appeared in 2001 **/33/**. The sweeping extension of the family is simply the trend at Linotype at the moment. You can do anything – even a true cursive – but then, often, it ceases to be a good typeface. The expansion and compression that we touched on earlier – when it doesn't spoil the typeface – works in all weights only really well in the oblique cut. Between you and me, what does the real cursive have that the inclined regular doesn't? The newly drawn italic of *Frutiger Next* **/32/** is not badly done. It has absolutely its own authority, but it doesn't belong in the family. To my

/37/
The Frutiger Next *type family from 2001. The three ultralight cuts added in 2007 brings it to 21 members.*

H
Frutiger Next
UltraLight

H
*Frutiger Next
UltraLight Italic*

H
Frutiger Next
UltraLight Condensed

H
Frutiger Next
Light

H
*Frutiger Next
Light Italic*

H
Frutiger Next
Light Condensed

H
Frutiger Next
Regular

H
*Frutiger Next
Regular Italic*

H
Frutiger Next
Regular Condensed

H
**Frutiger Next
Medium**

H
***Frutiger Next
Medium Italic***

H
**Frutiger Next
Medium Condensed**

H
**Frutiger Next
Bold**

H
***Frutiger Next
Bold Italic***

H
**Frutiger Next
Bold Condensed**

H
**Frutiger Next
Heavy**

H
***Frutiger Next
Heavy Italic***

H
**Frutiger Next
Heavy Condensed**

H
**Frutiger Next
Black**

H
***Frutiger Next
Black Italic***

H
**Frutiger Next
Black Condensed**

/38/
Overlaying Frutiger Next *in its various weights clearly shows the uniform progression of the letter shapes.*

/39/
The progression of weight of Frutiger LT *(top) and* Frutiger Next *(bottom) – the typeface* F Frutiger Book *(*) conforms broadly to the new Regular.*

eyes, there's a bit of dissonance going on there. There's something not quite right. There's a convergence toward the renaissance character that the original *Frutiger* just didn't have. This cursive was first shown to me in a letter. Right from the start, I wasn't happy about it at all. I don't know why Bruno Steinert, chief executive of Linotype, didn't have the strength to say that this cursive simply shouldn't make the cut. I never gave it my OK, indeed, I said 'no' quite clearly. Not forcefully, but it was clear what I meant. It wasn't my job to point the finger at anyone, but instead of messing with my cursive, Linotype should have encouraged the draughtswoman to design her own typeface. After I got no reply to my fax[22] /29/ saying 'no', I even wrote a letter,[23] /35/, in which I again made it clear that I wasn't giving it my approval. And I made some other suggestions about how Linotype could expand their type collection.[24] When I read this letter again, I'm dismayed that I didn't fight my corner more forcefully. Maybe I was just too soft to say what I really felt about this cursive. Maybe I should have said, "Herr Steinert, you do what you want, but this cursive isn't going out under the *Frutiger* banner". Bruno Steinert knew I was against it. We had talked about it. Later he apologised about the cursive, that he hadn't taken my letter seriously.

Has all this ultimately damaged my reputation? What coming generations will do with a piece of work – how are we going to control that? When *Frutiger Next* was being worked on by Linotype, I was already 70 years old. I just didn't have the strength and patience anymore to examine everything through a magnifying glass. I was tired. It was just too much. The fight, that I couldn't and wouldn't see through to the bitter end, that may be up to other people to carry on now. My time is over. But, as far as I'm concerned, one thing will remain: once upon a time there was a *Univers* and a *Frutiger,* and a couple of other

The digital versions   When comparing *Frutiger LT* and *Frutiger Next*, the differences between a drawn typeface family and one created by interpolation become obvious. In *Frutiger LT*, for instance, the lowercase a of the regular font features a rather round curve terminal compared to a fairly flat one in the ultrabold font. In *Frutiger Next*, however, the curve terminal is consistently flat /40/. A more pronounced difference can be identified in the counter of the g. In *Frutiger LT*, which is close to the original, the shape of the counters changes from an oval to a more rounded one. In *Frutiger Next* it is always oval /40/. There is almost no difference in the thin and ultrabold fonts of the two versions, which means that the differences in the other fonts are influenced by interpolation.

Besides a change in the basic construction /43/, *Frutiger Next* features many differences in the details, some of which are problematic. In the broader S-shape, for instance, the diagonal stroke appears to be too fine compared to the vertical curves /44/. Also too fine is the dot on the i, since it is of equal width to the stroke in *Frutiger Next* /51/. Furthermore, the strongly tapered curve junctures are not very pleasing /47/.[25]

The advantages of *Frutiger Next* lie mainly in the small capitals /53/ and the different types of numerals. Monospaced and proportional lining /56/, oldstyle /58/ and small cap figures /59/ are included respectively.[26]

/40/
In Frutiger LT *(left), dissimilar shapes of the bowls in the a and counters in the g; in* Frutiger Next *(right) they are identical.*

/42/
In comparison to the photo-set original *(left) and* Frutiger LT *(centre),* Frutiger Next *(right) has slightly different heights.*

/43/
In comparison to Frutiger LT *(top) the minuscule o and n of* Frutiger Next Medium *(right) are narrower and have higher contrast.*

/44/
In Frutiger LT *(top), the cap widths clearly vary; in* Frutiger Next Medium *(bottom) they are more similar.*

/45/
LT Univers, Frutiger LT *and* Frutiger Next *(l-r) in comparison – in the ampersand of* Frutiger Next *the t-shape is clearly de-emphasised.*

/46/
In comparison to Frutiger LT *(left),* Frutiger Next *displays flatter curve endings; furthermore, the e is cut on a slant.*

/47/
Strongly narrowed stroke at bowl joints and heightened stroke contrast in Frutiger Next *(right), in comparison with* Frutiger LT *(left).*

/48/
In contrast to the original, and to Frutiger LT *(left), the f and t of* Frutiger Next *have shortened crossbars and curve endings.*

/41/
In Frutiger Next *(black), the cuts penetrate more deeply than in* Frutiger LT *(brown).*

/49/
Compared to Frutiger LT *(left) the diaresis in* Frutiger Next *(right) exhibits both changed proportion and position.*

/50/
The inclined stroke in the Æ ligature in Frutiger LT *is straightened in* Frutiger Next.

/51/
Due to the stem and i-dot having the same width, the i-dot appears too small in Frutiger Next *(right) –* Frutiger LT *(left).*

Imitations of Frutiger Type manufacturers often have a problem with plagiarism. The outcome is always the same: the name of the typeface can be protected but its shape is regarded as being in the public domain and cannot therefore be protected.

One reason to call the typeface *Frutiger* was the additional protection afforded by a personal name. Copies that are released under a different name can no longer bear the label 'similar to', which is a popular reference to the original. *Frutiger* has been copied many times: under the name *Freeborn*, it was released at Scangraphic, Compugraphic's version was called *Frontiera*, URW's *Frutus*, Bitstream's *Humanist 777* **/54/**, Autologic's *Provencale* and Varityper released it under the name *Siegfried*. Type manufacturers had published guidelines for the legal use of their typefaces[27] but only with the advent of digitisation has the situation changed for the better. Now, a typeface can be protected as software.

Microsoft acted in a particularly audacious way by protecting their copy of *Frutiger Next* under the name *Segoe* **/54/** for their new operating system 'Vista'. In 2006, Linotype successfully appealed against this decision. Due to the similarities in the glyphs and construction of the type, *Segoe* was no longer classified as a new typeface. This was good news for Linotype because in the event of a negative decision, they could have been prevented from further distributing *Frutiger Next*.

typefaces besides. They are representative of a particular century. How many types of *Garamond* have emerged, how much were *Baskerville* or *Times* tinkered with? And how much, really, will *Frutiger* still get played around with?

My masterpiece is *Univers,* but my favourite typeface – if I'm being honest – is the original *Frutiger.* It's probably the typeface that holds the middle ground of the type landscape. It's like a nail that's been driven in, and on which you can hang everything. It corresponds, most likely, to my internal image, comparable with what I feel in the works of my favourite artist, Costantin Brâncuşi. *Frutiger* is a typeface that really is beautiful, one that sings.

/52/
In Frutiger Next *(right) the wider numerals align with the mathematical symbols – not so in* Frutiger LT *(left).*

01234 01234
+−×÷= +−×÷=
56789 56789

/53/
The enhanced OpenType version Frutiger Next Pro *contains corresponding small caps in all 21 fonts.*

SMALL CAPS
SMALL CAPS

/54/
Official versions compared with the look-alikes Frutiger LT *55,* Humanist 777, Frutiger Next *Regular,* Segoe *Regular (top to bottom).*

ABCDEFGHIJKLMNOPQRST
UVWXYZ&abcdefghijklmnop
qrstuvwxyzß1234567890

ABCDEFGHIJKLMNOPQRST
UVWXYZ&abcdefghijklmnop
qrstuvwxyzß1234567890

ABCDEFGHIJKLMNOPQRST
UVWXYZ&abcdefghijklmnop
qrstuvwxyzß1234567890

ABCDEFGHIJKLMNOPQRST
UVWXYZ&abcdefghijklmnop
qrstuvwxyzß1234567890

/55/
Unlike Frutiger LT *(left),* Frutiger Next *(right) has corresponding symbols for 'copyright', 'registered' and 'at'.*

©®@ ©®@

/56/
Alongside the old style figures (top), Frutiger Next Pro *also has proportional lining figures (bottom).*

0123456789
0123456789

/57/
In Frutiger Next *(right), the dollar and cent symbols conform to Frutiger's understanding of form.* Frutiger LT *(left).*

$¢ $¢

/58/
The range of symbols in Frutiger Next Pro *now contains lining figures (top) as well as small cap numerals (bottom).*

0123456789
0123456789

/59/
Frutiger Next Pro *has fractional numbers that sit on the baseline, as well as superior- and inferior-set variants.*

$0\,1\,2_{3}\,3^{3}\!/\!4\,4\,5\,6\,7\,8\,9$

ABCDEFGHIJKLMN
OPQRSTUVWXYZ&
abcdefghijklmnopqrs
tuvwxyzß1234567890

Optimal legibility in a sentence depends on different factors. The appearance of each typeface, no matter how well designed, can be destroyed through the wrong sentence parameters. To put it differently: in order to make a typeface sing, all parameters need to be harmonised.

The phrase 'colour of a sentence or typeface' is often used in regards to text type. For one thing, the colour is achieved through the typeface itself: stroke weight and contrast in particular are important in this context. In conversation Adrian Frutiger often repeated how fundamentally important, but also difficult, the definition of stroke weight is. For a typeface to have a regular colour, spacing is also crucial.

For another thing, the colour is defined through line parameters such as type size (see page 356), letter spacing (see page 312), word spacing and line spacing (see page 292).

The sample sentences set in *Frutiger LT* demonstrate the difference in appearance. The letter spacing must not be too narrow because then the letters run into each other; if letter spacing is too wide, however, the word images fall apart **/61/**. Word spacing should sufficiently separate individual words without tearing apart the line formation **/62/**. And the line spacing must provide a good horizontal guideline without compromising the coherence of the text **/63/**.

Sie fragen sich, warum es notwendig ist, so viele Schriften zur Verfügung zu haben. Sie dienen alle zum selben, aber machen die Vielfalt des Menschen aus. Diese Vielfalt ist wie beim Wein. Ich habe einmal eine

Sie fragen sich, warum es notwendig ist, so viele Schriften zur Verfügung zu haben. Sie dienen alle zum selben, aber machen die Vielfalt des Menschen aus. Diese Vielfalt ist wie beim Wein. Ich habe einmal eine

Sie fragen sich, warum es notwendig ist, so viele Schriften zur Verfügung zu haben. Sie dienen alle zum selben, aber machen die Vielfalt des Menschen aus. Diese Vielfalt ist wie beim Wein. Ich habe einmal eine

/61/
*The overall impression of a typeface
and its legibility can be adversely
affected by letter spacing that is either
too tight (top) or too loose (bottom).*

Sie fragen sich, warum es notwendig ist, so viele Schriften zur Verfügung zu haben. Sie dienen alle zum selben, aber machen die Vielfalt des Menschen aus. Diese Vielfalt ist wie beim Wein. Ich habe einmal eine

Sie fragen sich, warum es notwendig ist, so viele Schriften zur Verfügung zu haben. Sie dienen alle zum selben, aber machen die Vielfalt des Menschen aus. Diese Vielfalt ist wie beim Wein. Ich habe einmal eine

Sie fragen sich, warum es notwendig ist, so viele Schriften zur Verfügung zu haben. Sie dienen alle zum selben, aber machen die Vielfalt des Menschen aus. Diese Vielfalt ist wie beim Wein. Ich habe einmal eine

/62/
*Word spacing that is either too tight
(top) or too loose (bottom) also has
an adverse effect on the legibility of
a typeface.*

Sie fragen sich, warum es notwendig ist, so viele Schriften zur Verfügung zu haben. Sie dienen alle zum selben, aber machen die Vielfalt des Menschen aus. Diese Vielfalt ist wie beim Wein. Ich habe einmal eine

Sie fragen sich, warum es notwendig ist, so viele Schriften zur Verfügung zu haben. Sie dienen alle zum selben, aber machen die Vielfalt des Menschen aus. Diese Vielfalt ist wie beim Wein. Ich habe einmal eine

Sie fragen sich, warum es notwendig ist, so viele Schriften zur Verfügung zu haben. Sie dienen alle zum selben, aber machen die Vielfalt des Menschen aus. Diese Vielfalt ist wie beim Wein. Ich habe einmal eine

/63/
*The line spacing also changes the
optical grey and the overall
reading impression of a typeface.*

Font production
Adobe Font digitised by
Linotype

Font format:
PostScript Type 1

Also available in:
TrueType
OpenType Com
XSF

ABCDEFGHIJKLMN
OPQRSTUVWXYZ&
abcdefghijklmnopqrs
tuvwxyzß1234567890

You may ask w
hy so many differen
t typefaces. They all serve th
e same purpose but they express man's

diversity. It is the same diversity we find in wine. I once saw a list of Médoc wines featuring sixty different Médocs all of the same year. All of them were wines but each was different from the others. It's the nuances that are important. The same is true for typefaces. *Sie fragen sich, warum es notwen*

dig ist, so viele Schriften zur Verfügung zu haben. Sie dienen alle zum selben, aber machen die Vielfalt des Menschen aus. Diese Vielfalt ist wie beim Wein. Ich habe einmal eine Weinkarte studiert mit sechzig Médoc-Weinen aus dem selben Jahr. Das ist ausna hmslos Wein, aber doch nicht alles der gleiche Wein. Es hat eben gleichwohl Nuancen. So ist es auch mit der Schrift. *You may ask why so many different typefaces.* They all s erve the same purpose but they express man's diversity. It is the same diversity we fin d in wine. I once saw a list of Médoc wines featuring sixty different Médocs all of the

same year. All of them were wines but each was different from the others. It's the nuances that are important. The same is true for typefaces. *Pourquoi tant d'Alphabets différents!* Tous servent au même but, mais aussi à exprimer la diversité de l'homme. C'est cette même diversité que nous retrouvons da ns les vins de Médoc. J'ai pu, un jour, relever soixante crus, tous de la même année. Il s'agissait certes de vins, mais tous étaient différents. Tout est dans la nuance du bouquet. Il en est de même pour les caractères! *Sie fragen sich, warum es notwendig ist, so viele Schriften zur Verfügung zu haben.* Sie die

nen alle zum selben, aber machen die Vielfalt der Menschen aus. Diese Vielfalt ist wie beim Wein. Ich habe einmal eine Weinkarte studiert mit sechzig Médoc-Weinen aus dem selben Jah r. Das ist ausnahmslos Wein, aber doch nicht al les der gleiche Wein. Es hat eben gleichwohl N uancen. So ist es auch mit der Schrift. *You may ask why so many different typefaces.* They all s erve the same purpose but they express man's divesity. It is the same diversity we fi nd in win

65 pt | −35   48 pt | −30   32 pt | −10   22 pt | −5   14.5 pt | 19.5 pt | 0   10 pt | 13 pt | 5   7.2 pt | 10.2 pt | 10   5.8 pt | 8 pt | 15

ÅBÇDÈFG
HIJKLMÑ
ÔPQRŠTÜ
VWXYZ&
ÆŒ¥$£€
1234567890
åbçdéfghij
klmñôpqrš
tüvwxyzß
fi fl æ œ ø ł ð
[.,:;·'/-–—]
(¿¡"«‹›»"!?)
{§°%@‰*†}

45 Light

ÅBÇDÈFG
HIJKLMÑ
ÔPQRŠTÜ
VWXYZ&
ÆŒ¥$£€
1234567890
åbçdéfghij
klmñôpqrš
tüvwxyzß
fi fl æ œ ø ł ð
[.,:;·'/-–—]
(¿¡"«‹›»"!?)
{§°%@‰*†}

46 Light Italic

ÅBÇDÈFG
HIJKLMÑ
ÔPQRŠTÜ
VWXYZ&
ÆŒ¥$£€
1234567890
åbçdéfghij
klmñôpqrš
tüvwxyzß
fi fl æ œ ø ł ð
[.,:;·'/-–—]
(¿¡"«‹›»"!?)
{§°%@‰*†}

55 Roman

ÅBÇDÈFG
HIJKLMÑ
ÔPQRŠTÜ
VWXYZ&
ÆŒ¥$£€
1234567890
åbçdéfghij
klmñôpqrš
tüvwxyzß
fi fl æ œ ø ł ð
[.,:;·'/-–—]
(¿¡"«‹›»"!?)
{§°%@‰*†}

56 Italic

ÅBÇDÈFG
HIJKLMÑ
ÔPQRŠTÜ
VWXYZ&
ÆŒ¥$£€
1234567890
åbçdéfghij
klmñôpqrš
tüvwxyzß
fi fl æ œ ø ł ð
[.,:;·'/-–—]
(¿¡"«‹›»"!?)
{§°%@‰*†}

65 Bold

ÅBÇDÈFG
HIJKLMÑ
ÔPQRŠTÜ
VWXYZ&
ÆŒ¥$£€
1234567890
åbçdéfghij
klmñôpqrš
tüvwxyzß
fi fl æ œ ø ł ð
[.,:;·'/-–—]
(¿¡"«‹›»"!?)
{§°%@‰*†}

66 Bold Italic

Typeface comparison   The typefaces shown below – *Syntax, Frutiger* and *Praxis* – are generally attributed to the group of dynamic sans serifs. They share some characteristics with an oldstyle typeface such as the varying width of the capital letters and the open curve shapes. Adrian Frutiger himself, however, does not regard *Frutiger* as a typical representative of this group since b d p q feature oval counters and a vertical stress.

Syntax Antiqua, in comparison, was directly derived from humanist typefaces,[28] which becomes obvious, for instance, in the curves of the minuscule m, which lean to the right and are attached to the stem. In the case of *Praxis,* the curves feature angular connections to the stem but are kept very flat. In *Frutiger,* the curves have a round connection to the stem.

The stronger stroke contrast in *Praxis* is a reference to its relationship with *Demos,* its sister typeface with serifs.[29] The rounded terminals are an adaptation to CRT technology. This fact, however, makes *Praxis* appear slightly ambiguous. In comparison to *Praxis,* Frutiger's statement that with *Frutiger* he had designed a concise type becomes apparent: the horizontal terminals of the x-strokes, the straight terminal of the leg in the R and also the simple one-looped shape of the g all have clear and easily recognisable shapes with a definite line forming effect.

/64/

Measurements of the stroke widths and proportions of the Frutiger LT *regular weight.*

Roman					
Hh = 10.00 cm	nh = 7.34 cm	oh = 7.67 cm	Hh : Hw = 1 : 0.76	nh : nw = 1 : 0.88
Hw = 7.65	nw = 6.44	ow = 7.46	Hw : Hs = 1 : 0.86	nw : ns = 1 : 0.21
Hs = 1.42	ns = 1.33	os = 1.43	Hs : Hq = 1 : 0.89	nh : oh = 1 : 1.04
Hq = 1.27	nq = 1.09	oq = 1.09		nw : ow = 1 : 1.16

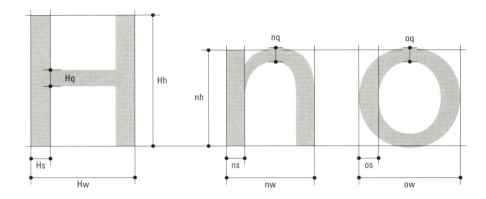

/65/

Frutiger LT *possesses, in comparison with the typefaces* Syntax *and* Praxis, *a rather strong roman font.*

Hofstainberg

Syntax
Hans Eduard Meier
1968

E G R a g m x 5 7

Hofstainberg

Frutiger
Adrian Frutiger
1976

E G R a g m x 5 7

E	G	R	a	g	m	x	5 7
Middle crossbar slightly shorter than overall width	With horizontal stroke on beard	Diagonal leg is curved where it exits bowl	Flattened curve on the belly	Oval counter, curve ends in a slightly diagonal cut	Rounded junctures, counters almost symmetrical	Diagonal strokes clearly offset	Strokes meet at a point in the 5; in the 7 they are chamfered

Hofstainberg

Praxis
Gerard Unger
1977

E G R a g m x 5 7

Comparison showing the
differents weights and angle of
of the obliques.

	Hh	Hw		Hs		Hq	
Light	10.00 cm	7.01	= 0.92	0.98	= 0.69	0.86	= 0.68
Roman	10.00	7.65	= 1	1.42	= 1	1.27	= 1
Bold	10.00	7.99	= 1.04	1.97	= 1.39	1.56	= 1.23
Black	10.00	8.49	= 1.11	2.64	= 1.86	1.87	= 1.47
Ultra Black	10.00	10.22	= 1.33	3.80	= 2.68	2.94	= 2.31
Italic	10.00	7.51	= 0.98	1.44	= 1.01	1.29	= 1.01

11.9°

Height comparison showing the
differences of x-heights to
ascenders and descenders – the cap
height is the starting point.

Syntax
41.3 pt

Frutiger
41 pt

Praxis
42.1 pt

ÅBÇDÈFG
HIJKLMÑ
ÔPQRŠTÜ
VWXYZ&
ÆŒ¥$£€
1234567890
åbçdéfghij
klmñôpqrš
tüvwxyzß
fi fl æœøłð
[.,:;·'/-–—]
(¿¡"«‹›»"!?)
{§°%@‰*†}

75 Black

ÅBÇDÈFG
HIJKLMÑ
ÔPQRŠTÜ
VWXYZ&
ÆŒ¥$£€
1234567890
åbçdéfghij
klmñôpqrš
tüvwxyzß
fi fl æœøłð
[.,:;·'/-–—]
(¿¡"«‹›»"!?)
{§°%@‰*†}

76 Black Italic

ÅBÇDÈFG
HIJKLMÑ
ÔPQRŠTÜ
VWXYZ&
ÆŒ¥$£€0
123456789
åbçdéfghij
klmñôpqrš
tüvwxyzß
fi fl æœøłð
[.,:;·'/-–—]
(¿¡"«‹›»"!?)
{§°%@‰*†}

95 UltraBlack

/72/
The stroke weight of Astra Frutiger
(black) lies somewhere between
Frutiger 57 (cyan) and Frutiger 67
(magenta).

Frutiger 57
Frutiger Astra
Frutiger 67

/68/
Construction drawings for the
production of the lowercase a b c d
of the standard typeface for the
Swiss road signage.

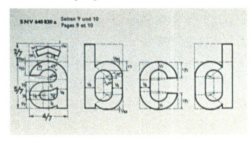

/69/
Construction drawings for the
word heights and line spacing, based
on a cap height of 7/7.

Neuchâtel
Biel/Bienne

Brugg
Aarau

/71/
Adjustment of Astra Frutiger to
the existing construction template
with increased line spacing
to accommodate the descenders.

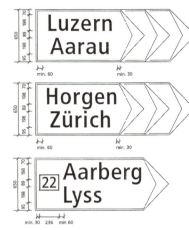

/73/
Examples of Astra Frutiger in use –
clearly words with descenders
are too close to the edges.

/70/
The standard typeface of the
VSS (left) and the new Astra Frutiger
(right) on road signage by day and
by night.

/74/
Astra Frutiger is set in a more
compressed way for the signage used
on main and trunk roads (top) than
that used on motorways (bottom).

Astra Frutiger Standard
Astra Frutiger Autobahn

Back to signage type – Astra Frutiger   In 2002, the new *Astra Frutiger* was introduced in Switzerland as the new type for road signage. It successively replaced the former *Normalschrift* of VSS **/68/**.[30]

In 1999, ASTRA[31] commissioned the graphic designer Viktor Stampfli to develop a typeface based on *Frutiger*.[32] He had a cut produced at Linotype Library that was between *Frutiger* 57 and 67 **/72/**. Only one cut was manufactured, which was not sufficient for use in positive, negative and backlit form. Black type on a light background appears thinner than white type on a dark background, which is why at least two cuts – for positive and negative use – are needed to guarantee good and consistent legibility.

Astra Frutiger had to be integrated into the existing layout system of the boards **/69/**. Given the different proportions of this typeface compared to the VSS one, this did not produce good results **/73/**. Compared to the line spacing, the distance to the edge of the panels is far too small. Since 2002 the typeface has been used in two different ways: with normal letter spacing for roads and with wide letter spacing for motorways **/74/**. In the case of very long words it can be compressed by 20 %.

As early as 1997, the narrow *Frutiger* became the starting point for a signage type. Reworked by MetaDesign into *FF Transit*,[33] it was implemented for signage in Berlin and later also in other German cities **/75/**.

/75/

FF Transit *by MetaDesign – based on* Frutiger *and conceived as a signage typeface – was first put into service in Berlin.*

FF Transit BackPositiv
FF Transit FrontPositiv
FF Transit FrontNegativ
FF Transit BackNegativ
FF Transit Print

/76/

The use of FF *Transit on the signage for the 'Berliner Verkehrs-betriebe' displays balanced letter spacing.*

47 Light Condensed

48 Light Condensed Italic

77 Black Condensed

78 Black Condensed Italic

57 Condensed

58 Condensed Italic

87 ExtraBlack Condensed

88 ExtraBlack Cond. Italic

67 Bold Condensed

68 Bold Condensed Italic

Name of typeface	Client	Designer	Design	Publication	Typesetting technology	Manufacturer	Weights
Glypha	D. Stempel AG	Adrian Frutiger	1976	1980	Photosetting, digital CRT typesetting	– D. Stempel AG	Linotype	10
					PostScript digital typesetting	– Adobe	Linotype	10

GLYPHA

Glypha was made at Mike Parker's request. In a conversation with him, in which Walter Greisner also took part, he said that he thought *Serifa* was too wide for a text face. He asked me whether I could imagine designing a narrower typeface derived from *Serifa* but with a different name. From 1977 *Serifa,* licensed by Wolfgang Hartmann from the Fundición Tipográfica Neufville, had been extended to five weights by D. Stempel AG. Three years later *Glypha* was released. This story was delicate.

In 1982, two years after *Glypha* appeared, Hartmann reacted and demanded that licensing rights should apply for *Glypha*. As far as he was concerned it was perfectly apparent that *Glypha* was derived from *Serifa*. He threatened D. Stempel AG with legal action if they didn't come to an amicable agreement. It was tricky because the people involved were all members of the Association Typographique Internationale (ATypI), the organisation for type designers and manufacturers. Eventually it was suggested the matter be handled internally at ATypI, which is what happened in 1983. A tribunal was convened, presided over by Gerrit Willem Ovink. Wolfgang Hartmann named Eckehart Schumacher-Gebler as adjudicator, while D. Stempel AG named Gerard Unger. Their verdict after two hours' deliberation was, in a nutshell, that *Glypha* is a copy of *Serifa*. It wasn't a case of a new idea, rather a modification of an existing typeface. D. Stempel AG accepted the decision and made a backdated licence payment to Hartmann. At least things quietened down after that.

Serifa and *Glypha* really are very similar in form. *Glypha* has been used more frequently since desktop publishing came about, more than *Serifa* at any rate because it is narrower with the same cap height. There are some small differences other than the tracking, such as the *Glypha* serifs being horizontal and no longer slightly drawn in, like the original *Serifa* foundry type version (see page 167). Actually, I regret doing that now, because an Egyptienne with slightly rounded serif transitions that taper off would have been much better. As opposed to other slab serif faces, *Glypha* is an engineered typeface. There's something contrived about it; I'm a little disappointed in it. It seems too harsh. Even though there is a certain quality in its construction, it isn't really evident, particularly in small point sizes. The eye doesn't want to love it. It's different when *Glypha* is used for headlines or large posters; then it works.

I came up with the name 'Glypha'. It was a word I had always liked. It's part of hieroglyph and is meant to remind people of Egypt. Many of the typefaces from the Egyptienne classification group have similar names, for instance *Karnak, Memphis* or *Pharaon*.[1] I was also thinking of glyphs, meaning the concrete graphic representation of a character.

Serifa versus Glypha In 1966 Adrian Frutiger transferred the exclusive copyright and usage rights for *Serifa* to Bauersche Giesserei in Frankfurt.[2] He made the contract with Walter Greisner, who was managing director there until 1967. In 1973 Wolfgang Hartmann of the Fundición Tipográfica Neufville S.A., successors to Bauersche Giesserei, extended the contract with Frutiger from 15 to 25 years. Thereafter, licences for photosetting versions were granted to H. Berthold AG, D. Stempel AG and Compugraphic.[3] Although D. Stempel AG did not receive the exclusive photosetting rights they desired for *Serifa*, they expanded the typeface family between 1975 and 1978. At the same time, the narrower *Glypha*, based on *Serifa*, was produced from 1976 on, although it was not released until 1980.[4]

In late 1982 Wolfgang Hartmann sent a letter from Barcelona to Walter Greisner, who in the meantime had become a board member at D. Stempel AG, expressing his surprise at *Glypha* and reminding him of the Code Morale of the ATypI.[5] Greisner replied that *Glypha*, though related to *Serifa*, was on the whole an independent typeface for text setting and for 'classified composition' such as reference works or catalogues, whereas *Serifa* was to be regarded as a headline or display face.[6]

As Neufville and Stempel could not reach an accord, they agreed to an internal arbitration tribunal at ATypI, of which they both were members. It was to be decided whether D. Stempel AG had broken the Code Morale[7] of the ATypI and whether *Glypha* was a plagiarised version of *Serifa*. Both parties declared their agreement agreed to accept the panel's decision. They put their positions in writing. Hartmann submitted a typeface comparison as part of his argument. He had a Spanish type house electronically narrow *Serifa* using a Linotype CRTronic machine and then expose it together with *Glypha* in order to demonstrate how they match. On 22 April 1983 the panel in Paris agreed with his view and unanimously judged in favour of Neufville, ruling "Glypha, though not a plagiarised version of Serifa in the sense of being nearly identical, is not a new creation but an adjustment of the existing Serifa. Glypha is unthinkable without Serifa."[8]

/01/
Serifa *(outlined) is the foundation of Glypha (black)* – uppercase characters are vertically distorted to 109.6 % and lowercase to 113.5 % *(red outlines).*

/02/
By vertically distorting Serifa *lowercase characters (outlined) to an x-height of 113.5 % (red outline),* Glypha *appears narrower.*

/03/
The vertical distortion of Serifa *(left) increases the horizontal serifs (middle) – in* Glypha, *however, the serifs are reduced slightly.*

/04/
The ascender and descender heights of Serifa *(left) are practically identical to those of* Glypha *(right).*

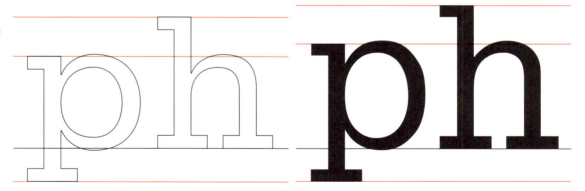

/05/
The character widths and weights of Glypha *(bottom) are the same as* Serifa *(top) – only the x-height is different.*

/06/
Character set of Glypha *for CRT (cathode ray tube) photosetting by Linotype.*

ABCDEFGHIJKLMN
OPQRSTUVWXYZ&
abcdefghijklmnopqrs
tuvwxyzß1234567890

Differences to Serifa In two letters, G.W. Ovink made further comments on the judgement: even though the case was decided in favour of Neufville, actually D. Stempel AG benefited from it. This is because they would be able to take action in the future if one of their own typefaces was electronically modified and sold without licence by another manufacturer.[9]

Indeed the only apparent distinction between *Glypha* and *Serifa* is their differing widths. Frutiger's design work for *Glypha* was confined to determining the new proportions of cap height and x-height. Apart from that, *Glypha* was entirely developed from 1976 to 1978 by Unternehmensberatung Rubow Weber (URW management consultancy) of Hamburg. Peter Karow and his colleagues first digitised *Serifa* 55, vertically distorting the cap height from 229 to 251 mm **/01/** and the x-height from 163 to 185 mm **/02/**.[10] The ascender and descender heights remained unchanged **/04/**. The *Glypha* serifs, however, became slightly lighter **/03/**. Since the character shapes were unaltered, the weights are the same as *Serifa*. A few characters required a minor reworking of the arc shapes, strength of diagonal strokes and character widths after the electronic distortion. For example, n and h appeared too narrow and were widened slightly. These corrections were undertaken by Adrian Frutiger.

/07/
Double page from the 1983 trilingual Linotype brochure Typefaces by Adrian Frutiger – *set in* Glypha.

/08/
Advertisement in the trade magazine Deutscher Drucker *no. 33, October 1980 set in* Glypha 45, 46, 65 *and* 66.

Eine Fotosetzmaschine ohne Schrift ist wie ein Klavier ohne Saiten:

Keine Botschaft für das Auge. Keine Botschaft für das Ohr. Schriften sollte man soviele haben, wie es Stimmen gibt. Mit mehr als eintausendzweihundert Schriften (jährlich kommen über hundert hinzu) bieten wir, was der Markt erwartet. Und aufnimmt.

Meinen Sie, daß mit einem Dutzend Schriften Ihre Marktchancen gesichert sind? (Ihre ausländischen Kollegen sehen fünfzig bis achtzig Schriften als Grundausstattung an.) Mit jedem neuen Font wachsen Rentabilität und Rendite, Wettbewerbsfähigkeit und Marktchance. Sie zahlen nur noch einen Bruchteil dessen, was noch vor einer Generation für eine Schriftfamilie ausgegeben wurde.

Unsere Schriftträger sind langlebig. Und kurzfristig abschreibbar. Die Aktion »profont« ist darüber hinaus an ein attraktives Preisangebot geknüpft.

Die Mergenthaler-Linotype-Firmengruppe steht für eine 400-jährige Schrifttradition. Die Unternehmen verfügen über Originalschnitte, die europäische Schriftgeschichte gemacht haben. Ebenso wie über das Angebot gegenwärtiger Schrifttrends. Eine bis ins vorige Jahrhundert zurückreichende Spezialerfahrung bei der D. Stempel AG in der Herstellung von Schriftträgern für alle Setzsysteme bedeutet eine hohe Selbstverpflichtung. Unsere Fonts werden von hundertfach vergrößerten Original-Vorlagen in moderner Computertechnik hergestellt.

Eine Schriften-Aktion für Linotype-Kunden

Linotype-Fotosetzmaschinen und -Systeme bieten in einem flexiblen, abgerundeten Programm Fotosatz hoher Qualität.

Unsere Schriftbibliothek umfaßt mehr als 1200 Schriften. Neben den zahlreichen Originalschnitten, für die wir ein gefragter Lizenzgeber sind, verfügen wir über den Schriftenfundus angesehener europäischer Schriftenhersteller bis zum aktuellen Schriftenprogramm der ITC (International Typeface Corporation). Hinzu kommen hunderte von Sonderlayouts für nichtlateinische Sprachen, mathematischen Satz, Katalogsatz und vieles andere.

Wir haben kürzeste Lieferzeiten. Das abrufbereite Lager führt 700 Schriften: davon 500 für den Direktabholdienst ab Frankfurt/Hedderichstraße oder für den Postversand, in der Regel innerhalb 24 Stunden. Und 200 weitere Schriften können kurzfristig geliefert werden.

Diese große Schriftenbibliothek bietet – verbunden mit dieser Aktion – Fonts zu einem attraktiven Preis. Rufen Sie unseren »profont«-service (06196) 403-246 an. Oder schicken Sie uns den Kupon dieser Anzeige. Die Aktion »profont« will Ihnen nicht nur Schrift näher bringen, sondern auch Auftrags-Chancen sichern.

Mergenthaler Linotype GmbH

An die
Mergenthaler Linotype GmbH
Frankfurter Allee 55–75
D-6236 Eschborn

☐ Bitte senden Sie mir kostenlos und unverbindlich Ihr Schriftenverzeichnis

☐ Ich wünsche eine ausführliche Beratung. Bitte rufen Sie mich an.

Name

Beruf/Firma

Straße

Plz/Ort

Telefon

Font Production:
Adobe Font digitised by
Linotype

Font format:
PostScript Type 1

Also available:
TrueType
OpenType Std

ABCDEFGHIJKLMN
OPQRSTUVWXYZ&
abcdefghijklmnopqrs
tuvwxyzß1234567890

Sie fragen sic
h warum es notw
endig ist, so viele Schriften
zur Verfügung zu haben. Sie dienen all

e zum selben, aber machen die Vielfalt des Menschen aus. Diese Vielfalt ist wie beim Wein. Ich habe einmal eine Wein karte studiert mit sechzig Médoc- Weinen aus dem selben Jahr. Das ist ausnahmslos Wein, aber doch nicht alles der g leiche Wein. Es hat eben gleichwohl Nuancen. So ist es au

ch mit der Schrift. *You may ask why so many different typefaces.* They all serve the sa me purpose but they express man's diversity. It is the same diversity we find in wine. I once saw a list of Médoc wines featuring sixty different Médocs all of the same year. All of them were wines but each was different from the others. It's the nuances that ar e important. The same is true for typefaces. *Pourquoi tant d'Alphabets différents!* Tou s servent au même but, mais aussi à exprimer la diversité de l'homme. C'est cette mê me diversité que nous retrouvons dans les vins de Mèdoc. J'ai pu, un jour, relever soix

ante crus, tous de la même année. Il s'agissait certes de vins, mais tous étaient différents. Tout est dans la nuance du bouquet. Il en est de même pour les caractères! *Sie fragen sich, warum es notwendig ist, so viele Sc hriften zur Verfügung zu haben.* Sie dienen alle zum selben, aber machen die Vielfalt des Menschen aus. Diese Vielfalt ist wie beim Wein. Ich habe einmal eine Weinkarte studiert mit sechzig Médoc-Weinen aus dem selb en Jahr. Das ist ausnahmslos Wein, aber doch nicht alles der gleiche Wei n. Es hat eben gleichwohl Nuancen. So ist es auch mit der Schrift. *You m*

ay ask why so many different typefaces. They all serve the same purose but they express m an's divesity. It is the same diversity we find i n wine. I once saw a list of Médoc wines featu ring sixty different Médocs all of the same ye ar. All of them were wines but each was differ ent from the others. It's the nuances that are i mportant. The same is true for typefaces. *Pou rquoi tant d'Alphabets différents!* Tous serve nt au même but, mais aussi à exprimer la dive

66 pt | −5   49 pt | −5   33 pt | −5   22 pt | 10   14 pt | 19 pt | 20   9.5 pt | 13 pt | 20   7.2 pt | 10.2 pt | 25   5.7 pt | 8 pt | 30

ÅBÇDÈFG HIJKLMÑ ÔPQRŠTÜ VWXYZ& ÆŒ¥$£€ 1234567890 åbçdéfghij klmñôpqrš tüvwxyzß fi fl æ œ ø ł ð [.,:;'/-–—] (¿¡"«‹›»"!?) {§°%@‰*†}
35 Thin

ÅBÇDÈFG HIJKLMÑ ÔPQRŠTÜ VWXYZ& ÆŒ¥$£€ 1234567890 åbçdéfghij klmñôpqrš tüvwxyzß fi fl æ œ ø ł ð [.,:;'/-–—] (¿¡"«‹›»"!?) {§°%@‰†}*
35 Thin Oblique

ÅBÇDÈFG HIJKLMÑ ÔPQRŠTÜ VWXYZ& ÆŒ¥$£€ 1234567890 åbçdéfghij klmñôpqrš tüvwxyzß fi fl æ œ ø ł ð [.,:;'/-–—] (¿¡"«‹›»"!?) {§°%@‰*†}
45 Light

ÅBÇDÈFG HIJKLMÑ ÔPQRŠTÜ VWXYZ& ÆŒ¥$£€ 1234567890 åbçdéfghij klmñôpqrš tüvwxyzß fi fl æ œ ø ł ð [.,:;'/-–—] (¿¡"«‹›»"!?) {§°%@‰†}*
45 Light Oblique

ÅBÇDÈFG HIJKLMÑ ÔPQRŠTÜ VWXYZ& ÆŒ¥$£€ 1234567890 åbçdéfghij klmñôpqrš tüvwxyzß fi fl æ œ ø ł ð [.,:;'/-–—] (¿¡"«‹›»"!?) {§°%@‰*†}
55 Roman

ÅBÇDÈFG HIJKLMÑ ÔPQRŠTÜ VWXYZ& ÆŒ¥$£€ 1234567890 åbçdéfghij klmñôpqrš tüvwxyzß fi fl æ œ ø ł ð [.,:;'/-–—] (¿¡"«‹›»"!?) {§°%@‰†}*
55 Oblique

Typeface comparison As in the *Serifa* chapter (see page 172), three static-style slab serif linear typefaces are compared here. All three have right-angled serifs. On the whole they appear matter-of-fact, strong and strict, virtually cold. These typefaces are often used for technical texts, such as instructional manuals.

Although *Glypha* is narrower than *Serifa*, it is somewhat broader than the 1980s typefaces shown below. The differences in tracking are slight, but Margaret Calvert's typeface *Calvert* appears narrower due to its taller x-height and an ascender height that tops the cap height. On the other hand, *Boton* by Albert Boton, Frutiger's erstwhile colleague at Deberny & Peignot in Paris, is narrower by design.

In the details the differences in shape of the three typefaces is considerable. The positioning of serifs is noticeably different. In *Glypha* they are seldom centred, while in *Calvert* some letters have outward-facing serifs on one side only. This produces more open counters, giving it a look originating from writing, also detectable in the asymmetric arcs and in the square transition to the stem. In *Boton* the serifs are optically centred, including the head serif in uppercase A.

/09/
Measurements of stroke widths and proportions of the Glypha *regular weight.*

Roman				
Hh = 10.00 cm	nh = 7.30 cm	oh = 7.65 cm	Hh : Hw = 1 : 0.72	nh : nw = 1 : 0.77
Hw = 7.19	nw = 5.60	ow = 6.78	Hw : Hs = 1 : 0.17	nw : ns = 1 : 0.20
Hs = 1.21	ns = 1.13	os = 1.21	Hs : Hq = 1 : 0.81	nh : oh = 1 : 1.05
Hq = 0.98	nq = 0.87	oq = 0.86		nw : ow = 1 : 1.21

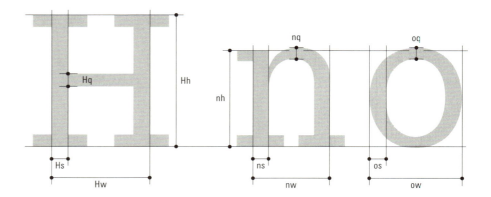

/10/
The character shapes of the three slab serif typefaces Glypha, Calvert *and* Boton *all vary in definition.*

Hofstainberg

Glypha
Adrian Frutiger
1980

A G K a m t x 4 5

A	**G**	**K**	**a**	**m**	**t**	**x**	**4 5**
No head serif, asymmetric foot serifs	Crossbar nearly centred	Diagonal strokes form a point where they join the stem	Elongated flat arc	Round arc opening, heavily tapered	Arc rises sharply	Serifs form negative arrow shapes	Short crossbar, crossbar without serif

Hofstainberg

Calvert
Margaret Calvert
1980

A G K a m t x 4 5

Hofstainberg

Boton
Albert Boton
1986

A G K a m t x 4 5

Comparison showing the
different weights and angle of
the Glypha obliques.

	Hh	Hw	Hs	Hq
Thin	10.00 cm	6.15 = 0.85	0.30 = 0.25	0.24 = 0.24
Light	10.00	6.70 = 0.93	0.75 = 0.62	0.67 = 0.68
Roman	10.00	7.19 = 1	1.21 = 1	0.98 = 1
Bold	10.00	7.87 = 1.09	1.90 = 1.57	1.25 = 1.27
Black	10.00	8.57 = 1.19	2.66 = 2.20	1.61 = 1.64
Oblique	10.00	7.11 = 0.99	1.20 = 0.99	0.99 = 1.01

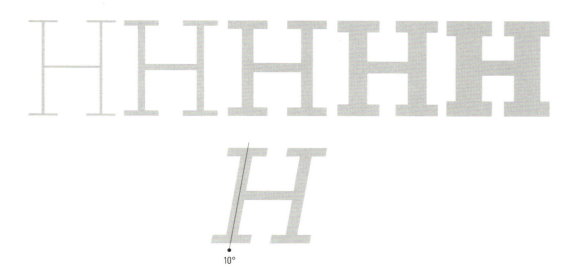

10°

/12/

Height comparison showing the
differences of x-heights to
ascenders and descenders – the cap
height is the starting point.

1.00
0

cm
Glypha
39.9 pt

131
100
73 3.7
10
−22 3.0

1.00
0

cm
Calvert
40.6 pt

127
105
76 3.8
10
−25 3.3

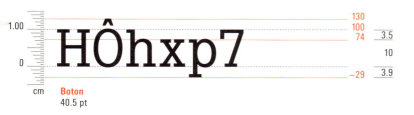

1.00
0

cm
Boton
40.5 pt

130
100
74 3.5
10
−29 3.9

ÅBÇDÈFG
HIJKLMÑ
ÔPQRŠTÜ
VWXYZ&
ÆŒ¥$£€
1234567890
åbçdéfghij
klmñôpqrš
tüvwxyzß
fi fl æ œ ø ł ð
[.,:;·'/-−—]
(¿¡"«‹›»"!?)
{§°%@‰*†}

65 Bold

ÅBÇDÈFG
HIJKLMÑ
ÔPQRŠTÜ
VWXYZ&
ÆŒ¥$£€
1234567890
åbçdéfghij
klmñôpqrš
tüvwxyzß
fi fl æ œ ø ł ð
[.,:;·'/-−—]
(¿¡"«‹›»"!?)
{§°%@‰*†}

65 Bold Oblique

ÅBÇDÈFG
HIJKLMÑ
ÔPQRŠTÜ
VWXYZ&
ÆŒ¥$£€
1234567890
åbçdéfghij
klmñôpqrš
tüvwxyzß
fi fl æ œ ø ł ð
[.,:;·'/-−—]
(¿¡"«‹›»"!?)
{§°%@‰*†}

75 Black

ÅBÇDÈFG
HIJKLMÑ
ÔPQRŠTÜ
VWXYZ&
ÆŒ¥$£€
1234567890
åbçdéfghij
klmñôpqrš
tüvwxyzß
fi fl æ œ ø ł ð
[.,:;·'/-−—]
(¿¡"«‹›»"!?)
{§°%@‰*†}

75 Black Oblique

Logos and wordmarks
1972–1978

Instruments Scientifiques
et Industriels
optical devices manufacturer
Paris (F)

Aéroport de Paris
Association of a Parisian Airport
Paris (F)

Réunion des musées nationaux
Association of
French National Museums
Paris (F)

Musée Rodin
Auguste Rodin Museum
Paris (F)

Autoroutes du Sud de la France
Association of Southern French
Motorways
Montélimar (F)

Institut Français de
Restauration des Œuvres d'Art
French Institute
for Art Restoration
Paris (F)

Société Industrielle des Charmilles
optical lens manufacturer
Villemomble (F)

National Institute of Design
Ahmedabad, India

Laboratoire National
de Métrologie et d'Essais
National Weights
and Measures Laboratory
Paris (F)

D. Stempel AG / Linotype
photosetting control element for
typeface production
Frankfurt am Main (D)

Collection 'Documents spirituels'
collection of Éditions Floyard
Paris (F)

Tribune de Genève
daily newspaper
Geneva (CH)
Design: Bruno Pfäffli

ASD
field of operation unknown
location unknown
Design: Helena Novak

Distribution pétrolière
petroleum distribution company
France

Pictogram
for the National-Zeitung
daily newspaper
Basel (CH)

Production of type
CRT setting

CRT (cathode ray tube) typesetting began in 1965 with Dr.-Ing. Rudolf Hell's Digiset, which replaced photosetting grids with digital characters stored in computer memory. Magnetic tape made typesetting faster, safer and more economical than punched tape. Mergenthaler Linotype's first CRT system, the Linotron 1010, was also introduced in the same year.

CRT typesetting is based on three factors: the cathode ray tube providing the light source for the electronic flash, the font master or data carrier, and the recording unit for positioning characters and changing sizes. Initially, Linotron technology used a cathode ray tube to scan characters from a grid. There were 11 or 24 grids available at any one time with 144 characters each. Widths were controlled digitally and there were many fonts to choose from that could be mixed and output to a maximum width of 60 ciceros (64 picas). The fonts could be modified electronically – slanted, condensed or expanded. This, however, brought with it the danger of exaggerated and inappropriate distortion.

The Linotron 303 output 300 000 characters per hour while the Linotron 505 S managed up to 2 million. Much faster speeds and precision could be achieved if the character image was stored as digital bitmaps. Typeface data were then generated by vertically scanning enlarged artwork and storing the scanlines **/03/** as originals for output.

Different size ranges could be generated and stored by increasing the scanner resolution. They could then be displayed as bitmaps on a screen. Editing applications could delete or add individual pixels and optimise character shapes.

CRT setting did not use a unit system, but there was a limit to the amount of scanlines per em. Coarse resolution would result in a stair-step effect on curves and diagonals that was referred to as 'the jaggies' **/04/**.

Later models like the Linotron 202 (1978) and the CRTronic (1979), the first compact digital CRT unit, stored the character outlines as vectors **/04/** instead of bitmaps, which brought about a significant saving of memory. Curves were divided into straight segments which were converted back into bitmaps for exposure.

In 1975 Peter Karow developed the Ikarus technology that could store font data independently of the output format: data could be processed as bitmaps, vectors or curves. The character artwork was captured by plotting points on the outlines **/06/**. Quality checks and corrections were carried out on a monitor **/07/**.

/01/
Schematic of the light path from the cathode ray tube via two mirrors that each deflect the beam of light by 90°.

/02/
Digitised character as bitmap artwork for output as well as representation on screen.

/03/
Schematic of the recording of a digitised character using a cathode ray.

/04/
Describing the shape with vertical scan lines (left) and outline description for output using vectors (right).

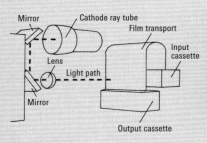

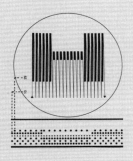

/05/
Digitising type – the artwork on a grid background is used for scanning the vertical lines.

/06/
Digitising type – the Ikarus system captures points on the outlines with a digitising tablet.

/07/
Ikarus software is used on a monitor to check digitised character outlines and correct them.

Name of typeface	Designer	Design | Publication	Typesetting technology	Manufacturer	Weights
Icone	Adrian Frutiger	1978 | 1980	CRT digital typesetting	– D. Stempel AG | Linotype	9
			PostScript digital typesetting	– Adobe | Linotype	9

ICONE

The influence technology has had on the written form has kept me occupied since redrawing *Bodoni* for Lumitype photosetting in the mid-fifties (see page 80). In the seventies while I was working for Linotype, I began to systematically study the written form and typesetting techniques. The result, alongside the digital-friendly modern-looking *Breughel* (see page 286) which appeared in 1981, was *Icone* in 1980. It was in response to the CRT typesetting modification possibilities, which sometimes disastrously distorted letters into caricatures. *Icone* was designed to withstand any distortion, be it character widths or angles of inclination. That's why I once called it a 'caoutchouc', or rubber typeface.

In the *Gutenberg-Jahrbuch 1985* I wrote that "the upcoming CRT typesetting upsets the conventional typographic definitions of quality in a much more profound way (than merely by breaking the typeface down into digital steps). [...] It's about the possibility of the original font being distorted through manipulation. It's no problem for the computer to numerically change the coordinate values of a digital character. In other words, to extend or reduce the width of a typeface in relation to its height. Inclining vertical rows to a desired angle is also a purely mathematical operation. However, wide, narrow or slanting typefaces produced this way fall short of the optical quality required of proper typographic expression. [...] The new machines' inexpert handling means that the expression of an original typeface is so altered as to be more recognisable as a distorted caricature. [...] The realisation that typefaces today can be manipulated by the user gave me an idea. The systematic changing of black and white values has the strongest effect on the typefaces with straight lines, particularly sans serif faces. So the idea arose for a new typeface, *Icone,* with highly modulated strokes in which the widths of the strokes are not at all clearly defined. From the illustration /02/, which shows the construction of the basic character as well as of the letters derived from it, it is evident that the disrupting proportional effect of mathematical distortion is no longer perceived as a corruption of the original form. For that reason *Icone* was suited to being produced largely with the aid of computers."[1]

So the basic premise of *Icone* was its ability to distort. Instead of strokes that are easily defined geometrically, it draws wilder ones. Curves and asymmetrically widened terminals are among its essential trademarks. Conventional serifs are missing, as they make inclination harder. The italic is tilted by calculation and slightly reworked afterwards. Normally automatic inclination causes swelling in the upper right-hand side of letters, for instance in lowercase o /11/. This doesn't happen with *Icone* /11/. I made two sketches in order to determine the slope, one with five and one with sixteen degrees, marking the minimum and maximum possibilities /05/.[2] I gave the number 556 to the design with the minimum slope, a combination of 55 and 56, that is, a version between upright

Technical development   At the ATypI general meeting in Basel in 1980, Adrian Frutiger gave a presentation in which he spoke about the technical developments in typesetting: "There was a mighty change when the relief of foundry type became redundant in offset printing. The emergence of photosetting meant that letters lost their 'base'. That is to say, their symmetrically stable, non-printing metal construction that designated a predetermined place for each character, line and also the all-important white space, ceased to be. The old terminology like width, left and right side bearing, body size or leading used to represent palpable space in the hands of typesetters. With the new process of photosetting, the floating letters made of light lost their own bodies. Their precise locations, so vital for readability, the spaces between them, as well as their size were now determined by moving lenses, prisms and film. [...] Photosetting itself, epoch-making to begin with, has now become 'historic'. Within the space of twenty years there have been giant steps in technical development. Without going into specific detail, one can say that in future the digitisation of text typesetting will continue its journey, posing the question of whether there will be a loss of quality due to type being broken down into points or lines. However, the experience of recent years and the knowledge of what is being prepared gives us reason to be optimistic of future developments. It is essential that the whole typesetting structure should once again receive a 'basic grid'. Type should be securely based on the digital grid, no longer floating around like in the first generation of photosetting. The process will be refined as the years pass. Vectors that are still somewhat disruptive today will soon be followed by curves, which the human eye desires. The practice of forcing character widths into crude unit systems has already been much refined for nearly all types of machines. Electronic storage technology will allow spaces between each character pair to be determined. [...] Therefore we can suppose that digital typesetting, still somehow insubstantial today, will become more manifest in the future and will assert itself as a new structural foundation."[3]

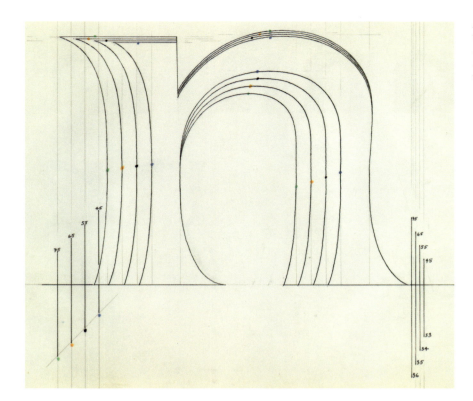

/01/
Weight diagram for Icone *showing character widths for 54 units per em quad – weights 45, 55, 65 and 75 were not made this way.*

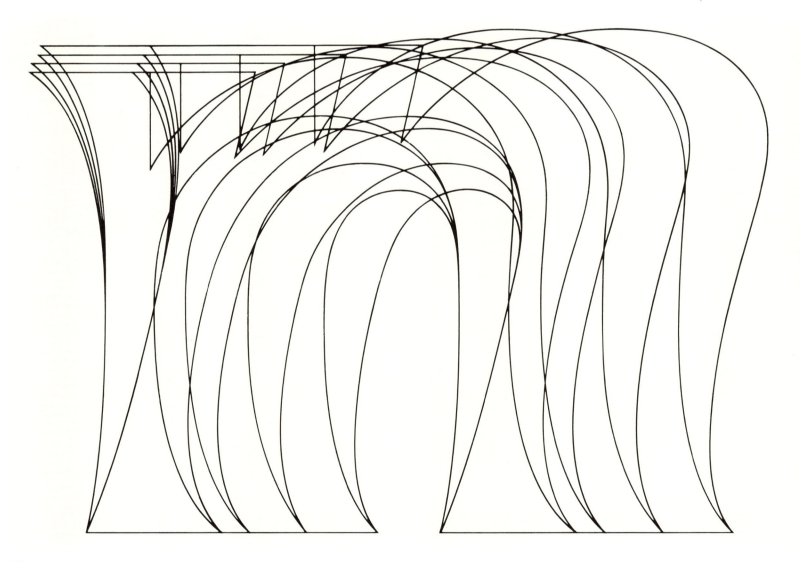

/02/
Thanks to its strongly modulated strokes, Icone *may be electronically distorted without being damaged.*

Hamburg

/03/
*Study of a slab serif latin face with
curved downstrokes – undated
design made with felt-tip pen on
tracing paper.*

/04/
*Paste-up with felt-tip pen on tracing
paper in six weights – the second
and fourth cuts from the left were
not produced.*

/05/
*Study of the slope of Icone italic –
5° with the weight description 556 (left),
16° with the description 56 (right).*

Icone
Icone *Icone* Icone

Icone

Icone

/06/
*Study from 1978 – in between
the 55 weight and the 16° inclined
56 is the 5° version, described
as 556.*

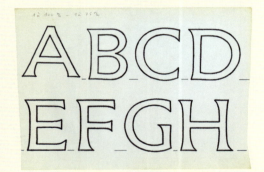

/07/
*Design of an outline version
of the regular weight of Icone –
the outlines are drawn with short
felt-tip pen strokes.*

/08/
*Undated design of Icone 55
with 46.5 mm x-height – pencil on
tracing paper mounted on
card stock.*

/09/
*Paste-up from reproductions
of reduced final artwork –
the lowercase l in 'bungalow' is cut
from the b.*

Honest man go into that fine
bungalow. Oversea mines
are Hambergs famouses rents
Imbricate a firestone into

The distortion of type The coarse resolution of CRT digital technology[4] produces steps in the curves /12/. It makes subtle tapering of the downstrokes /13/ and curved serifs extremely difficult. However, Frutiger did not avoid tapering *Icone*, instead he designed the stroke endings as swollen serifs, thus making the steps more evenly distributed.

Icone reasserted Adrian Frutiger's love of experimentation in addition to his studious examination of technical developments in typesetting. He was particularly interested in the distortion of type made possible by digitisation and its use in newspaper and magazine typesetting. Instead of altering the content of headlines, type could now be distorted to the given line width. This had a particularly negative effect on typefaces with a low stroke contrast. By compressing the width, the horizontal parts retain their strength, whereas the downstrokes become thinner and thus too delicate /11/, which contrasts with the Latin tradition of strong downstrokes. With linear typefaces, stretching the widths leads to an undesired stroke contrast. Electronic italicising or sloping is also unattractive. The curves, such as a and o of *Frutiger*, appear contorted rather than merely inclined /11/, while in *Méridien* the oblique becomes fat and broad with a notably overemphasised right leg of the K /11/.

and italic /06/. Those sorts of considerations were plentiful at the time, but weren't pursued. In the end we opted for around 12 degrees.

I came up with the name 'Icone', pronounced as in French. I was thinking of Russian icons, though not in reference to religion or churches. It was more to do with the look of icons. I felt a relationship between the roundness of *Icone* and the softness of the rounded faces in the pictures. *Icone* formally belongs to script or incised typefaces. Linotype filed it as an old-style variant, which is where everything ended up that was unclassifiable.[5]

We devised a system of weights with six grades for *Icone* /04/. At first three weights were planned but then four ended up being produced /06/. In hindsight the extra bold looks a little plump. Interestingly enough the whole appearance of *Icone* changes a bit in the light weight. Here the horizontal parts appear slightly stronger than vertical ones /06/. This was even more pronounced in the design than in the final result. The slightly curved endings are characteristic of *Icone*; the term 'tapered serifs' is therefore applied. However, these are not always the same. For example H has an emphasised curvy downstroke, while K has a straight and relatively short diagonal stroke with no reinforcement /17/. This was done on purpose. On the other hand the horizontals of some of the letters are straight and plain. A lively cross stroke on H, e or f would have been too kitschy /20/. The question mark was difficult. I sought long and hard for the right way to draw it. I don't like question marks that look like meathooks. All those curves would have given it an unlovely worm shape. In the end I chose a perhaps somewhat stubborn solution /22/.

At first glance a few of the letters, such as c e s t, recall *Antique Olive* /23/. I was once asked whether that typeface had influenced the design of *Icone*. No, I didn't copy anything

/10/
Comparison of Icone *design (top), cathode ray exposure (middle), and laser exposure of the PostScript font (bottom).*

/11/
Frutiger *(top),* Icone *(middle) and* Méridien *(bottom) in regular and italic weights and also electronically distorted in the second line.*

Huberts fantastic
Huberts fantastic
Huberts fantastic

Kano *Kano*
Kano Kano **Kano**

Kano *Kano*
Kano Kano **Kano**

Kano *Kano*
Kano Kano **Kano**

/12/
Compared to the digital Optima *(top),* Icone *(bottom) has finely graded curves at low resolution (right).*

/13/
The fine curvature of Optima *(top) is destroyed by CRT technology – the tapered serifs of* Icone *(bottom) are more suitable to the technology.*

Schrift

rschließt der typografischen G
gestalter, sondern auch die S
hriften. So ist es auch heute be
giset setzt seine Schriftzeichen

Schrift

es und unbearbeitetes Materi
auen oder aufgetragen. Sie w
nken. Mit dem zunehmender
ng des Gedankenaustausches

/14/
Electronic sloping widens the downstroke; the optically balanced stroke width of sans serif faces is destroyed.

Design-Gr.-Pt.	Garniturnummer Schriftnummer	Linse Zeichnung Bereich	Kamerastellung Korr. 606 Horizontal/Vertikal	Buchstaben-Nr.	Variations-Nr.	Einheiten 48*54	Frisketänderung Einheit Form Zurichtung Stellung	Datum: Name:
18	61413	E	O	*9	23	V30	* 54	☐☐☐☐☐

/15/
Frisket of Icone Bold Outline W –
*the digitised shape is cut
into the rubylith using a plotter.*

off Roger Excoffon. Yet you never really know what influences your own creation. When you get an image in your head, it can take some twenty years to come to fruition. *Antique Olive* by the Fonderie Olive in Marseille appeared between 1960 and 1969. To my mind it's the most beautiful piece of French type design. Daring and different. But whether it influenced *Icone*? Not consciously at any rate. With nine weights, Icone is well equipped. There are four stroke widths available, with their corresponding italics. I also designed a semi-bold outline weight.[6] That came about because Bruno Pfäffli needed something unusual of that sort for the exhibition catalogue *Mer Égée. Grèce des Îles.*[7] My suggestion was immediately approved at the Linotype Type Selection Meeting. All of the weights included oldstyle figures, plus the light and regular weights also had small caps. Work on *Icone* stretched from around 1978 to 1980. It was first introduced as paste-ups[8] /32/ in my book *Type Sign Symbol* /33/. Linotype were still using *Icone* as late as 1990. At the ATypI conference in Oxford an elaborately produced folding map was handed out with a sheet of artwork designed by myself. *Icone* took off quickly. I'm sure there were two reasons for its success; it was an unusual typeface and it had an extensive family.

/16/
Like Méridien *(left) and* Apollo *(middle), the* Icone *M (right) has splayed legs.*

MMM

/17/
The tapered serifs on the downstrokes of uppercase H are livelier and stronger than those of K.

HK

/18/
The tapered serif of 1 gives the impression of being added on, due to a lack of correspondence at the top; the 4 is also very rigid.

1114

/19/
Uppercase letters, numerals and the £ all have accentuated terminals – different ones – on the horizontal strokes.

EZ24£

/20/
In lowercase f and t, the cross-strokes have no accentuated terminal and look rather stuck-on because of it.

eftz

/21/
Lowercase b and q, and also d and p, have mirrored shapes with very minor alterations.

bdpq

/22/
The Icone *question mark has a slightly unusual shape with its curve ending in a vertical cut.*

?

/23/
The accentuated head sections and acute curve terminals are characteristic of Antique Olive *(left), as they are of* Icone *(right).*

cest cest

/24/
Albertus *(1932) by Berthold Wolpe and* Friz Quadrata *(1965) by Ernst Friz, are incised faces with reduced stroke contrast.*

Albertus
Friz Quadrata

/25/
Optima, *designed by Hermann Zapf and released in 1958 by Stempel, is an incised face with a strong stroke contrast.*

Optima

/26/
Roger Excoffon's Antique Olive, *designed for the Fonderie Olive in Marseille in 1962, is accentuated at the top.*

Antique Olive

/27/
Characters of Icone *normal*
for CRT (cathode ray technology)
photosetting by Linotype.

ABCDEFGHIJKLMN OPQRSTUVWXYZ& abcdefghijklmnopqrs tuvwxyzß1234567890

Creative counterattack   In order to come up with a solution to the disrespectful distortion of type, Frutiger designed *Icone* in 1978. Horst Heiderhoff wrote in the *Gutenberg-Jahrbuch 1985:* "These possibilities stimulated Adrian Frutiger, and the idea arose of designing a class of typeface that could withstand such manipulation. Thus *Icone* came to be, with its very personal, strongly modulated strokes. It reflects the successful search for a synthesis of historic development and the spirit of our times."[9]

However, Frutiger's originally positive outlook, which found expression at the 1980 ATypI presentation, turned somewhat negative in 1985 when he wrote that "for type designers, the mathematical alteration of basic data now made possible became something of a painful process as it turned the initial creation into a caricature or mutilation."[10] In 1988 Adrian Frutiger wrote of *Icone:* "An impulsive counterattack roused me, borne of a feeling of frustration. I imagined a typeface that could withstand distortion. ... It seemed to me that there had to be enough elasticity in the drawings so that the overall appearance, though contorted, wouldn't be destroyed."[11] The outcome was a self-contained typeface with shapes that echoed lettering of the Flower Power era of the late 1960s and early 1970s.[12]

/28/
Adrian Frutiger with the frisket
and drawing of the Icone 55 g *on*
his desk.

/29/
Capturing outline markers using
a digitising device – these are
transformed into digital data in
the CAD system.

/30/
Visual control and correction of
the digitally produced letter shapes
on the high resolution screen.

/31/
The letters are cut for production
into sheets (friskets) using a
plotter and a drawing/cutting
machine.

Hamburgefontsiv Hoffnung Organisation g ansaugen offensiv ruebensaftig turnverein frage begabt Hornisse tasse tee inserat i bagger bei ergeben mit baufenster bei te

Hamburgefontsiv Hoffnung Organisation ansaugen offensiv ruebensaftig turnvere frage begabt Hornisse tasse tee inserat bagger bei ergeben mit baufenster bei

Hamburgefontsiv Hoffnung Organisati offensiv ruebensaftig turnverein most frage begabt Hornisse tasse tee inserat sonnentau bagger baufenster

Hamburgefontsiv Hoffnung Organi offensiv ruebensaftig turnverein m frage begabt Hornisse tasse tee inserat sonnentau bagger baufenst

/33/
Transfer of Icone *– reproduction*
artwork with markings –
for Adrian Frutiger's book
Type Sign Symbol.

/32/
Dust jacket for Type Sign Symbol,
1960 by Adrian Frutiger –
the ox head in the hexagon at the
top is a nod to alef, the first letter in
the Phoenician alphabet.

Adrian Frutiger

Type Sign Symbol

Font production:
Digitised by Linotype

Font format:
PostScript Type 1

Also available:
TrueType
OpenType Com

ABCDEFGHIJKLMN OPQRSTUVWXYZ& abcdefghijklmnopqrs tuvwxyzß1234567890

Pourquoi tant
d'Alphabets différ
ents! Tous servent au même
but, mais aussi à exprimer la diversité de

l'homme. C'est cette même diversité que nous retrouvons dan
s les vins de Médoc. J'ai pu, un jour, relever soixante crus, tous
de la même année. Il s'agissait certes de vins, mais tous étaien
t différents. Tout est dans la nuance du bouquet. Il en est de m
ême pour les caractères! *Sie fragen sich, warum es notwendig*

ist, so viele Schriften zur Verfügung zu haben. Sie dienen alle zum selben, aber machen die
Vielfalt des Menschen aus. Diese Vielfalt ist wie beim Wein. Ich habe einmal eine Weinkar
te studiert mit sechzig Médoc-Weinen aus dem selben Jahr. Das ist ausnahmslos Wein, a
ber doch nicht alles der gleiche Wein. Es hat eben gleichwohl Nuancen. So ist es auch mit
der Schrift. *You may ask why so many different typefaces.* They all serve the same purpos
e but they express man's diversity. It is the same diversity we find in wine. I once saw a lis
t of Médoc wines featuring sixty different Médocs all of the same year. All of them were w

ines but each was different from the others. It's the nuances that are import
ant. The same is true for typefaces. *Pourquoi tant d'Alphabets différents! To
us servent au même but, mais aussi à exprimer la diversité de l'homme. C'es
t cette même diversité que nous retrouvons dans les vins de Médoc. J'ai pu,
un jour, relever soixante crus, tous de la même année. Il s'agissait certes de v
ins, mais tous étaient différents. Tout est dans la nuance du bouquet. Il en e
st de même pour les caractères! Sie fragen sich, warum es notwendig ist, so
viele Schriften zur Verfügung zu haben.* Sie dienen alle zum selben, aber mac

hen die Vielfalt des Menschen aus. Diese Vielfal
t ist wie beim Wein. Ich habe einmal eine Weink
arte studiert mit sechzig Médoc-Weinen aus de
m selben Jahr. Das ist ausnahmslos Wein, aber
doch nicht alles der gleiche Wein. Es hat eben g
leichwohl Nuancen. So is es auch mit der Schri
ft. *You may ask why so many different typeface
s.* They all serve the same purpose but they expr
ess man's diversity. It is the same diversity we fi
nd in wine. I once saw a list of Médoc wines fea

70 pt | −35 53 pt | −25 35 pt | −30 23 pt | −15 15 pt | 19 pt | −20 10 pt | 13 pt | 0 7.5 pt | 10.2 pt | 5 6 pt | 8 pt | 10

ÅBÇDÈFG HIJKLMÑ ÔPQRŠTÜ VWXYZ& ÆŒ¥$£€ 1234567890 åbçdéfghij klmñôpqrš tüvwxyzß fifl æ œ ø ł ð [.,:;·'/- – —] (¿¡"«‹›»"!?) {§°%@‰*†}
Light

ÅBÇDÈFG HIJKLMÑ ÔPQRŠTÜ VWXYZ& ÆŒ¥$£€ 1234567890 åbçdéfghij klmñôpqrš tüvwxyzß fifl æ œ ø ł ð [.,:;·'/- – —] (¿¡"«‹›»"!?) {§°%@‰†}*
Light Italic

ÅBÇDÈFG HIJKLMÑ ÔPQRŠTÜ VWXYZ& ÆŒ¥$£€ 1234567890 åbçdéfghij klmñôpqrš tüvwxyzß fifl æ œ ø ł ð [.,:;·'/- – —] (¿¡"«‹›»"!?) {§°%@‰*†}
Regular

ÅBÇDÈFG HIJKLMÑ ÔPQRŠTÜ VWXYZ& ÆŒ¥$£€ 1234567890 åbçdéfghij klmñôpqrš tüvwxyzß fifl æ œ ø ł ð [.,:;·'/- – —] (¿¡"«‹›»"!?) {§°%@‰†}*
Italic

ÅBÇDÈFG HIJKLMÑ ÔPQRŠTÜ VWXYZ& ÆŒ¥$£€ 1234567890 åbçdéfghij klmñôpqrš tüvwxyzß fifl æ œ ø ł ð [.,:;·'/- – —] (¿¡"«‹›»"!?) {§°%@‰*†}
Bold

ÅBÇDÈFG HIJKLMÑ ÔPQRŠTÜ VWXYZ& ÆŒ¥$£€ 1234567890 åbçdéfghij klmñôpqrš tüvwxyzß fifl æ œ ø ł ð [.,:;·'/- – —] (¿¡"«‹›»"!?) {§°%@‰*†}
Bold Italic

Typeface comparison Although neither its design nor production method bear any relation to inscriptions, *Icone* can still be classed stylistically as an incised face. In the German typeface classification DIN 16518 the group, which Maximilien Vox terms 'Incises', is not included as it had to make way for the generalised 'Antiqua Varianten' group, containing the decorative and display faces (see page 77). In the Italian classification by the typeface designer Aldo Novarese, it is called 'Lapidari'[13], whereas the American software and type manufacturer Adobe lists it as 'Glyphic'[14]. The historical significance of incised faces justifies a classification group for sans serif typefaces with tapered downstrokes and typefaces with swollen serifs. After all, the origins of Greek and Latin alphabets are to be found in stone inscription faces. *Poppl Laudatio* is a slightly less dynamic incised face than *Icone*. Its accentuated stroke endings with concave bases are symmetrically formulated, unlike *Icone*. *Romic* leaves a pronounced dynamic impression, like *Icone*. In this case it is not an incised face but an oldstyle one with a written feel. On the other hand, its emphasis on horizontal progression – noticeable in *Romic* by the serifs, which point left at the top and right at the bottom – as well as its rounded downstrokes show a kinship with *Icone*.

(see page 77)

/34/
Measurements of stroke widths and proportions of the Icone *regular weight.*

Roman				
Hh = 10.00 cm	nh = 6.98 cm	oh = 7.48 cm	Hh : Hw = 1 : 0.82	nh : nw = 1 : 0.90
Hw = 8.23	nw = 6.28	ow = 7.28	Hw : Hs = 1 : 0.58	nw : ns = 1 : 0.18
Hs = 1.30	ns = 1.12	os = 1.40	Hs : Hq = 1 : 0.82	nh : oh = 1 : 1.07
Hq = 1.07	nq = 1.13	oq = 0.97		nw : ow = 1 : 1.16

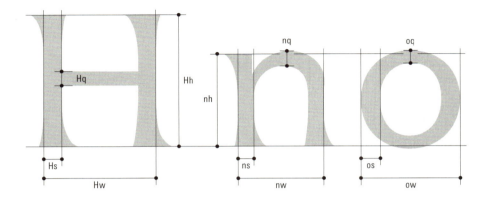

/35/
Compared to the two other typefaces Romic *and* Poppl Laudatio, Icone *appears to be wider and to have less stroke contrast.*

Hofstainberg

Romic
Colin Brignall
1979

DHNbnpy57

Hofstainberg

Icone
Adrian Frutiger
1980

DHNbnpy57

D
Centre of balance on the arc moved up slightly

H
Cross-stroke not tapered

N
Only slight asymmetric shape

b
Downstroke ends flat

n
Arc appears slightly heavier than tapered downstrokes

p
Oval counter

y
Swelling serifs point inwards on both sides

5 7
Strict appearance through lines being parallel

Hofstainberg

Poppl Laudatio
Friedrich Poppl
1982

DHNbnpy57

/36/

*Comparison showing the
different weights and angle of
the obliques.*

	Hh	Hw	Hs	Hq
Light	10.00 cm	7.92 = 0.96	0.86 = 0.66	0.78 = 0.73
Roman	10.00	8.23 = 1	1.30 = 1	1.07 = 1
Bold	10.00	9.35 = 1.14	2.36 = 1.81	1.76 = 1.64
Extra Black	10.00	10.83 = 1.31	3.77 = 2.90	2.67 = 2.49
Italic	10.00	8.04 = 0.98	1.28 = 0.98	1.09 = 1.02

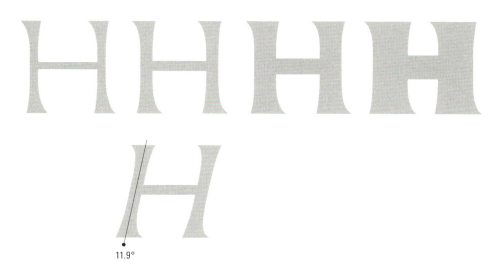

11.9°

/37/

*Height comparison showing the
differences of x-height to
descender and ascender – the cap
height is the starting point.*

Romic
40.1 pt

Icone
44 pt

Poppl Laudatio
40.7 pt

ÅBÇDÈFG
HIJKLMÑ
ÔPQRŠTÜ
VWXYZ&
ÆŒ¥$£€0
123456789
åbçdéfghij
klmñôpqrš
tüvwxyzß
fiflæœøłð
[.,:;·'/-–—]
(¿¡""«‹›»",!?)
{§°%@‰*†}

ExtraBlack

ÅBÇDÈFG
HIJKLMÑ
ÔPQRŠTÜ
VWXYZ&
ÆŒ¥$£€0
123456789
åbçdéfghij
klmñôpqrš
tüvwxyzß
fiflæœøłð
[.,:;·'/-–—]
(¿¡""«‹›»",!?)
{§°%@‰*†}

ExtraBlack Italic

ÅBÇDÉFGHIJ
KLMÑÔPQR
ŠTÜVWXYZ&

Light Small Caps

0123456789

Light Oldstyle Figures

0123456789

Light Italic Oldstyle Figures

ÅBÇDÉFGHIJ
KLMÑÔPQR
ŠTÜVWXYZ&

Regular Small Caps

0123456789

Regular Oldstyle Figures

0123456789

Regular Italic Oldstyle Figures

0123456789

Bold Oldstyle Figures

0123456789

Bold Italic Oldstyle Figures

0123456789

ExtraBlack OsF

0123456789

ExtraBlack Italic OsF

ÅBÇDÈFG
HIJKLMÑ
ÔPQRŠTÜ
VWXYZ&
ÆŒ€£$¥
0123456789
åbçdéfghij
klmñôpqr
štüvwxyzß
fiflæœøłð
(.,:;·'/-–—)
[¿¡""«‹›»",!?]
{§°%@‰*†}

Bold Outline

0123456789

Bold Outline OsF

Name of typeface	Designer	Design | Publication	Typesetting technology	Manufacturer	Weights
Breughel	Adrian Frutiger	1978 | 1982	Digital typesetting CRT	– D. Stempel AG | Linotype	6
			Digital typesetting PostScript	– Linotype	6

BREUGHEL

With *Breughel,* I actually managed to outsmart CRT technology. But running rings around the technology wasn't the main incentive, at least not consciously. First of all, I wanted to design beautiful, new typefaces. I always felt obliged, however, to bring something new to the type selection meetings at Linotype. There were two to three of these meetings per year and I never went there without some sketches or a glued sample character string. But neither D. Stempel AG nor Linotype explicitly commissioned the design of particularly technology-friendly typefaces. All these things developed in my thinking, in my head. Each day was different for me; each day brought a new idea. I was bubbling with ideas. There was an inner urge to do creative work. But I wasn't desperately trying to find something that was suited to the technology. That would have killed me. However, I could never totally ignore the technical aspects.

There were no systematic explorative studies for *Breughel.* During this period, however, many other sketches were developed. The calligraphic *'Breughel Script'* /04/, for instance, is a design in its own right. It shows a few similarities but there are also differences. If I had a good idea, I sketched it out for two to three days, polished it, filled the contours in with black and had the letters glued together to make a word image. The 'OHamburgefons' was only created once a proposal had been accepted in a meeting. After all, this represented a first business investment. All sketches and glued samples that I created at home were my own private explorations and didn't cost D. Stempel AG a penny.

Breughel's digitisation-friendly shape played an important role in the decision to implement it. The *Bodoni* shock with Lumitype during the mid-50s was followed by the *Méridien* shock at the beginning of the CRT age during the mid-70s. Back then, when I saw the results of digitisation with all those stepped edges I was horrified. That caricature of *Méridien* was totally unacceptable /12/. It was the beginning of a period that I once called the 'dark ages', the 'wandering in the wilderness'. Today I'd rather call it the 'experience of change'. I couldn't really accept IBM's philosophy that technology would be able to do everything one day, that it just needed a bit of patience. Should I have twiddled my thumbs and simply waited? It took almost 20 years to get from the disk-space hungry, cathode-ray-pixel technology to vector representation, which was considerably less data intensive, and then to the Bézier curves of the 80s.[1]

So I tried to circumvent the technological shortcomings by means of formgiving. The long curves of the slightly tapered downstrokes and concave serifs had to be avoided. Just as with *Méridien,* this would only have resulted in jagged pixels. Therefore, with *Breughel,* I kept the right contour of the downstroke vertical, while the left one was strongly concave /01/. Through the contrast between the straight line and the deep curve the typeface comes alive; additionally, this allows for it to be digitised without suffering any damage. The

Typographic designs for Breughel At the end of the 1970s and the beginning of the 1980s, Adrian Frutiger developed different but, in terms of shape, related typographic designs. The order in which they were created is not obvious since not all of the designs are dated. What they all have in common is a sturdy composition with strongly tapered strokes, which gives them a certain dynamic appearance. Emerging from these designs with differently shaped serifs came not only *Icone* (see page 276) but also *Breughel* /01/, which was conceived in three stroke weights /02/ with a corresponding cursive published in 1982.[2]

The name appears initially as *Breughel Script* and refers to a set of bold fonts in four weights dated May 1978. The set is shown in Adrian Frutiger's *Type Sign Symbol* /03/, where it is printed in red to differentiate it from the black upright cuts. There are outline drawings with a 12.5 cm x-height for some individual letters of *Breughel Script,* some in four different weights and some showing digitisation points /04/. This indicates that there were plans to implement this typeface.

Also, the sample string 'Hanover', drawn in pencil, bears similarities to the typeface *Breughel* /05/. There are differences, however, in the shape of the serifs, in the angle of the stress in the o and in the downstrokes, which are tapered on both sides. The same drawings also serve as templates for the adhesive letter set 'Hobnail business' /06/. On the same sheet there is a second, similar design called 'Irma's sombrero' /06/ with triangular instead of square serifs. The stress of the o is less oblique and closer to that of *Breughel.* It is also interesting to compare the lowercase a in both designs. In the top design, the upper terminal is rather pointed, and the transition from the bowl to the stem is strong and bent down in the interior /06/. In the bottom design, the upper terminal is pronounced, but the transition is fine and diagonal /06/. In the later design of *Breughel,* both parts are kept fine /18/.

The 1980 *'Ritual project'* /07/ is a slab serif in the shape of an italienne[3] but with slanted serifs as in *Breughel.* Typical for this kind of typeface are the more pronounced horizontal parts in comparison to the finer vertical ones and often also the narrow proportion of the typeface. In 1989, Adrian Frutiger designed an italienne with his *Westside* (see page 346).

Gemeine,
fi, fl, ß, ¢,
Hochst. Gemeine,

12p. Breughel 55

M: 253

Design-Gr. Pt.	Garniturnummer Schriftnummer	Linse Zeichnung Bereich	Kamerastellung Korr. 606 Horizontal/Vertikal		Buchstaben-Nr.	Variations-Nr.	Einheiten ✶'54	Friskеtänderung	
								☐ Einheit Datum:	
								☐ Form	
								☐ Zurichtung Name:	
								☐ Stellung	
								☐	
12	05 349	E	+0	✶+9	——	——	✶54		

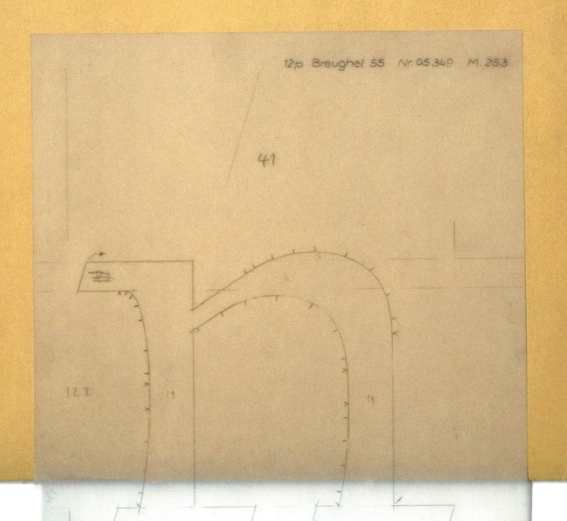

/01/
*Folder and final artwork for
Breughel 55 – Linotype archived a
character set in three folders.*

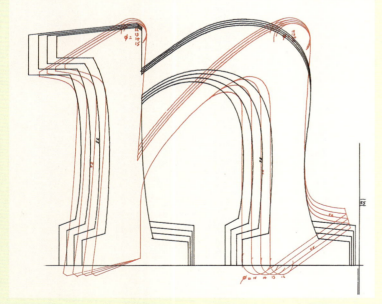

/02/
Proportional template of Breughel for the data capture of the steps – the strokes are tapered on one side, the serifs are slanted.

/04/
Pencil drawings for the design of 'Breughel Script' – the original drawings have an x-height of 12.5 cm.

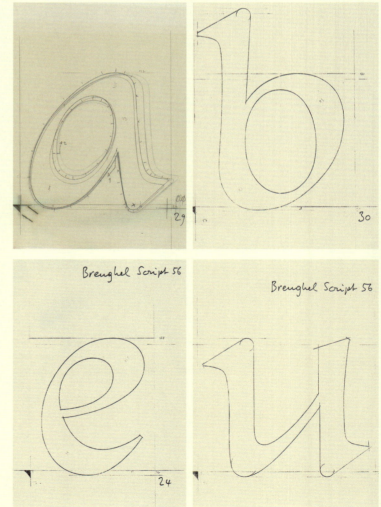

Breughel Script 56

Breughel Script 56

29

30

24

/03/
Proportional template of the design for 'Breughel Script' (red) and the regular font (black) in four weights each (1978).

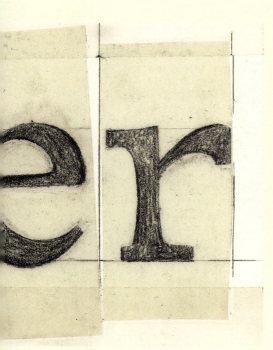

/05/
*A design similar to Breughel
with strokes tapered on both sides
and vertically cut serifs –
pencil drawing, original size.*

Hobnail business

How is your unbelievable Hobnail business in Hanover going over. Is your believable Home going over your Hanoverbus.
How is your unbelievable Hobnail business in Hanover going over. Is your believable Home going over your.
How is your unbelievable Hobnail business in Hanover going over. Is your believable Home going over your Hanover.

Hobnail business
Hanover

Irmas sombrero

Have one sombrero
when Irmas unborn boss
grave in Hamburgs gang

Irma
Hamburg

/06/
*Design of a typeface similar to
Breughel (top) and another version
derived from it with wedge serifs
(bottom).*

Ritual _____ project

min 1980
Af.

/07/
*The design of Ritual (1980)
is reminiscent of Breughel but also
of an italienne such as the later
Westside.*

Heimat deine Firne

Heimat deine Firne scheinen wie goldene
Flammen am abendlichen Firmament.
Hügelreihen ziehen sich wie bewaldete
Inseln vom nahen Flusse bis ins Hohland.

Ritual project

upper and lower contours of the serifs could not be curved either, but I gave them slanted side contours, so they wouldn't be too similar to an egyptienne.

In a brochure of my typefaces available at Linotype in 1983, Horst Heiderhoff wrote that *Breughel* was modelled on the early humanist typefaces, and in particular on *Jenson* /28/. I didn't say that. For a long time, I thought that this was an unsuitable statement but now I have to admit that there's some truth to it. If you compare a few lines from *Jenson* with the bold *Breughel,* the relationship becomes obvious /09/.[4] These sample sentences, developed at different times and using different technologies, also show that the quality of the stroke is less important than the quality of the whitespace. In the regular cut, the ratio of black to white in one line is approximately 25–30% black and 70–75% white.[5] Therefore, a typeface mainly consists of counters and sidebearings.

With *Breughel,* b d p q have oval counters /14/ while with h m n the transition from stem to shoulder is slightly angular /15/. Having a rounded transition here would have made the typeface altogether too soft. I could also have drawn an angle in the b, similar to the top part of the q in order to emphasise the movement even more /14/. That would perhaps conform more closely to the overall style because angles and edges are part of the basic shape of this typeface. The edginess, which is an intrinsic part, is missing in the lowercase b. What has always been problematic is the letter X, which is influenced so much by the Roman numeral. It is difficult to create a different X shape /16/. I would say that the upright ampersand is a compromise. It has neither my own nor a looped shape. It is a bit odd /17/.

Breughel was released in 1983, in six sets. There was a tendency at the time to extend typefaces to larger families so that they could be sold at a higher price.[6] A typeface with

Relationship to Jenson   *Breughel,* of course, is not a redesign of *Jenson;* the differences between the two typefaces are obvious /09/. There is also no indication that Frutiger deliberately used the 15th-century typeface as a starting point.[7] However, there are some characteristics that justify the comparison made by Horst Heiderhoff. Nicolas Jenson gave his antiqua a very even structure (see page 15). The serifs have a sturdy, asymmetrical shape and the second and third downstrokes in the lowercase m are concave on the left hand side. Through its asymmetrical alignment, there is a slightly inclined movement in Frutiger's typeface towards the reading direction, and through the sturdy serifs it clearly defines the line of text. This kind of design in typefaces goes back to the handwritten humanist minuscule /08/. Thus, at the beginning of the design process, we find the development of a hand-lettered typeface: *Breughel Script* /10/. A relationship in terms of shape to the earlier *Ondine* (see page 50) is obvious.

With *Apollo* /22/, Frutiger had already used slightly asymmetrical serifs and the italic *Opéra* /24/ already featured unidirectional serifs. The humanistic shape of the tapered downstrokes is another characteristic of many of Frutiger's serif typefaces. Similar to *Icone* – which was developed in parallel – the deep concave shape of the downstroke allows for a smaller radius, distributing pixellation over several steps. This results in a more agreeable appearance, shown in the subsequent comparison /11/.

/08/
A humanist minuscule from Ferrara (Italy), written on parchment, first half of 15th century.

/09/
Excerpt from the 1471 Fabius Quintilianus in the typography by Nicolas Jenson (top) and in comparison with Breughel *Bold.*

in primis exiſtimetur ueniſſe ad agendum ductus officio uel cognatio/ nis uel amicitiæ:maximeq; ſi fieri poteſt rei.pu.aut alicuius certe non mediocris exempli. Quod ſine dubio multo magis ipſis litigatoribus faciendum eſt: ut ad agendum magna atq; honeſta ratione:aut etiam

in primis exiſtimetur ueniſſe ad agendum ductus officio uel cognatio- nis uel amicitiæ:maximeq; ſi fieri poteſt rei.pu.aut alicuius certe non mediocris exempli. Quod ſine dubio multo magis ipſis litigatoribus faciendum eſt: ut ad agendum magna atq; honeſta ratione:aut etiam

/10/
Comparison between Breughel Script *(left),* Breughel Regular *(centre) and Regular Italic (right).*

bbb eee uuu

/11/
Majuscule I of Méridien, Icone *and* Breughel *at a low resolution of 300 dpi – comparison implemented using today's technology.*

I I I

/12/
CRT output of Méridien *showing the typical jagged steps – the tapered strokes look unattractive.*

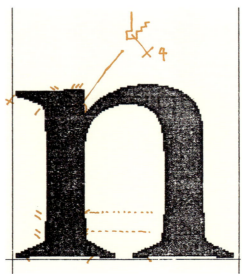

/13/
Humanist typeface suited for low resolution thanks both to the strokes being strongly tapered on one side only, and to flat, slanted serifs.

A typeface suited to digitisation In a letter bearing the greeting 'Lieber Freund Weidemann' (Dear friend Weidemann)[8] Frutiger responded to a 1984 survey[9] by Eurographic Press.[10] Among other points, the following excerpt was published: "When drawing or designing, it has become impossible for me to ignore or forget about the digitisation process. The grid of dividing a curve into single points has become second nature to me. The experience of pixellation has become part of my knowledge and therefore it is an inevitable aspect of the creative phase in the design process. Thus the creation of *Breughel* was the result of the idea of a digitisation-friendly typeface."[11] And in the *Gutenberg-Jahrbuch 1985*, Heiderhoff quoted Frutiger: "Very wide-sweeping curves were deliberately avoided, since the memories of the difficulties with the digital rendering of typefaces such as Meridien were still fresh in my mind. Nonetheless however, for a medieval antiqua, I was not prepared to replace the swelling and shrinking of a lively downstroke with a hard and straight line. This exploration resulted in the idea of having a concave curve on only the one side, although the concavity itself was more pronounced. The right-hand-side contour of the stem is thus a perfectly straight line, while the left-hand-side contour simulates a strong curve that is achieved through a relatively large number of pixellated steps. In the scaled-down version at reading size, however, the eye perceives the curvature of the downstroke as an organic whole."[12]

only three cuts wasn't worth much. Besides the marketing, the cost factor played an important role as well. It takes a lot of time and money before you get a roman, italic and bold right. Once these base shapes are done, further extension is easy.[13] I drew the regular and bold cuts completely myself; the medium one was done by interpolation. We also used the technological possibilities for the cursive. It was a mathematically sloped version, which, however, I refined manually. I only redrew the letters a e f g /18/. With its one-sided serifs for the lowercase letters, the cursive is a bit special. It's so consistent – and unique – that the left part of the r serif is also missing /20/. I didn't ask: what is allowed and what isn't? If I thought something was good, I did it. *Breughel* had oldstyle numerals and small capitals in the regular cut.[14] Linotype did the initial work for this and I then corrected the shapes. I designed only the oldstyle numerals 0, 1 and 2 myself, which have totally different proportions /21/ – that might have been a bit lazy.[15]

Apart from the technological aspects, *Breughel* has a character of its own. I used to call it 'rustic', 'gnarly'; I felt it had something in common with the pictures of the painter *Breughel*[16] – that's why I gave it his name. After *Méridien* and *Iridium* on the one hand, and the grotesque typefaces on the other, I wanted to go in a different direction. Instead of elegant and refined shapes, I was looking for something more grounded, with some meat on its bones, as it were, and with robust serifs. For a long time I used to look down on *Breughel* a bit, by seeing it as a transitional solution based on technological restrictions. When I look back at it today, I discover its quality: it is sturdy yet well formed with a strong character.

/14/
The transitions from the bowl to the stem in b d p q are round – the b appears a little soft due to its round shape at the bottom left.

bdpq

/15/
The curves of the lowercase h m n r u feature an angular transition into the stem, which strengthens the appearance of a handwritten shape.

hmnru

/16/
It is a typographic challenge to add some dynamic to the strokes of the symmetrical X-shape.

X

/17/
In the regular font, the & of Breughel *features a slightly pretentious, unlooped shape, which is not the case for the 8 and the italic version.*

&8&

/18/
Only a e f g were drawn from scratch for Breughel *Italic – all other shapes were inclined automatically and then refined.*

aefg*aefg*

/19/
While in the regular font the x has double serifs and the y has single serifs, this is exactly the opposite in the italic font.

xy*xy*

/20/
Humanist typeface suited for low resolution thanks both to strokes tapered on one side only, and flat, slanted serifs.

hr

/21/
As opposed to, for example, Garamond *(top), only 012 are different in the two figure sets of* Breughel *(bottom).*

0123456789
0123456789

0123456789
0123456789

/22/
Apollo *(top) and* Breughel *(bottom) display an obvious relationship in shape and construction.*

acehs
acehs

/23/
The letters of the italic versions of Opéra *(top) and* Breughel *(bottom) feature very similar shapes and serifs.*

abdgpq
abdgpq

/24/
Different to the earlier Opéra *(top), the transition from the curves to the stem is angular in* Breughel *(bottom).*

hmn
hmn

Characters of Breughel *normal in*
CRT (cathode ray technology)
photocomposition by Linotype.

ABCDEFGHIJKLMN
OPQRSTUVWXYZ&
abcdefghijklmnopqrs
tuvwxyzß1234567890

Leading of a typeface Leading plays a crucial part in the overall look and feel of a typeface. If the leading is too narrow, the beauty of a typeface has no room to unfold **/26/**. Additionally, a change in leading changes the optical colour of a typeface as well as the line rhythm, which is so important for legibility. Today, a rather light density is preferred **/27/**.

The amount of leading depends on the typeface, its size and the line width. While early printers used to set their typefaces with their long ascenders and descenders in a compact form, i.e. without additional space between the lines **/09/**, this would not be possible with most of today's typefaces, without a loss in the quality of the overall impression and legibility. Due to an increase in x-height over time, and with a simultaneous reduction in the length of the descender, line formation gets lost in a compact composition and is replaced by a difficult-to-read, dark block of text.

Typefaces with a vertical alignment, such as the modern ones, and those with a large x-height or with wide counters, need generous leading. Line spacing is also dependent on line width. In a narrow column the same line spacing is perceived to be more open than in a wide column **/28/**. Long lines therefore need more line spacing than short ones. One rule of thumb: the space between baseline and the following mean line should be at least equal to the x-height.

Adrian Frutiger's Breughel reflects its origin in the early Humanist typefaces of the 16th century; in particular, it has its roots in the Jenson type. In designing Breughel, with its assymetric serifs, Frutiger took into account the specific requirements of digitization. All vertical strokes are strictly rectangular on the right side, while ending in marked curves on the left side. The delicately modelled letterforms lend the typeface its dynamic, lively appearance.

Als Vorbild für die Breughel dienten die frühen humanistischen Schriften des 16. Jahrhunderts und dabei ganz besonders die »Jenson«. Frutiger hat bei der Zeichnungsanlage der Schrift die Probleme der verfeinerten Punkt- und Linienauflösung im digitalen Bereich mit eingeplant, indem er die Abstriche und Serifen asymmetrisch gestaltete. Die rechten Stammbegrenzungen sind senkrecht und rechtwinkelig geführt, während die linken in Kurven auslaufen und gut abgetastet und wiedergegeben werden können. Dadurch werden stark modellierte Formteile des Buchstabens betont und die Schrift erhält eine scheinbar nach rechts geneigte dynamische Schreib- und Lesebewegung.

Le Breughel reflète le tracé des premiers caractères humanistes du début du 16ème siècle, et plus particulièrement celui du »Jenson«. En le dessinant, Frutiger a tenu compte des contraintes auxquelles les formes sont astreintes par la digitalisation. Ainsi les montants sont délimités à droite d'une manière parfaitement rectiligne; à gauche par contre, ils sont fortement incurvés, donc facilement digitalisables. Ses traits bien modelés donnent au caractère un aspect dynamique et vivant.

/26/
*Set with far too narrow line
spacing – text on Breughel from the
trilingual Linotype brochure*
Typefaces by Adrian Frutiger *(1983).*

/27/
Breughel LT *Regular in 10.2 pt –
set solid with 1 pt, 2 pt und 3 pt
leading (from top to bottom).*

You may ask why so many different typefaces.
They all serve the same purpose but they express man's
diversity. It is the same diversity we find in wine.
I once saw a list of Médoc wines featuring sixty diffe

You may ask why so many different typefaces.
They all serve the same purpose but they express man's
diversity. It is the same diversity we find in wine.
I once saw a list of Médoc wines featuring sixty diffe

You may ask why so many different typefaces.
They all serve the same purpose but they express man's
diversity. It is the same diversity we find in wine.
I once saw a list of Médoc wines featuring sixty diffe

You may ask why so many different typefaces.
They all serve the same purpose but they express man's
diversity. It is the same diversity we find in wine.
I once saw a list of Médoc wines featuring sixty diffe

You may ask why
so many differ-
ent typefaces. They
all serve the same

You may ask why so many different
typefaces. They all serve the same
purpose but they express man's diversity. It is the same diversity we find

You may ask why so many different typefaces. They all serve the
same purpose but they express man's diversity. It is the same diversity we find in wine. I once saw a list of Médoc wines featuring
sixty different Médocs all of the same year. All of them were wines

/28/
Breughel LT *Regular in
10.2 pt size and 12.2 line spacing –
the line spacing appears to be
different*

Font production:
Digitised by Linotype

Font format:
PostScript Type 1

Also available:
TrueType
OpenType Com

Breughel™
Linotype
6 weights (6 SC | 6 OsF)

ABCDEFGHIJKLMN
OPQRSTUVWXYZ&
abcdefghijklmnopqrs
tuvwxyzß1234567890

Sie fragen sich
warum es notwen
dig ist, so viele Schriften zu
r Verfügung zu haben. Sie dienen alle zu

m selben, aber machen die Vielfalt des Menschen aus. Diese Vielfalt ist wie beim Wein. Ich habe einmal eine Weinkarte s tudiert mit sechzig Médoc- Weinenaus dem selben Jahr. Das ist ausnahmslos Wein, aber doch nicht alles der gleiche Wein. Es hat eben gleichwohl Nuancen. So ist es auch mit der Schri

ft. *You may ask why so many different typefaces.* They all serve the same purpose but t hey express man's diversity. It is the same diversity we find in wine. I once saw a list of Médoc wines featuring sixty different Médocs all of the same year. All of them we re wines but each was different from the others. It's the nuances that are important. The same is true for typefaces. *Pourquoi tant d'Alphabets différents!* Tous servent au même but, mais aussi à exprimer la diversité de l'homme. C'est cette même diversité que nous retrouvons dans les vins de Médoc. J'ai pu, un jour, relever soixante crus, t

ous de la même année. Il s'agissait certes de vins, mais tous étaient différe nts. Tout est dans la nuance du bouquet. Il en est de même pour les caractè res! *Sie fragen sich, warum es notwendig ist, so viele Schriften zur Verfügung zu haben.* Sie dienen alle zum selben, aber machen die Vielfalt des Mensch en aus. Diese Vielfalt ist wie beim Wein. Ich habe einmal eine Weinkarte st udiert mit sechzig Médoc-Weinen aus dem selben Jahr. Das ist ausnahmslo s Wein, aber doch nicht alles der gleiche Wein. Es hat eben gleichwohl Nua ncen. So is es auch mit der Schrift. *You may ask why so many different typef*

aces. They all serve the same purpose but they express man's diversity. It is the same diversit y we find in wine. I once saw a list of Médoc wines featuring sixty different Médocs all of t he same year. All of them were wines but each was different from the others. It's the nuances that are important. The same is true for typef aces. *Pourquoi tant d'Alphabets différents!* Tous servent au même but, mais aussi à exprimer la diversité de l'homme. C'est cette même retrou

69 pt | −25   53 pt | −5   35 pt | −5   23 pt | 0   15 pt | 19 pt | 5   10.5 pt | 13 pt | 10   7.5 pt | 10.2 pt | 20   6 pt | 8 pt | 30

ÅBÇDÈFG
HIJKLMÑ
ÔPQRŠTÜ
VWXYZ&
ÆŒ¥$£€
1234567890
åbçdéfghij
klmñôpqrš
tüvwxyzß
fi fl æ œ ø ł ð
[.,:;·'/-–—]
(¿¡"«‹›»"!?)
{§°%@‰*†}
Regular

ÅBÇDÈFG
HIJKLMÑ
ÔPQRŠTÜ
VWXYZ&
ÆŒ¥$£€
1234567890
åbçdéfghij
klmñôpqrš
tüvwxyzß
fi fl æ œ ø ł ð
[.,:;·'/-–—]
(¿¡"«‹›»"!?)
{§°%@‰*†}
Regular Italic

ÅBÇDÈFG
HIJKLMÑ
ÔPQRŠTÜ
VWXYZ&
ÆŒ¥$£€
1234567890
åbçdéfghij
klmñôpqrš
tüvwxyzß
fi fl æ œ ø ł ð
[.,:;·'/-–—]
(¿¡"«‹›»"!?)
{§°%@‰*†}
Bold

ÅBÇDÈFG
HIJKLMÑ
ÔPQRŠTÜ
VWXYZ&
ÆŒ¥$£€
1234567890
åbçdéfghij
klmñôpqrš
tüvwxyzß
fi fl æ œ ø ł ð
[.,:;·'/-–—]
(¿¡"«‹›»"!?)
{§°%@‰*†}
Bold Italic

ÅBÇDÈFG
HIJKLMÑ
ÔPQRŠTÜ
VWXYZ&
ÆŒ¥$£€
1234567890
åbçdéfghij
klmñôpqrš
tüvwxyzß
fi fl æ œ ø ł ð
[.,:;·'/-–—]
(¿¡"«‹›»"!?)
{§°%@‰*†}
Black

ÅBÇDÈFG
HIJKLMÑ
ÔPQRŠTÜ
VWXYZ&
ÆŒ¥$£€
1234567890
åbçdéfghij
klmñôpqrš
tüvwxyzß
fi fl æ œ ø ł ð
[.,:;·'/-–—]
(¿¡"«‹›»"!?)
{§°%@‰*†}
Black Italic

Typeface comparison All three typefaces shown below, *Raleigh, Garth Graphic* and *Breughel,* have a unique look and feel. In all three typefaces we can find letters, such as the capital K with its curved diagonal, that lend a very special note to the design **/30/**. Additionally, all three typefaces have a rather sturdy appearance and pronounced, oblique serifs. In terms of shape, these serifs differentiate themselves from the usual, symmetrical ones. The origin of the asymmetrical serifs can be traced back to the use of a broad pen in the 15th-century handwritten minuscule, as well as to Jenson's 1470 antiqua – a style that was soon to be replaced by the work of Aldus Manutius and Claude Garamont and that would only receive renewed attention with the 19th-century Arts and Crafts movement.

The most obvious difference to Adrian Frutiger's *Breughel* can be found in the straight downstrokes of *Raleigh*[17] and *Garth Graphic*[19] (named after Bill Garth,[18] founder of Compugraphic and former president of Photon). But there are also differences in the slanted serifs. In *Raleigh* the transition from the stem to the serifs is curved and the base flat, whereas it is concave in *Garth Graphic*. The serifs are also flatter. In *Breughel* the serif transitions are not concave which results in the serifs having a less three-dimensional appearance. Additionally, the ascender height and the cap height are identical in Frutiger's typeface **/32/**.

/29/

Measurements of stroke widths and proportions of the Breughel *regular weight.*

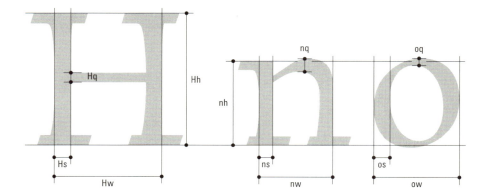

Roman				
Hh = 10.00 cm	nh = 6.39 cm	oh = 6.81 cm	Hh : Hw = 1 : 0.79	nh : nw = 1 : 0.85
Hw = 7.87	nw = 5.43	ow = 6.30	Hw : Hs = 1 : 0.15	nw : ns = 1 : 0.18
Hs = 1.17	ns = 0.98	os = 1.18	Hs : Hq = 1 : 0.61	nh : ch = 1 : 1.06
Hq = 0.72	nq = 0.99	oq = 0.53		nw : cw = 1 : 1.16

/30/

Due to the strokes being tapered on one side only, Breughel *appears softer and more fragile than the comparison typefaces* Raleigh *and* Garth Graphic.

Hofstainberg

Raleigh
Robert Norton
1978

K P W a b m y 3 6

Hofstainberg

Garth Graphic
Constance Blanchard / Renee Le Winter
1979

K P W a b m y 3 6

Hofstainberg

Breughel
Adrian Frutiger
1982

K P W a b m y 3 6

K	P	W	a	b	m	y	3 6
Stem tapered on one side, foot serif shorter on the right than on the left	Open counter, foot serifs elongated on the right	With centre serif	Terminal without emphasis	Stroke transitions directly into the curve	Angular transition into the stem, dynamic curves	Descender with vertical serif	Open shape, round counter

/31/

*Comparison showing the
different weights and angle of
the italics.*

	Hh	Hw	Hs	Hq
Roman	10.00 cm	7.87 = 1	1.17 = 1	0.72 = 1
Bold	10.00	8.49 = 1.08	1.77 = 1.51	0.92 = 1.28
Black	10.00	9.13 = 1.16	2.40 = 2.05	1.09 = 1.51
Italic	10.00	7.61 = 0.97	1.04 = 0.89	0.73 = 1.01

9.5°

1234567890
Å B Ç D É F G H I J
K L M Ñ Ô P Q R Š
T Ü V W X Y Z SS
Regular SC

*1234567890
Å B Ç D É F G H I J
K L M Ñ Ô P Q R Š
T Ü V W A X Y Z SS*
Regular Italic SC

**1234567890
Å B Ç D É F G H I J
K L M Ñ Ô P Q R Š
T Ü V W X Y Z SS**
Bold SC

***1234567890
Å B Ç D É F G H I J
K L M Ñ Ô P Q R Š
T Ü V W X Y Z SS***
Bold Italic SC

**1234567890
Å B Ç D É F G H I J
K L M Ñ Ô P Q R Š
T Ü V W X Y Z SS**
Black SC

***1234567890
Å B Ç D É F G H I J
K L M Ñ Ô P Q R Š
T Ü V W X Y Z SS***
Black Italic SC

/32/

*Height comparison showing the
differences of x-heights to
ascenders and descenders – the cap
height is the starting point.*

Raleigh
44.7 pt

Garth Graphic
41.9 pt

Breughel
40.5 pt

Dolmen
1980

Although we have already disclaimed all intention of treating fully on Ornamental turning, which would need several costly illustrations and a fractional increase in the size of this book, the two very Handy Instruments heading the present chapter seem to call for judicious attention.

/01/
Paste-up for the typeface design 'Dolmen' – in contrast to 'Delta', g r t are replaced by lowercase forms.

eine displayschrift von der unziale abgeleitet

/03/
Variants of the uncial design with Cassandre – in contrast to the designs of the 1950s, the lower-case a has a gap at the bottom.

tiens, mon unique enfant, mon fils, prends ce breuvaçe. sa chaleur te rendra ta force et ton couraçe. la mauve,

/02/
The early-to-mid 1950s typeface design for 'Delta' is the formal foundation for 'Dolmen'.

'Delta' and 'Dolmen' A dolmen is the simplest type of New Stone Age megalithic tomb.[1] Adrian Frutiger said that names from Antiquity have always appealed to him. The name was, however, already taken, since as early as 1922 the type foundry of Schelter & Giesecke (Leipzig) had produced a robust sans serif typeface with the name *Dolmen* **/08/**.

Frutiger went back to the hand drawings for *'Delta'*, produced at the start of the 1950s **/02/**, for one of his designs for *'Dolmen'* **/01/**. In contrast to the version from the time of Deberny & Peignot, the English-language paste-up – which presumably appeared around 1980 – was not conceived as a single-alphabet typeface. Rather, it was designed – as usual – with capitals and lower case characters. The three uncial forms are replaced by the lower-case g r and t, which makes the typeface more flexible. However, Adrian Frutiger had not fully given up on the uncial form, as a further modification of the *'Delta'* design shows **/03/**. The a is designed differently from the various attempts with Cassandre (see page 37). The letter curves are rounder and the previously closed counter is now open at the bottom. This design was not pursued further. However, *'Dolmen'* received several final designs **/04/** and a test exposure **/11/12/** before its development was halted, like *'Delta'* before it.

It was not until 2007 that *'Dolmen'*, under the name *Nami*, was completed by Linotype, more than fifty years after the first design (see page 402).

The idea had always been to create a lively sans serif type to sit alongside my grotesque typefaces. When I say lively, that should be understood in the sense of soft shapes, and not in the hard forms of a pure sans serif. I wanted to design a grotesque where you can feel the hand behind it, one that writes. Around the end of the seventies or early eighties, the various designs for *'Dolmen'* were created. At any rate, it was after *Frutiger* and the final artwork for *Icone* had been done. I found the *'Dolmen'* design 'Farbenschein' from January 1980 a little too soft with its rounded-off corners **/13/**.

The basis for *'Dolmen'* lies in my type design *'Delta'* from the mid-fifties (see page 36). At that time, I had already drawn a sans serif with a handwritten feel to it. Ideas that had been either rejected or never brought to fruition, I simply reworked and presented again. However, in contrast to *'Delta'* **/02/**, in *'Dolmen'* **/01/** there's no attempt at an uncial typeface.

My design seemed to have been accepted by D. Stempel AG / Linotype. At any rate, we had implemented the test word 'OHamburgefonstiv' and created the first test string **/10/**. In the light font *'Dolmen'* has a nice appearance. But the liveliness that's there in the light weight is all but lost in the bold **/12/**. This example shows that you can't extend all typefaces into families. The clearly more-robust aspect gives it another feeling. That was probably the reason why further development was stopped. But it's still not clear to me today why they rejected it. In my eyes the project could have taken wing if it had been pushed more. If somebody had pushed it, it would have been implemented, no matter whether Mergenthaler Linotype in the United States reacted positively to it or not. The Americans had their projects and we had ours. But no one pushed it. It just needed someone to say

/04/
Final artwork for 'Dolmen', with width specifications and digitising points for 'Dolmen' 45 narrow, 56 italique and 65 bold.

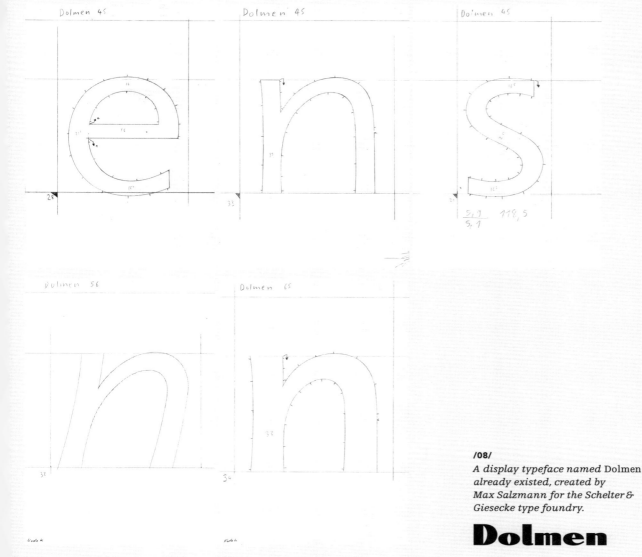

/05/
Letter comparison between 'Dolmen' (paste-up, top) and the less pronounced version in the test exposure (bottom).

aenrsv
aenrsv

/06/
The Art Nouveau typeface Hobo, designed in 1910 by Morris Fuller Benton, already exhibited the lower-case a with smooth bowl juncture.

Hobo a

/07/
Sans serif typefaces with a smooth bowl juncture on the a: Semplicità (1931), Chambord (1945) and Barmen / Barmeno (1983).

Semplicità
Chambord
Barmen

/08/
A display typeface named Dolmen already existed, created by Max Salzmann for the Schelter & Giesecke type foundry.

Dolmen

/09/
In ITC Eras (1976), Albert Boton's slightly oblique sans serif, the a has a gap at bottom right.

ITC Eras

Dolmen 45

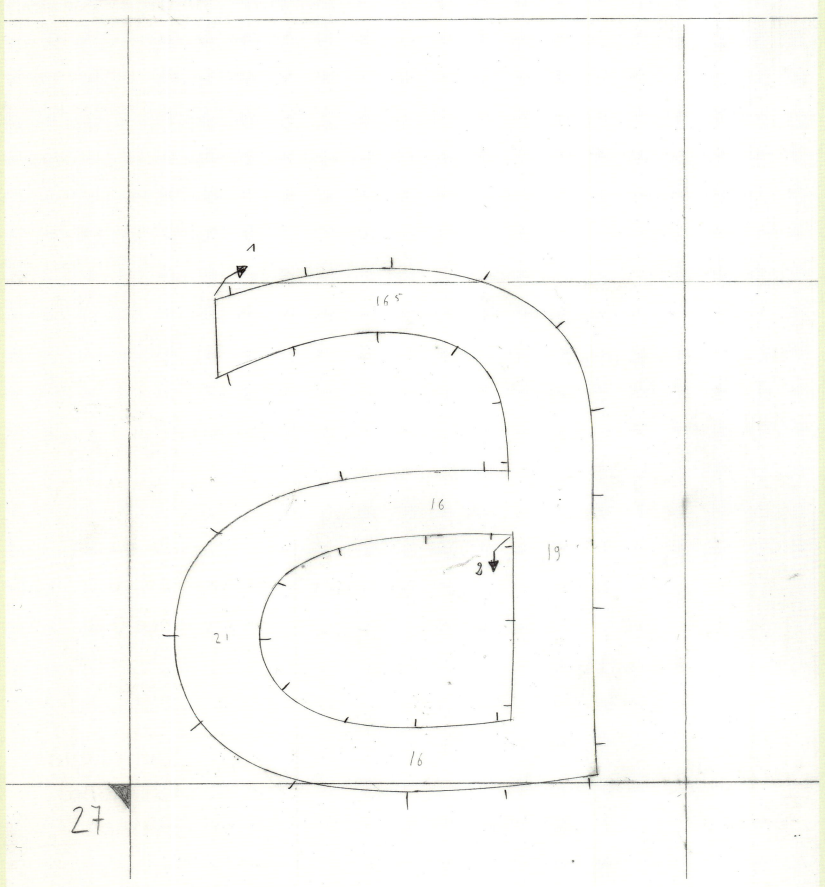

Curve junctures in 'Dolmen' There are some differences between the first design of *'Dolmen'* /01/ and its final version /04/. In the original design the hand-drawn ductus is more explicit. For example, the curve of the n and r begins further down and, in the r, has a slanted ending /05/. The legs of the diagonal letters, v w and y, also share this oblique termination. In the test exposure, however, they have horizontal terminations /11/. Since the curves of a and s are not as diagonal /05/, either, the exposed version gives a more austere, tamer impression. However, the appearance of a generous, handwritten sans serif is still maintained.

Besides the handwritten appearance of the ductus and the waisted stems, the clean junctures of a b d g p q are a distinguishing feature of the *'Delta'* and the *'Dolmen'* designs. This form element is – especially in the lower case a /10/ – unusual and, at the same time, charming. Amongst the few typefaces that exhibit this a-form is the Art Nouveau typeface *Hobo* (1910), by Morris Fuller Benton /06/. Other sans serif typefaces with this feature are *Semplicità*[2] (1931) by the Società Nebiolo type foundry and Roger Excoffon's *Chambord* (1945) /07/.

In the 1980's Adrian Frutiger's *'Dolmen'* might have found its niche: in 1983 H. Berthold AG brought out *Barmen* /07/ – known today as *FF Sari* – a typeface with smooth curve junctures.[3] However, Hans Reichel's typeface, in which m n r and u all share this feature, is not as fluid as *'Dolmen'*.

no forcefully; and all the other voices died down. I certainly had no say in the matter. But I didn't have to manufacture the typeface and get the investment together either – and in those days, getting a typeface as far as the matrix plate was a big investment.

The special thing about *'Dolmen'* – more than any other – is the shape of the lower case a. When you look at the word 'bagger' in the test exposure, you see straight away the formal relationship in the bowl junctures of a b and g /11/. But I'm not entirely happy with the situation on the bottom right of the a. It looks like the corner is jutting out slightly /10/. I've often asked myself if it wouldn't have been better if I'd left a small gap there. Similar to how Albert Boton, my former colleague at Deberny & Peignot, had done in 1976 with his slightly oblique *ITC Eras* /09/. Or, it would at least have been better to pull the bowl downwards a little more and let it rise more sharply to the right.

A stable grotesque, like *Frutiger* for instance, gives a type designer the possibility to use it as raw material for the development of further typefaces. *'Dolmen'*, in contrast, isn't raw material – its expression is less dispassionate, less neutral. It's already pointing in a certain direction.

OHamburgefonstiv HHOHOOHHOOH
nanmnbnunrngnenfnonsntninvnnnn
oaomobouorogoeofooosotoiovoooo
Hamburgefonstivt Oberforster Hornisse
Otto Hoffnung sonnentau tasse tee inserat
moostrauben monsunregen frage
abteigruft nortvone gabe turnverein
namensgebung miinnora bagger
baufenster torfing mutter Homberger
ff fi f ft tf rt rv tv vt
nnoono ss gg tt eemeem neen nein

/11/
*Sample text produced by the Ikarus
digitising system – the exposure of
the sample string serves to point out
any problems in letter shape,
stroke weight and letter spacing.*

OHamburgefonstiv HHOHOOHHOOH
nanmnbnunrngnenfnonsntninvnnnn
oaomobouorogoeofooosotoiovoooo
Hamburgefonstivt Oberforster Hornisse
Otto Hoffnung sonnentau tasse tee inserat
moostrauben monsunregen frage
abteigruft nortvone gabe turnverein
namensgebung miinnora bagger
baufenster torfing mutter Homberger
ff fi f ft tf rt rv tv vt
nnoono ss gg tt eemeem neen nein

OHamburgefonstiv HHOHOOHHOOH
nanmnbnunrngnenfnonsntninvnnnn
oaomobouorogoeofooosotoiovoooo
Hamburgefonstivt Oberforster Hornisse
Otto Hoffnung sonnentau tasse tee inserat
moostrauben monsunregen frage
abteigruft nortvone gabe turnverein
namensgebung miinnora bagger
baufenster torfing mutter Homberger
ff fi f ft tf rt rv tv vt
nnoono ss gg tt eemeem neen nein

OHamburgefonstiv HHOHOOHHOOH
nanmnbnunrngnenfnonsntninvnnnn
oaomobouorogoeofooosotoiovoooo
Hamburgefonstivt Oberforster Hornisse
Otto Hoffnung sonnentau tasse tee inserat
moostrauben monsunregen frage
abteigruft nortvone gabe turnverein
namensgebung miinnora bagger
baufenster torfing mutter Homberger
ff fi f ft tf rt rv tv vt
nnoono ss gg tt eemeem neen nein

/12/
*Sample strings of 'Dolmen' 65
exposed on photographic paper –
Frutiger's control sign developed for
Linotype in 1978 serves as a check
of exposure quality.*

/10/
*Final artwork for the lowercase a
of the typeface design 'Dolmen' 45 –
the bowl curve flows cleanly into
the stem at bottom right.*

Farbenschein

Heimat deine Firne scheinen goldenen Flammen gleich am abendlichen Firmament Inseln reihen sich wie Girlanden zwischen den bewaldeten Hügeln. Immer wenn der Herbst in seinem milden Farbenschein das Hohland verwandelt zauberhaft schön.

Januar 1980

/13/
January 1980 paste-up of 'Dolmen projekt'– the downstrokes are more strongly waisted and end in diagonals with rounded-off corners.

/14/
January 1980 paste-up of 'Dolmen projekt' in medium and bold weights with the corresponding oblique (here referred to as italic).

do!men medium

Heimat deine Firne scheinen wie goldene Flammen am abendlichen Firmament. Hügelreihen ziehen sich wie bewaldete Inseln vom nahen Flusse bis ins Hohland.

dolmen bold

Heimat deine Firne scheinen wie goldene Flammen am abendlichen Firmament. Hügelreihen ziehen sich wie bewaldete Inseln vom nahen Flusse bis ins Hohland.

dolmen italic

Heimat deine Firne scheinen wie goldene Flammen am abendlichen Firmament. Hügelreihen ziehen sich wie bewaldete Inseln vom nahen Flusse bis ins Hohland.

dolmen bold italic

Heimat deine Firne scheinen wie goldene Flammen am abendlichen Firmament. Hügelreihen ziehen sich wie bewaldete Inseln vom nahen Flusse bis ins Hohland.

A further 'Dolmen' project   Adrian Frutiger is also responsible for another design with the name 'Dolmen', dating from January 1980 and called 'Dolmen projekt' /13/. A second sheet shows paste-ups of the four fonts /14/. In conversation[4], Frutiger has labelled this typeface as somewhat soft – in comparison with the 'Dolmen' design shown earlier. This is understandable. The two typefaces are related, but in terms of character are very different. Which of the two was developed first is not clear. The skeleton of both designs is virtually identical, even if the curves in 'Dolmen projekt' are slightly more angular, and the lowercase a and d do not have the smooth juncture, exhibiting instead an incision. However, the 'clothing' – as Frutiger called it[5] – produces a wholly different feel. The 'Dolmen projekt' paste-up, with its more pronounced stroke endings, has an altogether somewhat heavier and, therefore, slightly narrower, appearance. In contrast to 'Dolmen' – and to *Icone* – it exhibits rounded-off corners and diamond-shaped dots.

Later, Frutiger undertook yet another formally very interesting approach. However, the undated study /17/ was shelved by Linotype. Its ductus is similar to a narrow *Frutiger* and the waisted strokes recall his design for 'Gespannte Grotesk' (see page 157). The smooth bowl junctures of b and g are from 'Dolmen', while the numerous studies for the stroke endings demonstrate, once more, Frutiger's joy in design /18/.

/15/
Photograph taken from the poster Adrian Frutiger á Íslandi: 24. nóvember 1987 – *in the background, at left, letters from* 'Dolmen projekt'.

/16/
The diagonally cut strokes of the n, in combination with the rounded-off corners, make the letters dance somewhat.

/17/
Synthesis of the typeface designs 'Gespannte Grotesk' *and* 'Dolmen' *with the ductus of the narrow* Frutiger – *presumably from the 1990s.*

nobe

Hanbeog

/18/
By varying the stroke ends, even with the same base form, a variety of different characters can be produced.

/19/
As usual, Adrian Frutiger always explored the impression of the typeface at various weights.

n n n n n   nn nn

n n

Name of typeface	Client	Designer	Design | Publication	Typesetting technology	Manufacturer	Weights
Tiemann	Die Zeit	Adrian Frutiger	1982 | 1982	Photosetting CRT, Lasersetting	– D. Stempel AG | Linotype	2
		(Walter Tiemann)	(1922 | 1923)	Digital setting TrueType	– Linotype	2

TIEMANN

I don't recall *Tiemann* as being a big contract. An employee of the German weekly newspaper *Die Zeit* came to me one day in Paris, and laid out what they wanted: it was to be a slight reworking of the typeface for CRT digital typesetting. *Die Zeit*'s headings would still be handset in *Tiemann*. My only job was to adjust it to the digital setting system that production was being switched over to at the beginning of the eighties. In the world of newspapers, these changes took place relatively late. As you can see here in the article 'A Farewell to Lead', announcing the event /01/: "Since its founding, around 192,000 tons of lead have been carried through the typesetting department in 'boats' by the metteurs (the graphic designers) at *Die Zeit*. Today, they and the typesetters sit in front of monitor screens and stay clean. But they, like the editors, got their joy from the sensory dimension of the job – being able to touch, to smell. This comes from something in the nature of many journalists: they like to recommend progress to others on a daily basis, but to experience progress themselves scares them. They worry for the good old days, and at the same time are scared of the new and unknown. Progressive journalists have a deeply conservative soul. The changeover at many other newspapers did, at first, flounder upon this contradiction. *Die Zeit* had it easier. The unwanted, but at the same time, inevitable change reached us only when it was a relatively mature technology."[1]

Tiemann was only used for headings and sub-headings. In well-known newspapers like this one, changing the look was always a thorny topic. The reader is acutely aware of that. The appearance of the paper gives it its face – the reader has had it in his head for decades. At *Die Zeit,* a proof of the alphabet was prepared for me as a starting point, probably already on newsprint, so that I could see the ink spread produced by the printing process. I changed hardly anything of the basic form of the letters, since I wanted it to remain a *Tiemann*. Otherwise, I would have been accused again of bringing my own hand to it. It was only a bread-and-butter job, not a creative one. Of course, for the photosetting, I had to draw the glyphs slightly less fragile. For this reason, I made the fine junctions and the serifs slighty bolder. With the c and e you can see that the terminals are a bit bolder than in the version for hot metal setting. First I made around ten test letters, with attempts at bolder and finer versions. I think Nicole Delamarre may also have worked on that. Actually, she wasn't employed at my studio at that time, but towards the end of my time in Paris in 1992, she was carrying out work for me from home. *Tiemann* was completed in 1982, and the reader was informed of the changeover in the edition of the 14 May /01/.

Tiemann-Antiqua at *Die Zeit* The liberal weekly newspaper *Die Zeit* was founded in bombed-out Hamburg nine months after the end of the Second World War, first appearing on 21 February 1946. Initially *Bodoni* was used as the headline face, but starting with Issue 10 in 1946, it was changed to Walter Tiemann's *Tiemann-Antiqua*. The foundry type was available from Gebrüder Klingspor. For the body type, set in Linotype line-casting, Stanley Morison's *Times Roman* was employed, a newspaper typeface specially developed in 1932 for *The Times* of London. Columns that were added later sometimes featured other headline typefaces, including even sans serifs.

The type most often used after *Tiemann-Antiqua* was *Ratio-Latein*[3] by Friedrich Wilhelm Kleukens /04/, which, only a few years after the appearance of the first issue, had replaced *Didot* in the supplement 'Feuilleton'. *Ratio-Latein* belongs, as does *Tiemann-Antiqua*, to the category of the 20th-century neoclassical antiquas /07/, but exhibits a lighter appearance. These two typefaces were still in use in 1982, the year of *Die Zeit*'s switchover to digital setting. The change of technology to the Linotron 606 CRT digital setting machines was also used to standardise the masthead typeface. Adrian Frutiger received the contract not only to adapt the normal *Tiemann-Antiqua* for CRT digital setting, but also to develop a lighter typeface /10/ as a replacement for *Ratio-Latein*. The two *Tiemann* fonts drawn by Adrian Frutiger were later adopted into the Linotype range, and can be seen in the 1984 type catalogue digital type faces, displayed in a design size of 18 pt.[4]

Also in 1988, at the request of *Die Zeit*, Linotype adapted *Tiemann* for desktop publishing. *Die Zeit* then had both digitised fonts reworked by Jovica Veljović,[5] who prepared them exclusively for the digital setting of the newspaper. He corrected their colour, adjusted the spacing and changed the kerning. Additionally, he expanded them to include Light Italic, Normal Italic, Normal Narrow and Normal Small Caps, as well as an inline version.[6] Since 1998 the two typefaces designed by Adrian Frutiger have been available from Linotype in TrueType format and now also in PostScript and OpenType format.

Polen fünf Monate nach dem Putsch: ein Aufruf zur Versöhnung (S. 25–28)

Stellenangebote
Neue Positionen – neue Aufgaben
Seiten 34–38

DIE ZEIT

Für Ihre Reise:
Angebote – Informationen
Seiten 53–61

Nr. 20 14. Mai 1982
37. Jahrgang. Preis 3,00 DM

WOCHENZEITUNG FÜR POLITIK · WIRTSCHAFT · HANDEL UND KULTUR

C 7451 C

Zeitverlag Gerd Bucerius KG
Postfach 10 68 20, 2000 Hamburg 1

Spätstart aus der Eiszeit

Reagans Abrüstungsvorschlag und Moskau

Von Christian Schmidt-Häuer

Mit neuem Elan hat sich Präsident Reagan auf die Suche nach der verlorenen Zeit begeben. Schon im Juni möchte er die Verhandlungen über strategische Waffen wieder beginnen. *Start* soll den Abbau der Interkontinentalwaffen beider Weltmächte einleiten, in der ersten Stufe um ein Drittel ihrer derzeitigen Feuerkraft. Kommt der Vorschlag noch rechtzeitig?

Das für Amerika günstige Salt-II-Abkommen, das den Kreml schon heute – vor dem in Moskau anstehenden Machtwechsel – zur Verringerung seines strategischen Potentials verpflichtet hätte, verkannte der Wahlkämpfer Reagan, verwarf der neue Präsident. Zu lange ließ er sich von jenen Falken blockieren, die Moskaus Militärmacht gezielt überbewerteten, aus ideologischen Bedenken gegen alle früheren Abrüstungsbemühungen. Kann sich der Präsident nun mit *Start* der Friedensbewegung im eigenen Land, den Europäern beim Nato-Gipfel am 9. Juni und vor allem den mißtrauischen Sowjets doch noch als der Mann präsentieren, der den ehrlichen Konsens einer Politik der Stärke voranstellt?

Mit neuem Elan hat der gesundheitlich angegriffene Leonid Breschnjew einem Ärztekongreß in London telegraphiert: „Damit das Licht über der Erde nicht erlischt, muß man dem Kernwaffenkrieg sofort unüberwindliche Schranken setzen. Die Sowjetunion ist zu den denkbar radikalsten Vereinbarungen in dieser Richtung bereit." Ist das die große Einladung zum Kompromiß – nachdem die Sowjetunion bisher entgegen ihren anderslautenden Bekundungen unermüdlich neue Raketen aufgestellt hatte?

„Nicht jede Zeit findet ihren großen Mann, und nicht jede große Fähigkeit findet ihre Zeit", schrieb Jacob Burckhardt. „Vielleicht sind jetzt sehr große Männer vorhanden für Dinge, die nicht vorhanden sind." In den letzten Jahren ist es umgekehrt gewesen: Es gab große Themen, die nicht ihren Mann fanden. Die objektiven Voraussetzungen für einen Rüstungsabbau sind günstiger, weil dringender als je zuvor. Aber die subjektiven Bedingungen stehen ihnen inzwischen fast unüberwindlich entgegen.

An unsere Leser

Die nächste Ausgabe der *ZEIT* (Nr. 21/82) wird wegen des Feiertags Christi Himmelfahrt früher gedruckt und ausgeliefert. Sie erhalten sie bereits am Mittwoch, dem 19. Mai, an Ihrem Kiosk.

Vor allem drei objektive Voraussetzungen könnten das Wettrüsten und die politische Konfrontation eingrenzen.

Erstens: Auf beiden Weltmächten lastet ein immer größerer wirtschaftlicher Druck. Der amerikanische Präsident hat seinen Haushalt in eine beispiellose Krise gesteuert. Der Budgetausschuß des Senats hat Reagans Etatvorlage gnadenlos zerpflückt; für die nächsten Jahre zeichnen sich bedrohliche Fehlbeträge in Höhe von weit über 100 Milliarden Dollar ab. Die sowjetische Wirtschaft schrumpfte 1981 auf die niedrigste Wachstumsrate seit der Oktoberrevolution. Seit 1979 hat das Land jedes Jahr drei Prozent weniger Lebensmittel erzeugt. Die Getreideimporte werden sich 1982 der Grenze dessen nähern, was sowjetische Häfen abfertigen können.

Zweitens: Waffentechnik und Zerstörungskapazität haben ein solches Ausmaß erreicht, daß US-Außenminister Haig und Moskaus Geheimdienstchef Andropow jüngst in sinngemäßer Übereinstimmung verkündeten: Die Rivalität der Systeme gehe weiter – aber sie werde durch die Kernwaffen begrenzt.

Drittens: Beide Supermächte haben mit der propagandistischen Ausmalung des gegnerischen Atompotentials – bei gleichzeitigen Rekordausgaben für die eigene Rüstung – neue, hausgemachte Friedensbewegungen herangezüchtet. Selbst Generalstabschef Ogarkow warnt neuerdings vor dem wachsenden Pazifismus der Sowjetjugend.

Den objektiven Voraussetzungen für einschneidende Raketen-Reduzierungen stehen freilich die subjektiven Bedingungen entgegen. Die Beziehungen zwischen Washington und Moskau sind im Kalten Krieg erstarrt. Das sowjetische Mißtrauen ist ins Uferlose gewachsen. Bei dieser Ausgangslage muß die Landmacht Sowjetunion Reagans neue Vorschläge als eindeutige Vorgabe für Washington ansehen. Denn die Reduzierungspläne zielen mit ihrer ersten Stufe einseitig auf den Abbau der schweren landgestützten sowjetischen Fernraketen. Dennoch reagiert der Kreml nicht mit brüsker Ablehnung wie bei Carters Abrüstungsvorschlägen von 1977. Er erkennt an, daß *Start* den amerikanischen Präsidenten zu einer entscheidenden Wendemarke geführt hat: Mit seiner Verhandlungsbereitschaft verzichtet Reagan auf die starre Doktrin vom *linkage* zwischen Rüstungsbegrenzung und politischem Wohlverhalten Moskaus. Die Sowjetführer werden sich deshalb nicht grundsätzlich weigern zu verhandeln.

Das bedeutet aber noch lange keine Annäherung, geschweige denn Einigung. Wenn die Amerikaner ehrlich die „historische Chance" suchen, von der Alexander Haig jüngst sprach, müssen sie sich jetzt vor allem auf den Machtwechsel einstellen, der im Kreml bevorsteht. Das erfordert für künftige Verhandlungen zwei Orientierungspunkte. Einerseits: Kein Nachfolger Breschnjews kann die Parität mit Amerika zurückstellen, ohne sich selbst aufzugeben. Andererseits: Militärs und Hochrüstung müssen bei und nach einem Machtwechsel nicht zwangsläufig triumphieren.

Bei den letzten beiden Wachablösungen in Moskau stand die Außenpolitik im Schatten der inneren Auseinandersetzungen. Im Jahre 1953 mußten Stalins Terror und sein monströses Despotenregime entschärft werden; 1964 ging es um den Wiederaufbau der Partei, die Chruschtschow mit seinem „Vertrauen in die Massen" gespalten hatte. Diesmal wird der Kreml die Wachablösung ungleich geschlossener, eingespielter vollziehen. Dafür wartet auf die Nachfolger Breschnjews eine andere Zerreißprobe: Sie werden zwischen ihrer Neigung zu konservativer Politik und dem Zwang zu wirtschaftlicher Innovation entscheiden müssen. Auf den sich zuspitzenden Verteilungskampf um die schrumpfenden Mittel werden die internationale Politik und die Rüstungsverhandlungen größeren Einfluß haben als früher.

Jeder Nachfolger Breschnjews, der nur den wirtschaftlichen Niedergang aufhalten und dafür bessere Rezepte suchen will, wird zwangsläufig in Konkurrenz mit den Generälen geraten. Denn die Militärausgaben, die unverändert um jährlich vier Prozent steigen, verschlingen die Lebensmittel. Doch westliche Behauptungen, daß jede neue Machtgruppierung im Kreml zwangsläufig an ungeschmälerter Aufrüstung festhalten müsse, lassen die ökonomische Zwangslage außer acht. Die entscheidenden Fragen lauten vielmehr: Unter welchen äußeren Bedingungen wird die Rüstungspolitik in die internen Auseinandersetzungen eingebracht? Welche Rolle können die Militärs spielen? Wird die Wachablösung alle Rüstungskontrollvorhaben der Supermächte ähnlich zurückwerfen, wie dies die amerikanischen Präsidentenwechsel die beiden letzten Male getan haben?

Die sowjetische Geschichte birgt da einige Hinweise. Die von Stalin am Ende angestrebte Entspannung in der Deutschlandpolitik wurde nach seinem Tode durch die Diadochenkämpfe aufgehalten. Auch Chruschtschows Entspannungsoffensive gegenüber Bonn, die er noch 1964 mit der spektakulären Deutschland-Reise seines Schwiegersohns Adschubej einzuleiten versuchte, wurde nach seinem Sturz erst einmal abgebrochen.

Am Anfang beider Duumvirate, die auf die Stalin-Ära folgten, kämpfte die Regierung für mehr Butter, die Partei für mehr Kanonen. Schon Ministerpräsident Malenkow verlangte – wie später Kossygin – größere Investitionen für Leichtindustrie und Konsumgüter. Parteichef Chruschtschow betrieb demgegenüber zunächst – wie später sein Nachfolger Breschnjew – einen Ausbau der Rüstung. Bei diesen Auseinandersetzungen hat die Armee aber keine eigenständige Rolle gespielt. In diesem Punkt hat sich der Kreml bis heute an die Tradition gehalten: Schon das Zarenreich wurde durch Militärpolitik zusammengehalten, aber nie von Offizieren beherrscht.

Vieles spricht dafür, daß die kommende Wachablösung einen relativ kontrollierten Machtkampf bringen wird. Und die wirtschaftliche Notlage der Sowjetunion räumt dem Westen diesmal die Chance ein, künftige Reformer – die sich vorsichtig an den ungarischen Experimenten orientieren – wirksamer zu unterstützen, als das zu Zeiten Malenkows 1953 und Kossygins 1964 möglich war. Die *Start*-Verhandlungen können ein Schritt nach vorn sein – wenn Ronald Reagan die Pose des antikommunistischen Kreuzzüglers ablegt und seinen kalifornischen Pragmatismus in die Gespräche einbringt.

Signal geben bei Ebbe

Kein Hinterausgang

Die FDP kann sich nicht aus der Koalition stehlen

Von Rolf Zundel

Die Freien Demokraten haben in den letzten Wochen manche ihrer Freunde irritiert. Dabei sind es nicht einmal so sehr ihre Angriffe auf den sozialdemokratischen Koalitionspartner, selbst wenn sie manchmal überhart und ungerecht ausfielen, die Grund zur Verwunderung geben; da stehen die beiden Lager einander nicht nach. Es ist vielmehr der Eindruck, daß die Partei durch ihr ungesteuertes und undiszipliniertes öffentliches Nachdenken, wie sie sich denn am besten aus der Affaire ziehen könne, beides verbaut: einen Erfolg in der Koalition – und, notfalls, ein begründbares Ende des Regierungsbündnisses.

Die Serie der Koalitionsgespräche in den letzten Tagen hat diese Sorge nicht beseitigt; immerhin haben sie *eines* bewirkt: Die Partner haben sich vorgenommen, ihre Differenzen etwas leiser, weniger öffentlich auszutragen, um die Haushaltsentscheidungen in den nächsten Wochen nicht noch weiter zu erschweren. Dieser Vorsatz wird gewiß auch dadurch gefördert, daß im Blick auf die Hamburger Wahlen weitere Demonstrationen der Zerstrittenheit nicht empfehlenswert sind, zumal Schmidt und Genscher dort selber kräftig in den Wahlkampf eingreifen. Insofern mag man tatsächlich, wie es der FDP-Generalsekretär Verheugen nahegelegt hat, von „Entwarnung" reden. Vorläufig wenigstens.

Wie lange? Die Liberalen verweisen verdächtig oft auf Hamburg – so als werde dort eine Art Gottesurteil über den Fortgang der Bonner Politik und den Fortbestand der Koalition gefällt. Aber wie könnte denn ein solches Urteil aussehen? Es gibt, so lassen die Umfragen vermuten, zwei wenig wahrscheinliche Möglichkeiten: SPD und FDP oder CDU und FDP erreichen zusammen die Mehrheit der Mandate. Das eine Ergebnis wäre der Stimmung in Bonn förderlich, das andere nicht. Beide jedoch lieferten keine stichhaltige Begründung für das Ende oder die Fortsetzung der Koalition.

Die realistischere Alternative für Hamburg aber lautet: Entweder kommt die FDP in die Bürgerschaft, wird jedoch neben den Grünen zur vierten Partei und kann keiner Mehrheit in den Sattel helfen, oder sie scheitert an der Fünf-Prozent-Klausel und ist überhaupt nicht in der Bürgerschaft vertreten. Die FDP hat also allen Grund, diese Wahl wichtig zu nehmen, denn es geht wieder einmal darum, ob sie ihre Rolle als dritte Kraft ausgespielt hat. Das Ergebnis wird auch für die Koalitionsentscheidung der hessischen Liberalen wichtig sein – etwa nach dem Motto: Mit der SPD reicht es nicht mehr, jetzt versuchen wir es mit der CDU. Das wäre lähmend für die Stimmung in Bonn, aber ebenfalls kein einleuchtendes Argument für das Ende der Koalition, das vom Wähler fröhlich akzeptiert würde und die FDP unbeschädigt ließe. Das Bild von den Ratten, die das sinkende Schiff verlassen, würde die FDP auf Jahre verfolgen.

Verdächtig oft ist auch von manchen Liberalen der Gedanke hin- und hergewendet worden, ob es aus staatspolitischen Gründen nicht wünschenswert wäre, wenn die SPD in die Opposition geriete und dann in ihrer neuen Rolle den Grünen so viele Wähler abjagte, daß diese Bewegung wieder zu einer unbedeutenden Randerscheinung der Politik würde. Abgesehen davon, daß bei diesen Betrachtungen die Grünen als bloße Protestpartei unterschätzt und die „Beweglichkeit des Tankers" SPD überschätzt wird – die Absicht, damit der FDP ihre profitable Stellung als dritte Kraft zu sichern, ist zu offenkundig, als daß die hehre Argumentation Eindruck machte. Und zwangsläufig wird damit der Verdacht geweckt, hier werde an einer eleganten Ausstiegshilfe aus der Koalition gebastelt.

Das gilt auch für den ebenfalls breitgewalzten, trauervollen Gedanken, leider sei, so wie sich die demoskopische Lage jetzt darstelle, die Wahrscheinlichkeit gering, daß Sozialdemokraten und Liberale bei der nächsten Bundestagswahl zusammen die Mehrheit gewönnen. Dann aber gerate die FDP möglicherweise in die höchst unkomfortable Rolle einer zweiten oder gar, falls die Grünen ins Bonner Parlament einzögen, dritten kleinen Oppositionspartei. Wäre es deshalb nicht besser, vorher den großen Sprung zu wagen?

Das alles sind legitime Überlegungen, nur taugen sie zu einem nicht: einen Koalitionswechsel vor dem Wähler zu begründen. Er fragt weniger nach dem Schicksal der FDP, so traurig es sein mag, sondern vielmehr nach dem Schicksal der Politik. Die ständige öffentliche Diskussion, wie denn, unter welchen Umständen, nach welchen Ereignissen, die FDP ohne allzu großen Schaden springen könne – nach Hamburg, nach Hessen oder vielleicht überhaupt nicht –, macht jedoch die einzig akzeptable Begründung, wenn es sie denn geben sollte, fadenscheinig, noch ehe sie gefunden ist: sachlich und ideologisch unvereinbare Positionen bei der Haushaltspolitik.

Noch aber gibt es in der FDP-Führung und in der Fraktion keine Mehrheit für einen Bruch, noch liefert die Regierungspolitik auch keinen Anlaß dazu. Die Auseinandersetzung mit den Parteitagsbeschlüssen der SPD, berechtigt in der Sache, weil die meisten Regierungsmitglieder der SPD diese Diskussion laufen ließen, als ginge sie das nichts an, reicht dazu nicht aus. Die Beschlüsse sind nicht Regierungspolitik.

Es reicht auf die Dauer für die FDP auch nicht, sich vor dem Hintergrund des SPD-Parteitags als die Partei der Steuererleichterungen profilieren zu wollen. Wenn die Haushaltsberatungen ernst werden, wenn über eine neue Finanzierung des Beschäftigungsprogramms, den Nachtrag für den Haushalt '82 und die Eckdaten für den Haushalt '83 entschieden wird, muß die FDP Farbe bekennen: Wieviel, wo soll gekürzt werden – bei den Sozialausgaben, bei den Subventionen? Dabei wird sich wahrscheinlich zeigen, daß die Freien Demokraten keineswegs so radikal, wie manche vermuten, die sozialen Leistungen beschneiden werden; wenn dann am Ende trotzdem eine Einigung nicht möglich ist, wenn Angenehmes und Unangenehmes auf dem Tisch liegt, dann erst ist die Frage erlaubt und notwendig: Kann die Koalition fortgesetzt werden? Aber diese Entscheidung wird erst glaubhaft, nachdem ernsthaft verhandelt worden ist, nicht vorher.

Es gibt keinen Hinterausgang aus der Koalition. Wenn die FDP die Suche danach nicht einstellt, hilft ihr am Ende weder das Verbleiben in der Koalition noch deren Verlassen. Beim Spiel mit den Optionen wird die FDP allmählich selber zum Verlierer. Die Tage bekömmlicher Schlauheit gehen für die Liberalen zu Ende.

DIESE WOCHE

Politik	1–11
Politische Woche	8
Länderspiegel	12–13
Politisches Buch	14–15
Themen der Zeit	16
Wirtschaft	17–31
Dossier	25–28
Bildung	33
Berufe	34–38
Theaterspielpläne	40
Feuilleton	41–47
Literatur	48–50
Leserbriefe	51
Impressum	46, 51
Kritik und Information	52
Reise	53–61
Wissenschaft	66
Modernes Leben	63–70

9–11 **Prags schwarzer Knödel-Kommunismus**
Hans Peter Riese über die Tschechoslowakei

17 **Mehr Gerüchte als Geschäfte**
Heinz Blüthmann und Wolfgang Gehrmann über den entthronten Abschreiber-Star Jürgen Amann

41/42 **„Das Imperium schlägt zurück"**
Hans-Christoph Blumenberg über zwei Filme zur Falkland-Krise

70 **Die Schuld wurde mir zugewiesen**
Ben Witters Spaziergang mit Albert Vietor, dem ehemaligen Chef der „Neuen Heimat"

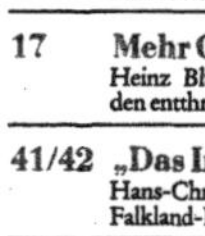

Ein Tierleben, damit Menschen leben
Diese Woche findet in Bonn ein Bundestags-Hearing über das emotionsgeladene Thema Tierversuche statt. Thomas von Randow sah sich in den Laboratorien um. Sein Urteil: ein notwendiges Übel

Abschied vom Blei

Aus dem konservativen Innenleben der *ZEIT*

Nun hat die Elektronik auch bei der *ZEIT* getan, was sie überall tut: Einzug gehalten. Dies ist unsere erste Ausgabe, die nicht mehr mit Hilfe von Bleilettern und Bleizeilen, sondern nach den Gesetzen von Computer und Lichtsatzmaschine entstanden ist.

Länger als 500 Jahre haben Gutenbergs Ideen gehalten. Sie haben die Arbeit der Journalisten, noch mehr der Schriftsetzer bestimmt – sie und Mergenthalers Linotype. Jetzt wurden sie ausrangiert. Rund 192 000 Tonnen Blei, schmierig von Druckerschwärze, haben die Metteure in „Schiffen" durch die Setzerei geschleppt, seit die *ZEIT* gegründet wurde. Heute sitzen sie und die Schriftsetzer am Bildschirm und bleiben sauber. Doch ihnen wie den Redakteuren ist das sinnliche Vergnügen an der Arbeit genommen, die Freude, anfassen zu können, riechen zu können.

Dies auch aus einem Grund, der in der Natur vieler Journalisten liegt: Sie empfehlen den Fortschritt gern und täglich anderen. Ihn am eigenen Leibe zu erleben, macht ihnen jedoch angst. Angst um das schöne Alte; Angst aber auch vor dem unbekannten Neuen. Progressive Journalisten haben ein höchst konservatives Innenleben.

An diesem Widerspruch ist die Umstellung bei manch anderer Zeitung zunächst gescheitert. Kopfarbeit und perfekte, allein an technischem Bedürfnis und kaufmännischem Kalkül ausgerichtete Organisation passen nun einmal schlecht zusammen. Da hatte es die *ZEIT* besser: Uns erreichte der ungewollte und doch unausweichliche Fortschritt erst, als er ziemlich ausgereift war. Die schlimmen Kinderkrankheiten mußten wir nicht mehr auskurieren. Außerdem hat die *ZEIT* keine eigene Technik. Und es ist immer schön, andere für die Fehler geradestehen zu lassen, die man sonst selbst gemacht hätte.

Wichtiger noch war, daß Zeit genug blieb, vom Alten zu retten, was rettenswert war. Für die Redakteure zum Beispiel ihre

Die Seite eins der *ZEIT*, zum letztenmal in Blei gesetzt

individuelle Arbeitsweise: Daß der technische Fortschritt den Journalisten – zumindest in diesem Stadium – keine Erleichterung brächte, war rasch klar. Daß er die Redaktionsarbeit, deren Organisationsprinzip das kreative Chaos ist, zumindest nicht beeinträchtigte, war das Ziel ungezählter Detailgespräche mit der Technik. Bis heute klappt es, nicht zuletzt mit Hilfe der neuen Schlußredaktion, die gegenläufige Interessen von Redaktion und Technik ausgleicht. Und kein Redakteur muß seine Berichte, Kommentare, Glossen und Leitartikel in ein Bildschirmgerät eintippen. Noch herrschen Bleistift, Kugelschreiber und Schreibmaschine.

Für die Leser zum Beispiel die Schriften: Die Bleibuchstaben sind zum letzten Male eingeschmolzen, die Setzkästen endgültig in die Wohnzimmer abgewandert, die Schrift kommt jetzt aus dem Computer. Dafür, wie sie hineinkommt, gibt es Verfahren, die die Eigenart haben, komplizierte, anspruchsvolle Schriftbilder zu glätten. Adrian Frutiger, ein in Paris lebender Schweizer, hat dies verhindert. Er hat die „Tiemann", die wir in der *ZEIT* als einzige große Zeitung für die Überschriften nutzen, so neu gezeichnet, daß sie auch im elektronischen Satz die alte bleibt.

Marginalien alles? Gewiß nicht. Wir haben versucht, die äußere und innere Identität der *ZEIT* zu erhalten – auch gerade unter dem Druck unabweisbarer technischer und kaufmännischer Zwänge. Gleichwohl: Das Leben dieser Zeitung hat sich geändert, weil sich die Form ihrer Entstehung geändert hat. Daran können wir uns nicht vorbeimogeln. Verharmlosend nennen wir die technische Revolution, die unsere Arbeit umgekrempelt hat, „Neue Technik". Das ist die Begriffsbildung des Euphemisten, der, aus Furcht vor dem Teufel, ihn den „Gottseibeiuns" nennt. *Rainer Frenkel*

/01/

/02/
Sample of the original Tiemann-Antiqua *and* Tiemann-Antiqua *Kursiv (italic) with ligatures and oldstyle numerals.*

Walter Tiemann, the type designer, painter and teacher, chiefly known as a creator of gothic typefaces, designed *Tiemann-Antiqua* /02/ in 1922–23.[7] This typeface, with its neoclassical bearing, was a product of the Gebr. Klingspor type foundry (Offenbach am Main), which regularly entrusted artists with the design of their typefaces.[8] In 1923–26 an italic was developed for *Tiemann-Antiqua* and in 1925–27 a bold font /05/. In 1921, Walter Tiemann had already designed *Narziss*, an inline typeface of the 20th-century neoclassical character, which in a 1938 sample string was assigned to the *Tiemann-Antiqua* family /05/. Julius Rodenberg declared *Tiemann-Antiqua* "the first German antiqua of the new age"[9] by which he meant the typefaces available in Germany at the beginning of the 20th century.

At that time in Germany there was a renewal movement,[10] triggered by the creations of William Morris in England, who confronted what he saw as the weakness of 19th-century type designs by redrawing the typefaces of the 15th century, so that they matched those of the current century in form and quality.[11] Under the influence of this movement, various artists designed typefaces in a neo-renaissance style, amongst them Peter Behrens with his *Behrens-Mediaeval* of 1909, Walter Tiemann with *Tiemann-Mediaeval* in the same year, and Jakob Erbar with *Erbar-Mediaeval* in 1920. In Germany the question still arose over the use of gothic or antiqua, and several type

/03/
Headers from Die Zeit, *handset in* Tiemann-Antiqua.

Weltpolitik auf der Seufzerbrücke Übers Ziel hinaus

/04/
The 20th-century neoclassical foundry typeface Ratio-Latein *in the 'Feuilleton' supplement of* Die Zeit.

Zürich eine glückliche Stadt…?

/05/
Sample strings of Tiemann-Antiqua *from 1938 in normal, italic and bold; and sample strings of the light* Narziss.

TIEMANN **Antiqua**
TIEMANN *Antiqua-Kursiv*
TIEMANN **Antiqua, halbfett**
TIEMANN **Narziß**

/06/
The neoclassical typefaces Bodoni, Didot *and* Walbaum, *developed at the end of the 18th century.*

Bodoni
Didot
Walbaum

/07/
Typefaces of the 20th-century neoclassical group: Ratio-Latein *(1923),* Tiemann-Antiqua *(1923),* Egmont *(1932) and* Caledonia *(1938).*

Ratio-Latein
Tiemann-Antiqua
Egmont
Caledonia

designers tried at the beginning of the 20th century to unite the two styles. This situation gave rise to Otto Eckmann's *Eckmann*-Schrift (1900) and Peter Behrens' *Behrens*-Schrift (1901). All of this had an indirect effect on the gothic typefaces themselves, and attempts were made at a simplification and renewal of these designs, giving rise to neo-gothic types[12] such as *Deutsche Schrift* by Rudolf Koch (1910), *Hupp-Fraktur* (1911) and *Tiemann-Fraktur* (1914).

The 20th-century neoclassical antiquas would shortly undergo a renewal as well **/05/**. The year 1921 saw the arrival of *Winkelmann-Antiqua*, and *Ratio-Latein* and *Tiemann-Antiqua* followed in 1923. They possess – as do their 18th-century forebears *Bodoni*, *Didot* and *Walbaum* **/06/**, which was popular in Germany – an upright stress and a strong contrast between bold and thin stroke weights. In contrast to those earlier typefaces, however, the curves at the transitions from bold to fine strokes are more softly drawn, and the proportions of the caps differ more strongly **/11/**, which lends them a certain warmth and grace. The typefaces also have – where available – a true italic, and in *Tiemann*, the serifs and endings of the lowercase letters have angular curves.

Simultaneously with the German renewal of 20th-century neoclassical typefaces, there was a return to the original ones. In 1913, H. Berthold AG published *Didot-Antiqua*, and the Bauersche foundry produced *Bauer Bodoni* and *Baskerville-Antiqua*, both in 1924.[13]

/08/
The original ck- and ch-ligatures were taken over by Frutiger – however, they were not used in Die Zeit.

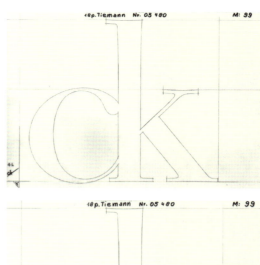

/09/
Headers from Die Zeit, *in Adrian Frutiger's CRT digital typeset version of* Tiemann.

Ein Hauch von rauher Wirklichkeit
Anfang oder Übergang?

/10/
Adrian Frutiger's newly drawn Tiemann light, *used in the 'Feuilleton' supplement of* Die Zeit.

Darf ich Ihnen die „Wolke" widmen?

/11/
*The 20th century neoclassical typeface (*Tiemann, top*) has differentiated cap widths – in the neoclassical (*Bodoni, bottom*) they are equal.*

/12/
Foundry Tiemann-Antiqua, *CRT digital type* Tiemann roman *and* light *(left to right) – the middle stroke of the E has been lengthened.*

/13/
Foundry Tiemann *(left) and CRT digital type* Tiemann roman *(right) – the angles of the W have changed to favour more white space.*

/14/
The descenders of p and q have been lengthened in the CRT digital type versions, and the serif of the q has been made the same as in p.

FGO on
FGO on

EEE

WW

pq pq

Typeface comparison The typefaces compared below were originally hot metal typefaces that were made available under new technologies. Walter Tiemann's *Tiemann-Antiqua* (1923), designed for handsetting for the Gebr. Klingspor foundry, was adapted for Linotype CRT digital typesetting by Frutiger in 1982, and was extended with a light version.

New Caledonia, based on William A. Dwiggins' *Caledonia*[14] (1938, Mergenthaler Linotype), was adapted for digital typesetting by John Quaranta in 1979.[15] *Fairfield*, designed in 1939 by Rudolf Růžička for Mergenthaler Linotype line-casting, was adapted for digital setting by Alex Kaczun in 1991. Both typefaces had other variants added to them.

All three typefaces can be classified under the 20th-century neoclassical group but have their own peculiarities. In *Tiemann-Antiqua*, the stem of the lowercase b and d ends with a rounding; and the M has splayed legs. Additionally – as is the case with *Fairfield* – the curve junctures are attached to the stem. *Fairfield*'s a c f and j show curve endings that display a thickening but do not end in a true teardrop serif. Also, in *New Caledonia* the teardrop serif is discrete, and the stem serifs are sometimes hairline and sometimes bracketed.[16]

In *Tiemann-Antiqua*, Adrian Frutiger made small changes between the hot metal and CRT digital type versions: the angles of W change in favour of lengthened hairlines **/13/**, and the middle stroke of the E is longer **/12/**.

A B C D E F G H I J K L M N O P Q R S T U V W X Y Z &
a b c d e f g h i j k l m n o p q r s t u v w x y z ß 1 2 3 4 5 6 7 8 9 0

/16/
Tiemann *exhibits the strongest connection to a 20th-century neoclassical antiqua through its marked thick/thin stroke contrast.*

Hofstainberg
New Caledonia
John Quaranta (William A. Dwiggins)
1979 (1938)

M Q W b f j n 2 5

Hofstainberg
Tiemann
Adrian Frutiger (Walter Tiemann)
1982 (1923)

M Q W b f j n 2 5

M	Q	W	b	f	j	n	2 5
Legs splayed	Vertical tail juncture	No middle serif	Angular juncture with stem, rounded serif juncture	Crossbar diagonally terminated	Small i-dot, termination without teardrop serif	Angular juncture with stem	Curves end both with and without teardrop serifs

Hofstainberg
Fairfield
Alex Kaczun (Rudolf Růžička)
1991 (1939)

M Q W b f j n 2 5

Font production:
Digitised by Linotype

Font format:
OpenType Com

Also available:
PostScript Type 1
TrueType

Tiemann™
Linotype
2 weights

ABCDEFGHIJKLMN
OPQRSTUVWXYZ&
abcdefghijklmnopqrs
tuvwxyzß1234567890

You may ask w hy so many differen t typefaces. They all serve th

e same purpose but they express man's di

versity. It is same diversity we find in wine. I once saw a list o f Médoc wines featuring sixty different Médocs all of the sa me year. All of them were wines but each was different from the others. It's the nuances that are important. The same is true for typefaces. Pourquoi tant d'Alphabets différents! To

us servent au même but, mais aussi à exprimer la diversité de l'homme. C'est cette m ême diversité que nous retrouvons dans les vins de Médoc. J'ai pu, un jour, relever s oixante crus, tous de la même année. Il s'agissait certes de vins, mais tous étaient dif férents. Tout est dans la nuance du bouquet. Il en est de même pour les caractères! S ie fragen sich, warum es notwendig ist, so viele Schriften zur Verfügung zu haben. Si e dienen alle zum selben, aber machen die Vielfalt des Menschen aus. Diese Vielfal t ist wie beim Wein. Ich habe einmal eine Weinkarte studiert mit sechzig Médoc-We

inen aus dem selben Jahr. Das ist ausnahmslos Wein, aber doch nicht alle s der gleiche Wein. Es hat eben gleichwohl Nuancen. So is es auch mit der Schrift. You may ask why so many different typefaces. They all serve the sa me purpose but they express man's diversity. It is the same diversity we fin d in wine. I once saw a list of Médoc wines featuring sixty different Médocs all of the same year. All of them were wines but each was different from the others. It's the nuances that are important. The same is true for typefac es. Pourquoi tant d'Alphabets différents! Tous servent au même but, mais

aussi à exprimer la diversité de l'homme. C'e st cette même diversité que nous retrouvons dans les vins de Médoc. J'ai pu, un jour, rele ver soixante crus, tous de la même année. Il s'agissait certes de vins, mais tous étaient di fférents. Tout est dans la nuance du bouquet. Il en est de même pour les caractères! Sie fr agen sich, warum es notwendig ist, so viele Schriften zur Verfügung zu haben. Sie diene n alle zum selben, aber machen die Vielfalt

ÅBÇDÈFG
HIJKLMÑ
ÔPQRŠTÜ
VWXYZ&
ÆŒ¥$£€
1234567890
åbçdéfghij
klmñôpqrš
tüvwxyzß
fi fl æ œ ø ł ð
[.,:;·'/‒–—]
(¿¡"«‹›»"!?)
{§°%@‰*†}

Light

ÅBÇDÈFG
HIJKLMÑ
ÔPQRŠTÜ
VWXYZ&
ÆŒ¥$£€
1234567890
åbçdéfghij
klmñôpqrš
tüvwxyzß
fi fl æ œ ø ł ð
[.,:;·'/‒–—]
(¿¡"«‹›»"!?)
{§°%@‰*†}

Roman

76 pt | −20   57 pt | −20   38 pt | −5   25 pt | 10   17 pt | 19 pt | 15   12 pt | 14 pt | 15   8.5 pt | 10.2 pt | 30   7 pt | 8 pt | 40

Name of typeface	Designer	Design | Publication	Typesetting technology	Manufacturer	Weights
Versailles	Adrian Frutiger	1982 | 1984	CRT and laser digital typesetting	– D. Stempel AG | Linotype	8
			PostScript digital typesetting	– Adobe | Linotype	8

VERSAILLES

Versailles came about from the realisation that there was a gap in the Linotype Type Library amongst the latin typefaces. Yes, *Méridien* (see page 60) is a latin typeface – and an elegant one at that – but it doesn't have the adornment that these typefaces exhibit. With *Versailles* I wanted to create a latin typeface that was well grounded historically. When I showed my design at one of the type selection meetings at Linotype /03/, Mike Parker[1] said: "That's it." It's not really heavily ornamented, without curlicues, just enough, so we can use it straight away. Linotype had been looking for gaps in the market, and my idea came along at just the right time. Actually, it came out of the conversations with Mike Parker during the meetings. We talked about whether *Méridien's* classical, tapered-end solution to the open curve of the a was better than, say, a more playful, horizontal solution /01/. The more playful solution with the thickening and the horizontal ending was chosen unanimously – and that was amongst about twelve people. This curve ending has practically the same weight as an a with a teardrop serif /17/. It's all about the regularity of the white space and the optical grey of the whole string.

Over a period of at least sixty years, from around 1840 right up to the Art Nouveau era, the latin typefaces were amongst the most widely used in France. At the start of my type design duties at Deberny & Peignot, I had spoken to Rémy Peignot about latin typefaces, and ever since then I'd had this style of typeface in the back of my mind, and I made studies of it repeatedly. I really wanted to design a true latin, at least once. I had the idea of raising the dead, reviving the elegance. When I was designing *Versailles,* I had Deberny & Peignot's type specimen book open before me, with its pages turned to *Latins Maigres* /10/ and *Latins Étroits* /11/. In terms of these templates, there were at least ten to twenty body typefaces in the type specimen book.

In my design, the curves of the letters a f g j r y have thickened horizontal endings. The s was also horizontal to start with /01/, but there I went back to the classical form with the half-serifs /17/. Even the c still had a horizontal termination in the original design. Later in the development that also became vertical. In one way, I suppose, that's of no consequence, but the c in classical typefaces has a teardrop serif, like a f j and r, and, in light of that, also had to have a horizontal ending. In the *Latins Étroits* by D&P, we find a c that has two different endings; horizontal in the larger point sizes, vertical in the smaller ones /11/. Perhaps that's where the influence comes from. A further explanation would be that the c with a horizontal ending could get confused with the e in the smaller point sizes. However, I think it was more of an intuitive solution, although, after the event, it's difficult to say what was due to gut instinct, and what was thought through. In any case, the readability wasn't the main reason for the reworking of *Versailles.* Whenever I've designed a typeface, I've always looked at the whole. The endings are a matter of optical balance with the weight.

Historically 'correct' latin typeface   The typeface *Versailles* has no particular connection with the palace southwest of Paris. The imposing compound at *Versailles* was already in existence at the beginning of neoclassicism in the 17th century, a good two hundred years before the development of latin typefaces. *Versailles* is, however, an embodiment of French culture and so is particularly suitable as the name for this typeface. Also, Frutiger is fond of strolling through the Palace grounds.

A historic Latin inscription can be found in another place: carved in marble at the *Opéra Garnier* – the *Grand Opéra* in Paris – on the Eugénie pavillion.[2]

With *Versailles,* Frutiger went back to the neoclassical forms. The 'Latines' index in the 1926 Deberny & Peignot *Spécimen Général* listed 14 Latin typefaces. In addition to these were 12 related typefaces, whose stroke endings exhibit (tri)angular emphases, but which are classified as Antique latinés, Orientales and Helléniques. However, in comparison with *Caractères Latins Maigres* /10/ and *Caractères Latins Larges* (see page 29), the inwards-arching curve endings are more reticently drawn in *Versailles.* In its proportions *Versailles* is closer to the *Latines Deuxième Série* /16/; however because of their clearly stronger stroke contrast, their orientation comes across as more vertical. Moreover, the serif junctures are somewhat less flowing, which lends them a harder edge.

In *Versailles,* Adrian Frutiger did not use his usual tapered strokes. This straightening might have been implemented for reasons of design alone, but could also be attributed to a consideration of the limitations of digital technology. Vectorisation, i. e. the description of curves through a series of short straight lines, did not yet allow for the same quality that had been a characteristic of earlier forms of production. However, compared to the beginning of the 1980s, some technological progress must have taken place, because Frutiger wrote in 1985: "Today I know about the refinement in reproduction and therefore my most recent typeface 'Versailles' – reconsidering earlier traditions of non-bitmapped setting technologies – has been deliberately designed using a more subtle stroke."[3]

In 1984 *Versailles* was released in 8 fonts for the Linotype CRT machines by D. Stempel AG; this release was followed slightly later by the additional publication of old style numerals and small capitals in the thin and regular fonts.[4] Since 1993 *Versailles* has been available as a PostScript font but without the aforementioned additions.

/02/
Versailles family concept – *the vertical stress and the horizontal curve endings allow for consistent extension.*

minim

minim minim

minim minim minim

minim minim

palme projekt

Heimat deine stimmen hallen im weitgeplanten friedlichen Hain. Inseln reihen sich wie girlanden zwischen den bewaldeten Hügeln. Immer wenn der Herbst in seinem milden farbenschein das Hohland verwandelt quillt ein klares Licht

/03/
Paste-up with reduced design sketches – the s and c still have a horizontal ending, and the w has a middle serif.

/04/
Test string of the typeface name – the transitions to the serifs are still uncupped, and the s still has a horizontal curve ending.

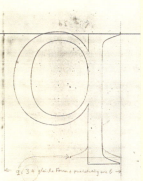

/06/
Five design drawings for ornaments and vignettes displaying a formal relationship to Versailles – these were never produced.

/05/
Design of the & (left) and the J with a playful variant (middle); and the lowercase q, derived from the b, with correction notes.

These days, I find the j a bit heavy in the bottom curve, almost plump /19/. There's too little contrast between the horizontal and vertical curve shapes. A similar criticism can be leveled at the top of the r /17/. It has a deep cut-in, but there, where it curves up to the horizontal, I find it too fat. It's just not elegant. For the lowercase g, I decided against the double-looped shape /18/. For me, the lowercase g, with its three counters is a classical form that belongs to a certain era. However, in *Versailles* I wanted to have a modern solution, even though I knew that the distinctive classical g is an aid to legibility. Even in Deberny & Peignot's *Latins Étroits,* the g has a single-looped shape /11/. Taken together with the legibility, maybe it wasn't the best choice, but when you see it in purely aesthetic terms as a line, then it works really well.

In the P and the Q there's a lot of tension, also in the curve of the D /20/. Look at the white space: it isn't symmetrical and yet it gives the impression of being so. And the fine junctures with the stem, you'll see what I mean. I'm surprised at my work – the D is just beautiful. The number 4 is unusual in that it is slightly convex /21/. The 2 and the 7 also exhibit curved diagonals /23/. I tried to inject a certain elegance there, so that it didn't look too hard in a line. That's something that the numbers all show, in contrast to the caps – they've got more verve. You can also see similar forms in the *Latins Maigres* /10/. The number 1 is a special case. For me, it has to be drawn a little stronger in the downstroke than in all the other numbers /21/. I always thought of lining figures based on the en width. Otherwise the 1, with its narrower form and the greater white space on both sides, would produce a lighter impression. The rounded guillemets – *Versaille's* quotation marks – are also a little unusual, I have to admit /22/. I found them more elegant: I found the pointed

Designing the curve endings A particular point to note in the latin typefaces is the make-up of the curve endings. These playful 'piglet's tails' – which is what they look like in, for example, the *Latines Deuxième Série* /16/ – did not sit well with Frutiger's ideas about a contemporary latin text type. The *Caractères Latins Maigres* /10/ were more what he had in mind. For *Versailles*, he chose similar curve endings, but terminated them horizontally rather than diagonally. While they were still strongly curved in the original design /01/, in the final version they are somewhat more relaxed. A further change between the original and the final design can be seen in the endings of lowercase c and s, which change from horizontal to vertical /17/. Therefore, for the c, Frutiger opted for the 'modern' form of the half-serif. This first appeared in lowercase c in the 19th century, as a formal harmonisation with capital C and lowercase s. Examples are *Caractères Latins Larges* and *Caractères Latins Étroits* /11/, the latter of which is, however, also available with inward curled curve ends. For the s, Frutiger opted for the usual half-serif shape. In contrast to the other round lowercase letters, the s had been drawn with half-serif endings in serif types for some time.

Historically, there has been a variety of ways of terminating these curve shapes. The a without emphasis /07/ derives from the handwritten form of the 15th century. The teardrop serif developed gradually over the next three centuries. /08/. The a also later got a half-serif /12/.

/07/
The form of the Renaissance a – as if written with a broad pen – was taken on by 20th-century typefaces.

/08/
Variations in curve endings from the 15th to the 18th centuries: Jenson, Garamond, Caslon, Fournier, Baskerville *and* Bodoni *(left to right).*

/09/
Stereotype for the packaging lettering from Deberny & Cie./Ch. Tuleu – the text in latin type was subsequently imprinted.

/10/
In Deberny & Peignot's Latins Maigres *the curve endings are cut diagonally, and only slightly curled.*

/11/
A type sample from Deberny & Peignot shows the upper curve ending of the lowercase c of Latins Étroits *in two variants.*

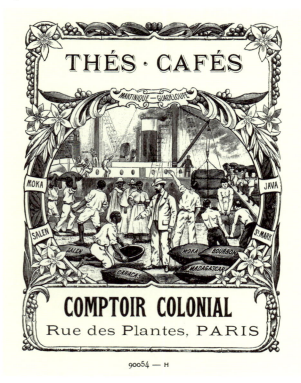

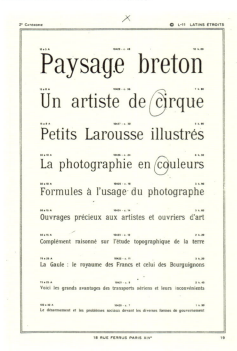

ITC latin typefaces at Linotype In the first half of the 20th century very few of the various type foundries were producing latin-style hot metal typefaces, and at the beginning of photosetting they played hardly any role. Founded in New York in 1970, the International Typeface Corporation (ITC) produced typefaces but not typesetting machines. They were, however, interested in bringing some of the more unusual designs into their catalogue. Subsequently, ITC sold licenses for their typefaces to the manufacturers of typesetting machines, for both their computer- and phototypesetting systems. One of ITC's licensees was Linotype. This gave them the rights to Ed Benguiat's *ITC Barcelona* (1981) **/28/** and Jovica Veljović's *ITC Veljovic* (1984) **/28/**, which was designed the same year as *Versailles*. Adrian Frutiger's *Versailles* was, therefore, not the only latin typeface available from Linotype that was designed in the 1980s, even if *ITC Veljovic* only appeared in their catalogue after 1984. The three typefaces each provide eight fonts, two sets of small caps and in addition to the lining figures either oldstyle – or small caps numerals. In addition, Adrian Frutiger must have considered providing *Versailles* with matching ornaments or vignettes. More than five design sketches were made but are not present in the final typeface **/06/**. Later, in *Linotype Didot* (see page 362), Frutiger was able to bring these ideas to fruition.

ones too hard. If anything should be criticised, it's that I simply drew an inclined font instead of a true italic **/18/**. In Deberny & Peignot's type catalogue, there are a few cursive latins, and I find the elegance of this typeface lies somewhere else.[5] Finally, I drew the letters a little lighter, since an italic is, of course, lighter than a roman.

Versailles appeared in 1983. Originally it was vectorised **/25/**. At the start, when you digitised a typeface, you'd get 'jaggies' – awful to look at, and way too much information needed to be stored for a single letter. Later, it was reduced by vectorising, since you could account for ten pixels with a single segment. Later came Bézier curves.[6] In spite of the technical shortcomings of the period, I still view *Versailles* in a very positive light. I never understood why it wasn't a success. Even though there was a comprehensive prospectus **/24/**, with all the typefaces that I had designed for Linotype – *Versailles* amongst them – maybe they just didn't advertise it enough.[7] It was a very well-constructed typeface, with four bold weights and the corresponding cursives, with lowercase numerals and also small caps in the normal and light versions **/26/**. In the era of CRT and laser typesetting you had all these things that people put a lot of store by in the early eighties. It brought money in: they could charge a good price for the fonts, since they were so comprehensive. Unfortunately, in the later PostScript version the lowercase numerals and the small caps were dropped.

/12/
Hooked curve endings in the lowercase a of the latins of the 19th century and half-serifs in typefaces of the 20th.

/13/
Tapered curve endings in Méridien (left), teardrop serifs in Iridium (middle) and uncial endings in Versailles (right).

aaa

/14/
Frutiger designed the curve endings of his three latin typefaces differently: Président, Méridien and Versailles (from left to right).

222

/15/
Varying shapes of the serifs and serif junctures in Frutiger's latin typefaces Président, Méridien and Versailles (from left to right).

/16/
Deberny & Peignot's Latins Deuxième Série exhibits a reduced stroke contrast and curve endings with a strong inward curl.

/17/
In the neoclassical Iridium (top), the c has a teardrop serif, in Versailles (bottom) the c and the s both exhibit half-serifs.

acrs
acrs

/18/
Versailles has an oblique, but no italic font, although a true cursive is available in Latins Noirs Italiques.

aeg
aeg

/19/
The curve endings of gj and y appear to be identical, but are different in terms of position, shape and weight.

gjy

/20/
Dynamic forms and counter-forms; the curves are not equal and the counters have no right angles.

DPQ

/21/
In order to lend it sufficient clarity in the lining figures, the stroke and serifs of the 1 are clearly heavier.

14

/22/
Round guillemets – like those in Versailles – already existed in Philippe Grandjean's Romain du Roi (1694–1714).

(( )) (( ))

ABCDEFGHIJKLMN OPQRSTUVWXYZ& abcdefghijklmnopqrs tuvwxyzß1234567890

Determining the letter spacing   Setting text using a computer forces the standard kerning value to be 0. However this setting is often not appropriate, since the letter spacing depends upon the style of typeface, its weight and its point size. In hot metal setting the relationship between these three parameters was resolved by the type designer and manufacturer, and was determined by the body size. However, since the introduction of non-mechanical photosetting, the user has been responsible for the letter spacing.

Unfortunately, the type manufacturers have failed to specify a consistently defined null value for their typefaces. They have also failed to provide any information about which point sizes are to be used with the standard kerning value of 0. For every typeface – even for every font – the letter spacing has to be determined by repeated trial and error. However, the letter spacing is crucial for legibility and for an appealing, harmonious composition. Basically, the letters must not clump together, and neither should they be too strung out.

Generally the rule is: smaller point sizes need wider letter spacing, and larger point sizes need narrower letter spacing (see facing page). For Frutiger's text types for Linotype this meant that in normal text sizes, they should always be set with a positive kerning value. Furthermore, light typefaces also need generous letter spacing, since large counters call for large spacing. On the other hand, bold and narrow typefaces can be set somewhat tighter.

/24/
Dustcover and inside front page – the 1983 brochure contains all of the Frutiger typefaces available from Linotype.

/25/
Greatly enlarged numeral 5 from the brochure – the vectors that make up the curves in CRT digital typesetting are clearly recognisable.

5

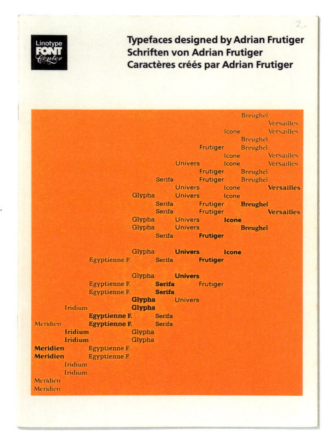

Versailles

ABCDEFGHIJKLMNO
PQRSTUVWXYZ
abcdefghijklmnopqrstu
vwxyz& 1234567890
.,:;?!-—'''»«*/§%

05311   Versailles™ 55 roman/normal/romain   12   **143**   (15)

abcdefghijklmnopqrstuvwxyz
ABCDEFGHIJKLMNOPQRSTUVW
XYZ 1234567890 1234567890 .,:;:''«»&!?

Håmbûrgefönstiv iam admodum Mɪᴛɪɢᴀᴛɪ Rᴀᴘᴛᴀʀᴜᴍ Aɴɪᴍɪ era
nt sed earum parentes tum maxime sordida veste lacrimisque et

Font production:
Adobe Font digitised by
Linotype

Font format:
PostScript Type 1

Also available:
TrueType
OpenType Com

Versailles™
Linotype
8 weights (+CE)

ABCDEFGHIJKLMN
OPQRSTUVWXYZ&
abcdefghijklmnopqrs
tuvwxyzß1234567890

Pourquoi tant
d'Alphabets différ
ents! Tous servent au mêm

e but, mais aussi à exprimer la diversité

de l'homme. C'est cette même diversité que nous retrouv
ons dans les vins de Médoc. J'ai pu, un jour, relever soixa
nte crus, tous de la même année. Il s'agissait certes de vi
ns, mais tous étaient différents. Tout est dans la nuance
du bouquet. Il en est de même pour les caractères! *Sie fr*

agen sich, warum es notwendig ist so viele Schriften zur Verfügung zu haben. Sie di
enen alle zum selben, aber machen die Vielfalt des Menschen aus. Diese Vielfalt ist
wie beim Wein. Ich habe einmal eine Weinkarte studiert mit sechzig Médoc-Weine
n aus dem selben Jahr. Das ist ausnahmslos Wein, aber doch nicht alles der gleich
e Wein. Es hat eben gleichwohl Nuancen. So ist es auch mit der Schrift. *You may a*
sk why so many different typefaces. They all serve the same purpose but they expre
ss man's diversity. It is the same diversity we find in wine. I once saw a list of Médo

c wines featuring sixty different Médocs all of the same year. All of th
em were wines but each was different from the others. It's the nuance
s that are important. The same is true for typefaces. *Pourquoi tant d'Al*
phabets différents! Tous servent au même but, mais aussi à exprimer
la diversité de l'homme. C'est cette même diversité que nous retrouvo
ns dans les vins de Médoc. J'ai pu, un jour, relever soixante crus, tous
de la même année. Il s'agissait certes de vins, mais tous étaient différe
nts. Tout est dans la nuance du bouquet. Il en est de même pour les! *Si*

e fragen sich, warum es notwendig ist, so vie
le Schriften zur Verfügung zu haben. Sie dien
en alle zum selben, aber machen die Vielfalt
des Menschen aus. Diese Vielfalt ist wie bei
m Wein. Ich habe einmal eine Weinkarte stu
diert mit sechzig Médoc-Weinen aus dem se
lben Jahr. Das ist ausnahmslos Wein, aber d
och nicht alles der gleiche Wein. Es hat eben
gleichwohl Nuancen. So ist es auch mit der
Schrift. *You may ask why so many different*

65 pt | –25   49 pt | –15   33 pt | –10   22 pt | –5   15 pt | 19 pt | 0   10 pt | 13 pt | 12   7.5 pt | 10.2 pt | 15   6 pt | 8 pt | 20

ÅBÇDÈFG
HIJKLMÑ
ÔPQRŠTÜ
VWXYZ&
ÆŒ¥$£€
1234567890
åbçdéfghij
klmñôpqrš
tüvwxyzß
fi fl æ œ ø ł ð
[.,:;·'/-–—]
(¿¡"«‹›»"!?)
{§°%@‰*†}

45 Light

ÅBÇDÈFG
HIJKLMÑ
ÔPQRŠTÜ
VWXYZ&
ÆŒ¥$£€
1234567890
åbçdéfghij
klmñôpqrš
tüvwxyzß
fi fl æ œ ø ł ð
[.,:;·'/-–—]
(¿¡"«‹›»"!?)
{§°%@‰†}*

46 Light Italic

ÅBÇDÈFG
HIJKLMÑ
ÔPQRŠTÜ
VWXYZ&
ÆŒ¥$£€
1234567890
åbçdéfghij
klmñôpqrš
tüvwxyzß
fi fl æ œ ø ł ð
[.,:;·'/-–—]
(¿¡"«‹›»"!?)
{§°%@‰*†}

55 Roman

ÅBÇDÈFG
HIJKLMÑ
ÔPQRŠTÜ
VWXYZ&
ÆŒ¥$£€
1234567890
åbçdéfghij
klmñôpqrš
tüvwxyzß
fi fl æ œ ø ł ð
[.,:;·'/-–—]
(¿¡"«‹›»"!?)
{§°%@‰†}*

56 Italic

ÅBÇDÈFG
HIJKLMÑ
ÔPQRŠTÜ
VWXYZ&
ÆŒ¥$£€
1234567890
åbçdéfghij
klmñôpqrš
tüvwxyzß
fi fl æ œ ø ł ð
[.,:;·'/-–—]
(¿¡"«‹›»"!?)
{§°%@‰*†}

75 Bold

ÅBÇDÈFG
HIJKLMÑ
ÔPQRŠTÜ
VWXYZ&
ÆŒ¥$£€
1234567890
åbçdéfghij
klmñôpqrš
tüvwxyzß
fi fl æ œ ø ł ð
[.,:;·'/-–—]
(¿¡"«‹›»"!?)
{§°%@‰*†}

76 Bold Italic

Typeface comparison   There is a large variation in the formal characteristics among the latin typefaces. Therefore a definitive description of their form is possible only with some difficulty. Along with their scarcity and lack of impact in the 1950s, this is perhaps one reason why the typefaces with (tri)angular serifs have been refused their own typeface classification. According to its serif weight and stroke contrast, each latin typeface was assigned to one of the following categories in the Vox, ATypI and DIN systems; renaissance-, baroque-, slab serif antiqua, antiqua variants or incises. Therefore, in the 1986 LinoType-Collection, *ITC Barcelona* is found under antiqua variants, Frutiger's *Versailles* under the baroque-antiquas and *ITC Veljovic* under the renaissance-antiquas – an altogether unsatisfactory classification.

With *ITC Barcelona*, Ed Benguiat had created a latin type with a light stroke contrast and with inward curled curve endings, combined with slab serifs, even in the lower case c. In contrast, with its flattened (tri)angular serifs and heavier stroke contrast, *ITC Veljovic* comes across as more pointed, and the asymmetrical curve forms lend it a dynamic appearance. *Versailles,* however, is static. Only the numerals introduce a playful element. Altogether the effect is peaceful, clear, balanced and elegant, but at the same time distant. Each letter stands alone, self-consistent, self-sufficient. It is wholly due to its courtly appearance that *Versailles* earns its name.

/27/
Measurements of stroke widths and proportions of the Versailles *regular weight.*

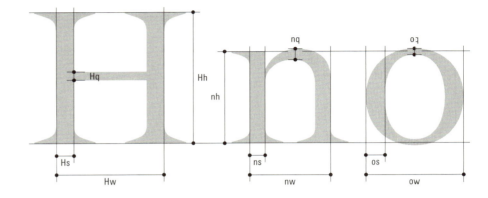

Roman					
Hh = 10.00 cm	nh = 6.96 cm	oh = 7.40 cm	Hh : Hw = 1 : 0.79	nh : nw = 1 : 0.85
Hw = 7.93	nw = 5.92	ow = 7.18	Hw : Hs = 1 : 0.16	nw : ns = 1 : 0.19
Hs = 1.30	ns = 1.14	os = 1.39	Hs : Hq = 1 : 0.49	nh : oh = 1 : 1.06
Hq = 0.64	nq = 0.85	oq = 0.48		nw : ow = 1 : 1.21

/28/
By eschewing the 'piglet's tails', Versailles *has a more balanced, peaceful aspect than either* ITC Barcelona *(top) or* ITC Veljovic *(bottom).*

Hofstainberg

ITC Barcelona
Edward Benguiat
1981

J K P a c j w 2 4

Hofstainberg

Versailles
Adrian Frutiger
1984

J K P a c j w 2 4

J
Curve ending with half-serif

K
Angle of the legs meets stem at a point

P
Angular juncture with the stem, below slightly rising

a
Curve end flared, terminated horizontally

c
Top curve ends with half-serif, bottom is tapered

j
Curve end flared, terminated horizontally

w
Apex lacks serif

2 4
Curved diagonals, horizontal crossbars only slightly flaring

Hofstainberg

ITC Veljovic
Jovica Veljović
1984

J K P a c j w 2 4

Comparison showing the different weights and angle of the obliques.

	Hh	Hw	Hs	Hq
Light	10.00 cm	7.69 = 0.97	0.94 = 0.72	0.49 = 0.76
Roman	10.00	7.93 = 1	1.30 = 1	0.64 = 1
Bold	10.00	8.71 = 1.10	1.97 = 1.51	0.78 = 1.22
Black	10.00	9.67 = 1.22	2.89 = 2.22	1.03 = 1.61
Italic	10.00	7.75 = 0.98	1.19 = 0.91	0.57 = 0.89

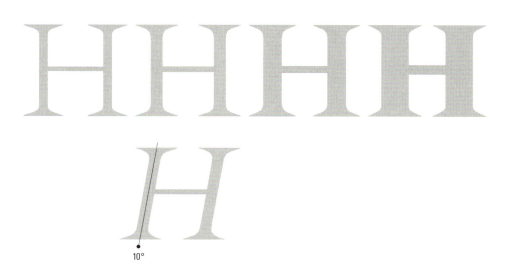

10°

ÅBÇDÈFG
HIJKLMÑ
ÔPQRŠTÜ
VWXYZ&
ÆŒ¥$£€0
123456789
åbçdéfghij
klmñôpqrš
tüvwxyzß
fi fl æ œ ø ł ð
[.,:;·'/-–—]
(¿¡"«‹›»"!?)
{§°%@‰*†}

95 Black

ÅBÇDÈFG
HIJKLMÑ
ÔPQRŠTÜ
VWXYZ&
ÆŒ¥$£€0
123456789
åbçdéfghij
klmñôpqrš
tüvwxyzß
fi fl æ œ ø ł ð
[.,:;·'/-–—]
(¿¡"«‹›»"!?)
{§°%@‰†}*

96 Black Italic

Height comparison showing the differences of x-heights to ascenders and descenders – the cap height is the starting point.

ITC Barcelona
42.9 pt

Versailles
40.1 pt

ITC Veljović
45.7 pt

Logos and wordmarks
1979–1983

Haas Fotocomposition Fonts
typeface manufacturer
Münchenstein (CH)
Design not implemented

Verband landeskirchlicher
Gemeinschaften des Kantons Bern
Christian organization
Bern (CH)

Atlantic Institute
international institute for
economic, political and cultural
procurement
Paris (F)

Sogreah-Sogelerg-Sedim
institute for engineering sciences
Paris (F)

Autoroute Rhône et Alpes
society for motorways of the
Rhône et Alpes département
Bron (F)

Association des
Sociétés Françaises d'Autoroutes
Association of
French motorway companies
Paris (F)
Design: Lucette Girard

Christlicher Sängerbund
der Schweiz
Christian organisation
Switzerland

PTT – Schweizer Reisepost
postal bus company
Bern (CH)

Animation des Autoroutes
Art et Archéologie
Paris (F)
Design: Brigitte Rousset
Design not implemented

Winkel Verlag
publishing house
Basel (CH)

CGE Novelerg
renewable energy sources
company
Paris (F)
Design: Brigitte Rousset

PTT – Post Telegraf Telefon
Swiss post and
telecommunications company
Bern (CH)

CGE Distribution
electrical appliance company
Montrouge (F)

Scoricentres – Société nationale
pour la vente des scories Thomas
State Company for
Mining Slag Exploitation
Paris (F)

Philippe Lebaud
publisher
Paris (F)

Musée National de la Renaissance
Château d'Écouen
Écouen (F)

400 years of the Haas'sche
type foundry
commemorative logo
Münchenstein (CH)

Collection Colibri
edition by Hallwag Verlag
Bern (CH)

Küppersbusch Systeme
construction of packing plants
Velbert (D)

Musée de Grenoble
art museum
Grenoble (F)

Domaine Universitaire
Pessac (F)
Design: Adrian Frutiger
and Gérard Ifert

Production of type
Lasersetting

The term 'laser' is an acronym for 'Light Amplification by Stimulated Emission of Radiation'. In laser printing a light beam is used to produce a small, sharp, intensely focused point of light on the material to be printed. The light concentration is many times higher than that of other light sources.

During exposure the light beam horizontally traverses the material (film, photographic paper, or, since 1993, computer-to-plate systems). As it does so, it is switched on and off, corresponding to the shape of the letter. In contrast to the vertical exposure in CRT systems, the laser system produces a better text appearance at the same resolution /03/. Varying the typeface, point size and line spacing have no affect on the speed of the light beam.

In 1976 the British Monotype Corporation introduced the Lasercomp, a pioneering machine for the laser exposure of digitised typefaces. In the United States Mergenthaler Linotype followed suit in 1979 with its compact Omnitech 2000 system. Exposure and setting were combined in a single unit. Linotronic 300,

a more affordable machine with a separate exposure unit was introduced in 1984 /01/. An upstream RIP (raster image processor) enabled the high-resolution output of PostScript data and provided a connection to a Apple Macintosh computer. A newer development, which provides greater economy and is more environmentally friendly, is the direct exposure of the printing plates – the 'Computer-to-Plate' process – rendering the film exposure stage unnecessary.

Essentially, every lasersetter consists of the RIP and recorder modules, which can be housed together or in separate units. The RIP consists of random access memory (RAM) and a processor that converts the raw PostScript data into commands that control the exposure laser. Additionally, storage units (hard disk) increase the number of typefaces that are available. The model A of the Linotronic 200P also held a 20 MB hard disk, which was capable of storing some 150 typefaces at resolutions of 250, 333 and 500 lines/cm. The 80 MB hard disk of the model B could store 1000

typefaces and offered the additional resolution of 666 lines/cm.

The recorder only started with the exposure when the entire calculation process had been completed. According to the desired quality, the exposure resolution could be set to either 1270 or 2540 dpi, and with some models up to 3251 dpi. As well as typefaces, lasersetters also offered the ability to render rules and halftones.

The light sources in laser imagesetters were originally based on the technically elaborate helium-neon gas laser. The necessary modulator interrupted the laser beam, corresponding to signals from the RIP and the desired scan-line length. This complex piece of machinery would often break down in the Linotronic 200P, and a more consistent performance was later achieved by replacing it with longer-lasting laser diodes.

/01/
The Linotype Linotronic 300 lasersetter (in front) can be directly connected to the developing machine (behind).

/02/
Diagram of the path of the light beam through a Linotronic 300 – the exposure can be achieved across the entire width of the photographic material.

/03/
Vertical CRT exposure (left) shows problems with steeply diagonal lines, lasersetting (right) with less steep ones.

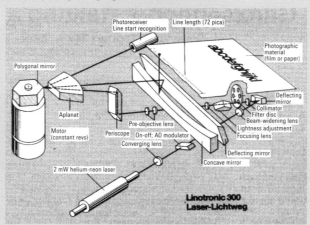

/04/
Digitising typefaces for lasersetting was done using the Ikarus system – tight radii need more closely clustered points.

/05/
In contrast to photosetting, where the exposure is done on a letter-by-letter basis, in lasersetting entire pages are set line-by-line.

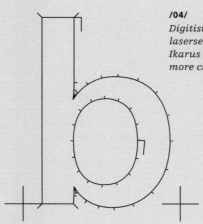

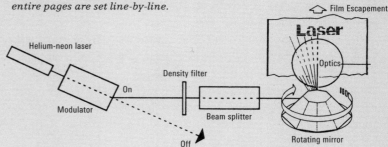

Name of typeface	Client	Designer	Design | Publication	Typesetting technology	Manufacturer	Weights
Linotype Centennial	Linotype	Adrian Frutiger	1985 | 1986	CRT and laser digital typesetting	– Linotype	8
				PostScript digital typesetting	– Adobe | Linotype	8

LINOTYPE
CENTENNIAL

Centennial was a commissioned typeface. Linotype wanted to release a new typeface in 1986 to celebrate the 100th anniversary of its linecasting machine.[1] It was supposed to be an all-purpose face in which any text could be set, like a rival to the ubiquitous *Times* by Monotype. Linotype already had *Excelsior* for newspapers, and paperback books in Germany relied heavily on Hermann Zapf's *Aldus.* Yet *Times* had a different status. If one didn't know which font to go for, *Times* was used. It was easy for graphic designers who were too lazy to think. That's the sort of typeface Linotype was after.

At the same time Olaf Leu[2] was looking for a 'more readable' *Bodoni.* He was very clear in formulating what kind of typeface it ought to be: a narrow, neoclassical serif face – strong, easily legible and not too contrasty.

Those were the starting points. With them in mind I drew the first sketches and test settings, which went relatively quickly. Olaf Leu was the critical eye, together we would discuss what worked and what didn't. Making *Centennial* was a considerable effort. There were two design sizes, 12 pt for body text and 18 pt for headlines /30/. In the end only eight months passed from the first draft through to the finished typeface. We had a fixed date, besides which 1986 was also a drupa[3] year. Accordingly, the typeface was pushed, marketing-wise, and a communications concept was worked out for its launch /12/.

It's interesting to look at *Centennial* with hindsight and see what lives up to the requirements and what doesn't. This has nothing to do with the quality of the typeface itself, but with the starting position. The job specification names ten criteria for the new typeface; it should be easily and quickly legible, normal, universal, lively, handy, robust, tight, proud, stable, and classical in the modern sense of the word.

'Easily and quickly legible' – that had to be defined more precisely. Is a neoclassical face ever appropriate for quick reading? Compared to other neoclassical faces like *Bodoni* /17/, as mentioned in the concept, or *Madison* /18/ it certainly is. *Centennial* has less of a marked thick-thin contrast, thus minimising the typical flickering effect which hampers legibility. 'Normal' is a pretty vague term. *Centennial* isn't really a normal reading face because it's so narrow, but on the other hand its attenuated contrast between hairline strokes and thick downstrokes, its open shapes and large x-height, make it good for normal text setting. 'Universal', what does that mean? There's no such thing as a universal typeface, seeing as there are two distinct groups to start with, sans serif and serif. *Centennial* can be employed universally, be it newspapers, magazines or books in any language based on the Latin alphabet, for any printing method or kind of paper. However, it's not truly universal, it's too influenced by the neoclassical style. 'Lively'? It's not very lively compared to a normal width transitional face, but still livelier than the strict *Bodoni.* 'Handy' is a term I like. Handy shapes are immediately recognised by the human eye. *Centennial* has

Linotype's demands The type manufacturer had high expectations for the success of *Linotype Centennial,* which has been confirmed by various sources. An 'internal communication' by René Kerfante, then department director of type production, on 21 February 1986 reads; "Linotype Centennial has to become as successful as the classic Times! The reason is that Linotype isn't releasing just any new typeface (to go with the many existing ones), but a type concept." /01/

To market this type concept, an outside consultant was employed, even though Linotype had an internal marketing department. Bodo Rieger produced a 16-page communication concept, in which he describes the requirements, starting position and needs, marketing and product concept, positioning of the typeface style and target groups, and how the concept applies to advertising wording /12/. These high expectations were echoed in the journal *DruckIndustrie,* where it was compared to *Helvetica:* "The aim was not merely to follow Helvetica, the classic modern typeface, with a modern classic typeface, but to stand up alongside it." [4] /03/

Linotype Centennial had to live up to a great many expectations. Economically, it was supposed to compete with *Times;* in its application it was supposed to be *Bodoni* with improved legibility; and it was supposed to be something exceptional to celebrate 100 years since the first Linotype typesetting machine was made in 1886. Its name is derived from the Latin word for a hundred, 'centum'. The addition of 'Linotype' to the name was made both to indicate its origin and to avoid confusion with *Bell Centennial,* a typeface designed by Matthew Carter for telephone directories, commissioned in 1976 to mark the centenary of AT&T, the American telephone company.[5]

Eight weights plus old style figures of Linotype Centennial are published in 1986. The 1987 catalogue does not contain the small caps for the 45 and 55 weights /32/ and they are missing altogether from the 1988 Linotype catalogue for PostScript fonts.[6] Initially mostly classic typefaces were adapted, and *Linotype Centennial* had not made an impact on the market in the two years that it had been available. *Bodoni* was the only neoclassical face to be included. *Linotype Centennial* was first made available as a PostScript typeface in 1992.

1986 Linotype internal communication concerning the rival typeface Times Roman.

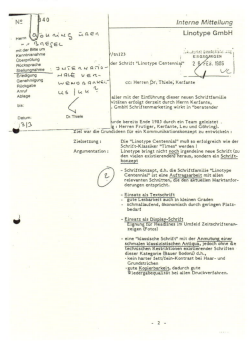

/02/

Page from a Linotype advertising portfolio comparing other neoclassical typefaces.

Die Schrift. die nichts weiter sein will als die Schrift. die sich nicht vordrängt, weil sie dem Wort Platz macht, die Schrift, die der Gestalt der Gedanken dient.

Bemerkenswert. weil sie nicht besonders bemerkt werden will. Sie hat Schriftzeiten hinter sich und Zeiten der Schrift vor sich. Sie schafft es, klassisch und digital zugleich zu sein. 100 Jahre Schrifterfahrung haben mitgewirkt, aus ihr die Antiqua fürs Digital-Zeitalter zu machen. Für alles Klein- und Großgedruckte, für alle Druckverfahren.

Jede Zeit hat ihre Schrift – jede Schrift hat ihre Zeit.

LinotypeCentennial.* Die Schrift.

Wenn Sie mehr über die Linotype Centennial wissen wollen, sprechen Sie mit Linotype. Telefon 069-6068 227.

/04/

Advertisement from one of the campaigns designed by Olaf Leu for Linotype Centennial.

Antiqua fürs Digital-Zeitalter

Zum 100jährigen Jubiläum von Ottmar Mergenthalers Erfindung stellt Linotype mit der «Centennial» ein neues Schriftkonzept vor. Befragungen in Verlagen und Werbeagenturen ergaben eine aktuelle Nachfrage nach einer klassischen und zugleich universellen Schrift. Ergänzende Untersuchungen von existierenden Schriften und eigenen Beständen an Originalvorlagen führten zu einem neuen Schriftkonzept. Mit der Umsetzung und Ausgestaltung wurde Adrian Frutiger beauftragt. Ziel war. der Helvetica, der Schrift der klassischen Moderne, eine Schrift der modernen Klassik nicht nur folgen zu lassen, sondern komplementär gegenüberzustellen. Der klassische Gestus der Antiqua sollte erhalten bleiben und zugleich den komplexen Anforderungen unseres Digital-Zeitalters entsprochen werden. Die technischen Gegebenheiten der modernen Laser- und CRT-Belichter wurden bei der Gestaltung benso berücksichtigt wie die Erfordernisse des Offset- und des Tiefdrucks.

/03/

Article from the trade journal 'DruckIndustrie' no.11/1986 – Helvetica *is used as a reference.*

/05/
Design drawing of a narrow weight, made to test the limits of what is possible.

/06/
Design and digitisation drawing for a bold extended version that was never realised.

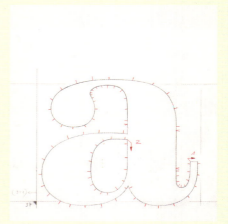

/07/
Sketch showing optimum serif thickness in the light weight, using the letter m, with three different thicknesses.

/08/
Fine-tuning of serif transition bracketing and upstroke, combined with different serif thicknesses.

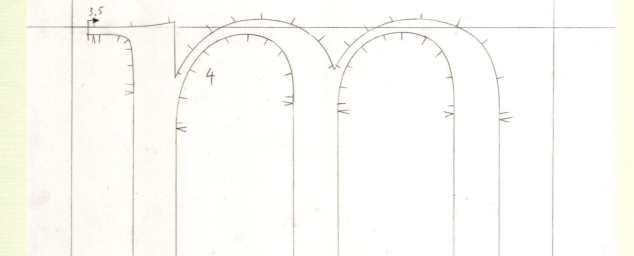

/09/
Self-made stencil from IBM material for drawing serifs and bowed stems for Linotype Centennial.

Characterisation of type Typographers believe that typefaces can influence our perception of words beyond their definition alone, drawing on emotions and associations. This has been scientifically confirmed.

In his 1957 book *The Measurement of Meaning,* psychologist and communication scientist Charles E. Osgood separated two different word definitions: denotative (main definition) and connotative. To measure connotative meaning, Osgood developed the semantic differential. A slight variation on the quantitative analysis of subjective meaning was developed by Peter Hofstätter. His polarity profiles are based on a mostly seven-step scale, in which the opposite poles have terms such as hot/cold and so on.[7]

In 1968 Dirk Wendt applied the semantic differential to typography and claimed that every typeface creates its own impression. For his experiment he selected twelve adjectives on a five-step scale from 'very' to 'not at all': elegant, classic, kitschy, dynamic, matter-of-fact, customary, natural, cumbersome, manly, harmonious, decorative, and technical.[8] More recently Christian Gutschi has worked on this subject.[9]

The 1986 communication concept for *Linotype Centennial* also used several adjectives to determine the positioning of the typeface and help place it in the market /12/.

Domverbau
Domverbau

/10/
Design for a waisted sans serif to complement Linotype Centennial *(top) – conceived in the 1990s as an extension into a typeface family (see page 157).*

/11/
Werner Schimpf and Adrian Frutiger discussing one of the designs.

/12/
Extract from the marketing concept by Bodo Rieger for the positioning of Linotype Centennial.

- 3 -

2. Die Ausgangssituation

Es werden am deutschen Markt etwa 2.500 verschiedene Schriften angeboten, verfügbar sind etwa 20.000, allein Linotype bietet zwischen 1.600 und 1.900 Schriftgarnituren an, das entspricht etwa 600 Schriftfamilien.

Angesichts dieses Überangebots an Schriften sind Marktlücken nicht ohne weiteres definierbar.

Deshalb ist man bei Linotype methodisch konsequent daran gegangen, zuerst die eigenen Schriften zu analysieren, um herauszufinden, welche für eine Aktualisierung und Renovation am besten geeignet sein könnten. Darüber hinaus hat man die sogenannte "Schatzkammer" durchforscht nach Schriften, die eine Entdeckung wert sind. Zum zweiten hat man das Angebot des Wettbewerbs gründlich untersucht und schließlich zum dritten mit führenden Köpfen das grafischen Gewerbes diskutiert, um herauszufinden, in welche Richtung die Nachfrage geht, wo noch Bedarf besteht.

Dabei stellte es sich heraus, daß durchaus eine aktuelle Nachfrage nach einer klassischen und zugleich universellen Schrift besteht.

Das führte zur Definition des Projektes Linotype-Centennial.

- 4 -

3. Die Bedarfssituation

Wir haben die Problematik des Überangebots an Schriften im Markt und zugleich die Tendenz, daß sich viele Schriften als Typus ähneln oder überschneiden. Es gibt übergenug Adaptionen und Imitationen. Viele Schrift-Angebote sind ganz einfach "me too".

Kein Schriftgestalter kann und wird dieses Riesen-Angebot in seinem vollen Umfang jemals nutzen.

"Ein Schriftgestalter braucht nicht mehr als 60 - 80 Schriftfamilien", sagt Professor Olaf Leu.

Daraus folgt, daß es nicht so sehr um ein Mehr an neuen Schriften geht - im Sinne echter Innovation -, sondern vielmehr darum, eine echte Erweiterung des Enssembles der Basisschriften anzuvisieren. Individualschriften gibt es reichlich, jedoch ist die Palette der Basisschriften begrenzt. Hier konnte die Marktlücke fixiert werden.

- 5 -

Es kommt ein weiteres spezifisches Antiqua-Problem hinzu - nämlich die Tatsache, daß reine Buchdruckschriften, wie z.B. die Bodoni, sich bislang schlecht für eine Digitalisierung eigneten, weil sie in ihrer Ursprungsform ideal für den Zeitungsdruck zugeschnitten waren. Das betrifft z. B. auch die "Times" mit ihren fetten Versalien. Diese Schriften sind für unsere heutigen Druck- und Lese-Verhältnisse zu kontrastreich und produzieren im Offset-Druck ein optisches Flimmern. Das war beim früheren Buchdruck unproblematisch und wurde vom Drucker mit seiner Erfahrung und seinem Fingerspitzengefühl ausgeglichen.

Die neue Werkschrift als Basisschrift soll für eine breitere Anwendung geeignet sein, vor allem, was die Ideal-Gerade zwischen 10 und 15 Punkt anbelangt. Gesucht ist eine Schrift für alle Text-Zwecke, von der Tabelle über den Katalog bis zum Zeitungs- und Anzeigensatz, eine Schrift für alle Druckverfahren. Sie soll so etwas wie eine universelle Problemlösung sein, indem sie die Vorzüge einer Antiqua-Schrift nutzt und zugleich die bereits erwähnten Nachteile eliminiert.

- 6 -

4. Das Marketing-Konzept

Eine Alternative zu dem bisherigen Marktführer für Antiqua-Schriften, der Times, zu schaffen, die als universelle Basis-Schrift gleichermaßen den Bedürfnissen nach klassischer Haltung und zeitgemäßer Technik-Entsprechung genügt.

Das neue Schrift-Konzept ist gefordert, nicht die absolut neue Schrift. Die Schrift als Produkt soll das Ergebnis konzeptioneller Arbeit sein, welche die Grundmuster für die Gestaltungsarbeit vorzeichnet.

- 7 -

5. Das Produkt-Konzept

Ausgangspunkt war die "Werk-Bodoni", eine Schrift die nicht den breiten Verlauf, also keine quadratischen Buchstaben als Gestalt hat, sondern schmaler und höher läuft, also eher zum Rechteck sich orientiert und dafür mehr Buchstaben in die Zeile bringt. Eine Schrift, die weniger Kontrast und damit weniger Flimmern verursacht. Gleichzeitig wurden die Madison und ihr Vorläufer, die Amts-Antiqua, sowie die Century in die Überlegungen mit einbezogen. Es sind acht Schnitte für Text und weitere acht für Display vorgesehen, die Kursiv-Formen in den vier Graden fein, normal, halbfett und fett.

Die meisten Leseschriften sind entweder zu glatt oder zu nüchtern oder zu stur, sie ermüden. Mit der Linotype-Centennial wurde das Ziel verfolgt, das Lesen lebendiger zu gestalten und damit auch eine Schrift zu machen, die jeder Texter gerne akzeptiert.

- 8 -

6. Die Positionierung

Die Marktlücke wird dort gesehen, wo ein Bedarf besteht für eine Schrift mit dem Gestus der klassischen Antiqua, die zugleich den komplexen Anforderungen unseres "Digital-Zeitalters" entspricht.

Das Anforderungsprofil für diese neue Basisschrift läßt sich in zehn Kriterien aufzeichnen:

- gut und schnell lesbar,
- normal,
- universell,
- lebendig,
- griffig,
- robust,
- straff,
- stolz,
- stabil,
- und im heutigen Sinne klassisch.

these handy shapes, whether a numeral or a k or an a. 'Robust' in the technical sense means that it should work well on CRT and lasersetters, in offset printing as well as in rotogravure, which it does. 'Tight'? *Centennial* is tight. It doesn't fidget. 'Proud' is something my typeface is not. It is, however, 'stable' and probably also 'classical in the modern sense of the word', although I'm not too sure exactly what that's supposed to mean. At any rate it's neither a romantic nor a fantasy typeface, to me it's more of an elegant one, more classical.

To characterise a typeface with zippy adjectives instead of formal criteria is certainly interesting but also difficult. Olaf Leu never told me the typeface had to be classical or lively. Nor did he describe how the numerals or other professional details ought to look. He merely told me to do it, and then we'll have a look at it together. He simply trusted his eyes, and when he agreed to something, it was done.

Centennial has a few special features. For instance, I made its x-height visibly higher than other neoclassical typefaces /23/, while I tended toward openness as far as width is concerned. That improves legibility because it appears bigger. In the beginning I experimented with different widths for lowercase letters such as n b a /05/. I tried to see how far I could reduce them. I tested the optimal serif strengths for lowercase m /07/, to find the limit. I've never gone that far with any of my other typefaces. In this case I really wanted to know what the proper serif strength was in order for it to remain neoclassical, not too thick and not too thin, and to avoid damage under exposure where possible. I made versions with three and a half, four and four and a half millimetre thickness, and chose the strongest.

A standard neoclassical typeface A typeface becomes a standard when it is used a lot. The most important aspects of a standard are versatility, availability for all printing or setting methods, and minimal required space. It must also possess good legibility, have a neutral appearance in order to convey all kinds of content, have a contemporary feel yet still be essentially timeless. A typical example of a standard typeface is *Times Roman*.[10] It meets all the requirements listed, and has achieved widespread use in the second half of the 20th century, not only for newspapers but generally as a text and display typeface. Due to the robustness of its shapes and their economical use of space, it became popular, and hence it became available for all typesetting methods and all major typesetting machine manufacturers[11] included it in their library. In time it started to outdo other Dutch oldstyle and transitional typefaces such as *Caslon* and *Baskerville*, or newspaper typefaces like *Excelsior*. Now that *Times* is a core font on PCs, it is also omnipresent in the office.

Both Didot's and Bodoni's typefaces from the 18th century are seminal influences within the neoclassical group. They set the standard for faces of their time with their formal quality, subtlety and technical perfection. *Bodoni* remains the most important representative of this group to this day.

At the request of Prof. Olaf Leu, a leading German graphic designer, the new typeface was to be a more legible

/13/
The Q tail is not centred (according to the stress) but offset slightly to the right.

Q

/14/
Iridium *(left)* and Linotype Centennial *(right) with looped ampersands; the latter also with a looped pound symbol.*

&£ &£

/15/
Iridium *and* Linotype Centennial: *different treatment of similar upper- and lowercase terminals.*

SLJ SLJ
ajr ajr

/16/
Three different possibilities for the AE ligature in Iridium *(left),* Breughel *(middle) and* Linotype Centennial *(right).*

Æ Æ Æ

/17/
The poorer legibility of the neoclassical typeface Bodoni *is evident, due to its low x-height and strong thick-thin contrast.*

Bodoni Book 8.8 pt
Sie fragen sich, warum es notwendig ist, so viele Schriften zur Verfügung zu haben. Sie dienen alle zum selben, aber machen die Vielfalt des Menschen aus. Diese Vielfalt ist wie beim Wein. Ich habe mal eine Weinkarte studiert mit sechzig Médoc-Weinen aus dem selben Jahr. You may ask why so many different typefaces. They all serve the same purpose but they express man's diversity. It is the same diversity we find in wine. I once saw a list of Médoc wines featuring sixty different Médocs all of the same year. Pourquoi tant d'Alphabets différents! Tous servent au même but, mais aussi à exprimer la diversité de l'homme. C'est cette même diversité que nous retrouvons dans les vins de Médoc.

/18/
The two narrow neoclassical faces Madison *and* Century Expanded, *both available by Linotype.*

Madison Roman 8 pt
Sie fragen sich, warum es notwendig ist, so viele Schriften zur Verfügung zu haben. Sie dienen alle zum selben, aber machen die Vielfalt des Menschen aus. Diese Vielfalt ist wie beim Wein. Ich habe mal eine Weinkarte studiert mit sechzig Médoc-Weinen aus dem selben Jahr. You may ask why so many different typefaces. They all serve the same purpose but they express man's diversity. It is the same diversity we find in wine. I once saw a list of Médoc wines featuring sixty different Médocs all of the same year. Pourquoi tant d'Alphabets différents! Tous servent au même but, mais aussi à exprimer la diversité de l'homme. C'est cette même diversité que nous retrouvons dans les vins de Médoc.

Century Expanded Roman 8 pt
Sie fragen sich, warum es notwendig ist, so viele Schriften zur Verfügung zu haben. Sie dienen alle zum selben, aber machen die Vielfalt des Menschen aus. Diese Vielfalt ist wie beim Wein. Ich habe mal eine Weinkarte studiert mit sechzig Médoc-Weinen aus dem selben Jahr. You may ask why so many different typefaces. They all serve the same purpose but they express man's diversity. It is the same diversity we find in wine. I once saw a list of Médoc wines featuring sixty different Médocs all of the same year. Pourquoi tant d'Alphabets différents! Tous servent au même but, mais aussi à exprimer la diversité de l'homme. C'est cette même diversité que nous retrouvons dans les vins de Médoc.

/19/
Universal application and minimal space requirement, like Times, *were the aims when creating* Linotype Centennial.

Times New Roman 8.6 pt
Sie fragen sich, warum es notwendig ist, so viele Schriften zur Verfügung zu haben. Sie dienen alle zum selben, aber machen die Vielfalt des Menschen aus. Diese Vielfalt ist wie beim Wein. Ich habe mal eine Weinkarte studiert mit sechzig Médoc-Weinen aus dem selben Jahr. You may ask why so many different typefaces. They all serve the same purpose but they express man's diversity. It is the same diversity we find in wine. I once saw a list of Médoc wines featuring sixty different Médocs all of the same year. Pourquoi tant d'Alphabets différents! Tous servent au même but, mais aussi à exprimer la diversité de l'homme. C'est cette même diversité que nous retrouvons dans les vins de Médoc.

and economic *Bodoni*. Linotype seized this opportunity – to coincide with the centenary of the typesetting machine – to make *Linotype Centennial* a new standard among neoclassical typefaces. The requirements of the new typeface led to differences between *Linotype Centennial* and *Bodoni*. *Linotype Centennial* has a calmer appearance overall, due to its low stroke contrast, tall x-height and strong serifs. This makes Adrian Frutiger's typeface extremely versatile, even for high speed printing on poor quality paper.

The neoclassical *Linotype Centennial* needs a little more space than the transitional *Times New Roman* for typesetting. *Linotype Centennial* achieves the same use of space as *Times New Roman* **/24/25/** when compressed by 5%, although this affects its legibility.

As an exclusive Linotype typeface – though only made available as a digital PostScript font two years after *Bodoni* was – *Linotype Centennial* never caught on like *Times* or *Helvetica*. This may be one reason why the success that Linotype so desired for the typeface continues to elude it.

I put a lot of sweat and toil into this typeface. There was the will to produce the best my hands were capable of, with all the details. Along with that there was the idea of making all vertical strokes slightly waisted – my way of bringing a typeface to life. For drawing connections and terminals I made a stencil for *Centennial* **/09/** out of IBM material[12] because something like that couldn't be bought in a shop. First I cut the shape out and then I sanded it down with very fine emery paper until it was absolutely right. I put a lot into the sanding. I wasn't too lazy to draw all the curves the same. This went one step further. I wanted to make sure that all joins were exactly the same. I had a whole collection of self-made stencils for *Centennial*. For the really small curves I used a Monotype stencil.

There were fundamental decisions to make with some of the letters. Where should the tail go on uppercase Q? It seemed to me that in a neoclassical typeface constructed over the vertical cross it ought to come more or less out of the middle. Here it's offset slightly to the right **/13/**, which one could criticise. The ampersand is equally classical **/14/**. Because the Americans insisted on 'their' ampersand, I opted for the traditional version. I also went for the classical solution for the pound symbol **/14/**, which means a loop belongs on the bottom. I can see in these details how strong the will was to bring little of my own personal preferences into the typeface. I only stayed true to my habits in uppercase J, where I just couldn't bring myself to use a teardrop shape **/15/**. The AE ligature is daring. I really wanted the A to be symmetrical. Because of this the upper part of the E is very long **/16/**. I had no set rules for these characters, each time it was simply a new typeface for me.

/20/
Change in the a-shape in the italic ae ligature in Iridium *(left), a-shape maintained in* Linotype Centennial *(right).*

ae ae
æ œ
œ œ

/21/
Different fl-connections and widths for Iridium *(left) and* Linotype Centennial *(right) – single letters (above), ligatures (below).*

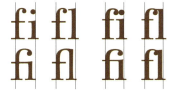

/22/
The tabular numeral 4 has a foot serif which the oldstyle numeral does not have, it ends in a swell serif.

4 4

/23/
The most important representatives of the neoclassical group – Bodoni, Didot *and* Walbaum *– in comparison with* Linotype Centennial.

Bodoni
Didot
Walbaum
Centennial

/24/
Type specimen of Linotype Centennial *in the same optical size as* Times, *and compressed to 95%, with the same tracking.*

/25/
Shape comparison between Linotype Centennial *and* Times *(bottom) – 100% width (top) and compressed to the width of* Times *(95%, middle).*

Linotype Centennial Roman 7.4 pt
Sie fragen sich, warum es notwendig ist, so viele Schriften zur Verfügung zu haben. Sie dienen alle zum selben, aber machen die Vielfalt des Menschen aus. Diese Vielfalt ist wie beim Wein. Ich habe mal eine Weinkarte studiert mit sechzig Médoc-Weinen aus dem selben Jahr. You may ask why so many different typefaces. They all serve the same purpose but they express man's diversity. It is the same diversity we find in wine. I once saw a list of Médoc wines featuring sixty different Médocs all of the same year. Pourquoi tant d'Alphabets différents! Tous servent au même but, mais aussi à exprimer la diversité de l'homme. C'est cette même diversité que nous retrouvons dans les vins de Médoc.

Centennial 7.7 pt – 5% verschmälert
Sie fragen sich, warum es notwendig ist, so viele Schriften zur Verfügung zu haben. Sie dienen alle zum selben, aber machen die Vielfalt des Menschen aus. Diese Vielfalt ist wie beim Wein. Ich habe mal eine Weinkarte studiert mit sechzig Médoc-Weinen aus dem selben Jahr. You may ask why so many different typefaces. They all serve the same purpose but they express man's diversity. It is the same diversity we find in wine. I once saw a list of Médoc wines featuring sixty different Médocs all of the same year. Pourquoi tant d'Alphabets différents! Tous servent au même but, mais aussi à exprimer la diversité de l'homme. C'est cette même diversité que nous retrouvons dans les vins de Médoc.

Hamburgefonstiv
Hamburgefonstiv
Hamburgefonstiv

In general one can ask oneself whether it makes any sense for a neoclassical face to try and compete with a renaissance or transitional face, but the requirements and the typeface description by Olaf Leu were very clear. There was no mention of old style, and anyway a narrow old style is pointless. Had the word transitional been mentioned, my pencil would have drawn something completely different. The relation to *Times* is down to success and Linotype's desire to counter the ever present *Times*.

I find *Centennial* to be a very good reading typeface, a good all-round typeface for text setting of which I'm really proud. Even though this time Linotype did work a lot on publicising and marketing the typeface, it didn't become quite the driving force Linotype were looking for. My world was sans serifs, that was obvious. I'd love to have designed a successful text face. That didn't work out, my serif faces never spread the way *Univers* or *Frutiger* did. Still, *Centennial* is one of my most professional typefaces; it was created on the back of 25 years' experience of type design, with absolute logic – and feeling, naturally.

100 years of Linotype typesetting   On 17 July 1886 Ottmar Mergenthaler, a German emigrant in the United States, received the first patent for his 'Blower' typesetting machine. It was the first functioning matrix setting and line casting machine. One of these machines was installed in the New York Tribune newspaper printing plant. Its publisher Whitelaw Reid inspired its future name with his cry of "A line of types!" In the same year the newspaper released the very first machine-set book, *The Tribune Book of Open Air Sports*.[13]

To mark the centenary of the machine in 1986, Linotype released its Mergenthaler type library in a new extensive grand edition. The LinoTypeCollection was conceived by Adrian Frutiger, Horst Heiderhoff, René Kerfante and Walter Wilkes, and was designed by Heinz Richter.[14] The collection is arranged into eight colour-coded classification groups /27/. Divided over six Perspex boxes and placed on a trolley made by Swiss furniture makers USM Haller /26/, the LinoTypeCollection contains over 1600 fonts on as many double-sided A4 landscape pages. Naturally, the eight *Linotype Centennial* weights by Adrian Frutiger are also included /28/. With its loose-leaf format the collection is flexible and easy to add to, and the laser-set Linotype typefaces are presented exquisitely.

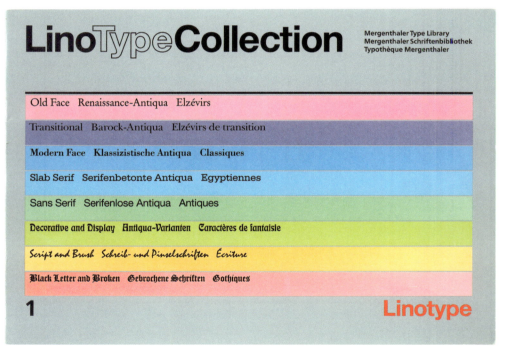

/27/
Title page of the accompanying brochure explaining the LinoType-Collection with colour codes.

/26/
Rolling cart with the LinoTypeCollection – six Perspex boxes containing 1600 weights on specimen sheets.

/28/
Front of the sheet for Linotype Centennial 55 *with character set, setting specimens and additional information.*

Mergenthaler Type Library Typefaces/Schriften/Caractères

Linotype Centennial™ 55
roman/normal/romain

05633 12 pt Design

Modern Face/Klassizistische Antiqua/Classiques
Adrian Frutiger 1986
Linotype

abcdefghijklmnopq
rstuvwxyz fiflß&
ABCDEFGHIJKLMN
OPQRSTUVWXYZ
1234567890 .,:;-——
1234567890 '' "" „" ‹›«»*
%‰!?¡¿0[]/†‡§$£¢ƒ

ÄÅÀÂÃÁÆÇĈËÉÈÊÉĞĨÍÎÏÑÖÓÔÒØ
ŒŒŠÜÚÛÙŪŽ
áàâäãåæçĉëéèêéğĩíîïñ̃öóôòøœœšüúûùūž

Small Caps/Kapitälchen/Petites Capitales
AABCDEFGHIJKLMNOPQRSTUVWXYZZ

Parameter for 10 pt/Parameter in 10 pt/Paramètre pour 10 pt
H2.50 mm   k2.62 mm   x1.74 mm   p0.76 mm   kp3.38 mm   Ép4.02 mm
H0.098 Inches k0.103 Inches x0.069 Inches p0.030 Inches kp0.133 Inches Ép0.158 Inches
Factor/Faktor/Facteur 1.00

* Given in pica point/Angaben in pica point/Toutes indications en points pica

---

△ 2.11 mm/6 pt* (2.25 mm^6pt) ▽ 2.50 mm (7 pt*) ◁ 0   H 1.50 mm
abcdefghijklmnopqrstuvwxyz abcdefghijklmnopqrstuvwxyz abcdefghijklmn 1234567890
In every type design the basic character is determined by the uniform design characteristic of all letters in the alphabet. However, this alone does not determine the standard of the typeface and the quality of composition set with it. The appearance is something complex whi ch forms itself out of many details, like form, proportion, rhythm etc. If everything harmoni
THE APPEARANCE IS SOMETHING COMPLEX WHICH FORMS ITSELF OUT OF MANY

△ 2.46 mm/7 pt* (2.63 mm^7pt) ▽ 2.75 mm (8 pt*) ◁ 0   H 1.75 mm
abcdefghijklmnopqrstuvwxyz abcdefghijklmnopqrstuvwxyz ab 1234567890
Bei jeder Schriftgestaltung wird der Grundcharakter eines Alphabets von ein
heitlichen Formmerkmalen der Buchstaben bestimmt. Er allein besagt noch
nichts über das Niveau einer Druckschrift und die Qualität des Satzgefüges
Das Erscheinungsbild ist etwas Komplexes, das sich aus vielen Einzelheiten
FORM UND PROPORTIONEN SIND DIE WICHTIGSTEN KRITERIEN BEI

△ 2.81 mm/8 pt* (3.00 mm^8pt) ▽ 3.25 mm (9.25 pt*) ◁ 0   H 2.00 mm
abcdefghijklmnopqrstuvwxyz abcdefghijklmnopqrst 1234567890
Le style de chaque caractère d'imprimerie se détermine par des car
actéristiques qui sont les mêmes pour toutes les lettres de l'alphabe
Dans tous les rapports formels et autres relations il s'agit de phéno
mènes optiques irréductibles aux règles mathématiques et que seul
D'AUTRE PART MALGRÉ TOUTES LES RESSOURCES DE MÉCA

△ 3.16 mm/9 pt* (3.38 mm^9pt) ▽ 3.50 mm (10 pt*) ◁ 0   H 2.25 mm
abcdefghijklmnopqrstuvwxyz abcdefghijklmn 1234567890
In every type design the basic character is determined by th
uniform design characteristics of all letters in the alphabet
However, this alone does not determine the standard of the
typeface and the quality of composition set with it. The appe
THE APPEARANCE IS SOMETHING COMPLEX WHICHS

△ 3.51 mm/10 pt* (3.75 mm^10pt) ▽ 4.00 mm (11.5 pt*) ◁ 0   H 2.50 mm
abcdefghijklmnopqrstuvwxyz abcdefghi 1234567890
Bei jeder Schriftgestaltung wird der Grundcharakter
eines Alphabets von einheitlichen Formmerkmalen de
Buchstaben bestimmt. Er allein besagt noch nichts üb
er das Niveau einer Druckschrift und die Qualität des
FORM UND PROPORTIONEN SIND DIE WICHTIGS

△ 3.87 mm/11 pt* (4.13 mm^11pt) ▽ 4.50 mm (12.75 pt*) ◁ 0   H 2.75 mm
abcdefghijklmnopqrstuvwxyz abcd 1234567890
Le style de chaque caractère d'imprimerie se dét
ermine par des caractéristiques qui sont les mêm
es pour toutes les lettres de l'alphabet. Dans tous
D'AUTRE PART MALGRÉ TOUTES LES RESSO

△ 4.22 mm/12 pt* (4.50 mm^12pt) ▽ 4.75 mm (13.5 pt*) ◁ 0   H 3.00 mm
abcdefghijklmnopqrstuvwxyz a 1234567890
In every type design the basic character is det
ermined by the uniform design characteristi
cs of all letters in the alphabet. However, this
THE APPEARANCE IS SOMETHING COMP

△ 4.92 mm/14 pt* (5.25 mm^14pt) ▽ 0   H 3.50 mm
In every type design the basic characte

△ 5.62 mm/16 pt* (6.00 mm^16pt) ▽ 0   H 4.00 mm
Bei jeder Schriftgestaltung wurde

△ 6.33 mm/18 pt* (6.75 mm^18pt) ▽ -1   H 4.50 mm
Le style de chaque caractère di

△ 7.03 mm/20 pt* (7.50 mm^20pt) ▽ -1   H 5.00 mm
För alla nya stilar bestämes

△ 8.44 mm/24 pt* (9.00 mm^24pt) ▽ -1   H 6.00 mm
In elk letterontwerp wo

△ 9.84 mm/28 pt* (10.50 mm^28pt) ▽ -1   H 7.00 mm
Em todo o desenhos

△ 12.65 mm/36 pt* (13.50 mm^36pt) ▽ -1   H 9.01 mm
In ciascuna ser

△ 16.87 mm/48 pt* (18.00 mm^48pt) ▽ -2   H 12.01 mm
En cada typ

△ 21.09 mm/60 pt* (22.50 mm^60pt) ▽ -2   H 15.01 mm
Den ensti

△ 25.31 mm/72 pt* (27.00 mm^72pt) ▽ -2   H 18.01 mm
Bestern

△ 29.52 mm/84 pt* (31.50 mm^84pt) ▽ -2   H 21.01 mm
Muotei

6
7
8
9
10
11
12
14
16
18
20
24
28
36
48
60
72
84

/29/
Character set of
Linotype Centennial *normal for*
lasersetting by Linotype.

Initially *Linotype Centennial* was made available in two design sizes, 12 pt for text setting and 18 pt for titling. Only the 12 pt design size is shown in the 1986 LinoTypeCollection, although the specimens go up to 84 pt type size /28/.

In the accompanying booklet Linotype comments on the design sizes: "Special care is taken in the production of photosetting typefaces to ensure that typeface drawings (design sizes) are applied which suit the particular requirements of the typeface. Most of our photosetting typefaces are applied so that all point sizes may be set from one design size. [...] However, there are typefaces which are especially sensitive (e.g. *Bodoni*). They cannot be enlarged or reduced at will without loss of quality, otherwise their characteristic serifs would become too thick or too thin, or the counter openings would become too wide or too narrow." Linotype made typefaces with a high stroke contrast available in two or more sizes. They recommend design 8 pt size for type size up to 10 pt, 12 pt design size for type sizes from 9 to 24 pt, and 18 pt design size for type sizes from 12 pt and over.

Linotype Centennial is now only available for digital typesetting in the slightly stronger 12 pt design size /30/. Moreover, the downstrokes appear to be straightened /31/.

ABCDEFGHIJKLMN
OPQRSTUVWXYZ&
abcdefghijklmnopqrs
tuvwxyzß1234567890

/30/
Outline of the current version
over the redrawn original drawing
in design size 18 pt.

/31/
The first version by Linotype
has slightly concave stems (left),
in the current version they
have all been straightened (right).

/32/
Linotype Centennial 55 is available
in two design sizes, 12 and 18 pt –
1987 (above) still without,
1992 (below) with small caps.

05633 Linotype Centennial 55 roman/normal/romain 12*/18 **138/129** (30)

abcdefghijklmnopqrstuvwxyz
ABCDEFGHIJKLMNOPQRSTUVWXYZ
1234567890 1234567890 .,;:'"«»&!?
Håmbûrgefönstiv iam admodum mitigati raptarum animi erant se
earum parentes tum maxime sordida veste lacrimisque et querelis

05633 Linotype Centennial 55 roman / normal / romain 12+ (100) **138** H 2.50 mm F 1.000
18 **129** H 2.50 mm F 1.000

abcdefghijklmnopqrstuvwxyz
ABCDEFGHIJKLMNOPQRSTUVWXYZ
1234567890 1234567890 .,;:'"«»ß&!?

Håmbûrgefönstiv. Since 1886 LINOTYPE HAS BEEN a leader in the fiel
of typeface development and today offers one of the finest selection

Font production:
Adobe Font digitised by
Linotype

Font format:
PostScript Type 1

Also available:
TrueType
OpenType Std

ABCDEFGHIJKLMN
OPQRSTUVWXYZ&
abcdefghijklmnopqrs
tuvwxyzß1234567890

Sie fragen sich

warum es notwen

dig ist, so viele Schriften zu

r Verfügung zu haben. Sie dienen alle zu

m selben, aber machen die Vielfalt des Menschen aus. Die
se Vielfalt ist wie beim Wein. Ich habe einmal eine Weinka
rte studiert mit sechzig Médoc-Weinen aus dem selben Ja
hr. Das ist ausnahmslos Wein, aber doch nicht alles der gl
eiche Wein. Es hat eben gleichwohl Nuancen. So ist es auc

h mit der Schrift. *You may ask why so many different typefaces.* They all serve the sa
me purpose but they express man's diversity. It is the same diversity we find in wine.
I once saw a list of Médoc wines featuring sixty different Médocs all of the same year.
All of them were wines but each was different from the others. It's the nuances that
are important. The same is true for typefaces. *Pourquoi tant d'Alphabets différents!*
Tous servent au même but, mais aussi à exprimer la diversité de l'homme. C'est cette
même diversité que nous retrouvons dans les vins de Médoc. J'ai pu, un jour, relever

soixante crus, tous de la même année. Il s'agissait certes de vins, mais to
us étaient différents. Tout est dans la nuance du bouquet. Il en est de mê
me pour les caractères! *Sie fragen sich, warum es notwendig ist, so viele
Schriften zur Verfügung zu haben.* Sie dienen alle zum selben, aber mach
en die Vielfalt des Menschen aus. Diese Vielfalt ist wie beim Wein. Ich ha
be einmal eine Weinkarte studiert mit sechzig Médoc-Weinen aus dem s
elben Jahr. Das ist ausnahmslos Wein, aber doch nicht alles der gleiche
Wein. Es hat eben gleichwohl Nuancen. So ist es auch mit der Schrift. *Yo*

u may ask why so many different typefaces.
They all serve the same purpose but they ex
press man's divesity. It is the same diversity
we find in wine. I once saw a list of Médoc wi
nes featuring sixty different Médocs all of th
e same year. All of them were wines but each
was different from the others. It's the nuance
s that are important. The same is true for typ
efaces. *Pourquoi tant d'Alphabets différents!*
Tous servent au même but, mais aussi à expr

66 pt | −30   50 pt | −15   33 pt | −15   22 pt | −10   15 pt | 19 pt | −5   10 pt | 13 pt | 2   7.5 pt | 10.2 pt | 5   6 pt | 8 pt | 15

ÅBÇDÈFG
HIJKLMÑ
ÔPQRŠTÜ
VWXYZ&
ÆŒ¥$£€
1234567890
åbçdéfghij
klmñôpqrš
tüvwxyzß
fi fl æ œ ø ł ð
[.,:;·'/-–—]
(¿¡"«‹›»"!?)
{§°%@‰*†}

45 Light

ÅBÇDÈFG
HIJKLMÑ
ÔPQRŠTÜ
VWXYZ&
ÆŒ¥$£€
1234567890
åbçdéfghij
klmñôpqrš
tüvwxyzß
fi fl æ œ ø ł ð
[.,:;·'/-–—]
(¿¡"«‹›»"!?)
{§°%@‰†}*

46 Light Italic

ÅBÇDÈFG
HIJKLMÑ
ÔPQRŠTÜ
VWXYZ&
ÆŒ¥$£€
1234567890
åbçdéfghij
klmñôpqrš
tüvwxyzß
fi fl æ œ ø ł ð
[.,:;·'/-–—]
(¿¡"«‹›»"!?)
{§°%@‰*†}

55 Roman

ÅBÇDÈFG
HIJKLMÑ
ÔPQRŠTÜ
VWXYZ&
ÆŒ¥$£€
1234567890
åbçdéfghij
klmñôpqrš
tüvwxyzß
fi fl æ œ ø ł ð
[.,:;·'/-–—]
(¿¡"«‹›»"!?)
{§°%@‰†}*

56 Italic

ÅBÇDÈFG
HIJKLMÑ
ÔPQRŠTÜ
VWXYZ&
ÆŒ¥$£€
1234567890
åbçdéfghij
klmñôpqrš
tüvwxyzß
fi fl æ œ ø ł ð
[.,:;·'/-–—]
(¿¡"«‹›»"!?)
{§°%@‰*†}

75 Bold

ÅBÇDÈFG
HIJKLMÑ
ÔPQRŠTÜ
VWXYZ&
ÆŒ¥$£€
1234567890
åbçdéfghij
klmñôpqrš
tüvwxyzß
fi fl æ œ ø ł ð
[.,:;·'/-–—]
(¿¡"«‹›»"!?)
{§°%@‰*†}

76 Bold Italic

Typeface comparison The vertical stress and balanced proportions of letter widths are characteristic of neoclassical typefaces. *ITC Fenice, Linotype Centennial* and *CorporateA* – the latter was originally an exclusive corporate type for Daimler-Benz company – are particularly noteworthy for the narrow feel of their character, without being narrow typefaces, as well as their tall x-height **/36/**. All three typefaces appear strict, with a sober elegance.

Compared to *Bodoni* and *Didot,* the influential neoclassical typefaces of the late 18th century, the x-height of *Linotype Centennial* is substantially higher. In this respect *Walbaum Antiqua,* cut by Justus Erich Walbaum around 1800, can be regarded as a model **/23/**.

While *ITC Fenice* has the most typical stylistic features of a neoclassical typeface when it comes to stroke contrast and serif shape – apart from its unique features – these are less obvious in *Linotype Centennial.* In *CorporateA* there are barely any neoclassical elements, particularly in the curved serif shapes. However, its even oval arcs with vertical stress are neoclassical.

Linotype Centennial regular weight is relatively strong right down to the hairlines, making it robust and versatile for typesetting, even under poor conditions.

/33/
Measurements of stroke widths and proportions of the Linotype Centennial *regular weight.*

Roman				
Hh = 10.00 cm	nh = 6.94 cm	oh = 7.42 cm	Hh : Hw = 1 : 0.72	nh : nw = 1 : 0.84
Hw = 7.29	nw = 5.81	ow = 6.47	Hw : Hs = 1 : 0.21	nw : ns = 1 : 0.24
Hs = 1.56	ns = 1.39	os = 1.62	Hs : Hq = 1 : 0.26	nh : oh = 1 : 1.07
Hq = 0.40	nq = 0.66	oq = 0.40		nw : ow = 1 : 1.11

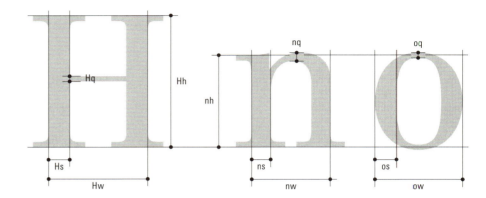

/34/
Of these three narrow-looking static typefaces, Linotype Centennial *is the widest and its shapes appear softer.*

Hofstainberg

ITC Fenice
Aldo Novarese
1977

AGRabns27

Hofstainberg

Linotype Centennial
Adrian Frutiger
1986

AGRabns27

A
Flat top, flat foot serif

G
Round transition from arc to stem, bracketed transition to foot

R
Curved right leg, terminal curves upwards

a
Upstroke with drop, entry into stem slightly sloping

b n
Flat upstroke rises very slightly, b has foot serif

s
Terminal with semi-serif

2
Curved diagonal, slanted terminal

7
Arched diagonal, round terminal

Hofstainberg

Corporate A
Kurt Weidemann
1990

AGRabns27

Comparison showing the
different weights and angle of
the italics.

	Hh	Hw	Hs	Hq
Light	10.00 cm	7.09 = 0.97	1.27 = 0.81	0.40 = 1
Roman	10.00	7.29 = 1	1.56 = 1	0.40 = 1
Bold	10.00	7.92 = 1.09	2.19 = 1.40	0.49 = 1.22
Black	10.00	8.39 = 1.15	2.62 = 1.68	0.49 = 1.22
Italic	10.00	6.92 = 0.95	1.48 = 0.95	0.42 = 1.05

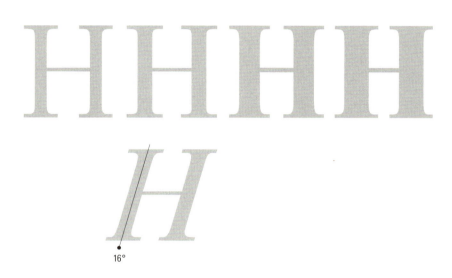

16°

/36/

Height comparison showing the
differences of x-heights to
ascenders and descenders – the cap
height is the starting point.

ITC Fenice
41.3 pt

Linotype Centennial
40.2 pt

Corporate A
43.5 pt

ÅBÇDÈFG HIJKLMÑ ÔPQRŠTÜ VWXYZ& ÆŒ¥$£€ 1234567890 åbçdéfghij klmñôpqrš tüvwxyzß fi fl æ œ ø ł ð [.,:;·'/-–—] (¿¡"«‹›»"!?) {§°%@‰*†}

95 Black

ÅBÇDÈFG HIJKLMÑ ÔPQRŠTÜ VWXYZ& ÆŒ¥$£€ 1234567890 åbçdéfghij klmñôpqrš tüvwxyzß fi fl æ œ ø ł ð [.,:;·'/-–—] (¿¡"«‹›»"!?) {§°%@‰†}*

96 Black Italic

1234567890 ÅBÇDÉFGHIJ KLMÑÔPQRŠ TÜVWXYZ&

45 Light OsF & SC

1234567890

46 Light Italic OsF

1234567890 ÅBÇDÉFGHIJ KLMÑÔPQRŠ TÜVWXYZ&

55 Roman OsF & SC

1234567890

56 Italic OsF

1234567890

75 Bold OsF

1234567890

76 Bold Italic OsF

1234567890

95 Black OsF

1234567890

96 Black Italic OsF

Name of typeface		Designer	Design | Publication	Typesetting technology	Manufacturer	Weights
Avenir		Adrian Frutiger	1987 | 1988	CRT and laser digital typesetting	– Linotype	6
Avenir Next[*]				PostScript digital typesetting	– Adobe | Linotype	12
				OpenType digital typesetting	– Linotype[*]	24

AVENIR

In the mid-80s, I looked back on some 40 years of ongoing work with sans serif typefaces. I felt, as it were, a duty – following on from the stylistic developments – to draw a geometric grotesque myself. First off, I carried out a study[1] on the grotesque typefaces that were available from Linotype at that time, and realised that a modern version of the constructivist grotesque was missing. There were the historic geometrics from the '20s, like *Futura* or *Kabel* /20/ – typefaces which were becoming popular again. I had seen the success of Herb Lubalin and Tom Carnase's *ITC Avant Garde Gothic* /27/, and I felt that a new graphic era had begun. These new geometric alphabets /32/, however, remained display faces; they weren't any use for setting printed body text. I started by comparing all existing typefaces of the same sort, so that with all that experience I could produce an independent alphabet, one that belonged in the present.

As a starting point, I set myself the task of rendering more human the circular shapes that had been drawn using compasses. I sat myself down in a small, quiet room, and first of all drew an o contained within a perfect circle – the first and most important letter. Then I refined it, always with the goal of forming an easily readable curvature that was also easy on the eye. Scientific investigations have shown that the human eye has been shaped by nature so that it's able to recognise danger, which comes more often from left or right than from above or below. You can use two fingers to demonstrate that your field of vision is stretched horizontally: hold them before your eyes and draw them away slowly – they'll stay in sight for longer when you move them sideways than when you move them up and down.[2] In contrast, a fish or a bird has fully round eyes, since danger can come from all sides. The insight here is that horizontal values are evaluated differently from vertical ones. Translated into typefaces, this means making the horizontal strokes thinner, and the vertical strokes thicker, as the type cutters have always done. From such considerations was the o of *Avenir* born. I looked at it for a long time, laid the perfect circle and my shape next to each other, and saw that the modulated o had a resonance, and that in comparison, the hard round circle was simply a geometric shape, not a letter /01/. I showed both to my wife, Simone, and to several other people – the reaction was always the same: everyone saw the modulated o as a letter immediately. This experience encouraged me to take things further.

With this o as a starting point, I drew the entire alphabet in a light weight. All the strokes had to sit with those of the o. It was about making the tiniest adjustments. In the horizontal and vertical stroke weights I made such slight differences that the eye actually couldn't see them any more, but would rather feel them. I began with the juncture of the n and saw how thin I could make it, while still staying true to my original ideas about the typeface /01/. From the first word I'd make a reduction, then check it all again. In this

Avenir – a humanist linear grotesque The 1988 edition of *Linotype Express* contained the passage: "Even a few years ago there were still rules about which typefaces must not be used together and a tendency towards sharply differentiated font sizes. The greatest contrast was always sought between large and small, thin and bold, coloured or plain. Today, however, typography is tending toward a soft and nuanced expression." And further down Adrian Frutiger writes: "Through a close examination of the stylistic developments of the past decades and a comparison of all existing typefaces,[3] I undertook the task of developing an alphabet that would be of its time. (…) The typeface that originated from this analysis, Avenir, tries neatly to encompass all the present fashions. Typographers will discover in it a typeface that – in spite of its strict construction – has a humanist appearance."[4]

With *Avenir*, Frutiger had seized upon the ideal of Ancient Greek stone inscriptions. "The circle, triangle and square are becoming … the dogma of a new religion. At its core is the belief in the alphabet. It is a manifestation of human endeavour, not divine dispensation," wrote Philipp Luidl.[5] How do we recognise the masterpiece in *Avenir* that Frutiger has mentioned in his interview?[6] Does not the most technical class of typeface, the constructed typeface, embody the renunciation of human qualities, and the embracing of the mechanical? Or is this only the case with those typefaces, constructed with ruler and compass by graduates of the Bauhaus? And would the technical, through the optical corrections of the circle, not simply be given a human face? When Le Corbusier wrote: "Geometry is the language of humanity"[7] he expressed a belief that geometry was deeply human.

On the one hand, the idea of geometric typefaces is based on the absoluteness of mathematical perfection, on the basic forms such as circle, square and triangle, as well as linear strokes. On the other hand, a typeface – especially a text typeface – should conform to certain optical criteria that render it pleasant to read. And here a contradiction raises its head. To find that balance, to recognise that moment when both aspects – the mathematical and the human – join together in equilibrium, that was for Adrian Frutiger the masterstroke in *Avenir*. Making that mathematically perfect form more pleasant to the human eye is what Frutiger considers his paramount achievement.

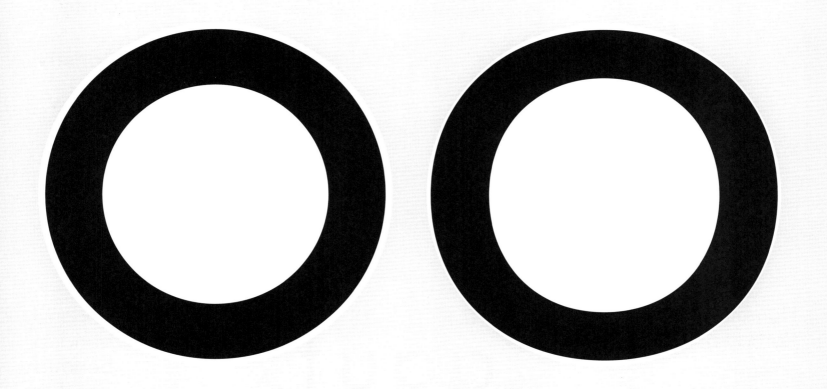

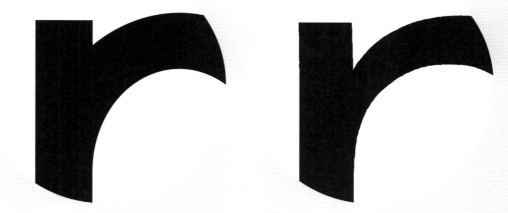

/01/
A perfect circle makes the upper and lower portions of the o appear too fat – the same is true for the juncture with the stem (left) – Adrian Frutiger's original design for Avenir (right).

Wo gibt es Marktlücken
im heutigen Schriften-Angebot ?

AVENIR
CLEAN

Eine Studie und ein Vorschlag
im Bereiche der Grotsk-Schriften.

⇒ Es fehlt eine moderne Fassung
einer konstruktivistischen Grotesk.

Januar 1987 Adrian Frutiger

Was ist mit "linear" und "konstruktivistisch" gemeint ?

Durch die Handhabung der Breitfeder während 1500 Jahren kaligraphischer Entwicklung werden die Silhouetten der Antiqua-Buchstaben in ihrer typischen an- und abschwellenden Liniengebung geprägt.

Garamond

In der Zeit der Industrialisierung erschien die rationale Überlegung einer mechanischen Zeichnung mit konstanter Liniendicke. Matrizen für Schreibmaschinen-Schriften z.B. wurden miteiner einzigen uniformen Fräse graviert.

Schreibmaschine

Im Schriftguss kam es nie zur sturen "Schnurlinie". Der Schriftschneider wusste um die feinen, morphologisch bedingten Reaktionen des menschlichen Auges, welches zum Beispiel horizontale Striche stärker einschätzt als vertikale.

Die Bestrebung absolut nüchterne Schriften zu konstruieren entsprach dem Zeitgeist der 20-30er Jahre (Erbar, Futura, Kabel etc.). Dieser Trend wurde jedoch von der Welle der mehr modulierten Akzidenz-Grotesk-Schriften der 50-60er Jahre verdrängt (Helvetica, Univers etc.). Letztere fanden im Soge des wirtschaftlichen Aufstieges eine immense Verbreitung und es bestehen von dieser Stilart eine Mengevon Varianten in allen Schriftmusterbüchern (siehe in beiliegender Zusammenstellung A).

Helvetica   Univers

Heute greift der Grafiker gerne zurück auf die frühen, nüchternen Typen zu einer "farbloseren" Aussage. Die Futura steht als solchen "Oldtimer" obenan.

Futura

Etliche moderne Schriftzeichner haben versucht, neue geometrische Alphabete zu entwerfen. Fast in allen Fällen blieben sie als Fantasie-Schriften unerreichbar für den Textbereich (siehe B). Eine der schlimsten dieser "Schnur-Schriften" ist die Avangarde Gothic, deren unerklärlicher Erfolg bekannt ist.

Avant Garde Gothic

Andererseits ist man auf der Suche nach markanteren, für die Lesbarkeit griffigeren und der Antiquaform ähnlicheren Schriften. Der anhaltende Erfolg der Gill spricht davon.

Gill Sans

Aus der Zusammenstellung der von der Linotype heute angebotenen Groteskschriften geht klar hervor, dass im Bereiche der neuen, konstruktivistischen Typen eine bestimmte Marktlücke besteht (siehe C).

Konstruktivistische Grotesk-Schriften im Linotype-Angebot

ALTE SCHRIFTEN
1. a.
OHamburgefonstiv
OHamburgefonstiv
b.
OHamburgefonstiv
2. a.
OHamburgefonstiv
b.
OHamburgefonstiv
3.
OHamburgefonstiv
OHamburgefonstiv

NEUE SCHRIFT
4.
OHamburgefonstiv

Vorschlag einer Synthese im Vergleich
mit den 3 gefragtesten Grotesk-Schriften dieser Art.

Hamburg
Hamburg

Hamburg

Hamburg

Hamburg

Hamburg fenster gang

Abweichungen von der klassischen Grundform

Beispiel an vier frequenzreichen Buchstaben

a g u t

Futura
agut

Avant Garde
ag t

Neuer Vorschlag A
agut

Neuer Vorschlag B
ag t

Die verschiedenen Schnitte

4 feinabgestimmte Fetten für den Textbereich

Leicht   45   bendup
Mager   45.5   bendup
Kräftig   55.5   bendup
Normal 55.5   bendup

Ein oder zwei fette Schnitte, so angelegt, dass keine Kompromisse in der Strich-Dicke bei gedrängten Buchstaben wie a,e etc. eingegangen werden müssen.

bendup

Eigentliche Kursiv-Schnitte sind in diesem Stil undenkbar. Aus wirtschaftlichen Überlegungen müssten trotzdem in jeder Fette ein geschwenkter Schnitt angeboten werden.

/02/
Adrian Frutiger's study for Avenir from 1987 contains a short historical overview and a comparison of the available typefaces.

/03/
Variants of Avenir 55 – double-storey g, diagonally terminated curve ends in rt and a with a spur (bottom).

Die griechische Kunst

Der kulturelle Zusammenhang der griechischen Klassik mit dem spateren Klassizismus

Die griechische Kunst

Der kulturelle Zusammenhang der griechischen Klassik mit dem spateren Klassizismus

Studies on the linear grotesque For Linotype's type selection meeting of February 1987, Adrian Frutiger had drafted the document: 'Wo gibt es Marktlücken im heutigen Schriftenangebot? (Where are there gaps in the current typeface market?)[8] **/02/** He conceived of the possibility of a modern, geometric sans suitable for body text. First, the foundations were laid. Adrian Frutiger showed *Garamond*, representative of all text typefaces with dynamic strokes, and which recalls writing with a broad pen. Against this he contrasted the typewriter face with its constant stroke weight – a result of the mechanically cut characters. Adrian Frutiger wrote that this was a rational consideration, derived from the age of industrialisation. Proportional typefaces with a 'rigid line' were not taken up by the foundries. On the other hand, a multitude of linear grotesque typefaces with optical correction were produced.[9]

In his study, Frutiger had compared the typefaces *Spartan, Futura, Neuzeit, DIN Neuzeit, Gill Sans, Kabel* and *ITC Avant Garde Gothic*. For *Avenir* he developed a synthesis of the aforementioned. He chose, in contrast to *ITC Avant Garde Gothic*, a normal x-height and ascenders that were not greatly exaggerated, as is the case with *Futura*.[10] For a g t u he adopted the distinctive shapes of *Gill Sans*. However, for g he finally adopted the single-storey form **/03/**. In the lowercase letters *Avenir* resembles most closely Wilhelm Pischner's *Neuzeit-Grotesk* 1929 **/20/**. In the capitals it is rather individual.

way, gradually, I built up an entire lowercase alphabet, with about ten additional capitals. It was always about the finest of nuances. *Avenir* is the typeface where I expended the most effort in getting it exactly right, and all by hand. In that sense I pushed it to the limit. It's the most precise typeface I've ever drawn.

Before I presented my new typeface to the type selection meeting, I had prepared myself well, as always. In a concept document **/02/** I illustrated Linotype's existing sans serif typefaces and identified gaps in the market. I showed, with the aid of the test string 'genova GENOVA' a whole collection of sans serif typefaces, put together sample texts and various weight gradations. For such meetings, I always wrote a report with explanations and also historical developments. But I'd hardly ever done this as thoroughly as with *Avenir*. It was really important to me to include all comparable typefaces. The conclusion was: "There is a need for a modern interpretation of the constructivist grotesque."**/02/**

The geometric sans was the fundamental idea behind *Avenir*. It's a variant form of the grotesque. I always felt a clear separation between antiqua and sans serif – they're two different worlds. The one world is that of the softer, rounder typefaces for poetry and literature. The other is that of the sober, clear typefaces for signage and information. It's a lot harder to design a grotesque; in a serif typeface you can hide your mistakes; use the serifs to fudge things, or the junctures. In contrast, the sans serif is like a slippery eel, always sliding through your fingers, it's very difficult to get a grip on it. I've always preferred the grotesque, I wanted to rework the entire spectrum. My approach was always: a typeface must be able to be expanded into a family. Alfred Willimann, my teacher at the Kunstgewerbeschule Zurich, never wanted to hear about semibold or bold; for him there

/04/
The oblique of Avenir LT *was created electronically, and contains no optical correction – the angle of inclination is 8°.*

OO

/05/
With its downstroke, the G of Avenir *follows the model of Roman capitals (right) rather than the geometric grotesques (left).*

GG GG

/06/
In Futura K *and* R *exhibit somewhat smaller counters –* ITC Avant Garde Gothic *and* Avenir *employ two different solutions to this (from left to right).*

KR KR KR

/07/
In contrast to Futura *(left) and* ITC Avant Garde Gothic *(centre), the* f r t *of* Avenir *are somewhat broader (right).*

ifrt ifrt ifrt

/08/
The stroke widths in Avenir *are not constant – this comparison makes the slightly varying widths in the O apparent.*

OODER
ODER

/09/
Even in a linear grotesque like Avenir, *the half serifs have a slightly lighter stroke weight than the downstrokes.*

AKNSV
AKNSV

/10/
Three equal stroke weights in the A (left), three varying stroke weights in the A of Avenir *(middle), as made clear in the mirrored version (right).*

A A A

/12/
Adrian Frutiger's concept of finely differentiated weights, enables text composition similar to a halftone screen.

/11/
The next heaviest weight of Avenir, *when viewed in negative, looks optically identical to the preceding, lighter weight.*

Avenir LT 35
Avenir LT 45
Avenir LT 55
Avenir LT 65

»Mehr als vierzig Jahre dauert nun schon meine Auseinandersetzung mit den serifenlosen Schriften. Ihre stilistische Weiterentwicklung sehe ich fast als eine ›Verpflichtung‹ an, so daß ich selbst eine Linear-Antiqua zu zeichnen begann. Dabei war mir klar, daß es sich nicht um eine herausragende Neuschöpfung handeln konnte. Durch genaues Verfolgen der stilistischen Entwicklungen der vergangenen Jahrzehnte und den Vergleich aller bestehenden Typen unternahm ich den Versuch, ein der Gegenwart entsprechendes Alphabet zu erarbeiten. **Die auf diese Weise entstandene Avenir versucht, allen gegenwärtigen Tendenzen sauber zu entsprechen. Die Typografen werden in ihr eine Schriftform entdecken, die trotz aller konstruktivistischen Strenge ein humanes Bild vermittelt.«**

von Hamburg Ost gibt
es feine manieren

**von Hamburg Obergau
gibt es feinste
manifestationen**

**von Hamburg
bis Ostern
ist Hoffnung
bei meiner**

/13/
*Avenir 35 and Avenir 95 represent
the upper and lower limits for
the interpolation of the intermediate
weights – original drawings with
guidelines and corrections.*

/14/
*Paste-up of two narrow fonts
and the ultrablack version 125 –
implemented by Linotype in
2004 in Avenir Next.*

/15/
*Original drawings with two
variants – Q with an orthogonal
tail that passes through into
the counter, and R with an open
counter.*

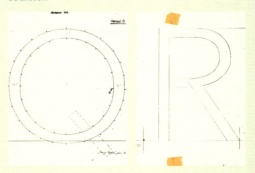

/16/
*Overlaid original drawings
for b d p q – the descenders are
somewhat shorter than the
ascenders.*

Early geometric sans serif   The first sans serif typeface, *Two Lines English Egyptian* /17/ appeared in 1816 in the type specimen book of William Caslon IV.[11] It drew upon the Greek design principle of circle, square and triangle. The vertical double square used by the Romans /19/ does not play a role here. As a seemingly geometrical sans serif it is unique amongst all the typefaces of the 19th century.[12]

It was only in 1916 with Edward Johnson's *Railway Type* that the idea of the geometric typeface was taken up again. It formed the basis for Eric Gill's *Gill Sans*, published in 1927, the alternate characters of which have a geometric appearance /18/. Around 1920, Wagner and Schmidt (Leipzig) released a typeface that would later come to be called *Kristall Grotesk* /20/.[13] For the German linear grotesques, the Roman double-square principle /19/ is absolutely characteristic, as can be seen in Jakob Erbar's *Erbar Grotesk* (1926), in Paul Renner's *Futura* /23/ and Rudolf Koch's *Kabel* (1927) /24/. In all these typefaces the inscriptional form is also evident, as can be seen from the sharp angles in A M N V W.

The elementary forms of circle, square and triangle were also dominant in the teaching of the Bauhaus.[14] However, these alphabets, developed from 1924 onwards, as well as Joost Schmidt's 'construction of a square-based grotesque' were never implemented. Their lack of optical correction made them unsuitable for longer texts. The Roman proportion played no role in these experiments.

was only ever the pure line. He totally rejected the idea of typeface families. That's where our ways parted, since I was a designer of typefaces destined for graphic design. *Avenir* emerged from the Willimann spirit but in the sense of his theory of inscriptional typefaces. In that theory I could bring the simple line to expression; additionally I could make all those slight differences between horizontal and vertical that were practically never seen, but only felt.

In the '80s, extremely fine, delicate fonts were in fashion. That was the case with *Avenir* as well, where, starting with a light version, I made subtle gradations, always using interim steps. The light version I labelled 45, then the following ones 45.5, then 55 and 55.5 /02/. It was almost like a colour gradient: graphic artists should be able to experiment with the finest gradations. I had no plans for a fully developed family. I just started out with the idea of designing a geometric typeface that was easy on the human eye.

There are details that I drew in a different way compared to my usual style. The base letter t, for example, has a horizontal stroke at the top /07/, since this is a constructed font. The i has a round dot instead of a rhomboid /07/, since it felt more 'right' in that context. I designed two alternatives for the lowercase a and g /02/, one leaning more towards *Futura* and *ITC Avant Garde Gothic,* the other more towards *Gill Sans.* For the a, I plumped for the classical form, since a circle with a stroke really isn't an a. The classical, double-eyed g, on the other hand, absolutely does not belong in such a pure, constructed typeface, so here I used the shape derived from the cursive. I also designed two variations for each of f r t, and the versions with the less diagonal terminations were used /02/. In contrast to *Futura* or *ITC Avant Garde Gothic, Avenir* doesn't have a completely round G /05/. I simply couldn't

---

/17/

The first sans serif printing typeface Two Lines English Egyptian *(1816), by William Caslon IV belongs to the geometric classification.*

W CASLON JUNR LETTERFOUNDER

/18/

The Monotype version of the dynamic Gill Sans also features some alternative shapes in the geometric style.

Gill Sans
AGMNRW
abdgpq
abdgpqtu

/19/

Conforming to the Roman Trajan *proportion, the E of* Futura *is a double square, unlike the 'Greek'* Avenir *(from top to bottom).*

AEHOP
AEHOP
AEHOP

/20/

In contrast to the Bauhaus alphabets, all geometric sans serifs of the 1920s exhibit optical correction.

Kristall Grotesk
Erbar-Grotesk
Futura
Kabel
Neuzeit-Grotesk

/21/

An alphabet based on perfect circles, Joost Schmidt's 'Construction of a grid-based grotesque' is typical of the Bauhaus-Dessau design school.

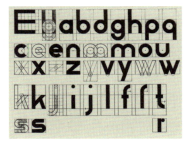

/22/

Around 1925, Paul Renner designed a variety of alternative characters for Futura *– however, they were not popular with the end users.*

/23/

Typeface samples of Futura *from the Bauersche foundry (1928) – the last line contains Paul Renner's alternative characters.*

/24/

The Roman formal ordering principle as the foundation of the constructed sans serif – Rudolf Koch's system for Kabel (1927).

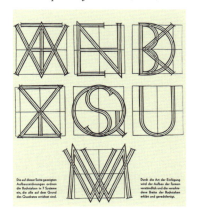

imagine that, since, for me, a G has always got a corner at the bottom right. The vertically cut circle is equally geometric. In the R, the juncture doesn't meet the stem like it does in the K /06/, since the counter at the bottom would have been too small.

The experiments for the narrow versions /14/ were never implemented. Neither was the oblique – there is no constructed oblique. In my concept document I said: "True obliques are impossible in this style. However, from purely economic considerations, an inclined version should be offered for every weight." Originally, *Avenir* was offered in six regular weights /53/. There were three slightly varying weights for body text, and in addition there were two bold weights that were constructed in such a way that no compromise had to be made for compact letters like a or e. Only later was an inclined form added to each weight. I was also later asked to have a go at an ultrabold *Avenir* /14/. I replied that if there was a demand for it, I would try it out. I was just being accommodating. Actually, there never was an ultrabold version, it was out of the question. I was always against any further extensions. But I never said that *Avenir* couldn't be extended – I just didn't want to do it myself.

Now, there's *Avenir Next*, with over 20 weights /60/. When it has been as well done as by Akira Kobayashi, the artistic director at Linotype – then you really can't say anything against it. Akira sent me a test string of each cut, to obtain my approval. There was really nothing to disagree with. It's so perfect that I ended up saying: Why not? But if the market demand hadn't been there, I wouldn't have agreed.

The name *Avenir* was, of course, a conscious allusion. I did that on purpose. 'Futura' is the Latin word for future, 'Avenir' the French equivalent. But there was never any question

A new constructed grotesque In his concept studies for *Avenir* /02/, Frutiger created 'a list of grotesque typefaces', ordered according to formal criteria. Within this group he further classified the typefaces into 'old ones', like *Erbar, Futura* etc. /20/ and 'new ones', to which he assigned *ITC Avant Garde Gothic* /27/. A further group, which likewise contained constructed typefaces Frutiger named 'Fantasy-Grotesque'. The majority of those are American types from the 1970s, whose shapes deviate in parts from the normal by having straight lines or corners replaced by curves, in the manner of *ITC Bauhaus* /32/.[15] What these typefaces have in common is an extremely fine version, thanks to improved photosetting technology. Herb Lubalin's 1968 masthead for *AvantGarde* marked the beginning of this trend /25/. Subsequently numerous circle-based types were created, among them Colin Brignall's *Premier* (1969) /32/ and the type family *ITC Avant Garde Gothic* (1970) /27/ by Herb Lubalin and Tom Carnase. [16] The ligatures made interesting title designs possible, while at the same time allowing tighter setting. Presumably in order to achieve a cohesive line formation for body text, the letter spacing of these (too-) thin sans serifs was reduced – with disastrous results. Many texts from the 1970s and 80s – even those in antiqua typefaces – are simply too tiring to read, and a generation of young type users were denied the opportunity of appreciating good typography.[17]

/25/
In 1968 Herb Lubalin, art director of the magazine Avant Garde *produced the distinct masthead – title page of issue no. 5, 1968.*

/26/
Herb Lubalin and Tom Carnase's ITC Avant Garde Gothic *first appeared in 1970 – page from the ITC catalogue (1974).*

/27/
Ed Benguiat developed the condensed fonts in 1974 – in 1977 A. Gürtler, C. Mengelt and E. Gschwind released the oblique fonts.

Avant Avant Avant **Avant** *Avant* Garde *Garde Garde Garde* ***Garde*** Gothic Gothic **Gothic** **Gothic**

/28/
Adrian Frutiger's corporate typeface Alpha BP *(1969) for the British Petroleum Company used* Futura *as a starting point.*

ABCDEFGHIJKLMN OPQRSTUVWXYZ abcdefghijklmnopq rstuvwxyz:;- 1234567890 !?/&()

/29/
Bank Gothic (1930) by Morris Fuller Benton and Micrograma *(1952) by Alessandro Butti and Aldo Novarese based on the rectangle.*

/30/
Aldo Novarese's Eurostile *(1962) and Dick Johnson's* Serpentine *(1972) both convey a constructed appeareance.*

/31/
Electronic – Letraset's Data Seventy *(1970); John Russel's* Russel Square *(1973); Alan Birch's* Letraset LCD *(1981).*

BANK GOTHIC
MICROGRAMMA

Eurostile
Serpentine

Data Seventy
Russel Square
LETRASET LCD

New Wave and Techno For *Avenir*, Frutiger drew on his experiences with his own *Alpha BP* (1969) **/28/**. He also, however, took on board the still-current trend of the 1970s extremely fine fonts. At the same time, he responded to the style of flowing transitions, which – in the form of weight transitions – was typical for many creative works of the 1980s New Wave **/33/**, by using six fine, graduated weights **/12/**. With these fonts, Frutiger produced a forerunner of the Multiple-Master idea. With this technology Adobe would, in 1991, offer the seamless generation of fonts along four design axes – 'weight', 'width', 'optical size' and 'style'. The weight axis, for example, allowed the user to generate, between two extremes, a multitude of weight gradations themselves. The first two Multiple Master typefaces appeared in 1992: *Myriad MM* (see page 257) and *Minion MM*.

As in the preceding decade, several constructed display typefaces were created in the 1980s **/36/**. In contrast to earlier attempts, the emphasis was now placed on angularity, and often extremely black fonts were used. Neville Brody's typefaces, designed for the magazine *The Face*, became very popular. *Typeface Two* and *Typeface Six* in particular became the trendsetters for the Techno style.[18] In his designs, Brody harks back to the Constructivism of the early 20th century and to 19th-century industrialisation. In contrast to *Avenir*, his typefaces and typography **/34/** display a brutish strength.

of wanting to compete with Paul Renner's or Herb Lubalin's typeface. I just wanted to bring a bit of humanity to the field of geometric types. *Avenir* wasn't a success at first. But I will say: what I did was the longest development period typeface, because there's so much purity in it. That I was able to design this typeface shows how finely honed my typographical sensibilities can get. *Univers* was a striking idea, as was *Frutiger*, but in *Avenir* there's a harmony that's much more subtle than in the others. When a letter shape really works, when you can say "that's it" – that really is a joy. And the joy is greater with *Avenir* than with *Univers*. You appreciate the o of *Univers* more quickly than the o of *Avenir*. It's all subjective, I can't describe it other than a feeling. The quality of the draughtsmanship in *Avenir* – rather than the intellectual idea behind it – is my masterpiece. To draw in all those nuances, so fine that you can hardly see them, but you know they're there, that really sapped my strength. It was the hardest typeface that I have worked on in my life. Working on it, I always had human nature in mind. And what's crucial is that I developed the typeface alone, in peace and quiet – no drafting assistants, no-one was there. My personality is stamped upon it. I'm proud that I was able to create *Avenir*.

/32/
Circle-based typefaces from the late 1960s onwards – Bauhaus *by Ed Benguiat and Victor Caruso was not designed at the Bauhaus.*

Premier
Washington
Horatio
Bauhaus
Blippo

/35/
Constructed alphabets with perfect circle O – ITC Busorama *was also designed by Tom Carnase.*

ITC BUSORAMA
PLAZA
FRANKFURTER
CHROMIUM ONE

/33/
This collage-like, colourful design (1983) by American graphic artist April Greiman is typical of the New Wave.

/36/
Typefaces from Émigré *– Zuzana Licko's* Modula *(1986), Zuzana Licko and Rudy VanderLans'* Variex *(1988); Jeffrey Keedy's* Keedy Sans *(1991).*

Modula
variex
Keedy Sans

/34/
Page from The Face 77/1986 *– logo, title and design by Neville Brody, set in* Monotype Baskerville *and* Futura.

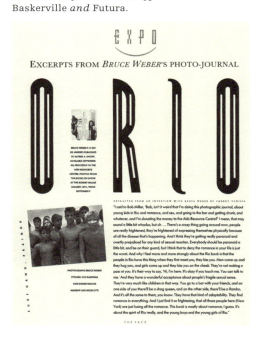

/37/
Lightly reworked versions of Neville Brody's TypefaceTwo *and* Typeface Six *were released by Linotype in 1989 as* Industria *and* Insignia.

Industria Industria
Insignia Insignia

Characters of Avenir *normal*
for laser digital typesetting by
Linotype Library.

ABCDEFGHIJKLMN
OPQRSTUVWXYZ&
abcdefghijklmnopqrs
tuvwxyzß1234567890

Production and marketing The type selection meeting took place in February 1987, and shortly after, Adrian Frutiger delivered the first sketches for the preparation of a test string. At the start of May, he produced print samples of *Avenir* 55 on various paper stocks, as well as examples of the planned weight gradations. In July the sample string 'OHamburgefonstiv' followed in master designs for 35 and 95. At this point a contract had not yet been finalised. This was eventually concluded in August. In February 1988 test exposures of 54 units of *Avenir* 35 were readied on the CRTronic, and the digitising of *Avenir* 95 was begun. In May 1988 the interpolation of the intermediate versions was carried out.[19]

The four finely graduated weights of *Avenir* offered not only nuanced possibilities in the area of body text, they were also suitable for positive-negative reproduction /11/. The two heavy weights were intended for titles and headlines. Although the concept was described, it hardly featured in specialist magazines, and was nowhere to be seen in the catalogue /39/.[20]

Oblique fonts were not offered by Linotype for laser- or CRT-setting. Instead, they were generated by the typesetter as requested. However, in 1989 oblique PostScript typefaces were available. Since these were sloped electronically and had no optical correction, the angle of inclination was limited to 8° /04/.

Avenir 125 ultrabold, planned in 1992, and the thin weights /14/ were only implemented in *Avenir Next*.

/40/
This marketing leaflet for Avenir *was given out at the Type 90 conference in Oxford in 1990 – the handwritten script contrasts with the geometrical typeface.*

/39/
The eight-page brochure (1988) was a missed opportunity: it showcased neither contemporary design nor the qualities of Avenir.

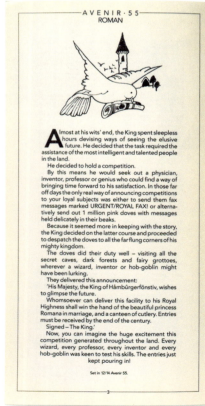

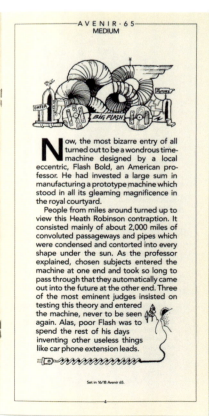

Font production:
Adobe Font digitised by
Linotype

Font format:
PostScript-Type-1

Also available:
TrueType
OpenType Com
XSF

ABCDEFGHIJKLMN
OPQRSTUVWXYZ&
abcdefghijklmnopqrs
tuvwxyzß1234567890

You may ask w

hy so many differen

t typefaces. They all serve the

same purpose but they express man's di

versity. It is the same diversity we find in wine. I once saw a li
st of Médoc wines featuring sixty different Médocs all of the
same year. All of them were wines but each was different fro
m the others. It's the nuances that are important. The same i
s true for typefaces. *Pourquoi tant d'Alphabets différents! To*
us servent au même but, mais aussi à exprimer la diversité de l'homme. C'est cette
même diversité que nous retrouvons dans les vins de Médoc. J'ai pu, un jour, relever
soixante crus, tous de la même année. Il s'agissait certes de vins, mais tous étaient di
fférents. Tout est dans la nuance du bouquet. Il en est de même pour les caractères!
Sie fragen sich, warum es notwendig ist, so viele Schriften zur Verfügung zu haben. S
ie dienen alle zum selben, aber machen die Vielfalt des Menschen aus. Diese Vielfalt
ist wie beim Wein. Ich habe einmal eine Weinkarte studiert mit sechzig Médoc-Weine

n aus dem selben Jahr. Das ist ausnahmslos Wein, aber doch nicht alles
der gleiche Wein. Es hat eben gleichwohl Nuancen. So ist es auch mit de
r Schrift. *You may ask why so many different typefaces.* They all serve the
same purpose but they express man's diversity. It is the same diversity w
e find in wine. I once saw a list of Médoc wines featuring sixty different M
édocs all of the same year. All of them were wines but each was different
from the others. It's the nuances that are important. The same is true for
typefaces. *Pourquoi tant d'Alphabets différents!* Tous servent au même b

ut, mais aussi à exprimer la diversité de l'h
omme. C'est cette même diversité que nou
s retrouvons dans les vins de Médoc. J'ai p
u, un jour, relever soixante crus, tous de la
même année. Il s'agissait certes de vins, ma
is tous étaient différents. Tout est dans la nu
ance du bouquet. Il en est de même pour l
es caractères! *Sie fragen sich, warum es not
wendig ist, so viele Schriften zur Verfügung
zu haben.* Sie dienen alle zum selben, aber

70 pt | –40   51 pt | –40   33 pt | –20   23 pt | –10   15 pt | 19 pt | 0   10.5 pt | 13 pt | 5   7.8 pt | 10.2 pt | 10   6.5 pt | 8 pt | 15

ÅBÇDÈFG
HIJKLMÑ
ÔPQRŠTÜ
VWXYZ&
ÆŒ¥$£€
1234567890
åbçdéfghij
klmñôpqrš
tüvwxyzß
fi fl æ œ ø ł ð
[.,:;·'/-–—]
(¿¡"«‹›»"!?)
{§°%@‰*†}

35 Light

*ÅBÇDÈFG
HIJKLMÑ
ÔPQRŠTÜ
VWXYZ&
ÆŒ¥$£€
1234567890
åbçdéfghij
klmñôpqrš
tüvwxyzß
fi fl æ œ ø ł ð
[.,:;·'/-–—]
(¿¡"«‹›»"!?)
{§°%@‰*†}*

35 Light Oblique

ÅBÇDÈFG
HIJKLMÑ
ÔPQRŠTÜ
VWXYZ&
ÆŒ¥$£€
1234567890
åbçdéfghij
klmñôpqrš
tüvwxyzß
fi fl æ œ ø ł ð
[.,:;·'/-–—]
(¿¡"«‹›»"!?)
{§°%@‰*†}

45 Book

*ÅBÇDÈFG
HIJKLMÑ
ÔPQRŠTÜ
VWXYZ&
ÆŒ¥$£€
1234567890
åbçdéfghij
klmñôpqrš
tüvwxyzß
fi fl æ œ ø ł ð
[.,:;·'/-–—]
(¿¡"«‹›»"!?)
{§°%@‰*†}*

45 Book Oblique

ÅBÇDÈFG
HIJKLMÑ
ÔPQRŠTÜ
VWXYZ&
ÆŒ¥$£€
1234567890
åbçdéfghij
klmñôpqrš
tüvwxyzß
fi fl æ œ ø ł ð
[.,:;·'/-–—]
(¿¡"«‹›»"!?)
{§°%@‰*†}

55 Roman

*ÅBÇDÈFG
HIJKLMÑ
ÔPQRŠTÜ
VWXYZ&
ÆŒ¥$£€
1234567890
åbçdéfghij
klmñôpqrš
tüvwxyzß
fi fl æ œ ø ł ð
[.,:;·'/-–—]
(¿¡"«‹›»"!?)
{§°%@‰*†}*

55 Oblique

Typeface comparison   With *Avenir*, Adrian Frutiger had clearly filled a gap in the market, since, as geometric comparison typefaces from the 1980s, there are only the examples of display typefaces such as *Litera* by Michael Neugebauer and *Insignia* by Neville Brody **/42/**. These two typefaces are not suited for body text, due to their extremely high x-heights and their (sometimes) rather unconventional glyphs. However, they possess lowercase characters, in contrast to other geometric display type-faces from the period. And in comparison to *Litera* and *Insignia*, *Avenir* appears a little less broad, not least due to its reduced x-height.

By looking at the o, the difference between *Avenir* and *Litera* and *Insignia* becomes immediately apparent: it is more balanced. The outer edge appears circular, but does, however, have minimal optical correction. The main opti-cal correction takes place on the inner edge. *Litera* has no such correction, and therefore appears to be more thinned-out at the sides than at top and bottom. In *Insignia*, the height is on the whole somewhat reduced in comparison to the width.

The three comparison typefaces clearly distinguish them-selves from each other. As opposed to *Avenir,* in *Litera* it is clearly more noticeable that it is a synthesis of earlier typefaces. The resemblance to *ITC Avant Garde Gothic* is particularly noticeable **/26/**, even if several letters have differing shapes, and the x-height is slightly higher. The diagonally terminated curve ends and the pointed di-agonals are further differences.

/41/
Measurement of stroke widths and proportions of the Avenir *normal weight.*

Roman				
	Hh = 10.00 cm	nh = 6.61 cm	oh = 6.95 cm	Hh : Hw = 1 : 0.77	nh : nw = 1 : 0.87
	Hw = 7.71	nw = 5.77	ow = 7.07	Hw : Hs = 1 : 0.15	nw : ns = 1 : 0.19
	Hs = 1.19	ns = 1.11	os = 1.20	Hs : Hq = 1 : 0.92	nh : oh = 1 : 1.05
	Hq = 1.10	nq = 1.02	oq = 1.02		nw : ow = 1 : 1.22

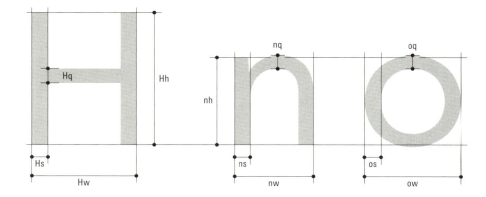

/42/
In contrast to Litera *and* Insignia, Avenir *exhibits a balanced relationship between its x-height and its cap height, one of the reasons for its increased legibility.*

Hofstainberg

Litera
Michael Neugebauer
1983

G M R a t o v 46

Hofstainberg

Avenir
Adrian Frutiger
1988

G M R a t o v 46

G
Curve ends in vertical throat without spur

M
Wide, right-angled proportion, V-form rests horizontally on the baseline

R
Diagonal leg clearly offset from stem

a
Classical shape, curve terminated diagonally

t
Stem cut horizontally at top, curved under

o
Stroke weight slighty reduced top and bottom

v
Angle horizontally terminated

4 6
Blunt termination of angles, diagonals horizontally terminated

Hofstainberg

Insignia
Neville Brody
1989

G M R a t o v 46

/43/

Comparison showing the different weights and angle of the oblique.

	Hh	Hw	Hs	Hq
Light	10.00 cm	7.44 = 0.96	0.93 = 0.78	0.85 = 0.77
Book	10.00	7.48 = 0.97	0.99 = 0.83	0.94 = 0.85
Roman	10.00	7.71 = 1	1.19 = 1	1.10 = 1
Medium	10.00	7.88 = 1.02	1.35 = 1.13	1.27 = 1.15
Heavy	10.00	8.23 = 1.07	1.77 = 1.49	1.60 = 1.45
Black	10.00	8.67 = 1.12	2.18 = 1.83	1.94 = 1.76
Italic	10.00	7.62 = 0.99	1.17 = 0.98	1.11 = 1.09

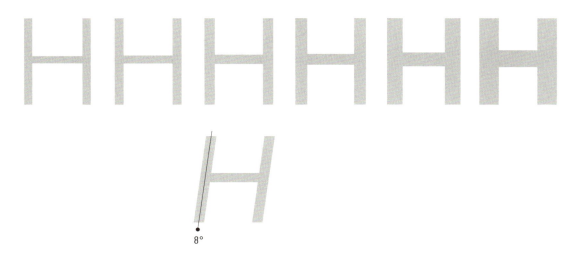

8°

/44/

Height comparison showing the difference of x-heights to ascenders and descenders – the cap height is the starting point.

Litera
42.8 pt

Avenir
40.3 pt

Insignia
45.5 pt

ÅBÇDÈFG HIJKLMÑ ÔPQRŠTÜ VWXYZ& ÆŒ¥$£€ 1234567890 åbçdéfghij klmñôpqrš tüvwxyzß fi fl æ œ ø ł ð [.,:;·'/-–—] (¿¡"«‹›»"!?) {§°%@‰*†}

65 Medium

ÅBÇDÈFG HIJKLMÑ ÔPQRŠTÜ VWXYZ& ÆŒ¥$£€ 1234567890 åbçdéfghij klmñôpqrš tüvwxyzß fi fl æ œ ø ł ð [.,:;·'/-–—] (¿¡"«‹›»"!?) {§°%@‰†}*

65 Medium Oblique

ÅBÇDÈFG HIJKLMÑ ÔPQRŠTÜ VWXYZ& ÆŒ¥$£€ 1234567890 åbçdéfghij klmñôpqrš tüvwxyzß fi fl æ œ ø ł ð [.,:;·'/-–—] (¿¡"«‹›»"!?) {§°%@‰*†}

85 Heavy

ÅBÇDÈFG HIJKLMÑ ÔPQRŠTÜ VWXYZ& ÆŒ¥$£€ 1234567890 åbçdéfghij klmñôpqrš tüvwxyzß fi fl æ œ ø ł ð [.,:;·'/-–—] (¿¡"«‹›»"!?) {§°%@‰*†}

85 Heavy Oblique

ÅBÇDÈFG HIJKLMÑ ÔPQRŠTÜ VWXYZ& ÆŒ¥$£€ 1234567890 åbçdéfghij klmñôpqrš tüvwxyzß fi fl æ œ ø ł ð [.,:;·'/-–—] (¿¡"«‹›»"!?) {§°%@‰*†}

95 Black

ÅBÇDÈFG HIJKLMÑ ÔPQRŠTÜ VWXYZ& ÆŒ¥$£€ 1234567890 åbçdéfghij klmñôpqrš tüvwxyzß fi fl æ œ ø ł ð [.,:;·'/-–—] (¿¡"«‹›»"!?) {§°%@‰*†}

95 Black Oblique

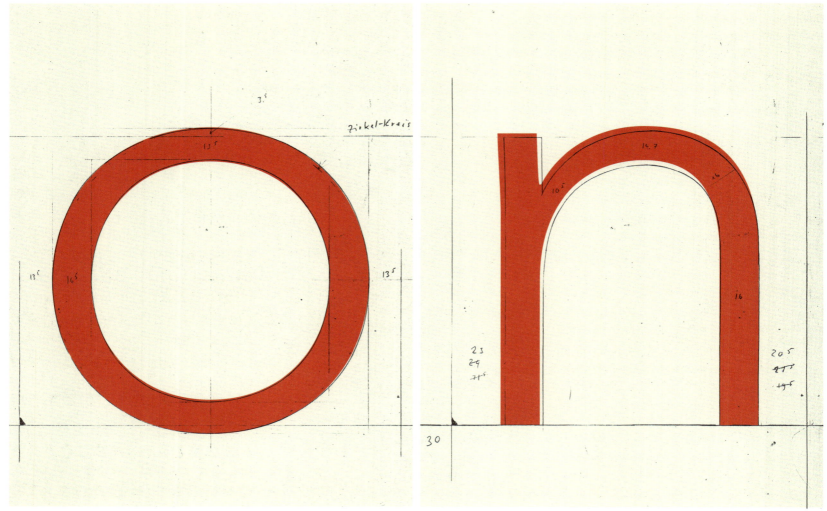

/45/
*Adrian Frutiger's orginal drawings
with measurements (background)
superimposed by the PostScript
version of* Avenir LT *35.*

/46/
In Avenir LT *(left) interior side on
the m is vertical, on the n it is
slightly inclined; in* Avenir Next
they are both the same.

/47/
On the K of Avenir LT *a short
bridge joins the diagonals
to the stem; in* Avenir Next *this
is absent.*

/48/
In Avenir LT *95 Black (left)
the e conforms less to a perfect
circle than it does in*
Avenir Next *Bold (right).*

/49/
In contrast to Avenir LT *(left),
the at-sign in* Avenir Next *(right) is
more harmonious and a little
more open.*

/50/
In Avenir LT *the horizontal strokes of
E F G are all at the same height –
in* Avenir Next *that of the F is slightly
lower and that of the G clearly lower.*

EFG EFG

/51/
*A skewing in the X-diagonal is
required optically – in* Avenir LT
*(left) this is far more noticeable
than in* Avenir Next *(right).*

/52/
In the 4 of Avenir LT *the diagonal
is the lightest stroke; in* Avenir Next
*(right) it is the horizontal – and
the 0 is also narrower.*

40 40

/53/
The original Avenir LT *with the
four finely graduated text weights
and the two blacker title and
signage fonts.*

Avenir Light
Avenir Book
Avenir Roman
Avenir Medium
Avenir Heavy
Avenir Black

Avenir Next In 2002 Linotype decided upon the reworking and extension of *Avenir*. In the marketing brochure **/59/** for *Avenir Next,* it stated: "Avenir's true potential as a contemporary typeface has not been appreciated." Akira Kobayashi, art director of Linotype, was quoted as saying: "There are some fonts missing that would make Avenir universally applicable."[21] Adrian Frutiger's idea of providing the layout designer with minimal shifts in weight in order to be able to produce gradations with text **/12/**, is no longer in fashion. More varied typefaces are demanded, as well as a broader spectrum from ultralight to black **/60/**. Furthermore, there is a demand for condensed fonts. *Avenir Next* was reworked by Akira Kobayashi, with Adrian Frutiger as consultant. The new version shows improvements. The arches of m and n are given the same shape and are not so strongly curved **/46/**. Originally Adrian Frutiger had drawn them vertical **/45/**. The angle of the uppercase K is set directly against the stem, and the bridge eliminated **/47/**. In the X, the offset of the diagonal is more conservative **/51/**, in the 4 the diagonal is strengthened, and the 0 receives a somewhat more oval, narrower shape **/52/**. There are now also oldstyle numerals **/56/** and small caps **/57/**.[22] Moreover, in *Avenir Next* the bold-fine contrast is slightly increased compared to *Avenir LT,* and the narrow fonts exhibit clearly tapered junctures. Because of this, in larger point sizes and also in its narrow versions, *Avenir Next* loses some of its linear character **/55/**.

/54/
Characters of Avenir Next *Regular for OpenType digital typesetting by Linotype.*

A B C D E F G H I J K L M N O P Q R S T U V W X Y Z &
a b c d e f g h i j k l m n o p q r s t u v w x y z ß 1 2 3 4 5 6 7 8 9 0

/55/
Especially in the narrow fonts, Avenir Next *has sharply tapering curve junctures, and therefore has a less linear appearance.*

Avenir Next Condensed

/56/
Avenir Next *contains oldstyle numbers (left) that differ formally from lining figures and small caps numerals.*

1234567890 1234567890

/57/
True small caps such as the ones for Avenir Next *are an enrichment and are increasingly used in sans serif types.*

SMALL CAPS

/58/
Avenir Next *OpenType Pro is equipped with a comprehensive set of accented characters for multilingual typesetting.*

áâàãäåāǎąćĉċč

/59/
Avenir Next *brochure in three languages (2004) – the 16 pages show sample strings and usage examples of all the fonts.*

/60/
The weight gradations of Avenir Next *encompass a wide spectrum – the weights with the same designation differ from those in* Avenir LT.

Avenir Next UltraLight
Avenir Next Regular
Avenir Next Medium
Avenir Next Demi
Avenir Next Bold
Avenir Next Heavy

/61/
Avenir LT *(top) and* Avenir Next *(bottom) have almost the same stroke weights – although light and roman are omitted.*

Font production:
Digitised by Linotype

Font format:
OpenType Pro

Å B Ç D È F G
H I J K L M Ñ
Ô P Q R Š T Ü
V W X Y Z &
Æ Œ ¥ $ £ €
1 2 3 4 5 6 7 8 9 0
å b ç d é f g h i j
k l m ñ ô p q r š
t ü v w x y z ß
fi fl æ œ ø ł ð
[. , : ; · ' / - – —]
(¿ ¡ " « ‹ › » " ! ?)
{ § ° % @ ‰ * † }

UltraLight Condensed

Å B Ç D È F G
H I J K L M Ñ
Ô P Q R Š T Ü
V W X Y Z &
Æ Œ ¥ $ £ €
1 2 3 4 5 6 7 8 9 0
å b ç d é f g h i j
k l m ñ ô p q r š
t ü v w x y z ß
fi fl æ œ ø ł ð
[. , : ; · ' / - – —]
(¿ ¡ " « ‹ › » " ! ?)
{ § ° % @ ‰ * † }

UltraLight Condensed Italic

Å B Ç D È F G
H I J K L M Ñ
Ô P Q R Š T Ü
V W X Y Z &
Æ Œ ¥ $ £ €
1 2 3 4 5 6 7 8 9 0
å b ç d é f g h i j
k l m ñ ô p q r š
t ü v w x y z ß
fi fl æ œ ø ł ð
[. , : ; · ' / - – —]
(¿ ¡ " « ‹ › » " ! ?)
{ § ° % @ ‰ * † }

Condensed

Å B Ç D È F G
H I J K L M Ñ
Ô P Q R Š T Ü
V W X Y Z &
Æ Œ ¥ $ £ €
1 2 3 4 5 6 7 8 9 0
å b ç d é f g h i j
k l m ñ ô p q r š
t ü v w x y z ß
fi fl æ œ ø ł ð
[. , : ; · ' / - – —]
(¿ ¡ " « ‹ › » " ! ?)
{ § ° % @ ‰ * † }

Condensed Italic

Å B Ç D È F G
H I J K L M Ñ
Ô P Q R Š T Ü
V W X Y Z &
Æ Œ ¥ $ £ €
1 2 3 4 5 6 7 8 9 0
å b ç d é f g h i j
k l m ñ ô p q r š
t ü v w x y z ß
fi fl æ œ ø ł ð
[. , : ; · ' / - – —]
(¿ ¡ " « ‹ › » " ! ?)
{ § ° % @ ‰ * † }

Medium Condensed

Å B Ç D È F G
H I J K L M Ñ
Ô P Q R Š T Ü
V W X Y Z &
Æ Œ ¥ $ £ €
1 2 3 4 5 6 7 8 9 0
å b ç d é f g h i j
k l m ñ ô p q r š
t ü v w x y z ß
fi fl æ œ ø ł ð
[. , : ; · ' / - – —]
(¿ ¡ " « ‹ › » " ! ?)
{ § ° % @ ‰ * † }

Medium Condensed Italic

Å B Ç D È F G
H I J K L M Ñ
Ô P Q R Š T Ü
V W X Y Z &
Æ Œ ¥ $ £ €
1 2 3 4 5 6 7 8 9 0
å b ç d é f g h i j
k l m ñ ô p q r š
t ü v w x y z ß
fi fl æ œ ø ł ð
[. , : ; · ' / - – —]
(¿ ¡ " « ‹ › » " ! ?)
{ § ° % @ ‰ * † }

UltraLight

UltraLight Italic

Regular

Italic

Medium

Medium Italic

1 2 3 4 5 6 7 8 9 0
Å B Ç D È F G
H I J K L M Ñ
Ô P Q R Š T Ü
V W X Y Z &
Æ Œ ¥ $ £ €

UltraLight Cond. OsF & SC

UltraLight Cond. Ital. OsF & SC

Condensed OsF & SC

Condensed Italic OsF & SC

Medium Cond. OsF & SC

Medium Cond. Ital. OsF & SC

1 2 3 4 5 6 7 8 9 0
Å B Ç D È F G
H I J K L M Ñ
Ô P Q R Š T Ü
V W X Y Z &
Æ Œ ¥ $ £ €

UltraLight OsF & SC

UltraLight Italic OsF & SC

Regular OsF & SC

Italic OsF & SC

Medium OsF & SC

Medium Italic OsF & SC

ÅBÇDÈFG ÅBÇDÈFG ÅBÇDÈFG ÅBÇDÈFG ÅBÇDÈFG ÅBÇDÈFG
HIJKLMÑ HIJKLMÑ HIJKLMÑ HIJKLMÑ HIJKLMÑ HIJKLMÑ
ÔPQRŠTÜ ÔPQRŠTÜ ÔPQRŠTÜ ÔPQRŠTÜ ÔPQRŠTÜ ÔPQRŠTÜ
VWXYZ& VWXYZ& VWXYZ& VWXYZ& VWXYZ& VWXYZ&
ÆŒ¥$£€ ÆŒ¥$£€ ÆŒ¥$£€ ÆŒ¥$£€ ÆŒ¥$£€ ÆŒ¥$£€
1234567890 1234567890 1234567890 1234567890 1234567890 1234567890
åbçdéfghij åbçdéfghij åbçdéfghij åbçdéfghij åbçdéfghij åbçdéfghij
klmñôpqrš klmñôpqrš klmñôpqrš klmñôpqrš klmñôpqrš klmñôpqrš
tüvwxyzß tüvwxyzß tüvwxyzß tüvwxyzß tüvwxyzß tüvwxyzß
fi fl æ œ ø ł ð

Demi Condensed | Demi Condensed Italic | Bold Condensed | Bold Condensed Italic | Heavy Condensed | Heavy Condensed Italic

Demi | Demi Italic | Bold | Bold Italic | Heavy | Heavy Italic

Demi Cond. OsF & SC | Demi Cond. Italic OsF & SC | Bold Cond. OsF & SC | Bold Cond. Italic OsF & SC | Heavy Cond. OsF & SC | Heavy Cond. Italic OsF & SC

Demi OsF & SC | Demi Italic OsF & SC | Bold OsF & SC | Bold Italic OsF & SC | Heavy OsF & SC | Heavy Italic OsF & SC

Name of typeface	Designer	Design | Publication	Typesetting technology	Manufacturer	Weights
Westside	Adrian Frutiger	1988 | 1989	CRT and laser digital typesetting	– Linotype	1
			OpenType digital typesetting	– Linotype	1

WESTSIDE

As a type designer I wanted to draw something in every style. It's a matter of professional pride. After having done oldstyle, latin, egyptienne and grotesque, italienne was still missing. *Westside* from 1989 is my contribution to this group. It was created during a period in which I felt a certain degree of emptiness. Up until the late seventies I had been working flat out on projects. After that came a quiet phase where I suddenly had time to think. I felt that I was through with the whole area of classic type, with or without serifs. I had rounded off my work nicely with *Linotype Centennial,* and I had no desire to do a *Garamond*-style typeface; it just wasn't my thing. Grotesque, too, seemed to be exhausted. What was missing was a cowboy typeface with bold serifs, like part of the 'corporate identity' of any Wild West movie. I found the existing italiennes with their big feet too harsh and strict /09/. Like so many times before, I was interested in the inner shapes. The fine curves in the serifs give *Westside* its own expression /10/. A text set in this typeface looks like a weaving pattern.

Another reason for trying an italienne may have been the fact that I had a consultancy contract with Linotype, and felt myself obliged not to show up at type selection meetings empty handed. This was also behind the steady search for new possibilities. Those were the things that drove me. When I presented my italienne design to the committee it aroused some interest. They found it to be both novel and classical at the same time. My concept for capitals was special: I made all horizontal strokes thick, and all verticals thin. It was a question of consistency. Making the horizontal strokes thick was only possible for capitals, it wouldn't work for lowercase a and e with their small counters /16/. As opposed to my design, the existing italienne versions only had thickened serifs and arcs, the cross-strokes themselves were left thin. Werner Schimpf, director of the Linotype type department at the time, always wrote detailed comments to the final artwork. He was quick to remark "H – cross-stroke too bold?"[1] However, my idea was to continue the horizontal band of the lowercase letters by using emphasised cross-strokes /16/. With the consistency of strokes and rounded serif transitions, I slowly developed an alternative design to the existing italiennes. One thing was typical of me: I didn't look first to see what others had done. I just drew it the way I wanted. I was always very self-absorbed in this phase of the type design process, although I did, of course, have the image of an italienne in mind.

The name 'Westside' was my idea. The typeface was part of a package consisting of four derivations; the concept was to complement *Westside* with '*Eastside*' and '*Gothic F*' versions, in addition to a few '*Fancy*' typefaces. The thick serifs made me want to try something playful. I delivered the basic version of *Westside* and Linotype then wanted to change only the serif shapes independently, though it never came to that. However, it was a big investment to produce an entire typeface with 120 characters. Unfortunately *Westside* was

Consistency in Westside Adrian Frutiger's *Westside* is a slab serif typeface in the italienne subgroup of slab serifs. In general italiennes, like the ornamental variety tuscans, are known as western typefaces[2] – a style of typeface that was not actually represented by Linotype in the 1989 Mergenthaler Type Library. Robert Harling's *Playbill* from 1938 is the only one to be included /09/. This may sound surprising for a type manufacturer based in the United States, but it is explained by the fact that Mergenthaler originally concentrated on body text typefaces.

In conversation Adrian Frutiger points out that his approach to italiennes was to emphasise the consistency of thick strokes. All horizontal parts of the letters are bold, the exceptions being the cross-strokes of lowercase a and e, which are thin. These bars cannot be emphasised for two reasons. First of all, the counters are too small for a bold stroke. Second, and more importantly, it would disrupt the horizontal bands of baseline and x-height /16/. It is this impression of bands that interests Frutiger most. For this reason he also thickened the lower converging diagonal strokes of the letters VWvw.[3] Even the y has this, albeit slightly less /15/. In addition, the bold cross-strokes of ABEFGHPRS continue the line of the x-height, but shifted down a little, since the optical middle of capitals is lower than the x-height. Finally, the ascenders and descenders form two other bands, with all four bands creating the weaving pattern mentioned by Frutiger /16/.

Adrian Frutiger kept in mind that capitals without bold middle strokes appear distinctly lighter /13/, leading to an unharmonious appearance /10/. Harmony is seldom achieved by other italienne typefaces, as light spots often appear in the heads or feet of diagonal letters /09/.

The concept of *Westside* as a basic typeface with extensions through different serif shapes might well have proved successful, as Adobe released some wood type fonts in 1990,[4] awaking interest in the genre /12/. There is barely any material available regarding Adrian Frutiger's '*Eastside*', '*Gothic F*' and '*Fancy*' typeface variants. All that exists is a written note of the aforementioned versions and a design for an English latin typeface /06/, plus a sketch with six tuscan variants /07/.[5]

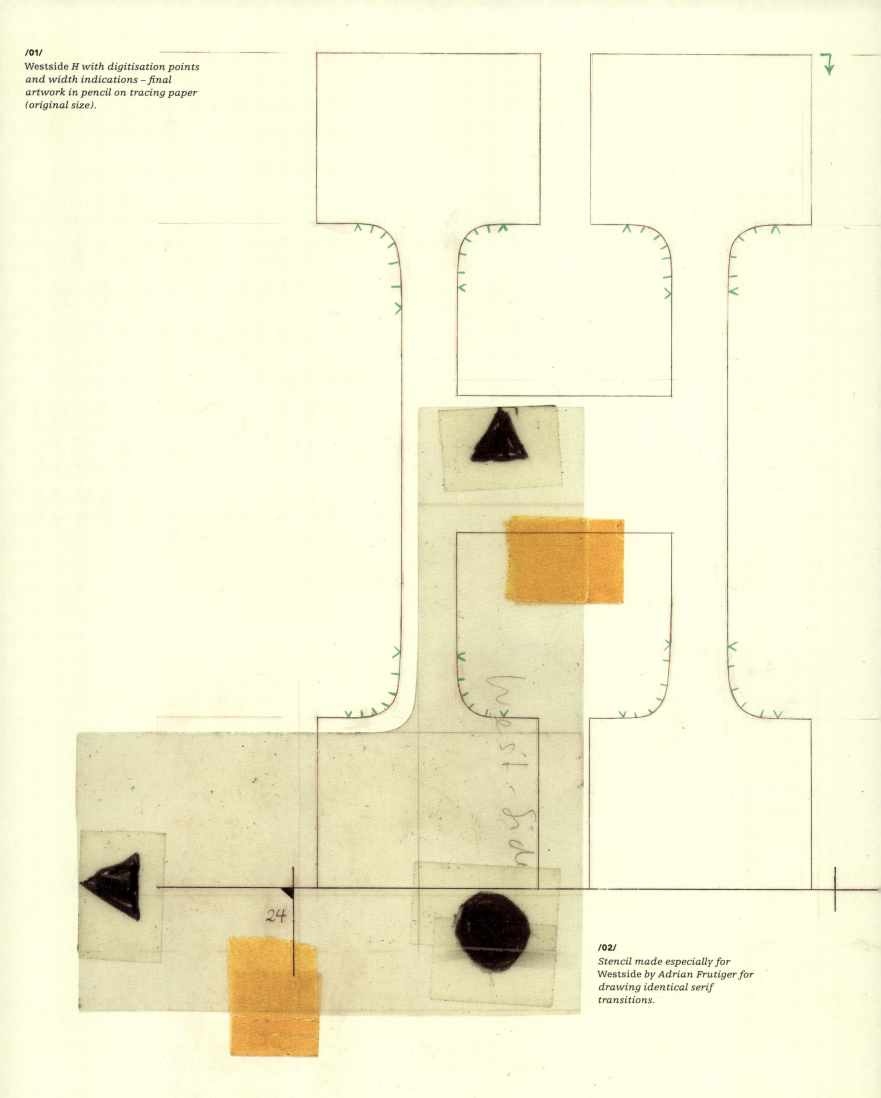

/01/
Westside *H with digitisation points and width indications – final artwork in pencil on tracing paper (original size).*

/02/
Stencil made especially for Westside by Adrian Frutiger for drawing identical serif transitions.

24

/03/
Sheet assembled by Adrian Frutiger
of very varied kinds of decorative
faces, including many tuscans.

/04/
*'Ritual' typeface design from
1980 is related to Breughel and also
to Westside, due to its fine
vertical strokes and accentuated
horizontals.*

Heimat deine Firne

Heimat deine Firne scheinen wie goldene
Flammen am abendlichen Firmament.
Hügelreihen ziehen sich wie bewaldete
Inseln vom nahen Flusse bis ins Hohland.

Ritual project

/05/
*Undated design for Westside –
the version realised in 1989 –
has approximately 30% narrower
proportions.*

/06/
*Undated design of a
Westside variant in the style of a
latin typeface with very heavy
serifs.*

bondum

/07/
*Adrian Frutiger's concept
includes extensions with variations
of the serif shapes of the basic
version of Westside.*

The italienne subgroup Italiennes (French Clarendon) are a subgroup of slab serif typefaces. These jobbing, and in particular, poster typefaces originated, like egyptians, in early 19th-century England.[6] The Italian Rustica from the 4th/5th century was the sole historical precedent (see page 387) for the unusual principle of accentuated horizontal strokes opposed to fine vertical strokes. Whether or not the term italienne refers to this relation is open. Generally, a historically formal reference is not made, particularly so as the other subgroups like egyptian and tuscan do not have this feature.[7]

According to František Muzika italiennes may be classed in two groups.[8] The newer form has accentuated heads and feet only /08/, whereas in the older form capitals with three horizontal strokes, such as B and R, have accentuated middle strokes /08/. Thus Westside /10/ belongs to the older form. Whether or not italienne serif transitions are angular or bracketed makes no difference for classification.[9] Rob Roy Kelly however makes a difference.[10]

Hans Rudolf Bosshard divides slab serif typefaces into five subgroups: Egyptienne[11], without curved serif transitions; clarendon, with curves; italienne, accentuated bold serifs opposite thinner stems; oldstyle (latin), triangular serifs; and toscanienne, with split serifs /11/.[12]

also not successful enough – much to our surprise. Perhaps it was just too meek compared to the 2000 or so very freeform fantasy typefaces of the 1980s.

Westside is very rarely associated with me, even though I really enjoyed drawing it. For one thing it was just great fun, yet it was also serious in the sense of having to execute all its details perfectly. In hindsight there are a few niggles: capital G is slightly too narrow /13/; C appears wider, more open, as does uppercase O – in other words, G could be broader; but in the end it proved impossible to give all letters the same width. The fact that letters like K L M N – in comparison with E F G H – appear visibly lighter due to their lacking emphasis in the middle is perhaps a bit irritating /13/. One could criticise the very large i and j dots /10/. Legibility is not exactly improved by them. Yet even this feature arose from the consistency of the dark horizontal bands /16/. A word like 'Pourquoi' /14/ doesn't look too bad because the missing ascenders surround the dot with enough white space.

On the whole, work on *Westside* went ahead swiftly and smoothly.[13] My procedure was the usual one. For the final artwork I first cut stencils and sanded their curves with emery paper /02/, then the drawings were done in a jiffy. After that Werner Schimpf added his suggestions for changes, and the last final artwork finishing was done on the individual shapes. *Westside* was released in 1989. It is a very consistent typeface.

/08/
19th-century French Clarendons – the older form (top) has heavy cross-strokes while the newer form (bottom) remains thin in the middle.

BROS
BROSE

/09/
Different designs of the heads and feet of the diagonal letters A and W: P.T. Barnum, Playbill *and* Figaro *(from left to right).*

WANTED wildwest

WANTED wildwest

WANTED wildwest

/10/
Westside *belongs to the older French Clarendons with its heavy cross-strokes and its consistently bold heads and feet.*

WANTED wildwest

/11/
Slab serif jobbing faces may be divided into the following five groups according to their serif shapes.

EGYPTIENNE
CLARENDON
ITALIENNE
LATIN
TOSCANIENNE

/12/
Wood types by Adobe from the early 1990s – all were derived from types shown in American Wood Type: 1828–1900 *by Rob Roy Kelly.*

COTTONWOOD IRONWOOD PONDEROSA
JUNIPER MESQUITE ROSEWOOD

/13/
Westside *capitals can be divided into two groups: those with bold middle sections (top) and those with thin middle sections (bottom).*

ABEFGHPRS
CKLMNOTZ

/14/
There are French Clarendon typefaces from narrow to wide – Westside *looks very different when electronically expanded by 200%.*

Pourquoi
Pourquoi

/15/
The converging lines in the diagonal letters are stressed: the A is given a single-sided serif.

AVWvwy

/16/
The accentuated sections form four horizontal bands – Westside's verticality creates a kind of weaving pattern.

ae bghipsv

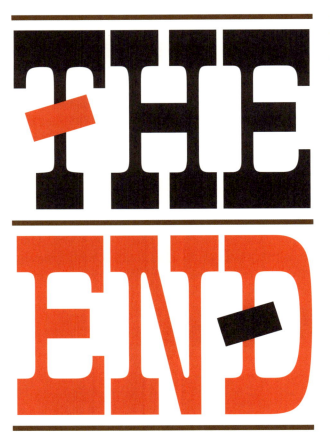

/17/
Design for a possible end of a film in Westside – *the absence of heavy cross-strokes can inspire exciting solutions.*

Typeface comparison   In the late 1980s personal computers became the instrument of choice among designers and typographers, and typefaces by various manufacturers were released for desktop publishing, then still in its infancy. Nevertheless, at the time there was a lack of well-known typefaces for PCs, although new ones were eagerly anticipated. The new type formats – independent of hardware but not of operating systems – presented the manufacturers with the opportunity of producing type for a much wider clientele.[14] Typefaces could also be produced that were intended for limited areas of use, or which followed short-lived trends.

Until the mid-1990s a conspicuously large number of 'western' or wood type fonts were produced. Along with a few mostly ornamental all caps alphabets by Adobe /12/, three other typefaces of that period had lowercase letters: *Westside, Buffalo Gal* and *Wanted* /18/. They also have accentuated serifs and a narrow proportion in common. While in *Westside* the band effect is emphasised, *Buffalo Gal* manages to produce another fine horizontal line with its double-sided points in the downstrokes, typical of a tuscan. The most traditional, and at the same time most 'modern' version of this historical genre was Letraset's *Wanted*, in which Robert Harling's typeface *Playbill* was imitated as worn-out wooden letters.

/18/
Westside *and* Buffalo Gal *have strict design concepts, whereas* Wanted *tends to impart a sense of casual coincidence.*

Hofstainberg
Westside
Adrian Frutiger
1989

> A > Q S < a < g > w ^ ^ y < 3 < 6

A	**Q**	**S**	**a**	**g**	**w**	**y**	**3 6**
Single one-sided head serif, accentuated cross-stroke	Tail vertically attached to the middle	Diagonal stroke accentuated, almost horizontal	Head section appears wide, horizontal arc connection	Single loop shape	Baseline accentuated by right-angled feet	Filled cup, descender attached vertically	Arc shape closed and open respectively

Hofstainberg
Buffalo Gal
Thomas A. Rickner
1994

A Q S a g w y 3 6

Hofstainberg
Wanted (Playbill)
Esselte Letraset (Robert Harling)
1995 (1938)

A Q S a g w y 3 6

Font production:
Digitised by Linotype

Font format:
PostScript Type 1

Also available:
TrueType

ABCDEFGHIJKLMN
OPQRSTUVWXYZ&
abcdefghijklmnopqrst
uvwxyzß1234567890

ÅBÇDÈFG
HIJKLMÑ
ÔPQRŠTÜ
VWXYZ&
ÆŒ¥$£€
1234567890
åbçdéfghij
klmñôpqrš
tüvwxyzß
fiflæœøłð
[.,:;·'/-–—]
(¿¡"«‹›»"!?)
{§°%@‰*†}

Regular

Pourquoi tant d'Alp habets différents! Tous s ervent au même but, mais aussi à exprimer la diversité de l'homme. C'est cette

même diversité que nous retrouvons dans les vins de Médoc. J'ai pu, un jour, relever soixante crus, tous de la même année. Il s'agissait certes de vins, mais tous étaient différents. Tout est dans la nuance du bouquet. Il en est de même pour les caractères! Sie fragen sich, warum es notwend ig ist, so viele Schriften zur Verfügung zu haben. Sie dienen alle zum sel

ben, aber machen die Vielfalt des Menschen aus. Diese Vielfalt ist wie beim Wein. Ich habe einmal eine Weink arte studiert mit sechzig Médoc-Weinen aus dem selben Jahr. Das ist ausnahmslos Wein, aber doch nicht alles der gleiche Wein. Es hat eben gleichwohl Nuancen. So ist es auch mit der Schrift. You may ask why so many di fferent typefaces. They all serve the same purpose but they express man's diversity. It is the same diversity we find in wine. I once saw a list of Médoc wines featuring sixty different Médocs all of the same year. All of them were wines but each was different from the others. It's the nuances that are important. The same is true for ty pefaces. Pourquoi tant d'Alphabets différents! Tous servent au même but, mais aussi à exprimer la diversité de

l'homme. C'est cette même diversité que nous retrouvons dans les vins de Médoc. J'ai pu, un jour, relever soixante crus, tous de la même année. Il s'agissait certes de vins, mais tous éta ient différents. Tout est dans la nuance du bouquet. Il en est de même pour les caractères! Sie fragen sich, warum es notwendig ist, so viele Schriften zur Verfügung zu haben. Sie di enen alle zum selben, aber machen die Vielfalt des Menschen aus. Diese Vielfalt ist wie bei m Wein. Ich habe einmal eine Weinkarte studiert mit sechzig Médoc-Weinen aus dem selb en Jahr. Das ist ausnahmslos Wein, aber doch nicht alles der gleiche Wein. Es hat eben gle ichwohl Nuancen. So ist es auch mit der Schrift. You may ask why so many different typefa

ces. They all serve the same purpose but they express man' s diversity. It is the same diversity we find in wine. I once saw a list of Médoc wines featuring sixty different Médocs all of the same year. All of them were wines but each was different from the others. It's the nuances that are import ant. The same is true for typefaces. Pourquoi tant d'Alphab ets différents! Tous servent au même but, mais aussi à ex primer la diversité de l'homme. C'est cette même diversité que nous retrouvons dans les vins de Médoc. J'ai pu, un jo ur, relever soixante crus, tous de la même année. Il s'agiss

81 pt | −20   63 pt | −10   44 pt | 0   33 pt | 10   19.5 pt | 19.5 pt | 15   12.5 pt | 13.2 pt | 20   9.5 pt | 10.2 pt | 30   7 pt | 8 pt | 50

Name of typeface	Designer	Design | Publication	Typesetting technology	Manufacturer	Weights
Vectora	Adrian Frutiger	1988 | 1991	Laser digital typesetting	– Linotype	4
			PostScript digital typesetting	– Adobe | Linotype	8

VECTORA

The stimulus for *Vectora* came from two directions: on the one hand, I had been thinking about the then-current trends, because I had seen the invitation to the 1988 ATypI conference, set in *Trade Gothic*. It looked as if the time of sleek grotesque typefaces was over for graphic designers. My thoughts wandered from the recently released *Avenir* to the American gothics. I made a sketch of how a *News Gothic* in a new guise might look /06/. On the other hand, there was this enquiry from the Schweizerische Volksbank. They wanted a new corporate typeface, and couldn't decide between *Helvetica* and *Univers;* the competition had switched to *Futura.* I suggested that they look more in the direction of *News Gothic* /04/, and prepared a further sketch /07/. The first design didn't seem appropriate to me: there's something hard-nosed about a bank, it's all about percentages and dividends, not literature or music. The consultation didn't result in a contract in the end, but those musings gave birth to my last typeface family, *Vectora.*

While I was developing this typeface, I thought about the closely set small ads in the newspapers, about the idea of 'classified news' that had always appealed to me. With *Franklin Gothic* /04/ Morris Fuller Benton had created an important reader-friendly typeface. And I always try and keep the reader foremost in my mind. So the question is: is a typeface readable? I had seen old people with thick glasses trying to decipher timetables, or businessmen reading the stock market reports in the papers, often at a size of 5 pt, or even smaller. I created *Vectora* for just such disparate needs.

The American gothics are characterised by the way the curves are attached to the stem – like gnarled branches that are joined together like girders. In smaller point sizes, they are simply easier to make out than a curve. I carried this over into *Vectora.* What's unique about *Vectora* is the elevated x-height. You find that as well in American gothics, but here it's based on the x-height of Roger Excoffon's *Antique Olive* /11/. While he was designing it, I had already discussed the proportion of the x-height to the cap height with him – we always showed our designs to each other. *Antique Olive* really was something new, and I was quite enthusiastic about what he was doing. I always regarded *Antique Olive* as a really beautiful yet daring design. The sharply raised x-height in *Vectora* caused a problem: I had to lower the crossbars of f and t. If I had left them at the x-height, the top counter of the f would have been too small /08/. However, ligatures like rt or tz seem to appear a bit unbalanced now /10/. Really, I didn't lose any sleep over those ligatures – they're not very common, and in small point sizes, like those found in telephone books, they really don't bother me.

The lowercase ascenders were stretched slightly higher than the cap height /11/, I didn't want to overdo it – in condensed settings it can get tricky when ascenders and descenders are bumping into each other. That's why I also drew the numbers at the cap height. In

General remarks on Vectora The naming of Adrian Frutiger's typeface, which was derived from American gothics,[1] merits an explanation. Frutiger referred to it as 'Relief' in the original designs from 1988, but this name is not ideal in English.[2] Adrian Frutiger made thirteen suggestions. Among them his favourites were 'Raster Gothic', 'Delta Gothic' and 'Grid'.[3] In a Linotype 'internal memorandum', his first and third suggestions were accepted, and three further names were added.[4] However, none of these was finally adopted, since an additional problem surfaced in the form of the Patent Office, which will not register typeface names with the suffix 'gothic'.[5] Finally, Linotype suggested 'Vektora' (initially written with a k) with the justification: "… relying on the geometric vector, which is mostly used as a mathematical description of the magnitude and direction of a physical quantity, for example speed or power."[6] The typeface was released in 1991 as *Vectora.*

While 'Relief' was being worked on, Otmar Hoefer expressed a wish to draw it in such a way that it would be compatible with *Linotype Centennial.* For Adrian Frutiger this idea was unfeasible, since the most noticeable feature of 'Relief' is its extremely tall x-height.[7] He had conceived his typeface for the field of 'classified news' which he understood to comprise text in small point sizes for newspapers, such as television guides, stock market reports and classified ads.

Although in the first test exposures the crossbars of f and t were placed at the x-height, over the course of the face's development Adrian Frutiger lowered them /08/. Reinhard Haus, art director of Linotype-Hell AG, experimented with placing the cap height at the same level as the height of the ascenders /08/. However, this approach was not implemented.

The initially planned range of weights from 45 to 85 was soon extended to 95, since headlines and titles appeared too light at 85. Adrian Frutiger eventually produced final drawings for the 45 and 95 versions, and the intermediate weights of 55 and 75 were interpolated. The typeface was available from the start as both laser- and digital (PostScript) setting; for lasersetting, however, it was produced – as was *Avenir* – without oblique versions. Instead, in all four weights, *Vectora* has small caps and lining figures /01/.

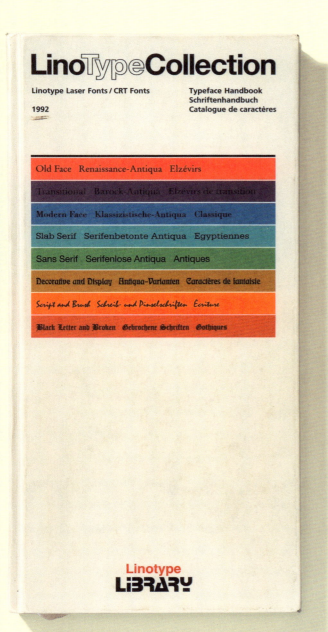

LinoTypeCollection

Linotype Laser Fonts / CRT Fonts   Typeface Handbook
Schriftenhandbuch
1992   Catalogue de caractères

Old Face Renaissance-Antiqua Elzévirs

Transitional Barock-Antiqua Elzévirs de transition

Modern Face Klassizistische-Antiqua Classique

Slab Serif Serifenbetonte Antiqua Egyptiennes

Sans Serif Serifenlose Antiqua Antiques

Decorative and Display Antiqua-Varianten Caractères de fantaisie

Script and Brush Schreib- und Pinselschriften Écriture

Black Letter and Broken Gebrochene Schriften Gothiques

Linotype
LIBRARY

/01/
*Cover and inside front cover of the
1992 Linotype Collection – the
version of Vectora for lasersetting
contains lining figures and
small caps.*

DONNERSTAG, DEN **20. JUNI, UM 16 UHR**

GUISEPPE **VERDI**

VORSPIEL 1. AKT DER OPER **LA TRAVIATA**

/02/
*Laser-set sample strings for Vectora
from 1991 – in the grotesque typefaces
of that time small caps and lining
figures were not common.*

02390   VAG Rounded light / leicht / maigre   18   **121**   H 2.53 mm   F 0.989

abcdefghijklmnopqrstuvwxyz
ABCDEFGHIJKLMNOPQRSTUVWXYZ
1234567890 .,:;"«»ß&!?

Håmbûrgefönstiv. Linotype have been

07390   VAG Rounded bold / halbfett / demi-gras   18   **127**   H 2.53 mm   F 0.989

**abcdefghijklmnopqrstuvwxyz
ABCDEFGHIJKLMNOPQRSTUVWXYZ
1234567890 .,:;"«»ß&!?**

Håmbûrgefönstiv. Linotype has been

09390   VAG Rounded black / fett / gras   18   **128**   H 2.54 mm   F 0.984

**abcdefghijklmnopqrstuvwxyz
ABCDEFGHIJKLMNOPQRSTUVWXYZ
1234567890 .,:;"«»ß&!?**

Håmbûrgefönstiv. Linotype has bee

02161   Vectora 45 light / leicht / maigre   12   (100)   **170**   H 2.51 mm   F 0.997

abcdefghijklmnopqrstuvwxyz
ABCDEFGHIJKLMNOPQRSTUVWXYZ
1234567890 1234567890 .,:;"«»ß&!?

Håmbûrgefönstiv. Since 1886 LINOTYPE HAS BEEN a leader in the field of typ
eface development and today offers one of the finest selections of typefa

05161   Vectora 55 roman / normal / romain   12   (100)   **170**   H 2.51 mm   F 0.997

abcdefghijklmnopqrstuvwxyz
ABCDEFGHIJKLMNOPQRSTUVWXYZ
1234567890 1234567890 .,:;"«»ß&!?

Håmbûrgefönstiv. Since 1886 LINOTYPE HAS BEEN a leader in the field of
typeface development and today offers one of the finest selections in

07161   Vectora 75 bold / halbfett / demi-gras   12   (100)   **170**   H 2.51 mm   F 0.997

**abcdefghijklmnopqrstuvwxyz
ABCDEFGHIJKLMNOPQRSTUVWXYZ
1234567890 1234567890 .,:;"«»ß&!?**

**Håmbûrgefönstiv. Since 1886 LINOTYPE HAS BEEN a leader in the fie
ld of typeface development and today offers one of the finest sel**

09161   Vectora 95 black / fett / gras   12   (100)   **170**   H 2.51 mm   F 0.997

**abcdefghijklmnopqrstuvwxyz
ABCDEFGHIJKLMNOPQRSTUVWXYZ
1234567890 1234567890 .,:;"«»ß&!?**

**Håmbûrgefönstiv. Since 1886 LINOTYPE HAS BEEN a leader in th
field of typeface development and today offers one of the fin**

publications that are consulted, like telephone books /17/ and timetables, the numbers are the most important glyphs. Their shapes in *Vectora* are open and distinctive, with a straight diagonal in 6 and 9 /14/ and a cross in the 8 /15/. I'm a little surprised at the down stroke of the 1, which is straight – it doesn't lean slightly to the right – so that the figure seems to be tilting slightly to the left /12/. Never in my life would I have put a serif on the 1, even if it did fill out the whitespace a little. On the other hand, I deliberately chose the classical g for *Vectora* /08/, since it's more readable in smaller point sizes than the single-storey form. When your eye runs across a line, a two-storey g is a feature, a reading aid. I distinguish quite clearly between a signage and a text face. You could, of course, say that the classical g is also a sign. However, when I think of how often g occurs, and of the overall picture it produces, a classical g in a signage face wouldn't, in this sense, be a direct aid to legibility.

For lasersetting I designed additional small caps and old style numerals. By that, I wanted to show that *Vectora* is not just a typeface for 'classified news', but that it's also suitable for jobbing composition such as invitations to a concert, as well as for telephone books /02/. It wasn't adopted for digital typesetting, however.

The working title for *Vectora* was 'Relief', but I suggested, amongst others, 'Raster Gothic' as well. The definitive name came from Linotype. For me, a vector was actually something ugly: but *Vectora* had a ring to it, it has something mathematical, modern about it: I think the name fits. The typeface came out in 1991. Its marketing – as far as I know – didn't go too well. The marketing people didn't really get the idea behind it. Its qualities weren't pointed out enough. When it was introduced, they should have concentrated more

American Gothics as the starting point Alongside Frederic W. Goudy, Morris Fuller Benton is regarded as the most important American type designer of the first half of the 20th century. In 1896, four years after 23 American type foundries were merged to form the American Type Founders Company, he started as an assistant to his father, Linn Boyd Benton, at the New Jersey head office of ATF.[8] Subsequently, he developed around 200 typefaces,[9] and was instrumental in the development of an important form of the grotesque, called American Gothics. The bold *Franklin Gothic* appeared in 1902, followed by the condensed bold *Alternate Gothic* in 1903, and in 1908 by both the regular *News Gothic* and the thin *Lightline Gothic*. Benton and ATF thought of these faces as a type family and marketed them as such. This /04/ relationship can no longer be discerned in the digital versions, *ITC Franklin Gothic* and *News Gothic,* since both have been developed into stand-alone type families. Other well-known typefaces are *Bell Gothic* /04/, which was developed in 1938 at Mergenthaler Linotype by Chauncey H. Griffith for the telephone directories of the American telephone company AT&T, and *Trade Gothic* /04/, developed by Jackson Burke in 1948, also at Linotype. Like the 1876 *Grotesque* by British type foundry Stephenson Blake, *Franklin Gothic* has an easily discerned stroke contrast /03/, but also exhibits differences typical of this new style. In American gothics the letters are somewhat narrower, and the junction between the curves and the

/03/
Grotesque *(1876) by Stephenson Blake (England),* Schelter Grotesk *(1880) by Schelter & Giesecke,* Akzidenz Grotesk *(1909) by Berthold, the latter two from Germany (top to bottom).*

Grotesque
Schelter Grotesk
Akzidenz Grotesk

/06/
An undated design for Vectora *shows waisted downstrokes and the curves of a and e have almost vertical terminations.*

/04/
American gothics (top to bottom):
Franklin Gothic *(1902),* News Gothic
(1908), Lightline Gothic *(1908),*
Bell Gothic *(1938),* Trade Gothic *(1948).*

Franklin Gothic
News Gothic
Lightline Gothic
Bell Gothic
Trade Gothic

/05/
19th century sans serif typefaces usually have the two-storey g shape:
Grotesque *and* Schelter Grotesk *compared with* Akzidenz Grotesk *(left to right).*

g g g

/07/
*Undated design by Adrian Frutiger for the Schweizerische Volksbank –
the typeface is based on* News Gothic.

stem is abrupt, or, when rounded, features a very small radius. In contrast to the British and American examples, the German grotesques from the 19th century, such as *Schelter Grotesk* (1870–80) and *Akzidenz Grotesk* (1898–1909) **/03/**, possess barely any stroke contrast, not even in the bold versions. However, the rounded bowl junctures share similarities with their British counterparts. A noticeable feature of the American gothics is the two-storey g. In the 19th century this was the prevailing form, and no geographical differences can be observed between American and German typefaces, as attested by *Schelter Grotesk*. The simpler g shape of the later *Akzidenz Grotesk* can therefore be seen as a modern development **/05/**.

The popularity of the American Gothics derives from their narrow, economical and therefore easily readable ductus. The elevated x-height **/11/** also contributes, which is an advantage, especially in the smaller point sizes. In *Antique Olive* (designed by French typographer Roger Excoffon) and in *Vectora*, the x-height was sharply raised, which results in a very small counter in the lowercase f. Roger Excoffon solved this problem in 1966 by simultaneously raising the ascender above the cap height, and by taking the crossbar of the f below the x-height. Adrian Frutiger stayed with this arrangement, but as a consequence also moved the crossbar of the t down. This change resulted in a somewhat unsettled composition, especially in combinations with r and z **/10/**.

on the readers, for them a typeface like that is useful and helpful. There were also hardly any marketing materials like brochures. These days you see it more often, for example in reference books or in the tabular setting of some daily newspapers.

In 2003, Kurt Wälti and I used *Vectora* as the basis for a logo design for the Zentrum Paul Klee in Bern **/16/**. For many years Wälti was responsible for the lettering for the Swiss Post office. The name of Paul Klee had to be used as the basis for the logo. We talked about the artistic works of the painter, and suddenly the idea of 'play' came to us. Looking at Klee's work, you get the feeling that somehow he always liked to play, even if his work is quite serious. Paul Klee is close to children's drawings, to simplification. The word 'tütschi' came to us – 'puzzle' in the German dialect spoken in Bern – and it was clear to me, that the right typeface for the logo should look like a puzzle – as if it had been made up out of individual pieces. And *Vectora* suggested itself, because it has these junctures set hard against the stem, and so it's one of the few of my typefaces where you can introduce gaps, without injuring the letters.

The starting design with the lightly waisted downstrokes would have made an interesting typeface **/06/**. It's not too sleek, there's something soft in there. If I were younger now, it would be nice to develop something like that, with the higher resolutions available today … I'd like to say that *Vectora* is, perhaps, the typeface where I had to invent least, since, of course, *Franklin Gothic, News Gothic* and *Trade Gothic* had already demonstrated their legibility.

/08/
Test sample for 'Relief', crossbars of f and t at x-height, simple g-shape, raised ascenders; 'Version RH' with higher H; Vectora 45 (top to bottom).

Hamburgefonstiv
Hamburgefonstiv
Hamburgefonstiv

/09/
The unrealised 85 version from the 1989 'Relief' sample (centre) between Vectora 75 (top) and Vectora 95 (bottom).

Hamburgefonstiv
Hamburgefonstiv
Hamburgefonstiv

/10/
Different positioning of the crossbars of t and f – News Gothic, Antique Olive *and* Vectora *(top to bottom).*

Hirtzfeld
Hirtzfeld
Hirtzfeld

/11/
News Gothic *already displayed a raised x-height, but in* Antique Olive *and* Vectora *it is even higher.*

Hlaep **Hlaep** Hlaep

/12/
The foot serif on the 1 is typical of American gothics like Bell Gothic *and* News Gothic. *No foot serif in* Vectora *(left to right).*

111

/13/
In Bell Gothic *the figure 3 has a dynamic shape,* News Gothic *and* Vectora *have a static shape (left to right).*

333

/14/
Bell Gothic *(left) and* Vectora *exhibit an open, diagonal shape for 6, whereas* News Gothic *is more closed.*

666

/15/
The shape of the 8 in Bell Gothic *is constructed from two broad ovals – in* News Gothic *and* Vectora *it features the looped shape.*

888

/16/

2003 logo design by Kurt Wälti and Adrian Frutiger for the Paul Klee Zentrum in Bern based upon Vectora *(not implemented).*

Paul Klee
Die Paul Klee Schrift

Size and impact of a typeface   In hot metal setting, the point size was determined by the body size, i.e. the lead slug on which the composition sat. This size can be measured, in points (ciceros), using a typometer. On the other hand, in digital typesetting the body size is only notional. It is not measurable, but is apparent in a condensed setting (e.g. 9 pt / 9 pt). A rough guide to point size – not always reliable – is the distance from the top of the ascender to the bottom of the descender **/18/**.

Apart from the point size, the only other metric that is standardised is the baseline – the cap height, ascender, x-height and descender are, in contrast, variable. This means that typefaces with the same point size can have very different heights **/18/**. For this reason, the type example pages of this book are each set with typefaces of the same optical size, not the same point size. Due to its increased x-height, *Vectora* looks far bigger than other typefaces, and bigger than the given point size would lead one to suppose. In the sample text (right), *Vectora* is therefore set in a slightly smaller point size than the sample text of *Avenir* (see page 339).

Also the overall text format, the page composition or the line width can alter the perception of type size. Small page sizes, tight margins and narrow line widths all make a typeface appear slightly larger. In contrast, generous space around a text makes a typeface appear slightly smaller **/19/**. Also, too-narrow letter spacing at small point sizes makes the type appear smaller.

/17/

Typefaces for small point sizes: Bell Gothic *(1938) by Chauncey H. Griffith,* Bell Centennial *(1978) by Matthew Carter and* Vectora *(left to right).*

Reimgarthauser Oliver Friaulbeerenstr. 68	273 11 46	**Reimgarthauser Oliver** Friaulbeerenstr. 68	273 11 46	**Reimgarthauser Oliver** Friaulbeerenstr. 68	273 11 46
– **Elisabeth Maria** Musikerin Havannaweg 452	561 38 20	– **Elisabeth Maria** Musikerin Havannaweg 452	561 38 20	– **Elisabeth Maria** Musikerin Havannaweg 452	561 38 20
Reimstrasser Monika Grafikerin Barbadostr. 17	121 67 98	**Reimstrasser Monika** Grafikerin Barbadostr. 17	121 67 98	**Reimstrasser Monika** Grafikerin Barbadostr. 17	121 67 98
Reinbüchel Hannelore Meeresblickstr. 793	669 43 72	**Reinbüchel Hannelore** Meeresblickstr. 793	669 43 72	**Reinbüchel Hannelore** Meeresblickstr. 793	669 43 72
– **Bruno** Hochbauzeichner Holunderbachstr. 4	547 32 33	– **Bruno** Hochbauzeichner Holunderbachstr. 4	547 32 33	– **Bruno** Hochbauzeichner Holunderbachstr. 4	547 32 33
Reinzach Robert u. Veronica Oranienburgstr. 96	785 90 12	**Reinzach Robert u. Veronica** Oranienburgstr. 96	785 90 12	**Reinzach Robert u. Veronica** Oranienburgstr. 96	785 90 12
Reinzmann Annarosa Visagistin Brissagostr. 191	643 01 41	**Reinzmann Annarosa** Visagistin Brissagostr. 191	643 01 41	**Reinzmann Annarosa** Visagistin Brissagostr. 191	643 01 41
– **Bastian** Apotheker Milanostr. 75	532 83 38	– **Bastian** Apotheker Milanostr. 75	532 83 38	– **Bastian** Apotheker Milanostr. 75	532 83 38
– **Orlando** Securitaswächter St. Petersburg-Str. 240	989 68 23	– **Orlando** Securitaswächter St. Petersburg-Str. 240	989 68 23	– **Orlando** Securitaswächter St. Petersburg-Str. 240	989 68 23
Reinzmichel Borchert Franca Buchsbaumgartenstr. 90	176 25 99	**Reinzmichel Borchert Franca** Buchsbaumgartenstr. 90	176 25 99	**Reinzmichel Borchert Franca** Buchsbaumgartenstr. 90	176 25 99
Reiores Sarah-Nina Paradiesvogelallee 6	340 24 47	**Reiores Sarah-Nina** Paradiesvogelallee 6	340 24 47	**Reiores Sarah-Nina** Paradiesvogelallee 6	340 24 47

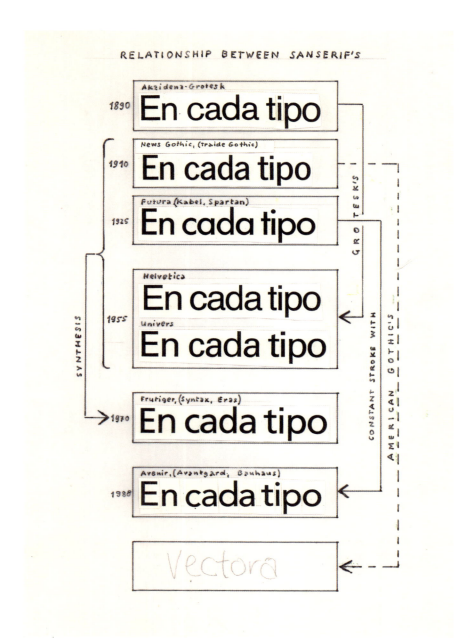

/20/

Sheet by Adrian Frutiger showing the relationships between his typefaces and other sans serifs.

/18/

A consequence of the varying x-heights is that Kabel, Avenir *and* Vectora *appear different in size, even at the same point size.*

Schriftgrad
Schriftgrad
Schriftgrad

Schriftgrad
Schriftgrad
Schriftgrad

/19/

A small margin makes a typeface look larger compared to the same point size with a more generous margin.

Schriftgrad

Schriftgrad

Font production:
Adobe Font digitised by Linotype

Font format:
PostScript Type 1

Also available:
TrueType
OpenType Com

ABCDEFGHIJKLMN
OPQRSTUVWXYZ&
abcdefghijklmnopqrs
tuvwxyzß1234567890

Sie fragen sich

warum es notwendi

g ist, so viele Schriften zur Ver

fügung zu haben. Sie dienen alle zum selb

en, aber machen die Vielfalt des Menschen aus. Diese Vielfalt is
t wie beim Wein. Ich habe einmal eine Weinkarte studiert mit se
chzig Médoc-Weinen aus dem selben Jahr. Das ist ausnahmslos
Wein, aber doch nicht alles der gleiche Wein. Es hat eben gleich
wohl Nuancen. So ist es auch mit der Schrift. *You may ask why*

so many different typefaces. They all serve the same purpose but they express man's diversi
ty. It is the same diversity we find in wine. I once saw a list of Médoc wines featuring sixty d
ifferent Médocs all of the same year. All of them were wines but each was different from t
he others. It's the nuances that are important. The same is true for typefaces. *Pourquoi tant
d'Alphabets différents!* Tous servent au même but, mais aussi à exprimer la diversité de l'h
omme. C'est cette même diversité que nous retrouvons dans les vins de Médoc. J'ai pu, un j
our, relever soixante crus, tous de la même année. Il s'agissait certes de vins, mais tous étai

ent différents. Tout est dans la nuance du bouquet. Il en est de même pour les caractères! *Sie fragen sich, warum es notwendig ist, so viele Schriften zur Ver fügung zu haben.* Sie dienen alle zum selben, aber machen die Vielfalt des Me nschen aus. Diese Vielfalt ist wie beim Wein. Ich habe einmal eine Weinkarte studiert mit sechzig Médoc-Weinen aus dem selben Jahr. Das ist ausnahmslos Wein, aber doch nicht alles der gleiche Wein. Es hat eben gleichwohl Nuancen. So ist es auch mit der Schrift. *You may ask why so many different typefaces.* T hey all serve the same purpose but they express man's diversity. It is the sam

e diversity we find in wine. I once saw a list of M édoc wines featuring sixty different Médocs all of the same year. All of them were wines but eac h was different from the others. It's the nuances that are important. The same is true for typeface s. *Pourquoi tant d'Alphabets différents!* Tous ser vent au même but, mais aussi à exprimer la dive rsité de l'homme. C'est cette même diversité qu e nous retrouvons dans les vins de Médoc. J'ai p u, un jour, relever soixante crus, tous ante crus,

63 pt │−5 45 pt │0 30 pt │10 21 pt │15 13.5 pt │19 pt │20 9 pt │13 pt │35 6.8 pt │10.2 pt │40 5.4 pt │8 pt │50

ÅBÇDÈFG
HIJKLMÑ
ÔPQRŠTÜ
VWXYZ&
ÆŒ¥$£€
1234567890
åbçdéfghij
klmñôpqrš
tüvwxyzß
fi fl æ œ ø ł ð
[.,:;·'/-—]
(¿¡"«‹›»"!?)
{§°%@‰*†}
45 Light

ÅBÇDÈFG
HIJKLMÑ
ÔPQRŠTÜ
VWXYZ&
ÆŒ¥$£€
1234567890
åbçdéfghij
klmñôpqrš
tüvwxyzß
fi fl æ œ ø ł ð
[.,:;·'/-—]
(¿¡"«‹›»"!?)
{§°%@‰†}*
46 Light Italic

ÅBÇDÈFG
HIJKLMÑ
ÔPQRŠTÜ
VWXYZ&
ÆŒ¥$£€
1234567890
åbçdéfghij
klmñôpqrš
tüvwxyzß
fi fl æ œ ø ł ð
[.,:;·'/-—]
(¿¡"«‹›»"!?)
{§°%@‰*†}
55 Roman

ÅBÇDÈFG
HIJKLMÑ
ÔPQRŠTÜ
VWXYZ&
ÆŒ¥$£€
1234567890
åbçdéfghij
klmñôpqrš
tüvwxyzß
fi fl æ œ ø ł ð
[.,:;·'/-—]
(¿¡"«‹›»"!?)
{§°%@‰†}*
56 Italic

ÅBÇDÈFG
HIJKLMÑ
ÔPQRŠTÜ
VWXYZ&
ÆŒ¥$£€
1234567890
åbçdéfghij
klmñôpqrš
tüvwxyzß
fi fl æ œ ø ł ð
[.,:;·'/-—]
(¿¡"«‹›»"!?)
{§°%@‰*†}
75 Bold

ÅBÇDÈFG
HIJKLMÑ
ÔPQRŠTÜ
VWXYZ&
ÆŒ¥$£€
1234567890
åbçdéfghij
klmñôpqrš
tüvwxyzß
fi fl æ œ ø ł ð
[.,:;·'/-—]
(¿¡"«‹›»"!?)
{§°%@‰*†}
76 Bold Italic

Typeface comparison The typefaces below (Kurt Weidemann's *Corporate S*, Erik Spiekermann's *Meta* and Adrian Frutiger's *Vectora*), were published in the early 1990s. They all feature a raised or sharply raised x-height and a somewhat narrow ductus. Thus, they correspond to the prevailing trend in typefaces of that time, which was also influenced by the digital adaptations of *Franklin Gothic* and *News Gothic* **/04/**, which in 1987 were among the first sans serif fonts from Adobe / Linotype in Post-Script format.

Despite similarities to the American gothics, neither *Corporate S* nor *Meta* belong to this group. *Meta's* open curves point towards a dynamic sans serif, while with *Corporate S* the difference lies in the rounded curve junctures. In 1984, Weidemann's concept of a corporate type was created in 1984. Two years later he proposed *Corporate A·S·E* to Daimler-Benz, and in 1989 it became the group's exclusive house style.[10] These days, this type family is freely available. It comprises three complementary type families: antiqua, sans and égyptienne.

In contrast to the American Gothics, the G of the three comparison typefaces has no spur, and the arms of the K form an angle. Additionally, in *Meta* and *Vectora*, the t is terminated diagonally. Initially, Frutiger designed his g in the single-storey form, derived from the cursive **/08/**. However, the final glyph is a two-storey version, typical of American gothics.

/21/

Measurements of stroke widths and proportions of the Vectora regular weight.

Roman				
$Hh = 10.00\,cm$	$nh = 8.29\,cm$	$oh = 8.65\,cm$	$Hh : Hw = 1 : 0.73$	$nh : nw = 1 : 0.73$
$Hw = 7.28$	$nw = 6.08$	$ow = 7.01$	$Hw : Hs = 1 : 0.17$	$nw : ns = 1 : 0.20$
$Hs = 1.28$	$ns = 1.22$	$os = 1.30$	$Hs : Hq = 1 : 0.80$	$nh : oh = 1 : 1.04$
$Hq = 1.03$	$nq = 1.12$	$oq = 0.99$		$nw : ow = 1 : 1.15$

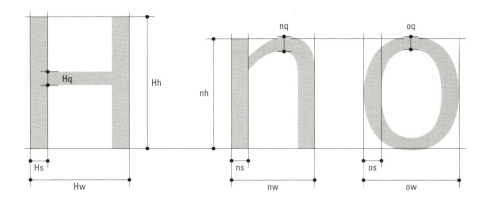

/23/

Static grotesque, dynamic grotesque, American static grotesque (top to bottom). In spite of their differing sub-classifications, similarities are obvious.

Hofstainberg

Corporate S
Kurt Weidemann
1990

GKMeghs16

Hofstainberg

Meta+
Erik Spiekermann
1991

GKMeghs16

Hofstainberg

Vectora
Adrian Frutiger
1991

GKMeghs16

G	K	M	e	g	h	s	1 6
Crossbar terminated vertically, curves end diagonally	Angle overlaps the stem	Legs vertical, wide proportions	Curve closes the shape optically	Horizontal ear, angular juncture between loop and diagonal	Angular juncture with stem, asymmetrical curve	Terminals have same angle as in e	Diagonals of 6 with emphasis, those of 1 without, no foot serif in 1

Comparison showing the
different weights and angle of
the obliques.

	Hh	Hw	Hs	Hq
Light	10.00 cm	6.85 = 0.94	0.88 = 0.69	0.72 = 0.70
Roman	10.00	7.28 = 1	1.28 = 1	1.03 = 1
Bold	10.00	8.08 = 1.11	2.09 = 1.63	1.59 = 1.54
Black	10.00	8.78 = 1.21	2.74 = 2.14	2.05 = 1.99
Italic	10.00	7.24 = 0.99	1.25 = 0.98	1.09 = 1.06

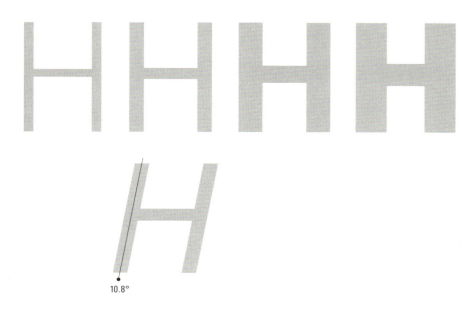

10.8°

ÅBÇDÈFG ÅBÇDÈFG
HIJKLMÑ HIJKLMÑ
ÔPQRŠTÜ ÔPQRŠTÜ
VWXYZ& VWXYZ&
ÆŒ¥$£€ ÆŒ¥$£€
1234567890 1234567890
åbçdéfghij åbçdéfghij
klmñôpqrš klmñôpqrš
tüvwxyzß tüvwxyzß
fiflæœøłð fiflæœøłð
[.,:;·'/-–—] [.,:;·'/-–—]
(¿¡"«‹›»"!?) (¿¡"«‹›»"!?)
{§°%@‰*†} {§°%@‰*†}

95 Black   96 Black Italic

Height comparison showing the
differences of x-heights to
ascenders and descenders – the cap
height is the starting point.

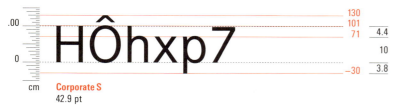

.00 / 0 / cm

130 / 101 / 71 / 4.4 / 10 / −30 / 3.8

Corporate S
42.9 pt

.00 / 0 / cm

132 / 105 / 73 / 4.4 / 10 / −28 / 3.8

Meta+
41.7 pt

.00 / 0 / cm

127 / 109 / 83 / 3.1 / 10 / −26 / 3.1

Vectora
40.1 pt

Logos and wordmarks
1984–1990

Filatures Fulmen Fribourg
car batteries / ball bearings /
transmissions
Fribourg (CH)

Filatures Fulmen Fribourg
car batteries / ball bearings /
transmissions
Fribourg (CH)

Lyven
grocery company
Colombelles (F)

Westiform
neon signs
Niederwangen (CH)

Ministère des Finances Recherches
Finance Ministry
France

Ministère des Finances Recherches
Service de l'Information
Finance Ministry
France

Ministère des Finances Recherches
Finance Ministry
France

Fonderie Lyonnaise Turbines
turbine manufacturer
Lyon (F)

Blanchard Editeur
publishers
Le Plessis-Robinson (F)

Circuit Dijon-Prenois
motor racing circuit
Prenois (F)

Frutiger Heimtextil
household textiles supplier
Interlaken (CH)

Johann Wolfgang Goethe-
Universität
university
Frankfurt am Main (D)

Édition de la Thièle
publishers
Yverdon (CH)

SEK – Schweizerischer
Evangelischer Kirchenbund
Swiss Christian organisation
75th anniversary logo
Design: Kurt Wälti

Arguments
theological magazine
France
Design: Bruno Pfäffli

Erdyn consultants
economic and technical
consultancy
Paris (F)

Compagnie Générale de Traveaux
de la Voierie
highways department
France

NEC – Nippon Electric Company
Tokyo (J)
Re-working of existing logo

Lyven
grocery company
Colombelles (F)

Production of type
Digital typesetting

In handsetting or in mechanical hot metal setting the typeface exists as a real, three-dimensional entity, and in photosetting it is a quasi two-dimensional image as a typeface disc or grid/matrix; there are no saved data. Although in OCR and lasersetting the typeface can be stored digitally, the term 'digital typesetting' will be used here only for the period from 1984 onwards when desktop publishing (DTP) ushered in a new era. Desktop publishing rapidly established itself in the area of pre-press, but was also promoted as an office solution.

In this revolution, three companies were at the forefront: Apple Computer, Inc. with its Macintosh computer with mouse and graphical user interface (GUI); Aldus Inc. with its PageMaker layout program; and Adobe Systems Inc. with its PostScript page description language. Also playing a role were Canon with its production of laser printers, and Linotype, with its PostScript RIP (raster image processor) and the high-resolution Linotronic 300 lasersetter. The pre-installed typefaces on the Macintosh came from Linotype and ITC (the International Typeface Corporation).

Desktop publishing laid the groundwork for electronic publishing. Unlike previous setting technologies, using graphical user interfaces permitted the placement of not only raw text, but also scanned pictures and graphics directly into a layout on a personal computer. As soon as the design of a page was finished, it could be output in high resolution on either a laser printer or lasersetter. The options afforded by DTP are largely due to the PostScript page-description language, developed by Adobe Systems, Inc. PostScript made possible the use of WYSIWYG (What You See Is What You Get) on the computer screen. In order to transfer this visual information to an output medium, a raster image processor (RIP) is necessary. The task of the RIP is to interpret the code generated by the page description language.

PostScript typefaces require two files: one for the display of bitmapped fonts on the computer screen (the screen font) and an 'outline file' (or printer font) for the output device. While the curve description in PostScript fonts is handled by Bézier curves /02/, in the TrueType format (jointly developed by Apple and Microsoft) they are handled by Q-splines /03/. These files can handle the task of both screen font and printer font. For the lower resolution of monitors and laserprinters – especially at smaller point sizes – a 'hinting' description is necessary, which give the typeface a more balanced appearance /04/.

Adobe and Microsoft's OpenType format has the advantage of being able to use the same font files for both Macintosh and Windows operating systems, and can additionally store more than 65000 glyphs per character set, rather than the 256-glyph ASCII limit of PostScript and TrueType fonts.

Font design programs like FontStudio, Fontographer, and Ikarus M became available in the 1980s and made possible the creation of typefaces directly on the computer. They have since been superseded by FontMaster and FontLab.

/01/
Various methods of digitising typefaces: original design, bitmap, vertical scanline, vector and horizontal scanline encoding.

/02/
PostScript Type1 Bézier curves – a quarter circle can be described using only two anchor points and two Bézier handles.

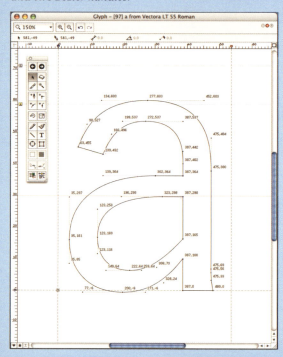

/03/
TrueType Q-splines – a quarter circle is defined using two anchor points and four control points.

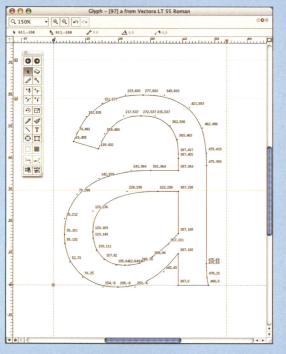

/04/
Outline drawings automatically converted into bitmaps: without hinting (top); with hinting (bottom).

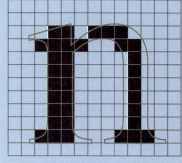

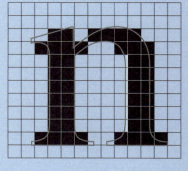

Name of typeface	Client	Designer	Design | Publication	Typesetting technology	Manufacturer	Weights
Linotype Didot	Linotype-Hell AG	Adrian Frutiger (Firmin Didot)	1990 | 1991	PostScript digital typesetting	– Adobe | Linotype	6

LINOTYPE
DIDOT

At the beginning of the nineties, exposure technology had advanced so much, that I wanted to see how far I could push this highly developed technology.[1] I was trying to come up with the most difficult task imaginable, and that's when I thought of *Didot*. With its extreme contrast between ultrafine hairlines and fat downstrokes, it was a real challenge – one reason why it had only been available in hot metal up until then, and why it had almost slid into obscurity. My suggestion was adopted at a Type Selection Meeting, so I sought some advice from Paul Jammes,[2] the foremost authority on the works of the Didot family, and bought from him a book by the name of *La Henriade* /01/. This book was set in Firmin Didot's original *Didot,* and I wanted to use it to show Linotype how beautiful this typeface was. The book was printed in 1819, and in the foreword, Firmin Didot confirms the use of the letters cut by him, which was an important proof of authenticity. It is an artistic high-point in the type design work of the Didot family, not only technically, but also aesthetically. It's also formally incredibly beautiful. The Didots were a distinguished dynasty: from François, the father, to his sons François Ambroise and Pierre François, and their sons Pierre and Firmin on the one side, and Henri and Saint-Léger on the other, and even their offspring, they were all successful in the type and printing industries, and were also involved in paper production.

I'd like to repeat here, what I once wrote about *Didot:* "In the development of the latin typeface, the classical antiqua, and above all, the later forms of the alphabet cut by Firmin Didot stand out as the most remarkable formal innovations. From Jenson to Baskerville, the strokes became finer, but their ductus remained tied to the written forms of renaissance calligraphy /04/. Bodoni and Didot consciously moved the stroke direction away from the skewed impact of the broad pen, by building the up- and downstrokes, the serifs and the junctures on a clear horizontal-vertical grid. This tendency towards a strongly objective means of letter construction exactly mirrored the zeitgeist of the revolution that was gathering momentum at the end of the 18th century."[3]

My idea was to newly interpret *Didot,* using *La Henriade* as a starting point. I did some really fine optical adjustments where I tried to not bring my own hand into it too much – an accusation that had been levelled at me during the adaptation of *Baskerville* to Lumitype photosetting. I straightened a few details out, and made the script overall somewhat more regular. The distortion of a few lines in the printed original /01/ looked to me as if it was due to manufacturing or technical reasons. That had something to do with either the type manufacture using punches, matrices and hot metal, or with the printing process or the paper. But that's what accounted for its liveliness, in spite of the rigidity that classical typefaces tend to have. I did not want to copy these things. Under no circumstances did I want to create a typeface that was technically flawed. That might result in the criticism

The genesis of Linotype Didot Since 1986, the idea had existed at Linotype of adding a *Didot* to its range. Under the heading 'Further Investigations', the production plan contains a *'Firmin Didot'* with the note: "Test font should be produced."[4] The typeface, produced c.1800 by Firmin Didot, is considered the most beautiful *Didot* typeface due to its immaculate cut, its open text appearance and the marked contrast between the fine hairlines and the weight of the main strokes. It has served as the basis for many imitations and copy cuts.

When the members of Linotype's Type Selection Meeting of 26 October 1989[5] adopted the suggestion for *Didot,* the time was absolutely right for this typeface. Until then, there had been no version available for the current setting systems or for DTP. Haas'sche Schriftgiesserei AG[6] requested *Didot* typefaces by Deberny & Peignot /09/ as the starting point for the adaptation, and in August 1990 these were made available in printed form.[7] However, whether the typefaces displayed in Deberny & Peignot's type catalogue were the originals by Firmin Didot, is not documented.[8] Adrian Frutiger was also advised by Paul Jammes, the Parisian bookseller and antiquarian. For Linotype, Adrian Frutiger bought from Paul Jammes a copy of Voltaire's[9] *La Henriade,* printed in 1819 and available only as an unbound book. The book contains a foreword in which Firmin Didot himself confirms the use of his typeface.

After preliminary test drawings, the *Didot* project was again tested for suitability for implementation. This was carried out by Adrian Frutiger, Reinhard Haus (artistic director at Linotype) and André Gürtler, on 13 March 1991.[10] André Gürtler suggested a three-part plan, by which *Didot* could be realised.[11] Frutiger found this interesting, but for reasons of time and marketing decided that it was not feasible, which was also Linotype's view. Linotype stuck to the initial concept to create a reworked new version of *Didot*.

Using *La Henriade* as a basis, Adrian Frutiger designed the roman and italic versions; he also drew a bold version. Furthermore, he drew a headline version, using as a starting point a typeface by Didot from Deberny & Peignot's collection. In 1991, at the ATypI Congress in Parma, the typeface was presented in four versions: roman, italic, bold and headline. Today, the family comprises some six fonts.

LA HENRIADE,

POËME ÉPIQUE

EN DIX CHANTS,

PAR FRANÇOIS-MARIE AROUET

DE VOLTAIRE.

PARIS,

DE L'IMPRIMERIE DE FIRMIN DIDOT,

IMPRIMEUR DU ROI, ET DE L'INSTITUT.

M. DCCC XIX.

that my typefaces are too slick or not 'lively' enough, but I absolutely rejected the idea of putting a curve in the L, just so that it looked as if the punch had been knocked into the matrix. I'm thankful that during my time at Deberny & Peignot, I got the chance to experience the foundry – what it really means to cut punches, to strike copper matrices and to pour hot metal type. Should I have considered all these technical influences? These days, our copying, setting and printing methods are totally different from those that were around in the late eighteenth and early nineteenth centuries. So, the starting point was the ideal of the classical *Didot,* rather than the flawed print image itself.

André Gürtler, who had been brought in as a consultant, suggested a three-part concept: an authentic *Didot,* true to the original, then a second version, slightly reworked for today's tastes and a third, a new classical antiqua that would take the original as its starting point, but which would comprise several weights, and could be expanded into a larger family. This suggestion, however, came too late; the project was already well under way. Also, sales and marketing wouldn't have wanted to run with it. To draw and implement an alphabet was a big investment; it needed a lot of consideration. So eventually *Linotype Didot* was slightly reworked and released in four weights, as originally planned.

Looking at the capital A, you can see that my version is more balanced than the original. I've added somewhat to the width; however it's still slightly too narrow /05/. In the original, the diagonal stroke of the uppercase N is taken through all the way to the serif at the top left, whereas in my version it terminates against the stem, which is set a little more over to the right. The point at the lower right therefore, dips below the baseline, so I was able to bring the right stem a little more over to the right /05/. I did that, because in the

In hot metal type, every point size of a typeface has its own design. Due to optical considerations, small sizes are drawn somewhat darker and broader than larger sizes. This changed with photosetting. Multiple point sizes could be produced through exposures from one original design. The formal differences between each typeface version simply ceased to exist. This was even more apparent in typefaces with strong contrasts between broad and fine strokes.

This problem was well known to the experts at Linotype who, for the technologies that followed hot metal setting, developed difficult typefaces in several point sizes. In their 1992 typeface catalogue for laser and CRT fonts, the topic was discussed and clarified by means of illustrations /02/.

Gerhard Höhl, head of typeface production, also noted this fact regarding *Linotype Didot,* and remarked in a memo that a headline version for setting larger sizes had to be developed.[12] Work began immediately, and the resulting headline version is a little less black in appearance than the bold face. Additionally, the letter shapes are narrower in construction. Based on the headline version, an initials font was soon developed, with slightly heavier main strokes, albeit with an identical glyph width.

/02/
Linotype's laser-set Bodoni *regular in the design sizes 8, 12 and 18 pt – at the same point size the differences are clearly visible.*

Hamburgefons
26 pt, Design Size 8 pt

Hamburgefons
26 pt, Design Size 12 pt

Hamburgefons
26 pt, Design Size 18 pt

/03/
A page from the 1819 version of La Henriade *with Firmin Didot's typeface (left) and the reset version in* Linotype Didot *(right).*

/04/
Development of the serif through use of a pen: Jenson, Garamond *and* Baskerville *– in neoclassicism, starting with* Didot, *the serif became independent of written forms.*

nnnn

/05/
Original print from La Henriade *(left) and* Linotype Didot *Roman: the A is broader, the N more balanced.*

/06/
The headline version (right) is narrower than the roman one (left) and exhibits different letter shapes in the a f *and* t.

/07/
The curves of the bowl of P and the tail of Q differ between roman (left) and headline (right).

/08/
Details of shape and the degree of curvature between roman (left) and headline (right).

ALN ALN afnt afnt PQ PQ 47 47

The originals The basis for *Linotype Didot* came from two different original sources. The book *La Henriade /01/* was the inspiration for the roman and italic faces. With a type size of some 18 pt, it was an ideal basis for the redrawings, which were developed for a design size of 18 point.

For the headline version (and later the initials), Firmin Didot's alphabet from Jan Tschichold's *Meisterbuch der Schrift* (A Treasury of Alphabets, 1965) was the starting point. According to the caption, the font originated from Deberny & Peignot and was also reproduced in the necessary point sizes, namely 48 pt */09/* and 72 pt. In terms of shape, Frutiger kept to the respective originals, and so the roman and headline versions exhibit varying letterforms, for instance in P Q */07/* 4 and 7 */08/*.

After *Linotype Didot* was completed, an elaborate booklet was produced for marketing purposes that was printed on handmade paper.[13] It consisted of a blind-embossed jacket and two inlay pages. These showed the title page */10/* and a page of text */03/* from the book *La Henriade* which brought the graceful historical printing back to life. The text on the inside back jacket stated, "A re-printing from the book *La Henriade,* set with the new Linotype Didot." However, the typeface used for the title page differed in details to the typeface of *Linotype Didot* that was actually delivered. It also differed from the original */11/*.

/09/
Firmin Didot *by Deberny & Peignot served as the basis for the headline version of Adrian Frutiger's* Linotype Didot.

Firmin Didot

ABCDEFGHIJ
KLMNOPQRS
TUVWXYZ
abcdefghijklmno
pqrstuvwxyz
1234567890
fi & fl
Imprimerie

176

LA HENRIADE,

POËME ÉPIQUE

EN DIX CHANTS,

PAR FRANÇOIS-MARIE AROUET

DE VOLTAIRE.

PARIS,

DE L'IMPRIMERIE DE FIRMIN DIDOT,

IMPRIMEUR DU ROI, ET DE L'INSTITUT.

M. DCCC XIX.

/10/
Title page of La Henriade, *reset with* Linotype Didot *that had been specially reworked for this edition.*

/11/
Comparison between the original Didot *from* La Henriade, *the reprint,* Linotype Didot *Bold and Headline (top to bottom).*

LA HENRIADE
LA HENRIADE
LA HENRIADE
LA HENRIADE

original the proportions of the white space are a little less evenly balanced. For the italic, I had all the italic words in *La Henriade* photographed, but they didn't make an entire alphabet. The f, with its strong overhang, was like the original /03/. It's not my invention – I would never have allowed myself to do that.

After that I drew the headline version. I used Deberny & Peignot's *Didot* as a starting point /09/, which differs clearly from the typeface in the book, *La Henriade*. The headline font runs narrower, and shows a stronger contrast /06/; additionally, some individual characters differ: the P, for example, has a different bowl juncture /07/. Then there's the tail of the Q /07/ and the 4 and the 7 /08/. For the headline version as well as for the regular one of *Linotype Didot,* only one design size of 18 pt was used. Amazingly, in the regular weight even the 8 pt size was still legible. But setting a text in *Linotype Didot* in that point size isn't realistic. However, the conclusion was: even this works, the laser typesetting machines at Linotype-Hell could produce such a fine output.

The ornaments for *Linotype Didot* aren't mine. The D&P type catalogue was used as a reference /12/. If I had to choose one out of all those, I would have chosen differently. I can't imagine who made that decision.

When I first proposed the *Didot* project, I thought that graphic designers would be interested in such a contrast-rich typeface. Unfortunately, in the end, nobody wanted it, although an exclusive PR brochure was produced – it was even embossed. For this brochure, the title page /10/ and an interior page /03/ of *La Henriade* were reset in *Linotype Didot*. Only later did we sell a few copies, and then Adobe took it over under licence.

Ornaments and decorative fonts   *Linotype Didot* was also provided with two additional fonts for ornamentation. Although this was a new concept in PostScript fonts, it has firm roots in traditional book printing. The 1926 Deberny & Peignot type catalogue alone shows nineteen pages of 'Vignettes Style Didot' /12/ next to five pages of 'Vignettes Elzéviriennes' and three of 'Vignettes XIXe Siècle'.

While the decorative forms of the end of the 18th century possessed a range of expression from simple to complex, at Linotype simpler forms were chosen for implementation. In their individual shapes, they corresponded to the rather geometrical design language of the 1980s. However, when these shapes are set in rows, they develop their full effect /13/.

Linotype Didot Bold was used as a basis for a lighter, shadowed decorative face, called *Linotype Didot Openface*. It was developed in 1992 and in 1995 included in a series of eight loose A4 pages /15/.[14] This version was not published until 2007. With its broad main strokes, the initials font provided the basis for another decorative design /14/. Such typefaces are very common in neoclassicism and are very sumptuously adorned. Two glyphs from the ornamental font were chosen for decoration, but the proposal never came to fruition.

Like the initials version, the ornamental and decorative versions were not the work of Adrian Frutiger. They were developed internally at Linotype.

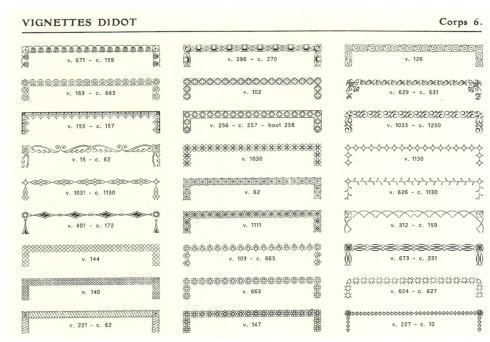

/12/
Section of a page showing Vignettes Didot *from* Deberny & Peignot's 1926 *type catalogue.*

/13/
Sample string with combinations of decorative glyphs from Linotype Didot *Ornaments.*

/14/
Didot Floriated Capitals *from* Pierre Didot l'Aîné *and the never-implemented design for a decorative font by Linotype (right).*

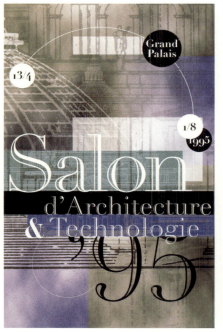

 Linotype Didot Openface

/15/
Sample setting from 1995 with Linotype Didot Openface *(designed in 1993 but not issued until 2007).*

ABCDE EFHIM

Font production:
Digitised by Linotype

Font format:
PostScript Type 1

Also available:
TrueType
OpenType Std

ABCDEFGHIJKLMN
OPQRSTUVWXYZ&
abcdefghijklmnopqrs
tuvwxyzß1234567890

You may ask w
hy so many differe
nt typefaces. They all serv

e the same purpose but they express
man's diversity. It is the same diversity we find in wine.
I once saw a list of Médoc wines featuring sixty different
Médocs all of the same year. All of them were wines but
each was different from the others. It's the nuances that
are important. The same is true for typefaces. *Pourquoi t*

ant d'Alphabets différents! Tous servent au même but, mais aussi à exprimer la
diversité de l'homme. C'est cette même diversité que nous retrouvons dans les
vins de Médoc. J'ai pu, un jour, relever soixante crus, tous de la même année. I
l s'agissait certes de vins, mais tous étaient différents. Tout est dans la nuance
du bouquet. Il en est de même pour les caractères! *Sie fragen sich, warum es not
wendig ist, so viele Schriften zur Verfügung zu haben.* Sie dienen alle zum selben,
aber machen die Vielfalt des Menschen aus. Diese Vielfalt ist wie beim Wein. I

ch habe einmal eine Weinkarte studiert mit sechzig Médoc-Weinen
aus dem selben Jahr. Das ist ausnahmslos Wein, aber doch nicht a
lles der gleiche Wein. Es hat eben gleichwohl Nuancen. So ist es a
uch mit der Schrift. *You may ask why so many different typefaces.* Th
ey all serve the same purpose but they express man's diversity. It is
the same diversity we find in wine. I once saw a list of Médoc wine
s featuring sixty different Médocs all of the same year. All of them
were wines but each was different from the others. It's the nuances

that are important. The same is true for
typefaces. *Pourquoi tant d'Alphabets différents!* Tous servent au même but, mais a
ussi à exprimer la diversité de l'homme.
C'est cette même diversité que nous ret
rouvons dans les vins de Médoc. J'ai pu,
un jour, relever soixante crus, tous de la
même année. Il s'agissait certes de vins,
mais tous étaient différents. Tout est da
ns la nuance du bouquet. Il en e est de

ÅBÇDÈFG
HIJKLMÑ
ÔPQRŠTÜ
VWXYZ&
ÆŒ¥$£€
1234567890
åbçdéfghij
klmñôpqrš
tüvwxyzß
fi fl æ œ ø ł ð
[.,:;·'/-–—]
(¿¡""«‹›»"!?)
{§°%@‰*†}
Roman

*ÅBÇDÈFG
HIJKLMÑ
ÔPQRŠTÜ
VWXYZ&
ÆŒ¥$£€
1234567890
åbçdéfghij
klmñôpqrš
tüvwxyzß
fi fl æ œ ø ł ð
[.,:;·'/-–—]
(¿¡""«‹›»"!?)
{§°%@‰*†}*
Italic

**ÅBÇDÈFG
HIJKLMÑ
ÔPQRŠTÜ
VWXYZ&
ÆŒ¥$£€
1234567890
åbçdéfghij
klmñôpqrš
tüvwxyzß
fi fl æ œ ø ł ð
[.,:;·'/-–—]
(¿¡""«‹›»"!?)
{§°%@‰*†}**
Bold

ÅBÇDÈFG
HIJKLMÑ
ÔPQRŠTÜ
VWXYZ&
ÆŒ¥$£€
1234567890
åbçdéfghij
klmñôpqrš
tüvwxyzß
fi fl æ œ ø ł ð
[.,:;·'/-–—]
(¿¡""«‹›»"!?)
{§°%@‰*†}
Openface

1234567890
ÅBÇDÉFGHIJ
KLMÑÔPQRŠ
TÜVWXYZ&
Oldstyle Figures & Small Caps

1234567890
Italic Oldstyle Figures

1234567890
Bold Oldstyle Figures

72 pt | –30   54 pt | –5   36 pt | 3   25 pt | 5   16 pt | 19 pt | 10   11 pt | 13 pt | 20   8.2 pt | 10.2 pt | 30   6.8 pt | 8 pt | 40

Typeface comparison   All three typefaces shown below are derived from Firmin Didot's types. They differ in form and construction, depending on which print original served as the basis for their adaptation.

While Adrian Frutiger's *Linotype Didot* Roman is derived from Firmin Didot's typefaces for the book *La Henriade* **/03/**, Jonathan Hoefler based his version of *Didot* – designed in 1991 for the magazine *Harper's Bazaar* and which was first used in 1992[15] – on Pierre and Jules Didot's 1819 *Spécimen de nouveaux caractères*[16]. As a starting point, he predominantly used the book's *Grosse Sans Pareille No. 206,* a typeface from Molé le jeune that is very similar to the sample contained in Jan Tschichold's *Meisterbuch der Schrift,* and, therefore, also to Firmin Didot's typeface. Jonathan Hoefler prepared *HTF Didot* in three weights, with corresponding italic versions, and in seven design sizes, ranging from 6 to 96 pt. Pictured below is the 16 pt size.

Didot LP, created in 1995 by Garrett Boge, is based on the version of *Didot* from the 1926 type catalogue by Ludwig & Mayer GmbH, which itself draws on the version of *Didot* from Deberny & Peignot **/09/**. This typeface can be traced back to an earlier Firmin Didot face c.1784. *Didot LP's* stroke contrast is less strongly emphasised, which leads to the conclusion that it was derived from a smaller point size than the other two versions shown here.

/16/
Measurement of stroke widths and proportions of the Linotype Didot *regular weight.*

Roman				
Hh = 10.00 cm	nh = 6.02 cm	oh = 6.39 cm	Hh : Hw = 1 : 0.79	nh : nw = 1 : 0.95
Hw = 7.50	nw = 5.71	ow = 6.55	Hw : Hs = 1 : 0.19	nw : ns = 1 : 0.21
Hs = 1.40	ns = 1.20	os = 1.42	Hs : Hq = 1 : 0.13	nh : on = 1 : 1.06
Hq = 0.19	nq = 0.20	oq = 0.20		nw : ow = 1 : 1.15

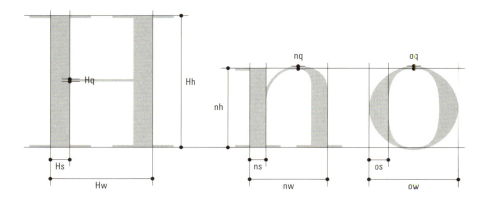

/17/
In comparison to other reworkings of Didot, *and unlike the orginal,* Linotype Didot *appears more balanced in its proportions.*

Hofstainberg
Linotype Didot
Adrian Frutiger (Firmin Didot)
1991 (c. 1800)

K N R a b f n 3 4

K
Leg with minimal juncture at stem

N
Counters are proportionally balanced against each other

R
Curved leg set to the right

a
Hairline flows steeply into the stem without sagging

b
More rounded transition from bowl to stem

f
Generous curve shape

n
Broad shape, elongated hairline

3 4
No teardrop serif at bottom, curved diagonal

Hofstainberg
HTF Didot Light 16
Jonathan Hoefler (Molé le jeune)
1992 (1819)

K N R a b f n 3 4

Hofstainberg
Didot LP
Garrett Boge (Firmin Didot)
1995 (c. 1784)

K N R a b f n 3 4

Comparison showing the different weights and angle of the italics.

	Hh	Hw	Hs	Hq
Roman	10.00 cm	7.50 = 1	1.40 = 1	0.19 = 0.1
Bold	10.00	8.12 = 1.08	2.01 = 1.44	0.20 = 1.05
Italic	10.00	6.66 = 0.89	1.20 = 0.86	0.20 = 1.05

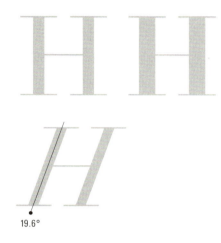

19.6°

/19/

Height comparison showing the differences of x-heights to ascenders and descenders – the cap height is the starting point.

Linotype Didot
40.2 pt

HTF Didot
40.3 pt

Didot LP
42.6 pt

ÅBÇDÈFG
HIJKLMÑ
ÔPQRŠTÜ
VWXYZ&
ÆŒ¥$£€
1234567890
åbçdéfghij
klmñôpqrš
tüvwxyzß
fi fl æ œ ø ł ð
[.,:;·'/- – —]
(¿¡""«‹›»"!?)
{§°%@‰*†}

Headline

1234567890

Headline Oldstyle Figures

ÅBÇDÉFG
HIJKLMÑ
ÔPQRŠTÜ
VWXYZ
ÆŒØŁD

Initials

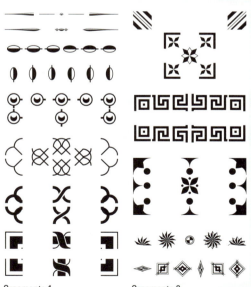

Ornaments 1   Ornaments 2

Name of typeface		Designer	Design | Publication	Typesetting technology	Manufacturer	Weights
Herculanum		Adrian Frutiger	1990 | 1991	Digital Typesetting PostScript	– Adobe | Linotype	1
					– Linotype	3

HERCULANUM

The basic idea for the 'Type before Gutenberg' project came from me. I suggested it in a 1989 type selection meeting. The whole concept was developed the same year and introduced in 1990. The brochure containing the first six alphabets /15/ – which were produced very quickly – was first distributed at Type 90 in Oxford and was out of stock immediately. The concept of this project was to re-interpret handwritten alphabets from ancient times until the era of Johannes Gutenberg, the mid-15th century. It was about establishing an alternative that would position something other than just adaptations of classic faces and funny new fantasy types at the beginning of desktop publishing. 'Type before Gutenberg' was about starting a project from which would arise expressive calligraphic types based on examples from history. Obviously, I am of the opinion that it is totally justified to try and imitate the gesture of handwriting using today's computers. If it's done well, why not?

The whole thing did not just come about overnight. When I got in touch with Aaron Burns, who co-founded The International Typeface Corporation ITC[1] in 1970, I suggested incorporating such faces into their programme. However, back then he didn't understand what I meant. It simply wasn't modern enough for him. So some 20 years later I re-introduced my old idea at the Linotype type selection meeting. Otmar Hoefer and some other people from German Linotype chose who was to work on the project. I wasn't totally happy with their selection. Although Karlgeorg Hoefer, Herbert Maring and Gottfried Pott certainly weren't bad calligraphers, they were perhaps a bit boring. What was missing were people like David Kindersley, André Gürtler or Hermann Zapf, who would have added a bit of pizzazz. I couldn't do that myself. I later suggested to Linotype that they ask André Gürtler but it didn't result in a contribution by him.

Palaeographer Prof. Peter Rück also wrote a report for the project.[2] He held a professorship for historical ancillary sciences at the University of Marburg (Germany) and checked everything very carefully. But the question has to be: Where does palaeography end and where does calligraphy start? We had lots of discussions about this subject and sometimes our views would differ quite significantly. As a scientist he had difficulties in adapting his thinking to the world of typography, typographers and graphic designers. But in places he was certainly right. For instance, he wrote that the designs had a German feel to them.

Apart from the palaeographic aspect, there is another fundamental issue when designing display faces for typesetting: How to maintain the gestural aspect of a handwritten alphabet? In hot metal setting people have tried very hard, for instance through using angled matrices,[3] to transfer the calligraphic gesture of handwritten alphabets into their typefaces. I'm thinking, for example, of Legende /13/ by F. H. Ernst Schneidler, which was released by the Bauer foundry of Frankfurt in 1937 and used all over the world.

'Type before Gutenberg'   On 26 October 1989 Adrian Frutiger presented his proposal for the project 'Type before Gutenberg' at the type selection meeting at Linotype AG in Eschborn near Frankfurt (Germany). To illustrate his idea, he included Victor Hammer's American Uncial in his paper,[4] a design that was released in 1953 by Schriftgiesserei Klingspor and has been available from Linotype since 1988 as Neue Hammer Unziale /13/.[5] On two other pages he showed about 30 handwritten examples by Hans Eduard Meier. These were interpretations of scripts from Ancient Greece to the 16th century, which can be found in Hans Eduard Meier's booklet The Development of Script and Type.[6] Adrian Frutiger did not add his own diploma thesis Lettering – The development of European letter types carved in wood[7] /01/.

"This great idea," as Otmar Hoefer referred to the project he headed at Linotype, was then handed over to three calligraphers, all from the Schreibwerkstatt Klingspor Offenbach,[8] "in order to create calligraphic designs for this subject based on important styles from the past and interpreted with a view to current reading habits."[9] Otmar Hoefer pointed out that these designs should be interpretations of historic scripts and not exact redrawings. Therefore, some criticism was expected when palaeographer Peter Rück submitted his report on the first six alphabets of the 'Type before Gutenberg' project. He criticised the ductus, the use of non-historic form elements and proportion and noted "that all six designs have a 'rather German' appearance". He attributed this to the way German calligraphers were trained. "In their imagination, scripts consist of clearly differentiated hairlines and stems as well as clearly marked heads and feet. One gets the impression that they think of blackletter even if they write antiqua …". And he went on: "All six sample types appear to be systematically rigid and cold, i.e. very different from the products of the organic script thinking of the Gothic period."[10]

In order to avoid a stereotypical repetition of shapes, Rück suggested a variety of ligatures, letter shapes and spacing. Adrian Frutiger liked the alternative letter shapes /02/ and – as he had done before with his first designs for Deberny & Peignot – included these. They were not yet part of the 1990 brochure /15/ that was distributed at the Type 90 in Oxford but were included in the 1991 release of Herculanum.[11]

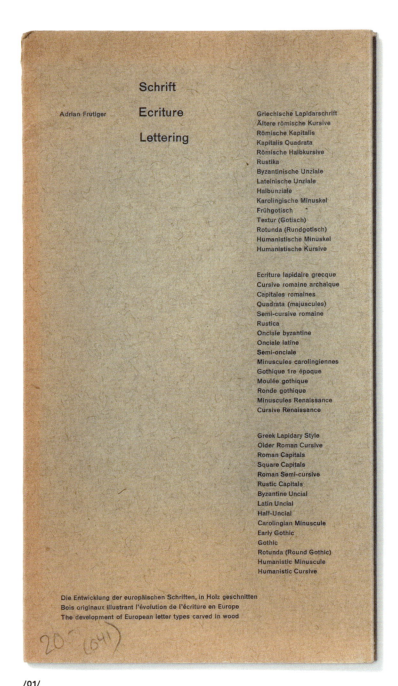

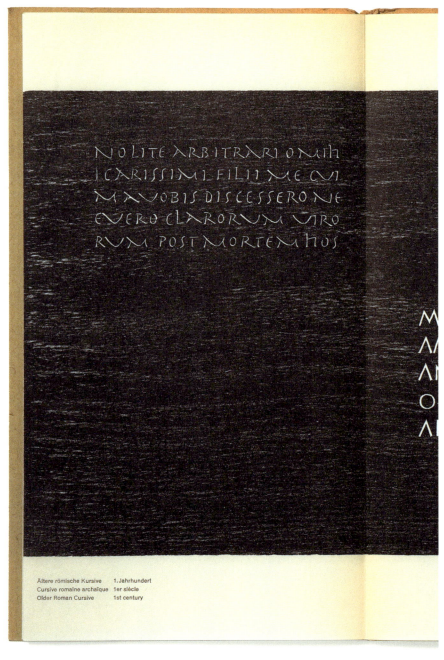

Schrift

Adrian Frutiger

Ecriture

Lettering

Griechische Lapidarschrift
Ältere römische Kursive
Römische Kapitalis
Kapitalis Quadrata
Römische Halbkursive
Rustika
Byzantinische Unziale
Lateinische Unziale
Halbunziale
Karolingische Minuskel
Frühgotisch
Textur (Gotisch)
Rotunda (Rundgotisch)
Humanistische Minuskel
Humanistische Kursive

Ecriture lapidaire grecque
Cursive romaine archaïque
Capitales romaines
Quadrata (majuscules)
Semi-cursive romaine
Rustica
Onciale byzantine
Onciale latine
Semi-onciale
Minuscules carolingiennes
Gothique 1re époque
Moulée gothique
Ronde gothique
Minuscules Renaissance
Cursive Renaissance

Greek Lapidary Style
Older Roman Cursive
Roman Capitals
Square Capitals
Roman Semi-cursive
Rustic Capitals
Byzantine Uncial
Latin Uncial
Half-Uncial
Carolingian Minuscule
Early Gothic
Gothic
Rotunda (Round Gothic)
Humanistic Minuscule
Humanistic Cursive

Die Entwicklung der europäischen Schriften, in Holz geschnitten
Bois originaux illustrent l'évolution de l'écriture en Europe
The development of European letter types carved in wood

20°(041)

Ältere römische Kursive   1. Jahrhundert
Cursive romaine archaïque 1er siècle
Older Roman Cursive   1st century

/01/
Cover and interior page of Adrian Frutiger's diploma thesis (1951) – the woodcut shows an interpretation of the Early Roman Cursive from the 1st century.

/02/
Undated collage – felt pen on tracing paper (original size) – single glyphs are still being reworked.

In order to understand the idea behind 'Type before Gutenberg' better it's useful to have a quick look into the typefaces of the Gutenberg period because a particular development took place during that time: a move away from the manual gesture. In the letters of Gotico-Antiqua[12] from the mid-15th century, which took up the handwritten humanist minuscule at the transition from gothic type to renaissance-antiqua, you can still clearly feel the manual gesture /06/. However, some 70 to 80 years later, in *Garamond* /08/, this wasn't really the case any more. This change happened within a span of 50 years. Nicolas Jenson's Antiqua from about 1470 already had serifs at the foot. You can still see the pen in the upper parts of the oblique serifs of the small letters. At the foot of the letters, however, the serifs are adjusted to the line of the hot metal setting /08/. That's different from a handwritten alphabet. Although the calligrapher puts some pressure on the pen in the lower parts in order to get more ink flowing, the terminal is either pointed or, at most, round due to the inclined position of the pen. For optical reasons, i.e. so that the terminals don't appear too short in comparison to the round and horizontal strokes, the point should be positioned slightly below the baseline.

Initially, I only contributed *Herculanum* to the 'Type before Gutenberg' project. *Pompeijana* (see page 384) and *Rusticana* (see page 390) were to follow later. I knew the Ancient Roman alphabets inside out and I admired them; they had been on my mind ever since I did my diploma /01/. *Herculanum* is an imitation of an inclined roman majuscule alphabet /03/. This antique alphabet is so beautiful – if I'd ever seen an original, I would have been overwhelmed by its beauty. If you think about when it was created … Originally, these alphabets were inscribed in wax using a stylus, or Latin 'stilus' /03/. The stylus is made from

Historical analysis of Herculanum   Besides Capitalis Monumentalis, which was inscribed in stone using a hammer and chisel, Cursive Majuscules and Early Roman Cursive were developed in the first century AD. Historical examples can be found inscribed in wax tablets, as graffiti engraved on walls or on papyrus /03/. "In contrast to 'stone inscriptions' the Early Roman Cursive is characterised by a fluid ductus, which mirrors the movement of the hand and thus appears very alive and not static," wrote Peter Rück.[13]

According to Peter Rück, Adrian Frutiger based his *Herculanum* on the script of *Carmen de bello Actiaco*, a song about the sea battle of Actium, which had been written on papyrus between 31 BC and 79 AD in *Herculaneum*. However, the original version was not used as a template for 'Remus' (the working title for *Herculanum*) but rather a redrawing form the 19th century created by English archaeologist John Hayter, based on a barely legible papyrus from Naples /04/. Palaeographer Jean Mallon called this version a very badly done redrawing.[14] Peter Rück agreed: "Therefore the 'Remus' design cannot be evaluated in comparison to the original – because, as a historic script it is actually a 'fake' – but only in comparison to John Hayter's redrawing. Although the dynamic of the mean line is rather well done through the use of variable letter heights (shortening of the O, lengthening of the S), the horizontal expression of the crossbars (which are inclined, i.e. dynamically rising upwards in the original)

/03/
The Roman majuscule cursive can be found inscribed with a stylus on wax tablets, on walls or on papyrus (top to bottom).

/04/
Roman majuscule cursive from the papyrus 'Carmen de bello Actiaco'; redrawing from the 19th century by John Hayter.

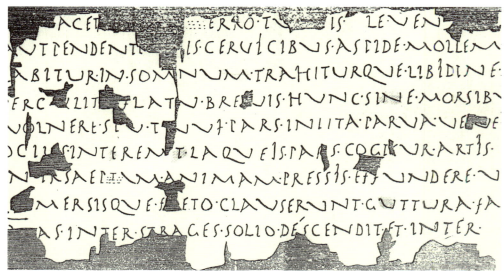

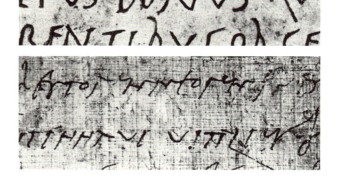

/05/
For each of the ten majuscules there are narrower alternative shapes on the minuscule keys (bottom).

AKMNRUVXYZ

AKMNRUVXYZ

in A E F H gives 'Remus' a static median, which does not conform to the original. The extremely wide M forms a soft garland while in the original it is more like a double gable. The choice of a purely oval O (which has various shapes in the original) and furthermore of the stretched uncial E is an unlucky one; this type of E only appears once in the original, usually it features rising crossbars, which are typical of the period. These elements altogether make 'Remus' rounder and softer ... than the original would suggest. The terminals of H are too strong, the same is true for the tongue of the G, which in the original is much finer and more strongly spread towards the right. Other individual contradictions arise from the 'wrong' ductus of 'Remus'; in the original, the A is not drawn in three movements but in two ... Additionally, the bodies of the letters are bent towards the left, whereas in 'Remus' they are vertical. Horizontality and verticality – in other words a general straightening of the letters – are modern characteristics ... from the 20th century. Therefore, the original appears much more lively, closer to handwriting and more cursive than 'Remus'. This cannot be changed completely, but at the very least an inclination of the crossbars could counteract the curves with a balancing angular pointedness."[15]

wood or metal with a pointed end for writing and a broad, flat one to smooth out the wax in case something had to be deleted. As a model, I used a sheet with an inclined roman majuscule alphabet from Naples, or Herculaneum /04/, the twin city of Pompeii, and hence the name.[16] Basically, I 'only' redrew it a bit more beautifully. I can say that without losing face. However, the aforementioned Swiss expert Peter Rück doubts, with reference to his well-known French colleague Jean Mallon, that the sheet I used was an authentic representation of the original. He wrote that it was based on a badly done imitation by Englishman John Hayter from the beginning of the 19th century. I, however, think that his work is well done, showing love and diligence. He even adopted the mistakes. No, I'm full of awe and I'm feeling closer to the person who did this than to the palaeographer who thinks it's just a bad imitation. After all, you could say that about every redrawn research document. Of course there was an element of interpretation but one that shows love and respect.

I drew initial sketches using – and this might sound a bit brutal – a thick felt pen /02/. I didn't choose an angular but a rounded one, which I could use for serifs but also for dabbing and filling in. I pre-sketched these designs using a 48 pt pencil in order to get the curves right and then I filled the contours using the felt pen. So they were actually drawn. But my very first sketches were written rather than drawn, at least they appear very fluid. Calligraphy, however, wasn't really in my nature; it was cutting that was. Taking bits away and leaving others, exactly like I did in my woodcarvings of plants.[17] This kind of thinking and feeling was rooted in my apprenticeship as a typesetter. If you become a typographer this will stay with you for the rest of your life.

/06/
Gotico-Antiqua from Cicero's
De oratore *by Konrad Sweynheim and Arnold Pannartz – printed in 1465 in Subiaco near Rome.*

Sed ín co genere ín quo quale ſit qu
ex ſcripti ínterpratione ſepe cōtent
mſi ex ambiguo controuerſia. Nā i
tēna diſcrepat · genus quoddā hab

/08/
In Gotico-Antiqua the movement of the pen is still obvious at the top and bottom; in Jenson and Garamond it is hardly visible, if at all (from left to right).

111

/07/
Test exposure of Herculanum *Regular with electronically fattened strokes for the definition of the bold version.*

OHAMBURGEFONSTIV

Fill and stroke 0.5 Punkt
OHAMBURGEFONSTIV

Fill and stroke 1 Punkt
OHAMBURGEFONSTIV

Fill and stroke 1.5 Punkt
OHAMBURGEFONSTIV

Fill and stroke 2 Punkt
OHAMBURGEFONSTIV

Fill and stroke 3 Punkt
OHAMBURGEFONSTIV

Fill and stroke 4 Punkt
OHAMBURGEFONSTIV

/09/
In contrast to John Hayter's redrawing, Herculanum *features horizontal crossbars in A E F H, and the E is not pointed.*

AEFH

/10/
For Adrian Frutiger, the shape of the T is like a punch, the U is pure gesture, and the N consists of two lines with a gesture in the middle.

TUN

/11/
The three versions of Herculanum: *Regular (1990) and Bold (1992) – based on a stroke weight of 1.5 – and Outline.*

OHAMBURGEFONSTIV
OHAMBURGEFONSTIV
OHAMBURGEFONSTIV

In *Herculanum* I, too, interpreted the letters. The sample sheet contained, for instance, a beautiful majuscule R with a slightly diagonally curved stem /04/, which I didn't adopt in the same style. Instead I designed two versions of the R with a straight stem, a narrow one and another one that runs a bit broader /05/. For me as a typographer and type designer it was obvious that a straight line is needed every now and then in order to get the ductus right for each single word image. The change between free movements and straight lines is necessary because otherwise everything falls apart. This was the reason why I chose a straight stroke instead of a curved one for the R – even if this wasn't true to the original.

The letters of *Herculanum* have both straight strokes and gestural, curved junctures. The T is like a punch, the U on the other hand is pure gesture, and the N consists of two straight lines with a gesture in between /10/. Some letters exist in two versions, a rigid one and a dynamic one /05/ as had already been the case with *Initiales Président* (see page 32) and *Ondine* (see page 55). Letters with diagonal strokes are well suited for this. For others, in particular for those that only consist of straight lines, I can't imagine any alternative versions, for example for the H. Nor can I see an alternative O. And for the E of *Herculanum* I didn't create an alternative version either. I could have drawn a historically documented angular version in addition to the round E, but I didn't. Peter Rück criticised my decision. He wrote that the round E was historically rare; that the most common shape was the angular E with rising crossbars /04/. I think that you have to see the E in connection with the S – it's a question of pulling and pushing. The writer from the 19th century never pushed, not with E and S either. I have a tendency of very lightly pushing, which isn't correct

'Type before Gutenberg' type sets The six calligraphic types from the project 'Type before Gutenberg' /14/ that were introduced in 1990 in Oxford were released in two sets. The first was published the same year. In addition to Adrian Frutiger's *Herculanum* it contained Karlgeorg Hoefer's *Omnia*, an uncial going back to the 8th-century, as well as *Duc de Berry* by Gottfried Pott, which is reminiscent of the 15th-century French Bastarda from the books of hours of the Duc de Berry /12/.

The second set became available from Linotype in 1991. It contains Gottfried Pott's *Carolina*, an interpretation of the Carolingian minuscule from the late 8th-century and another contribution by Karlgeorg Hoefer. Otmar Hoefer's father is represented with *San Marco*, an Italian Rotunda based on 14th-century styles. And finally there is Herbert Maring's *Clairvaux*, which goes back to the early German Gothic styles from the 13th-century /12/. The suggestions for the names of the six type all came, except for *Omnia*, from Rück. Hence he was not only involved in the project as a critic but also as a name designer.[18]

In 1991, Karlgeorg Hoefer designed another typeface based on calligraphic styles /14/. As indicated by the name *Beneta* it was inspired by the south Italian book and document script 'Littera beneventana' from the 10th to 12th-century. It was not part of the second original set of 'Type before Gutenberg' but is included today by Linotype as a fourth typeface.[19]

/13/
Scripts derived from historical calligraphy: Legende *(1937) by F. H. Ernst Schneidler;* Neue Hammer Unziale *(1953) by Victor Hammer.*

Legende
Neue Hammer Unziale

/14/
TBG 1 and 2: Omnia, San Marco (and Beneta) *by Karlgeorg Hoefer;* Carolina, Duc de Berry *by Gottfried Pott;* Clairvaux *by Herbert Maring.*

OMNIA
Carolina
Clairvaux
San Marco
Duc de Berry
Beneta

/15/
Brochure Type before Gutenberg *(1990) – besides* Herculanum *it contains five other calligraphic types (left).*

TYPE BEFORE GUTENBERG

Linotype
LIBRARY

/12/
Historic calligraphic scripts: uncial, 8th century; Carolingian minuscule, 8th century; Gothic minuscule, 13th century; rotunda, 14th century; bastarda, 15th century.

LIEBER ANWENDER,

ALS GESTALTER DER HERCULANUM MÖCHTE ICH IHNEN
EINIGES ÜBER IHRE HERKUNFT BERICHTEN UND EINE
KLEINE HILFESTELLUNG GEBEN IM UMGANG MIT DIESER
ETWAS UNGEWÖHNLICHEN SCHRIFT:

DAS VORBILD DER HERCULANUM IST KEINE KALLI-
GRAPHISCHE BUCHSCHRIFT, SONDERN DIE NACHBILDUNG
EINER VON EINEM RÖMISCHEN SCHRIFTKUNDIGEN
FLÜCHTIG AUFGEZEICHNETEN HANDSCHRIFT. ALS MATERIAL
FÜR DIESE AUFZEICHNUNGEN DIENTEN HAUPTSÄCHLICH
WACHSTAFELN. SELTENER WURDE ALS BESCHREIBSTOFF
PAPYRUS ODER PERGAMENT VERWENDET.

DER SCHREIBER GAB SEINER HANDSCHRIFT EINEN GANZ
PERSÖNLICHEN DUKTUS, INDEM ER DIE ZEICHEN IN
SCHRÄGBEWEGUNGEN MIT EINER GEWISSEN GROSSZÜGIGKEIT
WEITGEZOGEN HAT, WAS DER GESCHRIEBENEN SEITE EINEN
SEHR BEWEGTEN, EXPRESSIVEN AUSDRUCK VERLEIHT. ES IST
ABER KEINE STURE SYSTEMATIK IN DER ANWENDUNG
DIESER WEITEN ELEMENTE. EIN A ODER X ZUM BEISPIEL
STEHT EINMAL WEIT, DANN WIEDER GEDRÄNGT, UM EINE
INTERESSANTE, ABER HARMONISCHE BUCHSTABENREIHUNG
ZU ERZIELEN.

BEIM AUSARBEITEN DIESES ALPHABETES WURDE VON VIELEN
ZEICHEN EINE WEITE UND EINE SCHMALE VERSION
AUSGEFÜHRT. AUF DER TASTATUR STEHT IN DER VERSAL-
EBENE DAS ALPHABET MIT DEN SCHMALEN ZUSAMMEN
MIT DEN WEITEN ZEICHEN.

A B C D E F G H I J K L M N O P Q R S T U V W
X Y Z

IN DER POSITION DER KLEINBUCHSTABEN STEHT DAS GANZE
ALPHABET NOCHMALS, ABER NUR MIT SCHMALEN
FIGUREN. EINE AUSNAHME BILDEN DIE BUCHSTABEN A
UND R, WOBEI DAS BREITE R ALS REINE SCHLUSSFIGUR
ZU SEHEN IST.

A B C D E F G H I J K L M N O P Q R S T U V W
X Y Z

/16/
Setting instructions for Herculanum –
*Frutiger generally recommends using
the majuscule alphabet; repetition
of the same shapes is to be avoided
through the use of alternative glyphs.*

historically. You can do that with a stylus or felt pen but, of course, you can't with a pen. And here it is again, the sensitive issue of the right gesture. So, in the case of E and S, I was more of a draftsman and typesetter than a palaeographer or calligrapher. You can see that in almost all the letters of *Herculanum.*

Initially, one version of my typeface was implemented in 1990. You can find it in the first line of a sample exposure with different interpolated stroke weights. This sample was created at Linotype while looking for an additional version /07/. I also allowed myself the freedom to draw an outline version /11/ although I knew that, historically, this was stupid. But I've always felt attracted by outlines. Maybe that's an expression of the 'patissier spirit' that's part of our family history. *Herculanum* sold rather well. At least, in 2003, Linotype decided to release the semibold and outline versions as well. One day Akira Kobayashi sent over some samples and asked me whether I was OK with these versions. He's been art director at Linotype since 2001. As long as he's there you don't have to be afraid of any crimes against your typefaces.

Presumably, as calligraphers, my colleagues in the project would have done some things differently with *Herculanum,* in a freer, more calligraphic style. Because the calligrapher writes words whereas the typographer sets letters – this is a big difference. As a type designer my work is clearly committed to typography.

Typeface comparison With *Herculanum, Mission* and *Reliq* we can compare three interpretations of antique majuscule cursives /17/. Following their historical predecessors, Adrian Frutiger's *Herculanum* and Steve Miggas' *Mission* do not include a minuscule alphabet. For the same reason, the minuscules of Carl Crossgrove's *Reliq* are not shown.

So as not to appear too monotonous, *Herculanum* features a number of alternative glyphs. *Reliq* is comprised of three versions, each with alternative shapes. The version shown below – 'Active' – features more dynamic strokes and letters of different height, which seem to dance more than in the 'Calm' version. These features are even stronger in the 'ExtraActive' version.[20]

When comparing the three types, the difference in the shape of strokes becomes apparent. In *Herculanum*, Frutiger consistently emphasises the terminals of the downstrokes, which endows the stems with a slight waist. In *Mission* and *Reliq*, on the other hand, the strokes appear more linear and the downstrokes vary from emphatic to linear and tapered forms. The appearance of these two typefaces is thus rather reminiscent of the majuscule cursives engraved in wax or plaster, while *Herculanum* is similar to versions written with a broad pen. In terms of the skeleton shapes of the letters and numerals, however, the three typefaces appear very similar.

/17/
In comparison to Mission *and* Reliq, Herculanum *features waisted strokes and stronger terminals, which lends it a more calligraphic look.*

HOFSTAINBERG

Herculanum
Adrian Frutiger
1991

A	E	K	M	Q	U	2	5
Broad form, apex projects above upstroke	Narrow, round shape	Terminal emphasised, arms slightly offset, very wide at the bottom	Spread legs, centre diagonal high above baseline	Long, projecting tail drawn as an extension of the curve	Downstroke stronger than upstroke	Balanced shape, serif-like terminals	Dynamic shape, reaching below the baseline

HOFSTAINBERG

Mission
Steve Miggas
1998

HOFSTAINBERG

Reliq
Carl Crossgrove
1998

Font production:
Adobe Font digitised by
Linotype

Font format:
PostScript Type 1

Also available:
TrueType
OpenType Std

ABCDEFGHIJKLMN
OPQRSTUVWXYZ&
ABCDEFGHIJKLMNOPQR
STUVWXYZ1234567890

SIE FRAGEN SICH

WARUM ES NOTWEN

DIG IST, SO VIELE SCHRIFTEN ZU

R VERFÜGUNG ZU HABEN. SIE DIENEN ALLE

ZUM SELBEN, ABER MACHEN DIE VIELFALT DES MENSCHEN AUS. DIESE
VIELFALT IST WIE BEIM WEIN. ICH HABE EINMAL EINE WEINKARTE STU
DIERT MIT SECHZIG MÉDOC-WEINEN AUS DEM SELBEN JAHR. DAS IST AU
SNAHMSLOS WEIN, ABER DOCH NICHT ALLES DER GLEICHE WEIN. ES HAT
EBEN GLEICHWOHL NUANCEN. SO IST ES AUCH MIT DER SCHRIFT. YOU

MAY ASK WHY SO MANY DIFFERENT TYPEFACES. THEY ALL SERVE THE SAME PURPOSE BUT HEY EXPRE
SS MAN'S DIVERSITY. IT IS THE SAME DIVERSITY WE FIND IN WINE. I ONCE SAW A LIST OF MÉDOC WI
NES FEATURING SIXTY DIFFERENT MÉDOCS ALL OF THE SAME YEAR. ALL OF THEM WERE WINES B
UT EACH WAS DIFFERENT FROM THE OTHERS. IT'S THE NUANCES THAT ARE IMPORTANT. THE SAME IS
TRUE FOR TYPEFACES. POURQUOI TANT D'ALPHABETS DIFFÉRENTS! TOUS SERVENT AU MÊME BUT, M
AIS AUSSI À EXPRIMER LA DIVERSITÉ DE L'HOMME. C'EST CETTE MÊME DIVERSITÉ QUE NOUS RETROU
VONS DANS LES VINS DE MÉDOC. J'AI PU, UN JOUR, RELEVER SOIXANTE CRUS, TOUS DE LA MÊME AN

NÉE. IL S'AGISSAIT CERTES DE VINS, MAIS TOUS ÉTAIENT DIFFÉRENTS. TOUT EST DA
NS LA NUANCE DU BOUQUET. IL EN EST DE MÊME POUR LES CARACTÈRES! SIE FRAGE
N SICH, WARUM ES NOTWENDIG IST, SO VIELE SCHRIFTEN ZUR VERFÜGUNG ZU
HABEN. SIE DIENEN ALLE ZUM SELBEN, ABER MACHEN DIE VIELFALT DES MENSC
HEN AUS. DIESE VIELFALT IST WIE BEIM WEIN. ICH HABE EINMAL EINE WEINKARTE
STUDIERT MIT SECHZIG MÉDOC-WEINEN AUS DEM SELBEN JAHR. DAS IST AUSNAH
MSLOS WEIN, ABER DOCH NICHT ALLES DER GLEICHE WEIN. ES HAT EBEN GLEICH-
WOHL NUANCEN. SO IST ES AUCH MIT DER SCHRIFT. YOU MAY ASK WHY SO MA

NY DIFFERENT TYPEFACES. THEY ALL SERVE THE S
AME PURPOSE BUT THEY EXPRESS MAN'S DIVESIT
Y. IT IS THE SAME DIVERSITY WE FIND IN WINE.
I ONCE SAW A LIST OF MÉDOC WINES FEATURING
SIXTY DIFFERENT MÉDOCS ALL OF THE SAME YEA
R. ALL OF THEM WERE WINES BUT EACH WAS DI
FFERENT FROM THE OTHERS. IT'S THE NUANCES T
HAT ARE IMPORTANT. THE SAME IS TRUE FOR TY
PEFACES. POURQUOI TANT D'ALPHABETS DIFFERE
NTS! TOUS SERVENT AU MÊME BUT, MAIS AUSSI

65 pt | −75   45 pt | −40   31 pt | −35   21 pt | −25   13 pt | 19 pt | −25   9 pt | 13 pt | 0   6.8 pt | 10.2 pt | 10   5.7 pt | 8 pt | 25

ÅBÇDÈFG
HIJKLMÑ
ÔPQRŠTÜ
VWXYZ&
ÆŒ¥$£€
1234567890
ÅBÇDÉFGHIJ
KLMÑÔPQRŠ
TÜVWXYZß
FIFLÆŒØŁÐ
[.,:;·'/-——]
(¿¡"«‹›»"!?)
{§°%@‰*†}

Regular

ÅBÇDÈFG
HIJKLMÑ
ÔPQRŠTÜ
VWXYZ&
ÆŒ¥$£€
1234567890
ÅBÇDÉFGHIJ
KLMÑÔPQRŠ
TÜVWXYZß
FIFLÆŒØŁÐ
[.,:;·'/-——]
(¿¡"«‹›»"!?)
{§°%@‰*†}

Bold

ÅBÇDÈFG
HIJKLMÑ
ÔPQRŠTÜ
VWXYZ&
ÆŒ¥$£€
1234567890
ÅBÇDÉFGHIJ
KLMÑÔPQRŠ
TÜVWXYZß
FIFLÆŒØŁÐ
[.,:;·'/-——]
(¿¡"«‹›»"!?)
{§°%@‰*†}

Outline

SHISEIDO

It was June 1991. I was tired of type design and in the middle of planning our new house in Bremgarten near Berne and sifting through heaps of accumulated papers, when four Japanese turned up. They were from the cosmetics company Shiseido of Tokyo. They showed me a brochure with a wide headline face similar to the company logo, and a text set in *Optima* **/05/**. They told me that their brochures were printed like that, because *Optima* was known throughout the world. They asked whether I wouldn't care to develop a text face to match the logo. There was an all caps alphabet already **/02/**, although it had many flaws. The existing alphabet was to be reworked and extended to include lowercase letters, numerals and a few accents; the logo wasn't to be touched. I've never been able to say no to anything in my life, so I suggested a very high fee. Two days later I received a contract and an advance payment – I had to accept the contract.

I ditched my negative approach after the first sketches. It was enormous fun to work on the typeface. It's an interesting variety between grotesque and serif. One can create beautiful movements with a serif face, while a grotesque is much more static – *Shiseido* is somewhere in between the two. And it looks really elegant. A delicately printed page of type set in it literally smells of perfume **/07/**.

Fortunately I had a good graphic designer for the execution in Serge Cortesi.[1] If I hadn't had him I wouldn't have taken it on. He was trained as a type designer at the Atelier National de Création Typographique.[2] That's where I knew him from. However, I made the first drafts for *Shiseido* by myself, as ever in black and white. I used a thin felt-tip pen, and a thicker one for filling in. I can still see the sketches now, they were hung from a washing line in front of the wall during the entire holidays. Back in the Paris studio I had always hung up letters. I had to make the typeface slightly thinner than the logo, because one can see in the paste-up **/03/** that it was too thick in the body text. That decision was purely a matter of feeling. I was concerned with elegance. A whole block of text looks too heavy in semibold. The basic type for a cosmetic product ought to be something very delicate.

The middle E cross stroke in the text version is longer compared to the logo – my way of understanding type **/08/**. I simply don't like E with a short cross stroke. I also altered other letters slightly, like Q. All of my corporate typefaces, including *Shiseido,* have t with a flat, horizontal top. My text faces, including sans serifs (even the geometric *Avenir*), have an oblique top. As far as I'm concerned, there's no such thing as a straight t in a classic typeface because the stroke is derived from writing with a quill. However, a corporate typeface doesn't have the same significance as a book typeface, even when long texts are set in it. There's a difference, and that can be seen in a detail like that.

A whiff of a typeface Shiseido, founded in 1872, has a long tradition of engaging well-known designers to shape its visual appearance. This goes back to the founder's son who studied in Europe. He adapted European design trends for Shiseido advertisements,[3] which was very unusual for a Japanese company. In 1980 the Frenchman Serge Lutens,[4] who had previously worked for *Vogue* and Dior, became responsible for the international image of Shiseido.

The logo with Latin letters dates to the beginning of the 20th century, and rapidly developed into the form it has today. In the 1960s the logo was complemented by the similar-looking *Peignot* **/04/** for headlines, for example, on posters.[5] A kind of *Copperplate Gothic* was also employed for shorter body texts.[6]

In the early 1990s texts were set in *Optima* or *Times*. In addition there was an all-caps alphabet **/02/** which was used for headlines **/05/**. Helmut Schmid, a well-known designer of German origin, educated at the Schule für Gestaltung Basel and resident in Japan, was asked to rework this alphabet. Due to a lack of time, he suggested the job be carried out by someone he considered the greatest typedesigner of the time, Adrian Frutiger.[7]

In Frutiger's opinion the all-caps alphabet had to be completely reworked. He criticised the stroke contrast between thick and thin lines, the fact that the stroke width of hairlines was not the same in each letter, the wide proportions of certain letters, the Q tail, and much more. Also, the stroke width of the alphabet was slightly bolder than that of the logo, and the round letters were narrower **/06/**. Frutiger subsequently designed a complete alphabet in one light weight **/08/**. He also worked with Serge Cortesi on a bold weight for headlines and text emphasis followed immediately after. *Shiseido* was not the first sans serif typeface with a strongly defined stroke contrast that Frutiger had designed. As early as 1959 he conceived a typeface for signage at Orly airport based on *Peignot* and *Univers* (see page 134).

The *Shiseido* alphabet was extended over the course of time, also adapting Japanese type to the character of the Latin alphabet,[8] albeit without the participation of Adrian Frutiger.

/01/

The Shiseido *logo, used in a similar form since the beginning of the 20th century, is the basis of the alphabet.*

/02/

The predecessor alphabet to Shiseido *was capitals only, and was used as a titling face (unknown designer).*

ABCDEFGH IJKLMNOPQ RSſTUVWX YZ."""¯¯

/03/

Typeface design with a similar stroke width to the logo – paste-up by Serge Cortesi with corrections by Adrian Frutiger.

HOHDH
nanbnenfngn
ninmnonrnsn
utnvn

/04/

Peignot *(1937) by A.M.Cassandre is a typeface with a high stroke contrast and differentiated letter widths.*

ACHMQRS

/05/

Extract from a brochure set in the predecessor alphabet and Optima *(left); test exposure of* Shiseido roman *by Frutiger (right).*

CONTRASTES SUBTILS
PAR SERGE LUTENS

Printemps 1990

Quoi de plus charmant que

de porter parures, bijoux... issus des

voyages de la mémoire.

CONTRASTES SUBTILS
PAR SERGE LUTENS

Printemps 1990

Quoi de plus charmant que

de porter parures, bijoux... issus des

voyages de la mémoire.

/06/

Comparison between the logo, the predecessor alphabet and Shiseido *bold (from top to bottom).*

DO
DO
DO

/07/

Product brochure (undated) with, text set in Shiseido regular *and* bold.

Ich bin die Energie
Ihrer Haut.
Vertrauen Sie mir.

The Skincare

/08/

The Shiseido *alphabet by Adrian Frutiger in the regular weight; some characters below in* Shiseido *bold.*

ABCDEFGHIJKLMN
OPQRSſSTUVW YZ
ÆŒ1234567890
åbçdéfghijklmnôpqrs
ſtüvwxyzæœß&
.,:;'!?-()‹()›*/–¥£ƒ$

DHOabefn

FRUTIGER CAPITALIS

/01/
Undated drawing for 'Capitalis Outline' *– Adrian Frutiger cancels the open counter for the P, and later for the R as well.*

/02/
Extract from a 1992 test exposure of 14 letters of 'Symbolica', *originally* 'Capitalis Outline', *18 pt.*

/03/
Historic inscriptions; two Roman lapidary inscriptions from around the birth of Christ (top) and from the 1st century AD.

Another ancient roman typeface Adrian Frutiger contributed three new typefaces to the 'Type before Gutenberg' (TBG) project launched by Linotype in 1989; *Herculanum*, *Pompeijana* and *Rusticana*. All of these are based on ancient Roman scripts.

A further TBG design was produced in 1991, an outline face with additional symbols **/04/**. It, too, is based on ancient Roman lapidary scripts **/03/**, although like Frutiger's other TBG typefaces it is not necessarily historically accurate, but a free interpretation. While *Herculanum* is derived from pen writing, *Pompeijana* from reed pen writing and *Rusticana* from stone engraving, Frutiger's outline design has no apparent connection to any tool of antiquity. It looks as though it were drawn with a felt-tip pen. Designing this typeface came as something of a relief to Adrian Frutiger after having worked on so many serious and meticulous typefaces.[1]

The design was approved by the type selection meeting panel for the fourth TBG package under the working title 'Capitalis Outline'; and a business plan was drawn up. However, in 1992, after test exposures of the final artwork for 14 letters **/02/**, Linotype called a halt to the project, which by then had been renamed 'Symbolica'. Frutiger wrote in his memoirs that "another project was a Roman all caps outline face with a somewhat jolly expression … the project was never completed."[2]

In 2005 Linotype revived the design, reworked it and produced it under the name *Frutiger Capitalis*. However, the characters are not as fine and accurately formed as the design and test exposures from 1992 **/06/**. The orientation of some of the letters is different, such as A. In addition, the outlines are bolder and they get thicker at the corners. The uneven line widths appear to have been designed intentionally, which is especially noticeable in the larger point sizes **/05/**. In the regular weight, the visually small counters are conspicuous, which must have been due to filling in the outline weight. In general the typeface loses some of the joyousness which Frutiger so desired.

Frutiger Capitalis was released in 2005 as an OpenType font in regular and outline weights, extended to include the signs character set.

KAPITALIEN

IN RÖMISCHER SCHREIBFORM WURDEN IN
STEIN GEHAUEN · DER FLUSS DER GESTEN
ERWIRKT DIE LEBENDIGKEIT · KAPITALIEN
IN RÖMISCHER SCHREIBFORM WURDEN IN
STEIN GEHAUEN · DER FLUSS DER GESTEN
ERWIRKT DIE LEBENDIGKEIT·

/04/
'Capitalis Outline' design
with some symbols, presented to
the type selection meeting in
November 1991.

/05/
Adrian Frutiger's final artwork from
1991 (black) compared with the
digitised Frutiger Capitalis (red).

/06/
Comparison showing Frutiger's
design with the test exposure
from 1992 and Frutiger Capitalis
(top to bottom).

AEN
AEN
AEN

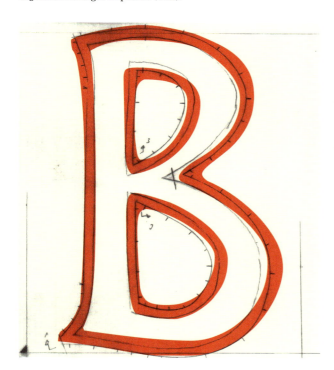

/07/
Test exposure from 1992 made
to harmonise Frutiger Signs
with the typeface then still called
'Symbolica'.

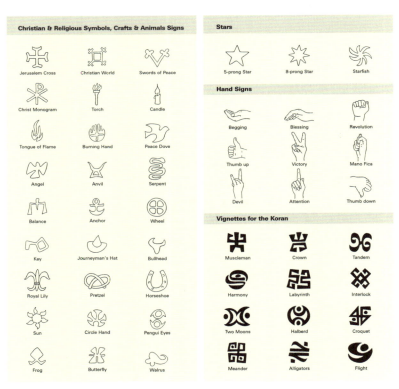

Christian & Religious Symbols, Crafts & Animals Signs

Jerusalem Cross	Christian World	Swords of Peace
Christ Monogram	Torch	Candle
Tongue of Flame	Burning Hand	Peace Dove
Angel	Anvil	Serpent
Balance	Anchor	Wheel
Key	Journeyman's Hat	Bullhead
Royal Lily	Pretzel	Horseshoe
Sun	Circle Hand	Pengui Eyes
Frog	Butterfly	Walrus

Stars

5-prong Star	8-prong Star	Starfish

Hand Signs

Begging	Blessing	Revolution
Thumb up	Victory	Mano Fica
Devil	Attention	Thumb down

Vignettes for the Koran

Muscleman	Crown	Tandem
Harmony	Labyrinth	Interlock
Two Moons	Halberd	Croquet
Meander	Alligators	Flight

/08/
*Two pages of the eight-page
Linotype brochure from
2005 – the signs are divided
into eight groups in total.*

Frutiger Capitalis Signs   Adrian Frutiger planned additional linear symbols when designing *'Capitalis Outline'*. He wrote of the origins of the characters: "The first stage consisted of producing drawings of printed characters from the book *Der Mensch und seine Zeichen*.[3] "[…] some 90 characters […] are currently being worked on with help from the digital system. […] The longer I spend on the project, the more the different areas and character variations spread out. For instance, I intended to draw two or three hand symbols. After some consideration they became over 20."[4]

In order to accommodate the intended range of 334 characters, the symbols were divided into four fonts and given the working title *Frutiger Signs*. Linotype's business plan gave precedence to its individuality over existing pi fonts,[5] yet the scheme was postponed.

While the symbols relate to the typeface /07/ in the 1992 test exposures, this is no longer the case for *Frutiger Capitalis* in 2005. Their line width and quality appear uneven and to have been rushed. They look as though they were computer generated after being scanned.

The intended range of characters and division into eight groups, which can be seen in the brochure /08/, was not feasible.[6] Linotype wrote that *Frutiger Capitalis* Signs was Adrian Frutiger's personal symbol cosmos.

/09/
*The three lapidary-like typefaces
all have flared, diagonally cut stroke
ends.*

HOFSTAINBERG

Hoffmann
Richard Lipton (Lothar Hoffmann)
1993

A B H M R X 3 8

HOFSTAINBERG

ITC Woodland
Akira Kobayashi
1997

A B H M R X 3 8

HOFSTAINBERG

Frutiger Capitalis
Adrian Frutiger
2005

A B H M R X 3 8

A	B	H	M	R	X	3	8
Dynamic curved downstroke, small counter	Bottom bow ends left of stem in a spur	Diagonal cross stroke	Curved V-shape	Closed counter	Rounded angles, flared stroke ends	Horizontal top shape	Crossing lines, pointed end of counters rounded

Font production:
Digitised by Linotype

Font format:
OpenType Std

ABCDEFGHIJKLMN
OPQRSTUVWXYZ&
ABCDEFGHIJKLMNOPQR
STUVWXYZ1234567890

POURQUOI TAN
T D'ALPHABETS DIFF
ÉRENTS! TOUS SERVENT A
U MÊME BUT, MAIS AUSSI À EXPRIM
ER LA DIVERSITÉ DE L'HOMME. C'EST CETTE MÊME DIVER
SITÉ QUE NOUS RETROUVONS DANS LES VINS DE MÉDOC.
J'AI PU, UN JOUR, RELEVER SOIXANTE CRUS, TOUS DE LA M
ÊME ANNÉE. IL S'AGISSAIT CERTES DE VINS, MAIS TOUS ÉT
AIENT DIFFÉRENTS. TOUT EST DANS LA NUANCE DU BOUQ

UET. IL EN EST DE MÊME POUR LES CARACTÈRES! SIE FRAGEN SICH, WARUM ES NOTWE
NDIG IST, SO VIELE SCHRIFTEN ZUR VERFÜGUNG ZU HABEN. SIE DIENEN ALLE ZUM SEL
BEN, ABER MACHEN DIE VIELFALT DES MENSCHEN AUS. DIESE VIELFALT IST WIE BEIM
WEIN. ICH HABE EINMAL EINE WEINKARTE STUDIERT MIT SECHZIG MÉDOC-WEINEN
AUS DEM SELBEN JAHR. DAS IST AUSNAHMSLOS WEIN, ABER DOCH NICHT ALLES DER GL
EICHE WEIN. ES HAT EBEN GLEICHWOHL NUANCEN. SO IST ES AUCH MIT DER SCHRIFT.
YOU MAY ASK WHY SO MANY DIFFERENT TYPEFACES. THEY ALL SERVE THE SAME PURP

OSE BUT THEY EXPRESS MAN'S DIVERSITY. IT IS THE SAME DIVERSITY WE FI
ND IN WINE. I ONCE SAW A LIST OF MÉDOC WINES FEATURING SIXTY DIFF
ERENT MÉDOCS ALL OF THE SAME YEAR. ALL OF THEM WERE WINES BUT E
ACH WAS DIFFERENT FROM THE OTHERS. IT'S THE NUANCES THAT ARE IM
PORTANT. THE SAME IS TRUE FOR TYPEFACES. POURQUOI TANT D'ALPHAB
ETS DIFFÉRENTS! TOUS SERVENT AU MÊME BUT, MAIS AUSSI À EXPRIMER
LA DIVERSITÉ DE L'HOMME. C'EST CETTE MÊME DIVERSITÉ QUE NOUS RET
ROUVONS DANS LES VINS DE MÉDOC. J'AI PU, UN JOUR, RELEVER SOIXANT

E CRUS, TOUS DE LA MÊME ANNÉE. IL S'AGISSAIT
CERTES DE VINS, MAIS TOUS ÉTAIENT DIFFÉREN
TS. TOUT EST DANS LA NUANCE DU BOUQUET. IL
EN EST DE MÊME POUR LES CARACTÈRES! SIE FR
AGEN SICH, WARUM ES NOTWENDIG IST, SO VIEL
E SCHRIFTEN ZUR VERFÜGUNG ZU HABEN. SIE D
IENEN ALLE ZUM SELBEN, ABER MACHEN DIE VI
ELFALT DES MENSCHEN AUS. DIESE VIELFALT IST
WIE BEIM WEIN. ICH HABE EINMAL EINE WEINK
ARTE STUDIERT MIT SECHZIG MÉDOC-WEINEN A

ÅBÇDÈFG
HIJKLMÑ
ÔPQRŠTÜ
VWXYZ&
ÆŒ¥$£€
1234567890
ÅBÇDÉFGHIJ
KLMÑÔPQRŠ
TÜVWXYZSS
FIFLÆŒØŁÐ
[.,:;·'/---]
(¿¡"«‹›»"!?)
{§°%Ⓐ‰*†}

Regular   Signs

ÅBÇDÈFG
HIJKLMÑ
ÔPQRŠTÜ
VWXYZ&
ÆŒ¥$£€
1234567890
ÅBÇDÉFGHIJ
KLMÑÔPQRŠ
TÜVWXYZSS
FIFLÆŒØŁÐ
[.,:;·'/---]
(¿¡"«‹›»"!?)
{§°%Ⓐ‰*†}

Outline

56 pt | –45   44 pt | –30   33 pt | –5   23 pt | 0   14 pt | 19 pt | 15   9 pt | 13 pt | 30   6.6 pt | 10.2 pt | 45   5 pt | 8 pt | 65

POMPEIJANA

After the first font pack for 'Type Before Gutenberg' shipped with *Herculanum* on it, it wasn't until the third pack that more of my fonts were included: *Pompeijana* in 1992, and *Rusticana* in 1993. The name *Pompeijana* was Linotype's suggestion.[1] It was taken from the ancient city, destroyed in 79 AD by the eruption of Vesuvius, and only later discovered and excavated in the 18th century. You'll find records of this type of script on the walls of the houses there **/05/**. But Capitalis Rustica was primarily written with a pen on parchment. The classical originals were actually written with a reed pen. It started with Capitalis Quadrata **/05/**, with its horizontal or very flat pen position, then came Rustica.[2] It got that name because of its somewhat rustic, countrified appearance when set against Capitalis Monumentalis. The pen is held in a steep position, and turned through an angle of 25° to 30° **/09/**.[3] That's what produces the change in the strokes – from the thin, slender down-strokes to the thick crossbars. Later scripts never got any steeper. For me that was an end-point in the history of the development of Latin script. The steep angle produced a majuscule script that's very closely spaced with a lively feel to it. A similar but much more rigid looking script came about later with the gothic minuscule (Textura) and its very narrow, pointed letter shapes **/05/**.

During the preliminary work on *Pompeijana,* I looked through Albert Kapr's Book *Schriftkunst,* and in *Hoffmanns Schriftatlas*.[4] I also wanted to see what was shown in Hans Eduard Meier's *The Development of Script and Type* **/08/**.[5] Basically I had the samples of my teacher, Alfred Willimann, on hand, although these on their own were certainly not enough.

The first sketches for *Pompeijana* were done with a broad pen on well-sized paper, at a height of around 30 pt, maybe a little bigger. Apart from *Ondine,* it's the only typeface where I actually wrote the originals, rather than drawing them. It would have been impossible for me to draw the curves in the same way that a pen can produce them. The types of curve you see in the D or the O can only be made with a pen. The thought of drawing them simply wouldn't have occurred to me. The letters have to flow, you see. I've written so much with it that the pen has come to feel like an extension of myself, and that probably adds something to the quality of a typeface. It's all about the correctly proportioned dynamic in the stroke. Everyone should try at least once, to write script with a pen, preferably under supervision. On the other hand, I would never have drawn the originals for an antiqua with a pen. In spite of that, the curves in *Méridien,* for example, came out well. I think, however, that I can safely state: a type designer who has never written a script by hand will never be able to produce proper curves. The junctures are always shaky. Writing by hand is, after all, somewhat different from drawing. You can recognise in the curves of *Pompeijana* a different liveliness and excitement than in *Méridien,* which has a more constructed, or rather, more drawn feel to it.

Further development of 'TBG' After the appearance of *Herculanum* (see page 370) in the first font pack of 'Type Before Gutenberg', and the absence of any Adrian Frutiger fonts in the second, the third font pack contained two: *Pompeijana* and *Rusticana* (see page 390). Once again, the theme was typefaces from Roman antiquity.

The name *Pompeijana* is derived from the ancient settlement of Pompeii, southeast of Naples, which was destroyed during the eruption of the volcano Vesuvius in 79 AD.[6] However, Adrian Frutiger did not base his calligraphic script directly on the historical inscriptions found there. **/05/** Rather, the connection lies more with the antique writing script **/05/**. This style of Capitalis Rustica, written with a quill or reed, appears – due to its greater stroke contrast – more pointed than the inscriptions at Pompeii, which were painted with a flat brush on the whitewashed walls. However, both the 1st-century brush script and the 4th-century pen script are not typical of calligraphic scripts: due to the steeply inclined angle at which the pen is held, the vertical strokes are thinner than the horizontal ones **/09/**. From a historical perspective this was, until well into the 19th century, somewhat unique among Latin scripts. Only with the so-called French Clarendon typefaces like Italienne (see page 346) did this unusual reversal of stroke weights find a counterpart.

For *Pompeijana* Adrian Frutiger could use his experience, gained in his calligraphic studies under Alfred Willimann at the Kunstgewerbeschule in Zurich, as he had done with *Herculanum,* the first calligraphic typeface for the 'Type Before Gutenberg' project. Indeed, his diploma submission featured a woodcut of Capitalis Rusticana **/01/**.[7] In addition, in his second year as a type designer at the Deberny & Peignot type foundry in Paris, he produced a woodcut of *Rusticana* **/02/**. It was used to print Deberny & Peignot's New Year's card for 1953.

To reproduce a historical script as accurately as possible was not Adrian Frutiger's goal with *Pompeijana*. To this end, he worked not only from photographs of a particular original, but he also consulted versions that had been rewritten later, one of which was by Hans Eduard Meier from the booklet *The Development of Script and Type* (1959) **/08/**. It was more important for him to create the most balanced typeface possible. *Pompeijana* was completed in 1992, and an additional decorative font was also supplied for border designs.

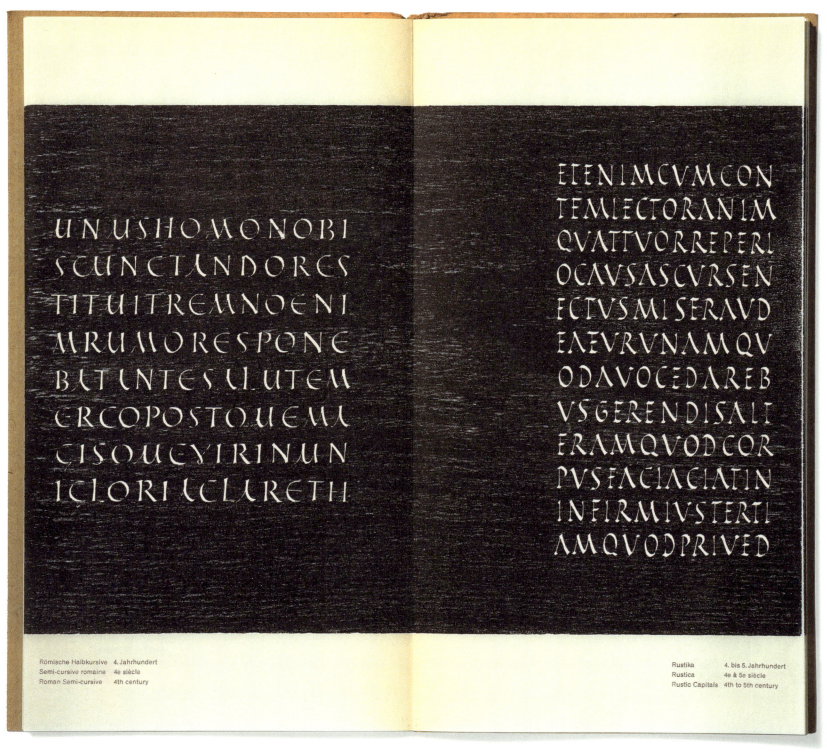

Römische Halbkursive   4. Jahrhundert
Semi-cursive romaine   4e siècle
Roman Semi-cursive   4th century

Rustika   4. bis 5. Jahrhundert
Rustica   4e à 5e siècle
Rustic Capitals 4th to 5th century

/01/
Diploma presentation (1951),
woodcut by Adrian Frutiger – the
right side of the accordion-fold
booklet shows a Rustica from the
4th to 5th century AD.

/02/
1953 New Year's greetings card
from Deberny & Peignot –
this woodcut, with text in Rustica,
was done by Adrian Frutiger,
their new staff member.

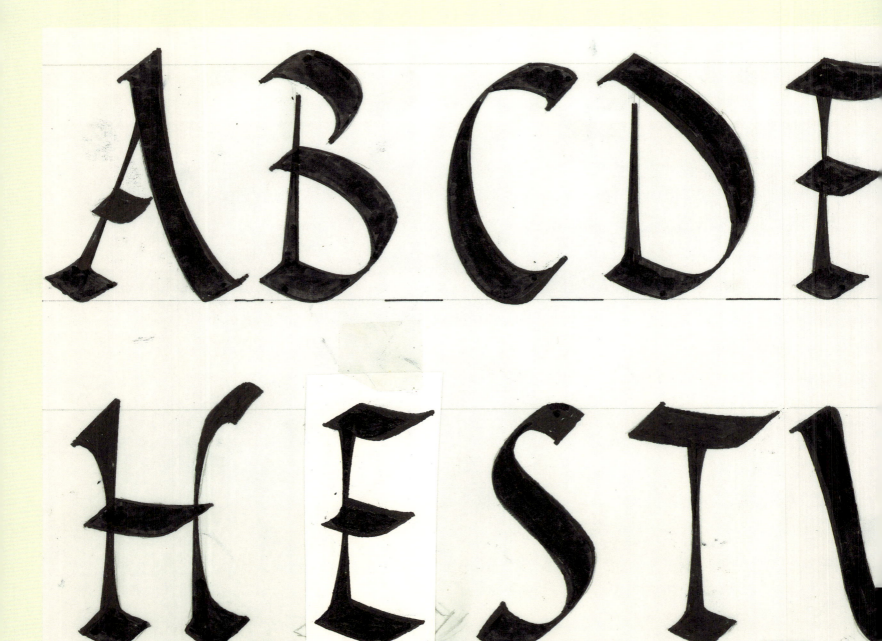

/03/
Undated felt-tip pen drawing for Pompeijana on tracing paper – the E on white paper has been glued on later (original size).

/04/
Pencil drawings on mounted tracing paper – mistakes have been scraped away with a scalpel (slightly smaller than original size).

The design of Pompeijana In conversation, Frutiger has mentioned that for the design of *Pompeijana* he had handwritten the letters.[8] His originals have not survived, and hardly any designs for the typeface are to be found. Only a few letters, drawn in felt-tip on tracing paper /03/, and the numerals and a few additional glyphs, drawn in pencil on tracing paper can be reproduced here /04/. In both preliminary designs the formal correspondence with the finished version is clear, and yet, in a few glyphs, there are obvious differences to be noted.

In many letters *Pompeijana* shows similarities to the Rustica in Frutiger's diploma submission /01/, while in others it clearly owes more to Hans Eduard Meier's version. That he co-opted both of these in the design has been confirmed in conversation, and can also be seen through reference to an enlarged copy.[9] The C, for example, compares with Meier's letter shape, the S also shows Meier's rather closed curve shape /08/ and the D is still diagonally oriented in Frutiger's design. The published version, however, features another shape: the D is now rounder, leaning more toward the shapes of his diploma thesis. The Q is striking with its short, curled-under tail, also the G with its 'beard' jutting down below the baseline. While the former can be seen around 500 AD in the script *Vergilius Palatinus* /05/, the latter is unusual. The backwards-sloping, diagonal beard was taken from Hans Eduard Meier's design /08/.[10]

I was careful to make sure that all the verticals were as fine as possible in order to create a contrast with the short, thick, horizontal strokes, which is why, in my typeface, the finer strokes dominate. The change from thick to thin is an awkward, but beautiful change in contrast. Consider the letters D and R of *Pompeijana* in the word 'Druckschrift', in the last line of the sample string /06/; it's apparent that the downstrokes are really fragile. A look at the handwritten originals of *Vergilius Palatinus* for example /05/, is interesting in this regard. There the thin strokes are even finer in places. It's also written very closely spaced, the letters almost melt into each other. *Pompeijana's* text image, on the other hand, is lighter; my typeface runs wider. You can see clearly here my way of setting script rather than writing it. Each letter has its own personality, but still, along with its neighbours, makes the whole word hang together.

There's a big difference, whether I write or set such a typeface or rather draw it in such a way that it can be set. That produces a couple of differences with regards to the originals from the 4th century. I evened out the width of the letters, so that the counters and sidebearings would be approximately equal. That's just become second nature to me. I can't change it. My E is wider, and therefore lighter, than the F /06/ – in the old written scripts that's not necessarily clear – and in *Pompeijana's* M, the angles are less steep than in the historical originals, and the letter is a little airier for that. Altogether, my letters run quite wide; in addition the serifs are very short: almost reduced to a point. That means that the rhythm of the line is not quite as marked as in the *Rustica* originals. The typeface has, however, better legibility.

/06/
1991 text sample – 'Rustica 1', corresponding to Frutiger's original drawings, and 'Rustica 2', a somewhat heavier version (top to bottom).

/05/
Handwritten scripts: Wall writing in Pompeii, 1st c. AD; Capitalis Rustica 'Vergilius Vaticanus' and 'Vergilius Palatinus', 4th c. AD; Capitalis Quadrata, 4th c. AD; Gothic minuscule, 15th c. AD (top to bottom).

/07/
In the original design the opening of the O is at the bottom, in the test exposure it is at the top and in the published version it is at the bottom again.

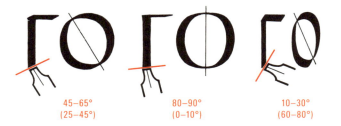

Typeface Comparison   In *Fontbook*, Fontshop International's comprehensive 2006 typeface catalogue, *Carus* and *Pompeijana* are designated as blackletter fonts, while *Virgile* is classified as a display font.[11] Although a formal relation to the blackletter type is given and the division as display type is possible, this very difficile and expense attribution is not really solved. Historically, as well as in terms of design, it would have been better to assign it to the category of scripts.[12]

These three typefaces belonging to the Capitalis Rustica classification were all published in the mid-1990s. Conforming to historical models these are majuscule types, since in the original handwritten Rusticas there were no lowercase forms, although these were already beginning to appear in scripts in the 4th–5th century AD.[13]

When comparing the scripts, differences in the letter shapes become evident. In keeping with the original, the A of *Virgile*, for example, has no crossbar. The composition of the typefaces is also different: *Virgile* is heavier and has less stroke contrast. It therefore appears less pointed than *Pompeijana* and *Carus*, both of which display hairline strokes. In *Carus*, the less-rigorous strokes and the often rather narrow counters lend it a somewhat messy text image, although this is not atypical of typefaces derived from handwritten scripts /10/.

/08/
Capitalis Rustica, calligraphy by Hans Eduard Meier, from his book Schriftentwicklung, *served as a model for* Pompeijana.

/09/
When writing with a broad pen, stroke weight and stroke contrast change according to the angle of the pen's front edge: Roman Capitalis, Capitalis Quadrata, Capitalis Rustica (left to right).

45–65°
(25–45°)   80–90°
(0–10°)   10–30°
(60–80°)

/10/
Compared with the two other interpretations of Rustica, Pompeijana *has a lighter, harder and more pointed appearance.*

HOFSTAINBERG

Virgile
Franck Jalleau
1991

HOFSTAINBERG

Pompeijana
Adrian Frutiger
1992

A	**B**	**F**	**G**	**K**	**Q**	**V**	**1 5**
Short crossbar, sitting on the left diagonal	Counters open and closed, minimal difference in size	Cap height not exceeded	Truncated curve shape, spur drops below baseline	Upper arm curved toward right	Short tail, curved back to left	Diagonals separated by gap	Rhomboid serifs, very pointed appearance

HOFSTAINBERG

Carus
Jürgen Brinckmann
1995

Font production:
Adobe Font digitised by
Linotype

Font format:
PostScript Type 1

Also available:
TrueType
OpenType Std

ABCDEFGHIJKLMN
OPQRSTUVWXYZ&
ABCDEFGHIJKLMNOPQR
STUVWXYZ1234567890

POURQUOI TANT
D'ALPHABETS DIFFÉRENT
S! TOUS SERVENT AU MÊME BUT, M
AIS AUSSI À EXPRIMER LA DIVERSITÉ DE L'HOM
ME. C'EST CETTE MÊME DIVERSITÉ QUE NOUS RETROUVONS DANS LES VI
NS DE MÉDOC. J'AI PU, UN JOUR, RELEVER SOIXANTE CRUS, TOUS DE LA
MÊME ANNÉE. IL S'AGISSAIT CERTES DE VINS, MAIS TOUS ÉTAIENT DIFFÉR
ENTS. TOUT EST DANS LA NUANCE DU BOUQUET. IL EN EST DE MÊME PO
UR LES CARACTÈRES! SIE FRAGEN SICH, WARUM ES NOTWENDIG IST, SO

VIELE SCHRIFTEN ZUR VERFÜGUNG ZU HABEN. SIE DIENEN ALLE ZUM SELBEN, ABER MACHEN D
IE VIELFALT DES MENSCHEN AUS. DIESE VIELFALT IST WIE BEIM WEIN. ICH HABE EINMAL EINE
WEINKARTE STUDIERT MIT SECHZIG MÉDOC-WEINEN AUS DEM SELBEN JAHR. DAS IST AUSNAH
MSLOS WEIN, ABER DOCH NICHT ALLES DER GLEICHE WEIN. ES HAT EBEN GLEICHWOHL NUANCEN.
SO IST ES AUCH MIT DER SCHRIFT. YOU MAY ASK WHY SO MANY DIFFERENT TYPEFACES. THEY AL
L SERVE THE SAME PURPOSE BUT THEY EXPRESS MAN'S DIVERSITY. IT IS THE SAME DIVERSITY
WE FIND IN WINE. I ONCE SAW A LIST OF MÉDOC WINES FEATURING SIXTY DIFFERENT MÉDOCS

ALL OF THE SAME YEAR. ALL OF THEM WERE WINES BUT EACH WAS DIFFER
ENT FROM THE OTHERS. IT'S THE NUANCES THAT ARE IMPORTANT. THE SAME
IS TRUE FOR TYPEFACES. POURQUOI TANT D'ALPHABETS DIFFÉRENTS! TOUS S
ERVENT AU MÊME BUT, MAIS AUSSI À EXPRIMER LA DIVERSITÉ DE L'HOMME.
C'EST CETTE MÊME DIVERSITÉ QUE NOUS RETROUVONS DANS LES VINS DE M
ÉDOC. J'AI PU, UN JOUR, RELEVER SOIXANTE CRUS, TOUS DE LA MÊME AN
NÉE. IL S'AGISSAIT CERTES DE VINS, MAIS TOUS ÉTAIENT DIFFÉRENTS. TOUT E
ST DANS LA NUANCE DU BOUQUET. IL EN EST DE MÊME POUR LES CARACTÈR

ES! SIE FRAGEN SICH, WARUM ES NOTWENDIG
IST, SO VIELE SCHRIFTEN ZUR VERFÜGUNG ZU H
ABEN. SIE DIENEN ALLE ZUM SELBEN, ABER MA
CHEN DIE VIELFALT DES MENSCHEN AUS. DIESE
VIELFALT IST WIE BEIM WEIN. ICH HABE EINM
AL EINE WEINKARTE STUDIERT MIT SECHZIG M
ÉDOC-WEINEN AUS DEM SELBEN JAHR. DAS IST
AUSNAHMSLOS WEIN, ABER DOCH NICHT ALLES
DER GLEICHE WEIN. ES HAT EBEN GLEICHWOHL
NUANCEN. SO IST ES AUCH MIT DER SCHRIFT. Y

ÅBCDĚFG
HIJKLMÑ
ÔPQRŠTÜ
VWXYZ&
ÆŒ¥$£€
1234567890
ÅBCDÉFGHIJ
KLMÑÔPQRŠ
TÜVWXYZSS
Fl FL Æ Œ Ø Ł ð
[.,:;·'/---]
(¿¡"«‹›»"!?)
{§°%@‰*†}

Roman

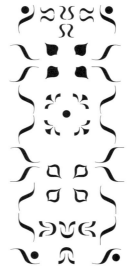

Borders

61pt|−5   42pt|0   28pt|8   20pt|25   13pt|19pt|30   9.5pt|13pt|50   7.5pt|10.2pt|60   6pt|8pt|70

RUSTICANA

Rusticana appeared in 1993, as a further addition to the 'Type Before Gutenberg' project. The basis for this typeface was the Roman inscriptional capitals from the 3rd to 2nd centuries BC, as shown in volume one of František Muzika's *Die Schöne Schrift* **/09/**.[1] But basically, *Rusticana* is my creation, or rather a mixture of the historically traditional and my own personal style. It's basically about working with the spirit of Roman antiquity, but converted into modern times. The name was Linotype's idea. The naming is probably a bit confusing, particularly for palaeographers. My *Pompeijana,* which had come out a year earlier, embodied the style of the so-called Capitalis Rustica (see page 387), while the typeface called *Rusticana* actually has more to do with the clearly older Roman inscriptional capitals, which were mostly chiselled on stone **/07/**.

I've never been to a type selection meeting where I didn't have something new to show them. It was almost expected that I would turn up with a new design. I felt somehow obliged not to turn up empty-handed. My suggestion for *Rusticana* was based on a paste-up string of letters. Mostly, at the beginning, I had used only the test word 'OHamburgefonstiv'. That was, of course, not yet perfectly well balanced. You can't draw any real conclusions about the spacing from this test word, since the forms and counterforms are far too different. Typically, you'd place each letter between two ms or ns, or with capital letter typefaces, between two Hs, in order to get a better idea of the spacing. There's a poster that my teacher Alfred Willimann did for an exhibition on ancient Roman portrait sculpture; the inscriptional capital there is very beautiful and lively but the spaces between the letters aren't right. That's what always amazed me about Willimann. Someone who's never spaced type using a composing stick just won't get it. In the meetings we often argued over the letterspacing. Reinhard Haus has an amazingly sharp eye, he could always deliver a ringing judgement. Arthur Ritzel, and his successor Werner Schimpf, they had that in their blood, they were used to being in contact with Linotype matrices. That's a smidgen too wide, that's how it went, or a smidgen too tight. Examining the first text sample, the word 'SONNENTAU' still falls apart, especially between the two Ns **/01/**.

My designs were developed using a felt-tip marker **/04/**; in parts I blotted them **/05/**. They display an emphasis on serif-style terminals. Characteristic of *Rusticana* is that the slightly widened terminals are cut virtually at right angles to the stroke direction. Also typical are the strongly varying letter widths. The round letters like C and S are very narrow, the rest are kept rather wide. I find the Q interesting; it has an archaic quality to it. And the numerals have a character all their own **/11/**.

'Type before Gutenberg' – Third instalment   For his third typeface for the Linotype project 'Type before Gutenberg' Adrian Frutiger again went back to a script from Roman antiquity. The originals were stone inscriptions from the 3rd and 2nd century BC **/07/**. The basis for *Rusticana* is, therefore, from an earlier period in the history of writing than that for either *Pompeijana* or *Herculanum*. The character of Frutiger's inscriptional capital (Latin 'lapis', 'lapidis', stone; 'lapidarius', carved in stone) appears, however, to be rather more contemporary in comparison to the other two typefaces, due to its graphic quality, the others being more calligraphic in character.

No script similar to *Rusticana* appeared in Frutiger's diploma submission. He cut the 'early Roman Capitals' in wood, without flared stroke endings.[2] Formally related, however, is a headline face whose terminals appear more accentuated and less moderated **/08/**. Frutiger drew the letters for the 1976 booklet *Le Louvre*.[3] The Parisian museum had regularly been a client at the studio Frutiger et Pfäffli, and it was Bruno Pfäffli who, over the years, designed many publications for the museum, including the booklet. He would often be the first to employ Frutiger's typefaces when working on these projects.

In February 1992, in a handwritten memo from Linotype, the question was put forward of whether there were any further suggestions other than the two names *Pompeijana* and *Rusticana*. According to the memo, up until that point both typefaces had gone under the name 'Rustica'. Frutiger's two folders containing the original design drawings also bore that designation.[4] The name *Rusticana* has been a problem. The confusion with *Pompeijana*, which is in the style of Capitalis Rustica, is simply too great. In addition, there is no intrinsic connection to the idea of a rustic, countrified script.

The third pack of the 'Type Before Gutenberg' project included Karlgeorg Hoefer's *Notre Dame* in addition to *Pompeijana* and *Rusticana* **/10/**. Appearing in 1993, it was derived from the gothic minuscule or *textura* of the 14th and 15th centuries AD. All three typefaces contain a set of standard glyphs and an extension. Adrian Frutiger produced the so-called border fonts for the design of borders and backgrounds, and Karlgeorg Hoefer produced a few ornamentations as well **/10/**.

From 1990 to 1993 Linotype published nine typefaces in the 'Type Before Gutenberg' project, which were also incorporated into the Adobe type library.

OHAMBURGEFONSTIV OBERFORSTER HORNISSE OTTO HOFFNUNG SONNENTAU
TASSE TEE INSERAT MOOSTRAUBEN MONSUNREGEN FRAGE ABTEIGRUFT
NORTVONE GABE TURNVEREIN NAMENSGEBUNG MIINNORA BAGGER
BAUFENSTER MUTTER HOMBERGER OHAMBURGEFONSTIV OBERFORSTER
HORNISSE OTTO HOFFNUNG SONNENTAU TASSE TEE INSERAT MOOSTRAUBEN
MONSUNREGEN OHAMBURGEFONSTIV OBERFORSTER HORNISSE OTTO
HOFFNUNG SONNENTAU TASSE TEE INSERAT MOOSTRAUBEN MONSUNREGEN

OHAMBURGEFONSTIV OBERFORSTER HORNISSE OTTO HOFFNUNG
SONNENTAUTASSE TEE INSERAT MOOSTRAUBEN MONSUNREGEN
FRAGE ABTEIGRUFT NORTVONE GABE TURNVEREIN
NAMENSGEBUNG MIINNORA BAGGER BAUFENSTER MUTTER
HOMBERGER OHAMBURGEFONSTIV OBERFORSTER HORNISSE OTTO
HOFFNUNG SONNENTAU TASSE TEE INSERAT MOOSTRAUBEN
MONSUNREGEN OHAMBURGEFONSTIV

OHAMBURGEFONSTIV OBERFORSTER HORNISSE OTTO
HOFFNUNG SONNENTAU TASSE TEE INSERAT
MOOSTRAUBEN MONSUNREGEN FRAGE ABTEIGRUFT
NORTVONE GABE TURNVEREIN NAMENSGEBUNG
MIINNORA BAGGER BAUFENSTER MUTTER HOMBERGER
OHAMBURGEFONSTIV OBERFORSTER HORNISSE OTTO

OHAMBURGEFONSTIV OBERFORSTER
HORNISSE OTTO HOFFNUNG SONNENTAU
TASSE TEE INSERAT MOOSTRAUBEN
MONSUNREGEN FRAGE ABTEIGRUFT
NORTVONE GABE TURNVEREIN
NAMENSGEBUNG MIINNORA BAGGER

OHAMBURGEFONSTIV
OBERFORSTER HORNISSE OTTO
HOFFNUNG SONNENTAU TASSE
TEE INSERAT MOOSTRAUBEN
MONSUNREGEN

/01/
Undated sample strings for
Rusticana in sizes from 10 to 24 pt –
the letter spacing is still not
satisfactorily resolved.

RUSTICANA   **391**

Poster by Alfred Willimann from 1953 – he designed this inscriptional typeface to accompany an exhibition on the subject of Ancient Roman Portrait Sculpture.

/03/
Title design for an article in the magazine Art de France, 1962, by André Gürtler in collaboration with Adrian Frutiger.

TRESOR ÇALLO-ROMAIN
DE ÇRAINCOURT

/04/
Undated designs for Rusticana – the terminals were subsequently made stronger and the glyphs underwent formal changes.

HOAMEBGFNT

URSCDLPJKQ

VXYZÆŒ&G

/05/
Undated design in felt-tip marker, 'blotted' onto smooth paper – the letter shapes recall Christian inscriptions from the 4th to 6th century AD.

AAAAABBBCCCD

Shape changes in the terminals In the early Greek inscriptionals the text image is very linear. The tapered, rounded terminals come about as a result of carving in stone /06/. The same characteristic is seen in Roman inscriptionals from the 6th to 4th centuries BC. Inscriptions that were produced more accurately show less-tapered and less-rounded terminals, and in the 4th century BC right-angled terminals appeared /06/ – a quality that was seen far earlier in the Greek inscriptionals. They formed the starting point of our sans serif typefaces.

As early as approximately 250 BC, the drive towards emphasising the terminals can already be discerned in the Roman inscriptionals. Carved with flared stroke endings had started to emerge /07/. Adrian Frutiger drew on this design approach for *Rusticana*. In his first designs, however, the strokes are more or less parallel /04/.

In the 200 years before the birth of Christ, stonemasons continued to develop inscriptions with serifs. The letters were, however, still of linear design /09/. From around 50 BC onwards, stroke modulation by painting the letterforms with a broad brush before chiselling became the standard. The result was Capitalis Monumentalis /09/. The linear character remained, however, and this characteristic is particularly evident in Christian inscriptions up to the 6th century AD /07/. One of Frutiger's sketches shows that this form of script with its actual serifs might have played a role in his design /05/.

/06/
The stroke endings of Roman inscriptions from the 6th to the 1st century BC show a development from tapered terminals to serifs.

/07/
Historical inscriptions: Roman inscriptional capitals from the 3rd century BC (top, middle) and a Christian inscription from the 5th century AD (bottom).

LE LOUVRE

/08/
Cover of a 1976 brochure for the Louvre in Paris, designed by Bruno Pfäffli and with a typeface design by Adrian Frutiger.

/09/
Roman inscriptions recorded by František Muzika: 250–150 BC, 1st century BC and 1st century AD (left to right).

/10/

*'Type before Gutenberg' 3 contained
Frutiger's* Pompeijana *and* Rusticana,
*each with a border font, and
Karlgeorg Hoefer's* Notre Dame *with
its own ornamentations.*

Typeface comparison   The common basis for the three inscriptionals shown below is their antique origin. They are not, however, copies of historical inscriptions, rather they exhibit their own stylistic characteristics.

The typefaces feature square-cut terminals. However, they display considerable differences in this regard. *Lithos* is based on Greek inscriptions from the 4th century BC; serifs had not yet developed in this period. The prototype for *Rusticana* are Roman inscriptionals from 200 BC, which have concave strokes /07/.[5] The terminals (they still cannot be called serifs at this time) are emphasised and lead via soft transitions to the middle of the stem, from where this concave shape derives. *Syntax Lapidar Serif* refers back to originals with prominent terminals that emerged around 200 BC. A shortened transition into the stem gives them the appearance of truncated triangles.

Lithos has strongly differing letter widths, something that is not often found in Greek inscriptions. In contrast, in *Syntax Lapidar Serif,* the widths are more even, which is unusual for an early Roman inscription. Compared to *Lithos* and *Rusticana, Syntax Lapidar Serif,* with its square proportions, shows a constant right-angled dimension. All three scripts possess our present-day number shapes. However, the Greeks and the Romans represented numerical quantities with letters.

/11/

With its flare serifs, Rusticana
sits between the sans serif Lithos
and Syntax Lapidar Serif *with
its distinctive serifs.*

HOFSTAINBERG

Lithos
Carol Twombly
1989

C L P Q U Y 3 4

HOFSTAINBERG

Rusticana
Adrian Frutiger
1993

C L P Q U Y 3 4

C	**L**	**P**	**Q**	**U**	**Y**	**3**	**4**
Very narrow curve shape, flared stroke endings	Rising crossbar	Counter open at bottom	Vertical tail	Up- and downstroke not vertical, acute curve	Asymmetrical shape, open angle, terminals cut diagonally	Shape above horizontal, below open	Open form, terminals cut diagonally

HOFSTAINBERG

Syntax Lapidar Serif Display
Hans Eduard Meier
2000

C L P Q U Y 3 4

Font production:
Adobe Font digitised by
Linotype

Font format:
OpenType Std

Also available:
PostScript Type 1
TrueType

ABCDEFGHIJKLMN
OPQRSTUVWXYZ&
ABCDEFGHIJKLMNOPQR
STUVWXYZ1234567890

YOU MAY ASK

WHY SO MANY DIF

FERENT TYPEFACES. THEY

ALL SERVE THE SAME PURPOSE BU

T THEY EXPRESS MAN'S DIVERSITY. IT IS THE SAME DIVER
SITY WE FIND IN WINE. I ONCE SAW A LIST OF MÉDOC
WINES FEATURING SIXTY DIFFERENT MÉDOCS ALL OF T
HE SAME YEAR. ALL OF THEM WERE WINES BUT EACH
WAS DIFFERENT FROM THE OTHERS. IT'S THE NUANCE T

HAT ARE IMPORTANT. THE SAME IS TRUE FOR TYPEFACES. POURQUOI TANT D'ALPHABETS D
IFFÉRENTS! TOUS SERVENT AU MÊME BUT, MAIS AUSSI À EXPRIMER LA DIVERSITÉ DE L'HOM
ME. C'EST CETTE MÊME DIVERSITÉ QUE NOUS RETROUVONS DANS LES VINS DE MÉDOC. J'AI PU,
UN JOUR, RELEVER SOIXANTE CRUS, TOUS DE LA MÊME ANNÉE. IL S'AGISSAIT CERTES DE VINS,
MAIS TOUS ÉTAIENT DIFFÉRENTS. TOUT EST DANS LA NUANCE DU BOUQUET. IL EN EST DE M
ÊME POUR LES CARACTÈRES! SIE FRAGEN SICH, WARUM ES NOTWENDIG IST, SO VIELE SCHRIFTE
N ZUR VERFÜGUNG ZU HABEN. SIE DIENEN ALLE ZUM SELBEN, ABER MACHEN DIE VIELFALT

DES MENSCHEN AUS. DIESE VIELFALT IST WIE BEIM WEIN. ICH HABE EIN
MAL EINE WEINKARTE STUDIERT MIT SECHZIG MÉDOC-WEINEN AUS DE
M SELBEN JAHR. DAS IST AUSNAHMSLOS WEIN, ABER DOCH NICHT ALLES
DER GLEICHE WEIN. ES HAT EBEN GLEICHWOHL NUANCEN. SO IST ES AU
CH MIT DER SCHRIFT. YOU MAY ASK WHY SO MANY DIFFERENT TYPEFAC
ES. THEY ALL SERVE THE SAME PURPOSE BUT THEY EXPRESS MAN'S DIVERS
ITY. IT IS THE SAME DIVERSITY WE FIND IN WINE. I ONCE SAW A LIST OF
MÉDOC WINES FEATURING SIXTY DIFFERENT MÉDOCS ALL OF THE SAME

YEAR. ALL OF THEM WERE WINES BUT EACH
WAS DIFFERENT FROM THE OTHERS. IT'S THE
NUANCES THAT ARE IMPORTANT. THE SAME I
S TRUE FOR TYPEFACES. POURQUOI TANT D'AL
PHABETS DIFFÉRENTS! TOUS SERVENT AU MÊ
ME BUT, MAIS AUSSI À EXPRIMER LA DIVERSIT
É DE L'HOMME. C'EST CETTE MÊME DIVERSITÉ
QUE NOUS RETROUVONS DANS LES VINS DE M
ÉDOC. J'AI PU, UN JOUR, RELEVER SOIXANTE CR
US, TOUS DE LA MÊME ANNÉE. IL S'AGISSAIT CER

ÅBÇDÈFG
HIJKLMÑ
ÔPQŘŠTÜ
VWXYZ&
ÆŒ¥$£€
1234567890
ÅBÇDÉFGHIJ
KLMÑÔPQR
ŠTÜVWXYZ
FIFLÆŒØŁÐ
[.,:;·'/-—]
(¿¡"«‹›»"!?)
{§°%@‰*†}
Roman

Borders

59pt|−110 43pt|−70 32pt|−50 23pt|−30 14pt|19pt|−30 8pt|13pt|−10 6.5pt|10.2pt|5 5pt|8pt|15

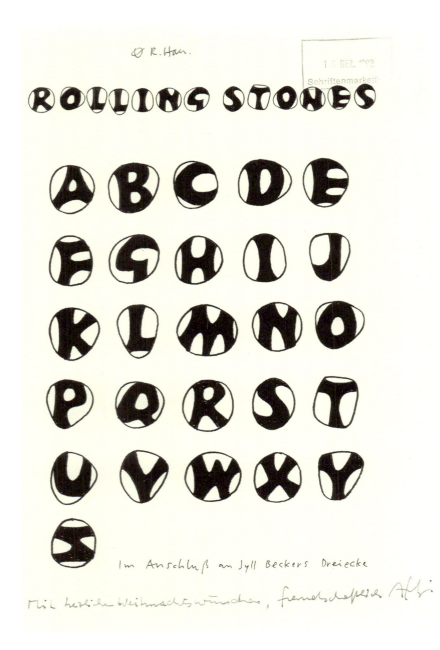

/01/
*1992 Christmas card
from Adrian Frutiger.*

From stone to type   Nature plays an important part in Adrian Frutiger's philosophy of life and work. Even during his early days as a student in Zurich he used to collect stones from the riverbed of the Sihl, scratching and writing shapes on their surfaces (see page 14). His artistic work has dealt intensively with primordial nature. Furthermore, having read histories of writing, Adrian Frutiger was familiar with the prehistoric stones of Mas d'Azil /02/,[1] on which characters are drawn. Their age is given as between 12000 and 6000 BC, and they represent a large number of developed characters.[2]

At a Linotype type selection meeting, a suggestion of Jyll Becker's was discussed, a design based upon triangular outlines with triangular letters within them /03/. The design was never brought to fruition, but Adrian Frutiger liked the idea of designing an alphabet within a variable basic shape. Ever since his time at Deberny & Peignot spent looking for display faces, he had been curious about creating playful types.

He sketched an alphabet in keeping with his style surrounded by amorphous outlines in allusion to Becker's design and sent it as a Christmas greeting to Otmar Hoefer /01/. The letter was filed away until Linotype went back to it in 1998 when looking for new typefaces. Typefaces by their most important designer – alongside Hermann Zapf – Adrian Frutiger sold well, and a Frutiger typeface such as that would be something new. In a 2002 conversation, Adrian Frutiger remarked that "Linotype dug out these old things and asked me whether they could do anything with them. I told them they ought to, because I wasn't going to do anything else."[3] Thus Linotype produced this unconventional typeface. Compared to Frutiger's design, the outline shapes in the digitised conversion are smoother. The N, for example, has a circular outer shape. The outlines of all characters also possess a consistently even stroke width, making the typeface lose some of its charm.

Called *Rolling Stones* by Frutiger, the typeface went by the working title *Frutiger Pebbles*[4] until it received the name *Frutiger Stones* when it was issued in 1998.

Lino tYpE Library GmbH

Du-Pont-Straße 1
D-61352 Bad Homburg
Internet: http://www.LinotypeLibrary.com
E-mail: Linotype@fonts.de

/04/
Type specimen brochure for
Frutiger Stones *and*
Frutiger Symbols, *designed by*
Leonardi.Wollein, Berlin.

/02/
Painted pebbles from the
Mesolithic era, found in the Mas
d'Azil cave in southern France.

/05/
Design drawings by
Adrian Frutiger for two different
ampersands – only the one on
the right was produced.

/03/
Jyll Becker's design titled 'Dreiecks-
variationen' (triangular variations)
made at Linotype in 1992, based
on a consistent basic shape.

/06/
The lowercase keyboard (below)
contains the capital forms,
which are staggered on the baseline
and partially rotated.

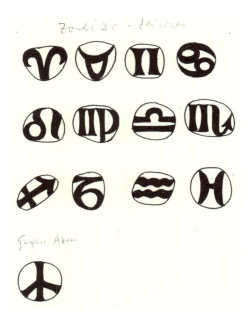

/07/
Some design drawings for
Frutiger Symbols *with handwritten*
notes by Adrian Frutiger.

/08/
Seven different representations of
the three existing faces (left)
are made possible by overlapping
them (right).

Frutiger Symbols *Frutiger Stones* was complemented with a symbol font in three weights. Symbols are Adrian Frutiger's speciality, as he has been busy with them for many years and published the three-volume book *Der Mensch und seine Zeichen* (Signs and symbols: their design and meaning) in 1978, 1979 and 1981.[5] Altogether, Adrian Frutiger designed 51 different symbols, divided into four groups: AF symbols (derived from his artistic work), animals, playing cards, signs of the zodiac /07/; and, by itself, an anti-nuclear symbol.

Thus, when Linotype came to produce *Frutiger Symbols*, they had a rich vein to mine. Some of the forms were taken from Adrian Frutiger's book and some were new designs; yet all were based on the concept of outlines and inner shapes, adapted to the characteristic style of *Frutiger Stones*.

Forms and counterforms are of particular importance in *Frutiger Symbols*, because the counterforms are defined by the outlines. This equal balance between both forms produces many variations on the combination of foreground and background /08/. The three different weights – regular (symbol with outline), positive (symbol without outline) and negative (counterform of the symbol) – may be combined by overlapping one another. The combination of all three variants is a further possibility. All three fonts have the same character width.

/09/
All three typefaces possess more or
less visible two-dimensional
limitations, giving the typeface
its shape.

HOFSTAINBERG

Cameo Solid
David Farey / Richard Dawson
1995

ABHKNRY50

HOFSTAINBERG

F2F Poison Flowers
Alessio Leonardi
1998

ABHKNRY50

Frutiger Stones
Adrian Frutiger
1998

A	**B**	**H**	**K**	**N**	**R**	**Y**	**5 0**
Asymmetrical legs	Axis slightly inclined to left	Upper counter slightly larger than lower counter	Emphasis on the upper section	Outline shape appears geometrically circular	Axis slightly inclined to the right	Vertical downstroke	Oval basic shape

Font production:
Adobe Font digitised by
Linotype

Font format:
PostScript Type 1

Also available:
TrueType

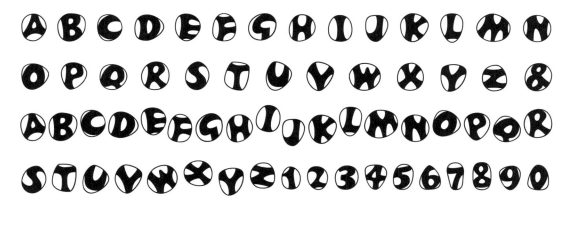

SIE FRAGEN SICH WARUM ES NOTWENDIG IST SO VI ELE SCHRIFTEN ZUR VERFUGUNG ZU HABEN. SIE DIENEN ALLE ZUM SELBEN, ABER MACHEN DIE VIELFALT DES MENSCHEN AUS DIE SE VIELFALT IST WIE BEIM WEIN. ICH HABE EI NMAL EINE WEINKARTE STUDIERT MIT SECHZ IG MEDOC·WEINEN AUS DEM SELBEN JAHR. DAS

IST AUSNAHMSLOS WEIN, ABER DOCH NICHT ALLES DER GLEICHE WEIN. ES HAT EBEN GLEICHWOHL NUANCEN. SO IST ES AUCH MIT DER SCHRIFT. YOU MAY ASK WHY SO MANY DIFFERENT TYPEFACES. THEY ALL SERVE THE SAME PURPOSE BUT THEY EXPRESS MAN'S DIVERSITY. IT IS THE SAME DIVERSITY WE FIND IN WINE. I ONCE SAW A LIST OF MEDOC WINES FEA TURING SIXTY DIFFERENT MEDOCS ALL OF THE SAME YEAR. ALL OF THEM WERE WINES BUT EACH WAS DIFFERENT FROM THE OTHERS. IT'S THE NUA

NCES THAT ARE IMPORTANT. THE SAME IS TRUE FOR TYPEFA CES. POURQUOI TANT D'ALPHABETS DIFFERENTS? TOUS SER VENT AU MEME BUT. MAIS AUSSI À EXPRIMER LA DIVERSITE DE L'HOMME. C'EST CETTE MEME DIVERSITE QUE NOUS RE TROUVONS DANS LES VINS DE MEDOC. J'AI PU, UN JOUR, REL EVER SOIXANTE CRUS, TOUS DE LA MEME ANNEE. IL S'AGIS SAIT CERTES DE VINS. MAIS TOUS ETAIENT DIFFERENTS. T OUT EST DANS LA NUANCE DU BOUQU BOUQUE QUET. IL EN ES

T DE MEME POUR LES CARACTÈRES! SIE FRAGEN SICH. WARUM ES NOT WENDIG IST. SO VIELE SCHRIFTEN ZUR VERFUGUNG ZU HABEN. SIE DI ENEN ALLE ZUM SELBEN. ABER MAC HEN DIE VIELFALT DES MENSCHEN AUS. DIESE VIELFALT IST WIE BEI M WEIN. ICH HABE EINMAL EINE W EINKARTE STUDIERT MIT SECHZI MEDOC·WEINEN AUS D SELBEN JAH

Stones Regular   Symbols Regular

Stones Positiv   Symbols Positiv

Stones Negativ   Symbols Negativ

58 pt | −95   42 pt | −70   30 pt | −60   21 pt | −55   14 pt | 19 pt | −35   9 pt | 13 pt | −25   7 pt | 10.2 pt | −18   6 pt | 8 pt | −15

Name of typeface	Client	Designer	Design | Publication	Typesetting technology	Manufacturer	Weights
Frutiger Neonscript	Westiform	Adrian Frutiger	1996 | 1996	Neon tubes	– Westiform	1
				TrueType digital typesetting	– URW	1

FRUTIGER NEONSCRIPT

Gebr. Klingspor, Offenbach am Main

Geschriebene Initialen zur Grotesk

ABCDE
FGHIJ
KLMN
OPQRS
TUVWX
YZ

74548 Zur 4 Cicero Satz, 4 A, etwa 6,8 Kilo fobaz

112/33

Made in Germany

/02/
Well-known connecting scripts in various styles: Künstlerschreib-schrift *(1902),* Kaufmann *(1936) and* Mistral *(1953).*

Künstlerschreibschrift

Kaufmann

Mistral

/01/
Scripted initials for Grotesk, *around 1930 by Rudolf Koch – with the linear strokes it is constructed to go with* Kabel.

/03/
Type designs with connecting glyphs from the early 1950s by Adrian Frutiger for Deberny & Peignot in the early 1950s (reduced).

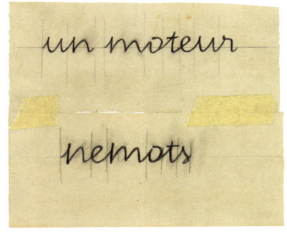

un moteur

nemots

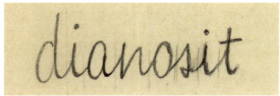

dianosit

Neon – A typeface for fluorescent lettering   Between 1952 and 1954 Adrian Frutiger had made several attempts to draw typefaces with connected glyphs, but *Frutiger Neonscript* (1996) is the only one in his career as a type designer that was implemented.

While working on new headline types – which would lead to the creation of *Initiales Phoebus* (see page 38) and *Ondine* (see page 50) – during his early days at Fonderies Deberny & Peignot, Adrian Frutiger produced three sketches, which he still retains **/03/**. They are written forms in which the widths and, therefore, the connection points between the letters are indicated by vertical strokes. This approach towards a connecting typeface was not pursued further.

Adrian Frutiger said of scripts, "For me, a typeface always consists of discrete letter elements. The scripts available at Deberny & Peignot, called calligraphiques, were very well done, but I knew what effort it entailed for a type founder to be able to produce them. Because of the accuracy needed in its production, a typeface like that would cost three times as much as a normal typeface. I was familiar with Roger Excoffon's *Mistral* **/02/**. This freedom of writing has always fascinated me, and I always thought I'd like to do a typeface like that. In the word 'moteur' **/03/** you can see the attempt at doing something more in the style of *Mistral*. That could have been taken further."[1] Connecting grotesques were also created in the field of printing typefaces, mostly for use in combination with sans serif typefaces **/01/**.

Certain things needed to happen before Frutiger started to develop a connecting typeface. In the 1980s he got to know Niklaus Imfeld,[2] the owner of Westineon,[3] a firm producing neon signs in which *Frutiger* and *Univers* had been employed for signage. A friendship soon developed, and in 1987, when the firm changed its name to Westiform, Frutiger developed the new logo (see page 360); and then in 1996 designed a connecting linear script to be used in the production of neon signs. As so often before, the technical challenges in producing this typeface were a prime motivation for Frutiger.

Frutiger Neonscript was also produced as a TrueType digital font **/04/** – to what end is not exactly clear.[4] It has never been freely available.

/04/
Character map of Frutiger
Neonscript *in TrueType digital
setting from URW.*

ABCDEFGHIJKLMN
OPQRSTUVWXYZ
abcdefghijklmnopq
rstuvwxyz1234567890

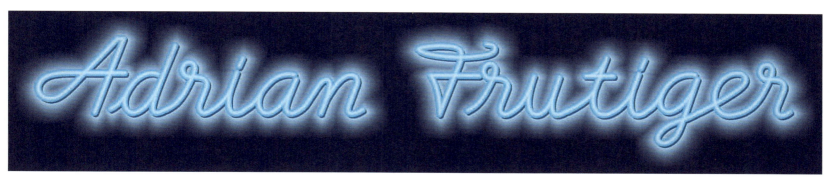

/05/
*Example of 3-dimensional
neon sign set in* Frutiger
Neonscript.

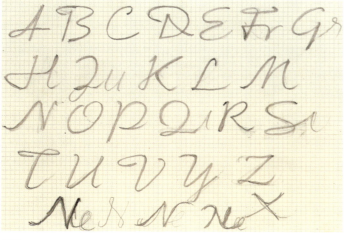

/06/
*Adrian Frutiger's sketches for
the capitals of* Frutiger Neonscript
*(left) and alternative shapes
(right).*

NAMI

/01/
*Undated pencil drawing by
Adrian Frutiger from the early 1950s –
several cuts were conceived for
the 'Delta' project.*

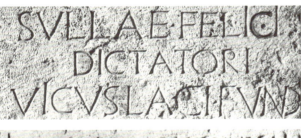

/02/
*Historical inscriptions: Roman
inscriptional capitals, 3rd century
BC (top); uncial stone inscription,
4th century AD (bottom).*

ITC Eras
FF Advert
Hoffmann

/03/
Typefaces related to Nami *in terms
of shape:* Eras *(1976) by Albert Boton,*
FF Advert *(1991) by Just van Rossum,*
Hoffman *(1993) by Lothar Hoffman
and Richard Lipton.*

LT Veto a
FF Dax
FF Signa

/04/
*Example of typefaces with flat curve
junctures in the lowercase a:*
Linotype Veto *(1994) by Marco Ganz,*
FF Dax *(1996) by Hans Reichel and*
FF Signa *(2000) by Ole Søndergaard.*

Half a century in the making At the beginning of his long career in type design at Deberny & Peignot in Paris, Adrian Frutiger designed *'Delta'* /01/, an uncial grotesque, as he himself christened this style of typeface. Frutiger derived the inspiration for it while studying under Alfred Willimann, whose teachings focused on historical aspects and from Willimann's work itself. More than 50 years later, the design was finally realised. Based on the initial design and the two pasted-up samples for *'Delta'* from 1952 /07/, *Nami* was issued in 2007. Therefore, it is actually the work of the 24-year-old Adrian Frutiger that Linotype realised for the then 79-year-old designer. Frutiger's pride in the late acknowledgement was correspondingly great.

The appearance of *'Delta'*, and therefore also for *Nami*, is indebted to the Roman inscriptional capitals from the 3rd century BC and the Roman uncials of the 4th–5th century AD /02/. The latter stands at the transition from majuscule to minuscule writing, uniting letter shapes from both in one alphabet. From today's viewpoint it would be called a single alphabet typeface.

Deberny & Peignot never put *Delta* into production, and the collaboration with Cassandre in 1954–55 did not come to fruition (see page 36). Adrian Frutiger did not take the proposal for a single alphabet typeface any further. On the other hand, during the development of several other grotesques, he often took up the waisted downstrokes that *'Delta'* featured. He also had no luck finding the necessary support to bring those faces – *'Gespannte Grotesk'* (1962), *'University'* and *'Primavera'*, from the early 1990s – into production (see page 157). Also, the first attempt to place *'Delta'* at Linotype without the uncial shapes produced only a few drawings and test exposures (1980) under the working title *'Dolmen'* (see page 296).

In 2006, the sample strings had the name *'Tectum'*. The original /05/ and final designs /06/ had been prepared in the preceding two years. According to Frutiger, Akira Kobayashi, art director at Linotype, and Adrian Frutiger worked hand in hand on the project.[1] The OpenType font appeared in 2007 in three weights: light, regular and bold. By then the name had changed to *Nami* (Japanese for 'wave'), recalling the devastating tsunami that, on 26 December 2004, caused the loss of 230 000 lives around the Indian Ocean, provoking widespread horror around the world.[2]

/05/
*Undated design drawings for Nami –
the curves of C and G, as well as
the downstrokes, and the tail of G
and Q, are not yet finalised.*

/06/
*Original designs for Nami:
a and b have a flat curve juncture;
the overall geometric shape is
not maintained in the c.*

/07/
*Paste ups of the two variants of the
'Delta' design from 1952 (top) –
reset with alternative glyphs in 2007's
Nami.*

Tiens, mon unique
enfant, mon fils,
prends ce breuvage.
sa chaleur te rendra

Tiens, mon unique
enfant, mon fils,
prends ce breuvage.
sa chaleur te rendra

Tiens, mon unique
enfant, mon fils,
prends ce breuvage.
sa chaleur te rendra

Tiens, mon unique
enfant, mon fils,
prends ce breuvage.
sa chaleur te rendra

Tiens, mon unique
enfant, mon fils,
prends ce breuvage.
Sa chaleur te rendra

TIENS, MON UNIQUE
ENFANT, MON FILS,
PRENDS CE BREUVAGE.
SA CHALEUR TE REND

/08/
Nami contains lining figures (left) and oldstyle figures (right) each of same widths (top) and proportions (bottom).

1234567890 1234567890
1234567890 1234567890

/09/
The alternative glyphs in Nami *are based on the Roman uncial and half-uncial from the 4th–5th century AD; two versions of the g exist.*

ʌᴇçǥhlmɴʀᴛu
Hofsᴛʌɪnbeʀç

/10/
Thanks to its large number of accented glyphs, Nami *is suited for typesetting in a wide range of languages.*

åċðę́ǵħĩĵķĺ'nő
ŕşťùŵÿž

There are at least two other typefaces that show a close relationship to Adrian Frutiger's *Nami*: *Skia*, developed in 1994 by Matthew Carter for Apple Computer, and Hans Eduard Meier's *Linotype Syntax Lapidar* from 2000. The shared starting point for all three typefaces is the linear stroke quality of the Roman inscriptional capitals **/02/**. *Linotype Syntax Lapidar* especially gets its archaic feel from the rudimentary, jagged shapes of a h m n r and from the slightly inclined composition, which does not always maintain a totally straight line **/11/**.

Syntax Lapidar and the alternative forms of *Nami* **/09/** lean toward the Roman uncials **/02/**, as shown by the A with no crossbar, the rounded, open E and the G with its downwards-pointing beard. In these letters the historic transition from majuscule to minuscule forms is particularly noticeable. In *Nami* this process has developed further, as can be seen in the lowercase h m n.

Similar to the majuscules, the minuscules of *Skia* and *Nami* have simple shapes. Additionally, their construction is broad, open and generous. A characteristic feature is the simplified shape of the a. Following on from a few earlier typefaces (see page 298), flat junctures were suddenly in fashion in the 1990s.[3] Other typefaces that appeared alongside Carter's *Skia* were, for example, Marco Ganz's *Linotype Veto*,[4] *FF Dax*[5] by Hans Reichel and *FF Signa* by Ole Søndergaard **/04/**.

/11/
The similarity of the three typefaces is obvious, especially when one recalls Nami's *alternative glyphs.*

Hofstainberg

Skia
Matthew Carter
1994

EMRaegn68

Hoϝsᴛʌɪnbeʀç

Linotype Syntax Lapidar
Hans Eduard Meier
2000

ᴇᴍʀʌєçɴ68

Hofstainberg

Nami
Adrian Frutiger, Akira Kobayashi
2007

EMRaegn68

E	M	R	a	e	g	n	6 8
Double-square proportion, middle crossbar more-sharply shortened	Diagonals are almost parallel, concave stroke endings	Waisted downstroke, blunt juncture of bowl curve to diagonal leg	Downward-sloping curve, flat juncture	Rounded transition	Flattened, almost horizontal, curves	Rounded transition from down stroke to curve	Closed counters, crossing lines

Font production:
Digitised by Linotype

Font format:
OpenType Com

Also available:
PostScript Type 1
True Type

Nami™
Linotype
3 weights

A B C D E F G H I J K L M N
O P Q R S T U V W X Y Z &
a b c d e f g h i j k l m n o p q r s
t u v w x y z ß 1 2 3 4 5 6 7 8 9 0

You may ask
why so many dif
ferent typefaces. They all se
rve the same purpose but they exp

ress man's diversity. It is the same diversity we find in win
e. I once saw a list of Médoc wines featuring sixty differe
nt Médocs all of the same year. All of them were wines b
ut each was different from the others. It's the nuances th
at are important. The same is true for typefaces. Pourquoi

tant d'Alphabets différents ! Tous servent au même but, mais aussi à exprimer la diver
sité de l'homme. C'est cette même diversité que nous retrouvons dans les vins de Mé
doc. J'ai pu, un jour, relever soixante crus, tous de la même année. Il s'agissait certes
de vins, mais tous étaient différents. Tout est dans la nuance du bouquet. Il en est de
même pour les caractères ! Sie fragen sich, warum es notwendig ist, so viele Schriften
zur Verfügung zu haben. Sie dienen alle zum selben, aber machen die Vielfalt des Me
nschen aus. Diese Vielfalt ist wie beim Wein. Ich habe einmal eine Weinkarte studiert

mit sechzig Médoc-Weinen aus dem selben Jahr. Das ist ausnahmslos Wein, aber doch nicht alles der gleiche Wein. Es hat eben gleichwohl Nuancen. So ist es auch mit der Schrift. You may ask why so many different typefaces. They all serve the same purpose but they express man's diversity. It is the sam e diversity we find in wine. I once saw a list of Médoc wines featuring sixty d ifferent Médocs all of the same year. All of them were wines but each was d ifferent from the others. It's the nuances that are important. The same is tru e for typefaces. Pourquoi tant d'Alphabets différents ! Tous servent au mêm

e but, mais aussi à exprimer la diversité de l'ho mme. C'est cette même diversité que nous retro uvons dans les vins de Médoc. J'ai pu, un jour, re lever soixante crus, tous de la même année. Il s' agissait certes de vins, mais tous étaient différen ts. Tout est dans la nuance du bouquet. Il en est de même pour les caractères ! Sie fragen sich, w arum es notwendig ist, so viele Schriften zur Ver fügung zu haben. Sie dienen alle zum selben, ab er machen die Vielfalt des Menschen aus. Diese

76 pt | –30   57 pt | –25   34 pt | –22   25 pt | –10   15 pt | 19 pt | 0   10 pt | 13 pt | 5   7.3 pt | 10 pt | 5   5.7 pt | 7.8 pt | 13

Å B Ç D È F G
H I J K L M Ñ
Ô P Q R Š T Ü
V W X Y Z &
Æ Œ ¥ $ £ €
1 2 3 4 5 6 7 8 9 0
å b ç d é f g h i j
k l m ñ ô p q r š
t ü v w x y z ß
fi fl æ œ ø ł ð
[. , : ; · ' / - – —]
(¿ ¡ " « ‹ › » " ! ?)
{ § ° % @ ‰ * † }

1 2 3 4 5 6 7 8 9 0
λ ∈ ς r τ
g h l m n u

Light

Å B Ç D È F G
H I J K L M Ñ
Ô P Q R Š T Ü
V W X Y Z &
Æ Œ ¥ $ £ €
1 2 3 4 5 6 7 8 9 0
å b ç d é f g h i j
k l m ñ ô p q r š
t ü v w x y z ß
fi fl æ œ ø ł ð
[. , : ; · ' / - – —]
(¿ ¡ " « ‹ › » " ! ?)
{ § ° % @ ‰ * † }

1 2 3 4 5 6 7 8 9 0
λ ∈ ς r τ
g h l m n u

Regular

Å B Ç D È F G
H I J K L M Ñ
Ô P Q R Š T Ü
V W X Y Z &
Æ Œ ¥ $ £ €
1 2 3 4 5 6 7 8 9 0
å b ç d é f g h i j
k l m ñ ô p q r š
t ü v w x y z ß
fi fl æ œ ø ł ð
[. , : ; · ' / - – —]
(¿ ¡ " « ‹ › » " ! ?)
{ § ° % @ ‰ * † }

1 2 3 4 5 6 7 8 9 0
λ ∈ ς r τ
g h l m n u

Bold

Logos and wordmarks
1991–2008

Association Française
de Communication
(name unconfirmed)
field of operation unknown
France

Reformiertes Pfarramt
Interlaken Ost
Parish
Interlaken (CH)

Sorec SA – Sté de Réalisation
Electronique du Centre
computer accessories
Paris (F)

Industrie de Béton
concrete industry association
France

Pro Bremgarten
cultural association
Bremgarten (CH)

FFT
field of operation unknown
location unknown

Fiduciaire – Michel Favre SA
fiduciary company
Echallens (CH)

Philip Raix
doctor
enamel plaque for entrance hall
Paris (F)

Congrès International
de Psychiatrie
international psychiatry
conference
location unknown

Psycho Thérapies
psychotherapy practice
location unknown

changer
biblical society magazine
Switzerland

La Poste / Die Post / La Posta
Swiss post and
telecommunications company
Bern (CH)

Paul Klee Zentrum
museum for artist Paul Klee
Bern (CH)
Design: Adrian Frutiger
and Kurt Wälti
Design not implemented

Haussmann
field of operation unknown
location unknown

Atelier 96
architecture and design
Lausanne / Vionnaz (CH)

"I am fascinated by the simplicity of abstract symbols, by the allure of letters,
which, by arranging them in a certain way, can make every thought in the world accessible."
Adrian Frutiger

Synopsis

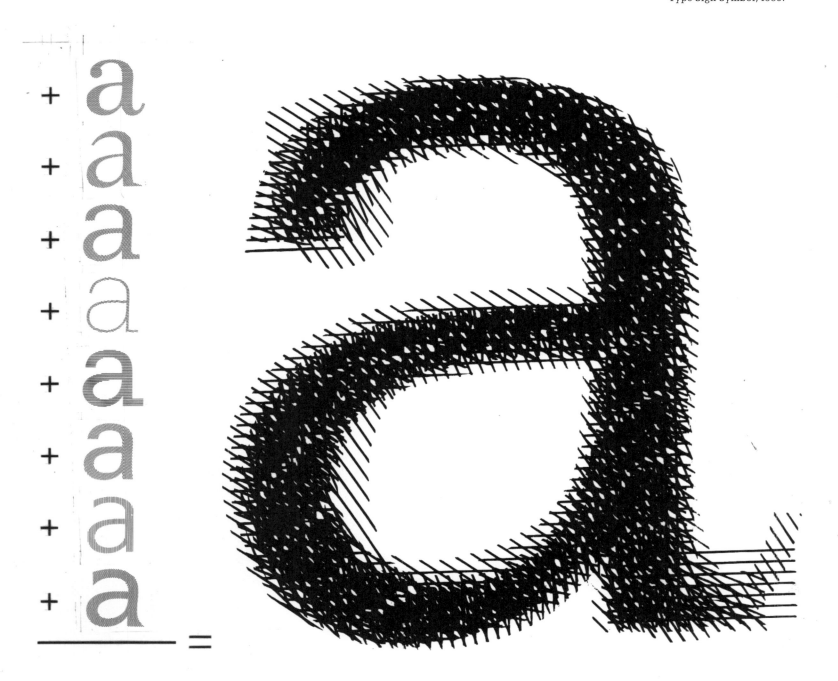

/01/
"The essence of a symbol is like a pure tone in music – the external appearance produces the sound" – *Adrian Frutiger in his book* Type Sign Symbol, *1980.*

/02/
Overlay of 17 text typefaces –
Frutiger's (top) have a more
consistent elementary form than
other well-known typefaces
(bottom).

Typeface classification

Adrian Frutiger's typefaces can be arranged into nine classification groups. The classification that has been undertaken here – using terms most familiar to the majority of readers – is specifically geared towards his typographical creations. The classification has no claim to completeness regarding roman typefaces, since Frutiger – in spite of having produced around 60 typefaces and typeface designs – has never produced typefaces in the Dutch oldstyle or transitional categories. Only *Opéra* (which is not available digitally) shows characteristics of a transitional face. The category of blackletter types also contains no contribution from Adrian Frutiger. True, *Ondine* and *Pompeijana* show leanings in this direction, but one is an uncial and the other a rustic. *Ondine*'s curves display no breaks; and the historical precedent for *Pompeijana* lies not in the Middle Ages, but in Roman Antiquity.

Compared to the familiar ATypI typeface classification, the one used here is expanded, especially in regard to the group of latins. These, as documented by Francis Thibaudeau in his 1924 typeface classification (see page 28), are important in understanding the typeface creations of Adrian Frutiger that display a French influence. Altogether five typefaces show the triangular serifs characteristic of latins. Also covered is the inscriptional group, whose markers include waisted vertical strokes, flared serifs, flared stroke endings or short serifs. In the mid-1950s the inscriptional group was included under the typeface classifications of Maximilian Vox, and also in that of Adrian Frutiger. However, in the German DIN 16518 typeface classification of 1964, this pronounced terminal is missing (see page 77). It is replaced by roman variants, and so serves as a dumping ground for typefaces that defy easy classification.

Adrian Frutiger adds a further level of classification: he draws a distinction between book types and corporate types, even when the latter can sometimes be used in longer passages of text. He does not believe that corporate typefaces should owe anything to the historical derivation of writing with a broad-nib pen, and this is evident, for example, in the abandonment of the triangle on the t. In addition, Frutiger draws a distinction between text typefaces and typefaces for signage. For him, good signage typefaces are as simple and clear as an arrow. For this reason he considers the two-storey lower case g to be too fussy.

In this book Frutiger's typefaces are further divided into body types and jobbing types. Although conceived for longer passages of text, the use of body types for signage and headlines is not ruled out.

	Text typefaces	Jobbing typefaces	Signage typefaces	Corporate typefaces
French oldstyle Garalde	Apollo Breughel			
Dutch oldstyle Transitional	Opéra			
Neoclassical Didone	Iridium Tiemann Linotype Centennial Linotype Didot			
Latin	Méridien Versailles Frutiger Serif	Président Phoebus		
Slab serif	Egyptienne F Serifa Glypha	Alphabet Algol Westside	Alphabet CGP	
Sans serif	LT Univers Concorde OCR-B Univers IBM Documenta Frutiger Avenir Vectora		Alphabet Orly Alphabet Roissy Alphabet Métro Astra Frutiger	Alphabet EDF-GDF Alpha BP Alphabet Facom Alphabet Brancher Alphabet Shiseido
Inscriptional Glyphic	Icone	Rusticana Frutiger Capitalis Nami		
Calligraphic Script		Ondine Herculanum Pompeijana	Frutiger Neonscript	
Decorative Graphic		Frutiger Stones		

АБВГДЕЖЗИЙКЛМНО
ПРСТУФХЦЧШЩЪЫЬЭЮЯ
агдежзийклмно
прстуфхцчшщъыьэюя

*АБВГДЕЖЗИЙКЛМНО
ПРСТУФХЦЧШЩЪЫЬЭЮЯ
агдежзийклмно
прстуфхцчшщъыьэюя*

АБВГДЕЖЗИЙКЛМНО
ПРСТУФХЦЧШЩЪЫЬЭЮЯ
агдежзийклмно
прстуфхцчшщъыьэюя

*АБВГДЕЖЗИЙКЛМНО
ПРСТУФХЦЧШЩЪЫЬЭЮЯ
агдежзийклмно
прстуфхцчшщъыьэюя*

**АБВГДЕЖЗИЙКЛМНО
ПРСТУФХЦЧШЩЪЫЬЭЮЯ
агдежзийклмно
прстуфхцчшщъыьэюя**

**АБВГДЕЖЗИЙКЛМНО
ПРСТУФХЦЧШЩЪЫЬЭЮЯ
агдежзийклмно
прстуфхцчшщъыьэюя**

**АБВГДЕЖЗИЙКЛМНО
ПРСТУФХЦЧШЩЪЫЬЭЮЯ
агдежзийклмно
прстуфхцчшщъыьэюя**

**АБВГДЕЖЗИЙКЛМНО
ПРСТУФХЦЧШЩЪЫЬЭЮЯ
агдежзийклмно
прстуфхцчшщъыьэюя**

АБВГДЕЖЗИЙКЛМНО
ПРСТУФХЦЧШЩЪЫЬЭЮЯ
агдежзийклмно
прстуфхцчшщъыьэюя

*АБВГДЕЖЗИЙКЛМНО
ПРСТУФХЦЧШЩЪЫЬЭЮЯ
агдежзийклмно
прстуфхцчшщъыьэюя*

АБВГДЕЖЗИЙКЛМНО
ПРСТУФХЦЧШЩЪЫЬЭЮЯ
агдежзийклмно
прстуфхцчшщъыьэюя

*АБВГДЕЖЗИЙКЛМНО
ПРСТУФХЦЧШЩЪЫЬЭЮЯ
агдежзийклмно
прстуфхцчшщъыьэюя*

АБВГДЕЖЗИЙКЛМНО
ПРСТУФХЦЧШЩЪЫЬЭЮЯ
агдежзийклмно
прстуфхцчшщъыьэюя

*АБВГДЕЖЗИЙКЛМНО
ПРСТУФХЦЧШЩЪЫЬЭЮЯ
агдежзийклмно
прстуфхцчшщъыьэюя*

**АБВГДЕЖЗИЙКЛМНО
ПРСТУФХЦЧШЩЪЫЬЭЮЯ
агдежзийклмно
прстуфхцчшщъыьэюя**

*АБВГДЕЖЗИЙКЛМНО
ПРСТУФХЦЧШЩЪЫЬЭЮЯ
агдежзийклмно
прстуфхцчшщъыьэюя*

**АБВГДЕЖЗИЙКЛМНО
ПРСТУФХЦЧШЩЪЫЬЭЮЯ
агдежзийклмно
прстуфхцчшщъыьэюя**

АБВГДЕЖЗИЙКЛМНО
ПРСТУФХЦЧШЩЪЫЬЭЮЯ
агдежзийклмно
прстуфхцчшщъыьэюя

АБВГДЕЖЗИЙКЛМНО
ПРСТУФХЦЧШЩЪЫЬЭЮЯ
агдежзийклмно
прстуфхцчшщъыьэюя

**АБВГДЕЖЗИЙКЛМНО
ПРСТУФХЦЧШЩЪЫЬЭЮЯ
агдежзийклмно
прстуфхцчшщъыьэюя**

**АБВГДЕЖЗИЙКЛМНО
ПРСТУФХЦЧШЩЪЫЬЭЮЯ
агдежзийклмно
прстуфхцчшщъыьэюя**

Univers Cyrillic
Frutiger Cyrillic

CEHORV abenosy
CEHORV abenosy

CEHORV abenosy
CEHORV abenosy
CEHORV abenosy
CEHORV abenosy

CEHORV abenosy
CEHORV abenosy
CEHORV abenosy

CEHORV abenosy
CEHORV abenosy
CEHORV abenosy

CEHORV abenosy
CEHORV abenosy
CEHORV abenosy
CEHORV abenosy
CEHORV abenosy

CEHORV abenosy

CEHORV
CEHORV

CEHORV abenosy

CEHORV
CEHORV
CEHORV abenosy

CEHORV abenosy
CEHORV
CEHORV

CEHORV ABENOSY

Principles of form

When designing his typefaces, Adrian Frutiger is always driven by the idea that his typefaces should be appropriate to the task – humanist typefaces, as he calls them. Body typefaces should be functional, as readable as possible, and at the same time beautiful, as much in reference and reading sizes as in headline sizes. For this reason Adrian Frutiger has often opted for waisted vertical strokes, to take away the hard edge of a typeface /03/.

An artistic expression or individual ductus is never Adrian Frutiger's primary goal. Nevertheless, it was apparent from the beginning that his typeface designs were imbued with a characteristic essence that is unmistakable.

Balance is a fundamental and defining principle that gives form to Frutiger's typefaces. The text image is defined as much by the well-balanced letter shapes /05/ as by the configuration of the white space, something upon which he places equal emphasis. His typefaces convey sobriety and neutrality, but at the same time presence and a pleasant coolness. They display elegance and modernity; they are possessed of an unpretentious style and a restrained elegance. In contrast, exuberance, emotiveness, showiness and pronounced heft have no place in his text typefaces.

With Adrian Frutiger, the guiding idea of creating humanist typefaces goes hand-in-hand with the awareness that typefaces must be designed with their setting technology in mind. This influences the shaping of his typefaces. On the one hand, typefaces like *Frutiger*, *Breughel* or *Linotype Centennial* demonstrate the necessary robustness that enables them to remain readable under difficult conditions. On the other, a typeface like *Iridium* shows a delicate charm, rarely seen in phototype faces.

Frutiger's typefaces always show their calligraphic roots. Alfred Williman's well-established calligraphic foundations can always be seen in the typefaces, as can the lettering and type design training Frutiger received under Walter Käch. And his text typefaces are always characterised by counters, something that his mentor, Emil Ruder, brought to *Univers* in the mid-1950s. This makes Frutiger's typefaces run slightly wide, something noticeable in comparison with the offerings of other designers /02/.

French oldstyle
Apollo, Breughel

Neoclassical
Iridium, Tiemann, LT Centennial, LT Didot

Latin
Président, Phoebus, Méridien, Versailles

Slab serif
Egyptienne F, Serifa, Glypha, Westside

Sans serif
LT Univers, OCR-B, Frutiger, Avenir, Vectora

Inscriptional
Icone, Rusticana, Frutiger Cap talis, Nami

Calligraphic
Ondine, Herculanum, Pompeijana

/03/
Certain of Adrian Frutiger's typefaces display waisted vertical strokes, which soften the appearance.

/04/
With or without serifs, asymmetrical or symmetrical, there is a wide variety apparent in the stroke endings.

/05/
Exemplar comparison: characteristic appearance for Frutiger's text typefaces (left) compared to other typefaces (right).

B B	Breughel	Berkeley
E E	Apollo	Baskerville
G G	Frutiger	Syntax

a a	Univers	Futura
e e	Méridien	Jenson
f f	Breughel	Bembo

/06/
Exemplar comparison: characteristic balance in Frutiger's text typefaces (left) compared to other typefaces (right).

A A	Univers	Imago
A		Eurostile

H H	Versailles	Benguiat
H		Bernhard Gothic

/07/
Exemplar comparison: characteristic similarity in curve endings in Adrian Frutiger's text typefaces (left) compared to other typefaces (right).

CGS acers	CGS acers
Méridien	Jenson
CGS acegs	CGS acegs
Avenir	Futura

/08/
Exemplar comparison: in Frutiger's text typefaces the cap width tends to be equal (left) compared to other typefaces (right).

DEHOS	DEHOS	Breughel	Mendoza
DEHOS	DEHOS	Méridien	Bembo
DEHOS	DEHOS	Frutiger	Gill Sans
DEHOS	DEHOS	Avenir	Avant Garde

Proportion

Adrian Frutiger's text typefaces – with a few exceptions – show a marked consistency in width at the same cap height **/09/**. In general, he draws generously proportioned typefaces, exhibiting a rather broad character, and the generally higher x-height gives an open appearance to the counters. This means that his typefaces are readable, even at small point sizes.

Frutiger does not harmonise the letter proportions of the caps of an alphabet directly. He never employs the extremes of a typeface, represented by the double-square capital E at the one end, and the circular capital O at the other. He either goes for a wider E, as in *Avenir* or for an oval O, as in *Frutiger*. Crucial for his harmonising principal is the idea of the properly developed typeface family, which he had already developed in 1954 with *Univers*. With four different widths – ultra-narrow, narrow, normal and wide – differing letter proportions would dilute the concept.

/09/
Frutiger's text typefaces – here overlaid with uniform cap height – often show similarities in their proportions.

/10/
In Frutiger's text typefaces equal cap and number heights are common – OCR-B, Serifa and Versailles.

Stroke weight

Adrian Frutiger developed his famous numbering system in 1954 for the new Lumitype photostetting machine while working at Deberny & Peignot in Paris. In one five-figure number it unites multiple specifications, amongst them a reliable method for ordering typefaces. This concept is also interesting from a typographical standpoint, since it contains at the same time a typeface classification system (see page 76).

From this five-figure number, Linotype reserved the last two numbers for Adrian Frutiger's typefaces (and for a few others). The numbering system was mostly used in conjunction with *Univers*. The first position of the number pair indicates the weight, and the second the width and type style of a typeface (see page 95). So the weight designation, for example 45 (light), is not seen as a mathematically fixed stroke weight. Rather, the number shows an approximate value for the quantity. With many typefaces the perceived weight often does not agree at all with the designating number. This is particularly evident with *Avenir* and *Icone*. With *Avenir* the reason lies with Adrian Frutiger's concept of developing intermediate weights in order to facilitate a flowing text progression. With *Icone*, in contrast, it is simply that a mistake crept in. However, these few faults in no way mitigate against the system in general **/13/**.

These days Linotype does not consistently use the numbering system for Adrian Frutiger's typefaces. The numerical designation for *Breughel*, for example, is nowhere to be seen, either in the *Typeface Catalogue*, or in the online version, although it was there previously. And *Icone* has its number listed in the Catalogue, but not when selecting the fonts in a layout programme. Linotype appears to prefer the designations to reside in the name of the typeface itself. One reason is that the Frutiger numbering system cannot cope with today's typographical demands. With the 63 weights of *Linotype Univers* the system has been expanded to a less manageable, but still-practical three digits. This solution could help to avoid the confusing tangle of weight designations.

	35	45	55	65	75	85	95
Apollo			H	H			
Breughel			H	H	H		
Iridium			H	H			
LT Centennial		H	H		H		H
Méridien			H	H	H		
Versailles		H	H		H		H
Egyptienne F			H	H	H		
Serifa		H	H	H	H		
Glypha	H	H	H	H	H		
LT Univers		H	H	H	H	H	
Frutiger		H	H	H	H		H
Avenir		H	H	H	H		H
Vectora		H	H		H		H
Icone		H	H	H		H	

/13/
Distribution of stroke weights using Adrian Frutiger's numbering system, developed in 1954.

/11/
In contrast to Frutiger with five weights, Avenir's six weights show a narrower spectrum of stroke contrast

/12/
In Linotype Centennial the serifs and crossbars remain the same, but in Glypha they grow with increasing stroke weight.

/14/
In Méridien the white space (counters) stay constant with increasing stroke weight; in Versailles they close up.

Formal considerations

Certain formal principles are evident in Adrian Frutiger's typefaces, which were present in his first typeface *Président,* and which delineate his entire typographical œuvre. These are formal characteristics that make most of Frutiger's typefaces easily recognisable.

The selection of typical letters listed on this double-page spread allows a comparative appraisal of Frutiger's available digital typefaces. With reference to these, his formal principles become apparent, but so, too, do the exceptions. By referring to Adrian Frutiger's statements in the separate typeface chapters, these exceptions become understandable. It is not often that he violates his own typeface principles or those of history (and which should not necessarily be considered a mistake), but even then, he has good reasons for doing so. These reasons may be technical in nature, as with *OCR-B.* Sometimes he is not totally free in the formulation of his typefaces, something that is clearly shown by the & (ampersand) in the Linotype typefaces **/38/.** At typeface publishing companies the people who run the business often exert considerable influence on the formal design.

Ultimately Frutiger adopted the stylistic characteristics of a classification group as the inspiration for his serif-accented romans. *Serifa, Glypha* and *Westside* are imbued with this characteristic **/17/.** Therefore they conform neither to the historical form of Capitalis Monumentalis nor to any principle of Frutiger's.

French oldstyle — Apollo, Breughel	J	J		
Neoclassical — Iridium, Tiemann, LT Centennial, LT Didot	J	J	J	J
Latin — Président, Phoebus, Méridien, Versailles	J	J	J	J
Slab serif — Egyptienne F, Serifa, Glypha, Westside	J	J	J	J
Sans serif — LT Univers, OCR-B, Frutiger, Avenir, Vectora	J J J J J
Inscriptional — Icone, Rusticana, Frutiger Capitalis, Nami	J J J J
Calligraphic — Ondine, Herculanum, Pompeijana	J J J

/15/
In Adrian Frutiger's typefaces the caps stand on the baseline – J is sometimes an exception, Q more often.

French oldstyle	Q	Q		
Neoclassical	Q	Q	Q	Q
Latin	Q	Q	Q	Q
Slab serif	Q	Q	Q	Q
Sans serif	Q Q Q Q Q
Inscriptional	Q Q Q Q
Calligraphic	Q Q Q

/16/
The tail of the Q never breaks into the counter – the only exception is the Q of OCR-B, which was necessary on technical grounds.

French oldstyle — Apollo, Breughel	a	a		
Neoclassical — Iridium, Tiemann, LT Centennial, LT Didot	a	a	a	a
Latin — Président, Phoebus, Méridien, Versailles	×	×	a	a
Slab serif — Egyptienne F, Serifa, Glypha, Westside	a	a	a	a
Sans serif — LT Univers, OCR-B, Frutiger, Avenir, Vectora	a a a a a
Inscriptional — Icone, Rusticana, Frutiger Capitalis, Nami	a	×	×	a
Calligraphic — Ondine, Herculanum, Pompeijana	a	×	×

/21/
In the characteristic Frutiger a, the central stroke meets the stem horizontally so that both counters appear optically balanced.

French oldstyle	g	g		
Neoclassical	g	g	g	g
Latin	×	×	g	g
Slab serif	g	g	g	g
Sans serif	g g g g g
Inscriptional	g	×	×	g
Calligraphic	s	×	×

/22/
Looking at the two-storey and simple g-shape, a clear separation between classical and modern typefaces is apparent.

French oldstyle — Apollo, Breughel	Cc	Cc		
Neoclassical — Iridium, Tiemann, LT Centennial, LT Didot	Cc	Cc	Cc	Cc
Latin — Président, Phoebus, Méridien, Versailles	×	×	Cc	Cc
Slab serif — Egyptienne F, Serifa, Glypha, Westside	Cc	Cc	Cc	Cc
Sans serif — LT Univers, OCR-B, Frutiger, Avenir, Vectora	Cc Cc Cc Cc Cc
Inscriptional — Icone, Rusticana, Frutiger Capitalis, Nami	Cc	×	×	Cc
Calligraphic — Ondine, Herculanum, Pompeijana	Cc	×	×

/27/
In classical typefaces different curve endings are common for the uppercase C and lowercase c – and also in Frutiger's typefaces.

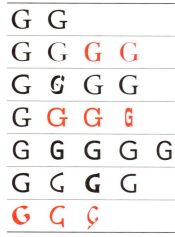

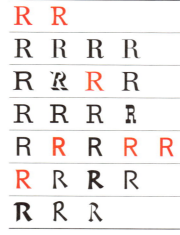

/17/
Just as in the Roman *Capitalis Monumentalis,* the uppercase G always has a vertical beard without a spur.

/18/
The arms of the upper case K always meet the stem together – rarely does Frutiger use offset diagonal strokes.

/19/
In the R the curve and the diagonal leg are usually formed in one continuous stroke – less often, the diagonal leg meets the horizontal stroke.

/20/
The W exhibits a simple shape – only in LT Didot do the diagonals meet below the apex – also, the vertex serif is rarely seen.

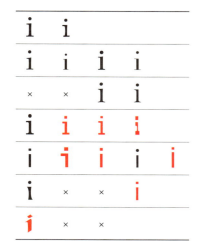

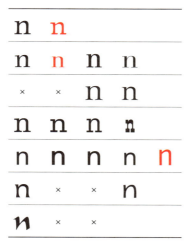

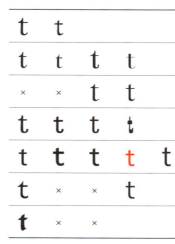

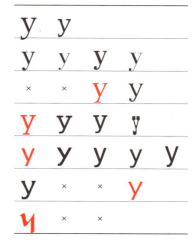

/23/
In classical typefaces Frutiger chooses the round dot on the i; elsewhere a rhomboid – in Ondine it has a calligraphic quality.

/24/
The juncture of the curve to the stem is almost always rounded – exceptions are Breughel, Tiemann *and* Vectora.

/25/
As in writing with a broad-nib pen, the termination of the t-stem is diagonal – with the exception of the geometrical Avenir.

/26/
The descender of the lower case y is usually curved, sometimes with a teardrop or half serif – Univers is an exception.

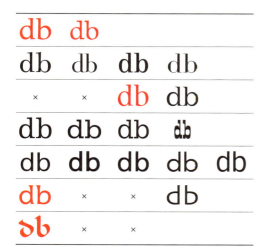

/28/
The reflected, static shape dominates – even in Egyptienne F *and* Frutiger – in dynamic typefaces d and b are far more different.

/29/
The shape of the g changes in only four typefaces – from two-storey in the roman to simple in the italic.

/30/
Frutiger's typefaces show two basic forms for the ampersand – the exceptions are those for Méridien *italic and* Rusticana.

Punctuation and special characters

A character set is many times larger than it may first appear. Alongside the 26 upper- and lowercase letters and the ten numerals, a font additionally comprises special characters for various European languages, including accented letters and ligatures. For example Æ æ and Œ œ /33/. Even the German esszett (ß) is a ligature, built from the union of long s (ſ) and round s (s) /39/. The standard character set of a digital font additionally contains the ligatures fi fl and the & (ampersand) /38/. The principle of currency symbols is similar, in formal regards, to the Icelandic Ð ð: the letters often receive an embellishment of one or two strokes. A typeface is filled out with approximately 30 punctuation marks, some 20 special characters such as @ § %, and a dozen or so additional mathematical symbols. A normally supplied font will have 160 constituent characters. Due to the process of internationalisation, and also to demands for quality typesetting, there is an increasing need for larger character sets. OpenType, the new digital type format, offers a basis for meeting this need. Fonts will therefore become more comprehensive, and the demand on the typeface designer ever greater.

French oldstyle Apollo, Breughel	
Neoclassical Iridium, Tiemann, LT Centennial, LT Didot	
Latin Président, Phoebus, Méridien, Versailles	
Slab serif Egyptienne F, Serifa, Glypha, Westside	
Sans serif LT Univers, OCR-B, Frutiger, Avenir, Vectora	
Inscriptional Icone, Rusticana, Frutiger Capitalis, Nami	
Calligraphic Ondine, Herculanum, Pompeijana	

/31/
Frutiger's typefaces for Linotype primarily have a continuous stroke going through the $ sign – although Frutiger prefers the character to be open.

/32/
Frutiger's characteristic £ sign is, more often than not, unadorned, with no loops or swooping strokes.

/36/
In Méridien the cedilla was originally unattached – this was changed at Linotype's insistence.

/37/
In the digital version of Ondine, Linotype kept the original form of the cedilla.

Numbers

For Adrian Frutiger, the forms of numerals have high artistic significance. It is extremely important to him that they be recognisable without ambiguity. This has been true at least since 1970 when he designed his signage typeface Alphabet for Paris-Roissy airport. His studies on the recognisability of number forms were very illuminating (see page 227). For instance, the number 1 was never drawn as a simple vertical stroke; it always had to have a prominent flag /40/. And with the 6 the recognition test made clear that the shape with an open curve rather than a diagonal stroke was the least ambiguous.

In his body types both static and dynamic number forms can be found /40/. A written form – asymmetrical and not always respecting the baseline – is almost never present. In the 6 the relationship between the static, closed shape (left) and the dynamic, open one (middle, right) is always counterbalanced. In the 8 the continuous-loop form (left) is more common than the form built from two ovals (right). In contrast, in the 3 it is the static form that dominates (left). One reason for this is that Adrian Frutiger has primarily designed static book faces.

Only rarely do Adrian Frutiger's typefaces contain oldstyle figures – and if they do, their form is closer to that of tabular figures.

/40/
The breakdown and overlaying of the various number shapes shows their uniformity in Frutiger's text typefaces.

/41/
In 2002, for the 'My Ego' watch from the Swiss watchmaker Ventura, Adrian Frutiger designed numerals that were specially harmonised to the round shape of the dial.

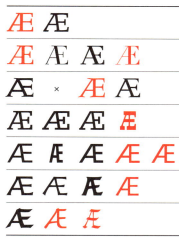

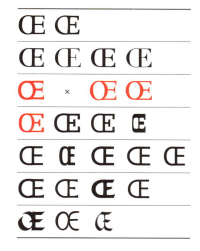

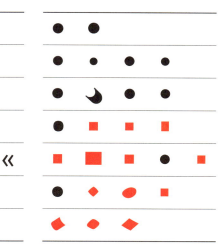

/33/

A wide variety of form in Æ and Œ – the combination can be balanced, but also dominated by either the left or the right side.

/34/

In classical French typefaces round guillemets are not unknown – Frutiger adopted these for Versailles.

/35/

The full stop (period) is round in the classical typefaces, mostly rhomboid in the modern ones and more free-form in the uncials.

/38/

In Linotype's typefaces the characteristic Frutiger & (ampersand) is rare – it is, however, present in Linotype Univers and Frutiger Next.

/39/

Also in the ß there was a change over time at Deberny & Peignot from the dynamic to the static form.

Italics

In German-language specialist publications a distinction is seldom found between a true cursive (italic) and an inclined form (oblique). The word 'cursive' (Lat. 'currere', to run or hasten) is used for both kinds of typefaces. In addition there is often a false interpretation of the term 'oblique'. Oblique does not mean an optically uncorrected version of a roman font sloped by electronic means. It is not a judgemental label representing a lack of quality. An oblique can be drawn inclined or it can be generated by electronic means. In the latter process a subsequent manual reworking of the design is unavoidable to correct the defects that result from the procedure.

The characteristic feature of the italic is its more free-flowing text image when compared to the upright face or roman. In January 1501 in Venice, Aldus Manutius published a small-format edition of the works of Virgil that had been set with an italic cut by Francesco Griffo. It was derived from the corsiva cancelleresca – or italic – used in the Papal chancery and by the Humanist scholars since the middle of the 15th century.

In the Renaissance italic the letters are not always joined, though they may touch. The letters differ from their roman counterparts in structure and proportion. They are narrower and the lower case a e f g k p v w x y z are distinctive.

Almost all of Adrian Frutiger's typefaces possess an italic or an oblique **/42/**.

French oldstyle			
Apollo, Breughel			

Neoclassical			
Iridium, Tiemann, LT Centennial, LT Didot			

Latin			
Président, Phoebus, Méridien, Versailles			

Slab serif			
Egyptienne F, Serifa, Glypha, Westside			

Sans serif			
LT Univers, OCR-B, Frutiger, Avenir, Vectora			

Inscriptional			
Icone, Rusticana, Frutiger Capitalis, Nami			

Calligraphic			
Ondine, Herculanum, Pompeijana			

				angles
aef	*aef*			15° / 14,5°
aef	×	*aef*	*aef*	19° / 16° / 19,5°
×	×	*aef*	*aef*	13,5° / 9,5°
aef	*aef*	*aef*	×	13,5° / 12° / 10°
aef	×	*aef*	*aef* *aef*	16° / 12° / 8° / 11°
aef	×	×	×	12°
×	×	×		

/42/

For classical typefaces Frutiger always draws an italic for the roman. For other typefaces he prefers an oblique.

/43/

Adrian Frutiger's italic cuts do not always show the same slope in the lower as in the upper case.

/44/
*The variety of asterisk shapes in
Adrian Frutiger's typefaces
is testament to his great joy in
designing.*

Career path →12

1 The information in this chapter is derived, in large part, from Adrian Frutiger's typed manuscript 'Aufzeichnungen aus dem Beruf', as well as from his book *Ein Leben für die Schrift*. Furthermore, information from the interviews with Erich Alb, Rudolf Barmettler and Philipp Stamm has been incorporated. The references to Walter Käch's teachers are based on the authors' own research.
2 Erich Alb (ed.), *Adrian Frutiger – Formen und Gegenformen / Formes et contreformes / Forms and counterforms.* Text by Roland Schenkel, Cham 1998, page 79.
3 Adrian Frutiger, *Ein Leben für die Schrift,* Interlaken 2003.
4 ALE, *Schrift – Signet – Symbol. Formgebung in Schwarz und Weiss. Ausstellung von Adrian Frutiger im Berner Gutenbergmuseum,* in an unknown publication, 1973 (probably a printing union journal).
5 Twenty-five years later the 6th edition of the 'Setzerbibel' was published. The total print run of all the editions was 27000 copies. – See Leo Davidshofer, Walter Zerbe, *Satztechnik und Gestaltung,* 6th ed., Zurich / Bern 1970.
At the end of the era of lead type, the printing house of the Bildungsverband Schweizerischer Typografen (The Swiss Typographers' Educational Union) published the two-volume *Setzerbibel*. – See Hans-Rudolf Bosshard, *Technische Grundlagen zur Satzherstellung,* vol. 1, Bern 1980. – Hans Rudolf Bosshard, *Mathematische Grundlagen zur Satzherstellung,* vol. 2, Bern 1985.
6 Based on the speech given by ensign Karl Hediger in Gottfried Keller's novella *Das Fähnlein der sieben Aufrechten.*
7 Ernst Jordi, 'Zum Geleit' (introduction), in Adrian Frutiger, *Die Kirchen am Thunersee,* Interlaken 1948, page 5.
8 *Claudius* is based on written examples by Rudolf Koch. While he was still alive, his son Paul produced one weight of the blackletter typeface in 1931–1934. The other weights were cut by Schriftgiesserei Gebr. Klingspor (Offenbach am Main) and published in 1937. – See Hans Adolf Halbey, *Karl Klingspor – Leben und Werk,* Offenbach am Main 1991, page 143.
9 The details of the typesetting and printing are listed at the back of Adrian Frutiger's book. – See Adrian Frutiger, *Die Kirchen am Thunersee,* Interlaken 1948, page 143.
10 Adrian Frutiger noted these details in *Ein Leben für die Schrift,* page 21. Max B. Kämpf is a graphic artist and not the painter Max Kämpf.
11 The special photography course at the Kunstgewerbeschule in Zurich was started in 1932. Hans Finsler was its head until 1958. Amongst those who later became famous, the Magnum photographers Werner Bischof, René Burri and Ernst Scheidegger all studied under Hans Finsler and Alfred Willimann.
12 Adrian Frutiger, 'Aufzeichnungen aus dem Beruf', typed manuscript, page 17.
13 Edward Johnston, *Writing and Illuminating and Lettering,* London 1906.
14 Edward Johnston, *Schreibschrift, Zierschrift & angewandte Schrift,* translated from the English by Anna Simons, Leipzig 1910.
15 Rudolf von Larisch, *Unterricht in ornamentaler Schrift,* Vienna 1905.
16 Fritz Helmut Ehmcke, *Ziele des Schriftunterrichts,* Jena 1911.
17 From 1925 to 1929 Walter Käch had already taught in the Applied Arts department of the Kunstgewerbeschule in Zurich. – See Friedrich Friedl, Nicolaus Ott, Bernard Stein, *Typography – when who how,* Cologne 1998, page 314.
18 Walter Käch, *Schriften Lettering Écritures – Geschriebene und gezeichnete Grundformen / The principle Types of running hand and drawn caracters / Principales familles d'écritures courantes et de letters dessinées,* Olten 1949. – Walter Käch, *Rhythmus und Proportion in der Schrift / Rhythm and Proportion in Lettering,* Olten 1956. – Walter Käch, *Bildzeichen der Katakomben,* Olten 1965.
19 Adrian Frutiger, 'Aufzeichnungen aus dem Beruf', typed manuscript, page 29.
20 Adrian Frutiger, 'Adrian Frutiger, der Typograf aus Leidenschaft', *NZZ Swiss made,* Zurich 2001.
21 Adrian Frutiger in conversation with Erich Alb, Rudolf Barmettler and Philipp Stamm, 25 March 2002.
22 Adrian Frutiger, *Schrift Ecriture Lettering – Die Entwicklung der europäischen Schriften, in Holz geschnitten / Bois originaux illustrant l'évolution de l'écriture en Europe / The development of European letter types carved in wood,* Zurich 1951.
23 Adrian Frutiger, *Der Mensch und seine Zeichen,* ed. Horst Heiderhoff, vol. 1, *Zeichen erkennen Zeichen gestalten,* Frankfurt am Main 1978; vol. 2, *Die Zeichen der Sprachfixierung,* Frankfurt am Main 1979; vol. 3, *Zeichen, Symbole, Signete, Signale,* Frankfurt am Main 1981.
24 Adrian Frutiger, *Der Mensch und seine Zeichen,* ed. Horst Heiderhoff, vol. 1, *Zeichen erkennen Zeichen gestalten,* Frankfurt am Main 1978.
25 Adrian Frutiger, *Type Sign Symbol,* Zurich 1980.
26 Adrian Frutiger's personal notes (typed manuscript).
27 Emil Ruder, *Typographie – Ein Gestaltungslehrbuch / Typography – A Manual of Design / Typographie – Un Manuel de Création,* Sulgen 1967.
28 European Computer Manufacturers' Association, Geneva.
29 Adrian Frutiger in conversation with Erich Alb, Rudolf Barmettler and Philipp Stamm, 26 January 2001.

Président →26

1 Adrian Frutiger, *Schrift Écriture Lettering – The development of European letter types carved in wood,* Zurich 1951.
2 In France, Initiales refers to all capital fonts, even those with small caps.
3 The term latins derives from Latium, and hence from inscriptions of Roman Antiquity.
4 Type specimen book of the Flinsch type foundry, Frankfurt am Main, not dated (c. late 1910s)
5 To choose the name of the Dutch printing dynasty Elzévier for the classification group we know today as oldstyle is bizarre, given the French tradition of Claude Garamont. It is also contradictory, since the Elzéviers were only active as printers in the late 16th century.
6 The term 'Antique', used in France for grotesque, refers to the origin of sans serif typefaces: Greek antiquity. In 19th-century England there were typefaces described as 'Antique'. The term is not used consistently though, both slab serif fonts and latins are described thus. – See Nicolete Gray, *Nineteenth Century Ornamented Typefaces,* London 1976.
7 The illustration shows the principle types of serif, placed one on top of another and in chronological order: The pointed shape of the latins in white, behind them in black like a shadow or a historical backdrop, the stronger serif shape of oldstyle with round brackets. Between them, screened back with the word ELZÉVIRS reversed-out, the square shape. – See Fonderies Deberny & Peignot, *Spécimen Général,* vol. II, Paris 1926.
8 František Muzika titles a chapter with this term and refers to the fact that in England as early as the 1840s, i.e. before William Morris and his Kelmscott Press, Caslon's Roman was increasingly employed in book typography. On the other hand Muzika barely mentions latin typefaces: only a *Renaissance-Antiqua* by the Genzsch & Heyse type foundry from 1882 is alluded to, yet not shown. – See František Muzika, *Die schöne Schrift,* vol. 2, Prague 1971, page 382 ff. – Paul Shaw remarks that the use of Caslon in the 1840s was limited primarily to the work of William Pickering.
9 See Nicolete Gray, *Nineteenth Century Ornamented Typefaces,* London 1976, page 78.
10 See Nicolete Gray, *Nineteenth Century Ornamented Typefaces,* London 1976, page 81.
11 See Albrecht Seemann, *Handbuch der Schriftarten. Eine Zusammenstellung der Schriften der Schriftgiessereien deutscher Zunge,* Leipzig 1926.
12 *Tiffany* by Deberny & Peignot is not the same as its namesake *ITC Tiffany* by Ed Benguiat from 1974.
13 *Copperplate Gothic* and *Monotype Spartan* (not to be confused with the sans serif *Spartan*) are the same typeface by different manufacturers. It is also known as *Mimosa*. – See Stempel Haas, *Universal-Schriftprobe,* Frankfurt am Main / Münchenstein 1974.
14 *Engravers Roman* is also known as *Hermes*. – See Stempel Haas, *Universal-Schriftprobe,* Frankfurt am Main / Münchenstein 1974.
15 See 'Textverarbeitung, Maschinenschreiben und E-Mails', in: *Duden 1 – Die Rechtschreibung,* Mannheim / Leipzig / Vienna / Zurich 2006, page 107.
16 See Jan Tschichold, *Formenwandlungen der et-Zeichen,* Frankfurt am Main 1953. – See also Andreas Stötzner, *Signa. Beiträge zur Signographie,* No. 2, Grimma 2001.
17 Conversation with Adrian Frutiger by Erich Alb, Rudolf Barmettler and Philipp Stamm, 1 January, 2001.

Delta (type-design project) →36

1 The foundation for the single case typeface is 4th and 5th century uncials, which represent the transition from capitals to lowercase script. *Delta* combines shapes from both cases.

Phoebus →38

1 Decorative faces are defined as typefaces whose appearance and character differ from that of text faces. Today they are normally considered ornamental or display fonts. In the typeface classification DIN 16518, all swash faces are placed in group VII, Antiqua varieties. Bosshard includes a 'swash face typology'. There he divides them into the following main groups: outline, inline, engraved, tinted, stencilled, cameo, bevelled, 3-dimensional, ornamental and perspective faces. *Phoebus* is shown as an example of the 'shadow face' subgroup of the 'plastic' main group. – See Hans Rudolf Bosshard, *Technische Grundlagen zur Satzherstellung,* Bern 1980, pages 94–103.
R. S. Hutchings uses the following categories: Inlines and Outlines, Three-Dimensional (which includes shaded, shadow, and open designs), Embellished (which refers to ornamented designs), Engraved, Halftone and Shaded (in this instance shaded means some form of tinting achieved through parallel lines, crosshatching or stippling), Cameo (white letters on a dark background), and Stencil. *Phoebus* belongs in the Three-Dimensional category. – See R. S. Hutchings, *A Manual of Decorated Typefaces,* London 1965.
2 In conversation, Adrian Frutiger often referred to the comprehensive and well-documented *Encyclopaedia of Type Faces* by W. Turner Berry, A. F. Johnson and W. P. Jaspert. The first edition (without Jaspert) was published 1953 in London.
3 *Caractère. Revue mensuelle des industries graphiques,* Paris.
4 Many publications, including some of Adrian Frutiger's own, list *Ondine* as the second typeface after *Président*.
5 These are the extremely light weight, available today in digital form, formerly known as *Gill Sans Shadow No. 1* (Monotype Series No. 406), the slightly stronger weight with deep shadows, *Gill Sans Shadow No. 2* (No. 408), and *Gill Sans Shadow No. 3* (No. 338). Weights nos. 406 and 408 were made in 1936, no. 338 is from 1932 without the participation of Eric Gill, according to *Monotype Recorder* New Series 8, 1990. – See Max Caflisch: *Schriftanalysen,* vol. 2, St. Gallen 2003, page 37.
6 *Umbra* from 1935 by Robert Hunter Middleton for the Ludlow Typograph Company, Chicago, is based on his own geometric sans serif *Tempo*. Only a few letters are different from *Gill Sans Shadow No. 1* by Monotype from 1936. Even the oldest of these very similar shadow typefaces, *Plastica* from 1928/29 by the H. Berthold AG type foundry, based on *Berthold Grotesque,* and also *Semplicità Ombra* by Società Nebiolo, Turin, demonstrate the same relation between stroke width and shadow depth. – See W. P. Jaspert, W. Turner Berry, A. F. Johnson: *The Encyclopaedia of Type Faces,* London 1970.
7 Rudolf Wolf also made a shadow version, *Memphis Luna,* of his slab serif *Memphis* for D. Stempel AG in 1937. – See Georg Kurt Schauer, *A Chronicle of D. Stempel AG type foundry – sixty years in the service of letters.* – W. Turner Berry, A. F. Johnson, W. P. Jaspert, *The Encyclopaedia of Type Faces,* London 1962 it is called *Luna*. – The 'Schriftprobe der Unionsdruckerei Bern' incorrectly calls it *Lumina*. But this is the name of an outline typeface designed by Jakob Erbar.
8 The posters made for the Phoebus-Palast in 1927 can be seen in Martijn F. Le Coultre, Alston W. Purvis, *Jan Tschichold. Posters of the Avantgarde,* Basel 2007.
9 In addition, there was also the *'Konturlose Schattenschrift'* design by the Bauhaus typographer Herbert Bayer from 1930. The design was not produced as foundry type, although it is available today as a digital font, *Bayer Shadow*. – See Magdalena Droste (ed.): *Herbert Bayer. Das künstlerische Werk 1918–1938,* Berlin 1982, page 134 f. – See also www.p22.com (May 2008).
10 There was no complete character set available for Dalton Maag of London in 2003 when making the Beta version of *Phoebus*. This, together with conceptual reasons, is why in 2006 Heidrun Osterer and Philipp Stamm commissioned Rainer Gerstenberg, Schriftenservice D. Stempel GmbH in Frankfurt am Main, to recast *Initiales Phoebus* in 36 pt size. Walter Fruttiger AG of Münchenstein near Basel supplied the original matrices by Deberny & Peignot. In Spring 2007 Romano Hänni in Basel produced the foundry type and printed the character set on baryta paper, thus enabling reworking and extension of the font in the best possible quality.

Element-Grotesk (type-design project) →46

1 The name 'Element Grotesk' was given by the publishers, with Adrian Frutiger's consent. In a manuscript, Frutiger called this design 'A composable typeface'.
2 Typefaces by Marcel Jacno which were released by Deberny & Peignot include *Initiales Film* 1934 (see page 40), *Scribe* 1936 and *Jacno* 1948.
3 Marcel Jacno created *Chaillot* 1950 as the house face for the Théâtre National Populaire in Paris. In 1954 it was adapted for the Typophane process by Deberny & Peignot.

Federduktus (type-design project) →48

1 A minimum is the smallest amount of foundry type you can order with different amounts of letters per character. These are calculated according to the average frequency of characters used in a text. The composition of a minimum varies for each language.

Ondine →50

1 Deberny & Peignot had *Scribe* in their library, a spontaneous looking script by Marcel Jacno from 1937. It fared poorly compared to Roger Excoffon's lively brush script *Mistral* from 1953. *Scribe* remained the only typeface of its kind at Deberny & Peignot until 1954, when *Améthyste* and *Bolide* by Georges Vial were released.

2 Erich Alb's trilingual book *Adrian Frutiger – Forms and counterforms* published 1998 by Syndor Press in Cham comprehensively documents Frutiger's uncommissioned artistic work.

3 See *Brockhaus Enzyklopädie in vierundzwanzig Bänden,* 19th completely revised edition, vol. 22, Mannheim 1993, page 620.

4 The foundry font range of several type foundries is still available today, among them that of Deberny & Peignot, Haas'sche type foundry, D. Stempel AG, Fonderie Olive and Nebiolo. The fonts may be purchased from Walter Fruttiger AG, Münchenstein, Switzerland, or from Schriften-Service D. Stempel GmbH, Rainer Gerstenberg, Darmstadt, Germany.

5 Uncials, or Uncialis, a Roman book script written with a broad quill, developed from 2nd century Roman mixed book scripts into its final form in the 4th century. Although still technically considered to be capitals, many uncial letters hint at lowercase shapes, especially because of the presence of ascenders and descenders. – See FRANTIŠEK MUZIKA, *Die schöne Schrift,* vol. 1, Prague 1965, pages 173 ff.

6 In the 20th century, traditional writing tools like the broad quill and the pointed quill increasingly gave way to the Redis pen (similar to a Speedball B-series pen), brush, pencil, felt-tip and ballpoint pens. Typefaces which suggest the spontaneity of brush strokes were frequently made into fonts in the 1950s.

7 Typophane dry transfer sheets (see page 223) were first advertised by Deberny & Peignot in *Caractère,* no. 3, March 1954.

8 Roger Excoffon married Albert Olive's daughter. Albert ran Fonderie Olive in Marseille from 1914 to 1938, after which his son Marcel took over. Excoffon was the foundry's artistic advisor from 1945 to 1959. In 1978 Fonderie Olive was bought by the Haas'sche type foundry. – See PHILIPP BERTHEAU, *Buchdruckschriften im 20. Jahrhundert. Atlas zur Geschichte der Schrift,* Darmstadt 1995, pages 555 ff.

9 *Calligraphiques Noires* by Deberny & Peignot is a pointed quill script face in the style of English writing and engraving scripts from the 18th and 19th centuries.

10 The typeface classification DIN 16518 of the German Industry Norm long ago ceased to fulfil the requirements of contemporary type classification – too much has changed in the world of type design since its introduction in 1964. Nevertheless it's still helpful for understanding Adrian Frutiger's work, as it was relevant during the period of this design.

11 Hans Rudolf Bosshard's 'Neuer Vorschlag für eine Klassifikation der lateinischen Druckschriften' (New suggestions for the classification of latin typefaces) proposes merging groups VIII and IX to form 'latin script typefaces' – with four subdivisions: pointed quill, broad quill, Redis pen and brush faces. – See HANS RUDOLF BOSSHARD, *Technische Grundlagen zur Satzherstellung,* Bern 1980, pages 72 f.

Méridien →60

1 In conversation Adrian Frutiger says January to May 1953, which is unlikely seeing as he only arrived in Paris in the late summer of 1952, and three typefaces were made before *Méridien: Initiales Président* (3–4 months), *Initiales Phoebus* (2 months) and *Ondine* (6 weeks). He was also involved in the final artwork for *Initiales Cristal* by Rémy Peignot. The idea was for Frutiger to get acquainted with the company and the whole production process by being present at each stage. – Conversation with Adrian Frutiger by Erich Alb, Rudolf Barmettler, Philipp Stamm, 26 February 2001.

2 In 1912/13 Georges Peignot drew the upright and the italic weights of the *Caractères Garamont* (the spelling with a t is witnessed by the title of a book published by Claude Garamont in 1545). His son Charles finished the typeface in the 1920s; it was published in 1930. Literature lists differing facts as to the original used for Peignot's *Garamont.* Philipp Bertheau, on the one hand, writes that Garamont's printed books served as originals. Max Caflisch, on the other hand, notes that this face, like many other versions from the 20th century, actually goes back to Jean Jannon's *Caractères de l'Université* from 1621, original types of which are kept at the Imprimerie Nationale in Paris. – See PHILIPP BERTHEAU: *Buchdruckschriften im 20. Jahrhundert. Atlas zur Geschichte der Schrift,* Darmstadt 1995, page 418. – MAX CAFLISCH: *Schriftanalysen,* volume 1, St. Gallen 2003, pages 117 ff.

3 In April 1949 René Higonnet and Louis Moyroud, together with Bill Garth, demonstrated the Photon prototype at the annual general meeting of the American Newspaper Publishers Association ANPA. The presentation to a selected audience at the Waldorf Astoria Hotel in New York was aimed at finding financial sponsors to develop the Photon until it was ready for production. – See ALAN MARSHALL, *Du plomb à la lumière,* Paris 2003.

4 *Brockhaus Enzyklopädie,* 19th edition, volume 14, Mannheim 1991, page 481.

5 In 1972 Haas'sche Schriftgiesserei acquired Deberny & Peignot along with the rights to their typefaces. Haas'sche Schriftgiesserei was partly owned by D. Stempel AG, who took on and expanded *Méridien* for photosetting. In 1989 Linotype in turn acquired Haas and the rights to their typefaces. The type foundry workshop was eventually liquidated and sold to Walter Fruttiger who has operated it since as Fruttiger AG. – See PHILIPP BERTHEAU, *Buchdruckschriften im 20. Jahrhundert. Atlas zur Geschichte der Schrift,* Darmstadt 1995, pages 555 ff.

6 The French writer Pierre Augustin Caron de Beaumarchais (1732–1799) was also active as royal watchmaker, harp instructor, poet, publicist, secret agent, merchant, business venturer and publisher (co-publisher of the first edition of the complete works of Voltaire). – See *Brockhaus Enzyklopädie,* 19th ed., volume 14, Mannheim 1991, page 689.

7 *La Folle Journée ou Le Mariage de Figaro* was rapturously received on its premiere, while the book had 15 new editions in its first year. Its content is symptomatic of the mood in prerevolutionary France. – See JOHN CARTER, PERCY H. MUIR (Ed.), *Printing and the Mind of Man, a Descriptive Catalogue Illustrating the Impact of Print on the Evolution of Western Civilization During Five Centuries,* London 1967.

8 In 1946 the engineers René A. Higonnet and Louis M. Moyroud first presented their idea for an electronic photosetting machine to an interested specialist audience at the École Estienne in Paris. Eight years later the Photon photosetting machine was shown for the first time in Europe by Deberny & Peignot at the Salon TPG in Paris. This is not the French version of the Lumitype. That machine was only shown for the first time in 1956 (with Frutiger's first typeface for Lumitype, *Méridien*). – See ALAN MARSHALL, *Du plomb à la lumière,* Paris 2003.

9 See WALTER KÄCH, *Rhythm and Proportion in Lettering / Rhythmus und Proportion in der Schrift,* Olten 1956, page 22 ff.

10 ibid.

11 ADRIAN FRUTIGER, 'The Latines, a style of Latin typeface' in *Swiss Typographic Magazine* 10/1977, St. Gallen 1977, page 6.

12 In foundry type every font size has its particular width. (Letterspacing, i.e. increasing the tracking, may be easy, but inserting spaces is laborious. Decreasing the tracking, on the other hand, is only possible by shaving off the side of the lead body.)
In photosetting and in today's digital setting tracking is variable, and it has to be adjusted when scaling the font. Unfortunately type manufacturers stopped taking responsibility for tracking and instead delegated it to the user. In photosetting this was still left to specialists (which was by no means a guarantee of good typesetting, as typography from the 1970s and '80s attests), but now, with digital setting on personal computers, it is delegated to laymen, too.
It would be desirable if type manufacturers today made it known for which type size for a given typeface the standard tracking of 0 applies. Unfortunately this remains unlikely as most typefaces do not even have the same tracking for the same size in all weights.
It could be that Adobe has the solution with 'optical kerning'. For quick usage in office applications, automatic tracking will surely achieve better typesetting. For high quality typesetting, however, 'optical kerning' remains insufficient.

13 The *Swiss Typographic Magazine* 3/1958, page 147, on the one hand reports on the first book set on the Lumitype, *Le Mariage de Figaro,* set in *Méridien,* while separately introducing *Méridien.*

14 Karl Schmid (1914–1998), teacher (department director 1964–72) for technical illustration at the Kunstgewerbeschule Zurich and wood engraver for Jean Arp.

15 ADRIAN FRUTIGER, '"Les Latines" a style of Latin typefaces' in *Swiss Typographic Magazine* 10/1977, St. Gallen 1977, pages 6 f.

16 ibid. page 4

Caractères Lumitype →74

1 In order to find more sponsors in addition to Bill Garth, a very rudimentary prototype was presented to some of the invited guests at the American Newspaper Publishers Association (ANPA) annual conference in 1949 at New York's Waldorf-Astoria Hotel. The sponsors gained via this presentation were made members, with signed contracts, of the specially created Graphic Arts Research Foundation (GARF). – See ALAN MARSHALL, *Du plomb à la lumière,* Paris 2003, pages 104 f.

2 The Photon-Lumitype project was eagerly followed up and commented upon in the trade press right from the start. For example *La France Graphique* No. 31, July 1949, pages 27–30, and No. 55, July 1951, pages 22–23. So Charles Peignot would have known about the project from trade publications at the least. It's likely that he would already have known about it through his association with the École Estienne, where a prototype of the photosetting machine was presented in 1946. After a trip to the USA in 1950, and after several talks, Charles Peignot submitted a draft contract to the inventors in 1952. Both parties were in agreement in 1953. However, due to clarification required by a third party, the contract was not signed until 30 March 1954. – See ALAN MARSHALL, *Du plomb à la lumière,* Paris 2003, pages 200 f.

3 A Photon 100 was shipped from the United States to Paris, which was then presented by Deberny & Peignot at the Salon TPG in 1954.

4 'Association Typographique Internationale', founded in 1957 by Charles Peignot with the involvement of John Dreyfus. Charles Peignot presided over it for the first sixteen years. – See www.atypi.org

5 The name 'Garaldes' is a mixture of the names Garamont and Aldus (Manutius). 'Didones', likewise, is a mix of a Didot and Bodoni.

6 On 2. 5. 1953 Aldro Gaul's book was presented by Vannevar Bush on behalf of GARF to Karl Compton, the president of MIT. This important event reverberated in the American daily newspapers, most of whose members sat on the GARF board of advisors. In reality, the book had been set on the earlier 'Petunia' model, as the Photon 100 was not ready for production. – See ALAN MARSHALL, *Du plomb à la lumière,* Paris 2003, pages 136 f.

7 Deberny & Peignot donated the original Photon 100 to the Gutenberg Museum in Mainz. Their Lumitype 200 can be seen at the Musée de l'imprimerie in Lyon.

8 The following publications have comprehensive articles on the history of Photon-Lumitype: – ALAN MARSHALL, *Du plomb à la lumière,* Paris 2003. – ALAN MARSHALL, *La Lumitype-Photon,* Lyon 1995. – L. W. WALLIS, *A Concise Chronology of Typesetting Developments 1886–1986,* Worcestershire 1988.

9 Adrian Frutiger, 'Determination des bases pour l'étude et le dessin des caractères à utiliser pour la Lumitype', 14 June 1954.

10 The ATypI recognised the 'Vox Classification' as the standard in 1960. The adjudicating committee was composed of Maximilien Vox, Walter Tracy, Gerrit W. Ovink, Adrian Frutiger, Aaron Burns and Hermann Zapf. In 1962 the 'ATypI Classification', extended from 9 to 10 groups, was adopted. Broken type (blackletter) was now included in a separate group. The following countries adopted the classification, even though the style descriptions are inconsistent: France, Federal Republic of Germany, Italy, Netherlands, United Kingdom, Spain and Portugal. – See GEORG KURT SCHAUER, *Klassifikation. Bemühungen um eine Ordnung im Druckschriftenbestand,* Darmstadt 1975, pages 15 ff and 52 ff.

I	Venetian | Humanist		
II	Old Style | Garalde		
III	Transition | Transitional		
IV	Modern | Didone		
V	Egyptienne | Slab serif		
VI	Lineale | Sans serif		
VII	Display | Glyphic		
VIII	Script		
IX	Hand-Lettered | Graphic		
X	Blackletter	Xa	Textura
		Xb	Rotunda
		Xc	Schwabacher
		Xd	Fraktur
		Xe	Fraktur variations
XI	Non-latin alphabets		

11 Monotype fonts may well have served as originals, particularly due to their division into 18 units. However, from a technical point of view Deberny & Peignot's fonts seem the more likely source, since they were readily at hand and also corresponded to clients' desires to have their familiar lead fonts turned into photosetting fonts.
12 "Ce disque remplace 3 tonnes de matrices dont le prix serait de 40 millions de Fr. environ. Il pèse 1.000 grammes et son diamètre est de 20 cm." – DEBERNY & PEIGNOT, *La Lumitype Possibilités Exemples,* Paris c.1957.
13 Floating accents have the advantage over fixed accented letters that only one character space per accent is used, and that, in theory, every accent can go on every letter. Lumitype had fixed as well as floating accents, probably so as not to affect the exposure speed.
14 *Garamont* is spelled differently in historical documents. In Garamont's lifetime it was written with a t on the title page of the book *L'histoire de Thucydide Athenie* in the printer's imprint: "Imprimé a Paris par Pierre Gaultier pour Ichan Barbé & Claude Garamont. 1545." – GERDA FINSTERER-STUBER (ed.), *Geistige Väter des Abendlandes,* Stuttgart 1960, chapter 35.
15 According to the letter 'Type Face & Machine Data' sent by Photon Inc. on 23 February 1955, *Cambridge Garamond* is an adaptation of *ATF Garamond* (by Morris Fuller Benton). In the 'Technical Memorandum No. 62' by Photon Inc. dated 7 March 1956 claims that *Paris Garamont* is an adaptation of Georges Peignot's *Garamont.*
16 In the typeface specimen of the International Photon Corporation *Times 451–55* ff. is noted as being a Photon font.
17 On the Photon em size was chosen – as it was in metal setting –, meaning that there was no visibly uniform height. Frutiger's groundbreaking decision was to standardise the cap heights for Lumitype. Unfortunately Frutiger's innovation wasn't included for the introduction of Adobe PostScript in 1983. To this day the cap heights and x-heights are inconsistent in digital fonts.
18 Gradually the font range of both manufacturers was expanded. The following typefaces, in alphabetical order, were produced for Lumitype after 1961: *Beauchamp, Bodoni Book, Century, Clarendon, Imprint, Modern, Olympic, Plantin, Gras Vibert* and *Neo Vibert,* as well as *Weiss Antiqua.* Frutiger's *Président* was also adapted for Lumitype. At International Photon Corporation, where Ladislas Mandel became artistic director, the following were produced: *Aster, Candida, Edgware, Gill, Haverhill, Sofia Latin, Textype, Thomson,* another *Times,* as well as *Univad,* a *Univers* adaptation for the smallest point sizes by Ladislas Mandel. Furthermore, a few non-latin alphabets were produced: a Greek *Univers* in four weights, for example, and a cyrillic *Univers* called *Mir* in seven weights, both drawn by Ladislas Mandel. To meet the demand for Photon-Lumitype faces, the American Dymo Graphic Systems included fonts by Photon and Lumitype or International Photon Corporation in its font brochure from 1976.
19 A sheet titled 'Deberny & Peignot 1956/57', signed by Albert Boton in 2003, shows photographs of the people listed, for example Ladislas Mandel working on *Caslon* italique.
In an article in English by Ladislas Mandel about the International Photon Corporation studio it is said of Annette Blanchard (nee Celsio) that "[...] Since 1959 [corrected by hand to 1954], she has taken part in realizing a great number of alphabets in the Lumitype-Photon catalogue." – LADISLAS MANDEL, 'Our IPC Type Design Studio in Paris', in unknown source, page 5.
20 Giambattista Bodoni, *Manuale Tipografico,* vol. 1, Parma 1818, page 41 (Filosofia 4 / Cadice), page 100 (Parangone 2 / Velteri), page 103 (Ascendonica 2 / Chieri). – See OCTAVO CORPORATION, ‹Giambattista Bodoni: Manuale Tipografico›, Oakland 1998 (CD-ROM).
21 The *Bodoni* adaptations are often much more rigid than the originals. The curves are nearly always straightened, the proportions of the counters aligned and the ascenders and descenders significantly shortened. In particular the lively, somewhat playful elegance and grace of the larger *Bodoni* sizes are mostly missing.

Univers →88

1 ADRIAN FRUTIGER, 'Der Werdegang der Univers' in *TM/STM, Sondernummer Univers (Univers special edition),* 1/1961, page 10. Set in Monotype *Univers.*
2 EMIL RUDER, 'Univers, eine Grotesk von Adrian Frutiger' in *TM/STM* 5/1957, pages 364 f.
3 Hans-Rudolf Lutz writes: "With Univers, Adrian Frutiger has created the first real typeface system. His working method differs from the usual process of completing typeface families only once after a few initial weights have been successful." – HANS-RUDOLF LUTZ, *Typoundso,* Zurich 1996, page 43.
4 The design was originally dated February 1951 in pencil. Adrian Frutiger erased this in the '90s, correcting it to 1950, the date he started working on it. – See ADRIAN FRUTIGER, *Type Sign Symbol,* page 12.
5 EMIL RUDER, 'Univers, eine Grotesk von Adrian Frutiger' in *TM/STM* 5/1957, page 362.
6 In relation to the Allgemeine Gewerbeschule Basel, the following books set in *Univers* should be mentioned: EMIL RUDER, *Typography,* Sulgen 1967; HANS WICHMANN (ed.), *Armin Hofmann: His Work, Quest and Philosophy,* Basel 1989. On the other hand, Armin Hofmann's book, *Graphic Design Manual,* Heiden 1965, is set in Akzidenz Grotesk. HELMUT SCHMID's book, *the road to Basel,* Tokyo 1997, has works by other Basel students; as does RICHARD HOLLIS's (*Swiss Graphic Design) Schweizer Grafik,* Basel 2006, pages 251 ff. He lists former Basel students such as Daniel Friedman, April Greiman and Willi Kunz, who were or are active in the USA.
7 In ADRIAN FRUTIGER, *Type Sign Symbol,* Zurich 1979, page 19.
8 An undated design with a pencil drawing of the lowercase n is titled 'Antique DP'.
9 Adrian Frutiger applies form principles which Walter Käch describes and demonstrates, and partly illustrates these in his own books. Frutiger and Käch make sure that the Q tail does not affect the counter, for example. Käch also writes about moving the strokes of the M, thereby opening the sharp-angled counters, to prevent a patchy text appearance. Frutiger's designs have finer details than those of Käch. For example, the cross strokes of the E have different stroke widths; the shorter the bar, the thinner. Käch too has different lengths for the three bars, but his all have the same stroke width. – See WALTER KÄCH, *Schriften Lettering Ecritures,* pages XVII ff.
10 A letter dated 02/27/1956 sent to people involved in the Photon-Lumitype project by Louis Rosenblum, responsible for type at Photon Inc., reads: "Atttached is a display showing the 14 widths and weights of the typeface designed by D&P that is known in Europe as 'ANTIQUE'. For obvious reasons we should like to select a new family name. Among the suggestions that have been made are 'UNIVERSAL', 'CONSTELLATION' and 'COSMOS'." The display shows the 14 upright weights of what was to be *Univers.*
11 'Memorandum: Sans serif design by Deberny et Peignot' by Louis Rosenblum, dated 27 February, 1956.
12 EMIL RUDER, 'Univers, eine Grotesk von Adrian Frutiger' in *TM/STM* 11/1963, page 690 f.
13 Adrian Frutiger says in conversation on 28 March 2001 that the diagram stems from Rémy Peignot. Rudolf Hostettler (TM publisher) named Frutiger, but in the sense of being ultimately responsible. In *TM/STM* 5/1957, page 361 ff.
14 The angle tends to be 16.5°, depending on weight and character. *Linotype Univers* was also tilted furtherto 16.3°.
15 The advertisements and posters that Hans-Rudolf Lutz designed in 1964 were part of a series for English Monotype. – See HANS-RUDOLF LUTZ, *Ausbildung in typografischer Gestaltung* Zürich 1996, page 168 ff. He made a series of typographic portraits for typesetters Ernst Gloor in Zurich in 1967/68, of which the Karl Marx portrait is set in *Univers.* – See HANS-RUDOLF LUTZ, *Typoundso,* Zürich 1996, page 38 ff. – Ernst Gloor also produced a *Univers* brochure in 1966 with typographic broadsheets by Fridolin Müller.
16 ADRIAN FRUTIGER, 'Der Werdegang der Univers' in *TM/STM, Univers special edition,* 1/1961, page 11.
17 Type casting was discontinued at Deberny & Peignot in 1972. The Haas'sche type foundry took over the company and its typeface range.
18 The *Grotesque* has different dates attributed to it – the typefaces shown are not identical: 1834 in NICOLETE GRAY, *Nineteenth Century Ornamented Typefaces,* London 1976, page 39. – Or 1832 in JASPERT, BERRY, JOHNSON, *Encyclopaedia of Type Faces,* London 1970, page 287.
19 *Breite Magere Grotesk* by Schelter & Giesecke, Leipzig has different dates attributed to it: 1870 in GEORG KANDLER, *Alphabete. Erinnerungen an den Bleisatz,* vol. 2, page 37. – Or 1840 in PHILIPP BERTHEAU, *Buchdruckschriften im 20. Jahrhundert. Atlas zur Geschichte der Schrift,* Darmstadt 1995, page 218. This last source does not mention whether lowercase letters were included at such an early date. It is shown on page 2 with the comment "Bauer & Co, Stuttgart 1895". It's not apparent whether these are indeed the same typeface. This is not surprising, given that the typefaces were produced in near-identical form by different foundries. On page 512 *Breite Fette Grotesk* is named as being a Bauer & Co typeface from 1880. However, on page 218 it's by Schelter & Giesecke from 1902. Neither of them are shown. A semi-bold weight from 1890 is also mentioned. – *Breite Fette Grotesk* by Schelter & Giesecke is shown and dated 1880 at: http://www.fontshop.de/fontblog/C420185419/E430231085/index.html (January 2008).
20 See Wolfgang Beinert: http://www.typolexikon.de/g/grotesk.html (May 2007).
21 Karl Gerstner, co-founder of well-known advertising agency GGK (Gerstner, Gredinger, Kutter) developed *Akzidenz Grotesk* into a systematic family of typefaces in the 1960s, similar to the *Univers* system. It was released by H. Berthold AG as *Gerstner Programm.* – See KARL GERSTNER, *Programme entwerfen,* Teufen 1968, page 29 ff. – See KARL GERSTNER, *Rückblick auf 5×10 Jahre Graphik Design etc.,* Ostfildern-Ruit 2001, page 96 ff. (In the USA, *Gerstner Program* is available from Visual Graphic Corporation).
22 HELMUT SCHMID, the road to Basel, Tokyo 1997, page 65.
23 EMIL RUDER, 'Univers, eine Grotesk von Adrian Frutiger' in *TM/STM* 5/1957, page 361.
24 This group of static grotesques with horizontal curve ends is often referred to as Neo-Grotesk in German. *Folio,* released by Bauersche Giesserei in Frankfurt in 1956–63, was created by Konrad F. Bauer and Walter Baum. It is known in France as *Caravelle. Mercator,* from 1957–61 by Lettergieterij Amsterdam, was by Dick Dooijes. The Haas'sche Schriftgiesserei released Zurich graphic designer Max Miedinger's *Neue Haas Grotesk* in 1957. It was constantly extended, from 1961 called *Helvetica* onward by D. Stempel AG / Linotype. Aldo Novarese's *Recta* from 1958–61 is by the Nebiolo type foundry in Torino. *Permanent* is by Karlgeorg Hoefer from 1962, made for the Ludwig & Mayer foundry in Frankfurt and the Italian Simoncini company.
25 *Maxima* by Gert Wunderlich from 1970, designed for East German Typoart, is closely related in form to the original idea of *Univers.* Its capitals have a more versatile rhythm though, similar in proportion to Capitalis Monumentalis. Team 77 – André Gürtler, Christian Mengelt and Erich Gschwind – were behind *Haas Unica.* It was released in 1980 as a reworking of the original *Neue Haas Grotesk.* Team 77 analyzed the original *Helvetica* by Haas'sche Schriftgiesserei, the Linotype *Helvetica, Akzidenz Grotesk* by Berthold and *Univers* by Deberny & Peignot. The name *Unica* could be seen as a reference to *Univers* and *Helvetica.* – See GÜRTLER, MENGELT, GSCHWIND, 'Von der Helvetica – zur Haas Unica', in *TM/STM* 4/1980, page 189 ff.
26 Monotype Newsletter no. 140, last page, Berne, October 1966.
27 OLIVER NINEUIL, 'Ladislas Mandel – explorateur de la typo française' in *Etapes Graphiques* no. 10, 1999, page 44.
28 Unknown author, 'Caractèristique de l'Antique Presse (version Mandel)', 11/14/1962. Musée de l'imprimerie, Lyon, Fonds Mandel.
29 ADRIAN FRUTIGER, 'Historique des caractères par Adrian Frutiger (pour mémoire)', 4/27/1988.
30 Letter from 02/28/1973 sent by Adrian Frutiger to Dr. Walter Greisner, "I think it's right that a typeface style whose letter shapes have changed from those of the Latin alphabet to the extent of say, Cyrillic or Greek, ought to be considered as a new independent creation, even though its character is based on an existing typeface style."
31 The question of copyright is not entirely clear regarding *Univers* extensions. Walter Greisner at Stempel learned that Compugraphic intended to ask André Gürtler to make an adaptation of *Univers Cyrillic* for them, and sent a letter dated June 20th 1973 to Alfred Hoffmann, director of the Haas'sche Schriftgiesserei, stating that Gürtler wasn't authorized to do so. The Haas foundry replied that, although he agreed with Greisner, the same should apply to the *Univers Cyrillic* weights which Frutiger had drawn for D. Stempel AG. The Haas foundry wrote in letter dated June 29th 1973: "Taking effect from 01/01/1973, Haas acquired the unlimited rights to Univers by DP, and is thereby exclusively entitled to its use."
32 Note from Adrian Frutiger to Dr. Walter Greisner with an attached alphabet of a Cyrillic *Univers* by Ladislas Mandel called *Mir.*
33 Adrian Frutiger drew a Cyrillic alphabet for the IBM Composer as early as 1971. He mentions in a letter to Walter Greisner that "the drawings can't be used for another purpose, first of all because I don't own the rights, and secondly because the system of units is too untypographic."
34 An outcome of the agreement between Monotype and Deberny & Peignot from 01 April 1965 was that Adrian Frutiger was to draw the Greek and Cyrillic versions of *Univers* for Monotype. However, according to Robin Nicholas (in January 2007), artistic director at Monotype, their archives contain drawings of the Greek version only. The Cyrillic version exists solely as copies of drawings made for Stempel / Linotype from 1973 on which served as the blueprint for the Monotype version.
35 Asher Oron is an Israeli graphic designer who teaches at the Bezalel Academy of Arts and Design in Jerusalem.
36 The process of making *Oron* is documented in Asher Oron, 'A new Hebrew sans serif for bilingual printing' in an unidentified publication on pages 16/17.
37 In the 'Typography' typeface catalogue by Hell, 9th ed./1989, *Univers* is listed as *Swiss 722* among the Bitstream typefaces. In later Bitstream publications (folded poster 'Bitstream Typeface Library' 1992) it is renamed *Zurich.*

38 In addition to the original 21 *Univers* weights, there are the 69, 85, and 86 weights, 53 oblique, 63 oblique, 73 oblique, 93 and 93 oblique, the reversed weights 65, 75, 76, and the outline weights 65, 67, 73.

39 It is surprising that there is such confusion in the thoroughly conceived *Univers*, of all things. Linotype's type specimens of digital fonts from 1984, 1987 and 1992 show the oblique weights angled at 16°, yet the narrow obliques are 12°. In 1969 *Univers* began to be adapted for photosetting by Mergenthaler Linotype. The first weights – 55, 56, 65 and 66 (all fitted to the same widths) – have 16° obliques, while the narrow obliques (also duplexed) made at the same time are 12°. The principal reason for this was technical: the narrow oblique weights were supposed to be as space-saving as possible. The range of 12° obliques was extended to include the regular width as well. This was done to achieve the uniformity that had been a goal in photosetting and line-casting since 1973. Further 16° weights (46 and 76) were added in 1982.

40 The sharp corner of the number 7 in the regular weight of the PostScript version from 1987 is obviously not correct for *Univers*. – See Erik Spiekermann, 'Mr. Univers' in *Page* 3/1990, page 62 ff.

41 Letter dated 10/19/1993 from Linotype-Hell and Gerhard Höhl to Adrian Frutiger. Unfortunately there's nothing left of that comprehensive project in the new *Linotype Univers*. Even the old-style figures and small capitals advertised in that brochure remain unavailable to this day.

42 The f-ligatures are not real ligatures, but unconnected pairs of letters placed on the same 'body'.

43 Adrian Frutiger was delighted with the refreshing *Univers Flair* which hung on his studio wall for years and which he reproduced. – See Adrian Frutiger, 'L'histoire des Antiques' in *TM/RSI* 1/1988, page 9. Along with *Univers Flair*, Phil Martin designed *Helvetica Flair* in 1970 for the VGC Photo Typositor photosetting machine by Visual Graphic Corporation. Martin founded Alphabet Innovations in 1969 and Type Spectra in 1974. He took well known typefaces and changed – improved in his opinion – their shapes, whilst neither having a license to use the fonts nor paying royalties for them. – See www.roostertypes.com/articles.asp (May 2007).

44 The Linotype type specimen catalog has included 35 weights (numbered according to the original *Univers* system) of *Neue Helvetica* since 1988. The (old) *Helvetica* is available in 47 weights.

45 The three-digit system was devised by Hans Peter Dubacher, Reinhard Haus and Otmar Hoefer.

46 The fonts by Deberny & Peignot, Fonderie Olive and Nebiolo among others, are stored at Haas'sche Schriftgiesserei's successor, Walter Fruttiger's office in Münchenstein, Switzerland. They can still be cast on demand today.

47 Undated typescript, c. 1998.

48 The first *Folio* weight, the bold condensed, was released in 1956 by Bauersche Giesserei. The regular and the light, shown here, and also the semi-bold and semi-bold wide were released in 1957. – See Philipp Bertheau, *Buchdruckschriften im 20. Jahrhundert. Atlas zur Geschichte der Schrift,* Darmstadt 1995, pages 484 and 540.

49 *Helvetica* was extended unsystematically by D. Stempel AG. The eight weights of *Neue Haas Grotesk*, renamed *Helvetica*, were joined by six adapted weights from previous Haas sets and five new weights by D. Stempel AG itself. – See Philipp Bertheau, *Buchdruckschriften im 20. Jahrhundert. Atlas zur Geschichte der Schrift,* Darmstadt 1995, pages 501 and 509. In 1983 *Helvetica* was given an overhaul at Stempel and released under the name *Neue Helvetica* with a unified design and coordinated weights. – See http://de.wikipedia.org/wiki/Helvetica_%28Schriftart%29 (May 2007)

Egyptienne F →118

1 There was an exhibition of Frutiger's work in 1964 at Monotype House in Salfords, Redhill, Surrey. The brochure documents part of the exhibited work.

2 In the English and French texts the date is given as 1958, the German text says 1956.

3 Horst Heiderhoff, 'Forms and Counterforms. Design and life of type artist Adrian Frutiger', in Stephan Füssel (ed.), *Gutenberg-Jahrbuch 1985,* page 29.

4 The fact that Charles Peignot was interested in the progress of French typography and was always looking for something unusual is reflected in a text by Maximilien Vox praising Charles Peignot's efforts and ambition: "One ambition was to continue his father's work, another was to leave a legacy that owed nothing to tradition. Receptive to new ideas […], endlessly searching for personalities and temperaments […], Peignot knew how to forge a passionate belief in type and print in France, with the promise of great success." – Maximilien Vox, 'Das halbe Jahrhundert', in Georg Kurt Schauer (ed.), *Internationale Buchkunst im 19. und 20. Jahrhundert,* page 252.

5 The compo dp type specimen book from 1961 contains only one typeface alongside Egyptian typefaces from the 19th century, *Pharaon* from 1933, a not very harmonious face similar in style to *Rockwell* and *Memphis*.

6 Letter from Adrian Frutiger to Dr. Walter Greisner, 4.9.1973.

7 Bockwitz writes that "after the Napoleonic campaign in Egypt which brought attention to the ancient land of the Nile after centuries of oblivion, England became fascinated with all things Egyptian, culminating in 1802 with the arrival in London, taken from the captured French ship Egyptienne, of the trilingual Rosetta stone […]." Hans H. Bockwitz, *Beiträge zur Kulturgeschichte des Buches,* page 31.

8 This is the shadow face *Two-line pica in shade* from 1815/17. In 1832 Blake & Stephenson released an Outline Clarendon, and in 1848 Thorowgood released *Two Lines English Clarendon*. – See Nicolete Gray, *Nineteenth Century Ornamented Typefaces,* London 1976, pages 26, 41, 67.

9 See Nicolete Gray, *Nineteenth Century Ornamented Typefaces,* London 1976, page 38, fig. 44, *Two Lines English Egyptian,* William Caslon IV, 1816. – Bollwage uses examples to demonstrate that this was the first sans serif in print, type without serifs having been used throughout previous centuries on coins and inscriptions. Max Bollwage, 'Serifenlose Linearschriften gibt es nicht erst seit dem 19. Jahrhundert', in Stephan Füssel (ed.), *Gutenberg-Jahrbuch 2002,* pages 212 ff.

10 Some digital fonts today also have several design sizes available, for example *ITC Bodoni* (1994), *ITC Founders Caslon* (1998), *MvB Sirenne* (2002) and *Cycles* (1990–2004).

11 Hans Rudolf Bosshard, *Technische Grundlagen der Satzherstellung,* page 90.

12 Hans Peter Willberg, *Wegweiser Schrift,* pages 57 and 67.

Opéra →130

1 In the four-page type specimen brochure 'Opéra' (undated, c. 1960), 8 pt alone is mentioned.

2 Letter dated 27 March 1958 from Alfred Devolz, owner of Sofratype, to Charles Peignot, owner of Fonderies Deberny & Peignot, confirming the oral agreement between the two Parisian companies regarding Adrian Frutiger's work for Sofratype.

3 ibid.

4 Letter dated 25 March 1958 from Adrian Frutiger to Alfred Devolz with sender's address: Privé: 11, rue Roger Salengro, Montrouge.

5 *Informations TG* no. 47, 1 July 1960, page 2.

Alphabet Orly →134

1 An announcement in the 'échos' section of *Informations TG* says that a new typeface has been created for the reopening of Orly airport on 24 February 1961 based on *Univers* and *Peignot* and designed by Adrian Frutiger. – See *Informations TG,* No. 76, 3 March 1961, page 1.

2 The archive of Aéroports de Paris is located at Orly airport.

3 Only two fonts of *Alphabet Orly* remain: the regular and italic capitals and numerals in normal width. The two expanded fonts cannot be found. Ladislas Mandel, a former colleague of Frutiger's at Deberny & Peignot, kept the microfilms until his death in 2006. He cooperated in the creation of the final artwork. Today the negatives are at Musée de l'imprimerie in Lyon, France.

4 The photographs of Orly airport show varying typefaces from the 1950s onwards. The typeface thought to be the predecessor of *Alphabet Orly* can still be seen in 1961. It shows a certain similarity with *Alphabet Orly* in terms of approach. In particular the round shape of the G, which is typical neither for *Peignot* nor *Univers,* points to a formal connection.

Apollo →138

1 The first patents regarding a typecasting machine for single letters were granted to the American Tolbert Lanston in 1887. The Lanston Monotype Company was subsequently founded in Washington D.C. After a start-up phase from 1890 until 1894, however, there was no more money to carry on. Lord Dunraven, an Englishman, bought the rights to Monotype and in 1897 the Lanston Monotype Corporation Ltd was founded in London. In 1898 the first two machines were installed in London and in Washington D.C. – See www.monotypeimaging.com/aboutus/timeline.aspx (March 2008).
A Monotype installation consists of two separate machines, the keyboard (for perforating the punch-tape) and the single letter caster, which is controlled by the punch-tape.

2 Apart from the Photon-Lumitype, others such as the Linofilm by Linotype (1954), the ATF Typesetter (1958) and Berthold's Diatype (1958) are worth mentioning. In 1961 Compugraphic also introduced their first machine.

3 Monotype recorded the production process in a document titled 'History of Preparation for Apollo; London Order E. 585'.

4 In the 'List of Monophoto Faces available' *Apollo 645* Roman / Italic and *Apollo 665* Semi-Bold are mentioned in 6–24 pt sizes with short descenders. In The Monotype Corporation Limited, *Specimen Book of 'Monophoto' Filmsetter Faces,* Salfords, England, undated.

5 The *Monotype Recorder* No. 1 (December 1979) announces "'Monophoto' APOLLO was used for six of the books selected for the National Book League exhibition of British Book Design and Production this year. Apart from six others set in 'Monophoto' Plantin, no single typeface was used for as many of the selected books as APOLLO."

6 Alongside Frutiger's typefaces, various logotypes and numerous book covers for Éditions Hermann of Paris were displayed. His diploma project also formed part of the exhibition, as did the *Genesis* and *Partages* books featuring his woodcuts.

7 The Monophoto catalog is mostly comprised of text faces, among them the well-known Monotype classics *Bembo, Perpetua, Poliphilus, Spectrum* and *Times* and many American typefaces. It also includes a few slab serif and sans serif faces.

8 Monotype Corporation: *Graphismes by Frutiger. Monotype House,* London 1964.

9 *Apollo* was referred to or shown in the following editions: *Monotype Newsletter:* No. 74, Nov. 1964; No. 78, March 1966; No. 81, May 1967; *Monotype Recorder* Vol. 43 No. 2, 1965; Vol. 43 No. 3, 1968; New Series No. 1, 1979.

10 Allan Hutt: 'Monophoto Apollo', in *British Printer,* December 1964, page 84.

11 Memo dated 5 November 1970 from the offices of the Typographical Committee.

12 See Hans Widmann, *Gutenberg-Jahrbuch 1971,* Mainz 1971, page 423 f.

13 Jan Middendorp, *Dutch Type,* Rotterdam 2004, page 145 f.

14 ibid.

Alphabet Bouygues (type-design project) →148

1 Frigidaire, an American manufacturer of fridges, formerly part of General Motors, became well-known and very successful. Raymond Loewy, the American pioneer of industrial design and ardent proponent of streamline forms, took on the design for Frigidaire from 1939. Bosch and Hoover were other well-known manufacturers that also offered fridges featuring the typical rounded corners through the 1950s. Christoph Bignens writes, "For some companies, the major engagement in advertising and design pays off in an area that marketing had not originally targeted: in art. In the case of Frigidaire it was the Swiss Dadaist, Jean Tinguely, who lifted the brand into the cultural domain in 1960. He had bought himself a used Frigidaire and adapted it to play a fire-engine's siren on opening the door. Tinguely called his piece 'Frigo Duchamp', an hommage to his artistic hero, Marcel Duchamp, in whose New York studio that siren was once supposed to have been installed." – Christoph Bignens, *American Way of Life. Architektur Comics Design Werbung,* Sulgen / Zurich 2003, page 106 ff.

2 Bruno Pfäffli, Adrian Frutiger's longstanding colleague and later studio partner, made a few designs for advertisements, which appeared briefly or not at all. He thought that if the typeface hadindeed ever made, it would have been used for only a short time. There are no longer any documents pertaining to this project at the company's archives.

Concorde →150

1 Letter (5 June 1961) from Alfred Devolz (Sofratype) to 'Monsieur le Directeur' at Deberny & Peignot. This was a response to a letter from 20 April 1961 with the reference AF/TE, which suggests that 'Monsieur le Directeur' refers to Adrian Frutiger. It is also obvious from this document that Adrian Frutiger's work was carried out in agreement with Deberny & Peignot, as had already been the case with *Opéra*.

2 Heidrun Osterer, Philipp Stamm and their assistant Andrea Näpflin in conversation with André Gürtler on 23 May 2005. Recording and transcription are archived at Swiss Foundation Type and Typography.

3 A smoke proof is generated by holding the engraved, untempered punch over a candle flame, producing a thin coating of soot on the face. When the soot-blackened punch is applied on baryte paper, the result is an exact impression of the face. This method is used for final checking of the punch before hardening.

4 Heidrun Osterer, Philipp Stamm in conversation with Günter Gerhard Lange on 24 July 2004 in Leipzig (Germany).

5 Eric Gill took calligraphy lessons from renowned calligraphy teacher Edward Johnston. This developed into a deep friendship. In 1913 the two designers were asked to develop a signage face for London Transport, i. e. for the London Underground. In 1915 Johnston started this work on his own since Gill had declined. He participated, however, as a freelance consultant in the development of this novel sans serif. – See Max Caflisch, *Schriftanalysen,* vol. 2, St. Gallen 2003, page 7 ff.

6 Besides many other typefaces, Jan van Krimpen designed *Romulus*, a comprehensive type family. It was developed between 1931 and 1937. The Renaissance antiqua was released in a roman, sloped roman, and semi-bold cut as well as in a semi-bold condensed one. This was extended by *Cancelleresca Bastarda*, a very elegant cursive with narrow letterfit. A Greek version was also cut. Of particular interest here is *Romulus Sans Serif* in the four cuts (light, regular, semibold and bold), which were, however, only implemented in 12 pt. – See John Dreyfus, *The Work of Jan van Krimpen*, London 1952, page 36 ff; Paul A. Bennett, *Jan van Krimpen. On Designing and Devising Type*, New York 1957, page 51 ff.
7 This issue is superbly described and represented in the brochure on Hans Eduard Meier's *Syntax-Antiqua*. – See Erich Schulz-Anker, *Formanalyse und Dokumentation einer serifenlosen Linearschrift auf neuer Basis: Syntax Antiqua*, Frankfurt am Main, 1969.

Serifen- / Gespannte Grotesk (type-design project) →156

1 In his letter to Gerhard Höhl of Linotype dated 4 May 1993, Adrian Frutiger wrote: "I have also enclosed the two projects Primavera and Cooperline (these are working titles). I am sending them to you without any further explanations, we can talk about them when the occasion arises."
2 With the working title *'Cooperline'* Frutiger acknowledged the relationship to *Copperplate Gothic*. The reference to Oswald B. Cooper and his *Cooper Black*, however, seems to be unintentional.
3 In 1962 Deberny & Peignot were still working on the completion of *Univers* for handsetting. As far as phototypesetting for Linotype was concerned, other adoptions of existing typefaces were paramount. Furthermore, another large sans-serif family would have created competition for *Univers*.
4 A letter from Adrian Frutiger dated 29 November 1991 and addressed to Linotype's Reinhard Haus, which accompanied the designs for his multiple-master project *'University'*, has a note attached to it by Reinhard Haus for his colleagues: "… look at … the individual shapes! After a first look through I'm not thrilled!"

Alphabet Algol →160

1 See L. Bolliet, N. Castinel, P. J. Laurent, *un nouveau langage scientifique. algol. manuel pratique*, Paris 1964.
2 *Microgramma*, 1952, created by Alessandro Butti and Aldo Novarese for Società Nebiolo, Turin (Italy).
3 See http://de.wikipedia.org/wiki/Algol_60 (July 2007).
4 Éditions Hermann, founded in 1876, was bought out in 1956 by the publisher and antiquarian bookseller Pierre Berès. One of the preconditions was the takeover of the scientific book stock. This included publications by important mathematicians such as Élie Joseph Cartan, Jules Henri Poincaré, Paul Langevin and even Albert Einstein. In 1961 the first comprehensive catalogue, designed by Adrian Frutiger, was published.
5 Before taking care of the book covers, Frutiger designed a company logo and the shop sign.
6 From 1960 onwards Bruno Pfäffli and André Gürtler assisted Adrian Frutiger in his work for Éditions Hermann, mainly on *Art de France*.
7 The glyphs are listed on page 11 of *algol:* numerals (10), letters (52), further base symbols (54; including 6 punctuation marks, 4 parentheses, 19 mathematical symbols and 25 words).
8 See André Gürtler, 'Schrift im Lichtsatz' in *TM* No. 3/1966, page 209.

Serifa →162

1 In February 1961 René Higonnet, his son René-Paul Higonnet and Louis Moyroud bought Deberny & Peignot. Charles Peignot was replaced by René-Paul Higonnet around 1962. – See Alan Marshall, *Du plomb à la lumière*, Paris 2003, page 214 ff.
2 Fundición Tipográfica Neufville changed its name to Bauer Types in 2007 and now does not just administer licensing rights for its own fonts, but also distributes fonts from other manufacturers.
3 Conversation between Heidrun Osterer, Philipp Stamm, their colleague Andrea Näpflin and André Gürtler on 23 May 2005. Cassette recording and transcription are archived at the Swiss Foundation Type and Typography.
4 American Type Founders.
5 Mentioned by Bruno Pfäffli on 27 August 2007.
6 Conversation between Heidrun Osterer, Philipp Stamm and Walter Greisner on 12 August 2002.
7 The contract between Adrian Frutiger and Bauersche Giesserei from June 24/29, 1966 mentions the intended completion of four weights: book, semibold, bold and bold condensed, with possible later extensions such as light, italic, light condensed and bold extended. The letter dated 27 November 1975 from D. Stempel AG to the Fundición Tipográfica Neufville, successor to Bauersche Giesserei, also includes four weights to be licensed. Reference books, however, mention only two *Serifa* weights for foundry type. Thus *Buchdruckschriften im 20. Jahrhundert* notes that *Serifa* appeared in light (later described as regular) and semibold weights. The *Encyclopaedia of Type Faces* (4th ed.) shows both of these weights. Max Caflisch, on whose initiative *Serifa* was released by Bauersche Giesserei, writes in his book Schriftanalysen that *Serifa* was being made in regular and italic. A letter from Walter Greisner to Prof. Dr. G. W. Ovink dated 3 March 1983 gives yet another account: "Serifa was made by Adrian Frutiger for foundry type in light, semibold and bold condensed weights for Bauersche Giesserei in 1966 and 1967." Exactly how many and which *Serifa* weights were produced for foundry type is also uncertain according to Wolfgang Hartmann of Bauer Types. – See Philipp Bertheau, *Buchdruckschriften im 20. Jahrhundert. Atlas zur Geschichte der Schrift*, Darmstadt 1995, page 524; W. Pincus Jaspert, W. Turner Berry, A. F. Johnson, *The Encyclopaedia of Type Faces*, London 1970, page 205; Max Caflisch, *Schriftanalysen*, vol. 2, St. Gallen 2003, page 95.
8 Swiss Typographic Magazine 10/1977, page 587.
9 The extension of the weights was helped along by Dr. Peter Karow's Ikarus program.
10 After many years of collaboration, Linotype acquired D. Stempel AG in 1985.
11 Of the two well-known manufacturers of transfer typefaces, Letraset and Mecanorma, only the first had *Serifa*, and only the regular weight. – See the type catalogue *Mecanorma Graphic Book 14*, Versailles 1988; *Letraset*, Glattbrugg 1990.
12 Adrian Frutiger, 'Über die Planung einer Schrift: Beispiel Serifa', in Adrian Frutiger, *Type Sign Symbol*, Zurich 1980, page 36 f. The illustrations referred to appeared in the article by Hans Kuh, 'Aus der Werkstatt einer Schriftgiesserei in Sonderdruck Serifa aus der Gebrauchsgraphik Juni 1968'.
13 Because the illustrations appear in a different order in both publications, we have taken the liberty of selecting our own order for optical reasons. – See Hans Kuh, 'Aus der Werkstatt einer Schriftgiesserei in Sonderdruck Serifa aus der Gebrauchsgraphik Juni 1968'; Adrian Frutiger, 'Der Konstruktivismus in der Schrift', in *Type Sign Symbol*, Zurich 1980, page 34 f.
14 The German typeface classification standard DIN 16518 describes Group V ('slab serif linear old style') thus: "The hairlines and stems of slab serif linear old style faces have similar widths or are indeed, including serifs, optically the same (linear). All typefaces in this group share a conspicuous emphasis on the serifs." *Clarendon, Volta, Schadow, Pro Arte* and *Memphis* are shown as examples. The linear aspect of up- and downstroke in the stroke widths of the typefaces shown applies only to *Memphis;* all the others have a distinct stroke contrast. Also, the formulation about serif width is rather ambiguous. – See Georg Kurt Schauer, *Klassifikation – Bemühungen um eine Ordnung im Druckschriftenbestand*, Darmstadt 1975, page 90.
15 Serif typefaces made for lower-quality paper (so-called newspaper faces) are especially difficult to classify, as they appear heavier in both stroke widths and serifs.
16 The five groups are: Egyptienne, non-concave serifs; Clarendon, concave serifs; Italienne (reversed weight), oversized, bold (concave or non-concave) serifs with thinner stems; Renaissance, wedge serifs (Latin types); Toscanienne (Tuscan), split or bifurcated serifs. – See Hans Rudolf Bosshard, *Technische Grundlagen zur Satzherstellung*, Berne 1980, page 79 f.
17 Unfortunately the description of subgroup A, 'slab serif linear old style, derived from neoclassical old style' is very one-sided and seems to be based entirely on typefaces of the Clarendon kind. It only applies in part to *Serifa:* "Their shapes derive from neoclassical old style by broadening the hairline strokes. However, the stroke widths remain easily differentiated. The serifs are heavily bracketed." The typeface examples do not always match either. Thus *PMN Caecilia* is placed in this subgroup, even though it is blatantly derived from Renaissance old style faces. – See Sauthoff, Wendt, Willberg, *Schriften erkennen*, Mainz 1998, page 36 ff.
18 Typefaces are considered according to two aspects, form and style. The principal formal groups are old style, sans serif, Egyptienne, cursives and blackletter; the main sylistic groups are dynamic, static, geometric and decorative. – See Hans Peter Willberg, *Wegweiser Schrift*, Mainz 2001, page 49.
19 Some recent Dutch typefaces in this style are *Curvisium* 1986 by Jelle Bosma, *Oranda* 1987 by Gerard Unger and *PMN Caecilia* 1990 by Peter Matthias Noordzij. Also worth mentioning are *ITC Officina* Serif by Erik Spiekermann 1990 and Sumner Stone's *Silica* 1993. – See Max Caflisch, *Schriftanalysen*, vol. 2, St. Gallen 2003, pages 96 ff., 100 ff., 111 ff.
20 Hans Kuh, 'Aus der Werkstatt einer Schriftgiesserei' in *Sonderdruck Serifa aus der Gebrauchsgraphik Juni 1968*.
21 ibid.
22 Hans Peter Willberg, *Wegweiser Schrift*, Mainz 2001, page 66 ff.
23 According to Günter Gerhard Lange (in a telephone call on 10 September 2007), Bauer's sans serif *Venus* is used on maps by the German cartographic institutes. In order to complement this typeface – which was declared the standard typeface for maps – with a seriffed version, *Venus Egyptienne* was designed. The booklet *Schriftmusterbuch – Schriften, Ziffern, Zeichen und Ligaturen der Stempelei der HVA X* includes both of these as map typefaces. It was released by the cartography subdepartment of the chief surveying department X, Bad Godesberg – dated in pencil 1948. H. Berthold AG produced this typeface for their Diatype photosetting machine in the 1960s. In the 1974 *Berthold Fototypes E1* type specimen it is shown as a text face.

OCR-B →176

1 ECMA was founded on 17 May 1961; the founding members were: Aktiebolaget ADDO, Compagnie des Machines Bull, N.V. Electrologica, English Electric-Leo-Marconi Computers LTD, IBM-WTEC, ICT International Computers and Tabulators Ltd, ITT Europe Inc, NCR The National Cash Register Company Ltd, Ing. C. Olivetti & Co. S.p.A, SEA Société d'Electronique et d'Automatisme, Siemens & Halske AG, Sperry Rand International Corp. and Telefunken Aktiengesellschaft.
2 In 1967 Gilbert Weill was an engineer at the École Polytechnique and Directeur de Programme au Centre National d'Études Spatiales, Paris. – See also *TM* 1/1967, page 29.
3 Since the abbreviation of the name International Organisation for Standardisation would have led to different acronyms in different languages, the name agreed upon was ISO, based on the Greek isos, meaning equal.
4 In addition to the national commissions for standardisation there are also standards-setting organisations formed by private companies and based around a particular subject. ECMA is one of those. In order to gain international acknowledgement, all organisations have to submit their applications and receive certification through ISO.
5 See also 'Monotype mit OCR-Schriften', in: *Deutscher Drucker* No. 21, 1971, page VII.
6 Ruedi Rüegg, Godi Fröhlich, *Basic Typography*, Zurich 1972, page 220.
7 Today, the digital version of *OCR-B* is available from Adobe, Bitstream, Elsner+Flake and Linotype.
8 How fashionable *OCR-B* was in the 1990s is demonstrated by the fact that besides *OCRBczyk* from 1994 in regular and bold, there is another version called *FF OCR-F* by Albert-Jan Pool from 1995 in light, regular and bold.

Univers IBM Composer →190

1 The slab serif *Pyramid* shows formal similarities to *Rockwell* 1934 and *Scarab* 1937 by Monotype and Stephenson Blake respectively.
2 European Computer Manufacturers Association.
3 Justified and centred text are very difficult to set without the memory unit since each line has to be typed twice for proper composition.
4 According to Frutiger, further classic typefaces such as *Janson, Garamond* and *Baskerville* were implemented subsequently. In 1968, IBM was in a position to draw new typefaces that were suited to the technology of the Composer, which resulted in Frutiger's design for a semi-egyptienne, *'Delta'*.
According to Identifont, Adrian Frutiger also adapted the typewriter face *Courier* – designed by Howard Kettler in 1956 – for the IBM Selectric Series. – See www.identifont.com (accessed August 2007).
5 According to Frutiger's collected written memoirs.
6 Adrian Frutiger gave talks to IBM employees, for example in Southampton (England) in September 1967; Barcelona (Spain) in April 1968, and Milan (Italy) in September 1968.
7 During the 1980s, Frutiger was again asked to work for IBM, in this case in Sindelfingen (Germany). He had to check typefaces punched on film.
8 Besides traditional typewriters with monospace fonts, IBM had typewriters that use fonts with four or five units even before the Composer.
9 From *Der IBM Magnetband-Composer. Eine neue Technik der Satzherstellung*, IBM Germany, Sindelfingen (no date).

10 Golfballs in the following cuts and sizes were produced in *Univers* for the IBM Composer: Light 8, 10, 11 pt; Medium 7, 8, 10, 11 pt; Medium Italic 8, 10, 11 pt; Bold 8, 10, 11 pt; Light Condensed 10, 11, 12 pt; Medium Condensed 10, 11 and maybe 12 pt; Medium Italic Condensed 10, 11 pt; and Bold Condensed 10, 11, 12 pt.
11 Undated letter by Emil Ruder with the title "Qualities of 'Delta'". He wrote, "An adaptation of a book-printing face to typewriter faces. The beauties of a typewriter face with the qualities of a typeface for book printing. – Created for a typesetting system limited by 7 units. Not a limitation but a typical characteristic. – The technical aspects are paramount, thus a new aesthetic is created, a technical aesthetic that is exemplary of all typesetting machines. […] – With 'Delta', the formal characteristics based on language of the so-called national typefaces (Garamond, Baskerville, Bodoni et al.) have been overcome. This typeface has good legibility in the main languages without any limitations. […] – 'Delta' is based on the contemporary idea that form arises from material and technology".

Alphabet EDF-GDF →198
1 This chapter contains informationfrom a manuscript by Horst Heiderhoff for *form,* the German design magazine. It is an edited version of a 1975 text by Adrian Frutiger on the EDF-GDF project.
2 The conversation with Adrian Frutiger took place on 14 January 2002. In 2005 EDF reworked their company logo again: the capital E was replaced by a lowercase e and the blue rectangle by an orange, brushstroke-style sun positioned above the monogram.
3 In 1964 the Directorate General of EDF commissioned its department Service Création-Diffusion to develop a programme for a consistent corporate branding. It was planned to seek expert input from the areas of graphic design and architecture. Under the direction of Jacques Veuillet and Francis Boucrot, the architect Nicolas Karzis, the graphic designer Giulio Confalonieri, and the typographer Adrian Frutiger were involved. – See: Louis Flach, 'L'image de Firme d'Électricité de France EDF', in: *Contacts électriques,* No. 84, July 1970, page 10.
4 An internal memo titled 'Communiqué interne N° 7. Une nouvelle identité pour EDF' from 28 June 2005 features the 1958 EDF monogram with rounded corners and combined with two blue triangles.
5 Flyer by Électricité de France (title unknown, no date) from the archive of Swiss Foundation Type and Typography.

Katalog (type-design project) →202
1 From the typed 'Note sur le Cheltenham' it does not become clear what exactly had been reviewed. Erich Schulz-Anker, however, mentioned an inclined font and a possible true cursive, which seems to indicate that the latter did not yet exist.
2 The A4 sheet with the title 'Katalog (in Richtung Cheltenham)' bears the number 3 of a series of similar sheets with glued-on typeface designs – No. 1 is 'Serifen Grotesk' and No. 2 is 'Gespannte Grotesk'.
3 In a letter dated 15 March 1968 and addressed to Adrian Frutiger, Erich Schulz-Anker – art director of D. Stempel AG – mentioned the receipt of comparison sheets of *Candida, Excelsior* and *Melior.* In a further letter dated 11 December 1968 he wrote: "While I'm dictating this letter, the comparison sheets of your new newsprint face with *Excelsior, Melior* and *Candida* are being put on my desk […]." This book only shows a small excerpt from the comparison copies, which contain the complete set of glyphs in addition to the v.
4 Erich Schulz-Anker criticizes the newsprint face with the following words: "During a first superficial look through these sheets I made a few notes in the margins, which I shall repeat here without edits: 1) typeface altogether too fat. 2) x-heights decidedly too high (it's not about achieving a slim look but a narrow letter-spacing). 3) The rounded, short serifs give the typeface a somewhat 'squeezed' look. As far as Cheltenham is concerned, the rounded, stubby look is part of its character, therefore it does not create this impression. For the F-Type the drawings themselves are very exact – this might cause this optical illusion. By the way, the Cheltenham has very low x-heights." Erich Schulz-Anker continued to make the point that a newsprint face should be as unobtrusive as possible. It should appear neither too wide nor too narrow. The idea of using short serifs should be developed further when the typeface became finer and the x-heights lower.
5 In 1968 Arthur Ritzel designed *Rotation.* Linotype commissioned D. Stempel AG to manufacture the matrices for the setting machines. – See also: Philipp Bertheau (ed.), *Buchdruckschriften im 20. Jahrhundert,* Darmstadt 1995, page 531.
6 The four typeface designs set in the sample phrase 'une pomme du monde' are combined on a barite paper copy. On the copy bearing the handwritten note 'Konzept von 1969' the comparison line in *Méridien* is cut off.
7 The similarity with *Cheltenham* is not necessarily obvious since Adrian Frutiger's design is stronger with less stroke contrast. The relationship is, however, expressed in the short serifs and in the proportions of the characters – even though in Frutiger's design the ascenders and x-height are higher in relation to the cap height.
8 Most newsprint faces, apart from *Times New Roman* and *Rotation,* appear to be significantly wider indeed when compared to Frutiger's design.

Devanagari / Tamil →206
1 The idea for the founding of the National Design Institute goes back to Charles and Ray Eames. They were commissioned by the Indian government to suggest solutions for creating an industrialised and modern future for India without neglecting its traditions. In the Indian Report from 1958 they suggested, among other things, the establishmentof a state-sponsored design institute, which was founded in 1961 and subsequently became independent.
2 See *Poster Collection 07 – Armin Hofmann,* Baden 2003, page 72.
3 The exact number of script systems in India is difficult to establish because conflicting numbers can be found in the relevant literature. In his 1991 book *Universalgeschichte der Schrift,* Harald Haarmann mentions 19 officially recognised scripts for 14 officially recognised languages on page 523; on page 527, however, he speaks of 15 officially recognised languages. Eli Franco and Karin Preisendanz mention 11 scripts for 16 official languages in their article 'Die indischen Schriften' in *Der Turmbau zu Babel,* vol. IIIa, page 296. Mahendra Patel speaks of 11 scripts. On the currency notes 11 scripts are represented (in 13 languages), which is the number that can be found most often when looking at script representations in specialist journals. – See Harald Haarmann: *Universalgeschichte der Schrift,* Frankfurt 1991, pages 523, 527. Eli Franco, Karin Preisendanz: 'Die indischen Schriften', in *Der Turmbau zu Babel. Ursprung und Vielfalt von Sprache und Schrift,* vol. IIIa, Vienna 2003, page 296.
4 In Sanskrit, words are written together without any spaces but there are also exceptions from this rule.
5 The Calam is an Indian pen, made from a bamboo stick, the tip of which is cut flat at a special angle similar to a broad pen.
6 Adrian Frutiger: *Type Sign Symbol,* Zurich 1980, page 91.
7 Today called Varanasi.
8 First evidence of the Brāhmī script can be traced back to roughly the 3rd century BC. In the religious tradition of the Hindus, the genesis of this script is attributed to the god Brahmā. Indian scientists are trying to establish a derivation from the Indus script – an as yet not completely deciphered script that emerged at about 2400 BC in the Northwest of India and vanished again around 1500 BC. Any interim versions have not been discovered so far. German scientists have put forward the as yet most plausible thesis that India with its oral traditions (re)-developed its scripts only later on. The Kharoṣṭhī script, which only emerged shortly before the Brāhmī script, shows a clear relationship to the Aramaic script.
9 Over the course of time, increasingly more languages have been officially recognised in the Constitution. The first version of 1947 lists 13 languages, and currently there are 22; the latest addition is Maithilī, which was added in 2003.
10 Mahendra Patel: *Letters for Tomorrow.* Experiments in Type-Form Development. National Institute of Design, Ahmedabad, no date, page 3.
11 According to his email from 23 August 2005, Mahendra Patel worked in Adrian Frutiger's studio in Arcueil, near Paris, from December 1970 to January 1972.
12 Adrian Frutiger: 'Brief aus Indien', offprint from TM / STM, 6/7 1967.
13 Adrian Frutiger: *Type Sign Symbol,* Zurich 1980, page 92.

Alpha BP →214
1 The design studio was originally founded in 1962 by Alan Fletcher, Colin Forbes and Bob Gill. The latter left the company in 1965 and Theo Crosby became a new partner. From 1969 onwards Georg Staehelin ran the Zurich office. In 1972 Crosby, Fletcher, Forbes became Pentagram, with the addition of Kenneth Grange and Mervyn Kurlansky as partners. The firm subsequently established additional offices in New York c. 1976, San Francisco in the 1980s and Austin in the 1990s.
2 Heidrun Osterer held a conversation with Alan Fletcher on his cooperation with Adrian Frutiger on 6 April 2005 in Basel. During this conversation a telephone call with Colin Forbes also took place. Before this conversation a meeting was held with Georg Staehelin in Ottenbach near Zurich on 31 March 2005.
3 See: 'Identity design: Corporate programmes', in Pentagram: *Living by design*, London 1978, page 27 ff.
4 As Emil Ruder defined *Univers* as a universal typeface for all Latin languages and for all sorts of applications (see page 88), so Bauhaus master Herbert Bayer did likewise with *'Universal'.* In 1925/26 Bayer designed several variations of his single-case alphabet. The designs partly bear handwritten notes, in which the greater context of this typeface is explained. Bayer saw the constructed shape of the type as universally applicable to different typesetting technologies, and also as a 'world type' for 'supra-national communication'. – See: Ute Brüning, 'Zur Typographie Herbert Bayers', in *Herbert Bayer – Das künstlerische Werk 1918–1938,* Berlin 1982, page 118 ff.
5 This also differentiates Adrian Frutiger's typeface from the 1964 corporate type of American oil giant Mobil designed by the studio Chermayeff & Geismar (New York) and based on *Futura.* – See www.cgstudionyc.com (accessed June 2008).

Documenta →218
1 The exclusivity of the typeface is debatable. It is listed in the brochure *Lintoype Fotosatz Schriften – im 18-Einheiten-System für Linocomp, Linofilm VIP und Linotron* by Mergenthaler Linotype and could thus be ordered. A note in pencil dates the brochure to 1974.
2 Telephone conversation between Heidrun Osterer and Fritz Sutter on 28 May 2001.
3 The working title features a k for *Documenta;* in the published brochure, however, it is written using a c, which is why we have adopted this version. – See *Linotype Fotosatz Schriften – im 18-Einheiten-System für Linocomp, Linofilm VIP und Linotron,* Eschborn, Germany, approx. 1974.
4 The widths of the individual glyphs of Linotype faces for phototypesetting were originally between 5 and 18 units. With *Documenta* all glyphs were set to the same width of 12 units.
5 According to Fritz Sutter, *Documenta* was used in the printing of documents for the construction of the motorway through the St Gotthard Tunnel; furthermore it was used in the printing of share price listings, as well as for radio and television programmes.

Alphabet Facom →220
1 Bruno Pfäffli, initially an employee of Atelier Frutiger, and from 1974 onwards co-owner of Atelier Frutiger & Pfäffli, designed and laid out the 200- to 350-page catalogues. Adrian Frutiger designed the catalogue covers and the corporate typeface for Facom. Also for Facom, Adrian Frutiger implemented a 'Kunst am Bau' piece (art within architecture). A marble relief 9 metres long (about 29.5 feet) was installed in the foyer of the factory in Morangis (France). – See Erich Alb (ed.): *Adrian Frutiger – Forms and counterforms,* Cham 1998, page 100.
2 The French tool manufacturer Facom (established in 1918) was one of the first clients of the newly founded Atelier Frutiger. André Mosès, son of the company founder Louis Mosès, took over the company in 1924. He died 50 years later, and presumably the cooperation with Atelier Frutiger & Pfäffli ended with his death. Therefore, afterwards only the anniversary catalogue from 1978 features a cover designed by Frutiger.
3 In a conversation with the editors (23 July 2001), Bruno Pfäffli mentioned that the contact was established via the company Victor-Michel, photolithography and text setting.
4 Adrian Frutiger's remarks probably relate to the Facom catalogue F67 (1964) or maybe to the later F68 catalogue (1967). The latter was set in *Univers* and not yet in *Alphabet Facom.* Heavily stylised contour drawings can already be found in earlier catalogues but the F64 catalogue (1960) was set in *Antique Olive Nord* and *Gill Sans.*
5 Facom's director came across Frutiger's exclusive typeface for EDF and also commissioned a corporate typeface, according to Bruno Pfäffli in a conversation with the editors (23 July 2001).
6 Lucette Girard designed the logo while working for Agence Raymond Loewy in Paris. It was not yet part of the Facom catalogue F64 (1960) but it was definitely featured on the cover of the F67 catalogue. As opposed to the pictogram version on page 221 (reproduced from a letterhead dated 11 May 1984), only half of the centreline is cut diagonally in the original version.
7 In reply to an inquiry by Adrian Frutiger, Günter Gerhard Lange wrote in a letter dated 22 June 1983 that, after ten years, there were no more original drawings and papers from the Facom project. It is not clear from that letter why Frutiger had asked for the original artwork and documentation. – The letter is archived at Swiss Foundation Type and Typography.
8 See www.facom.fr/fr/index.htm (November 2007).
9 In 1974, the Facom catalogue offered more than 4000 items. See www.facom.de (September 2007).

10 Horst Heiderhoff reports comprehensively on the typographic organisation of the Facom tool catalogue by Atelier Frutiger & Pfäffli, Paris. Described and pictured is the F73 catalogue (1973). – See HORST HEIDERHOFF: 'Der Katalog als didaktischer Mittler zwischen Angebot und Nachfrage' in form, 1975-III-71, page 19 ff.
11 ibid, p.19.
12 ibid, p. 23.

Alphabet Roissy →224

1 The colour expert was Jacques Filacier, a French interior designer.
2 In addition to the people named in the text and Jacques Filacier, the French designer J. A. Motte was responsible for the interior design. – See ADRIAN FRUTIGER: 'The Signage of Paris-Roissy Airport', in TM/STM, 1/1977, page 9.
3 ADRIAN FRUTIGER, HORST HEIDERHOFF: ‚Das Beschriftungssystem des größten Flughafens Europas – Der neue "Aéroport Charles de Gaulle" in Roissy', in form. Zeitschrift für Gestaltung, No. III-67, 1974, page 25 ff.
4 See ADRIAN FRUTIGER: 'The Signage of Paris-Roissy Airport' in TM/STM, 1/1977, page 9 ff.
5 See ERICH ALB (ed.): Adrian Frutiger – Forms and counterforms, Cham 1998, page 100 ff.
6 The association with Assistance Publique (the social services and the orphanages or shelters for the poor) was so strong that the employees of the airport threatened to go on strike rather than wear their uniforms bearing the AP monogram. – According to Bruno Pfäffli in a conversation with the editors on 23 July 2001.
7 Bruno Pfäffli designed typographic illustrations, for instance in the shapes of a sun or snow crystals. Additionally, there were abstracted geographic maps showing flight connections. – See ADRIAN FRUTIGER, BRUNO PFÄFFLI: 'Neugestaltung des Air-France-Flugplans', in TM/STM, 1/1971, page 9 ff.
8 See WALTER DIETHELM: Signet Signal Symbol, Zurich 1970, page 32.
9 Initially used exclusively for the Paris airports, the signage face was adopted by Jean Widmer (1972), another successful Swiss designer in Paris, for the brown tourist information boards along the French motorways.
10 ADRIAN FRUTIGER: 'The Signage of Paris-Roissy Airport', in TM/STM, 1/1977, page 11.
11 ADRIAN FRUTIGER: 'The Signage of Paris-Roissy Airport', in TM/STM, 1/1977, page 13.
12 The handwritten sheet '17. Mai 79 – Corrections Alphabet Roissy' is archived at Swiss Foundation Type and Typography.

Alphabet Brancher →230

1 In an email (8 March 2005) Bruno Pfäffli wrote that the name 'Brancher' has eight letters and that their colour fan 'Multiset 500' contains eight base colours. It was therefore an obvious solution to use the eight base colours for the eight letters.
2 Quoted from a manuscript by Horst Heiderhoff (14 August 1975) that referred to the articles 'Facom', 'Brancher' and 'EDF' for the magazine form. The basis for the heavily-edited text was a manuscript by Adrian Frutiger. – Both manuscripts are archived at Swiss Foundation Type and Typography.
3 Erich Alb, Rudolf Barmettler and Philipp Stamm in conversation with Adrian Frutiger (14 January 2002) on the topic of his corporate typefaces.
4 Frutiger's serif jobbing type Algol from 1963 (see page 160) also follows the same style. Not following this style, however, is the 1968 corporate typeface Alpha BP for British Petroleum Co. Its round style was determined by the clients' guidelines (see page 214).
5 Examples of corporate typefaces with a rectangular base shape for O: majuscule and minuscule alphabet for 3M (USA), 1961 based on Georg Trump's City (1931), designer not known. See Design Industrie, No. 84–85/1967, page 22, No. 87/1969, page 19. – Minuscule alphabet for Berliet (France) before 1962, designer not known. See Esthétique Industrielle, No. 56-57/1962, page 44. – Majuscule alphabet for IBM (USA), 1966 by Paul Rand; also based on City. See Design Industrie, No. 81/1966, page 23. – Majuscule alphabet for Benrus Watch Company (USA), 1967 by Rudolph de Harak. See HENRI HILLEBRAND (ed.): große designer in der werbegraphik, vol. 6, Munich 1971, page 117.
6 Adrian Frutiger listed these implementations of the logo in an undated manuscript. – The manuscript is archived at Swiss Foundation Type and Typography.
7 In the modified wordmark 'Brancher' the letters are narrower and therefore less aesthetic; the now symmetrical N is not as clearly recognisable. The stylised beehive is slightly smaller and more restrained. – See www.brancher.com (October 2007).

Iridium →234

1 See GEORG KURT SCHAUER, Chronik der Schriftgiesserei D. Stempel AG, Frankfurt a. M. – Sechzig Jahre im Dienste der Lettern. 1895-1955, Frankfurt am Main 1954. The company chronicle was continued until 2001 and can be accessed at: http://www.systemarchitektur.de/stempel/ChronikStempel.pdf (October 2007).
2 Linotype Germany only started the manufacture of phototypesetting machines in 1967, as opposed to Mergenthaler Linotype in the USA, who had launched their first Linofilm machine as early as 1954.
3 In an interview by Kurt Kohlhammer with Dr Walter Greisner it says in a caption that the camera was mounted on a 16 tonne granite block measuring 300 by 200 by 60 cm. – See 'D. Stempel AG: Auch die Zukunft der Schrift steht auf zwei Beinen, dem Bleisatz und dem Fotosatz', in Deutscher Drucker, No. 19, 15 May 1975, page 6.
4 See Brockhaus Enzyklopädie in vierundzwanzig Bänden, 19th, revised edition, vol. 10, Mannheim 1991, page 631.
5 Scangraphic has a less noble name for their copy of Iridium: Iron. – See LAWRENCE W. WALLIS, Modern Encyclopedia of Typefaces 1960-90, London 1990, page 91.
6 See 'D. Stempel AG mit Auftragseingängen zufrieden', in Deutscher Drucker, 6 June 1968, page X.
7 See 'Linotype GmbH: 1970 brachte Erfolgsrekord', in Deutscher Drucker, 3 December 1970, page VIII.
8 Conversation between the authors and Dr Walter Greisner on 12 August 2002.
9 Linotype used duplex type matrices: each glyph exists in two different fonts of one typeface per matrix. This allows for type differentiation within a document, without having to change the matrix drum. Usually, either the regular and italic, or the regular and semibold fonts were combined.
10 Rubylith film (also known as Ulano film after its manufacturer) consists of a transparent back sheet, which is covered by a thinner, red-coloured foil that is UV-safe. A scalpel is used to cut shapes into the red membrane, and the parts that need to be exposed are then peeled off.
11 See ERICH SCHULZ-ANKER, 'Iridium-Antiqua – eine spezifische Fotosatzschrift auf klassizistischer Basis', in Deutscher Drucker, No. 14, 12 April 1973, page 22. – In Typografische Monatsblätter 5/1973, page 410.
12 As opposed to typefaces for mechanical and electronic phototypesetting, where usually only one design size exists (optimised for 12 pt as was the case with Iridium, or 18 pt), typefaces for hand composition are cut in a different manner for the various sizes. The small sizes are wider, have a greater x-height and less stroke contrast, which improves legibility. The large sizes are designed in a more condensed style and appear finer. Exceptions to this can be found with some neoclassical typefaces, since a loss in quality would be most obvious in these. For example, Bauer Bodoni was offered by Linotype in 1987 in the design sizes 8, 12 and 18 pt. – See LinoTypeCollection. Mergenthaler Type Library, 1987, page 38 and page 274 ff.
13 In France, the neoclassical typefaces Bodoni and Didot were still used frequently in book printing in the mid-20th century, this was true of Bodoni in the USA from 1910 on; but not of Didot, which was barely used until the 1990s. In Germany the use of typefaces from the renaissance antiqua group was more common.
14 In 1895, David Stempel founded a company in Frankfurt am Main (Germany) for the manufacture of spacing material for hand composition and plates for book printing. In 1897, he took over the first foundry – more were to follow – and his brother-in-law, the engineer Wilhelm Cunz, joined the company, becoming co-owner the following year. From 1900 onwards, matrices for Linotype machines were produced. – See GEORG KURT SCHAUER, Chronik der Schriftgiesserei D. Stempel AG, Frankfurt a. M. – Sechzig Jahre im Dienste der Lettern. 1895-1955, Frankfurt am Main 1954.
15 German Linotype GmbH introduced its first phototypesetting machine, the Linofilm-Europa, only in 1970. At American Mergenthaler Linotype Company the age of phototypesetting had already started in 1954 with the Linofilm-System. This was followed in 1964 by the Linofilm-Quick, in 1968 by the Linofilm-Super-Quick, and in 1970 by the Linofilm VIP. Early cathode ray (CRT) machines for phototypesetting were developed with the advent of the American Linotron 1010 (1965) and Linotron 505 (1967) by English sister company Linotype-Paul Ltd. – See LAWRENCE W. WALLIS, A Concise Chronology of Typesetting Developments 1886-1986, Severn, Worcestershire.
16 Arthur Ritzel (1910-2002) was a master craftsman in punchcutting and type cutting.
From 1963 onwards he headed the department for typeface design and punchcutting at D. Stempel AG. In 1971 he designed Rotation, a typeface for newspaper use.

17 Hans Gutenberg Stempel, son of company founder David Stempel, joined the company in 1925, followed by Walter H. Cunz, son of co-owner Wilhelm Cunz, in 1927. – See GEORG KURT SCHAUER, Chronik der Schriftgiesserei D. Stempel AG Frankfurt a. M., 1954. – PHILIPP BERTHEAU, EVA HANEBUTT-BENZ, HANS REICHARDT, Buchdruckschriften im 20. Jahrhundert, Darmstadt 1995, page 571 ff.
18 The following typefaces (among others) by Hermann Zapf were released by D. Stempel AG: Gilgengart, completed in 1941 but only published in 1950; Novalis Antiqua 1947 (cut in metal but never issued); Palatino Antiqua 1948; Michelangelo 1950; Sistina 1951; Virtuosa, Melior and Saphir 1952, Kompakt, Linotype Aldus and Linotype Mergenthaler Antiqua 1954; Optima 1958; and Noris Script 1976. Mergenthaler Linotype Company in New York issued (among others): Linofilm Venture 1969 and Linofilm Medici 1971. – See KNUT ERICHSON, JOHN DREYFUS (eds): ABC-XYZapf. Fünfzig Jahre Alphabet Design, Offenbach / London 1989, page 251.
19 Erich Schulz-Anker's article on Iridium-Antiqua was published in a number of German-language professional journals: Druck Print 3/1973, page 160 ff., Deutscher Drucker, No. 14, 12 April 1973, page 22, Typografische Monatsblätter 5/1973, page 410.

Translation of the article: 'Iridium-Antiqua: A Typeface Conceived Specifically for Phototypesetting'

As far as text type is concerned, the brand new photosetting technology has so far been limited to the adoption of existing typefaces for hot metal setting into the photoset type programme. Soon, however, it became apparent that any direct adoption was not going to produce satisfactory results. Typefaces that had been designed for a different technology, had to be reworked and adapted to the new technologies and materials. The manner of the adoption, and the extent to which a type was adopted, were dependent on the specific structure of the glyphs, i.e. the style of the typeface. Some typefaces are particularly sensitive when it comes to changes caused by reproduction in photosetting. This is particularly true for typefaces that feature a strong contrast between thin and bold weights, for example those in the style of a Bodoni, Walbaum or Didot Antiqua.

The task of making a neoclassical antiqua suitable for photosetting cannot be solved by simply adapting a pre-existing type. Hence D. Stempel AG has opted for a different solution right from the start and, with Iridium by Adrian Frutiger (Paris), has developed and released a classical type that has been specially designed for photosetting. Thus, the designer was in a position to work towards a solution suited for photosetting right from the inception of the design and could produce appropriate drawings.

In contrast to hot metal setting, many phototypesetting systems render the entire point size range that can be produced with a specific machine by scaling up or down one character size. To continue to guarantee a true reproduction of all sizes of a classical typeface with its typical richness in stroke contrast, it is, however, necessary to carefully ascertain and define stroke relationships through preliminary experiments. For the development of Iridium, the perfectly equipped manufacturing labs of D. Stempel AG were used for this purpose. Under these optimal conditions, in combination with the very close cooperation between Adrian Frutiger and the in-house experts, it was thus possible to achieve a solution suitable for phototypesetting from the very inception of the design.

The concept of Iridium

However, the special task that Frutiger had set himself with Iridium went beyond even that: it referred to the expression and the feel of the typeface. In terms of construction, classical types are often rather strict, sober and cool. The aim was to mellow these characteristics in Iridium.

The razor-sharp reproduction of glyphs in phototypesetting, however, exactly reinforces the impression that was to be deliberately avoided in this case. Therefore, this effect had to be clearly counterbalanced by suitable means. Frutiger solved the problem in two ways: first, through a suitable shape construction and additionally through manually cutting the large reproduction templates himself.

The concept of Iridium: in accordance with the overall aim of the design, the starting point was the classical base shape with its elegant expression. In comparison to its historical predecessors, the x-height of Iridium is increased slightly, giving a slightly taller appearance, the ductus is less strict and all form characteristics are finely balanced. This is true for the basic strokes as well as for the transitions in weight, the delicate connecting elements and the terminating serifs. What is true for the details of this typeface is also true for its overall structure and expression: the appearance of Iridium features the clarity and elegance of a classical typeface while displaying a pleasant suppleness.

The qualities of a typeface for photosetting are based not solely on the concept and the drawings but also on the adequate implementation of the reproduction templates. With Iridium, the designer himself took on the production of the large templates, called friskets. This means that Adrian Frutiger cut out the glyphs himself following the corrected initial drawings. He cut them manually out of the usual two-layered film. Thus, the final design is clearly informed by the designer's intentions and his hand guiding the tool.
With Iridium, D. Stempel AG has delivered a modern version of the classical typeface character that is suited for photosetting. It is available in three sets of thin, oblique and semibold for the phototypesetting machines from Mergenthaler-Linotype. *Erich Schulz-Anker*

20 See Friedrich Friedl, Nicolaus Ott, Bernard Stein (eds), *Typographie – when who how,* Cologne 1998, page 275 ff.
21 See Adrian Frutiger, Horst Heiderhoff, 'Das Beschriftungssystem des grössten Flughafens Europas – Der neue "Aéroport Charles de Gaulle" in Roissy' in *form. Zeitschrift für Gestaltung,* 1974-III-67, page 25 ff. – Horst Heiderhoff, 'Der Katalog als didaktischer Mittler zwischen Angebot und Nachfrage' in *form,* 1975-III-71, page 19 ff. – Horst Heiderhoff, 'Formen und Gegenformen. Gestaltungseinheiten im Leben des Schriftkünstlers Adrian Frutiger' in *Gutenberg-Jahrbuch 1985,* Mainz 1985, page 29 ff.
22 Adrian Frutiger talks about this in the handwritten notes to his memoirs, page 45 ff.
23 When asked, Bruno Pfäffli stated that Adrian Frutiger hardly did any teaching after 1966. Bruno Pfäffli himself took over Frutiger's teaching committments.
24 The second, reworked and extended edition was published in 1989 by Fourier as a single volume and set in the computer font *Linotype Centennial.* In 2004, the 9th edition of the book was published, this time at Marix-Verlag. It has been translated into six languages (Spanish, English, Italian, Portuguese, French and Korean).
25 Autologic Switzerland and USA (formerly known as Bobst Graphic Lausanne) took over André Gürtler's *Basilia* in 1977. It turned out, however, that it had to be re-designed for phototypesetting, which is why it was only published one year later. In 1984 Linotype added *Basilia* to its range of typefaces. – See André Gürtler, *'Basilia – eine klassizistische Type' in Officina. Mitteilungen des Hauses Schwabe & Co. AG,* Basel, November 1989, page 27 ff.

Alphabet Métro →244
1 The extensive picture gallery of the London Transport Museum bears witness to the beginnings of the London Underground. – See www.ltmcollection.org/photos/index.html (july 2008).
2 Edward Johnston (1872–1944) was a calligrapher, type designer, teacher and author. In 1906 his authoritative textbook *Writing and Illuminating and Lettering* appeared. This was translated into German by his pupil Anna Simons under the title *Schreibschrift, Zierschrift & angewandte Schrift* in 1910. Type designs: *Hamlet-Type* 1912–1927, *Imprint Antiqua* (with E. Jackson, G. Meynell and J. H. Mason) 1913, and *Johnston Railway Sans* 1916.
3 In 1979, *Johnston Railway Sans* was re-worked by Eiichi Kono of Banks & Miles into *New Johnston,* and was extended to 9 weights. Two weights (book and book italic) were added later by the Banks & Miles design office. – Cf. Max Caflisch, *Schriftanalysen,* vol. 2, St. Gallen 2003, page 7 ff.
4 Hector Guimard (1867–1942) was a leading French exponent of the Art Nouveau movement.

Alphabet Centre Georges Pompidou →248
1 Jean Widmer trained at the Kunstgewerbeschule Zürich (Zurich School of Arts and Crafts) and then moved to Paris in 1953 to work as an art director and graphic designer. He opened the Jean Widmer studio in 1970, which was renamed Visual Design Association (VDA) in 1974 when Ernst Hiestand joined (due to the competition for Centre Georges Pompidou). After Hiestand left, the name was changed again to Visuel Design. From 1961 until 1995 Widmer was a teacher at the École Nationale Supérieure des Arts Décoratifs in Paris.
2 Ernst Hiestand trained at the Kunstgewerbeschule Zürich. From 1980 to 1986 he was director of graphic design at the school. He currently lives and works in Zurich.
3 Based on an initiative by president Georges Pompidou, the Centre Pompidou was developed by the architects Richard Rogers and Renzo Piano, who won the 1971 competition. After a six-year building period the Centre opened in 1977. Its complete official name, which was rarely used in full, was Centre national d'art et de culture Georges Pompidou. The Centre itself used the short form Centre Georges Pompidou in its publications. In 1999, along with the redesign of the corporate identity by Intégral Ruedi Baur et associés, the name was shortened to Centre Pompidou.
4 The naming of the typeface is not totally clear. Both the working title and the official name are still used today. According to Catherine de Smet, the names are used on a case by case basis. – See Catherine de Smet, 'Histoire d'un rectangle rayé. Jean Widmer et le logo du Centre Pompidou', in: *Les Cahiers du Musée national d'art moderne,* No. 89, Autumn 2004, page 15). According to Hans-Jürg Hunziker, the name of the typeface is *Centre Georges Pompidou, CGP* and *Beaubourg* is only an unofficial name. Frutiger consistently calls it *Alphabet Beaubourg* and in the design guidelines for the 1999 redesign of the corporate identity it is called *Beaubourg*.
5 Frutiger refers to the IBM Machine de Direction, which is called the IBM Executive Typewriter in English, an electric typewriter, which had typefaces with four units. The machine had been available since 1946.
6 Frutiger's manuscript 'Alphabet Beaubourg' was attached to a letter by Marc Piel from Groupe ENFI Design dated 10 February 1978, in which it was being returned to him.
7 Adrian Frutiger was also invited to submit a proposal. However his proposal, developed together with Leen Averink, was rejected in the first round.
8 One of the tasks for those taking part in the competition was to comment on the question of whether the Centre needed a logo. Many of the participating agencies responded by suggesting that a logo was not necessary because at that time, after the events of 1968, logos were seen as symbols for commercial activities and therefore incompatible with the mission of a cultural institution. Shortly before the Centre's opening, however, an argument about this point broke out among the Centre's management, and in 1977 Jean Widmer designed the later well-known 'stripes' logo, the shape of which is based on the building's facade.
9 The basic elements of the wayfinding system are the typeface, the colours, the vertical direction and the verbal constants. The colours are assigned according to the following system: yellow for the Centre itself and grey for the head office. Each of its four departments has its own color: green stands for the 'Bibliothèque publique d'information', blue for the 'Centre de Création Industrielle' (CCI), purple for the 'Institut de Recherche et de Coordination Acoustique / Musique' (IRCAM) and red for the 'Musée national d'art moderne'.
10 Catherine de Smet gives a detailed account of the development of the visual concept for Centre Georges Pompidou including the story of the competition. – See Catherine de Smet, 'Histoire d'un rectangle rayé. Jean Widmer et le logo du Centre Pompidou', in: *Les Cahiers du Musée national d'art moderne,* No. 89, Autumn 2004, page 6 ff.
11 Hans-Jörg Hunziker worked at Frutiger's studio from 1971 to 1975. After that he followed this project and joined Centre Pompidou in order to work on the implementation and further development of the corporate design defined by Visuel Design. After the Centre's opening in 1977, he established an in-house studio and in the same year he set up his own studio in Paris. – See Hans-Jürg Hunziker, *Siemens. Brand Notebook 1. Our Typeface,* Munich 2001, page 37 ff.
12 The transfer characters were manufactured at Mecanorma. There were individual glyphs as well as the complete names of the departments and the Centre itself, which – set as complete words and justified – could be applied directly.
13 On the occasion of the Centre's 20th anniversary in 1995, the typeface was extended by a bold version and the overall character set was extended.
14 On the website of Centre Pompidou it says in point 11. Identité visuelle: '– la typographie (le DIN et le caractère Beaubourg)'. – See www.centrepompidou.fr/rapport99/index.htm (December 2007).

Frutiger →250
1 Hans-Jürg Hunziker achieved further renown, particularly for his exclusive typeface family for Siemens. – See *Siemens Brand Notebook 1 – Our Typeface,* Munich 2001.
2 See Font Shop, *100 Best Typefaces of all Time,* Berlin 2007. www.100besteschriften.de (January 2008).
3 According to the author and expert Silvia Werfel, from 2005 the newspaper *Trouw* has used Gerard Unger's typeface *Swift*.
4 In his book *Frutiger: Die Wandlung eines Schriftklassikers* and in an interview in *typeforum,* Erik Faulhaber conveys the impression that the idea and the total development of *Frutiger Next* came from him. On the 23 February 2006, in a response to the interview, Linotype's Bruno Steinert said, "… Without this follow-up, many of the countless admirers of Frutiger's typefaces would have believed that Faulhaber (with Adrian Frutiger as his mentor) had created Frutiger Next. And that's not exactly the case … Mr Faulhaber has little claim on Frutiger Next, and can, in no way, make the assertion that the initiative or the sole authorship was his alone, although he certainly made a contribution; that can't be denied." – See 'Interview: Faulhaber's Transformation of Frutiger', at www.typeforum.de/news_254.htm (January 2008).
5 See Erik Faulhaber, *Frutiger: Die Wandlung eines Schriftklassikers,* Sulgen / Zurich 2004, page 60.
6 Also in 1985, Adrian Frutiger additionally produced the Cyrillic version of *Frutiger* in 14 weights. – See Linotype Typeface Catalogue A–Z, Bad Homburg 2006.
7 The drawings for the regular-width typefaces were given the designation *Roissy.* These were later crossed out and replaced with the name *Frutiger.* The rights to *Alphabet Roissy* were held by Aéroports de Paris ADP, the airport operating company.
8 According to Walter Greisner, alongside the legal reasons, linguistic reasons were also decisive. The French name was never given much consideration, since it is difficult for English speakers to pronounce.
9 See *Linotype Library – Schriftenhandbuch,* PostScript typefaces, Linotype AG, Eschborn bei Frankfurt 1988.
10 Apart from *Ondine,* Adrian Frutiger's earlier typefaces – *Méridien, Univers, Egyptienne F* and *Apollo* – all have the soft curved shape of the esszett, which developed from the ss-ligature. When Adrian Frutiger first produced a typeface for a German foundry – *Serifa* – he changed to the harder shape, which was based on the sz-ligature. Only *Linotype Didot,* a French typeface, and *Nami,* which goes back to the earlier type design *Delta,* still have this curved shape. Adrian Frutiger's statement is surprising, however, because with *Univers* he proved that even in the black font, a good, curved ligature is possible.
11 See Kurt Winterhager, 'Zur Frutiger-Schrift', in *form,* 95-III-1981, page 1. In the same issue Kurt Weidemann wrote an introduction with the title 'Zu Adrian Frutiger'.
12 The re-design of *form* was documented in a separate, 58-page supplement. It containes, amongst other things, an interview with Adrian Frutiger, as well as an article about Lucas de Groot and the interpolated *F Frutiger* Book. – See Andreas Liedtke, Lucas de Groot, 'Befragt: Adrian Frutiger, Schriftentwerfer. "Ich bin der Backsteinbrenner"', in: *form 150 Dossier reform,* 2/1995, page 47 ff. – Ines Wagemann, 'Mit Hilfe mathematischer Formeln', ibid. page 50.
13 Reinhard Haus to Dr Stückradt: 'Concerning the Frutiger design for the magazine form' (internal memo, Linotype-Hell, 25 August 1995).
14 By evaluating the intermediate cuts of *Frutiger* while under contract to Studio Dumbar, Lucas de Groot developed his interpolation model. Also on behalf of the agency, de Groot created *Corpid* (originally *Agrofont*) for a Dutch government ministry. The previous corporate typeface *Frutiger* was the starting point for the new typeface, whose stroke weights and proportions recall *Frutiger* 55. Additionally, de Groot was contracted as type director at Meta Design in Berlin, where he worked on *FF Transit,* a variant of *Frutiger,* for the Berlin Transport authorities. – See Jan Middendorp, *Dutch Type,* page 219 ff.
15 Kurt Wälti was responsible for the design and signage on Swiss postal vehicles, as a member of the advertising department of the Swiss post office. He decided, after visiting one of the seminars given by Adrian Frutiger at the Bern School of Design from 31 January to 4 February 1977, to propose the *Frutiger* typeface to his employers. From 1978 onwards, this typeface was applied to all postal vehicles. From 1980 on, the Swiss PTT also took on *Frutiger* for the signage on its post office counters before, in 1993, it was finally adopted as the typeface for the entire organisation. Through Kurt Wälti, Adrian Frutiger also received the contract to redesign the post office's logo. In contrast to the 1969 version by the graphic designer Werner Mühlemann, Frutiger curled the posthorn in a different way, closing the winding to the mouth of the horn and detaching the mouthpiece (see page 316). Kurt Wälti quoted Frutiger as saying: "Since the character of the horn is derived, naturally, from the end where the sound comes out." Frutiger was also given the brief to redesign the logo of the PTT. The design from 1976, by in-house graphic designer Martin Altenburger was reworked, and the three letters PTT redrawn and positioned offset from the open-ended cross (see page 316). This striking logo replaced the previous coat-of-arms emblem from 1982 onwards. In 1997 Wälti and Frutiger worked together one more time on the wordmarks LA POSTE DIE POST LA POSTA (see page 406). – Information from 'Document collection of Kurt Wälti' 7 December 2007. – See also Adrian Frutiger, *Ein Leben für die Schrift,* Interlaken 2003, page 106 ff.
16 Conversation, 25 March 2002 between Adrian Frutiger, Erich Alb, Rudolf Barmettler and Philipp Stamm.
17 *Linotype Ergo,* by Gary Munch, was brought into the Linotype range in 1997; *Linotype Projekt,* by Andreas Koch, was added in 1999.

18 In an internal memo from 7 October 1993 with comparison strings, Linotype-Hell's Reinhard Haus wrote: "The typeface 'Myriad', from Adobe is, from an aesthetic overall impression, a copy of our 'Frutiger'. Certainly, Adobe has no doubt figured out that they should equip this copy with 'Myriad', minimal changes in form and an altered proportionality […] Certainly, in the whole concept of 'Myriad', the intent is absolutely clear, with this copy, to ride on the coattails of the success of our 'Frutiger' typeface, which is used the world over." Adobe had to be contacted later, since on 2 February 1993, a letter was sent to Adrian Frutiger, detailing the individuality of *Myriad*. The letter was signed by Fred Brady, manager of New Typographic Development, and by the two type designers, Robert Slimbach and Carol Twombly.

19 Handwritten observations by Adrian Frutiger on a Linotype-Hell internal memo from 7 October 1992.

20 Akira Kobayashi is a type designer, and has since 2001 been the artistic director of Linotype GmbH.

21 Erik Faulhaber wrote, "My employers [Linotype Library GmbH] want, as a bonus for the market, a true cursive. Even though Adrian Frutiger has distanced himself from this development, it will be pushed through." It did not remain a bonus typeface, but became part of the standard family. – See Erik Faulhaber, *Frutiger: Die Wandlung eines Schriftklassikers,* Sulgen / Zurich 2004, page 76.

22 Fax from 7 April 1999 from Adrian Frutiger to Linotype: "Dear friends, I am looking at the cursive version by Silja Bilz. It is a beautiful, refined version. I see however, the following snags: for one thing, in my opinion, a grotesque with a written appearance is only conceivable in narrow and normal – in heavier versions the typeface loses its charm. – For another, a version like this would only be a minor contribution to the whole family. – I'm thinking of gaps in the market. The market is at saturation point with regular typefaces. I found these lines in my old papers. But I'm no longer of the generation that's willing to try new things. – Forgive the criticism. Kind regards, Adrian F."

23 Letter dated 14 April 1999 from Adrian Frutiger to Linotype's Bruno Steinert: "Dear Herr Steinert, a week ago, Reinhard Haus asked me to take part in a project from one of his students for a livelier *Frutiger* cursive. My faxed answer must not have been satisfactory, since I have heard nothing more. I permitted myself to express my long-held opinions concerning gaps in the market. I think that it is correct to base the education of young people on existing, good typefaces. – I have, therefore, the feeling that the coming generation – well-schooled and versed in the rules of legibility – should seek out new directions. The possibilities are by no means exhausted. I'm not thinking for the moment of all the goings-on with exotic typefaces, but rather of typefaces with which text can be set, since these are the bread and butter of a company like yours (ours, I should say). I have searched amongst my many old papers for thoughts in this direction. Unfortunately I have found not much more than all the putative ideas that were argued about in the Type Selection meetings. I have some (unfortunately bad) copies that I have stuck together and enclose herewith. – I am doing this, not in the hope that something should come of it – I don't want to 'foist' any new typefaces on anyone! I'd just like to give a signpost, to point out the new directions in typography, in which I can steer young people. – I don't want to hurt anyone's feelings – just take it as a simple exchange of ideas. – With friendly greetings to you, Herr Steinert, to your wife and to all our co-workers. I remain, cordially yours, A. Frutiger."

24 A third sheet is attached to the two-page letter, with various typeface designs for *Delta* (see page 36) and the sans serif design *Dolmen,* which had already been worked into two weights, but which eventually never made it to market (see page 296).

25 In the detail comparisons in this book, the roman font of *Frutiger LT* is not compared to the regular, but to the medium typeface of *Frutiger Next,* since their stroke weights are more similar.

26 *Frutiger Next Pro* is an OpenType version by Linotype with an extended character set. The type family is also available as Central European Font CE with the accents for East European languages.

27 Time and again, appeals have been made to the sense of fair play of the typeface user, and that is the case even today. A few examples: ATypI was founded in 1957 to bring type producers and users together and to establish a 'moral code' in typographical relations. Linotype-Hell AG published an undated pamphlet titled 'Typography between Art and Commerce', in which examples of two Linotype typefaces were given, and in which it was explained how demanding it is to develop an alphabet, what intellectual piracy is, and what the consequences of it are. In 1992, FontShop International launched, together with other type houses, an education campaign with the title 'Kulturgut Schrift' (Type as a cultural good) and in 2000 produced the brochure *'Alles was Recht ist'* (Legitimate use), which appeared in a third, completely re-edited edition in 2001.

28 *Syntax Antiqua* had its dynamic form principle in common with Renaissance Antiqua. The difference lies in the variation of stroke weight with serifs in the Renaissance Antiqua, in contrast to the uniform stroke weight without serifs in *Syntax Antiqua*. Erich Schulz-Anker oustandingly traced and explained the historical development of the Renaissance Antiqua [Venetian old-style roman] to the Classical Antiqua [Neoclassical roman], and further to conventional linear typefaces (static grotesques) and to *Syntax Antiqua*. – See Erich Schulz-Anker: *Formanalyse und Dokumentation einer serifenlosen Linearschrift auf neuer Basis: Syntax-Antiqua*, D. Stempel AG, Frankfurt am Main, 1969.

29 In 1976, the serif typeface *Demos* was the first from the Dutch type designer Gerard Unger for the CRT technology of the Dr. Ing. Rudolf Hell company in Kiel. This was followed in 1977 by the sans serif typeface *Praxis* and, in 1984, by the almost perpendicular sans serif italic, *Flora*. – See Jan Middendorp, *Dutch Type,* Rotterdam, 1976, page 167 ff.

30 VSS is the Swiss body for road and traffic specialists. In 1993 a VSS expert committee decided on the reworking of the constructed VSS typeface. Adrian Frutiger was approached and cast a critical eye over the existing typefaces and showed, using certain changes in letter shape, how the legibility of the signage could be bettered. The VSS took its time coming to a decision, and in 1998, when Frutiger was again approached, he turned down the offer of further collaboration.

31 The ASTRA Federal Roads Agency was founded in 1998.

32 Viktor Stampfli worked from 1973 to 1975 in Paris with Jean Widmer on the tourist signage for the Autoroute du Sud, for which *Roissy* was employed. On the strength of this, in 1999 he was invited to take over the conception of *Astra Frutiger,* since *Frutiger* was not available.

33 *FF Transit* was, in contrast to *Astra Frutiger,* brilliantly realised. The base typefaces were *FF Transit* Back, positive and negative, and *FF Transit* Front, positive and negative, each in normal, italic and bold (12 typefaces altogether). In addition, there was also *FF Transit* Print in 5 fonts. The typefaces were filled out with pictograms and extra fonts for the numbers on the underground and S-Bahn.

Glypha →268

1 *Karnak* by Robert Hunter Middleton was released by Ludlow; *Memphis* was designed by Rudolf Wolf for D. Stempel AG; and *Pharaon* is a Deberny & Peignot typeface. With almost the same name, *Pharaoh* is a copy of *Glypha* by Varityper. Frutiger's typeface was released by Scangraphic under the name *Gentleman.* See Lawrence W. Wallis, *Modern Encyclopedia of Typefaces 1960–90,* London 1990.

2 Contract for a new Egyptienne with the working name *'Champion'* between Bauersche Giesserei (Frankfurt) and Adrian Frutiger, 24 June 1966.

3 The Fundición Tipográfica Neufville S.A. gave licences of their fonts to different machine manufacturers, according to demand. Up until the introduction of personal computers, typesetting machines were closed systems. Fonts were not transferable from one machine to another. Hence the choice of fonts was an important selling point for the machine manufacturers.

4 *Glypha* was made in 1976 and finished in 1977. As far as we know it was not marketed until 1980. It was first introduced in the index of the *Linotype Fotosatz Schriften Teil 3* catalogue in July 1980. According to Walter Greisner, *Glypha* was held back because D. Stempel AG lacked the capacity for adapting the existing fonts for photosetting.

5 Letter sent 25 November 1982 from Wolfgang Hartmann at Fundición Tipográfica Neufville S.A. to Dr. Walter Greisner at D. Stempel AG.

6 Reply sent 8 December 1982 from Greisner to Hartmann.

7 Paragraph 2 of the *Code Morale,* reedited in 1975, reads, "Members consider it to be incompatible with their professional ethics to make a reproduction of another member's typeface, whether identical or slightly modified, irrespective of the medium, technique, form or size used …". – Wolfgang Hartmann to Professor G. W. Ovink in a letter of 24 February 1983, page 2. The *Code Morale* was discontinued when ATypI was registered in New Jersey, USA in 2004.

8 Verdict of ATypI regarding *Serifa* versus *Glypha,* Paris, 22 April 1983, signed by the permanent ATypI adjudicator for questions of plagiarism, Gerrit Willem Ovink, as well as by Eckehart Schumacher-Gebler and Gerard Unger, acting as supplied adjudicators.

9 Statement of 28 April 1983 by G. W. Ovink to Adrian Frutiger, and of 4 May 1983 to Dr. Walter Greisner.

10 The process of producing *Glypha* from *Serifa* 55 is described in a memo dated 5 November 1976 from Werner Schimpf at D. Stempel AG.

Icone →276

1 Adrian Frutiger, 'Das Miterleben einer Wandlung. Schriftzeichen für die Satztechnik der Gegenwart', in: Hans-Joachim Koppitz (ed.), *Gutenberg-Jahrbuch 1985,* Mainz 1985, page 22.

2 It is hard to determine the slope of *Icone* italic, but in the designs shown it is more like 6 degrees (left) and 18 or even 19 degrees (right).

3 Adrian Frutiger, 'Type, paper and man today'. Presentation to the general assembly of the Association Typographique Internationale (ATypI) in Basel, 22 September 1980, in *Swiss Typographic Magazine (STM)* 5/1980, page 277 ff: trilingual publication set in *Icone*.

4 In photosetting, characters are no longer negatives, they are digital data. Letters are broken down into pixels or vertical stripes and exposed onto film or paper. This makes electronically modified type possible.

5 In the Linotype classification, typefaces that do not clearly belong to a certain group are placed in group 6, 'Decorative and Display'. In German the group is called 'Antiqua-Varianten' and in French, 'Caractères de fantaisie'.

6 *Icone* Outline Bold had not been yet introduced on the double-page advertisement by Mergenthaler Linotype Company in the American magazine *U&lc,* no. 1, March 1980, of ITC.

7 The outline version was only used for catalogue and chapter titles, including posters and invitations. The catalogue *Mer Égée. Grèce des Îles* appeared in April 1979. At that point *Icone* was not yet available in Linotype's product range. The necessary letters were drawn with felt-tip pen on parchment paper. Bruno Pfäffli, type designer and studio partner of Adrian Frutiger, was usually the first to employ Frutiger's new typefaces. He used them many times for Paris museum catalogue designs.

8 Paste-ups were made from reduced reproductions of original character drawings, with individual letters cut to their widths and stuck together into a sample text.

9 Horst Heiderhoff, 'Formen und Gegenformen. Gestaltungseinheiten im Leben des Schriftkünstlers Adrian Frutiger' in: Hans-Joachim Koppitz (ed.), *Gutenberg-Jahrbuch 1985,* Mainz 1985, page 59.

10 Quote from a survey by specialist magazine Eurographic Press; 'Über die Zukunft von Schrift und Typografie', in *Druckindustrie,* no. 12 / 27 June 1985, page 9.

11 Quote from Adrian Frutiger; 'Adrian Frutiger himself'. Presentation given at 'Type 87' in New York, in *Der Druckspiegel,* 8/1988, page 922 f.

12 The psychedelic rock posters by Bonnie MacLean and Wes (Robert Wesley) Wilson may be named as examples. – See Lewis Blackwell, *20th century type (remix),* Corte Madera 1998, page 110.

13 In the Italian 'Classificazione Novarese' from 1957, the group 'Lapidari' is at the beginning. However, in order to conform with the ATypI classification it was listed as group VII in 1965. The term 'lapidari' refers to 'lapis' (Latin for stone) and Italian 'lapide' (headstone). – See Georg Kurt Schauer, *Klassifikation. Bemühungen um eine Ordnung im Druckschriftenbestand,* page 43 ff., page 54.

14 The trilingual Adobe type catalogue lists 'incised' fonts as 'Glyphic' and 'Polices Glyphiques'. – See *Adobe Type Library. Reference Book,* San Jose 2000, page 40.

Breughel →286

1 The first photocomposition machine was the 1965 Digiset by Dr.-Ing. Rudolf Hell KG in Kiel, Germany. The cathode ray tube (CRT) transferred the digitised typeface, which was broken down into pixels or vertical lines, onto film. With vector representation, a later CRT technology, it was no longer the vertical lines of the letter that were described as black and white values, but rather the contours. In order to save storage space, curve descriptions were divided into several straight segments. The precise representation of typefaces became possible again only in 1980 with the combination of Bézier curves (originally developed in 1960 by Pièrre Bézier for the French car manufacturer Renault) and high resolution lasers. These typefaces are also known as vector fonts.

2 Linotype cites 1981 as the year in which *Breughel* was designed. It is possible, however, that Frutiger's typeface was not completed until 1982. René Kerfante, then the director of the type manufacturing division at D. Stempel AG, is quoted as having said in conversation: "We will soon introduce 'Breughel', the new typeface for text setting by Adrian Frutiger in the style of a renaissance antiqua." – See 'Dem Schriftschaffen verpflichtet. Zu Gast bei der D. Stempel AG' in: *Der Druckspiegel,* No. 9/1982, page 687.
3 Hans Rudolf Bossard divides group V Slab Serif into five subgroups: 'Va Egyptienne, serifs without bracketing; Vb Clarendon, serifs with bracketing; Vc Italienne, serifs thicker than the stems (with or without bracketing); Vd Renaissance, wedge serifs; Ve Toscanienne [Tuscan], split serifs.' – HANS RUDOLF BOSSHARD: *Technische Grundlagen zur Satzherstellung,* Berne 1980, page 79.
4 Not all characters of the comparison string to *Jenson,* set in *Breughel* 65, correspond to the text sample. It is rather a visual comparison. This is also the reason why the lowercase f had been cut to mimic a 'long s'.
5 In our conversations, Adrian Frutiger gave slightly varying details concerning the stroke weight of a text face. He also said: "What is perceived as pleasant is subject to change. Today, we would therefore classify Jenson as a semibold cut."
6 Walter Greisner, chairman of D. Stempel AG, saw the extension to larger typeface families as a benefit for graphic designers. – See 'Dem Schriftschaffen verpflichtet. Zu Gast bei der D. Stempel AG' in *Der Druckspiegel,* No. 9/1982, page 680.
7 The brochure *Typefaces designed by Adrian Frutiger* by Linotype Font Center, which was published in 1983 by D. Stempel AG, incorrectly says the 16th century (see page 292).
8 Letter from Adrian Frutiger to typographer and graphic designer Kurt Weidemann, dated 18 February 1984. Frutiger and Weidemann had known each other since early in their careers. As director of typography for the German professional journal *Der Druckspiegel* for example, Weidemann published an article on Frutiger's logo designs in 1961.
9 Six type designers, seven typeface manufacturers and six graphic designers participated in the 1985 survey by Eurographic Press. – See 'Über die Zukunft von Schrift und Typographie' in *DruckIndustrie,* No. 12, St. Gallen, 27 June 1985, page 3 ff.
As early as 1976 Eurographic Press carried out a survey among fourteen type designers. See 'Die Zukunft unserer Druckschriften' in *Deutscher Drucker* Nos. 1–2/8 January 1976, page 2 ff. Part 2 of the survey is in *Deutscher Drucker* No. 3/22 January 1976.
10 Eurographic Press, established in 1959, is currently an association of fifteen European professional journals of the graphic design industry. – See: www.eurographicpress.com (December 2007).
11 Quoted in *DruckIndustrie,* No. 12, St. Gallen, 27 June 1985, page 9.
12 ADRIAN FRUTIGER: 'Das Miterleben einer Wandlung. Schriftzeichen für die Satztechnik der Gegenwart' in HANS-JOACHIM KOPPITZ (ed.), *Gutenberg-Jahrbuch 1985,* Mainz 1985, page 20.
13 In particular the manufacture of typefaces using Peter Karow's 'Ikarus' digitisation system at Unternehmensberatung Rubow Weber URW enabled a simplification of production and a reduction in production time.
14 Linotype's 1983 and 1984 typeface sample catalogues did not yet contain small capitals and lining figures for *Breughel.* They are shown in the *LinoTypeCollection 1987,* published in 1986.
15 This practical approach is not uncommon for Frutiger's typefaces. It does not, however, correspond to the way this is usually done by type designers because, more often than not, all figures of the two sets of lining figures and old style figures respectively are different in terms of shape, proportion and width.
16 Pieter Bruegel the Elder (b. c. 1525/30 in Breda (?), Netherlands; d. 9 September 1569 in Brussels, Belgium), also nicknamed 'Peasant Bruegel'. Known for his representations of rural life in 16th-century Flanders.
17 *Raleigh* (1977 but dated 1978 at Linotype) is based on *Cartier* by Canadian type designer Carl Dair. He designed *Cartier* for the 1967 Montreal World's Fair. Adrian Williams subsequently extended it with three cuts for display purposes while Robert Norton developed a text version.
18 William (Bill) Garth, president and majority shareholder of Lithomat, which produced offset printing plates from paper, was also president of the Graphic Arts Research Foundation. The foundation was established in the USA in 1949 by René Higonnet and Louis Moyroud to advance the development of the Lumitype-Photon. In 1950 Lithomat was renamed Photon Inc. Garth left Photon Inc. in 1960 and, together with Ellis Hanson, set up Compugraphic Corporation, a manufacturer of machines for phototypesetting. – See ALAN MARSHALL, *Du plomb à la lumière,* Paris 2003.
19 The drawings for *Garth Graphic* were originally done by John Matt around the mid-1960s. Before the typeface could be published, however, American Typefounders ATF abandoned their plans for phototypesetting. In the late 1970s, Renee Le Winter and Constance Blanchard of Compugraphic redesigned the almost-forgotten *Matt Antique* and extended it. The new name was based on that of Bill Garth, founder of Compugraphics and former president of Photon Inc. – See www.myfonts.com (December 2007). – See also LAWRENCE W. WALLIS *The Encyclopedia of Modern Typefaces 1960–90,* London 1990.

Dolmen (type-design project) →296
1 Dolmen: prehistoric monument usually consisting of several great stone slabs set edgewise in the earth to support a flat stone, which served as a roof. Designed as a burial chamber, the structure is typical of the Neolithic Period in Europe. The word is Celtic in origin but probably is not Breton. Dolmens, although found in covered form as far east as Japan, are mainly confined to Europe, the British Isles, and northern Africa. – See *Encyclopædia Britannica,* CD 2000 Edition.
2 The identity of the designer of Società Nebiolo's *Semplicità* is not known. The shadowed version, *Semplicità Ombra,* is by Alessandro Butti. – See www.klingspor-museum.de/Klingspor Kuenstler/Schriftdesigner/Butti/ABUtti.pdf (February 2008).
3 Hans Reichel's typeface for H. Berthold AG first appeared in 1983 under the name of *Barmen* before it was re-named *Barmeno* in 1990. In 1999, six years after H. Berthold AG ceased trading, Font Shop (Berlin) republished the typeface under the name *FF Sari.* – See www.sanskritweb.net/forgers/barmen.pdf (February 2008).
4 Conversation between Adrian Frutiger, Erich Alb, Rudolf Barmettler and Philipp Stamm on 24 April 2003.
5 Adrian Frutiger draws a distinction between the base form, the skeleton of a letter, which ensures its recognisability, and its overall shape, which generates its appearance. He wrote in 1994: "The work of a type designer is like that of a couturier, dressing an untouched, naked body". – See ADRIAN FRUTIGER, *Denken und Schaffen einer Typografie,* Villeurbanne 1994, page 17. Frutiger also sometimes makes a comparison to music: "The nucleus of the character is like the pure tone in music, while the outer form provides the sound." – See ADRIAN FRUTIGER, *Type Sign Symbol,* Zurich 1980, page 69.

Tiemann →302
1 RAINER FRENKEL, 'Abschied vom Blei. Aus dem konservativen Innenleben der Zeit'. In *Die Zeit,* No. 20, Hamburg 14 May 1982, page 1.
2 Walter Tiemann (1876–1951) studied fine arts in Leipzig and Dresden and made study visits to the Rhineland and Paris. From 1898 he was active in publishing houses; from 1903 he taught at the Staatliche Akademie für Graphische Künste Leipzig (State Academy for Graphic Arts); from 1905 he collaborated with Karl Klingspor; founded the Janus-Presse in 1907 with Carl Ernst Poeschel (1920–1941); and 1945–1946 he was the director of the Staatliche Akademie für Graphische Künste Leipzig. He was awarded an honorary doctorate in 1946.
3 F. W. Kleukens' *Ratio-Latein* was manufactured in 1923–24 by D. Stempel AG. From 1925 it was additionally available from Linotype.
4 In 1956, D. Stempel AG, as majority shareholder in the type foundry of Gebr. Klingspor, discontinued that company's hot metal programme and brought a selection of Klingspor's typefaces into their own catalogue. *Tiemann-Antiqua* was not one of those typefaces. In 1984 D. Stempel AG was taken over by Linotype and the rights to those typefaces passed to them.
5 Jovica Veljović is a calligrapher, type designer, typographer, graphic designer and teacher of type design and typography in Hamburg. – See FRIEDRICH FRIEDL, NICOLAUS OTT, BERNHARD STEIN, *Typography – when who how,* Cologne 1998, page 529 ff.
6 At the same time, a complete redesign of the layout was undertaken by Marco Garcia, the renowned South American newspaper designer. Among other changes, he introduced *Garamond* as a body typeface, after many years of the *Tiemann/Times Roman* combination.
7 Tiemann's first typeface for Gebr. Klingspor, *Tiemann Medieval* (1909), based on the style of a renaissance antiqua, was a reworking of a typeface created by Walter Tiemann and Carl Ernst Poeschel in 1907 for their jointly founded Janus Press. After that, Tiemann turned his attention to his preferred gothic typefaces. He developed *Tiemann-Fraktur* (1914), *Peter Schlemihl* (1914), *Tiemann-Gotisch* (1924), *Kleist-Fraktur* (1928) and *Fichte-Fraktur* (1935). Later typefaces were *Orpheus* (1928), *Daphnis* (1931) and *Euphorion* (1935). All the typefaces designed by Tiemann were cast at Gebr. Klingspor. – See JULIUS RODENBERG, *In der Schmiede der Schrift,* Berlin 1940, page 121 ff.
8 Artist Otto Eckmann and architect Peter Behrens also worked for Gebr. Klingspor.
9 See JULIUS RODENBERG, *In der Schmiede der Schrift,* Berlin 1940, page 127.
10 William Morris studied theology and worked as an architect, then as a painter, before he founded the Kelmscott Press. His aim was the renaissance of craft as art. He designed, among others, *Golden Type* based on Nicolas Jenson's typeface. The type was cut by Edward Prince.
11 See page 26: 'About Président'.
12 Johann Gottlob Immanuel Breitkopf and Johann Friedrich Unger had already tried to simplify the gothic forms at the end of the 18th century in an attempt to carve a niche for gothic scripts in opposition to antiquas. – See GUSTAV BOHADTI, *Von der Romain du Roi zu den Schriften J. G. Justus Erich Walbaums,* H. Berthold AG, Berlin/Stuttgart 1957, page 40.
13 This may have been sparked by the success of *ATF Bodoni* in 1910.
14 Caledonia is the Latin name for Scotland. 1938, *Caledonia* – known in Germany as *Cornelia* – was based on *Scotch Roman* (1907) and *Bulmer* – also manufactured by Monotype. *Scotch Roman* is a consolidation of Richard Austin's neoclassical typeface of 1810, itself based on *Bodoni* and *Didot,* and which was manufactured by the Wilson Foundry in Glasgow and by William Miller & Co. in Edinburgh. This typeface was known abroad as *Scotch* Populär. – See PHILIPP BERTEAU, *Buchdruckschriften im 20. Jahrhundert. Atlas zur Geschichte der Schrift,* Darmstadt 1995, pages 91, 397, 482.
15 The exact year of the reworking is not entirely clear. The *LinoTypeCollection* of the Mergenthaler Type Library from 1986 gives the year as 1979. – L. W. Wallis gives the year as 1981. See LAURENCE W. WALLIS, *Type Design Developments 1970 to 1985,* Arlignton 1985, page 77. – In Linotype GmbH's *Typeface Catalogue* from 2006, the year is noted as 1982.
16 Based on the criteria mentioned earlier, *Fairfield* and *New Caledonia* can also be assigned to the neo-baroque typefaces. In particular, the lower case b, with its slightly skewed stroke ending on top and slightly diagonal one at the bottom, as well as the lower case e of *Fairfield* with its open curve shape, point in this direction.

Versailles →308
1 Mike Parker studied architecture and graphic design at Yale. From 1950 to 1980 he was employed at the Mergenthaler Linotype Company in New York, first as assistant to Jackson Burke, later as Director of Typographic Development. It was his responsibility to oversee the migration and further development of line-cast typefaces to photo- and CRT setting. In 1981, together with Matthew Carter, Cherie Cone and Rob Friedmann, he founded Bitstream, Inc. – See www.fontbureau.com/people/MikeParker (November 2007).
Matthew Carter studied type design at Charterhouse, Surrey (Great Britain). In 1960 he met Mike Parker. In 1963 he joined Crosfield Electronics, the company responsible for the Photon/Lumitype photosetting machines. He met Adrian Frutiger in Paris. From 1965 to 1971 he worked as a type designer at the Mergenthaler Linotype Company in the USA, and then until 1981 for American, British and German Linotype. In 1981, together with Mike Parker, Cherie Cone and Rob Friedmann, he founded BitStream, Inc. In 1991 he and Cherie Cone founded Carter & Cone Type, Inc. Well-known typefaces by Carter include, amongst others, *Olympian* 1970, *Galliard* 1978, *Bell Centennial* 1978, *Charter* 1987, *Verdana* 1996. – See MARGARET RE, *Typographically Speaking. The Art of Matthew Carter,* New York 2003.
2 Reinhard Haus – employed at Atelier Frutiger 1978–1982 – mentioned that he had brought this Napoleonic inscription to Frutiger's attention. In 1958, the French Emperor Napoleon III decided to commission the building of a new opera house. The young architect Charles Garnier was the surprise winner of the competition, although the young Empress Eugénie spoke out against the design. The construction of the imposing opera house – today known as 'Opéra National de Paris' – took place between 1861 and 1875. In the years after the French Revolution (1789–1799), the title 'Grand Opéra' referred to a style of opera that mixed elements of comic opera with the serious. – See JULIA DROSTE-HENNINGS, THORSTEN DROSTE, *Paris: Eine Stadt und ihr Mythos,* Cologne 2005, page 307 ff.
3 See the Euro Graphic Press survey, 'Über die Zukunft von Schrift und Typografie' (On the future of type and typography), in *DruckIndustrie,* No. 12, St. Gallen 1985, page 9.
4 In the 1984 Linotype typeface catalogue, Digital Typefaces, the oldstyle numerals and small caps are still present. The latest that these can be seen is on the typeface sheets contained in the plexiglass box of the 1986 LinoTypeCollection.
5 The type sample *Spécimen Géneral* (Deberny & Peignot, vol. 2, 1926) lists only the *Caractères Latins Noirs Italiques* and *Caractères Antiques Italiques Latinés.* The latter was a grotesque with dynamic strokes.
6 See *Breughel,* note 1, page 432.

7 For the marketing of *Versailles,* Linotype placed a bilingual advertisement in the American magazine, *U&lc.* An article entitled 'Eine neue Schrift von Adrian Frutiger' (A New Typeface by Adrian Frutiger), appeared in the German professional journal, *Novum Gebrauchsgraphik* 1985, vol. 5, page 67 ff. It was written by Reinhard Haus, head of the Linotype typeface studio, and dealt with *Versailles* and additionally with latin typefaces. A significant marketing tool was, however, the 28-page brochure published by Linotype in three languages and entitled *Typefaces by Adrian Frutiger* (1983). This was made available free of charge. On double-page spreads, the brochure presented the ten Frutiger typefaces that were available from Linotype: *Meridien, Iridium, Egyptienne F, Glypha, Serifa, Univers, Frutiger, Icone, Breughel* and *Versailles* (the order in which they appeared in the brochure). It was reviewed in the specialist publication *Der Druckspiegel* (1984, vol. 5, page 54). Additionally, in autumn 1984 Linotype began 'The Great Frutiger Typeface Offer' campaign. The brochure was included in the offer portfolio, along with an order form and price list. A typeface for the CRTronic or Linotype 202 cost 1080 German marks in lots of four (then around US $ 380); additionally, ordering one or more extra typeface families guaranteed a further 5 % discount. Today, in comparison, Linotype sells a digital font of *Versailles* for $ 33, or the entire type family for $ 259 (prices as of February 2008).

Linotype Centennial →318

1 Ottmar Mergenthaler, who emigrated to the United States from Germany, unveiled the first matrix setting and line-casting machine, named 'Blower', in New York in 1886. The Mergenthaler Linotype Company was founded in 1890.

2 Olaf Leu, born in 1936 in Chemnitz (Germany), is a graphic designer. He was a professor of corporate design at Mainz University from 1986 to 2003.

3 drupa, the German abbreviation for Druck und Papier (print and paper), is the trade fair of the printing and communication industry which takes place every four years in Düsseldorf. It is one of the most important and largest trade fairs in the world.

4 See *DruckIndustrie,* 11/1986, page 42.

5 *Bell Centennial* was released in 1978 for CRT photosetting on the Linotron 606. It is based on *Bell Gothic,* drawn in 1938 by Chauncey H. Griffith for AT&T and for Mergenthaler Linotype. See www.myfonts.com/fonts/adobe/bell-centennial/ (March 2008). – Jaspert, Berry, Johnson: *The Encyclopaedia of Type Faces,* London 1970, page 252.

6 See *Linotype Library. Typeface Handbook,* Eschborn 1988.

7 The semantic differential was introduced by Charles E. Osgood in 1952 and published in 1957. Peter Hofstätter adopted the methodology in a slightly altered form, which he called polarity profiles, in Germany in 1955. – See Charles E. Osgood, G. J. Suci, P. H. Tannenbaum: *The Measurement of Meaning,* Urbana 1957. – http://en.wikipedia.org/wiki/Semantic_differential (March 2008).

8 In 1965 Dirk Wendt examined the legibility of typefaces at the psychological institute of the University of Hamburg. In 1968 he examined the qualities of impression of 18 different typefaces, among them Frutiger's *Univers* and *Serifa.* – See Dirk Wendt: *Untersuchungen zur Lesbarkeit von Druckschriften,* Bericht Nr. 2, Hamburg 1965 (reproduced manuscript). – Dirk Wendt: 'Semantic Differentials of Typefaces as a Method of Congeniality Research' in *The Journal of Typographic Research,* vol. II, Cleveland 1/1968. – Peter Karow: *Schriftentechnologie. Methoden und Werkzeuge,* Berlin/Heidelberg 1992, p. 405 ff.

9 Christian Gutschi, M.A. in media psychology at the University of Vienna, decided on a polarity profile with 23 pairs of adjectives for his examination. – See Christian Gutschi: 'Psychologie der Schriften', part 1, in *Page* 8/1996, page 54 ff.; part 2 in *Page* 9/1996, page 64 ff.; part 3 in *Page* 10/1996, page 74 ff.; part 4 in *Page* 12/1996, page 66 ff.; part 5 in *Page* 1/1997, page 52 ff. – See www.medienpsychologie.at (March 2008).

10 *Times New Roman,* which belongs to the transitional typeface group, was created in 1932 by Stanley Morison for the British newspaper 'The Times'. Linotype's version of the typeface was called *Times Roman.*

11 Linotype and Monotype are without doubt the two major typesetting machine manufacturers. *Times New Roman* was also an important element in the type library of Berthold, Compugraphic, Hell, IBM, Intertype, Ludlow, Photon-Lumitype et al where it was called *Times Roman* or simply *Times.* Both Letraset and Mecanorma sold *Times* as dry transfer.

12 When he says 'IBM material', Adrian Frutiger is referring to very strong, standard-size polyethylene sheets that IBM used at the time for test exposures of IBM typefaces.

13 See http://en.wikipedia.org/wiki/Ottmar_Mergenthaler (march 2008).

14 See LinoTypeCollection – Mergenthaler Type Library, Eschborn 1986.

Avenir →330

1 The 'Zusammenstellung der Linotype-Grotesk-Schriften' was part of Adrian Frutiger's study 'Wo gibt es Marktlücken im heutigen Schriftenangebot?' from January 1987. This list was additionally available in several publications. – See Adrian Frutiger, 'L'histoire des Antiques', in *TM/RSI* 3/1988 (a continuation of the article in *TM/RSI* 1/1988). – Adrian Frutiger: *Nachdenken über Zeichen und Schrift,* Bern 2005, page 94 ff. (The dates given in this publication are not correct. The article was written not in 1975 but in 1985, and published not in 1978 but in 1988.)

2 The space that can be perceived by one eye without any eye movements is called the field of vision. For adults the dimension of the horizontal field of vision of both eyes is approximately 170°, the vertical is about 110°. At the edges (roughly 10° for both) only moving objects can be perceived. – See http://de.wikipedia.org/wiki/Gesichtsfeld (April 2008.)

3 This means a 'comparison of all existing linear typefaces'.

4 Adrian Frutiger, 'Konstruktivistisch und human. Avenir – eine neue serifenlose Linear-Antiqua von Adrian Frutiger' in *Linotype express,* 2/1988, page 2.

5 Philipp Luidl, *Schrift – die Zerstörung der Nacht,* Munich 1993, page 75.

6 The conversation with Adrian Frutiger on *Avenir* was held by Erich Alb, Rudolf Barmettler and Philipp Stamm on 25 March 2002 and continued on 22 April 2002.

7 Le Corbusier, *Kommende Baukunst,* Stuttgart, Berlin, Leipzig 1926, page 55. Quoted in Kimberly Elam, *Proportion und Komposition: Geometrie im Design,* New York 2006, page 5 (*Geometry of Design: Studies in proportion & composition,* New York 2001).

8 Adrian Frutiger, 'Wo gibt es Marktlücken im heutigen Schriften-Angebot? Eine Studie und ein Vorschlag im Bereiche der Grotesk-Schriften. Es fehlt eine moderne Fassung einer konstruktivistischen Grotesk', January 1987, 10 pages.

9 The *Encyclopedia of Type Faces* lists numerous geometrical typefaces. Besides *Erbar Grotesk,* 1926 by Jakob Erbar; *Futura,* 1927 by Paul Renner and *Kabel (Cable),* 1927 by Rudolf Koch there are: *Elegant-Grotesk,* 1928 by Hans Möhring; *Bernhard Gothic,* 1929 by Lucian Bernhard; *Super,* 1930 by Arno Drescher; *Tempo,* 1930 by Robert Hunter Middleton. However, *Neuzeit Grotesk* (1928) co-designed by Wilhelm Pischner is missing, for instance. – See Jaspert, Berry, Johnson: *Encyclopaedia of Type Faces,* London 1970.

10 As can be seen in Philipp Bertheau's book, Paul Renner's *Futura Buchschrift* for hot metal setting by Bauersche Giesserei features strongly differing ratios between x-height and ascenders. In large sizes, x-height and ascenders appear to be almost the same, at 48 pt the ratio is approximately 10:8,5. In body text and small sizes the ratio of the ascenders is significantly reduced, which greatly aids legibility. At 10 pt the ratio is approximately 10:7, at 6 pt it is only 10:6. – See Philipp Bertheau: *Buchdruckschriften im 20. Jahrhundert. Atlas zur Geschichte der Schrift,* Darmstadt 1995, page 303. – Unfortunately only one design size was implemented later for photosetting and digital setting. The 1992 *LinoTypeCollection* lists 12 pt as the design size. Here, the ratio is approximately 10:7.6. – See *LinoTypeCollection,* Eschborn 1992, page 233.

11 The use of *Two Lines English Egyptian* has not been documented in any printed publication so far. However, this typeface is known in architecture. According to Max Bollwage it is derived from the inscriptions on Greek temples. He goes on to demonstrate a continual use of sans serif majuscules as inscriptions on coins, tombs and buildings. – See Max Bollwage, 'Serifenlose Linearschriften gibt es nicht erst seit dem 19. Jahrhundert. Mutmassungen eines Typografen', in Stephan Füssel (ed.), *Gutenberg-Jahrbuch 2002,* Mainz 2002, page 212 ff.

12 The 19th-century sans serifs are mainly based on rectangular and oval shapes, thus expressing neoclassical design principles.

13 Unfortunately, there is no exact date available for the geometrical grotesque cut by Wagner & Schmidt in Leipzig and extended to ten sets. Neither are there any references as to who the designer was. In 1922 it was published using partly different shapes under the name *Universal* by the Prague state printing press; in 1930 as *Polar Grotesk* by Schriftgiesserei J. John Söhne in Hamburg and in 1931 as *Rund Grotesk* by C. E. Weber in Stuttgart. The Norddeutsche Schriftgiesserei in Berlin called their 1937 version *Kristall Grotesk,* the name by which it was later also available at Johannes Wagner in Ingolstadt. The foundry Berlinska in Lund (Sweden) listed it as *Saxo* and José Iranzo in Barcelona as *Predilecta.* – See Philipp Bertheau, *Buchdruckschriften im 20. Jahrhundert. Atlas zur Geschichte der Schrift,* Darmstadt 1995, page 191.

14 The Bauhaus was founded in 1919, one year after the end of World War I, in Weimar. In 1920 the preliminary course was established and headed by the Swiss teacher and artist Johannes Itten, who used the basic shapes of circle, square and triangle in creative exercises. In his article 'Elementar Schule' J. Abbott Miller writes on page 21: "Itten, Klee and Kandinsky wanted to discover the origins of 'visual language'; they tried to find these origins in elementary geometry, in pure colours and in abstraction." From 1923 onwards, the square, circle and triangle increasingly influenced the Bauhaus design. For example, László Moholy-Nagy, who by that time had become head of the preliminary course, designed a logo for publications of the Bauhaus press using geometrical base shapes. Josef Albers, too, developed preliminary designs of an elementary template type and Herbert Bayer produced initial designs that would later become the *'Universal'* alphabet. In 1924 the Bauhaus lost support from the city of Weimar for political reasons and moved to Dessau in 1925 where, in 1932, it was closed by the city council following a petition by the Nazi party NSDAP. For a short period the Bauhaus managed to continue teaching in Berlin but was closed for good in 1933. Adolf Hitler had taken power and the works by Bauhaus artists and sympathisers were ostracised as degenerate, which resulted in the emigration of many Bauhaus teachers and students. – See Ellen Lupton, J. Abbott Miller (eds), *The ABCs of (Triangle Square Circle): The Bauhaus and Design Theory from Preschool to Post-Modernism,* New York 1993. – See also: www.bauhaus.de/bauhaus1919/zeittafel1919.htm (April 2008).

15 Besides Tom Carnase's *ITC Busorama* (1965) and *ITC Bauhaus* (1975) by Ed Benguiat and Victor Caruso, further examples could be mentioned such as *Churchward* (1970) by Joseph Churchward; *ITC Ronda* (1970) by Tom Carnase; *Premier* (1970) by Colin Brignall; *Washington* (1970) by Russell Bean; *Blippo* or the almost identical *Pump* (1970) by Bob Newman; *Horatio* (1971) also by Bob Newman; and *Plaza* (1975) by Alan Meeks.

16 In a first step, Herb Lubalin's colleague Tom Carnase extended the 1968 *Avant Garde* magazine masthead to a majuscule alphabet, which was again extended by additional majuscule ligatures. In 1970 the fully fledged typeface *ITC Avant Garde Gothic* was published by Lubalin, Burns & Co. Inc. In cooperation with Tom Carnase, the three weights x-light, medium and demi were implemented first. Also in 1970, Aaron Burns, Herb Lubalin and Edward Rondthaler set up the International Typeface Corporation (ITC) in New York. *ITC Avant Garde Gothic* was, of course, part of the portfolio and two further weights, Book and Bold, were developed. These were followed in 1974 by four condensed fonts by Ed Benguiat and in 1977 by five oblique versions designed by André Gürtler, Christian Mengelt and Erich Gschwind.

17 At this time, most foundries and print shops used to set typefaces with a reduced intercharacter spacing and passed this practice on to their apprentices. Even typeface manufacturers such as H. Berthold AG communicated this principle in their type sample books. All typefaces were shown in five widths: wide, regular, condensed, extra condensed and ultra condensed. The regular font already appeared quite compact but a tighter kerning was sometimes recommended for job composition: "The regular width is the one that a reader will perceive as pleasant and right even when reading long texts. A sentence should neither have gaps nor appear to be squashed. A typeface should not attract attention itself but should serve as a medium of knowledge or information. Short pieces of text in advertising, on labels or flyers appear to be wider compared to longer texts, especially in narrow columns with small margins. In these cases condensed or even extra condensed fonts should be used, not only for aesthetic reasons but also for better legibility." – See *Berthold Fototypes E2, Body Types,* Berlin / Munich 1980, page XV f.

18 As art director of the British magazine *The Face* Neville Brody designed several alphabets, among them his 1984 *Typeface Two.* In 1989 it was published as *Industria* by Linotype in a solid and inline version both for a regular and alternate font. *Typeface Five* from 1985/86, which was published as *Arcadia* by Linotype, and *Typeface Six* (1986), which was renamed *Insignia,* both have an alternate font. All three typefaces are clearly different from their original versions. – See Jon Wozencroft, *The Graphic Language of Neville Brody,* Munich / Lucerne 1988, page 26 ff. – See also www.fontshop.com (July 2008).

19 According to Walter Schimpf's interpolation table from 10 May 1988, the six *Avenir* weights from thin to bold are graded such: 0 %, 11.25 %, 24.5 %, 38.1 %, 68.5 %, 100 %.

20 There is a fairly large amount of published material on *Avenir*. A comprehensive, handwritten manuscript by Adrian Frutiger served as the foundation for articles in the various German professional journals. Articles were published in the following journals (among others): *Linotype express* [Ger.] 2/1988, page 2; *Linotype express* [Engl.] autumn 1988; *Graphic Repro* 12/1988, page 22 ff.; *Deutscher Drucker* 15 December 1988, page g21; *DruckIndustrie* 3/1989, page 32; *World-Wide Printer* 6/1989, page 68 f.; *Page* [Ger.] 6/1992, page 50 ff. Additionally, Linotype published flyers, supplements and brochures. - See ADRIAN FRUTIGER, 'Eine neue konstruktivistische Schrift', Eschborn no date (circa 1988); - TYPOGRAPHICS OF CHELTENHAM: 'The King who glimpsed the future', Cheltenham 1988; - LINOTYPE: 'Avenir - A new sans serif from Adrian Frutiger', Eschborn no date (c. 1990).

21 See *Linotype Library, Platinum Collection: Avenir Next by Adrian Frutiger,* Bad Homburg 2004/2006, pages 3 and 4.

22 The pro-version of *Avenir Next* also comprises a larger set of diacritics for foreign language setting. *Avenir LT* was also extended to accommodate European languages. However, for these purposes, the 12 separate CE (Central European) fonts are needed.

Westside →346

1 Werner Schimpf, director of the type studio at Linotype, posed the question in a letter to Adrian Frutiger dated 10 January 1989. Later he notes, "This question touches upon the overall concept of capitals," challenging the general principle of accentuated middle strokes in *Westside*. He was responding to the first settings from the digitised test drawings.

2 In the United States only italiennes, which are called French Clarendons or French Egyptians, are commonly associated with Western movies. Tuscans are more closely associated with circuses.

3 Stefan Schlesinger's *Hidalgo,* released by the Amsterdam type foundry in 1939, also has this feature. - See JASPERT, BERRY, JOHNSON: *Encyclopaedia of Type Faces,* London 1970, page 113.

4 The typefaces based on designs found in: ROB ROY KELLY, *American Wood Type: 1828-1900,* New York 1970.

5 In his letter from 10 January 1989 to Adrian Frutiger, Schimpf included *'Eastside', 'Gothic F'* and *'Fancy'* typefaces alongside *Westside.* The copy of the letter unfortunately does not have any test letters attached, meaning that the undated design drawings depicted cannot be properly classified. Schimpf showed interest in the *'Eastside'* test letters, which are a modification of *Westside.* He writes of *'Gothic F'*: "We had the test letters with added corners exposed in different typesetting qualities. Precisely in low resolution the corners are disruptive and start looking like serifs." A possible selection of *'fancy'* typefaces was to be discussed at the subsequent type meeting on 25 January. At Frutiger's request electronic modifications of *Westside* – reduced or widened to 80%, 90%, 120%, 140% and 160% – were included in the letter.

6 Nicolete Gray lists one French Clarendon and one tuscan, both dated 1821. The first is *Italian* by Caslon & Catherwood, the second is *Two-line english Tuscan* by the Thorowgood foundry. - See NICOLETE GRAY: *Nineteenth Century Ornamented Typefaces,* London 1976, pages 32 f.

7 František Muzika writes, "Another kind ... of 19th-century jobbing typeface is one which was christened *Tuscan* in England. This term is equally as coincidental and unfounded as the terms egyptienne, antique, French antique, italienne and so on. Just as egyptienne has nothing to do with Egypt, nor italienne with Italy, so the tuscan typefaces have no relation to the Italian province of Tuscany nor to the Tuscan order of Roman architecture. Its description may only be attributed to commercial reasons [...]." - FRANTIŠEK MUZIKA: *Die schöne Schrift in der Entwicklung des lateinischen Alphabets,* volume 2, Prague 1965, page 338.

8 See FRANTIŠEK MUZIKA: *Die schöne Schrift in der Entwicklung des lateinischen Alphabets,* volume 2, Prague 1965, pages 332 ff.

9 In general there is little point in subdividing slab serif typefaces into subgroups with angular or curved serif transitions, as they are not defining features. Nor should this be applied to egyptian typefaces. On the other hand it would be interesting to separate slab serif typefaces into those with and those without stroke contrast. Typefaces of the Clarendon group would be included in the latter. See page 168.

10 The term egyptian must not be confused with the general description of slab serif typefaces of the same name.

11 Kelly says the French Clarendons were always bracketed while the French Antiques were not. - See ROB ROY KELLY, *American Wood Type: 1828-1900,* New York 1970, page 130.

12 See HANS RUDOLF BOSSHARD: *Technische Grundlagen zur Satzherstellung,* Berne 1980, page 79.

13 Three months after the first exposures of the test letters, Schimpf confirmed, in a letter to Adrian Frutiger from 13 April 1989, that he had received the upper- and lowercase letters for *Westside.* In a letter dated 5 August 1989. Frutiger made some corrections and also altered a few drawings. On the whole, however, the typeface appears to have been ready.

14 At the time, Apple Macintosh, Windows PC and Unix Workstations and their printers still required different type formats: PostScript Type 1, TrueType and PostScript Type 3.

Vectora →352

1 The term 'gothic' was first used in the USA in 1837 for a sans serif typeface.

2 In English, 'relief' refers not only to 'three-dimensional representation' but is also used to mean 'freedom from pain and assistance with necessities such as food or money for the socially disadvantaged'.

3 According to a letter of 12 April 1990 from Adrian Frutiger to W. Glathe, the other suggested names were Grid Gothic, Regular Gothic, Register, Scan Gothic, Alpha, Omega, Sigma, Data Gothic, Digest Gothic and Register Gothic.

4 According to a letter from A. Semmelbauer dated 25 June 1990 the five suggested names are ordered according to priority: Raster Gothic, Grid Gothic, Formula, Tartan Gothic, Villa Gothic.

5 The Patent Office understands the term 'gothic' to be a designation for a particular sort of typeface, which is why it cannot be protected.

6 See REINHARD HAUS, 'American Blend' in *Page* 6/1991, page 80.

7 According to a letter from Adrian Frutiger to Otmar Hoefer, 23 January 1990.

8 Linn Boyd Benton was the inventor of several machines for the cutting of steel letter punches, amongst them being the pantograph. His first machine was patented in the United States in 1885. In 1894 he was appointed one of the directors of the newly founded ATF. In the same year his famous typeface *Century,* developed in cooperation with Theodore Low De Vinne, and designed for 'The Century magazine', was released. His son, Morris Fuller Benton, started working at the foundry in 1896, and by 1900 had already been appointed chief type designer. He, too, became a managing director of ATF. - See WOLFGANG BEINERT: www.typolexikon.de (as accessed June 2008). - See PATRICIA A. COST, 'Linn Boyd Benton, Morris Fuller Benton, and Typemaking at ATF' in *Printing History,* nos. 31–32/2002, pages 27–44.

9 The approximately 200 font series were produced between 1896 and 1937. The font series, today called a font, contains the cutting of the various point sizes.

10 See YVONNE SCHWEMER-SCHEDDIN, 'Ästhetik der Technik. Zur neuen Corporate-Schrift von Daimler-Benz und deren Gestalter Kurt Weidemann' in *Page* 7/1990, page 54 ff.

Linotype Didot →362

1 Since 1986 it has been possible, using the Linotronic 500 Laser RIP (Raster Image Processor), to produce daily newspapers and glossy magazines at the highest level of printing technology. - See www.typolexikon.de/l/linotype.html (May 2008).

2 In his Parisian antiquarian bookshop, Paul Jammes keeps a large collection of original prints by the Didot family. In 1998, with the help of Pierre Firmin-Didot (the great-great-great grandson of Firmin Didot), Paul Jammes' son André was able to mount an exhibition and produce a catalogue on the life and works of this distinguished family. - See ANDRÉ JAMMES, *Les Didot. Trois siècles de typographie et de bibliophilie 1698-1998,* Paris 1998.

3 Quote from one of Frutiger's undated manuscripts, which served as the basis for an article in the professional journal *Page.* The manuscript is kept in the archive of the Swiss Foundation Type and Typography. - See REINHARD HAUS, 'Klassizistisches Erbe', in *Page,* 12/1991, page 66.

4 Linotype's *typeface production plan 1986,* page 9, 'subject for further investigation = 4' mentioned a *Didot* typeface.

5 In a 22 August 1990 Linotype GmbH internal memorandum to Otmar Hoefer and two other Linotype employees, A. Plowright mentions that at the Type Selection Meeting of October 1989 *Didot* had been chosen to go into production. However, *Didot* is not mentioned in the minutes of the meeting, whereas 'Type before Gutenberg' is.

6 The range of hot metal type from Parisian foundry Deberny & Peignot was carried by Haas'sche Schriftgiesserei AG (Münchenstein / Basel), and all rights passed to them after the closure of Deberny & Peignot in 1974.

7 Linotype AG internal memorandum by Anja Plowright, 22 August 1990.

8 The company's long history and the mergers of various type foundries (Didot's own among them) meant that there were many typefaces at Deberny & Peignot with the name Didot. The typeface catalogue does not list the names of the designers, and only rarely is the designer's name mentioned in the typeface name.
Peignot's (of Deberny & Peignot) lineage can be traced back to the Fonderie Générale in Paris. Here the lines of three type foundries came together: the first goes back to Vibert and his descendants, the second goes – through Pierre and Firmin Didot – back to François Ambroise Didot, and the third line started with Molé. Therefore, all the most important French type foundries of the late 18th and early 19th centuries were united under the roof of Deberny & Peignot. - See PHILIPP BERTHEAU, *Buchdruckschriften im 20. Jahrhundert,* Darmstadt 1995, page 56 ff.

9 Voltaire (the pen name of François Marie Arouet) is one of France's most important writers and philosophers. His work *La Henriade,* begun in 1717 while he was under arrest in the Bastille and completed in 1723, is an epic poem about the French king, Henry IV. It appeared in many editions besides that of Firmin Didot.

10 Linotype AG internal note from Reinhard Haus to Gerhard Höhl, 9 April 1991.

11 Letter from André Gürtler to Linotype AG Günter Zorn, head of typeface development, 29 December 1990.

12 Linotype AG internal note from Gerhard Höhl to M. Tannrath, 22 July 1991.

13 Booklet with two inlaid pages, handmade paper, A4, two-colour, black-red, blind embossed.

14 According to Otmar Hoefer's memo of 20 May 2008, the eight pages with test versions of various type faces were subjected to evaluation by a client survey in 1993. On the basis of the results, *Linotype Didot Openface* was not implemented. In addition to *Didot,* the typefaces *Herculanum, Notre Dame+, Grace, Koch Antiqua+, Pine, Terazzo* and *Noodles* are shown on the eight sheets. The first three were implemented shortly thereafter. They appear in the 1996 Linotype catalogue. The remaining four, however, do not. *Pine* first appeared in 2003 as *Linotype Pine.*

15 Jonathan Hoefler created his *HTF Didot* in 1991 in response to a commission from *Harper's Bazaar* magazine. It was first used in 1992. Hoefler was contacted because, until that time, there had been no *Didot* on the American market for modern typesetting machines. *Linotype Didot,* which was released in Europe in 1991, only made it to the American market in 1992. Hoefler pointed out that *HTF Didot* was not derived from Frutiger's *Linotype Didot.* – Emails from Jonathan Hoefler to Heidrun Osterer, 16 August 2006 and 6 December 2006.

16 Pierre Didot had composed his print ed works in the typefaces of his brother Firmin, until he established his own foundry, in collaboration with the punchcutter Vibert, in 1809 - See GUSTAV BOHADTI, *Von der Romain du Roi zu den Schriften J. G. Justus Erich Walbaums,* Berlin / Stuttgart 1957, page 19 ff.

Herculanum →370

1 The International Typeface Corporation (ITC) was founded in 1970 by Aaron Burns, Herb Lubalin and Ed Rondthaler. Its aim was to make typefaces available independently of any setting system. Designs were bought from type designers, and very successfully sold via licensing to type manufacturers. From 1973 to 1999, ITC published its magazine *U&lc* (Upper and lower case) as a marketing tool. In 1986 ITC was bought by Letraset and in 2000 it was taken over by Agfa-Monotype. The ITC library still exists today. - See http://de.wikipedia.org/wiki/ International_Typeface_Corporation (May 2008).

2 From 1980/81 onwards, Prof. Peter Rück (1934-2004) held a professorship for historical ancillary sciences and archiving science at Philipps University Marburg (Germany). In 1990 Linotype asked him to develop a palaeographic evaluation of the first six type designs for the 'Type before Gutenberg' project. He participated in a project meeting at the beginning of June 1990 at Linotype AG in Eschborn. Peter Rück sent his comprehensive analysis of the six calligraphic designs (dated 10 July 1990) to Günter Zorn, the Senior Department Manager at Linotype. In his accompanying letter he wrote, "I hope you don't mind that I discuss and criticise the designs in as objective a manner as possible. I'm fully aware of the fact that a company like Linotype has to take into account aspects other than just historical ones when launching a new product. However, my task was to give my opinion as a palaeographer and not as a marketing strategist." - For a biography of the Swiss paleographer Peter Rück see www.peterrueck.ch/cv.htm (May 2008).

3 In order to avoid the overhangs of script type from breaking off the metal body, casting type with matrices cut at an angle was introduced by Firmin Didot in the 19th century. – See Gustav Bohadti: *Die Buchdruckletter. Ein Handbuch für das Schriftgiesserei- und Buchdruckgewerbe,* Berlin 1954, page 156.

4 For the presentation of his project proposal Adrian Frutiger compiled a five-page report with the title *Type before Gutenberg* in October 1989. In the introduction he stated that handwritten letterforms had a fascinating expression and that many of these faces could easily be adapted to modern setting technologies.

5 A first version of *Hammer-Unziale* was cut as early as 1923/24 and registered by Schriftgiesserei Klingspor in 1925. As can be seen from his correspondence with Karl Hermann Klingspor, Victor Hammer considered a later reworked version, *American Uncial,* which was released in 1953, a big step forward. – See Hans Adolf Halbey, *Karl Klingspor – Leben und Werk,* Offenbach am Main 1991, page 134f. – Victor Hammer's goal was different from that of the 'Type before Gutenberg' project. He believed that uncial was the most readable and harmonious letterform and set out to create the perfect version. He was not making calligraphic typefaces per se. Statements by Hammer about uncial can be found in a small booklet by The Typophiles and also in a two-volume book published by David R. Godine.

6 See Hans Eduard Meier, *Die Schriftentwicklung / The Development of Script and Type / Le développement des caractères,* Zurich 1959, Cham 1994.

7 See Adrian Frutiger, *Schrift Ecriture Lettering. The development of European letter types carved in wood,* Zurich 1951. – A reprint of the booklet appeared under the title: *Schriften des Abendlandes in Holztafeln geschnitten / Bois originaux illustrant l'évolution de l'écriture en Occident / The Development of Western Type carved in wood plates,* Cham 1996.

8 The association Schreibwerkstatt Klingspor Offenbach, Förderkreis internationaler Kalligraphie e.V. (Lettering Workshop Klingspor Offenbach for the Development of International Calligraphy) was founded in 1987. Its predecessor was the Schreibwerkstatt für Jedermann (Lettering Workshop for Everyone), founded in 1982 by Karlgeorg Hoefer and his wife Maria. In 1946 Karlgeorg Hoefer started his post as 'teacher for typography' at Werkkunstschule Offenbach, Germany. Towards the end of his 33 years of teaching he became professor in 1979. Like Hoefer, Gottfried Pott and Herbert Maring ran courses and workshops on calligraphy. – See www.schreibwerkstatt-klingspor.de – and www.kghoefer.de/KgHoefer_Lebensabschnitte.html (May 2008).

9 Statement by Otmar Hoefer about the 'Type before Gutenberg' project, from an internal memo of Linotype AG from 24 January 1990, page 1.

10 'Paläographische Bemerkungen zu Type before Gutenberg von Professor Dr. Peter Rück', Philipps University Marburg Germany, Expert Evaluation dated 10 July 1990, page 1.

11 The 16-page brochure *Type before Gutenberg* exists in different versions. The 1990 version by Linotype AG did not yet contain the alternative characters for *Herculanum.* In the 1991 version by Linotype Hell AG three alternative glyphs are prominently displayed on page 5.

12 At the beginning of the development of the Renaissance typefaces, there were many transitional forms, which are subsumed under the term 'Gotico-Antiqua'. "This collective name therefore does not refer to typefaces of a particular drawn style, but to a whole group of types in which are contained elements of both styles to varying degrees. This also includes types which still feature obvious gothic characteristics, as well as others whose gothic origins are often debatable …" And four pages further, František Muzika wrote: "In its motherland Italy, the Gotico-Antiqua was replaced very early as a handwriting style, and as a typeface it appeared very spontaneously. However, it featured almost no gothic characteristics, so that its attribution to this class of typefaces is still a controversial one." – František Muzika, *Die schöne Schrift,* vol. 2, Prague 1965, pages 92, 96.

13 'Paläographische Bemerkungen zu Type before Gutenberg von Professor Dr. Peter Rück', Philipps University Marburg Germany, Expert evaluation dated 10 July 1990, page 3.

14 See Jean Mallon, *Paléographie romaine,* Madrid 1952, page 174.

15 'Paläographische Bemerkungen zu Type before Gutenberg von Professor Dr. Peter Rück', Philipps-University Marburg Germany, Expert evaluation dated 10 July 1990, page 3f.

16 Herculaneum (Latin Herculanum) was an ancient city (the remains of which still exist) at the western foot of Mount Vesuvius in Italy. It is located nearby (and partly underneath) the modern-day seaside town of Ercolano. According to legend, Herculaneum was founded by Hercules. In 63 AD an earthquake destroyed the elegant villas of Herculaneum and only 16 years later, in 79 AD, Herculaneum and Pompeii were buried through a volcanic eruption. In 1709 Herculaneum was rediscovered by chance. – See *Brockhaus Enzyklopädie in vierundzwanzig Bänden,* vol. 9, Mannheim 1989, page 696.

17 In Karl Schmid's course at the Kunstgewerbeschule Zurich Frutiger created several plant motifs carved in wood (1949). – See Erich Alb (ed.), *Adrian Frutiger – Forms and counterforms,* Cham 1998, page 16f.

18 'Paläographische Bemerkungen zu Type before Gutenberg von Professor Dr. Peter Rück', Philipps University Marburg Germany, Expert evaluation dated 10 July 1990, Appendix 2.

19 See www.linotype.com (May 2008).

20 See www.adobe.com/de/type/ (May 2008).

Shiseido →378

1 Serge Cortesi completed a two-year advanced typography course under Hans-Jürg Hunziker among others at the Atelier National de Création Typographique (ANCT). Through them he subsequently worked as a freelancer for Adrian Frutiger on the *Shiseido* alphabet and other smaller projects, and also helped support Bruno Pfäffli on jobs for Frutiger. From an email from Serge Cortesi to Heidrun Osterer, 27 May 2008. – See www.sergecortesi.com (May 2008).

2 Atelier National de Création Typographique (ANCT), later the Atelier National de Recherche Typographique (ANRT), an institute founded in 1984 in Paris for the advancement of typography and transferred to Nantes about 2002. It was closed in 2006. Aside from Hans-Jürg Hunziker, other well-known lecturers were André Baldinger, Albert Boton, Peter Keller (director after 1990) and Jean Widmer. From a telephone conversation on 16 June 2008 between Peter Keller and Heidrun Osterer.

3 Shinzo Fukuhara, son of company founder Arinobu Fukuhara, travelled for years through America and Europe, which made a great impression on him. This was evident in his aesthetic approach to product design and advertising which was previously unknown in Japan. In 1916 he formed a design department composed of young people who exclusively dealt with advertising and design, despite the fact that Shiseido only had one single cosmetics outlet at the time. The design was heavily influenced by Art Nouveau, and also by Art Deco and arabesque elements. Their creative interpretations of European design steadily developed into the Shiseido style. – See www.shiseido.co.jp/e/story/html/sto21600.htm (May 2008).

4 Serge Lutens, whose professional training consisted solely of an aborted hairdressing apprenticeship, worked for *Vogue* from 1963 and for Dior from 1968, before being able to transform his visions into reality at Shiseido starting in 1980. Under his directorship the company received a new image as well as expanding its range of perfumes. Lutens himself created the fragrances and installed the in-house shop 'Les Salons du Palais Royal Shiseido' in Paris, where the perfumes were sold. – See Renate Wolf: 'Betäubend', in *Die Zeit,* no. 40, Hamburg 1996, page 91. – See http://en.wikipedia.org/wiki/Serge_Lutens (July 2008).

5 On a 1966 poster entitled 'Beauty Cake', *Peignot* is used for the headline. – See www.shiseido.co.jp/e/story/html/sto21600.htm (May 2008).

6 Small package with multicoloured illustrations for the Shiseido beauty salon. – See *Graphis,* no. 122, vol. 21, Zurich 1965, page 503.

7 According to a conversation between Helmut Schmid and Philipp Stamm from 22 February 2005 in Basel, and also an email from Helmut Schmid on 22 August 2005.

8 Telephone call conversation 30 January 2007 with Ms Tomoko, assistant creative director, Shiseido Paris.

Frutiger Capitalis →380

1 See the Linotype brochure *Fonts in Focus 2,* Bad Homburg 2006, page 4.

2 Adrian Frutiger wrote his memoirs between 1996 and 1998. They are kept in the archives of the Swiss Foundation Type and Typography.

3 See Adrian Frutiger: *Der Mensch und seine Zeichen,* 3 vols., Frankfurt 1978, 1979, 1981. (Adrian Frutiger: *Signs and symbols: their design and meaning.* New York 1989.)

4 Five-page letter from Adrian Frutiger to Otmar Hoefer, January 1993.

5 The business plan drawn up by Anja Plowright of Linotype on 19 June 1992 explains the intention of this pi font, its target market, competition and distribution.

6 The eight groups are: 'Signs from Various Cultures', 'The Song of Solomon', 'Christian & Religious Symbols', 'Crafts & Animals Signs', 'Signs of the Zodiac', 'Hand Signs', 'Vignettes for the Koran' and 'Life Signs'.

Pompeijana →384

1 The survey 'Paläographische Bemerkungen zu Type before Gutenberg von Professor Dr. Peter Rück' (Palaeographic Remarks on Type before Gutenberg by Dr. Peter Rück) from 10 July 1990 lists two alternative names for Adrian Frutiger's typeface *Herculanum,* among which was Pompeii. The naming of *Pompeijana* may have been influenced by this.

2 Based on the graffiti at Pompeii dating from the 1st century CE, today, Capitalis Rustica is generally placed prior to Capitalis Quadtrata.

3 Adrian Frutiger's angle specification is typographically oriented. It goes from an upright form with 0 degree, and not as is usual, from the horizontal. The slope of a cursive is defined by the angle of the pen, a steep pen angle, like that seen in Rustica, produces a shallower slope. Anders Stan Knight, he writes that the vertical strokes of the rustica of 'Vergilius Platinus' are written at an angle of 80 deg., the curves at 60 deg. and the diagonals at 45 deg. – See Stan Knight, *Historical Scripts,* New Castle, Delaware 1998, page 25.

4 See Alfred Finsterer (Ed.), *Hoffmanns Schriftatlas. Ausgewählte Alphabete und Anwendungen aus Vergangenheit und Gegenwart,* Stuttgart 1952, page 3. – See Albert Kapr: *Schriftkunst. Geschichte, Anatomie und Schönheit der lateinischen Buchstaben,* Dresden 1971, page 33. (English edition: Albert Kapr: *Art of Lettering: the History, Anatomy and Aesthetics of the Roman Letter Forms,* Munich 1983.)

5 See Hans Eduard Meier, *Die Schriftentwicklung / The Development of Script and Type / Le développement des caractères,* Zurich 1959, Natick 1984, Cham 1994.

6 Pompeii, in Italian Pompei, lies southeast of Vesuvius and Naples. The ancient city was inhabited succesively by Oscans, Etruscans and Samnites, and became a Roman colony under Sulla. The city was badly damaged by an earthquake on 5 February 62 (or 63) CE, and had been only partially rebuilt when, on 24 August 79 CE, it was completely destroyed by a volcanic eruption, along with its neighbouring city of Herculaneum. See *Brockhaus Enzyklopädie in vierundzwanzig Bänden,* vol. 17, Mannheim 1992, page 349.

7 See Adrian Frutiger, *Schrift Ecriture Lettering. The Development of Western Type Carved in Wood Plates,* Zurich 1951, Cham 1996.

8 The conversation with Adrian Frutiger about *Pompeijana* was conducted by Erich Alb, Rudolf Barmettler and Philipp Stamm on 18 March 2003.

9 The enlarged copy of the Rustica written by Hans Eduard Meier forms part of the documents for *Pompeijana* donated by Adrian Frutiger to the Swiss Foundation for Type and Typography.

10 On the last page of his 48-page booklet *The Development of Script and Type,* Hans Eduard Meier cites as the original for his version of Rustica a reproduction of 'Vergilius Palatinus' from the book by Herman Degering. A G with a descender is the only exception. It is an embellishment found only on the last line of a page. – See Hermann Degering, *Lettering,* Berlin 1929, London 1965, page 29.

11 *Virgile* is classified as a *display* font on page 508, *Carus* and *Pompeijana* as *Blackletter* fonts on pages 6 and 23 respectively. – See Mai-Linh Thi Truong, Jürgen Siebert, Erik Spiekermann, *FontBook. Digital Typeface Compendium,* Berlin 2006.

12 In the 'Font Book' a rough classification of the typefaces into the eight groups Sans, Serif, Slab, Script, Display, Blackletter, Symbols and Non-Latin was used. In the 1963 Vox classification and in the DIN 16518 printing type classification, scripts that is, printing typefaces with a handwritten appearance are divided into two groups. Group VIII written scripts (scriptes) contain the current (Letters) and the chancery typefaces (Documentaires). Typefaces that were derived from antiquas or cursives that had been personally modified were placed in Group IX (handwritten antiquas). A considerable component of this group are however the historical book faces. Adrian Frutiger's *Herculanum* is assigned to Scriptes, while *Ondine* and *Pompeijana* and handwritten antiquas. – See Mai-Linh Thi Truong, Jürgen Siebert, Erik Spiekermann, *FontBook. Digital Typeface Compendium,* Berlin 2006. – See Georg Kurt Schauer, *Klassifikation. Bemühungen um eine Ordnung im Druckschriftenbestand,* Darmstadt 1975.

13 Parallel pathways can be discerned in the development of various types of script in Roman antiquity. A newer script would not automatically replace an older one; there would instead be an extension of the script's characters. In addition, there were different areas of use that existed side-by-side and in which the scripts would develop further according to the medium they were written on, and the implements used to write them. The areas can be clearly distinguished: inscriptions, book scripts and scripts for correspondence.

As writing became faster, the majuscule scripts developed ascenders and descenders and the angles of the letters became rounder. Naturally, minuscule scripts developed first in the area of hastily written scripts, the so-called Roman cursives. Towards the end of the 1st century CE isolated minuscule forms are found in majuscule cursives. By the 3rd century CE these are much more prevalent. The Roman mixed book script of the 2nd and 3rd centuries CE also exhibits these lowercase forms. A continuation of this development can be seen in the Roman uncial of the 4th and 5th centuries CE, and moreso in the half-uncial of the 5th century CE, where they dominate the composition. The contemporaneous book script, Capitalis Rustica, shows no lowercase forms. The lowercase forms that are still in use today finally appear in the Carolingian minuscule of the late 8th century CE.

Rusticana →390

1 See FRANTIŠEK MUZIKA, *Die schöne Schrift in der Entwicklung des lateinischen Alphabets*, vol. 1, Prague 1965, page 96 and table 11.
2 See ADRIAN FRUTIGER, *Schrift Ecriture Lettering. The development of European letter types carved in wood*, Zurich 1951.
3 See PIERRE QUONIAM, *Le Louvre*, Éditions de la Réunion des musées nationaux, Paris 1976.
4 Two thin files containing the original design drawings for *Pompeijana* and *Rusticana* were passed on to the Swiss Foundation Type and Typography by Adrian Frutiger. Both were labelled 'Rustica'.
5 František Muzika named the script form that around 250–150 BC featured fattened terminals 'Roman monumental script, concave transitional'. - See FRANTIŠEK MUZIKA, *Die schöne Schrift in der Entwicklung des lateinischen Alphabets,* vol. 1, Prague 1965, page 96.

Frutiger Stones / Frutiger Symbols →396

1 Adrian Frutiger demonstrates his knowledge of the Mas d'Azil stones in the third volume of his trilogy *Der Mensch und seine Zeichen*, where they are depicted. - See ADRIAN FRUTIGER, *Der Mensch und seine Zeichen. Zeichen, Symbole, Signete, Signale,* Frankfurt 1981, pages 97, 111. - ADRIAN FRUTIGER, *Signs and symbols: their design and meaning,* New York 1989.
2 Harald Haarmann and Károly Földes-Papp classify them as mesolithic (c. 10000 to 6000 BC). Hans Jensen dates them from 12000 to 8000 BC and thus as palaeolithic. - See HARALD HAARMANN, *Universalgeschichte der Schrift,* Frankfurt / New York 1991, page 63. - KÁROLY FÖLDES-PAPP, *Vom Felsbild zum Alphabet,* Stuttgart 1966, page 36 f. - HANS JENSEN, *Die Schrift in Vergangenheit und Gegenwart,* Berlin 1969, page 30.
3 Adrian Frutiger in conversation with Erich Alb, Rudolf Barmettler and Philipp Stamm on 25 February 2002.
4 In an undated summary of Frutiger typefaces produced by Linotype, it is presented under the working title *Frutiger Pebbles.*
5 See ADRIAN FRUTIGER, *Der Mensch und seine Zeichen,* edited by Horst Heiderhoff, 3 vols., Frankfurt am Main, 1978, 1979, 1981. - ADRIAN FRUTIGER, *Signs and symbols: their design and meaning,* New York 1989.

Frutiger Neonscript →400

1 Adrian Frutiger, 26 January 2001, in conversation about *Ondine* with Erich Alb, Rudolf Barmettler and Philipp Stamm.
2 Adrian Frutiger wrote in his memoirs that he was introduced to Niklaus Imfeld by Kurt Wälti. The latter was working for the signage department of the Swiss post office, in collaboration with Westineon. When Imfeld learned that Wälti was in touch with Frutiger, he asked to be introduced. Through the resulting friendship Frutiger received contracts for the logo and typeface and was also appointed to Westiform's board of directors.
3 Westineon, an offshoot of Westinghouse, an American electrical products company, produced high-voltage neon tubes. Today Westineon produces electrical lamps and lighting. The signage business has been taken over by Westiform. - See www.westiform.com (June 2008).
4 Due to fears about font and intellectual property theft, Westiform is unwilling to give any further information on *Frutiger Neonscript* and its use.

Nami →402

1 Letter from Adrian Frutiger to Heidrun Osterer and Philipp Stamm 16 June 2007, containing sample strings of *Nami.*
2 The undersea Sumatra-Andaman earthquake of 26 December 2004, with a force of 9.1 on the Richter scale, unleashed several tidal waves. The tsunami (Japanese, *tsu:* harbour, *nami:* wave) brought enormous devastation to Western Indonesia, Thailand, India and East Africa. It caused 230000 deaths, injured 110000 and made more than 1.7 million people homeless. The term *tsunami* comes from Japanese fishermen who, returning from a fishing trip, found their harbour devastated, even though they had not noticed any unusual wave activity while they were at sea. - See http://en.wikipedia.org/wiki/Tsunami. - See http://geology.com/articles/tsunami-geology.shtml (July 2008).
3 The flat curve junctures were already incorporated in sans serif types at the beginning of the 20th century - among others, in Morris Fuller Benton's 1910 Art Nouveau typeface *Hobo. Gill Sans* (1928–32) also shows this distinguishing characteristic, but only in the lowercase b d p q. It is, therefore, mostly sans serifs derived from renaissance antiquas that show these flat curve junctures, often only in the lowercase b and q. In the 1980s, and more noticeably in the 1990s, typefaces with this characteristic appeared, marking a trend. How many and which of the letters a b d g m n p q r u were given this treatment varies between the following typefaces: *FF Dax, Linotype Ergo, Fedra Sans, Formata, Generica, Lux Sans, PTL Manual Sans, DTL Prokyon, Raldo, FF Sari (Barmen), Sassoon Sans, Skia, Linotype Veto.*
4 *Linotype Veto,* by the Zurich-based graphic designer Marco Ganz, was released in 1994, originally under the name of *Evo,* from H. Berthold Systeme GmbH, the successor company to H. Berthold AG. - See YVONNE SCHWEMER-SCHEDDIN, 'Evo - A mirror of everyday culture', in *Typografische Monatsblätter TM* 1/1996, page 1 ff.
5 With *FF Dax* Hans Reichel continued the style of his 1983 typeface *Barmen,* which was re-issued by FontShop International in 1999 under the new name of *FF Sari.*

"The essence of a sign is like a pure tone in music.
 The exterior form, however, is what makes the sound."
 Adrian Frutiger

Biography

1928
Adrian Johann Frutiger, born 24 May
in Unterseen, near Interlaken, Switzerland.

1944-48
Typesetting apprenticeship at Otto Schlaefli AG,
printers, Interlaken, Switzerland.

1944-48
Studied at Kunstgewerbeschule
(School of Arts and Crafts) Bern, Switzerland.
Lecturer: Walter Zerbe.

1948-49
Employed as compositor at Gebr. Fretz AG,
Zurich, Switzerland.

1949-51
Further studies at the Kunstgewerbeschule
(School of Arts and Crafts) Zurich, Switzerland.
Lecturers: Walter Käch, Karl Schmid,
Alfred Willimann.

1951-52
Studio with the scientific draughtsman
Willi Urfer, Zurich, Switzerland.

1952
Married Paulette Flückiger from Porrentruy,
Switzerland.

1952-60
Employed as type designer
at Deberny & Peignot, Paris, France.

1952-60
Taught at the École Estienne, Paris, France
(training school for the graphic industries).

1954
Birth of son Stéphane, death of wife Paulette.

1954-58
Head of the Type Design Studio
at Deberny & Peignot, Paris, France.

1954-66
Taught at the École Nationale Supérieure
des Arts Décoratifs, Paris, France.
Visiting lecturer until 1968.

1955
Married Simone Bickel from Geneva,
Switzerland, a friend of Paulette's.

1956
Birth of daughter Anne-Sylvie.

1957-67
Artistic director at Éditions Hermann, Paris,
France. Publisher: Pierre Berès.

1958
Birth of daughter Annik.

1958
First journey to the USA, to Photon Inc.,
to resolve problems caused by the reworked
drawings for the Photon photosetting machine.

1958-60
Artistic director at Deberny & Peignot, Paris,
France.

1960
With Remy Peignot, founded and led internal
Atelier de composition at Deberny & Peignot,
Paris, France.

1961-65
Self employed, Atelier Frutiger, Place d'Italie,
Paris, France.

1961-67
External artistic director at Deberny & Peignot,
Paris, France.

1963-64
Taught at the École Nationale Supérieure des
Beaux-Arts, Paris, France.

1963-73
Collaboration with ECMA, Geneva, Switzerland
on the development of *OCR-B* and other
projects.

1963-81
Consultant at IBM for typewriter typefaces;
adapted existing typefaces for the golfball in
Lexington, USA and Orléans, France. Instructed
employees worldwide on type history and
typeface development.

1965
First trip to Japan for an ECMA conference
in Tokyo. On the return leg visited the National
Institute of Design in Ahmedabad, India at the
invitation of Armin Hofmann.

1965-68
Atelier Frutiger, Villa Moderne, à la Vache Noire,
Arcueil, France.

1967
Three-week residency at the
National Institute of Design, Ahmedabad, India.

1968-85
Worked as consultant to D. Stempel AG,
Frankfurt am Main, Germany.

1969-74
Atelier Frutiger+Pfäffli, Villa Moderne,
à la Vache Noire, Arcueil, France.

1972
Death of daughter Anne-Sylvie.

1974-92
Atelier Frutiger / Atelier Pfäffli, Villa Moderne,
à la Vache Noire, Arcueil, France.

1980
Death of daughter Annik.

Since 1985
Consultant at Linotype, Eschborn and
Bad Homburg, Germany.

1992
Moved to Bremgarten near Bern, Switzerland.

2008
Death of wife Simone.

Awards and prizes

1950
Federal Department of the Interior Prize, Bern,
Switzerland.

1960
Advertising campaign award, given by
De Arbeiderspers, Amsterdam, Netherlands,
for the 1959 Citroën advertising campaign
'La joie de vivre', designed in conjunction with
Bruno Pfäffli.

1968
Chevalier dans l'ordre des Arts et des Lettres,
Ministère de la Culture et de la Communication,
Paris, France.

1970
Award in competition for 'Most Beautiful
Swiss Books' with Bruno Pfäffli for *Im Anfang
Au commencement In the beginning*,
Bern, Switzerland.

1971
Silver medal in competition for 'Most Beautiful
International Books' with Bruno Pfäffli for
Das Hohe Lied Salomos, International Book Art
Exhibition, Leipzig, Germany.

1974
Honoured with a coat of arms by the city of
Interlaken, Switzerland.

1984
Paul-Haupt Prize from the city of Bern,
Switzerland.

1986
Gutenberg Prize from the
International Gutenberg Society and
the city of Mainz, Germany.

1987
Gold medal from the Type Directors Club,
New York, USA.

1989
Jäggi Prize from the Jäggi bookshop,
Basel, Switzerland.

1990
Officier de l'ordre des Arts et des Lettres,
Ministère de la Culture et de la Communication,
Paris, France.

1993
Grand Prix National de la Culture, Graphic Arts
Section, Paris, France.

2006
SOTA Typography Award, The Society
of Typographic Aficionados, Boston, USA.

2007
Prix Designer 2007, Federal Office of Culture,
Bern, Switzerland.

Lectures
A selection

1956
**First lecture on Univers and the Classification
of Book Typefaces**
École Estienne, Paris, France.

17 November 1960
**'Nos caractéres sont ils l'expression de notre
epoche?'**
École Estienne, Paris, France.

20 September 1964
Lecture in Heritage of the Graphic Arts Series
Gallery 303, New York, USA.

3 May 1966
'Technik und Schriftform'
Allgemeine Gewerbeschule, Basel, Switzerland
Given during a one-week guest lectureship

19 May 1966
**'Grundsätzliche Betrachtungen über den
Buchdruck'**
Typographical forum during the yearly ATypI
conference, Gutenberg Museum, Germany.

25 September 1966
**Lecture on the Technical Developments
in Printing Type**
Gallery 303, New York, USA.

22 November 1966
**Lecture on the Technical Developments in
Printing Type**
Given during the Cours Magistraux at the École
Estienne, Paris, France.

September 1967
Lecture on Typography
IBM, Southampton, UK.

9 November 1967
Lecture on Typefaces in India
Given during the ATypI yearly conference in the
Unesco Building, Paris, France.

10 November 1967
**'Alphabets pour la lecture automatique,
magnétique et optique'**
Given during the ATypI yearly conference in the
Unesco Building, Paris, France.

April 1968
'La Typographie'
IBM, Barcelona, Spain.

September 1968
**Lecture on typographic possibilities in the
age of the computer**
Given during the yearly ATypI conference,
Frankfurt am Main, Germany.

September 1968
'La Typographie'
IBM, Milan, Italy.

27 November 1968
**Paper on the reworking of metal type
for photosetting**
Press reception at D. Stempel AG and Linotype,
Frankfurt am Main, Germany.

June 1969
**'Entwurf von Buchstaben für Kathoden-
strahlröhren-Systeme'**
Given during the yearly ATypI conference,
Charles University, Prague, Czechoslovakia.

October 1973
**'Typographic Training for Technicians and
Technical Training for Typographers'**
Given during the yearly ATypI conference,
Copenhagen, Denmark.

Exhibitions

A selection

28 May 1974
'Die Verantwortung des Schriftenherstellers gegenüber dem Unterbewusstsein des Lesers'
Given during the yearly ATypI conference, Unesco building, Paris, France.

29 November 1979
'Schrift in der Umwelt / Zukunft der Schrift, Schrift in der Zukunft der neuen Medien'
Two lectures at the Hochschule für bildende Künste, Braunschweig, Germany.

5 February 1980
'Datenprogramme und Laserstrahlen – die neuen Schreibwerkzeuge'
Typographical Society, Munich, Germany.

22 September 1980
'Schrift und Papier – der Mensch heute'
Given during the yearly ATypI conference in Basel, Switzerland.

26 January 982
'Textschriften und Buchtypografie heute'
Organised by the Frankfurt Publishers' Working Party in the offices of the Stiftung Buchkunst, Frankfurt am Main, Germany.

24 February 1984
'Mensch und Schrift'
Kantonale Schule für Gestaltung, Biel, Switzerland.

30 May 1985
Lecture on the beauty and readability of a typeface
Venue unknown, Gothenburg, Sweden.

November 1986
'Technik und Schriftform'
Organised by Linotype at the Centre Georges Pompidou, Paris, France.

10 December 1986
'Schriftqualität für den digitalen Fotosatz'
Schule für Gestaltung, Bern, Switzerland.

May 1987
Lecture on the beauty and readability of a typeface
Arbeitskreis Forum Typographie, Offenbach, Germany.

28 June 1987
Lecture on the beauty and readability of a typeface
Tokyo, Japan.

October 1987
Speech given at the presentation of the Gold Medal, Type Directors Club of New York
New York, USA.

24 November 1987
'Fyrsta alþjóðlega letursamsætið á Íslandi'
Iceland.

18-19 February 1988
'Sequential Design'
14th Icograda Student Seminar, London, UK.

5 September 1988
'Zeichen und Gefühl, Zeichen und Verstand'
Bałtyskie Centrum (Baltic Centre), Gdansk, Poland.

20 October 1988
'Du caractère manuscrit au caractère d'imprimerie'
La société française de graphologie, Paris, France.

8 November 1988
Lecture on sans serif typefaces
Organised by Linotype, London, UK.

8 December 1988
'Modern-day type and design'
Lecture given on the 20th anniversary of the Frederic W. Goudy Award at the Rochester Institute of Technology, New York, USA.

May 1989
'Zur inhaltlichen Harmonie von Text und Bild. Das Hohelied Salomos / Die Schöpfungsgeschichte'
Lecture given during a symposium at the International Book Art Exhibition (IBA), Leipzig, Germany.

April 1989
Research Paper
Given during the HRP-Media Seminars at the Hotel Intercontinental, Oerlikon, Switzerland.

19 October 1989
'Zeichen erkennen, mit dem Gefühl – mit dem Verstand'
Schule für Gestaltung, Bern, Switzerland.

November 1989
Lecture
At the Type & Typo event, Hamburg, Germany.

November 1989
Lecture
Cantonal Library, St. Gallen, Switzerland.

2 September 1990
'The designer's response'
Given during the yearly ATypI conference, Oxford, UK.

27 October 1990
'Von der Type zur Typografie'
Lecture given on Tag der Typografie, Hotel Bern, Bern, Switzerland.

1 November 1991
'Gibt es die Ideale DTP-Schrift?'
Given during theTypo ade!? symposium, organised by abc-Winterthur Textbildtechnik in Technorama Winterthur, Winterthur, Switzerland.

16 January-11 February 1961
Deux cents ans de création de caractères
École Estienne, Paris, France.

5-16 October 1963
L'Œuvre graphique de Adrian Frutiger
Galerie Pierre Berès, Paris, France.

10 June-30 October, 1964
'Graphismes by Frutiger'
Monotype House, London, England.

3 May-28 May 1966
Adrian Frutiger, Paris - Schriftkünstler
Gewerbeschule, Basel, Switzerland.

21 September 1973-...
Schrift - Signet - Symbol. Formgebung in Schwarz und Weiss
Gutenberg Museum, Bern, Switzerland.

21 November 1976-2 January 1977
Adrian Frutiger - Zeichen Schriften Symbole
Gutenberg Museum, Mainz, Germany.

3 June-26 June 1988
Freie Arbeiten
Könizer Gallery, Köniz, Switzerland.

Autumn 1988
Litera, Znak, Symbol
Travelling exhibition through the cities of Thorn, Warsaw, Cracow and Breslau, Poland (during the ATypI conference).

15 April-12 September 1994
Adrian Frutiger, son œuvre typographique et ses écrits
Maison du Livre, de l'Image et du Son, Villeurbanne, France.

September 1994
Adrian Frutiger, Denken und Schaffen einer Typographie
Unterseen, Switzerland.

19 October-19 November 1994
Hommage an die Schrift
Schule für Gestaltung Bern, Switzerland. Organised by: Gesellschaft der Freunde des Gutenbergmuseums (Society of the Friends of the Gutenberg Museum), Freiburg.

6 November–29 November 1994
'Adrian Frutiger, son œuvre typographique et ses écrits'
Atrium, école des arts visuel de l'Université Laval édifice la Fabrique, Quebec, Canada.

February 1995
Title unknown
Ecole des arts décoratifs, Geneva, Switzerland.

25 April-23 June 1996
Adrian Frutiger, his typographic work and his writings
Design Exchange Resource, Toronto, Canada.

October to mid-December 1996
Adrian Frutiger: Gesang der Wandlungen
Basler Papiermühle, Basel, Switzerland.

October 1997
Symbole und Zeichen - freie grafische Arbeiten
Parish hall, Bremgarten bei Bern, Switzerland.

Beginning 1998
Formen und Gegenformen
Travelling exhibition. Idea and concept: Erich Alb.
  18 June-....August 1998
Heidelberger Druckmaschinen AG, (Heidelberg Printing Machines, AG), Heidelberg, Germany (coincided with the celebrations of Adrian Frutiger's 70th birthday)
  9 October-11 October 1998
Rat für Formgebung, (Design Council) Frankfurt, Germany, coincided with Frankfurt Book Fair
  4 February-19 March 1999
Design Zentrum Thüringen, Weimar, Germany
  19 May-30 June 2000
Basler Papiermühle (Basel Paper Mill), Basel, Switzerland
  1 November 2000-30 May 2001
Gutenberg Museum, Fribourg, Switzerland
  14 June-10 August 2001
Institut für Medien und Kunst (Insitute for Media and Art), Lage-Hörste, Germany
  28 February-14 April 2002
Gutenberg Museum, Mainz, Germany, last call for the exhibition. Adrian Frutiger then donated it to the Museum.

Beginning 1999
Read me - mit Adrian Frutiger durch die Welt der Zeichen und Buchstaben
Travelling exhibition. Idea and concept: Anja Bodmer and Jürg Brühlmann
  17 June-1 August 1999
Forum für Medien und Gestaltung (Forum for Media and Design), Kornhaus, Bern, Switzerland
  13 January-27 February 2000
Gewerbemuseum, Winterthur, Switzerland
  21 June-3 September 2000
19th International Biennale of Graphic Design, Brno, Czech Republic
  20 November-10 December 2000
National Institute of Design, Ahmedabad, India
  8-25 May 2002
Grafist 6, The Sixth International Istanbul Graphic Design Week, Istanbul, Turkey
  1 June-1 July 2004
Berner Fachhochschule - Hochschule für Architektur, Bau und Holz HSB, Biel, Switzerland
  12 August-31 October 2005
Aargauer Kantonsbibliothek, (Library of the Canton of Aarau) Aarau, Switzerland.

21 October-3 November 99
Okakura. Adrian Frutiger. Typoarchitektur.
Fachhochschule für Technik und Wirtschaft FHTW (School of Technology and Economics), organised by The International Design Centre, Berlin, Germany.

29 April–30 October 2000
'Adrian Frutiger: Gesang der Wandlungen'
Symbols, signs, watermarks. Klostermühle Thierhaupten, Thierhaupten, Germany.

19 May-5 September 2004
Off Side Art 2: Adrian Frutiger - Type Designer
Haus Konstruktiv, Zurich, Switzerland.

Publications by Adrian Frutiger

Specialist articles by Adrian Frutiger
A selection

Die Rede des jungen Hediger
Work done in 4th year of typesetting apprenticeship, Gewerbeschule der Stadt Bern, 1947.

Die Kirchen am Thunersee
Final submission for typesetting apprenticeship, with woodcuts by Adrian Frutiger; text, setting and printing by Adrian Frutiger, Otto Schlaefli AG, printers, Interlaken 1948.

Schrift - Écriture - Lettering. Die Entwicklung der europäischen Schriften, in Holz geschnitten - Bois originaux illustrant l'évolution de l'écriture en Europe - The development of European script carved in wood
Final submission at the Kunstgewerbeschule Zurich, published by the Bildungsverband Schweizerischer Buchdrucker, Zurich 1951.

Au commencement
Text from the first chapter of Genesis, hand set in *Univers* 55, 24 pt, with 15 woodcuts by Adrian Frutiger, printed in a run of 140 copies, Atelier Frutiger, published by Pierre Berès, Éditions Hermann, Paris 1962.

partages
26 woodcuts by Adrian Frutiger, printed in a run of 75 copies, published by Pierre Berès, Éditions Hermann, Paris 1962.

Univers
With contributions by Adrian Frutiger and Emil Ruder, Ernst Gloor (ed.) handsetting room, Zurich 1966.

Cantique des Cantiques de Salomon – Das Hohe Lied Salomos – The Song of Songs which is Solomon's – אשר לשלמה שיר השירים
With illustrations by Adrian Frutiger, typography by Bruno Pfäffli, Winterthur Printing Press AG, Winterthur 1966 / Flamberg-Verlag, Zurich 1967.

Im Anfang – Au commencement – In the beginning – בראשית
With illustrations by Adrian Frutiger, typography by Bruno Pfäffli, Winterthur Printing Press AG, Winterthur 1966 / Flamberg-Verlag, Zurich 1969.

Typographic Training for Technicians and Technical Training for Typographers
Booklet, Copenhagen 1973.

Der Mensch und seine Zeichen
Edited: Horst Heiderhoff. D. Stempel AG Frankfurt am Main / Heiderhoff Verlag, Echzell. First edition, Volume 1: *Zeichen erkennen Zeichen gestalten*, 1978. Volume 2: *Die Zeichen der Sprachfixierung*, 1979. Volume 3: *Zeichen, Symbole, Signete, Signale*, 1981. – now in 10th edition (three volumes combined): Marix Verlag, Wiesbaden 2006. Translations: Spanish: *Signos Símbolos Marcas Señales*, Barcelona 1981. French: *Des signes et des hommes*, Lausanne, 1983; *L'Homme et ses signes*, Reillanne 1999. English: *Signs and Symbols: Their Design and Meaning*, London 1989 and 1998; New York 1998. Italian: *Segni & Simboli*, Viterbo 1996. Portuguese: *Sinais & Símbolos*, São Paulo 1999. Polish: *Czowiek i jego znaki*, Warsaw 2003. Korean: *l'Homme et ses signes, Der Mensch und seine Zeichen*, both Seoul 2007.

Type - Sign - Symbol
With articles by Maurice Besset, Emil Ruder and Rudolf Schneebeli, ABC-Verlag, Zurich 1980.

Zur Geschichte der linearen, serifenlosen Schriften
Brochure by Linotype AG, c.1986.

Der Prophet Jona
Picture cycle, Könizer Gallery, Köniz, Switzerland 1988.

Zeichen
Design: Jost Hochuli, Typotron AG, St.Gallen 1989 (Issue 7 from the series Typotron-Hefte).

Adrian Frutiger, son œuvre typographique et ses écrits
Exhibition catalogue, text by Jost Hochuli and Adrian Frutiger with articles by Andrew Blum, Roger Chatelain, Martin Enzensberger, Horst Heiderhoff, Emil Ruder, Hans Schneebeli and Kurt Weidemann, Maison du Livre, de l'Image et du Son, Villeurbanne 1994.

Adrian Frutiger. Denken und Schaffen einer Typografie
Exhibition catalogue, text by Jost Hochuli and Adrian Frutiger with articles by Andrew Blum, Roger Chatelain, Martin Enzensberger, Horst Heiderhoff, Emil Ruder, Hans Schneebeli and Kurt Weidemann, Maison du Livre, de l'Image et du Son, Villeurbanne 1994.

Eine Typografie
New edition of *Adrian Frutiger. Denken und Schaffen einer Typografie*, Vogt-Schild-Verlag, Solothurn 1995 – 5th edition, Syndor Press GmbH, Cham 2001.

Schriften des Abendlandes in Holztafeln geschnitten
Reprint of final diploma submission from 1951, Syndor Press GmbH, Cham 1996.

Gesang der Wandlungen
Symbols by Adrian Frutiger, turned into watermarks by Markus Müller, Basler Papiermühle, Basel 1996.

Song of Changes
Symbols by Adrian Frutiger, turned into watermarks by Markus Müller, Basler Papiermühle, Basel 1996.

Symbole Zeichen. Wanderungen
Fold-out map of symbols, fashioned after the standardised Hallwag street map symbols, self-published / personal distribution, Bern 1996.

Symbole Zeichen. Wanderungen
Fold-out map of symbols, fashioned after the standardised Hallwag street map symbols, Syndor Press, Cham, 1997.

Symbols and Signs. Explorations
Map of symbols, fashioned after the standardised Hallwag street map symbols, Syndor Press, Cham, 1997.

de Symboles en Signes. promenades
Fold-out map of symbols, fashioned after the standardised Hallwag street map symbols, Syndor Press, Cham, 1997.

Formen und Gegenformen – Formes et contreformes – Forms and Counterforms
Text by Ronald Schenkel, printed in a run of 1400 copies in 17-colour offset printing, 98 copies signed and numbered by the author, accompanied by an embossed colour print on handmade paper. Produced to celebrate Adrian Frutiger's 70th birthday. Published by Erich Alb, Syndor Press GmbH, Cham 1998. Paperback edition: Syndor Press GmbH, Cham 1999.

Worte für einen Strich – Paroles pour un trait – Words for Line Drawings
Supplement to *Formen und Gegenformen*, text by Adrian and Simone Frutiger, published by Erich Alb, Syndor Press GmbH, Cham 1998.

Geometrie der Gefühle – Géométrie des sentiments – Geometry of Feelings
Published by Erich Alb, Syndor Press GmbH, Cham 1998.

Lebenzyklus – Cycle de la vie – Life Cycle
Extract from *Formen und Gegenformen*, published by Erich Alb, Syndor Press GmbH, Cham 1999.

À bâtons rompus. Ce qu'il faut savoir du caractère typographique
Text by Adrian Frutiger, Roger Chatelain, Marcelle Charrière, Horst Heiderhoff, Yves Perrousseaux and Emil Ruder, Atelier Perrousseaux, Reillanne 2001.

Ein Leben für die Schrift
Verlag Schlaefli & Maurer AG, Interlaken 2003.

Entstehung und Wandel unserer Schrift
Text by Adrian Frutiger and Hans Flück, Verlag Wegwarte, Bolligen 2003.

Une vie consacré à l'écriture typographique
Based on *Ein Leben für die Schrift*, Atelier Perrousseaux, Reillanne 2004.

Nachdenken über Zeichen und Schrift
Haupt-Verlag, Bern 2005.

Adrian Frutiger's Buch der Schriften
Marix Verlag, Wiesbaden 2005.

Anfangsgeschichten
Woodcuts, drawings and collages by Adrian Frutiger, Marix Verlag, Wiesbaden 2006.

Symbole: Geheimnisvolle Bilder-Schriften, Zeichen, Signale, Labyrinthe, Heraldik
Haupt-Verlag, Bern 2008.

'Der Werdegang der Univers' in *Typographische Monatsblätter, Univers special edition*, 1/1961, page 10a.

'Die Herstellung einer Drucktype' in *Typographische Monatsblätter, Univers special edition*, 1/1961, page 13 – in *Typorama. Rund um das graphische Gewerbe*, Basel 1964, page 39 ff.

'How I came to design Univers' in *Print in Britain*, January 1962, vol. 9, page 263.

'un livre jeune et courageux sur la typographie' in *Informations TG*, no. 134, 25 March 1962, page 3.

Foreword to: Emil Ruder: *Typographie - Ein Gestaltungslehrbuch. Typography – A Manual of Design. Typographie – Un Manuel de Création*, Sulgen/Zurich 1967.

'OCR-B: normalisierte Schrift für optische Lesbarkeit' in *Typographische Monatsblätter*, 1/1967, page 29.

'Composeuse Multipoint' in *Typographische Monatsblätter*, 1/1967.

'OCR-B: A Standardized Character for Optical Recognition' in *The Journal of Typographic Research*, vol. 1, no. 2, 1967, page 137 ff. (with André Gürtler and Nicole Delamarre).

'Typography with the IBM Selectric Composer' in *The Journal of Typographic Research*, vol. 1, no. 3 1967, no page details available.

'Brief aus Indien', offprint from *Typographische Monatsblätter*, 6-7/1967.

'Les alphabets pour la lecture automatique magnétique et optique' in *Caractère*, 12/1967, page 47 f. - in *Arts et Techniques Graphiques*, no. 75, 3-6/1968, page 198 ff.

'IBM Composer' in *IBM Journal*, New York, USA 1968.

'Letter Forms in Photo-typography' in: *The Journal of Typographic Research*, Cleveland, Ohio, Vol. 4, no. 4, 1970.

'The Evolution of Composition Technology' in *IBM Journal of Research and Development*, vol. 12, 1/1968. Also available as an offprint, 1974.

'Die Herstellung von Schriftträgern für Fotosatzsysteme mit hohen Belichtungsgeschwindigkeiten' in *Typografische Monatsblätter*, 01/1969, page 9 ff.

'Über die Zukunft der Schrift für automatische optische Lesbarkeit' in *Typografische Monatsblätter*, 3/1970, page 203 ff.

'La forme des caractères à l'âge de la photocomposition', in *Informations TG*, no. 500, 1970, page 3 ff. - in *Typografische Monatsblätter*, 2/1970, page 141 ff.

'Neugestaltung des Air-France-Flugplans' in *Typografische Monatsblätter*, 1/1971, page 9 ff. (with Bruno Pfäffli).

'L'évolution des caractères pour la lecture optique automatique' in *Informations TG*, No. 535, January 1971, page 3 ff.

'Die Verantwortung des Schriftenherstellers dem Unterbewusstsein des Lesers gegenüber' in *Typografische Monatsblätter,* 8-9/1974, page 607 ff.

'Schreiben und Lesen' in *Typografische Monatsblätter,* 11/1974.

'Das Beschriftungssystem des grössten Flughafens Europas – Der neue Aéroport Charles de Gaulle in Roissy' in *form. Zeitschrift für Gestaltung,* no. III-67, 1974, page 25 ff. (with Horst Heiderhoff).

'Holzschnitte zum ersten Kapitel der Bibel' in *Das Hardermannli,* no. 23, Interlaken 1974.

'Schrift am Röntgenbildschirm' in *Deutscher Drucker,* 23/1975, page 6 f.

'A.Typ.I Arbeitsseminar in Basel' in *Typografische Monatsblätter,* 8-9/1975, page 499 ff.

'Die Beschriftung des Flughafens Paris-Roissy' in *Typografische Monatsblätter,* 1/1977, page 9.

'Die Etienne-Schriften – ein Erscheinungsbild der lateinischen Schrift' in *Typografische Monatsblätter,* 10/1977, page 1 ff.

'Das Schriftbild: Kleid der Lesebotschaft' in *Deutscher Drucker,* 35/1978, page 4 ff.

'Schrift und Papier – der Mensch heute' in *Typografische Monatsblätter,* 5/1980, page 272. Also available as an offprint. Offprint of the address given to the Association Typographique Internationale (AtypI) in Basel, 22 September 1980.

'Type, Paper and You', in *Champion: The Printing Salesman's Herold,* Book 4, Stamford, Connecticut 1982.

'Das Miterleben einer Wandlung. Schriftzeichen für die Satztechnik der Gegenwart' in Hans-Joachim Koppitz (ed.), *Gutenberg-Jahrbuch 1985,* Mainz 1985, page 19.

'L'histoire des Antiques' (History of the Antiquas), part 1 in *Typografische Monatsblätter* 1/1988, page 9. Part 2 in *Typografische Monatsblätter* 3/1988, page 35. Also available as an offprint for Linotype France.

'Konstruktivistisch und human. Avenir – eine neue serifenlose Linear-Antiqua von Adrian Frutiger' in *Linotype express* [ger.] 2/1988, in *Linotype express* [engl.] autumn 1988, in *Graphic Repro* 12/1988, in *Deutscher Drucker* 15.12.1988, in *DruckIndustrie* 3/1989, in *World-Wide Printer* 6/1989, in *Page* 6/1992.

Eine neue konstruktivistische Schrift, Eschborn near Frankfurt, c. 1988.

'Adrian Frutiger Himself' in *Der Druckspiegel,* 8/1988, page 919. Exclusive offprint of Adrian Frutiger's address given at the presentation of the Gold Medal, Type Directors Club of New York.

Foreword to Van Nostrand Reinhold Company: *The International Type Book,* New York 1990.

Foreword to Christopher Perfect, Gordon Rookledge: *Rookledge's international type-finder: the essential handbook of typeface recognition and selection,* New York 1991.

'Gibt es die Ideale DTP-Schrift?' (Is There an Ideal DTP Typeface?) in *Typo ade!? symposium,* Winterthur 1992, part 2, p. 4 ff. Offprint of a paper given at the Typo ade!? symposium.

'Die Schriftfamilie Univers' in *Officina,* June 1992, page 18 ff.

'Was ich für die Zukunft sagen möchte...' in *Heidelberg Nachrichten,* 1/1998.

Foreword to Philip Jodidio: *Paul Andreu, architect,* Basel 2004.

'Adrian Frutiger', in *Le musée Gutenberg à Fribourg. Das Gutenberg Museum in Freiburg,* Gesellschaft der Freunde des Gutenbergmuseums, Fribourg 2004.

Adrian Frutiger. Bemerkungen zum Schriftentwerfen
Interview conducted 10 April 1996 by Erik Spiekermann. Font Shop 1996 (video, 33 minutes). Language: German.

Adrian Frutiger. Schriftengestalter
Documentary film. Director: Anne Cuneo, Fama Film AG, Zurich 1998 (video, 54 minutes), with contributions from Max Caflisch, Marco Ganz, Bruno Pfäffli, Rieder Saluz, Bernard Campiche, Roger de Weck, Reinhard Haus, Bruno Steinert, Flavia Mosele, Sascha Graf, Tobias Krauser. Languages: French, German, Italian. Subtitles: German and English.

Adrian Frutiger: Racine – Fais-moi un signe
Video, 1998/1999. Broadcast on Télévision Suisse Romande. Language: French.

Frutiger
Short portrait for the Alliance Graphique Internationale (AGI). Director: Peter Knapp, Paris 2001 (DVD, 8 minutes). Language: French.

Adrian Frutiger, der Typograf aus Leidenschaft
in NZZ Swiss made, produced by Beat Rauch (video, 6 minutes). Language: German. Broadcast on Swiss television SF 2 on Sunday, 11 March 2001 at 21.30.

Adrian Frutiger. Der Mann von Schwarz und Weiss
Documentary film. Directors: Christine Kopp and Christoph Frutiger. Interlaken 2004 (DVD, 47 minutes). Languages: Swiss-German dialect, German, French, English.

Title unknown
Interview on 18.11.1984, broadcaster unknown, 20 minutes, language: Swiss-German dialect.

Der Stradivari der Buchstaben. Adrian Frutiger – Berner Schriftgestalter mit Weltruf
Producer Luzia Stettler, broadcast on 2.5.2002 on Schweizer Radio DRS 1, 50 minutes, language: German.

Publications about Adrian Frutiger's work
A selection

Articles on Adrian Frutiger's work
A selection

Schweizerischer Typographenbund (ed.)
Univers Special Edition
Typografische Monatsblätter 1/1961.

Kurt Weidemann
Atelier Adrian Frutiger, Paris. Schrift und Schriftmarke
Der Druckspiegel, December 1961,
typographic supplement 12a.

Kurt Weidemann
Atelier Adrian Frutiger, Paris. Marques et Typographie
Der Druckspiegel, December 1961,
typographic supplement 12a.

The Monotype Corporation
Monotype Newsletter
No.130, April 1963, *Univers special edition.*

Maurice Besset
A propos de recherches récentes d'Adrian Frutiger
Special offprint from *Typographische Monatsblätter,* 8–9/1963, page 537 ff.

John Dreyfus
Graphismes by Frutiger. The graphic work of Adrian Frutiger
Exhibition catalogue, London 1964.

Stanislav Souček
Sondernummer Frutiger – Zapf
typografia, no. 9, Prague 1965.

Ove Andersson and Sture Löfberg
Bokstavsgestaltning. Stjärnreminariet Adrian Frutiger
Grafiska Institutet, Stockholm 1967.

Bauersche Giesserei (ed.)
Serifa Vorprobe
With contributions by Emil Ruder and
Hermann Zapf, Frankfurt am Main 1967.

Hans Kuh
Aus der Werkstatt einer Schriftgießerei
Serifa special offprint from *Gebrauchsgraphik,* June 1968.

Walter Zerbe
Schrift, Signet, Symbol: Formgebung in Schwarz und Weiss
Exhibition catalogue, Bern 1973.

Gutenberg-Gesellschaft (ed.)
Adrian Frutiger. Zeichen, Schriften, Symbole
Fold-out brochure to the exhibition of the same name, Mainz 1976. Text by Kurt Weidemann.

D. Stempel AG
Typefaces designed by Adrian Frutiger. Schriften von Adrian Frutiger. Caractères crées par Adrian Frutiger
Text by Horst Heiderhoff, Frankfurt 1983.

Horst Heiderhoff
Formen und Gegenformen. Gestaltungseinheiten im Leben des Schriftkünstler Adrian Frutiger
Special offprint from the *Gutenberg-Jahrbuch* 1985, Mainz 1985.

Gutenberg-Gesellschaft, Mainz
Adrian Frutiger. Gutenberg-Preisträger 1986
With contributions by Dr Anton M. Keim,
Dr Walter Greisner, Adrian Frutiger.
Gutenberg-Gesellschaft, Mainz 1986 (no.107
in the series Kleine Drucke der Gutenberg-
Gesellschaft).

Linotype Library
Linotype Didot. Die Wiederentdeckung des Klassizismus
Special offprint from *Der Druckspiegel* 11/1992
and 12/1992, Eschborn 1992.

Reinhard Haus
Linotype Univers
Special edition from *Columnum*-Journal by
Linotype, No. 22, May 1997, first presentation of
the Linotype Univers.

Friedrich Friedl
Die Univers von Adrian Frutiger
Published by Volker Fischer, Verlag form,
Frankfurt 1998 (from the series Design-
Klassiker.)

Friedrich Friedl
L'Univers d'Adrian Frutiger
Published by Volker Fischer, Verlag form,
Frankfurt 1998 (from the series Design-
Klassiker).

Friedrich Friedl
The Univers by Adrian Frutiger
Published by Volker Fischer, Verlag form,
Frankfurt 1998 (from the series Design-
Klassiker).

Friedrich Friedl
zum siebzigsten geburtstag adrian frutiger
Celebratory speech by Friedrich Friedl on
the occasion of Adrian Frutiger's 70th birthday,
held in the Heidelberg Schloss,
Verlag Hermann Schmidt, Mainz 1998.

Erik Faulhaber
Frutiger. Die Wandlung eines Schriftklassikers
Niggli Verlag, Sulgen 2004.

Anja Bodmer and Jürg Brühlmann
Read me – mit Adrian Frutiger durch die Welt der Zeichen und Buchstaben
Published for travelling exhibition,
Verlag Hochparterre, Zurich 2008.

AUTHOR UNKNOWN: 'Langholzschnitte von
Adrian Frutiger, Glattbrugg / Zürich, gedruckt
ab Galvanos', in *Typographische Monatsblätter,* 12/1951. First publication of his 'Oats',
'Pasture', 'Pine' and 'Horsetail' woodcuts,
accompanied by poetry.

EMIL RUDER: 'Eine Entwicklungsgeschichte der
Schrift', in *Typographische Monatsblätter,*
12/1951, page 536. Presentation of Frutiger's
diploma thesis.

AUTHOR UNKNOWN: no title, in *Typographische
Monatsblätter,* 11/1954, page 560.
Announcement of the publication of the
three new typefaces: *Phoebus, Ondine,*
and *Président* by Deberny & Peignot in the
production year 1953/1954.

EMIL RUDER: 'Univers, eine Grotesk von Adrian
Frutiger', in *Typographische Monatsblätter,*
5/1957, page 364 ff.

E. MAUDUIT: 'Les artistes du graphisme.
Adrian Frutiger', in *L'imprimerie nouvelle,*
no. 29, June 1958, page 18 ff.

EMIL RUDER: 'Zu den Arbeiten von Adrian
Frutiger', in *Typographische Monatsblätter,*
7–8/1959, page 445 ff.

AUTHOR UNKNOWN: 'La création d'une nouvelle
typographie', in *L'imprimerie Nouvelle,*
page 57 ff.

ALFRED WILLIMANN: 'Adrian Frutiger', in
Caractère Noël, 1959. Frutiger's career and
an illustration of the humanist minuscule
from his final diploma submission.

AUTHOR UNKNOWN: 'Du caractère français
Univers', in *L'imprimerie Nouvelle,* no. 52
(June 1960), page 111.

AUTHOR UNKNOWN: 'Une nouvelle typographie,
l'Univers d'Adrian Frutiger', in *Esthétique
Industrielle,* 45/1960, page 12 ff.

EMIL RUDER: 'Die Univers in der Typographie',
in *Typographische Monatsblätter, Univers
special edition,* 1/1961, page 69 ff.

PAUL HEUER: 'Matrix production for Monotype
Systems – Problems in the Production
of Monotype Univers', in *Typographische
Monatsblätter, Univers special edition,*
1/1961, page 21 ff.

EMIL O. BIEMANN: 'Univers… a New Concept
in European Type Design', in *Print,* XV:1
(Jan./Feb. 1961), page 32 ff.

AUTHOR UNKNOWN: 'Univers ou la forme au
service de la fonction' in: *Informations TG,*
no. 36 (March-April 1961), page 25.

JOHN DREYFUS: 'Univers in Action', in *Penrose
Annual,* 55/1961, page 15 ff.

CHARLES PEIGNOT: 'Méridien and the Univers
Family', in *Art de France,* Paris 1961,
page 431 f.

WALTER AMSTUTZ (ed.): 'Frutiger Adrian, France',
in *Who's Who in Graphic Art,* Zurich 1962,
page 161.

Eurographic Press: 'Designer's profile:
Adrian Frutiger', in *Print in Britain,* vol. 9
(January 1962), page 258 ff.

PAUL HEUER: 'Zwischenbericht über den Schnitt
der Monotype-Univers', in *Typographische
Monatsblätter,* 1/1962, page 10.

AUTHOR UNKNOWN: 'Werbung für Citroën.
Publicité pour Citroën. Atelier Adrian Frutiger,
Paris', in *Typographische Monatsblätter,*
1/1962, page 35 ff.

AUTHOR UNKNOWN: 'Who is who:
Adrian Frutiger', in *Informations TG,* no.124,
16 March 1962, page 4.

M. C. L.: 'Adrian Frutiger', in *Le Monde,*
18 October 1962. Article about the exhibition
of his artistic works in the Galerie Berès,
Paris.

AUTHOR UNKNOWN: 'Un nouvel alphabet:
L'Algol', in *Informations TG,* 2nd quarter 1963,
page 2 ff.

AUTHOR UNKNOWN: 'Univers', in *Monotype
Technical Bulletin,* no. 57 (October 1963),
page 2 ff.

FREDERICK LAMBERT (ed.): Title unknown,
in *Letter Forms: 110 Complete Alphabets,*
London 1964.

DENNIS CHEETHAM, BRIAN GRIMBLY:
'Design Analysis: Typeface', in *Design,* no.186
(June 1964), page 61 ff. Report on *Univers,*
Interview with Adrian Frutiger by
Matthew Carter.

PIERRE DESCARGUES: 'Les graphistes
suisses font la loi à Par s', in *Feuille d'avis
de Lausanne,* 13 October 1964, page 58.
Report on four leading Swiss designers
in Paris. In this edition, Albert Hollenstein
and Adrian Frutiger.

JOHN DREYFUS: 'Monophoto Apollo. A New
Face by Frutiger', in *Monotype Newsletter,*
no. 74 (November 1964), page 10.

ALLAN HUTT: 'Monophoto Apollo',
in *British Printer* (December 1964), page 84 f.

AUTHOR UNKNOWN: 'Monophoto Apollo – eine
neue Schrift Frutigers', in *Typographische
Monatsblätter,* 2/1965, page 96 f.

AUTHOR UNKNOWN: Caractère Univers Deberny
Peignot, in *Esthétique Industrielle,* 74/1965,
page 27 ff.

MONOTYPE CORPORATION (Publ.): 'Correct
specification of Univers', in *Monotype
Newsletter,* 75/1965.

AUTHOR UNKNOWN: 'Face to face with Univers',
in *Print Design and Production,* vol. 2
(March / April 1966), page 23 ff.

AUTHOR UNKNOWN: 'Some Vital Facts About
Univers', in *Monotype Newsletter,* no. 80
(December 1966), page 12 f.

AUTHOR UNKNOWN: 'Stilskapare', in *Dagens
Nyheter,* 2 June 1967. Short newspaper
article with photo about Frutiger in a
Swedish daily newspaper.

EUGENE M. ETTENBERG: 'Frutiger's Serifa:
Timely Display face and legible Text Type',
in *Inland Printer/American Lithographer,*
vol.163, no. 2 (May 1969), page 56.

EMIL RUDER: 'Actualités graphiques. Le Serifa, d'Adrian Frutiger', in *Typografische Monatsblätter*, 1/1970, page 79.

MARCELLE CHARRIÈRE: 'Rencontre: Adrian Frutiger', in *Informations TG* (15-22 June 1970), page 4 ff.

LOUIS FLACH: 'L'image de firme d'Électricité de France EDF', in *Contacts électriques*, no. 84, July 1970. Report on the firm's new public image, with reference to its designer, Adrian Frutiger.

FRANZ KNUCHEL: 'Über das Werk Adrian Frutigers', in *Jahrbuch vom Thuner- und Brienzersee*, Interlaken 1971, page 60 ff.

WALTER TAPPOLET: 'Adrian Frutiger und seine Genesis', in *Quatember*, 4/1970-71, page 2.

ALE: 'Schrift - Signet - Symbol', in an unknown printing trades union publication (Autumn 1973). Brief report on the exhibition of the same name at the Gutenberg Museum, Fribourg, Switzerland, with detailed career history.

ERICH SCHULZ-ANKER: 'Iridium-Antiqua - eine spezifische Fotosatzschrift auf klassizistischer Basis', in *Deutscher Drucker*, no. 14, 12 April 1973, p. 22. - in *Druck Print* 3/1973, page 160 f. - in *Typografische Monatsblätter* 5/1973, page 410.

AUTHOR UNKNOWN: '"Devanagari" - Frutigers neue Schrift', in *Deutscher Drucker*, no. 1, 10 January 1974, page V.

S.B.: 'Eine zeitgemässe Devanagari. Adrian Frutiger, Paris', in *Novum Gebrauchsgraphik*, 4/1975, page 44 ff.

HORST HEIDERHOFF: 'Der Katalog als didaktischer Mittler zwischen Angebot und Nachfrage', in *form*, 1975-III-71, page 19 ff. Report on the design of the product catalogue for the Facom tool company carried out by Atelier Frutiger + Pfäffli.

JOHN DREYFUS, FRANÇOIS RICHAUDEAU: 'Frutiger Adrian', in *La chose imprimée, Les Encyclopédies du savoir moderne*, Paris 1977, page 161. Short career history with photo.

HORST HEIDERHOFF: 'Erste Frutiger-Ausstellung in der Bundesrepublik', in *Wandelhalle der Bücherfreunde*, 1/1977, page 21 ff. Report on the exhibition 'Adrian Frutiger – Zeichen Schriften Symbole'.

HEINRICH BECK: 'Schriftform, Lesbarkeit, Lesemechanik', in *Deutscher Drucker*, 1/1979, page 14. Reader's commentary on the article 'Das Schriftbild: Kleid der Lesebotschaft' in 35/1978, page 4 ff.

MARCELLE CHARRIÈRE (translated from the French by Helen Reshetnik and Pam Manfried): 'Adrian Frutiger. Type and I', in *Typographic*, vol. 11, no. 2 (June 1979), page 8 ff.

AUTHOR UNKNOWN: 'Interview with Adrian Frutiger', in *Graphics World*, no. 9 (September 1979), page 22 ff.

ROGER CHATELAIN: 'Adrian Frutiger', in *Revue Suisse de l'imprimerie*, 4/1980, page 221 ff. Report on Frutiger's work connected with the publication of his book *Type Sign Symbol*.

ELI REIMER: 'Frutiger Grotesk', in *Bogtrykkerbladet*, 3/1981, page 77 ff.

TONY BISLEY (?): 'Adrian Frutiger', in *Baseline*, 4/1981, page 3 ff.

A. J. BISLEY: 'Typefaces + Corporate Identity Systems' in *Graphics World*, no. 32 (September 1981), page 49 ff. Covers *Alphabet EDF-GDF, Alphabet Métro* and *Alpha BP*.

KURT WEIDEMANN: 'Zu Adrian Frutiger' in *form*, 95-III-1981, page 3.

KLAUS WINTERHAGER: 'Zur Frutiger-Schrift', in *form* 95-III-1981, page 1.

JORGE FRASCARA: 'Frutiger Adrian', in *Contemporary Designers*, Macmillan Publishers, London 1984, page 212 ff.

HORST HEIDERHOFF: 'Der Gestaltungswille des Schriftdesigners Adrian Frutiger', in *Linotype Express*, 3/1984, page 9.

GEORG RAMSEGER: 'Verdiente Ehrung für verdienstvollen Mann', in *Börsenblatt*, no. 96, 30 November 1984, page 2824 ff.

LOTHAR KONIETZKA: 'Der Weg durch die Wüste ist vorüber …', in *Grafik Design + Technik*, (c. 1985), page 86 ff. Interview with Adrian Frutiger.

REINHARD HAUS: 'Eine neue Schrift von Adrian Frutiger', in *Novum Gebrauchsgraphik*, May 1985, page 67 ff. Report on *Versailles*.

EUROGRAPHIC PRESS: 'Über die Zukunft von Schrift und Typografie', in *DruckIndustrie*, No. 12, 27 June 1985, page 3 ff. Survey of 14 leading type designers and typographers by the industry body Eurographic Press, formed from the merger of ten European specialist printing publications.

COLIN COHEN: 'The Letters Page', in *Creative Review*, September 1986, page 70 f. Report on Frutiger's design work leading to the publication of *Linotype Centennial*.

CARYL HOLLAND: 'Typography, Technology & Adrian Frutiger', in *Graphics World*, no. 62, September-October 1986, page 69 ff.

WALTER GREISNER: 'Adrian Frutiger: Laudatio auf den Träger des Gutenberg-Preises 1986', in *BDG-Mitteilungen*, no. 79, October 1986, page 12 ff.

BERGNER: 'Internationales Schriftschaffen. Adrian Frutiger', in *Papier und Druck*, 35/1986, page 407 ff.

KURT WOLFF: 'Der Druckspiegel im Gespräch mit Adrian Frutiger', in *Der Druckspiegel*, 12/1986, page 1477 ff.

SEBASTIAN CARTER: 'Adrian Frutiger', in *Twentieth Century Type Designers*, Trefoil Publications Ltd., London 1987, page 156 ff.

CHARLES BIGELOW: 'Philosophies of Form in Seriffed Typefaces of Adrian Frutiger', in *Fine Print On Type*, Bedford Arts, London 1988, page 171 ff.

CARRIE BACKFORD: 'Face to Face with Adrian Frutiger', in *Hot Graphics International*, 1988, page 14 f.

ROGER CHATELAIN: 'Les Antiques dans l'œuvre d'Adrian Frutiger', in *Revue Suisse de l'imprimerie*, 1/1988, page 1.

ROGER CHATELAIN: 'Les caractères dessinés par Adrian Frutiger', in *Typografische Monatsblätter*, 3/1988, page 33.

ANDREAS BELLASI: 'Adrian Frutiger. Ein Leben für die schöne Schrift', in *Tages-Anzeiger Magazin*, no. 25, 25.6.1988, page 24 ff.

AUTHOR UNKNOWN: 'Frutiger's New Face', in *Linotype Express*, 14/1988. Report on *Avenir* in Linotype's house magazine.

MANFRED KLEIN: 'TypoNews Univers / Helvetica', in *Der Druckspiegel*, 6/1988, page 674. Comparison of *Univers* with *Helvetica* to coincide with the release of *Univers* for the Apple Macintosh.

AUTHOR UNKNOWN: 'Frutiger Looks to the Future', in *Graphic Repro*, December 1988, page 22 ff.

AUTHOR UNKNOWN: 'Avenir - eine neue serifenlose Linear-Antiqua von Adrian Frutiger', in *Deutscher Drucker*, no. S2, 15 December 1988, page g21 - in *DruckIndustrie*, no. 3, 7 February 1989, page 32. - in *Der Polygraph*, 4/1989, page 253.

ECKEHART SCHUMACHERGEBLER (ed.): 'Adrian Frutiger. Frutiger 55', in *26 Lettern*, Munich 1989. September / October in two-weeks-to-a-page calendar with short description of 26 typefaces.

GRET HEER, THOMAS P. HERMANN: 'Du sollst die Schrift nicht verhunzen', in *Tages-Anzeiger*, 12 May 1989, page 69 f.

AUTHOR UNKNOWN: 'Sanserif - Gone Digital', in *World-Wide Printer*, 6/1989, page 68 f.

ERIK SPIEKERMANN: 'Mr. Univers', in *Page*, 3/1990, page 62 ff.

AUTHOR UNKNOWN: Der Schlüssel Macher, in *Cicero*, 3/1990, page 16 ff. Interview with Frutiger about the adoption of *Linotype Centennial* as body type for the magazine.

REINHARD HAUS: 'Type before Gutenberg', in *Page*, 1/1991, page 58 ff.

REINHARD HAUS: 'American Blend', in *Page*, 6/1991, page 78 ff. Report on *Vectora*.

REINHARD HAUS: 'Klassizistisches Erbe'. Part 1 in *Page*, 11/1991, page 82 ff. Part 2 in *Page*, 12/1991, page 66 ff. Report on *Linotype Didot*.

ECKEHART SCHUMACHERGEBLER (ed.): 'Iridium. Adrian Frutiger', in *26 Lettern*, Munich 1992. February / March in two-weeks-to-a-page calendar with short description of 26 typefaces.

REINHARD HAUS: 'Moderner Konstruktivismus', in *Page*, 6/1992, page 50 ff. Report on *Avenir*.

AUTHOR UNKNOWN: 'Frutiger - ein Synonym für zeitgemässe Groteskschriften', in *Desktop Dialog*, 7/1993, page 30 f.

HERMANN PFEIFFER: 'Vom Zeichen zur Schrift in der Handschrift des Adrian Frutiger', in *Der Druckspiegel*, 9/1993, page 775 ff.

REINHARD HAUS: 'Le nouveau Didot', in *Revue Suisse de l'imprimerie*, 2/1994, page 8 ff.

AUTHOR UNKNOWN: 'Didot', in *Druckspiegel*, 2/1994.

GIOVANNI LUSSU: 'Adrian verso il Duemila', in *Linea Grafica* no. 292, 4/1994, page 10 ff.

JOST HOCHULI: 'Adrian Frutiger', in *Druck-Industrie* no. 11, 31 May 1994, page 15 ff. Reprint of the foreword from the exhibition catalogue *Adrian Frutiger, His Typographical Work and His Writings*.

SABINE PIROLT: 'Adrian Frutiger, l'homme qui créa l'Univers', in *L'Hebdo*, 26 January 1995, page 54 f.

ANDREAS LIEDTKE, LUCAS DE GROOT: 'Befragt: Adrian Frutiger, Schriftentwerfer. "Ich bin der Backsteinbrenner"', in *form 150 Dossier reform*, 2/1995, page 46 ff.

ROGER CHATELAIN: 'Adrian Frutiger raconte', in *Revue Suisse de l'imprimerie* 2/1995, page 1 ff. Reprint of a synopsis by Adrian Frutiger given in 1994 at an international symposium on photosetting at the Musée lyonnais de l'imprimerie et de la banque in Lyon.

MICHAEL DÜBLIN: 'Schriften für Menschen', in *Basler Magazin*, no. 3, 18 January 1997, page 12 f.

ALESSIO LEONARDI: 'Familienplanung', in *Page*, 8/1997, page 46 ff. Report on the reworked *Univers* family.

PATRICK BACHMANN, NORBERT RICHTER: 'Schrift ist ein Werkzeug, nicht eine Mode', in *X-Time Die grosse Zeitung*, 4/1998, page 78 f.

HERMANN PFEIFFER: 'Atelierbesuch beim Schriftkünstler Adrian Frutiger', in *Deutscher Drucker*, no. 39, 15 October 1998, page 22.

STEFAN BETTSCHON: 'Der PC ist keine Schreibmaschine. Adrian Frutiger und der technische Wandel der Typographie', in *Neue Zürcher Zeitung*, no. 156, 9 July 1999, page 71.

YVONNE SCHWEMER-SCHEDDIN: 'Reputations. Adrian Frutiger', in *eye*, 31/1999, page 18 ff. Reprint of an interview by Yvonne Schwemer-Scheddin with Adrian Frutiger, conducted during the 1998 ATypI Conference in Lyon.

ROGER CHATELAIN: 'Adrian Frutiger. Une œuvre protéiforme', in *Étapes*, no. 60, March 2000, page 50 ff.

HELMUT KRAUS: 'Original und Originaler', in *Page*, no. 12/2001, page 58 ff. Article about *Frutiger Next*.

KONRAD RUDOLF LIENERT: 'Wege durch Adrian Frutigers Privatarchiv', in *Tages-Anzeiger*, 24 May 2003, page 51.

KLAUS-PETER NICOLAY: 'Schrift - dem Leben angepasst', in Druckmarkt, No. 19, October 2004, page 10 ff.

MANUEL KREBS, CORNEL WINDLIN: 'ASTRA Frutiger-Autobahn', in *soDA #27*, vol. 5, March 2005, page 17.

GERRIT TERSTIEGE: 'Meine Schriften sollen klingen', in *form. The Making of Design*, no. 221, August 2008, page 74 ff.

Typefaces
by Adrian Frutiger

Adrian Frutiger's typefaces in chronological order, giving years of design and publication, and type

1952 | 1954
Initiales Président
Jobbing typeface

1953 | 1953
Initiales Phoebus
Jobbing typeface

1953 | 1954
Ondine
Jobbing typeface

1953 | 1957
Méridien
Text typeface

1953 | 1957
Univers
Text typeface

c. 1956 | c. 1958
Egyptienne F
Text typeface

1958 | 1960
Opéra
Text typeface

1959 | 1961
Alphabet Orly
Signage typeface

1960 | 1964
Apollo
Text typeface

1961 | 1964
Concorde
Text typeface

1962 | 1964
Antique Presse
Jobbing typeface

1963 | 1963
Algol
Jobbing typeface

from 1963 | from 1965
OCR-B
Text typeface

1963 | 1967
Serifa
Text typeface

1964 | 1966
Univers
IBM Composer
Text typeface

1964 | 1967
Alphabet EDF-GDF
Corporate typeface

1967 | 1967
Univers Greek
Text typeface

1967 | 1973
Devanagari / Tamil
Text typeface

1968 | 1969
Alpha BP
Corporate typeface

1969 | 1970
Documenta
Text typeface

1970 | 1971
Alphabet Facom
Corporate typeface

1970 | 1972
Alphabet Roissy
Signage typeface

1971 | 1972
Alphabet Brancher
Corporate typeface

1972 | 1972
Iridium
Text typeface

1973 | 1973
Alphabet Métro
Signage typeface

1973 | 1974
Roissy-Solaris
Split-flap typefaces

1973 | 1976
Univers Cyrillic
Text typeface

1974 | 1976
Alphabet Centre
Georges Pompidou
Signage typeface

1974 | 1976
Frutiger
Text typeface

1976 | 1980
Glypha
Text typeface

1978 | 1979
Caractères TVP
Screen typeface

1978 | 1980
Icone
Text typeface

1978 | 1982
Breughel
Text typeface

1982 | 1982
Tiemann
Text typeface

1982 | 1984
Versailles
Text typeface

1985 | 1985
Frutiger Cyrillic
Text typeface

1985 | 1986
Linotype Centennial
Text typeface

1987 | 1988
Avenir
Text typeface

1988 | 1989
Westside
Jobbing typeface

1988 | 1991
Vectora
Text typeface

1990 | 1991
Linotype Didot
Text typeface

1990 | 1991
Herculanum
Jobbing typeface

1991 | 1991
Shiseido
Corporate typeface

1991 | 2005
Frutiger Capitalis
Jobbing typeface

1992 | 1992
Pompeijana
Jobbing typeface

1992 | 1993
Rusticana
Jobbing typeface

1992 | 1998
Frutiger Stones /
Frutiger Symbols
Jobbing typeface

1996 | 1996
Frutiger Neonscript
Signage typeface

1996 | 1998
Linotype Univers
Text typeface

1998 | 2001
Frutiger Next
Text typeface

1999 | 2002
Astra Frutiger
Signage typeface

2002 | 2004
Avenir Next
Text typeface

(1952) | 2007
Nami
Jobbing typeface

(1954) | 2008
Frutiger Serif
Text typeface

Typeface
manufacturers

Adrian Frutiger's type-design projects in chronological order, giving year of design.

1952 | (2007)
Delta
Typedesign project

1953 | –
Element-Grotesk
Typedesign project

1953 | –
Federduktus
Typedesign project

1961 | –
Alphabet Entreprise
Francis Bouygues
Typedesign project,
Corporate typeface

1962 | –
Serifen-Grotesk
Typedesign project

1962 | –
Gespannte Grotesk
Typedesign project

1965 | –
Katalog
Typedesign project

1969 | –
Delta
IBM Composer
Typedesign project

1980 | –
Dolmen
Typedesign project

1991 | –
University
Typedesign project

1993 | –
Cooperline
Typedesign project

1993 | –
Primavera
Typedesign project

France

Deberny & Peignot (1923–1972)
The Parisian foundry was formed through the merger of two traditional and well-established type foundries. The first branch, Deberny, traced its roots back to the firms of Joseph Gillé (1748–1789), J. F. Laurent (1818–1823) and J. L. Duplat (17…–1824). These three foundries amalgamated in 1827 under the name of Laurent, [Honoré] Balzac & Barbier. In 1923, after several more name and ownership changes, the foundry finally settled on Girard & Cie. The other branch, Peignot, went back to François Ambroise Didot (established c. 1775) and his son Firmin Didot. In the mid-1830s the family firm, after branching out greatly, was absorbed into the Fondérie Générale, which, in turn, was bought by Peignot & Fils in 1912. Deberny & Peignot was formed in 1923 through the merger of Girard & Cie and Peignot & Cie. It was led by Henri Menut. Charles Peignot was director from 1939 to 1962 (1964?). Louis Moyroud and René A. Higonnet, along with the latter's son René-Paul Higonnet, bought the firm. The foundry was run by the younger Higonnet. Deberny & Peignot went into liquidation in 1972 with Higonnet fils still at the helm. The foundry programme and typeface licences were taken over by the Haas type foundry.

Typefaces by Adrian Frutiger for Deberny & Peignot:
    Initiales Président
    Initiales Phoebus
    Ondine
    Méridien
    Univers
    Antique Presse

Société Lumitype (1955–1960)
The company was founded in Paris in 1945 by Louis Moyraud and René A. Higonnet. It was based at Deberny & Peignot. Its goal was to build the Lumitype photosetting machine in Paris and to distribute it throughout Europe. In 1960 the Société Lumitype, together with American Photon Inc. were amalgamated into the International Photon Corporation.
Typefaces by Adrian Frutiger for the Lumitype photosetting machine:
    Adaptations of other designers' typefaces
    Méridien
    Univers
    Egyptienne
    Algol

Sofratype (19…–1969)
The Swiss Alfred Devolz founded the Sofratype company in Paris. The small firm produced and distributed matrices for line-casting machines. In 1969 it was bought out by the Mergenthaler Linotype Company.
Typefaces by Adrian Frutiger for Sofratype:
    Opéra
    Concorde (with André Gürtler)

USA

Photon Inc. (1950–1960)
Bill Garth, owner of the Lithomat offset printing-plate company in Cambridge, Massachusetts, USA, met French engineers René A. Higonnet and Louis M. Moyroud through contacts at the Massachusetts Institute of Technology (MIT) in 1946. Shortly after, he became involved in their attempts to develop a photosetting machine. In 1950 Lithomat changed its name to Photon Inc. and in 1960 Photon Inc. merged with Société Lumitype to become the International Photon Corporation.
Typefaces by Adrian Frutiger for the Photon photosetting machine:
    Latine (Méridien)
    Univers

IBM (1896–present)
The business company dates back to Herman Hollerith's Tabulating Machine Company, founded in 1896, which produced machines that gathered data and output data based on punch cards. In 1924 the company's name was changed to International Business Machines. In the 1950s and '60s the company produced its first computers. IBM is a founding member of the European Computer Manufacturers' Association (ECMA).
Typefaces by Adrian Frutiger for the IBM Composer:
    Univers IBM Composer
    Adaptation of other designers' typefaces and foreign-language typefaces

United Kingdom

Monotype (1895–1985)

Tolbert Lanson, inventor of the Monotype setting and casting machine, founded his first Lanston Monotype Machine Company in 1887. By 1897 a machine had been produced that would lay the foundations for all future Monotype machines. To secure funds for its further development, the British and Colonial patent rights (excepting Canada) were sold to British investors and the Lanston Monotype Corporation Ltd. was founded in Salfords, Surrey. From the 1920s on, the British Monotype Corporation gained ever-more technical and economic prominence, overshadowing its American counterpart. In 1966 the latter was bought by the United States Banknote Corporation, and then liquidated in 1969. Agfa, the successor to Compugraphic, bought the Monotype Corporation in 1999, giving the new company the name Agfa Monotype. In 2006 Monotype Imaging – as Agfa Monotype was renamed in 2004 after being purchased by TA Associates – bought Linotype Imaging GmbH.

Typefaces by Adrian Frutiger for Monotype:
Univers
Apollo
Univers Greek
Devanagari / Tamil (with Mahendra Patel)

Switzerland

ECMA (1961–present)

The European Computer Manufacturers' Association (ECMA) is a private organisation with responsibility for the standardisation of information and communication systems with headquarters in Geneva. It was founded on 17 May 1961 by 13 computer and typewriter manufacturers. The founding members were: Aktiebolaget ADDO, Compagnie des Machines Bull, N.V. Electrologica, English Electric-Leo-Marconi Computers Ltd, IBM-WTEC, ICT International Computers and Tabulators Ltd, ITT Europe Inc, NCR (The National Cash Register Company Ltd.), Ing. C. Olivetti & Co. S.p.A., SEA Société d'Electronique et 'Automatisme, Siemens & Halske AG, Sperry Rand International Corp., and Telefunken Aktiengesellschaft. In 1994 the organisation changed its name to ECMA International, to better reflect the body's international direction.

Typeface by Adrian Frutiger for ECMA:
OCR-B

Westiform (1948–present)

The Swiss family firm emerged from Westinghouse Electric Corporation, an American lighting company in 1948. Under the name of Westineon, it produced high-voltage neon tubes. In 1959 the Imfeld family took over the 'neon' department and continued to expand and develop it. The name was changed to Westiform in 1987.

Typefaces by Adrian Frutiger for Westiform:
Frutiger Neonscript

Germany

Bauersche Schriftgiesserei (1837–1972)

Johann Christian Bauer established the type foundry in 1837 in Frankfurt am Main. The business was taken over by his son and sold in 1873. In 1898 Georg Hartmann took possession of the firm and, in addition, bought several other type foundries. After Hartmann's death in 1954, his son-in-law, Ernst Vischer, ran the company until his own death in 1962. Walter Greisner was managing director from 1964 until 1967. After the firm's liquidation in 1972 the casting division was taken over by Fundición Tipográfica Neufville and its owner, Wolfgang Hartmann, grandson of Georg Hartmann, has led the company ever since. They distribute digital typefaces under the name of Bauer Type.

Typefaces by Adrian Frutiger for the Bauer Type Foundry:
Serifa

D. Stempel AG (1895–1985)

Founded by David Stempel in 1895, D. Stempel AG produced matrices for Linotype linecasting machines. After much buying and selling of assets, as well as investment in other type foundries, Walter Greisner took over as managing director in 1967. In 1973 he became head of the board of directors. In 1983 Stempel ceased matrix production and in 1985 the firm went into liquidation. The matrix-plate production was taken over by Linotype GmbH. The material assets, the punches and matrices, were sent to the Darmstadt Technische Hochschule, where a typecasting workshop was set up, led by Rainer Gerstenberg. Today, this is incorporated into the Printing Museum, which is itself a part of the Hessisches Museum in Darmstadt.

Typefaces by Adrian Frutiger for D. Stempel AG:
Adaptation of other designers' typefaces
Documenta
Iridium
Frutiger
Univers Cyrillic (with Alexei Chekoulaev)
Glypha
Icone
Breughel
Versailles
Frutiger Cyrillic

Linotype (1886–present)

The Mergenthaler Linotype Company was founded in 1890 in Brooklyn, N.Y., with the aim of producing the line-casting machine invented by Ottmar Mergenthaler. Shortly after the firm's founding, subsidiaries were set up in England (1890) and Germany (1896). From 1900 onwards, matrices, which up until then had been produced only in the United States, were produced by D. Stempel AG in Germany. The subsidiaries in the three countries operated independently in their respective markets. After the Second World War the German headquarters was moved from Berlin to Frankfurt. In 1973 Mergenthaler Casting Machine GmbH and Linotype GmbH merged to form Mergenthaler-Linotype GmbH. Meanwhile, in the United States, the Mergenthaler Linotype Company was purchased by the Eltra Corporation in 1963, which, in turn, was bought by Allied Chemical Corporation in 1979. Frankfurt became the headquarters for all of the Linotype companies in 1983. Two years later, D. Stempel AG, along with its entire typeface portfolio, was absorbed into Linotype. Linotype now possessed the rights to the typefaces of the former firms of the Benjamin Krebs, Klingspor and Haas type foundries; and, at the same time, the typeface rights of Deberny & Peignot, Fonderie Olive and Società Nebiolo. (Haas type foundry's typefaces are still available today in hot-metal form from Walter Fruttiger, and are cast in Rainer Gerstenberg's type workshop.) In 1987 Linotype became a public company when a German bank purchased it from Allied Chemical Corporation and renamed it Linotype AG. A merger in 1990 with Dr.-ing Rudolf Hell led to Linotype-Hell AG. Heidelberg Druckmaschinen bought the company in 1997 and changed its name to Linotype Library. Then, in 2006, Linotype was purchased by Monotype Imaging.

Typefaces by Adrian Frutiger for Linotype:
Tiemann (original by Walter Tiemann)
Linotype Centennial
Avenir
Vectora
Westside
Herculanum
Linotype Didot (orignal by Firmin Didot)
Frutiger Stones / Frutiger Symbols
Pompeijana
Rusticana
Linotype Univers
Frutiger Next
Avenir Next
Frutiger Capitalis
Nami
Frutiger Serif

Places of work and co-workers

Over the course of his career – whether as an employee, freelance or in his own studio – Adrian Frutiger has worked with in-house and external co-workers who have supported him in the realisation of his commissions.
They are listed here in the following overview according to the current state of our knowledge.

1952–1960
Deberny & Peignot
Paris, France

Charles Peignot – Director
Rémy Peignot – Graphic designer

Harry Boller – Typographer
Albert Boton – Type draughtsman
Annette Celsio – Type draughtswoman
Lucette Girard – Type draughtswoman
Ladislas Mandel – Type draughtsman
Robert Meili – Typographer
Jean Mentha – Typographer
Marcel Mouchel – Leader, Gravure dept.
Marcel Nebel – Typographer

External co-workers
A. M. Cassandre – Artist

1960
Deberny & Peignot – Atelier de composition
Paris, France

André Gürtler – Typographer
Rémy Peignot – Graphic designer
Bruno Pfäffli – Typographer

1961–1964
Atelier Frutiger
Place d'Italie, Paris, France

Suzanne Curtil – Secretary
Nicole Delamarre – Type draughtswoman
André Gürtler – Type designer
Bruno Pfäffli – Typographer

External co-workers
Rudolf Mumprecht – Artist
Peter Willi – Photographer

1965–1968
Atelier Frutiger
Villa Moderne, Arcueil, France

Martin Altenburger – Occupation unknown
Suzanne Curtil – Secretary
Nicole Delamarre – Type draughtswoman
Bruno Pfäffli – Typographer
Verena Pfäffli – Co-worker, compositor
Sylvain Robin – Type draughtsman
Brigitte Rousset – Draughtswoman and layout artist

External co-workers
Nadine Bonnier – Co-worker type
Françoise – Frisket cutter
Mahendra Patel – Type designer, National Institute of Design, Ahmedabad, India
Peter Willi – Photographer

1969–1974
Atelier Frutiger+ Pfäffli
Villa Moderne, Arcueil, France

Bruno Pfäffli – Typographer
Nicole Delamarre – Type draughtswoman
Hans-Jürg Hunziker – Type designer
Verena Pfäffli – Co-worker, compositor
Brigitte Willay (née Rousset) – Draughts-woman and layout artist

External co-workers
Leen Averink – Designer
Gérard Ifert – Graphic designer
Rudolf Mumprecht – Artist
Mahendra Patel – Type designer, National Institute of Design, Ahmedabad, India
Sylvain Robin – Type draughtsman
Peter Willi – Photographer
Françoise … – Frisket cutter

1975–1992
Atelier Frutiger / Atelier Pfäffli
Villa Moderne, Arcueil, France

Bruno Pfäffli – Typographer
Helena Nowak – Draughtswoman
Verena Pfäffli – Co-worker, compositor

External co-workers
Serge Cortesi – Type draughtsman
Lucette Girard – Type draughtswoman
Sylvain Robin – Type draughtsman

Collaborations with other companies

Adrian Frutiger has produced typefaces for numerous firms. In the following overview – complete according to the current state of our knowledge – the dates of collaboration is listed, as well as the names of Frutiger's contacts at those firms.

1954–1960
Société Lumitype
Paris, France
… Bernard – Photographer
René Gréa – Engineer

1954–1960
Photon Inc.
Cambridge, Massachusetts, USA
René A. Higonnet – Engineer, developer
Louis M. Moyroud – Engineer, developer
Louis Rosenblum – Head of the typographic studio

1957–1967
Éditions Hermann
Paris, France
Pierre Berès – Publisher

1959–c. 1965
Sofratype
Paris, France
Alfred Devolz – Owner

1960–1962
Monotype Corporation
Salfords, Surrey, England
John Dreyfus – Typographic consultant
Stanley Morison – Typographic consultant

1960–1974
Brancher
Vélizy, France
Pierre Brancher (father) – Owner
Olivier Brancher (son) – Owner

1961–ca. 1963
Synergie, advertising agency
Paris, France

1963–1973 (plus further collaborations)
ECMA
European Computer Manfacturers Association, Geneva, Switzerland
Dara Hekimi – General secretary
Gilbert Weill – Compagnie des Machines Bull

1966–1968
Bauersche Type Foundry
Frankfurt am Main, Germany
Konrad F. Bauer – Artistic director
Walter Greisner – Member, board of directors

1963–1978
Facom
Morangis, France
André Moses – Owner

1964–1981
IBM
International Business Machines, Armonk, USA / Orléans, France
André Bonnier – Departmental head, golfball production
Max Caflisch – External typographic consultant
Henri Friedlaender – Type designer
Fritz Kern – Departmental head, graphics products
J. François Leblanc – Departmental head, typeface department

1965–1967
EDF-GDF
Paris, France
Jacques Veuillet – Project leader
Francis Boucrot – Project leader
Nicolas Karzis – Architect
Giulio Confalonieri – Graphic artist

1967–1972
National Institute of Design
Ahmedabad, India
Mahendra Patel – Typographic draughtsman
Gira Sarabhai – Founder and principal, design department

1968–1969
Crosby / Fletcher / Forbes
London, England
Alan Fletcher – Designer
Colin Forbes – Designer
Georg Staehelin – Designer

1968–1985
D. Stempel AG
Frankfurt am Main, Germany
Walter Cunz – Member, board of directors
Walter Greisner – Member, board of directors
Reinhard Haus – Typographic draughtsman
Horst Heiderhoff – Artistic director
Arthur Ritzel – Head, typeface department
Erich Schulz-Anker – Artistic director

1969–1970
National-Zeitung
Basel, Switzerland
Fritz Sutter – Head, photosetting department

1970–1976
Aéroport de Paris
Paris, France
Paul Andreu – Architect
Jacques Filacier – Colour consultant

1973
Régie Autonome des Transports Parisiens
Paris, France
Paul Andreu – Architect
… Ebeling – Director

1982
Die Zeit
Hamburg, Germany

since 1985
Linotype / Mergenthaler Linotype Company
Eschborn / Bad Homburg, Germany
Reinhard Haus – Head, typographic studio, Artistic director
Hans Wolfgang Glathe – Head of type licences
Otmar Hoefer – Marketing director
Gerhard Höhl – Head, typeface department
René Kerfante – Head, matrix-plate production
Akira Kobayashi – Artistic director
Werner Schimpf – Head typeface department, Artistic director
Bruno Steinert – Director

Brooklyn, USA
Matthew Carter – Type designer
Mike Parker – Typographic director

since 1987
Westiform
Niederwangen, Switzerland
Niklaus Imfeld – Owner

1991
Shiseido
Tokyo, Japan
Yutaka Kobayashi – Artistic director

List of illustrations

We would like to extend our thanks to all copyright holders and to those who have made books, magazines and other materials available to us. And we would similarly like to thank them for the right to reproduce the aforementioned material. All picture rights remain the property of the respective copyright holders. Any images that are not listed below were produced or reproduced by the editors. Unless stated otherwise, the first entry is the lender/owner of the image, the second the person responsible for its reproduction.

All material relating to Adrian Frutiger can be found (unless otherwise stated) in the archive of the Swiss Foundation Type and Typography, Bern.

We have tried, as far as possible, and with the information available to us, to make the picture copyright as easy as possible to trace. Should you require further information, please contact the editors.

Foreword
/01/ Photography: Hansueli Trachsel.

Career path
/01/ Adrian Frutiger.
/02/ from Bätschmann, Oskar. *Schreibkunst. Schulkunst und Volkskunst in der deutschsprachigen Schweiz 1548 bis 1980.* Zurich: Kunstgewerbemuseum der Stadt Zürich, Museum für Gestaltung, 1981.
/03/ Adrian Frutiger, Bremgarten / Bern.
/04/ Frutiger, Adrian. *Die Kirchen am Thunersee.* Interlaken: Otto Schlaefli, Buch- und Kunstdruckerei AG, 1948.
/05/ Davidshofer, Leo and Walter Zerbe. *Satztechnik und Gestaltung.* Zurich / Bern: Bildungsverband Schweizerischer Buchdrucker, 1970. Photography: Philippe Karrer, Angelo A. Lüdin, Basel.
/06/07/ Adrian Frutiger, Bremgarten / Bern.
/08/ from Tschichold, Jan. *Meisterbuch der Schrift.* Ravensburg: Otto Maier Verlag, 1965.
/09/ January 1950. Zürcher Hochschule der Künste ZHdK, Medien- und Informationszentrum MIZ-Archiv. Museum für Gestaltung Zurich. Photography: Margo Koch-Ruthke.
/10/ from *Neue Graphik* 12/1962.
/11/ Museum für Gestaltung Zurich, poster collection.
/12/ Lent by Leni Willimann-Thöny, Münsingen / Bern.
/13/ Photography: Peter Stähli.
/14/ Käch, Walter. *Rhythmus und Proportion / Rhythm and Proportion.* Olten: Verlag Otto Walter AG, 1956. Photography: Philippe Karrer, Angelo A. Lüdin.
/15/16/17/ Käch, Walter. *Schriften Écriture Lettering.* Olten: Verlag Otto Walter AG, 1949. Photography: Philippe Karrer, Angelo A. Lüdin, Basel.
/18/ Fritz Kern. Photography: Philippe Karrer, Angelo A. Lüdin.
/19/ Adrian Frutiger, Bremgarten / Bern.
/20/ from *Typographische Monatsblätter* 4 (1970).
/21/ *Typographische Monatsblätter* 1 (1961); title page design: Emil Ruder.
Ruder, Emil. *Typographie.* Sulgen: Verlag Niggli AG, 2001. Photography: Philippe Karrer, Angelo A. Lüdin.
/22/ from Frutiger, Adrian. *Der Mensch und seine Zeichen,* vol. 1. Frankfurt am Main: D. Stempel AG, 1978.
/23/ Frutiger, Adrian. *Der Mensch und seine Zeichen,* vol. 1. Frankfurt am Main: D. Stempel AG, 1978.
Type Sign Symbol. Zurich: ABC-Verlag, 1980. Alb, Erich, ed. *Adrian Frutiger – Forms and counterforms.* Cham: Syndor Press, 1998. Photography: Philippe Karrer, Angelo A. Lüdin, Basel.

Président
/01/18/22/ St Bride Library, London.
/02/ from *La France Graphique,* no. 115 (Juli 1956).
/03/ from Deberny & Peignot: title unknown, n.d.
/04/ Adrian Frutiger, Bremgarten / Bern.
/07/ from *Manuel Français de Typographie Moderne.* Paris: Bureau de l'Édition, 1924.
/10/ Adrian Frutiger, Bremgarten / Bern.
/21/22/ from Deberny & Peignot. *Initiales fantaisies.* Lyon: Musée de l'Imprimerie, 1956.
/27/ Musée de l'Imprimerie, Lyon.

Delta
/01/ Museum für Gestaltung Zurich, poster collection.
/02/05/06/ Adrian Frutiger.
/07/ Photography: unknown

Phoebus
/01/02/09/12/21/ Photography: Philippe Karrer, Angelo A. Lüdin.
/03/ from Deberny & Peignot. *typographie.* c.1957.
/05/ Adrian Frutiger, Bremgarten / Bern.
/07/ from Bertheau, Philipp. *Buchdruckschriften im 20. Jahrhundert.* Darmstadt: Technische Hochschule, 1995.

Element-Grotesk
/01/02/03/ Adrian Frutiger, Bremgarten / Bern.

Federduktus
/01/04/ Adrian Frutiger, Bremgarten / Bern.
/02/ Photography: unknown.

Ondine
/02/ Adrian Frutiger, Bremgarten / Bern.
/04/ Adrian Frutiger; André Gürtler, Basel. – Gotische Halbkursiv from Bosshard, Hans Rudolf. *Technische Grundlagen zur Satzherstellung.* Bern: Verlag des Bildungsverbandes Schweizerischer Typografen, 1980.
/08/ Lent by Jean Mentha, Cortaillod. Photography: Philippe Karrer, Angelo A. Lüdin, Basel.
/10/11/ Lent by Papiermühle Basel.
/12/ Illustration: St Bride Library, London.

Méridien
/01/03/04/05/06/07/08/ Adrian Frutiger, Bremgarten / Bern.
/02/38/ Photography: Philippe Karrer, Angelo A. Lüdin, Basel.
/09/ Beaumarchais. *Le mariage de Figaro.* Paris: Berger-Levrault, 1957. Photography: Philippe Karrer, Angelo A. Lüdin, Basel.
/10/ André Gürtler, Basel.
/10/ André Gürtler, Basel.
/10/ André Gürtler, Basel.
/11/ from Johannes Gutenberg. *Biblia Latina,* Facsimile edition of the incunabula Inc.1 in the Bibliothèque Mazarine, Paris.
/14/ from Tschichold, Jan. *Meisterbuch der Schrift.* Ravensburg: Otto Maier Verlag, 1965.
/15/ from Käch, Walter. *Schriften Écriture Lettering.* Olten: Verlag Otto Walter AG, 1949.
/36/37/39/ Swiss Foundation Type and Typography, Bern.
/41/ Bibliothèque Forney, Paris.
/42/ Swiss Foundation Type and Typography, Bern.

Caractères Lumitype
/01/ Photography: Philippe Karrer, Basel.
/02/ from *Caractère* (December 1975).
/03/08/28/30/35/39/ Musée de l'Imprimerie, Lyon.
/05/ from Friedl, Friedrich. *Typografie. when who how.* Cologne: Könemann Verlagsgesellschaft, 1998.
/06/ Yves Perrousseaux, Reillanne.
/09/10/12/13/14/16/20/ Swiss Foundation Type and Typography, Bern.
/11/ from *Techniques Graphiqes,* no. 6/1957.
/40/ from *Atlantis,* 1954, no. 7.
/41/ from Burkhardt, Richard. *grafische technik – heute und morgen.* Stuttgart: Industriegewerkschaft Druck und Papier, 1959.
/42/ from *Imprimerie Nouvelle* (June 1958).
/43/ Bibliothèque Forney, Paris. Photography: J-H. M.
/44/ Bibliothèque Forney, Paris. Photography: J. Mourreau.

Univers
/02/12/15/18/ from *Typographische Monatsblätter* 5 (1957).
/03/ Photography: Albert Boton.
/04/05/06/07/08/16/33/39/51/52/53/55/ Adrian Frutiger.
/09/ Photography: André Gürtler, Basel. Capitalis Monumentalis from: Muess, Johannes. *Das römische Alphabet.* Munich: Callwey, 1989.
/10/ from Frutiger, Adrian. *Denken und Schaffen einer Typografie.* Villeurbanne: Maison du Livre, de l'Image et du Son, 1994.
/17/41/42/ Musée de l'Imprimerie, Lyon.
/20/ from Schweizerische Verlagsdruckerei G. Boehm: *Schrift- und Druckproben.* Basel, n.d.
/36/ Tania Prill Lutz – from *Typographische Monatsblätter* 9 (1967).
/37/ Jean Mentha, Cortaillod and Alfred Hoffmann, Basel.
/38/ from *Deutscher Drucker* 3 (1972).
/40/ above: Ladislas Mandel, Le Paradou. Middle, bottom: Musée de l'Imprimerie, Lyon.
/43/45/ Linotype AG, Bad Homburg.
/44/ Monotype Images, Salfords, Surrey.
/46/47/ Papiermühle, Basel.
/50/ from *Typografische Monatsblätter* 1 (1988).
/54/ Photography: Erich Alb, Cham.
/57/ Photography: Philippe Karrer, Angelo A. Lüdin, Basel.

Egyptienne F
/01/03/ Adrian Frutiger.
/02/ Photography: Georges Dudognon – from *Informations TG.* no. 526 (November 1970).
/16/ Swiss Foundation Type and Typography, Bern.
/20/23/ Linotype AG, Bad Homburg.

Opéra
/01/02/03/04/07/ Ladislas Mandel, Le Paradou.

Alphabet Orly
/01/03/06/ Aéroports de Paris.
/05/ Ladislas Mandel, Le Paradou.

Apollo
/01/03/04/05/ Adrian Frutiger. Monotype Images, Salfords, Surrey.
/02/14/ Monotype Images, Salfords, Surrey.
/06/ from Tschichold, Jan. *Meisterbuch der Schrift.* Ravensburg: Otto Maier Verlag, 1965.
/23/ Swiss Foundation Type and Typography, Bern. Photography: Philippe Karrer, Angelo A. Lüdin, Basel.
/25/ from *Gutenberg-Jahrbuch 1971.*
/26/ from *Monotype Recorder* 1 (1979). St. Bride Library, London.

Alphabet Entreprise Francis Bouygues
/01/02/04/05/06/07/08/ Adrian Frutiger, Bremgarten / Bern.
/03/ from Käch, Walter. *Schriften Écriture Lettering.* Olten: Verlag Otto Walter AG, 1956.

Concorde
/01/ Papiermühle, Basel.
/02/03/12/15/ André Gürtler, Basel.
/04/ from Muess, Johannes. *Das römische Alphabet.* Munich: Callwey, 1989.
/05/ from Caflisch, Max. *Schriftanalysen,* vol. 2. St. Gallen: Typotron AG, 2003.
/10/ André Gürtler, Basel. Photography: Philippe Karrer, Angelo A. Lüdin, Basel.

Serifen-Grotesk / Gespannte Grotesk
/01/02/04/05/06/09/10/14/15/16/ Adrian Frutiger, Bremgarten.
/11/ Photography: Viktoria Juvalta.

Alphabet Algol
/01/ Bolliet, L., N. Gastinel and P. J. Laurent. *Un nouveau langue scientifique algol.* Paris: Éditions Hermann, 1964. Photography: Philippe Karrer, Angelo A. Lüdin, Basel.
/03/ Adrian Frutiger, Bremgarten / Bern.

Serifa
/01/06/07/30/ Swiss Foundation Type and Typography, Bern. Photography: Philippe Karrer, Angelo A. Lüdin, Basel.
/02/03/04/05/08/14/29/ Adrian Frutiger, Bremgarten / Bern.
/32/33/34/ Bauer Types, Barcelona. Design: Bruno Pfäffli.

OCR-B
/01/10/21/23/24/28/36/ Adrian Frutiger, Bremgarten / Bern.
/25/26/ from Bosshard, Hans Rudolf. *Technische Grundlagen zur Satzherstellung.* Bern: Verlag des Bildungsverbandes Schweizerischer Typografen, 1980.
/17/18/19/20/ ECMA. *ECMA Standard for the alphanumeric Character Set OCR-B for Optical Recognition.* 1963.
/27/32/ Swiss Foundation Type and Typography, Bern.
/38/ from *Arts et Techniques Graphiques* no. 75 (1968).
/39/ Swiss Confederation identity card.
/40/ from *Typografische Monatsblätter* 11 (1974).

Univers IBM Composer
/01/ Swiss Foundation Type and Typography, Bern. Photography: Philippe Karrer, Angelo A. Lüdin, Basel.
/07/10/14/ Adrian Frutiger, Bremgarten / Bern.
/09/10/11/ from *IBM Journal of Research and Development,* vol. 12, no. 1 (1968).
/12/ IBM. *IBM Composer-Schriften.* n.d.
/13/ Hans-Jürg Hunziker, Paris.
/14/ Adrian Frutiger, Bremgarten / Bern.

Alphabet EDF-GDF
/01/ from: Electricité de France Gaz de France. Memoires de la Communication. Paris, 1994. - www.edf.fr.
/03/08/09/ Electricité de France Gaz de France. *La reception du public dans les unites de la distribution.* Paris 1968. Photography: Philipp Karrer, Angelo A. Lüdin, Basel.
/04/05/06/07/ Adrian Frutiger, Bremgarten / Bern.

Katalog
/01/02/03/04/05/07/10/ Adrian Frutiger, Bremgarten / Bern.
/08/ Swiss Foundation Type and Typography, Bern.

Devanagari / Tamil
/03/ Photographer unknown.
/06/ Photography: André Gürtler.
/07/ from *Typographische Monatsblätter* 6-7 (1967).
/08/ Unknown publication.
/11/ from Monotype Corporation. *Specimen Book of 'Monotype'
    Non-Latin Faces.* Salfords, Redhill: Monotype Corporation,
    c.1972.
/13/16/17/18/19/22/23/29/ Adrian Frutiger, Bremgarten / Bern.
/20/24/ Adrian Frutiger, Bremgarten / Bern.
    Photography: Philippe Karrer, Angelo A. Lüdin, Basel.
/21/ Photography: Bruno Pfäffli, Paris.
/26/27/28/29/ Mahendra Patel.

Alpha BP
/01/09/ Adrian Frutiger, Bremgarten / Bern.
/02/ from *Graphics World* 32 (1981). – www.bp.com.
/03/04/ from *Graphics World* 32 (1981).
/05/ Bauhaus-Archiv, Berlin. VG Bild-Kunst Bonn.
/08/ from Blackwell, Lewis. *Schrift als Experiment.* Basel:
    Birkhäuser Verlag, 2004.
/10/ Georg Staehelin, Ottenbach. Photography: Pentagram.
/11/ Photography: Pentagram.

Documenta
/03/ Adrian Frutiger, Bremgarten / Bern.
/07/ Linotype AG, Bad Homburg.

Alphabet Facom
/02/03/ Adrian Frutiger, Bremgarten / Bern.
/04/05/ Swiss Foundation Type and Typography, Bern.

Alphabet Roissy
/01/02/28/ Photography: Erich Alb, Cham.
/03/05/06/07/08/10/11/13/14/19/20/21/22/23/26/
    Adrian Frutiger, Bremgarten / Bern.
/04/ *Typographische Monatsblätter* 1 (1977).
    Photography: Philippe Karrer, Angelo A. Lüdin, Basel.
/09/ from Caflisch, Max. *Schriftanalysen,* vol. 2.
    St. Gallen: Typotron AG, 2003.
/25/ Photography: Philippe Karrer, Angelo A. Lüdin, Basel.
/27/ Photography: Jean-J. Moreau.

Alphabet Brancher
/01/ from Weidemann, Kurt. *Der Druckspiegel,* 12a
    (December 1961), Typographical supplement.
/02/04/ Adrian Frutiger, Bremgarten / Bern.
/03/05/07/ Bruno Pfäffli, Paris.
/06/ from *Caractère* 1 (1967).
    From *Informations TG,* no. 578 (March 1972).

Iridium
/05/ Linotype AG, Bad Homburg.
/16/23/ Swiss Foundation Type and Typography, Bern.
/17/ Gutenberg Bibliothek Mainz.
/22/21/ Adrian Frutiger, Bremgarten / Bern.
/25/ Adrian Frutiger, Bremgarten / Bern.
    Photography: Philippe Karrer, Angelo A. Lüdin, Basel.

Alphabet Métro
/06/08/09/10/11/13/14/15/ Adrian Frutiger, Bremgarten / Bern.
/07/ Photography: Pio Corradi.

Alphabet Centre Georges Pompidou
/01/ Ernst Hiestand, Zurich.
/03/ from Widmer, Jean. *Jean Widmer.*
    Villeurbanne: Maison du Livre, de l'Image et du Son, 1991.
/04/ Hans Jürg Hunziker, Paris.

Frutiger
/04/ from Conways. *Quick name a sans.* London, n.d.
/05/06/07/23/ Adrian Frutiger, Bremgarten / Bern.
/24/25/33/70/ Photography: Philippe Karrer, Angelo A. Lüdin.
/29/35/ Linotype AG, Bad Homburg.
/30/ Swiss Foundation Type and Typography, Bern.
/68/69/ from Schweizerische Normenvereinigung. Normalschrift
    für Signale, Zurich 1972. Photography: Viktor Stampfli.
/71/ from Schweizerischer Verband der Strassen-
    und Verkehrsfachleute. Strassensignale. Zurich 2002.
/75/ MetaDesign Berlin.

Glypha
/07/ from D. Stempel AG. *Typefaces designed by Adrian Frutiger.
    Schriften von Adrian Frutiger. Caractères créés par
    Adrian Frutiger.* Frankfurt am Main: D. Stempel AG, 1983.

Icone
/01/02/03/04/05/06/07/08/09/33/ Adrian Frutiger.
/15/ Linotype AG, Bad Homburg.
/28/ from *Linotype Express* 14 (1988).
/29/30/31/ from *Der Polygraph,* special edition 1988.
/32/ Photography: Philippe Karrer, Angelo A. Lüdin, Basel.

Breughel
/01/ Photography: Philippe Karrer, Angelo A. Lüdin, Basel.
/02/03/04/05/06/07/12/13/ Adrian Frutiger, Bremgarten / Bern.
/08/ Photography: André Gürtler.
/09/ from Faulmann, Karl. *Die Erfindung der Buchdruckerkunst
    nach den neuesten Forschungen.* Vienna: A. Hartlebens
    Verlag, 1891.

Dolmen
/01/02/03/04/10/11/12/13/14/16/17/18/19/ Adrian Frutiger.
/15/ Photographer unknown.

Tiemann
/01/ *Die Zeit* archive, Hamburg.
/02/ Gutenberg Bibliothek, Mainz.
/03/ from *Die Zeit,* 26 (1980).
/04/ from *Die Zeit,* 25 (1980).
/05/ Klingspor-Museum, Offenbach.
/08/ Adrian Frutiger.
/09/ from Die Zeit, 40 (1982), 40 (1983).
/10/ from Die Zeit, 46 (1982).

Versailles
/01/02/03/04/05/06/ Adrian Frutiger, Bremgarten / Bern.
/09/ from Deberny & Peignot. Title unknown, n.d.
/10/11/16/ from Deberny & Peignot. *Spécimen Général,* Tome II.
    Paris: Deberny & Peignot, 1926.
/24/ D. Stempel AG. *Typefaces designed by Adrian Frutiger.
    Schriften von Adrian Frutiger. Caractères créés par
    Adrian Frutiger.* Frankfurt am Main: D. Stempel AG, 1983.
    Photography: Philippe Karrer, Angelo A. Lüdin, Basel.
/26/ from Linotype AG. LinoTypeCollection. Mergenthaler Type
    Library / Mergenthaler Schriftenbibliothek / Typothèque
    Mergenthaler. Eschborn bei Frankfurt: Linotype AG, 1987.

Linotype Centennial
/01/12/ Linotype AG, Bad Homburg.
/02/ Swiss Foundation Type and Typography, Bern.
/04/ Publication unknown.
/05/06/07/09/10/27/28/ Adrian Frutiger, Bremgarten / Bern.
/08/11/ from *Der Polygraph,* 5 (1988), special edition.
/26/27/28/ Linotype GmbH. *LinoTypeCollection – Mergenthaler
    Type Library / Mergenthaler Schriftenbibliothek / Typo-
    thèque Mergenthaler.* Eschborn: Linotype GmbH, 1986.

Avenir
/02/14/15/16/45/ Adrian Frutiger, Bremgarten / Bern.
/03/13/ Linotype AG, Bad Homburg.
/12/ from *Der Polygraph,* 4 (1989).
/21/ Bauhaus archive, Berlin.
/22/33/ from *Typo. when who how.* Cologne: Könemann
    Verlagsgesellschaft, 1998.
/23/24/ from Bertheau, Philipp. *Buchdruckschriften im
    20. Jahrhundert.* Darmstadt: Technische Hochschule, 1995.
/25/ from Hillebrand, Henri. *grosse designer in der werbe-
    graphik band fünf.* Munich: Schuler Verlagsgesellschaft,
    1971.
/34/ from Wozencroft, Jon. *The graphic language
    of Neville Brody.* Munich: C. J. Bucher GmbH, 1988.
/39/40/ Swiss Foundation Type and Typography, Bern.
/59/ Photography: Philippe Karrer, Angelo A. Lüdin, Basel.

Westside
/01/02/03/04/05/06/07/ Adrian Frutiger, Bremgarten / Bern.

Vectora
/01/ Photography: Philippe Karrer, Angelo A. Lüdin, Basel.
/02/06/07/20/ Adrian Frutiger, Bremgarten / Bern.
/16/ Kurt Wälti, Urtenen-Schönbühl.

Linotype Didot
/01/03/ Paul Jammes, Paris.
/09/ from Tschichold, Jan. *Meisterbuch der Schrift.*
    Ravensburg: Otto Maier Verlag, 1965.
/14/ from Berry, W. Turner, *Encyclopedia of Type Faces.*
    London: Blandford Press, 1970.

Herculanum
/01/15/ Photography: Philippe Karrer, Angelo A. Lüdin, Basel.
/02/07/16/ Adrian Frutiger, Bremgarten / Bern.
/03/ from Hochuli, Jost. *Kleine Geschichte der geschriebenen
    Schrift.* St. Gallen: Typotron AG, 1991. –
    Photography: André Gürtler, Basel.
/04/ Steffens, Franz. *Lateinische Paläographie.*
    Fribourg: B. Veith, 1903.
/06/ from Muzika, František. *Die schöne Schrift,* vol. II.
    Prague: Artia Verlag, 1965.
/12/ Roman Uncials from Mittler, Elmar. *Biblioteca Palatina.*
    Heidelberg: Edition Braus, 1986. – Carolingian minuscules
    and Bastarda: Photography: André Gürtler, Basel. –
    Gothic minuscules from Bosshard, Hans Rudolf. *Technische
    Grundlagen zur Satzherstellung.* Bern: Verlag des
    Bildungsverbandes Schweizerischer Typografen, 1980.

Alphabet Shiseido
/03/05/08/ Adrian Frutiger.
/07/ Photography: Philippe Karrer, Angelo A. Lüdin, Basel.

Frutiger Capitalis
/01/02/04/05/06/ Adrian Frutiger, Bremgarten / Bern.
/03/ from Degering, Hermann. *Die Schrift.* Berlin: Verlag Ernst
    Wasmuth, 1929.
/07/08/ Swiss Foundation Type and Typography, Bern.

Pompeijana
/01/ Photography: Philippe Karrer, Angelo A. Lüdin, Basel.
/02/03/04/06/ Adrian Frutiger, Bremgarten / Bern.
/05/ Photography: André Gürtler, Basel.
    Vergilius Palatinus und Vergilius Vaticanus from Degering,
    Hermann. *Die Schrift.* Berlin: Verlag Ernst Wasmuth, 1929.
/08/ from Meier, Hans Eduard. *Die Schriftentwicklung.*
    Cham: Syntax Press, 1994.
/09/ from Korger, Hildegard. *Schrift und Schreiben.*
    Leipzig: Fachbuchverlag 1991.

Rusticana
/01/03/04/05/08/ Adrian Frutiger, Bremgarten / Bern.
/02/ Museum für Gestaltung Zurich, Plakatsammlung.
/07/ Photography: André Gürtler, Basel.
/08/ Réunion des musées nationaux, Paris.
    Adrian Frutiger, Bremgarten / Bern.
/09/ from Muzika, František. *Die schöne Schrift,* vol. II.
    Prague: Artia Verlag, 1965.

Frutiger Stones
/01/07/ Adrian Frutiger, Bremgarten / Bern.
/02/ from Földes-Papp, Károly. *Vom Felsbild zum Alphabet.*
    Stuttgart: Belser Verlag, 1966.
    Photography: André Gürtler, Basel.
/03/ Linotype AG, Bad Homburg.

Frutiger Neonscript
/01/ Klingspor-Museum Offenbach.
/02/06/ Adrian Frutiger, Bremgarten / Bern.
/05/ Westiform AG, Niederwangen.

Nami
/01/05/06/07/ Adrian Frutiger, Bremgarten / Bern.
/02/ Photography: André Gürtler, Basel.

For the illustrations in the technical parts we would like to
extend our thanks to:
Fritz Antenen, IBM, Linotype AG, Monotype Imaging,
Peter Karow, Musée de l'imprimerie Lyon, Polygraph Verlag
Press Medien GmbH & Co KG, Wikimedia Commons
(Ian Ruotsala).

List of literature

The publications and articles by Adrian Frutiger as well as the publications and articles about Adrian Frutiger that were used in the preparation of this book are listed on pages 444–447.

A

Aicher, Otl. *typographie.* Berlin: Ernst & Sohn, 1989.

Arbeitsgemeinschaft für grafische Lehrmittel, ed. *Filmsatzausbildung für Schriftsetzer.* Solothurn: Arbeitsgemeinschaft für grafische Lehrmittel, 1972.

Association Typographique Internationale. *Lettres Françaises.* Redhill, Surrey: ATypI, 1998.

B

Bain, Peter and Paul Shaw. *Blackletter: Type and National Identity.* New York: Princeton Architectural Press and The Cooper Union for the Advancement of Science and Art, 1998.

Baines, Phil and Andrew Haslam. *Lust auf Schrift! Basiswissen Typografie.* Mainz: Verlag Hermann Schmidt, 2002.

Barthel, Gustav. *Konnte Adam schreiben? – Weltgeschichte der Schrift.* Cologne: M. Dumont Schauberg, 1972.

Basel School of Arts and Crafts / Kunstgewerbeschule Basel / École des arts et métiers de Bâle. *graphic design. Schriften des Gewerbemuseums Basel,* no. 6 (1967).

Bauer, Konrad F. *Aventur und Kunst. Eine Chronik des Buchdruckgewerbes von der Erfindung der beweglichen Letter bis zur Gegenwart.* Frankfurt am Main: Bauersche Giesserei, 1940.

Bauer, Konrad F. *Wie eine Buchdruckschrift entsteht.* Frankfurt am Main: Bauersche Giesserei, n.d.

Baufeldt, Uwe, Manfred Dorra, Hans Rösner, Jürgen Scheuermann and Hans Walk. *Informationen übertragen und drucken.* Itzehoe: Verlag Beruf + Schule, 1989.

Beaumarchais. *La Folle Journée ou Le Mariage de Figaro.* Paris: Berger-Levrault, 1957. (Reprint from 1785 with 4-page insert on Lumitype). Also available from Berger-Levrault as a special edition (two-colour printed, quarto bound in Solander box).

Bennett, Paul A. *J. van Krimpen: On Designing and Devising Type.* New York: The Typophiles, 1957.

Berry, W. Turner, A. F. Johnson and W. P. Jaspert. *The Encyclopaedia of Type Faces.* London: Blandford Press, 1962.

Bertheau, Philipp, Eva Hanebutt-Benz and Hans Reichardt. *Buchdruckschriften im 20. Jahrhundert. Atlas zur Geschichte der Schrift.* Darmstadt: Technische Universität Darmstadt, 1995.

Bignens, Christoph. *'Swiss Style'. Die grosse Zeit der Gebrauchsgrafik in der Schweiz 1914–1964.* Zurich: Chronos Verlag, 2000.

Bignens, Christoph. *American Way of Life. Architektur Comics Design Werbung.* Sulgen/Zurich: Verlag Niggli AG, 2003.

Bishop, D. A. et al. 'Development of the IBM Magnetic Type Selectric Composer,' in *IBM Journal of Research and Development* (September 1968).

Blackwell, Lewis. *Schrift als Experiment. Typographie im 20. Jahrhundert.* Basel: Birkhäuser, 2004.

Blanchard, Gérard. *Aide au choix de la typo-graphie.* Reillanne: Atelier Perrouseaux, 1998.

Bockwitz, Hans H. *Beiträge zur Kulturgeschichte des Buches.* Leipzig: Harrassowitz Verlag, 1956.

Bohadti, Gustav. *Die Buchdruckletter. Ein Handbuch für das Schriftgiesserei- und Buchdruckgewerbe.* Berlin: Ullstein Verlag, 1954.

Bohadti, Gustav. *Von der Romain du Roi zu den Schriften J. G. Justus Erich Walbaums.* Berlin / Stuttgart: H. Berthold AG, 1957.

Bohadti, Gustav. *Justus Erich Walbaum. Ein Lebensbild.* Berlin: Berlin Staatliches Lehrinstitut für Graphik, Druck und Werbung, 1964.

Bolliet, L., N. Gastinel and P. J. Laurent: *un nouveau langage scientifique – algol. manuel pratique.* Paris: Editions Hermann, 1964.

Bollwage, Max. 'Formen und Strukturen. Gedanken über eine moderne Klassifikation der Druckschriften,' in *Gutenberg-Jahrbuch 2000.*

Bollwage, Max. 'Serifenlose Linearschriften gibt es nicht erst seit dem 19. Jahrhundert. Mutmassungen eines Typografen,' in *Gutenberg-Jahrbuch 2002.*

Bose, Günter and Erich Brinkmann, eds. *Jan Tschichold: Schriften 1925–1974.* 2 vols. Berlin: Brinkmann & Bose, 1992.

Bosshard, Hans Rudolf. *Technische Grundlagen zur Satzherstellung.* vol. 1. Bern: BST, Fachbücher für die graphische Industrie, 1980.

Bosshard, Hans Rudolf. *Mathematische Grundlagen zur Satzherstellung.* vol. 2. Bern: BST, Fachbücher für die graphische Industrie, 1985.

Bosshard, Hans Rudolf. *Typografie Schrift Lesbarkeit.* Sulgen: Verlag Niggli AG, 1996.

Brockhaus, F. A. *Brockhaus Enzyklopädie in vierundzwanzig Bänden,* 19., völlig neubearbeitete Auflage. Mannheim: F. A. Brockhaus, 1986–1994.

Brüning, Ute. 'Zur Typografie Herbert Bayers,' in *Herbert Bayer – Das künstlerische Werk 1918–1938.* Berlin: Gebr. Mann, 1982.

Buchmann, Mark, ed. *Walter Käch. Schriftgrafiker und Lehrer.* Zurich: Kungstgewerbemuseum der Stadt Zürich, 1973.

Bulcourt, R. 'La Lumitype et ses possibilités,' in *Graphê* no. 18 (Juli / August / September 1960).

Burkhardt, Richard. *grafische technik – heute und morgen.* Stuttgart: Vereinsdruckerei Heilbronn, 1959.

C

Caflisch, Max. *Schriftanalysen.* 2 vols. St. Gallen: Typotron AG, 2003.

Carter, John and Percy H. Muir, eds. *Bücher die die Welt verändern.* Munich: Deutscher Taschenbuch Verlag, 1968.

Carter, Sebastian. *Twentieth century type designers.* London: Trefoil, 1987.

Centre d'Étude et de Recherche Typographiques. *De plomb d'encre & de lumière.* Paris: Imprimerie Nationale, 1982.

Cheongju Early Printing Museum. *Koreas alte Schriftkunst. Begegnungen – Koreanischer Buchdruck vor Gutenberg.* Cheongju, 2005.

Cheng, Karen. *Anatomie der Buchstaben.* Mainz: Verlag Hermann Schmidt, 2005.

Cost, Patricia A. 'Linn Boyd Benton, Morris Fuller Benton, and Typemaking at ATF,' in *Printing History* 31–32 (2002).

D

Davidshofer, Leo and Walter Zerbe. *Satztechnik und Gestaltung.* Zurich / Bern: Bildungsverband Schweizer, 1970.

Degering, Hermann. *Die Schrift. Atlas der Schriftformen des Abendlandes vom Altertum bis zum Ausgang des 18. Jahrhunderts.* Berlin: Wasmuth, 1929.

Diehl, Ernst. *Inscriptiones Latinae. Tabulae in usum scholarum.* vol. 4. Bonn: A. Marcus, 1912.

Diehl, Robert. *Beaumarchais als Nachfolger Baskervilles.* Frankfurt am Main: Privately printed by Bauersche Giesserei, 1925.

Diethelm, Walter. *Signet Signal Symbol / Emblème Signal Symbole / Signet Signal Symbol.* Zurich: ABC-Verlag, 1970.

Dreyfus, John. *The Work of Jan van Krimpen.* London: Museum House, Sylvan Press, 1952.

Droste, Magdalena, ed. *Herbert Bayer. Das künstlerische Werk 1918–1938.* Berlin: Mann, 1982.

Dudenredaktion. *Duden 1 – Die deutsche Rechtschreibung.* Mannheim / Leipzig / Vienna / Zurich: Duden, 2006.

Dürer, Albrecht. *Konstruktion der Antiquamajuskeln.* Frankfurt am Main: Polygraph Verlag, 1971 (extract reprinted from Unterweisung der Messung mit dem Zirkel und Richtscheit [1525]).

E

European Computer Manufacturers Associaton. *ECMA Standard for the Alphanumeric Character Set OCR-B for Optical Recognition.* Geneva: ECMA, 1965.

Ehmcke, Fritz Helmut. *Ziele des Schriftunterrichts.* Jena: Eugen Diederich, 1911.

Ehmcke, Fritz Helmut. *Schrift – ihre Gestaltung und Entwicklung in neuerer Zeit.* Hanover: Günther Wagner, 1925.

Ehmcke, Fritz Helmut. *Die historische Entwicklung der Abendländischen Schriftformen.* Ravensburg: Otto Maier Verlag, 1927.

Ehrle, Franz and Paul Liebaert. *Specimina Codicum Latinorum Vaticanorum.* Tabulae in usum scholarum. vol. 3. Berlin: Walter de Gruyter, 1927.

Eidenbenz, Hermann. 'Magdeburg, 1926–1932. Ein systematischer schriftunterricht,' in *Typografische Monatsblätter* 2 (1978).

Elam, Kimberly. *Proportion und Komposition: Geometrie im Design.* New York: Princeton Architectural Pres, 2006.

Erichson, Knut and John Dreyfus, eds. *ABC-XYZapf. Fünfzig Jahre Alphabet Design.* Offenbach / London: Wynken de Worde Society, 1989.

Eurographic Press. 'Die Zukunft unserer Druckschriften', in *Deutscher Drucker* no. 1–2 (8 January, 1976). Part 2 of the survey appears in *Deutscher Drucker* no. 3. (January 22, 1976).

Eurographic Press. 'Über die Zukunft von Schrift und Typografie,' in *DruckIndustrie* no. 12 (27 June, 1985).

F

Faulmann, Carl. *Das Buch der Schrift – enthaltend die Schriftzeichen und Alphabete aller Zeiten und aller Völker des Erdkreises.* Nördlingen: Greno, 1985. (Reprint of 1880 edition).

Faulmann, Karl. *Die Erfindung der Buchdruckerkunst.* Vienna: A. Harlebens Verlag, 1891.

Fineder, Martina, Eva Kraus and Andreas Pawlik, eds. *postscript – Zur Form von Schrift heute A/CH/D.* Stuttgart: Hatje Cantz, 2004.

Finsterer, Alfred, ed. *Hoffmanns Schriftatlas.* Stuttgart: Julius Hoffmann, 1952.

Finsterer-Stuber, Gerda, ed. *Geistige Väter des Abendlandes.* Stuttgart: C. Belser, 1960.

Fleischmann, Gerd. *bauhaus – drucksachen typografie reklame.* Stuttgart: Oktagon, 1995.

Földes-Papp, Károly. *Vom Felsbild zum Alphabet.* Stuttgart: C. Belser, 1966.

Franco, Eli and Karin Preisendanz. 'Die indischen Schriften', in Wilfried Seipel, ed. *Der Turmbau zu Babel. Ursprung und Vielfalt von Sprache und Schrift.* vol. IIIa. Vienna: Kunsthistorisches Museum Wien, 2003.

Frenkel, Rainer. 'Abschied vom Blei. Aus dem konservativen Innenleben der Zeit', in *Die Zeit* no. 20 (14 May, 1982).

Friedl, Friedrich, Nicolaus Ott and Bernard Stein, eds. *Typography – when who how / Typographie – wann wer wie / Typographie – quand qui comment.* Cologne: Könemann, 1998.

Friedl, Friedrich. 'Zwischen Tradition und Experiment. Aspekte typografischen Formwillens im 20. Jahrhundert', in *Gutenberg-Jahrbuch 2000.*

Füssel, Stephan. *Gutenberg und seine Wirkung.* Frankfurt am Main: Insel Verlag, 1999.

G

Geck, Elisabeth. *Das Wort der Meister. Bekenntnisse zu Schrift und Druck aus fünf Jahrhunderten.* Berlin / Frankfurt: Mergenthaler Verlag Linotype, 1966.

Gerstner, Karl. *Programme entwerfen.* Teufen: Verlag Arthur Niggli, 1968.

Gerstner, Karl. *Kompendium für Alphabeten. Systematik der Schrift.* Heiden: Verlag Arthur Niggli, 1990.

Gerstner, Karl. *Rückblick auf 5 × 10 Jahre Graphik Design etc.* Stuttgart: Hatje Cantz, 2001.

Gray, Nicolete. *Nineteenth Century Ornamented Typefaces.* Berkeley: University of California Press, 1976.

Gray, Nicolete. *A History of Lettering.* Oxford: Phaidon, 1986.

Gürtler, André. 'Schrift im Lichtsatz', in *Typographische Monatsblätter* no. 3 (1966).

Gürtler, André. 'Basilia – eine klassizistische Type,' in *Officina. Mitteilungen des Hauses Schwabe & Co. AG* (November 1989).

Gürtler, André. 'Die Entwicklungsgeschichte der Zeitung / L'histoire du développement du journal / History of the development of the newspaper.' (Special report in *Typografischen Monatsblätter,* spread over several issues, 1983–1988).

Gürtler, André. *Die Entwicklung der lateinischen Schrift / L'évolution de l'écriture latine / The Development of the Roman Alphabet.* St. Gallen: Bildungsverband Schweizerischer Buckdrucker, 1969.

Gürtler, André, Christian Mengelt and Erich Gschwind. 'Von der Helvetica – zur Haas Unica,' in *Typografische Monatsblätter* 4 (1980).

Gutenberg-Gesellschaft Mainz, ed. *Giovanni Mardersteig. Typograph Verleger Humanist.* Mainz, 1990.

Gutschi, Christian. 'Psychologie der Schriften,' part 1 in *Page* 8 (1996); part 2 in *Page* 9 (1996); part 3 in *Page* 10 (1996); part 4 in *Page* 12 (1996); part 5 in *Page* 1 (1997).

H

Haarmann, Harald. *Universalgeschichte der Schrift.* Frankfurt / New York: Campus Verlag, 1991.

Haas'sche Schriftgiesserei. *Die Type.* Münchenstein: Haas'sche Schriftgiesserei, 1959.

Haas'sche Schriftgiesserei. *Die Drucktype. Rückblick, Gegenwart, Ausblick.* Basel: Haas'sche Schriftgiesserei, 1980.

Halbey, Hans Adolf. *Karl Klingspor – Leben und Werk.* Offenbach am Main: Vereinigung 'Freunde des Klingspor-Museum', 1991.

Haley, Allan. *Schriftdesign – Menschen, Typen und Stile.* Bonn: MITP-Verlag, 2002.

Hammer, Victor. *The Forms of Our Letters.* Typophile Monographs, New Series no. 6. New York: The Typophiles, 1989.

Handover, P.M. *Geschichtliches über die endstrichlose Schrift, die wir Grotesk nennen.* London: Monotype Corporation, 1962.

Harzmuseum der Stadt Wernigerode. *Paul Renner. Dem Schöpfer der Futura zum 125. Geburtstag.* Wernigerode: Urachhaus, 2003.

Herrmann, Ralf. *index schrift.* Bonn: MITP-Verlag, 2003.

Hillebrand, Henri, ed. *große designer in der werbegraphik.* vol. 5 USA I. Munich: Schuler, 1971.

Hillebrand, Henri, ed. *große designer in der werbegraphik.* vol. 6 USA II. Munich: Schuler, 1971.

Hochuli, Jost. 'Die schrift in der ausbildung des grafikers,' in *Typografische Monatsblätter* 6-7 (1975).

Hochuli, Jost. *Das Detail in der Typografie.* Wilmington, MA: Compugraphic, 1978.

Hochuli, Jost. *Kleine Geschichte der geschriebenen Schrift.* St. Gallen: Typotron AG, 1991.
Hofmann, Armin. *Methodik der Form und Bildgestaltung / Manuel de Création Graphique / Graphic Design Manual.* Niederteufen: Verlag Arthur Niggli, 1965.
Hollis, Richard. *Schweizer Grafik. Die Entwicklung eines internationalen Stils 1920–1965.* Basel: Birkhauser, 2006.
Hölscher, Eberhard. *Anna Simons. Monographien künstlerischer Schrift.* vol. 2. Berlin / Leipzig: Heintze & Blanckertz, n.d. (c. 1937)
Hölscher, Eberhard. *Rudolf von Larisch und seine Schule / Rudolf von Larisch and his School.* Monographien künstlerischer Schrift. vol. 5. Berlin / Leipzig: Heintze & Blanckertz, n.d. (c. 1938).
Holt, G.A. 'The IBM Selectric Composer – Philosophy of Composer Design,' in *IBM Journal of Research and Development* (January 1968).
Hostettler, Rudolf. *Type – A Selection of Types / Une Sélection de Caractères d'Imprimerie / Eine Auswahl guter Druckschriften.* St. Gallen / London: FGB Books, 1949.
Hunziker, Hans-Jürg. *Siemens. Brand Notebook 1. Unsere Schrift.* Munich: Siemens, 2001.
Hurm, Otto. *Johnston, Larisch, Koch – Drei Erneuerer der Schreibkunst.* Basel: Buchdruckerei A. Apel, 1955.
Hutchings, R.S. *A Manual of Decorated Typefaces.* New York / London: Hastings House, 1965.

I

IBM Deutschland. *Der IBM Magnetband-Composer. Eine neue Technik der Satzherstellung.* Sindelfingen, n.d.
International Business Forms Industries. *optical character recognition, and the years ahead.* Elmhurst, IL., 1959.

J

Jammes, André. *Les Didot. Trois siècles de typographie et de bibliophilie 1698–1998.* Paris: Agence culturelle de Paris, 1998.
Jaspert, W.P., W. Turner Berry and A.F. Johnson. *The Encyclopaedia of Type Faces.* London: Blandford Press, 1970. 4th ed.
Jensen, Hans. *Die Schrift in Vergangenheit und Gegenwart.* Berlin: VEB Deutscher Verlag der Wissenschaften, 1969.
Johnston, Edward. *Writing and Illuminating and Lettering.* London: John Hogg, 1906.
Johnston, Edward. *Schreibschrift, Zierschrift & angewandte Schrift.* Translated by Anna Simons. Leipzig: Klinkhardt & Biermann, 1910.
de Jong, Cees W., Alston W. Purvis and Friedrich Friedl. *Creative type.* London: Thames & Hudson, 2005.
Jubert, Roxane. *graphisme typographie histoire.* Paris: Flammarion, 2005.

K

Käch, Walter. *Schriften Lettering Écritures.* Olten: Walter-Verlag, 1949.
Käch, Walter. *Rhythm and Proportion in Lettering / Rhythmus und Proportion in der Schrift.* Olten: Walter-Verlag, 1956.
Käch, Walter. *Bildzeichen der Katakomben.* Olten: Walter-Verlag, 1965.
Kandler, Georg. *Alphabete. Erinnerungen an den Bleisatz.* 2 vols. Kornwestheim: Minner-Verlag, 1995 and 2001.
Kapr, Albert. *Deutsche Schriftkunst.* Dresden: Verlag der Kunst, 1955.
Kapr, Albert. *Schriftkunst. Geschichte, Anatomie und Schönheit der lateinischen Buchstaben.* Dresden: Verlag der Kunst, 1971.
Kapr, Albert and Detlef Schäfer. *Fotosatzschriften – Type-Design und Schriftherstellung.* Leipzig: VEB Fachbuchverlag, 1989.
Karow, Peter. *Schrifttechnologie. Methoden und Werkzeuge.* Berlin / Heidelberg: Springer Verlag, 1992
Kelly, Rob Roy. *American Wood Type: 1828–1900.* New York: Van Nostrand & Reinhold, 1970.
Kern, Otto. *Inscriptiones Graecae, Tabulae in usum scholarum.* vol. 7. Bonn: A. Marcus and E. Weber, 1913.
Kirschgarten-Druckerei AG, ed. *Typorama – Rund um das graphische Gewerbe.* Basel, 1964.
Knight, Stan. *Historical Scripts.* New Castle, DE: Oak Knoll Press, 1998.
Korger, Hildegard. *Schrift und Schreiben.* Leipzig: VEB Fachbuchverlag, 1991.
Kuckenburg, Martin. *Die Entstehung von Sprache und Schrift.* Cologne: DuMont Buchverlag, 1990.
Kunstgewerbemuseum der Stadt Zurich. *Gründung und Entwicklung – 1878–1978: 100 Jahre Kunstgewerbeschule der Stadt Zürich.* Zurich: Schule für Gestaltung, 1978.

L

Larisch, Rudolf von. *Unterricht in ornamentaler Schrift.* Vienna: K.K. Hof- und Staatsdruckerei, 1905.
Le Coultre, Martijn F. and Alston W. Purvis: *Jan Tschichold. Plakate der Avantgarde.* Basel: Birkhäuser, 2007.
Luidl, Philipp. *Paul Renner.* TGM-Bibliothek. Munich: Typographische Gesellschaft München, 1978.
Luidl, Philipp. *Schrift – die Zerstörung der Nacht.* Munich: Typographische Gesellschaft München, 1993.
Lupton, Ellen and J. Abbott Miller, eds. *Dreieck, Quadrat und Kreis. Bauhaus und Design-Theorie heute.* Basel, 1994.
Lutz, Hans-Rudolf. *Ausbildung in typografischer Gestaltung.* Zurich: Verlag Lutz, 1996.
Lutz, Hans-Rudolf. *Typoundso.* Zurich: Verlag Lutz, 1996.

M

Macmillan, Neil. *An A–Z of type designers.* London: Laurence King Publishing, 2006.
Mallon, Jean. *Paléographie romaine.* Madrid: Consejo Superior de Investigaciones Cientificas, Instituto Antonio de Nebrija de Filologia, 1952.
Malsy, Victor and Lars Müller, eds. *Helvetica Forever. Geschichte einer Schrift.* Baden: Lars Müller Publishers, 2008.
Mandel, Ladislas. 'Our IPC Type Design Studio in Paris,' in unknown journal.
Marshall, Alan. *La Lumitype-Photon.* Lyon: Musée de la imprimerie et de la banque, 1995.
Marshall, Alan. Du plomb à la lumière. Paris: Maison des sciences de l'homme, 2003.
Meggs, Philip B. *A History of Graphic Design,* New York: John Wiley & Sons, Inc., 1998. 3rd ed.
Meier, Hans Eduard. 'Beiträge zur Ausbildung in Schrift / Contributions to Education in Letterform / Contributions pour l'enseignement de la letter,' in *Typografische Monatsblätter* 4 (1991).
Meier, Hans Eduard. *Die Schriftentwicklung / The Development of Script and Type / Le développement des caractères.* Zurich: Graphis Press, 1959. Reprint Cham: Syndor Press, 1994.
Middendorp, Jan. *Dutch Type.* Rotterdam: 010 Publishers, 2004.
Mittler, Elmar, ed. *Bibliotheca Palatina.* 2 vols. Heidelberg: Edition Braus, 1986.
Muess, Johannes. *Das römische Alphabet. Entwicklung, Form und Konstruktion.* Munich: Verlag Callwey, 1989.
Müller-Brockmann, Josef. *Geschichte der visuellen Kommunikation / A History of Visual Communication.* Niederteufen: Verlag Niggli AG, 1986. 2nd ed.
Lars Müller Publishers. *Poster Collection 07 – Armin Hofmann.* Baden: Lars Müller Publishers, 2003.
Museum für Gestaltung Zürich. *Frische Schriften / Fresh Type.* Zurich, 2004.
Muzika, Frantisek. *Die schöne Schrift.* 2 vols. Prague: Artia, 1971.

N

Newark, Quentin. *Was ist Grafik-Design?* Mies: Stiebner Verlag GmbH, 2006.
Nineuil, Olivier. 'Ladislas Mandel – explorateur de la typo française,' in *Etapes Graphiques* no. 10 (1999).
Noordzij, Gerrit. *Letterletter.* Vancouver: Hartley & Marks, 2000.

O

Oron, Asher. 'A new Hebrew sans serif for bilingual printing,' in unknown journal.

P

Patel, Mahendra. *Letters for Tomorrow. Experiments in Type-Form Development.* Ahmedabad: National Institute of Design, n. d.
Peignot, Jerôme. *Typoésie.* Paris: Imprimerie Nationale, 1993.
Pentagram. *the work of five designers / l'œuvre de cinq designers / fünf Designer und ihre Arbeiten.* London: Lund Humphries, 1972.
Pentagram. *Living by Design.* London: Lund Humphries, 1978.
Pott, Gottfried. 'Schriftkunst – Faszination des Originals. Kalligraphie als Impulsgeber und Kontrapunkt des Typedesigns,' in *Gutenberg-Jahrbuch 2000.*
Poynor, Rick. *Grafik-Design von den Achtzigern bis heute.* Basel: Birkhäuser, 2003.

Q

Quoniam, Pierre. *Le Louvre.* Paris: Éditions de la Réunion des musées nationaux, 1976.

R

Re, Margaret. *Typographically Speaking: The Art of Matthew Carter.* New York: Princeton Architectural Press, 2003.
Renner, Paul. *mechanisierte grafik. Schrift Typo Foto Film Farbe.* Berlin: Verlag Hermann Reckendorf, 1931.
Renner, Paul. *Die Kunst der Typographie.* Berlin: Frenzel & Engelbrecher, 1939
Robinson, Andrew. *Die Geschichte der Schrift.* Bern / Stuttgart / Vienna: Paul Haupt, 1996.
Rodenberg, Julius. *In der Schmiede der Schrift.* Berlin: Büchergilde Gutenberg, 1940.
Rothenstein, John. *Victor Hammer, Artist and Craftsman.* Boston: David R. Godine, Publisher, 1978.
Ruder, Emil. *Typographie – Ein Gestaltungslehrbuch / Typography – A Manual of Design / Typographie – Un Manuel de Création.* Sulgen: Verlag Niggli AG, 1967.
Rüegg, Ruedi and Godi Fröhlich. *Typografische Grundlagen / Bases Typographiques / Basic Typography.* Zurich: ABC-Verlag, 1972.

S

Sauthoff, Daniel, Gilmar Wendt and Hans Peter Willberg. *Schriften erkennen.* Mainz: Verlag Hermann Schmidt, 1998.
Schauer, Georg Kurt. *Chronik der Schriftgiesserei D. Stempel AG Frankfurt a. M. – Sechzig Jahre im Dienste der Lettern. 1895–1955.* Frankfurt am Main: D. Stempel AG, 1954.
Schauer, George Kurt, ed. *Internationale Buchkunst im 19. und 20. Jahrhundert.* Ravensburg: Otto Maier Verlag, 1969.
Schauer, Georg Kurt. *Klassifikation. Bemühungen um eine Ordnung im Druckschriftenbestand.* Darmstadt: Technische Hochschule, 1975.
Schmid, Helmut. *der Weg nach Basel / the road to Basel / Basel e no michi.* Tokyo: Robundo, 1997.
Schmitt, Günter. *Typographische Gestaltungsepochen.* Bellach: Arbeitsgemeinschaft für graphische Lehrmittel, 1983.
Schubart, Wilhelm. *Papyri Graecae Berolinensis, Tabulae in usum scholarum,* vol. 2. Bonn: A. Marcus and E. Weber, 1911.
Schulz-Anker, Erich. *Formanalyse und Dokumentation einer serifenlosen Linearschrift auf neuer Basis: Syntax Antiqua.* Frankfurt am Main: D. Stempel AG, 1969.
Schwemer-Scheddin, Yvonne. 'Ästhetik der Technik. Zur neuen Corporate-Schrift von Daimler-Benz und deren Gestalter Kurt Weidemann,' in *Page* 7 (1990).
Schwemer-Scheddin, Yvonne. 'Die Evo – Spiegel der Alltagskultur,' in *Typografische Monatsblätter,* Zurich 1 (1996).
Seemann, Albrecht. *Handbuch der Schriftarten. Eine Zusammenstellung der Schriften der Schriftgiessereien deutscher Zunge.* Leipzig: A. Seemann, 1926.
Seipel, Wilfried, ed. *Der Turmbau zu Babel. Ursprung und Vielfalt von Sprache und Schrift.* 3 vols. Vienna: Kunsthistorisches Museum, 2003.
Simoneit, Manfred and Wolfgang Zeitvogel. *Satzherstellung. Vom Bleisatz zum Computer Publishing.* Frankfurt am Main: Polygraph Verlag, 1979.
Simons, Anna. *Edward Johnston und die englische Schriftkunst / Edward Johnston and English Lettering.* Monographien künstlerischer Schrift, vol. 1. Berlin / Leipzig: Heintze & Blanckertz, 1937.
de Smet, Catherine. 'Histoire d'un rectangle rayé. Jean Widmer et le logo du Centre Pompidou,' in *Les Cahiers du Musée national d'art moderne* no. 89 (Herbst 2004).
Spiekermann, Erik. *Ursache & Wirkung: ein typografischer Roman.* Berlin: H. Berthold GmbH, 1982.
Spiekermann, Erik. *Studentenfutter oder: Was ich schon immer über Schrift & Typografie wissen wollte, mich aber nie zu fragen traute.* Nürnberg: Context GmbH, 1989.
Spiekermann, Erik. *Über Schrift.* Mainz: Verlag Hermann Schmidt, 2004.
Stamm, Philipp. 'schrift gleich sprache. Erweiterung des lateinischen alphabetes für die deutsche sprache / Extension of the Latin alphabet for the German language,' in *Typografische Monatsblätter* 1 (1997).
D. Stempel AG, ed. *Altmeister der Druckschrift.* Frankfurt am Main: D. Stempel AG, 1940.
Stötzner, Andreas. *Signa. Beiträge zur Signographie.* issue 2. Grimma: Denkmalschmiede Höfgen, 2001.
Sutton, James and Alan Bartram. *Typefaces for Books.* London: British Library, 1990.

T

Lehrdruckerei der Technischen Hochschule Darmstadt, ed. *Hermann Zapf – Ein Arbeitsbericht.* Hamburg: Maxmimilian-Gesellschaft, 1984.
Thibaudeau, Francis. *Manuel Français de Typographie Moderne.* Cœuvres-&-Valsery: Ressouvenances, 2005. (Facsimile of 1924).
Tschichold, Jan. *Formenwandlungen der et-Zeichen.* Frankfurt am Main: D. Stempel AG, 1953.
Tschichold, Jan. *Meisterbuch der Schrift.* Ravensburg: Otto Maier Verlag, 1965.
Tschichold, Jan. *Leben und Werk des Typographen Jan Tschichold.* Dresden: Verlag der Kunst, 1977.

U

Updike, Daniel Berkeley. *Printing Types: Their History, Forms, and Use.* 2 vols. Cambridge, MA: The Belknap Press of Harvard University, 1966. 3rd ed.

V

Vox, Maximilien. 'Das halbe Jahrhundert 1914–1964', in Georg Kurt Schauer, ed. *Internationale Buchkunst im 19. und 20. Jahrhundert.* Ravensburg: Otto Maier Verlag, 1969.

W

Wagemann, Ines. 'Mit Hilfe mathematischer Formeln',
in *form* 150 Dossier reform, 2 (1995).

Wallis, Lawrence W. *Type Design Developments 1970 to 1985.*
Arlington, VA: National Composition Society, 1985.

Wallis, Lawrence W. *Modern encyclopedia of typefaces 1960–90.*
London: Lund Humphries, 1990.

Wallis, Lawrence W. *A Concise Chronology of Typesetting
Developments 1886–1986.* London: Wynken de Worde
Society with Lund Humphries, 1988.

Wanner, Gustaf Adolf. '400 Jahre Haas'sche Schriftgiesserei,'
contribution to *Gutenberg-Jahrbuch 1979.*

Weidemann, Kurt. *Wo der Buchstabe das Wort führt.*
Stuttgart: Verlag Cantz, 1994.

Wendt, Dirk. *Untersuchungen zur Lesbarkeit von Druckschriften,*
Bericht no. 2. Hamburg, 1965 (photocopied/mimeographed
manuscript).

Wendt, Dirk. 'Semantic Differentials of Typefaces as a Method of
Congeniality Research,' in *The Journal of Typographic
Research.* vol. II, no. 1 (1968).

Wetzig, Emil. *Ausgewählte Druckschriften.*
Leipzig: Verlag Leipziger Buchdrucker Besitzer, 1925.

Wichmann, Hans, ed. *Armin Hofmann: His Work, Quest and
Philosophy / Werk Erkundung Lehre.*
Basel: Birkhäuser Verlag, 1989.

Wilkes, Walter. *Das Schriftgiessen. Von Stempelschnitt,
Matrizenfertigung und Letternguss.*
Darmstadt: Technische Hochschule, 1990.

Willberg, Hans Peter. 'Schrift und Typographie im 20. Jahrhundert', in *Gutenberg-Jahrbuch 2000.*

Willberg, Hans Peter. *Wegweiser Schrift.*
Mainz: Verlag Hermann Schmidt, 2001.

Windisch, Albert. *Professor Dr. h. c. Walter Tiemann.*
Mainz: Gutenberg-Gesellschaft, 1953.

Wingler, Hans M. and Magdalena Droste. *Herbert Bayer. Das
künstlerische Werk 1918–1938.* Berlin: Bauhaus-Archiv, 1982.

Wolf, Renate. 'Betäubend', in *Die Zeit* no. 40 (1996).

Wozencroft, Jon. *The Graphic Language of Neville Brody.*
London: Thames & Hudson, 1988.

Z

Zapf, Hermann. *William Morris. Sein Leben und Werk
in der Geschichte der Buch- und Schriftkunst.*
Lübeck: Klaus Blanckertz Verlag, 1949.

Zapf, Hermann. 'Vom Stempelschnitt zur Digitalisierung von
Schriftzeichen. Die technischen Veränderungen der
Schriftherstellung', in *Gutenberg-Jahrbuch 2000.*

Zeitler, Julius. *Emil Rudolf Weiss,* Archiv für Buchgewerbe und
Gebrauchsgraphik Sonderheft. Leipzig: Archiv für
Buchgewerbe und Gebrauchsgraphik, 1922.

Periodicals

The following periodicals and yearbooks were consulted:

Art de France
Bulletin officiel des cours professionnels
Caractère. Revue mensuelle des industries graphiques
Caractère Noël
Deberny & Peignot, Bulletin d'information
Der Druckspiegel
Der Polygraph
Design Industrie
Deutscher Drucker
DruckIndustrie
Esthétique Industrielle
Etapes Graphiques
form
Graphê
Graphis
Gutenberg-Jahrbuch
Informations TG
L'Imprimerie Nouvelle
La France Graphique
Métiers graphiques
Monotype Newsletter
Monotype Recorder
Neue Graphik
Officina. Mitteilungen des Hauses Schwabe & Co AG, Basel
Page
Techniques graphiques
Typografische Monatsblätter / Revue Suisse de l'imprimerie /
Swiss Typographic Magazine
U&lc (Upper and lower case)
Visible Language
Werk

Internet (a selection)

http://de.wikipedia.org
http://en.wikipedia.org
http://fr.wikipedia.org
http://ellie.rit.edu:1213/dphist1.htm
http://sammlungen-archive.hgkz.ch
www-05.ibm.com
www.100besteschriften.de
www.adobe.com
www.atypi.org
www.bauhaus.de
www.bitstream.com
www.bleisetzer.de
www.brancher.com
www.centrepompidou.fr
www.cgstudionyc.com
www.edf.fr
www.emigre.com
www.eurographicpress.com
www.facom.fr / www.facom.de
www.fontbureau.com
www.fontinform.de
www.fonts.com
www.fontshop.de
www.houseoftype.com
www.identifont.com
www.itcfonts.com
www.kghoefer.de
www.klingspor-museum.de
www.letraset.com
www.linotype.com
www.medienpsychologie.at
www.monotypeimaging.com
www.imprimerie.lyon.fr
www.myfonts.com
www.obib.de
www.p22.com
www.proz.com
www.perrousseaux.com
www.peterrueck.ch
www.porcheztypo.com
www.sanskritweb.net
www.schreibwerkstatt-klingspor.de
www.sergecortesi.com
www.shiseido.co.jp
www.stbride.org
www.systemarchitektur.de
www.typofonderie.com
www.typeforum.de
www.typography.com
www.typolexikon.de
www.westiform.com

Typeface catalogues

The following were consulted for the research texts and typeface
comparisons (typeface brochures are not listed).

Adobe Systems Incorporated. *Adobe Type Library. Reference
Book / Adobe-Schriftenbibliothek. Referenzhandbuch /
Guide de Référence de la Typothèque Adobe.*
San Jose: Adobe Systems, 2000.

Agfa Monotype. *Creative Alliance 9.0.*
Wilmington, MA: Agfa Monotype, 1999.

Bauersche Giesserei. *Schriftenprobe.*
Frankfurt am Main: Bauersche Giesserei, 1960.

Bauersche Giesserei. *Des Buchdruckers Schatzkästlein.*
Frankfurt am Main: Bauersche Giesserei, n.d.

H. Berthold AG. Berthold-Schriften. Hauptprobe no. 428.
Berlin: H. Berthold AG, n.d.

H. Berthold AG. *Berthold Fototypes E1.*
Berlin: H. Berthold AG, 1974.

H. Berthold AG. *Berthold Fototypes E2: Body Types.*
Berlin / Munich: H. Berthold AG, 1980.

H. Berthold AG. *Berthold Fototypes E3.*
Berlin: H. Berthold AG, 1982.

Bitstream. *Bitstream Typeface Library – PostScript.*
Cheltenham, Gloucestershire: Bitstream, 1989.

Compugraphic Corporation. *A portfolio of text & display type.*
Wilmington, MA: Compugraphic Corporation, 1980.

Compugraphic Corporation. *Compugraphic Typefaces* 2 vols.
Wilmington, MA: Compugraphic Corporation, 1985.

Deberny & Peignot. *Spécimen Général.* 2 vols. Paris, 1926.

Deberny & Peignot. *La Lumitype Possibilités Exemples.*
Paris, c. 1957.

Deberny & Peignot. *typographie.* Paris, n.d.

Deberny & Peignot. *Liste des Caractères Lumitype.* Paris, n.d.
(c. 1961).

Deberny & Peignot. *compo dp.* Paris, n.d. (c. 1961).

Emigre. *Emigre.* Nuth, 1998.

Schriftgiesserei Flinsch. Frankfurt am Main: Schriftgiesserei
Flinsch, n.d. (c. 1910).

FontShop International. *FontBook. Digital Typeface Compendium.* Berlin: FontShop International, 1998 and 2006.

Haas'sche Schriftgiesserei. *Hauptprobe.*
Münchenstein: Haas'sche Schriftgiesserei, n.d.

Haas France. *Spécimen de Caractères.* Paris: Haas France, n.d.

Haas Stempel. *Universal-Schriftprobe.*
Münchenstein / Frankfurt am Main: Haas Stempel, 1974.

Handsetzerei Ernst Gloor. *Univers mit typografischen Blättern
von Fridolin Müller.* Zurich, 1966.

Dr.-Ing. Rudolf Hell GmbH. *Typography 9.* Kiel: 1989.

IBM. *IBM Composer-Schriften.* Sindelfingen, n.d.

Imprimerie Nationale. *Le Cabinet des Poinçons de l'Imprimerie
Nationale.* Paris, 1963.

International Photon Corporation. *Typefaces.* year of publication
unknown.

International Typeface Corporation. *The ITC Typeface Collection.*
New York: International Typeface Corporation, 1980.

Intertype Company. *InterType Faces.* Brooklyn, NY: Intertype,
1958.

Letraset. *Letraset.* Glattbrugg: 1990.

Lettergieterij Amsterdam. *Auslese Moderner Druckschriften /
Choix de caractères modernes.* Amsterdam, n.d.

Linotype GmbH. *Linotype-Schriften.* Berlin / Frankfurt, 1967.

Linotype. *Linotype Fotosatz Schriften – im 18-Einheiten-System
für Linocomp, Linofilm VIP und Linotron.* Eschborn, c. 1974.

Linotype Font Center. *Digital Type Faces / Digitale Schriften /
Caractères digitalisés.* Eschborn bei Frankfurt, 1984.

Linotype AG. *LinoTypeCollection. Mergenthaler Type Library /
Mergenthaler Schriftenbibliothek / Typothèque Mergenthaler.* Eschborn bei Frankfurt, 1986 and 1987.

Linotype AG. *Linotype Library – Typeface Handbook /
Schriftenhandbuch / Catalogue de Caractères (PostScript).*
Eschborn bei Frankfurt, 1988.

Linotype-Hell AG. *LinoTypeCollection. Linotype Laser Fonts /
CRT Fonts.* Eschborn bei Frankfurt, 1992.

LinotypeLibrary. *Typeview Font Catalog 6.0.* Eschborn, 1996.

LinotypeLibrary. *FontExplorer Font Catalog.*
Bad Homburg, 1998 and 2001.

Linotype GmbH. *Typeface Catalog A–Z,* Bad Homburg, 2006.

Matrotype. *Matrotypefaces.* n.d.

Mecanorma. *Mecanorma Graphic Book 14.* Versailles, 1988.

Mergenthaler Linotype. *mergenthaler vip typeface.* 2 vols.
New York, 1980.

Mergenthaler Linotype Stempel Haas. *54 unit General Typefaces.*
c. 1976.

Mergenthaler Linotype Stempel Haas. *Display Typefaces.* c. 1976.

Mergenthaler Linotype Stempel Haas. *Text Typefaces.* c. 1976.

Mergenthaler Linotype Stempel Haas. *digital typeface directory.*
Eschborn, 1983.

Monotype Corporation. *Specimen Book of 'Monotype' Printing
Types.* 2 vols. Salfords, Redhill, 1970.

Monotype Corporation. *Specimen Book of 'Monotype'
Non-Latin Faces.* Salfords, Redhill, 1972.

Monotype Corporation. *Specimen Book of 'Monophoto'
Filmsetter Faces.* Salfords, Redhill, n.d.

Photon Inc. *Photon Phototypesetting Typefaces.* Wilmington MA,
c. 1972.

Schweizerische Verlagsdruckerei G. Böhm. *Schrift- und
Druckproben.* Basel, n.d.

Società Nebiolo. *Caratteri Indispensabili alla Tipografia Moderna.*
Turin, n.d.

D. Stempel AG. *Gesamtprobe der lieferbaren Schriften.*
Frankfurt am Main: D. Stempel AG, 1974.

Unionsdruckerei Bern. *Schriftprobe der Unionsdruckerei Bern.*
Bern, n.d.

Unterabteilung Kart der Hauptvermessungsabteilung X, ed.
*Schriftmusterbuch – Schriften, Ziffern, Zeichen und
Ligaturen der Stempelei der HVA X.* Bad Godesberg, 1948.

CD-ROM

See Octavo Corporation. *Giambattista Bodoni: Manuale
Tipografico.* Oakland: Octavo, 1998.

Our thanks

We would like to offer our heartfelt thanks
to the following institutions, companies and individuals
for their help and support with the publication. Without their
contribution this book would not have been possible.

For financial help and support:
Adrian Frutiger, Bremgarten, Switzerland
Sandoz-Familienstiftung, Pully, Switzerland

With the support of Pro Helvetia, Swiss Arts Council

swiss arts council
prohelvetia

For donation in kind:
Arctic Paper Deutschland GmbH, Germany
  (Wolfgang Lübbert)
Dr. Cantz'sche Druckerei GmbH & Co. KG, Stuttgart, Germany
  (Hermann Kuhnhäuser)
Klingspor-Museum Offenbach am Main, Germany
  (Stefan Soltek, Andrea Weiss)
Musée de l'imprimerie, Lyon, France
  (Alan Marshall, Pierre-Antoine Lebel)
MetaDesign, Berlin, Germany
polygraph, Press Medien GmbH & Co. KG, Detmold, Germany

For help and support with hot metal type and digital typefaces:
Elsner + Flake – Barcelona, Carus, Columna, Egyptian 505,
  Playbill
Fontbureau – Agenda, Hoffmann
Fonthaus (Mark Solsburg) – Cameo
FontShop – FF Advert, FF Bau, FF Dax, FF Signa
form – F Frutiger
Walter Fruttiger – Méridien, Ondine, Initiales Phoebus,
  Initiales Président, Univers
Hoefler & Frere-Jones (Jonathan Hoefler)
  HTF Didot light 16
Letterperfect – Didot LP
Linotype AG – Avenir Next, Basilia, Beneta, Linotype Didot
  Openface, Frutiger LT, Frutiger Next, Frutiger Cyrillic,
  Frutiger Serif, Litera, Nami, Linotype Syntax Lapidar,
  Linotype Univers, Vendome, Vialog
Monotype Imaging – Albertina, Buffalo Gal, Figaro, Virgile
Typos, Peter H. Singer – Boton, Poppl Laudatio
URW++ – Corporate A, Legende

For help and support with material and information:
Paul Andreu, Paris, France
Aéroports de Paris, Orly, France (Stefania Bator, Photothèque)
Albert Boton, Paris, France
Basler Papiermühle, Basel, Switzerland
  (Alfred Hoffmann, Stefan Meier, Markus Müller)
Basler Zeitung, Basel, Switzerland
  (Fritz Sutter, Heinrich Schanner)
Bauer Types, Barcelona, Spain (Wolfgang Hartmann)
Pierre Berès †, Paris, France
Bibliothèque Forney, Paris (Martine Guillermaine Boussoussou)
Bibliothèque nationale de France, Paris
Bouygues, Paris, France (Hubert Engelmann)
Brancher, Tremblay-les-Villages, France (Sebastien Brancher)
Max Caflisch †, Meilen, Switzerland
Dr. Cantz'sche Druckerei GmbH & Co. KG, Stuttgart, Germany
  (Hermann Kuhnhäuser)
Roger Chatelain, Mont-sur-Lausanne, Switzerland
Comedia, Bern, Switzerland (Hans Kern)
Serge Cortesi, Paris, France
Die Zeit, Hamburg, Germany
  (Andrea Beekmann, Ulrike Pieper, Ruth Viebrock)
EDF-GDF, Paris, France (Damien Kuntz)
ETH-Bibliothek, Zurich, Switzerland
Fachbibliothek der Schule für Gestaltung Basel, Switzerland
Facom, Morgangis, France (Thierry Givone)
Dave Farey, London, UK
Alan Fletcher †, London, UK
Colin Forbes, Westfield NC, USA
Rainer Frenkel, Hamburg, Germany
Friedrich Friedl, Frankfurt am Main, Germany
Jürg Fritzsche, St. Gallen, Switzerland
Adrian Frutiger, Bremgarten, Switzerland
Erich Frutiger, Interlaken, Switzerland
Simone Frutiger †, Bremgarten, Switzerland

Rainer Gerstenberg, Darmstadt, Germany
Walter Greisner, Königstein, Germany
André Gürtler, Basel, Switzerland
Gutenberg-Bibliothek Mainz, Germany
  (Claus Maywald-Pitellos, Wolfgang Steen, André Horch)
Gutenberg-Gesellschaft, Mainz, Germany (Gertraude Benöhr)
Romano Hänni, Basel, Switzerland
Reinhard Haus, Maintal, Germany
Jost Hochuli, St. Gallen, Switzerland
Hans-Jürg Hunziker, Paris, France
Peter Keller, Paris, France
Fabian Kempter, Basel, Switzerland
André Jammes, Paris, France
Günther Gerhard Lange, Grosshesselohe, Germany
Olaf Leu, Wiesbaden, Germany
Günther Lieck, Zurich, Switzerland
Linotype, Bad Homburg, Germany (Bruno Steinert,
  Otmar Hoefer, Bernd Hofmacher, Hans Reichardt)
Bruno Maag, London, UK
Ladislas Mandel †, Le Paradou, France
Jean Mandel, Arles, France
Jean Mentha, Cortaillod, Switzerland
Monotype Imaging, Salfords, Surrey, UK (Robin Nicholas)
Luis Murschetz, Munich, Germany
Marcel Nebel, Basel, Switzerland
Mike Parker, Portland ME, USA
Mahendra Patel, Ahmedabad, India
Yves Perrousseaux, Reillanne, France
Bruno Pfäffli, Paris, France
Tania Prill, Zurich, Switzerland
François Rappo, Lausanne, Switzerland
Rochester Institute of Technology, USA
  (Amelia Hugill-Fontanel)
Fiona Ross, London, UK
Helmut Schmid, Osaka, Japan
Christian Schmidt-Häuer, Hamburg, Germany
Werner Schneider, Wiesbaden, Germany
Jonas Schudel, Gockhausen, Switzerland
Yvonne Schwemer-Scheddin, Planegg, Germany
Pierre di Sciullo, Paris, France
Paul Shaw, New York, USA
Martin Sommer, Basel, Switzerland
Georg Staehelin, Ottenbach, Switzerland
Viktor Stampfli, Winikon, Switzerland
St Bride Library, London, UK (Nigel Roche)
Typemuseum London, UK (Duncan Avery)
URW++, Hamburg, Germany (Stefan Einkopf, Peter Rosenfeld)
Jovića Veljovic, Hamburg, Germany
Gregory Vines, Basel, Switzerland
Kurt Wälti, Urtenen-Schönbühl, Switzerland
Westiform AG, Niederwangen, Switzerland (Niklaus Imfeld)

For help and support with layout, photography, repro,
proofreading and production:
Kaspar Elsaesser, Michael Hartmann, Simon Hauser,
Philippe Karrer, Barbara Lüdi, Angelo A. Lüdin,
Andrea Näpflin, Tamara Nakhutsrishvili, Sandra Rizzi,
Sybille Schaub, Matthias Schneider, Esther Stamm,
Daniela Stolpp

Credits

Book idea
Friedrich Friedl, Adrian Frutiger, Erich Alb

Book concept, design, layout, project organisation
feinherb, Visuelle Gestaltung. Basel, Switzerland
Heidrun Osterer & Philipp Stamm

Conversations with Adrian Frutiger about his work
Erich Alb. Rudolf Barmettler, Philipp Stamm

Texts
Interviews with Adrian Frutiger
Silvia Werfel in collaboration with Heidrun Osterer and
Philipp Stamm
Research sections
Heidrun Osterer and Philipp Stamm
Printing technology sections
Peter Karow, René Kerfante, Heidrun Osterer,
Hermann Pfeiffer, Philipp Stamm

Technical editors
Erich Alb, Adrian Frutiger, Bruno Pfäffli, Paul Shaw

Adaptation from German into English
Susanne Dickel, Cologne, Germany
Chapters Serifen-Grotesk / Gespannte Grotesk, Orly,
Alphabet Algol, OCR-B, IBM-Univers, Concorde to Frutiger,
Breughel, Herculanum
Dylan Spiekermann, London, UK and
Erik Spiekermann, Berlin, Germany
Chapters Président to Apollo, Serifa, Glypha, Icone, Linotype
Centennial, Shiseido, Frutiger Stones / Frutiger Symbols,
Frutiger Capitalis, technology pages Transfer type, Linofilm
photosetting, CRT setting
Tim Danaher, Cologne, Germany
Prefaces, introduction, opening chapter, Alphabet Métro,
Dolmen, Tiemann, Versailles, Avenir, Linotype Didot,
Pompeijana, Rusticana, Vectora, Neonscript, Nami,
Logos and Wordmarks, all other technology pages, synopsis,
appendix

Copy editing of the English edition
Paul Shaw, New York, USA

Proofreading of the English edition
Monica Buckland, Basel, Switzerland

Typefaces used
Avenir, Avenir Next, Egyptienne F, Linotype Univers,
all Linotype GmbH, Bad Homburg,
various other typefaces from their respective publishers

Reproductions
feinherb, Visuelle Gestaltung. Basel, Switzerland
weissRaum (Kaspar Elsaesser). Basel, Switzerland

Paper
Munken Pure, 130 g/m² (Arctic)
f-color / schwarz (Zanders)
Peyer Princesse

Printing
VVA / Konkordia / Wesel Kommunikation,
Baden-Baden, Germany

Bookbinding
Grossbuchbinderei Josef Spinner GmbH,
Ottersweier, Germany

Library of Congress Control Number:
2007943315

Bibliographic information published by the
German National Library
The German National Library lists this publication in the
Deutsche Nationalbibliografie; detailed bibliographic data
are available on the Internet at http://dnb.d-nb.de.

This book is also available
in the original German language edition:
Adrian Frutiger – Schriften. Das Gesamtwerk
(ISBN 978-3-7643-8576-7)
and in a French language edition
Adrian Frutiger – Caractères. L'Œuvre complète
(ISBN 978-3-7643-8582-8).

Copyright
© 2009 Birkhäuser Verlag AG
Basel · Boston · Berlin
P.O. Box 133, CH-4010 Basel, Switzerland
Part of Springer Science+Business Media

Printed on acid-free paper produced from chlorine-free pulp.
TCF ∞

Printed in Germany

ISBN 978-3-7643-8581-1

9 8 7 6 5 4 3 2 1

www.birkhauser.ch